Contemporary Authors®

NEW REVISION SERIES

ISSN 0275-7176

Contemporary

Authors®

A Bio-Bibliographical Guide to Current Writers in Fiction, General Nonfiction, Poetry, Journalism, Drama, Motion Pictures, Television, and Other Fields

NEW REVISION SERIES
volume 131

THOMSON

GALE

Detroit • New York • San Francisco • San Diego • New Haven, Conn. • Waterville, Maine • London • Munich

Contemporary Authors, New Revision Series, Vol. 131

Project Editor
Tracey Watson

Editorial
Katy Balcer, Sara Constantakis, Natalie Fulkerson, Michelle Kazensky, Julie Keppen, Joshua Kondek, Lisa Kumar, Mary Ruby, Lemma Shomali, Susan Strickland, Maikue Vang

Permissions
Margaret Chamberlain, Jacqueline Key, Sheila Spencer

Imaging and Multimedia
Leslie Light, Michael Logusz

Composition and Electronic Capture
Carolyn Roney

Manufacturing
Lori Kessler

LIBRARY OF CONGRESS CATALOG CARD NUMBER 81-640179

ISBN 0-7876-6723-4
ISSN 0275-7176

Printed in the United States of America
10 9 8 7 6 5 4 3 2 1

Contents

Indexing note: All *Contemporary Authors* entries are indexed in the *Contemporary Authors* cumulative index, which is published separately and distributed twice a year.

As always, the most recent Contemporary Authors cumulative index continues to be the user's guide to the location of an individual author's listing.

Preface

Contemporary Authors (CA) provides information on approximately 115,000 writers in a wide range of media, including:

- Current writers of fiction, nonfiction, poetry, and drama whose works have been issued by commercial publishers, risk publishers, or university presses (authors whose books have been published only by known vanity or author-subsidized firms are ordinarily not included)

- Prominent print and broadcast journalists, editors, photojournalists, syndicated cartoonists, graphic novelists, screenwriters, television scriptwriters, and other media people

- Notable international authors

- Literary greats of the early twentieth century whose works are popular in today's high school and college curriculums and continue to elicit critical attention

A *CA* listing entails no charge or obligation. Authors are included on the basis of the above criteria and their interest to *CA* users. Sources of potential listees include trade periodicals, publishers' catalogs, librarians, and other users.

How to Get the Most out of *CA*: Use the Index

The key to locating an author's most recent entry is the *CA* cumulative index, which is published separately and distributed twice a year. It provides access to *all* entries in *CA* and *Contemporary Authors New Revision Series (CANR)*. Always consult the latest index to find an author's most recent entry.

For the convenience of users, the *CA* cumulative index also includes references to all entries in these Thomson Gale literary series: *Authors and Artists for Young Adults, Authors in the News, Bestsellers, Black Literature Criticism, Black Literature Criticism Supplement, Black Writers, Children's Literature Review, Concise Dictionary of American Literary Biography, Concise Dictionary of British Literary Biography, Contemporary Authors Autobiography Series, Contemporary Authors Bibliographical Series, Contemporary Dramatists, Contemporary Literary Criticism, Contemporary Novelists, Contemporary Poets, Contemporary Popular Writers, Contemporary Southern Writers, Contemporary Women Poets, Dictionary of Literary Biography, Dictionary of Literary Biography Documentary Series, Dictionary of Literary Biography Yearbook, DISCovering Authors, DISCovering Authors: British, DISCovering Authors: Canadian, DISCovering Authors: Modules* (including modules for Dramatists, Most-Studied Authors, Multicultural Authors, Novelists, Poets, and Popular/ Genre Authors), *DISCovering Authors 3.0, Drama Criticism, Drama for Students, Feminist Writers, Hispanic Literature Criticism, Hispanic Writers, Junior DISCovering Authors, Major Authors and Illustrators for Children and Young Adults, Major 20th-Century Writers, Native North American Literature, Novels for Students, Poetry Criticism, Poetry for Students, Short Stories for Students, Short Story Criticism, Something about the Author, Something about the Author Autobiography Series, St. James Guide to Children's Writers, St. James Guide to Crime & Mystery Writers, St. James Guide to Fantasy Writers, St. James Guide to Horror, Ghost & Gothic Writers, St. James Guide to Science Fiction Writers, St. James Guide to Young Adult Writers, Twentieth-Century Literary Criticism, 20th Century Romance and Historical Writers, World Literature Criticism,* and *Yesterday's Authors of Books for Children.*

A Sample Index Entry:

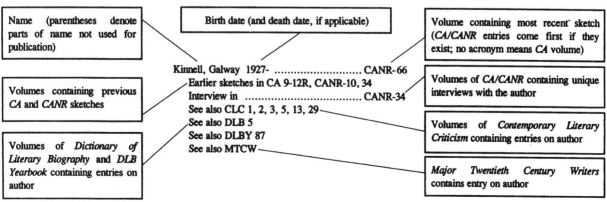

vii

How Are Entries Compiled?

The editors make every effort to secure new information directly from the authors; listees' responses to our questionnaires and query letters provide most of the information featured in *CA*. For deceased writers, or those who fail to reply to requests for data, we consult other reliable biographical sources, such as those indexed in Thomson Gale's *Biography and Genealogy Master Index,* and bibliographical sources, including *National Union Catalog, LC MARC,* and *British National Bibliography.* Further details come from published interviews, feature stories, and book reviews, as well as information supplied by the authors' publishers and agents.

An asterisk (*) at the end of a sketch indicates that the listing has been compiled from secondary sources believed to be reliable but has not been personally verified for this edition by the author sketched.

What Kinds of Information Does An Entry Provide?

Sketches in *CA* contain the following biographical and bibliographical information:

- **Entry heading:** the most complete form of author's name, plus any pseudonyms or name variations used for writing

- **Personal information:** author's date and place of birth, family data, ethnicity, educational background, political and religious affiliations, and hobbies and leisure interests

- **Addresses:** author's home, office, or agent's addresses, plus e-mail and fax numbers, as available

- **Career summary:** name of employer, position, and dates held for each career post; resume of other vocational achievements; military service

- **Membership information:** professional, civic, and other association memberships and any official posts held

- **Awards and honors:** military and civic citations, major prizes and nominations, fellowships, grants, and honorary degrees

- **Writings:** a comprehensive, chronological list of titles, publishers, dates of original publication and revised editions, and production information for plays, television scripts, and screenplays

- **Adaptations:** a list of films, plays, and other media which have been adapted from the author's work

- **Work in progress:** current or planned projects, with dates of completion and/or publication, and expected publisher, when known

- **Sidelights:** a biographical portrait of the author's development; information about the critical reception of the author's works; revealing comments, often by the author, on personal interests, aspirations, motivations, and thoughts on writing

- **Interview:** a one-on-one discussion with authors conducted especially for *CA,* offering insight into authors' thoughts about their craft

- **Autobiographical essay:** an original essay written by noted authors for *CA,* a forum in which writers may present themselves, on their own terms, to their audience

- **Photographs:** portraits and personal photographs of notable authors

- **Biographical and critical sources:** a list of books and periodicals in which additional information on an author's life and/or writings appears

- **Obituary Notices** in *CA* provide date and place of birth as well as death information about authors whose full-length sketches appeared in the series before their deaths. The entries also summarize the authors' careers and writings and list other sources of biographical and death information.

Related Titles in the *CA* Series

Contemporary Authors Autobiography Series complements *CA* original and revised volumes with specially commissioned autobiographical essays by important current authors, illustrated with personal photographs they provide. Common topics include their motivations for writing, the people and experiences that shaped their careers, the rewards they derive from their work, and their impressions of the current literary scene.

Contemporary Authors Bibliographical Series surveys writings by and about important American authors since World War II. Each volume concentrates on a specific genre and features approximately ten writers; entries list works written by and about the author and contain a bibliographical essay discussing the merits and deficiencies of major critical and scholarly studies in detail.

Available in Electronic Formats

GaleNet. *CA* is available on a subscription basis through GaleNet, an online information resource that features an easy-to-use end-user interface, powerful search capabilities, and ease of access through the World-Wide Web. For more information, call 1-800-877-GALE.

Licensing. *CA* is available for licensing. The complete database is provided in a fielded format and is deliverable on such media as disk, CD-ROM, or tape. For more information, contact Thomson Gale's Business Development Group at 1-800-877-GALE, or visit us on our website at www.galegroup.com/bizdev.

Suggestions Are Welcome

The editors welcome comments and suggestions from users on any aspect of the *CA* series. If readers would like to recommend authors for inclusion in future volumes of the series, they are cordially invited to write the Editors at *Contemporary Authors*, Thomson Gale, 27500 Drake Rd., Farmington Hills, MI 48331-3535; or call at 1-248-699-4253; or fax at 1-248-699-8054.

Contemporary Authors Product Advisory Board

The editors of *Contemporary Authors* are dedicated to maintaining a high standard of excellence by publishing comprehensive, accurate, and highly readable entries on a wide array of writers. In addition to the quality of the content, the editors take pride in the graphic design of the series, which is intended to be orderly yet inviting, allowing readers to utilize the pages of *CA* easily and with efficiency. Despite the longevity of the *CA* print series, and the success of its format, we are mindful that the vitality of a literary reference product is dependent on its ability to serve its users over time. As literature, and attitudes about literature, constantly evolve, so do the reference needs of students, teachers, scholars, journalists, researchers, and book club members. To be certain that we continue to keep pace with the expectations of our customers, the editors of *CA* listen carefully to their comments regarding the value, utility, and quality of the series. Librarians, who have firsthand knowledge of the needs of library users, are a valuable resource for us. The *Contemporary Authors* Product Advisory Board, made up of school, public, and academic librarians, is a forum to promote focused feedback about *CA* on a regular basis. The seven-member advisory board includes the following individuals, whom the editors wish to thank for sharing their expertise:

- **Anne M. Christensen,** Librarian II, Phoenix Public Library, Phoenix, Arizona.

- **Barbara C. Chumard,** Reference/Adult Services Librarian, Middletown Thrall Library, Middletown, New York.

- **Eva M. Davis,** Youth Department Manager, Ann Arbor District Library, Ann Arbor, Michigan.

- **Adam Janowski, Jr.,** Library Media Specialist, Naples High School Library Media Center, Naples, Florida.

- **Robert Reginald,** Head of Technical Services and Collection Development, California State University, San Bernadino, California.

- **Stephen Weiner,** Director, Maynard Public Library, Maynard, Massachusetts.

International Advisory Board

Well-represented among the 115,000 author entries published in *Contemporary Authors* are sketches on notable writers from many non-English-speaking countries. The primary criteria for inclusion of such authors has traditionally been the publication of at least one title in English, either as an original work or as a translation. However, the editors of *Contemporary Authors* came to observe that many important international writers were being overlooked due to a strict adherence to our inclusion criteria. In addition, writers who were publishing in languages other than English were not being covered in the traditional sources we used for identifying new listees. Intent on increasing our coverage of international authors, including those who write only in their native language and have not been translated into English, the editors enlisted the aid of a board of advisors, each of whom is an expert on the literature of a particular country or region. Among the countries we focused attention on are Mexico, Puerto Rico, Spain, Italy, France, Germany, Luxembourg, Belgium, the Netherlands, Norway, Sweden, Denmark, Finland, Taiwan, Singapore, Malaysia, Thailand, South Africa, Israel, and Japan, as well as England, Scotland, Wales, Ireland, Australia, and New Zealand. The sixteen-member advisory board includes the following individuals, whom the editors wish to thank for sharing their expertise:

- **Lowell A. Bangerter,** Professor of German, University of Wyoming, Laramie, Wyoming.

- **Nancy E. Berg,** Associate Professor of Hebrew and Comparative Literature, Washington University, St. Louis, Missouri.

- **Frances Devlin-Glass,** Associate Professor, School of Literary and Communication Studies, Deakin University, Burwood, Victoria, Australia.

- **David William Foster,** Regent's Professor of Spanish, Interdisciplinary Humanities, and Women's Studies, Arizona State University, Tempe, Arizona.

- **Hosea Hirata,** Director of the Japanese Program, Associate Professor of Japanese, Tufts University, Medford, Massachusetts.

- **Jack Kolbert,** Professor Emeritus of French Literature, Susquehanna University, Selinsgrove, Pennsylvania.

- **Mark Libin,** Professor, University of Manitoba, Winnipeg, Manitoba, Canada.

- **C. S. Lim,** Professor, University of Malaya, Kuala Lumpur, Malaysia.

- **Eloy E. Merino,** Assistant Professor of Spanish, Northern Illinois University, DeKalb, Illinois.

- **Linda M. Rodríguez Guglielmoni,** Associate Professor, University of Puerto Rico—Mayagüez, Puerto Rico.

- **Sven Hakon Rossel,** Professor and Chair of Scandinavian Studies, University of Vienna, Vienna, Austria.

- **Steven R. Serafin,** Director, Writing Center, Hunter College of the City University of New York, New York City.

- **David Smyth,** Lecturer in Thai, School of Oriental and African Studies, University of London, England.

- **Ismail S. Talib,** Senior Lecturer, Department of English Language and Literature, National University of Singapore, Singapore.

- **Dionisio Viscarri,** Assistant Professor, Ohio State University, Columbus, Ohio.

- **Mark Williams,** Associate Professor, English Department, University of Canterbury, Christchurch, New Zealand.

CA Numbering System and Volume Update Chart

Occasionally questions arise about the *CA* numbering system and which volumes, if any, can be discarded. Despite numbers like "29-32R," "97-100" and "223," the entire *CA* print series consists of only 282 physical volumes with the publication of *CA* Volume 224. The following charts note changes in the numbering system and cover design, and indicate which volumes are essential for the most complete, up-to-date coverage.

CA First Revision	• 1-4R through 41-44R (11 books) *Cover:* Brown with black and gold trim. There will be no further First Revision volumes because revised entries are now being handled exclusively through the more efficient *New Revision Series* mentioned below.
CA Original Volumes	• 45-48 through 97-100 (14 books) *Cover:* Brown with black and gold trim. 101 through 224 (124 books) *Cover:* Blue and black with orange bands. The same as previous *CA* original volumes but with a new, simplified numbering system and new cover design.
CA Permanent Series	• *CAP*-1 and *CAP*-2 (2 books) *Cover:* Brown with red and gold trim. There will be no further Permanent Series volumes because revised entries are now being handled exclusively through the more efficient *New Revision Series* mentioned below.
CA New Revision Series	• CANR-1 through CANR-131 (131 books) *Cover:* Blue and black with green bands. Includes only sketches requiring significant changes; **sketches are taken from any previously published CA, CAP, or CANR volume.**

If You Have:	You May Discard:
CA First Revision Volumes 1-4R through 41-44R and *CA Permanent Series* Volumes 1 and 2	*CA* Original Volumes 1, 2, 3, 4 and Volumes 5-6 through 41-44
CA Original Volumes 45-48 through 97-100 and 101 through 224	**NONE:** These volumes will not be superseded by corresponding revised volumes. Individual entries from these and all other volumes appearing in the left column of this chart may be revised and included in the various volumes of the *New Revision Series*.
CA New Revision Series Volumes *CANR*-1 through *CANR*-131	**NONE:** The *New Revision Series* does not replace any single volume of *CA*. Instead, volumes of *CANR* include entries from many previous *CA* series volumes. All *New Revision Series* volumes must be retained for full coverage.

A Sampling of Authors and Media People Featured in This Volume

Dave Barry

Barry is a nationally syndicated columnist who has won a wide following with his lighthearted, often outrageous observations on life in middle America. A Pulitzer Prize-winner based at the *Miami Herald,* Barry looks at the most ordinary experiences of everyday life and extracts unexpected humor and irony in books like his best-seller *Dave Barry Slept Here: A Sort of History of the United States.* In 2002 he published *Boogers Are My Beat: More Lies, but Some Actual Journalism,* and the novel *Tricky Business.*

William Boyd

Boyd, a British novelist, playwright, and critic, is widely read on both sides of the Atlantic for his darkly humorous fiction, laced with biting satire and social commentary, but also with a warm regard for his characters. His long list of literary honors began with the prestigious Whitbread and Somerset Maugham awards for his first novel, *A Good Man in Africa.* Among his recent works is the 2002 novel *Any Human Heart: The Intimate Journals of Logan Mountstuart.*

Patricia Cornwell

Cornwell is a reporter-turned-novelist whose first outing, *Postmortem,* introduced forensic pathologist/sleuth Dr. Kay Scarpetta and won five of the most prestigious awards in the realm of mystery fiction. A highly successful "Scarpetta" series followed, noted for its authentic, grisly science and fast-paced action. In a departure from the popular series, Cornwell produced a real-crime study in 2002, identifying a new culprit in *Portrait of a Killer: Jack the Ripper—Case Closed.* Her latest Scarpetta novel is *Blow Fly,* published in 2003.

Clive Cussler

Cussler is the author of the best-selling novel series featuring Dirk Pitt, a handsome, witty, devil-may-care adventurer—in short, a cross between Indiana Jones and James Bond. Once an awarding-wining adman, Cussler has a passion for collecting classic cars and searching for lost ships that is also a hallmark of his fictional hero in stories like *Raise the Titanic* and *Flood Tide.* Cussler added *The Trojan Odyssey* to Dirk Pitt's repertoire in 2003.

Umberto Eco

Eco is a highly respected Italian scholar who specializes in semiotics, the study of how cultures communicate through signs. He took the literary world by storm—and by surprise—with his internationally acclaimed semiotic murder mystery *Name of the Rose.* Combining intriguing slices of history with many layers of meaning, his novels, including *Foucault's Pendulum* and *The Island of the Day Before,* inspire a wide range of critical responses—from mystified to mesmerized. In 2004, Eco published the nonfiction title *On Literature.*

Nadine Gordimer

Gordimer, born and raised in South Africa, has gained an international reputation with numerous novels, short stories, and essays in which she writes of her homeland and the sufferings of its citizens under apartheid. Regarded as the preeminent recorder of life under apartheid, Gordimer is praised for her insight, integrity, and compassion in books like *Burger's Daughter* and *The Conservationist.* Gordimer published the novel *The Pickup* in 2001 and *The Loot : And Other Stories* in 2003.

Muriel Spark

Spark, a Scottish writer of fiction, poetry, biography, and criticism, may be best known for her novels, like the popular *The Prime of Miss Jean Brodie.* Considered an intellectual writer, Spark favors the play of ideas over florid description and matches her technical virtuosity with an elegant, acerbic wit. Yet, she defies easy classification by critics who find her a serious and accomplished writer, a moralist engaged with the human predicament, and wildly entertaining. Her most recent book is *The Ghost Stories of Muriel Spark,* published in 2003.

Alice Walker

Walker is recognized as one of the best-selling writers of literary fiction in the United States and a focal spokesperson and symbol for black feminism. Her reputation was firmly establshed with her third novel, *The Color Purple,* which earned a Pulitzer Prize and an American Book Award, followed by a popular motion picture. In 2003 Walker published *Absolute Trust in the Goodness of the Earth: New Poems,* followed by the novel *Now Is the Time to Open Your Heart,* in 2004.

Acknowledgments

Grateful acknowledgment is made to those publishers, photographers, and artists whose work appear with these authors' essays. Following is a list of the copyright holders who have granted us permission to reproduce material in this volume of *CA*. Every effort has been made to trace copyright, but if omissions have been made, please let us know.

Photographs/Art

Edward Abbey: Abbey, photograph. © Jonathan Blair/Corbis. Reproduced by permission.

William Baker: Baker, photograph. Reproduced by permission.

Dave Barry: Barry, photograph. AP/Wide World Photos. Reproduced by permission.

James Bennett: Bennett, photograph. Reproduced by permission of James Bennett.

Lucy Jane Bledsoe: Bledsoe, photograph by Phyllis Christopher. Reproduced by permission of Lucy Jane Bledsoe.

William Boyd: Boyd, photograph. © Jerry Bauer. Reproduced by permission.

Stephen R. Braun: Braun, photograph. Reproduced by permission.

William Bryson: Bryson, photograph. Copyright © by Jerry Bauer. Reproduced by permission.

Eoin Colfer: Colfer, photograph. The O'Brien Press Ltd., 2001. Reproduced by permission of the O'Brien Press.

Patricia Cornwell: Cornwell, photograph. AP/Wide World Photos. Reproduced by permission.

Clive Cussler: Cussler, photograph by Ron Semrod. AP/Wide World Photos. Reproduced by permission.

Robert Darnton: Darnton, photograph. © Jerry Bauer. Reproduced by permission.

Diane di Prima: di Prima, photograph by Chris Felver. Copyright © by Chris Felver. Reproduced by permission.

Penelope Fitzgerald: Fitzgerald, photograph. © Jerry Bauer. Reproduced by permission.

Sid Fleischman: Fleischman, photograph by Damon Webster. Courtesy of Sid Fleischman. Reproduced by permission of Sid Fleischman.

Philip Glass: Glass, photograph. AP/Wide World Photos. Reproduced by permission.

Nadine Gordimer: Gordimer, photograph. AP/Wide World Photos. Reproduced by permission.

Sheila Ellen Green: Green, photograph by Carlo Carnivalli. Reproduced by permission of Sheila Ellen Green.

Vartan Gregorian: Gregorian, photograph. AP/Wide World Photos. Reproduced by permission.

Kent Haruf: Haruf, photograph. Copyright © by Jerry Bauer. Reproduced by permission.

A

Indicates that a listing has been compiled from secondary sources believed to be reliable, but has not been personally verified for this edition by the author sketched.

ABBEY, Edward 1927-1989

PERSONAL: Born January 29, 1927, in Home, PA; died of internal bleeding due to a circulatory disorder, March 14, 1989, in Oracle, AZ; buried in a desert in the southwestern United States; son of Paul Revere (a farmer) and Mildred (a teacher; maiden name, Postlewaite) Abbey; married Jean Schmechalon, August 5, 1950 (divorced, 1952); married Rita Deanin, November 20, 1952 (divorced, August 25, 1965); married Judith Pepper, 1965 (died, July 4, 1970); married Renee Dowling, February 10, 1974 (divorced, 1980); married Clarke Cartwright, May 5, 1982; children: (with Deanin) Joshua Nathanael, Aaron Paul; (with Pepper) Susannah Mildred; (with Cartwright) Rebecca Claire, Benjamin Cartwright. *Education:* University of New Mexico, B.A., 1951, M.A., 1956; attended University of Edinburgh. *Politics:* "Agrarian anarchist." *Religion:* Piute.

CAREER: Writer. Park ranger and fire lookout for National Park Service in the southwest United States, 1956-71; University of Arizona, Tuscon, teacher of creative writing, beginning 1981, became full professor, 1988. *Military service:* U.S. Army, 1945-46.

AWARDS, HONORS: Fulbright fellow, 1951-52; Wallace Stegner Creative Writing Fellowship, Stanford University, 1957; Western Heritage Award for Best Novel, 1963, for *Fire on the Mountain;* Guggenheim fellow, 1975; American Academy of Arts and Letters award, 1987 (declined).

Edward Abbey

WRITINGS:

NOVELS

Jonathan Troy, Dodd (New York, NY), 1956.

1

The Brave Cowboy, Dodd (New York, NY), 1958, reprint published as *The Brave Cowboy: An Old Tale in a New Time,* University of New Mexico Press (Albuquerque, NM), 1977.

Fire on the Mountain, Dial (New York, NY), 1962.

Black Sun, Simon & Schuster (New York, NY), 1971, published as *Sunset Canyon,* Talmy (London, England), 1972.

The Monkey Wrench Gang, Lippincott (Philadelphia, PA), 1975.

Good News, Dutton (New York, NY), 1980.

Confessions of a Barbarian (bound with *Red Knife Valley* by Jack Curtis), Capra (Santa Barbara, CA), 1986, revised edition published as *Confessions of a Barbarian: Selections from the Journals of Edward Abbey, 1951-1989,* edited and with an introduction by David Petersen, Little, Brown (Boston, MA), 1994.

The Fool's Progress, Holt (New York, NY), 1988.

Hayduke Lives!, Little, Brown (Boston, MA), 1990.

NONFICTION

Desert Solitaire: A Season in the Wilderness, illustrated by Peter Parnall, McGraw (New York, NY), 1968, reprint published as *Desert Solitaire,* University of Arizona Press (Tucson, AZ), 1988.

Appalachian Wilderness: The Great Smoky Mountains, photographs by Eliot Porter, Dutton (New York, NY), 1970.

(With Philip Hyde) *Slickrock: The Canyon Country of Southeast Utah,* Sierra Club, 1971.

(With others) *Cactus Country,* Time-Life (New York, NY), 1973.

The Journey Home: Some Words in Defense of the American West, illustrated by Jim Stiles, Dutton (New York, NY), 1977.

Back Roads of Arizona, photographs by Earl Thollander, Northland Press, 1978, published as *Arizona's Scenic Byways,* 1992.

The Hidden Canyon: A River Journey, photographs by John Blaustein, Viking (New York, NY), 1978.

(With David Muench) *Desert Images: An American Landscape,* Chanticleer (New York, NY), 1979.

Abbey's Road: Take the Other, Dutton (New York, NY), 1979.

(Self-illustrated) *Down the River,* Dutton (New York, NY), 1982.

(With John Nichols) *In Praise of Mountain Lions,* Albuquerque Sierra Club (Albuquerque, NM), 1984.

Beyond the Wall: Essays from the Outside, Holt (New York, NY), 1984.

(Editor and illustrator) *Slumgullion Stew: An Edward Abbey Reader,* Dutton (New York, NY), 1984, published as *The Best of Edward Abbey,* Sierra Club Books (San Francisco, CA), 1988.

One Life at a Time, Please, Holt (New York, NY), 1988.

Vox Clamantis in Deserto: Some Notes from a Secret Journal, Rydal Press (Santa Fe, NM), 1989, published as *A Voice Crying in the Wilderness: Essays from a Secret Journal,* illustrated by Andrew Rush, St. Martin's Press (New York, NY), 1990.

The Serpents of Paradise: A Reader, edited by John Macrae, Holt (New York, NY), 1995.

OTHER

(Essayist) Thomas Miller, *Desert Skin,* University of Utah Press (Salt Lake City, UT), 1994.

Earth Apples: The Poetry of Edward Abbey, collected and introduced by David Peterson, illustrated by Michael McCurdy, St. Martin's Press (New York, NY), 1994.

Also author of introductions for books, including *Walden,* by Henry D. Thoreau, G. M. Smith (Salt Lake City, UT), 1981; *Ecodefense: A Field Guide to Monkeywrenching,* edited by Dave Foreman, Ned Ludd Books, 1987; *The Land of Little Rain,* by Mary Austin, Viking (New York, NY), 1988; and *Wilderness on the Rocks,* by Howie Wolke, Ned Ludd Books, 1991. Contributor to books, including *Utah Wilderness Photography: An Exhibition,* Utah Arts Council, 1978; *Images from the Great West,* edited by Marnie Walker Gaede, Chaco Press (La Cañada, CA), 1990; *Late Harvest: Rural American Writing,* edited by David R. Pichaske, Paragon House (New York, NY), 1991; and *The Best of Outside: The First 20 Years,* Vintage Departures (New York, NY), 1998. A collection of Abbey's manuscripts is housed at the University of Arizona, Tucson.

ADAPTATIONS: The Brave Cowboy was adapted for film and released as *Lonely Are the Brave,* starring Kirk Douglas and Walter Matthau, 1962; *Fire on the Mountain* was adapted for film, 1981.

SIDELIGHTS: Edward Abbey was best known for his hard-hitting, frequently bitter, and usually irreverent defense of the world's wilderness areas. Anarchistic and outspoken, he was called everything from America's crankiest citizen to the godfather of modern environmental activism. Abbey himself strenuously resisted any attempt to classify him as a naturalist, environmentalist, or anything else. "If a label is required," Burt A. Folkart quoted him as saying in the *Los Angeles Times,* "say that I am one who loves the unfenced country." His favorite places were the deserts and mountains of the American West, and the few people who won his respect were those who knew how to live on that land without spoiling it. The many targets of his venom ranged from government agencies and gigantic corporations responsible for the rape of the wild country, to cattle ranchers grazing their herds on public lands, to simple-minded tourists who, according to Abbey, defile the solitude with their very presence.

Born on a small farm in Appalachia, Abbey hitchhiked west in 1946, following one year of service in the U.S. Army. Captivated by the wide-open spaces of Arizona, New Mexico, and Utah, he stayed there, studying philosophy and English at the University of New Mexico. His first novel, *Jonathan Troy,* shows the influence of the philosophical works he was reading in college, including the writings of William Godwin, Pierre-Joseph Proudhon, Karl Marx, and Michael Bakunin. Published in 1954, *Jonathan Troy* is the story of a self-involved young man who yearns to escape his Pennsylvania home for the open spaces of the West. He finally realizes his dream, but not without overcoming many problems first. The greatest difficulty is the loss of his anarchist father, Nat, who is wrongly killed by a rookie policeman. Jonathan's dreams are also imperiled by a shallow young woman who tries to trap him into marriage. He is threatened by his friendship with his English teacher, who reinforces in him his father's radical politics. Ultimately, Jonathan sees that life in the East has become impossible for him, and the story ends with him heading West, lured by the promise of a new way of life there. The novel is notable for its depiction of the conflict between wilderness and civilization, a theme that would always be central to Abbey's work. It is also distinguished by "Abbey's descriptions of an industrial wreckage visited on the Pennsylvania coal country," remarked an essayist for the *Dictionary of Literary Biography.* "These descriptions are important because they mark the first expressions of Abbey's environmental awareness. The dialogue is the weak element of the novel, particularly Jonathan's ponderous interior monologues."

Abbey's next novel, *The Brave Cowboy,* enjoyed somewhat greater success than *Jonathan Troy*—

particularly after it was adapted into the film *Lonely Are the Brave.* The novel features Jack Burns, a nineteenth-century-style cowboy whose rugged individualism has become anachronistic in modern New Mexico. Burns rides his horse into modern Duke City, intent on helping his friend Paul Bondi, a draft resister serving a jail term. Burns undertakes this rescue by getting arrested so that he will be imprisoned with Bondi. The plot twists when Bondi will not follow Burns into the night and to freedom. Burns then runs for Mexico, pursued by the authorities, in a compelling chase story that includes his bringing down a helicopter with a small-caliber rifle. In a similar story, *Fire on the Mountain,* Abbey explores the struggles of John Vogelin as he attempts to prevent the White Sands Missile Range from encroaching on his ranch land in southern New Mexico.

Desert Solitaire, published in 1968, is drawn from Abbey's experiences as a forest ranger and fire lookout. His first nonfiction work was also one of his greatest successes. *Desert Solitaire* opens with a truculent preface, in which the author expresses his hope that serious critics, librarians, and professors will intensely dislike his book. In the body of the book, which compresses many of Abbey's experiences with the Park Service and Forest Service into the framework of one cycle of the seasons, readers find both harsh criticism and poetic description, all related to the landscape of the West and what mankind is doing to it. Freeman Tilden, reviewing *Desert Solitaire* in *National Parks,* recommended the book, "vehemence, egotism, bad taste and all. Partly because we need angry young men to remind us that there is plenty we should be angry about. . . . Partly because Abbey is an artist with words. There are pages and pages of delicious prose, sometimes almost magical in their evocation of the desert scene. . . . How this man can write! But he can do more than write. His prehension of the natural environment—of raw nature—is so ingenuous, so implicit, that we wonder if the pre-Columbian aborigines didn't see their environment just that way."

In a review of *Desert Solitaire* for the *New York Times Book Review,* Pulitzer Prize-winning writer Edwin Way Teale noted that Abbey's work as a park ranger brought him to the wilderness before the invasion of "the parked trailers, their windows blue tinged at night while the inmates, instead of watching the desert stars, watch TV and listen to the canned laughter of Hollywood." Calling the book "a voice crying in the wilderness, for the wilderness," Teale warned that it is also "rough, tough and combative. The author is a rebel, an eloquent loner. In his introduction, he gives fair warning that the reader may find his pages 'coarse, rude, bad-tempered, violently prejudiced.' But if they are all these, they are many things besides. His is a passionately felt, deeply poetic book. It has philosophy. It has humor. It has sincerity and conviction. It has its share of nerve tingling adventure in what he describes as a land of surprises, some of them terrible." Teale concluded: "Abbey writes with a deep undercurrent of bitterness. But as is not infrequently the case, the bitter man may be the one who cares enough to be bitter and he often is the one who says things that need to be said. In *Desert Solitaire* those things are set down in lean, racing prose, in a close-knit style of power and beauty. Rather than a balanced book, judicially examining in turn all sides, it is a forceful presentation of one side. And that side needs presenting. It is a side too rarely presented. There will always be others to voice the other side, the side of pressure and power and profit."

While it never made the best-seller lists, *Desert Solitaire* is credited as being a key source of inspiration for the environmental movement that was growing in the late 1960s. Abbey's no-holds-barred book awakened many readers to just how much damage was being done by government and business interests to so-called "public" lands, as did the many other essay collections he published throughout his career. But an even greater influence may have come from his 1975 novel, *The Monkey Wrench Gang*. Receiving virtually no promotion, it nonetheless became an underground classic, selling half a million copies. Within the comic story, which follows the misadventures of four environmentalist terrorists, is a serious message: peaceful protest is inadequate; the ecology movement must become radicalized. The ultimate goal of the Monkey Wrench Gang—blowing up the immense Glen Canyon Dam on the Colorado River—is one Abbey seemed to endorse, and his book provides fairly explicit instructions to anyone daring enough to carry it out. The novel is said to have inspired the formation of the real-life environmental group Earth First!, which impedes the progress of developers and loggers by tactics such as sabotaging bulldozers and booby-trapping trees with chainsaw-destroying spikes. Their term for such tactics: monkeywrenching.

National Observer reviewer Sheldon Frank called *The Monkey Wrench Gang* a "sad, hilarious, exuberant, vulgar fairy tale filled with long chase sequences and careful conspiratorial scheming. As in all fairy tales, the characters are pure cardboard, unbelievable in every respect. But they are delightful." A contributor to the London *Times* observed that the book is "less a work of fiction . . . than an incitement to environmentalists to take the law into their own hands, often by means of vandalizing whatever they considered to be themselves examples of vandalism and overkill."

The Monkey Wrench Gang is possibly Abbey's best-known work, but the author's personal favorite of his more than twenty books was the bulky, largely autobiographical novel *The Fool's Progress*. "From the outset of this cross-country story it seems almost impossible to separate Edward Abbey from his narrator," observed Howard Coale in the *New York Times Book Review*. "The harsh, humorous, damn-it-all voice of Henry Lightcap is identical to the voice in the author's many essays." In Coale's opinion, the book was too "self-involved" to be a really successful work of fiction, although it contained some excellent descriptive passages. Other commentators agreed that the book was flawed. John Skow wrote in *Time*, "Abbey . . . is feeling sorry for his hero and probably for himself too. What saves the book is that he is skilled enough to pull sympathetic readers into his own mood of regret." "Abbey is not for everybody," summarized Kerry Luft in his *Chicago Tribune* assessment. "He's about as subtle as a wrecking ball. Some might call him sexist or downright misogynistic and point out that his female characters tend to be shallow stereotypes. I can only agree. But for those readers with the gumption and the stomach to stay with him, Abbey is a delight."

Abbey's last act contributed to his legend as a rugged individualist. When he realized he was terminally ill, he left the care of his doctors and checked himself out of the hospital. Following instructions he had set down years earlier in his journal, his wife and friends took him into the desert so that he could die under the stars. After one night went by and he was still alive, Abbey was taken back to his cabin home until the end came. Then his body was taken back into the desert and buried illegally there in a secret location.

Shortly before his death, Abbey had completed a sequel to *The Monkey Wrench Gang*, titled *Hayduke Lives!* Published posthumously, *Hayduke Lives!* finds most of the cast of the earlier novel settled comfortably into middle-class lives, only to be galvanized into action again by the reappearance of their leader, thought to be long dead. Critical assessment of the sequel varied widely. Grace Lichtenstein, reviewing it in the *Washington Post Book World,* found "the entire theme of ecotage" to be "shopworn," while *Chicago Tribune* editor David E. Jones stated that "the fun-loving bawdiness [of the original] is still there, and the camaraderie and dedication," along with "an unexpected darker side."

Excerpts from Abbey's journals and a collection of his essays were also published posthumously. *Confessions of a Barbarian: Selections from the Journals of Edward Abbey, 1951-1989* includes 368 pages from the writer's copious journals. His acid pen ranges over subjects such as aging, suicide, music, and literature. Assessing the book in *Backpacker,* Peter Lewis observed that Abbey proves his ability to "inspire and infuriate. . . . It's spirited stuff. Some of the highlights center around his closely observed, tack-sharp sketches of places he knew and loved. Abbey was as nimble as they come when summoning emotions surrounding a landscape, and the desert Southwest has had few who could better sing its praises." Roland Wulbert concurred in *Booklist* that Abbey is "both compelling and infuriating," and added, "His journals show that he didn't so much find a voice as mature the one he always had."

The Serpents of Paradise: A Reader is a collection of essays, travel pieces, and works of fiction by Abbey, organized to parallel events in Abbey's own life. His fiction is represented by excerpts from *The Brave Cowboy, The Fool's Progress,* and *The Monkey Wrench Gang,* while the nonfiction is drawn from *Desert Solitaire* and numerous other sources. The pieces here reveal Abbey as "a true independent, a self-declared extremist and 'desert mystic,'" as well as "a hell of a good writer," observed Donna Seaman in *Booklist.* "Irreverent about man and reverent toward nature, Abbey wielded his pen as a weapon in the battle for freedom and wilderness and against arrogance and greed." A *Publishers Weekly* reviewer commented that *The Serpents of Paradise* "makes for a splendid summary of his best work—though it does not slight his faults," which include "occasional outbursts of xenophobia and old-fashioned sexism," as well as "gleefully overweening destructive fantasies. . . . Anyone who doesn't already know his work will find this volume, culled from more than a dozen books of fiction and nonfiction, an addictive introduction."

Reflecting in the *New York Times Book Review* on Abbey's body of work, Edward Hoagland called him "the nonpareil 'nature writer' of recent decades." Hoagland went on: "He was uneven and self-indulgent as a writer and often scanted his talent by working too fast. But he had about him an authenticity that springs from the page and is beloved by a rising generation of readers." "*Desert Solitaire* stands among the towering works of American nature writing," stated Lichtenstein. "Abbey's polemic essays on such subjects as cattle subsidies and Mexican immigrants, scattered through a half-dozen volumes, remain so angry, so infuriating yet so relevant that they still provoke arguments among his followers. As for his outdoors explorations, no one wrote more melodic hymns to the red rocks and rivers of the Southwest; no one ever defended them with more elan. It is in those nonfiction odes to the wilderness, by turns cantankerous and lyrical . . . that Abbey lives, forever."

Speaking for himself in the essay "A Writer's Credo," Abbey declared, "I write to entertain my friends and exasperate our enemies. I write to record the truth of our time as best I can see it. To investigate the comedy and tragedy of human relationships. To oppose, resist, and sabotage the contemporary drift toward a global technocratic police state, whatever its ideological coloration. I write to oppose injustice, to defy power, and to speak for the voiceless. I write to make a difference."

BIOGRAPHICAL AND CRITICAL SOURCES:

BOOKS

Abbey, Edward, *Confessions of a Barbarian: Selections from the Journals of Edward Abbey, 1951-1989,* edited by David Petersen, original drawings by Abbey, Little, Brown (Boston, MA), 1994.

Abbey, Edward, *One Life at a Time,* Holt (New York, NY), 1988.

Balassi, William, and others, editors, *This Is about Vision: Interviews with Southwestern Writers,* University of New Mexico Press (Albuquerque, NM), 1990.

Berry, Wendell, *What Are People For?,* North Point (San Francisco, CA), 1990.

Bishop, James, Jr., with Charles Bowden, *Epitaph for a Desert Anarchist: The Life and Legacy of Edward Abbey,* Atheneum (New York, NY), 1994.

Calahan, James M., *Edward Abbey: A Life,* University of Arizona Press (Tucson, AZ), 2001.

Contemporary Literary Criticism, Gale (Detroit, MI), Volume 36, 1986, Volume 59, 1990.

Dictionary of Literary Biography, Volume 256: Twentieth-Century Western Writers, Third Series, Gale (Detroit, MI), 2002.

Foreman, Dave, *Confessions of an Eco-Warrior,* Harmony Books (New York, NY), 1991.

Hafen, Lyman and Milo McCowan, *Edward Abbey: An Interview at Pack Creek Ranch,* Vinegar Tom (Santa FE, NM), 1991.

Hepworth, James, and Gregory McNamee, editors, *Resist Much, Obey Little: Some Notes on Edward Abbey,* Dream Garden (Salt Lake City, UT), 1985.

Loeffler, Jack, *Adventures with Ed—A Portrait of Abbey,* University of New Mexico Press (Albuquerque, NM), 2002.

McCann, Garth, *Edward Abbey,* Boise State University (Boise, ID), 1977.

McClintock, James, *Nature's Kindred Spirits: Aldo Leopold, Joseph Wood Krutch, Edward Abbey, Annie Dillard, and Gary Snyder,* University of Wisconsin Press (Madison, WI), 1994.

Quigley, Peter, editor, *Coyote in the Maze: Tracking Edward Abbey in a World of Words,* University of Utah Press (Salt Lake City, UT), 1998.

Ronald, Ann, *The New West of Edward Abbey,* University of New Mexico Press (Albuquerque, NM), 1982.

St. James Encyclopedia of Popular Culture, St. James Press (Detroit, MI), 2000.

Scribner Encyclopedia of American Lives, Volume 2: 1986-1990, Scribner (New York, NY), 1999.

Stegner, Wallace, and Richard W. Etulain, *Conversations with Wallace Stegner on Western History and Literature,* revised edition, University of Utah Press (Salt Lake City, UT), 1990.

PERIODICALS

Albuquerque Journal, November 4, 2001, "Book Attempts to Release Edward Abbey from Myth," p. F8.

America, April 9, 2001, Thomas J. McCarthy, "The Ultimate Sanctum," p. 6.

Audubon, July, 1989, pp. 14, 16.

Backpacker, December, 1994, Peter Lewis, review of *Confessions of a Barbarian,* p. 115.

Best Sellers, June 15, 1971.

Booklist, August, 1994, John Mort, review of *Earth Apples: The Poetry of Edward Abbey,* p. 2018; September 15, 1994, Roland Wulbert, review of *Confessions of a Barbarian,* p. 100; March 1, 1995, Donna Seaman, review of *The Serpents of Paradise: A Reader,* p. 1173.

Canadian Dimension, May, 2001, Louis Proyect, "Lonely Are the Brave," p. 43.

Chicago Tribune, February 14, 1988, section 14, p. 3; November 29, 1988; March 15, 1989; February 12, 1990.

Chicago Tribune Book World, November 30, 1980, section 7, p. 5.

Christian Science Monitor, July 27, 1977.

Growth and Change, summer, 1995, Nathanael Dresser, "Cultivating Wilderness: The Place of Land in the Fiction of Ed Abbey and Wendell Berry," p. 350.

Harper's, August, 1971; February, 1988, pp. 42-44.

Library Journal, January 1, 1968; July, 1977; August, 1994, Frank Allen, review of *Earth Apples: The Poetry of Edward Abbey,* p. 90; September 1, 1994, Tim Markus, review of *Confessions of a Barbarian,* p. 181; February 15, 1995, Cathy Sabol, review of *The Serpents of Paradise,* p. 155.

Los Angeles Times, October 22, 1980.

Los Angeles Times Book Review, June 17, 1979; May 16, 1982, p. 1; November 29, 1987, p. 10; January 24, 1988, p. 12; May 15, 1988, p. 14; November 20, 1988, p. 3; September 2, 1989, p. 8; January 7, 1990, p. 1; March 26, 1995, p. 6.

Nation, May 1, 1982, pp. 533-535.

National Observer, September 6, 1975, p. 17.

National Parks, February, 1968, pp. 22-23.

National Review, August 10, 1984, pp. 48-49.

New Yorker, July 17, 1971.

New York Times, June 19, 1979; March 15, 1989; May 11, 1997, Lesley Hazleton, "Arguing with a Ghost in Yosemite," p. XX37; February 10, 2002, T. Coraghessan Boyle, "A Voice Griping in the Wilderness," p. 8; April 29, 2002, Blaine Harden, "A Friend, Not a Role Model: Remembering Edward Abbey, Who Loved Words, Women, Beer and the Desert," p. E1.

New York Times Book Review, January 28, 1968, p. 7; July 31, 1977, pp. 10-11; August 5, 1979, pp. 8, 21; December 14, 1980, p. 10; May 30, 1982, p. 6; April 15, 1984, p. 34; December 16, 1984, p. 27; February 28, 1988, p. 27; May 1, 1988; December 18, 1988, p. 22; May 7, 1989, Edward Hoagland, "Standing Tough in the Desert," pp. 44-45; February 4, 1990, p. 18; July 8, 1990, p. 28; January

27, 1991, p. 32; December 11, 1994, Tim Sandlin, review of *Confessions of a Barbarian,* p. 11; June 11, 1995, p. 18; March 17, 1996, p. 32.

Publishers Weekly, October 5, 1984, p. 85; August 12, 1988, p. 439; November 11, 1988, pp. 34-36; July 25, 1994, p. 44; September 12, 1994, p. 75; January 23, 1995, review of *The Serpents of Paradise,* p. 52.

Seattle Times, January 20, 2002, Anne Stephenson, "Straight-on Look at Writer Edward Abbey," p. J9.

Southwest Review, winter, 1976, pp. 108-111; winter, 1980, pp. 102-105.

Time, November 28, 1988, p. 98.

Washington Post, December 31, 1979; January 5, 1988.

Washington Post Book World, March 24, 1968; June 25, 1979; May 30, 1982, p. 3; April 1, 1984, p. 9; April 3, 1988, p. 12; December 31, 1989, p. 12; January 28, 1990, p. 5; April 1, 1990, p. 8; April 22, 1990, p. 12; June 10, 1990, p. 15.

Western American Literature, fall, 1966, pp. 197-207; May, 1989, pp. 37-43; May, 1993, Paul T. Bryant, "The Structure and Unity of *Desert Solitaire,*" pp. 3-19.

Wilson Library Bulletin, March, 1994, Preston Hoffman, review of *Hayduke Lives!* (sound recording), p. 116.

Zephyr, April-May, 1999, interview with Edward Abbey.

ONLINE

Edward Abbey, http://www.abbeyweb.net/ (July 20, 2003).

OTHER

Edward Abbey: A Voice in the Wilderness (documentary film), 1993.

OBITUARIES:

PERIODICALS

Chicago Tribune, March 15, 1989.
Detroit Free Press, March 15, 1989.
Los Angeles Times, March 16, 1989; May 22, 1989.
New York Times, March 15, 1989.

Times (London), March 28, 1989.
Washington Post, March 17, 1989.*

* * *

ADELBERG, Doris
See ORGEL, Doris

* * *

AGEE, James (Rufus) 1909-1955

PERSONAL: Born November 27, 1909, in Knoxville, TN; died of a heart attack, May 16, 1955, in New York, NY; son of Hugh James and Laura (Tyler) Agee; married Olivia Saunders, January 28, 1933 (divorced); married Alma Mailman, 1939 (divorced); married Mia Fritsch, 1946; children: (second marriage) Joel; (third marriage) Julia Teresa. *Education:* Harvard University, A.B., 1932.

CAREER: Poet, novelist, screenwriter, and reviewer. Staff member of *Fortune* magazine, c. 1930s. Actor in motion pictures, including *The Bride Comes to Yellow Sky,* 1953.

AWARDS, HONORS: Literary Award from American Academy and Institute of Arts and Letters, 1949; nomination for Academy Award for best screenplay adaptation, Academy of Motion Picture Arts and Sciences, 1951, for *The African Queen;* Pulitzer Prize for fiction (posthumous), 1957, for *A Death in the Family.*

WRITINGS:

Permit Me Voyage (poetry), foreword by Archibald MacLeish, Yale University Press (New Haven, CT), 1934.

Let Us Now Praise Famous Men, photographs by Walker Evans, Houghton Mifflin (Boston, MA), 1941, new edition, with an introduction by John Hersey, 1969, enlarged edition, 2000.

The Quiet One (documentary), Museum of Modern Art, 1949.

The Morning Watch (novel), Houghton Mifflin (Boston, MA), 1951.

A Death in the Family (novel), McDowell, Obolensky, 1957, prologue published separately as *Knoxville, Summer of 1915,* Caliban Press, 1986, reprinted, Vintage Books (New York, NY), 1998.

Agee on Film: Reviews and Comments, McDowell, Obolensky, 1958, published as *Agee on Film: Criticisms and Comments on the Movies,* introduction by David Denby, Modern Library (New York, NY), 2000.

Agee on Film, Volume 2: *Five Film Scripts* (includes *The African Queen,* wirtten with John Huston and adapted from C. S. Forester's novel, United Artists, 1951; *The Bride Comes to Yellow Sky,* adapted from a story by Stephen Crane and included in *Face to Face,* R.K.O., 1953; *White Mane,* Rembrandt Films/Contemporary Films, 1953; *The Night of the Hunter,* adapted from Davis Grubb's novel, United Artists, 1955; and *Green Magic,* Italian Film Exports, 1955), McDowell, Obolensky, 1960.

Letters of James Agee to Father James Flye, edited by James H. Flye, Brazilier (New York, NY), 1962, 2nd edition, Houghton Mifflin (Boston, MA), 1971.

Four Early Stories by James Agee (contains "Boys Will Be Boys," "Death in the Desert," "They That Sow in Sorrow Shall Reap," and "You, Andrew Volstead"), compiled by Elena Harap, etchings by Keith Achepohl, Cummington Press, 1964.

The Collected Short Prose of James Agee, edited by Robert Fitzgerald, Houghton Mifflin (Boston, MA), 1968.

The Collected Poems of James Agee, edited by Robert Fitzgerald, Houghton Mifflin (Boston, MA), 1968.

The Last Letter of James Agee to Father Flye, Godine (Boston, MA), 1969.

Selected Journalism, edited by Paul Ashdown, University of Tennessee Press (Knoxville, TN), 1985.

(Author of poems) Dan Welcher, *Evening Scenes* (printed music), T. Presser (Bryn Mawr, PA), 1986.

Agee: Selected Literary Documents, edited by Victor A. Kramer, Whitston (Troy, NY), 1996.

James Agee: Literary Notebooks and Other Manuscripts, edited by Michael A. Lofaro and Hugh Davis, James Agee Press (Ridgewood, NJ), 2002.

James Agee Rediscovered: The Notebooks for "Let Us Now Praise Famous Men," and Other New Manuscripts, edited by Michael A. Lofaro and Hugh Davis, University of Tennessee Press (Knoxville, TN) 2004.

Work by Agee included in Helen Levitt's *A Way of Seeing,* Duke University Press, 1989. Contributor of scripts to television program *Omnibus,* NBC-TV. Book reviewer for *Time,* 1938-48; film reviewer for *Nation,* 1942-48. Contributor to periodicals, including *Botteghe Oscure, Films,* and *Politics.*

ADAPTATIONS: A Death in the Family was adapted by Tad Mosel as the play *All the Way Home* in 1960 and by Robert W. Lenski in 2001 as a screenplay produced for PBS *Masterpiece Theatre's American Collection,* directed by Gil Cates; *All the Way Home* and passages from *Let Us Now Praise Famous Men* were adapted as an opera by William Mayer in 1983 and recorded on CD as *A Death in the Family,* Albany Records, 2000; "Knoxville, Summer of 1915" (prologue to *A Death in the Family*) was set to music by Samuel Barber; various poems were set to music by David Diamond as *The Fall: A Cycle of Nine Songs for Voice and Piano,* King's Crown Music Press, 1983; "In Memory of My Father," "The Storm," and "A Lullaby" were set to music by Dan Welcher as *Songs for High Voice, Flute, Clarinet, Piano, Percussion, Violin, and Violoncello,* T. Presser, 1986.

SIDELIGHTS: James Agee is described as a wide-ranging, rather self-destructive writer who distinguished himself in poetry, screenplays, and both fiction and nonfiction before dying prematurely at age forty-five. Kenneth Seib, in his volume *James Agee: Promise and Fulfillment,* described Agee as "a versatile and accomplished artist whose mind played freely over all possible media of expression and whose ability with the English language was exceeded by none of his contemporaries."

Agee was born in Knoxville, Tennessee, in 1909, and when he reached age six his father died in an automobile accident. His father's death eventually inspired Agee's autobiographical novel *A Death in the Family,* which ranks among the author's finest works. In his youth Agee attended an Episcopalian boarding school, where he befriended cleric James Harold Flye—his correspondence with Flye was eventually published as *Letters of James Agee to Father James Flye.* Agee then entered Phillips Exeter Academy in New Hampshire, where he developed an enthusiasm for writing. Later, at Harvard University, he showed promise in both poetry and prose. While at Harvard he also became acquainted with visiting instructor I. A. Richards, a literary critic whose notions of narrative immediacy would powerfully influence Agee's own work.

After graduating from Harvard, Agee obtained work as a writer for *Fortune* business magazine. According to W. M. Frohock in *The Novel of Violence in America*, Agee's *Fortune* writings "revealed a craftsman who could lose himself, with complete detachment, in any ephemeral piece of writing which happened to challenge his skill."

The steady income from *Fortune* enabled Agee to concentrate on his poetry. In 1934 he issued *Permit Me Voyage,* a volume that reveals his flair for both stylistic precision and American subject matter. In his introduction to *Permit Me Voyage,* poet and fellow *Fortune* writer Archibald MacLeish commented on Agee's "delicate and perceptive ear" and acknowledged his "technical apprenticeship successfully passed." Horace Gregory, in his *Poetry* review of *Permit Me Voyage,* tempered MacLeish's assessment, but nonetheless acknowledged that "MacLeish's general enthusiasm for James Agee's work is visibly justified," and he called Agee "a genuine poet."

With *Permit Me Voyage,* Agee had made an impressive beginning to his literary career. But he would not yet leave *Fortune,* even though the publication's ardent pro-capitalism was contrary to the beliefs of the leftist Agee. It was through *Fortune* that Agee came to write one of his greatest works, *Let Us Now Praise Famous Men. Fortune* teamed Agee with photographer Walker Evans in 1936, sending the pair to Alabama to do a report on tenant farmers there. The duo's work provided enough material for a sizeable volume and provided a sympathetic look at a way of life rife with suffering, squalor, and economic hardship.

While Evans, in *Let Us Now Praise Famous Men,* documents the tenant farmers with moving, objective photographs, Agee evokes that same way of life in quasi-fictional pieces incorporating shifting narratives and nonchronological episodes. Furthermore, Agee includes comments relating his own concerns in rendering his subjects. "What this technique achieves," Robert E. Burkholder wrote in the *Dictionary of Literary Biography,* "is the feeling that the writer is working from a sincere concern for the peole with whom he has lived and labored."

Upon publication in 1941, *Let Us Now Praise Famous Men*—with Evans's harshly realistic photographs and Agee's technically ambitious prose style—failed to engage an American public increasingly preoccupied with World War II. More recently the book has received recognition not only as a stirring portrait of farm life but as an incisive expression of the artist's dilemma in fashioning that portrait. William Stott, for instance, wrote in his *Documentary Expression and Thirties America* that "*Let Us Now Praise Famous Men* is confessional in a way no documentary had been" and that "Agee's extraordinary participation in the narrative . . . set the book apart from other documentary writing of the thirties." An expanded edition of the book, included sixty-four new archival photographs, was published in 2000. Upon reading the new edition, a *Creative Review* contributor noted that the book remains a classic and commented, "Stylistically, Agee veers from the compact sections describing with minute fascination the physical environment and the waking, sleeping, eating, working, social lives of his hosts, to long, meandering almost stream-of-consciousness passages, expressing his personal response to the situation of the sharecroppers."

While still at work on *Let Us Now Praise Famous Men* in the late 1930s, Agee began writing book reviews for *Time,* and a few years later he became a film critic for *Nation.* His film reviews are distinguished by what Manny Farber, writing in *New Leader,* deemed "an excessive richness." Agee's reviews have been collected in *Agee on Film: Reviews and Comments* and *Agee on Film: Criticism and Comment on the Movies.* In a review of the latter volume for *Library Journal,* Michael Rogers simply stated, "Film heads will jump on this."

In the 1940s, particularly after leaving *Fortune,* Agee supported himself largely through his various magazine writings, including film reviewing. He eventually decided to undertake his own film work, and in 1951 he collaborated with filmmaker John Huston on the script for *The African Queen.* The popular drama tells the story of the unlikely bond that develops between a prim missionary and a profane ship captain in German-occupied Africa. The film, which Agee and Huston adapted from C. S. Forester's novel, received Academy Award nominations for screenplay and direction.

In 1951 Agee also released a modest novel, *The Morning Watch,* about an introspective boy who is preoccupied with spiritual matters and is consequently ostracized by his fellow students. By killing a snake the youthful protagonist gains a measure of acceptance from his peers, but also forfeits a measure of saintliness. "Throughout *The Morning Watch*," Victor A. Kramer noted in *Renascence*, "Agee is most concerned with evoking the complex emotions of particular imagined moments."

During 1951, as Agee worked on *The African Queen* and issued *The Morning Watch*, he suffered a heart attack; others followed the following year, prompting his doctors to advise Agee to temper his alcohol intake and his fast-paced lifestyle. For many months afterward, Agee's health seemed to improve. He continued his work as a screenwriter, penning the short film *The Bride Comes to Yellow Sky*, based on a screenplay he adapted from a story by Stephen Crane. *The Bride Comes to Yellow Sky*, which is included in the two-part film *Face to Face*, concerns a group of citizens in a western town. Among the residents is a kindly ex-convict, played by Agee.

In 1955 Agee was again plagued with heart attacks, sometimes several a day. In early March of that year he endured a particularly painful series of attacks, and died in New York City on May 16, 1955, while riding in a taxi cab. His death came the same year as the release of *The Night of the Hunter*, a film Agee had adapted from Davis Grubb's novel. The movie, directed by noted actor Charles Laughton and starring Lillian Gish and Robert Mitchum, focuses on two children who are terrorized by a psychopath posing as a preacher.

At his death Agee left incomplete an autobiographical novel, *A Death in the Family*. In the novel, a family much like Agee's own must contend with the father's untimely death in an automobile accident. Like *Let Us Now Praise Famous Men*, *A Death in the Family* is narratively complex, focusing on both the death itself and on the son's memories of his father. Robert E. Burkholder, writing in the *Dictionary of Literary Biography*, observed that "the reader is aware of two levels of time working concurrently in the novel." Burkholder noted that "much of the action in *A Death in the Family* is created by an exploration of tensions." He added: "At the center of all these tensions is young Rufus Follet, whom we are led to believe is the narrator. . . . His disguise is that of a young boy, but he is actually a fully-grown and developed artist who will not be limited by speaking through an adolescent persona." The revelation of the narrator as an adult renders *A Death in Family* a tale not just about death, and a

family's consequent reactions to it, but about maturation and the emotional growth of an individual through experiences both good and bad.

A Death in the Family, though incomplete, nonetheless won the 1957 Pulitzer Prize for fiction, and was adapted into both a play and a film airing on the Public Broadcasting System's *Masterpiece Theatre's American Collection* series in 2001. In the years since his death, other of Agee's writings have appeared in print. A collection of screenplays was published in 1960, followed by volumes of poems, short prose, and journalism. With these posthumous publications came recognition for Agee not only as an accomplished stylist and innovative storyteller but also as a profound artist whose works poignantly reflect the human condition. As Victor A. Kramer noted in his book *James Agee*, "the quality of [Agee's] moral vision is a final reason why [his] works have enduring value. He was a writer for whom there was little separation between moral and aesthetic judgments. There was never a question of anything being right if it did not honor the human spirit."

BIOGRAPHICAL AND CRITICAL SOURCES:

BOOKS

Agee, James, *Permit Me Voyage*, foreword by Archibald Macleish, Yale University Press (New Haven, CT), 1934.

Barson, Alfred, *A Way of Seeing: A Critical Study of James Agee*, University of Massachusetts Press, 1972.

Bergreen, Laurence, *James Agee: A Life*, Dutton (New York, NY), 1984.

Boger, Astrid, *Documenting Lives: James Agee's and Walker Evans's "Let Us Now Praise Famous Men,"* P. Lang (New York, NY), 1994.

Dictionary of Literary Biography, Gale (Detroit, MI), Volume 2: *American Novelists since World War II*, 1978, Volume 26: *American Screenwriters*, 1984.

Doty, Mark, *Tell Me Who I Am: James Agee's Search for Selfhood*, Louisiana State University Press, 1981.

Frohock, W. M., *The Novel of Violence in America*, revised edition, Southern Methodist University Press (Austin, TX), 1957, pp. 212-230.

Hynes, Samuel, *Landmarks of American Writing*, edited by Hennig Cohen, Basic Books (New York, NY), pp. 328-330.

Kramer, Victor A., *James Agee*, Twayne (New York, NY), 1975.

Larsen, Erling, *James Agee,* University of Minnesota Press, 1971.

Lowe, James, *The Creative Process of James Agee,* Louisiana State University Press, 1994.

Macdonald, Dwight, *Against the American Grain,* Random House (New York, NY), 1962, pp. 143-159.

Madden, David, editor, *Remembering James Agee,* Louisiana State University Press, 1974.

Moreau, Genevieve, *The Restless Journey of James Agee,* translated by Miriam Kleiger and Morty Schiff, Morrow (New York, NY), 1977.

Seib, Kenneth, *James Agee: Promise and Fulfillment,* University of Pittsburgh Press (Pittsburgh, PA), 1969.

Snyder, John J., *James Agee: A Study of His Film Criticism,* Arno Press (New York, NY), 1977.

Stott, William, *Documentary Expression and Thirties America,* Oxford University Press (New York, NY), 1973, pp. 290-314.

Twentieth-Century Literary Criticism, Gale (Detroit, MI), Volume 1, 1978, Volume 19, 1986.

PERIODICALS

America, December 21, 1991, pp. 490-491.

Antioch Review, winter, 1999, Bruce Jackson, "The Deceptive Anarchy of *Let Us Now Praise Famous Men,*" p. 38.

Chicago Tribune Books, April 30, 1989, pp. 1, 4.

Commonweal, September 12, 1958, pp. 591-592.

Creative Review, July, 2001, "Let Us Praise a Famous Book," p. 68.

Library Journal, February 15, 2000, review of *Agee on Film: Criticism and Comment on the Movies,* p. 203.

Los Angeles Times Book Review, January 12, 1986.

New Leader, December 8, 1958.

New Republic, December 9, 1957, pp. 25-26; December 1, 1958, pp. 18-19; August 13, 1962, pp. 23-24.

Poetry, April, 1935, pp. 48-51; September, 1969.

Publishers Weekly, January 24, 2000, "Let Us Now Praise Evans and Agee," p. 307.

Renascence, summer, 1975, pp. 221-230.

Rolling Stone, March 23, 1989.

Time, April 23, 1951, pp. 119-120.

Village Voice, August 29, 1989, pp. 58-60.

Western Humanities Review, autumn, 1961, pp. 359-367.*

*   *   *

ALTMAN, Suzanne
See ORGEL, Doris

B

BAKER, William 1944-

PERSONAL: Born July 6, 1944, in Shipston-on-Stout, Warwickshire, England; naturalized U.S. citizen; son of Stanley Cohen (a publisher) and Mabel (a homemaker; maiden name, Woolf) Baker; married Rivka Frank (a nurse), November 16, 1969; children: Sharon, Karen. *Education:* University of Sussex, B.A. (with honors), 1966; Royal Holloway College, London, M.Phil., 1970; University of London, Ph.D., 1973; Loughborough University of Technology, postgraduate diploma in library and information studies, 1981, M.L. S., 1987. *Religion:* Jewish. *Hobbies and other interests:* Collecting books and manuscripts, music, opera, walking, cricket.

ADDRESSES: Home—DeKalb, IL. *Office*—Department of English, University Libraries, Northern Illinois University, DeKalb, IL 60115-2868; fax: 815-753-2003. *E-mail*—wbaker@niu.edu.

CAREER: City Literary Institute, London, England, lecturer in English, 1967-71; Ben-Gurion University of the Negev, Beersheva, Israel, lecturer, 1971-77; University of Kent at Canterbury, Canterbury, England, lecturer, 1977-78; West Midlands College of Higher Education, senior lecturer, 1978-85; Clifton College, Bristol, England, housemaster, 1986-89; Northern Illinois University, DeKalb, associate professor, 1989-94, professor of English, 1994—. Thurrock Technical College, lecturer, 1969-71; Hebrew University of Jerusalem, lecturer, 1973-75; Pitzer College, visiting professor, 1981-82.

MEMBER: Modern Language Association of America (member of executive committee of Discussion Group on Bibliographical and Textual Studies, 1994-98; chair,

William Baker

1997-98), American Library Association, Society for Textual Scholarship, Bibliographical Society of America (founding chair of English and American Literature Section, 1992-93; member of council, 2002-05), British Library Association, George Eliot Fellowship, Wilkie Collins Society.

AWARDS, HONORS: British Academy, fellowship, 1978-79, grant, 1981; Ball Brothers Foundation fellow at Lilly Library, Indiana University—Bloomington,

1993; fellow, Bibliographical Society of America, 1994-95; Illinois Cooperative Collection grant, 1997; grant from American Philosophical Society, 1997; book of the year award, *Choice*, 2000, for *The Letters of Wilkie Collins;* fellow of National Endowment for the Humanities, 2002-03.

WRITINGS:

(With others) *Harold Pinter,* Oliver & Boyd (Edinburgh, Scotland), 1973.

Critics on George Eliot, Allen & Unwin (London, England), 1973.

George Eliot and Judaism, University of Salzburg (Salzburg, Austria), 1975.

Some George Eliot Notebooks: An Edition of the Carl H. Pforzheimer Library's George Eliot Holograph Notebooks, Mss 707, 708, 709, 710, 711, four volumes, University of Salzburg (Salzburg, Austria), 1976-85.

The George Eliot—George Henry Lewes Library, Garland Publishing (New York, NY), 1977.

The Libraries of George Eliot and G. H. Lewes, University of Victoria (Victoria, British Columbia, Canada), 1981.

Shakespeare: The Merchant of Venice, Pan Brodie (London, England), 1985.

Shakespeare: Antony and Cleopatra, Pan Books (London, England), 1985, revised edition, 1991.

(With John Kimber and M. B. Kinch) *F. R. Leavis and Q. D. Leavis: An Annotated Bibliography,* Garland Publishing (New York, NY), 1989.

The Early History of the London Library, Edwin Mellen (Lewiston, NY), 1992.

(Editor) *The Letters of George Henry Lewes,* University of Victoria (Victoria, British Columbia, Canada), Volumes 1-2, 1995, Volume 3 (with new letters by George Eliot), 1999.

(Editor, with J. H. Alexander) *Sir Walter Scott: Tales of a Grandfather; The History of France,* Second Series, Northern Illinois University Press (DeKalb, IL), 1996.

(Editor, with J. Wolfreys) *Literary Theories: A Case Study in Critical Performance,* New York University Press (New York, NY), 1996.

(With Kenneth Womack) *Recent Work in Critical Theory, 1989-1995: An Annotated Bibliography,* Greenwood Press (Westport, CT), 1996.

(Associate editor) *New Dictionary of National Biography,* Clarendon Press (Oxford, England), 1996-2005.

(Editor, with Kenneth Womack) *Dictionary of Literary Biography,* Volume 184: *Nineteenth-Century British Bibliographers and Book Collectors,* Gale (Detroit, MI), 1997.

(Editor, with William M. Clarke) *The Letters of Wilkie Collins,* St. Martin's Press (New York, NY), 1999.

(Editor, with Kenneth Womack) *Dictionary of Literary Biography,* Volume 213: *Pre-Nineteenth-Century British Book Collectors and Bibliographers,* Gale (Detroit, MI), 1999.

(Editor, with Kenneth Womack) *Dictionary of Literary Biography,* Volume 201: *Twentieth-Century British Book Collectors and Bibliographers,* Gale (Detroit, MI), 1999.

(Compiler, with Kenneth Womack) *Twentieth-Century Bibliography and Textual Criticism: An Annotated Bibliography,* foreword by T. H. Howard-Hill Greenwood Press (Westport, CT), 2000.

(Editor, with Kenneth Womack) George Eliot, *Felix Holt, the Radical,* Broadview Press (Peterborough, Ontario, Canada), 2000.

(With John C. Ross) *George Eliot: A Bibliographical History,* Oak Knoll Press (London, England), 2002.

Wilkie Collins's Library: A Reconstruction, Greenwood Press (Westport, CT), 2002.

(Editor, with Kenneth Womack) *Companion to the Victorian Novel,* Greenwood Press (Westport, CT), 2002.

(Editor, with Kenneth Womack) Ford Madox Ford, *The Good Soldier: A Tale of Passion,* Broadview Press (Peterborough, Ontario, Canada), 2003.

(Editor) *Nineteenth-Century Travels, Explorations, and Empires: Writings from the Era of Imperial Consolidation, 1835-1910,* Volume 2: *North America,* Pickering & Chatto (London, England), 2003.

Contributor to encyclopedias and other reference books. Contributor of more than 150 articles and reviews to periodicals, including *Library Review, Style, Notes and Queries, English Studies, Analytical and Enumerative Bibliography,* and *Thackeray Newsletter.* Editor, *George Eliot—George Henry Lewes Studies,* 1982—; coeditor, *The Year's Work in English Studies,* 2002; member of editorial advisory board, *Interdisciplinary Studies,* 1999—.

WORK IN PROGRESS: Editing *Wilkie Collins's Letters,* four volumes, for Pickering & Chatto (London, England); editing *The Merchant of Venice,* for "Shakespeare the Critical Tradition Series," Continuum (London, England); *Harold Pinter: A Bibliographical History,* British Library (London, England); *Reading Shakespeare: A Study of Responses to Shakespeare.*

SIDELIGHTS: William Baker once told *CA:* "Since the early 1970s I have been engaged in nineteenth- and twentieth-century British literary study. My emphasis has been on the description, interpretation, discovery, and editing of unique and important primary documents from the period, the scholarly reconstruction from the primary evidence of the libraries (that is, the books owned) of famous writers, and the authoritative itemization of the achievements of some of the most distinguished literary figures of the period. My research has been primarily embodied in monographs, analytical and descriptive bibliographies, bibliographical histories, and more than 150 articles, as well as a large number of reviews and notes. I have also edited several scholarly volumes.

"In 1997 *Nineteenth-Century British Bibliographers and Book-Collectors* was published. The volume, the first of its kind, contains original essays from thirty-two scholars drawn from three continents: the Americas, Europe, and the Antipodes. This is the first to be published of three volumes that will analyze, assess, and describe the achievements of British book collectors and bibliographers. I have commissioned contributions from all over the world for what are pioneering studies, to which I have also contributed. This project allows me to combine my avocational and professional interests: book and manuscript collecting and bibliography. I am fortunate professionally to hold a joint university appointment in the English department and the university libraries. This allows me to research, teach, and acquire and maintain research materials.

"I enjoy reviewing, which I regard as a neglected art. Reviewing hones writing skills, keeps one abreast of the latest developments, and of course provides a source for books and CD-ROM discs. I try to produce around a thousand words a day on something or other. That at least is my aim, and I feel satisfied when such a goal has been achieved. I am excited by discovery, editing, transcribing documents (especially letters), reconstructing libraries, and writing about book collecting and bibliography." More recently Baker added, "Bibliographical history—represented for instance by the well-received *George Eliot: A Bibliographical His-*

tory—is a fascinating challenge. This work took over twenty-five years to complete. I am now engaged in a similar task on Harold Pinter. It will also be a product of more than twenty-five years of work and engagement."

In his original comments to *CA,* Baker also wrote: "I love classical music and opera—discovered in America. Opera was inaccessible in England: too expensive or limited primarily to London. The Chicago Lyric season is wonderful and not to be missed. Truth to me is preferable to fiction. I suppose I am a frustrated novelist and poet. The novels I have within me would be based on experience, though many wouldn't believe them! Research and writing satisfy a deep inner need for self-expression."

BIOGRAPHICAL AND CRITICAL SOURCES:

PERIODICALS

Choice, October, 1997, p. 291.
New York Times Book Review, February 13, 2000, Sarah Harrison Smith, review of *The Letters of Wilkie Collins,* p. 20.
Nineteenth-Century Literature, March, 1997, p. 565; June, 2000, review of *The Letters of Wilkie Collins,* p. 145.
Scottish Literary Journal, spring, 1997, pp. 23-25.
Spectator, August 7, 1999, B. Hillier, review of *The Letters of Wilkie Collins,* pp. 27-33.
Sunday Times (London, England), August 15, 1999, D. Grylls, review of *The Letters of Wilkie Collins,* pp. 6-7.
Times Literary Supplement, February 14, 1997, p. 24; October 8, 1999, J. Bowen, review of *The Letters of Wilkie Collins,* p. 26; October 25, 2002, p. 30.
Victorian Periodicals Review, winter, 2000, George V. Griffith, review of *The Letters of George Henry Lewes,* Volume 3, pp. 413-414.
Wilkie Collins Society Newsletter, summer, 1999, P. Lewis and A. Gasson, review of *The Letters of Wilkie Collins,* pp. 1-2.

*   *   *

BARRY, Dave 1947-

PERSONAL: Born July 3, 1947, in Armonk, NY; son of David W. and Marion Barry; married Elizabeth Lenox Pyle, 1975 (marriage ended); married Michelle Kaufman, 1996; children: Robert, Sophie. *Education:* Haverford College, B.A., 1969.

Dave Barry

ADDRESSES: Office—*Miami Herald,* 1 Herald Plaza, Miami, FL 33132-1693.

CAREER: Daily Local News, West Chester, PA, reporter, 1971-75; worked for Associated Press, Philadelphia, PA, 1975-76; lecturer on effective writing for businesses for R. S. Burger Associates (consulting firm), 1975-83; freelance humor columnist, beginning 1980; *Miami Herald,* Miami, FL, humor columnist, 1983—.

AWARDS, HONORS: Distinguished Writing Award, American Society of Newspaper Editors, 1986; Pulitzer Prize for commentary, 1988.

WRITINGS:

The Taming of the Screw: Several Million Homeowners' Problems Sidestepped, illustrated by Jerry O'Brien, Rodale Press (Emmaus, PA), 1983.

Babies and Other Hazards of Sex: How to Make a Tiny Person in Only Nine Months, with Tools You Probably Have around the Home, illustrated by Jerry O'Brien, Rodale Press (Emmaus, PA), 1984.

Bad Habits: A 100-Percent Fact-Free Book, Doubleday (New York, NY), 1985.

Stay Fit and Healthy until You're Dead, illustrated by Jerry O'Brien, Rodale Press (Emmaus, PA), 1985.

Claw Your Way to the Top: How to Become the Head of a Major Corporation in Roughly a Week, illustrated by Jerry O'Brien, Rodale Press (Emmaus, PA), 1986.

Dave Barry's Guide to Marriage and/or Sex, illustrated by Jerry O'Brien, Rodale Press (Emmaus, PA), 1987.

Dave Barry's Greatest Hits, Crown (New York, NY), 1988.

Homes and Other Black Holes: The Happy Homeowner's Guide, illustrated by Jeff McNelly, Fawcett (New York, NY), 1988.

Dave Barry Slept Here: A Sort of History of the United States, Random House (Garden City, NY), 1989.

Dave Barry Turns Forty, Crown (New York, NY), 1990.

Dave Barry Talks Back, Crown (New York, NY), 1991.

Dave Barry's Only Travel Guide You'll Ever Need, Fawcett (New York, NY), 1991.

Davy Barry's Guide to Life, illustrated by Jerry O'Brien, Wings Books (New York, NY), 1991.

Dave Barry Does Japan = Deibu Bari ga "Nihon o Suru," Random House (Garden City, NY), 1992.

Dave Barry Is Not Making This Up, cartoons by Jeff MacNelly, Crown (New York, NY), 1994.

Dave Barry's Gift Guide to End All Gift Guides, Crown (New York, NY), 1994.

The World According to Dave Barry, Wings Books (New York, NY), 1994.

Dave Barry's Complete Guide to Guys: A Fairly Short Book, Random House (Garden City, NY), 1995.

Dave Barry in Cyberspace, Crown (New York, NY), 1996.

(With Jeff MacNelly) *A Golf Handbook: All I Ever Learned I Forgot by the Third Fairway,* Triumph Books (Chicago, IL), 1997.

Dave Barry Is from Mars and Venus, Crown (New York, NY), 1997.

Dave Barry's Book of Bad Songs, Andrews McMeel (Kansas City, MO), 1997.

Dave Barry Turns Fifty, Crown (New York, NY), 1998.

Big Trouble, Putnam (New York, NY), 1999.

Dave Barry Is Not Taking This Sitting Down!, Crown (New York, NY), 2000.

The Greatest Invention in the History of Mankind Is Beer; and Other Many Insights from Dave Barry, Andrews McMeel (Kansas City, MO), 2001.

My Teenage Son's Goal in Life Is Making Me Feel 3,500 Years Old; and Other Thoughts on Parenting from Dave Barry, Andrews McMeel (Kansas City, MO), 2001.

Dave Barry Hits below the Beltway: A Vicious and Unprovoked Attack on Our Most Cherished Political Institutions, Random House (New York, NY), 2001.

Tricky Business (novel), Putnam (New York NY), 2002.

Boogers Are My Beat: More Lies, but Some Actual Journalism, Crown (New York, NY), 2002.

ADAPTATIONS: Big Trouble was adapted as a motion picture, directed by Barry Sonnenfeld, starring Tim Allen and Rene Russo, and released by Touchstone in 2001.

WORK IN PROGRESS: A children's book collaboration with suspense novelist Ridley Pearson.

SIDELIGHTS: Dave Barry ranks as one of America's most popular humor columnists; his lighthearted and often outrageous observations on the foibles of middle-class America helped to win him the 1988 Pulitzer Prize for commentary. Barry is based at the *Miami Herald,* but since 1986 his column has been syndicated in more than 150 newspapers nationwide. The humorist attracts a large, loyal readership because he finds and exaggerates the irony in situations average people experience on a daily basis. The subjects of his columns are limitless; any event or popular trend that strikes Barry as silly or worthy of ridicule can become the focus of his scrutiny—the adventures of buying and maintaining a home, raising children, or facing rush-hour traffic.

Before becoming a full-time columnist, Barry worked as a journalist for the *Daily Local News* in West Chester, Pennsylvania, and the Associated Press, then spent several years conducting writing seminars for businesspeople. The opportunity to contribute humor columns to the *Daily Local News* as a freelancer gave Barry the chance to indulge in his satirical observations. By 1983 his column appeared in the *Miami Herald.* That same year he published his first book of humor, *The Taming of the Screw: Several Mil-*

lion Homeowners' Problems Sidestepped. Barry has since produced many other books, including *Dave Barry's Greatest Hits,* a collection of previously published columns, and two titles that reached the *New York Times* best-seller list, *Dave Barry Slept Here: A Sort of History of the United States* and *Dave Barry Turns Forty.*

Dave Barry Slept Here offers Barry's unorthodox history of the United States, spoofing, among other things, history textbooks and classes and Americans'—including the author's—general ignorance of the subject. Barry boasts that the book skips most wars, is completely free of facts which he considers boring, and offers an ingenious cure for remembering historical dates: all events occur on October 8, which coincides with his son's birthday. Further humor derives from amusing chapter headings, useless footnotes, outrageous discussion questions, and an unusual index, with such helpful references as "Louis the Somethingth." *Washington Post* reviewer John Sladek pronounced the book "a dazzling performance" and *New York Times Book Review* critic Richard Lingeman lauded Barry's "irreverent eye." *Dave Barry Turns Forty* describes, from Barry's very personal point of view, the problems that arise when facing middle age.

A family trip to Japan became the inspiration for *Dave Barry Does Japan.* Jonathan Rauch commented in the *Washington Post Book World* that Barry "is funny on Japan, but like all good humorists he is also, in his twisted way, truthful and merciless." Barry comments on the strangeness of Japanese society and custom with satirical description of bathhouses, Japanese business ethos, Tokyo taxis, the exorbitant expenses associated with daily life, and the peculiar assimilation of Western culture in Japan. *New York Times Book Review* critic Robert J. Collins noted, "As Mr. Barry makes clear, Japanese and Americans do the same things for different reasons, and different things for the same reason." Barry's observations of Japan's "alien culture" are presented "with style, grace, true wit and a sense of humanity (though slightly warped)," according to Collins.

Barry branched out from his series of nonfiction humor books to write the novels *Big Trouble* and *Tricky Business.* *Big Trouble* is set in the criminal underworld of Miami, and *Tricky Business* takes place on a casino cruise. Both novels have a huge cast of characters, all of whom are involved in arresting, killing, influencing, or lusting after one another, and who all end up in various absurd situations. In the *Houston Chronicle,* Jim Barlow noted, "Plot is not a strong point with Barry. Funny is." Some critics, however, found that Barry's humor did not overcome his lack of strong plots and roundly depicted characters. In the *New York Times,* John Leland wrote that in *Tricky Business,* Barry's use of stock details to characterize people and institutions "serves him well in his columns, which tame the chaos of an unruly world by reducing it to a familiar comedy of manners," but that in fiction, this technique makes the story feel "mechanical and enclosed." Bob Longino wrote in the *Atlanta Journal-Constitution* that both novels were "fast-paced, bullet-riddled and steeped with Barry's cynical wit," and in the same publication, Phil Kloer commented that *Big Trouble* "is a very funny novel, with more laughs per chapter than most of Barry's twenty or so nonfiction books."

Barry's 2003 collection of columns, *Boogers Are My Beat: More Lies, but Some Actual Journalism,* continues in his trademark humorous vein, this time in discussions of everything from the Olympic games, the Florida election recall, income taxes, and Gary Condit to airport security, guest towels, Yorkshire terriers, and Humvees. "For the most part, the humor is in the title," remarked *Library Journal* reviewer Necia Parker-Gibson, "but it is intended to get the audience's attention so that Barry can make his political or personal points rather than shock his audience." In *Booklist,* Kristine Huntley commented that "Barry has never been as funny as he is in this rip-roaring new collection of columns." On a rare serious note, Barry includes two essays written after the September 11, 2001 attacks on the World Trade Center. Of these essays, and the book in general, Huntley concluded, "Whether funny or serious, Barry is always on target."

"What makes Mr. Barry funny? Easy," wrote *New York Times Book Review* contributor Alison Teal in a review of *Dave Barry's Greatest Hits.* "He grew up in an all-WASP upper-middle-class neighborhood, played Little League baseball, mowed his parents' lawn and . . . attended the Episcopal Church. . . . He gets his humor from the blandest slice of American pie." Teal added of Barry, "He has a gift for taking things at face value and rendering them funny on those grounds alone, for squeezing every ounce of humor out of a perfectly ordinary experience."

Barry once told an interviewer: "I always wanted to write when I was a kid; it just never occurred to me

that you could have a job that didn't involve any actual work. When I wrote for my high school and college newspapers, I pretty much made stuff up. . . . I felt it would be fun to have a job like that where you could make stuff up and be irresponsible and get paid for it, but there were no openings for making stuff up when I got out of college, so I went to work for a small newspaper called the *Daily Local News. . . .* The result was that I wrote several years' worth of stories that nobody read but me, and sometimes even I didn't read all the way to the end of them. After a few years in this small-time newspaper business, I went briefly to the Associated Press. I really didn't like that. It was very restrictive." Once he turned from straight journalism to column-writing, things turned more interesting. "Just about anything's a topic for a humor column: any event that occurs in the news, anything that happens in daily life driving, shopping, reading, eating," Barry explained. "You can look at just about anything and see humor in it somewhere. The hard part is getting the jokes to come, and it never happens all at once for me. I very rarely have any idea where a column is going to go when it starts. It's a matter of piling a little piece here and a little piece there, fitting them together, going on to the next part, then going back and gradually shaping the whole piece into something. . . . That's what writing is. That's why it's so painful and slow. But that's more technique than anything else. You don't rely on inspiration I don't, anyway, and I don't think most writers do. The creative process is just not an inspirational one for most people. There's a little bit of that and a whole lot of polishing. . . . I don't worry about running out of ideas, drying up. The world's too full of things to write about for that to ever happen."

BIOGRAPHICAL AND CRITICAL SOURCES:

PERIODICALS

American Spectator, September, 1989; December 1993, p. 25.
Atlanta Journal-Constitution, September 19, 1999, review of *Big Trouble,* p. L15; October 17, 2002, Bob Longino, review of *Tricky Business,* p. E1.
Book, November-December, 2002, Steve Wilson, review of *Tricky Business,* p. 87.
Booklist, August, 1999, Brad Hooper, review of *Big Trouble,* p. 1984; August, 2000, Gilbert Taylor, review of *Dave Barry Is Not Taking This Sitting*

Down!, p. 2068; August, 2001, Kristine Huntley, review of *Dave Barry Hits below the Beltway: A Vicious and Unprovoked Attack on Our Most Cherished Political Institutions,* p. 2043; September 1, 2002, Kristine Huntley, review of *Tricky Business,* p. 4; July, 2003, Kristine Huntley, review of *Boogers Are My Beat: More Lies, but Some Actual Journalism,* p. 1842.

Chicago Tribune, June 16, 1989; May 14, 1990.

Entertainment Weekly, September 10, 1999, L.S. Klepp, review of *Big Trouble,* p. 143; April 12, 2002, Lisa Schwarzbaum, review of *Big Trouble,* p. 49.

Houston Chronicle, September 19, 1999, Jim Barlow, review of *Big Trouble,* p. 23.

Kirkus Reviews, September 15, 1999, A. J. Anderson, review of *Big Trouble,* p. 110; August 15, 2001, review of *Dave Barry Hits below the Beltway,* p. 1180; August 15, 2002, review of *Tricky Business,* p. 1155; July 15, 2003, review of *Boogers Are My Beat,* p. 960.

Knight Ridder/Tribune News Service, October 9, 2002, Charles Matthews, review of *Tricky Business,* p. K7414; November 6, 2002, Chauncey Mabe, review of *Tricky Business,* p. K0634.

Library Journal, September 15, 2000, Joe Accardi, review of *Dave Barry Is Not Taking This Sitting Down!,* p. 74; October 1, 2001, A. J. Anderson, review of *Dave Barry Hits below the Beltway,* p. 97; September 15, 2002, A. J. Anderson, review of *Tricky Business,* p. 88; August, 2003, Necia Parker-Gibson, review of *Boogers Are My Beat,* p. 82.

Los Angeles Times, September 12, 1999, review of *Big Trouble,* p. NA.

Los Angeles Times Book Review, August 21, 1994, p. 6; July 23, 1995, p. 6.

New York Times, April 5, 2002, Elvis Mitchell, review of *Big Trouble,* p. E10; October 6, 2002, John Leland, review of *Tricky Business,* p. 2; October 14, 2002, Christopher Buckley, review of *Tricky Business,* p. E1.

New York Times Book Review, April 28, 1985, p. 25; October 9, 1988; June 18, 1989; October 25, 1992, p. 17; June 19, 1994, p. 33; October 13, 1996, p. 68.

People, September 11, 1989.

Publishers Weekly, August 26, 1996, p. 86; July 19, 1999, review of *Big Trouble,* p. 180; September 4, 2000, review of *Dave Barry Is Not Taking This Sitting Down!,* p. 94; September 9, 2002, review of *Tricky Business,* p. 42; October 21, 2002, Daisy Marylea, review of *Tricky Business,* p. 20; June 23, 2003, review of *Boogers Are My Beat,* p. 56; September 15, 2003, John F. Baker, "Authors Team Up for Kids' Book," p. 14.

St. Louis Post-Dispatch, April 5, 2002, Harper Barnes, review of *Big Trouble,* p. E3.

School Library Journal, February, 2002, Pam Johnson, review of *Dave Barry Hits below the Beltway,* p. 155.

Time, July 3, 1989; October 4, 1999, interview with Barry, p. 111.

Tribune Books (Chicago, IL), April 23, 1995, p. 51.

Washington Post, July 1, 1988; June 12, 1989; November 8, 1992, p. 9.

ONLINE

Dave Barry's Official Web site, http://www.davebarry.com/ (November 17, 2003).

Miami Herald Online, http://www.miami.com/ (November 26, 2003), "Columnists: Dave Barry."

Random House Web site, http://www.randomhouse.com/ (November 26, 2003).

Sacramento Bee Online, http://www.sacbee.com/ (November 26, 2003), "Opinion: Dave Barry."*

*   *   *

BAUCHART
  See CAMUS, Albert

*   *   *

BEAN, Normal
  See BURROUGHS, Edgar Rice

*   *   *

BENNETT, James (W.) 1942-

PERSONAL: Born 1942; married; wife's name Judith; children: Jason. *Education:* Wesleyan University, B.A., 1964; attended graduate school at Illinois State University, 1966. *Hobbies and other interests:* Mythology, photography.

ADDRESSES: Home—306 West Division St., Normal, IL 61761. *E-mail*—jwbnnt@aol.com.

James Bennett

CAREER: Writer. Worked as a teacher of creative writing at a community college until 1976; aide to high school-aged mentally handicapped students, Bloomington, IL, 1983-95. Writer-in-residence, Illinois secondary schools.

AWARDS, HONORS: "1995's Finest YA Novel" citation, *Voice of Youth Advocates,* 1996, for *The Squared Circle.*

WRITINGS:

A Quiet Desperation, Thomas Nelson (Nashville, TN), 1983.
The Flex of the Thumb, Pin Oak Press (Springfield, IL), 1996.
Old Hoss: A Fictional Baseball Biography of Charles Radbourn, McFarland (Jefferson, NC), 2002.

YOUNG ADULT NOVELS

I Can Hear the Mourning Dove, Houghton Mifflin (Boston, MA), 1990.
Dakota Dream, Scholastic (New York, NY), 1994.

The Squared Circle, Scholastic (New York, NY), 1995.
Blue Star Rapture, Simon & Schuster (New York, NY), 1998.
Plunking Reggie Jackson, Simon & Schuster (New York, NY), 2001.
Faith Wish, Holiday House (New York, NY), 2003.

SIDELIGHTS: Writer James Bennett draws heavily on personal experience in his novels for young adult readers. His high school-aged protagonists are often emotionally or intellectually confused individuals unable to summon the emotional strength to deal with the circumstances that confront them in school, at home, and in other social situations. Only the caring, compassionate support of others can provide Bennett's characters with a resilient lifeline to adulthood. "I would like my readers to recognize that the handicapped are not throw-away people," Bennett told *Publishers Weekly* interviewer Lynda Brill Comerford. "Within them lies enormous courage and a strong nourishing drive."

Bennett's experiences as an intern for a local newspaper during his undergraduate studies in Illinois prompted his first thoughts of becoming a writer. Subsequent graduate studies in English at Illinois State University led Bennett to a career teaching creative writing to community college students. In 1975, however, Bennett suffered an emotional breakdown; during his recovery in a psychiatric hospital, he began to view writing as a way of expressing his feelings and promoting an increased awareness of the plight of many who are challenged by mental and emotional disorders.

During the period of his own hospitalization in the late 1970s, Bennett was particularly troubled by the acquaintance of a young woman, a fellow patient who was notably emotionally withdrawn. *I Can Hear the Mourning Dove,* his first novel, is based on his impressions of that young woman. "I knew nothing about the girl's background or diagnosis," Bennett explained to Comerford. "She was difficult to approach, but I realized that it was worth the effort to get through her shy exterior and discover the human being inside." In addition to recreating the young patient's speech and mannerisms—both on and off medication—in his novel, Bennett had to do some extensive research into the world of female adolescents to realistically portray his young heroine. Three years of effort culminated in

Bennett's first highly praised work for young adults. Published in 1990, *I Can Hear the Mourning Dove* is the story of Grace Braun, a sixteen-year-old "crazy wild" adolescent attempting to return to the outside world after spending several weeks in the supportive environment of a hospital psychiatric unit following her most recent unsuccessful attempt at suicide. This was not Grace's first stay in a psychiatric ward: she has suffered from periods of depression for many years. The recent death of her father and the stressful transition to a new school add to the young woman's difficulties in readjusting to "normal" teen life after her release; unfortunately, it takes only the hateful actions of a group of rowdy, uncaring teens to send her back to the hospital in a highly depressed state. Fortunately, Grace's condition improves with the help of her psychiatrist, her mother, and Luke Wolf, a brash and angry teen hospitalized in police custody after he knowingly killed a paralyzed friend. "Few novels written for teenagers have dared to probe as deeply into mental illness" as *I Can Hear the Mourning Dove,* according to Stephanie Zvirin, who praised Bennett's novel in *Booklist.* "With tenderness and remarkable insight, Bennett identifies the causes and effects of Grace's suffering," noted a *Publishers Weekly* reviewer.

In the novel *Dakota Dream,* teen protagonist Floyd Rayfield has replaced his early childhood memories of his natural mother and father with those of a long sequence of foster families and group homes. With a desperate need to belong somewhere, fifteen-year-old Floyd creates an internal sense of being a part of something by convincing himself that he is really a misplaced Dakota Indian; his main goal now becomes escaping the foster care system and joining "his people." Stealing a motorcycle, the young man makes an eight-hundred-mile journey to the Dakota tribe's Pine Ridge Reservation, where a vision quest taken with Chief Bear-in-Cave and the active intervention of a naive but compassionate social worker help him to understand the real reasons for his fight against inflexible teachers and insensitive social workers. A *Kirkus Reviews* critic praised *Dakota Dream,* writing that the "dynamics between a thoughtful boy struggling to keep his unique spark alive and the oblivious public employees doing their best to quench it are poignantly realized." Deborah Stevenson of the *Bulletin of the Center for Children's Books* maintained that "this is a measured, serious story and Floyd, not your stereotypical problem kid, is admirable in his devotion and application." *Voice of Youth Advocates* contributor Shirley Carmony added: "Floyd is finely drawn and comes painfully alive for the reader."

Like Bennett's other novels, 1995's *The Squared Circle* features a teen struggling to deal with a series of emotional problems. This time, though, Sonny Youngblood must also try to cope with his mother's mental breakdown as she spirals toward hospitalization. Basketball provides the eighteen-year-old high school senior with an escape, and when his obsession with the game helps him to earn a sports scholarship to a university, it appears that he is on the verge of burying his troubles for good. But life becomes more complicated as a growing friendship with his cousin, a university art professor, and Sonny's firsthand freshman-year experience with big-time college sports and all of its trappings propel him toward self-understanding and maturity. "Interwoven around gritty, occasionally brutish, guys-only scenes of fraternity hazing, basketball team practice, and tension-filled games is an acutely perceptive account of a young man's emotional and intellectual awakening," asserted a *Publishers Weekly* reviewer. Calling the novel "a sobering read," Tom S. Hurlburt recommended in a *School Library Journal* review that *The Squared Circle* "should be thrust into the hands of any high school students who are contemplating playing revenue-producing sports" at large colleges or universities. "It is difficult to adequately describe the power of this book," exclaimed Dorothy M. Broderick in *Voice of Youth Advocates.* "It is a masterpiece."

In *Blue Star Rapture,* Bennett further examines issues related to unrealistic demands placed on teenagers and on corruption in scouting and recruiting of collegiate athletes. In the book, T. J. Nucci and his friend Tyron receive invitations to attend a high-profile basketball camp swarming with reporters, college recruiters, and others all making tempting offers to budding college stars. Though Tyron suffers from a learning disability, the six-foot-nine ballplayer is a talented athlete, with a natural skill that heralds a promising future in the professional ranks. T. J. lacks Tyron's innate abilities with the ball but is still approached by several recruiters and agents. Suspicious of their motives, T. J. soon realizes that the coaches and recruiters are interested in him not for any athletic ability but for his influence over the sometimes volatile Tyron. They want T. J. to help persuade Tyron to accept particular offers or attend particular schools. Overwhelmed by the pressure and the blatant unethical behavior surrounding him, T. J. goes for a walk to clear his thoughts and in the process meets LuAnn, a troubled attendee at a religious camp adjacent to the basketball camp. The camp that LuAnn attends is little more than a religious cult, and her own fragile psychological condition, out-of-wedlock pregnancy, and intense manipulation by the cult lead her to commit suicide. T. J. finds the unethical sports recruiting to be as despicable as the religious brainwashing and confronts issues of his own self-preservation versus his long-term role as T. J.'s unofficial protector. "Rarely in YA fiction is a protagonist as authentic as T. J.," thought Roger Leslie in *Booklist.* "He is an admirable, thoroughly believable character with a solid moral core." A *Publishers Weekly* reviewer noted that "while the pitfalls of religious fanaticism are clearly drawn, the ills of sports recruitment are more ambiguous." Although Mary Ann Capan, writing in *Voice of Youth Advocates,* remarked that the individual issues of the book were not explored in sufficient depth, she went on to claim, "This issue-laden novel honestly explores the politics of college sports recruitment."

Plunking Reggie Jackson also addresses the harmful effects of a too-deep obsession with sports and athletic achievement. Coley Burke is on top of the world at his central Illinois high school. One of the popular kids, Coley is a talented baseball player with a beautiful girlfriend and a promising future of a college athletic scholarship, or maybe an offer to join a pro team directly from high school. But when Coley's grades begin to slip, jeopardizing his scholastic eligibility to play, his world begins to collapse around him. His difficult and overbearing father—a man so obsessed with baseball that he keeps a life-sized bronze statue of Reggie Jackson in his back yard—begins to criticize and pressure him intensely. Unresolved issues surrounding the earlier death of his older brother, Patrick—a major league ballplayer—threaten to damage Coley and his family. Eventually, Coley's poor grades and a severe ankle injury confine him to the bench and make him ineligible to play during some critical games. Coley must find a way to overcome the abundant guilt, sadness, and pressure facing him from all sides or be destroyed before his career can even begin. "The ambitious novel borders on soap opera at times," commented Shelle Rosenfeld in *Booklist.* However, Rosenfeld praised the "straightforward prose," the appeal of the baseball background, and the "portrait of a teen's self-doubts." A *Publishers Weekly* reviewer remarked that Bennett "provides a frank, insightful psychological study of a troubled teen." Elizabeth Bush, reviewing the book in *Bulletin of the Center for Children's Books,* commented that *Plunking Reggie Jackson* relies too much on "stock plotlines pumped dry for dramatic effect and then swept tidily under the carpet." Despite that complaint, however, Bush noted that "There's just enough genuine baseball action, however, to keep sports enthusiasts turning the pages, and teens whose tastes run to daytime drama might even find some guilty pleasures here." Although Todd Morning, writing in *School Library Journal,* found the ending "abrupt and simplistic," he found that Bennett nonetheless "presents characters that are compelling and real, against a realistic background of high school life and sports action."

BIOGRAPHICAL AND CRITICAL SOURCES:

PERIODICALS

Booklist, January 15, 1991, Stephanie Zvirin, review of *I Can Hear the Mourning Dove,* p. 1052; January 15, 1994, p. 918; December 15, 1995, Susan Dove Lempke, review of *The Squared Circle,* p. 697; April 15, 1998, Roger Leslie, review of *Blue Star Rapture,* p. 1438; April 1, 2001, Shelle Rosenfeld, review of *Plunking Reggie Jackson,* p. 1458.
Book Report, January-February, 1999, Harolyn Legg, review of *Blue Star Rapture,* p. 59.
Bulletin of the Center for Children's Books, February, 1994, Deborah Stevenson, review of *Dakota Dream,* p. 192; February, 2001, Elizabeth Bush, review of *Plunking Reggie Jackson,* pp. 214-215.
Kirkus Reviews, February 1, 1994, review of *Dakota Dream,* p. 138; November 1, 1995; March 1, 1998, p. 334.
Publishers Weekly, July 13, 1990, review of *I Can Hear the Mourning Dove,* p. 57; December 21, 1990, Lynda Brill Comerford, "Flying Starts: New Faces of 1990," interview with James W. Bennett, p. 15; November 20, 1995, review of *The Squared Circle,* p. 79; March 30, 1998, review of *Blue Star Rapture,* pp. 83-84; January 1, 2001, review of *Plunking Reggie Jackson,* p. 94.
School Library Journal, December, 1995, Tom S. Hurlburt, review of *The Squared Circle,* p. 128; February, 2001, Todd Morning, review of *Plunking Reggie Jackson,* p. 117.
Voice of Youth Advocates, October, 1990, pp. 213-214; April, 1994, Shirley Carmony, review of *Dakota Dream,* pp. 22-23; February, 1996, Dorothy M. Broderick, review of *The Squared Circle,* p. 379; December, 1998, Mary Ann Capan, review of *Blue Star Rapture,* p. 352.

ONLINE

James W. Bennett Home Page, http://www.jamesw bennett.com/ (March 21, 2004).*

*   *   *

BETANCOURT, Jeanne 1941-

PERSONAL: Born October 2, 1941, in Burlington, VT; daughter of Henry (a certified public accountant) and Beatrice (a secretary; maiden name, Mario) Granger; married second husband, Lee Minoff (a writer and psychoanalyst), March 5, 1983 (divorced); children: (first marriage) Nicole. *Education:* College of St. Joseph the Provider, B.S., 1964; New York University, M.A., 1974. *Hobbies and other interests:* "I spend my time gardening, drawing, and oil painting. I've never been good in competitive sports, probably because I have terrible eye/hand coordination; so I swim, cross-country ski, do yoga, and ride my bike around the countryside. I still love to dance."

ADDRESSES: Home—New York, NY. *Agent*—c/o Author Mail, Scholastic, 557 Broadway, New York, NY 10012.

CAREER: Teacher at St. Peters School, Rutland, VT, 1961-63, St. Francis deSales Academy, Bennington, VT, 1963-64, Edmunds Junior High School, Burlington, VT, 1964-65, East Islip High School, East Islip, NY, 1965-66, High School for Pregnant Teens, Bronx, NY, 1967-69, Tetard Junior High School, Bronx, 1969-70, John Jay High School, Brooklyn, NY, 1970-71, Prospect Heights High School, Brooklyn, 1971-76, and Edward R. Murrow High School, Brooklyn, 1976-80; New School for Social Research, New York, NY, faculty member, 1977-80; Tomorrow Entertainment/ Medcom Company, New York, NY, director of development, 1980-81; full-time writer, 1981—. Member of preview committee of first International Film Festival, 1972, of reviewing committee of film division at Brooklyn Public Library, 1974-79, and of board of directors of the Media Center for Children, New York, NY, 1977-87. Developer of workshops for librarians and educators on the topic of film programming for adolescents.

MEMBER: New York Women in Film (president, 1981-82).

AWARDS, HONORS: Outstanding Science Trade Book for Children, National Science Teachers Association/ Children's Book Council, 1982, for *SMILE! How to Cope with Braces;* Emmy nomination for Outstanding Children's Special, 1986, for *I Want to Go Home* and *Don't Touch,* 1987, for *Teen Father,* and 1988, for *Supermom's Daughter;* Emmy nomination for Best Children's Script, 1986, and Humanitarian Award, Los Angeles Council on Assaults against Women, 1987, both for *Don't Touch;* Humanitas Award finalist, 1986, for *Don't Touch,* and 1987, for *Teen Father;* National Psychology Award for Excellence in the Media, American Psychological Association, and Nancy Susan Reynolds Award, Center for Population Options, both 1987, for *Teen Father;* Children's Choice Award, International Reading Association/Children's Book Council, 1987, for *Sweet Sixteen and Never . . . ;* Commendation Award, American Women in Radio and Television, and Mentor Award, National Association for Youth, both 1988, for *Supermom's Daughter;* Lifetime Achievement Award, Hamilton School at Wheeler, 2004.

WRITINGS:

FICTION; FOR YOUNG PEOPLE

The Rainbow Kid, Avon (New York, NY), 1983.
Turtle Time, Avon (New York, NY), 1985.
Puppy Love, Avon (New York, NY), 1986.
Crazy Christmas, Bantam (New York, NY), 1988.
Valentine Blues, Skylark, 1990.
Ten True Animal Rescues, Scholastic (New York, NY), 1998.

"PONY PALS" SERIES

I Want a Pony, Scholastic (New York, NY), 1995.
A Pony for Keeps, Scholastic (New York, NY), 1995.
A Pony in Trouble, Scholastic (New York, NY), 1995.
Give Me Back My Pony, Scholastic (New York, NY), 1995.
Pony to the Rescue, Scholastic (New York, NY), 1995.
Too Many Ponies, Scholastic (New York, NY), 1995.
Runaway Pony, Scholastic (New York, NY), 1995.
Good-Bye Pony, Scholastic (New York, NY), 1996.
The Wild Pony, Scholastic (New York, NY), 1996.
The Baby Pony, Scholastic (New York, NY), 1996.

Don't Hurt My Pony, Scholastic (New York, NY), 1996.
Circus Pony, Scholastic (New York, NY), 1996.
Keep Out, Pony!, Scholastic (New York, NY), 1996.
The Girl Who Hated Ponies, Scholastic (New York, NY), 1997.
Pony-Sitters, Scholastic (New York, NY), 1997.
The Story of Our Ponies, Scholastic (New York, NY), 1997.
The Blind Pony, Scholastic (New York, NY), 1997.
The Missing Pony Pal, Scholastic (New York, NY), 1997.
The Ghost Pony, Scholastic (New York, NY), 1997.
Detective Pony, Scholastic (New York, NY), 1997.
The Saddest Pony, Scholastic, 1997.
Moving Pony, Scholastic (New York, NY), 1999.
Stolen Ponies, Scholastic, 1999.
The Winning Pony, Scholastic (New York, NY), 1999.
Western Pony, Scholastic (New York, NY), 1999.
The Pony and the Bear, Scholastic (New York, NY), 1999.
Unlucky Pony, Scholastic (New York, NY), 2000.
The Lonely Pony, Scholastic (New York, NY), 2000.
Movie Star Pony, Scholastic (New York, NY), 2000.
The Pony and the Missing Dog, Scholastic (New York, NY), 2000.
The Newborn Pony, Scholastic (New York, NY), 2000.
Lost and Found Pony, Scholastic (New York, NY), 2001.
Pony-4-Sale, Scholastic (New York, NY), 2001.
Ponies from the Past, Scholastic (New York, NY), 2001.
He's My Pony!, Scholastic (New York, NY), 2001.
What's Wrong with My Pony?, Scholastic (New York, NY), 2001.
The Fourth Pony Pal, Scholastic (New York, NY), 2002.
The Pony and the Lost Swan, Scholastic (New York, NY), 2002.
Magic Pony, Scholastic (New York, NY), 2002.
The Pony and the Haunted Barn, Scholastic (New York, NY), 2002.
Pony Problem, Scholastic (New York, NY), 2003.
No Ponies in the House!, Scholastic (New York, NY), 2003.
Ponies on Parade, Scholastic (New York, NY), 2003.
The Last Pony Ride, Scholastic (New York, NY), 2004.

"Pony Pals" books have been translated into French and German.

"CHEER USA" SERIES

Fight, Bulldogs, Fight, Scholastic (New York, NY), 1999.
We've Got Spirit, Scholastic (New York, NY), 1999.
Go, Girl, Go!, Scholastic (New York, NY), 1999.
Ready, Shoot, Score, Scholastic (New York, NY), 1999.

"THREE GIRLS IN THE CITY" SERIES

Self-Portrait, Scholastic (New York, NY), 2003.
Exposed, Scholastic (New York, NY), 2003.
Black and White, Scholastic (New York, NY), 2004.
Close-Up, Scholastic (New York, NY), 2004.

NOVELS; FOR YOUNG ADULTS

Am I Normal? (film novelization), Avon (New York, NY), 1983.
Dear Diary (film novelization), Avon (New York, NY), 1983.
The Edge, Scholastic (New York, NY), 1985.
Between Us, Scholastic (New York, NY), 1986.
Sweet Sixteen and Never . . . , Bantam (New York, NY), 1986.
Home Sweet Home, Bantam (New York, NY), 1988.
Not Just Party Girls, Bantam (New York, NY), 1988.
More Than Meets the Eye, Bantam (New York, NY), 1990.
Kate's Turn, Scholastic (New York, NY), 1992.
My Name Is Brain Brian, Scholastic (New York, NY), 1993.

TELEPLAYS; PRODUCED AS "AMERICAN BROADCASTING COMPANIES (ABC) AFTERSCHOOL SPECIALS"

I Want to Go Home, ABC (New York, NY), 1985.
Don't Touch, ABC (New York, NY), 1985.
Are You My Mother, ABC (New York, NY), 1986.
Teen Father, ABC (New York, NY), 1986.
Supermom's Daughter, ABC (New York, NY), 1987.
Tattle, ABC (New York, NY), 1988.

OTHER

Women in Focus (adult nonfiction), Pflaum (Dayton, OH), 1974.
Smile! How to Cope with Braces (for children), illustrated by Mimi Harrison, Knopf (New York, NY), 1982.

Author of feature film script *Rosie,* based on a novel by Anne Lamott; of ABC's movie of the week script *The Passion of Mary Francis;* of three teleplay scripts based on "The Baby-sitters Club" series for Scholastic and Home Box Office Corporation; of the teleplay script *A Place Called Home;* and, with Lee Minoff, of screenplay *Carolyn and Maggie,* based on a novel by Norma Klein. Contributor of articles and reviews to periodicals, including *Women in Film, Film Library Quarterly, Media Methods,* and *Sightlines.* Contributing editor, *Channels,* 1981-82.

SIDELIGHTS: Jeanne Betancourt brings an understanding of both country and city life to her books for young readers. The author of the "Pony Pals" series for elementary school-age readers that follows the adventures of young horse-lovers, Betancourt is also the author of several books and "Afterschool Special" teleplays for teens that concern some of the harsh realities faced by some youngsters: drug abuse, racial prejudice, cocaine addiction, homelessness, and teen parenting. "I know that my reader/viewers are either experiencing some of these difficult and challenging situations personally, through their friends and neighbors, or through the media," the author once told *CA.* "I want to show, in a story, the aspects of the 'issue' that I feel kids should be aware of. These are important issues that the media sometimes exploits. I want to explore them. I want to help kids grow stronger and wiser through the experiences of my stories, to see that they have responsibility and power. Through role models from their own age group I want to show kids what they can and should do for themselves and for others."

Betancourt was raised in rural Vermont, across the road from a dairy farm, where she spent much of her time playing, helping work in the barns, or spending time with the Swedish farm owner and his family. "Those years I never thought of being a writer," she once confided to *CA.* "I loved my tap dancing classes and wanted to be a Rockette at Radio City Music Hall."

Then, in high school, Betancourt and her family moved to the city of Burlington, where she attended a Catholic girls school. Her dreams of becoming a Rockette were finally dashed when she learned that, at five feet eight inches in height, she was too tall to be a Rockette. Betancourt transferred her energy from dreams of

dancing to pursuing a religious calling that began in her junior year of high school. After graduation, she moved to Rutland, Vermont, and entered a teaching order of nuns called the Sisters of Saint Joseph. Over the next six years, she earned her teaching certification and taught at high schools in Vermont. After leaving the order, she took her skills as a teacher to New York City; part of her new life there included getting married and having a child.

While raising her daughter, Nicole, Betancourt taught in New York's inner-city public high schools. She also found the time to pursue her interest in film and, in 1974, earned an advanced college degree in film studies from New York University that enabled her to design courses in film studies and filmmaking for secondary school students. Her first published book, 1974's *Women in Focus,* was based on her master's degree project.

"I wrote my first children's book, *Smile! How to Cope with Braces,* when my daughter, Nicole, was having orthodontic treatment," Betancourt once recalled. "I couldn't find the right book to help her with this new experience, so I researched and wrote one. By the time the book was published, Nicole was out of braces, but her picture is on the cover of the book."

In fact, Nicole has been the inspiration for many of Betancourt's books. "But when it comes down to writing the story and getting into the head and heart of . . . my characters, I have to become the character myself," the author once noted. "Nicole can't do that for me." Betancourt was, however, inspired to write a series of books featuring the young protagonist Aviva Granger, she once remembered, "when, at nine, Nicole first became a joint-custody kid and began to split her life—two weeks at a time—with me and her father. I've given Aviva my maiden name, Granger, and set the stories in Burlington, Vermont." The four books featuring Aviva Granger—*The Rainbow Kid, Turtle Time, Puppy Love, Crazy Christmas,* and *Valentine Blues*—appeared between 1983 and 1990.

Despite having a real child on which to base her books, Betancourt also does a great deal of research for each new book. For 1988's *Home Sweet Home,* the author tackled the subject of young Tracy Jensen's move from New York City to her Grandmother Tilly's farm in a quiet New England country town. Tracy's feelings of alienation in her new environment are reflected by the situation of Anya, a Russian foreign exchange student she meets during her junior year in high school. "I read many books about the Soviet Union, visited dairy farms, and interviewed farmers," Betancourt once said about writing the novel. And "for *Between Us*—a mystery novel that makes a connection between drugs used for medical reasons and drugs sold illegally for recreational use—I spent many mornings in the pharmacy of our local hospital in Sharon, Connecticut, learning about drugs and how a hospital pharmacy works."

In *Sweet Sixteen and Never . . . ,* sixteen-year-old Julie is faced with a different kind of problem when she starts dating a young man with a reputation for being "fast." She knows his desire to begin a sexual relationship with her is imminent, and she needs to decide how she is going to react when the time comes. Learning that her mother had a child when she was Julie's age but gave it up for adoption complicates things between mother and daughter after Julie's mother discovers birth control pills in her daughter's room. Fortunately, the lines of communication are open between each of the book's protagonists—Julie, her mom, and boyfriend Sam—and Julie is able to make the decision that is best for her. Writing in *School Library Journal,* contributor Nancy P. Reeder noted that Betancourt "effectively conveys Julie's turmoil." In a *Kliatt* review, Rita M. Fontinha applauded Betancourt's "believable plot and engaging characters," going on to say that the novel offers young girls "an excellent introduction to the real world."

Not Just Party Girls, which Betancourt published in 1988, draws on the author's experiences as a nun. Sixteen-year-olds Anne, Kate, and Janet are the Party Girls, a group that arranges birthday parties for younger children in their neighborhood. When Anne becomes concerned with the meaninglessness of her life after working in a local homeless shelter, she begins to consider joining a religious order—but her newfound desire to save others ends up hurting both her friends and her family. The down-to-earth wisdom of Anne's religious guide, Sister Mary, as well as "some highly unsettling practical experiences provide a strong antidote to self-righteousness and day dreams," noted Libby K. White in her positive review of the novel for *School Library Journal.* The author's life-long love of dancing is reflected in *Kate's Turn,* in which the young teen protagonist follows her dream of becoming a ballerina to a New York dance school and learns about the real rigors of the profession first-hand.

Betancourt has dyslexia, a learning disability that makes ordering letters for the correct spelling of words difficult and also makes remembering dates and names a challenge. "I also have trouble following special directions and am a very slow reader," she once explained to *CA.* "To compensate for my disability, I have developed a sharply tuned attention to conversation (particularly the rhythms and emotional content of dialogue), heightened visual acuity and memory, and empathy." Her personal experiences of overcoming her disability were the focus of her 1993 work, *My Name Is Brain Brian.* In the novel, the sixth-grader Brian deals with his learning disability as well as all the other typical problems that arise during adolescence. He begins to reexamine his longtime friendships with pals John, Rich, and Dan, as well as his relationship with his authoritarian father, his new teachers who are able to diagnose and help Brian adapt to his dyslexia, and other students at school. Even the "class brain," Isabel, gets a new impression of him after she is forced to work with Brian on a science class project. "Betancourt's depiction of Brian's emotional and psychological growth is believable and involving," noted Janice Del Negro in a *Booklist* review. A *Kirkus Reviews* contributor called the novel "a skillfully structured, entertaining story" and acknowledged that "Brian himself . . . is drawn with real insight."

Aimed at a younger audience, the "Pony Pals" books reflect Betancourt's love for animals, and with dozens of titles, the series is perhaps her best-known work. The author told *Kids Care Clubs* interviewer Maureen Byrne that these stories were inspired by her mostly unfulfilled desire to ride horses as a child. Introduced in 1995 in *I Want a Pony,* the "Pony Pals" are Pam, Anna, and Lulu, three girls who live in a small town like the one Betancourt grew up in. The author called the girls "strong, smart, independent, kind, and fun loving. They are the kinds of girls I would have liked for friends." Their ponies, Lightning, Acorn, and Snow White, are the animal friends she dreamed of as a child.

Shifting to an urban setting, Betancourt began the "Three Girls in the City" series in 2003 with *Self-Portrait,* in which the shy teenager Carolyn moves from the Wyoming countryside to Manhattan. In the city, she makes friends with Maya, a confident extrovert from Harlem, and the more cynical, withdrawn Joy. The girls share an interest in photography but have very different home lives and perspectives. Carolyn's mother died recently, and she feels her father is overprotective of her. Maya has a happy family life but is torn between her new pals and friends from her neighborhood. Joy's parents have divorced, so she must divide her time between two homes. A *Publishers Weekly* reviewer called the story "pleasant if predictable" and credited the author with defining "distinct, credible voices" while she "gently contrasts their developmental differences." Reviewing the book for *Time Out New York*, Barbara Aria commended Betancourt for the "subtlety with which [she] portrays her characters' insecurities." Other volumes in the series that have followed include *Exposed, Black and White,* and *Close-Up.*

"Some people think that a writer's life is lonely," Betancourt once explained to *CA*. "When I'm writing a story, I don't feel lonely because I am actively involved with lots of interesting people—the characters in my books. I love knowing that some day—in the private moment of reading—other people will get to know and care about these people too." Despite the enjoyment she gets from her work, she continues to take her responsibility as a writer for young people seriously. "I believe that the antidote to our human problems is based in human values—those little things we can do for one another to alleviate the pain. I've learned, as children must, that bad things happen to good people and good people have no choice but to become better through the process of coping. This is where the writer comes in. Samuel Johnson said it best when he wrote, 'The only end of writing is to enable the reader to enjoy life better or better to endure it.'"

BIOGRAPHICAL AND CRITICAL SOURCES:

PERIODICALS

Booklist, January 15, 1988, p. 854; January 15, 1989, p. 858; April 1, 1993, Janice Del Negro, review of *My Name Is Brain Brian,* p. 1430.
Bulletin of the Center for Children's Books, December, 1982, review of *Smile! How to Cope with Braces,* pp. 61-62; April, 1983, review of *Dear Diary,*

p. 143; February, 1992, Zena Sutherland, review of *Kate's Turn,* p. 148; April, 1993, Kathryn Jennings, review of *My Name Is Brain Brian,* p. 241.
Kirkus Reviews, January 1, 1992, p. 48; February 11, 1993, review of *My Name Is Brain Brian,* p. 142.
Kliatt, April, 1987, Rita M. Fontinha, review of *Sweet Sixteen and Never . . . ,* p. 5.
Publishers Weekly, June 9, 2003, review of *Self-Portrait,* p. 51.
School Library Journal, August, 1982, Hannah Pickworth, review of *Smile!,* p. 111; June, 1987, Nancy P. Reeder, review of *Sweet Sixteen and Never . . . ,* p. 104; February, 1988, Susan H. Williamson, review of *Home Sweet Home,* p. 84; January, 1989, Libby K. White, review of *Not Just Party Girls,* pp. 90-91.
Time Out New York, July 3-10, 2003, Barbara Aria, review of *Self-Portrait,* p. 65.
Voice of Youth Advocates, October, 1982, Susan B. Madden, review of *Smile!,* p. 53; August, 1983, Elizabeth G. Paddock, review of *Dear Diary,* p. 144; August-September, 1987, Judith A. Sheriff, review of *Sweet Sixteen and Never . . . ,* p. 118; April, 1988, p. 21; February, 1989, pp. 282-283; October, 1990, p. 214; April, 1992, p. 22.

ONLINE

Kids Care Clubs, http://www.kidscare.org/ (July, 2002), Maureen Byrne, interview with Betancourt.

*   *   *

BIRDSEYE, Tom 1951-

PERSONAL: Born July 13, 1951, in Durham, NC; son of Irving Earl (a minister) and Mary Hughes (a librarian; maiden name, Carmichael) Birdseye; married Debbie Holsclaw (an educator), May 18, 1974; children: Kelsey, Amy. *Education:* Attended University of Kentucky, 1969-72; Western Kentucky University, B.A. (mass communications), 1974, B.A. (elementary education), 1977. *Hobbies and other interests:* Skiing, hiking, canoeing, camping, mountain climbing.

ADDRESSES: Home and office—511 Northwest 12th St., Corvallis, OR 97330. *Agent*—Jean V. Naggar, 216 East 75th St., New York, NY 10021.

CAREER: Writer. Ocean Lake School, Lincoln City, OR, teacher, 1977-83; Washington Elementary School, Sandpoint, ID, teacher, 1985-88. Has also taught English in Japan.

MEMBER: Authors Guild, Authors League of America, Society of Children's Book Writers and Illustrators.

AWARDS, HONORS: Children's Choice Book Award, International Reading Association, 1989, for *Air Mail to the Moon,* and 1995, for *A Regular Flood of Mishap;* Missouri Show Me Readers Award for grades 1-3, Nebraska Golden Sower Award for grades K-3, Washington Children's Choice Picture Book and Sasquatch Reading Awards for grades K-3, all 1996, and Maryland Black-Eyed Susan Award for picture books, 1997, all for *Soap! Soap! Don't Forget the Soap!;* Lampman Award, Oregon Library Association, 1999, for contributions to children's literature; Storytelling World Gold Award, 2002, for *Look Out, Jack! The Giant Is Back!*

WRITINGS:

I'm Going to Be Famous, Holiday House (New York, NY), 1986.

Air Mail to the Moon, illustrated by Stephen Gammell, Holiday House (New York, NY), 1988.

A Song of Stars: An Asian Legend, illustrated by Ju-Hong Chen, Holiday House (New York, NY), 1990.

Tucker, Holiday House (New York, NY), 1990.

Waiting for Baby, illustrated by Loreen Leedy, Holiday House (New York, NY), 1991.

Just Call Me Stupid, Holiday House (New York, NY), 1993.

A Kids' Guide to Building Forts, illustrated by Bill Klein, Harbinger House (Tucson, AZ), 1993.

(Reteller) *Soap! Soap! Don't Forget the Soap! An Appalachian Folktale,* illustrated by Andrew Glass, Holiday House (New York, NY), 1993.

A Regular Flood of Mishap, illustrated by Megan Lloyd, Holiday House (New York, NY), 1994.

(With wife, Debbie Holsclaw Birdseye) *She'll Be Comin' round the Mountain,* illustrated by Andrew Glass, Holiday House (New York, NY), 1994.

Tarantula Shoes, Holiday House (New York, NY), 1995.

(With Debbie Holsclaw Birdseye) *What I Believe: Kids Talk about Faith,* photographs by Robert Crum, Holiday House (New York, NY), 1996.

(With Debbie Holsclaw Birdseye) *Under Our Skin: Kids Talk about Race,* photographs by Robert Crum, Holiday House (New York, NY), 1997.

The Eye of the Stone, Holiday House (New York, NY), 2000.

Look Out, Jack! The Giant Is Back!, illustrated by Will Hillenbrand, Holiday House (New York, NY), 2001.

Attack of the Mutant Underwear, Holiday House (New York, NY), 2003.

Oh Yeah!, illustrated by Ethan Long, Holiday House (New York, NY), 2003.

WORK IN PROGRESS: Middle-grade novel set in rural Kentucky.

SIDELIGHTS: Tom Birdseye readily admits that he never aspired to be a writer. As a young man growing up in North Carolina and Kentucky, he was more interested in sports, crawdads, mud balls, forts built in the woods, secret codes, bicycles without fenders, butter pecan ice cream, and snow. Birdseye, however, became published at the age of thirty-five after ten years of teaching, a year of living in Japan, and two unrelated degrees. The author once commented, "Life, it seems, is full of who'd-a-thought-its."

"At times it still amazes me that writing is my profession," Birdseye once said. "It was such a difficult process for me when I was a kid; I can really identify with the reluctant writer in school today." The author recalled how difficult it was for him to complete stories because of his poor grammatical skills. He acknowledges that if it were not for certain people offering him encouragement, he would not have prospered as a writer. Birdseye now carries a small notebook around just in case he comes across any new ideas or characters.

"True, I still labor through my stories," Birdseye once admitted, "wrestling with the spelling beast and the punctuation monster, writing and rewriting, then rewriting some more, until I glean my best, but the process has become one of pleasure instead of pain. I love doing it, and I love sharing it with others. The boy who couldn't imagine himself a writer, now can't imagine himself anything else."

Birdseye's first published work for children, *I'm Going to Be Famous,* appeared in 1986. In this story, a fifth grader, Arlo, focuses all of his energy on breaking the world record for eating bananas, which is seventeen bananas in two minutes. Arlo's feat begins as a personal endeavor but quickly becomes a major event at his school. He starts to wonder if breaking the record is worth the attention, especially since his parents disapprove. Arlo lies about the outcome, leaving him in an awkward position with his friends. Calling *I'm Going to Be Famous* a "furiously funny story," *Booklist* contributor Ilene Cooper stated that the work has a "built-in appeal and a certain silliness that middle graders will adore."

Tucker addresses issues of divorce, sibling rivalry, and unemployment. The title character, eleven-year-old Tucker Renfro, lives with his divorced father, apart from his mother and nine-year-old sister, Olivia. When Olivia comes to visit Tucker after seven years of absence, they do not get along. With time, however, the siblings grow more comfortable with each other. Olivia makes Tucker hopeful by telling him that their parents are getting back together. His hopes are crushed, however, after learning that his sister has been lying. The book also touches upon Tucker's passion to become a hunter. He shoots a deer with his homemade bow and arrow despite being too young to receive a hunting license. After watching the deer suffer before dying, Tucker regrets killing the animal. The young boy's dilemmas are "treated sensitively and realistically," according to *School Library Journal* contributor Susan H. Williamson. Deborah Abbott, a reviewer for *Booklist,* contended that "readers will identify with the problems and the positive ending."

Waiting for Baby is another of Birdseye's well-known children's stories. In anticipation of becoming a big brother, a young boy envisions the fun he and his new sibling will have playing games, wrestling, and reading stories—but the activities he imagines are not appropriate for an infant. When his baby sister arrives, the older child is not disappointed because he likes to snuggle and hold her close to him. *Booklist*'s Ellen Mandel asserted that *Waiting for Baby* is "a beautifully executed, reassuring read for expectant families." "This idealized view of a new sibling is a good choice for sharing aloud," Virginia E. Jeschelnig noted in *School Library Journal.*

Just Call Me Stupid tells the struggle of a fifth-grader, Patrick, who reads below his grade level. Published in 1993, the book details the effects that parental verbal abuse and neglect have on a child. Every time Patrick tries to read, he begins to hyperventilate and the words blur together. His alcoholic father makes matters worse with his negative comments. The only people who seem to care about Patrick are his teacher, Mrs. Romero, and his next door neighbor and classmate, Celina. Celina is bubbling with enthusiasm and motivates Patrick to explore his creativity. Thus, he recites an original story to Celina, which she records and secretly submits to a contest. When he wins, Patrick is furious with her. The boy later conquers his fear of books with his mother's unconditional love, Celina's confidence, and Mrs. Romero's encouragement. A contributor to *Kirkus Reviews* remarked that the book is "lively and well plotted, with funny . . . scenes and a satisfying upbeat ending." Describing *Just Call Me Stupid* as a "dramatic, insightful novel," a *Publishers Weekly* reviewer proclaimed the book "may also spark classroom discussion about self-esteem, disabilities, and talents."

In 1993, Birdseye turned his attention to folklore, in *Soap! Soap! Don't Forget the Soap! An Appalachian Folktale.* Plug Honeycut is a forgetful little boy who is sent to the store by his mother to purchase soap. Since the young man is easily distracted, he has to repeat, "Soap! Soap! Don't forget the soap!" Unfortunately, Plug ends up repeating whatever he hears from other people along the way. Each time he picks up a new phrase, he tells it to the next person he comes in contact with, unintentionally offending the stranger. When someone mentions soap again, Plug finally remembers his initial mission. A *Kirkus Reviews* contributor described Birdseye's retelling of the book as "colorful and comical." *Booklist* reviewer Janice Del Negro added that the "book will also work well in read-aloud programs . . . or as a source for more traditional library storytelling."

What I Believe: Kids Talk about Faith, written with wife Debbie Holsclaw Birdseye, explores in a candid, encouraging way the varied religious beliefs of six children aged twelve to thirteen. A Christian, Jewish, Hindu, Buddhist, Muslim, and Native American child each discuss their religious practices, their feelings about their religions, and how their religions function as an integral part of their daily lives. Beginning with a questionnaire originally given to adults, the Birdseyes revised the questionnaire for children and went seeking answers from their six subjects. "Despite what some adults think of the youth of today—that they are only interested in video games, rock stars, TV, and when dinner will be ready—our job turned out to be quite easy," Birdseye wrote on his Web site. "The world, it seems, is brimming with wonderful kids from all walks of life who are giving a great deal of thought to their spirituality." The book includes the children's views on God and discussion of how and why they pray. The "first-hand and refreshing" responses of the children reveal "a depth of perception and commitment," observed a reviewer in *Teacher Librarian.*

The companion book to *What I Believe, Under Our Skin: Kids Talk about Race,* addresses children's views and concepts of race and racial identity. As in *What I Believe,* the book records the candid responses of six children, aged twelve to thirteen, of Hispanic, Arabic, African-American, Native American, Caucasian, and Asian descent. Spurred by their success in getting middle-school-aged children to talk about religion, the Birdseyes sought out children willing to discuss their ideas and experiences with race. Mindful of the potential volatility of the subject, the authors asked about experiences as a member of a particular race, about experiences with prejudice, and the general issue of race relations in the United States, especially in relation to young people. "Not only were they willing to talk, but with great honesty and feeling, giving us very personal portraits of themselves in the process," Birdseye remarked on the his Web site. Yapha Nussbaum Mason, writing in *School Library Journal,* commented that *Under Our Skin* "gives readers a chance to see what life is like through someone else's eyes, and in someone else's skin."

Birdseye turns again to fiction with *The Eye of the Stone.* Thirteen-year-old Jackson Cooper has his share of troubles. His schoolmates consider him a wimp, his father is unemployed, and as he tries to work up the courage to ride his bike down a steep incline on his thirteenth birthday, he knows that he will chicken out again. When he dozes off in the woods behind his home, however, he wakes up in a magical, ancient world where he is hailed as a mighty hero. The people of the village of Timmran adore him and count on him for protection against a warring village, which he provides with the powers of a magic stone. During a battle, Jackson inadvertently unleashes a destructive demon called the Baen, which causes untold deaths and injuries. Heavily burdened with the disappointment of having let down the people who relied on

him, particularly the village girl Tessa, Jackson finds within himself the courage and resolve to seek out an enchanted flute that will defeat the demon and bring peace to his new world. After doing so, Jackson is returned to his real home, where his newfound maturity, courage, and wisdom remain to let him face the challenges of his own world. "This novel is a predictable but fairly interesting science fiction-fantasy tale," with elements of time travel and *Romeo and Juliet,* wrote Nicole A. Cooke in *Voice of Youth Advocates.* Despite finding "the time-travel element . . . not entirely convincing," *Booklist*'s Carolyn Phelan, nonetheless remarked that *The Eye of the Stone* "provides plenty of excitement for adventure fans."

Birdseye revisits a familiar fairy tale in *Look Out, Jack! The Giant Is Back!* Picking up the story about ten minutes after Jack dispatched the giant in the original *Jack and the Beanstalk, Look Out, Jack!* tells what happens when the original giant's brother slides down the beanstalk, looking for Jack and a little revenge. Mr. Giant, bigger and meaner than the original, pursues Jack and his mother to the mountains of North Carolina, where heaps of delicious southern food—and smelly feet—stave off the giant's vengeance. Eventually Mr. Giant becomes angry and stomps so hard that the mountains collapse and swallow him up as easily as the giant swallowed mounds of fried chicken, biscuits, and mashed potatoes. Janie Schomberg, reviewing the book in *School Library Journal,* remarked that "readers will love this tale about Jack." Writing in *Kirkus Reviews,* a critic noted that Birdseye's "folksy style of storytelling uses an American vernacular full of tall-tale exaggerations and dramatic page turns," concluding that the book is "great fun."

Oh Yeah!, Birdseye's 2003 book, is also based on exaggerations, this time the escalating dares and counterdares issued by two boys during a creepy campout in their back yard. Safely tucked inside their pup tent, the boys boast of their ability to stay out in the yard no matter what. The first could stay outside in the dark even if there were spiders hanging over his head; the second could stay out in the dark even if there were spiders over his head and snakes crawling around his feet. With shouts of "Oh Yeah?," each boy increases the risk and intensity of fear he could withstand, through crocodiles, dragons, and monsters. Finally they exit the tent, leaving their stuffed animals inside to demonstrate their amazing bravery. When a "kid-eating monster" shows up on the scene, they're frightened into the house—until they realize they left their stuffed friends behind, and muster up the courage to rescue their toys from the monster, which turns out to be the family dog. "Children who enjoy a good scare will delight in the imaginary big-eyed, slithering, stalking, dangling critters that crowd the pages in increasing numbers," wrote Marge Loch-Wouters in *School Library Journal,* while a *Kirkus Reviews* critic noted that *Oh Yeah!* "will probably strike a chord and tickle the funny bone of many young 'brave' campers."

BIOGRAPHICAL AND CRITICAL SOURCES:

PERIODICALS

Booklist, December 1, 1986, Ilene Cooper, review of *I'm Going to Be Famous,* pp. 574-575; July, 1990, Deborah Abbott, review of *Tucker,* p. 2086; November 1, 1991, Ellen Mandel, review of *Waiting for Baby,* p. 530; March 15, 1993, Janice Del Negro, review of *Soap! Soap! Don't Forget the Soap! An Appalachian Folktale,* p. 314; January 15, 1994, p. 930; July, 1994, p. 1952; February 15, 2001, Carolyn Phelan, review of *The Eye of the Stone,* p. 1136; September 1, 2001, Stephanie Zvirin, review of *Look Out, Jack! The Giant Is Back!,* p. 112; January 1, 2004, Ilene Cooper, review of *Attack of the Mutant Underwear,* p. 852.
Kirkus Reviews, March 15, 1988, p. 450; May 1, 1993, review of *Soap! Soap! Don't Forget the Soap!,* p. 593; November 1, 1993, review of *Just Call Me Stupid,* p. 1386; September 1, 2001, review of *Look Out, Jack! The Giant Is Back!,* p. 1285; July 15, 2003, review of *Oh Yeah!,* p. 961.
Publishers Weekly, March 18, 1988, p. 86; April 27, 1990, p. 60; October 25, 1993, review of *Just Call Me Stupid,* p. 62; August 1, 1994, p. 78; September 10, 2001, review of *Look Out, Jack! The Giant Is Back!,* p. 92; August 11, 2003, review of *Oh Yeah!,* p. 279; December 8, 2003, review of *Attack of the Mutant Underwear,* p. 62.
School Library Journal, May, 1988, p. 76; June, 1990, Susan H. Williamson, review of *Tucker,* p. 116; November, 1991, Virginia E. Jeschelnig, review of *Waiting for Baby,* p. 90; April, 1998, Yapha Nussbaum Mason, review of *Under Our Skin: Kids Talk about Race,* p. 141; December, 2000, Valerie Diamond, review of *The Eye of the Stone,* p. 138; October, 2001, Janie Schomberg, review of *Look Out, Jack! The Giant Is Back!,* p. 104; August,

2003, Marge Loch-Wouters, review of *Oh Yeah!,* p. 122; January, 2004, Kathy Krasniewicz, review of *Attack of the Mutant Underwear,* p. 124.
Teacher Librarian, May, 1999, review of *What I Believe: Kids Talk about Faith,* p. 51.
Voice of Youth Advocates, April, 2001, Nicole A. Cooke, review of *The Eye of the Stone,* p. 50.

ONLINE

Tom Birdseye Home Page, http://www.tombirdseye.com/ (January 25, 2004).

* * *

BLEDSOE, Lucy Jane 1957-

PERSONAL: Born February 1, 1957, in Portland, OR; daughter of John P. and Helen (Wieman) Bledsoe; companion of Patricia E. Mullan. *Education:* Attended Williams College, 1975-77; University of California-Berkeley, B.A., 1979. *Hobbies and other interests:* Cycling, mountaineering, literacy programs.

ADDRESSES: Agent—c/o Author Mail, Holiday House, 425 Madison Ave., New York, NY 10017-1110.

CAREER: Author. Martin Luther King Junior High, Berkeley, CA, California Poets in the Schools residency, 1990; Tenderloin Women Writers Workshop, San Francisco, CA, facilitator, 1990-92; George Lucas Education Foundation, Skywalker Ranch, Marin County, CA, script and story writer, 1992; Globe Book Company, Paramus, NJ, textbook and story writer, 1992-95. Conducts creative writing workshops for adult literacy programs in Richmond, San Francisco, Oakland, and Berkeley, CA. Curriculum writer for organizations, including National Geographic and the Seti Institute.

MEMBER: PEN, National Writers Union, Media Alliance.

AWARDS, HONORS: Youth grant, National Endowment for the Humanities, 1982; PEN Syndicated Fiction Award, 1985; semifinalist, San Francisco Foundation's Joseph Henry Jackson Award for Fiction,

Lucy Jane Bledsoe

1987 and 1988; Poets and Writers Readings/Workshop grant, 1989; creative writing fellowship, Money for Women/Barbara Deming Memorial Fund, 1989; honorable mention, *Literary Lights* fiction contest, 1990; honorable mention, *New Letters Literacy Awards,* 1995, for essay "Above Treeline"; Lambda Literary Award finalist, c. 1995, for *Sweat: Stories and a Novella;* American Library Association Literature Award, 1998, for *Working Parts;* Individual Fellowship in Literature, California Arts Council, 2002; National Science Foundation Artists and Writers grant, 2003.

WRITINGS:

Break Away, David S. Lake Publishers (Belmont, CA), 1986.

A Question of Freedom, David S. Lake Publishers (Belmont, CA), 1987.

A Matter of Pride, Fearon Education (Belmont, CA), 1989.

Colony of Fear, Fearon Education (Belmont, CA), 1989.

The Journey Home, Fearon Education (Belmont, CA), 1989.

Two Kinds of Patriots, Fearon Education (Belmont, CA), 1989.

(With others) *Combat Zone,* Fearon Education (Belmont, CA), 1990.

Fearon's Amazing Adventures, Fearon/Janus/Quercus (Belmont, CA), 1993.

Sweat: Stories and a Novella (adult fiction), Seal Press (Seattle, WA), 1995.

The Big Bike Race (juvenile fiction), illustrated by Sterling Brown, Holiday House (New York, NY), 1995.

(Editor) *Heatwave: Women in Love and Lust: Lesbian Short Fiction,* Alyson Publications (Los Angeles, CA), 1995.

Working Parts (adult novel), Seal Press (Seattle, WA), 1997.

Tracks in the Snow (middle-grade novel), Holiday House (New York, NY), 1997.

(Editor) *Gay Travels: A Literary Companion,* Whereabouts Press (San Francisco, CA), 1998.

(Editor) *Lesbian Travels: A Literary Companion,* Whereabouts Press (San Francisco, CA), 1998.

Cougar Canyon (middle-grade novel), Holiday House (New York, NY), 2001.

Hoop Girlz (middle-grade novel), Holiday House (New York, NY), 2002.

This Wild Silence (adult novel), Alyson Books (Los Angeles, CA), 2003.

The Antarctic Scoop (middle-grade novel), Holiday House (New York, NY), 2003.

SIDELIGHTS: Lucy Jane Bledsoe's interests in the outdoors, sports, and literacy have often informed her fiction for adults and young readers. She got her start as an author of textbooks, which, as she once explained to *CA,* was something she did to earn an income: "I write textbooks for a living. About fifty percent of the textbook writing I do is in the sciences. I love reading about physics and earth science, both of which teach me what a blip we are in the history of the universe. We don't have time for anything but the truth. So I try to tell the truth. I do that better with fiction than with nonfiction."

Bledsoe's first work of fiction was the story collection *Sweat: Stories and a Novella.* The ten works in *Sweat* focus on lesbian relationships, usually set against a backdrop of sports and/or the outdoors. "State of Grace," for example, relates a tale of first love between two high-school softball teammates; "Sweat" is the story of a physical education instructor who considers a career change in order to maintain her relationship with her lover; and "Solo" revolves around a woman who challenges herself on a trip as homage to her now dead partner. The single novella in *Sweat,* "The Place before Language," centers on a woman who has been left by her lover of ten years for another. Partially set in the outdoors, the work has been praised by critics for showing the healing powers of the wilderness. A writer for *Publishers Weekly* called *Sweat* "an outstanding novella" with "rich and satisfying stories," and described Bledsoe as "a smart and savvy writer." In *Library Journal,* Lisa Nussbaum lauded Bledsoe's work as "bold" and "exciting."

Sports and other physical activities often intertwine with lesbian themes in Bledsoe's work, which is a reflection of how the two combined in her own early life. She enjoyed sports as a young student, and her admiration for the women who taught her eventually led to her realization about her sexual orientation. As she remembered in a *Gay and Lesbian Review Worldwide* article, "That's just the feeling I had about my coaches and older teammates or camp counselors. My reaction was entirely from the gut. At nine years old, I didn't really think, 'Ah! Finally women who are smashing stereotypes.' I just wanted to be close to them. I guess that's how I knew I was a lesbian!" As she further commented, "A huge part of being a lesbian—for me, anyway—is having the opportunity to redefine how I view, and also how I use, my body. That means being a wild mountain woman if I want. It means playing basketball until I'm sweaty and exhausted. Not having to worry about what men think of our bodies is very much still a huge difference between many (not all) lesbians and straight women."

Bledsoe drew on both her love of the outdoors and her experience as a literacy educator in her first novel for adults, *Working Parts.* The book features a lesbian protagonist, Lori Taylor, who is very active and whose job is repairing bikes. Lori also happens to be illiterate, but has managed to fake her way through school and most of life's situations. But when her friend Mickey pushes her to become his business partner, Lori is forced to acknowledge her disability. With Mickey's prodding, she enrolls in an adult literacy course, but she does not like her teacher, Deirdre Felix, whom she perceives to be an affluent "do-gooder." The other difference that divides teacher and student is that Deirdre is straight. Furthermore, Lori, who did not attend college and comes from a blue-collar back-

ground, confronts other difficulties, too, when she joins a lesbian business organization and runs into elitist attitudes from the college-educated people there; the lack of a college education also disrupts her relationship with her girlfriend.

This class prejudice was one of the themes that *Lambda Book Report* critic Trisha Collopy admired in the novel, and she also praised Bledsoe's descriptions of what it is like to be illiterate in modern America: "[Bledsoe] clearly knows her subject. Her descriptions of Lori's panic and resentment towards reading provide some of the most vivid passages of the book." Although, according to Collopy, *Working Parts* lacks the "rawness" of *Sweat,* she concluded, "Anyone looking for a well-written novel with a mix of fascinating characters, both straight and gay, will enjoy *Working Parts.*" Whitney Scott, writing in *Booklist,* also praised this debut novel, which he described as "funny and sad, moving and thoughtful, smoothly written and eminently enjoyable." And *Library Journal* contributor Ina Rimpau asserted that the novel "is important reading for anyone interested in adult literacy."

Bledsoe's second adult novel, *This Wild Silence,* explores the pain caused by family secrets. The story involves two sisters: Liz, who has had a long marriage to an educational book publisher named Mark, and Christine (Tina), who is a lesbian and cannot seem to maintain a relationship. When Liz and Mark invite Tina to go camping with them in the Sierra Nevada Mountains, Tina takes them up on it, thinking this will be a chance to reconnect with her sister. But the presence at the camp of Mark, as well as his foster child and a coworker named Melody, make it hard for Tina to find any private time with Liz. And private time is needed, because a secret that the two sisters have kept for years about the death of their little brother when they were all kids has created a deep rift in their relationship. *Library Journal* reviewer Lisa Nussbaum found *This Wild Silence* to be "a thought-provoking examination of the bond between sisters."

The Big Bike Race, a book for young children, is about Ernest and his sister, Melissa, who are being raised by their grandmother in Washington, D.C. Ernest desperately wants a sleek, new, racing bicycle for his tenth birthday, so his grandmother scrapes enough money together to buy him a bike. Although the big, clunky, yellow bike initially embarrasses Ernest, he is touched by his grandmother's generosity and is determined to win the Citywide Cup race with his new bicycle. Critics have praised *The Big Bike Race* for its depiction of a loving African-American family whose members succeed despite poverty. Lauren Peterson, writing in *Booklist,* called it "a strong, dignified portrayal." "Bledsoe's likable characters and enjoyable story [are] a good choice," added a critic in *Horn Book.*

Bledsoe's middle grade novels often concern outdoors life or sports. *Tracks in the Snow,* her first foray into the genre, pits two young girls against the elements in a tale that might remind some readers of a Gary Paulsen book. Although Susan Dove Lempke, writing in *Booklist,* felt this tale about two girls who brave the elements to find a missing babysitter was too predictable, the critic admired "Bledsoe's thorough outdoor knowledge" and appreciated that this adventure featured girls instead of boys battling the elements. *Cougar Canyon* also features a girl protagonist in an adventure story. Izzie Ramirez is an ambitious thirteen year old who has started her own gardening business. One of her clients, the Gray family, has a yard that abuts a park where, it is rumored, there is a cougar. Initially frightened by the idea of working so near a wild predator, Izzie researches cougars and becomes sympathetic to their plight. When a poacher shoots the cougar dead, however, a mystery ensues in which Izzie seeks to find out who killed the animal. *Cougar Canyon* was called a "thematically rich story" by Janet Gillen in *School Library Journal,* and the reviewer added that although the characters are a little two dimensional, Bledsoe's "consistently engaging style" makes for "an entertaining adventure story." Denise Wilms further noted in a *Booklist* review that *Cougar Canyon* would be "a good choice for junior-high-school students with reading problems," even though the book was written for younger readers.

With *Hoop Girlz* Bledsoe wrote a traditional kind of sports story that is distinguished by its female characters. Set in Azalea, Oregon, the tale is about a group of sixth-grade girls who form the Hoop Girlz basketball team after they have been rejected by their school's organized team—which was created to select a girl athlete for basketball camp—for not being good enough. While *School Library Journal* writer Renee Steinberg felt that the story was full of "platitudes about perseverance, dedication, and the need to follow your dreams," Bill Ott asserted in his *Booklist* review that although *Hoop Girlz* shares some of the themes of the old "Bad News Bears" stories, "Bledsoe cleverly

avoids most of the cliches," and he complimented the author on a unique ending and interesting subplots and supporting characters.

More recently, Bledsoe completed yet another middle-grade novel, *The Antarctic Scoop,* which combines her interest in science with some of her personal experiences of having traveled to the Antarctic on a National Science Foundation Artists and Writers grant. The story features a twelve-year-old girl who goes to the frozen continent so that she can see through an amazing telescope constructed near the South Pole. In addition to her children's and adult novels, though, Bledsoe has also edited two books of travel essays written by homosexual writers: *Gay Travels: A Literary Companion* and *Lesbian Travels: A Literary Companion.*

Bledsoe once told *CA:* "My primary motivation for writing is to make sense of the world. Creating—stories, paintings, dance, music, art of any kind—is the only way I know how to combat forces of destruction and feelings of alienation. I am also motivated to write as a way to explore topics that intrigue me. For example, most of the stories in my first [fiction] book, *Sweat,* are about the relationship between the body and language. They are about sport, wilderness, survival, crossing boundaries, and sex, but more importantly, they are about how our deepest understanding of life comes from our bodies, from the centers of our cells. While *Sweat* is often about the *limits* of language, my novel *Working Parts* is a celebration of the vast possibilities of language.

"I read widely and am influenced by everything I read. Each month I have different favorite authors, both contemporary and classic. I teach creative writing classes in literacy—that's literacy, not literary—programs, and I sincerely believe adults who are learning to read and write for the first time are the best writing teachers I have had. They teach me about the bones of language and about the absolute necessity of a story.

"I write fiction every day and all morning. I am not an outline writer, though I usually try to write a string of scenes before beginning a first draft. (These synopses always change drastically in the course of writing a story or book.) Then I write the first draft pretty much all the way through. The real work begins after the first draft is complete. I rewrite a tremendous amount:

every story or chapter goes through dozens of drafts. I am also inspired by courageous people and nutty people, and most of all, by people who are both."

BIOGRAPHICAL AND CRITICAL SOURCES:

William Boyd

PERIODICALS

Booklist, September 15, 1995; April 1, 1997, Whitney Scott, review of *Working Parts,* p. 90; August, 1997, Susan Dove Lempke, review of *Tracks in the Snow,* p. 1900; February 1, 2002, Denise Wilms, review of *Cougar Canyon,* p. 938; September 1, 2002, Bill Ott, review of *Hoop Girlz,* p. 128; April 15, 2003, Whitney Scott, review of *This Wild Silence,* p. 1447.

Gay and Lesbian Review Worldwide, July, 2001, "Sports and Lesbian Culture," p. 9.

Horn Book, January-February, 1996, Margaret A. Bush, review of *The Big Bike Race,* p. 72.

Kirkus Reviews, October 15, 1995.

Lambda Book Report, October, 1997, Trisha Collopy, review of *Working Parts,* p. 16; April, 1999, Lora-lee Macpike, review of *Lesbian Travels: A Literary Companion,* p. 25.

Library Journal, October 1, 1995; April 1, 1997, Ina Rimpau, review of *Working Parts,* p. 120; May 15, 2003, Lisa Nussbaum, review of *This Wild Silence,* p. 122.

Publishers Weekly, August 7, 1995.

School Library Journal, November, 1995, Christina Dorr, review of *The Big Bike Race,* p. 96; July, 1997, Susan W. Hunter, review of *Tracks in the Snow,* p. 90; February, 2002, Janet Gillen, review of *Cougar Canyon,* p. 129; December, 2002, Renee Steinberg, review of *Hoop Girlz,* p. 132.

ONLINE

Lucy Jane Bledsoe Home Page, http://www.lucyjanebledsoe.com/ (July 16, 2004).

*   *   *

BOYD, William 1952-

PERSONAL: Born March 7, 1952, in Accra, Ghana; son of Alexander Murray (a physician) and Evelyn (a teacher; maiden name, Smith) Boyd; married Susan Wilson (a magazine editor), 1975. *Education:* University of Nice, diploma (French studies), 1971; University of Glasgow, M.A. (with honors), 1975; postgraduate study at Jesus College, Oxford, 1975-80.

ADDRESSES: Home—London, England. *Agent*—Lemon, Unna & Durbridge Ltd., 24 Pottery Lane, Holland Park, London W11 4LZ, England.

CAREER: Novelist and screenwriter. St. Hilda's College, Oxford, England, lecturer in English literature, 1980-83; *New Statesman,* London, England, television critic, 1981-83.

MEMBER: Royal Society of Literature (fellow, 1992).

AWARDS, HONORS: Whitbread Literary Award for best first novel, Booksellers Association of Great Britain and Ireland, 1981, and Somerset Maugham Award, Society of Authors, 1982, both for *A Good Man in Africa;* John Llewelyn Rhys Memorial Prize and Booker McConnell Prize nomination, National Book

League, both 1982, both for *An Ice-Cream War;* James Tait Black Memorial Book Prize, 1991, for *Brazzaville Beach;* Chevalier de l'Ordre des Arts et des Lettres, 1991; *Sunday Express* Book of the Year Award, 1983; *Los Angeles Times* Book Prize for fiction, 1995, for *The Blue Afternoon;* honorary Litt.D., University of St. Andrews, 1997, University of Stirling, 1997, and University of Glasgow, 2000.

WRITINGS:

NOVELS

A Good Man in Africa, Hamish Hamilton (London, England), 1981, Morrow (New York, NY), 1982.

An Ice-Cream War: A Tale of the Empire, Hamish Hamilton (London, England), 1982, Morrow (New York, NY), 1983.

Stars and Bars, Morrow (New York, NY), 1985, reprinted, Vintage (New York, NY), 2001.

School Ties, Hamish Hamilton (London, England), Morrow (New York, NY), 1985.

The New Confessions, Morrow (New York, NY), 1988.

Brazzaville Beach, Morrow (New York, NY), 1990.

Cork, Ulysses (London, England), 1994.

Transfigured Night, One Horse Press (London, England), 1995.

The Blue Afternoon, Knopf (New York, NY), 1995.

Visions Fugitives, Cuckoo Press for John Sandoe (London, England), 1997.

Armadillo, Knopf (New York, NY), 1998.

Nat Tate: An American Artist, 1928-1960, 21 Publishing (Cambridge, England), 1998.

Protobiography, Bridgewater (London, England), 1998.

Any Human Heart: The Intimate Journals of Logan Mountstuart, Hamish Hamilton (London, England), 2002, Knopf (New York, NY), 2003.

SHORT-STORY COLLECTIONS

On the Yankee Station and Other Stories, Hamish Hamilton (London, England), 1981, expanded edition published as *On the Yankee Station: Stories,* Morrow (New York, NY), 1984, reprinted, Vintage (New York, NY), 2001.

The Destiny of Nathalie "X," Sinclair-Stevenson (London, England), 1994, expanded edition published as *The Destiny of Nathalie "X" and Other Stories,* Knopf (New York, NY), 1997.

PLAYS

Care and Attention of Swimming Pools, and Not Yet Jayette, produced in London, England, 1985.

On the Yankee Station, (adapted for radio from short-story collection), 1985.

School Ties: "Good and Bad at Games" (television play; broadcast by Channel Four Television, 1984), Hamish Hamilton (London, England), 1985, Morrow (New York, NY), 1986.

School Ties: "Dutch Girls" (television play; London Weekend Television, 1985), Hamish Hamilton (London, England), 1985, Morrow (New York, NY), 1986.

Scoop (television play; adapted from Evelyn Waugh's novel), ITV, 1986.

Stars and Bars (screenplay; adapted from novel), Columbia Pictures, 1988.

Aunt Julia and the Scriptwriter (screenplay; adapted from the novel by Mario Vargas Llosa), Cinecom, 1990, released as *Tune in Tomorrow,* Hobo, 1990.

Mister Johnson (screenplay; adapted from the novel by Joyce Cary), Avenue Pictures, 1991.

(With Bryan Forbes and William Goldman) *Chaplin,* (adapted from *My Autobiography* by Charles Chaplin), Carolco, 1992.

A Good Man in Africa (adapted from his novel), Gramercy (New Brunswick, NJ), 1994.

Homage to AB: A Masque (adapted for radio from the novel), BBC Radio, (Scotland), 1994, Gramercy (New Brunswick, NJ), 1994.

The Trench (screenplay), Bonaparte Films, 1999.

Armadillo (television play; adapted from his novel), BBC, 2001, A & E, 2002.

OTHER

(Author of introduction) Joyce Cary, *Mister Johnson,* Penguin (Harmondsworth, England), 1985.

(Author of introduction) *Graham Sutherland, Modern British Masters,* Volume 9, Bernard Jacobson Gallery (London, England), 1993.

(Author of introduction) Charles Dickens, *Martin Chuzzlewit,* Knopf (New York, NY), 1994.

(Author of introduction) Ken Saro-Wiwa, *A Month and a Day: A Detention Diary,* Penguin Books (New York, NY), 1995.

(Author of introduction) Frederic Manning, *Her Privates We,* Serpent's Tail (London, England), 1999.

Television critic for *New Statesman*, 1981-83; fiction reviewer for London *Sunday Times*, 1982-83; contributor of stories and reviews to periodicals, including *Books and Bookmen, Daily Telegraph, Harper's, London Magazine, London Review of Books, New Republic, New York Times Book Review, Spectator, Times Literary Supplement*, and *Washington Post*.

SIDELIGHTS: British novelist and critic William Boyd has found a wide readership for his darkly humorous fiction on both sides of the Atlantic. Boyd's work addresses subjects from expatriation to modern mathematical theory, reflecting the author's own view that life's events are completely unpredictable and even the most banal folk can be buffeted by fate. Boyd is "an intellectual who wears his learning lightly, when he does not toss it aside completely," remarked *Time* magazine reviewer Martha Duffy. Writing for the *Washington Post Book World*, columnist Jonathan Yardley maintained that Boyd "writes more often than not about the conflict of alien cultures, but he invariably does so in ways that are unpredictable and imaginative; he is heir to an established tradition of English comic fiction, yet within it he is clearly his own man; he is a biting satirist and social commentator, yet he regards his characters with an affection that is too rare in such fiction. There's hardly a writer around whose work offers more pleasure and satisfaction."

With the publication of his comic first novel, *A Good Man in Africa*, Boyd won acclaim as one of England's brightest young literary talents, earning two of Britain's top literary prizes, the Whitbread and Somerset Maugham awards. The novel's protagonist, Morgan Leafy, is a British junior diplomat in a dusty outpost of post-colonial West Africa whose misadventures—stemming from his fondness for alcohol and women and his frustrated career ambitions—are comically exacerbated by his foreign environment. "Leafy wants to improve his life, and his ambitions are endearingly average," wrote Mona Simpson in the *New York Times Book Review*. "Of course, as a comic hero Leafy gets nothing of the sort."

Many reviewers allowed that, as a rollicking farce, *A Good Man in Africa* succeeds admirably. "It lack[s] depth, perhaps, but not finesse or wit," Anne Tyler commented in the *Detroit News*. "Boyd's control of a fairly complicated plot reveals him as a most accomplished *farceur*," remarked A. N. Wilson in a *Spectator*

critique, "and he puts Morgan through his paces with all the assurance of a circus trainer making a poodle jump through hoops."

For his second award-winning novel, *An Ice-Cream War: A Tale of the Empire*, Boyd explores the stories of six characters swept up in the conflict of war, including an American expatriate sisal farmer, his German officer neighbor, a young British military officer, and his artistic younger brother. It is through the experiences of the last, Felix Cobb, that Boyd most conspicuously advances his theme that war is "chaotic and absurd. It is the romance of *war* that Boyd wants to destroy, and the hideous chaos of the war in Africa . . . is recreated with . . . a fine balance of satire, black comedy and horror," reported Harriett Gilbert in a *New Statesman* review.

Commending the novel's historical detail, critics professed even greater praise for the sureness and skill with which Boyd developed his ambitious theme and complex narrative. "Using an almost cinematic technique, Mr. Boyd cuts back and forth between the exploits of different characters, building narrative suspense with brisk assurance." "The scenes and characters shift with admirable dispatch," commented Robert Towers in the *New York Review of Books*. Michiko Kakutani concluded in the *New York Times*, "*An Ice-Cream War* . . . represents Mr. Boyd's discovery of his own voice—an elastic voice that is capable not only of some very funny satire but also of seriousness and compassion." The single weakness detected by some critics in Boyd's historical drama lies in the realm of character development. Towers noted, "Whatever is ultimately mysterious or unpredictable in the human personality is largely missing—and yet we hardly notice its absence, so effective are the strong, quick outlines he provides." The tales in Boyd's collection of short stories, *On the Yankee Station*, vary widely in subject matter and narrative technique. Reviewing the collection for the *Spectator*, Paul Ableman asserted, "Here is a collection of short stories which are, with one exception, formidably accomplished."

Largely traditional narratives, the stories portray innocents and misfits struggling in an indifferent world: a faded child-star-turned-parking-attendant who dreams of meeting a celebrity, a young boy tortured by his mother's adulteries, a bullied soldier obsessed with revenge. *Los Angeles Times Book Review* critic Malcolm Boyd described *On the Yankee Station* as a look "at life's underside instead of its smiling face." Kakutani related that "Boyd's people are not an overly introspective lot: Instead of looking into their own souls for answers, they tend to project their needs and frustrations outward to the world at large." Andrew Motion reiterated this assessment when writing for the *Times Literary Supplement.* "Boyd does not show his characters receiving impressions. . . . They exist primarily in terms of narrative event: for all the frequency with which circumstances conspire against them, they seldom form a speculative or philosophical attachment to their worlds. The greatest virtue of this narrative method is a certain kind of readability—Boyd's stories race along, confident and competent. The disadvantage, though, is a degree of sameness."

In *Stars and Bars* Boyd returned to the comic tradition of the hapless Englishman abroad, introducing Henderson Dores, a timid London art appraiser who takes a new job with a Manhattan auction house, eager to lose his inhibitions and reserve in the bold, impetuous world of America. Frequently daunted by New York City manners and conventions, the Englishman surrenders all comprehension when in the end he finds himself stranded on Park Avenue wearing only a cardboard box. Perceived as a madman by fellow pedestrians, he abdicates his responsible self to an irrational world—and feels sudden kinship. "This 'America' by which he has hoped to be liberated," observed Yardley in a *Washington Post Book World* critique, "turns out to be a far more complex and difficult place than he bargained for."

Reviewing *Stars and Bars* for the *New York Times Book Review,* Caroline Seebohm determined that Boyd's "talent in evoking a place, which worked so well in his earlier two novels, serves him brilliantly here." Yardley concurred, lauding the author's sense of "the American landscape, both physical and psychological" and contending that Boyd "recreates American speech with the aplomb of a born mimic." While Boyd pokes fun at "American food, accents, adolescents, motels with their conventions, hotels with interior forests and lakes," opined *Newsweek* reviewer Peter S. Prescott, he never loses sight of his "primary target," the transplanted Englishman who cannot assimilate. "Can this British author get all this American arcana right?" the critic pondered. "Alas, he can."

In Boyd's novel *The New Confessions,* a Scottish expatriate filmmaker named John James Todd looks back over a life than spans much of the twentieth century.

"I wanted this to be like a life," Boyd explained in the *Washington Post.* "I wanted the graininess, the texture of life, with the blind alleys and circlings that a real life has. I wanted [the character] to seem like a real person. That type of genial egomaniac is his own worst enemy."

In the *Los Angeles Times Book Review,* Ronald Gottesman observed that in *The New Confessions* "Boyd has created an important and complex character in a vividly evoked series of settings. He has told a tale that we cannot not believe in (in spite of its many astonishing turns). He has written a subtle and provocative history of our time."

Boyd's next novel, *Brazzaville Beach,* won the James Tait Black Memorial Book Prize. The story follows a scientist named Hope Clearwater as she observes chimpanzee behavior in Africa and ruminates on her unsuccessful marriage to a troubled mathematician. Hope's discovery that groups of chimpanzees in the game reserve are actually waging war upon each other threatens to refute the many popular publications of the reserve's leading scientist. "Strong or interesting characters give *Brazzaville Beach* its color, impetus, and bite, but Hope is its dynamo," wrote Michael Bishop in the *Washington Post Book World.* "She sets things going—from her courtship of John Clearwater, who attracts her because he has a cast of mind beyond her own understanding, to the necessary dismantling of a great primatologist's self-deluding theories about the chimpanzees." The critic concluded that *Brazzaville Beach*'s "people convince, its contrapuntal story unfolds with a complex inevitability that does not preclude surprises, and its intellectual music, honestly grounded in the workaday lives of its characters, resonates from the earth up rather than from the sky down."

Critics once again applauded Boyd for *The Destiny of Nathalie "X" and Other Stories.* The collection showcases what *New York Times Book Review* contributor Michael Upchurch called Boyd's "pleasing variousness as a writer." Containing eleven stories that span geography and era, the book taps its author's comic sensibilities while also reflecting a broad knowledge and an intricate way with a storyline. In the title story, the protagonist, a West African film director, visits Hollywood and remains implacable amid the hype, stress, and superficiality of the Hollywood culture. "Cork" finds a young widow inheriting a cork-processing plant after her husband's untimely death; a subsequent affair with the plant manager proves ultimately unsatisfying, due to his request that they only meet once a year. And in "Loose Continuity," Boyd juxtaposes his protagonist's war-torn romance in World War II Germany with her success as a designer in the United States less than a decade later, when reflections on her former life in Germany become almost unfathomable. Chicago's *Tribune Books* reviewer Sandra Scofield positively described the volume as "a collection of marvelously realized characters, deftly sketched in full, compressed, intelligent, eminently readable tales."

In the novel *The Blue Afternoon* Boyd weaves a story through the interaction of a confident and successful thirty-something woman named Kay Fischer and the stranger who enters her life and claims to be her natural father. The heart of the novel offers the flashback memories of the father, Salvador Carriscant, narrated by Kay who tells her father's story shortly after meeting him in 1936. "Several years ago a critic wrote that 'no book by Boyd is ever a failure,' and this is true," recognized Donna Rifkind in *Washington Post Book World*, "but neither can [*The Blue Afternoon*] . . . be called an unequivocal triumph." Calling *The Blue Afternoon* both "clever" and "exasperating," *Los Angeles Times Book Review* contributor Richard Eder also withheld enthusiastic praise from the work, which he contended has "loose ends." Boyd "has set out to write a book about life, death and narrative itself," Eder continued: "His trouble is that he has written too well. He has constructed too beautifully to be able effectively to de-construct. He has not blown up his story, he has pitted it and scratched it."

In a return to the absurd that is his trademark, Boyd's *Armadillo* is a satire about chance and life. The protagonist is Lorimer Black, an insurance adjuster with a dark secret that begins to spiral out of control along with his career and life. Jason Cowley in a *New Statesman* critique considered *Armadillo* to be "a genuine puzzle and an enigma. Is it serious satire about fragmented identity or an exercise in burlesque? A literary novel or a simple, undemanding genre piece?" According to *Publishers Weekly*, "Boyd's comic writing is zesty and brilliantly on-target . . . Lorimer's adventures have enough of an alarming edge to keep a reader constantly, and delightedly, off balance." Yet some of the same critics found the novel flawed. "With each new book," Cowley opined, Boyd "seems to take

fewer and fewer risks . . . apparently uninterested in writing against his own successful formula, in extending the limits of his craft."

It is possible, even probable, that history will witness Boyd's most remembered work as an elaborate April Fools' joke. In 1998 *Nat Tate: An American Artist, 1928-1960* was published, complete with credible period photographs and paintings. According to contributor Andrew Biswell of the *Dictionary of Literary Biography, Nat Tate* "achieved the rare distinction of being written about on the news pages rather than the review sections of newspapers." The character Nat Tate was revealed to be a figment of Boyd's imagination by David Lister in the *Independent* of London. Lister claimed that "some of the biggest names in the art world have been the victims of a literary hoax." Boyd's explanation of the joke demonstrated his intention that the book be quickly revealed as a hoax, "The book was . . . studded with covert and cryptic clues and hints as to its real, fictive status." *Newsweek* described the book that caused the furor as a satirical charmer in which "Boyd is spot-on with details [while] other features . . . are slightly—and deliciously—wrong." According to Biswell, "It is a joyously disrespectful performance that stands up to repeated close readings, and it promises to become a key reference point in the recent history of fakes and faking."

Any Human Heart: The Intimate Journals of Logan Mountstuart was pronounced by a *Publishers Weekly* critic as "one of the most beguiling books of this season . . . rich sophisticated, often hilarious and disarming." This book chronicles the life of Logan Clinton, a globetrotting author and adventurer whose fictional life spans most of the twentieth century. The "tale is lively and likable, if awfully anecdotal," said a *Kirkus Reviews* contributor, "and perversely given to serial name-dropping. A rich, unruly work, intermittently skimpy and chaotic. . . . And, in its best pages . . . a nearly irresistible entertainment." Written as a journal complete with footnotes and an index, *Any Human Heart* "is shot through with Boyd's customary black humor," explained Toby Clements in the London *Daily Telegraph*, "combining a dry and sophisticated wit with a love for the embarrassing and the absurd."

Regardless of what fictional avenues he traverses, Boyd has established himself as a renowned writer of farce and a practical joker of international caliber. According to Cowley, "he is the supreme chronicler of contemporary contingency, of randomness and uncertainty." Boyd would doubtless agree, because for him, "Writing fiction is absolute freedom. As an art form it is so boundlessly generous. Novels literally have no boundaries. You can write a two-thousand-page novel covering billions of years, if that's what you decide to do. Anything is possible."

BIOGRAPHICAL AND CRITICAL SOURCES:

BOOKS

Contemporary Literary Criticism, Gale (Detroit, MI), Volume 28, 1984, Volume 53, 1989, Volume 70, 1992.

Dunn, Douglas, "Divergent Scottishness: William Boyd, Alan Massie, Ronald Frame," in *The Scottish Novel since the Seventies: New Visions, Old Dreams,* edited by Gavin Wallace and Randall Stevenson, Edinburgh University Press (Edinburgh, Scotland), 1993.

Hargis, Margaret Finley, *William Boyd Family,* M. F. Hargis (Warrenton, VA), 1995.

PERIODICALS

Books, spring, 1999, review of *Armadillo,* p. 23.

Books and Bookman, October 1995, p. 19.

Boston Review, September, 1985, Judith Wynn, review of *A Good Man in Africa,* pp. 27-28; June, 1988, p. 28.

British Book News, January, 1986, p. 54.

Daily Telegraph (London, England), April 20, 2002, Toby Clements, "He Made the Whole Thing Up; A Mock Journal with Spot-on Mimicry Almost Convinces Toby Clements," review of *Any Human Heart: The Intimate Journals of Logan Mountstuart,* p. 6.

Detroit Free Press, August 26, 1984.

Detroit News, August 12, 1984.

Guardian, April 9, 1998, John Mullan, "Sting in Manhattan," p. 11; February 19, 1998, Mark Lawson, "Frozen Assets" (interview), pp. 11-12; April 20, 2002, Giles Foden, review of *Any Human Heart,* p. 9.

Hudson Review, winter, 1986; autumn, 1988; winter, 1992; winter, 1996.

Kirkus Reviews, November 15, 2002, review of *Any Human Heart,* p. 1636.

London Review of Books, October 1, 1987; June 4, 1998, Alex Ivanovitch, "Onomastics," pp. 28-29; September 27, 1990, pp. 19-20; September 23, 1993, p. 22.

Los Angeles Times Book Review, March 27, 1983; August 26, 1984; May 26, 1985; June 19, 1988, p. 2, 8; July 7, 1991, pp. 2, 7; February 26, 1995, pp. 3, 9; January 19, 1997, p. 11.

New Republic, April 25, 1983; Jack Beatty, review of *An Ice-Cream War: A Tale of the Empire,* p. 37; July 8, 1985, Gerald Epps, review of *Stars and Bars,* pp. 41-42; June 13, 1988, Thomas R. Edwards, audio of *The New Confessions,* pp. 32-34; January 25, 1993, Stanley Kauffmann, review of *Chaplin* (movie review), p. 28.

New Scientist, October 13, 1990, Robin McKie, review of *Brazzaville Beach,* p. 47.

New Statesman, January 30, 1981, Alan Hollinghurst, review of *A Good Man in Africa,* p. 19; July 17, 1981, Bill Greenwell, review of *On the Yankee Station,* p. 21; September 17, 1982, Harriett Gilbert, review of *An Ice Cream War,* p. 21; September 21, 1984, Roger Lewis, review of *Stars and Bars,* p. 29; December 6, 1985, Alan Brien, review of *Stars and Bars,* p. 110; October 2, 1987; March 6, 1998, Jason Cowley, review of *Armadillo,* p. 48; April 17, 1998, Jessica Smerin, review of *Nat Tate: An American Artist, 1928-1960,* p. 43; September 20, 1999, Jonathan Romney, review of *The Trench,* p. 48; April 1, 2002, review of *Any Human Heart,* p. 55.

New Statesman and Society, September 14, 1990, Sean French, review of *Brazzaville Beach,* p. 38; September 24, 1993, p. 24.

Newsweek, January 14, 1985; David Lehman, review of *On the Yankee Station,* p. 104; May 6, 1985, Peter S. Prescott, review of *Stars and Bars,* p. 80; July 8, 1991, Peter S. Prescott, review of *Brazzaville Beach,* p. 59; April 20, 1998, Malcolm Jones, "The Late Great Tate: An Artist Is Rediscovered; April Fool," p. 62; February 24, 2003, Malcolm Jones, review of *Any Human Heart,* p. 66.

New Yorker, April 12, 1982, review of *A Good Man in Africa,* p. 153; April 25, 1983, review of *An Ice Cream War,* p. 154; October 15, 1984, review of *On the Yankee Station,* p. 177; May 20, 1985, review of *Stars and Bars,* p. 125; April 8, 1991, Terrence Rafferty, movie review of *Mister Johnson,* p. 82; October 21, 1991, John Updike, review of *Brazzaville Beach,* p. 129; March 27, 1995, Zoe Heller, review of *The Blue Afternoon,* pp. 100-101.

New York Review of Books, June 2, 1983, Robert Towers, review of *An Ice Cream War,* pp. 42-43; October 10, 1991, Thomas R. Edwards, review of *Brazzaville Beach,* p. 33-34.

New York Times, April 6, 1982, Michiko Kakutani, review of *A Good Man in Africa,* p. 25; April 25, 1982, Mona Simpson, review of *A Good Man in Africa,* p. 12; December 5, 1982, review of *A Good Man in Africa,* p. 87; February 27, 1983, Michael Gorra, review of *An Ice Cream War,* p. 8; April 5, 1983, Michiko Kakutani, review of *An Ice Cream War,* p. C13; May 21, 1983; July 2, 1984, Michiko Kakutani, review of *On the Yankee Station,* p. 15; August 5, 1984; Bernard McCabe, review of *On the Yankee Station,* p. 12; April 14, 1985, Caroline Seebohm, review of *Stars and Bars,* p. 17; August 9, 1986, Michiko Katutani, review of *School Ties,* p. 11; March 18, 1988, Vincent Canby, movie review of *Stars and Bars,* p. 20; April 27, 1988, Michiko Kakutani, review of *The New Confessions,* p. 18; December 28, 1990, John J. O'Connor, television review of *Scoop,* p. B4; May 31, 1991, Michiko Kakutani, review of *Brazzaville Beach,* p. C29; December 25, 1992, Vincent Canby, movie review of *Chaplin,* p. B6; April 11, 1995, Michiko Kakutani, review of *The Blue Afternoon,* p. B2; April 9, 1998, Sarah Lyall, review of *Nat Tate,* p. E6; November 3, 1998, Richard Bernstein, review of *Armadillo,* p. E6; November 19, 2000, William Boyd, "Seeking Answers down in the Trenches," movie review of *The Trench,* p. AR13; November 22, 2000, Stephen Holden, movie review of *The Trench,* p. B3; August 2, 2002, Julie Salamon, television review of *Armadillo,* p. B1.

New York Times Book Review, August 31, 1986, Patricia T. O'Conner, review of *Stars and Bars,* p. 20; May 29, 1988, Michael Wood, review of *The New Confessions,* p. 5; June 23, 1991, Blanche d'Alpuget, review of *Brazzaville Beach,* p. 14; April 2, 1995; Thomas Keneally, review of *The Blue Afternoon,* p. 6; January 12, 1997; January 19, 1997, Michael Upchurch, audio review of *An Ice Cream War,* pp. 9-10; June 14, 1998, Paul Mattick,"Imagining Imaginary Artists," p. 35; November 14, 1999, review of *An Ice Cream War,* p. 38; February 16, 2003, review of *Any Human Heart,* p. 9; March 2, 2003, review of *Any Human Heart,* p. 26; March 16, 2003, review of *Any Human Heart,* p. 26

Observer (London, England), September 12, 1982, p. 32; October 27, 1985; August 28, 1988; September 27, 1987; October 2, 1988; September 16, 1990, p. 55; June 18, 1995; February 7, 1999, review of *Armadillo,* p. 14; December 30, 2001, review of *Any Human Heart,* p. 14; September 2, 2001, review of *Armadillo,* p. 18; April 14, 2002, review of *Any Human Heart,* p. 17.

Publishers Weekly, February 26, 1982, review of *A Good Man in Africa,* p. 140; January 28, 1983, Barbara A. Bannon, review of *An Ice Cream War,* p. 71; April 8, 1983, review of *A Good Man in Africa,* p. 57; May 18, 1984, review of *On the Yankee Station,* p. 143; February 15, 1985, review of *Stars and Bars,* p. 88; June 6, 1986; April 15, 1988, Sybil Steinberg, review of *The New Confessions,* p. 74; April 29, 1988, Amanda Smith, "William Boyd" (interview), pp. 56-57; April 5, 1991, Sybil Steinberg, review of *Brazzaville Beach,* p. 136; January 9, 1995, review of *The Blue Afternoon,* p. 55; January 9, 1995, Paul Nathan, "Times Past," p. 24; January 27, 1997, review of *The Destiny of Nathalie "X" and Other Stories,* p. 80; July 27, 1998, review of *Armadillo,* p. 50; December 2, 2002, review of *Any Human Heart,* p. 34; March 3, 2003, Sybil Steinberg, "William Boyd: Resisting the Last Word" (interview), p. 49.

Punch, October 3, 1984; August 24, 1990, pp. 46-47.

Quill & Quire, May, 1985; November, 1990, p. 25.

Sewanee Review, fall, 1999, review of *Armadillo,* p. 600.

Southern Review, winter, 1998, Thomas Keneally, review of *Brazzaville Beach,* p. 76.

Spectator, February 28, 1981; August 8, 1981, pp. 21-22; November 28, 1981; September 11, 1982, pp. 23-24; December 18, 1982; January 1, 1983; October 6, 1984; October 3, 1987; September 15, 1990, Anita Brookner, review of *Brazzaville Beach,* p. 38; June 1, 1991; November 23, 1991; May 20, 1995; April 20, 2002, review of *Any Human Heart,* p. 41.

Texas Studies in Literature and Language, spring, 2000, Pierre Vitoux,"The Uses of Parody in William Boyd's *The New Confessions*," p. 79.

Time, July 30, 1984, Pico Iyer, review of *On the Yankee Station,* p. 103; May 20, 1985, Martha Duffy, review of *Stars and Bars,* p. 82; May 30, 1988, Martha Duffy, review of *The New Confessions,* p. 62; June 24, 1991, Martha Duffy, review of *Brazzaville Beach,* p. 64; February 6, 1995, Martha Duffy, review of *The Blue Afternoon,* p. 74; February 17, 2003, Lev Grossman, review of *Any Human Heart,* p. 76.

Times (London, England), October 28, 1981; February 28, 1983; September 20, 1984; September 28, 1987.

Times Literary Supplement, January 30, 1981, D. A. N. Jones, review of *A Good Man in Africa,* p. 106; July 17, 1981, Andrew Motion, review of *On the Yankee Station,* p. 803; September 17, 1982, p. 993; October 22, 1982; September 21, 1984; September 25, 1987; September 14, 1990, p. 970; May 19, 1995; April 19, 2002, James Campbell, review of *Any Human Heart,* p. 22.

Tribune Books (Chicago, IL), May 8, 1988, pp. 5, 9; February 2, 1997, p. 3.

Village Voice Literary Supplement, September, 1984; May, 1985.

Virginia Quarterly Review, summer, 1999, review of *Armadillo,* p. 94.

Vogue, May, 1988, Rhoda Koenig, "Rude Confessions: England's Best Storyteller Gives His Characters an Absurdly Hard Time," p. 16; June, 1991, Christopher Hitchens, review of *Brazzaville Beach,* p. 84; February, 1995, Rhoda Koenig, review of *The Blue Afternoon,* p. 161.

Wall Street Journal, July 25, 1988, Susan Vigliante, review of *The New Confessions,* p. 11; June 26, 1991, Lee Lescaze, review of *Brazzaville Beach,* p. A9; December 24, 1992, Julie Salamon, movie review of *Chaplin,* p. A5.

Washington Post, May 31, 1988, April 10, 1998, Paula Span, review of *Nat Tate,* p. B1; September 6, 1998, review of *Armadillo,* p. 10; July 28, 2002, Martie Zad, "A & E's *Armadillo*: Who's in the Shell?," p. Y04.

Washington Post Book World, March 20, 1983; July 10, 1983; August 5, 1984; April 28, 1985, pp. 3, 9; November 24, 1985; August 17, 1986; May 8, 1988; June 4, 1989; June 2, 1991, pp. 1, 14; February 19, 1995, p. 5.

Woman's Journal, March, 1999, review of *Armadillo,* p. 18.*

*   *   *

BRAUN, Stephen R. 1957-

PERSONAL: Born February 13, 1957, in Wilmington, DE; son of Robert A. (an organic chemist and counselor) and Janet (Laird) Braun; married Susan Redditt (a professor of education), September 19, 1987; children: Isa R., Aurora R. *Ethnicity:* "Caucasian." *Education:*

Stephen R. Braun

St. John Fisher College, B.A. *Religion:* Buddhist (Zen). *Hobbies and other interests:* Hiking, skiing, bicycling, sailing.

ADDRESSES: Home and office—180 Lincoln Ave., Amherst, MA 01002. *Agent*—Gail Ross, LSTR, 1666 Connecticut Ave., Washington, DC 20009. *E-mail*—stephenbraun@attbi.com.

CAREER: Writer. New England Research Institutes, Boston, MA, executive producer, beginning 1994.

AWARDS, HONORS: First-place award, American Medical Writers Book Competition, 1997.

WRITINGS:

Buzz: The Science and Lore of Alcohol and Caffeine, Oxford University Press (New York, NY), 1996.
The Science of Happiness: Unlocking the Mysteries of Mood, Wiley (New York, NY), 2000.

WORK IN PROGRESS: Coping with Depression and Anxiety in Uncertain Times, for Houghton Mifflin (Boston, MA).

SIDELIGHTS: Science writer Stephen R. Braun chose a subject—or rather two subjects—of almost universal interest for his book *Buzz: The Science and Lore of Alcohol and Caffeine.* Those two legal drugs have been used in cultures around the world from ancient times to modern, and their role in history provides a glimpse of continuities and differences from era to era and country to country. Medical and mental health professionals have traditionally found both help and harm in these substances, and Braun illuminates the positive and negative aspects of caffeine and alcohol by relating some of his own experiences "under the influence" during the writing of his book. (According to *Entertainment Weekly,* Braun credits caffeine as an "invaluable tool" for his own writing.) Braun also includes in his book considerable information about the chemistry and physiological effects of alcohol and caffeine.

Library Journal contributor Eris Weaver found that Braun had treated the technical side of his material "engagingly." Similarly, a *Publishers Weekly* critic reported that Braun's "presentation of complicated scientific concepts is understandable without being condescending." The reviewer also cited the historical, sociological, and anecdotal portions of the text. An *Entertainment Weekly* reviewer pointed out the "stimulating dash of related cultural tidbits" in the "zippy" work.

BIOGRAPHICAL AND CRITICAL SOURCES:

PERIODICALS

Booklist, August, 1996, p. 1867.
Entertainment Weekly, October 11, 1996, review of *Buzz: The Science and Lore of Alcohol and Caffeine.*
Kirkus Reviews, June 1, 1996, p. 794.
Library Journal, July, 1996, Eris Weaver, review of *Buzz,* p. 148.
Publishers Weekly, June 10, 1996, review of *Buzz,* p. 80.
Science, August 9, 1996, p. 738.

*   *   *

BRINDLE, Max
See FLEISCHMAN, (Albert) Sid(ney)

BRYSON, Bill
See BRYSON, William

*   *   *

BRYSON, William 1951(?)-
(Bill Bryson)

PERSONAL: Born c. 1951, in Des Moines, IA; son of William Bryson (a sports columnist); married; wife's name Cynthia (a nurse); children: four. *Education:* Attended Drake University.

ADDRESSES: Home—Hanover, NH, and Norfolk, England. *Agent*—c/o Author Mail, Broadway Books/Doubleday, c/o Random House, 15400 Broadway, New York, NY 10036.

CAREER: Journalist and author. Worked at a newspaper in Bournemouth, England, beginning 1977, and for business sections of *Times* and *Independent,* London, England. Guest on television programs, including *Good Morning America* and *Sunday Morning.* Appointed an English Heritage Commissioner, 2003.

WRITINGS:

AS BILL BRYSON, EXCEPT AS INDICATED

The Facts on File Dictionary of Troublesome Words, Facts on File (New York, NY), 1984, revised edition, 1988, published as *The Penguin Dictionary of Troublesome Words,* Penguin (New York, NY), 1984, revised edition, Viking, (New York, NY) 1988, published as *Bryson's Dictionary of Troublesome Words,* Broadway Books (New York, NY), 2002.
(As William Bryson) *The Palace under the Alps, and Over Two Hundred Other Unusual, Unspoiled, and Infrequently Visited Spots in Sixteen European Countries,* Congdon & Weed (New York, NY), 1985.
The Lost Continent: Travels in Small-Town America, Harper (New York, NY), 1989.
The Mother Tongue: English and How It Got That Way, Morrow (New York, NY), 1990.

William Bryson

Neither Here nor There: Travels in Europe, Secker & Warburg (London, England), 1991, Morrow (New York, NY), 1992.

The Penguin Dictionary for Writers and Editors, Viking (New York, NY), 1992.

Made in America: An Informal History of the English Language in the United States, Morrow (New York, NY), 1994.

Notes from a Small Island: An Affectionate Portrait of Britain, Morrow (New York, NY), 1995.

A Walk in the Woods: Rediscovering America on the Appalachian Trail, Broadway Books (New York, NY), 1998.

I'm a Stranger Here Myself: Notes on Returning to America after Twenty Years Away, Broadway Books (New York, NY), 1999.

(Editor, with Jason Wilson) *The Best American Travel Writing, 2000,* Houghton Mifflin (Boston, MA), 2000.

In a Sunburned Country, Broadway Books (New York, NY), 2000, published as *Down Under,* Doubleday (London, England), 2000.

Bill Bryson's African Diary, Broadway Books (New York, NY), 2002.

Author of "Notes from a Big Country," a weekly column in *Mail on Sunday.* Contributor to periodicals, including *Travel and Leisure, National Geographic,* and *New York Times.*

ADAPTATIONS: Neither Here nor There was adapted for audio recording by Random House (New York, NY), 1999. *In a Sunburned Country* was adapted for audio recording by BDD Audio (New York, NY), 2000.

SIDELIGHTS: William Bryson's works can be divided into two categories, according to some reviewers. "In his adoptive Britain," Norman Oder explained in *Publishers Weekly,* "Bryson reached best-seller status with wiseacre travelogues. . . . In the United States, he's best known for excursions into the lore of the English language."

For the first of the travelogues, the American-born journalist returned from his home in North Yorkshire, England, to his native Iowa and set out on a journey by car across the North American continent to write *The Lost Continent: Travels in Small-Town America.* The work is an account of a thirty-eight-state tour Bryson began in 1987, having decided to embark on the kind of motor trip his family once took in their blue Rambler station wagon. Bryson's quest was to find the perfect small town in which, as he explains in *The Lost Continent,* "Bing Crosby would be the priest, Jimmy Stewart mayor, Fred MacMurray the high school principal, Henry Fonda a Quaker farmer. Walter Brennan would run the gas station, a boyish Mickey Rooney would deliver groceries, and somewhere, at an open window, Deanna Durbin would sing."

Throughout his travels, however, Bryson offers descriptions of what he finds as "parking lots and tallish buildings surrounded by a sprawl of shopping centers, gas stations and fast-food joints." His observations about small-town America are laced with a sharp-edged humor; at one point he notes that "talking about a scenic route in southeast Iowa is like talking about a good Barry Manilow album," which alienated some reviewers. *Los Angeles Times Book Review* contributor Wanda Urbanska termed *Lost Continent* "merely a forum for the put-down humor so popular these days." A *Newsweek* critic, however, noted that the book "is paradoxically touching—a melancholy memoir in the form of a snide travelogue." *The Lost Continent* proved more popular with readers, becoming a Book-of-the-Month Club alternate selection. "You have to be able to laugh at yourself to understand this book, and I know that is asking a lot of some people," Bryson explained in the *Chicago Tribune.* "It really is a fond portrait."

Bryson again took to the road with his next book, although this time journeying the European continent. *Neither Here nor There: Travels in Europe* describes his adventures in places such as France, Italy, Norway, and Turkey. As with *The Lost Continent,* some reviewers expressed reservations about *Neither Here nor There,* complaining that the book's humor sometimes wears thin. A *Los Angeles Times* critic, however, found some of Bryson's descriptions "amusing and accurate" and noted that Bryson occasionally "provides the perfect telling detail." Dervla Murphy in the *Times Literary Supplement* found that "sometimes Bill Bryson's humour recalls [P. G.] Wodehouse, sometimes Flann O'Brien. More often it is distinctive, depending on his cunning use of flamboyant exaggerations, grotesque but always successful metaphors and the deft juxtapositions of incongruous images—the whole presented in a style that boldly veers from laid-back colloquial American to formal clean-cut English."

In the mid-1990s, Bryson moved back to the United States, where he settled with his family in Hanover, New Hampshire. Before leaving England, where he had lived for more than twenty years, the author toured the island one last time, confining himself to public transportation and foot travel. *Notes from a Small Island: An Affectionate Portrait of Britain* represents what some reviewers have likened to a fond farewell. "This affectionate valediction lauds British eccentricity, endurance, and genius for adversity," Oder wrote. British critic Boyd Tonkin reported in *New Statesman and Society* that, beneath the humor of Bryson's "all-smiles, easy reading jaunt," there flows an undercurrent of lament for days gone by. "The Britain he loves is quaint, quiet and deeply welfare-statist," Tonkin wrote, and Bryson's criticisms of "the damage wrought by market-minded dogmas," however witty, left the critic "unpersuaded. . . . He seldom reads our mustn't-grumble tolerance as a sign of surrender, not just of civility." In the United States, on the other hand, some reviewers were delighted with Bryson's "trenchant, witty and detailed observations," as a *Publishers Weekly* critic noted. *Publishers Weekly* recommended *Notes from a Small Island* as an "immensely

entertaining" account, and *Booklist* reviewer Alice Joyce hailed Bryson's writing as "delightfully irreverent."

Bryson marked his return to the land of his birth with an exploration of one of America's longest and oldest footpaths—the Appalachian Trail. His goal was to walk the entire trail, more than two thousand miles long, from Georgia to Maine. He set out optimistically from a Georgia state park with a companion of his boyhood and completed the first hundred miles with relative ease. "Initially, it didn't seem an impossible task," Bryson told Oder in an interview. "But your expectations cannot match reality." Citing difficulties ranging from "drudgery" to the whimsical reliability of maps and map makers to the defection of his partner, Stephen Katz, Bryson abridged his plan. According to *New Statesman* critic Albert Scardino, "He decides he doesn't have to walk the whole trail to absorb its spirit." In various segments over a period of time, Bryson eventually completed more than eight hundred miles of hiking and observation. *A Walk in the Woods: Rediscovering America on the Appalachian Trail* is the memoir of his journey. A *Forbes* reviewer remarked that the author's "humor is winning and succinct" and displays a talent "for boiling down his observations to their absurd essences." *Library Journal* critic Nancy J. Moeckel wrote, "Bryson shares some truly laugh-out-loud moments" in his "amiable" account of the journey and the people he met along the way. A British reviewer for the *Economist* compared Bryson's talents to the "droll American mix of folksy intelligence and aw-shucks wit" of Garrison Keillor, and Ron Antonucci recommended the memoir to *Booklist* readers as "a marvelous description and history of the trail."

Oder suggested that *A Walk in the Woods* represents a combination of both sides of Bryson's career: "picaresque traveler and lore-gatherer." The lore-gatherer emerges in several books about words and language, beginning with *The Penguin Dictionary of Troublesome Words.* A third edition of the *Penguin Dictionary* was released in 2002 as *Bryson's Dictionary of Troublesome Words* and contains "some sixty percent" of new or updated material, according to the author. Created initially by Bryson as an editorial tool for personal use, it remains a concise guide to common English language problems. Features include lists of words and phrases often misused, clarification of differences between British and American English, redundant wording, examples of blatant errors found in prominent publications, and a glossary of punctuation and grammatical terms. A *Booklist* reviewer described this book as "admittedly narrow in range" but a "pithy guide [that] will work fine in conjunction with a full-blown style manual." Lilli McCowan of the *European Business Journal* concluded, "Bryson can help us to get stylish and even better, understood."

The Mother Tongue: English and How It Got That Way is an anecdotal, historical survey of what Bryson calls "the most important and successful language in the world." *The Mother Tongue* was warmly received by critics, who considered the book lively and engaging. *New York Times Book Review* contributor Burt Hochberg found reading Bryson's presentation of such topics as etymology, pronunciation, spelling, dialects, grammar, origins of names, and wordplay "an enthralling excursion." *Los Angeles Times Book Review* contributor Fred S. Holley called the volume "a vastly informative and vastly entertaining consideration, not only of the language's history but also of its position today."

In *Made in America: An Informal History of the English Language in the United States,* Bryson, according to Oder, "uses the evolution of American English to slalom through American history and culture." The *Economist* described Bryson as "an easy, intelligent and good-humoured writer" but warned, "Towards its end the book threatens to become little more than a history of consumption and consumer goods: how the automobile, shopping mall, aeroplane, hamburger, came to America." That reviewer also warned of errors—a caution echoed by other critics as well. In *People,* Elaine Kahn identified some of the mistakes that could lead an unwary reader astray. Others reviewers were less critical, however. Albert Kim of *Entertainment Weekly* was engaged by Bryson's "unabashed curiosity" about the English language and the "sheer delight" he derives from transmitting the information to his readers. George W. Hunt summarized the work in *America* as, overall, "a leisurely history . . . of a nation's growth as dramatized by its changing vocabulary," and a *Publishers Weekly* reviewer called the book "a treasure trove of trivia about American culture past and present."

Bryson revisited his favored genre of travel writing and his editorial past for *The Best American Travel Writing, 2000.* As guest-editor, Bryson shared duties with series editor Jason Wilson to publish this volume of Houghton Mifflin's "Best American" series. This collection of travel anthologies was described by Nicholas Howe in the *New Republic* as "'testosterone travel' or 'exploraporn' . . . today's versions of the adventure stories that ran thirty or fifty years ago in barbershop or cigar-store magazines." Bryson chose travel pieces he liked for this collection, penned by writers who, according to a *Publishers Weekly* contributor, "share a love of a place, a moment, a people," and who have written tales to "remind us of how amazing the world truly is."

Bryson recorded his return to the world of his roots in a collection of essays originally written for the British magazine *Night and Day.* The book *I'm a Stranger Here Myself: Notes on Returning to America after Twenty Years Away* is filled with funny anecdotes describing contemporary American life from the absurd, witty, and unique vantage of Bryson who chose to make his birth land home after twenty years as an expatriate. "This is humor writing at its sharpest," noted Brad Hooper in *Booklist,* who went on to say, "his saving grace is that he does more laughing with us than at us." Wilda Williams of *Library Journal* reported that the book is filled with Bryson's "trademark humor," but also "a bit slight and choppy," a small criticism that she does not expect to have any impact on the book's popularity.

In a Sunburned Country is Bryson's appropriately eccentric and humorous depiction of Australia, the continent he claims "has more things that will kill you than anywhere else," an opinion he expands, saying, "If you are not stung or pronged to death in some unexpected manner, you may be fatally chomped by sharks or crocodiles, or helplessly carried out to sea by irresistible currents, or left to stagger to an unhappy death in the baking outback." Harry Levins writing in the *St. Louis Dispatch* warned that "*In a Sunburned Country* is not a travel guide or tour book," yet he recommended Bryson's "witty, curious, and fiendishly observant" book as good traveling company. Robert Zeller in *Antipodes* reported that "Bryson is at his best in portraying the various characters he encounters . . . and in conveying his sense of wonder at his discoveries."

Not all reviewers found *In a Sunburned Country* to be Bryson's most sterling book. David Gates in *Newsweek* found Bryson's "leaden whimsy and faux-conversational tone" to be annoying and "the wealth of gee-whiz factoids [to be] almost . . . worth the trip."

Perhaps the most accurate description of the book, its author, and the subject was from a reviewer in *Publishers Weekly* who commented that "a land as vast as Australia needs a primer to make it accessible, and Bryson has accomplished that with humor and relentless curiosity."

Reviewers from the *Boston Herald* and other newspapers have compared Bryson's writing to that of a "somewhat sedate" or "smarter, more sarcastic" Dave Barry, but Gloria Maxwell of *Library Journal* provided a more concise definition of Bryson's writing: "What makes Bryson the most entertaining and interesting travel writer around is his singular facility to fashion a unique whole from historical facts, topographical observations and geographical ramblings." A *Publishers Weekly* critic agreed, claiming that Bryson's "strength lies in his ability to incorporate astounding facts about the country with nutty personal anecdotes."

BIOGRAPHICAL AND CRITICAL SOURCES:

BOOKS

Bryson, Bill, *The Lost Continent: Travels in Small-Town America,* Harper (New York, NY), 1989.
Bryson, Bill, *The Mother Tongue: English and How It Got That Way,* Morrow (New York, NY), 1990.

PERIODICALS

America, November 25, 1995, George W. Hunt, review of *Made in America: An Informal History of the English Language in the United States,* p. 2.
Antipodes, December, 2000, Robert Zeller, review of *In a Sunburned Country,* p. 175.
Booklist, May 1, 1996, Alice Joyce, review of *Notes from a Small Island: An Affectionate Portrait of Britain,* p. 1486; April, 1998, Ron Antonucci, review of *A Walk in the Woods: Rediscovering America on the Appalachian Trail,* pp. 1297-1299; April 1, 1999, Brad Hooper, review of *I'm a Stranger Here Myself: Notes on Returning to America after Twenty Years Away,* p. 363; August,

1999, Karen Harris, review of *Neither Here nor There: Travels in Europe,* p. 2075; September 15, 1999, Whitney Scott, review of *A Walk in the Woods,* p. 276; September 15, 2000, Mary Frances Wilkens, audiobook review of *In a Sunburned Country,* p. 263; September 15, 2000, Brad Hooper, review of *The Best American Travel Writing, 2000,* p. 97; July, 2002, Joanne Wilkinson, review of *Bryson's Dictionary of Troublesome Words: A Writer's Guide to Getting It Right,* p. 1805.
Boston Herald, June 6, 1999, Erica Noonan, review of *I'm a Stranger Here Myself,* p. 064; June 29, 2000, review of *In a Sunburned Country,* p. 62.
Chicago Tribune, September 20, 1989, pp. 1, 10; July 11, 1990, section 5, p. 3.
Economist, August 20, 1994, review of *Made in America,* p. 69; November 15, 1997, review of *A Walk in the Woods,* pp. S5-S7.
Entertainment Weekly, May 5, 1995, Albert Kim, review of *Made in America,* p. 63; June 7, 1996, Curt Feldman, review of *Notes from a Small Island,* p. 54.
European Business Journal, spring, 2002, Lilli McCowan, review of *Bryson's Dictionary of Troublesome Words,* p. 53.
Forbes, September 26, 1994, Katherine A. Powers, audiobook review of *The Mother Tongue,* p. S32; May 4, 1998, review of *A Walk in the Woods,* p. S140.
Fortune, July 10, 2000, "The Books of Summer," review of *In a Sunburned Country,* p. 314.
Guardian, October 16, 1999, review of *I'm a Stranger Here Myself,* p. 11; December 21, 2002, review of *In a Sunburned Country,* p. 14.
Houston Chronicle, July 30, 2000, review of *In a Sunburned Country,* p. 14.
Insight on the News, October 16, 2000, Rex Roberts, review of *In a Sunburned Country,* p. 33.
Library Journal, April 1, 1998, Nancy J. Moeckel, review of *A Walk in the Woods,* pp. 114-116; May 15, 1999, Wilda Williams, review of *I'm a Stranger Here Myself,* p. 114; September 1, 1999, Carolyn Alexander, review of *Neither Here nor There,* p. 255; March 1, 2000, review of *In a Sunburned Country,* p. S1; June 1, 2000, Joseph L. Carlson, review of *In a Sunburned Country,* p. 174; November 15, 2000, Gloria Maxwell, audiobook review of *In a Sunburned Country,* p. 118; December, 2000, Robert Zeller, review of *In a Sunburned Country,* p. 175; September 15, 2001, Nancy Pearl, review of *A Walk in the Woods,* p. 61;

August, 2002, review of *Bryson's Dictionary of Troublesome Words.*

Los Angeles Times, August 23, 1990, section E, pp. 1, 13.

Los Angeles Times Book Review, September 3, 1989, pp. 1, 5; September 30, 1990, p. 8; February 16, 1992, p. 6.

New Republic, August 6, 2001, Nicholas Howe, review of *The Best American Travel Writing, 2000,* p. 34.

New Statesman, December 12, 1997, Albert Scardino, review of *A Walk in the Woods,* pp. 43-45.

New Statesman & Society, October 4, 1991, Marek Kohn, review of *Neither Here nor There,* pp. 35-36; September 15, 1995, Boyd Tonkin, review of *Notes from a Small Island,* p. 34.

Newsweek, August 14, 1989, Jim Miller, review of *The Lost Continent,* p. 51; June 5, 2000, David Gates, review of *In a Sunburned Country,* p. 73.

New York, September 18, 1989, Chris Smith, review of *The Lost Continent,* p. 26.

New York Times, July 16, 1990; June 5, 2000, Janet Maslin, review of *In a Sunburned Country,* p. B6.

New York Times Book Review, September 17, 1989, Michele Slung, review of *The Lost Continent,* p. 26; August 5, 1990, Burt Hochberg, review of *The Mother Tongue,* p. 8; May 30, 1999, Elizabeth Gleick, review of *I'm a Stranger Here Myself,* p. 10; August 20, 2000, Annette Kobak, review of *In a Sunburned Country,* p. 105; December 3, 2000, "Travel Review," p. 58.

People, April 17, 1995, Elaine Kahn, review of *Made in America,* p. 32.

Publishers Weekly, February 13, 1995, review of *Made in America,* p. 71; March 4, 1996, review of *Notes from a Small Island,* p. 40; February 23, 1998, review of *A Walk in the Woods,* p. 57; May 4, 1998, Norman Oder, "Bill Bryson: An Ex-expat Traveling Light" (interview), pp. 191-193; March 22, 1999, review of *I'm a Stranger Here Myself,* p. 76; May 15, 2000, review of *In a Sunburned Country,* p. 95; August 7, 2000, audiobook review of *In a Sunburned Country,* p. 42; September 18, 2000, review of *The Best American Travel Writing 2000,* p. 96; June 3, 2002, review of *Bryson's Dictionary of Troublesome Words,* p. 75.

St. Louis Post-Dispatch, May 30, 2001, review of *In a Sunburned Country,* p. E1; June 18, 2000, review of *In a Sunburned Country,* p. F8.

Spectator, July 22, 2000, Michael Davie, review of *Down Under,* p. 35; December 15, 2001, Christopher Howse, review of *Bryson's Dictionary of Troublesome Words,* p. 61.

Times (London, England), September 25, 1991, p. 13; July 5, 2000, James Bone, "Our Rumpled Tour-Guide to the Familiar," p. B12.

Times Literary Supplement, October 18, 1991, p. 28; July 28, 2000, Robert Drewe, review of *Down Under,* p. 8.

Times Saturday Review (London, England), October 5, 1991, p. 57.

U.S. News and World Report, June 12, 2000, Holly J. Morris, review of *In a Sunburned Country,* p. 69.

Wall Street Journal, May 14, 1999, Kate Flatley, review of *I'm a Stranger Here Myself,* p. W9.

Washington Post, October 18, 2000, Elizabeth Ward, review of *In a Sunburned Country,* p. C08.

Washington Post Book World, September 3, 1989, p. 3.

ONLINE

Random House Web site, http://www.randomhouse. com/ (November 9, 2003), "Bill Bryson."*

*   *   *

BURROUGHS, Edgar Rice 1875-1950
(Normal Bean, John Tyler McCulloch)

PERSONAL: Born September 1, 1875, in Chicago, IL; died March 19, 1950; son of George Tyler (a distiller and battery manufacturer) and Mary Evaline (Zeiger) Burroughs; married Emma Centennia Hulbert, January 1, 1900 (divorced, 1934); married Florence Dearholt, 1935 (divorced, 1942); children: Joan, Hulbert, John Coleman. *Education:* Michigan Military Academy, graduated, 1895.

CAREER: Writer, 1912-50. Michigan Military Academy, Orchard Lake, MI, instructor and assistant commandant, 1895-96; owner of stationery store, Pocatello, ID, 1898; associated with American Battery Company, Chicago, IL, 1899-1903; associated with Sweetser-Burroughs Mining Company, ID, 1903-04; Oregon Short Line Railroad Company, Salt Lake City, UT, railroad policeman, 1904; Sears, Roebuck & Company, Chicago, manager of stenographic department, 1906-08; Burroughs and Dentzer (advertising agency), Chicago, partner, 1908-09; Physicians Co-operative Association, Chicago, office manager, 1909; State-Burroughs Company (sales firm), Chicago, partner,

1910-11; System Service Bureau, Chicago, manager, 1912-13; mayor, Malibu Beach, CA, 1933; United Press war correspondent in the Pacific during World War II. Founder of Edgar Rice Burroughs, Inc. (publishing house), Burroughs-Tarzan Enterprises, and Burroughs-Tarzan Pictures. *Military service:* U.S. Cavalry, 1896-97.

WRITINGS:

NOVELS

Tarzan of the Apes, McClurg (Chicago, IL), 1914, reprinted, Modern Library (New York, NY), 2003.

The Return of Tarzan, McClurg (Chicago, IL), 1915.

The Beasts of Tarzan, McClurg (Chicago, IL), 1916.

The Son of Tarzan, McClurg (Chicago, IL), 1917.

A Princess of Mars, McClurg (Chicago, IL), 1917, reprinted, Modern Library (New York, NY), 2003.

The Gods of Mars, McClurg (Chicago, IL), 1918.

Tarzan and the Jewels of Opar, McClurg (Chicago, IL), 1918.

The Warlord of Mars, McClurg (Chicago, IL), 1919.

Thuvia, Maid of Mars, McClurg (Chicago, IL), 1920.

Tarzan the Terrible, McClurg (Chicago, IL), 1921.

The Chessmen of Mars, McClurg (Chicago, IL), 1922.

At the Earth's Core, McClurg (Chicago, IL), 1922, reprinted, Dover Publications (Mineola, NY), 2001.

Pellucidar, McClurg (Chicago, IL), 1923, reprinted, Dover Publications (Mineola, NY), 2002.

Tarzan and the Golden Lion, McClurg (Chicago, IL), 1923.

The Girl from Hollywood, Macaulay, 1923.

Tarzan and the Ant Men, McClurg (Chicago, IL), 1924.

The Bandit of Hell's Bend, McClurg (Chicago, IL), 1925.

The War Chief, McClurg (Chicago, IL), 1927.

The Outlaw of Torn, McClurg (Chicago, IL), 1927.

Tarzan, Lord of the Jungle, McClurg (Chicago, IL), 1928.

The Master Mind of Mars, McClurg (Chicago, IL), 1928.

The Monster Men, McClurg (Chicago, IL), 1929.

Tarzan and the Lost Empire, Metropolitan, 1929.

Tarzan at the Earth's Core, Metropolitan, 1930.

Tanar of Pellucidar, Metropolitan, 1930.

A Fighting Man of Mars, Metropolitan, 1931.

Tarzan the Invincible, Burroughs (Tarzana, CA), 1931.

Tarzan the Triumphant, Burroughs (Tarzana, CA), 1931.

Jungle Girl, Burroughs (Tarzana, CA), 1932, published as *The Land of Hidden Men,* Ace Books, 1963.

Tarzan and the City of Gold, Burroughs (Tarzana, CA), 1933.

Apache Devil, Burroughs (Tarzana, CA), 1933.

Tarzan and the Lion-Men, Burroughs (Tarzana, CA), 1934.

Pirates of Venus, Burroughs (Tarzana, CA), 1934, reprinted, University of Nebraska Press (Lincoln, NE), 2001.

Lost on Venus, Burroughs (Tarzana, CA), 1935, reprinted, University of Nebraska Press (Lincoln, NB), 2004.

Tarzan and the Leopard Men, Burroughs (Tarzana, CA), 1935.

Tarzan's Quest, Burroughs (Tarzana, CA), 1936.

Swords of Mars, Burroughs (Tarzana, CA), 1936.

Back to the Stone Age, Burroughs (Tarzana, CA), 1937.

The Oakdale Affair: The Rider, Burroughs (Tarzana, CA), 1937.

Tarzan and the Forbidden City, Burroughs (Tarzana, CA), 1938.

The Lad and the Lion, Burroughs (Tarzana, CA), 1938.

Carson of Venus, Burroughs (Tarzana, CA), 1939.

The Deputy Sheriff of Comanche County, Burroughs (Tarzana, CA), 1940.

Synthetic Men of Mars, Burroughs (Tarzana, CA), 1940.

Land of Terror, Burroughs (Tarzana, CA), 1944.

Escape on Venus, Burroughs (Tarzana, CA), 1946.

Tarzan and the Foreign Legion, Burroughs (Tarzana, CA), 1947.

The People That Time Forgot, Ace Books (New York, NY), 1963.

Tarzan and the Madman, Canaveral Press (New York, NY), 1964.

Beyond the Farthest Star, Ace Books (New York, NY), 1964.

The Girl from Farris's, House of Greystoke, 1965.

The Efficiency Expert, House of Greystoke, 1966.

I Am a Barbarian, Burroughs (Tarzana, CA), 1967.

(Under pseudonym John Tyler McCulloch) *Pirate Blood,* Ace Books (New York, NY), 1970.

Out of Time's Abyss, Tandem (London, England), 1973.

Tarzan: The Lost Adventure, Dark Horse Comics (Milwaukie, OR), 1995.

Marcia of the Doorstep, Donald M. Grant (Hampton Falls, NH), 1999.

STORY COLLECTIONS

Jungle Tales of Tarzan, McClurg (Chicago, IL), 1919.

Tarzan the Untamed, McClurg (Chicago, IL), 1920.

The Mucker, McClurg (Chicago, IL), 1921, published as *The Man without a Soul,* two volumes, Methuen (London, England), 1921-1922.

The Land That Time Forgot, McClurg (Chicago, IL), 1924, reprinted, Modern Library (New York, NY), 2002.

The Eternal Lover, McClurg (Chicago, IL), 1925, published as *The Eternal Savage,* Ace Books (New York, NY), 1963.

The Cave Girl, McClurg (Chicago, IL), 1925.

The Moon Maid, McClurg (Chicago, IL), 1926, abridged edition published as *The Moon Men,* Canaveral Press (New York, NY), 1962, reprinted, University of Nebraska Press (Lincoln, NE), 2002.

The Monster Men, Canaveral Press (New York, NY), 1962.

The Mad King, McClurg (Chicago, IL), 1926.

Tarzan the Magnificent, Burroughs (Tarzana, CA), 1939.

Llana of Gathol, Burroughs (Tarzana, CA), 1948.

Beyond Thirty, privately printed, 1955, published as *The Lost Continent,* Ace Books (New York, NY), 1963, reprinted, University of Nebraska Press (Lincoln, NE), 2001.

The Man-Eater, privately printed, 1955.

Savage Pellucidar, Canaveral Press (New York, NY), 1963.

Tales of Three Planets, Canaveral Press (New York, NY), 1964.

John Carter of Mars, Canaveral Press (New York, NY), 1964.

Tarzan and the Castaways, Canaveral Press (New York, ,NY), 1964.

The Wizard of Venus, Ace Books (New York, NY), 1970.

Forgotten Tales of Love and Murder, Guidry & Adkins (New Orleans, LA), 2001.

OTHER

The Tarzan Twins (juvenile), Volland, 1927.

Tarzan and the Tarzan Twins, with Jad-Bal-Ja, the Golden Lion (juvenile), Whitman Publishing, 1936.

Official Guide of the Tarzan Clans of America, privately printed, 1939.

A Romantic Play in Three Acts, Donald M. Grant (Hampton Falls, NH), 1999.

Author of column "Laugh It Off," *Honolulu Advertiser,* 1941-42 and 1945. Contributor, sometimes under pseudonym Normal Bean, to *All-Story, Writer's Digest, New York World,* and other publications.

ADAPTATIONS: The story of Tarzan has been adapted into motion picture and video formats, along with coloring books and children's books.

SIDELIGHTS: As the creator of Tarzan, one of the most enduring characters of popular adventure fiction, Edgar Rice Burroughs has earned a lasting place in twentieth-century American literature. Tarzan, the loin-clothed, bare-chested "King of the Jungle," ranks with such fictional characters as Sherlock Holmes and Dracula in sheer name recognition and archetypal power. He has appeared in scores of motion pictures, television programs, comic books, and related media, and he has given birth to many imitators over the years, none of whom have achieved the same level of success. Despite the immense popularity of Tarzan, the character has never been a favorite with librarians, teachers, or literary critics, all of whom relegate the jungle monarch to the realm of cheap pulp adventure. Yet Burroughs's primary goal as a writer—to entertain his readers—was remarkably well satisfied with his Tarzan books. As for why he created Tarzan, Burroughs was always honest about his need for money. "I had a wife and two babies," he once explained.

Burroughs first turned to writing fiction following a series of unsuccessful careers as a railroad policeman, a partner in several businesses, a miner in Idaho, and as a manager for Sears, Roebuck. None of these positions gave him financial security. By 1912 Burroughs, an avid reader of adventure fiction, decided to try writing as a career. His first story, "Under the Moons of Mars," features interplanetary adventurer John Carter and sold almost immediately to *All-Story* magazine for four hundred dollars. It was printed under the pseudonym Normal Bean because Burroughs thought the story of Martian adventure might get him branded crazy if he used his real name. He also wanted to let his readers know that he was sane, with a "normal bean." His fears were unfounded. Readers demanded more stories of Mars and due to his success, Burroughs at last complied. By 1914 Burroughs was earning a reported twenty thousand dollars a year writing for the pulp magazines.

Discussing Burroughs's Mars novels, *Dictionary of Literary Biography* contributor John Hollow noted that "if one looks more closely at these novels, what emerges" from the action-driven plot that usually finds a young heroine's virtue imperiled, "is the far more universal threat of death. Burroughs's original Martian trilogy [*A Princess of Mars, The Gods of Mars,* and *The Warlord of Mars*] is a particularly fine instance of science fiction's attempt to cope with what Burroughs himself called 'the stern and unalterable cosmic laws,' the certainty that both individuals and whole races grow old and die."

Although his initial success lay with his Mars adventures, Burroughs's most popular character was undoubtedly Tarzan. An instant best-seller from his introduction in the October, 1912, issue of *All-Story,* Tarzan caught the imagination of the American public like few other characters ever had. Orphaned in the African jungle as a baby, Tarzan was raised by apes and was therefore able to communicate with all of the jungle's animals. His courage, strength, and primitive sense of justice served him well when confronted with treacherous villains, dangerous animals, or wild terrain. His adventures took him to lost cities and into the hollow center of the Earth. By the 1930s Tarzan had made Burroughs wealthy enough to found his own publishing house and motion picture company.

The overwhelming commercial success of the "Tarzan" books was somewhat dampened by the critical hostility Burroughs received. Throughout his career critics were less than kind to Burroughs, labeling his books as little more than crudely written entertainment. Some have even found, just beneath the surface of his fiction, clear signs of fascism, racism, and anti-intellectualism. However, as George P. Elliott noted in the *Hudson Review,* Burroughs's "prejudices are so gross that no one bothers to analyze them out or to attack them. . . . They were clear-eyed, well-thewed prejudices arrayed only in a loin cloth; you can take them or leave them, unless *your* big prejudice happens to be anti-prejudice. What matters is the story, which tastes good." Brian Attebury agreed, writing in *The Fantasy Tradition in American Literature: From Irving to Le Guin* that "Burroughs was neither more nor less than a good storyteller, with as much power—and finesse—as a bulldozer." Writing in *Esquire,* Gore Vidal claimed that, although Burroughs "is innocent of literature," he nonetheless "does have a gift very few writers of any kind possess: he can describe action vividly. . . . Tarzan *in action* is excellent."

Michael Orth, denying Burroughs's own claims that he wrote only to provide his readers with entertain-

ment, discovered far more important themes in the prolific author's books. Burroughs, Orth stated in *Extrapolation,* "wrote stories about the value of an individual in relation to society, the value of progress, the problems and possibilities of advanced technologies, humans' relation to their environment, the proper role of religion, sexual and class politics, and a hundred other typically utopian concerns."

Perhaps the best case for the value of Burroughs's work is presented by Richard A. Lupoff in his *Edgar Rice Burroughs: Master of Adventure.* "When an author," wrote Lupoff, "survives for half a century, not only without the support of the critical or academic community, but in the face of these communities' adamant condemnation, it is time to begin asking if a legitimate folk-author has not been here. It is time to start thinking of permanence."

BIOGRAPHICAL AND CRITICAL SOURCES:

BOOKS

Attebury, Brian. *The Fantasy Tradition in American Literature: From Irving to Le Guin,* Indiana University Press (Bloomington, IN), 1980.

Brady, Clark A., *The Burroughs Cyclopaedia: Characters, Places, Fauna, Flora, Technologies, Languages, Ideas, and Terminologies Found in the Works of Edgar Rice Burroughs,* McFarland (Jefferson, NC), 1996.

Day, Bradford M., *Edgar Rice Burroughs Bibliography,* Science Fiction and Fantasy Publications, 1956.

Dictionary of Literary Biography, Volume 8: *Twentieth-Century American Science Fiction Writers,* Gale (Detroit, MI), 1981, pp. 87-92.

Farmer, Philip José, *Tarzan Alive,* Doubleday (New York, NY), 1972.

Fenton, Robert, *Big Swingers: Biography of Edgar Rice Burroughs,* Prentice-Hall, 1967.

Fury, David, *Kings of the Jungle: An Illustrated Reference to "Tarzan" on Screen and Television,* McFarland (Jefferson, NC), 1994.

Harwood, John, *The Literature of Burroughsiana,* Camille Cazedessus, Jr. (Baton Rouge, LA), 1963.

Heins, Henry Hardy, *A Golden Anniversary Bibliography of Edgar Rice Burroughs,* Donald M. Grant (West Kingston, RI), 1964.

Lupoff, Richard A., *Edgar Rice Burroughs: Master of Adventure,* Canaveral Press (New York, NY), 1965.

Porges, Irwin, *Edgar Rice Burroughs: The Man Who Created Tarzan,* Brigham Young University Press (Provo, UT), 1975.

Twentieth-Century Literary Criticism, Gale (Detroit, MI), Volume 2, 1979, Volume 32, 1989.

Zaidan, Samira H., *A Comparative Study of Haiu Bnu Yakdhan, Mowgli, and Tarzan,* Red Squirrel Books, 1998.

Zeuschner, Robert B., *Edgar Rice Burroughs: The Exhaustive Scholar's and Collector's Descriptive Bibliography of Periodical, Hardcover, Paperback, and Reprint Editions,* McFarland (Jefferson, NC), 1996.

PERIODICALS

Booklist, November 15, 2000, p. 657.

Chicago, December, 1989, p. 168.

Dalhousie Review, spring, 1976, pp. 83-92.

Esquire, December, 1963.

Extrapolation, Fall, 1986, Michael Orth, "Utopia in the Pulps: The Apocalyptic Pastoralism of Edgar Rice Burroughs," pp. 221-223.

Harpers Bazaar, May, 1981, p. 38.

Hudson Review, autumn, 1959.

Journal of American Culture, summer 1979, David Cowart, "The Tarzan Myth and Jung's Genesis of the Self," pp. 220-230.

Journal of Popular Culture, winter, 1957, pp. 263-275; fall, 1973, pp. 280-287.

Library Journal, October 1, 1992, p. 123, December, 1992, p. 192.

Maclean's, April 2, 1984, p. 65.

New Yorker, April 2, 1984, p. 119.

Publishers Weekly, October 18, 1999, p. 73.

School Library Journal, August 1982, p. 112.

Smithsonian, March, 2001, p. 63.

Spectator, October 16, 1999, p. 11.*

C

CAMUS, Albert 1913-1960
(Bauchart, Albert Mathe; Saetone, a joint pseudonym)

PERSONAL: Born November 7, 1913, in Mondovi, Algeria; died after an automobile accident, January 4, 1960, near Paris, France; son of Lucien (a farm laborer) and Catherine (a charwoman; maiden name, Sintes) Camus; married Simone Hie, 1933 (divorced); married Francine Faure, 1940; children: (second marriage) Jean (son) and Catherine (twins). *Education:* University of Algiers, diplome d'etudes superieures, 1936. *Religion:* "Atheistic humanist."

CAREER: Novelist, essayist, and playwright. Worked as meteorologist, stockbroker's agent, and civil servant; actor, writer, and producer of stage productions with Theatre du travail (later Theatre de l'equipe), 1935-38; journalist with *Alger-Republicain,* 1938-40; teacher in Oran, Algeria, 1940-42; journalist in Paris, France, 1942-45; Editions Gallimard, Paris, reader, 1943-60, director of Espoir collection; *Combat* (daily newspaper), cofounder, 1945, editor, 1945-47. Staff member of *Paris Soir,* 1938. Founder of Committee to Aid the Victims of Totalitarian States. *Military service:* Member of French Resistance during World War II.

AWARDS, HONORS: Medal of the Liberation; Prix de la Critique, 1947, for *La Peste;* Nobel Prize for literature, 1957; Prix Algerian du Roman.

WRITINGS:

NOVELS

L'Etranger, Gallimard (Paris, France), 1942, translation by Stuart Gilbert published as *The Stranger,* Knopf (New York, NY), 1946, reprinted, Vintage (New York, NY), 1972, translation by Matthew Ward published under same title, Knopf (New York, NY), 1988, published as *The Outsider,* Hamish Hamilton (London, England), 1946.

La Peste, Gallimard (Paris, France), 1947, translation by Stuart Gilbert published as *The Plague,* Knopf (New York, NY), 1948, reprinted, Vintage (New York, NY), 1991, translation by Robin Buss, Allen Lane (London, England), 2001.

La Chute, Gallimard (Paris, France), 1956, translation by Justin O'Brien published as *The Fall,* Knopf (New York, NY), 1957, reprinted, Vintage (New York, NY), 1991.

Le Premier homme, Gallimard (Paris, France), 1994, translation by David Hapgood published as *The First Man,* Knopf (New York, NY), 1995.

PLAYS

Le Malentendu [and] *Caligula* (also see below; former, three-act, first produced at Theatre des Mathurins, 1944; latter, four-act, first produced at Theatre Hebertot, 1945), Gallimard (Paris, France), 1944, translation by Stuart Gilbert published as *Caligula* [and] *Cross Purpose* (former produced in New York, NY 1960), New Directions (New York, NY), 1947.

L'Etat de siege (first produced 1948; also see below), Gallimard (Paris, France), 1948, translation published as *State of Siege* in *Caligula and Three Other Plays,* 1958.

Les Justes (first produced at Theatre Hebertot, 1949), Gallimard (Paris, France), 1950, translation by

Elizabeth Sprigge and Philip Warner published as *The Just Assassins,* Microfilm, 1957, published in *Caligula and Three Other Plays,* 1958.

La Devotion à la croix (title means *Devotion to the Cross*; adaptation of work by Calderon de la Barca), Gallimard (Paris, France), 1953.

Les Esprits (title means *The Wits*; adaptation of work by Pierre de Larivey), Gallimard (Paris, France), 1953.

Un Cas interessant (title means *An Interesting Case*; adaptation of work by Dino Buzatti; first produced at Theatre La Bruyere, 1955), L'Avant-scene, 1955.

Requiem pour une nonne (adaptation of novel *Requiem for a Nun* by William Faulkner; first produced at Theatre des Mathurins, 1956), Gallimard (Paris, France), 1956.

Caligula and Three Other Plays (contains *State of Siege, Cross Purpose,* and *The Just Assassins*), translated by Stuart Gilbert, Knopf (New York, NY), 1958.

Les Possedes (adaptation of novel *The Possessed* by Fyodor Dostoyevsky; first produced at Theatre Antoine, 1955), Gallimard (Paris, France), 1959, translation by Justin O'Brien published as *The Possessed: A Modern Dramatization of Dostoevsky's Novel,* Knopf (New York, NY), 1964.

Also author of unfinished play "Don Juan."

ESSAYS

L'Envers et l'endroit (title means "Inside and Out"), Charlot Alger, 1937.

Le Mythe de Sisyphe, Gallimard (Paris, France), 1942, translation by Justin O'Brien published as *The Myth of Sisyphus and Other Essays,* Knopf (New York, NY), 1955, reprinted, Vintage (New York, NY), 1991.

Lettres à un ami allemand, Gallimard (Paris, France), 1945.

Noces (title means "Nuptials"), Charlot Alger, 1945.

L'Existence, Gallimard (Paris, France), 1945.

Le Minotaur, ou La Halte d'Oran (title means "The Minotaur; or, Stopping at Oran"), Charlot Alger, 1950.

Actuelles I: Chroniques, 1944-1948 (title means "Now I: Chronicles, 1944-1948"), Gallimard (Paris, France), 1950.

L'Homme révolté, Gallimard (Paris, France), 1951, translation by Anthony Bower published as *The Rebel: An Essay on Man in Revolt,* Knopf (New York, NY), 1954, revised edition, 1956, reprinted, Vintage (New York, NY), 1991.

Actuelles II: Chroniques, 1948-1953 (title means "Now II: Chronicles, 1948-1953"), Gallimard (Paris, France), 1953.

L'Ete (title means "Summer"), Gallimard (Paris, France), 1954.

(With Arthur Koestler) *Reflexions sur la peine capitale* (contains "Reflexions sur la guillotine"; translation by Richard Howard published separately as *Reflections on the Guillotine: An Essay on Capital Punishment,* Fridtjof-Karla Publications, 1960), Calman-Levy (Paris, France), 1957.

Actuelles III: Chronique algerienne, 1939-1958 (title means "Now III: Algerian Chronicle, 1939-1958"), Gallimard (Paris, France), 1958.

Discours de suede, Gallimard (Paris, France), 1958, translation by Justin O'Brien published as *Speech of Acceptance upon the Award of the Nobel Prize for Literature, Delivered in Stockholm on the Tenth of December, 1957,* Knopf (New York, NY), 1958.

Neither Victims nor Executioners, translated from the French by Dwight Macdonald, Liberation, 1960.

Resistance, Rebellion, and Death, translated from the French by Justin O'Brien, Knopf (also see below), Calman-Levy (Paris, France), 1957.

Meditations sur le theatre et la vie, P. Alberts, 1961.

Théâtre, récits, nouvelles, Gallimard (Paris, France), 1962, reprinted, preface by Jean Grenier, 1991.

Essais, Gallimard (Paris, France), 1965.

Lyrical and Critical Essays, edited by Philip Thody, translated from the French by Ellen Conroy Kennedy, Knopf (New York, NY), 1968.

Between Hell and Reason: Essays from the Resistance Newspaper "Combat," 1944-1947, translated and edited by Alexandre de Gramont, University Press of New England (Hanover, NH), 1991.

OTHER

L'Exil et le royaume (short stories; contains "Le Renegat," "Jonas," "La Femme adultere," "Les Muets," "L'Hôte," and "La Pierre qui pousse"), Gallimard (Paris, France), 1957, translation by Justin O'Brien published as *Exile and the Kingdom,* Hamish Hamilton (London, England), 1960, reprinted, Vintage (New York, NY), 1991; "L'Hôte" translated as *The Guest,* Creative Education (Mankato, MN), 1991.

Carnets: mai 1935-fevrier 1942, Gallimard (Paris, France), 1962, translation published as *Notebooks: Volume I, 1935-1942* (also see below), Knopf (New York, NY), 1963, published as *Carnets: 1935-1942,* Hamish Hamilton (London, England), 1963).

Lettre à Bernanos, Minard, 1963.

Carnets: janvier 1942-mars 1951, Gallimard (Paris, France), 1964, translation by Justin O'Brien published as *Notebooks: 1942-1951* (also see below), Modern Library (New York, NY), 1970, reprinted, Paragon House (New York, NY), 1991.

La Mort heureuse, Gallimard (Paris, France), 1971, translation by Jean Sarocchi published as *A Happy Death,* Vintage (New York, NY), 1973, translated by Richard Howard, notes by Sarocchi, Vintage (New York, NY), 1995.

Le Premier Camus, suivi de ecrits de jeunesse d'Albert Camus, Gallimard (Paris, France), 1973, translation by Ellen Conroy Kennedy published as *Youthful Writings,* Knopf (New York, NY), 1976, reprinted, Marlow (New York, NY), 1990.

Fragments d'un Combat: 1938-1940, Alger Republicain, Le Soir Republicain (articles), two volumes, edited by Jacqueline Lévi-Valensi and Andre Abbou, Gallimard (Paris, France), 1978.

Journaux de voyage, edited by Roger Quillot, Gallimard (Paris, France), 1978, translation by Hugh Levick published as *American Journals,* Paragon House (New York, NY), 1987.

Albert Camus, Jean Grenier: Correspondance: 1932-1960 (letters), edited by Marguerite Dobrenn, Gallimard (Paris, France), 1981.

Oeuvres completes d'Albert Camus, five volumes, Club de l'Honnete Homme, 1983.

Carnets: mars 1951-decembre 1959, Gallimard (Paris, France), 1989.

Notebooks, 1935-1951 (includes *Notebooks: Volume I, 1935-1942* and *Notebooks: 1942-1951*), Marlowe (New York, NY), 1998.

(With Pascal Pia) *Correspondance: 1939-1947,* edited by Yves Marc Ajchenbaum, Gallimard (Paris, France), 2000.

Camus à Combat: Éditoriaux et articles d'Albert Camus, 1944-1947, edited by Jaqueline Lévi-Valensi, Gallimard (Paris, France), 2002.

(With Jean Grenier) *Correspondence, 1932-1960,* translation by Jan F. Rigaud, University of Nebraska Press (Lincoln, NB), 2003.

Author of prefaces to many works. Contributor to *Combat* (under pseudonyms Bauchart and Albert Mathe, and under joint pseudonym Saetone), to *Alger-Republicain, Soir-Republicain, L'Express,* and many other newspapers and magazines.

SIDELIGHTS: The first major writer to emerge from modern North Africa, Albert Camus was imbued with a "Mediterranean sensibility," wrote Rima Drell Reck in her *Literature and Responsibility: The French Novelist in the Twentieth Century,* a sensibility that profoundly influenced his writings. The author of the novel *The Stranger* and numerous so-called existentialist writings during the mid-twentieth century, Camus saw the Algeria of his youth as a place of perpetual summer. Those memories would contrast with his experiences in Europe during World War II.

Camus's father, a native Algerian of Alsatian descent, had been killed at the first battle of the Marne when Camus was just a year old. Because she was partially deaf and much affected by her husband's death, Camus's illiterate mother left the rearing of her sons to her own strong-willed mother. That Camus still focused his love on his mother later becomes evident in some of his writings, such as his unfinished novel, *Le Premier homme (The First Man).*

Camus was a superior student at school. An instructor, Louis Germain, recognized his potential and urged Camus to vie for the scholarship that allowed him to attend high school—in 1957 Camus would dedicate his Nobel Prize acceptance speech to Germain. At age seventeen Camus contracted tuberculosis, making him a target for depression and flu. Undaunted by his illness, he attended the University of Algiers and studied Greek literature, poetry, and philosophy. He also joined a young intellectual group known as the North Africa Literary School.

In 1936, Camus earned his diplome d'etudes superieures in philosophy and began a career in journalism, writing first for the *Alger-Republicain.* He also joined the Communist party, although he quickly became disillusioned with the party and broke all ties with it. By 1942 he had moved to Paris and joined the French Resistance against German occupation. Camus worked on writing his novels *The Plague* and *The Rebel* while simultaneously working as a reader at Paris-based Gallimard publishing company during the day and writing for the underground newspaper *Combat* at night. Jean-Paul Sartre and Simone de Beauvoir were also on the *Combat* staff, as were André Malraux and Michel Gallimard, all of whom became Camus's friends. At *Combat,* Camus wrote clandestinely under the names Albert Mathe, Bauchart, and the joint pseudonym Saetone. By the end of World War II *Combat* had became a daily newspaper, with Camus as editor, but in 1944, Camus left journalism to focus entirely on other forms of writing.

In his writings, declared a *Time* contributor, Camus "was the authentic voice of France's war generation." In the 1940s, values were being challenged as no longer relevant. With the atrocities and resulting feelings of hopelessness brought about by World War II, many people concluded that human existence is pointless. While Camus perceived life's absurdity, he did not adopt this point of view. As the *Time* reviewer observed, "Because Camus articulated despair so eloquently, a generation bred in depression, surrender and occupation chose him its leader in its quest for something to believe in." Typically pictured in a rumpled trenchcoat with a cigarette dangling from his mouth, Camus was also deeply admired by the generation following his own. In response to the international acclaim that seemed to greet him overnight, Camus asks in *L'Ete* simply: "What else have I done but meditate on an idea I found in the streets of my time?"

In his search to break through the pervading sense of meaninglessness to discover happiness, Camus charted a plan of writing that eventually encompassed at least three cycles. He named each cycle after a figure in mythology, calling the first Sisyphus, the second Prometheus, and the third Nemesis. The novel *The Stranger,* the play *Caligula,* and the essay *The Myth of Sisyphus* together form cycle one, which is concerned with a certain duality in man's nature: the love of life versus the hatred of death.

In *The Stranger,* perhaps Camus's most famous work, a man named Meursault shoots an Arab for no apparent reason and is subsequently convicted. His punishment, however, appears to be less the result of his murder than the consequence of his refusal to conform to society's expectations of appropriate emotional behavior. Because Meursault seems indifferent to human relationships and lacks contrition and the ability to feel grief, he is alienated from his society. Approaching his execution, Meursault accepts life as an imperfect end in itself and resolves to die happily and with dignity. He finds consolation in resigning himself to what Camus called the "benign indifference of the universe."

Meursault is portrayed as a "stranger" in life because he does not parrot conventional cant—neither at his mother's funeral nor as the defendant in the courtroom. When his mother dies, for example, he feels little emotion and does not pretend otherwise. Then when his lawyer tries to induce him to respond to judicial questions in the socially acceptable way, Meursault refuses to do so. Those around him are threatened by his candor. He is subsequently sentenced, shunning last of all the chaplain's offer of God. Meursault is ultimately saved by death, which at the same time causes his destruction.

When *The Stranger* first appeared in print, Jean-Paul Sartre predicted it would become a classic. Often required reading for literature classes, *The Stranger* has been viewed as Camus's only nihilist novel. R. Barton Palmer, examining the form of the novel, noted in *International Fiction Review* that Camus eschews the causality typical of conventional narratives and instead presents "a slice of the daily routine, devoid of intention and plot as it must be, a procession of events linked only by chronology. Event succeeds event, perception replaces perception, without any values by which the process may be interpreted."

In *Caligula,* the concept of the absurd is taken further than in *The Stranger.* The title character is based on Caius Caesare Augustus Germanicus, who became emperor of Rome at the age of twenty-five. A gentle man at the onset of his reign, Caligula gradually evolved into a cruel and heartless ruler who was eventually assassinated. In Camus's portrayal of Caligula, the emperor is transformed into a tyrant after the death of his sister—and lover—Drusilla. It becomes clear to the emperor that "men die and they are unhappy." Like Meursault, Caligula rebels, but his revolt takes a far more extreme form. Since life is absurd, Caligula reasons, every act is equally senseless. He then proceeds to prove his point by destroying accepted conventions. For instance, he seduces a man's wife, with the man himself as witness, causes a famine, and tortures his subjects with the aim of educating the self-deluding patricians. A revolt culminates in the assassination of the emperor, whose last utterances include the lament, "I didn't take the right road, I came out nowhere. My freedom is not the right kind."

Sisyphus is another survivor. According to the legend, he is eternally condemned to push a boulder the full height of a mountain only for it to roll back down to the starting point. Sisyphus "is the absurd hero," explains Camus in the essay "The Myth of Sisyphus." "He *is,* as much through his passions as through his torture. His scorn of the gods, his hatred of death, and his passion for life won him that unspeakable penalty in which the whole being is exerted toward accomplishing nothing. This is the price that must be paid for the passions of this world." For Camus, Sisyphus represents all men.

The Fall links the idea of the absurd to Camus's second cycle of writing. Written in the first person, as are all of Camus's novels, *The Fall* is a monologue delivered by Jean Baptiste Clamence, a one-time lawyer who has abandoned a lucrative practice in Paris. Although formerly self-satisfied, Clamence now suffers from guilt and can no longer in good conscience judge other people without viewing himself as a hypocrite: "Who is to say he is not equally guilty?" he asks himself. Clamence ends up confessing his own transgressions to anyone who will listen in a Dutch bar frequented by sailors. "In short," he confesses, "I never bothered with larger concerns except in the intervals between my little flings." His frankness evokes similar disclosures from his listeners, and to Clamence, this proves that all men are inherently wicked.

Revolt is the theme of Prometheus, the mythological hero who represents Camus's second cycle. Prometheus loves man and leads him to battle against the gods, whom Prometheus despises. Eventually, man begins to question his mission, but Prometheus avows his belief in their actions: "Those who doubt will be thrown out into the desert, nailed on a rock, offered as prey to cruel birds. All others shall walk in the dark behind the pensive and solitary master." As Camus puts it, Prometheus has thus become Caesar engaged in a metaphysical kind of revolt against the human condition.

The Plague is Camus's most complex work, although while the book met with popular acclaim in 1947, its message was lost on many readers. The story takes place in the Algerian town of Oran, where life is very predictable and routine. As the tale progresses, one rat dies, then more rats, then one human, and before long a pestilence has almost imperceptibly ravaged the city. The pain the plague causes elicits real feeling from the normally sedate townspeople. The actions of the characters illustrate that the complacent can be moved to take heroic action when faced with an emergency

situation. Therefore, there is hope for the human condition, as long as the transition is not forgotten when life returns to normal.

The events in *The Plague* are related in the third person by Dr. Rieux, who is not revealed as the narrator until the end of the book. Throughout the story Rieux fervently strives to aid the plague victims as a way of resolving his own fears about the purpose of his life. Rieux's friend, the artist Tarrou, also combats the disease, and chronicles in his diary the events taking place in Oran. In one entry he states, "I know with a certain knowledge that each man carries a plague within"; rather than fighting his fears about death, Tarrou attempts through his work to transcend them.

The Plague has been viewed as Camus's most anti-Christian novel, especially as it confronts fascism, Naziism, and the horrors of World War II. In Reck's opinion, Camus "suggests that faith is questionable, that man's torments are unjustifiable, that religion offers no answers to the travail of quotidian existence." Emphasizing Camus's own assertion that *The Plague* "was to be a more positive book" than *The Stranger,* however, Patrick McCarthy noted in the book *Albert Camus: The Stranger* that "Rieux and his friends demonstrate the moral values of courage and fraternity which do not defeat the plague but which bear witness against it." Sartre and Roland Barthes identified a flaw in Camus's allegory, observed McCarthy. "Camus had asserted the need to act but he had not treated the more difficult problems of which action one chooses. . . . The occupation was far from nonhuman [unlike Camus's fictional plague] and it involved agonizing choices."

Although the personification of evil in the symbolic play *The State of Siege* is named "King Plague," and though there are surface similarities to the novel, the play is not an adaptation of *The Plague,* but is more similar to *Caligula,* due to its focus on death. Diego, the rebel in the play, energizes the population of Cadiz and prompting them to revolt against their oppressors. *The State of Siege* was one of Camus's favorite works, although it did not fare well on the Paris stage. Camus remarked in the introduction to the English translation of the play that *The State of Siege* "had without effort achieved critical unanimity" and "a complete cutting up."

The Just Assassins (Les Justes) was greeted with more opposing reactions in the French press. The play deals with Russian terrorism in the early 1900s, specifically a plot involving a Socialist group that plans to assassinate the grand duke. A young poet, Kaliayev, who is totally committed to the cause of the organization, is chosen to throw the bomb that will kill the duke. Seeing himself as an avenger against the oppressed, Kaliayev dies for his actions without regret. But his death raises the question, Is the sacrifice of one person worth the promise of a better future for mankind?

While the composition of *The Rebel* (*L'Homme révolté*), the last volume in the cycle of Prometheus, was not an easy task for Camus, the author felt that the task was his responsibility: afterward he could freely devote his time to creating more literature. In his *Notebooks* he states: "For my own part, I should not have written *L'Homme révolté* if in the forties I had not found myself face to face with men whose acts I did not understand. To put it briefly, I did not understand that men could torture others without ever ceasing to look at them." In *The Rebel*, Camus defines revolt as the "impulse that drives an individual to the defense of a dignity common to all men." He takes the phrase by Descartes, "I think, therefore I am," and turns it into "I revolt, therefore we are." Citing paths of rebellion chosen by numerous figures throughout history, Camus illustrates how each was unsuccessful according to his own definition of revolt. The Marquis de Sade's actions were too calculated, too intellectual; Rimbaud's too individualized. But Camus criticized Hegel's method of rebellion above all because its absence of limitations would inevitably lead to anarchy and dictatorship.

A highly political novel, *The Rebel*'s "structural and rational flaws are glaring," Reck contended, but even so, it sparked more controversy than any other writing by Camus. It is "the only thing written by Camus resembling a political philosophy," said Reck. Probably one of the major conflicts was fostered by Camus's condemnation of Marxism: "End satisfies the means? Is this possible? But what will justify the ends?" Camus's assertion that the Left should oppose Stalinism led to a much-publicized rift between Camus and Sartre. "The break between these two leading French writers touched off literary pyrotechnics vivid even for Paris," wrote the *New York Times*.

Camus never completed the third cycle of his writing, which was to be called Nemesis, concerning measure. He had just emerged from a period of writer's block when he died in an automobile accident on January 4, 1960, at age forty-six. "News of the death stunned the French literary world of which M. Camus was one of the brightest lights," wrote a *New York Times* contributor.

At the time of his death, Camus had completed approximately one hundred pages of the rough draft of his epic novel, *The First Man,* based on the first French settlers in Algeria. A draft of the work—and Camus's notes for further chapters—was found in the crashed car in which Camus perished. While Camus's widow decided not to circulate the work due to its incomplete form, following her death his children saw to the book's publication. Critics recognized Camus himself in novel's protagonist, Jacques Cormier, a prominent French literary figure who is on a quest to learn more about his late father while also attempting to come to terms with the disconnection between his elite status as a writer and a childhood Richard Eder described in the *Los Angeles Times Book Review* as "constrained by poverty but wonderfully free in exploration and sensuous discovery." Praising the novel, Eder asserted that *The First Man* "has an overwhelming emotional integrity." Nicholas Delbanco in the Chicago *Tribune Books* observed that, while the novel "betrays the haste of its composition throughout, . . . the overwhelming impression is of how well Camus wrote, how natural and unforced was his eloquence."

The publication of any work by Camus was closely critiqued by reviewers, both in its original French and in translation. But as literature, Reck remarked, Camus's fiction is "conceptually thin," his novels mere essays in fictional form. Reck added that "Camus's originality as a novelist lay in his ability to state his insights ambiguously, that is, with the density and complexity of human existence."

The posthumous translation of Camus's *American Journals* has contributed greatly to reexaminations of the writer's life and thought. Originally published in 1978 as *Journaux de voyage, American Journals* describes Camus's impressions of the United States and South America during the 1940s. Reviewers have noted that the value of the journals is not in their descriptive power as travel documents, but in the insight they provide into Camus's character and works. They highlight aspects of the writer's personal life, such as his obsession with and fear of death and his guilt-ridden, but repeated, episodes of infidelity. Throughout, he documents feelings of despondency and unhappiness, along with notes he eventually uses in published works, such as *The Plague. American Journals* "show us how Camus passed from anguish to creativity, willing his pain into art," commented Gail Pool in the *Christian Science Monitor.* Patrick McCarthy, in the *Times Literary Supplement,* also emphasized the illumination of Camus's political views provided in *American Journals,* noting that the author "reveals a strong sense of belonging to the working class and a frustration at not knowing how to transform that sense into a political vision."

BIOGRAPHICAL AND CRITICAL SOURCES:

BOOKS

Anderson, David, *The Tragic Protest,* John Knox, 1969.

Beauclair, Michelle, *In Death's Wake: Mourning in the Works of Albert Camus and Marguerite Duras,* P. Lang (New York, NY), 1996.

Bloom, Harold, editor, *Albert Camus,* Chelsea House (New York, NY), 1989.

Bree, Germaine, and Margaret Guiton, *The French Novel from Gide to Camus,* Harcourt, Brace (New York, NY), 1957, revised edition published as *An Age of Fiction: The French Novel from Gide to Camus,* Rutgers University Press (Rutgers, NJ), 1968.

Bree, Germaine, *Camus and Sartre: Crisis and Commitment,* Delacorte (New York, NY), 1972.

Bronner, Stephen Eric, *Albert Camus: The Thinker, the Artist, the Man,* Franklin Watts (New York, NY), 1996.

Bree, Germaine, editor, *Camus: A Collection of Critical Essays,* Prentice-Hall (New York, NY), 1962, revised edition, Rutgers University Press (Rutgers, NJ), 1964.

Champigny, Robert, *A Pagan Hero: An Interpretation of Meursault in Camus' "The Stranger,"* University of Pennsylvania Press, 1969.

Contemporary Literary Criticism, Gale (Detroit, MI), Volume 1, 1973, Volume 2, 1974, Volume 4, 1975, Volume 9, 1978, Volume 11, 1979, Volume 14, 1980, Volume 32, 1985, Volume 63, 1991, Volume 69, 1992.

Cruickshank, John, *Albert Camus and the Literature of Revolt,* Galaxy, 1960.

Dictionary of Literary Biography, Volume 72: *French Novelists, 1930-1960,* Gale (Detroit, MI), 1988.

Drama Criticism, Volume 2, Gale (Detroit, MI), 1992.

Falk, Eugene H., *Types of Thematic Structure,* University of Chicago Press (Chicago, IL), 1967, pp. 52-116.

Fitch, Brian T., *The Narcissistic Text: A Reading of Camus' Fiction,* University of Toronto Press (Toronto, Ontario, Canada), 1982.

Fitch, Brian T., *The Fall: A Matter of Guilt,* Twayne (New York, NY), 1994.

Frohock, W. M., *Style and Temper: Studies in French Fiction, 1925-1960,* Harvard University Press (Cambridge, MA), 1967, pp. 78-117.

Hanna, Thomas, *The Thought and Art of Albert Camus,* Regnery (Washington, DC), 1958.

Jackson, Tommie Lee, *The Existential Fiction of Ayi Kwei Armah, Albert Camus, and Jean-Paul Sartre,* University Press of America (Lanham, MD), 1996.

Kazin, Alfred, *Contemporaries,* Little, Brown (Boston, MA), 1962.

Kellogg, Jean Defrees, *Dark Prophets of Hope: Dostoevsky, Sartre, Camus, Faulkner,* Loyola University Press, 1975.

Lazere, Donald, *The Unique Creation of Albert Camus,* Yale University Press (New Haven, CT), 1973.

Lebesque, Morvan, *Portrait of Camus,* Herder & Herder (London, England), 1971.

Lottman, Herbert R., *Albert Camus: A Biography,* Doubleday (New York, NY), 1979.

Maquet, Albert, *Albert Camus: The Invincible Summer,* Humanities Press, 1972.

Mauriac, Claude, *The New Literature,* translated from the French by Samuel I. Stone, Braziller (New York, NY), 1959.

McCarthy, Patrick, *Camus: A Critical Study of His Life and Work,* Hamish Hamilton (London, England), 1982.

McCarthy, Patrick, *Albert Camus: The Stranger,* Cambridge University Press (New York, NY), 1988.

Merton, Thomas, *The Literary Essays of Thomas Merton,* edited by Patrick Hart, New Directions (New York, NY), 1985, pp. 292-301.

Nadeau, Maurice, *The French Novel since the War,* translated from the French by A. M. Sheridan-Smith, Methuen (London, England), 1967.

O'Brien, Conor Cruise, *Albert Camus of Europe and Africa,* Viking (New York, NY), 1970.

Oxenhandler, Neal, *Looking for Heroes in Postwar France: Albert Camus, Max Jacob, Simone Weil,* University Press of New England (Hanover, NH), 1995.

Panichas, George A., editor, *The Politics of Twentieth-Century Novelists,* Hawthorne, 1971.

Parker, Emmet, *Albert Camus: The Artist in the Arena,* University of Wisconsin Press (Madison, WI), 1966.

Peyre, Henri, *French Novelists of Today,* Oxford University Press (Oxford, England), 1967.

Podhoretz, Norman, *Doings and Undoings,* Farrar, Straus (New York, NY), 1964.

Pollman, Leo, *Sartre and Camus: Literature of Existence,* Ungar (New York, NY), 1970.

Reck, Rima Drell, *Literature and Responsibility: The French Novelist in the Twentieth Century,* Louisiana State University Press, 1969.

Rhein, Philip H., *The Urge to Live: A Comparative Study of Franz Kafka's "Der Prozess" and Albert Camus' "L'etranger,"* University of North Carolina Press (Chapel Hill, NC), 1964.

Rhein, Philip H., *Albert Camus,* Twayne (New York, NY), 1969.

Rizzuto, Anthony, *Camus' Imperial Vision,* Southern Illinois University Press, 1981.

Sartre, Jean-Paul, *Situations I,* Gallimard (Paris, France), 1947.

Scott, Nathan A., Jr., editor, *Forms of Extremity in the Modern Novel,* John Knox Press, 1965.

Short Story Criticism, Volume 9, Gale (Detroit, MI), 1992.

Showalter, English, Jr., *Exiles and Strangers: A Reading of Camus's "Exile and the Kingdon,"* Ohio State University Press, 1984.

Sprintzen, David, *Camus: A Critical Examination,* Temple University Press (Philadelphia, PA), 1988.

Sprintzen, David, and Adrian van den Hoven, editors and translators, *Sartre and Camus: A Historic Confrontation,* Humanity Books (Amherst, NY), 2004.

Tarrow, Susan, *Exile from the Kingdom: A Political Rereading of Albert Camus,* University of Alabama Press, 1985.

Thody, Philip, *Albert Camus, 1913-1960,* Macmillan (New York, NY), 1962.

Thody, Philip, *Albert Camus: A Study of His Work,* Grove Press (New York, NY), 1959, revised edition, 1989.

Ullman, Stephen, *The Image in the Modern French Novel,* Basil Blackwell (London, England), 1963, pp. 239-299.

Viallaneix, Paul, *The First Camus: An Introductory Essay and Youthful Writings by Albert Camus,* translated from the French by Ellen Conroy Kennedy, Knopf (New York, NY), 1976.

Willhoite, Fred H., *Beyond Nihilism: Albert Camus's Contribution to Political Thought,* Louisiana State University Press, 1968.

World Literature Criticism, Gale (Detroit, MI), 1992.

PERIODICALS

America, April 4, 1998, John F. Kavanaugh, review of *The Fall,* p. 28.

American Imago, winter, 1988, p. 359.

American Poetry Review, January-February, 1973.

Cambridge Quarterly, March, 1999, Geoffrey Wall, review of *The First Man,* p. 65.

Chicago Tribune, September 24, 1995.

Choice, November, 2003, J. P. Cauvin, review of *Correspondence, 1932-1960,* p. 547.

Christian Science Monitor, August 7, 1987, p. B4.

Contemporary Literature, fall, 1983, pp. 322-348.

Explicator, fall, 1997, Alice J. Strange, review of *The Stranger,* p. 36; spring, 2001, Arthur Scherr, review of *The Stranger,* p. 149.

Forum for Modern Language Studies, July, 1984, pp. 228-246.

French Cultural Studies, June, 1998, Nancy Wood, "Colonial Nostalgia and *Le Premier homme,*" p. 167.

French Review, winter, 1970, pp. 158-167; October, 1986, pp. 30-38; April, 2000, p. 834; December, 2002, p. 328.

French Studies, January, 1998, Marc Orme, "The Theme of Revolt in Albert Camus' *Ecrits de jeunesse,*" p. 5; January, 2002, p. 29; April, 2002, Jill Beer, review of *L'Hôte,* p. 179.

Historian, winter, 1999, George Cotkin, "French Existentialism and American Popular Culture, 1945-1948," p. 327.

International Fiction Review, summer, 1980, p. 123.

Journal of European Studies, June, 2003, Jennifer Lefevre, "Men of Ideas, Men of Action: French Intellectuals' Impact on Post-war Politics," p. 177.

Journal of Politics, May, 1999, Cecil L. Eubanks, "Reconstructing the World: Albert Camus and the Symbolization of Experience," p. 293.

London Review of Books, September 8, 1994, pp. 6-7.

Los Angeles Times Book Review, May 29, 1988; September 3, 1995.

Michigan Law Review, May, 2000, Kenji Yoshino, review of *The Fall,* p. 1399.

Modern Fiction Studies, autumn, 1964, pp. 232-244 and 265-273; summer, 1973; spring, 1978.

Modern Language Review, July, 2002, Mark Orme, review of *La Peste,* p. 723.

Neophilologus, October, 1977, pp. 523-533.

New Republic, November 23, 1992, p. 32.

Newsweek, May 9, 1994, p. 68.

New York Review of Books, June 15, 1972; October 6, 1994, pp. 3-5; November 29, 2001, Tony Judt, review of *The Plague,* p. 6.

New York Times, February 3, 1986; April 18, 1988; October 20, 1989.

New York Times Book Review, August 16, 1987, p. 17.

PMLA, December, 1956, pp. 865-887; December, 1963, pp. 606-621; December, 1964, pp. 519-533.

Quadrant, October, 2003, Russell Blackford, "Sisyphus and the Meaning of Life," p. 54.

Renascence, winter, 1976.

Research in African Literatures, fall, 1999, Edward J. Hughes, "Building the Colonial Archive: The Case of Camus' *Le Premier homme,*" p. 176.

Sartre Studies International, December, 2001, Ronald Aronson, "Sartre, Camus, and the Caliban Articles," p. 1; June, 2002, "Camus and Revolt," p. 85; December, 2003, p. 9.

Scandinavian Studies, summer, 1976.

Symposium, summer, 2002, p. 97.

Time, March 19, 1979; May 16, 1994, p. 91.

Times (London, England), February 2, 1989; September 1, 1989.

Times Literary Supplement, April 17, 1981; September 1-7, 1989, p. 954; June 24, 1994, p. 26.

Washington Post Book World, November 5, 1995.

Wilson Quarterly, winter, 2004, "Camus' Dynamite," p. 108.

Yale French Studies, June, 2000, Dbarati Sanyal, "Broken Engagements," p. 29.

OBITUARIES:

PERIODICALS

Commonweal, February 12, 1960.

France-Observateur, January 7, 1960.

New Republic, January 18, 1960.

New Statesman, January 9, 1960.

Newsweek, January 18, 1960.

New Yorker, January 16, 1960.

New York Times, January 5, 1960.

Time, January 18, 1960.*

*   *   *

CAVALLO, Evelyn
    See SPARK, Muriel (Sarah)

CHAMBERS, Jessie
    See LAWRENCE, D(avid) H(erbert Richards)

*   *   *

CHESTERTON, G(ilbert) K(eith) 1874-1936

PERSONAL: Born May 28, 1874, in London, Campden Hill, Kensington, England; died of complications resulting from an edematous condition, aggravated by heart and kidney trouble, June 14, 1936, in Beaconsfield, Buckinghamshire, England; son of Edward (a house agent) and Mary Louise (Grosjean) Chesterton; married Francis Blogg, June 28, 1901. *Education:* Attended Colet Court School, London; St. Paul's School, London, 1887-92; Slade School of Art, London, 1893-96. *Religion:* Converted to Roman Catholicism, 1922.

CAREER: Author, social and literary critic, poet and illustrator. Worked for Redway (publisher), 1896, and T. Fisher Unwin, 1896-1902. Leader of the Distributist movement, and president of Distributist League. Lecturer at Notre Dame University, 1930; radio broadcaster during the 1930s.

MEMBER: Royal Society of Literature (fellow), Detection Club (president, 1928-36).

AWARDS, HONORS: Knight Commander with Star, Order of St. Gregory the Great, 1934.

WRITINGS:

NOVELS

The Napoleon of Notting Hill (also see below), illustrated by W. Graham Robertson, John Lane (New York, NY), 1904, with an introduction by Andrew M. Greeley, Paulist Press (New York, NY), 1978, with an introduction by Martin Gardner, Dover (New York, NY), 1991, edited and with an introduction by Bernard Bergonzi, Oxford University Press (New York, NY), 1994.

The Man Who Was Thursday: A Nightmare, (also see below) Dodd, Mead (New York, NY), 1908, with an introduction by Garry Wills, Sheed & Ward (New York, NY), 1975, edited and with an introduction by Stephen Medcalf, Oxford University Press (New York, NY), 1996, edited by Josef Kraus, Wexford College Press (Palm Springs, CA), 2001, with an introduction by Jonathan Lethem, Modern Library (New York, NY), 2001, published as *The Annotated Thursday: G. K. Chesterton's Masterpiece, The Man Who Was Thursday,* annotated by Martin Gardner, Ignatius Press (San Francisco, CA), 1999.

The Ball and the Cross, John Lane (New York, NY), 1909, with an introduction by Martin Gardner, Dover (New York, NY), 1995.

Manalive, Nelson (New York, NY), 1912, Dover (Mineola, NY), 2000.

The Flying Inn (also see below), John Lane (New York, NY), 1914, Dover (Mineola, NY), 2001.

The Return of Don Quixote, Dodd, Mead (New York, NY), 1926, Dufour Editions (Philadelphia, PA), 1963.

A G. K. Chesterton Omnibus (includes *The Napoleon of Notting Hill, The Man Who Was Thursday,* and *The Flying Inn*), Methuen (London, England), 1936.

Basil Howe (Chesterton's first novel, written in 1893, discovered in 1989), New City (London, England), 2001.

SHORT STORIES

The Tremendous Adventures of Major Brown, Shurmer Sibthorp, 1903.

(Self-illustrated) *The Club of Queer Trades,* Harper (New York, NY), 1905, with an introduction by Martin Gardner, Dover (New York, NY), 1987, Thorndike Press (Waterville, ME), 2004.

The Innocence of Father Brown, illustrated by Will F. Foster, Cassell (New York, NY), 1911, annotated edition published as *The Annotated Innocence of Father Brown,* edited by Martin Gardner, Oxford University Press (New York, NY), 1987, Dover Publications (Mineola, NY), 1998.

The Wisdom of Father Brown, Cassell (New York, NY), 1914, MacroPrintBooks (Chesterfield, MO), 2000.

The Perishing of the Pendragons, Paget (New York, NY), 1914.

The Man Who Knew Too Much and Other Stories, Cassell (New York, NY), 1922, abridged edition published as *The Man Who Knew Too Much,* illustrated by W. Hatherell, Harper (New York, NY), 1922, Dover (Mineloa, NY), 2003.

Tales of the Long Bow, Cassell (New York, NY), 1925, Dufour Editions (Philadelphia, PA), 1963, selections published as *The Exclusive Luxury of Enoch Oates* [and] *The Unthinkable Theory of Professor Green,* Dodd, Mead (New York, NY), 1925, and *The Unprecedented Architecture of Commander Blair,* Dodd, Mead (New York, NY), 1925.

The Incredulity of Father Brown, Cassell (New York, NY), 1926, G. K. Hall (Boston, MA), 1984.

The Secret of Father Brown, Cassell (New York, NY), 1927, G. K. Hall (Boston, MA), 1985.

The Sword of Wood, Elkin Mathews, 1928, Norwood Editions (Norwood, PA), 1978.

Stories, Harrap, 1928.

The Poet and the Lunatics: Episodes in the Life of Gabriel Gale, Dodd, Mead (New York, NY), 1929, Dufour Editions (Philadelphia, PA), 1963.

The Moderate Murderer [and] *The Honest Quack* (also see below), Dodd, Mead (New York, NY), 1929.

The Father Brown Stories, Cassell (New York, NY), 1929, 12th edition, 1974, published as *The Father Brown Omnibus,* Dodd, Mead, 1933, new and revised edition, 1951, with a preface by Auberon Waugh, 1983.

The Ecstatic Thief (also see below), Dodd, Mead (New York, NY), 1930.

Four Faultless Felons (includes *The Moderate Murderer, The Honest Quack, The Ecstatic Thief,* and *The Loyal Traitor*), Dodd, Mead (New York, NY), 1930, with an introduction by Martin Gardner, Dover (New York, NY), 1989.

The Scandal of Father Brown, Dodd, Mead (New York, NY), 1935, G. K. Hall (Boston, MA), 1986.

The Paradoxes of Mr. Pond, Dodd, Mead (New York, NY), 1937, with an introduction by Martin Gardner, Dover (New York, NY), 1990.

The Pocket Book of Father Brown, Pocket Books (New York, NY), 1943.

The Vampire of the Village, privately published, 1947.

Father Brown: Selected Stories, edited and with an introduction by Ronald Knox, Oxford University Press, 1955.

The Amazing Adventures of Father Brown, Dell (New York, NY), 1961.

Father Brown Mystery Stories, selected and edited by Raymond T. Bond, Dodd, Mead (New York, NY), 1962.

G. K. Chesterton: Selected Stories, edited by Kingsley Amis, Faber (New York, NY), 1972.

Daylight and Nightmare: Uncollected Stories and Fables, edited by Marie Smith, Dodd, Mead (New York, NY), 1986.

Thirteen Detectives: Classic Mystery Stories, edited by Marie Smith, Dodd, Mead (New York, NY), 1987.

Seven Suspects, edited by Marie Smith, foreword by H. R. F. Keating, Carroll & Graf (New York, NY), 1990.

Best of Father Brown, selected and with an introduction by H. R. F. Keating, C. E. Tuttle (Rutland, VT), 1991.

Favorite Father Brown Stories, Dover Publications (New York, NY), 1993.

Father Brown—a Selection, edited by W. W. Robson, Oxford University Press (New York, NY), 1995.

Father Brown of the Church of Rome: Selected Mystery Stories, edited and with an introduction by John Peterson, Ignatius Press (San Francisco), 1996.

POEMS

Greybeards at Play: Literature and Art for Old Gentlemen, Rhymes and Sketches (also see below), Johnson, 1900, Sheed & Ward (London, England), 1930.

The Wild Knight and Other Poems, Richards (London, England), 1900, 4th revised edition, Dutton (New York, NY), 1914.

The Ballad of the White Horse, John Lane (New York, NY), 1911, edited by Sister Mary Bernadette, Brother John Totten and Brother George Schuster, illustrated by Addison Burbank, Catholic Authors Press (Kirkwood, MO), 1950, edited by Bernadette Sheridan, illustrated by Robert Austin, Ignatius Press (San Francisco, CA), 2001.

Poems, John Lane (New York, NY), 1915.

Wine, Water and Song, Methuen (London, England), 1915, 1945.

A Poem, privately published, 1915.

Old King Cole, privately published, 1920.

The Ballad of St. Barbara and Other Verses, Palmer (London, England), 1922, Putnam (New York, NY), 1923.

Poems, Dodd, Mead (New York, NY), 1922.

G. K. Chesterton (collected poems), E. Benn, 1925, Methuen (London, England), 1933.

The Queen of Seven Swords, Sheed & Ward (London, England), 1926.

The Collected Poems of G. K. Chesterton, Palmer (London, England), 1927, Dodd, Mead (New York, NY), 1932, revised edition, Methuen (London, England), 1933, Dodd, Mead (New York, NY), 1966, with an introduction by Daniel B. Dodson, 1980.

Gloria in Profundis, wood engravings by Eric Gill, Faber (London, England), 1927.

Ubi Ecclesia, drawings by Diana Murphy, Faber (London, England), 1929.

Lepanto, Federal Advertising Agency (New York, NY), 1929, Ignatius Press (San Francisco, CA), 2004.

The Grave of Arthur, Faber (London, England), 1930.

Graybeards at Play and Other Comic Verse, edited by John Sullivan, Elek (London, England), 1974.

LITERARY CRITICISM AND ESSAYS

The Defendant (essays), Johnson (London, England), 1901, Dodd, Mead (New York, NY), 1902, Books for Libraries Press (Freeport, NY), 1972.

(With J. E. Hodder Williams) *Thomas Carlyle,* Hodder & Stoughton (London, England), 1902, Pott (New York, NY), 1903, R. West (Philadelphia, PA), 1978.

Twelve Types, Humphreys (London, England), 1902, published as *Twelve Types: A Collection of Mini-Biographies,* IHS Press (Norfolk, VA), 2002, enlarged edition published as *Varied Types,* Dodd, Mead (New York, NY), 1903, Books for Libraries Press (Freeport, NY), 1968, abridged edition published as *Five Types: A Book of Essays,* Humphreys (London, England), 1910, Holt (New York, NY), 1911, Books for Libraries Press (Freeport, NY), 1969, new abridged edition published as *Simplicity and Tolstoy,* Humphreys (London, England), 1912.

(With W. Robertson Nicoll) *Robert Louis Stevenson* (also see below), Pott (New York, NY), 1903, Norwood Editions (Norwood, PA), 1976.

(With G. H. Perris and Edward Garnett) *Leo Tolstoy,* Pott (New York, NY), 1903, Norwood Editions (Norwood, PA), 1978.

(With F. G. Kitton) *Charles Dickens,* Pott (New York, NY), 1903.

Robert Browning, Macmillan (New York, NY), 1903, St. Martin's Press (New York, NY), 1951.

(With Richard Garnett) *Tennyson,* Hodder & Stoughton (London, England), 1903.

(With Lewis Melville) *Thackeray,* Pott (New York, NY), 1903, R. West (Philadelphia, PA), 1978.

G. F. Watts, Dutton (New York, NY), 1904.

Heretics (essays; also see below), John Lane (New York, NY), 1905, Books for Libraries Press (Freeport, NY), 1970.

Charles Dickens: A Critical Study, Dodd, Mead (New York, NY), 1906, new edition, with a foreword by Alexander Woolcott, published as *Charles Dick-*

ens: The Last of the Great Men, Readers Club Press, 1942, with an introduction by Steven Marchus, Schocken Books (New York, NY), 1965, Burns & Oates (London, England), 1975.

All Things Considered (essays), John Lane (New York, NY), 1908, Books for Libraries Press (Freeport, NY), 1971.

George Bernard Shaw, John Lane (New York, NY), 1909, revised edition, Bodley Head (London, England), 1950, Folcroft Library Editions (Folcroft, PA), 1978.

Orthodoxy (essays; also see below), John Lane (New York, NY), 1909, Ignatius Press (San Francisco, CA), 1995.

Alarms and Discussions (essays), Methuen (London, England), 1910, enlarged edition, Dodd, Mead (New York, NY), 1911.

William Blake, Dutton (New York, NY), 1910, R. West (Philadelphia, PA), 1978.

What's Wrong with the World (essays), Dodd, Mead (New York, NY), 1910, with a tutorial introduction by F. J. Sheed, Sheed & Ward (New York, NY), 1942, Ignatius Press (San Francisco, CA), 1994.

Appreciations and Criticisms of the Works of Charles Dickens, Dutton (New York, NY), 1911, introduction by Michael Slater, C. E. Tuttle (Rutland, VT), 1992.

A Defence of Nonsense and Other Essays, Dodd, Mead (New York, NY), 1911.

The Victorian Age in Literature, Williams & Norgate, 1913, Oxford University Press (New York, NY), 1966.

Utopia of Usurers and Other Essays, Boni & Liveright, 1917, IHS Press (Norfolk, VA), 2002.

Charles Dickens Fifty Years After, privately published, 1920.

The Uses of Diversity: A Book of Essays, Methuen (London, England), 1920, Dodd, Mead (New York, NY), 1921.

Eugenics and Other Evils (essays), Cassell (London, England), 1922, published as *Eugenics and Other Evils: An Argument against the Scientifically Organized State,* edited by Michael W. Perry, with additional articles by Francis Galton, C. W. Saleeby, Marie Stopes, and others, Inkling Books (Seattle, WA), 2000.

William Cobbett, Dodd, Mead (New York, NY), 1925.

The Everlasting Man (essays), Dodd, Mead (New York, NY), 1925, Ignatius Press (San Francisco, CA), 1993.

Robert Louis Stevenson, Hodder & Stoughton (London, England), 1927, Dodd, Mead (New York, NY), 1928.

Generally Speaking: A Book of Essays, Methuen (London, England), 1928, Dodd, Mead (New York, NY), 1929, Books for Libraries (Freeport, NY), 1968.

Essays, Harrap, 1928.

Come to Think of It . . . : A Collection of Essays, Methuen (London, England), 1930, Dodd, Mead (New York, NY), 1931, Books for Libraries Press (Freeport, NY), 1971.

All Is Grist: A Book of Essays, Methuen (London, England), 1931, Dodd, Mead (New York, NY), 1932, Scholarly Press (St. Clair Shores, MI), 1971.

Chaucer, Farrar & Rinehart (New York, NY), 1932, Greenwood Press (New York, NY), 1969.

Sidelights on London and Newer York and Other Essays, Sheed & Ward (New York, NY), 1932, Scholarly Press (St. Clair Shores, MI), 1970.

All I Survey: A Book of Essays, Methuen (London, England), 1933, Books for Libraries Press (Freeport, NY), 1967.

Avowals and Denials: A Book of Essays, Methuen (London, England), 1934, Dodd, Mead (New York, NY), 1935.

The Well and the Shallows (essays), Sheed & Ward (New York, NY), 1935.

As I Was Saying: A Book of Essays, Dodd, Mead (New York, NY), 1936, Books for Libraries Press (Freeport, NY), 1966.

Essays, edited by John Guest, Collins, 1939.

Selected Essays, edited by Dorothy Collins, Methuen (London, England), 1949.

Essays, edited by K. E. Whitehorn, Methuen (London, England), 1953.

A Handful of Authors: Essays on Books and Writers, edited by Dorothy Collins, Sheed & Ward (New York, NY), 1953.

The Glass Walking-Stick and Other Essays from the "Illustrated London News," 1905-1936, edited by Dorothy Collins, Methuen (London, England), 1955.

Lunacy and Letters (essays), edited by Dorothy Collins, Sheed & Ward (New York, NY), 1958, Books for Libraries Press (Freeport, NY), 1972.

The Spice of Life and Other Essays, edited by Dorothy Collins, Finlayson, 1964, Dufour Editions (Philadelphia, PA), 1966.

Chesterton on Shakespeare, edited by Dorothy Collins, introduction by John Sullivan, Dufour Editions (Philadelphia, PA), 1971.

The Apostle and the Wild Ducks and Other Essays, edited by Dorothy Collins, Elek (London, England), 1975.

Heretics [and] Orthodoxy, T. Nelson (Nashville, TN), 2000.

OTHER

Tremendous Trifles, Dodd, Mead (New York, NY), 1909, reprinted, Dufour Editions (Philadelphia, PA), 1968.

(Editor) *Thackeray* (selections), Bell, 1909.

The Ultimate Lie, privately published, 1910.

(Editor, with Alice Meynell) *Samuel Johnson* (selections), Herbert & Daniel, 1911.

A Chesterton Calendar, Kegan Paul, 1911, Gordon Press (New York, NY), 1976, published as *Wit and Wisdom of G. K. Chesterton,* Dodd, Mead (New York, NY), 1911, published as *Chesterton Day by Day,* Kegan Paul, 1912, published as *Chesterton Day by Day: The Wit and Wisdom of G. K. Chesterton,* edited by Michael W. Perry, Inkling Books (Seattle, WA), 2002.

The Future of Religion: Mr. G. K. Chesterton's Reply to Mr. Bernard Shaw, privately published, 1911.

The Conversion of an Anarchist, Paget (New York, NY), 1912.

A Miscellany of Men, Methuen (London, England), 1912, enlarged edition, Dodd, Mead (New York, NY), 1912, with an introduction by Dorothy E. Collins, Dufour Editions (Philadelphia, PA), 1969, reprinted, IHS Press (Norfolk, VA), 2003.

Magic: A Fantastic Comedy (play; first produced in London, England, 1913; produced in New York, 1917), Putnam (New York, NY), 1913.

Thoughts from Chesterton, edited by Elsie E. Morton, Harrap (London, England), 1913.

The Barbarism of Berlin, Cassell (New York, NY), 1914, published as *The Appetite of Tyranny, including Letters to an Old Garibaldian,* Dodd, Mead (New York, NY), 1915.

London, photographs by Alvin Langdon Coburn, privately published (Minneapolis, MN), 1914.

Prussian versus Belgian Culture, Belgian Relief and Reconstruction Fund, 1914.

Letters to an Old Garibaldian, John Lane (New York, NY), 1915.

The So-Called Belgian Bargain, National War Aims Committee, 1915.

The Crimes of England, Palmer & Hayward (London, England), 1915, John Lane (New York, NY), 1916.

Divorce versus Democracy, Society of SS. Peter and Paul (London, England), 1916.

Temperance and the Great Alliance, True Temperance Association, 1916.

The G. K. Chesterton Calendar, edited by H. Cecil Palmer, Palmer & Hayward, 1916.

A Shilling for My Thoughts, edited by E. V. Lucas, Methuen (London, England), 1916.

A Short History of England, John Lane (New York, NY), 1917, reprinted, Chatto & Windus (London, England), 1930.

Lord Kitchener, privately published, 1917.

How to Help Annexation, Hayman Christy & Lilly, 1918.

Irish Impressions, Collins (London, England), 1919, John Lane (New York, NY), 1920, reprinted, IHS Press (Norfolk, Va), 2002.

(Editor, with Holbrook Jackson and R. Brimley Johnson) Charles Dickens, *The Personal History of David Copperfield,* C. Chivers (London, England), 1919.

The Superstition of Divorce, John Lane (New York, NY), 1920.

The New Jerusalem, Hodder & Stoughton (London, England), 1920, Doran (New York, NY), 1921.

What I Saw in America, Hodder & Stoughton (London, England), 1922, with an introduction by George Harmon Knoles, Da Capo Press (New York, NY), 1968.

Fancies versus Fads, Dodd, Mead (New York, NY), 1923.

St. Francis of Assisi (biography), Hodder & Stoughton (London, England), 1923, Doran (New York, NY), 1924.

The End of the Roman Road: A Pageant of Wayfarers, illustrated by T. H. Robinson, preface by A. St. John Adcock, Classic Press (London, England), 1924.

The Superstitions of the Sceptic (lecture), Herder (London, England), 1925.

A Gleaming Cohort, Being Selections from the Works of G. K. Chesterton, edited by E. V. Lucas, Methuen (London, England), 1926.

(Editor) *Essays by Divers Hands 6,* Oxford University Press (Oxford, England), 1926.

The Outline of Sanity, Sheed & Ward (New York, NY), 1926, reprinted, IHS Press (Norfolk, VA), 2001.

The Catholic Church and Conversion, Macmillan (New York, NY), 1926.

Selected Works, nine volumes, Methuen (London, England), 1926.

Social Reform versus Birth Control, Simpkin Marshall, 1927.

The Judgement of Dr. Johnson: A Comedy in Three Acts (play; first produced in London, England, 1932), Sheed & Ward (New York, NY), 1927.

Culture and the Coming Peril (lecture), University of London Press (London, England), 1927.

(With George Bernard Shaw) *Do We Agree? A Debate between G. K. Chesterton and Bernard Shaw, with Hilaire Belloc in the Chair,* Mitchell (Hartford, CT), 1928, R. West (Philadelphia, PA), 1977.

A Chesterton Catholic Anthology, edited by Patrick Braybrooke, Kenedy, 1928.

The Thing, Sheed & Ward (New York, NY), 1929, 1957, published as *The Thing: Why I Am a Catholic,* Dodd, Mead (New York, NY), 1930.

G. K. C. As M. C., Being a Collection of Thirty-seven Introductions, selected and edited by J. P. de Foneska, Methuen (London, England), 1929, reprinted, Books for Libraries Press (Freeport, NY), 1967.

The Turkey and the Turk, St. Dominic's Press, 1930.

At the Sign of the World's End, Harvest Press, 1930.

The Resurrection of Rome, Dodd, Mead (New York, NY), 1930.

(With E. Haldeman-Julius) *Is There a Return to Religion?,* Haldeman-Julius, 1931.

(Contributor) *The Floating Admiral,* Hodder & Stoughton (London, England), 1931, Doubleday, Doran (New York, NY), 1932, with an introduction by Christianna Brand, Gregg Press (Boston, MA), 1979.

Christendom in Dublin, Sheed & Ward (London, England), 1932, (New York, NY), 1933.

St. Thomas Aquinas (biography), Sheed & Ward (New York, NY), 1933, with an introduction by Ralph McInerny and Joseph Pearce, Ignatius Press (San Francisco, CA), 2002.

G. K. Chesterton (selected humor), edited by E. V. Knox, Methuen (London, England), 1933, published as *Running after One's Hat and Other Whimsies,* McBride, 1933.

(Editor) *G. K.'s* (miscellany from *G. K.'s Weekly*), Rich & Cowan, 1934.

Explaining the English, British Council, 1935.

Stories, Essays, and Poems, Dent (London, England), 1935, Dutton (New York, NY), 1957.

Autobiography, Hutchinson (London, England), 1936, with an introduction by Anthony Burgess, 1969, published as *The Autobiography of G. K. Chesterton,* Sheed & Ward (New York, NY), 1936.

The Man Who Was Chesterton: The Best Essays, Stories, Poems and Other Writings of G. K. Chesterton, compiled and edited by Raymond T. Bond, Dodd, Mead (New York, NY), 1937, reprinted, Books for Libraries Press (Freeport, NY), 1970.

(Self-illustrated) *The Coloured Lands,* Sheed & Ward (New York, NY), 1938.

The End of the Armistice, compiled by F. J. Sheed, Sheed & Ward (New York, NY), 1940, reprinted, Books for Libraries Press (Freeport, NY), 1970.

(Contributor) Ellery Queen, editor, *To the Queen's Taste,* Little, Brown (Boston, MA), 1946.

The Common Man, compiled by F. J. Sheed, Sheed & Ward (New York, NY), 1950.

The Surprise (play; first produced in Hull, England, 1953), preface by Dorothy L. Sayers, Sheed & Ward (New York, NY), 1952.

G. K. Chesterton: An Anthology, edited and with an introduction by D. B. Wyndham Lewis, Oxford University Press, 1957.

Essays and Poems, edited by Wilfrid Sheed, Penguin Books (Harmondsworth, England), 1958.

Where All Roads Lead, Catholic Truth Society, 1961.

The Man Who Was Orthodox: A Selection from the Uncollected Writings of G. K. Chesterton, edited by A. L. Maycock, Dobson (London, England), 1963.

G. K. Chesterton: A Selection from His Non-Fictional Prose, edited by W. H. Auden, Faber (London, England), 1970.

The Spirit of Christmas: Stories, Poems, Essays, edited by Marie Smith, Dodd, Mead (New York, NY), 1985.

The Collected Works of G. K. Chesterton, Ignatius Press (San Francisco, CA), 1986-2001.

G. K.'s Weekly: A Sampler, edited by Lyle W. Dorsett, Loyola University Press, 1986.

Collected Nonsense and Light Verse, edited by Marie Smith, Dodd, Mead (New York, NY), 1987.

As I Was Saying . . . : A Chesterton Reader, edited by Robert Knille, Eerdmans (Grand Rapids, MI), 1987.

The Essential G. K. Chesterton, edited by P. J. Kavanagh, Oxford University Press (New York, NY), 1987.

More Quotable Chesterton: A Topical Compilation of the Wit, Wisdom, and Satire of G. K. Chesterton, edited by George J. Marlin, Richard P. Rabatin, and John L. Swan, with a foreword by George William Rutler, Ignatius Press (San Francisco, CA), 1988.

Brave New Family: G. K. Chesterton on Men and Women, Children, Sex, Divorce, Marriage and the Family, edited and with an introduction by Alvaro de Silva, Ignatius Press (San Francisco, CA), 1990.

On Lying in Bed and Other Essays, edited and with an introduction by Alberto Manguel, Bayeux Arts (Calgary, Alberta, Canada), 2000.

G. K. Chesterton's Sherlock Holmes: Original Illustrations: A Facsimile of the Original Unpublished Drawings, edited and with an introduction by Steven Doyle, Baker Street Irregulars (New York, NY), 2003.

Essential Writings, edited by William Griffin, Orbis Books (Maryknoll, NY), 2003.

Contributor to London *Daily News,* 1901-13, *Illustrated London News,* 1905-36, and London *Daily Herald,* 1913-14. Editor, *The Debater* (St. Paul's School publication), 1891-93; coeditor, *Eye Witness,* 1911-12; editor, *New Witness,* 1912-23; editor, *G. K.'s Weekly,* 1925-36. Editor, with H. Jackson and R. B. Johnson, "Readers' Classics" series, 1922. Illustrator of works, including *Great Inquiry,* by Hilaire Belloc, 1903; *Emmanuel Burden, Merchant, of Thames St., in the City of London, Exporter of Hardware,* by Hilaire Belloc, 1904; *Missing Masterpiece,* by Belloc, 1929; *Clerihews Complete,* by E. C. Bentley, 1951; *Complete Clerihews of E. Clerihew Bentley,* 1981; and *First Clerihews,* 1982.

Many of Chesterton's papers are held in the Robert John Bayer Memorial Chesterton Collection, John Carroll University Library, Cleveland, Ohio; other materials are at Columbia University, Marquette University, and the British Library.

ADAPTATIONS: John Longenbaugh adapted *The Man Who Was Thursday* for the stage, produced by Taproot Theatre Company, Seattle, 2002.

SIDELIGHTS: G. K. Chesterton was one of the dominating figures of the London literary scene in the early twentieth century. Not only did he get into lively discussions with anyone who would debate him, including his friend, frequent verbal sparring partner, and noted Irish playwright George Bernard Shaw, but he wrote about seemingly every topic, in every genre, from journalism to plays, poetry to crime novels. "He said something about everything and he said it better than anyone else," declared Dale Ahlquist, president

of the American Chester Society, on the society's Web site. Most of Chesterton's literary output was nonfiction, including thousands of columns for various periodicals, but today he is best remembered for his fictional work—a mystery series about Father Brown, a Catholic priest and amateur detective.

Chesterton began his literary career as a manuscript reader for a London publishing house, but he soon moved into writing art criticism. When his friends formed a journal, the *Speaker,* Chesterton contributed a series of articles, and soon began writing for the London *Daily News* and *Bookman* as well. Before long, people were taking notice of his work. Ian Boyd explained in the *Dictionary of Literary Biography,* "He belonged to that category of writer which used to be called the man of letters, and like the typical man of letters he wrote journalism which included a wide variety of literary forms and literature which possessed many of the characteristics of journalism."

Chesterton's first published books were of poetry, seemingly a far cry from his column-writing. But Boyd noticed a "close connection between his poetry and his everyday journalism." Boyd concluded: "In this sense, T. S. Eliot's description of Chesterton's poetry as 'first-rate journalistic balladry' turns out to have been particularly perceptive, since it is a reminder about the essential character of all Chesterton's work. In his verse, as in all his writings, his first aim was to comment on the political and social questions of the day."

Chesterton's first novel, the manuscript of which was discovered in a steamer trunk in 1989, was published for the first time in 2001. *Basil Howe* was written in 1893, shortly after Chesterton graduated from school. Although, as critics noted, the book is clearly the work of an inexperienced, unformed writer, it shows hints of Chesterton's future style—including the witticisms for which he would later become famous—and provides insights into his frame of mind during this stage in his life. It has long been known that Chesterton underwent a period of philosophical soul-searching during his young adulthood that was so intense that some of his friends thought he was losing his mind, and *Basil Howe* is assumed to have been written during that time. "Those familiar with Chesterton's teenage years will see much of the author in" the book, Mark Knight commented in *English Literature in Transition, 1880-1920,* although he cautioned against reading the book as autobiography rather than as a novel.

Although best known nowadays for his detective fiction, Chesterton first gained public attention as a journalist and social philosopher; he actually wrote the popular, lucrative Father Brown mysteries in part to bankroll his less financially rewarding work. Questions of religion and morality were prominent in his writings. His book *What's Wrong with the World* advocated Distributism, a social philosophy that divided property holders into small communities, trying to foster neighborliness. Chesterton viewed Distributism as a counter to Socialism and Capitalism, ideologies that, he felt, reduced people to inhumane units. Stephen Metcalf, writing in the *Times Literary Supplement,* pointed out that this philosophy, also expounded in the 1904 novel *The Napoleon of Notting Hill,* more accurately reflects modern society's problems than does George Orwell's classic *1984:* "It is not only . . . that Chesterton cared passionately for what ordinary humanity feels and thinks," Metcalf stated. "It is also that he had particular convictions about how one should understand humanity."

Much of Chesterton's work reflected his social concern. Using literary devices such as parable and allegory, he sought to bring about social changes that embodied his religious and political beliefs. His novels, reported Brian Murray in the *Dictionary of Literary Biography,* "are as frequently called romances, extravaganzas, fantasies, parables, or allegories. For while they are thick with the details of everyday life, Chesterton's hastily written book-length fictions are outlandishly plotted and, in the main, unabashedly didactic."

This didacticism has alienated modern readers from some of Chesterton's fiction. His detective stories, however, remain popular. Chesterton himself was very fond of the detective story and recognized that much of his writing was pedantic and would probably not survive him. "Chesterton assumed that he would never be considered a novelist of enormous importance," asserted Murray; "that, as a writer of fiction, he would always remain best known for the long series of Father Brown stories he began with *The Innocence of Father Brown* in 1911—stories he sometimes tossed off in a day or two."

Chesterton was raised in a theologically liberal family and did not convert to Catholicism until the age of 48, more than a decade after the first Father Brown stories were published. Loosely based upon Chesterton's friend, the Roman Catholic priest John O'Connor, Father Brown "drops typical Chestertonian quips as he solves ghastly transgressions not with Holmes-sharp logic but by 'getting inside' the criminal mind," according to Murray. Rather than using deductive methods to discover the perpetrator of a crime, Father Brown—whom Chesterton depicted in his *Autobiography* as "shabby and shapeless [in appearance], his face round and expressionless, his manners clumsy"—bases his conclusions on his knowledge of human nature. This knowledge is drawn in part from his experience in the confessional box, but also from his recognition of his own capacity for evil. "The little priest could see," stated Ronald Knox in his introduction to *Father Brown: Selected Stories,* "not as a psychologist, but as a moralist, into the dark places of the human heart; could guess, therefore, at what point envy, or fear, or resentment would pass the bounds of the normal, and the cords of convention would snap, so that a man was hurried into crime." "To Father Brown," wrote Eric Routley in *The Puritan Pleasures of the Detective Story: A Personal Monograph,* "any criminal is a good man gone wrong. He is not an evil man who has cut himself off from the comprehension or sympathy of those who labour to be good." To this end, Brown is not primarily interested in solving the case, but in getting the criminal to confess his sin and repent, thereby saving his soul.

Father Brown remains, in the minds of most readers, Chesterton's greatest creation, although his contribution to the art of mystery writing is also recognized. "If Chesterton had not created Father Brown," Leitch declared, "his detective fiction would rarely be read today, but his place in the historical development of the genre would still be secure." Even in his own day, Chesterton was considered to be the father of the detective tale. As Leitch noted, when the Detection Club was founded in 1928, "Chesterton, not Conan Doyle [creator of Sherlock Holmes] . . . became its first president and served in this capacity until his death." Not only did Chesterton write detective stories, he also wrote several critical essays about the proper form and style of such works.

Under the influence of Chesterton's Father Brown, the mystery story became less a portrait of the detective's personality, and more a puzzle that the detective and the reader could both solve. "Chesterton's determination to provide his audience with all the clues available to his detectives," stated Leitch, "has been so widely imitated as to become the defining characteristic of the formal or golden age period (roughly 1920-1940) in detective fiction. . . . Modern readers, for whom the term *whodunit* has become synonymous with *detective story,* forget that the concealment of the criminal's identity as the central mystery of the story is a relatively modern convention." In the end, H. R. F. Keating (himself a prominent mystery writer) concluded in the *St. James Guide to Crime and Mystery Writers,* "Chesterton's fame rests on the priest with 'the harmless, human name of Brown' and it will endure."

BIOGRAPHICAL AND CRITICAL SOURCES:

BOOKS

Barker, Dudley, *G. K. Chesterton: A Biography,* Stein & Day, 1973.

Belloc, Hilaire, *The Place of Gilbert Chesterton in English Letters,* Sheed & Ward (New York, NY), 1940.

Bogaerts, Anthony Mattheus Adrianus, *Chesterton and the Victorian Age,* Rozenbeek en Venemans, 1940.

Boyd, Ian, *The Novels of G. K. Chesterton: A Study in Art and Propaganda,* Barnes & Noble (New York, NY), 1975.

Canovan, Margaret, *G. K. Chesterton: Radical Populist,* Harcourt (New York, NY), 1977.

Carol, Sister M., *G. K. Chesterton: The Dynamic Classicist,* Morilal Banarsidass, 1971.

Chesterton, Cecil, *Gilbert K. Chesterton: A Criticism,* John Lane (New York, NY), 1909.

Chesterton, G. K., *Autobiography,* Hutchinson (London, England), 1936, published as *The Autobiography of G. K. Chesterton,* Sheed & Ward (New York, NY), 1936.

Clemens, Cyril, *Chesterton As Seen by His Contemporaries,* Mark Twain Society, 1939.

Clipper, Lawrence J., *G. K. Chesterton,* Twayne, 1974.

Coates, John, *Chesterton and the Edwardian Cultural Crisis,* Hull University Press, 1984.

Concise Dictionary of British Literary Biography, Volume 6: *Modern Writers, 1914-1945,* Gale (Detroit, MI), 1991.

Conlon, D. J., editor, *G. K. Chesterton: A Half Century of Views,* Oxford University Press, 1987.

Dale, Alzina Stone, *The Outline of Sanity: A Life of G. K. Chesterton,* Eerdmans (Grand Rapids, MI), 1982.

Dictionary of Literary Biography, Gale (Detroit, MI), Volume 10: *Modern British Dramatists, 1900-1945,* 1982, Volume 19: *British Poets, 1880-1914,* 1983, Volume 34: *British Novelists, 1890-1929: Traditionalists,* 1985, Volume 70: *British Mystery Writers, 1860-1919,* 1988, Volume 98: *Modern British Essayists, First Series,* 1990, Volume 149: *Late Nineteenth- and Early Twentieth-Century British Literary Biographers,* 1995, Volume 178: *British Fantasy and Science-Fiction Writers before World War I,* 1997.

Encyclopedia of World Biography, 2nd edition, seventeen volumes, Gale (Detroit, MI), 1998.

Fagerberg, David W., *The Size of Chesterton's Catholicism,* University of Notre Dame Press (Notre Dame, IN), 1998.

Hollis, Christopher, *The Mind of Chesterton,* Hollis & Carter, 1970.

Hunter, Lynette, *G. K. Chesterton: Explorations in Allegory,* St. Martin's Press (New York, NY), 1979.

Kenner, Hugh, *Paradox in Chesterton,* Sheed & Ward (New York, NY), 1947.

Knox, Ronald, editor and author of introduction, *Father Brown: Selected Stories* by G. K. Chesterton, Oxford University Press, 1955.

O'Connor, John, *Father Brown on Chesterton,* Muller/Burns, Oates, 1937.

Peters, Thomas C., *Battling for the Modern Mind: A Beginner's Chesterton,* CPH (St. Louis. MO), 1994.

Rauch, Rufus William, *A Chesterton Celebration,* Notre Dame University Press (Notre Dame, IN), 1983.

Reference Guide to English Literature, 2nd edition, St. James Press (Detroit, MI), 1991.

Routley, Eric, *The Puritan Pleasures of the Detective Story: A Personal Monograph,* Gollancz (London, England), 1972.

St. James Guide to Crime and Mystery Writers, 4th edition, St. James Press (Detroit, MI), 1996.

St. James Guide to Fantasy Writers, St. James Press (Detroit, MI), 1996.

Short Story Criticism, Volume 1, Gale (Detroit, MI), 1988.

Sprug, Joseph W., editor, *An Index to G. K. Chesterton,* Catholic University of America Press, 1966.

Sullivan, John, *G. K. Chesterton: A Bibliography,* University of London Press (London, England), 1958.

Sullivan, John, *Chesterton Continued: A Bibliographic Supplement,* University of London Press (London, England), 1968.

Tadie, Andrew A. and Michael H. MacDonald, *Permanent Things: Toward the Recovery of a More Human Scale at the End of the Twentieth Century,* William B. Eerdmans (Grand Rapids, MI), 1995.

Titterton, W. R., *G. K. Chesterton: A Portrait,* Organ, 1936.

Twentieth-Century Literary Criticism, Volume 6, Gale (Detroit, MI), 1982.

Ward, Maisie, *Gilbert Keith Chesterton,* Sheed & Ward (New York, NY), 1943.

Winks, Robin W., editor, *Mystery and Suspense Writers: The Literature of Crime, Detection, and Espionage,* two volumes, Scribner (New York, NY), 1998.

PERIODICALS

Chesterton Review, fall/winter, 1974—.

Christian History, August, 2002, special issue devoted to Chesterton.

Commonweal, August 14, 1992, A. W. R. Sipe and B. C. Lamb, "Chesterton's Brown and Greeley's Blackie: Two Very Different Detectives," pp. 18-21.

English Literature in Transition, 1880-1920, fall, 2002, Mark Knight, review of *Basil Howe,* pp. 464-467.

National Review, September 6, 1985, M. D. Aeschliman, review of *As I Was Saying: A Chesterton Reader,* pp. 54-55; August 14, 1987, James E. Person, Jr., review of *Daylight and Nightmare: Uncollected Stories and Fables,* p. 53.

Renascence, spring, 2001, Joseph Schwartz, "Chesterton on the Idea of Christian Tragedy," p. 227.

Spectator, June 30, 2001, P. J. Kavanagh, review of *Basil Howe,* p. 45.

Times Literary Supplement, December 25-31, 1987.

ONLINE

American Chesterton Society Web site, http://www.chesterton.org/ (April 22, 2004).*

*   *   *

COLFER, Eoin 1965-

PERSONAL: First name is pronounced "Ow-en"; born May 14, 1965, in Wexford, Ireland; son of Billy (a primary school teacher, artist, and historian) and Noreen (a drama teacher, actress, and writer) Colfer; married, 1991; wife's name Jackie; children: Finn, Seán.

Eoin Colfer

Education: Teacher's training course, Dublin, Ireland, graduated 1986. *Hobbies and other interests:* Reading, theater, parachuting.

ADDRESSES: Home—Wexford, Ireland. *Agent*—c/o Author Mail, Hyperion Books, 77 West 66th St., 11th Fl., New York, NY 10023.

CAREER: Writer. Primary school teacher, 1987-2001.

AWARDS, HONORS: White Raven Award, 1998, for *Benny and Omar;* Bisto Children's Book of the Year nomination, 2000, for *Benny and Babe;* Bisto Children's Book of the Year Merit Award, 2001, for *The Wish List;* Whitbread Children's Book of the Year shortlist, and Children's Book of the Year, British Book Awards, both 2001, Bisto Children's Book of the Year nomination, and Children's Book of the Year, W. H. Smith Book Awards, both 2002, all for *Artemis Fowl.*

WRITINGS:

Benny and Omar, O'Brien Press (Dublin, Ireland), 1998.

Benny and Babe, O'Brien Press (Dublin, Ireland), 1999.

The Wish List, O'Brien Press (Dublin, Ireland), 2000, Hyperion (New York, NY), 2003.

Artemis Fowl, Hyperion (New York, NY), 2001.

Artemis Fowl: The Arctic Incident, Hyperion (New York, NY), 2002.

Artemis Fowl: The Eternity Code, Hyperion (New York, NY), 2003.

Artemis Fowl: The Seventh Dwarf (written for the Irish World Book Day celebration), Puffin (London, England), 2004.

The Legend of Spud Murphy, Hyperion (New York, NY), 2004.

The Supernaturalist, Hyperion (New York, NY), 2004.

"O'BRIEN FLYERS" SERIES

Going Potty, O'Brien Press (Dublin, Ireland), 1999.

Ed's Funny Feet, O'Brien Press (Dublin, Ireland), 2000.

Ed's Bed, O'Brien Press (Dublin, Ireland), 2001.

Colfer's work has been translated into Danish, Dutch, French, German, Italian, Portuguese, and Spanish.

ADAPTATIONS: Artemis Fowl has been optioned for a film by Miramax.

WORK IN PROGRESS: Another book in the "Artemis Fowl" series; a musical.

SIDELIGHTS: Described by its author as "*Die Hard* with fairies," the young adult fantasy *Artemis Fowl* burst onto the book scene in 2001, set to take over where the "Harry Potter" books left off and to make its creator, Irish schoolteacher Eoin Colfer, the new wunderkind of children's literature. As Kate Kellaway noted in the London *Observer,* a line from the novel about a boy in search of fairy gods—"Irish people skulking around rainbows hoping to win the supernatural lottery"—-was prescient. Kellaway remarked, "What Eoin Colfer did not know at the time was that he was about to strike gold himself." Colfer's humor-

ous, high-tech fantasy about a twelve-year-old who kidnaps a leprechaun started a bidding war among publishers, was optioned for a film, and has been projected as the first in a series of novels about young Mr. Fowl. "It's just like a dream," Colfer told Heather Vogel in a *Publishers Weekly* interview. "[A] fellow from a small town gets a big break. You never think it's going to happen to you."

The second of five sons born to school teachers, Colfer grew up in Wexford, in the southeast of Ireland. His mother, Noreen, was a drama teacher and actress while his father taught primary school and was an artist and historian. "Understandably," Colfer wrote on his Web site, "there was never a shortage of discussions, projects, artistic pursuits, or stimuli for the Colfer boys." They spent memorable summer holidays at the seaside village of Slade where Colfer's father was born. Young Colfer attended the grammar school where his father taught and early on developed a love of writing and of illustrating the stories he penned.

In secondary school, Colfer continued with his writing and began to read widely, enjoying especially the thrillers of Robert Ludlum and Jack Higgins. At a dance at a local girls school, he met his future wife, Jackie. Inspired by his parents, Colfer decided to go into teaching, entering a three-year degree course in Dublin to qualify as a primary school teacher. In 1986, he returned to his native Wexford to teach, writing by night, both stories and plays, many of which were performed by a local dramatic group. He also wrote a novel which he sent to publishers "with visions of black sedans pulling up to the house the next day," as he told Jeff Chu in *Time Atlantic.* "I thought I was the best writer on the planet." However, the publishers did not quite agree. Colfer's breakthrough was put on hold.

In 1991, Colfer and Jackie married, and the couple left Ireland for four years, teaching in Saudi Arabia, Italy, and Tunisia. When they returned to Ireland in the mid-1990s, Colfer and his wife settled once again in Wexford, and he resumed teaching, squeezing in writing after school. A son was born in 1997, by which time Colfer had begun processing some of the experiences of his four years abroad and saw how they might very well fit into a juvenile novel, an obvious fit for this teacher who was familiar with the reading habits of the young.

The result of Colfer's labors was his first published novel, *Benny and Omar,* brought out by Dublin's O'Brien Press in 1998. The novel recounts the madcap adventures of a young Irish boy and his Tunisian friend in North Africa. Benny Shaw is a champion athlete at Saint Jerome's school in Wexford, Ireland, and is quite content with his life. Then his parents tell him they have decided to move to Tunisia where the locals have never heard of his sport, hurling. The village school where Benny ends up "is taught by feel-good hippies and filled with students actually bent on learning," according to Linda Bindner in *School Library Journal.* Benny is miserable until he meets up with Omar, a street-smart kid who lives by his wits and takes Benny under his wing. Benny at first loves the thrill of the havoc they cause, going from one scrape to the next until he meets Omar's younger sister, a drug addict in a local institution, and he suddenly understands the costs of Omar's life. Benny sees that his friend's life is much more tragic than he at first thought.

Bindner felt that Colfer does a "masterful job of mixing humor and tragedy" in this "funny, fast-paced read . . . that takes a wonderful glimpse into some very non-American worlds." A reviewer for *Publishers Weekly* similarly found that Colfer "smoothly layers adventure, moments of poignancy and subtle social commentary, and his comic timing is pitch-perfect." *Booklist* contributor Frances Bradburn also had praise for this first novel that became a best-seller in Ireland, calling it "an interesting and eye-opening study in contrasts" and a "comic adventure" that "likely will spawn a sequel."

Colfer did indeed reprise Benny for the 1999 *Benny and Babe* in which the irrepressible protagonist is back in Ireland and visiting his grandfather in the country for the summer holiday. Benny is considered a "Townie" by the local kids and has trouble finding a buddy until he meets up with the village tomboy, Babe, who has proven herself with the tough boys of the area. She and Benny hit it off, working together in Babe's business of finding lost fishing lures and flies and then reselling them. Things are going great for Benny and Babe until the bully Furty Howlin decides he wants part of their business. "Humor, sensitivity, and candor underscore this coming-of-age story that features incredibly well-drawn characters," wrote Renee Steinberg in a *School Library Journal* review of *Benny and Babe.* Steinberg went on to note that Colfer's second novel "has it all—an absorbing story, vibrant characters with whom readers will surely identify, and an on-target narrative voice." *Benny and Babe* was nominated for Ireland's prestigious Bisto Children's Book of the Year Award.

Next, Colfer turned his hand to a series for young readers aged five to seven. Ed Cooper is the character that figures in each of the titles: *Going Potty, Ed's Funny Feet,* and *Ed's Bed.* These tales find Ed alternately learning how to use a strange new toilet, having to wear corrective shoes, and dealing with a bedwetting incident. In 2000, Colfer also published *The Wish List,* a somewhat bizarre tale of "life, death and an unexpected hereafter," as he described the novel on his Web site. Winner of a Bisto Merit Award, the book tells the story of an angry adolescent girl, Meg Finn, who sets out on a short-lived career of crime. Killed in the first chapter, Meg is given the rest of the novel as a chance to redeem herself; a moral tug of war ensues as the forces of good and evil battle for her soul. *School Library Journal* critic Janet Hilbun found *The Wish List* "an entertaining and compelling read," while *Booklist*'s Ilene Cooper called the work "surprisingly thought-provoking."

Dealing with fantasy of a sort for *The Wish List,* Colfer was encouraged to try more of the same, but this time with more humor and with the possibility of reaching a larger audience. As was noted on Colfer's Web site, "every child Eoin Colfer has ever taught will testify to his love of traditional magical Irish legends. They will also attest to his innate ability to make these legends come alive for them on a daily basis. It was in this genre he found his inspiration, but then took a unique slant on this well known underworld civilisation." Colfer blended this world of fairies and leprechauns with another constant interest, the *Die Hard* movies of Bruce Willis. "I really liked . . . [the film's] self-deprecating humor," Colfer told Heather Vogel in *Publishers Weekly.* "They were big-budget action movies, but very much tongue-in-cheek, and I wanted to create an adventure with one foot in the comedy zone." So Colfer sat down to see how he could put these two genres together and knew that he had to do so employing a protagonist "original and different enough to make his mark and not just be the latest in line of clean-cut heroes," as he remarked to Vogel. He decided on "a bit of a villain," and set him to kidnap a leprechaun and demand a ransom in gold. "The twist being that these weren't the fairies you were used to reading about, but were actually quite futuristic," he explained. "It all fell into place after that." Colfer admitted to Vogel that he did not consciously set out to write a book that would appeal to both kids and adults, but he did "make a conscious effort to engage clever kids. The book doesn't talk down to them."

The finished manuscript, *Artemis Fowl,* was sent to a London agent in hopes of breaking out of the more confined Irish market. No one was more surprised than Colfer when his agent let him know that a bidding war on the novel was won by Penguin Puffin, with a six-figure film deal sold to Miramax in the United States and rights sold in at least twenty other markets. The total package meant well over a million dollars for the book even before publication. "I was on yard duty worried about kids trying to blow their noses on my pants and others trying to jump off the roof, and I got this message," he told Matthew Dorman in the *Hollywood Reporter.* "I understood all the words, but I didn't really know what it meant when I put them all together."

From its prepublication success, *Artemis Fowl* proceeded to publication. Antihero Artemis is something of a boy genius and the last in a long line of a famous crime family who have lately fallen on hard times. Enlisting the help of his bodyguard, Butler, Artemis determines to restore the Fowl family wealth by capturing a fairy and then holding her ransom for all of the legendary fairy gold. He kidnaps Captain Holly Short, a leprechaun from LEPrecon, a branch of the Lower Elements Police and absolutely the wrong mark for Artemis to choose. He is set upon by a "wisecracking team of satyrs, trolls, dwarfs and fellow fairies," according to a reviewer for *Publishers Weekly,* who want to rescue Holly. These rescuers employ a good deal of elfin technology in their pursuit, while Artemis has to translate the arcana of the fairy folk's sacred book, employing a computer.

Reviewers made the inevitable comparisons to the "Harry Potter" books, as both have twelve-year-old protagonists and both employ types of magic. However, there the similarity ends. Colfer, in fact, had not read the "Harry Potter" novels before writing *Artemis Fowl.* Critical response was as varied as the plot of the book itself. Some found the novel less than successful. A *Horn Book* reviewer, for example, felt that Colfer's "revisioning of the fairy world as a sort of wisecracking police force . . . steal[s] focus from the one truly intriguing character, Artemis himself." The same reviewer noted that there is "a lot of invention here, but it's not used enough in service to the story, and may be deployed to better effect in the feature film." Daniel Fierman, writing in *Entertainment Weekly,* felt that things turn "leaden" in the final "Die Hard-style standoff," and also found comparisons to J. K. Rowling's work specious, concluding that this dem-

onstrates the difference "between a great children's book and a simply good one." Andrea Sachs, reviewing the novel in *Time,* wrote that "parents who might be worried about their children's reading a book glorifying extortion don't know the half of what's wrong with *Artemis Fowl.*" Sachs felt that the writing "is abysmal." Writing in *School Library Journal,* Eva Mitnick found Artemis to be "too stiff and enigmatic to be interesting," while the contributor for *Publishers Weekly* concluded that "the series is no classic in the making."

Other critics found more to like in the novel. *Library Journal* reviewer Jennifer Baker commented that the "quirky characters and delightful humor . . . will undoubtedly delight American readers." Baker further described the novel as "fun to read" and "full of good humor." *Family Life*'s Sara Nelson similarly called the book "action-packed" and "perfect for long, lazy summer days." Yvonne Zipp noted in the *Christian Science Monitor* that after a slow first chapter, "the action kicks into high gear and never stops." *Time International*'s Elinor Shields added to the chorus of praise, describing the book as "pacy, playful and very funny, an inventive mix of myth and modernity, magic and crime." And Kellaway found *Artemis Fowl* "a smart, amusing one-off" with "flashes of hi-tech invention."

Artemis Fowl goes into action for a second time in *Artemis Fowl: The Arctic Incident,* in which the brilliant criminal teenager returns as does Colfer's magical underground world of fairies, trolls, satyrs, and gnomes who usually find themselves on the other side of the fence metaphorically from the "Mud People," or humans, who chased them underground. In the first installment, Artemis thought he had lost his beloved father, but via a video e-mail he sees a man who looks like his father sitting in the Arctic wasteland of Russia. Artemis wants to rescue this man, but not before he turns to his former enemies for some magical assistance. Meanwhile, below ground things are in a state of chaos after someone arms a band of trolls who wreaks havoc on the citizenry. Certain clues lead Captain Holly Short to Artemis, and in a turnaround from the first adventure, she kidnaps him in hopes of stopping the chaos. When she discovers Artemis is not responsible, the two former enemies join forces to fight both battles. Colfer's gun-toting, motorized fairies are back in action.

"Once again," noted a reviewer for *Publishers Weekly* of this second installment, "the roller coaster of a plot introduces a host of high jinks and high-tech weaponry as Colfer blends derring-do with snappy prose." Writing in *School Library Journal*, Steven Engelfried found "the action . . . brisk, with fiendish plots, ingenious escapes, and lively battle scenes."

A year older, Artemis Fowl returns for a third adventure in *Artemis Fowl: The Eternity Code*. This time, the teenager vies with a dangerous businessman over the supercomputer Artemis built using technology stolen from the fairy world. Hoping to earn a few dollars before destroying the C Cube machine, Fowl plans to deceive the millionaire Jon Spiro, but the businessman doublecrosses Artemis, threatening the existence of the fairy world. Calling again for help from his underground friends, the young trickster battles Spiro in a tale filled with "agile prose . . . , rapid-fire dialogue, and wise-acre humor," remarked a *Publishers Weekly* critic, who predicted that "readers will burn the midnight oil to the finish." Writing in *Booklist*, Sally Estes favorably compared *Artemis Fowl: The Eternity Code* to the two previous books, claiming, "The action is fast and furious, the humor is abundant, [and the] characterizations are zany."

BIOGRAPHICAL AND CRITICAL SOURCES:

BOOKS

Colfer, Eoin, *Artemis Fowl*, Hyperion (New York, NY), 2001.

PERIODICALS

Booklist, August, 2001, Frances Bradburn, review of *Benny and Omar*, p. 2118; May 1, 2002, Sally Estes, review of *Artemis Fowl: The Arctic Incident*, p. 1518; June 1, 2003, Sally Estes, review of *Artemis Fowl: The Eternity Code*, p. 1759; October 1, 2003, Ilene Cooper, review of *The Wish List*, p. 330.
Christian Science Monitor, March 22, 2001, Yvonne Zipp, "The Un-Potter at the Rainbow's End," p. 20.
Entertainment Weekly, July 20, 2001, Daniel Fierman, review of *Artemis Fowl*, p. 62.

Family Life, June 1, 2001, Sara Nelson, "Summer Reads," p. 70.
Hollywood Reporter, May 29, 2001, Matthew Dorman, "Storybook Beginnings," pp. 14-15.
Horn Book, July-August, 2001, review of *Artemis Fowl*, p. 449; January-February, 2002, Patty Campbell, "YA Scorecard 2001," p. 117.
Library Journal, June 15, 2001, Jennifer Baker, review of *Artemis Fowl*, p. 102; November 1, 2001, Nancy Pearl, "Not Just for Kids," p. 160.
New York Times Book Review, June 17, 2001, Gregory Maguire, review of *Artemis Fowl*, p. 24.
Observer (London, England), May 13, 2001, Kate Kellaway, "Elf and Happiness."
Publishers Weekly, April 9, 2001, review of *Artemis Fowl*, p. 75; April 23, 2001, Heather Vogel, "'Die Hard' with Fairies," pp. 25-26; July 9, 2001, review of *Benny and Omar*, p. 68; April 15, 2002, review of *Artemis Fowl: The Arctic Incident*, p. 65; March 31, 2003, review of *Artemis Fowl: The Eternity Code*, p. 68; October 13, 2003, review of *The Wish List*, p. 81.
School Library Journal, May, 2001, Eva Mitnick, review of *Artemis Fowl*, p. 148; December, 2001, Linda Bindner, review of *Benny and Omar*, pp. 132-133; March, 2002, Renee Steinberg, review of *Benny and Babe*, p. 226; July, 2002, Steven Engelfried, review of *Artemis Fowl: The Arctic Incident*, p. 118; July, 2003, Tim Wadham, review of *Artemis Fowl: The Eternity Code*, p. 128; December, 2003, Janet Hilbun, review of *The Wish List*, p. 148.
Time, April 30, 2001, Andrea Sachs, "A Case of Fowl Play," p. 76.
Time Atlantic, May 7, 2001, Jeff Chu, "Legends of the Fowl," p. 56.
Time International, May 7, 2001, Elinor Shields, "A Magical Myth," p. 56.
Times Educational Supplement, May 11, 2001, Jan Mark, review of *Artemis Fowl*.

ONLINE

Artemis Fowl Web site, http://www.artemisfowl.com/ (March 22, 2004).
Eoin Colfer Home Page, http://www.eoincolfer.com/ (March 22, 2004).*

CORNWELL, Patricia (Daniels) 1956-

PERSONAL: Born June 9, 1956, in Miami, FL; daughter of Sam (an attorney) and Marilyn (a secretary; maiden name, Zenner) Daniels; married Charles Cornwell (a college professor), June 14, 1980 (divorced, 1990). *Education:* Davidson College, North Carolina, B.A., 1979. *Religion:* Presbyterian. *Hobbies and other interests:* Tennis.

ADDRESSES: Home—Greenwich, CT. *Office*—Cornwell Enterprises, P.O. Box 35686, Richmond, VA 23235. *Agent*—International Creative Management, 40 West 57th St., New York, NY 10019.

CAREER: Novelist. *Charlotte Observer,* Charlotte, NC, police reporter, 1979-81; Office of the Chief Medical Examiner, Richmond, VA, computer analyst and technical writer, 1985-91. President of Bell Vision Productions (film production company); worked as a volunteer police officer.

MEMBER: International Crime Writers Association, International Association of Chiefs of Police, International Association of Identification, National Association of Medical Examiners, Authors Guild, Authors League, Mystery Writers of America, Virginia Writers Club.

AWARDS, HONORS: Investigative reporting award, North Carolina Press Association, 1980, for a series on prostitution; Gold Medallion Book Award for biography, Evangelical Christian Publishers Association, 1985, for *A Time for Remembering: The Story of Ruth Bell Graham;* John Creasey Award, British Crime Writers Association, Edgar Award, Mystery Writers of America, Anthony Award, Boucheron/World Mystery Convention, and Macavity Award, Mystery Readers International, all for best first crime novel, all 1990, and French Prix du Roman d'Aventure, 1991, all for *Postmortem;* Gold Dagger award, for *Cruel and Unusual.*

WRITINGS:

NOVELS

Postmortem, Scribner (New York, NY), 1990.
Body of Evidence, Scribner (New York, NY), 1991.
All That Remains, Scribner (New York, NY), 1992.

Patricia Cornwell

Cruel and Unusual, Scribner (New York, NY), 1993.
The Body Farm, Scribner (New York, NY), 1994.
From Potter's Field, Scribner (New York, NY), 1995.
Cause of Death, Putnam (New York, NY), 1996.
Hornet's Nest, Putnam (New York, NY), 1997.
Unnatural Exposure, Putnam (New York, NY), 1997.
Three Complete Novels: Postmortem, Body of Evidence, All That Remains, Smithmark Publishers (New York, NY), 1997.
Point of Origin, Putnam (New York, NY), 1998.
Southern Cross, Putnam (New York, NY), 1998.
Black Notice, Putnam (New York, NY), 1999.
The Last Precinct Putnam (New York, NY), 2000.
Isle of Dogs, Little, Brown (Boston, MA), 2001.
Blow Fly, Putnam (New York, NY), 2003.

OTHER

A Time for Remembering: The Story of Ruth Bell Graham (biography), Harper & Row (San Francisco, CA), 1983.
Scarpetta's Winter Table, Wyrick (Charleston, SC), 1998.

Life's Little Fable (children's book), illustrated by Barbara Leonard Gibson, Putnam (New York, NY), 1999.

(With Marlene Brown) *Food to Die For: Secrets from Kay Scarpetta's Kitchen,* Putnam (New York, NY), 2001.

Portrait of a Killer: Jack the Ripper—Case Closed, Putnam (New York, NY), 2002.

ADAPTATIONS: Brilliance Corp. released a sound recording of *Body of Evidence* in 1992; sound recordings are also available for *Postmortem, All That Remains, Cruel and Unusual, The Body Farm,* and *From Potter's Field;* negotiations are in progress for the film rights to *From Potter's Field;* Columbia Pictures is planning a film treatment of *Cruel and Unusual* and *Unnatural Exposure.*

SIDELIGHTS: Since 1990 Patricia Cornwell's novels have followed Dr. Kay Scarpetta, a medical examiner called upon to solve murders with forensic sleuthing. The "Scarpetta" novels are praised for their accurate detail based upon research Cornwell did in the Virginia medical examiner's office, witnessing scores of autopsies. In addition to this, Cornwell also went out on police homicide runs. "I'm not sure I could have read my last book if I hadn't written it," Cornwell told Sandra McElwaine in *Harper's Bazaar.* "The violence is so real, I think it would have scared me to death."

Cornwell began her book-writing career in 1983 with a biography of Ruth Graham, wife of evangelist Billy Graham. It was Graham who encouraged her to pursue writing. "I felt she had real ability," Graham told Joe Treen in *People.* "I've kept every note I ever got from her." With Graham's encouragement, Cornwell went back to school at Davidson College in North Carolina, majoring in English. Right after graduation she married Charles Cornwell, one of her former professors, and began working as a crime reporter for the *Charlotte Observer.*

"I had a compulsion to get close to every story. I really wanted to solve crimes," Cornwell told McElwaine. In 1980, Cornwell received an investigative reporting award from the North Carolina Press Association for a series she did on prostitution. Unfortunately, just when she felt her career was getting underway, her husband decided that he wanted to become a minister, and the couple moved to Richmond,

Virginia, where he attended Union Theological Seminary. "I did not want to give up the *Observer,*" she told Treen. "It was a very bad time for me."

Cornwell began working on a biography of her good friend Graham, which kept her busy for a few years until it was published in 1983. She had always pictured herself as a novelist, so she decided to try writing crime novels with the information she had gathered as a reporter. She realized that she would need to do more in-depth research to make her murder plots seem more believable. A friend recommended that she might try talking to the deputy medical examiner at the Virginia Morgue. Cornwell took the advice.

At her first appointment with Dr. Marcella Fierro, Cornwell was introduced to a whole world of high-tech forensic procedures that she knew nothing about. "I was shocked by two things," Cornwell told Joanne Tangorra in *Publishers Weekly.* "One, by how fascinating it was, and two, by how absolutely little I knew about it. I realized I had no idea what a medical examiner would do—Did they put on gloves, wear lab coats and surgical greens? They do none of the above." After a short time, Cornwell began doing technical writing for the medical examiner's office.

Cornwell soon became a regular visitor at the forensic center and also took on technical writing projects for the morgue to absorb more of the forensic knowledge she craved. Working at the morgue led Cornwell to write her first novel, *Postmortem,* featuring the fictional investigative forensic pathologist, Dr. Kay Scarpetta.

Postmortem focuses on the rape and murder of several Richmond women by a serial killer. The book charts the work of Scarpetta, the chief medical examiner of Virginia, as she attempts to uncover the killer's identity. Frequently faced with sexism regarding her ability to handle a "man's job," Scarpetta aptly displays her knowledge of the innovative technologies of today's forensic medicine to crack the case. "Dr. Scarpetta has a terrible time with the chauvinists around her, one of whom in particular is malevolently eager for her to fail," wrote Charles Champlin in the *Los Angeles Times Book Review.* "These passages have the ring of truth as experienced, and so does the portrait of an investigative reporter who abets the solving."

Postmortem "won just about every mystery fiction award," declared *New York Times Book Review* contributor Bill Kent. "The follow-up novel, *Body of Evi-*

dence, proved that Ms. Cornwell's success wasn't mere beginner's luck." *Body of Evidence* centers on Beryl Madison, a young woman who is writing a controversial book for which she has received death threats. Shortly after she reports these events she is murdered—apparently after allowing the killer to enter her home. Scarpetta must once again use tiny bits of evidence to track down the murderer.

In *Cruel and Unusual,* Cornwell introduces Temple Gault, a serial killer with intelligence to match Scarpetta's. Gault, who specializes in the murder of children, only narrowly escapes being captured by Scarpetta herself. "With his pale blue eyes and his ability to anticipate the best minds of law enforcement," wrote Elise O'Shaughnessy in the *New York Times Book Review,* "Gault is a 'malignant genius' in the tradition of Hannibal Lecter," the cannibalistic character in Thomas Harris's *The Silence of the Lambs.* "Like Lecter's bond with Clarice Starling," O'Shaughnessy concluded, "Gault's relationship with Scarpetta is *personal.*"

Gault appears again in the 1995 novel *From Potter's Field,* when he murders a young girl on Christmas Eve in Central Park. Scarpetta is called in to investigate the murder and ends up in a face-to-face confrontation with Gault. Critics again noted the research involved in the novel, as Mary B. W. Tabor commented in the *New York Times:* "There is something especially savory about novels set in real places, with real street names, real shops, real sights and smells that ring true for those who know the territory." *Booklist* reviewer Emily Melton compared reading *From Potter's Field* to "riding one of those amusement-park roller coasters . . . [that leave] the rider gasping and breathless." Melton lauded Cornwell's "magnificent plotting, masterful writing, and marvelous suspense," rating her among the top crime fiction writers.

Cornwell continued the Scarpetta series with *Cause of Death, Unnatural Exposure,* and *Point of Origin.* In the 1999 novel *Black Notice,* Scarpetta falls into an international mystery involving "the Werewolf," a killer named Jean-Baptiste Chandonne. *Library Journal* reviewer Leslie Madden observed, "This novel focuses on the features that made Cornwell's earliest novels so interesting—the slow unraveling of a mystery using Scarpetta's skill and intelligence." A reviewer for *Publishers Weekly* declared, "The forensic sequences boom with authority; the brief action se-

quences explode on the page." Cornwell continues the *Black Notice* storyline in *The Last Precinct* and *Blow Fly.* "Cornwell writes, as usual, with unwavering intensity in this grisly, fast-paced thriller. The effect: utterly chilling," concluded *Entertainment Weekly* reviewer, Jennifer Reese about *Blow Fly.*

In a column for *Mystery Scene* magazine, Cornwell shed some light on the nature of her heroine, Dr. Scarpetta. "Violence is filtered through her intellectual sophistication and inbred civility, meaning that the senseless cruelty of what she sees is all the more horrific," the author explained. She added that Dr. Scarpetta "approaches the cases with the sensitivity of a physician, the rational thinking of a scientist, and the outrage of a humane woman who values, above all else, the sanctity of life. Through Dr. Scarpetta's character I began to struggle with an irony that had eluded me before: the more expert one gets in dismantling death, the less he understands it."

Cornwell has written several other novels in addition to the Scarpetta series. *Hornet's Nest, Southern Cross,* and *Isle of Dogs* feature Judy Hammer and Andy Brazil as Virginia police officers. These books do not have the technical forensic writing of Cornwell's Scarpetta novels. In addition to her novels, Cornwell has coauthored a book of recipes titled *Food to Die For: Secrets from Kay Scarpetta's Kitchen,* and a similar novella called *Scarpetta's Winter Table,* which breaks down the ingredients for some of Scarpetta's favorite dishes, but lacks detailed recipes. She also wrote a children's book called *Life's Little Fable,* about a boy named Jarrod who lives in a land filled with sunlight, but whose curious nature leads him to explore a mysterious pond.

In 2002 Cornwell released the nonfiction book *Portrait of a Killer: Jack the Ripper—Case Closed.* The book is based on the infamous killer known as Jack the Ripper, who murdered prostitutes and terrorized London in the late 1880s. The book discusses Cornwell's forensic research and findings. Cornwell paints vivid pictures of Victorian London, specifically the crime scenes left behind by Jack the Ripper. In the book, Cornwell fingers artist Walter Sickert as the notorious killer. Though Cornwell has been criticized for basing her conclusion largely on circumstantial evidence, a *Publishers Weekly* reviewer described the book as "compassionate, intense, superbly argued, fluidly written and impossible to put down."

BIOGRAPHICAL AND CRITICAL SOURCES:

BOOKS

American Women Writers: A Critical Reference Guide: From Colonial Time to the Present, St. James Press (Detroit, MI), 2000.

Beahm, George W., *The Unofficial Patricia Cornwell Companion,* St. Martin's Press (New York, NY), 2002.

Contemporary Southern Writers, St. James Press (Detroit, MI), 1999.

Mystery and Suspense Writers: The Literature of Crime, Detection, and Espionage, Scribner (New York, NY), 1998.

Newsmakers, Issue 1, Gale (Detroit, MI), 2003.

PERIODICALS

Armchair Detective, winter, 1991, p. 32.

Book, September, 1999, review of *Black Notice,* p. 70.

Booklist, May 1, 1995; December 15, 1999, Karen Harris, audio book review of *Southern Cross,* p. 798; May 1, 2000, Karen Harris, audio book review of *Black Notice,* p. 1626; September 1, 2000, Stephanie Zvirin, review of *The Last Precinct,* p. 6; October 15, 2001, Mark Knoblauch, review of *Food to Die For: Secrets from Kay Scarpetta's Kitchen,* p. 370; April 15, 2002, audio book review of *Isle of Dogs,* p. 1423; December 1, 2002, Brad Hooper, review of *Portrait of a Killer: Jack the Ripper—Case Closed,* p. 626.

Books, autumn, 1999, review of *Black Notice,* p. 18; Christmas 2001, review of *Isle of Dogs,* p. 18.

Bookseller, November 8, 2002, "Retailers Tied by Cornwell Embargo," p. 7.

Book World, October 17, 1999, review of *Black Notice,* p. 13.

Children's Book Review Service, August, 1999, review of *Life's Little Fable,* p. 157.

Children's Bookwatch, August, 1999, review of *Life's Little Fable,* p. 3.

Detroit Free Press, October 14, 2001, review of *Isle of Dogs,* p. 4E; April 14, 2002, review of *From Potter's Field,* p. 5E.

Economist (U.K.), June 19, 1999, review of *Black Notice,* p. S4.

Entertainment Weekly, June 26, 1992, p. 73; January 25, 2002, Matthew Flamm, "Between the Lines: The Inside Scoop on the Book World," p. 97; October 17, 2003, Jennifer Reese, review of *Blow Fly,* p. 86.

Europe Intelligence Wire, November 11, 2002, "Patricia Cornwell Fingers Painter As Jack the Ripper."

Globe and Mail (Toronto, Ontario, Canada), February 13, 1999, review of *Southern Cross,* p. D13; August 28, 1999, review of *Black Notice,* p. D17; October 20, 2001, review of *Isle of Dogs,* p. D22; November 24, 2001, audio book review of *Isle of Dogs,* p. D27.

Guardian, December 8, 2001, Fiachra Gibbons, "Does This Painting by Walter Sickert Reveal the Identity of Jack the Ripper?," p. 3; December 8, 2001, Mark Lawson, "A Novelist at the Scene of the Crime," p. 20.

Harper's Bazaar, August, 1992, pp. 46, 148.

Independent, November 17, 2001, Dina Rabinovitch, "Anatomy of a Gentle Ghoul," p. WR10.

Kirkus Reviews, June 1, 1995; January 1, 1999, review of *Southern Cross,* p. 30; July 1, 1999, review of *Black Notice,* p. 837.

Kliatt Young Adult Paperback Book Guide, November, 1999, audio book review of *Black Notice,* p. 48; March, 2001, audio book review of *The Last Precinct,* p. 52; March, 2002, audio book review of *Isle of Dogs,* p. 49.

Knight Ridder/Tribune News Service, August 4, 1999, Linda B. Blackford, review of *Black Notice,* p. K6581; October 18, 2000, Connie Ogle, review of *The Last Precinct,* p. K4862; November 1, 2000, Jeff Guinn, "Dissecting Patricia Cornwell," p. K1359; November 1, 200, Jeff Guinn, review of *The Last Precinct,* p. K2261; December 11, 2002, Oline H. Cogdill, audio book review of *Portrait of a Killer,* p. K4617.

Library Journal, September 1, 1994, p. 213; February 15, 1999, audio book review of *Point of Origin,* p. 126; April 15, 1999, Leslie Madden, review of *Point of Origin,* p. 142; July 1999, Leslie Madden, review of *Black Notice,* p. 129; September 1, 1999, Joyce Kessel, audio book review of *Southern Cross,* p. 252; November 15, 1999, Jennifer Belford, audio book review of *Black Notice,* p. 116; October 15, 2000, Leslie Madden, review of *The Last Precinct,* p. 101; February 15, 2001, audio book review of *Isle of Dogs,* p. 194; March 1, 2001, audio book review of *The Last Precinct,* p. 152; April 1, 2003, Joyce Kessel, audio book review of *Portrait of a Killer,* p. 147.

Los Angeles Times, March 28, 1991, p. F12; February 2, 2003, Eugen Weber, review of *Portrait of a Killer,* p. R11.

Los Angeles Times Book Review, February 11, 1990, p. 5; February 10, 1991, p. 9; September 20, 1992, p. 8; February 1, 1999, review of *Southern Cross,* p. 9.

M2 Best Books, April 18, 2002, Darren Ingram, review of *Food to Die For.*

Mystery Scene, January, 1990, pp. 56-57.

National Post, January 18, 2003, Lynn Crosbie, "Relentless Pursuit of the Elusive Ripper," review of *Portrait of a Killer,* p. SP4.

New Straits Times, February 6, 2001, Martin Spice, "In Better (If Not Best) Form," review of *The Last Precinct;* August 6, 2001, Manveet Kaur, review of *The Last Precinct.*

Newsweek, August 3, 1992; July 5, 1993.

New York Times Book Review, January 7, 1990; February 24, 1991; August 23, 1992; April 4, 1993, p. 19; July 4, 1993; September 16, 1994, pp. 38-39; January 10, 1999, Marilyn Stasio, review of *Southern Cross,* p. 18; August 8, 1999, Marilyn Stasio, review of *Black Notice,* p. 21; November 5, 2000, Marilyn Stasio, review of *The Last Precinct,* p. 32; December 15, 2002, Caleb Carr, review of *Portrait of a Killer,* p. 15.

Observer (London, England), February 28, 1999, review of *Southern Cross,* p. 12.

People, August 24, 1992, pp. 71-72; October 3, 1994, pp. 37-38; November 5, 2001, review of *Isle of Dogs,* p. 51; December 9, 2002, Galina Espinoza, "Killer Instinct: Author Patricia Cornwell Thinks She Has Unmasked a Notorious Serial Killer. Critics Say She Doesn't Know Jack," p. 101; October 27, 2003, Edward Karam, review of *Blow Fly,* p. 50.

Publishers Weekly, December 7, 1990, p. 76; February 15, 1991, pp. 71-72; June 15, 1992, p. 89; September 12, 1994; January 4, 1999, review of *Southern Cross,* p. 76; June 14, 1999, review of *Black Notice,* p. 52; September 25, 2000, review of *The Last Precinct,* p. 90; January 1, 2001, audio book review of *The Last Precinct,* p. 42; January 8, 2001, review of *The Last Precinct,* p. 35; October 15, 2001, review of *Food to Die For,* p. 65; November 11, 2002, review of *Portrait of a Killer,* p. 52; November 11, 2002, Jeff Zaleski, "On the Trail of Jack the Ripper," p. 53; January 6, 2003, audio book review of *Portrait of a Killer,* p. 20.

School Library Journal, December, 1992, pp. 146-147; July, 1999, review of *Life's Little Fable,* p. 68.

Scientist, February 10, 2003, Terry Melton, review of *Portrait of a Killer,* p. 16.

Skeptical Inquirer, March-April, 2003, Joe Nickell, review of *Portrait of a Killer,* p. 27.

Spectator, November 9, 2002, Richard Sloane, review of *Portrait of a Killer,* p. 84.

Sunday Times (London, England), August 13, 2000, John Harlow, "Thriller Queen Is World's Top Woman Writer," p. 20; November 18, 2001, Joan Smith, review of *Isle of Dogs,* p. C48.

Time, September 14, 1992; October 3, 1994.

Times (London, England), November 27, 2001, Penny Wark, "I'm over Sex and Fame," p. S4.

Times Educational Supplement (London, England), December 17, 1999, review of *Black Notice,* p. 19.

Times Literary Supplement (London, England), July 16, 1993, p. 22; January 22, 1999, review of *Southern Cross,* p. 21; October 1, 1999, Lucy Atkins, review of *Black Notice,* p. 21; October 27, 2000, Heather O'Donoghue, review of *The Last Precinct,* p. 23.

Times of India, December 10, 2001, "Ripper: Mystery Unfolds Yet Again."

Wall Street Journal, August 27, 1999, Bob Hughes, review of *Black Notice,* p. W7.

Washington Post Book World, January 21, 1990, p. 6.

Wilson Library Bulletin, December, 1993.

Women's Quarterly, summer, 2001, Charlotte Hays and Ivy McClure Stewart, "Politically Correct Private Eyes," p. 18.

ONLINE

ABC News Web site, http://www.abcnews.com/ (October 29, 2003), "Stalking Jack the Ripper: A Crime Novelist Is Obsessed with a 113-Year-Old Case."

BookReporter.com, http://www.bookreporter.com/ (April 24, 2003).

Patricia Cornwell Web site, http://www.patriciacornwell.com/ (October 28, 2003).

Richmond Review Online, http://www.richmondreview.co.uk/ (April 24, 2003), Chris Wood, review of *Black Notice.*

Tangled Web UK Web site, http://www.twbooks.co.uk/ (October 29, 2003).

USA Weekend Online, http://www.usaweekend.com/ (October 29, 2003), Jeffrey Zaslow, "Straight Talk."*

* * *

CUSSLER, Clive (Eric) 1931-

PERSONAL: Born July 15, 1931, in Aurora, IL; son of Eric E. and Amy (Hunnewell) Cussler; married Barbara Knight, August 28, 1955; children: Teri, Dirk, Dayna. *Education:* Attended Pasadena City College,

Clive Cussler

1949-50, and Orange Coast College. *Politics:* "Non-partisan." *Hobbies and other interests:* Collecting automobiles, searching for historic shipwrecks.

ADDRESSES: Home—Telluride, CO, and Paradise Valley, AZ. *Agent*—Peter Lampack, The Lampack Agency, 551 Fifth Ave., New York, NY 10017.

CAREER: Bestgen and Cussler Advertising, Newport Beach, CA, owner, 1961-65; Darcy Advertising, Hollywood, CA, creative director, 1965-68; Mefford, Wolff and Weir Advertising, Denver, CO, vice president and creative director of broadcast, 1970-75; Aquatic Marine Dive Equipment, Newport Beach, CA, member of sales staff; National Underwater and Marine Agency, founder and chair. Discoverer of more than sixty shipwrecks. Worked for a supermarket and a gas station. *Military service:* U.S. Air Force, 1950-54; served as aircraft mechanic, became sergeant.

MEMBER: National Society of Oceanographers (fellow), Classic Car Club of America, Royal Geographic Society (London, England; fellow), Explorers Club of New York (fellow).

AWARDS, HONORS: Ford Foundation Consumer Award, 1965-66, for best promotional campaign; first prize, Chicago Film Festival, 1966, for best thirty-second live action commercial; International Broadcasting Awards, 1964, 1965, 1966, 1972, 1973, for year's best radio and TV commercials; first place award, Venice Film Festival, 1972, for sixty-second live commercial; Clio Awards, 1972, 1973, 1974, for TV and radio commercials; Lowell Thomas Award, Explorers Club of New York, for underwater exploration; numerous honors for work in shipwreck discoveries and marine archaeology, including NUMA's receiving a Lightspan Academic Excellence Award for outstanding contribution to education in the field of marine archaeology and historic preservation.

WRITINGS:

"DIRK PITT" ADVENTURE NOVELS

The Mediterranean Caper, Pyramid (New York, NY), 1973, also published as *May Day.*
Iceberg, Dodd, Mead (New York, NY), 1975.
Raise the Titanic, Viking (New York, NY), 1976.
Vixen 03, Viking (New York, NY), 1978.
Night Probe, illustrations by Errol Beauchamp, Bantam (New York, NY), 1981.
Pacific Vortex!, Bantam (New York, NY), 1983.
Deep Six, Simon & Schuster (New York, NY), 1984.
Cyclops, Simon & Schuster (New York, NY), 1986.
Treasure, Simon & Schuster (New York, NY), 1988.
Dragon, Simon & Schuster (New York, NY), 1990.
Sahara, Simon & Schuster (New York, NY), 1992.
Inca Gold, Simon & Schuster (New York, NY), 1994.
Shock Wave, Simon & Schuster (New York, NY), 1996.
Flood Tide, Simon & Schuster (New York, NY), 1997.
Atlantis Found, Putnam (New York, NY), 1999.
Valhalla Rising, Putnam (New York, NY), 2001.
Two Complete Novels (contains *Cyclops* and *Flood Tide*), Wings Books (New York, NY), 2001.
Trojan Odyssey, Putnam (New York, NY), 2003.

"KURT AUSTIN" SERIES

(With Paul Kemprecos) *Serpent: A Novel from the NUMA Files,* Pocket (New York, NY), 1999.
(With Paul Kemprecos) *Blue Gold: A Novel from the NUMA Files,* Pocket (New York, NY), 2000.

(With Paul Kemprecos) *Fire Ice,* Putnam (New York, NY), 2002.

(With Paul Kemprecos) *White Death,* Putnam (New York, NY), 2003.

"OREGON FILES" SERIES

(With Craig Dirgo) *Golden Buddha,* Putnam (New York, NY), 2003.

OTHER

(With Craig Dirgo) *The Sea Hunters: True Adventures with Famous Shipwrecks,* Simon & Schuster (New York, NY), 1996.

(With Craig Dirgo) *Clive Cussler and Dirk Pitt Revealed,* Pocket (New York, NY), 1998.

(With Craig Dirgo) *The Sea Hunters II: Diving the World's Seas for Famous Shipwrecks,* Putnam (New York, NY), 2002.

Some novels adapted for young adult audiences beginning 1999.

ADAPTATIONS: Raise the Titanic, based on Cussler's novel and starring Jason Robards and Richard Jordan as Dirk Pitt, was released by Associated Film Distribution in 1980; Eco-Nova (Halifax, Canada) and *National Geographic* documentary series, "Clive Cussler's 'The Sea Hunters'"; *Sahara* was adapted into a screenplay for a movie starring Matthew McConaughey, released in 2004; Cussler's books are available on audiotape.

SIDELIGHTS: Clive Cussler began writing novels to while away the time when his wife took a night-time job, but earned his living writing award-winning advertising copy until the success of his underwater adventure novels featuring his hero, Dirk Pitt, enabled him to leave the business world and pursue his writing interests full time. Since then, his adventure tales have sold over seventy million copies in more than forty languages and a hundred countries. Some sources cite the best-selling author as having more than ninety million fans, a number of which eagerly attend his book-signings and ask for his "famous" "personalized inscription[s]," wrote Daisy Maryles in a 1999 *Publishers Weekly* article recognizing the remarkable

initial demand for Cussler's fifteenth Dirk Pitt novel, *Atlantis Found.* In a *People* review of that book, J. D. Reed described Cussler's writing—that it has two-dimensional characters, predictable story-lines, and "dialogue as sticky as Mississippi mud." "Still," qualified Reed, "we can't put down a Cussler Opus." Noting that Cussler "typically [exerts a] make-no-apologies enthusiasm," a *Publishers Weekly* critic declared: "For muscle-flexing, flag-waving, belief-suspending fare, [Cussler] has no equal." The *Publishers Weekly* critic's review specifically referred to *Atlantis Found* as "another wickedly engrossing yet predictably scripted tale of bravery against all odds."

"There are many things I'd rather be doing than writing a book," Cussler once said, according to Rebecca Ascher-Walsh in a 1997 *Entertainment Weekly* article. Acquiring cars and discovering shipwrecks are among his passions. Cussler has built a premier collection of over eighty-five classic and vintage automobiles. From European classic body styles to American town cars to 1950s convertibles, they are all carefully restored by Cussler and his crew of experts to concours d'elegance condition.

Cussler lives almost the same sort of adventurous life as his best-selling protagonist, Dirk Pitt: tramping the Southwest deserts and mountains in search of lost gold mines and ghost towns, as well as funding and leading more than thirty expeditions in search of lost ships and aircraft. He and his team of NUMA scientists and engineers (his fictional National Underwater and Marine Agency became a reality) have discovered and surveyed nearly seventy historically significant shipwrecks around the world, including the long-lost Confederate submarine *Hunley,* the German submarine *U-20* which sank the *Lusitania,* the famous Confederate raider *Florida,* the Navy dirigible *Akron* which crashed at sea during a storm in 1933, the troop transport *Leopoldville* which was torpedoed on Christmas Eve of 1944 off the coast of Cherbourg, France, killing over eight hundred American soldiers, and the *Carpathia,* which braved icebergs to rescue passengers of the *Titanic.* Cussler has donated all of his recovered artifacts from the archaeological sites to museums and universities.

Cussler's chosen genre, his avocations, and even his entry into publishing reveal his willingness to take risks. Almost thirty years ago, after his first manuscript received numerous rejections, the author created a clever ploy to promote his second work: he printed up stationery with the name of a fabricated West Coast literary agent and used it to send recommendations for his books to major New York agencies. Within a month he had a contract, and has remained with the same (real) agent, Peter Lampack, ever since. After *Flood Tide,* his fourteenth Dirk Pitt adventure, however, he split with his longtime publisher Simon & Schuster. The Phoenix, Arizona, *Business Journal* reported that he left his former publisher in hopes of getting more respect through his new contract with G. P. Putnam and Sons: "Cussler would joke that Simon & Schuster executives lavished their attention on Mary Higgins Clark. . . . Cussler said. 'I get less respect than Rodney Dangerfield.'"

Cussler's widely read "Dirk Pitt" novels relate the adventures of a handsome, witty, courageous, devil-may-care character who, like his creator, collects classic cars and searches for lost ships. *Armchair Detective* reviewer Ronald C. Miller offered this description: "Dirk Pitt has the archeological background of Indiana Jones and the boldness of James Bond. He is as skilled and comfortable underwater as Jacques Cousteau, and, like Chuck Yeager, he can fly anything with wings." Yet Pitt is far from superhuman, Chicago's *Tribune Books* contributor David E. Jones observed: "Cussler has created a caring, cared-about, flesh and blood human being" who takes wrong turns and suffers from lapses in judgment, but who "also thinks faster on his feet than most and has an uncanny ability to turn negative situations into positive ones." This combination has proved to be tremendously appealing to readers, even though reviewers have often faulted Cussler's writing style and his improbable story lines. *New York Times Book Review* critic Newgate Callendar cited Cussler as "the cliche expert nonpareil" in a review of *Raise the Titanic* and asserted that "Cussler has revived the cliche and batters his reader with choice specimens: 'the cold touch of fear'; 'a set look of determination in the deep green eyes'; 'before death swept over him'; 'narrow brush with death.'" *Best Sellers* contributor Ralph A. Sperry dismissed the author's prose in *Cyclops* as "the prosaic in the service of the implausible."

Cussler shrugs off negative responses to his work. "Because I was locked in for eighteen years writing the short, snappy ad copy, I could never sit down and write a Fitzgerald-Hemingway-Bellow-type Great American Novel," he once told *CA.* "But [that experi-ence] did prepare me to write easy, understandable prose, and also to look at writing and publishing from a marketing angle."

Cussler once recalled to *CA* that at the beginning of his writing career, "blood and guts adventure" was not universally accepted in the publishing field. Initially he was told that his adventures would never sell and that critical opinion was against him, but these views have softened with the growth of the author's popular appeal. When Cussler complained to his agent, Peter Lampack, about negative reviews, Lampack, Cussler said, "came back with a classic statement: 'Listen, when we start getting good literary reviews, we're in big trouble.'"

While early reviews of Cussler may have been dismissive, reviews of his later works have recognized his stories as full of action, fun to read—and extremely popular, while nonetheless pointing out the incredibility of his plots. Discussing *Dragon,* the author's 1990 release, *Publishers Weekly* critic Sybil Steinberg admitted that although the story line was "improbable," Cussler had still come up with "a page-turning romp that achieves a level of fast-paced action and derring-do that . . . practitioners of modern pulp fiction might well envy." Peter L. Robertson, in his *Tribune Books* review of *Treasure,* placed Cussler's stories "in the tradition of Ian Fleming's James Bond," and added, "Cussler has developed and patented a vibrant, rollicking narrative style that seldom shows signs of relenting." *Inca Gold,* which finds Pitt in the Amazonian jungles on a quest to thwart a group of smugglers, is "pure escapist adventure, with a wry touch of humor and a certain self-referential glee (Cussler himself makes a cameo appearance)," a *Publishers Weekly* reviewer noted, "but the entertainment value meets the gold standard." *Booklist* reviewer Joe Collins noted that the author's fans "are already familiar with his gift for hyperbole," and recommended that new readers take Cussler's "breathless approach with a grain of salt and just relax and enjoy the adventures of Pitt and company" in *Inca Gold.*

In 1997's *Flood Tide* Pitt's vacation plans go by the wayside as he uncovers a Chinese immigrant smuggling ring in waters near Seattle—an operation that is linked, through its leader, Qin Shang, to an attempt to cause "ecological and economic destruction from New Orleans to eastern Texas," related a *Publishers Weekly* reviewer, who also noted Cussler was tapping into "right-wing fears of a flood tide of nonwhite immigrants." The *Publishers Weekly* reviewer, as well as many other critics, determined that *Flood Tide* will please Cussler's fans. As Gilbert Taylor concluded in *Booklist,* "This bombastically scripted tale will satisfy Cussler faithfuls." The story is "packed with meticulous research and wonderfully quirky characters," remarked *People* contributor Cynthia Sanz, judging *Flood Tide* to be "as fun as it is formulaic." "Cussler's story is entertaining, but suspending disbelief may be a problem," asserted Ray Vignovich in a *Library Journal* assessment of an audiobook edition of the novel.

In an interview with Connie Lauerman in the *Chicago Tribune,* Cussler reflected on his work. "I look upon myself more as an entertainer than merely a writer. It's my job to entertain the reader in such a manner that he or she feels that they received their money's worth when they reach *the end* of the book." Cussler also considers the impact of his books on young adults. "I have quite a large following of young people," he once told *CA.* "That's why I don't believe in using four-letter words, and any sex is simply alluded to, never detailed. I've had letters from kids as young as eight who enjoy Pitt and his adventures. And because I try to write my stories in a simple, forward manner, I'm especially pleased by letters from mothers and school teachers, who tell me their children and students had refused to read before they were given one of my books. Now they read everything in sight and are hooked on reading."

Cussler found that his readers enjoy the pictures of Pitt's cars included on the backs of his book jackets. *Clive Cussler and Dirk Pitt Revealed* provides a guide to the world of Pitt, including summaries of each novel of the Dirk Pitt series as well as details on weapons, vehicles, and locations from the writings. Cussler also once told *CA* that he has great fun with his cameo appearances. He and Pitt always meet up, with Cussler often supplying his hero with vital information before sending him on his way to subdue the villains. While his stories may seem tailor-made for Hollywood, Cussler emphasized that he refuses to sell them for adaptation until he can be assured of a quality production.

Asked how he comes up with his intricate plots, the author once told *CA:* "First comes the overall concept. This is, of course, the old cut-and-dried, time-tested *What-if.* What if, for example, they raise the *Titanic?* In *Night Probe,* what if Canada and the United States became one country? I also use a prologue that describes something in the past that sets up the plots in the present. Then I end with an epilogue that sews all the corners together. My plots are pretty convoluted; I usually juggle one main plot and as many as four subplots. Then the trick is to thread the needle in the end and give the readers a satisfying conclusion." Cussler has continually succeeded in giving readers a plot to escape in—even with his fifteenth "Dirk Pitt" adventure, published in 1999, twenty-three years after the series debut. Of *Atlantis Found,* Ronnie H. Terpening proclaimed in *Library Journal:* "Brilliantly conceived and boldly plotted. . . . his most imaginative yet. . . . A fascinating story . . . backed by meticulous research."

After *Atlantis Found,* Cussler continued with two more novels in the Dirk Pitt series but, as Mark Graham in the *Rocky Mountain News* noted, he decided to add a couple of younger figures in a spinoff series planned by Cussler, written by Paul Kemprecos, and revised by Cussler, the "Kurt Austin" series which began publication in 1999: "Clive Cussler's James Bondesque undersea hero Dirk Pitt has starred in sixteen novels over the last four decades. And although Pitt is still capable of amazing feats, his bones are starting to creak, and he isn't quite as quick as he once was. If Pitt's National Underwater Marine Agency is going to keep up with the times, it obviously needs new blood. Recognizing this, the prolific Colorado author has not only taken on a partner (Paul Kemprecos, a Shamus Award-winning author of undersea thrillers in his own right), but created a new protagonist. Kurt Austin takes over as the 21st century Dirk Pitt clone." Finding—with four novels in the series at the top of charts immediately on publication—that this formula for success worked well, in 2003, Cussler added another series, the "Oregon Files," written by the man who coauthored the two volumes of *The Sea Hunters* with him, Craig Dirgo, and starring "cool, brainy Chairman" of "the Corporation," Juan Cabrillo. Graham found himself disappointed that "the only differences between Dirk Pitt and Kurt Austin are their names and ages" but acknowledged that "the key word here is fun. Like most of Dirk Pitt novels, what happens in *Fire Ice* is almost ludicrous in its improbability. Yet watching Cussler and Kemprecos maneuver around possible pitfalls (pun intended) in plot, action and setting makes for enjoyable light reading."

Serpent: A Novel from the NUMA Files tells of the adventures of Kurt Austin and his NUMA colleague

Joe Zavala. A *Publishers Weekly* reviewer described the duo as "two young bucks without the seasoning and panache of Pitt but worthy successors, nonetheless." The coauthors used "the 1956 sinking of the Andrea Doria as the springboard for [this] thriller," stated Roland Green in *Booklist.* In *Serpent,* Austin and Zavala "are trying to find out why top archeologists are being killed, some of them butchered, at dig sites," recounted the writer for *Publishers Weekly* who judged the novel to be "great fun, if not a little top-heavy at times from flabby subplots and excessive detail." In the fourth adventure, *White Death,* as a *Publishers Weekly* reviewer stated, "All the villains have satanic smiles and pitiless eyes, and snarl their dialogue. If it all sounds highly preposterous, it is, but Cussler manages with his usual aplomb, impressively juggling his plots and bringing everyone home in an action-fueled, rip-roaring finale in which evil doers are soundly defeated and swashbuckling heroes reign supreme."

Rave reviews by avid readers are balanced by others who take a more jaundiced view of Cussler's productions. A *Publishers Weekly* reviewer of *White Death,* noted the way in which some of the villains are described, such as "swarthy, black-clad, facially tattooed Eskimos of the evil Kiolya tribe who guard the company's many operations." A. D. Sullivan in *Scrap Paper Review,* remarked of *Flood Tide,* that "Cussler waves the American flag so often one questions whether this is a novel or a bullfight. His facts—inserted to raise the peril of Japanese sovereignty over America—are often wrong or distorted, and his villains simplistic and cruel without attempt at understanding the complexity of America's addiction to foreign money." Cussler does, however, also slate a megalomaniac U.S. oil baron among his villains, as in *Valhalla Rising.*

Cussler's enormous popularity worldwide as a writer of American patriotic adventure stories is not to be denied. A *Publishers Weekly* review of *Golden Buddha* quotes from the book's hero, Juan Cabrillo: "We [the Corporation] were formed to make a profit, that's for sure, but as much as we like the money, we are also cognizant of the chances that arise for us to somehow right the wrongs of others." The reviewer added, "They've been secretly hired by the U.S. government to find and acquire an ancient statue known as the Golden Buddha, stolen from the Dalai Lama upon his ouster from Tibet by the Chinese in 1959. An intricate

plan is then set in motion culminating in the defeat of the Chinese in Tibet and the ascension of the Dalai Lama to his rightful place as the leader of the country. The list of characters, both good and evil, is long and sometimes confusing, but a useful directory is supplied. Cabrillo and crew are adept at high finance and diplomacy, playing the Russians off against the Chinese and winning over the United Nations." The "good guys" are certainly most often Americans and the "bad guys" as often not.

Cussler held off on selling movie rights to Hollywood after, as he described it to *BookReporter.com*'s interviewer Ann Bruns, "They made such a botch of [*Raise the Titanic*]." He sold the movie rights to the Dirk Pitt novels in 2001 after, as he says, Hollywood "finally . . . gave me script and casting approval. So that's why I'm reading the script the screenwriter came up with. If it fails this time, it's my fault." The first movie to be produced will be *Sahara.*

BIOGRAPHICAL AND CRITICAL SOURCES:

BOOKS

Valero, Wayne, *The Collector's Guide to Clive Cussler,* 2000.

PERIODICALS

Americana, September-October, 1987, p. 10.
Armchair Detective, fall, 1994, p. 496.
Best Sellers, August, 1981; May, 1986.
Booklist, April 1, 1992, p. 1411; April 1, 1994, p. 1404; December 15, 1995, p. 667; August, 1997, p. 1846; June 1, 1999, p. 1741; November 15, 1999, p. 579; June 1, 2001, p. 1796; April 1, 2002, p. 1282; June 1, 2003, p. 1710; September 1, 2003, George Cohen, review of *Golden Buddha,* p. 53; November 1, 2003, David Pitt, review of *Trojan Odyssey,* p. 458.
Books and Bookmen, May, 1984.
Buffalo News, April 23, 2000, p. F6.
Business Journal (Phoenix, AZ), December, 1999, p. 8.
Chicago Tribune, February 10, 1980; August 13, 1984.
Christian Science Monitor, October 10, 1996, p. 10.
Courier-Mail (Brisbane, Australia), February 1, 2003, p. M07.

Critic, summer, 1977.

Defense Week, August 14, 2000, p. 4.

Denver Business Journal, May 27, 1994, p.14A.

Entertainment Weekly, October 17, 1997, p. 66; September 7, 2001, p. 158; November 28, 2003, Jennifer Reese, review of *Trojan Odyssey,* p. 128.

Far Eastern Economic Review, December 18, 1997, p. 47.

Globe and Mail (Toronto, Ontario, Canada), August 10, 1985.

Grand Rapids Press, September 22, 2002, p. J5.

Inside Books, November, 1988, pp. 31-34.

Kirkus Reviews, October 15, 2003, review of *Trojan Odyssey,* p. 1239.

Library Journal, July, 1981, p. 1442; June 1, 1984, p. 1144; October 15, 1990, p. 116; November 1, 1990, p. 139; April 15, 1994, p. 111; April 1, 1995, p. 142; February 1, 1996, p. 97; September 1, 1996, p. 229; November 1, 1997, p. 130; November 15, 1999, p. 97; July 2001, p. 121; May 1, 2002, p. 132; September 15, 2003, Jeff Ayers, review of *Golden Buddha,* p. 90.

Los Angeles Magazine, September, 1990, p. 183; September, 1981, p. 259.

Los Angeles Times, June 21, 1979; September 25, 1981; March 21, 1986.

Los Angeles Times Book Review, August 5, 1984; March 20, 1988.

New Choices for the Best Years, March, 1991, p. 58.

New Yorker, June 27, 1994, p. 87.

New York Times Book Review, December 19, 1976; September 25, 1977; October 18, 1981, p. 46; February 16, 1986, p. 16; May 29, 1988, p. 14; June 17, 1990, p. 19; May 22, 1994, p. 39; January 21, 1996, p. 21.

Observer (London, England), July 20, 2003, p. 17.

People, July 2, 1984, p. 61; July 27, 1992, p. 25; September 21, 1992, p. 93; December 16, 1996, p. 36; November 10, 1997, p. 41; March 20, 2000, p. 47.

Playboy, April, 1986, p. 32.

PR Newswire, November 27, 2000, p. 4806; May 10, 2002.

Publishers Weekly, August 23, 1976; June 12, 1981, p. 46; February 26, 1982, p. 146; November 12, 1982, p. 64; April 13, 1984, p. 50; August 31, 1984, p. 312; January 3, 1986, p. 41; January 15, 1988, p. 69; March 18, 1988, p. 71; September 2, 1988, p. 71; May 4, 1990, p. 51; July 6, 1990, p. 46; April 13, 1992, p. 40; August 3, 1992, p. 26; March 28, 1994, p. 80; July 11, 1994, p. 58; September 19, 1994, p. 11; October 9, 1995, p. 18; December 18, 1995, p. 42; May 20, 1996, p. 37; August 26, 1996, p. 87; August 25, 1997, p. 46; March 16, 1998, p. 10; September 28, 1998, p. 20; March 1, 1999, p. 14; May 31, 1999, p. 65; November 22, 1999, p. 44; December 20, 1999, p. 17; July 30, 2001, p. 61; August 21, 2000, p. 24; August 27, 2001, p. 17; May 13, 2002, p. 50; June 17, 2002, p. 18; May 12, 2003, p. 40; June 30, 2003, p. 15; August 25, 2003, p. 37; October 27, 2003, review of *Trojan Odyssey,* p. 44.

Rocky Mountain News (Denver, CO), August 17, 2001, p. 25D; July 12, 2002, p. 30D.

School Library Journal, October, 1981, p. 160; October, 1990, p. 150; March, 1997, p. 217; December, 1997, p. 150; April, 1999, p. 130; May, 2000, p. 192.

Skin Diver, November, 1984, p. 20; May, 1987, p. 151.

Star Tribune (Minneapolis, MN), February 2, 2003, p. 18F.

Tribune Books (Chicago, IL), March 20, 1988; June 21, 1992, p. 6; May 22, 1994, p. 6.

U.S. News and World Report, August 27, 1984, p. 45.

Washington Post, October 24, 1978; August 10, 1981; June 22, 1984; April 11, 1988.

Washington Post Book World, March 2, 1986; June 7, 1992, p. 8.

Writer, September, 1996, p. 15.

Writer's Digest, April, 1988, p. 31.

ONLINE

BookReporter.com, http://www.bookreporter.com/ (September 11, 2001), interview with Cussler.

Scrap Paper Review, http://www.hourwolf.com/ (January 1998), "Clive Cussler's Japan."*

D

DARNTON, Robert (Choate) 1939-

PERSONAL: Born May 10, 1939, in New York, NY; son of Byron (a journalist) and Eleanor (a journalist; maiden name, Choate) Darnton; married Susan Lee Glover (a homemaker), June 29, 1963; children: Nicholas, Catherine, Margaret. *Education:* Harvard University, B.A. (magna cum laude), 1960; Oxford University, B.Phil., 1962, D.Phil., 1964.

ADDRESSES: Home—6 McCosh Circle, Princeton, NJ 08540. *Office*—Department of History, 129 Dickinson Hall, Princeton University, Princeton, NJ 08540.

CAREER: New York Times, New York, NY, stringer in Oxford, England, 1960-64, temporary foreign correspondent in the London bureau, 1963-64, reporter in New York City, 1964-65; City College (now of the City University of New York), New York, NY, lecturer in European history, spring, 1965; Harvard University, Cambridge, MA, junior fellow in the history department, 1965-68; Princeton University, Princeton, NJ, assistant professor, 1968-71, associate professor, 1971-72, professor of history, 1972-85, Shelby Cullom Davis Professor of European History, 1985—, director of Program in European Cultural Studies, 1987-95, director of Center for the Study of Books and Media, 2002—. Director of studies at the Sixth Section of the École Pratique des Hautes Etudes, Paris, France, 1971, 1981, 1985; fellow, Center for Advanced Study in the Behavioral Sciences in Stanford, CA, 1973-74; fellow, Netherlands Institute for Advanced Study, 1976-77; visiting professor, Oxford University, 1986-87; lecturer, Collège de France, 1987; fellow, Institute for

Robert Darnton

Advanced Study, Berlin, Germany, 1989-90, 1993-94; associate member, All Souls College, Oxford, 1996—. Member of Princeton University's Institute for Advanced Study, 1971-81; executive board member, Center for the Book, Library of Congress, 1978-81; executive board member, Arbeitskreis für Geschichte des Buchwesens, Wolfenbüttel, Germany, 1981; board of directors, Voltaire Foundation, Oxford, England, 1987-

9l, and Social Science Research Council, l988-9l; director, East-West Seminar in Eighteenth-Century Studies, 1987-95; vice president and member of board of directors, Internationaler Beirat der Forschungsstätte Europäische Aufklärung, Halle, 1989-94; board member, *Correspondance de Mme de Graffigny,* the Papers of Thomas Jefferson, and the Papers of Benjamin Franklin; member of fellowship board, French-American Foundation; member of boards of trustees, Center for Advanced Study in the Behavioral Sciences, Stanford, CA, New York Public Library, Oxford University Press, Wissenschaftlicher Beirat, Wissenschaftskolleg zu Berlin, and Forschungszentrum Europäischer Aufklärung, Potsdam.

MEMBER: International Society for Eighteenth-Century Studies (first vice president, 1983-87, president, 1987-91), American Historical Association (president, 1997—), American Academy of Arts and Sciences (fellow), American Philosophical Society, American Antiquarian Society, American Society for Eighteenth-Century Studies (national executive board, 1977-80), Academia Europaea, Académie Royale de Langue et de Littérature Françaises (Belgium), Phi Beta Kappa.

AWARDS, HONORS: Rhodes scholarship, 1960-62; Guggenheim fellowship, 1970-71; award for best article in eighteenth-century studies, American Society for Eighteenth-Century Studies (ASECS), 1971, for "The High Enlightenment and the Low-Life of Literature in Prerevolutionary France," and 1973, for "The *Encyclopedie* Wars of Prerevolutionary France"; Koren Prize for best article in French history, Society for French Historical Studies, 1973, for "The *Encyclopedie* Wars of Prerevolutionary France"; Leo Gershoy Prize, American Historical Association, 1979, for *The Business of Enlightenment;* MacArthur Prize fellowship, John D. and Catherine T. MacArthur Foundation, 1982; American Book Award nomination, 1983, for *The Literary Underground of the Old Regime; Los Angeles Times* Book Prize in history, and National Book Critics Circle Award nomination for general nonfiction, both 1984, both for *The Great Cat Massacre and Other Episodes in French Cultural History;* National Book Critics Circle Award for Criticism, 1995, for *Forbidden Best Sellers of Pre-Revolutionary France;* honorary professor, University of Warwick, 1996; honorary doctorates, Université de Neuchâtel, 1986, LaFayette College, 1989, University of Bristol, 1991, and University of Warwick, 2001.

WRITINGS:

Mesmerism and the End of the Enlightenment in France, Harvard University Press (Cambridge, MA), 1968.

The Business of Enlightenment: A Publishing History of the "Encyclopedie," 1775-1800, Harvard University Press (Cambridge, MA), 1979.

The Literary Underground of the Old Regime, Harvard University Press (Cambridge, MA), 1982.

The Great Cat Massacre and Other Episodes in French Cultural History, Basic Books (New York, NY), 1984.

The Kiss of Lamourette: Reflections on Cultural History, W. W. Norton (New York, NY), 1989.

(Editor, with Daniel Roche) *Revolution in Print: The Press in France, 1775-1800,* University of California Press (Berkeley, CA), 1989.

What Was Revolutionary about the French Revolution?, Baylor University Press (Waco, TX), 1990.

Edition et sédition: L'Univers de la littérature clandestine au XVIIIe siècle, Gallimard (Paris, France), 1991.

Berlin Journal, 1989-1990, W. W. Norton (New York, NY), 1992.

Gens de lettres, gens du livre, Editions Odile Jacob (Paris, France), 1992.

The Forbidden Bestsellers of Pre-Revolutionary France, W. W. Norton (New York, NY), 1995.

The Corpus of Clandestine Literature in France, 1769-1789, W. W. Norton (New York, NY), 1995.

(Contributor of chapter and interview) *Luz y contraluz de una historia antropologica,* Editorial Biblos (Buenos Aires, Argentina), 1995.

(Compiler and author of introduction) *Denkende Wollust,* Eichborn Verlag (Frankfurt-am-Main, Germany), 1996.

(Writer and editor, and codirector with Olivier Duhamel) *Démocratie/Democracy* (television series), La Ciniuème-Arte), 1998, published as *Democratie,* Editions de Rocher (Paris, France), 1998.

(Contributor) *The Darnton Debate: Books and Revolution in the Eighteenth Century,* edited by Haydn Mason, Voltaire Foundation (Oxford, England), 1998.

J.-P. Brissot: His Career and Correspondence (1779-1987), Voltaire Foundation (Oxford, England), 2001.

Poesie und Polizei: Öffentliche Meinung und Kommunkiationsnetzwerke im Paris des 18 Jahrhunderts, Suhrkamp (Frankfurt am Main, Germany), 2002.

Pour les lumières: Défense, illustration, méthode, Presses universitaires de Bordeaux (Bordeaux, France), 2002.

George Washington's False Teeth: An Unconventional Guide to the Eighteenth Century, Norton (New York, NY), 2003.

El Coloquio de los lectores: Ensayos sobre autores, manuscritos, editors y lectores, Fonda de Cultura Económica, 2003.

Mademoiselle Bonafon and the Private Life of Louis XV: What the Butler Saw and What the Public Read in Eighteenth-Century France, Egham (Surrey, England), 2003.

Die Wissenschaft des Raubdrucks: Ein zentrales Element im Verlagswesen des 18. Jahrhunderts, Carl Friedrich von Siemens Stiftung (Munich, Germany), 2003.

Contributor to books, including *Historical Studies Today,* edited by Felix Gilbert and Stephen Graubard, [New York, NY], 1972; *Studies in Eighteenth-Century Culture,* American Society of Eighteenth-Century Studies, 1973; *The Dictionary of Scientific Biography,* 1975; *The Widening Circle: Essays on the Circulation of Literature in Eighteenth-Century Europe,* edited by Paul J. Korshin, University of Pennsylvania Press (Philadelphia, PA), 1976; *Essays on the Age of Enlightenment in Honor of Ira O. Wade,* edited by Jean Macary, Droz (Geneva, Switzerland), 1977; *Structure, Consciousness, and History,* edited by Richard H. Brown and Stanford M. Lyman, Cambridge University Press (Cambridge, England), 1978; *Vom ancien Regime zur franzosischen Revolution: Forschungen und Perspektiven,* edited by Ernest Hinrichs, Eberhard Schmitt, and Rudolf Vierhaus, Vandenhoeck & Ruprecht (Göttingen, Germany), 1978; *The Past before Us: Contemporary Historical Writing in the United States,* edited by Michael Kammen, Cornell University Press (Ithaca, NY), 1980; *Cinq siècles d'imprimerie genevoise,* edited by Jean-Daniel Candaux and Bernard Lescaze, Societe d'Histoire et d'Archeologie (Geneva, Switzerland), 1981; *Sozialgeschichte der Aufklärung in Frankreich,* edited by Hans Ulrich Gumbrecht, Rolf Reichardt, and Thomas Schleich, R. Oldenbourg Verlag (Munich, Germany), 1981; *Books and Society in History,* edited by Kenneth Carpenter, [New York, NY], 1983; *Gelehrte Bücher vom Humanismus biz zur Gegenwart,* edited by Bernhard Fabian and Paul Raabe, [Wiesbaden, Germany], 1983; *Histoire de l'édition française: Tome II: Le livre triomphant (1660-1830),* edited by Roger Chartier and Henri-Jean Martin, [Paris, France], 1984; *Pratiques de la lecture,* edited by Roger Chartier, Editions Rivages (Paris and Marseille, France), 1985; *Aspects du livre neuchâtelois,* edited by Jacques Rychner and Michel Schlup, [Neuchâtel, Switzerland], 1986; *Censures: De la bible aux larmes d'éros,* edited by Martine Poulain and Françoise Serre, [Paris, France], 1987; *The Political Culture of the Old Regime,* edited by Keith Baker, [Oxford, England], 1987; *Enlightenment Essays in Memory of Robert Shackleton,* edited by Giles Barber, Voltair Foundation (Oxford, England), 1988; *Drei Vorschläge Rousseau zu lesen,* by Ernst Cassirer, Jean Starobinski, and Robert Darnton, Fischer Taschenbuch (Frankfurt am Main, Germany), 1989; *L'Image de la Révolution française,* edited by Michel Vovelle, Pergamon Press (Paris, France, and Oxford, England), 1989; *Don Giovanni: Myths of Seduction and Betrayal,* edited by Jonathan Miller, [New York, NY], 1990; *Rewriting the French Revolution,* edited by Colin Lucas, Clarendon Press (Oxford, England), 1991; *Intellektuellendämmerung: Beiträge zur neuesten Zeit des Geistes,* edited by Martin Meyer, Carl Hanser Verlag (Munich, Germany), 1992; *Publishing and Readership in Revolutionary France and America,* edited by Carol Armbruster, [Westport, CT], 1993; *Historical Change and Human Rights: The Oxford Amnesty Lectures,* edited by Oliver Hufton, Basic Books (New York, NY), 1994; *Tre letture di Rousseau,* Editore Laterza (Rome, Italy), 1994; *Histoire du livre, nouvelles orientations,* edited by Hans Erich Bödeker, [Paris, France], 1995; *André Morellet (1727-1819) in the Republic of Letters and the French Revolution,* edited by Jeffrey Merrick and Dorothy Medlin, [New York, NY], 1995; *Historia a debate,* edited by Carlos Barros, [Santiago de Compostela], 1995; *L'Histoire grande ouverte: Hommages à Emmanuel Le Roy Ladurie,* edited by Andre Burguière, Joseph Goy, and Marie-Jeanne Tits-Dieuaide, [Paris, France], 1997; *Le Livre et l'historien: Etudes offertes en l'honneur du Professeur Henry-Jean Martin,* edited by Frédé Barbier and others, [Paris, France, and Geneva, Switzerland], 1997; and *La Recherche dix-huitiémiste objets, méthodes et institutions (1945-1995),* edited by Michel Delon and Jochen Schlobach, [Paris, France], 1998.

Contributor to literary and scholarly journalis, including *Annales: Economies, Societes, Civilisations; Annales Historiques de la Revolution Francaise; Journal of Modern History; English Historical Review; Daedalus; New York Review of Books; Past and Present; American Historical Review; Revue Francaise d'Histoire du Livre; Quarterly Journal of the Library of Congress; American Scholar; New Republic;* and

Harper's Magazine. Member of editorial board, Princeton University Press, 1977-81, and *American Scholar*, 1981-86, *Revue de Synthè, History of the Human Sciences, Wilson Quarterly, Communication, Intellectual History Newsletter, Actes de la Recherche en Sciences Sociales, Dix-Huitième Siècle, Mana, Estudios de Anthropologia Social, Book History, European Review,* and *Rethinking History*. Darnton's works have been translated into French, Italian, German, Japanese, Hungarian, Korean, Dutch, Swedish, and Portuguese.

SIDELIGHTS: Robert Darnton, a Princeton University professor of history, has established himself as an authority on the French Revolution and the Enlightenment. Often discussing the relationship between the two, he has, according to Lynn Hunt in the *New Republic,* "always taken a sensible middle-of-the-road position on the influence of the Enlightenment" on the revolution. His interest, instead, has led him to explore the less-trod ground of figures often less well-known than luminaries like Voltaire and Rousseau, and he has especially written a considerable volume of material on Jacques-Pierre Brissot, as well as the popular literature in France of the time that shunned such now-famous works as *Emile* in favor of everything from antigovernment pamphlets to pornography. Considered by many to be, as Hunt put it, "one of the pioneers of 'the history of the book,'" Darnton has researched eighteenth-century France by examining police reports, book circulation figures, and the popularity of songs, creating histories that identify the culturally significant in the apparently tangential.

In his first book, *Mesmerism and the End of the Enlightenment in France,* Darnton studies the influence of eighteenth-century Viennese physician Franz Mesmer on the two decades immediately preceding the French Revolution. Mesmer, who developed the theory of animal magnetism, believed that magnetic forces could be used to heal physical ailments. He credited the force of his own magnetism with the results that he achieved through hypnotizing his patients. This hypnotic healing, or "mesmerism," as it was called during the eighteenth century, forms the basis for Darnton's book, which the *Virginia Quarterly Review* deemed "a skillful exploration of the various psychological factors that made mesmerism a widely accepted attitude during [the Enlightenment]."

Darnton's next book, *The Business of Enlightenment: A Publishing History of the "Encyclopedie," 1775-1800,* grew out of the author's research in the Neuchâ-

tel Archives in Switzerland, where he unearthed letters and documents dating back to the eighteenth century that pertained to the way books were written, published, and distributed at that time. Among these records, Darnton found the papers of the Societé Typographique de Neuchâtel, the Swiss publishing house that collaborated during the late eighteenth century with French entrepreneur Charles Joseph Panckoucke to revise, print, and distribute popularly priced editions of Denis Diderot's famed *Encyclopedie*.

The *Encyclopedie* was an encyclopedic series that furnished, in systematic fashion, scientific, factual information infused with progressive philosophic and political doctrine. It is generally considered an influential organ of the Age of Enlightenment, the term "Enlightenment" referring to a movement in late-eighteenth-century Europe to publicly promote reason and science as tools to resolve social, political, and economic issues; proponents of the Enlightenment sought to end unquestioning reliance on traditional religious and political authorities. This movement is often cited by historians as one of the forces behind the dissatisfaction and demands for social and economic reform that culminated in the French Revolution.

The *philosophes,* those responsible for spreading the attitudes and theories of the Enlightenment to the general populace, were condemned by most French political and religious leaders, who considered their progressive ideas seditious. And, as J. M. Roberts explained in his *New York Review of Books* critique of *The Business of Enlightenment,* as "early as 1759 the Parlement of Paris saw behind the *Encyclopedie* a plot against church—indeed, religion—and the state; a royal prohibition (the second) on publication followed. In the same year came the special *cachet* of Papal condemnation." Darnton does not discuss these early years of the *Encyclopedie* when Diderot and his colleagues—among them such literary giants as Voltaire, Montesquieu, and Rousseau—worked on the book's production as an expensive *in folio* publication. Rather, Darnton focuses on the history of the *Encyclopedie*'s publication under the direction of Panckoucke, who acquired the publication rights to the encyclopedia in 1768 and during the 1770s worked to publish revised, less expensive (and thus more accessible) editions of Diderot's work. Nonetheless, the *Encyclopedie* was still outlawed in France, and much of what Darnton's book reveals concerns Panckoucke's various methods of evading this prohibition.

In his review of the book, Roberts described *The Business of Enlightenment* as "an immensely rich and complicated story which can be read with profit in many different ways. One way is simply for the economic and social realities of publishing history which are uncovered in astonishing detail, showing us who did the printing, made the paper, distributed the books, and how they did it." Among the practices revealed by Darnton's book are those of bribery, embezzlement, smuggling, promoting books through false advertising, pirating books, arranging collusive agreements among publishers, and soliciting favors from nobles and officials able to circumvent publishing regulations. As Roberts commented, "Publishing history, as told by Professor Darnton, turns out to be much meatier and livelier than might be expected, although without his wide-ranging scholarship the story might have become mere bibliography and antiquarianism."

In discussing the publication and distribution of the *Encyclopedie,* Darnton also illuminates the issue of who might have read the *Encyclopedie* and how they might have been influenced by it. According to Roberts, as "described by Darnton, the impact of the *Encyclopedie* turns out to be more complicated and qualified, and much less easy to summarize than the traditional mythology allows." For instance, the often conservative bent of the editorial revisions made to the various editions of the *Encyclopedie* to some extent mitigate its status as an anticlerical, antiestablishment publication. Moreover, Darnton's research shows that the majority of subscribers to both the initial and later editions were members of the French Old Regime's sociopolitical elite or those who aspired to elite status, rather than members of the merchant or industrial classes commonly associated with eighteenth-century progressive politics and beliefs. Part of the reason for this, according to *The Business of Enlightenment,* was that the publishers of the *Encyclopedie* appealed to its aristocratic subscribers by claiming to provide all-encompassing knowledge in a systematic fashion, and it thus became a symbol of intellectual taste among the upper classes.

In response to the idea that Darnton's book challenges the *Encyclopedie*'s reputation as a major force in the Enlightenment's education of the general populace and, as such, as a contributor to the revolutionary movement in France, Roberts asserted that there is another way to read Darnton's findings: "What we need to do, perhaps, is to make an adjustment in our conception of the readiness and receptiveness of the world which awaited [the Enlightenment] and to grasp that the 'Enlightenment' had more than one message. That it was faith in systematic knowledge rather than skepticism which was important now seems clear. This is perhaps the most general of the conclusions which this study of publishing history supports and the one which takes the reader furthest away from its rich and fascinating detail." Commenting that Darnton's "seemingly limited approach" to the history of the *Encyclopedie* "reveals more of the scope and limits of the *Encyclopedie*'s influence than any other has done," Roberts concluded that Darnton's *Business of Enlightenment* "is a major achievement of American scholarship and in the first rank of those which have been transforming our view of French history during the last twenty years."

Like *The Business of Enlightenment,* Darnton's *The Literary Underground of the Old Regime* draws on the resources of the Neuchâtel Archives to illuminate certain aspects of publishing in the late eighteenth century—the Age of Enlightenment. But *The Literary Underground* also relies on police records and the archives of the Parisian printers' and booksellers' guild, and rather than focusing on the history of one prohibited publication, Darnton's third book is concerned with the illegal book trade as a whole in pre-evolutionary France. In particular, Darnton discusses in this book the clandestine writing, publication, and sale of works that were censored or prohibited by France's Old Regime and the relationship between the illicit book trade and the fall of the Old Regime in 1789. He does this in six chapters—five of which were previously published as essays and one of which was originally a lecture. In the first chapter of *The Literary Underground of the Old Regime,* titled "High Enlightenment and the Low Life in Literature," Darnton delineates the differences between such established, well-known eighteenth-century authors as Montesquieu, Voltaire, and Rousseau and what Darnton calls the "Grub Street" writers of Paris—those who came to the French capital in the late-eighteenth century determined to achieve the literary success of a Voltaire or Rousseau but who finally, after failing to gain a livelihood through legitimate literary endeavors, resorted to performing hack work. According to Darnton the disappointment and degradation of these hack writers made them bitter toward the literary and political entities that rejected them. The disappointment of these Grub Street writers also made them likely to embrace subversive views, not out of ideological conviction but out of vengeance. Concluded Darnton, "It was from [Grub Street's] visceral hatred, not from the refined abstractions of the contented cultural elite, that the extreme . . . revolution found its authentic voice."

In the next four chapters of *The Literary Underground of the Old Regime,* Darnton develops his idea that the disaffected writers and publishers, disillusioned by their exclusion from the restricted, privileged world of legitimate French publishing, acted as a force in the French Revolution through the French literary underground, by lampooning the Old Regime and promoting the revolutionary ideals of liberty and equality. Darnton illustrates this proposition by examining the lives of four individuals who participated in the literary underground. One of them, Jacques-Pierre Brissot, was a journalist who, according to documentation discovered by Darnton, turned police informer in 1784 after serving time in the Bastille prison for allegedly publishing pornography. Darnton explains in *The Literary Underground* that Brissot's imprisonment in Paris and employment as a police spy pushed him to become a leader in the Revolution: "It corrupted him, and in the corrupting it confirmed his hatred of the Old Regime. How he must have hated it! How he must have raged inwardly against the system of arbitrary power that first struck him down and then enlisted him in its service. How he must have reviled the men in control of the system, who first blocked his attempts to win honor for himself and then dishonored him by making him their agent." Darnton's other illustrative studies focus on the careers of an underground bookseller, a printer, and a hack pamphleteer. And Darnton's closing chapter, titled "Ready, Writing, and Publishing," addresses the issue of what was read by whom in the years just prior to the French Revolution.

Critical reception of *The Literary Underground of the Old Regime* as a whole was positive, although some critics questioned a few of Darnton's methods and conclusions. Raymond Birn, who critiqued the book in the *American Historical Review,* expressed concern that Darnton "may fit writers . . . too neatly into defined social categories, and at times . . . substitutes what writers 'must have felt' for what they actually wrote." Norman Hampson voiced similar concerns in his *New York Review of Books* critique of *The Literary Underground of the Old Regime* and further noted Darnton's dependence on the production and sale of books as indications of their import: "He is generally content to treat books as commodities rather than as expressions of ideas. . . . [An] examination of what people like Brissot . . . actually wrote might have changed his views about what they 'must have' felt." Moreover, Hampson continued, when it comes to "Darnton's conclusion that by 1789 the literary underworld had made a significant contribution to undermining the old order . . . everyone is on dangerous ground since we still do not know with any precision what books were sold or who bought them." And even if scholars did know, concluded Hampson, "we might still be a long way from understanding their effects."

Hampson conceded, however, that to "suggest that things were rather more complicated and untidy" than Darnton depicts in *The Literary Underground* "is not to imply that Darnton is wrong, merely that one must bring in factors that he excludes and that his truths have to coexist with others." This said, the *New York Review of Books* critic deemed the book "splendid historical writing" and remarked of Darnton: "His imaginative reconstruction of the [Parisian] Grub Street world, and its enforced subordination of principle to the need for survival, illuminates the later revolutionary press, whose editors came mostly from the literary underground. All this has earned Darnton a well-justified reputation as one of the most original contributors to our understanding of life in pre-revolutionary Paris." Margaret Peters similarly commented in the *New York Times Book Review:* "The reader who wants a glimpse of the world behind a very unusual literature and an enlightening look at a famous time in history will get an eyeful in this surprising and entertaining volume." With regard to Darnton's use of the Neuchâtel Archives, Hampson noted, "He has an enviable gift for reading between the lines, extracting meaning and life from unpromising material, and finding relations between things that have no obvious connection with each other. Whatever he writes is stimulating to read." In his *American Historical Review* critique, Raymond Birn deemed Darnton a "superb storyteller" and remarked of *The Literary Underground* that "Darnton has clearly unearthed a human, multifaceted Enlightenment. What lies ahead is a systematic, compelling book on the cultural origins of the Revolution. Darnton surely possesses the vision to write it." And Hampson concluded that Darnton "has made good use of his gold mine [of documents] and left us all greatly in his debt. Thanks to him we know a good deal more about the ecology of *ancien regime* society. . . . The French Revolution was a continuous conflict between people, as well as a battle of ideas, and anyone who wants to understand the people had better start with the work of Robert Darnton."

Darnton examines an even more specialized literary genre in *The Forbidden Bestsellers of Pre-Revolutionary France* and its companion volume, *The Corpus of Clandestine Literature in France, 1769-1789,* both published in 1995. Clandestine books, ranging in subject matter from futuristic utopian novels and pornography to unauthorized biographies of wealthy and influential members of the aristocracy, influenced the common people of prerevolutionary France far more than did the high-minded *Encyclopedie,* according to the historian. Lumped with works by Voltaire and Rousseau into a censored classification called *livres philosphiques*—books that undermined the authority of Church, the King, or of commonly held moral values—were such volumes as the lascivious *Memoirs about the Affair between Father Dirrag and Mademoiselle Eradice* and other pornographic novels, as well as Louis-Sebastien Mercier's forward-looking *The Year 2440: A Dream If Ever There Was One.* Smuggled into France by various means—including a method called "larding" whereby pages of a non-censored book were interleaved with pages of a censored "philosophical" tract—these books became commonplace throughout the country despite their prohibition. Out of a list of 720 titles in circulation during this time (analyzed at great length in *The Corpus of Clandestine Literature*), Darnton's list of the thirty-five best-selling volumes of the period shows Mercier's book in top place, followed by a risque biography of Madame du Barry; interestingly, Voltaire's *Questions about the Encyclopedie* holds up surprisingly well at eleventh, even a notch or two above the translation of Cleland's *Fanny Hill.*

Through his continuing research at Neuchâtel, Darnton has become fascinated with the relationship between this literature, which had a heavy demand, despite the fact that it had to be smuggled into the country. Determining, as he did in *The Businesss of the Enlightenment,* that the *Encyclopedie* and other heavily politicized works circulated mainly within the socioeconomic class that the revolution ultimately sought to overthrow, the question remains, as Peter Brooks noted in the *New Republic:* "Do books make revolutions? If so, how?" Darnton "wants to answer yes, books do make revolutions," added Brooks. "But that is true, he wishes to show, only if one extends the list of books, beyond those the historians normally hold responsible for creating a fire in men's minds . . . [to] the true best-sellers." While finding Darnton's premise fascinating—particularly the historian's assertion that in eighteenth-century France the concept of "liberty" was closely linked to that of "libertinism"—Brooks expressed concern that the historian's purposes may have masked the larger fascination: that such serious *philosophes* as Voltaire, Rousseau, and d'Holbach were almost as widely read as "frivolities" in a society whose lower classes so greatly outnumbered the *ancien regime.* However, Frederic Tuten maintained in his appraisal of *Forbidden Bestsellers* in the *Los Angeles Times Book Review* that Darnton correctly gauges the "living network of the culture's sentiment," of which such books were a part. "What he finds in the literature," Tuten explained of Darnton, "is a growing disaffection from the monarchy from the time of Louis XV, a disaffection which by 1789 led some to lose faith in the legitimacy of the monarchy itself." John Sturroch added in the *New York Times Book Review* that "Darnton makes good on his case that 'dangerous' literature cashed in on attitudes more than it create them, and that it supported an informal confederation of the potentially subversive."

Darnton would further contribute to the discussion of the role of books in the French Revolution in *Revolution in Print: The Press in France, 1775-1800,* which he edited with Daniel Roche. Designed to accompany the Bicentenary exhibit "Revolution in Print" that was held at the New York Public Library in 1989, the book is comprised of essays on bookmaking and distribution, the production of pamphlets and newspapers, and other aspects of the publishing trades prior to and during the French uprising. Containing numerous illustrations, the volume also includes a discussion of such issues as freedom of the press, written in a manner that is "scholarly without being in the least arcane," according to *Times Literary Supplement* reviewer Allan Forest.

In *The Great Cat Massacre and Other Episodes in French Cultural History,* Darnton delves even further back into historical records to examine the attitudes of people living in pre-Enlightenment France. As Darnton, quoted in the *New York Times Book Review,* explained, "The human quest underlying the tales in this book" was "how other people were thinking two centuries ago." And in introducing *The Great Cat Massacre* Darnton elaborated on his aim, stating: "This book investigates ways of thinking in eighteenth-century France. It attempts to show not merely what people thought but how they thought—how they construed the world, invested it with meaning, and infused it with emotion." He does this by investigating the accounts given of their era in police dossiers, letters, and other documents by individuals alive in the early eighteenth century, as well as the literature and folklore produced at the time.

Two of the essays in *The Great Cat Massacre* concern the folklore of pre-Enlightenment France. In the title essay Darnton studies printer Nicolas Contat's recollection of a mock trial and slaughter of cats that occurred while he was a printer's apprentice in Paris during the 1730s. Two of Contat's fellow apprentices, frustrated by the overwork and poor living conditions imposed by their master, gleefully turned permission given by their master to eliminate some of the stray cats who disturbed the apprentices' sleep into a license to conduct a mass round-up, mock trial, torture, and hanging of the animals. Particularly cruel was their torture and execution of the mistress's favorite cat, whom the master had specifically ordered the apprentices to exempt from their purge. According to Stanley Hoffman, reviewing *The Great Cat Massacre* in the *New Republic,* this essay on Nicolas Contat's remembrance is one of the chapters in Darnton's book that tells us "mainly about the differences between Frenchmen then and Frenchmen now. Nobody today would find a slaughter of cats funny, unlike the printing apprentices of the rue Saint-Severin. As Darnton tells us the story, it is a gruesome case of workers' revenge against the master and his wife, a symbolic sexual violation of his wife (a cat lover), a humiliation of the boss . . . an expression of 'working-class militancy' within the confines of *artisinat* (craft) and artisanal culture: 'a popular rebellion, though it remained restricted to the level of symbolism,' insofar as human beings were concerned." And writer Eve Drobot, critiquing *The Great Cat Massacre* for Toronto's *Globe and Mail,* remarked: "The point of the [cat massacre] incident, in Darnton's account, is not that dissatisfied workers revolted against their masters, but that they found the whole experience utterly hilarious. The massacre lives on in the annals of the printing shop where it was repeated endlessly in mime and ritualized in story telling. 'Yet,' Darnton writes, 'it strikes the modern reader as unfunny, if not downright repulsive.' The discrepancy in perception is precisely his territory, and one that he mines most effectively 'When you realize that you are not getting something—a joke, a proverb, a ceremony—that is particularly meaningful to the natives, you can see where to grasp a foreign system of meaning in order to unravel it.'"

In the next essay, Darnton reinterprets traditional French fairy tales, stripping away the glosses and alter-

ations that have accumulated during the past two hundred years to reveal the tales—as nearly as possible—as they were first told. Among the tales examined by Darnton is one known today as "Little Red Riding Hood," although in its original form the heroine's hood is not red, a revelation that challenges certain modern analyses of the tale that are based on the hood's redness as a symbol for menstruation and puberty. Another difference between the version revealed by Darnton and the modern-day version of "Little Red Riding Hood" is that the modern tale ends happily with the heroine alive and well, while in the original the girl is eaten by the wolf. This reflects what Darnton shows to be a general tendency—that the original French fairy tales were harsher than those that have evolved out of them, and the originals stressed the need for people to be cunning and resourceful in order to survive the brutal conditions of peasant life in eighteenth-century France. As Mavis Gallant explained in *New York Times Book Review,* "The bare bones of the fairy tales that reach us . . . are nearly all we can know about 'the mental world of the unenlightened during the Enlightenment.'" And what they convey is "a dark world without warmth or compassion, in which families starve and children are a burden to be deserted when they cannot be fed. Dupery and cunning, not love or justice, are to be relied upon and practiced, for they are the only props of the poor. Generations of the illiterate and the dispossessed learned—from a small core of stories that were told aloud—how to 'live mistrustfully ever after.'"

Darnton's third study in *The Great Cat Massacre* relates an anonymous bourgeois's description of the social order of his hometown of Montpellier, France, and is followed by what Drobot described as the "wittiest chapter in the book." This latter looks at the files of an eighteenth-century police inspector charged with the responsibility of keeping records on the literary community of Paris between 1748 and 1753. His files include more than five hundred dossiers on both prestigious and hack writers. In the dossiers the inspector evaluates the style and content of the writers' works, the writers' private lives, their sources of financial support, and their physical appearance. He also provides anecdotes and gossip that circulated about the writers at the time.

Darnton's next essay analyzes the editorial strategies used by Denis Diderot and his colleague Jean Le Rond d'Alembert in propagating through their *Encyclopedie* ideas that would come to characterize the Enlightenment. And in the final episode of *The Great Cat Massacre,* Darnton relates the contents of a cache of forty-seven letters and book orders sent to a Swiss publisher and printer by a French merchant with a passion for the writings of Jean-Jacques Rousseau. Darnton discovered these letters in Swiss archives and used them to show how the writings of Rousseau influenced the lives of the merchant, his family, and others.

Winner of the 1984 *Los Angeles Times* Book Prize, *The Great Cat Massacre and Other Episodes in French Cultural History* prompted William S. McFeely to commend Darnton in the *Washington Post Book World,* where he noted: "The job description for the historian is simple; he must read well. Darnton does. He will read anything, take it seriously, and, applying a fertile imagination, write beautifully about what he has learned." Hoffman similarly praised Darnton's work in the *New Republic:* "Robert Darnton has the inquisitiveness of a first-rate investigative reporter, the thoroughness of a rigorous scholar, and the sensitivity of a novelist. Rarely have these very different gifts been so deliciously combined." And of Darnton's essays in *The Great Cat Massacre,* Hoffman concluded: "Each one of his stories is a gem," together comprising a "most rewarding book . . . for those of us who like to study France, and whose enjoyment of social science is at its peak whenever the gap between it and good literature is at its narrowest."

In *The Kiss of Lamourette: Reflections on Cultural History,* Darnton steps back and views the role of historians in understanding, interpreting, and using history to educate in the present. Spreading his inquiry from France during the age of revolution to the modern day, his essays cover such things as the history of reading and history's relationship with other sciences, such as anthropology and psychology. Informed by his early work as a journalist, he meshes the media of today with the Terror of the eighteenth century, a Terror that was stilled only by brief moments of "fraternite," such as that from which the book draws its title. Speaking before the revolutionary Assembly in 1782, Antoine Adrien Lamourette's suggestion that political troubles could be solved through affection was followed by what *Los Angeles Times Book Review* critic Scott Mahler deemed "one of the most improbable scenes from European political history"—assemblymen rising to their feet and hugging and kissing their fellow legislators. "Darnton daydreams about history the way other people daydream about taking a vacation or finding true love," wrote Mahler, who found the volume to be the product of "a rich intelligence." "Whether exploring the high plains of scholarly debate or the fertile lowlands of popular culture, he makes an excellent guide for all."

In an uncharacteristic change of pace, Darnton the cultural historian turns journalist in *Berlin Journal, 1989-1990,* a record of an academic year spent in Germany for a German think tank. He had intended to immerse himself in the study of the eighteenth century, but, as Gordon A. Craig explained in the *New York Review of Books,* "unexpectedly . . . found himself in the middle of something that looked like a revolution and decided to try to produce a journalistic account of events as they occurred." Traveling from his base in West Berlin into communist East Germany after the Berlin Wall came down in November of 1989, the historian records the details of his interactions with the people he meets on his travels: "His reportage of changing moods, conversations, arguments, and above all, people in particular situations, is direct and vivid," noted Steven Lukes of Darnton's book in the *Times Literary Supplement,* while adding that Darnton the historian is never far behind Darnton the journalist, asking questions and "drawing analogies and disanalogies" with revolutionary France, and possessing "a keen eye for the strange significance of books under communism." Craig praised the volume as "an attractive and highly readable book," although he later added that "one is left wondering why a 'Berlin journal' should say so little about the western half of the city." *Berlin Journal* is "not without repetition," Anthony Ailey stated in *New York Times Book Review,* but he added that the volume "makes us appreciate something of what it felt like for Germans East and West as [their formerly bisected] world ended."

Darnton added to his oeuvre on the Enlightenment with the 2003 publication of his essay collection *George Washington's Teeth: An Unconventional Guide to the Eighteenth Century.* The subtitle seems to indicate a broader scope, though the historian mostly focuses on his favorite subject, France in the years before the revolution. However, he does spend time discussing the influences of what was happening in France upon the American colonies, as well as his usual romps through bits of cultural trivia that bring the eighteenth-century to life. As Hunt, writing in the *New Republic,* noted, "Darnton has a knack for breaking open an old chestnut and finding the meat still clinging inside." Although Hunt became frustrated with the book because it refuses to adequately connect the Enlightenment with the French Revolution—or, on the other hand, take the position that they were not strongly connected, the critic maintained that *George Washington's Teeth* "is good history, because it is so richly documented. It is also captivating history." Marie Marmo Mullaney, writing in *Library Journal,* seconded that opinion, declaring Darnton's book "a refreshing and stimulating collection of essays by one of the preeminent historians of the eighteenth century."

Hunt, summing up the historian's contributions to the discipline, noted that "Darnton never focused on the ideas of the Enlightenment itself. He wanted to show how those ideas diffused outward and downward, and above all he was fascinated by the low life of literature, the publishers and the smugglers of forbidden books, the pamphleteers and the pornographers who gnawed away at the beams holding up the *ancien regime.* Darnton has done more than anyone else to illuminate this story and to show how it matters. *The Business of Enlightenment* and *The Forbidden Bestsellers of Pre-Revolutionary France* are rightly considered classics in the field."

Darnton once told *CA:* "I write history books, so my publications express a continuing process of archival research and a commitment to a professional vocation. Still, I attempt to write the books in such a way that they could interest the general educated reader. That attempt has not succeeded as well as I would hope in the United States, but I do find it possible to reach a 'grand public' through translations in Europe." Regardless of the readership, Darnton has enjoyed his excursions into history, especially his delvings into the Societé Typographique de Neuchâtel's papers. Calling himself an "archival historian," he revealed to *Publishers Weekly* writer Gary M. Kramer, "What really excites me as a historian . . . is how to get inside the mental world that existed hundreds of years ago, to roam around and understand how people made sense of things."

BIOGRAPHICAL AND CRITICAL SOURCES:

PERIODICALS

American Historical Review, October, 1969; October, 1980; June, 1983.
Atlantic Monthly, February, 1984.

Business History Review, winter, 1981.
Contemporary Review, January, 1997, Linda Kirk, review of *The Forbidden Bestsellers of Pre-Revolutionary France,* p. 49.
Detroit News, December 13, 1984.
Globe and Mail (Toronto, Ontario, Canada), April 21, 1984.
History Today, February, 1982.
Insight on the News, July 3, 1995, Stephen Goode, review of *The Forbidden Bestsellers of Pre-Revolutionary France,* p. 29.
Journal of Interdisciplinary History, spring, 1984.
Journal of Modern History, September, 1970; June, 1981; March, 1997, Jeremy D. Popkin, review of *The Corpus of Clandestine Literature in France, 1769-1789,* p. 154.
Library Journal, March 1, 1995, T. J. Schaeper, review of *The Forbidden Bestsellers of Pre-Revolutionary France,* p. 88; June 15, 2003, Marie Marmo Mullaney, review of *George Washington's False Teeth: An Unconventional Guide to the Eighteenth Century,* p. 86.
London Review of Books, December 2, 1982.
Los Angeles Times Book Review, March 25, 1984; September 23, 1984; November 4, 1984; November 19, 1989, pp. 1, 15; April 2, 1995, p. 3.
Modern Language Review, January, 1984.
Nation, March 12, 1990.
National Review, June 8, 1979.
New Republic, April 16, 1984; July 31, 1989, pp. 26-33; July 17, 24, 1995, pp. 51-53; October 6, 2003, Lynn Hunt, review of *George Washington's False Teeth,* p. 35.
Newsweek, February 27, 1984.
New York Review of Books, February 7, 1980; October 7, 1982; November 1, 1991, pp. 31-37; June 8, 1995, P. N. Furbank, review of *The Corpus of Clandestine Literature in France, 1769-1789* and *The Forbidden Bestsellers of Pre-Revolutionary France,* p. 51, pp. 51-55; July 13, 2003, David Walton, review of *George Washington's False Teeth,* p. 24.
New York Times, February 15, 1983; April 14, 1983.
New York Times Book Review, November 21, 1982; February 12, 1984; July 14, 1991, pp. 15-16; April 2, 1995, p. 13.
Publishers Weekly, January 30, 1995, review of *The Forbidden Bestsellers of Pre-Revolutionary France,* p. 90; March 13, 1995, Gary M. Kramer, "Robert Darnton: 'The Vulgar Element Is Crucial,'" p. 50.
Review of Metaphysics, June, 1981.

Science, March 21, 1969.

Time, February 13, 1984.

Times Literary Supplement, December 14, 1979; October 6-12, 1989, pp. 1097-1098; March 29, 1991, p. 7; May 22, 1993, p. 33.

Virginia Quarterly Review, summer, 1969; spring, 1980.

Voice Literary Supplement, May 1995, pp. 7-8.

Washington Post Book World, February 12, 1984.

Wilson Quarterly, spring, 1995, review of *The Forbidden Bestsellers of Pre-Revolutionary France,* p. 85.

*   *   *

DAVISON, Lawrence H.
    See LAWRENCE, D(avid) H(erbert Richards)

*   *   *

di PRIMA, Diane 1934-

PERSONAL: Born August 6, 1934, in Brooklyn, NY; daughter of Francis and Emma (Mallozzi) di Prima; married Alan S. Marlowe (an actor, model, and director), November 30, 1962 (divorced, 1969); married Grant Fisher (a poet), 1972 (divorced, 1975); children: Jeanne, Dominique, Alexander, Tara, Rudra. *Education:* Attended Swarthmore College, 1951-52; studied Zen Buddhism with Master Shunryu Suzuki-Roshi. *Politics:* "Anarchist." *Religion:* Buddhist.

ADDRESSES: Home—584 Castro St., San Francisco, CA 94114. *Office*—c/o Wingbow Press, 2940 West Seventh St., Berkeley, CA 94710.

CAREER: Poet, editor, and educator. *Floating Bear* (magazine), New York, NY, coeditor with LeRoi Jones (Imamu Amiri Baraka), 1961-63, editor, 1963-69; *Signal Magazine,* associate editor, 1963-65; Poets Press, New York, NY, publisher and editor, 1963-69; Eidolon Editions, Point Reyes, CA, editor and publisher, 1972-76; formerly affiliated with Wingbow Press, Berkeley, CA. Naropa Institute School of Poetics, instructor, 1974—; New College of California, San Francisco, CA, poetry instructor, 1980-87; instructor at California College of Arts and Crafts, 1990-93, San Francisco Art Institute, 1992, California Institute of Integral

Diane di Prima

Studies, 1993-95, and Napa State Hospital. Director and cofounder, New York Poets Theatre, 1961-65; cofounder and instructor, San Francisco Institute of Magical and Healing Arts, 1983-90; cofounder, American Theatre for Poets; founder, Poets Institute.

AWARDS, HONORS: Grant from National Endowment for the Arts, 1973, 1979.

WRITINGS:

POETRY

This Kind of Bird Flies Backward, Totem Press (New York, NY), 1958.

The Monster, Penny Poems (New Haven, CT), 1961.

The New Handbook of Heaven, Auerhahn (San Francisco, CA), 1963.

Unless You Clock In, Patchen Cards (Palo Alto, CA), 1963.

Combination Theatre Poem and Birthday Poem for Ten People, Brownstone Press (New York, NY), 1965.

Poems for Freddie, Poets Press (New York, NY) 1966, published as *Freddie Poems,* Eidolon Editions (Berkeley, CA), 1974.

Some Haiku, Love Press (Topanga, CA), 1967.

Earthsong: Poems 1957-1959, edited by Alan S. Marlowe, Poets Press (New York, NY) 1968.

Hotel Albert: Poems, Poets Press (New York, NY) 1968.

New Mexico Poem, June-July 1967, Roodenko (New York, NY), 1968.

The Star, the Child, the Light, privately printed, 1968.

L.A. Odyssey, Poets Press (New York, NY), 1969.

New As . . . , privately printed, 1969.

The Book of Hours, Brownstone Press (San Francisco, CA), 1970.

Kerhonkson Journal: 1966, Oyez (Berkeley, CA), 1971.

Prayer to the Mothers, privately printed, 1971.

So Fine, Yes Press (Santa Barbara, CA), 1971.

XV Dedications: Poems, Unicorn Press (Santa Barbara, CA), 1971.

Revolutionary Letters, City Lights (San Francisco, CA), 1971, revised edition published as *Revolutionary Letters, Etc.,* Karus Reprint, 1973.

The Calculus of Letters, privately printed, 1972.

Loba: Part I, Capra Press (Santa Barbara, CA), 1973.

North Country Medicine, privately printed, 1974.

Brass Furnace Going Out: Song after an Abortion, Pulpartforms Unlimited/Intrepid Press (Syracuse, NY), 1975.

Selected Poems, 1956-1975, North Atlantic Books (Plainfield, VT), 1975, enlarged edition, 1977.

Loba As Eve, Phoenix Book Shop (New York, NY), 1975.

Loba: Part II, Eidolon Editions (Point Reyes, CA), 1977.

Loba: Parts I-VIII, Wingbow Press (Berkeley, CA), 1978, expanded edition published as *Loba,* Penguin (New York, NY), 1998.

Wyoming Series, Eidolon Editions (Point Reyes, CA), 1988.

The Mysteries of Vision, Am Here Books (Santa Barbara, CA), 1988.

Pieces of a Song: Selected Poems, City Lights (San Francisco, CA), 1990.

Seminary Poems, Floating Island (Point Reyes, CA), 1991.

The Mask Is the Path of the Star, Thinker Review International (Louisville, KY), 1993.

Twenty-two Death Poems, Backwoods Broadsides (Ellsworth, ME), 1996.

Poetry has been collected in anthologies.

PLAYS

Murder Cake, first produced in New York, NY, by Living Theatre, 1960.

Paideuma, first produced in New York, NY, by Living Theatre, 1960.

The Discontentment of a Russian Prince, first produced in New York, NY, 1961.

Like, first produced by New York Poets Theatre, 1964.

Poets Vaudeville (first produced in New York, NY, 1964), music by John Herbert McDowell, Feed Folly Press (New York, NY), 1964.

Monuments, first produced in New York, NY, by Caffe Cino, 1968.

Discovery of America, first produced in New York, NY, by Theatre for the New City, 1972.

Whale Honey, first produced in San Francisco, CA, by Intersection, 1975, produced in New York, NY, 1976.

Zip Code: Collected Plays, Coffee House Press (Minneapolis, MN), 1994.

OTHER

(Editor) *Various Fables from Various Places,* Putnam (New York, NY), 1960.

Dinners and Nightmares (short stories), Corinth (New York, NY), 1961, revised edition, 1974.

(Translator, with others) Jean Genet, *The Man Condemned to Death,* Poets Press (New York, NY), 1963.

(Translator) *Seven Love Poems from the Middle Latin,* Poets Press (New York, NY), 1965.

The Calculus of Variation (autobiographical novel) Poets Press (New York, NY), 1966.

Spring and Autumn Annals (novel), Frontier Press (San Francisco, CA), 1966.

(Author of introduction) Arthur Edward White, editor, *The Hermetic and Alchemical Writings of . . . Paracelsus,* University Books (New Hyde Park, NY), 1967.

(Editor) *War Poems,* Poets Press (New York, NY) 1968.

(Author of introduction) Audre Lord, *The First Cities,* Poets Press (New York, NY) 1968.

Notes on the Summer Solstice: June 21, 1969, [San Francisco, CA], 1969.

Memoirs of a Beatnik (novel), Olympia Press (New York, NY), 1969, reprinted, Penguin (New York, NY), 1998.

(Editor, with LeRoi Jones, and author of introduction) *The Floating Bear: A Newsletter, Nos. 1-37, 1961-1969,* Laurence McGilvery (La Jolla, CA), 1973.

(Coauthor) *City for Sale: Ed Koch and the Betrayal of New York,* Harper & Row (New York, NY), 1988.

Only in America: The Life and Crimes of Don King, Morrow (New York, NY), 1995.

Recollections of My Life As a Woman: The New York Years: A Memoir, Viking (New York, NY), 2001.

Contributor to *Love on a Trampoline,* by Sybah Darrich, Olympia Press (Paris, France), 1968; and *Of Sheep and Girls,* Traveller's Companion (Paris, France), 1968. Columnist for *Mama Bear's News and Notes,* 1987-92, and *Harbin Quarterly,* 1992-93. Contributing editor, *Kulchur* (magazine), 1961-62.

Di Prima's work has been translated into over twenty languages.

SIDELIGHTS: Diane di Prima has been called the most important female poet to come out of the Beat generation of the mid-twentieth century. Writing verses since the 1950s, she has been a major influence not only through her poems but also as a teacher and magazine publisher. Her poetry, according to Gretchen H. Munroe in the *Dictionary of Literary Biography,* "is the expression of a strong, sensitive, intelligent woman during more than two decades of social and artistic ferment. Unfettered by the conventions of academia or society, she speaks of life outside the mainstream of middle-class America: the life of bohemia, of the counterculture. Involvement with and concern for the people in her life is central in her work. As she moves from the early years of Greenwich Village pads, the Beat, jazz, drug culture of the 1950s into the revolutionary currents of the flower children and Vietnam War protests of the 1960s and early 1970s, through Buddhism, Hinduism, and Zen to the emerging social consciousness of women in the 1970s, [di Prima's] work charts the shifting streams of America's fringe culture."

While di Prima "has never stated her poetics formally," explained George F. Butterick in another *Dictionary of Literary Biography* essay, "she has a poem titled 'Poetics' toward the end of [*Earthsong: Poems 1957-1959*] that presumably can stand as a partial statement or reflection of her poetic thinking from that time, especially because it is written in the first person. The narrator speaks of herself as having 'deserted her post' as an appointed 'rearguard' whose responsibility it had been 'to preserve the language/lucidity'—a not unreasonable task for a poet (although 'rearguard' is a curious choice, since most of her generation would have seen themselves as fighting an 'avant-garde' action)." Di Prima's "position would seem to be the anarchist one," continued Butterick. "She would rather enact the language as poetry than preserve it, and ['Poetics'] concludes with the speaker as a 'hoodlum fish' plunged in a language more naturally elemental, moving about in it gracefully, totally immersed, breathing it in. . . . Di Prima never proposed that her work embody theories of literature. She is more committed to life-styles than to poetic styles."

Born to Italian-American parents in Brooklyn, di Prima inherited her taste for rebellion from her grandfather, Domenico Mallozzi, a man of anarchist political sentiments. She began writing when she was seven and discovered poetry when she was thirteen; within a year she was writing every day. As she explained more fully in her autobiography, *My Life As a Woman: The New York Years: A Memoir,* di Prima began to see her life with her family as a sort of prison, and her independent spirit would not abide it. She wanted to "embrace this new thing, my Will. Fierce, silent love of Self, my angel." She became so committed to making her way as a poet that she left Swarthmore College in 1953 before finishing her degree and moved to a Lower East Side apartment to focus on her craft, or, as she put it, her "calling. The holiest life that was offered in our world: artist." During the next four years she wrote and studied her craft, becoming influenced by art forms such as jazz music, abstract art, and avant garde theatre and dance.

The 1950s were an amazing time for di Prima, who had the chance to meet poet Ezra Pound in 1956 while Pound was held in a mental hospital as a consequence of his support of Italian fascist dictator Benito Mussolini; was inspired that same year by Allen Ginsberg's *Howl;* actually met Ginsberg and other famous writers in New York; and generally enjoyed the atmosphere and Beat culture of the time. By the end of the decade she had prepared enough as a poet to get her first book, *This Kind of Bird Flies Backward,* published through Totem Press, a small press started by Imamu Amiri Baraka. Di Prima's early poems, as Monroe stated, are concerned mostly with love—"her love for her daughter and for her lovers, androgynous love, sensual love, physical love." Of the poet's style, Monroe wrote that, like the jazz music of the time, "her poetry rejects traditional formal restraints, seeking new forms of expression in design, rhyme, and meter." But di Prima was not satisfied with just writing poetry; she wanted to help other counterculture writers such as herself, so she teamed up with Baraka to found *Floating Bear* magazine, which published works by such authors as William Burroughs, Jack Kerouac, Richard Wright, and Frank O'Hara. The avant-garde publication was mailed out to many people for free. Seeing the norms of "good taste" as a kind of cultural oppression, the works published in *Floating Bear* were considered by some to be offensive, and both di Prima and Baraka were charged by the FBI with distributing obscene material through the U.S. Post Office. Di Prima's attorney was able to win the sympathy of the court because the poet was pregnant, and she was soon released. Baraka, on the other hand, fought his case and won by pointing out how many works of literature, such as Irish novelist James Joyce's *Ulysses,* have been considered obscene by some critics prior to becoming esteemed as classics.

When *Floating Bear* shut down in 1963, di Prima moved on to found other small presses, including The Poets Press and Eidolon Editions. By the 1960s she became caught up in new interests, including Eastern religions, especially Buddhism, and these influences can be seen in collections such as *The New Handbook of Heaven* and *Earthsong: Poems 1957-1959.* She also took up art, working in collage and assemblage art forms. Like many of her contemporaries, di Prima also experimented with sex and drugs during the 1960s, and she was part of Timothy Leary's Millbrook, New York, community. While her lifestyle during this period could be considered extremely reckless, di Prima argues in her autobiography: "It was not that I held my life so cheap, but held experience, the savoring of life so dear."

The poet's passion for life can clearly be seen in her verses, especially those captured in her "Loba" books: *Loba: Part I, Loba As Eve, Loba: Part II, Loba: Parts 1-VIII,* and 1998's *Loba.* The central voice in these books is that of woman as female wolf, expressing love and savagery, civilization and anarchy, nature and art. The poems, which draw on folklore and mythology, mark a transition in which, according to Munroe, di Prima "no longer . . . accept[s] womanhood as passive and masochistic, for she insists that women are able to see into realms which surpass masculine sensibilities." As the poet explained in an interview in *Whole Earth, Loba* is "about the feralness of the core of women, of the feminine in everything. In everyone."

BIOGRAPHICAL AND CRITICAL SOURCES:

BOOKS

Contemporary Poets, 7th edition, St. James Press (Detroit, MI), 2001.
Dictionary of Literary Biography, Gale (Detroit, MI), Volume 5: *American Poets since World War II, First Series,* 1980, pp. 202-205, Volume 16: *The Beats: Literary Bohemians in Post-War America,* 1983.

PERIODICALS

Book, May, 2001, Denise Gess, review of *Recollections of My Life As a Woman: The New York Years: A Memoir,* p. 77.
Booklist, April, 2001, Donna Seaman, review of *Recollections of My Life As a Woman,* p. 1444; March 1, 2002, Donna Seaman, review of *Recollections of My Life As a Woman,* p. 1084.
Intersection, spring, 1980.
Library Journal, April 15, 1992, William Gargan, review of *Zipcode: Collected Plays,* p. 89; August, 1998, William Gargon, review of *Loba,* p. 94.
New York Times, May 6, 2001, Barbara Grizzuti Harrison, review of *Recollections of My Life As a Woman.*
New York Times Book Review, October 17, 1976; May 6, 2001, "Barefoot in the Park: As Diane di Prima Recalls in Her Memoir, She Was Determined to Be a Poet, Whatever the Hardships," p. 25.
Publishers Weekly, June 29, 1990, Penny Kaganoff, review of *Pieces of Song: Selected Poems,* p. 96; May 7, 2001, review of *Recollections of My Life As a Woman,* p. 240.
Rocky Ledge, February-March, 1981.

San Francisco Chronicle, May 26, 1996, Stephen Schwartz, "A Poet's Take on Life and Learning: San Francisco's Diane di Prima Looks Back on Her Time with Some of the Literary Lights and the Visionary Souls of the Beat Generation," p. 3; April 22, 2001, James Sullivan, "Diane di Prima: Beat Poet and New York Single Mom," p. 5.

Washington Post, June 10, 2001, "Bohemian Rhapsody."

Whole Earth, fall, 1999, interview with Diane di Prima, p. 20.*

*   *   *

DOOLITTLE, Hilda 1886-1961
(H. D., John Helforth)

PERSONAL: Born September 10, 1886, in Bethlehem, PA; died of a heart attack, September 27, 1961, in Zurich, Switzerland; daughter of Charles Leander (a professor of mathematics and astronomy) and Helen Eugeneia (Woole) Doolittle; married Richard Aldington (a writer), October, 1913 (separated, 1919; divorced, 1938); children: Perdita (Mrs. John Schaffner). *Education:* Attended Bryn Mawr College, 1900-06.

CAREER: Poet, playwright, novelist, and translator. Literary editor of *Egoist,* 1916-17; contributing editor of *Close-Up* (cinema journal), 1927-31. Actress with Paul Robeson in film "Borderline," c. 1930.

AWARDS, HONORS: Guarantors Prize from *Poetry,* 1915; Levinson Prize, 1938, and Harriet Monroe Memorial Prize, 1958, both for verse published in *Poetry;* Brandeis University Creative Arts Medal, 1959, for lifetime of distinguished achievement; Award of Merit Medal for poetry, National Institute and American Academy of Arts and Letters, 1960.

WRITINGS:

UNDER INITIALS H. D.

Sea Garden (poems), Constable (London, England), 1916, reprinted, St. Martin's Press (New York, NY), 1975.

(Translator) *Choruses from the "Iphigenia in Aulis" by Euripides,* Clerk's Private Press, 1916.

The Tribute and Circe: Two Poems, Clerk's Private Press, 1917.

Hymen (poems), Holt (New York, NY), 1921.

Heliodora and Other Poems, Houghton Mifflin (New York, NY), 1924.

Collected Poems of H. D., Boni & Liveright (New York, NY), 1925.

H. D. (poems), edited by Hugh Mearns, Simon & Schuster (New York, NY), 1926.

Palimpsest (novel), Houghton Mifflin (New York, NY), 1926, revised edition, Southern Illinois University Press (Carbondale, IL), 1968.

Hippolytus Temporizes: A Play in Three Acts, Houghton Mifflin (New York, NY), 1927, revised edition, 1985.

Hedylus (novel), Houghton Mifflin (New York, NY), 1928, revised edition, 1980.

Red Roses for Bronze (poems), Random House (New York, NY), 1929, reprinted, AMS Press, 1970.

Borderline—A Pool Film with Paul Robeson, Mercury, 1930.

Kora and Ka (novel), Darantiere (Dijon, France), 1934, Bios (Berkeley CA), 1978.

The Usual Star (poems), Darantiere (Dijon, France), 1934.

The Hedgehog (children's fiction), Brendin (London, England), 1936.

(Translator) Euripides, *Ion* (play), Houghton Mifflin (New York, NY), 1937, revised edition, 1985.

What Do I Love? (poems), Brendin (London, England), 1944.

The Walls Do Not Fall (poems; also see below), Oxford University Press (New York, NY), 1944.

Tribute to the Angels (poems; also see below), Oxford University Press (New York, NY), 1945.

The Flowering of the Rod (poems; also see below), Oxford University Press (New York, NY), 1946.

By Avon River (poetry and prose), Macmillan (New York, NY), 1949, revised edition, 1986.

Tribute to Freud, with Unpublished Letters to Freud by the Author, Pantheon (New York, NY), 1956, enlarged edition, McGraw-Hill (New York, NY), 1975, 2nd edition published as *Tribute to Freud: Writing on the Wall,* New Directions (New York, NY), 1984.

Selected Poems, Grove (New York, NY), 1957.

Bid Me to Live: A Madrigal (novel), Grove (New York, NY), 1960, revised edition, 1983.

Helen in Egypt (poem), Grove (New York, NY), 1961.

Two Poems (originally published in *Life and Letters Today*, 1937), Arif (San Francisco, CA), 1971.

Temple of the Sun, Arif (San Francisco, CA), 1972.

Hermetic Definition, New Directions (New York, NY), 1972.

Trilogy: The Walls Do Not Fall, Tribute to the Angels, The Flowering of the Rod, New Directions (New York, NY), 1973.

The Poet and the Dancer (originally published in *Life and Letters Today*, December, 1935), Five Trees Press, 1975.

(Contributor) Eric Walter White, *Images of H. D.*, Enitharmon (London, England), 1976.

End to Torment: A Memoir of Ezra Pound, edited by Norman Holmes Pearson and Michael King, New Directions (New York, NY), 1979.

HERmione, New Directions (New York, NY), 1981, published as *Her*, Virago, 1984.

The Gift (memoir), New Directions (New York, NY), 1982.

Collected Poems, 1912-1944, edited by Louis L. Martz, New Directions (New York, NY), 1983.

Notes on Thought and Vision and The Wise Sappho, City Lights Books, 1983.

Priest [and] A Dead Priestess Speaks (two poems), Copper Canyon Press (Port Townsend WA), 1983.

Selected Poems, edited by Louis L. Martz, Carcanet Press (Manchester, England), 1989.

Richard Aldington and H. D.: The Later Years in Letters, Manchester University Press (Manchester, England), 1995, revised edition published as *Richard Aldington and H. D.: Their Lives in Letters, 1918-1961*, edited and with an introduction and commentary by Caroline Zilboorg, 2003.

Between History and Poetry: The Letters of H. D. and Norman Holmes Pearson, edited by Donna Krolik Hollenberg, University of Iowa Press (Iowa City, IA), 1997.

Pilate's Wife, edited and with an introduction by Joan A. Burke, New Directions (New York, NY), 2000.

Analyzing Freud: Letters of H. D., Bryher, and Their Circle, edited by Susan Stanford Friedman, New Directions (New York, NY), 2002.

Hippolytus Temporizes [and] Ion: Adaptations of Two by Euripides, introduction by Carol Camper, New Directions (New York, NY), 2003.

OTHER

(Under pseudonym John Helforth) *Nights*, Darantiere (Dijon, France), 1935.

Work represented in anthologies, including *Des Imagistes: An Anthology*, edited by Ezra Pound, A. & C. Boni, 1914; *Some Imagist Poets: An Anthology*, edited by Amy Lowell, Houghton Mifflin (New York, NY), 1915-17; and *Contact Collection of Contemporary Writers*, edited by Robert McAlmon, Contact Editions, 1925. Contributor to *Poetry* and other periodicals. Translator of Euripides's *Hippolytus*, 1919.

Collections of H. D.'s papers are housed at the Beinecke Library, Yale University.

SIDELIGHTS: As one of the founders of Imagism, Hilda Doolittle (known as H. D.) became known as much for her poetry as for her association with the group's distinguished writers. Yet her own stark and concrete poetry typified the demands of Imagism as set forth by Ezra Pound and a core of other avant-garde poets. By the mid-1920s, however, after a series of personal crises and the passing of the Imagist years, H. D. sought a more secluded life in Switzerland. But the events of her time—her psychoanalysis with Sigmund Freud, World War II, her advancing age and growing Christian faith—continued to be reflected in her writing. Although in many ways she wrote more productively and diversely than ever before, the influence she held early in her career has not been forgotten. H. D. remains known to many as "the perfect Imagist."

Clearly the most influential figure in H. D.'s early years was Ezra Pound. The two met when H. D. was fifteen, he sixteen, reported Melody Zajdel in the *Dictionary of Literary Biography*, and they were briefly engaged to be married until H. D.'s father broke up the relationship. Still, they continued to share their love of literature, classical as well as modern, with Pound encouraging H. D. by bringing books for her to read. Pound also introduced her to a close friend, William Carlos Williams. Pound, Williams, H. D., and H. D.'s Bryn Mawr classmate, Marianne Moore, as undergraduates discussed and developed the literary theories that would lead each of them to play a distinct role in changing the course of American poetry.

In 1906 H. D. left Bryn Mawr because of poor health. She continued to study on her own and began to write seriously for the first time. When Pound left the United States for Europe in 1908, publishing his first book in Venice and joining the literary circles in London, H. D. stayed behind, contributing poems, stories, and articles to a variety of newspapers and small journals.

She fell under Pound's influence again in 1911. She had left on a summer vacation to Europe, where she eventually settled permanently, and met Pound in London. There she was introduced to many of his literary friends, among them Ford Maddox Ford, William Butler Yeats, F. S. Flint, and Richard Aldington. But Pound, at first, remained most influential: "I had never heard of *verse libre*," she once noted of this time.

H. D., Pound, Flint, and Aldington formed the core of what became known as the Imagist movement. Living in Europe and publishing in the United States through *Poetry,* the group shaped the course of modern poetry. They abandoned the formalities of the poetry of the time as they set forth their Imagist tenets, calling for an economical verse in the language of common speech, composed "in sequence of the musical phrase, not in sequence of a metronome." Many saw the Imagists as innovators of poetic form. But to many readers, the new poetry was scandalous. In fact, the Imagists made poetry news and *Poetry* the subject of newspaper editorials and indignant letters.

Though H. D. wrote in the Imagist mode throughout much of her career, the movement itself was short-lived. Pound, who by some accounts invented the school solely to bring attention to H. D.'s work, drifted away from the movement's center and was replaced by Amy Lowell. (Disgusted with Lowell's influence in the group, Pound then dubbed the school "Amygism.") When the last of the group's collections, *Some Imagist Poets,* was published in 1917, it was accompanied with an explanation that its contributors could better establish their own direction as writers independent of the Imagist label. H. D. herself would later place the movement that had given her a name in a lowered perspective.

The highlight of H. D.'s personal life during these years was her relationship with fellow Imagist Richard Aldington. The two married in 1913, bonded by what Zajdel called a "mutual interest in classical literature, a mutual contempt of middle-class hypocrisy, and a mutual dedication to careers in poetry." They appeared to those around them as happy, but that joy was interrupted by World War I. Aldington went into service in 1916 while H. D. assumed his post as literary editor of the *Egoist.* Upon his return, however, their relationship began to deteriorate, leaving H. D. alone to endure a most difficult period of her life.

In addition to her marital problems, H. D. faced other serious personal crises. In 1918 her brother was killed in action in France. Later that year, in poor health and pregnant for the second time—her first pregnancy had ended in miscarriage—H. D. separated from Aldington. Her daughter Perdita was born in 1919; but also in that year H. D.'s father died. H. D.'s despondency was broken only with the help of a new friend, Winifred Ellerman, known pseudonymously as Bryher.

H. D.'s relationship with Bryher was the "single bright spot" of the time, reported Zajdel. Bryher stabilized her friend during her emotional crises, and offered H. D. encouragement as a writer as well. The two had met after Bryher had sent H. D. a letter praising *Sea Garden,* and Bryher continued to compliment H. D.'s work. In her book *The Heart to Artemis: A Writer's Memoirs,* Bryher called H. D.'s collection *Hymen* "a beacon to those who, in a destructive age, believe in life." H. D., in turn, provided Bryher the encouragement she needed to pursue her own writing, and Bryher eventually became a successful novelist. Between 1919 and 1923 the two also traveled extensively, to Greece, Egypt, and America, spending most of their time in London between travels. H. D. finally settled in Switzerland in 1924.

By that time, the publication of *Hymen* and *Heliodora* had given H. D.'s poetry a significant platform from which to be judged. Readers praised her work for its economy of language and its precision but also detected hints of emotion uncharacteristic of much Imagist work. Whether she chose as her subjects symbols from the Hellenic world or objects taken from nature, she fused her abilities to create and to control.

The publication of *Collected Poems* in 1925 is considered a watershed in H. D.'s career. The book helped establish her reputation by bringing into one volume all of her poems and translations. To some, such as William Carlos Williams, *Collected Poems* was warmly received for presenting all of H. D.'s work together. But at the same time, as Vincent Quinn suggested in *Hilda Doolittle (H. D.),,* the book did H. D. one particular disservice: "The title suggests the end rather than the beginning of her career."

Aside from the publication of *Collected Poems,* the mid-1920s was marked by several other shifts in H. D.'s career. During this time she abandoned the active literary life of the expatriate circles and moved to Switzerland, which would remain her "permanent" home. Also during the 1920s H. D. changed the focus of her writing, broadening into some different types of poetry as well as into drama and fiction.

Though H. D. impressed some readers with her first two books of fiction, critics at the same time found them lacking. Her three-story collection *Palimpsest* "is a repository for the themes H. D. would explore throughout the rest of her career," declared Zajdel. Specifically, H. D. was concerned with the artist's search for identity and the role of the artist in society. In her second work of fiction, *Hedylus,* she explored a mother-son relationship. Praise for these works centered around her "exquisite" prose and the beauty of her presentation. Reservations about them, on the other hand, pointed to their difficult and exclusive nature. For example, writing in the *New York Times,* Babette Deutsch called *Palimpsest* a book "for poets and patient intellectuals." Deutsch added, however, that "to dismiss it as caviar would be to emphasize its delicacy at the expense of its indubitable strength."

During the 1930s H. D. published little while living privately in Switzerland. A major influence on her during this time was the psychoanalysis she submitted to under the guidance of Sigmund Freud. H. D. first sought Freud's help in 1933 and visited him again a year later, and she published her recollections of the experience in her 1956 book, *Tribute to Freud.* "Essentially," said Quinn, "the work is a self-portrait brought into focus by her confrontation with Freud." Freud helped H. D. to understand her dreams, Quinn reported, but the two differed in their beliefs regarding immortality. As H. D. herself wrote, Freud's argument was that a "belief in the soul's survival, in a life after death . . . was the last and greatest phantasy." H. D., in contrast, longed "for the Absolute," said Quinn. "She clung to the faith that the shortcomings of time would be overcome in eternity."

H. D. regained some attention as a poet with the release of the separate volumes of her "war trilogy" in the mid-1940s. Her most recent major publication before that, *Red Roses for Bronze* (1929), had been noted for some stylistic innovations, but the volume had also, according to Zajdel, "marked the end of H. D.'s popularity with the public." While the trilogy did not bring her immediate fame, it was evidence of a renewed creative vigor.

In *The Walls Do Not Fall,* the first volume of the trilogy, H. D. asserts her idealism—her belief in man's union with God—in the face of war. *Tribute to the Angels* follows that same theme, focusing on the conflict between faith and war. With her faith firmly established, H. D. then seeks in *Flowering of the Rod* to achieve a mystical vision, "a transcendental union with God." This section of the trilogy has been criticized for being too mystical; but, as Quinn noted, "although the reader may be dismayed by H. D.'s theology, his sympathy is almost certain to be aroused by the candor and intensity of her quest for a religious experience."

Corresponding with the power of H. D.'s vision was an equally strong poetic presentation. In *A Short History of American Poetry,* Donald Barlow Stauffer remarked: "There are in these poems the same qualities found in the verse written more than a decade earlier, precision of image and word, directness of statement, but with a sureness and evenness of tone that show how firmly she was in control of the world she had chosen to re-create."

After World War II H. D. returned to Switzerland, where she wrote her third major work of fiction, *Bid Me to Live.* The novel is her roman à clef about life in London in the 1920s. "I am Julia," she told *Newsweek* interviewer Lionel Durand of her connection with the novel's protagonist in 1960, "and all the others are real people." Specifically, "all the others" include D. H. Lawrence, his wife, and Aldington. In the novel Julia's marriage dissolves and she becomes involved in a platonic relationship with another man. When that man withdraws from her, Julia's solution, said Zajdel, "is a dedication to her life as an artist and an affirmation of her identity as a creator and poet. As a result, the theme of artist as hero who will prevail if the artist remains dedicated to his or her art is prevalent throughout H. D.'s work."

H. D. offered a different sort of optimism in her last major poetic work, *Helen in Egypt.* A book-length mixture of poetry and prose composed in three parts, *Helen in Egypt* is the author's recreation of the Helen-Achilles myth. Her theme, said Quinn, "is stark and transcendental: the perfect love that she and Achilles seek is to be found in death: 'the dart of Love / is the dart of Death.'" Horace Gregory reinforced this notion in his introduction to the 1974 edition of *Helen in Egypt* when he said "her overlying theme . . . is one of rebirth and resurrection." *Helen in Egypt* is also important as a representative display of the themes and techniques H. D. employed throughout her career. Many critics agreed with Emily Stipes Watts who wrote in *The Poetry of American Women from 1632 to 1945* that "*Helen in Egypt* is the climax of H. D.'s career both intellectually and poetically."

Interestingly, a novel H. D. had written around 1930 but never published was finally made available in 2000. *Pilate's Wife* tells the story of Pontius Pilate from the viewpoint of his wife, Claudia, who H. D. calls "Veronica" in the novel. Bored with her life in the Roman court, Veronica has various lovers and intrigues. When she finally seeks the help of a seer, her life is changed to the point that Veronica determines to help Jesus escape execution. *Library Journal* contributor Melanie C. Duncan noted that, "Although the story would have been shocking had it been published in its time, today it will interest only H. D. scholars at best." Writing on the *Elima Books* Web site, B. Renner noted, "The novel, much less a reinvestigation of Christian origins than a character study, moves as Veronica herself moves, languidly, with dignity, detachment, and an ironic suspicion of the ineffable."

Though few would argue about H. D.'s importance as an influence on modern poetry, there continues to be debate regarding the lasting merits of her work. Readers have been deterred from much of H. D.'s writing because of the preciousness of her language, the abundance of mythology, and the limited world of her focus. And though she did broaden her subject range after World War II, she did so at the expense of the clarity and conciseness that had been her trademark. Still, her technical achievements, her poignant portrayals of her personal struggles, and the beauty of her work continue to earn her poetry and fiction a significant amount of praise.

To many, H. D. will be remembered as "a poets' poet." "To be 'a poets' poet,'" said Gregory, "has few tangible rewards, for this means that the poet who holds that title must often wait upon the future for true recognition." For the time being, however, H. D.'s achievement has been measured in comparison with the "major poets of the twentieth century," asserted Hyatt H. Waggoner in *American Poets from the Puritans to the Present*, "or at least with those in some sort of second category, like [Conrad] Aiken or [Archibald] MacLeish or [John Crowe] Ransom." And in the process of gaining her stature, "the notes she made in her journey, in her poems, compose one of the really distinguished bodies of work of this century."

BIOGRAPHICAL AND CRITICAL SOURCES:

BOOKS

Aldington, Richard, *Life for Life's Sake: A Book of Reminiscences,* Viking (New York, NY), 1941.

Bryher, *The Heart to Artemis: A Writer's Memoirs,* Harcourt (New York, NY), 1962.

Coffman, Stanley K., *Imagism: A Chapter for the History of Modern Poetry,* University of Oklahoma Press (Norman, OK), 1950.

Contemporary Literary Criticism, Gale (Detroit, MI), Volume 3, 1975, Volume 8, 1978, Volume 14, 1980, Volume 31, 1985, Volume 34, 1985.

Dictionary of Literary Biography, Gale (Detroit, MI), Volume 4: *American Writers in Paris, 1920-39,* 1980, Volume 45: *American Poets, 1880-1945,* 1986.

Edmunds, Susan, *Out of Line: History, Psychoanalysis, and Montage in H.D.'s long poems,* Stanford University Press (Palo Alto, CA), 1994.

Ellmann, Richard, and Robert O'Clair, editors, *The Norton Anthology of Modern Poetry,* Norton (New York, NY), 1973.

Foster, Damon S., *Amy Lowell,* Houghton Mifflin (New York, NY), 1935.

Gregory, Eileen, *H. D. and Hellenism: Classic Lines,* Cambridge University Press (New York, NY), 1997.

Gregory, Horace, and Marya Zaturenska, *A History of American Poetry: 1900-1940,* Harcourt (New York, NY), 1942.

Guest, Barbara, *Herself Defined: The Poet H. D. and Her World,* Doubleday (New York, NY), 1984.

H. D., *Helen in Egypt,* introduction by Horace Gregory, New Directions (New York, NY), 1974.

Holland, Norman N., *Poems in Persons: An Introduction to the Psychoanalysis of Literature,* Norton (New York, NY), 1973.

Hughes, Glenn, *Imagism and the Imagists,* Humanities Press (Atlantic Highlands, NJ), 1931.

Laity, Cassandra, *H. D. and the Victorian Fin de Siècle: Gender, Modernism, Decadence,* Cambridge University Press (New York, NY), 1996.

Lawrence, D. H., *A Composite Biography,* three volumes, University of Wisconsin Press (Madison, WI), 1957-59.

Perkins, David, *A History of Modern Poetry: From the 1890s to the High Modernist Mode,* Harvard University Press (Cambridge, MA), 1976.

Quinn, Vincent, *Hilda Doolittle (H. D.),* Twayne (New York, NY), 1967.

Robinson, Janice S., *H. D.: The Life and Work of an American Poet,* Houghton Mifflin (Boston, MA), 1982.

Stauffer, Donald Barlow, *A Short History of American Poetry,* Dutton (New York, NY), 1974.

Swann, Thomas Burnett, *The Classical World of H. D.,* University of Nebraska Press (Lincoln, NE), 1962.

Sword, Helen, *Engendering Inspiration: Visionary Strategies in Rilke, Lawrence, and H. D.,* University of Michigan Press (Ann Arbor, MI), 1995.

Waggoner, Hyatt H., *American Poets from the Puritans to the Present,* Houghton Mifflin (Boston, MA), 1968.

Watts, Emily Stipes, *The Poetry of American Women from 1632 to 1945,* University of Texas Press (Austin, TX), 1977.

White, Eric Walter, *Images of H. D.,* Enitharmon (London, England), 1976.

PERIODICALS

Agenda, autumn, 1974.
Best Sellers, February 15, 1974; June, 1975.
Books, February 14, 1932.
Christian Science Monitor, October 26, 1961.
College English, March, 1975.
Commonweal, April 18, 1958.
Contemporary Literature, autumn, 1969; spring, 1978.
Essays in Criticism, July, 1977.
Library Journal, June 1, 2000, Melanie C. Duncan, review of *Pilate's Wife,* p. 106.
Mississippi Quarterly, fall, 1962.
Nation, April 26, 1922, November 12, 1924; August 19, 1925; October 8, 1973.
Literary Review, May 23, 1925; November 27, 1926.
New Republic, January 2, 1929; February 16, 1974.
Newsweek, May 2, 1960.
New York Herald Tribune Book Review, November 28, 1926; June 12, 1960.
New York Times, August 31, 1924; November 21, 1926; November 18, 1928; January 31, 1932; July 31, 1949; September 22, 1957.

New York Times Book Review, May 1, 1960; December 24, 1961.
Poetry, March, 1922; November, 1932; April, 1947; January, 1958; June, 1962; June, 1974.
Poetry Nation, number 4, 1975.
Saturday Review, May 28, 1960.
Saturday Review of Literature, January 1, 1927; December 22, 1928; December 29, 1945; February 22, 1947; August 20, 1949.
Sewanee Review, spring, 1948.
Spectator, February 25, 1922; December 31, 1931.
Times Literary Supplement, July 3, 1924; July 27, 1946; March 23, 1973; March 15, 1974.
Triquarterly, spring, 1968.
Weekly Book Review, October 1, 1944.

ONLINE

Elimae Books, http://elimae.com/ (April 4, 2004), B. Renner, review of *Pilate's Wife.*

OBITUARIES:

PERIODICALS

Newsweek, October 9, 1961.
New York Times, September 29, 1961.
Publishers Weekly, October 23, 1961.
Time, October 6, 1961.*

*   *   *

DOYLE, A. Conan
    See DOYLE, Arthur Conan

*   *   *

DOYLE, Arthur Conan 1859-1930
    (A. Conan Doyle, Conan Doyle)

PERSONAL: Born May 22, 1859, in Edinburgh, Scotland; died of a heart attack, July 7, 1930, in Crowborough, Sussex, England; son of Charles Altamont (a civil servant and artist) and Mary (Foley) Doyle; married Louise Hawkins, August 6, 1885 (died, 1906); married Jean Leckie, September 18, 1907; children:

(first marriage) Mary Louise, Kingsley; (second marriage) Denis, Adrian Malcolm, Lena Jean. *Education:* Edinburgh University, B.M., 1881, M.D., 1885.

CAREER: Novelist and physician. Assistant to physician in Birmingham, England, 1879; ship's surgeon on whaling voyage to Arctic, 1880; ship's surgeon on voyage to west coast of Africa, 1881-82; physician in Southsea, Portsmouth, England, 1882-90; ophthalmologist in London, England, 1891; writer. Lectured on spiritualism in Europe, Australia, the United States, and Canada, 1917-25, South Africa, 1928, and Sweden, 1929. *Wartime service:* Served during the Boer War as chief surgeon of a field hospital in Bloemfontein, South Africa, 1900.

MEMBER: British Society for Psychical Research.

AWARDS, HONORS: Knighted, 1902.

WRITINGS:

"SHERLOCK HOLMES" SERIES; DETECTIVE FICTION

A Study in Scarlet (novel; first published in *Beeton's Christmas Annual,* November, 1887; also see below), illustrated by father, Charles Doyle, Ward, Lock (London, England), 1888, Lippincott (Philadelphia, PA), 1890, published as *A Study in Scarlet: The First Book about Sherlock Holmes,* Ward, Lock, 1920, illustrated by Joseph A. Brown, Hart (New York, NY), 1976, introduction by Hugh Greene, Doubleday (Garden City, NY), 1977, edited and with an introduction by Owen Dudley Edwards, Oxford University Press (New York, NY), 1994, with an introduction by Iain Sinclair, Penguin (New York, NY), 2001, with an introduction by Anne Perry and notes by James Danly, Modern Library (New York, NY), 2003.

The Sign of Four (novel; first published in *Lippincott's Monthly,* February, 1890; also see below), Blackett, 1890, Collier (New York, NY), 1891, bound with *The Big Bow Mystery,* by Israel Zangwill, Scribner (New York, NY), 1928, introduction by Graham Greene, Doubleday (New York, NY), 1977, published as *The Sign of the Four,* Conkey, 1900, abridged version, edited by Elizabeth Fowler, illustrated by Leonard Vosburgh, Hart (New York, NY), 1960, illustrated by Frank Bolle,

Lion Books, 1973, published as *The Sign of the Four; or, The Problem of the Sholtos,* introduction by P. G. Wodehouse, Ballantine (New York, NY), 1975, edited and with an introduction by Christopher Roden, Oxford University Press (New York, NY), 1994, with an introduction by Peter Ackroyd and notes by Ed Glinert, Penguin (New York, NY), 2001.

The Adventures of Sherlock Holmes (short stories; also see below), illustrated by Sidney Paget, Harper (New York, NY), 1892, with a new introduction, A & W Visual Library, 1975, with an introduction by Steven Marcus, Schocken (New York, NY), 1976, illustrated by Richard Lebenson, with an afterword by Fred Strebeigh, Reader's Digest (Pleasantville, NY), 1987, with an afterword by Peter Glassman, illustrated by Barry Moser, Morrow (New York, NY), 1992, edited and with an introduction by Richard Lancelyn Green, Oxford University Press (New York, NY), 1994.

The Memoirs of Sherlock Holmes (short stories; also see below), illustrated by Sidney Paget, Newnes (London, England), 1893, revised edition, illustrated by W. H. Hyde and Sidney Paget, Harper (New York, NY), 1894, with an introduction by Kingsley Amis, J. Murray (London, England), 1974, with an introduction by Leslie Fielder, Schocken (New York, NY), 1976, with an afterword by George Fletcher and illustrated by Sergio Martinez, Reader's Digest (Pleasantville, NY), 1988, edited and with an introduction by Christopher Roden, Oxford University Press (New York, NY), 1994.

A Scandal in Bohemia (also see below), Munro (New York, NY), 1895.

Sign of the Four, a Scandal in Bohemia, and Other Stories, Burt (New York, NY), 1900.

The Hound of the Baskervilles (novel; serialized in *Strand* magazine, 1901-02), illustrated by Sidney Paget, McClure, Phillips (New York, NY), 1902, with an introduction by Frank Condie Baxter, Doubleday, Page (Garden City, NY), 1926, illustrated by Gil Walter, Looking Glass Library (New York, NY), 1961, with an introduction by James Nelson, Dodd, Mead (New York, NY), 1968, published as *The Hound of the Baskervilles: Another Adventure of Sherlock Holmes: A Facsimile of the Adventure As It Was First Published in the Strand Magazine, London,,* introduction by Samuel Rosenberg, Schocken (New York, NY), 1975, with foreword and afterword by John Fowles, Doubleday (Garden City, NY), 1977, with photographs by Michael Kenna, Arion Press (San Francisco, CA), 1985, illustrated by Sidney Paget and Sergio Martinez, Portland House Illustrated Classics (New York, NY), 1988, published as *The Hound of the Baskervilles: Another Adventure of Sherlock Holmes,* edited and with an introduction by W. W. Robson, Oxford University Press (New York, NY), 1994, edited with an introduction and notes by Christopher Frayling, Penguin Books (New York, NY), 2001, with an afterword by Anne Perry, Signet (New York, NY), 2001, excerpt published as *The Hound of the Baskervilles: Chapter 11,* Baker Street Irregulars (New York, NY), 2001, with an introduction by Laurie R. King and notes by James Danly, Modern Library (New York, NY), 2002.

The Return of Sherlock Holmes (short stories; also see below), illustrated by Charles Raymond Macauley, McClure, Phillips (New York, NY), 1905, with an introduction by Angus Wilson, J. Murray (London, England), 1974, Penguin (New York, NY), 1987, illustrated by David Johnson, with an afterword by John L. Cobbs, Reader's Digest (Pleasantville, NY), 1991, published as *The Return of Sherlock Holmes: A Facsimile of the Stories As They Were First Published in the Strand Magazine, London,* with an introduction by Samuel Rosenberg, Schocken (New York, NY), 1975.

Study in Scarlet, and, The Sign of Four, with a note by Dr. Joseph Bell, Appleton (New York, NY), 1902, reprinted, Dover (Mineola, NY), 2003.

Stories of Sherlock Holmes, Harper (New York, NY), 1904.

The Valley of Fear (novel; serialized in *Strand* magazine, 1914-15; also see below), illustrated by Arthur I. Keller, Doran (New York, NY), 1914, with an introduction by Len Deighton, Doubleday (Garden City, NY), 1977, with an introduction by Owen Dudley Edwards, Oxford University Press (New York, NY), 1994, published as *The Valley of Fear: A Sherlock Holmes Novel,* illustrated by Arthur I. Keller, Doran, 1915.

His Last Bow: Some Reminiscences of Sherlock Holmes (short stories; also see below), J. Murray (London, England), 1917, with an introduction by Julian Symons, 1974, edited and with an introduction by Owen Dudley Edwards, Oxford University Press (New York, NY), 1994, published as *His Last Bow: A Reminiscence of Sherlock Holmes,* Doran (New York, NY), 1917, reprinted, Sun Dial Press (Garden City, NY), 1937.

The Case-Book of Sherlock Holmes (short stories; also see below), Doran (New York, NY), 1927, illus-

trated by Don Irwin, Children's Press (Chicago, IL), 1968, with an introduction by C. P. Snow, J. Murray (London, England), 1974, with an introduction by W. W. Robson, Oxford University Press (New York, NY), 1994.

Sherlock Holmes: His Adventures, Memoirs, Return, His Last Bow, and The Case-Book, J. Murray (London, England), 1929.

Sherlock Holmes: A Study in Scarlet, The Sign of Four, The Hound of the Baskervilles, The Valley of Fear, the Complete Long Stories, J. Murray (London, England), 1929.

The Complete Sherlock Holmes, Doubleday, Doran (Garden City, NY), 1930, reprinted, Doubleday (New York, NY), 1953.

Tales of Sherlock Holmes, Burt (New York, NY), 1906, with an afterword by Clifton Fadiman, illustrated by Harvey Dinerstein, Macmillan (New York, NY), 1963.

Sherlock Homes and Dr. Watson: A Textbook of Friendship, edited by Christopher Morley, Harcourt (New York, NY), 1944.

Cases of Sherlock Holmes, Webster (St. Louis, MO), 1947.

Sherlock Holmes: Selected Stories, edited and with an introduction by S. C. Roberts, Oxford University Press (New York, NY), 1951, reprinted, 1998.

The Later Adventures of Sherlock Holmes, definitive text, corrected and edited by Edgar W. Smith, illustrated by Frederic Dorr Steele, Sidney Paget, and others, Limited Editions Club (New York, NY), 1952.

A Treasury of Sherlock Holmes, Hanover House (Garden City, NY), 1955.

Sherlock Holmes Investigates, selected and with an introduction by Michael Hardwick and Mollie Hardwick, illustrated by Sidney Paget, J. Murray (London, England), 1963, Lothrop, Lee & Shephard (New York, NY), 1967.

Sherlock Holmes, Detective, with a preface by Raymond T. Bond, Dodd, Mead (New York, NY), 1965.

Sherlock Holmes' Greatest Cases, introduction by Howard Haycraft, F. Watts (New York, NY), 1966.

The Annotated Sherlock Holmes: The Four Novels and the Fifty-six Short Stories Complete, edited with introduction, notes, and bibliography by William S. Baring-Gould, illustrated by Charles Doyle and others, C. N. Potter (New York, NY), 1967.

Red-headed League, and The Adventure of the Speckled Band (also see below), illustrated by Paul

Spina, F. Watts (New York, NY), 1968, reprinted, Creative Education (Mankato, MN), 1990.

My Life with Sherlock Holmes: Conversations in Baker Street by John H. Watson, M.D., edited by J. R. Hamilton, Murray (London, England), 1968, Hawthorn Books (New York, NY), 1976.

The Illustrated Sherlock Holmes Treasury, Avenel Books (New York, NY), 1976, published as *The Illustrated Sherlock Holmes Treasury,* illustrated by Sidney Paget, George Hutchingon, and Frank H. Townsend, C. N. Potter (New York, NY), 1984, revised and expanded edition published as *Great Works of Sir Arthur Conan Doyle: The Illustrated Sherlock Holmes Treasury,* Chatham River Press (New York, NY), 1986.

The Sherlock Holmes Illustrated Omnibus, illustrated by Sidney Paget, with introductions by Steven Marcus, Leslie Fiedler, and Samuel Rosenberg, Schocken (New York, NY), 1976.

The Best of Sherlock Holmes, Franklin Library (Franklin Center, PA), 1977.

The Sherlock Holmes Book of Quotations: Being a Compilation of the Words of Wit and Wisdom Spoken by the World's First Consulting Detective: And Including the Observations of His Friend and Biographer, John H. Watson, M.D.: With a Selection of the More Memorable Remarks Made by Their Intimates and Acquaintances, compiled and classified by Bruce R. Beaman, Gaslight (Bloomington, IN), 1980.

The Uncollected Sherlock Holmes (short stories), compiled by Richard Lancelyn Green, Penguin Books, 1983.

Sherlock Holmes (selections), illustrated by Sidney Paget, George Hutchinson, and Frank H. Townsend, Chatham River Press (New York, NY), 1983.

Mysteries of Sherlock Holmes, New American Library (New York, NY), 1985, illustrated by Paul Bachem, Grosset & Dunlap (New York, NY), 1996.

A Study in Scarlet [and] The Hound of the Baskervilles, illustrated by Greg Spalenka, afterword by G. K. Chesterton, Reader's Digest (Pleasantville, NY), 1986.

Baker Street Dozen, edited by P. J. Doyle and E. W. McDiarmid, Congdon & Weed (New York, NY), 1987.

The Speckled Band, illustrated by Dean Morrissey, St. Martin's Press (New York, NY), 1987.

Sherlock Holmes Reader (includes "The Red-headed League" and "The Adventure of the Speckled Band"), Courage Books (Philadelphia, PA), 1994, published as *The Sir Arthur Conan Doyle Reader: From Sherlock Holmes to Spiritualism,* edited by Jeffrey Meyers and Valerie Meyers, Cooper Square Press (New York, NY), 2002.

Sherlock Holmes: Two Complete Adventures (miniature edition), Running Press (Philadelphia, PA), 1989.

Six Great Sherlock Holmes Stories, Dover (Mineola, NY), 1992.

The Best Sherlock Holmes Stories, Hearthstone (Munslow, Shropshire, England), 1995.

Sherlock Holmes, illustrated by Sidney Paget, Knopf (New York, NY), 1996.

Selected Adventures of Sherlock Holmes, introduction by E. D. Hirsch, Jr., Core Knowledge Foundation (Charlottesville, VA), 1997.

The Quotable Sherlock Holmes, selected and with an introduction by John H. Watson III, Mysterious Press (New York, NY), 2000.

Favorite Sherlock Holmes Detective Stories, Dover (Mineola, NY), 2000.

Sherlock Holmes: The Complete Illustrated Short Stories, Chancellor Press (London, England), 2000.

The Valley of Fear and Selected Cases, introduction by Charles Palliser, notes by Ed Gliners, Penguin (New York, NY), 2001.

Sherlock Holmes: The Complete Illustrated Novels, Chancellor Press (London, England), 2001.

The Adventures of Sherlock Holmes and The Memoirs of Sherlock Holmes, Penguin (New York, NY), 2001.

Quotable Sherlock, compiled and edited by David W. Barber, illustrated by Sidney Paget, Quotable Press (Toronto, Ontario, Canada), 2001.

A Study in Scarlet; and, The Sign of Four, Dover (Mineola, NY), 2003.

Collected Sherlock Holmes, with an introduction and notes by Kyle Freeman, Barnes & Noble Classics (New York, NY), 2003.

A Study in Scarlet, and, The Sign of Four, Dover (Mineola, NY), 2003.

The New Annotated Sherlock Holmes, edited and with a preface and noted by Leslie S. Klinger, introduction by John le Carré, Norton (New York, NY), 2004.

NOVELS

Beyond the City, Wm. L. Allison (New York, NY), c. 1870s, published as *Beyond the City: The Idyll of a Suburb,* illustrated by Pamela Mattix, afterword by Howard Lachtman, Gaslight (Bloomington, IN), 1982.

The Mystery of Cloomber, Ward & Downey, 1889, Munro (New York, NY), 1895, illustrated by Paul M. McCall, afterword by Jack Tracy, Gaslight (Bloomington, IN), 1980.

The Firm of Girdlestone (semiautobiographical), Lovell (New York, NY), 1890, illustrated by Paul M. McCall, afterword by Jack Tracy, Gaslight (Bloomington, IN), 1980.

The Doings of Raffles Haw (serialized in *Answers,* 1891-92), Lovell (New York, NY), 1891, illustrated by Paul M. McCall, afterword by John Bennett Shaw, Gaslight (Bloomington, IN), 1981.

The Parasite, Constable (London, England), 1894, published as *The Parasite: A Story,* illustrated by Howard Pyle, Harper (New York, NY), 1895.

The Stark Munro Letters: Being a Series of Sixteen Letters Written by J. Stark Munro, M.B., to his Friend and Former Fellow-Student, Herbert Swanborough, of Lowell, Massachusetts, during the Years 1881-1884 (autobiographical; also see below), Appleton (New York, NY), 1895, with an afterword by C. Frederick Kittle, illustrated by Lisa Rivard, Gaslight (Bloomington, IN), 1982.

Rodney Stone, illustrated by Sidney Paget, Appleton (New York, NY), 1896, reprinted, J. Murray (London, England), 1963.

The Tragedy of the Korosko (see also below), illustrated by Sidney Paget, Smith, Elder, 1898, reprinted, Gaslight (Bloomington, IN), 1983, published as *A Desert Drama: Being the Tragedy of the Korosko,* Lippincott (Philadelphia, PA), 1898.

A Duet with an Occasional Chorus, Appleton (New York, NY), 1899, with an afterword by Peter E. Blau, illustrated by Michele Lauber, Gaslight (Bloomington, IN), 1990.

Tragedy of the Korosko, and The Green Flag, and Other Stories of War and Sport, Appleton (New York, NY), 1902.

The Lost World: Being an Account of the Recent Amazing Adventures of Professor George E. Challenger, Lord John Roxton, Professor Summerlee, and Mr. E. D. Malone of the Daily Gazette (also see below), Burt (New York, NY), 1912, illustrated by Gil Walker, Looking Glass Library (New York, NY), 1959, with an introduction and notes by Robert L. Wilson and Richard Adams, Longman (London, England), 1980, edited and with an introduction and notes by Ian Duncan, Oxford University Press (New York, NY), 1995, with an introduction

by Michael Crichton and notes by Julia Houston, Modern Library (New York, NY), 2003.

The Poison Belt (also see below), illustrated by Harry Rountree, Doran (New York, NY), 1913, with an introduction by John Dickson Carr and epilogue by Harlow Shapley, Macmillan (New York, NY), 1964, with an introduction by Katya Reimann, University of Nebraska Press (Lincoln, NE), 2001.

The Adventure of the Six Napoleons, Collier (New York, NY), 1917.

The Dealings of Captain Sharkey, Doran (New York, NY), 1925.

The Land of Mist, Hutchinson (London, England), 1925, Doran (New York, NY), 1926.

Sir Arthur Conan Doyle: Three Adventure Novels (contains *The Lost World, The Poison Belt,* and *The White Company*), Gramercy (Avenel, NJ), 1996.

The Lost World; and, The Poison Belt: Professor Challenger Adventures, introduction by William Gibson, Chronicle Books (San Francisco, CA), 1989.

Sir Arthur Conan Doyle: Three Adventure Novels, Gramercy Books (Avenel, NJ), 1996.

The Haunted Grange of Goresthorpe, Arthur Conan Doyle Society (Ashcroft, British Columbia, Canada), 2000.

HISTORICAL NOVELS

Micah Clarke: His Statement As Made to His Three Grandchildren, Joseph, Gervas, and Reuben, during the Hard Winter of 1734, Harper (New York, NY), 1889, edited by Virginia Kirkus, illustrated by Henry C. Pitz, 1929.

The White Company (serialized in *Cornhill* magazine, 1891), Lovell (New York, NY), 1891, illustrated by George Willis Bardwell, Harper (New York, NY), 1922, illustrated by N. C. Wyeth, Cosmopolitan Book (New York, NY), 1922, illustrated by James Daughtery, Harper, 1929, with an introduction by Donald J. Harvey, Dodd, Mead (New York, NY), 1962, with an introduction by Anthony Burgess, J. Murray (London, England), illustrated by N. C. Wyeth, Morrow (New York, NY), 1988.

The Refugees: A Tale of Two Continents (serialized in *Harper's Monthly* magazine, 1893), illustrated by T. De Thulstrup, Harper (New York, NY), 1893, reprinted, Inheritance Publications (Pella, IA), 2004.

The Great Shadow (first published in *Arrowsmith's Christmas Annual,* 1892), Harper (New York, NY), 1893, reprinted, 1920.

Uncle Bernac: A Memory of the Empire, illustrated by Robert Sauber, Appleton (New York, NY), 1897, illustrated by John Mackay, J. Murray (London, England), 1968.

Sir Nigel: Boyhood of the Commander of the White Company (sequel to *The White Company;* serialized in *Strand* magazine, 1905-06), illustrated by Arthur Twidle, Smith, Elder (London, England), 1906, illustrated by the Kinneys, McClure, Phillips, 1906, illustrated by James Daugherty, Doubleday (Garden City, NY), 1931, with an introduction by Mary Renault, J. Murray (London, England), 1975, Hart Publishing (New York, NY), 1976.

Sir Arthur Conan Doyle: The Historical Romances, two volumes, New Orchard Editions (New York, NY), 1986.

SHORT STORIES

Mysteries and Adventures, Scott, 1890, published as *The Gully of Bluemansdyke and Other Stories,* 1892, published as *My Friend the Murderer and Other Mysteries and Adventures,* Lovell, Coryell (New York, NY), 1893, reprinted, Books for Libraries Press (Freeport, NY), 1971.

The Captain of the Polestar and Other Tales, Longmans, Green (London, England), 1890, Books for Libraries Press (Freeport, NY), 1970.

(With Campbell Rae Brown) *An Actor's Duel* [and] *The Winning Shot* (the former by Brown, the latter by Doyle), Dicks, 1894.

Round the Red Lamp: Being Facts and Fancies of Medical Life (horror; also see below), Appleton (New York, NY), 1894, reprinted, Books for Libraries Press (Freeport, NY), 1969.

The Surgeon of Gaster Fell (also see below), Ivers (New York, NY), 1895.

The Exploits of Brigadier Gerard (adventure), illustrated by W. B. Wollen, Appleton (New York, NY), 1896, reprinted, J. Murray (London, England), 1976, edited and with an introduction by Owen Dudley Edwards, Canongate Press (Edinburgh, Scotland), 1991.

The Green Flag and Other Stories of War and Sport (see also above), McClure (New York, NY), 1900, Books for Libraries Press (Freeport, NY), 1969.

The Stark-Munro Letters and Round the Red Lamp, Appleton (New York, NY), 1902.

Adventures of Gerard, illustrated by W. B. Wollen, McClure, Phillips (New York, NY), 1903, with an introduction by Elizabeth Longford, J. Murray (London, England), 1976, with an introduction by George MacDonald Fraser, published as *Exploits and Adventures of Brigadier Gerard,* New York Review Books (New York, NY), 2001.

Round the Fire Stories, McClure (New York, NY), 1908, reprinted, Chronicle Books (San Francisco, CA), 1991.

The Last Galley: Impressions and Tales, illustrated by N. C. Wyeth, Rountree, Paget (New York, NY), 1910, reprinted, J. Murray (London, England), 1931.

One Crowded Hour (also see below), Paget (New York, NY), 1911.

Danger! And Other Stories, J. Murray (London, England), 1918, Doran (New York, NY), 1919.

Three of Them: About Naughtiness and Frogs and Historical Pictures, Doran (New York, NY), 1919.

Tales of the Ring and Camp, J. Murray (London, England), 1922, published as *The Croxley Master and Other Tales of the Ring and Camp,* Doran (New York, NY), 1925.

Tales of Terror and Mystery, J. Murray (London, England), 1922, with an introduction by Nina Conan Doyle Harwood, illustrated by Barbara Ninde Byfield, Doubleday (Garden City, NY), 1977, reprinted, Trident Press International (Naples, FL), 2001, published as *The Black Doctor and Other Tales of Terror and Mystery,* Doran (New York, NY), 1925, reprinted, Buccaneer Books, 1982.

Tales of Twilight and the Unseen, J. Murray (London, England), 1922, published as *The Great Keinplatz Experiment and Other Tales of Twilight and the Unseen,* Doran (New York, NY), 1925.

Tales of Adventure and Medical Life, J. Murray (London, England), 1922, published as *The Man from Archangel and Other Tales of Adventure,* Doran (New York, NY), 1925, reprinted, Books for Libraries Press (Freeport, NY), 1969.

Tales of Long Ago, J. Murray (London, England), 1922, published as *The Last of the Legions and Other Tales of Long Ago,* Doran (New York, NY), 1925.

The Three of Them: A Reminiscence, J. Murray (London, England), 1923.

The Story of Spedegue's Dropper, Doubleday, Doran (New York, NY), 1929.

The Macarot Deep and Other Stories (also see below), Doubleday, Doran (New York, NY), 1929.

Conan Doyle's Stories for Boys, Cupples & Leon (New York, NY), 1938.

Sherlock Holmes, and Other Detective Stories, Illustrated Editions (New York, NY), 1941.

The Professor Challenger Stories (includes *The Lost World, The Poison Belt, The Land of Mist, The Disintegration Machine,* and *When the World Screamed*), J. Murray (London, England), 1952, published as *Complete Professor Challenger Stories,* Transatlantic, 1952.

Tales of Brigadier Gerard, illustrated by Eileen M. Hill, J. Murray (London, England), 1968.

The Ring of Thoth, and Other Stories, J. Murray (London, England), 1968.

The Maracot Deep, with an introduction by John Dickson Carr, Norton (New York, NY), 1968.

The Best Supernatural Tales of Arthur Conan Doyle, selected and with an introduction by E. F. Bleiler, Dover (New York, NY), 1979.

The Edinburgh Stories of Arthur Conan Doyle, Polygon Books (Edinburgh, Scotland), 1981.

Uncollected Stories: The Unknown Conan Doyle, compiled and with an introduction by John Michael Gibson and Richard Lancelyn Green, Doubleday (Garden City, NY), 1982.

Masterworks of Crime and Mystery, edited by Jack Tracy, Dial (New York, NY), 1982.

Conan Doyle Stories, Hippocrene Books, 1985.

Supernatural Tales of Sir Arthur Conan Doyle, edited and with an introduction by Peter Haining, W. Foulsham (New York, NY), 1987.

Strange Studies from Life and Other Narratives: The Complete True Crime Writings of Sir Arthur Conan Doyle, selected and edited by Jack Tracy, introduction by Peter Ruber, illustrated by Sidney Paget, Gaslight (Bloomington, IN), 1988.

The Best Horror Stories of Arthur Conan Doyle, edited by Frank D. McSherry, Martin H. Greenberg, and Charles G. Waugh, Academy Chicago (Chicago, IL), 1989.

Tales for a Winter's Night, Academy Chicago (Chicago, IL), 1989.

When the World Screamed and Other Stories, J. Murray (London, England), 1968, Chronicle Books (San Francisco, CA), 1990.

The Horror of the Heights and Other Tales of Suspense, Chronicle Books (San Francisco, CA), 1992.

The Collected Brigadier Gerard Stories, Hearthstone (Munslow, Shropshire, England), 1995.

The Lost World and Other Thrilling Tales, edited and with an introduction and notes by Philip Gooden, Penguin (New York, NY), 2001.

PLAYS

(With J. M. Barrie) *Jane Annie; or, The Good Conduct Prize* (comic opera; first produced in London, England, 1893), Chappell (London, England), 1893.

Foreign Policy (one-act; based on Doyle's short story "A Question of Diplomacy"), first produced in London, England, 1893.

Waterloo (one-act; based on Doyle's short story "A Straggler of '15"; first produced as *A Story of Waterloo* in Bristol, England, 1894), Samuel French (New York, NY), 1907.

Halves (prologue and three acts; based on the story by James Payn), first produced in Aberdeen, Scotland, 1899.

(With William Gillette) *Sherlock Holmes* (four-act; based on Doyle's short story "The Strange Case of Miss Faulkner"; first produced in London, England, 1899), Samuel French (New York, NY), 1922, Doubleday, Doran (New York, NY), 1932, definitive text corrected and edited by Edgar W. Smith, with an introduction by Vincent Starrett, Heritage Press (New York, NY), 1957.

A Duet (A Duologue) (one-act comedy; based on Doyle's novel *A Duet with an Occasional Chorus;* first produced in London, England, 1902), Samuel French (New York, NY), 1903.

Brigadier Gerard (four-act comedy; first produced in London, England, 1906), Gaslight (Bloomington, IN), 1986.

The Fires of Fate (four-act; based on Doyle's novel *The Tragedy of the Korosko*), first produced in Liverpool, England, 1909.

The House of Temperley, first produced in London, England, 1910.

A Pot of Caviare (one-act; based on Doyle's short story), first produced in London, England, 1910.

The Speckled Band: An Adventure of Sherlock Holmes (three-act; based on Doyle's short story "The Adventure of the Speckled Band"; first produced in London, England, 1910), Samuel French (New York, NY), 1912.

The Crown Diamond (one-act; first produced in Bristol, England, 1921), privately printed, 1958.

It's Time Something Happened (one-act), Appleton (New York, NY), 1925.

Exile: A Drama of Christmas Eve (one-act), Appleton (New York, NY), 1925.

Angels of Darkness: A Drama in Three Acts: A Facsimile of the Original Manuscript, edited by Peter E. Blau, Baker Street Irregulars in Cooperation with the Toronto Public Library (New York, NY), 2001.

Also author of *Sir Charles Tregellis, Admiral Denver, The Stonor Case, The Lift,* and *Mrs. Thompson* (based on the novel of the same title by W. B. Maxwell).

SPIRITUALISM

The New Revelation, Metropolitan Magazine (New York, NY), 1917, with introduction and afterword by George J. Lankevich, SquareOne Classics (Garden City, NY), 2001.

The Vital Message, Doran (New York, NY), 1919.

Spiritualism and Rationalism, Hodder & Stoughton (London, England), 1920.

The Wanderings of a Spiritualist, Doran (New York, NY), 1921, reprinted, Ronin (Berkeley, CA), 1988.

The Evidence for Fairies, Doran (New York, NY), 1921.

Fairies Photographed, Doran (New York, NY), 1921.

The Coming of the Fairies, Doran (New York, NY), 1922, reprinted, Weiser, 1972.

(With others) *The Case for Spirit Photography,* preface by Fred Barlow, Hutchinson (London, England), 1922, Doran (New York, NY), 1923.

Our American Adventure, Doran (New York, NY), 1923.

(Compiler) *The Spiritualists' Reader,* Two Worlds, 1924.

Our Second American Adventure, Little, Brown (Boston, MA), 1924.

(Contributor) James Marchant, editor, *Survival,* Putnam (New York, NY), 1924, Doyle's contribution published separately as *Psychic Experiences,* 1925.

The History of Spiritualism, two volumes, Doran (New York, NY), 1926, reprinted, Arno Press (New York, NY), 1975.

Pheneas Speaks: Direct Spirit Communications in the Family Circle, Doran (New York, NY), 1927.

Our African Winter, J. Murray (London, England), 1929.

The Roman Catholic Church: A Rejoinder, Psychic Press (London, England), 1929.

The Edge of the Unknown (essays), Putnam (New York, NY), 1930, reprinted, Time-Life Books (Alexandria, VA), 1991.

OTHER

Songs of Action (poetry; also see below), Doubleday & McClure (New York, NY), 1898.

The Great Boer War, McClure, Phillips (New York, NY), 1900, reprinted, Struik, 1976.

The War in South Africa: Its Cause and Conduct, McClure, Phillips (New York, NY), 1902.

The Story of Mr. George Edalji, privately printed, 1907, published as *The Case of Mr. George Edalji,* Blake, 1907.

Through the Magic Door (criticism), illustrated by W. Russell Flint, Smith, Elder (London, England), 1907, McClure (New York, NY), 1908, reprinted, Doubleday, Page (Garden City, NY), 1925.

The Crime of the Congo, Doubleday, Page (New York, NY), 1909.

The "Arch Adept" of the "First Degree," De Laurence, Scott (Chicago, IL), 1910.

Songs of the Road (poetry; also see below), Doubleday, Page (New York, NY), 1911.

The Passing of the Legions, Paget (New York, NY), 1911.

The Case of Oscar Slater, Hodder & Stoughton (New York, NY), 1912.

Great Britain and the Next War, Small, Maynard, 1914.

To Arms!, preface by F. E. Smith, Hodder & Stoughton (London, England), 1914.

The German War (essays), Hodder & Stoughton (London, England), 1914.

The Story of British Prisoners, Central Committee for National Patriotic Organization (London, England), 1915.

Western Wanderings, Doran (New York, NY), 1915.

A Visit to Three Fronts: June, 1916, Hodder & Stoughton (London, England), 1916, published as *A Visit to Three Fronts: Glimpses of the British, Italian, and French Lines,* Doran (New York, NY), 1916.

The Origin and Outbreak of the War, Doran (New York, NY), 1916.

The British Campaign in France and Flanders, six volumes, Doran (New York, NY), 1916-20, enlarged edition published as *The British Campaigns in Europe, 1914-1919,* Bles, 1928.

The Guards Came Through and Other Poems (also see below), J. Murray (London, England), 1919, Doran (New York, NY), 1920.

Fairies Photographed, Doran (New York, NY), 1921.

The Poems of Arthur Conan Doyle: Collected Edition (contains *Songs of Action, Songs of the Road,* and *The Guards Came Through and Other Poems*), J. Murray (London, England), 1922.

Memories and Adventures (autobiography), Little, Brown (Boston, MA), 1924, with a foreword by Richard Lancelyn Green, Greenhill Books (London, England), 1988.

(Translator from the French) Leon Denis, *The Mystery of Joan of Arc,* J. Murray (London, England), 1924, Dutton (New York, NY), 1925.

The Works of A. Conan Doyle: One Volume Edition, W. J. Black (New York, NY), 1928.

Strange Studies from Life: Containing Three Hitherto Uncollected Tales Based on the Annals of True Crime, additional material by Philip Trevor, edited and with an introduction by Peter Ruber, Candlelight Press, 1963.

Essays on Photography: The Unknown Conan Doyle, compiled with an introduction by John Michael Gibson and Richard Lancelyn Green, Secker & Warburg (London, England), 1982.

33, compiled and with an introduction by John Michael Gibson and Richard Lancelyn Green, Avenel Books (New York, NY), 1982.

The Adventure of the Priory School: A Facsimile of the Original Manuscript in the Marvin P. Epstein Sherlock Holmes Collection, introduction by Len Deighton, Santa Teresa Press (Santa Barbara, CA), 1985.

Letters to the Press, edited with an introduction by John Michael Gibson and Richard Lancelyn Green, University of Iowa Press (Iowa City, IA), 1986.

A Regimental Scandal: A Facsimile of the Manuscript, edited by Christopher Roden and Barbara Roden, with a foreword by Dame Jean Conan Doyle and an introduction by Richard Lancelyn Green, Arthur Conan Doyle Society (Penyffordd, Chester, England), 1995.

Contributor of works such as "The Truth sbout Sherlock Holmes" in a variety of genres to many magazines and newspapers, including *Strand, Chambers's Journal, Harper's, Blackwood's, Saturday Evening Post, McClure's, London Society, Cornhill, Lippincott's, Boston Herald, Philadelphia Inquirer, St. Louis Post-Dispatch,* and *New York Times.* Contributor to *What Irish Protestants Think: Speeches on Home Rule,* Irish Press Agency (Westminster, England).

ADAPTATIONS: Many of Doyle's works have been adapted for film, including *A Study in Scarlet, The Adventures of Sherlock Holmes, The Hound of the Baskervilles, His Last Bow, The Firm of Girdlestone,* and *The Exploits of Brigadier Gerard.* Doyle's writings have also been adapted for plays, television (including a series based on *The Lost World*), and filmstrips. Several stories, novels, and children's books have been based on the characters of Sherlock Holmes and others created by Doyle.

SIDELIGHTS: Arthur Conan Doyle is not considered to have been a great writer, but his work was great in one regard: he created one of the most famous characters in the history of fiction. Indeed, the name of Sherlock Holmes is synonymous with detective, and the deerstalker cap and calabash pipe suggest Holmes to people all over the world, even to those who have never read any of the four novels and fifty-six short stories Doyle wrote about him. Yet those kinds of cap and pipe are not mentioned and the phrase "Elementary, my dear Watson" is never uttered in any of the sixty tales. Interestingly, Holmes's more recognizable features were not even Doyle's creation; the hat was the creation of illustrator Sidney Paget; the pipe came from an actor who frequently performed the role of Sherlock Holmes in plays.

Many who are familiar with Sherlock Holmes have never heard of Doyle; to countless others, Doyle is known only as the author of the "Holmes" stories, despite the many other works he wrote during his career. What is true decades later was also very largely true during Doyle's lifetime, and this fact did not make him happy. He felt that he had better things to offer the world of literature than a series of detective stories; in particular, he considered his greatest achievements in fiction to be his historical novels. Outside the realm of fiction, Doyle believed that his most important writings were those in which he attempts to prove the truth of spiritualism and communication with the dead, a cause to which he devoted the last eleven years of his life. Doyle was so afraid that Holmes would distract his own and his readers' attention from what he considered his more important work that he killed the detective in one story, only to be forced by public demand to resurrect him later.

Although Doyle was not a great writer who communicated profound truths about the human condition, he was a good writer, with four principal areas of strength. First, his style is vigorous, clear, and readable. In fact, as he himself declared in a 1923 *Collier's* essay, "The Truth about Sherlock Holmes," his style might have been too clear: "I cultivate a simple style and avoid long words so far as possible, and it may be that this surface of ease has sometimes caused the reader to underrate the amount of real research which lies in all my historical novels." As Doyle biographer Ronald Pearsall put it in *Conan Doyle: A Biographical Solution:* "Doyle's style hardly altered for forty years. He sat down and wrote, unworried by the hesitations and concern for literary propriety that make 'artistic' novelists of his time (such as

George Moore) almost unreadable. He was never brainwashed by 'fine writing.'" Judging by the almost complete absence of revisions in his extant manuscripts, this style was as easy for him to write as it is to read.

Second, Doyle was able, through concise, sensuous description, to evoke atmosphere and a sense of place. Even today, tourists who visit London for the first time after reading the "Sherlock Holmes" stories often experience a feeling of familiarity, as though they had been there before. In the most famous of the "Holmes" novels, *The Hound of the Baskervilles,* the eeriness of the moors is vividly conveyed, and in certain passages of Doyle's historical novels, the reader is almost thrust bodily into the clang and crash of medieval hand-to-hand combat.

Third, Doyle could create memorable characters who, though not realistically drawn, are endowed with such striking personalities that they seem more real than many actual people. This believability applies not only to Sherlock Holmes, to whom mail, bearing his fictitious address, 221B Baker Street, London, is still sent, but applies also to such other Doyle heroes as Brigadier Etienne Gerard, Professor George Edward Challenger, and Sir Nigel Loring. At the same time, however, many of the minor characters in Doyle's fiction are not well defined or seem to be mere stock types: the innocent young woman, the unregenerate villain, the loyal companion, the stolid but bumbling Scotland Yard official.

Fourth, and perhaps most important, Doyle was a master storyteller. Even his weaker fictional efforts hold reader interest; when his plots are hackneyed and contain no real surprises—which is sometimes the case, even though Doyle prided himself on his ability to devise ingenious plots—the reader is carried along by the sheer power of the storyteller's art. In fact, this talent, like his lucid style, produced repercussions that were unwanted by Doyle: his historical novels, which he intended as authentic recreations of life in earlier periods and which were supposed to educate Englishmen in the history of their country, were treated by reviewers only as exciting adventure yarns.

Doyle was a professional writer, in the most complete sense of that term. After he gave up the practice of medicine in 1891, he lived and supported a large family on the income from his writing alone. By the 1920s he was the most highly paid writer in the world, commanding ten shillings a word. Market considerations occasionally entered into his decisions about what to write—especially in regard to the "Sherlock Holmes" stories, for which he was offered so much money that he was virtually forced to write them. But for the most part, he wrote what he wanted to write, and his choice was usually in harmony with what the public in Britain and America wanted to read. Most of his works appeared first in magazines and then in book form, so he was paid twice for each. His short stories were published in magazines and then collected in books; his novels were usually serialized in periodicals before appearing between hard covers. Doyle was also a professional author in the sense that he wrote almost constantly: on trains, in cabs, while posing for photographs, while carrying on a conversation at a party. According to his biographers, in his younger days, he could write without being distracted by one of his daughters crawling across his desk or even tearing up his manuscripts; later, he spent long hours behind a closed study door through which his children knew better than to try to enter. He kept diaries and notebooks, and most of his experiences and travels sooner or later provided material for published articles and books.

Doyle was also a professional in that he wrote in virtually every form and genre: detective stories, historical novels, science fiction, horror stories, domestic comedy, sports stories, poetry, and plays; he even collaborated on an operetta—one of his few failures. A significant portion of his writing is nonfiction, to which he brings the same stylistic and storytelling skills that made his fiction so popular. He was knighted not, as many people suppose, for writing the "Sherlock Holmes" stories, but for his pamphlet defending British actions in South Africa during the Boer War of 1899 to 1902. He also wrote histories of that war and of World War I, articles on military preparedness, literary criticism, histories and defenses of spiritualism, and vindications of men unjustly convicted of crimes.

In spite of his prodigious literary output, Doyle was by no means a retiring, closeted intellectual. He was a man of action, large in stature—six feet two inches tall, two hundred ten pounds in his prime—and an all-around athlete, proficient in rugby, boxing, and cricket; Doyle, his biographers claim, introduced the sport of skiing into Switzerland. Too old to fight in the Boer

War, he served as a surgeon with a privately financed hospital near the front in South Africa. During World War I he organized a volunteer rifle company—the forerunner of the modern Home Guard—and toured the front lines to gather material for his history of the conflict.

Doyle was a true man of his time: until his obsession with spiritualism began to make him look somewhat foolish, he was regarded on both sides of the Atlantic as the very symbol of British probity, stolidity, and common sense. He shared the prejudices of his time and place in his unswerving support of the British Empire, his steadfast opposition to women's suffrage, his unquestioning acceptance of the class system, and his hostility to labor unions and Mormons. On the other hand, he was a man behind his time in that he believed in and guided his behavior by a knightly code of honor. But he was also ahead of his time: he kept abreast of scientific discoveries, and he wrote articles and stories predicting the advent of such phenomena as television and submarine warfare.

Doyle's original career as a doctor gave him the inspiration for some of his later works. While attending Edinburgh University in the late 1870s, he met Dr. Joseph Bell, a surgeon who was able to deduce his patients' occupations and other information from observing their appearance. Bell became the model for Sherlock Holmes, as professor of physiology William Rutherford did for another Doyle character, Professor Challenger. The actual practice of medicine, which at that time was in the process of becoming a true science, may also have inspired Doyle. The very deductive skills—the ability to piece together seemingly unconnected bits of information—that allowed doctors to make proper diagnoses also allowed Doyle's fictional detective to solve crimes.

To help pay for his education, Doyle worked during vacations as an assistant to various doctors. The nephew of one of these physicians told Doyle that his letters were so vivid he ought to try to write something to sell. This encouragement launched Doyle's professional writing career. His first story was rejected, but the second, "The Mystery of Sasassa Valley," appeared anonymously in *Chambers's Journal* in 1879. It is the tale of three young adventurers in South Africa who investigate a native superstition about a demon with a glowing red eye and discover a huge diamond. Another story, "The American's Tale," written in imitation of the style of Bret Harte, was published in the Christmas, 1880, issue of *London Society*.

Doyle indulged his taste for real-life adventure by signing on as a ship's surgeon on a seven-month Arctic whaling and sealing expedition in 1880. As Pearsall commented, "His whaler types crop up time and time again in his stories, sometimes dressed up in army uniform." After receiving his bachelor of medicine degree in 1881, he sailed to Africa as a surgeon on a freighter. On his return, he wrote an account of the voyage for the *British Journal of Photography* and submitted short stories for publication in *London Society* and *Blackwood's*.

In 1886 Doyle decided to try his hand at penning a detective novel. He said later that all the detective fiction he had read was unsatisfactory because the solution of the mystery was made to depend on chance or on some flash of intuition by the detective. Doyle, as he declared in "The Truth about Sherlock Holmes," wanted to try to "reduce this fascinating but unorganized business to something nearer to an exact science." Influenced by Edgar Allen Poe's "Dupin" stories, the "Lecoq" novels of Emile Gaboriau, and Sergeant Cuff in Wilkie Collins's *The Moonstone*, Doyle began work on a novel he called "A Tangled Skein." His notes reveal that his detective protagonist was originally to be called "Sherrinford Holmes" and the narrator "Ormond Sacker"; but these names were quickly replaced by "Sherlock Holmes" and "John H. Watson, M.D." The title of the novel became *A Study in Scarlet*.

Doyle wrote the novel in three weeks during March and April, 1886, and sent it to the *Cornhill;* the editor, James Payn, liked but rejected it because it was too long to publish in one issue and too short to serialize. The novel was accepted by Ward, Lock for publication in their *Beeton's Christmas Annual* for 1887, more than a year away. They paid Doyle twenty-five pounds for the complete rights to the story—the only money he ever received for it. When *A Study in Scarlet* appeared, it caused no great stir; but the 1887 edition of *Beeton's Christmas Annual* sold out—it is now one of the rarest and most valuable publications in the world—and the novel received complimentary reviews in minor journals and newspapers. Ward, Lock republished it in book form in 1888 with six illustrations by Doyle's father, who had been in an asylum suffering from alcoholism since 1879.

In July of 1887 Doyle started work on the first of his historical novels, *Micah Clarke*, dealing with the duke of Monmouth's rebellion against his father, Charles II, in the seventeenth century. According to John Dickson Carr in *The Life of Sir Arthur Conan Doyle*, "The power of *Micah Clarke*, aside from its best action scenes—the bloodhounds on Salisbury Plain, the brush with the King's Dragoons, the fight in Wells Cathedral, the blinding battlepiece at Sedgemoor—still lies in its characterization: that other imagination, the use of homely detail, by which each character grows into life before ever a shot is fired in war." Charles Higham pointed out in *The Adventures of Conan Doyle: The Life of the Creator of Sherlock Holmes* that "the descriptions of war have a remarkable intensity, being alive with the author's love of battle"—at this time Doyle had never experienced a real war—but added that "the book suffers from deliberately antiquated 'period' diction in the dialogue and some of the descriptive material." Like many of Doyle's fictional works, the novel is narrated in the first person—in this case by Micah, a supporter of Monmouth. Doyle later claimed to have spent two years in research and five months in writing the book.

Micah Clarke received enthusiastic reviews when it was published in February, 1889, and Doyle immediately began work on another historical novel, *The White Company*, set in the fourteenth century. Between researching and writing *The White Company*, he received an offer from the American editor of *Lippincott's* magazine, which was published in both Philadelphia and London, for another "Sherlock Holmes" story. The proposal was made at a dinner in London that was also attended by Oscar Wilde; out of this meeting came both Doyle's *The Sign of Four* and Wilde's *The Picture of Dorian Gray*. *The Sign of Four*—published in the United States as *The Sign of the Four*—is set in 1888 and involves an Indian treasure, a one-legged man, a vicious Pygmy with a deadly blowgun, a character closely modeled on Oscar Wilde, and a chase down the Thames River in a motor launch. *The Sign of Four* appeared complete in one issue of *Lippincott's* and also in book form in 1890. It was well received, particularly in America, but the sensational popularity of Sherlock Holmes was yet to come.

After writing *The Sign of Four*, Doyle went back to *The White Company*. The novel follows the adventures in England, France, and Spain of the knight Sir Nigel Loring, his squire Alleyne Edricson, Edricson's friend

John of Hordle, and the bowman Samkin Aylward. As Higham noted, the novel is "somewhat dated" by modern standards but is "vigorously told and scrupulously accurate." Doyle felt that the novel illuminates the national traditions of England and reveals for the first time the significance of the rise of the longbowman, and was disturbed that critics regarded it simply as a rousing adventure story. *The White Company* was serialized in the *Cornhill* before appearing in book form in 1891, and went through numerous editions.

In 1891 Doyle set himself up as an eye specialist in London, though he never attracted a single patient. Instead, he contributed a humorous story about a phonograph, "The Voice of Science," to the March, 1891, issue of a new illustrated monthly, the *Strand*. Doyle soon realized that a series of stories with a continuing central character could build reader loyalty for the magazine; since he had already created Sherlock Holmes, he quickly wrote six short stories featuring the detective. When the first of these, "A Scandal in Bohemia," appeared in the July, 1891, issue of the *Strand*, the phenomenal popularity of Sherlock Holmes began. Doyle received thirty-five pounds for each story.

The *Strand* stories were illustrated by Sidney Paget, whom the editors had hired by mistake, thinking that they were getting his better-known brother Walter. Sidney Paget did as much as Doyle to establish the image of Sherlock Holmes that stands today. He made Holmes handsomer than Doyle's original conception; he also introduced the deerstalker cap, which actually appears in illustrations for only eight of the thirty-eight stories for which Paget provided art work before his death in 1908. In the rest of the pictures Holmes wears various types of headgear, including toppers, felt hats, bowlers, homburgs, and even a straw boater; Doyle himself gives his detective a "close-fitting cloth cap" in one story and an "ear-flapped traveling cap" in another.

After the first few "Holmes" stories had appeared in the *Strand*, Doyle found himself nationally famous. He therefore decided to give up medicine, take up residence in the suburbs, and live entirely by his pen. When the editors of the *Strand* asked for more "Holmes" stories beyond the original six, Doyle, who had other projects in mind, set a price for the work he was sure would be rejected. Instead, his demand for fifty pounds per story was immediately accepted. He dashed off six more stories at the rate of about two per week, then turned to another historical novel, *The Refugees,* which was serialized and then published in book form in 1893. Doyle was never very happy with the novel, though Carr said that "the adventure-scenes in the great forests have never been surpassed for sheer vividness and power of action. They have diabolical reality, as though painted Indian-faces really did look through a suburban window." But even Carr admitted that "it is an uneven book," and Pearsall wrote that "readers of the *Strand* and posterity did not give, and have not given, a button for the epoch of Louis XIV and the boring misadventures of the Huguenots as laid out, in all their detail, in *The Refugees.*" In the same period Doyle wrote his first dramatic work: a one-act play based on his short story "A Straggler of '15," which had appeared in *Harper's Weekly* in March, 1891. He sent the play to actor and theatre manager Henry Irving, who changed the title to *A Story of Waterloo* and performed it successfully on tour in 1894 and at London's Lyceum Theatre in 1896.

The first twelve "Holmes" stories were collected as *The Adventures of Sherlock Holmes,* and the *Strand* asked for more. Hoping to quiet the editors' requests, Doyle demanded what he considered an outrageous amount, 1,000 pounds sterling for another dozen stories. Again, the editors accepted. While working on these stories, the incredibly productive Doyle wrote a novel about suburban life, *Beyond the City,* and another historical novel, *The Great Shadow.* Higham called the latter work "tedious," though Carr wrote that the description of the Battle of Waterloo at the end "rings in the ears and stifles the nostrils with gun smoke." Doyle also helped his friend James Barrie, who had fallen ill, complete an operetta, *Jane Annie; or, The Good Conduct Prize,* which was a resounding failure when it was performed at the Savoy Theatre in May, 1893.

In the fall of 1893, Doyle's wife, Louise, was diagnosed as having tuberculosis and given only months to live; in fact, she survived for thirteen years. Burdened with concern for his wife, tired of inventing new plots for Holmes, and convinced that his detective was consuming the time and attention due his "better" work, Doyle killed Holmes in "The Final Problem," the last of the twelve stories he had promised the *Strand.* In this story, set in April, 1891, Holmes and Watson are pursued to Switzerland by arch-criminal Professor James Moriarty, whose gang has been destroyed

through Holmes's efforts. Watson returns to the brink of the Reichenbach Falls, after having been called away on a ruse, to find a note from Holmes and evidence that he and Moriarty have struggled and then fallen over the precipice to their deaths. When the story appeared in the *Strand* in December, 1893, twenty thousand readers canceled their subscriptions, businessmen dressed in mourning, and Doyle received letters addressing him as "You Brute." Unremorseful, Doyle collected the second twelve Holmes stories as *The Memoirs of Sherlock Holmes* and wrote *The Stark-Munro Letters,* an autobiographical novel, based on Doyle's experiences with Dr. Budd, that contains some of his best comedy but ends when the protagonist and his wife are killed in a railroad accident.

Doyle then wrote the first series of "Brigadier Gerard" stories for the *Strand.* Gerard is based on the real-life French General Baron de Marbot, whose memoirs Doyle had read in 1892. The two series of stories, collected as *The Exploits of Brigadier Gerard* and *Adventures of Gerard,* form in Carr's judgment "the finest picture he ever did of the Napoleonic campaigns. And the reason is this: that he saw it through the eyes of a Frenchman." Gerard's "naive boasting, his complacence, his firm conviction that every woman is in love with him, all blind the reader with mirth. Above everything, his serene good nature never fails. He curls his side-whiskers, gives his mustache the Marengo twist, and rides living out of the page." The stories are exciting and frequently hilarious—sometimes with a grim humor, as characters are run through with swords or decapitated—and Gerard is one of Doyle's most memorable creations.

In 1897 Doyle wrote a play about Holmes and sent it to actor Beerbohm Tree. When Tree wanted the part of Holmes rewritten to suit himself, Doyle refused. His agent then sent the manuscript to a New York impresario, who gave it to American actor William Gillette. Gillette rewrote the play as a melodrama based on several of Doyle's stories; Doyle's original manuscript has since been lost. According to Carr and Higham, Gillette cabled Doyle, "May I marry Holmes?" Doyle replied, "You may marry him or murder him or do whatever you like with him." Gillette did not write into the play a marriage for Holmes, although—equally out of character for the reasoning machine Doyle had created—Gillette's Holmes does fall in love.

In the spring of 1898 Doyle began a new series of stories for the *Strand* that were collected as *Round the*

Fire Stories. One of these, "The Lost Special," in which a train vanishes without a trace between stations, is, according to Carr, "by far his finest mystery." In the fall he wrote *A Duet with an Occasional Chorus*, a warm, gentle, humorous look at the ordinary life of a middle-class suburban couple. The book remained among his favorites, and he refused to allow it to be serialized because he thought serialization would ruin it. Though H. G. Wells and poet Algernon Charles Swinburne admired it, the novel was too great a departure from what the public and critics expected from Doyle, and it was not successful.

When fighting broke out in South Africa between the governing British colonists and the Dutch-descended settlers known as the Boers, Doyle was too old at age forty-one to enlist as a soldier. He instead served for three months in 1900 as a doctor in a private military hospital in Bloemfontein, South Africa. On his return to England he wrote *The Great Boer War*, an accurate and impartial history of the conflict up to that time. The book remains highly respected; but its final chapter advocating the modernization of the British army—an argument he had earlier presented in the *Cornhill*—predictably earned him the scorn of the military establishment (Interestingly, all the reforms he proposed were subsequently adopted). Later, angered by charges that the British committed atrocities during the Boer War, Doyle wrote in one week a sixty-thousand-word pamphlet in rebuttal. Published in January, 1902, *The War in South Africa: Its Cause and Conduct* sold for sixpence per copy in Britain; thousands of translations were given away in France, Russia, Germany, and other countries. All profits from the sale of the book were donated to charity. For producing this propaganda triumph, Doyle was knighted on August 9, 1902.

In March of 1901 Doyle went on a golfing holiday with Fletcher Robinson, who told him the legend of a ghostly hound from Robinson's native Dartmoor, in Devonshire. After a trip to Dartmoor with Robinson, Doyle began writing what he called "a real creeper" of a novel based on the legend. Almost as an afterthought, he decided to use Sherlock Holmes in the novel, titled *The Hound of the Baskervilles;* but he was careful to set the story in 1899, before Holmes's death in the Reichenbach Falls. According to Carr, *The Hound of the Baskervilles* "is the only tale, long or short, in which the story dominates Holmes rather than Holmes dominating the story; what captures the reader is less

the Victorian detective than the Gothic romance." The story is one of Doyle's most popular: it "is a brilliant book, without a spare word, as deftly constructed as a sonata," William Cook wrote in the *New Statesman*. It has been reprinted numerous times, and an illustration of the hound from the original publication of the story in the *Strand* was selected for the wall of the London Underground station at Baker Street.

While *The Hound of the Baskervilles* was being serialized in the *Strand*, Gillette's play, *Sherlock Holmes,* which had already been a hit in the United States, opened in London with equal success. Gillette went on to make a career of portraying Holmes, which he did until he was an elderly man. It was he who was responsible for the popular conception of the detective puffing on a curved-stem pipe, which he adopted because it was easy for him to use on stage; over the years, cartoonists exaggerated the pipe into the monstrous calabash. In fact, the only pipes mentioned in the Doyle stories are a brier, a long-stemmed cherrywood, and an oily black clay.

In 1903 *McClure's* magazine in New York offered Doyle five thousand dollars per story if he would bring Sherlock Holmes back to life, and the *Strand* offered more than half that amount for the British rights. Persuaded by these astronomical sums, Doyle agreed. In "The Empty House" Holmes reappears in London and tells the shocked Watson that his knowledge of the Japanese martial art of baritsu enabled him to slip through Moriarty's grasp and that the evil professor had plunged into the Reichenbach Falls alone. For reasons that, upon close examination, do not make a great deal of sense, Holmes decided to fake his own death and disappear. He has returned in "The Empty House" to apprehend Moriarty's last remaining henchman, Colonel Sebastian Moran, "the most dangerous man in London." The story is set in April, 1894, meaning that Holmes had been away for three years; in actual time, it had been ten years since he had last shown himself in "The Final Problem."

The appearance of "The Empty House" in the *Strand* in October of 1903 created a sensation. Along with twelve more stories, which ran in the magazine until December, 1904, it was collected in *The Return of Sherlock Holmes*. Holmes was as popular as ever, though some critics have contended that the stories written after what is known as "the Great Hiatus" are generally not up to the standard of the earlier ones.

Doyle was aware of this opinion, and although he disagreed with it, he enjoyed reporting—as he did in "The Truth about Sherlock Holmes"—the words of the Cornish boatman who said to him: "I think, sir, when Holmes fell over that cliff, he may not have killed himself, but all the same he was never quite the same man afterwards." Stephen Knight noted, in *Form and Ideology in Crime Fiction,* that some of the changes in the later "Holmes" stories correspond to changes in Doyle's own situation: "The older Doyle was a much more prosperous and prestigious man, and the later Sherlock Holmes becomes more respectable. . . . Holmes gives up cocaine, goes for healthy walks, gets on better with the police and is much less barbed towards Watson." Some of the stories Doyle wrote after reintroducing Holmes are set in the period after Holmes's return; others are purportedly records of cases that occurred before his disappearance.

Doyle very quickly wrote the tales that make up *The Return of Sherlock Holmes,* then turned to another historical novel. After a year of research and a year of writing, *Sir Nigel* began to run in the *Strand* in December, 1905. The book is what would now be called a "prequel" to *The White Company* and begins with Nigel Loring as a young man setting out to do three great deeds in order to be worthy of his lady. Doyle always considered the two novels about the fourteenth century to be his greatest work; but *Sir Nigel,* like its predecessor, was praised merely as an exciting adventure tale.

Inspired by the discovery near his home in Sussex of fossilized dinosaur footprints, Doyle in the fall and winter of 1911 wrote *The Lost World,* the story of four adventurers who find living prehistoric animals and people on an isolated mesa in Brazil. The young, naive journalist-narrator Edward Malone; the thin, sardonic, pipe-puffing Professor Summerlee; the dashing hunter Lord John Roxton; and above all, the squat, powerful, bellowing sarcastic genius Professor George Edward Challenger are all vividly and memorably drawn characters. *The Lost World* presents scenes of high comedy, as when Malone tries to pass himself off as a scientist on his first meeting with Challenger but is trapped by the professor's pseudoscientific doubletalk, and scenes of high adventure on the mesa. Furthermore, Doyle's descriptions of the pterodactyls and dinosaurs are scientifically accurate. At the end of 1912, Doyle produced another novel about Professor Challenger and his three friends. In *The Poison Belt,*

the earth passes through a poisonous zone in the "ether," and everyone in the world except the four heroes—who are supplied with oxygen in an airtight room—appears to have died. In the end, what seemed to be death turns out to have been suspended animation.

Doyle had completed by April, 1914, his final full-length "Sherlock Holmes" novel, *The Valley of Fear,* a locked-room murder mystery. As in *A Study in Scarlet,* a long central section, told in the third person, details the events in the past that led up to the crime; this section is set in the Pennsylvania coal fields and involves a terrorist labor organization, the "Scowrers," based on the real-life Molly Maguires. Though the interpolated section is a fine adventure story in itself, some critics have objected to the obvious antilabor bias displayed by Doyle here. The first part of the novel, in which the murder is solved by Holmes, was praised by Carr as "a very nearly perfect piece of detective-story writing" and "our clearest example of Conan Doyle's contribution to the detective story." According to Carr, Doyle "invented the enigmatic clue, . . . the trick by which the detective—while giving you perfectly fair opportunity to guess—makes you wonder what in sanity's name he is talking about." Pearsall, on the other hand, pointed out that although the murder takes place in a moated manor house, "there is something lacking in atmosphere. . . . Darkest Sussex was different from the darkest Devon of *The Hound of the Baskervilles.* . . . The action is restricted to the manor house, with the actors moving around, occasionally displaying emotion, searching a room or making pregnant remarks. . . . There is no need for Watson's trusty revolver." Pearsall concluded that the novel's "killer in a yellow coat riding a bicycle" is far from menacing. The story, set in the period before Holmes's disappearance at the Reichenbach Falls, gives Professor Moriarty a backstage role.

Doyle's response to the outbreak of World War I was characteristic: he both took direct action—forming a volunteer rifle company in his area and visiting the front—and wrote about it in articles, lectures, and several books, including the six-volume *The British Campaign in France and Flanders.* He brought Holmes into the war in "His Last Bow," in which the sixty-year-old detective comes out of retirement—he has been keeping bees on the Sussex downs since 1903—to capture a German spy. (While working undercover, Holmes uses the alias "Altamont," Doyle's father's middle name.) The story was written in 1917 but is set just before the outbreak of the war in August, 1914. It was made the title piece in a collection of stories that had been appearing in the *Strand* at long intervals since 1908.

Sherlock Holmes stories continued to appear at irregular intervals over the years, and in 1927 the last twelve of them were collected as *The Case-Book of Sherlock Holmes*. In the book's preface Doyle announced his intention to write no more of the stories: "I fear that Mr. Sherlock Holmes may become like one of those popular tenors who, having outlived their time, are still tempted to make repeated farewell bows to their indulgent audiences. This must cease and he must go the way of all flesh, material or imaginary." To stop writing the Holmes narratives had also been Doyle's intention when he wrote "The Final Problem" in 1893, but thirty-four years later he held to his resolution.

Exhausted from his travels and suffering from heart disease, Doyle died on July 7, 1930. The historical novels of which he was so proud are rarely read, but enjoyment is still derived from the "Brigadier Gerard" stories and *The Lost World*. The latter was made into a still well-regarded silent film in 1925 and has been the inspiration for other science-fiction films, including the classic "King Kong." But above all, of course, Doyle remains known for the "Sherlock Holmes" novels and short stories, which have remained continually in print more than half a century after his death and have been translated into at least fifty-six languages. The characters of Holmes and Watson have been depicted in plays, motion pictures, radio and television programs, a musical comedy, a ballet, cartoons, and comic strips; and the instantly recognizable figure of Holmes has been used in advertisements for all sorts of products. Holmes is referred to in such literary works as James Joyce's *Finnegan's Wake;* poet T. S. Eliot's "Macavity: The Mystery Cat" is obviously based on Professor Moriarty; and the dialogue between Becket and the Second Tempter in Eliot's blank-verse play *Murder in the Cathedral* was consciously based on the Musgrave Ritual in Doyle's 1893 story of that name.

Perhaps the most remarkable aspect of the Holmes phenomenon is the tongue-in-cheek pseudoscholarship that has grown up around the stories. The practitioners of this elaborate game—who call themselves Sherlock-ians or, in Britain, Holmesians—are educated, usually professional people. Adopting the pretense that Holmes really existed, that the stories are actual case reports written by Watson—or in two instances by Holmes himself—and that Doyle was merely Watson's literary agent, they study the sixty tales—called "the Canon (or Conan)"—to develop theories about unrecorded parts of the characters' lives and to try to explain away the main inconsistencies Doyle carelessly introduced into the stories. Among the questions that have been discussed are exact chronology of the cases, which university Holmes attended, the number of times Watson was married, the location of Watson's war wound or wounds (in *A Study in Scarlet* it is clearly in his shoulder; in *The Sign of Four* it is just as clearly in his leg), and why Watson's wife calls him "James" in "The Adventure of the Engineer's Thumb" when it was established in *A Study in Scarlet* that his name was John. Another perennial problem has been the exact location of Holmes's house on Baker Street, since the address 221B did not exist in the nineteenth century. Each theory is based on some hint in the stories—no matter how slender—and is buttressed with argument and evidence, including research in Victorian and Edwardian newspapers and almanacs. This tradition began in 1911 with Ronald Knox's paper "Studies in the Literature of Sherlock Holmes" and has been carried on in countless articles and books since then. In his two massive bibliographies, Ronald De Waal listed 4,457 such items. Some Sherlockians also try their hands at writing pastiches, or imitation "Sherlock Holmes" stories, copying the style of the originals as closely as possible. Some book-length pastiches, such as Nicholas Meyer's *The Seven-per-Cent Solution*, have been commercially successful.

Beginning with the 1933 founding in New York of the Baker Street Irregulars—named for the street urchins who assist Holmes in three of the stories—Sherlock-ians have been organized in clubs in at least thirteen countries, including Australia, Burma, Denmark, Germany, Holland, New Zealand, Venezuela, Sweden, and Japan. In the United States, the clubs are known as "scion societies" and take their names from titles of the stories, from cases alluded to by Watson but never recorded, or from something somehow connected with the stories: for example, the Greek Interpreters of East Lansing, Michigan; the Hounds of the Baskervilles of Chicago; the Naval Treaty of St. Louis; and the Redheaded League of Westtown, Pennsylvania. In addition, two periodicals are devoted entirely to Sherlockian scholarship: the *Baker Street Journal,* published by the Baker Street Irregulars, and the *Sherlock Holmes Journal,* published by the Sherlock Holmes Society of London.

The "Sherlock Holmes" stories have also been the subject of analysis more serious than the playful pseudoscholarship of the Sherlockians. Stephen Knight, writing in *Form and Ideology in Crime Fiction,* for example, looked at them from a sociological perspective and concluded that the stories became popular because they gave fictional form to the world view, the hopes, and the fears of the late-Victorian middle-class readers of the *Strand.* According to Knight, Holmes represents the power of individualistic, scientific rationality to impose order on an increasingly chaotic world. In some of the stories Knight also found symbolism personal to Doyle: in "The Man with the Twisted Lip," for instance, a respectable reporter discovers that he can earn more money for his family by disguising himself as a deformed beggar; the reporter's situation, Knight argued, represents Doyle's recognition that he had prostituted his own literary talent by writing the Holmes stories strictly for money. Doyle himself, as well as his most famous character, continues to be an object of fascination. In 1983, John Hathaway Winslow and Alfred Meyer, in a *Science '83* article, proposed the theory that Doyle was the perpetrator of the famous Piltdown Man hoax in 1912. His motive was ostensibly to get revenge on the scientists who scoffed at his beloved spiritualism.

Although his "serious" fiction did not attract the attention he desired, Doyle's creation of Sherlock Holmes ensured his immortality as a writer. No other character in the history of fiction has ever inspired such devotion and enthusiasm, and this fact must stand as a tribute to Doyle's talent. The "Holmes" stories were written carelessly, hastily, and almost always purely for money; but the unstudied and spontaneous nature of the narratives allowed Doyle's creative abilities to be exemplified more fully than did the historical novels for which he prepared so carefully and on which he labored so arduously.

BIOGRAPHICAL AND CRITICAL SOURCES:

BOOKS

Atkinson, Michael, *The Secret Marriage of Sherlock Holmes, and Other Eccentric Readings,* University of Michigan Press (Ann Arbor, MI), 1996.

Baring-Gould, William S., *Sherlock Holmes of Baker Street: A Life of the World's First Consulting Detective,* C. N. Potter (New York, NY), 1962.

Bell, H. W., *Baker Street Studies,* O. Penzler Books (New York, NY), 1995.

Blackbeard, Bill, *Sherlock Holmes in America,* Abrams (New York, NY), 1981.

Booth, Martin, *The Doctor, the Detective and Arthur Conan Doyle: A Biography of Arthur Conan Doyle,* Hodder & Stoughton (London, England), 1997.

Brend, Gavin, *My Dear Holmes: A Study in Sherlock,* Allen & Unwin (London, England), 1951.

Brown, Ivor, *Conan Doyle: A Biography of the Creator of Sherlock Holmes,* Hamilton (London, England), 1972.

Bullimore, Tom, *Baker Street Puzzles,* Sterling (New York, NY), 1994.

Bunson, Matthew, *Encyclopedia Sherlockiana: An A-to-Z Guide to the World of the Great Detective,* Macmillan (New York, NY), 1994.

Butters, Roger, *First Person Singular: A Review of the Life and Work of Sherlock Holmes, the World's First Consulting Detective,* Vantage (New York, NY), 1984.

Carr, John Dickson, *The Life of Sir Arthur Conan Doyle,* Harper (New York, NY), 1949.

Cawelti, John G., *Adventure, Mystery, and Romance: Formula Stories As Art and Popular Culture,* University of Chicago Press (Chicago, IL), 1976.

Concise Dictionary of British Literary Biography, Volume 5: *Late Victorian and Edwardian Writers, 1890-1914,* Gale (Detroit, MI), 1991.

Cox, Dan R., *Arthur Conan Doyle,* Ungar (New York, NY), 1985.

Dakin, D. Martin, *A Sherlock Holmes Commentary,* Drake (New York, NY), 1972.

De Waal, Ronald Burt, *The World Bibliography of Sherlock Holmes and Dr. Watson,* Bramhall House (New York, NY), 1974.

De Waal, Ronald Burt, *The International Sherlock Holmes: A Companion to the World Bibliography of Sherlock Holmes and Dr. Watson,* Archon Books (Hamden, CT), 1980.

De Waal, Ronald Burt, and George A. Vanderburgh, *The Universal Sherlock Holmes,* G. A. Vanderburgh (Shelburne, Ontario, Canada), 1994.

Dictionary of Literary Biography, Gale (Detroit, MI), Volume 18: *Victorian Novelists after 1885,* 1983, Volume 70: *British Mystery Writers, 1860-1919,* 1988, Volume 156: *British Short-Fiction Writers,*

1880-1914: The Romantic Tradition, 1996, Volume 178: *British Fantasy and Science-Fiction Writers before World War I,* 1997.

Doyle, Adrian Conan, *The True Conan Doyle,* J. Murray (London, England), 1945.

Doyle, Arthur Conan, *My Memories and Adventures,* Little, Brown (Boston, MA), 1924, reprinted, Darby, 1983.

Dudley-Edwards, Owen, *The Quest for Sherlock Holmes: A Biographical Study of Arthur Conan Doyle,* B & N Imports, 1983.

Encyclopedia of Occultism and Parapsychology, 5th edition, Gale (Detroit, MI), 2001.

Eyles, Allen, *Sherlock Holmes: A Centenary Celebration,* Harper (New York, NY), 1987.

Frost, Mark, *The Six Messiahs,* Morrow (New York, NY), 1995.

Gut, Patricia, *Bacchus at Baker Street: Observations on the Bibulous References of Mr. Sherlock Holmes and His Associates,* Players Press (Studio City, CA), 1995.

Haining, Peter, editor, *The Sherlock Holmes Scrapbook,* New English Library (London, England), 1973.

Haining, Peter, editor, *A Sherlock Holmes Compendium,* Castle (New York, NY), 1980.

Haining, Peter, editor, *The Final Adventures of Sherlock Holmes,* Castle (New York, NY), 1981.

Haining, Peter, *The Television Sherlock Holmes,* revised and updated edition, Virgin (Secaucus, NJ), 1994.

Hall, Trevor H., *Sherlock Holmes: Ten Literary Studies,* Duckworth (London, England), 1969.

Hall, Trevor H., *The Late Mr. Sherlock Holmes and Other Literary Studies,* Duckworth (London, England), 1971.

Hall, Trevor H., *Sherlock Holmes and His Creator,* St. Martin's Press (New York, NY), 1977.

Hammer, David L., *The Before-Breakfast Pipe of Sherlock Holmes,* Gasogene Press (Dubuque, IA), 1995.

Hardwick, Michael, and Mollie Hardwick, *The Man Who Was Sherlock Holmes,* J. Murray (London, England), 1964.

Hardwick, Michael, and Mollie Hardwick, *The Sherlock Holmes Companion,* Bramhall House (New York, NY), 1977.

Harrison, Michael, *In the Footsteps of Sherlock Holmes,* Cassell (London, England), 1958.

Harrison, Michael, *The World of Sherlock Holmes,* Muller (London, England), 1973.

Higham, Charles, *The Adventures of Conan Doyle: The Life of the Creator of Sherlock Holmes,* Norton (New York, NY), 1976.

Hjortsberg, William, *Nevermore,* Atlantic Monthly Press (New York, NY), 1994.

Holroyd, James Edward, editor, *Seventeen Steps to 221B: A Collection of Sherlockian Pieces by English Writers,* Allen & Unwin (London, England), 1967.

Holroyd, James Edward, *Baker Street By-ways,* O. Penzler Books (New York, NY), 1994.

Hyder, William, *From Baltimore to Baker Street: Thirteen Sherlockian Studies,* [Toronto, Ontario, Canada], 1995.

Jann, Rosemary, *The Adventures of Sherlock Holmes: Detecting Social Order,* Twayne (New York, NY), 1995.

Jenkins, William D., *The Adventure of the Detected Detective: Sherlock Holmes in James Joyce's "Finnegan's Wake,"* Greenwood Press (Westport, CT), 1994.

Kaye, Marvin, *The Game Is Afoot: Parodies, Pastiches, and Ponderings of Sherlock Holmes,* St. Martin's Press (New York, NY), 1995.

Keating, H. D. F., *Sherlock Holmes: The Man and His World,* Thames & Hudson (New York, NY), 1979.

Kestner, Joseph A., *Sherlock's Men: Masculinity, Conan Doyle, and Cultural History,* Ashgate (Aldershot, Hampshire, England), 1997.

King, Joseph A. Cutshall, and others, *Sherlock Holmes: From Victorian Sleuth to Modern Hero,* Scarecrow Press (Lanham, MD), 1996.

Klinefelter, Walter, *The Origins of Sherlock Holmes,* Gaslight (Bloomington, IN), 1983.

Knight, Stephen, *Form and Ideology in Crime Fiction,* Indiana University Press (Bloomington, IN), 1980.

Lachtman, Howard, *Sherlock Slept Here: A Brief History of the Singular Adventures of Sir Arthur Conan Doyle in America, with Some Observations upon the Exploits of Mr. Sherlock Holmes,* Capra (Santa Barbara, CA), 1985.

Lamond, John, *Arthur Conan Doyle: A Memoir,* J. Murray (London, England), 1931.

Literature and Its Times: Profiles of 300 Notable Literary Works and the Historical Events That Influenced Them, Volume 2: *Civil Wars to Frontier Societies (1800-1880s),* Gale (Detroit, MI), 1997.

Morley, Christopher, editor, *Sherlock Holmes and Dr. Watson: A Textbook of Friendship,* Harcourt (New York, NY), 1944.

Mystery and Suspense Writers: The Literature of Crime, Detection, and Espionage, two volumes, Scribner (New York, NY), 1998.

Park, Orlando, *The Shelock Holmes Encyclopedia,* Carol Publishing Group (Secaucus, NJ), 1994.

Pearsall, Ronald, *Conan Doyle: A Biographical Solution,* St. Martin's Press (New York, NY), 1977.

Pearson, Hesketh, *Conan Doyle: His Life and Art,* Methuen (London, England), 1943, Taplinger (New York, NY), 1977.

Pointer, Michael, *The Public Life of Sherlock Holmes,* David & Charles (Newton Abbott, England), 1975.

Pointer, Michael, *The Sherlock Holmes File,* C. N. Potter (New York, NY), 1976.

Reference Guide to English Literature, 2nd edition, St. James Press (Detroit, MI), 1991.

Reference Guide to Short Fiction, St. James Press (Detroit, MI), 1994.

Roberts, S. C., *Holmes and Watson: A Miscellany,* O. Penzler Books (New York, NY), 1994.

Rodin, A. E., and Jack D. Key, *Medical Casebook of Doctor Arthur Conan Doyle: From Practitioner to Sherlock Holmes and Beyond,* Krieger (Melbourne, FL), 1984.

Rosenberg, Samuel, *Naked Is the Best Disguise: The Death and Resurrection of Sherlock Holmes,* Bobbs-Merrill (Indianapolis, IN), 1974.

Ross, Thomas Wynne, *Good Old Index: The Sherlock Holmes Handbook,* Camden House (Rochester, NY), 1996.

St. James Guide to Crime and Mystery Writers, 4th edition, St. James Press (Detroit, MI), 1996.

St. James Guide to Horror, Ghost, and Gothic Writers, St. James Press (Detroit, MI), 1998.

St. James Guide to Science-Fiction Writers, 4th edition, St. James Press (Detroit, MI), 1996.

St. James Guide to Young Adult Writers, 2nd edition, St. James Press (Detroit, MI), 1999.

Satterthwait, Walter, *Escapade,* St. Martin's Press (New York, NY), 1995.

Sayers, Dorothy L., *Unpopular Opinions,* Gollancz (London, England), 1946.

Science Fiction Writers, 2nd edition, Scribner (New York, NY), 1999.

Shreffler, Philip A., editor, *The Baker Street Reader: Cornerstone Writings about Sherlock Holmes,* Greenwood Press (Westport, CT), 1984.

Starrett, Vincent, editor, *221B: Studies in Sherlock Holmes,* Macmillan (New York, NY), 1940.

Starrett, Vincent, *The Private Life of Sherlock Holmes,* University of Chicago Press (Chicago, IL), 1906, reprinted, Haskell House (New York, NY), 1971.

Tracy, Jack, *The Encyclopedia Sherlockiana,* Doubleday (New York, NY), 1977.

Twentieth-Century Literature Criticism, Volume 7, Gale (Detroit, MI), 1982.

Twentieth-Century Romance and Historical Writers, 3rd edition, St. James Press (Detroit, MI), 1994.

Van Liere, Edward J., *A Doctor Enjoys Sherlock Holmes,* Vantage (New York, NY), 1959.

PERIODICALS

American Scholar, autumn, 1968.

Atlantic Monthly, January, 1994, Nancy Cadwell Sorel, "Harry Houdini and Arthur Conan Doyle," p. 103.

Blue Book, July, 1912; May, 1953.

Bookman, December, 1892; February, 1901; July, 1901; May, 1902; August, 1903; November, 1912; July, 1914; July, 1922; October, 1927; August, 1929.

Collier's, August 15, 1908; December 29, 1923.

English Literature in Transition, 1880-1920, spring, 2002, Rosamund Dalziell, "The Curious Case of Sir Everard im Thurn and Sir Arthur Conan Doyle: Exploration and the Imperial Adventure Novel, *The Lost World,*" pp. 131-157; spring, 2004, Benjamin Fisher, "*The Hound of the Baskervilles* 100 Years After: A Review Essay," pp. 181-190.

Harper's, May, 1948.

Hudson Review, winter, 1949.

Journal of Popular Culture, winter, 2003, Derham Groves, "Better Holmes and Gardens: Sense of Place in the Sherlock Holmes Stories," pp. 466-471.

Living Age, March 22, 1919; November 28, 1925.

Los Angeles Times, January 14, 1987, Tyler Marshall, "Sherlock—Myth Blurs the Reality: Sleuth's Centennial," p. 1; January 18, 1987, Nicholas Meyer, "Most Rational Mr. Holmes on a Singular Anniversary," p. 1.

Medical Times, July, 1971.

Modern Fiction Studies, spring, 1969.

New England Journal of Medicine, October 1, 1953.

New Statesman, December 17, 2001, William Cook, "The Dog That Barked in the Night: William Cook on the Enduring Appeal of *The Hound of the Baskervilles,* 100 Years after First Publication," pp. 118-119.

Newsweek, August 24, 1959; November 18, 1974.

New Yorker, February 17, 1945.

New York Review of Books, August 17, 1978.

New York Times, March 9, 1952; January 17, 1987.

New York Times Book Review, April 2, 1944; January 21, 1968.
Pacific Quarterly, January, 1978.
Paris Match, August 8, 1959.
Playboy, December, 1966; January, 1975.
Punch, June 20, 1951.
Quarterly Review, July, 1904.
Reader, August, 1905.
San Francisco Review of Books, December, 1976; February, 1977; March, 1977.
Saturday Review, April 27, 1968.
Saturday Review of Literature, July 19, 1930; August 2, 1930; April 29, 1939; February 17, 1940.
Science '83, September, 1983.
Sports Illustrated, March 19, 1973.
Strand, August, 1892; September, 1930; August, 1943.
Texas Quarterly, summer, 1968.
Twentieth Century, May, 1901.
West Coast Review of Books, April, 1975.
Woman's Home Companion, November, 1930.
World and I, June, 2002, Laurie Morrow, "The Doctor and the Detective: Arthur Conan Doyle's Creative Journey," p. 256.*

*   *   *

DOYLE, Conan
    See DOYLE, Arthur Conan

*   *   *

DRABBLE, Margaret 1939-

PERSONAL: Born June 5, 1939, in Sheffield, England; daughter of John Frederick (a judge) and Kathleen Marie (Bloor) Drabble; married Clive Walter Swift (an actor with the Royal Shakespeare Company), June, 1960 (divorced, 1975); married Michael Holroyd (an author), 1982; children: (first marriage) Adam Richard George, Rebecca Margaret, Joseph. *Education:* Newnham College, Cambridge, B.A. (first class honors), 1960. *Hobbies and other interests:* Walking, dreaming.

ADDRESSES: Agent—Peters, Fraser, and Dunlop, 5th Floor, The Chambers, Chelsea Harbour, Lots Road, London SW10 0XF, England.

CAREER: Novelist, biographer, critic, editor, and short-story writer. Member of Royal Shakespeare Company for one year.

MEMBER: National Book League (deputy chair, 1978-80; chair, 1980-82).

AWARDS, HONORS: John Llewelyn Rhys Memorial Award, 1966, for *The Millstone;* James Tait Black Memorial Book Prize, 1968, for *Jerusalem the Golden;* Book of the Year Award from *Yorkshire Post,* 1972, for *The Needle's Eye;* E. M. Forster Award from National Institute and American Academy of Arts and Letters, 1973; *The Middle Ground* named a notable book of 1980 by the American Library Association, 1981; honorary fellow of Sheffield City Polytechnic, 1989; D.Litt. from University of Sheffield, 1976, University of Manchester, 1987, University of Keele, 1988, University of Bradford, 1988, University of Hull, 1992, University of East Anglia, 1994, and University of York, 1995.

WRITINGS:

NOVELS

A Summer Bird-Cage, Weidenfeld & Nicolson (London, England), 1963, Morrow (New York, NY), 1964.
The Garrick Year, Weidenfeld & Nicolson (London, England), 1964, Morrow (New York, NY), 1965.
The Millstone, Weidenfeld & Nicolson (London, England), 1965, Morrow (New York, NY), 1966, published with new introduction by Drabble, Longman (London, England), 1970, published as *Thank You All Very Much,* New American Library (New York, NY), 1973.
Jerusalem the Golden, Morrow (New York, NY), 1967.
The Waterfall, Knopf (New York, NY), 1969.
The Needle's Eye, Knopf (New York, NY), 1972.
The Realms of Gold, Knopf (New York, NY), 1975.
The Ice Age, Knopf (New York, NY), 1977.
The Middle Ground, Knopf (New York, NY), 1980.
The Radiant Way (first novel in a trilogy), Knopf (New York, NY), 1987.
A Natural Curiosity (second novel in a trilogy), Viking (New York, NY), 1989.

The Gates of Ivory (third novel in a trilogy), Viking (New York, NY), 1991.

Margaret Drabble in Tokyo, edited by Fumi Takano, Kenkyusha (Tokyo, Japan), 1991.

The Witch of Exmoor, Viking (New York, NY), 1996.

The Peppered Moth, Harcourt (New York, NY), 2001.

The Seven Sisters, Harcourt (New York, NY), 2002.

OTHER

Laura (television play), Granada Television, 1964.

Wadsworth (criticism), Evans Brothers (London, England), 1966, Arco, 1969.

(Author of dialogue) *Isadora* (screenplay), Universal, 1968.

Thank You All Very Much (screenplay; based on Drabble's novel *The Millstone*), Columbia, 1969, released as *A Touch of Love,* Palomar Pictures, 1969.

Bird of Paradise (play), first produced in London, 1969.

(Editor, with B. S. Johnson) *London Consequences* (group novel), Greater London Arts Association, 1972.

Virginia Woolf: A Personal Debt, Aloe Editions (New York, NY), 1973.

Arnold Bennett (biography), Knopf (New York, NY), 1974.

(Editor) *Jane Austen, Lady Susan, the Watsons and Sanditon,* Penguin (New York, NY), 1975.

(Editor, with Charles Osborne) *New Stories 1,* Arts Council of Great Britain (London, England), 1976.

(Editor) *The Genius of Thomas Hardy,* Knopf (New York, NY), 1976.

For Queen and Country: Britain in the Victorian Age, Deutsch (Berlin, Germany), 1978, published as *For Queen and Country: Victorian England,* Houghton Mifflin (New York, NY), 1979.

A Writer's Britain: Landscape and Literature, photographs by Jorge Lewinski, Knopf (New York, NY), 1979.

(Editor) *The Oxford Companion to English Literature,* 5th edition, Oxford University Press (Oxford, England), 1985, 6th edition, 2000.

(Editor, with Jenny Stringer) *The Concise Oxford Companion to English Literature,* Oxford University Press (New York, NY), 1987, 2nd edition, 2004.

Stratford Revisited, Celandine Press (Shipston-on-Stour, Warwickshire, England), 1989.

Safe As Houses, Chatto & Windus (London, England), 1990.

(Editor) Emily Brontë, *Wuthering Heights, and Poems,* Charles E. Tuttle, 1993.

Angus Wilson: A Biography, St. Martin's Press (New York, NY), 1996.

(Author of introduction) Thomas Hardy, *The Woodlanders,* Knopf (New York, NY), 1997.

Contributor to *Contemporary Fiction,* selected by Lorna Sage, Book Trust, 1988. Author of story for "A Roman Marriage," Winkast Productions. Contributor to numerous anthologies.

SIDELIGHTS: On the strength of her first three novels, *A Summer Bird-Cage, The Garrick Year,* and *The Millstone,* Margaret Drabble made her reputation in the early 1960s as the preeminent novelist of the modern woman, and she has gone on in subsequent novels to reaffirm her standing. Sister of fellow novelist A. S. Byatt, Drabble focuses her fiction on women attempting to make something of themselves in modern England, moving, as in novels ranging from the early *A Summer Bird-Cage* to the more recent *A Peppered Moth* and *The Seven Sisters,* the concerns of her protagonist to align with her own. As Stephanie Foote noted in a review of the 2004 novel *The Seven Sisters* for *Book:* "A master of quirky, richly drawn characters, Drabble is attuned to people on the brink of unexpected change." In addition to her fiction, Drabble has also made her mark as a biographer and has served as editor for several highly respected literary reference works.

Drabble's characters Sarah Bennett of *A Summer Bird-Cage* and Rosamund Stacey of *The Millstone,* are, like the author herself, Oxbridge graduates. Sarah has given up the notion of going on to get a higher degree because "you can't be a sexy don," and she has spent a year rather aimlessly looking for something to do that is worthy of her talents and education. In the course of the novel, she considers her options, partly represented by her beautiful sister Louise, who has sacrificed any ambition she had to marry a rich, fussy, rather sexless man, and partly by her Oxford friends, most of whom are working at dull jobs in London and falling short of their ambitions almost as badly as Louise is. In the end, Sarah is preparing to marry her long-time Oxford boyfriend, though she insists that she will "marry a don" as opposed to becoming "a don's wife." Rosamund, a Cambridge graduate, is more determined and less conventional. Not only does she earn her doctorate in English literature during the course of the novel, but she also becomes pregnant, has the baby on her own, and experiences mother-love at the same time.

At age twenty-six, somewhat older than the other two characters and the mother of two small children, Emma Evans of *The Garrick Year* experiences other problems. Having just been offered a chance to escape from the domestic routine for part of the day by reading the news on television, she finds that she must move her family from London to Hereford, where her actor husband has a year's engagement with a provincial theatre company. There she tries to escape the even more intense boredom by having an affair with her husband's director. Like Rosamund, Emma finds that motherhood is the dominant factor in her life and that both she and her husband are bound to their marriage by that most important factor, the children.

Drabble's approach is realistic in her early novels because she explores the extreme ambivalence her characters feel toward motherhood and the enforced domesticity accompanying it. As Valerie Myer put it in *Margaret Drabble: Puritanism and Permissiveness*, "The woman undergraduate's interest is divided between her academic work and her feminine destiny, which at the university stage appears as though it will take the conventional social forms. The conflict is between the duty of the self-imposed task and instinct." The early Drabble heroine is constantly fighting the opposing forces of ambition—the need to do something in the world, "the greater gifts, greater duty to society line," as she described it in *A Summer Bird-Cage*—and the social and biological urge to get married and/or have babies.

The two novels that followed these early treatments of women, *Jerusalem the Golden* and *The Waterfall*, represent a considerable development for Drabble as a novelist. Ellen Cronan Rose contended in *Critical Essays on Margaret Drabble* that *Jerusalem the Golden* is Drabble's "first wholly realized novel, economical in its construction, finely precise in its characterization of the heroine. In later novels she will be more profound; never will she be more completely in control of her material than in this relatively early work."

The Waterfall returns to the solipsistic protagonist but treats her in a much more self-conscious way. The most experimental of Drabble's novels, *The Waterfall*

has as its primary stylistic characteristic a divided narrative point of view. The first half of the book is written in the third person, narrated from the point of view of protagonist Jane Grey, a young woman on the verge of agoraphobia. She is the mother of a small child, and her husband has left her during the sixth month of her second pregnancy. The novel opens with the birth of Jane's second child and her falling in love with her cousin's husband and continues with Jane's experience of the ensuing affair, which is presented as the highest and most consuming of passions. In the middle of the novel, however, Jane breaks out in the first person, exclaiming, "Lies, lies, it's all lies. A pack of lies. . . . What have I tried to describe? A passion, a love, an unreal life, a life in limbo, without anxiety, guilt, corpses." The two voices then alternate, the third-person narrator creating an intense and unreal story of passionate love and the first-person narrator training an objective, almost cynical eye on the novel's events and characters. In one sense, this split expresses a division that runs throughout Drabble's fiction, between a romantic yearning for coherence through love and a realistic skepticism prompted by the awareness of conflict and incoherence.

Critics have been divided both on the nature of the split in point of view and on its success. Writing in the *Journal of Narrative Technique*, Caryn Fuoroli maintained that it results from Drabble's "inability to control narration" and that the novel fails because the technique keeps her from realizing "the full potential of her material." Rose believed that the novel works because its point of view is a dramatization of the conflict of the woman artist: "She has divided herself into Jane, the woman (whose experience is liquid), and Jane Grey, the artist (who gives form, order, and shapeliness to that experience)." Rose contends in *Contemporary Literature* that this is the fundamental truth the novel succeeds in expressing: "In order to be whole (and wholly a woman), Drabble suggests, a woman must reconcile these divisions. And if a woman writer is to articulate this experience of what it is to be a woman, she must devise a form, as Drabble has done in *The Waterfall*, which amalgamates feminine fluidity and masculine shapeliness."

Jerusalem the Golden's broader canvas and *The Waterfall*'s self-conscious narration were perhaps necessary first steps toward Drabble's full development in the mid-1970s. Her two biggest novels, *The Needle's Eye* and *The Realms of Gold*, were written during this period, and together they represent her fullest exploration of substantial themes: *The Needle's Eye* of personal morality and *The Realms of Gold* of the possibilities for individual achievement despite limitations beyond the individual's physical, social, familiar, psychological, and spiritual control.

The Needle's Eye reflects both Drabble's deep interest in ethics and morality and her lack of orthodoxy. Like her, the novel's heroine, Rose Vassiliou, is unsure of her theology but possessed of a conviction that she must do right. As a young heiress she achieved a certain amount of notoriety by giving up her inheritance to marry Christopher Vassiliou, an unsavory and radical young immigrant. After their marriage, she infuriates Christopher by giving away a thirty-thousand-pound legacy to a rather dubious African charity and refusing to move out of their working-class house into a more fashionable middle-class neighborhood when he begins to make his own fortune. At the time of the novel, Rose is living in her house with her children and has divorced the violent Christopher, who is trying to get her back or to get custody of the children.

Marion Vlastos Libby wrote in *Contemporary Literature* that *The Needle's Eye* is a "complex and passionate evocation of a fatalism deriving from the human condition and the nature of the world" and that its greatness "lies in portraying the tension, real and agonizing, between the hounds of circumstance and the force of the individual will." The best Drabble can say for Rose is that she has been "weathered into identity" by the hostile forces she confronts. In other words, she has developed a soul and found a way to grace, and in that sense she has won her battle. But she has "ruined her own nature against her own judgment, for Christopher's sake, for the children's sake. She had sold them for her own soul . . . the price she had to pay was the price of her own living death, her own conscious lying, her own lapsing, slowly, from grace."

If *The Needle's Eye* represents the human will at its weakest and circumstance at its strongest, Drabble moves to the opposite extreme in *The Realms of Gold.* The protagonist in this novel, Frances Wingate, is the apotheosis of the high-powered heroine. A celebrated archaeologist in her mid-thirties, Frances has divorced the wealthy man she married at an early age and is raising their four children on her own. She has a satisfying love affair with Karel Schmidt, an historian and survivor of the Holocaust, whom she eventually

marries. She is rich, accomplished, and a little smug, recognizing in herself "amazing powers of survival and adaptation," and openly admits to herself that she is a "vain, self-satisfied woman."

Frances has her frailties, but is not affected by her limitations in any fundamental way, because she does not allow them to affect her. She is Drabble's quintessential personification of will: "I must be mad, she thought to herself. I imagine a city, and it exists. If I hadn't imagined it, it wouldn't have existed." She is an obvious extreme, and Drabble sets her in opposition to the other extremes in the novel. While she makes her mark on her family, her profession, her society, even—in discovering a lost city in the desert—upon nature, she is surrounded by people who are destroyed by circumstances: environment, heredity, psychology, and fate. As Mary Hurley Moran noted in *Margaret Drabble: Existing within Structures,* "Drabble's fiction portrays a bleak, often menacing universe, ruled over by a harsh deity who allows human beings very little free will." Drabble's emphatic statement in *The Realms of Gold,* however, is that the will does count for something, that what hope there is for survival lies precisely in the individual's exercise of will in the face of what may seem overwhelming external forces.

The Ice Age and *The Middle Ground* present what has become the typical struggle of the individual in Drabble's work to survive and to maintain an identity in the face of a disintegrating social order. Drabble remarked that *The Ice Age* is in one sense a novel about money. Its protagonist, Anthony Keating, is a thoughtful man who made a fortune in real estate development during the boom times of the 1960s and lost it during the recession of the early 1970s. At the beginning of the novel he is recuperating from a heart attack and trying to come to terms with his new position in life. Meanwhile, the spoiled teenaged daughter of his fiancee, Alison Murray, has gotten herself into trouble in an eastern European country, and his former partner, Len, has landed himself in prison through his shady dealings. The novel is about money in many senses: about the failing British economy, about the effects that making a lot of money has on people, about the interaction of old money and new money, and about the class structures that underlie everyone's thinking about money. However, it is also about the forces that individuals in contemporary Britain are up against, from the natural fact of Alison's retarded younger daughter to the threat that an alien totalitarian government poses to her older one.

The interesting artistic fact about *The Ice Age* is that its narrative is not centered in one character, but is divided among Anthony, Alison, Len, and Len's girlfriend, Maureen. This is in part a reflection of the general disintegration going on in the world Drabble is presenting, in part a somewhat ironic move toward community. Not one of these characters has the force of will that makes Frances Wingate the central presence she is. Each of them is severely handicapped in some way, but they do manage to function in concert. There is some power in community.

The Middle Ground returns to a central character who is very much like Frances Wingate. Kate Armstrong is a successful writer with teenaged children who lives a very comfortable expense-account life. Because she resides in the world of *The Ice Age,* however, Kate is less confident than Frances of her future. In one sense *The Middle Ground* is about middle age. After the ending of a ten-year love affair and the abortion of a fetus with spina bifida, Kate at age forty-one is asking what is left for her to do with the rest of her life: "Work? Living for others? Just carrying on, from day to day, enjoying as much of it as one could? Responding to demands as they came, for come they would?" Faced with the decay of urban London, the realities of the Third World visited upon her in the shape of a house-guest called Mujid, the apparent failure of the women's movement, and the turning off of the youth in her world, Kate is not sure what course she should take.

In addition to stand-alone novels, Drabble has authored a trilogy that follows the lives of three women whose friendship began while they were students at Cambridge in the 1950s. In the first book, *The Radiant Way,* Drabble introduces Liz, a successful psychotherapist; Alix, an idealist whose socialistic principles have led her to work at low-paying, altruistic jobs; and Esther, a scholar whose main interest lies with minor artists of the Italian Renaissance. By following these three characters through the years in *The Radiant Way* and into their middle age in *A Natural Curiosity,* the author "also attempts to show us how a generation managed (or mismanaged) its hopes and dreams," commented Michiko Kakutani in the *New York Times.* Kakutani found this approach similar to that of Mary McCarthy's *The Group,* a novel about former Vassar

students, and criticized the tendency in both books "to substitute exposition for storytelling, sociological observation for the development of character and drama." But in a *Newsweek* review by Laura Shapiro, the critic approved of Drabble's willingness to explore all the facets of her characters' lives "at a time when skimpy prose, skeletal characterizations, frail plots and a sense of human history that stops sometime around last summer have become the new standards for fiction." Shapiro concluded: "Drabble reminds us here as in all her books exactly why we still love to read."

The Gates of Ivory, which completes the trilogy, differs from *The Radiant Way* and *A Natural Curiosity* in several significant ways. For example, "in *The Gates of Ivory,*" declared *Concise Dictionary of British Literary Biography* contributor Barbara C. Millard, "Drabble eschews a conventional plot in favor of a compelling scrutiny of her ongoing characters." Also, while the first two books centered on crime—the murder of one of Alix's students in *The Radiant Way* and Alix's attempts to understand the murderer's motivation in *A Natural Curiosity*—*The Gates of Ivory* follows Liz's actions on behalf of her friend, journalist Stephen Cox, in his attempt to interview Khmer Rouge leader Pol Pot. Cox disappears while traveling through rural Cambodia, and Liz becomes involved in the situation first in London, when she tries to trace his route and then in Cambodia itself, when she travels there to look for him. In the process, Drabble combines elements of the traditional domestic novel, for which she is celebrated, with journalism and literary criticism and examines such diverse topics as the Vietnam War, the novels of Joseph Conrad, and the restoration of the ancient temple complex at Angkor Wat. "The novel," stated Mary Kaiser in *World Literature Today,* "is multilayered, breathtaking in its ability to connect the First and Third Worlds." Disappointed with the novel's unrealized potential, the reviewer concluded: "Although Drabble has flirted with the explosive possibilities of leaving the domestic novel and inventing a new form, her allegiance to traditional realism prevents her from breaking the form in order to engage fully the undomesticated facts of our complex and violent times."

In *The Peppered Moth* Drabble tells the fictionalized story of her mother, Bessie Bawtry Baron, who was born and raised in a coal-mining town in South Yorkshire. Despite her working-class background and the prejudices against women at the time, she attends

Cambridge University on a scholarship, becomes a teacher, and eventually marries her longtime boyfriend. In the book's afterword, Drabble comments, "I wrote this book to try and understand my mother better." Except for Bessie, none of the other characters in the novel is based on real people, and the subplots of the book are also invented. In the *Houston Chronicle,* Shelby Hearon commented that the subplots, one of which involves the tracing of 8,000-year-old DNA, "seem forced," and "come alive only as they relate to the central story." Charles Matthews wrote in a *Knight-Ridder/Tribune News Service* review that Drabble's use of a "neo-Victorian omniscient narrator" who often intrudes on the reader can be "irritating and coy" and noted that "there are evasions and compromises in Drabble's storytelling." Overall, however, he found "much that is sharp and insightful in the novel." A *Booklist* reviewer praised the novel, noting, "Drabble glories in the musicality and pliancy of language in this exuberant, intelligent, and thoroughly entertaining saga." In the *New York Times,* Daphne Merkin called *The Peppered Moth* "one of the more absorbing novels I have read in a long time, both for its sheer storytelling ability and for its powers of imaginative conjecture."

Drabble's models have been the great British novelists of the nineteenth century—George Eliot, Anthony Trollope, the Brontës, Arnold Bennett, and to a lesser extent Jane Austen and Virginia Woolf—as well as Henry James. Elaine Showalter quoted her in *A Literature of Their Own* as saying, "I don't want to write an experimental novel to be read by people in fifty years, who will say, oh, well, yes, she foresaw what was coming. I'm just not interested." It is this kind of thinking that has led Drabble to be seen, as Michael F. Harper noted in *Contemporary Literature,* "as a late twentieth-century novelist who writes what many reviewers have taken to be good, solid nineteenth-century novels."

While some reviewers have criticized her approach as anachronistic, Harper maintained that Drabble's style "is not the result of unthinking acceptance of Victorian conventions, or of nostalgia for 'the riches of the past.' It is rather a working back to a reconstituted realism, in which Drabble begins with modernism and subjects it to a critique that is profound and contemporary." Drabble's realistic world, he said, "is something painfully and with difficulty constructed by the author and

her characters, something not assumed but affirmed in an act of faith, achieved at the end of an odyssey of doubt and questioning of both the world and the self."

Drabble's realism may very well be her personal mediation between two extreme visions that permeate her world: the vestigial yearning for a transformation of the ordinary into an ideal unity and the postmodernist view that contemporary society has disintegrated beyond the possibility of unity or coherence, beyond the possibility of even a coherent description of its disintegration. She continues to insist both on the reality of the writer and on the reality of the world she describes. And while she sees very clearly the extreme tensions in our society—from the contrary pulls on a talented woman who wants both to be a mother and to make her mark on the world to the economic and political forces that threaten the precarious stability of our social institutions—she continues to believe in the human striving for something transcendent, something spiritual or ideal.

In addition to her novels, Drabble has also written well-regarded works of criticism and biography and has edited several influential volumes, including two editions of the esteemed *Oxford Companion to English Literature.* Her biographies include 1974's *Arnold Bennett* and 1996's *Angus Wilson: A Biography.* In the latter work, Drabble chronicles the life of Angus Wilson, a well-known British writer who became a friend of Drabble's during the 1960s. While some reviewers felt that Drabble fails to offer a fully realized portrait of Wilson's inner life, others remarked that her own training as a novelist assisted her in analyzing Wilson's character and his writing. Commenting in the *London Review of Books,* Frank Kermode stated, "Altogether, with the assistance and consent of [Wilson's longtime companion] Tony Garrett, . . . she has given a minute, intimate and candid account . . . of Wilson's hectic life."

BIOGRAPHICAL AND CRITICAL SOURCES:

BOOKS

Allan, Tuzyline Jita, *Womanist and Feminist Aesthetics: A Comparative Review,* Ohio University Press (Athens, OH), 1995.

Blain, Virginia, Patricia Clements, and Isobel Grundy, *The Feminist Companion to Literature in English,* Yale University Press (New Haven, CT), 1990.

Bokat, Nicole Suzanne, *The Novels of Margaret Drabble: This Freudian Family Nexus,* Peter Lang (New York, NY), 1998.

Concise Dictionary of British Literary Biography: Contemporary Writers, 1960 to the Present, Gale (Detroit, MI), 1992.

Contemporary Literary Criticism, Gale (Detroit, MI), Volume 2, 1974, Volume 3, 1975, Volume 5, 1976, Volume 8, 1978, Volume 10, 1979, Volume 22, 1982, Volume 53, 1989.

Creighton, Joanne V., *Margaret Drabble,* Methuen (London, England), 1985.

Dictionary of Literary Biography, Gale (Detroit, MI), Volume 14: *British Novelists since 1960,* 1983, Volume 155: *Twentieth-Century British Literary Biographers,* 1995.

Drabble, Margaret, *A Summer Bird-Cage,* Weidenfeld & Nicolson (London, England), 1963, Morrow (New York, NY), 1964.

Drabble, Margaret, *The Middle Ground,* Knopf (New York, NY), 1980.

Drabble, Margaret, *The Realms of Gold,* Knopf (New York, NY), 1975.

Drabble, Margaret, *The Waterfall,* Knopf (New York, NY), 1969.

Moran, Mary Hurley, *Margaret Drabble: Existing within Structures,* Southern Illinois University Press (Carbondale, IL), 1983.

Myer, Valerie Grosvenor, *Margaret Drabble: Puritanism and Permissiveness,* Vision Press (London, England), 1974.

Packer, Joan Garrett, *Margaret Drabble: An Annotated Bibliography,* Garland (New York, NY), 1988.

Quiello, Rose, *Breakdowns and Breakthoughts: The Figure of the Hysteric in Contemporary Novels by Women,* Peter Lang (New York, NY), 1996.

Rose, Ellen Cronan, *The Novels of Margaret Drabble: Equivocal Figures,* Barnes & Noble (New York, NY), 1980.

Rose, Ellen Cronan, editor, *Critical Essays on Margaret Drabble,* Hall, 1985.

Roxman, Susanna, *Guilt and Glory: Studies in Margaret Drabble's Novels, 1963-1980,* Almquist & Wiksell (Stockholm, Sweden), 1984.

Sadler, Lynn Veach, *Margaret Drabble,* Twayne (New York, NY), 1986.

Schmidt, Dory, and Jan Seale, editors, *Margaret Drabble: Golden Realms,* Pan American University (Edinberg, TX), 1982.

Showalter, Elaine, *A Literature of Their Own,* Princeton University Press (Princeton, NJ), 1977.

Soule, George, *Four British Women Novelists: Anita Brookner, Margaret Drabble, Iris Murdoch, Barbara Pym; An Annotated and Critical Secondary Bibliography,* Salem Press (Pasadena, CA), 1998.

Staley, Thomas F., editor, *Twentieth-Century Women Novelists,* Barnes & Noble (New York, NY), 1982.

Stovel, Nora Foster, *Margaret Drabble: Symbolic Moralist,* Borgo Press (San Bernardino, CA), 1989.

Todd, Janet, *Gender and Literary Voice,* Holmes & Meier (New York, NY), 1980.

Wojcik-Andrews, Ian, *Margaret Drabble's Female Bildungsroman: Theory, Genre, and Gender,* Peter Lang (New York, NY), 1995.

Wynne-Davies, Marion, editor, *The Bloomsbury Guide to English Literature,* Prentice Hall General Reference (Paramus, NJ), 1990.

PERIODICALS

American Scholar, winter, 1973.

Atlantic, January, 1976; December, 1977; November, 1980; April, 2001, p. 106; November, 2002, review of *The Seven Sisters,* pp. 125-126.

Book, November-December, 2002, review of *The Seven Sisters,* p. 85.

Booklist, February 15, 2001, Donna Seaman, review of *The Peppered Moth,* p. 1084.

Books and Bookmen, September, 1969.

Bookview, January, 1978.

Canadian Forum, November, 1977.

Chicago Tribune Book World, August 31, 1980.

CLA Journal, September, 1984.

College Literature, fall, 1982.

Commentary, December, 1977.

Commonweal, June 18, 1976; February 13, 1981.

Comparative Literature Studies, February, 1998, p. 116.

Contemporary Literature, Volume 14, 1973; Volume 16, 1975; Volume 21, 1980; Volume 23, 1982.

Contemporary Review, April, 1972; January, 1976; January, 1978.

Critic, August, 1979.

Critique, number 15, 1973; number 21, 1980.

Daily Telegraph (London, England), February 12, 2000, p. 6.

Detroit News, October 19, 1980.

Economist, July 13, 1974; February 14, 1976.

English Review, November, 2001, p. 35.

English Studies, number 59, 1978.

Frontiers, number 3, 1978.

Globe and Mail (Toronto, Ontario, Canada), April 11, 1987; October 7, 1989.

Guardian, May 29, 1969; January 15, 1972; April 8, 1972; May 13, 1972; July 20, 1974; October 4, 1975; November 11, 1979; July 13, 1980; June 26, 1999, p. S6; October 14, 2000, p. 9; December 16, 2000, P. S38; December 8, 2001, p. 3.

Harper's, November, 1969; October, 1977; October, 1980.

History Today, March, 1980.

Houston Chronicle, May 13, 2001, Shelby Hearon, "Margaret Drabble's Mother: Paradise Gained and Lost," p. 13.

Hudson Review, winter, 1970; winter, 1973; winter, 1975; summer, 1975; spring, 1978; spring, 1981.

Journal of Narrative Technique, spring, 1981.

Knight-Ridder/Tribune News Service, May 2, 2001, Charles Matthews, review of *The Peppered Moth,* p. K4997.

Library Journal, June, 1, 1998, p. 187; February 1, 2001, p. 125; November 1, 2002, Starr E. Smith, review of *The Seven Sisters,* p. 128; March 1, 2004, Marilyn Lary, review of *The Concise Oxford Companion to Literature,* p. 64.

London Review of Books, June 8, 1995, p. 3.

Los Angeles Times, December 28, 1980; November 25, 1982; June 21, 1987; October 23, 1989; April 9, 2001, p. E3.

Los Angeles Times Book Review, October 18, 1987; September 24, 1989; June 9, 1996, p. 3.

Maclean's, September 29, 1980.

Midwest Quarterly, Volume 16, 1975.

Modern Fiction Studies, Volume 25, 1979-80.

Modern Language Review, April, 1971.

Ms., August, 1974; July, 1978; November, 1980.

Nation, October 23, 1972; April 5, 1975.

National Review, December 23, 1977; March 20, 1981.

New Leader, July 24, 1972; April 26, 1976; January 30, 1978; September 22, 1980.

New Republic, July 8, 1972; September 21, 1974; October 22, 1977.

New Statesman, May 23, 1969; March 31, 1972; July 12, 1974; September 26, 1975; March 19, 1976; September 9, 1977; December 7, 1979; July 11, 1980; May 26, 1995, p. 24.

Newsweek, September 9, 1974; October 17, 1977; October 6, 1980; November 2, 1987.

New Yorker, October 4, 1969; December 16, 1972; December 23, 1974; January 12, 1976; December 26, 1977; July 11, 1980.

New York Review of Books, October 5, 1972; October 31, 1974; November 27, 1975; November 10, 1977; July 19, 1979; November 20, 1980; July 5, 2001, p. 33.

New York Times, October 31, 1975; October 4, 1977; July 4, 1985; October 21, 1987; August 22, 1989; May 6, 2001, Daphne Merkin, "Unnatural Selection."

New York Times Book Review, November 23, 1969; June 11, 1972; December 3, 1972; September 1, 1974; December 1, 1974; December 7, 1975; April 18, 1976; June 26, 1977; August 21, 1977; October 9, 1977; November 20, 1977; December 23, 1977; September 7, 1980; February 14, 1982; November 7, 1982; July 14, 1985; November 1, 1987; September 3, 1989; May 30, 1993; May 28, 2001, p. E1; June 3, 2001, p. 26.

New York Times Magazine, September 11, 1988.

Novel, Volume 11, 1978.

Observer, April 2, 1972; September 23, 1973; July 14, 1974; September 28, 1975; December 14, 1975; March 21, 1976; April 17, 1977; September 4, 1977; December 18, 1977; June 29, 1980; July 13, 1980.

Partisan Review, number 46, 1979.

People, October 13, 1980.

Prairie Schooner, spring-summer, 1981.

Progressive, January, 1981.

Publishers Weekly, May 31, 1985; February 26, 2001, p. 55.

Regionalism and the Female Imagination, number 4, 1978.

Saturday Review, November 15, 1975; January 10, 1976; February 21, 1976; August 20, 1977; January 7, 1978.

Sewanee Review, January, 1977; April, 1978; January, 1982.

Spectator, April 1, 1972; July 20, 1974; September 27, 1975; February 7, 1976; February 14, 1976; July 5, 1980; May 27, 1995, p. 38; January 6, 2001, p. 29.

Studies in the Literary Imagination, Volume 11, 1978.

Time, September 9, 1974; November 3, 1975; June 26, 1976; October 17, 1977; September 15, 1980; November 16, 1987.

Times (London, England), June 30, 1980; April 25, 1985; April 27, 1987; April 30, 1987; July 8, 1987.

Times Literary Supplement, July 12, 1974; September 26, 1975; September 2, 1977; July 11, 1980; April 26, 1985; July 12, 1985; May 1, 1987; September 29, 1989; June 9, 1995, p. 24; January 12, 2001, p. 22.

Tribune Books (Chicago, IL), November 8, 1987; August 20, 1989.

Victorian Studies, spring, 1978.

Village Voice, November 24, 1975; October 24, 1977.

Virginia Quarterly Review, spring, 1976; summer, 1976; summer, 1978.

Voice Literary Supplement, May, 1982.

Washington Post, January 1, 1980.

Washington Post Book World, September 14, 1980; June 2, 1985; September 21, 1986; October 25, 1987; August 27, 1989.

Women's Studies, Volume 6, 1979.

World Literature Today, spring, 1993.

Yale Review, March, 1970; June, 1978.*

E

ECO, Umberto 1932-

PERSONAL: Born January 5, 1932, in Alessandria, Italy; son of Giulio and Giovanna (Bisio) Eco; married Renate Ramge (a teacher) September 24, 1962; children: Stefano, Carlotta. *Education:* University of Turin, Ph.D., 1954.

ADDRESSES: Office—Universita di Bologna, Via Toffano 2, Bologna, Italy.

CAREER: Italian Radio-Television (RAI), Milan, Italy, editor for cultural programs, 1954-59; University of Turin, Turin, Italy, assistant lecturer, 1956-63, lecturer in aesthetics, 1963-64; Casa Editore Bompiani (publisher), Milan, Italy, nonfiction senior editor, 1959-75; University of Milan, lecturer in architecture, 1964-65; University of Florence, Florence, Italy, professor of visual communications, 1966-69; Milan Polytechnic, professor of semiotics, 1969-71; University of Bologna, Bologna, Italy, associate professor, 1971-75, professor of semiotics, 1975—, director of doctorate program in semiotics, 1986—, chair of Corso di Laurea in Scienze della comunicazione, 1993—, founder of publishing-studies program, 2003. Visiting professor, New York University, 1969, 1976, Northwestern University, 1972, University of California, San Diego, 1975, Yale University, 1977, 1980, 1981, and Columbia University, 1978; visiting fellow at Italian Academy and Columbia University. Lecturer on semiotics at various institutions throughout the world, including Tanner Lecturer, Cambridge University, 1990, Norton Lecturer, Harvard University, 1992-93, University of Antwerp, École Pratique des Hautes Etudes, University of London, Nobel Foundation, University of Warsaw, University of Budapest, University of Toronto, Murdoch University/Perth, and Amherst College. Member of the Council for the United States and Italy. *Military service:* Italian Army, 1958-59.

MEMBER: International Association for Semiotic Studies (secretary-general, 1972-79; vice president, 1979—), James Joyce Foundation (honorary trustee).

AWARDS, HONORS: Premio Strega and Premio Anghiari, both 1981, both for *Il Nome della rosa;* named honorary citizen of Monte Cerignone, Italy, 1982; Prix Medicis for best foreign novel, 1982, for French version of *Il Nome della rosa; Los Angeles Times* fiction prize nomination, 1983, and best fiction book award from Association of Logos Bookstores, both for *The Name of the Rose;* Marshall McLuhan Teleglobe Canada Award from UNESCO's Canadian Commission, 1985, for achievement in communications; Commandeur de l'Ordre des Arts et des Lettres (France), 1985; Chevalier de la Legion d'Honneur (France), 1993; Golden Cross of the Dodecannese, Patmos (Greece), 1995; Cavaliere di Gran Croce al Merito della Repubblica Italiana, 1996; honorary degrees from Catholic University, Leuven, 1985, Odense University, 1986, Loyola University, Chicago, 1987, State University of New York at Stony Brook, 1987, Royal College of Arts, London, 1987, Brown University, 1988, University of Paris, Sorbonne Nouvelle, 1989, University of Glasgow, 1990, University of Tel Aviv and University of Buenos Aires, both 1994, and University of Athens, Laurentian University at Sudbury, Ontario, and Academy of Fine Arts, Warsaw, all 1996.

WRITINGS:

IN ITALIAN

Filosofi in liberta, Taylor (Turin, Italy), 1958, 2nd edition, 1959.

Apocalittici e integrati: Comunicazioni di massa e teoria della cultura di massa, Bompiani (Milan, Italy), 1964, revised edition, 1977.

Le Poetiche di Joyce, Bompiani (Milan, Italy), 1965, 2nd edition published as *Le Poetiche di Joyce dalla "Summa" al "Finnegan's Wake,"* 1966.

Appunti per una semiologia delle comunicazioni visive (also see below), Bompiani (Milan, Italy), 1967.

(Author of introduction) Mimmo Castellano, *Noi vivi,* Dedalo Libri, 1967.

(Coeditor) *Storia figurata delle invenzioni. Dalla selce scheggiata al volo spaziale,* Bompiani (Milan, Italy), 1968.

La Struttura assente (includes *Appunti per una semiologia delle comunicazioni visive*), Bompiani (Milan, Italy), 1968, revised edition, 1983.

La Definizione dell'arte (title means "The Definition of Art"), U. Mursia, 1968, reprinted, Garzanti, 1978.

(Editor) *L'Uomo e l'arte,* Volume 1: *L'Arte come mestiere,* Bompiani (Milan, Italy), 1969.

(Editor, with Remo Faccani) *I Sistemi di segni e lo strutturalismo sovietico,* Bompiani (Milan, Italy), 1969, 2nd edition published as *Semiotica della letteratura in URSS,* 1974.

(Editor) *L'Industria della cultura,* Bompiani (Milan, Italy), 1969.

(Editor) *Dove e quando? Indagine sperimentale su due diverse edizioni di un servizio di "Almanacco,"* RAI, 1969.

(Editor) *Socialismo y consolacion: Reflexiones en torno a "Los Misterios de Paris" de Eugene Sue,* Tusquets, 1970, 2nd edition, 1974.

Le Forme del contenuto, Bompiani (Milan, Italy), 1971.

(Editor, with Cesare Sughi) *Cent'anni dopo: Il ritorno dell'intreccio,* Bompiani (Milan, Italy), 1971.

Il Segno, Isedi, 1971, 2nd edition, Mondadori (Milan, Italy).

(Editor, with M. Bonazzi) *I Pampini bugiardi,* Guaraldi, 1972.

(Editor) *Estetica e teoria dell'informazione,* Bompiani (Milan, Italy), 1972.

(Editor) *Eugenio Carmi: Una Pittura de paesaggio?,* G. Prearo, 1973.

Il Costume di casa: Evidenze e misteri dell'ideologia italiano, Bompiani (Milan, Italy), 1973.

Beato di Liebana: Miniature del Beato de Fernando I y Sancha, F. M. Ricci, 1973.

Cristianesimo e politica: Esame della presente situazione culturale, G. B. Vico, 1976.

(Coeditor) *Storia di una rivoluzione mai esistita l'esperimento Vaduz,* Servizio Opinioni, RAI, 1976.

Dalla periferia dell'impero, Bompiani (Milan, Italy), 1976.

Come si fa una tesi di laurea, Bompiani (Milan, Italy), 1977.

(Coeditor) *Le Donne al muro: L'Immagine femminile nel manifesto politico italiano, 1945-1977,* Savelli, 1977.

Il Superuomo di massa: Studi sul romanzo popolare, Cooperativa Scrittori, 1976, revised edition, Bompiani (Milan, Italy), 1978.

(Coauthor) *Informazione: Consenso e dissenso,* Saggiatore, 1979.

(Coauthor) *Strutture ed eventi dell'economia alessandrina: Cassa di risparmio di Alessandria: Umberto Eco, Carlo Beltrame, Francesco Forte,* La Pietra, 1981.

Testa a testa, Images 70, 1981.

Sette anni di desiderio, Bompiani (Milan, Italy), 1983.

Conceito de texto, Queiroz, 1984.

(Coeditor) *Cremonini: Opere dal 1960 al 1984,* Grafis, 1984.

(Coauthor) *Carnival!,* Mouton Publishers (Hague, Netherlands), 1984.

L'Espresso, 1955/85, Editoriale L'Espresso, 1985.

La Rosa dipinta: Trentuno illustratori per "Il Nome della rosa," Azzurra, 1985.

Sugli specchi e altri saggi, Bompiani (Milan, Italy), 1985.

De bibliotheca, Echoppe, 1986.

Faith in Fakes: Essays, Secker & Warburg (London, England), 1986.

(Coauthor) *Le Ragioni della retorica: Atti del Convegno "Retorica, verita, opinione, persuasione": Cattolica, 22 febbrario-20 aprile 1985,* Mucchi, 1986.

(Coauthor) *Le Isole del tesoro: Proposte per la riscoperta e la gestione delle risorse culturali,* Electa, 1988.

(Author of introduction) Maria Pia Pozzato and others, *L'Idea deforme: Interpretazioni esoteriche di Dante,* Bompiani (Milan, Italy), 1989.

Lo Strano caso della Hanau 1609, Bompiani (Milan, Italy), 1989.

(Coauthor) *Leggere i promessi sposi: Analisi semiotiche,* Bompiani (Milan, Italy), 1989.

I Limiti dell'interpretazione, Bompiani (Milan, Italy), 1990.

Stelle e stellette, Melangolo, 1991.

Vocali, Guida, 1991.

(Coauthor) *Enrico Baj: Il Giardino delle delizie,* Fabbri, 1991.

Semiotica: Storia, teoria, interpretazione: Saggi intorno a Umberto Eco, Bompiani (Milan, Italy), 1992.

(With Eugenio Carmi) *Gli gnomi di gnu,* Bompiani (Milan, Italy), 1992.

(Coeditor) Flaminio Gualdoni, *La Ceramica di Arman,* Edizioni Maggiore, 1994.

(Editor) *Povero Pinocchio,* Comix, 1995.

(Coauthor) *Carmi,* Edizioni L'Agrifoglio, 1996.

Incontro, Guernica Editions, 1997.

La Bustina di Minerva, Bompiani (Milan, Italy), 1999.

Contributor to books, including *Momenti e problema di storia dell'estetica,* Marzorati, 1959; *Documenti su il nuovo medioevo,* Bompiani (Milan, Italy), 1973; *Convegno su realta e ideologie dell'informazione,* 1978, Il Saggiatore, 1979; *Carolina Invernizio, Matilde Serao, Liala,* La Nuova Italia, 1979; and *Perche continuiamo a fare e a insegnare arte?,* Cappelli, 1979.

Eco's works have been translated into several languages, including Spanish and French.

IN ENGLISH TRANSLATION

Il Problema estetico in San Tommaso, Edizioni di Filosofia, 1956, 2nd edition published as *Il Problema estetico in Tommaso d'Aquino,* Bompiani (Milan, Italy), 1970, translation by Hugh Bredin published as *The Aesthetics of Thomas Aquinas,* Harvard University Press (Cambridge, MA), 1988.

(Editor, with G. Zorzoli) *Storia figurata delle invenzioni: Dalla selce scheggiata al volo spaziali,* Bompiani (Milan, Italy), 1961, 2nd edition, 1968, translation by Anthony Lawrence published as *The Picture History of Inventions from Plough to Polaris,* Macmillan (New York, NY), 1963.

Opera aperta: Forma e indeterminazione nelle poetiche contemporanee (includes *Le poetiche di Joyce;* also see below), Bompiani (Milan, Italy),

1962, revised edition, 1972, translation by Anna Cancogni published as *The Open Work,* Harvard University Press (Cambridge, MA), 1989.

Diario minimo, Mondadori (Milan, Italy), 1963, 2nd revised edition, 1976, translation by William Weaver published as *Misreadings,* Harcourt (San Diego, CA), 1993.

(Editor, with Oreste del Buono) *Il Caso Bond,* Bompiani (Milan, Italy), 1965, translation by R. Downie published as *The Bond Affair,* Macdonald (London, England), 1966.

I Tre cosmonauti (juvenile), illustrated by Eugenio Carmi, Bompiani (Milan, Italy), 1966, revised edition, 1988, translation published as *The Three Astronauts,* Harcourt (New York, NY), 1989.

La Bomba e il generale (juvenile), illustrated by Eugenio Carmi, Bompiani (Milan, Italy), 1966, revised edition, 1988, translation by William Weaver published as *The Bomb and the General,* Harcourt (New York, NY), 1989.

(Editor, with Jean Chesneaux and Gino Nebiolo) *I Fumetti di Mao,* Laterza, 1971, translation by Frances Frenaye published as *The People's Comic Book: Red Women's Detachment, Hot on the Trail, and Other Chinese Comics,* Anchor Press (New York, NY), 1973.

Trattato di semiotica generale, Bompiani (Milan, Italy), 1975, translation published as *A Theory of Semiotics,* Indiana University Press (Bloomington, IN), 1976.

Lector in fabula: La Cooperazione interpretative nei testi narrativa, Bompiani (Milan, Italy), 1979, translation published as *The Role of the Reader: Explorations in the Semiotics of Texts,* Indiana University Press (Bloomington, IN), 1979.

Il Nome della rosa (novel), Bompiani (Milan, Italy), 1980, translation by William Weaver published as *The Name of the Rose,* Harcourt (New York, NY), 1983.

Semiotica e filosofia del linguaggio, G. Einaudi, 1984, translation published as *Semiotics and the Philosophy of Language,* Indiana University Press (Bloomington, IN), 1984.

Postscript to "The Name of the Rose" (originally published in Italian), translation by William Weaver, Harcourt (New York, NY), 1984.

Art and Beauty in the Middle Ages (originally published in Italian), translation by Hugh Bredin, Yale University Press (New Haven, CT), 1986.

Travels in Hyper Reality (originally published in Italian), edited by Helen Wolff and Kurt Wolff, translation by William Weaver, Harcourt (New York, NY), 1986.

Il Pendolo di Foucault (novel), Bompiani (Milan, Italy), 1988, translation by William Weaver published as *Foucault's Pendulum,* Harcourt (New York, NY), 1989.

The Aesthetics of Chaosmos: The Middle Ages of James Joyce (originally published in Italian), translation by Ellen Esrock, Harvard University Press (Cambridge, MA), 1989.

La Quete d'une langue parfaite dans l'histoire de la culture europeenne: Lecon inaugurale, faite le vendredi 2 octobre 1992, College de France, 1992, published in Italian as *La Ricerca della lingua perfetta nella cultura europea,* Laterza (Bari, Italy), 1993, translation by James Fentress published as *The Search for the Perfect Language,* Blackwell (Oxford, England), 1994.

How to Travel with a Salmon and Other Essays (originally published in Italian as *Il Secondo diario minimo*), translation by William Weaver, Harcourt (New York, NY), 1994.

L'Isola del giorno prima (novel), Bompiani (Milan, Italy), 1994, translation by William Weaver published as *The Island of the Day Before,* Harcourt (New York, NY), 1995.

Kant e l'ornitorinco, Bompiani (Milan, Italy), 1997, translation by Alastair McEwen published as *Kant and the Platypus: Essays on Language and Cognition,* Harcourt Brace (New York, NY), 2000.

Cinque scritti morali, Bompiani (Milan, Italy), 1997, translation by Alastair McEwen published as *Five Moral Pieces,* Harcourt (New York, NY), 2001.

Serendipities: Language and Lunacy, translation by William Weaver, Columbia University Press (New York, NY), 1998.

Baudolino, Bompiani (Milan, Italy), 2000, translation by William Weaver, Harvard University Press (Cambridge, MA), 2002.

Experiences in Translation, translation by Alastair McEwen, University of Toronto Press (Toronto, Canada), 2001.

On Literature, translation by Martin McLaughlin, Harcourt (Orlando, FL), 2004.

IN ENGLISH

(Coauthor) *Environmental Information: A Methodological Proposal,* UNESCO, 1981.

(Editor, with Thomas A. Sebeok) *Sign of the Three: Dupin, Holmes, Peirce,* Indiana University Press (Bloomington, IN), 1984.

(Editor, with others) *Meaning and Mental Representations,* Indiana University Press (Bloomington, IN), 1988.

(Editor, with Costantino Marmo) *On the Medieval Theory of Signs,* John Benjamins, 1989.

The Limits of Interpretation, Indiana University Press (Bloomington, IN), 1990.

(With Richard Rorty, Jonathan Culler, and Christine Brooke-Rose) *Interpretation and Overinterpretation,* Cambridge University Press (Cambridge, England), 1992.

Misreadings, Harcourt (New York, NY), 1993.

Apocalypse Postponed: Essays, Indiana University Press (Bloomington, IN), 1994.

Six Walks in the Fictional Woods, Harvard University Press (Cambridge, MA), 1994.

(Author of text) *Leonardo Cremonini: Paintings and Watercolors, 1976-1986,* Claude Bernard Gallery, 1987.

The Cult of Vespa, Gingko Press, 1997.

(Coauthor) *Conversations about the End of Time: Umberto Eco . . . [and others],* produced and edited by Catherine David, Frederic Lenoir, and Jean-Philippe de Tonnac, Fromm International (New York, NY), 2000.

(With Carlo Maria Martini) *Belief or Nonbelief?: A Confrontation,* translation by Minna Proctor, Arcade (New York, NY), 2000.

Contributor to numerous encyclopedias, including *Enciclopedia filosofica* and *Encyclopedic Dictionary of Semiotics.* Also contributor to proceedings of First Congress of the International Association for Semiotic Studies. Columnist for *Il Giorno, La Stampa, Corriere della sera,* and other newspapers and magazines. Contributor of essays and reviews to numerous periodicals, including *Espresso, Corriere della sera, Times Literary Supplement, Revue internationale de sciences sociales,* and *Nouvelle revue française.* Member of editorial board, *Semiotica, Poetics Today, Degres, Structuralist Review, Text, Communication, Problemi dell'informazione,* and *Alfabeta;* editor, *VS-Semiotic Studies.*

ADAPTATIONS: Jean-Jacques Annaud directed a 1986 film adaptation of Eco's novel *The Name of the Rose,* starring Sean Connery as William of Baskerville.

SIDELIGHTS: No one expected *The Name of the Rose* to become an internationally acclaimed best-seller, least of all its author, Umberto Eco. A respected Italian scholar, Eco has built his literary reputation on specialized academic writing about semiotics: the study of how cultures communicate through signs. Not only was *The Name of the Rose* Eco's first novel, it was also a complex creation, long on philosophy and short on sex—definitely not blockbuster material, especially not in Italy where the market for books is small.

Some experts attribute the novel's success to the rising interest in fantasy literature. "For all its historical accuracy, *The Name of the Rose* has the charm of an invented world," Drenka Willen, Eco's editor at Harcourt, told *Newsweek.* Others chalk it up to snob appeal. "Every year there is one great *unread* bestseller. A lot of people who will buy the book will never read it," Howard Kaminsky, president of Warner Books, suggested in that same *Newsweek* article.

But perhaps the most plausible explanation is the one offered by Franco Ferrucci in the *New York Times Book Review:* "The answer may lie in the fact that Mr. Eco is the unacknowledged leader of contemporary Italian culture, a man whose academic and ideological prestige has grown steadily through years of dazzling and solid work."

On one level *The Name of the Rose* is a murder mystery in which a number of Catholic monks are inexplicably killed. The setting is an ancient monastery in northern Italy, the year is 1327, and the air is rife with evil. Dissension among rival factions of the Franciscan order threatens to tear the church apart, and each side is preparing for a fight. On one side stand the Spiritualists and the emperor Louis IV who endorse evangelical poverty; on the other stand the corrupt Pope John XXII and the monks who believe that the vow of poverty will rob the church of earthly wealth and power. In an effort to avoid a confrontation, both sides agree to meet at the monastery—a Benedictine abbey that is considered neutral ground. To this meeting come William of Baskerville, an English Franciscan empowered to represent the emperor, and Adso, William's disciple and scribe. Before the council can convene, however, the body of a young monk is discovered at the bottom of a cliff, and William, a master logician in the tradition of Sherlock Holmes, is recruited to solve the crime, assisted by Adso, in Watson's role.

Nowhere is the importance of decoding symbols more apparent than in the library—an intricate labyrinth that houses all types of books, including volumes on pagan rituals and black magic. The secret of the maze is known to only a few, among them the master librarian whose job it is to safeguard the collection and supervise the circulation of appropriate volumes. William suspects that the murder relates to a forbidden book—a rare work with "the power of a thousand scorpions"—that some of the more curious monks have been trying to obtain. "What the temptation of adultery is for laymen and the yearning for riches is for secular ecclesiastics, the seduction of knowledge is for monks," William explains to Adso. "Why should they not have risked death to satisfy a curiosity of their minds, or have killed to prevent someone from appropriating a jealously guarded secret of their own?"

If William speaks for reason, Adso—the young novice who, in his old age, will relate the story—represents the voice of faith. Ferrucci believed that Adso reflects the author's second side: "The Eco who writes *The Name of the Rose* is Adso: a voice young and old at the same time, speaking from nostalgia for love and passion. William shapes the story with his insight; Adso gives it his own pathos. He will never think, as William does, that 'books are not made to be believed but to be subjected to inquiry'; Adso writes to be believed."

Another way *The Name of the Rose* can be interpreted is as a parable of modern life. The vehement struggle between church and state mirrors much of recent Italian history with its "debates over the role of the left and the accompanying explosion of terrorist violence," wrote Sari Gilbert in the *Washington Post.* Eco acknowledges the influence that former Italian premier Aldo Moro's 1978 kidnapping and death had on his story, telling Gilbert that it "gave us all a sense of impotence," but he also warned that the book was not simply a *roman à clef.* "Instead," he told Herbert Mitgang in a *New York Times Book Review* article, "I hope readers see the roots, that everything that existed then—from banks and the inflationary spiral to the burning of libraries—exists today. We are always approaching the time of the anti-Christ. In the nuclear age, we are never far from the Dark Ages."

As with his first novel, Eco's second novel was an international best-seller. Published in 1989 in English as *Foucault's Pendulum,* the book is similar to *The Name of the Rose* in that it is a semiotic murder mystery wrapped in several layers of meaning. The plot revolves around Casaubon, the narrator, and two Milan editors who break up the monotony of reviewing manuscripts on the occult by combining information from all of them into one computer program called the Plan. Initially conceived as a joke, the Plan connects the Knights Templar—a medieval papal order that fought in the Crusades—with other occult groups throughout history. The program produces a map indicating the geographical point at which the powers of the earth can be controlled. That point is in Paris, France, at Foucault's Pendulum. When occult groups, including Satanists, get wind of the Plan, they go so far as to kill one of the editors in their quest to gain control of the earth. Beyond the basic plot, readers will also encounter William Shakespeare, Rene Descartes, Tom and Jerry, Karl Marx, Rhett Butler and Scarlett O'Hara, Sam Spade, and Frederick the Great of Prussia, as well as assorted Nazis, Rosicrucians, and Jesuits. Eco orchestrates all of these and other diverse characters and groups into his multilayered semiotic story.

Some of the interpretations of *Foucault's Pendulum* critics have suggested include reading it as nothing more than an elaborate joke, as an exploration of the ambiguity between text as reality and reality as text, and as a warning that harm comes to those who seek knowledge through bad logic and faulty reasoning. Given this range of interpretation and Eco's interest in semiotics, *Foucault's Pendulum* is probably best described as a book about many things, including the act of interpretation itself.

Foucault's Pendulum generated a broad range of commentary. Some critics faulted it for digressing too often into scholarly minutia, and others felt Eco had only mixed success in relating the different levels of his tale. Several reviewers, however, praised *Foucault's Pendulum.* Comparing the work to his first novel, Herbert Mitgang, for example, said in the *New York Times* that the book "is a quest novel that is deeper and richer than *The Name of the Rose.* It's a brilliant piece of research and writing—experimental and funny, literary and philosophical—that bravely ignores the conventional expectations of the reader." Eco offered his own opinion of his novel in *Time:* "This was a book conceived to irritate the reader. I knew it would provoke ambiguous, nonhomogeneous responses because it was a book conceived to point up some contradictions."

Eco's third novel, *The Island of the Day Before,* like *The Search for the Perfect Language,* explained Toronto *Globe and Mail* contributor Patrick Rengger, "is

also, and in more ways than one, attempting to excavate truths by sifting language and meaning." The book takes place during the early seventeenth century and tells the story of an Italian castaway, Roberto della Griva, who is marooned on an otherwise deserted ship in the South Pacific. "While exploring the ship," stated Mel Gussow in the *New York Times,* "the protagonist drifts back into his past and recalls old battles as well as old figments of his imagination." *The Island of the Day Before* "is dazzling in its range," *Los Angeles Times Book Review* contributor Marina Warner declared, "its linguistic fireworks ('Babelizing' as Eco calls it) and sheer learning."

In *Baudolino* Eco draws readers back into the early thirteenth century to tell the life story of a man involved in most major events of the period, including the search for the Holy Grail and the fourth Crusade. An admitted liar, Baudolino tells his story to Byzantine scribe Niketas Choniates, a member of the court of Frederick Barbarossa, while all around the two men the city of Constantinople is undergoing destruction. "The implicit contrast between the refined civilization of Byzantium and the barbarity of the Crusaders who willfully put it to the torch is as forceful now as ever," noted Ingrid D. Rowland in a review for the *New Republic;* "the destruction of Constantinople in *Baudolino,* like the destruction of the library in *The Name of the Rose,* threatens to slay civility itself." Noting that the novel leaves the reader puzzling over what is fact and what is fiction—Niketas Choniates was an actual person, whereas Baudolino is not—*Seattle Times* contributor Terry Tazioli wrote that the novel "becomes so fun, so fanciful and so intricate that Eco must be chuckling all the way to the corner trattoria, simply anticipating his readers' befuddlement and fun." Calling *Baudolino* both "beguiling and exasperating," *Time* reviewer Richard Lacayo maintained that through his novel Eco once again illustrates that "the thing we call knowledge—of ourselves, one another, the world at large— . . . [is] mostly a matter of which illusions we choose to believe."

Apart from his novels, Eco has been a prolific contributor to Italian letters, and many of his works have been translated into English. *The Search for the Perfect Language* is a history of the attempts to reconstruct a "natural" original language. *London Review of Books* contributor John Sturrock called it "a brisk, chronological account of the many thinkers about language, from antiquity onwards, who have conceived programmes for undoing the effects of time and either recovering the ur-language that they believed must once have existed only later to be lost, or else inventing a replacement for it." Eco pursues this search as a semiotician, because he believes language is the most common human symbol. However, as *The Search for the Perfect Language* reveals, more often than not the thinkers only reveal their own linguistic prejudices in their conclusions. This search for the primal tongue is, Sturrock continued, a "history of a doomed but often laudably ingenious movement to go against the linguistic grain and rediscover a truly natural language: a language of Nature or of God as it were, the appropriateness of whose signs there could be no denying."

Eco's *Apocalypse Postponed* is a collection of essays on culture written between the 1960s and the 1980s. The book discusses a variety of topics, including cartoons, literacy, Federico Fellini, and the counterculture movement, and reflects the alarm of many intellectuals at the proliferation of pop culture during the period. Divided into four parts, which reflect the topics of mass culture, mass media, countercultures, and Italian intellectualism, the book was summarized by a *Kirkus* reviewer as "substantial, lucid, humane, and a great deal of fun." *Serendipities: Language and Lunacy* is, as Tom Holland reported in the *New Statesman,* "really nothing more than a collection of footnotes to an earlier and much more detailed work," *The Search for the Perfect Language.* In *Booklist,* Michael Spinella wrote, "This slim but pithy volume offers an approachable introduction to the intellectual history of language and the foundation of linguistic study."

In *Kant and the Platypus* Eco considers questions of meaning: how do we identify and classify something that is totally new to us? The book revisits and revises ideas of semiotics that Eco previously discussed in *A Theory of Semiotics* and *Semiotics and the Philosophy of Language.* According to Simon Blackburn in the *New Republic,* Eco said, "This is a hard-core book. It's not a page-turner. You have to stay on every page for two weeks with your pencil. In other words, don't buy it if you are not Einstein." However, in *World Literature Today,* Rocco Capozzi commented that the author has "an outstanding talent for teaching and entertaining at the same time, even as he examines complicated theoretical, philosophical, linguistic, and cultural issues." And in *Publishers Weekly,* a reviewer called *Kant and the Platypus* "valuable and pleasurable for anyone seeking a gallant introduction to the

philosophy of language." In *Five Moral Pieces,* Eco presents five essays on ethical principles in postmodern culture. The essays originated as lectures and were each prompted by a social crisis—such as the Gulf War, the trial of a Nazi criminal, or the rise of extreme conservatives in Europe—or by an invitation for Eco to contribute his thoughts on a topic. In *Library Journal,* Ulrich Baer wrote that the collection "cogently argues and periodically sparkles with . . . wit and insight."

Eco, who directs programs for communication sciences and publishing at the University of Bologna, frequently travels to the United States and elsewhere to speak and teach. He continues to produce scholarly treatises, contributes to several Italian and foreign newspapers, and edits a weekly column for the magazine *L'Espresso.*

BIOGRAPHICAL AND CRITICAL SOURCES:

BOOKS

Bondanella, Peter E., *Umberto Eco and the Open Text: Semiotics, Fiction, Popular Culture,* Cambridge University Press (New York, NY), 1997.
Capozzi, Rocco, editor, *Reading Eco: An Anthology,* Indiana University Press (Bloomington, IN), 1997.
Contemporary Literary Criticism, Gale (Detroit, MI), Volume 28, 1984, Volume 60, 1991.
Inge, Thomas M., editor, *Naming the Rose: Essays on Eco's "The Name of the Rose,"* University Press of Mississippi (Jackson, MS), 1988.
Santoro-Brienza, Liberato, editor, *Talking of Joyce: Umberto Eco, Liberato Santoro-Brienza,* University College Dublin Press (Dublin, Ireland), 1998.
Tanner, William E., Anne Gervasi, and Kay Mizell, editors, *Out of Chaos: Semiotics; A Festschrift in Honor of Umberto Eco,* Liberal Arts Press (Arlington, TX), 1991.

PERIODICALS

America, August 3, 1983.
American Historical Review, June, 1997, p. 776.
American Scholar, autumn, 1987.
Antioch Review, winter, 1993, p. 149.
Atlantic, November, 1989; November, 1998, p. 138.

Bloomsbury Review, September, 1992.

Booklist, April 15, 1998, p. 1369; February 15, 1997, p. 1038; October 15, 1998, p. 377; April 1, 2000, p. 1414; April 15, 2000, p. 1502; September 1, 2001, p. 43; March 15, 2003, Ted Hipple, review of *Baudolino,* p. 1338.

Books, autumn, 1999, p. 18.

Books in Canada, December, 2002, David Solway, review of *Baudolino,* p. 10.

Boston Book Review, July, 1999, p. 32; December, 1999, p. 33.

Boston Globe, March 30, 1994, p. 75.

Choice, December, 2000, p. 720; September, 2001, p. 108.

Corriere della sera, June 1, 1981.

Critique, spring, 2001, p. 271; summer, 2003, Thomas J. Rice, "Mapping Complexity in the Fiction of Umberto Eco," pp. 349-369.

Daily Telegraph (London, England), December 18, 1999, p. 3.

Drama Review, summer, 1993.

Economist, October 28, 1989.

Emergency Librarian, May, 1997, p. 9.

Esquire, August, 1994, p. 99.

Globe and Mail, (Toronto, Ontario, Canada), January 6, 1996, p. C7.

Guardian, March 24, 1998; December 18, 1999, p. 1.

Harper's, August, 1983; May, 1993, p. 24; January, 1995, p. 33.

International Philosophical Quarterly, June, 1980.

Interview, November, 1989.

Journal of Communication, autumn, 1976.

Kirkus Reviews, March 15, 1994; September 1, 1998, p. 1253; November 1, 1999, p. 1705; August 1, 2001, p. 1085.

Language, Volume 53, number 3, 1977.

Language in Society, April, 1977.

Library Journal, October 15, 1998, p. 70; November 1, 1999, p. 86; December, 1999, p. 158; April 15, 2000, p. 96; August, 2001, p. 107.

London Review of Books, October 5, 1995, p. 8; November 16, 1995; December 9, 1999, p. 9.

Los Angeles Times, November 9, 1989; June 1, 1993, p. E4; March 18, 2000, p. B2; December 3, 2001, p. E3.

Los Angeles Times Book Review, June 4, 1989; April 13, 1994; November 13, 1994, p. 6; December 17, 1995.

Maclean's, July 18, 1983.

Medieval Review, July 3, 1998.

Nation, January 6, 1997, p. 35.

National Review, January 22, 1990.

New Republic, September 5, 1983; November 27, 1989; February 7, 2000, p. 34; November 18, 2002, Ingrid D. Rowland, review of *Baudolino,* p. 33.

New Scientist, April 3, 1999, p. 50.

New Statesman, December 15, 1989; April 22, 1994; February 26, 1999, p. 54.

Newsweek, July 4, 1983; September 26, 1983; September 29, 1986; November 13, 1989.

New Yorker, May 24, 1993, p. 30; August 21-28, 1995, p. 122.

New York Review of Books, July 21, 1983; February 2, 1995; June 9, 1994, p. 24; June 22, 1995, p. 12; April 10, 1997, p. 4; June 15, 2000, p. 62.

New York Times, June 4, 1983; December 13, 1988; October 11, 1989; January 9, 1991, p. C15; November 28, 1995, pp. B1-B2.

New York Times Book Review, June 5, 1983; July 17, 1983; October 15, 1989; July 25, 1993, p. 17; October 22, 1995; March 14, 1993, p. 31; November 3, 2002, Peter Green, review of *Baudolino,* p. 14.

Observer (London, England), February 7, 1999, p. 13.

People, August 29, 1983.

Publishers Weekly, February 24, 1989, p. 232; September 28, 1998, p. 83; October 25, 1999, p. 61; March 27, 2000, p. 59; September 10, 2001, p. 69; November 4, 2002, Daisy Maryles, review of *Baudolino,* p. 18.

Quadrant, January, 1997, p. 113.

Reference and Research Book News, February, 1999, p. 153.

Review of Contemporary Fiction, spring, 1999, p. 180.

San Francisco Chronicle, December 12, 1999, p. 11.

San Francisco Review of Books, spring, 1991, pp. 18-19.

Seattle Times, November 13, 2002, Terry Tazioli, review of *Baudolino.*

Sight and Sound, November, 1994, p. 37.

Spectator, June 12, 1993, pp. 49-50; November 19, 1994, p. 48; March 27, 1999, p. 41; January 15, 2000, p. 35.

Time, June 13, 1983; March 6, 1989; November 6, 1989; November 4, 2002, Richard Lacayo, review of *Baudolino,* p. 86.

Times (London, England), September 29, 1983; November 3, 1983.

Times Higher Education Supplement, January 23, 1998, p. 18; January 22, 1999, p. 33.

Times Literary Supplement, July 8, 1977; March 3, 1989; April 7-13, 1989, p. 380; February 1, 1991, p. 9; December 6, 1991, p. 12; July 30, 1993, p. 8; June 11, 1999, p. 26; February 25, 2000, p. 7;

September 21, 2001, p. 31; May 2, 2003, Peter Hainsworth, "Dialects and Ecos: Italian Fiction Is in Good Shape," p. 14-15.

UNESCO Courier, June, 1993.

U.S. News and World Report, November 20, 1989.

Voice Literary Supplement, October, 1983; November, 1989.

Wall Street Journal, June 20, 1983; November 14, 1989.

Washington Post, October 9, 1983; November 26, 1989.

Washington Post Book World, June 19, 1983; October 29, 1989.

Washington Times, November 11, 2001, p. 6.

World Literature Today, spring, 1999, p. 313; autumn, 2000, p. 877.

ONLINE

The Modern Word, http://www.themodernword.com/ (January 18, 2002), "Umberto Eco."*

*   *   *

ENDO, Shusaku 1923-1996

PERSONAL: Born March 27, 1923, in Tokyo, Japan; died September 29, 1996; son of Tsuneshia and Iku (Takei) Endo; married Junko Okado, September 3, 1955; children: Ryunosuke (son). *Education:* Keio University, Tokyo, B.A., 1949; Lyon University, Lyon, France, student in French literature, 1950-53.

CAREER: Writer.

MEMBER: International PEN (president of Japanese Centre, 1969), Association of Japanese Writers (member of executive committee, 1966).

AWARDS, HONORS: Akutagawa prize (Japan), 1955, for *Shiroihito;* Tanizaki prize (Japan), 1967, and Gru de Oficial da Ordem do Infante dom Henrique (Portugal), 1968, both for *Chinmoku;* Sancti Silvestri, awarded by Pope Paul VI, 1970; Noma prize, 1980.

WRITINGS:

IN ENGLISH TRANSLATION

Umi to Dokuyaku (novel), Bungeishunju, 1958, translation by Michael Gallagher published as *The Sea and Poison,* P. Owen (London, England), 1971, Taplinger, 1980.

Kazan (novel), [Japan], 1959, translation by Richard A. Schuchert published as *Volcano,* P. Owen (London, England), 1978, Taplinger, 1980.

Obaka-san, [Japan], 1959, translation by Francis Mathy published as *Wonderful Fool,* Harper (New York, NY), 1983, reprinted, Dufour Editions (Chester Springs, PA), 2000.

Chinmoku (novel), Shinkosha, 1966, translation by William Johnston published as *Silence,* P. Owen (London, England), 1969, Taplinger, 1979.

Ougon no Ku (play), Shinkosha, 1969, translation by Francis Mathy published as *The Golden Country,* Tuttle (Tokyo, Japan), 1970.

Iseu no shogai, [Japan], 1973, translation by Richard A. Schuchert published as *A Life of Jesus,* Paulist Press, 1978.

Kuchibue o fuku toki (novel), [Japan], 1974, translation by Van C. Gessel published as *When I Whistle,* Taplinger, 1979.

Juichi no iro-garasu (short stories), [Japan], 1979, translation published as *Stained Glass Elegies,* Dodd (New York, NY), 1985.

Samurai (novel), [Japan], 1980, translation by Van C. Gessel published as *The Samurai,* Harper (New York, NY), 1982.

Scandal, translation by Van C. Gessel, Dodd (New York, NY), 1988.

Foreign Studies, translation by Mark Williams, P. Owen (London, England), 1989.

The Final Martyrs, translation by Van C. Gessel, New Directions (New York, NY), 1994.

Deep River, translation by Van C. Gessel, New Directions (New York, NY), 1994.

Watashi ga suteta onna (see also below), translation by Mark Williams published as *The Girl I Left Behind,* New Directions (New York, NY), 1995.

Five by Endo: Stories, translation by Van C. Gessel, New Directions (New York, NY), 2000.

Song of Sadness (originally published as *Kanashimi no uta*), translation by Teruyo Shimizu, University of Michigan Center for Japanes Studies (Ann Arbor, MI), 2003.

IN JAPANESE

Shiroihito (novel), Kodansha (Tokyo, Japan), 1955.

Seisho no Naka no Joseitachi (essays; title means "Women in the Bible"), Shinchosha (Tokyo, Japan), 1968.

Bara no Yakat (play), Shinchosha (Tokyo, Japan), 1969.

Yumoa shosetsu shu (short stories), Kodansha (Tokyo, Japan), 1974.

France no daigakusei (essays on travel in France), Kadokawashoten, 1974.

Kitsunegata tanukigata (short stories), Kodansha (Tokyo, Japan), 1976.

Watashi ga suteta onna, Kodansha (Tokyo, Japan), 1976.

Yukiaru kotoba (essays), Shinchosha (Tokyo, Japan), 1976.

Nihonjin wa Kirisuto kyo o shinjirareru ka, Shogaku-kan, 1977.

Kare no ikikata, Shinchosha (Tokyo, Japan), 1978.

Kirisuto no tanjo, Shinchosha (Tokyo, Japan), 1978.

Ningen no naka no X (essays), Shuokoronsha, 1978.

Rakuten taisho, Kodansha (Tokyo, Japan), 1978.

Ju to jujika (biography of Pedro Cassini), Shuokoronsha, 1979.

Marie Antoinette (fiction), Asahi Shinbunsha, 1979.

Chichioya, Shinchosha (Tokyo, Japan), 1980.

Kekkonron, Shufunotomosha, 1980.

Sakka no nikki (diary excerpts), Toju-sha, 1980.

Endo Shusaku ni yoru Endo Shusaku, Seidosha, 1980.

Meiga Iesu junrei, Bungei Shunju, 1981.

Onna no issho (fiction), Asahi Shinbunsha, 1982.

Endo Shusaku to Knagaeru, PHP Kekyujo, 1982.

Fuyu no yasashisa, Bunka Shuppakyoku, 1982.

Enishi no ito: bunshu, Sekai Bunkasha (Tokyo, Japan), 1998.

Also author of *Watakusi no Iesu,* 1976, *Usaba kagero nikki,* 1978, *Shinran,* 1979, *Tenshi,* 1980, *Ai to jinsei o meguru danso,* 1981, and *Okuku e no michi,* 1981.

SIDELIGHTS: Of all leading twentieth-century Japanese novelists, Shusaku Endo is considered by many critics as the most accessible to Western readers. Endo's Roman Catholic upbringing is often cited as the key to his accessibility, for it gave him a philosophical background shaped by Western traditions rather than those of the East. Christianity is a rarity in Japan, where two sects of Buddhism predominate. As Garry Wills explained in the *New York Review of Books,* "Christ is not only challenging but embarrassing [to the Japanese] because he has absolutely no 'face'. . . . He will let anyone spit on him. How can the Japanese ever honor such a disreputable figure?" While strongly committed to his adopted religion, Endo often described the sense of alienation felt by a Christian in Japan. Most of his novels translated into

English address the clash of Eastern and Western morals and philosophy, as well as illustrate the difficulty and unlikelihood of Christianity's establishment in Japan.

John Updike wrote in the *New Yorker* that Endo's first novel in English translation, *Silence,* is "a remarkable work, a somber, delicate, and startlingly empathetic study of a young Portuguese missionary during the relentless persecution of the Japanese Christians in the early seventeenth century." The young missionary, Rodrigues, travels to Japan to investigate rumors that his former teacher, Ferreira, has not only converted to Buddhism, but is even participating in the persecution of Christians. As Updike noted, "One can only marvel at the unobtrusive, persuasive effort of imagination that enables a modern Japanese to take up a viewpoint from which Japan is at the outer limit of the world."

Rodrigues is captured soon after his clandestine entry into Japan, and is handed over to the same jailer who effected Ferreira's conversion. Rodrigues is never physically harmed but is forced to watch the sufferings of native converts while repeatedly being told that his public denouncement of Christ is the only thing that will save them. At first he resists, anticipating a glorious martyrdom for himself, but eventually a vision of Christ convinces him of the selfishness of this goal. He apostatizes, hoping to save at least a few of the Japanese converts by his example. This "beautifully simple plot," wrote Updike, "harrowingly dramatizes immense theological issues."

Endo sought to illustrate Japan's hostility toward a Christ figure in another of his translated novels, *Wonderful Fool.* Set in modern times, this story centers on a Frenchman, Gaston Bonaparte. Gaston is a priest who longs to work with missionaries in Japan; after being defrocked, he travels there alone to act as a lay missionary. Completely trusting, pure-hearted, and incapable of harming anyone, Gaston is seen only as a bumbling fool by the Japanese. At their hands he is "scorned, deceived, threatened, beaten and finally drowned in a swamp," reported *Books Abroad* contributor Kinya Tsuruta. "In the end, however, his total faith transforms all the Japanese, not excluding even a hardened criminal. Thus, the simple Frenchman has successfully sowed a seed of good will in the corrupting mud swamp, Endo's favorite metaphor for non-Christian Japan."

Wonderful Fool was seen by some reviewers as Endo's condemnation of his country's values. "What shocks him . . . ," noted a *Times Literary Supplement* contributor, "is the spiritual emptiness of what he calls 'mud-swamp Japan,' an emptiness heightened by the absence of any appropriate sense of sin. . . . [But] is it not, perhaps, too self-righteous to ask whether Japan needs the sense of sin which the author would have it assume?" Addressing this issue in a *New Republic* review, Mary Jo Salter believed that "ultimately it is the novelist's humor—slapstick, corny, irreverent—that permits him to moralize so openly."

Louis Allen concurred in the *Listener* that Endo "is one of Japan's major comic writers." Praising the author's versatility, Allen went on to write: "In *When I Whistle,* he explores yet another vein, a plain realism behind which lingers a discreet but clear symbolism." *When I Whistle* tells two parallel stories, that of Ozu and his son, Eiichi. Ozu is an unsuccessful businessman who thinks nostalgically of his childhood in pre-war Japan and his youthful romance with the lovely Aiko. Eiichi is a coldly ambitious surgeon who "despises his father—and his father's generation—as sentimentally humanist," explained Allen. The parallel stories merge when Eiichi, in the hopes of furthering his career, decides to use experimental drugs on a terminal cancer patient—Ozu's former sweetheart, Aiko.

Like *Wonderful Fool, When I Whistle* presents "an unflattering version of postwar Japan," noted Allen, adding that while *Wonderful Fool* is marked by its humor, "Sadness is the keynote [of *When I Whistle*], and its symbol the changed Aiko: a delicate beauty, unhoused and brought to penury by war, and ultimately devoured by a disease which is merely a pretext for experiment by the new, predatory generation of young Japan." *When I Whistle* differs from many of Endo's novels in its lack of an overtly Christian theme, but here as in all his fiction, maintained *New York Times Book Review* contributor Anthony Thwaite, "what interests Mr. Endo—to the point of obsession—are the concerns of both the sacred and secular realms: moral choice, moral responsibility. . . . *When I Whistle* is a seductively readable—and painful—account of these issues."

Endo returned to the historical setting of *Silence*—the seventeenth century—with *The Samurai.* This novel—his most popular work among Japanese readers—is, like *Silence,* based on historical fact. Whereas *Silence* gave readers a Portuguese missionary traveling to Ja-

pan, *The Samurai* tells of a Japanese warrior journeying to Mexico, Spain, and finally the Vatican. The samurai, Hasekura, is an unwitting pawn in his shogun's complex scheme to open trade routes to the West. Instructed to feign conversion to Christianity if it will help his cause, Hasekura does so out of loyalty to the shogun, although he actually finds Christ a repulsive figure. Unfortunately, by the time he returns to Japan five years later, political policy has been reversed, and he is treated as a state enemy for his "conversion." Finally, through his own suffering, Hasekura comes to identify with Jesus and becomes a true Christian.

Geoffry O'Brien judged *The Samurai* to be Endo's most successful novel, giving particular praise to its engrossing storyline and to the novelist's "tremendously lyrical sensory imagination" in a *Village Voice* review. *Washington Post Book World* contributor Noel Perrin agreed that *The Samurai* functions well as an adventure story but maintained that "Endo has done far more than write a historical novel about an early and odd encounter between East and West. Taking the history of Hasekura's embassy as a mere base, he has written a really quite profound religious novel. . . . It is calm and understated and brilliantly told. Simple on the surface, complex underneath. Something like a fable from an old tapestry. . . . If you're interested in how East and West really met, forget Kipling. Read Endo."

In *Scandal,* Endo relates the self-referential story of Suguro, an aging Japanese-Catholic novelist who, upon receiving crowning accolades in a public ceremony, is accused of leading a double life in the brothels of Tokyo. Haunted by his striking semblance in a portrait displayed in a sordid hotel, and hounded by Kobari, a muckraking journalist, Suguro immerses himself in the Tokyo underworld to pursue his doppelganger. Here Suguro is introduced to Mrs. Naruse, a sadomasochist nurse who engages the author's lurid yearnings and arranges for him to view his double as he engages in sex with Mitsu, a young girl. The distinction between reality and illusion becomes ambiguous as Suguro discovers his shocking other self and struggles to reconcile the moral dichotomy. According to Charles Newman in the *New York Times Book Review,* "Suguro is left with a knowledge more complex than that of a moral hypocrite and more human than that of a writer who had commonly confused the esthetic dualism with the spiritual," reflecting instead "the irreducible evil at the core of his own character." In the end, as Louis Allen observed in the *Times Literary Supplement,* "The sure grip Suguro thought he had on his world is gradually pried loose. His relationship to his wife is falsified, and his art is seen to be built on self-deception. He realizes that 'sin' and the salvation which can arise from it are somehow shallow and superficial things." Nicci Gerrard praised *Scandal* in the London *Observer,* writing that Endo "is fastidious and yet implacable in exposing the dark side of human nature and is painstakingly lucid about unresolvable mysteries."

Foreign Studies, originally published in Japan in 1965, is a collection of three tragic stories that portray the reception of Japanese students in Europe, reflecting Endo's own education in France. The first, "A Summer in Rouen," describes a Japanese student's stay with a Catholic family in postwar France. Kudo, the student, is viewed as a reincarnation of the hostess's dead son and is even called by his name. Unable to express himself because of his poor French and taciturn nature, Kudo retreats into quiet misery among his European sponsors. The brief second piece, "Araki Thomas," anticipates the themes of *Silence* and *The Samurai* in the story of a seventeenth-century Japanese student who travels to Rome to study theology. Upon his return to Japan, however, a changed political climate and torture induce Araki Thomas to apostatize his new religion. As a result he suffers from his dual betrayal of self and his fellow Christians who continue to receive punishment.

The third and longest story in *Foreign Studies,* "And You, Too," is generally regarded as the most significant. Described by Endo as "a prelude to *Silence,*" "And You, Too" conveys the acute psychological pain caused by acculturation. Tanaka, a Japanese student, visits Paris in the mid-1960s to study literature, in particular the writings of the Marquis de Sade. His preference for European writers is the source of scorn among the other Japanese expatriates, except for a failed architecture student whom he befriends until tuberculosis forces the friend's premature departure. Isolated and disconsolate in Paris, Tanaka ventures to Sade's castle near Avignon where, in a highly symbolic denouement, he wanders about the ruins and coughs blood onto the snow as he leaves, signifying his final inability to reconcile the cultures of East and West and his imminent return to Japan. As John B. Breslin noted in a *Washington Post Book World* review, Endo's prefatory comments for the English translation indicated his belief that "East and West could never really understand one another on the deep level of 'culture,' only on the relatively superficial level of 'civilization.'" Marleigh Grayer Ryan praised the collection in *World Literature Today,* writing that "the three pieces taken together constitute a strong statement of the abyss that separates the Japanese mind and the sensibility from the West."

The Final Martyr is a collection of eleven short stories produced by Endo between 1959 and 1985. However, as Karl Schoenberger qualifies in the *Los Angeles Times Book Review,* "these are not short stories at all, but rather character sketches and rambling essays in the confessional *zuihitsu* style," some with extensive footnotes that display Endo's incorporation of historical detail. As several reviewers observe, the collection reveals Endo's frequent use of the short story to develop themes and characters for later novels. Joseph R. Graber wrote in the *San Francisco Review of Books* that "*The Final Martyrs* is a fascinating study of how the writer's mind works." The title story, originally published in 1959, describes the persecution of nineteenth-century Catholic villagers in southern Japan and foreshadows the novel *Silence.* Here the central figure is a weak-minded villager who renounces Christianity under torture and experiences acute guilt as he betrays both state and God. Endo also offers unabashed autobiographic examination in *A Sixty-Year-Old Man,* written upon the author's sixtieth birthday, which describes an aging Catholic writer's lust for a young girl he encounters at the park. In the final story, *The Box,* Endo contemplates whether talking to plants encourages their growth as he recounts wartime events revealed in an old box of postcards and photographs. Paul Binding concluded in a *New Statesman* review, "It is Endo's triumph that his sense of the totalitarian power of suffering does not diminish his insights into quotidian, late-twentieth-century urban life—and vice versa."

In *Deep River,* set in India along the Ganges, Endo describes the spiritual quest of Otsu, a rejected Catholic priest who carries corpses to the funeral pyres, and a Japanese tourist group, including a recently widowed businessman who pursues the reincarnation of his wife, a former soldier who survived the Burmese Highway of Death during World War II, a nature writer, and Mitsuko, a cynical divorced woman who once seduced and spurned Otsu. Through their experiences Endo explores the transcendent wisdom and salvation of

Hinduism, Buddhism, and Catholicism, symbolically reflected in Mitsuko's characterization of God as an onion. Robert Coles commented in the *New York Times Book Review* that "Endo is a master of the interior monologue, and he builds 'case' by 'case,' chapter by chapter, a devastating critique of a world that has 'everything' but lacks moral substance and seems headed nowhere." Praising the novel as among Endo's most effective, Andrew Greeley wrote in the *Washington Post Book World* that "this moving story about a pilgrimage of grace, must be rated as one of the best of them all."

The Girl I Left Behind, written some thirty-five years earlier but not published until a year before its author's death in 1996, recounts lifelong encounters between Yoshioka Tsutomu, a Japanese salesman, and Mitsu, a simple country girl whom he seduced as a college student. Though Endo himself acknowledges the immaturity of this early work in an afterword, the sentimental story adumbrates the author's skill for characterization and powerful Christian allusions, here represented by Mitsu's Christ-like goodness and charity. Confined to a leprosarium managed by Catholic nuns until informed of her misdiagnosis, Mitsu learns to live among the lepers and devotes her life to their care. Despite its noted awkwardness and technical shortcomings, P. J. Kavanagh regarded the novel as "remarkably convincing" in a review for the *Spectator,* and a *Publishers Weekly* reviewer concluded that Endo's writing is redeemed by "moments of sparkling intelligence and clarity."

BIOGRAPHICAL AND CRITICAL SOURCES:

BOOKS

Contemporary Literary Criticism, Gale (Detroit, MI), Volume 7, 1977, Volume 14, 1980, Volume 19, 1981, Volume 54, 1989.
Dictionary of Literary Biography, Volume 182: *Japanese Fiction Writers since World War II,* Gale (Detroit, MI), 1997.
Rimer, J. Thomas, *Modern Japanese Fiction and Its Traditions: An Introduction,* Princeton University Press (Princeton, NJ), 1978.

PERIODICALS

America, June 21, 1980; February 2, 1985; October 13, 1990; August 1, 1992; November 19, 1994, pp. 18, 28.
Antioch Review, winter, 1983.
Best Sellers, November, 1980.
Books Abroad, spring, 1975.
Chicago Tribune Book World, October 7, 1979.
Christian Century, September 21, 1966.
Christianity Today, March 17, 1989.
Commonweal, November 4, 1966; September 22, 1989; May 19, 1995.
Contemporary Review, April, 1978.
Critic, July 15, 1979.
Kirkus Reviews, October 1, 1995.
Listener, May 20, 1976; April 12, 1979.
London Magazine, April-May, 1974.
London Review of Books, May 19, 1988.
Los Angeles Times, November 13, 1980; December 1, 1983.
Los Angeles Times Book Review, December 5, 1982; September 18, 1994.
New Republic, December 26, 1983.
New Statesman, May 7, 1976; April 13, 1979; April 30, 1993.
Newsweek, December 19, 1983.
New Yorker, January 14, 1980.
New York Review of Books, February 19, 1981; November 4, 1982.
New York Times Book Review, January 13, 1980; June 1, 1980; December 26, 1982; November 13, 1983; July 21, 1985; August 28, 1988; May 6, 1990; May 28, 1995.
Observer (London, England), April 24, 1988.
Publishers Weekly, July 4, 1994, p. 25; September 11, 1995, p. 72.
San Francisco Review of Books, October-November, 1994.
Saturday Review, July 21, 1979.
Spectator, May 1, 1976; April 14, 1979; May 15, 1982; November 19, 1994.
Times (London, England), April 18, 1985.
Times Literary Supplement, July 14, 1972; January 25, 1974; May 5, 1978; May 21, 1982; October 26, 1984; April 29, 1988; October 28, 1994.
Vanity Fair, February, 1991.
Village Voice, November 16, 1982.
Washington Post Book World, September 2, 1979; October 12, 1980; October 24, 1982; June 23, 1985; May 6, 1990; June 25, 1995.
World Literature Today, summer, 1979; winter, 1984; winter, 1990; winter, 1996.*

F

FITZGERALD, Penelope 1916-2000

PERSONAL: Born December 17, 1916, in Lincoln, England; died of complications from a stroke, April 28, 2000, in Highgate, London, England; daughter of Edmund Valpy (editor of *Punch*), and Christina (Hicks) Knox; married Desmond Fitzgerald, August 15, 1953 (died, 1976); children: Edmund Valpy, Maria. *Education:* Somerville College, Oxford (first-class honors), 1939. *Religion:* Christian.

CAREER: Writer. Broadcasting House (British Broadcasting Corporation), London, England, recorded program assistant, 1939-53; also worked in a bookstore and as a teacher affiliated with Westminster Tutors, London.

AWARDS, HONORS: Booker Prize shortlist for fiction, 1978, for *The Bookshop;* Booker Prize for fiction, 1979, for *Offshore;* Heywood Hill Literary Prize for lifetime achievement in literature, 1996; National Book Critics Circle Prize, 1998, for *Blue Flower.*

WRITINGS:

NOVELS

The Golden Child, Scribner (New York, NY), 1977.
The Bookshop, Duckworth (London, England), 1978, Houghton Mifflin (Boston, MA), 1997.
Offshore, Collins (London, England), 1979, Holt (New York, NY), 1987.

Penelope Fitzgerald

Human Voices, Collins (London, England), 1980, Houghton Mifflin (Boston, MA), 1999.
At Freddie's, Collins (London, England), 1982, Godine (Boston, MA), 1985.
Innocence, Holt (New York, NY), 1986, Houghton Mifflin (Boston, MA), 1998.

The Beginning of Spring, Collins (London, England), 1988, Holt (New York, NY), 1989.

The Gate of Angels, Collins (London, England), 1990, Doubleday (Garden City, NY), 1992.

The Blue Flower, Flamingo (London, England), 1996, Houghton Mifflin (Boston, MA), 1997.

BIOGRAPHIES

Edward Burne-Jones, M. Joseph (London, England), 1975, Sutton (Stroud, Gloucestershire, England), 1998.

The Knox Brothers, Macmillan (London, England), 1977, published as *The Knox Brothers: Edmund (Evoe), 1881-1971, Dillwyn, 1883-1943, Wilfred, 1886-1950, Ronald, 1888-1957,* Coward, McCann & Geoghegan (New York, NY), 1977.

Charlotte Mew and Her Friends, Collins (London, England), 1984, published as *Charlotte Mew and Her Friends: With a Selection of Her Poems,* Addison-Wesley (Reading, MA), 1988.

OTHER

Means of Escape (short stories), Houghton Mifflin (Boston, MA), 2000.

The Afterlife, edited by Terrence Dooley, Christopher Carduff, and Mandy Kirkby, Houghton Mifflin (Boston, MA), 2000.

Contributor to *Modern Women's Short Stories,* Penguin (New York, NY), 1998. A collection of Penelope Fitzgerald's papers are held at the Harry Ransom Humanities Research Center at the University of Texas at Austin.

ADAPTATIONS: The Gate of Angels has been adapted as an audiobook.

SIDELIGHTS: Penelope Fitzgerald published her first novel when she was fifty-nine years old. Some two decades and a Booker Prize later, she had established a reputation as an ironic, spare, and richly comic author. Even when the settings for her novels range as far afield as Florence, pre-revolutionary Moscow, and Germany in the 1790s, she is praised for her sense of detail and her clear observations of human nature. In the *Spectator,* Anita Brookner characterized Fitzgerald

as "one of the mildest and most English of writers," adding: "Mild, yes, but there is authority behind those neat, discursive and unresolved stories of hers. . . . She is so unostentatious a writer that she needs to be read several times. What is impressive is the calm confidence behind the apparent simplicity of utterance." *Los Angeles Times Book Review* contributor Richard Eder noted that Fitzgerald's writing is "so precise and lilting that it can make you shiver . . . an elegy that nods at what passes without lamentation or indifference."

Some of Fitzgerald's early novels are loosely based upon her own work experiences. Born of a "writing family," she was educated at Oxford and was employed by the British Broadcasting Corporation during World War II. After her marriage in 1953, she worked as a clerk in a bookstore in rural East Suffolk; later she and her family lived on a barge on the Thames. These episodes in her life helped Fitzgerald to present, in her fiction, "a small, specialist world which she opens for the reader's inspection," to quote *Dictionary of Literary Biography* contributor Catherine Wells Cole. In *The Bookshop,* for instance, a courageous entrepreneur named Florence Green defies the stuffy prejudices of her town, Hardborough, by stocking Vladimir Nabokov's novel *Lolita. The Bookshop* was described by Valentine Cunningham in the *Times Literary Supplement* as "on any reckoning a marvelously piercing fiction. . . . There are the small circumstances that give rise naturally to a Hardy-like gothic, complete with a rapping poltergeist, and to a fiction where character inevitably comes to 'characters.' And Penelope Fitzgerald's resources of odd people are impressively rich."

Offshore, published in 1979 in England, presents a community of eccentric characters living in barges (much as the author did at one time) on Battersea Reach on the Thames River. As the tide ebbs and flows, so do the lives in the unconventional community, in both comic and tragic ways. *Offshore* won the Booker Prize in 1979 for Fitzgerald, who, at sixty-three, was still something of a novice writer. In *Books and Bookmen,* reviewer Mollie Hardwick described the work as "a delicate water-colour of a novel . . . a small, charming, Whistler etching." Similar praises greeted *Human Voices,* Fitzgerald's novelistic take on wartime work at Broadcasting House in London. There, one character wishes for a quick peace because he might be called upon to provide more typewriters than he has available; another one muses about the challenge of recording the sounds of tanks rolling across a beach. In *Encounter,* correspondent Penelope Lively found the novel "a clever fictional rendering of the way in which a random selection of people, flung together for impersonal reasons, will set up a pattern of relationships and reactions . . . told in a voice that is both idiosyncratic and memorable."

Beginning in 1986 with the publication of *Innocence,* Fitzgerald began to range farther afield for her stories. Set in Florence, Italy, during the postwar era, *Innocence* follows the fortunes of a patrician family in decline. In a *Times Literary Supplement* review of the work, Anne Duchene wrote of Fitzgerald: "Her writing, as ever, has a natural authority, is very funny, warm, and gently ironic, and full of tenderness towards human beings and their bravery in living." *The Beginning of Spring* presents an off-beat comedy of manners set in the household of a British expatriate in 1913 Moscow. As the thoughtful and upright Frank Reid faces the sudden departure of his wife—leaving him with three young children—he receives dubious assistance from some of his friends, both English and Russian. To quote *New York Times Book Review* correspondent Robert Plunket, with *The Beginning of Spring* Fitzgerald has become "that refreshing rarity, a writer who is very modern but not the least bit hip. Ms. Fitzgerald looks into the past, both human and literary, and finds all sorts of things that are surprisingly up to date. Yet as *The Beginning of Spring* reaches its triumphant conclusion, you realize that its greatest virtue is perhaps the most old-fashioned of all. It is a lovely novel."

Fitzgerald produced the well-received novels *The Gate of Angels* and *The Blue Flower* (for which she was the surprise recipient of the U.S. National Book Critics Circle Prize) in the 1990s. *The Gate of Angels,* published in the United States in 1992, concerns a fictitious Cambridge college for physicists in Edwardian England, and describes how the cloistered academy changes after one of its junior fellows, Fred Fairly, suffers a bicycle accident. "This funny, touching, wise novel manages, despite its brevity, to seem leisurely," remarked Nina King in the *New York Times Book Review.* "It is vibrant with wonderful minor characters, ablaze with ideas." *Listener* reviewer Kate Kellaway noted that, in *The Gate of Angels,* Fitzgerald "unostentatiously fills her story with quietly original observations so that you are constantly recognising and dis-

covering through her eyes." John Bayley in the *New York Review of Books* observed that "Penelope Fitzgerald is not only an artist of a high order but one of immense originality, wholly her own woman. She composes with an innocent certainty which avoids any suggestion that she might have a feminist moral in mind, or a dig against science, or a Christian apologetic. The translucent little tale keeps quite clear of such matters, and yet it is certainly about goodness, and . . . successful at giving us the experience and conviction of it."

In *The Blue Flower,* according to Adam Begley of *People:* "Penelope Fitzgerald squeezes tragedy, history and philosophy into a short, beautifully written, desperately sad novel." Set in the eighteenth century, the novel is based on a true story: the spontaneous and overwhelming infatuation of twenty-two-year-old poet prodigy Friedrich von Hardenberg (later to become renowned under the pen name Novalis) with a young girl named Sophie whom he sees standing by a window. Novalis is a penniless aristocrat who nevertheless has attended the best universities. "Sophie," as described by Begley, "is an empty-headed twelve-year-old whose best feature is a guileless laugh." Fitzgerald chronicles their tragic three-year courtship, contrasting Novalis's aristocratic background with Sophie's thoroughly middle-class one. At the same time she brings to life the era in which they lived. A *Publishers Weekly* reviewer commented: "There's scads of research here, into daily life in Enlightenment-era Saxony, German reactions to the French Revolution and Napoleon, early-nineteenth-century German philosophy. . . . But history aside, this is a smart novel. Fitzgerald . . . witty and poignant . . . has created an alternately biting and touching exploration of the nature of Romanticism—capital 'R' and small."

The Means of Escape, published just after Fitzgerald's death in 2000, is a collection of eight short-short stories set in many places and times—Tasmania, England, France, Turkey and from the present back to the seventeenth century. In the *Spectator,* Philip Hennsher argued of Fitzgerald's writing in general and the title story in particular, "The interest in farce is constant; one of her best short stories, 'The Means of Escape,' is revealed, only at the very end, to be a farce, as well as, as the reader had always suspected, a crime story, a miniature psychological thriller." He added that she draws the farce into reality by describing her characters with minute realism. Additionally, *World and I* commentator Maude McDaniel noted that Fitzgerald "refuses to take sides herself" with her characters in *The Means of Escape*. "In these stories, she seems curiously detached from her own creatures, leaving readers to make of things what they will—a surrender of authority that has always annoyed me with other writers. Somehow it seems right with these offerings, which are less inclined to heavy preaching than individual nuancing," and, as McDaniel continued, often turning the reader's expectations on their head. "The reader cannot be sure of anything in ['The Red-Haired Girl']—except that in some way, lives have been touched and consequences changed." McDaniel quoted Fitzgerald in an interview: "I have remained true to my deepest convictions. I mean the courage of those who are born to be defeated, the weaknesses of the strong, and the tragedy of misunderstandings and lost opportunities, which I have done my best to treat as comedy—for otherwise how can we manage to bear it?"

In addition to her many novels, Fitzgerald published several biographies, including one of Pre-Raphaelite painter Edward Coley Burne-Jones, and one titled *The Knox Brothers*, which recounts the lives of her father and his brothers, each of whom contributed to British society in a special—and individual—way. Her 1984 biography *Charlotte Mew and Her Friends* examines the life and work of a British poet that Fitzgerald feels contemporary critics have for the most part overlooked. Once praised by novelist Thomas Hardy as "far and away the best living woman poet," Charlotte Mew (1869-1928) did not lead a happy life. Throughout her childhood her family's fortunes descended increasingly into poverty. She saw three of her brothers die before the age of five, and another brother and sister institutionalized for schizophrenia. Only her younger sister Anne, a painter of decorative screens, accompanied her into adulthood. In addition, Mew was a lesbian with the unfortunate habit of forming attachments to women who were not, attachments that invariably remained unfulfilled. Mew began writing short stories at an early age and soon became a regular contributor to *Yellow Book*, one of the popular periodicals of the day. Her fiction is consciously imitative of other writers of the era, such as Henry James, and has been dismissed by most critics as inferior work. In her poetry, however, Mew found her own voice, a distinct and original one of considerable power. April Bernard of the *New Republic* stated, "The poems are masterpieces of the lyric macabre, throat-catching, heart-stopping effulgences of rage and despair and love. . . .

Mew's work is really only like itself, busting drunkenly out of whatever scheme it seems the poem has set, into long flailing lines and unsuspected rhymes." In her forties, Mew saw her work recognized and praised by writers who congregated around London's influential Poetry Bookshop. Her readings at the Poetry Bookshop were considered mesmerizing and the shop's owners published her first collection in 1916. The poverty Mew had experienced throughout her life was relieved when she received both a government artist's pension and a small inheritance from an uncle. However, after the death of her mother and sister, both of whom she'd lived with all her life, Mew's grief led to her confinement in a nursing home where she committed suicide. Phoebe-Lou Adams, reviewing *Charlotte Mew and Her Friends* for the *Atlantic*, felt that "Ms. Fitzgerald reconstructs her Mew's sad story with grace and intelligence, while the selection of poems the American edition appended to the biography makes it clear that Mew at her best was, if not a great poet, decidedly a good one." Bernard noted, "It is greatly to Penelope Fitzgerald's credit that she has not turned this biography into one of those ghoulish mystery stories reserved for suicides, wherein the entire life is cast retrospectively in the shadow of the subject's death."

In an essay for the *Contemporary Authors Autobiography Series*, Fitzgerald wrote of herself: "Biographies and novels are the forms which I feel I can just about manage. They are the outcome of intense curiosity about other people and about oneself." That "intense curiosity" has produced a body of work that casts an eye on such intangibles as personal relationships, social institutions, history, and the interactions between them. "On a superficial reading Fitzgerald's novels may appear slight," concluded Catherine Wells Cole, "but their real strength lies in what they omit, in what has been pared away. Their skill and grace is not simply displayed technical achievement, but derives instead from Fitzgerald's absolute concern, often conveyed through humor and comedy, for the moral values of the tradition she follows so precisely."

Fitzgerald once told *CA*: "I've begun to write at rather a late stage in life because I love books and everything to do with them. I believe that people should write biographies only about people they love, or understand, or both. Novels, on the other hand, are often better if they're about people the writer doesn't like very much."

BIOGRAPHICAL AND CRITICAL SOURCES:

BOOKS

Contemporary Authors Autobiography Series, Volume 10, Gale (Detroit, MI), 1989, pp. 101-109.

Contemporary Literary Criticism, Gale (Detroit, MI), Volume 19, 1981, pp. 172-175; Volume 51, 1989, pp. 123-127; Volume 61, 1989, pp. 114-124.

Dictionary of Literary Biography, Volume 14: *British Novelists since 1960,* Gale (Detroit, MI), 1983, pp. 302-308.

PERIODICALS

America, November 11, 2000, p. 22.

Atlanta Journal-Constitution, March 26, 1998, p. E2.

Atlantic, August, 1988, p. 80.

Austin American-Statesman, June 1, 1997, p. D6; November 12, 2000, p. L6.

Australian (Sydney, New South Wales, Australia), September 13, 2000, p. B20.

Birmingham Post (Birmingham, England), October 10, 1998, p. 37.

Booklist, September 1, 1997, p. 57; October 1, 2000, p. 321; November 15, 2003, Donna Seaman, review of *The Afterlife,* p. 563.

Books and Bookmen, December 1979, pp. 16-17.

Christian Science Monitor, June 26, 1997, p. B1; May 6, 1999, p. 20.

Commonweal, June 19, 1998, p. 27; September 10, 1999, p. 32; June 16, 2000, p. 20; November 3, 2000, p. 32.

Courier-Mail (Brisbane, Australia), February 24, 1996, p. 007.

Dickens Studies Annual: Essays on Victorian Fiction, 1982, p. 143.

Encounter, January 1981, pp. 53-59.

Essays in Arts and Sciences, October 1997, p. 1.

Explicator, summer, 2001, p. 204.

Financial Times, October 7, 2000, p. 4.

Guardian (London, England), March 27, 1998, p. 21; December 16, 2000, p. 10; December 21, 2002, p. 31.

Harper's, June 1999, p. 76.

Herald (Glasgow, Scotland), November 4, 2000, p. 20.

Independent (London, England), January 26, 2002.

Independent on Sunday (London, England), September 1, 1996, p. 37; October 1, 2000, p. 73; January 26, 2002, p. 11.

International Herald Tribune, March 26, 1998, p. 20.

Journal of the William Morris Society, autumn, 1998, p. 25.

Kirkus Reviews, October 1, 2003, Donna Seaman, review of *The Afterlife,* p. 1218.

Knight Ridder/Tribune News Service, November 29, 2000, p. K5334; January 3, 2001, p. K3072.

Library Journal, September 1, 1997, p. 217; May 1, 1998, p. 144; May 1, 1999, p. 109; October 15, 2000, p. 107.

Listener, August 23, 1990, p. 24.

London Review of Books, October 13, 1988, pp. 20-21; October 5, 1995, p. 7; May 23, 2002, p. 17.

Los Angeles Times Book Review, April 23, 1989, p. 3; January 12, 1992, pp. 3, 7; April 13, 1997, p. 5; December 24, 1997, p. 11; October 15, 2000, p. 11.

New Criterion, March 1992, p. 33.

New Republic, August 22, 1988, p. 36; August 2, 1999, p. 39.

New Statesman, October 3, 1980, p. 24; November 6, 2000, p. 52.

New Statesman and Society, October 6, 1995, p. 38; January 28, 2002, p. 54.

New Yorker, February 7, 2000, p. 80.

New York Review of Books, April 9, 1992, p. 13; October 5, 1995, p. 7; July 17, 1997, p. 4; June 10, 1999, p. 28.

New York Times, September 8, 1985, p. 24; April 28, 1987, p. C17; March 26, 1998, p. B11; May 5, 1999, p. E9; August 31, 2000, p. E8.

New York Times Book Review, April 1, 1979, p. 21; June 29, 1980, p. 3; September 8, 1985, p. 24; May 10, 1987, p. 20; September 13, 1987, p. 51; August 7, 1988, p. 15; May 7, 1989, p. 15; March 1, 1992, pp. 7, 9; April 13, 1997, p. 9; September 7, 1997, p. 11; December 7, 1997, p. 12; May 9, 1999, p. 22; November 26, 2000, p. 8; September 16, 2001, p. 32.

New York Times Magazine, August 15, 1999, p. 30.

Observer (London, England), September 17, 1995, p. 15; September 8, 1996, p. 18; October 29, 2000, p. 11; December 24, 2000, p. 19.

People, April 14, 1997, p. 29.

Publishers Weekly, March 10, 1997, p. 51; July 21, 1997, p. 183; April 5, 1999, p. 219; May 17, 1999, p. 51; September 4, 2000, p. 28; September 25, 2000, p. 88.

St. Louis Dispatch, October 5, 1997, p. 05C.

San Francisco Chronicle, March 30, 1997, p. 5; April 6, 1997, p. 11; August 24, 1997, p. 5; March 3, 1998, p. B3; March 25, 1998, p. E2; May 30, 1999, p. 11.

Scotsman (Edinburgh, Scotland), February 28, 1998, p. 3; November 4, 2000, p. 4.

Seattle Post-Intelligencer, March 25, 1998, p. E5.

Seattle Times, April 20, 1997, p. M3; March 25, 1998, p. E6; September 6, 1998, p. M9; June 6, 1999, p. M11; September 26, 1999, p. M9.

Spectator, October 1, 1988, pp. 29-30; September 23, 1995, p. 38; April 11, 1998, p. 33; October 21, 2000, p. 44.

Star Ledger (Newark, NJ), July 12, 1997, p. 006; July 4, 1999, p. 004.

Sunday Herald (Glasgow, Scotland), October 15, 2000, p. 6.

Sunday Times (London, England), May 7, 2000, p. 18; October 15, 2000, p. 50.

Time, May 15, 2000, p. 35.

Time International, April 6, 1998, p. 13.

Times (London, England), April 13, 1998, p. 10, interview with Fitzgerald; August 8, 1998, p. 20; October 11, 2000, pp. 17; December 29, 2000, p. 27.

Times Literary Supplement, November 17, 1978, p. 1333; September 12, 1986, p. 995.

Wall Street Journal, April 8, 1997, p. A20; May 28, 1999, p. W6; September 26, 2000, p. A24.

Washington Post, October 1, 2000, p. X15.

Washington Post Book World, February 23, 1992, pp. 1, 8; June 1997, pp. 3, 13.

Women's Review of Books, October, 1997, p. 6.

World and I, January, 2001, p. 254.

World Literature Today, spring, 1998, p. 371.

ONLINE

Second Circle, http://www.thesecondcircle.com/ (March 9, 2004), review of *The Blue Flower.*

OBITUARIES:

PERIODICALS

Guardian (London, England), May 3, 2000, p. 22; May 24, 2000, p. 24.

Herald Sun (Melbourne, Australia), May 15, 2000, p. 109.

Independent (London, England), May 3, 2000, p. 5; May 9, 2000, p. 6.

Los Angeles Times, May 4, 2000, p. A8.

Milwaukee Journal-Sentinel, May 5, 2000, p. 04.

New York Times, May 3, 2000, p. A29.

Seattle Times, May 3, 2000, p. A19.

Times (London, England), May 6, 2000, p. 24; October 11, 2000, p. 22.*

*   *   *

FLEISCHMAN, (Albert) Sid(ney) 1920-
(Carl March, Max Brindle)

PERSONAL: Born March 16, 1920, in Brooklyn, NY; son of Reuben and Sadie (Solomon) Fleischman; married Betty Taylor, January 25, 1942; children: Jane, Paul, Anne. *Education:* San Diego State College (now University), B.A., 1949. *Hobbies and other interests:* Magic, gardening.

ADDRESSES: Home—305 Tenth St., Santa Monica, CA 90402.

CAREER: Writer for children and adults. Is also a screenwriter and has been a professional magician. Worked as a magician in vaudeville and night clubs, 1938-41; traveled with Mr. Arthur Bull's Francisco Spook Show (magic act), 1939-40; *Daily Journal,* San Diego, CA, reporter and rewrite man, 1949-50; *Point* (magazine), San Diego, associate editor, 1950-51; full-time writer, 1951—. Author of scripts for television show *3-2-1 Contact,* 1979-82. *Military service:* U.S. Naval Reserve, 1941-45; served as yeoman on destroyer escort in the Philippines, Borneo, and China.

MEMBER: Authors Guild, Authors League of America, Writers Guild of America West, Society of Children's Book Writers and Illustrators.

AWARDS, HONORS: Children's Spring Book Festival Honor Book, *New York Herald Tribune,* and Honor Book, *Boston Globe-Horn Book,* both 1962, both for *Mr. Mysterious and Company;* Spur Award, Western Writers of America, Southern California Council on Literature for Children and Young People Award, and Junior Book Award, Boys' Clubs of America, all 1964, Recognition of Merit Award, George C. Stone Center

Sid Fleischman

for Children's Books, 1972, and Friends of Children and Literature (FOCAL) Award, Los Angeles Public Library, 1983, all for *By the Great Horn Spoon!*; Juvenile Book Award, Commonwealth Club of California, 1966, for *Chancy and the Grand Rascal*; Lewis Carroll Shelf Award, 1969, for *McBroom Tells the Truth*; Children's Spring Book Festival Honor Book, *Book World*, and Notable Books selection, American Library Association (ALA), both 1971, both for *Jingo Django*; Southern California Council on Literature for Children and Young People Award, 1972, for "Comprehensive Contribution of Lasting Value to the Literature for Children and Young People"; Golden Kite Honor Book, Society of Children's Book Writers and Illustrators, 1974, for *McBroom the Rainmaker*; Mark Twain Award, Missouri Association of School Libraries, and Charlie May Simon Children's Book Award, Arkansas Elementary School Council, both 1977, and Young Hoosier Award, Association for Indiana Media Educators, 1979, all for *The Ghost on Saturday Night*; National Book Award finalist, and Award for Fiction, *Boston Globe-Horn Book*, both 1979, both for *Humbug Mountain*; Newbery Medal, ALA, and Children's Books of the Year selection, Child Study Association of America, both 1987, both for *The Whipping Boy*; Paul A. Witty Award, International Reading Association, and Children's Picturebook Award, *Redbook*, 1988, both for *The Scarebird*; Parents' Choice Award, 1990, for *The Midnight Horse*, and 1992, for *Jim Ugly*; Nene Award, 1992, for *The Whipping Boy*; Jo Os-

bourne Award for Humor in Children's Literature, 1997; Children's Literature Council of Southern California Award, 1997, for *The Abracadabra Kid: A Writer's Life*; Charley May Simon Children's Book Award, Arkansas Elementary School Council, and Black-Eyed Susan Award (Maryland), both 1998, and California Young Reader Medal, 1999, all for *The 13th Floor: A Ghost Story*; John and Patricia Beatty Award, California Library Association, 1999, and FOCAL Award, Los Angeles Public Library, 2002, both for *Bandit's Moon*; Golden Dolphin Award, Southern California Children's Booksellers Association; Literary Fellowship, Magic Castle's Academy of Magical Arts, 2002; establishment of Sid Fleischman Humor Award, Society of Children's Book Writers and Illustrators, 2003.

WRITINGS:

FOR CHILDREN AND YOUNG ADULTS

Mr. Mysterious & Company, illustrated by Eric von Schmidt, Little, Brown (Boston, MA), 1962, reprinted, Greenwillow Books (New York, NY), 1997.

By the Great Horn Spoon!, illustrated by Eric von Schmidt, Little, Brown (Boston, MA), 1963, published as *Bullwhip Griffin,* Avon (New York, NY), 1967.

The Ghost in the Noonday Sun, illustrated by Warren Chappell, Little, Brown (Boston, MA), 1965, new edition illustrated by Peter Sis, Greenwillow Books (New York, NY), 1989.

Chancy and the Grand Rascal, illustrated by Eric von Schmidt, Little, Brown (Boston, MA), 1966, reprinted, Greenwillow Books (New York, NY), 1997.

McBroom Tells the Truth, illustrated by Kurt Werth, Norton (New York, NY), 1966, new edition illustrated by Walter Lorraine, Little, Brown (Boston, MA), 1981, new edition illustrated by Amy Wummer, Price Stern Sloan (New York, NY), 1998.

McBroom and the Big Wind, illustrated by Kurt Werth, Norton (New York, NY), 1967, new edition illustrated by Walter Lorraine, Little, Brown (Boston, MA), 1982.

McBroom's Ear, illustrated by Kurt Werth, Norton (New York, NY), 1969, new edition illustrated by Walter Lorraine, Little, Brown (Boston, MA), 1982.

Longbeard the Wizard, illustrated by Charles Bragg, Little, Brown (Boston, MA), 1970.

Jingo Django, illustrated by Eric von Schmidt, Little, Brown (Boston, MA), 1971, reprinted, Dell (New York, NY), 1995.

McBroom's Ghost, illustrated by Robert Frankenberg, Grosset (New York, NY), 1971, new edition illustrated by Walter Lorraine, Little, Brown (Boston, MA), 1981, new edition illustrated by Amy Wummer, Price Stern Sloan (New York, NY), 1998.

McBroom's Zoo, illustrated by Kurt Werth, Grosset (New York, NY), 1972, new edition illustrated by Walter Lorraine, Little, Brown (Boston, MA), 1982.

The Wooden Cat Man, illustrated by Jay Yang, Little, Brown (Boston, MA), 1972.

McBroom's Wonderful One-Acre Farm (includes *McBroom Tells the Truth, McBroom and the Big Wind,* and *McBroom's Ghost*), illustrated by Quentin Blake, Chatto & Windus (London, England), 1972, Greenwillow Books (New York, NY), 1992.

McBroom the Rainmaker, illustrated by Kurt Werth, Grosset (New York, NY), 1973, new edition illustrated by Walter Lorraine, Little, Brown (Boston, MA), 1982, new edition illustrated by Amy Wummer, Price Stern Sloan (New York, NY), 1999.

The Ghost on Saturday Night, illustrated by Eric von Schmidt, Little, Brown (Boston, MA), 1974, new edition illustrated by Laura Cornell, Greenwillow Books (New York, NY), 1997.

Mr. Mysterious's Secrets of Magic (nonfiction), illustrated by Eric von Schmidt, Little, Brown (Boston, MA), 1975, published as *Secrets of Magic,* Chatto & Windus (London, England), 1976.

McBroom Tells a Lie, illustrated by Walter Lorraine, Little, Brown (Boston, MA), 1976, new edition illustrated by Amy Wummer, Price Stern Sloan (New York, NY), 1999.

Here Comes McBroom (includes *McBroom Tells a Lie, McBroom the Rainmaker,* and *McBroom's Zoo*), illustrated by Quentin Blake, Chatto & Windus (London, England), 1976, Greenwillow Books (New York, NY), 1992.

Kate's Secret Riddle Book, F. Watts (New York, NY), 1977.

Me and the Man on the Moon-Eyed Horse, illustrated by Eric von Schmidt, Little, Brown (Boston, MA), 1977, published as *The Man on the Moon-Eyed Horse,* Gollancz (London, England), 1980.

Humbug Mountain, illustrated by Eric von Schmidt, Little, Brown (Boston, MA), 1978.

Jim Bridger's Alarm Clock and Other Tall Tales, illustrated by Eric von Schmidt, Dutton (New York, NY), 1978.

McBroom and the Beanstalk, illustrated by Walter Lorraine, Little, Brown (Boston, MA), 1978.

The Hey Hey Man, illustrated by Nadine Bernard Westcott, Little, Brown (Boston, MA), 1979.

McBroom and the Great Race, illustrated by Walter Lorraine, Little, Brown (Boston, MA), 1980.

The Bloodhound Gang in the Case of the Flying Clock, illustrated by William Harmuth, Random House/Children's Television Workshop (New York, NY), 1981.

The Bloodhound Gang in the Case of the Cackling Ghost, illustrated by Anthony Rao, Random House (New York, NY), 1981.

The Bloodhound Gang in the Case of Princess Tomorrow, illustrated by Bill Morrison, Random House (New York, NY), 1981.

The Bloodhound Gang in the Case of the Secret Message, illustrated by William Harmuth, Random House (New York, NY), 1981.

The Bloodhound Gang's Secret Code Book, illustrated by Bill Morrison, Random House (New York, NY), 1982.

The Bloodhound Gang in the Case of the 264-Pound Burglar, illustrated by Bill Morrison, Random House (New York, NY), 1982.

McBroom's Almanac, illustrated by Walter Lorraine, Little, Brown (Boston, MA), 1984.

The Whipping Boy, illustrated by Peter Sis, Greenwillow Books (New York, NY), 1986, HarperTrophy (New York, NY), 2003.

The Scarebird, illustrated by Peter Sis, Greenwillow Books (New York, NY), 1988.

The Ghost in the Noonday Sun, illustrated by Peter Sis, Greenwillow Books (New York, NY), 1989.

The Midnight Horse, Greenwillow Books (New York, NY), 1990.

Jim Ugly, illustrated by Joseph A. Smith, Greenwillow Books (New York, NY), 1992.

The 13th Floor: A Ghost Story, illustrated by Peter Sis, Greenwillow Books (New York, NY), 1995.

The Abracadabra Kid: A Writer's Life (nonfiction), Greenwillow Books (New York, NY), 1996.

Bandit's Moon, illustrated by Joseph A. Smith, Greenwillow Books (New York, NY), 1998.

A Carnival of Animals, illustrated by Marylin Hafner, Greenwillow Books Books (New York, NY), 2000.

Bo and Mzzz Mad, Greenwillow Books (New York, NY), 2001.

Disappearing Act, Greenwillow Books (New York, NY), 2003.

The Giant Rat of Sumatra, Greenwillow Books (New York, NY), in press.

NOVELS; FOR ADULTS

The Straw Donkey Case, Phoenix Press (New York, NY), 1948.

Murder's No Accident, Phoenix Press (New York, NY), 1949.

Shanghai Flame, Fawcett Gold Medal (New York, NY), 1951.

Look behind You, Lady, Fawcett Gold Medal (New York, NY), 1952, published as *Chinese Crimson,* Jenkins (Austin, TX), 1962.

Danger in Paradise, Fawcett Gold Medal (New York, NY), 1953.

Counterspy Express, Ace Books (New York, NY), 1954.

Malay Woman, Fawcett Gold Medal (New York, NY), 1954, published as *Malaya Manhunt,* Jenkins (Austin, TX), 1965.

Blood Alley, Fawcett Gold Medal (New York, NY), 1955.

Yellowleg, Fawcett Gold Medal (New York, NY), 1960.

The Venetian Blonde, Fawcett Gold Medal (New York, NY), 1963.

SCREENPLAYS

Blood Alley (starring John Wayne and Lauren Bacall), Batjac Productions, 1955.

Goodbye, My Lady (based on a novel by James Street), Batjac Productions, 1956.

(With William A. Wellman) *Lafayette Escadrille,* Warner Bros., 1958.

The Deadly Companions (based on his novel *Yellowleg*), Carousel Productions, 1961.

(With Albert Maltz) *Scalawag,* Byrna Productions, 1973.

(Under pseudonym Max Brindle) *The Whipping Boy,* Disney, 1994.

OTHER

Between Cocktails, Abbott Magic Company (Colon, MI), 1939.

(Under pseudonym Carl March) *Magic Made Easy,* Croydon (New York, NY), 1953.

(Contributor) Paul Heins, editor, *Crosscurrents of Criticism,* Horn Book (Boston, MA), 1977.

The Charlatan's Handbook, L & L Publishing (Tahoma, CA), 1993.

Fleischman's books have been translated into sixteen languages.

ADAPTATIONS: By the Great Horn Spoon! was filmed as *Bullwhip Griffin* by Walt Disney, 1967; *The Ghost in the Noonday Sun,* starring Peter Sellers, was filmed by Cavalcade Films, 1974.

SIDELIGHTS: "While my books rarely draw upon my personal experience," commented author Sid Fleischman in the *St. James Guide to Children's Writers,* "I catch ghostly glimpses of my presence on almost every page. The stories inevitably reveal my interests and enthusiasms—my taste for the comic in life, my love of adventure, the seductions (for me) of the nineteenth-century American frontier, and my enchantment with the folk speech of that period. Language is a wondrous toy and I have great literary fun with it." Regarded as a master of the tall tale as well as one of the most popular humorists in American children's literature, Fleischman is noted for writing action-filled adventure stories that weave exciting plots, rollicking wit, and joyous wordplay with accurate, well-researched historical facts and characterizations that reveal the author's insight into and understanding of human nature. He is perhaps best known as the author of *The Whipping Boy,* a Newbery Medal-winning story that features a spoiled prince and the stoical lad who takes his punishment, and a comic series of tall tales about blustery Iowa farmer Josh McBroom and his amazingly productive one-acre farm. Compared to such writers as Mark Twain, Charles Dickens, and Leon Garfield, Fleischman is praised for his ingenuity, vigorous literary style, polished craftsmanship, and keen sense of humor.

His works, which often draw on American folklore and pioneer history and use backgrounds such as the California Gold Rush, seventeenth-century piracy, and rural life from Ohio to Vermont, are consistently acknowledged for their diversity of subjects and settings. Formerly a professional magician, Fleischman fills his books with mystery, elements of surprise, and quick-witted characters. His young protagonists, who are regarded as figures with whom young readers can quickly identify, often embark on quests, noted Emily Rhoads Johnson in *Language Arts,* "for land or treasure or missing relatives," where "the heroes meet up with every imaginable kind of trouble, usually in the form of villains and cut-throats, impostors and fingle-fanglers." In his *Written for Children,* John Rowe Townsend asserted that, like Garfield, Fleischman "is fond of flamboyant, larger-than-life characters, and of mysteries of origin and identity; a recurrent Fleischman theme is the discovery of a father or father-substitute." Although he frequently styles his stories as farces, Fleischman underscores his works with a positive attitude toward life and a firm belief in such values as courage, loyalty, and perseverance. The author's love of language—an attribute for which he is often lauded—is evident in the flamboyant names he gives to his characters, his use of wild metaphors and vivid images, and the colorful expressions that dot his stories. Johnson explains that Fleischman's "words don't just sit there on the page; they leap and cavort, turn somersaults, and sometimes just hang suspended, like cars teetering at the top of a roller coaster." Acknowledged as exceptional to read aloud, Fleischman's works are often considered effective choices for reluctant readers.

Reviewers usually provide Fleischman with a warm critical reception. Johnson noted that he has "produced some of the funniest books ever for children," while Jane O'Connor claimed in the *New York Times Book Review,* "When it comes to telling whopping tall tales, no one can match Sid Fleischman." Writing in the same publication, Georgess McHargue said that Fleischman "can put more action into thirty-two pages than some authors of 'explosive best sellers' can put into seventy-five turgid chapters." Writing in *Horn Book,* Mary M. Burns added that although Fleischman's books are expectedly funny, his "transforming setbacks into comic situations and seeing possible triumphs where others with lesser gifts see only disasters . . . [is perhaps] what makes his books so popular." Observing that Fleischman's characters care deeply about each other, Johnson noted, "This, I feel, is what gives his books their substance and strength. To know Sid Fleischman, in person or through his work, is to experience an affirmation of life." In *Twentieth Century Children's Writers,* Jane Yolen concluded that Fleischman "has made the particular voice of the tall tale so much his own that, if any one author could be said to be master of the genre, it is he. . . . [He has made] highly original contributions to the literature of childhood, at least in this critic's opinion."

Born in Brooklyn, New York, Fleischman was raised in San Diego, California. He credits his father, Reuben, a Russian Jewish immigrant whom his son calls "an airy optimist with nimble skills," and his mother, Sadie, a "crackerjack penny-ante card player," with fostering his interest in storytelling. "My earliest literary memories," wrote Fleischman in *Horn Book,* "were funny ones. I remember most vividly the woodman's wife with the link sausages attached to her nose in 'The Three Wishes.' That had me rolling in the aisles—or on the living-room carpet. A little later came Lewis Carroll's Cheshire Cat and the Mad Hatter." Fleischman recalls *Aesop's Fables* and *Uncle Tom's Cabin* being read to him by his mother; however, the book that he claims affected him most profoundly was *Robin Hood,* which he calls "my first great reading experience, and my favorite of those early years." As a minority in San Diego due to his faith, Fleischman developed an identity with underdogs. "I can see this," he told *Language Arts,* "in the dynamics of my choice of characters to write about. The butler in *By the Great Horn Spoon!* The gypsies in *Jingo Django.* And children, of course, are every generation's underdogs." As a small boy, Fleischman developed a strong interest in magic, voraciously reading books on the subject, perfecting tricks to perform, and creating inventions of his own. At the age of seventeen, he decided to write a book of his original tricks, *Between Cocktails;* published when Fleischman was nineteen, the book was still in print over fifty years later. "When I saw my name on the cover," Fleischman once recalled, "I was hooked on writing books."

After graduating from high school, Fleischman traveled around the country with stage acts—such as Mr. Arthur Bull's Francisco Spook Show—during the last days of vaudeville. This experience, during which he heard folktales and folk speech in small towns throughout America, is often thought to have influenced the improvisational quality of the author's works; Fleischman's son, Paul, himself a Newbery Award-winning writer, called his father "a prestidigitator of words" in *Horn Book,* while Fleischman referred to his own writing as "sleight-of-mind" in an interview with Sybil S. Steinberg in *Publishers Weekly.* During the Second World War, Fleischman served in the U. S. Naval Reserve on a destroyer escort in the Philippines, Borneo, and China. In 1942, he married Betty Taylor; the couple has three children: Jane, Paul, and Anne. After the war, Fleischman began writing detective stories, suspense tales, and other pulp fiction for adults, learning, he says, "to keep the story pot boiling, to manage tension and the uses of surprise." In 1949, he graduated from San Diego State College and began working as a reporter for the San Diego *Daily Journal.* A year later, Fleischman became associate editor of *Point* magazine, a position he held until 1951 when he became a full-time writer. In 1955, he began a continuing career as a screenwriter when his novel *Blood Alley* was adapted to film.

When his children were young, Fleischman related in *Publishers Weekly,* they "didn't understand what I did for a living. So one day I sat down and wrote a story for children and read it to them." This book, *Mr. Mysterious & Company,* which includes Fleischman and his family as characters, became his first published book for children. Describing the warm relationship of the Hackett family, *Mr. Mysterious* includes the concept of Abracadabra Day, an annual event where children are allowed to be as bad as they want to be without fear of reproach. "A marvelous institution that may well sweep the country," wrote Dorothy M. Broderick in the *New York Times Book Review,* while *Horn Book* reviewer Ruth Hill Viguers called *Mr. Mysterious* "wholly delightful. . . . It is hard to imagine a child who would not enjoy it."

The "McBroom" series about the Iowan and his fertile farmland was prompted during the writing of *Chancy and the Grand Rascal,* a story about a young boy and his "coming-and-going" uncle that Jane Yolen called a "perfect blend of one part quest story and two parts tall tale" in the *New York Times Book Review.* "For all readers who adore braggadocio and consider Paul Bunyan and Pecos Bill the apogee of American humor," Yolen continued, "*Chancy and the Grand Rascal* is a godsend." While coming up with two tall tales for *Chancy,* Fleischman was so amused by his initial invention that he turned it into the first McBroom book, *McBroom Tells the Truth.* Although he did not intend to write another story about McBroom, Fleischman has written a dozen books about the folksy character who entertains young readers with a succession of wild impossibilities on, as Zena Sutherland described it in the *Bulletin of the Center for Children's Books,* "the marvelous McBroom farm, where instantaneous growth from superfertile soil and blazing Iowa sun provide magnificent crops of food and stories"; in addition to his tales about the farmer and his eleven children, Fleischman has written a compendium of McBroom's homespun advice in almanac format. McBroom's shaggy dog stories are usually considered

to be as funny as they are unlikely. In *Now upon a Time: A Contemporary View of Children's Literature,* Myra Pollack Sadker and David Miller Sadker noted that "Fleischman has created a tall tale hero who delights younger independent readers and also provides a grand vehicle for storytelling and reading aloud." Another of Fleischman's most popular series features the Bloodhound Gang, a team of three multiethnic junior detectives. Based on Fleischman's scripts for the *3-2-1 Contact* television show for the Children's Television Workshop, the books are fast-paced, fun-to-solve mysteries directed to middle graders and early adolescents that include short chapters filled with plenty of action. In each book, as Judith Goldberger noted in *Booklist,* "a neatly worked out plot is based on simple, believable gimmicks."

With *The Whipping Boy,* Fleischman departs from his characteristic yarns with American settings to write a story, in the words of *Horn Book* reviewer Ethel L. Heins, in "the manner of Joan Aiken and Lloyd Alexander [that is] set in an undefined time and place." Reminiscent of *The Prince and the Pauper* and written in a style that harkens back to that of nineteenth-century melodramas, *The Whipping Boy* describes how spoiled Horace, nicknamed Prince Brat because of his behavior, runs away with Jemmy, the street-smart orphan who takes the punishment for the things that the prince refuses to do, like learn to read. When they are kidnapped by villains Cutwater and Hold-Your-Nose Billy, the boys switch roles; after escaping the scoundrels in an exciting chase through a rat-filled sewer, Horace and Jemmy return to the palace as friends. Jemmy has learned to sympathize with the prince's restricted life and to admire his courage while realizing his own desire for knowledge, while Horace, who takes a whipping for Jemmy, discovers his personal strength and ability to change. "Like much of the author's writing," maintained Heins, "beneath the surface entertainment, the story also speaks of courage, friendship, and trust." Janet Hickman of *Language Arts* noted that besides "its lively entertainment value and stylistic polish, the story has much to say about human nature and the vagaries of justice." Writing in the *New York Times Book Review,* Martha Saxton concluded, "This is indisputably a good, rollicking adventure, but in its characterizations *The Whipping Boy* offers something special."

It took almost ten years for Fleischman to write *The Whipping Boy.* The initial idea for the book came to the author from some historical research he was doing for another book. In his Newbery Medal acceptance speech printed in *Horn Book,* Fleischman said, "I stumbled across the catapulting idea for *The Whipping Boy.* . . . I checked the dictionary. 'A boy,' it confirmed, 'educated with a prince and punished in its stead.'" Fleischman thought he could write the book quickly, but "after about eighteen months," he recalled in *Horn Book,* "I was still trying to get to the bottom of page five." Eventually, Fleischman realized the problem. "My original concept for the story was wrong," he explained. "Wrong, at least, for me. I saw *The Whipping Boy* as a picture book story." One day he read over the manuscript and discovered that his work needed to be much longer: "Once I took the shackles off, the story erupted. Scenes, incidents, and characters came tumbling out of a liberated imagination. Within a few months, I had it all on paper." When told that *The Whipping Boy* had won the Newbery Medal, Fleischman was elated. "I don't happen to believe in levitation, unless it's done with mirrors, but for a few days I had to load my pockets with ballast. The Newbery Medal is an enchantment. It's bliss. It should happen to everyone."

Following *The Whipping Boy,* Fleischman published *The Scarebird,* which contains illustrations by Peter Sis, who has also provided the pictures for several of the author's other works. The story and pictures describe how Lonesome John, whose sole companion is the scarecrow in his yard, slowly makes friends with Sam, an orphan looking for work who comes to John's farm. In her review in the *Bulletin of the Center for Children's Books,* Betsy Hearne stated, "In a period of thin picture books, this has much to teach about the substance of story and the complement of illustration." With *The Midnight Horse,* Fleischman returns to the adventure story genre with a novel that is, in the worlds of Ethel R. Twichell of *Horn Book,* "a mixture of tall tale, folktale, and downright magic." The story outlines how Touch, an orphan boy who comes to the town of Cricklewood, New Hampshire—where the entry sign reads "Population 217. 216 Fine Folks and 1 Infernal Grouch"—and reclaims his rightful inheritance from his wicked great-uncle with the help of a ghostly magician. "The enjoyment of the book," Twichell concluded, "lies in Fleischman's exuberant narrative flow and his ingenuity in dispatching his scoundrels." A *Publishers Weekly* critic called *The Midnight Horse* a "deftly told tale of innocence and villainy."

Fleischman's next novel, *Jim Ugly,* is a parody set in the Old West that includes such thinly disguised movie stars of the time as Mary Pickford, Douglas Fairbanks, Mae West, and W. C. Fields. In this story, twelve-year-old Jake discovers that the father that he thought he had buried is alive and is accused of stealing some missing diamonds; with his father's dog—which Jake describes as "part elkhound, part something else, and a large helping of short-eared timber wolf"—as companion, Jake and Jim Ugly travel by baggage car from town to town, trying to escape a villainous bounty hunter; in the end, Jake and his father are reunited in San Francisco and the mystery of the diamonds is solved. In the *Bulletin of the Center for Children's Books,* Zena Sutherland wrote: "Lively, clever, and humorous, this must have been as much fun to write as it is to read," while *School Library Journal* contributor Katherine Bruner added, "With a little silent-movie piano accompaniment, this rollicking parody of Western melodrama would effortlessly unfold across any stage." With *The 13th Floor: A Ghost Story,* Fleischman makes his first contribution to the time-travel genre of fantasy literature. In this work, twelve-year-old Buddy and his lawyer-sister Liz are left penniless when their parents are killed in a plane crash. Liz disappears after meeting a client on the thirteenth floor of an old building, and the client turns out to be their ancestor, a young girl accused of witchcraft in Puritan Boston. When Buddy goes after Liz, he is taken by magic elevator to a pirate ship captained by another ancestor and, after being cast adrift, is reunited with Liz, who defends—and acquits—ten-year-old Abigail in court; at the end of the book, the siblings return safely to the twentieth century with a treasure in hand. A critic from *Publishers Weekly* advised, "Hold on to your hats—there's never a dull moment when Fleischman is at the helm." "An easy, lighthearted adventure," maintained Ann A. Flowers in *Horn Book,* "yet the author's note also points out the serious consequences of ignorance and superstition."

The Abracadabra Kid: A Writer's Life is Fleischman's autobiography for young readers. Considered as lively and eminently readable as his fiction, *The Abracadabra Kid* includes Fleischman's personal information as well as his advice on writing; each chapter is introduced with quotes from children's letters to the author, ended with a cliff-hanging episode from his life, and illustrated with black-and-white family photographs. "Sid Fleischman is a pro," asserted Betsy Hearne in the *Bulletin of the Center of Children's Books,* "and it shows in this autobiography as much as it does in his fiction." A *Kirkus Reviews* contributor claimed that Fleischman "offers a gold mine of interesting reflections of writing," from one who has "lived adventurously and thoughtfully." Mary J. Arnold, reviewing the book in *Kliatt,* called it an "engaging memoir that serves as proof positive that writing flows from life experience." For Arnold, Fleischman's autobiographical sketch was "nonstop funny and entertaining." Writing in *Voice of Youth Advocates,* Candace Deisley commented, "The reader is rewarded with an appreciation for the author's art, and spurred with the desire to read more of his works." Carolyn Phelan of *Booklist* concluded, "From cover to cover, a treat."

Although more than eighty years old, Fleischman continues to entertain young readers with his raucous tales. With *Bandit's Moon,* he tells a tale of a Mexican bandit and an orphan girl during the California Gold Rush. Annyrose Smith is left in the care of a man who turns out to be less than honorable. Disguised as a boy, she makes her escape, only to be swept up by the outlaw band of legendary Joaquin Murrieta. Murrieta, it turns out, is badly in need of someone to teach him how to read, and he protects the young girl to that end. For her part, Annyrose is shocked by the behavior of the gang, but then she begins to discover the wrongs that have been done to Murrieta and other Mexicans at the hands of the whites. The plot includes the usual combination of fast pace and twists and turns which Fleischman typically employs; Annyrose slowly begins to be won over by Murrieta, saving his life at various times. In the end, however, believing he was responsible for the death of her brother, Lank, she turns on him. Murrieta manages to escape and slip away—unlike what actually happened to him historically. Writing in *School Library Journal,* Marlene Gawron called the book "classic Sid Fleischman: a quick read, with lots of twists, wonderful phrasing, historical integrity, and a bit of the tall tale thrown in." For a contributor to *Publishers Weekly,* the novel was more than just "thundering hooves and gunfire." Fleischman, according to this reviewer, "expertly crafts a fictionalized tale that takes a clear-eyed look at bigotry and racism, while steering away from the twin pitfalls of pedantry and sermonizing." Similarly, *Horn Book*'s Ann A. Flowers felt that Fleischman managed to "clothe issues of loyalty and honesty in a roaring adventure story, smartly written and chock full of humor and derring-do."

Published in 2000, *A Carnival of Animals* is a compilation of a half-dozen tall tales about the effects on various animals of a tornado that hits Barefoot Mountain. In "The Windblown Child," for example, a strange pink creature is blown in with the tornado; hairless, her fleece has been whisked away to take the place of missing hair on a bald farmer. "Emperor Floyd" tells of a rooster who develops a peculiar affliction as a result of the storm, and in "Stumblefrog," the amphibian in question gets jumping fever after eating the contents of a sack of Mexican jumping beans, torn open by the tornado. A reviewer for *Publishers Weekly* noted that "the glee with which [Fleischman] relates his outrageous yarns is infectious." *Booklist*'s Gillian Engberg had similar praise for the book of stories, commenting that "as usual, Fleischman writes about the fantastic and absurd with a captivating balance of casual assuredness and precise detail." Grace Oliff, reviewing the collection in *School Library Journal,* called Fleischman "a master of the tall tale."

Returning to the novel form with *Bo and Mzzz Mad,* Fleischman serves up another "classic . . . tale," according to a contributor for *Publishers Weekly,* offering a starred review. When twelve-year-old Bo Gamage's parents die, the youth decides to visit long-lost relatives in the Mojave Desert, separated by a family feud involving a lost gold mine. Arriving in Queen of Sheba, California, Bo finds a town that is little more than an old movie set, and its only residents are said relatives. A former actor in Westerns, great-uncle Charlie, alias Paw Paw, is now a full-time grump and tired of life. There is also an aunt and his cousin, Madeleine, who prefers to call herself Mzzz Mad. These two, of course, discover mutual dislike at first sight. Aunt Juna is the only one to take any interest in Bo; she talks him into tricking Paw Paw with a fake treasure map in order to restore his love of life. The map is supposedly one that shows the gold mine which set off the feud between the two sides of the family. But when some modern bandits arrive on the scene, Bo and his feuding relatives get more than they expected and need to pull together to survive. "The narrative speeds along with enough plot twists to keep readers flipping pages," observed Steve Clancy in a *School Library Journal* review. A contributor for *Publishers Weekly* also found the book a "thumping good page-turner spiced with humor, snappy descriptions . . . and a lickety-split plot." The same reviewer felt that Fleischman was "in top form" with *Bo and Mzzz Mad.* For a *Horn Book* critic, the novel was "a light-as-cotton-candy concoction," while *Booklist*'s Stephanie Zvirin pronounced the book a "quick, enjoyable read that will fly off the shelves."

More orphans appear in Fleischman's 2003 title, *Disappearing Act.* Kevin and Holly Kidd have just lost their archaeologist mother in an earthquake in Mexico. Now their home in Albuquerque, New Mexico, is struck by burglars and they think someone is stalking them. They escape memories and their fears and run off to southern California, living near the Venice boardwalk and renaming themselves Gomez. Kevin becomes Pepe and takes up fortune-telling on the boardwalk, while his older sister, a fledgling opera singer, becomes Chickadee. They slowly establish themselves in this strange new life, making friends with all the local characters, including a juggling medical student, a human mannequin, a screenwriter with a penchant for bugs, and a benevolent landlady. Holly even gets a role in a production of *La Boheme.* Then the stalker from New Mexico shows up, and all is put into jeopardy again. *Booklist*'s John Peters thought that Fleischman mixed "themes both comic and serious" in this story, and was able to pull together the manifold plot lines of "his twisty, nail-biter to an untidy, but satisfying, conclusion." Many critics found that the cast of secondary characters was the primary draw in this novel. Betty Carter, for example, writing in *Horn Book,* wrote that the book "primarily paints vivid character sketches" but "fails to sustain a coherent plot." For Steven Engelfried, writing in *School Library Journal,* the "characters and the setting are the main draws," though he also noted that "Fleischman neatly frames the conclusion into something more thoughtful and meaningful" than a mere potboiler. And a critic for *Kirkus Reviews* also praised "the colorful assemblage of secondary characters," concluding, "Realistic fiction it's not, but good, quick, and smart fun—definitely."

"Novels are written in the dark," Fleischman commented in an essay for *Children's Books and Their Creators.* "At lcast minc arc. Unlike many sensible authors, I start Chapter One with rarely a notion of the story that's about to unfold. It's like wandering down a pitch-black theater and groping around for the lights. One by one the spots and floodlights come on, catching a character or two against a painted backdrop. I sit back and enjoy the show. When the final curtain falls a year or two later, the stage is ablaze with lights, and I have a new novel."

BIOGRAPHICAL AND CRITICAL SOURCES:

BOOKS

Beacham's Guide to Literature for Young Adults, Volume 4, Beacham Publishing (Osprey, FL), 1990, Volume 11, Gale (Detroit, MI), 2001.

Cameron, Eleanor, *The Green and Burning Tree,* Atlantic/Little, Brown (Boston, MA), 1969.

Children's Literature Review, Gale (Detroit, MI), Volume 1, 1976, Volume 15, 1988.

Fleischman, Sid, in *Children's Books and Their Creators,* edited by Anita Silvey, Houghton Mifflin (Boston, MA), 1995.

Huck, Charlotte S., and Doris Young Kuhn, *Children's Literature in the Elementary School,* 2nd edition, Holt (New York, NY), 1968.

Meigs, Cornelia, and others, editors, *A Critical History of Children's Literature,* revised edition, Macmillan (New York, NY), 1969.

Sadker, Myra Pollack and David Miller Sadker, *Now upon a Time: A Contemporary View of Children's Literature,* Harper (New York, NY), 1977.

St. James Guide to Children's Writers, 5th edition, St. James Press (Detroit, MI), 1999.

Townsend, John Rowe, *Written for Children: An Outline of English Language Children's Literature,* revised edition, Lippincott (Philadelphia, PA), 1974.

Twentieth-Century Children's Writers, 4th edition, St. James Press (Detroit, MI), 1995.

PERIODICALS

Booklist, September 15, 1976, Barbara Elleman, review of *McBroom Tells a Lie,* p. 174; April 15, 1981, Judith Goldberger, review of *The Bloodhound Gang in the Case of the Cackling Ghost* and *The Bloodhound Gang in the Case of Princess Tomorrow,* p. 1159; September 1, 1996, Carolyn Phelan, review of *The Abracadabra Kid: A Writer's Life,* p. 126; March 1, 1999, Sally Estes, review of *Bandit's Moon,* p. 1212; September 1, 2000, Gillian Engberg, review of *A Carnival of Animals,* p. 113; May 15, 2001, Stephanie Zvirin, review of *Bo and Mzzz Mad,* p. 1750; June 1, 2003, John Peters, review of *Disappearing Act,* pp. 1774-1775.

Bulletin of the Center for Children's Books, May, 1970, Zena Sutherland, review of *McBroom's Ear,* p. 143; September, 1988, Betsy Hearne, review of *The Scarebird,* pp. 6-7; March, 1992, Zena Sutherland, review of *Jim Ugly,* p. 179; October, 1995, p. 53; September, 1996, Betsy Hearne, review of *The Abracadabra Kid,* pp. 11-12; September 1, 2000, Gillian Engberg, review of *A Carnival of Animals,* p. 113; May 15, 2001, Stephanie Zvirin, review of *Bo and Mzzz Mad,* p. 1750.

Horn Book, June, 1962, Ruth Hill Viguers, review of *Mr. Mysterious & Company,* p. 279; October, 1976, pp. 465-470; May-June, 1986, Ethel L. Heins, review of *The Whipping Boy,* pp. 325-326; July-August, 1987, Sid Fleischman, "Newbery Medal Acceptance," pp. 423-428; July-August, 1987, Paul Fleischman, "Sid Fleischman," pp. 429-432; November-December, 1990, Ethel R. Twichell, review of *The Midnight Horse,* p. 744; November-December, 1995, Ann A. Flowers, review of *The 13th Floor: A Ghost Story,* pp. 741-742; September-October, 1996, p. 567; November-December, 1996, Mary M. Burns, review of *The Abracadabra Kid,* p. 759; November, 1998, Ann A. Flowers, review of *Bandit's Moon,* p. 728; May, 2001, review of *Bo and Mzzz Mad,* p. 323; May-June, 2003, Betty Carter, review of *Disappearing Act,* p. 345.

Kirkus Reviews, October 1, 1972, review of *McBroom's Zoo,* p. 1144; April 1, 1992, p. 463; October 1, 1995, p. 1427; July 1, 1996, review of *The Abracadabra Kid,* p. 967; March 1, 2003, review of *Disappearing Act,* p. 383.

Kliatt, September, 1998, Mary J. Arnold, review of *The Abracadabra Kid,* p. 35.

Language Arts, 1982, Emily Rhoads Johnson, "Profile: Sid Fleischman," pp. 754-759; December, 1986, Janet Hickman, review of *The Whipping Boy,* p. 822.

New York Times Book Review, May 13, 1962, Dorothy M. Broderick, review of *Mr. Mysterious & Company,* p. 30; November 6, 1966, Jane Yolen, review of *Chancy and the Grand Rascal,* p. 40; October 17, 1971; September 11, 1977, Jane O'Connor, review of *Me and the Man on the Moon-Eyed Horse,* p. 32; January 20, 1980, Georgess McHargue, review of *The Hey Hey Man,* p. 30; February 22, 1987, Martha Saxton, review of *The Whipping Boy,* p. 23.

Publishers Weekly, February 27, 1978, Sybil S. Steinberg, "What Makes a Funny Children's Book?: Five Writers Talk about Their Method," pp. 87-90; August 10, 1990, review of *The Midnight Horse,* p. 445; October 9, 1995, review of *The 13th Floor,* p. 86; August 3, 1998, review of *Bandit's Moon,* p. 86; August 28, 2000, review of *A Carnival of Animals,* p. 83; March 26, 2001, review of *Bo & Mzzz Mad,* p. 94.

Reading Teacher, April, 1998, review of *The Ghost on Saturday Night,* pp. 588-589; October, 1999, review of *McBroom Tells the Truth,* p. 178; June-July, 2003, review of *Disappearing Act,* p. 32.

Reading Today, June-July, 2003, Lynne T. Burke, review of *Disappearing Act,* p. 32.

School Library Journal, April, 1992, Katherine Bruner, review of *Jim Ugly,* pp. 113-114; September, 1998, Marlene Gawron, review of *Bandit's Moon,* pp. 200-202; October 2000, Grace Oliff, review of *A Carnival of Animals,* p. 124; May, 2001, Steve Clancy, review of *Bo and Mzzz Mad,* p. 149; May, 2003, Steven Engelfried, review of *Disappearing Act,* pp. 150.

Voice of Youth Advocates, April, 1997, Candace Deisley, review of *The Abracadabra Kid,* pp. 52, 54.

Wilson Library Bulletin, April, 1987, Frances Bradburn, review of *The Whipping Boy,* p. 48.

ONLINE

Sid Fleischman Home Page, http://www.sidfleischman.com/ (January 12, 2004).*

*　　　*　　　*

FOOTE, Shelby 1916-

PERSONAL: Born November 17, 1916, in Greenville, MS; son of Shelby Dade (a business executive) and Lillian (Rosenstock) Foote; married Gwyn Rainer, September 6, 1956; children: Margaret Shelby, Huger Lee. *Education:* Attended University of North Carolina, 1935-37.

ADDRESSES: Agent—c/o Author Mail, Dial Press, Dell Publishing, 1540 Broadway, New York, NY 10036.

CAREER: Novelist, historian, and playwright. Novelist-in-residence, University of Virginia, Charlottesville, 1963; playwright-in-residence, Arena Stage, Washington, DC, 1963-64; writer-in-residence, Hollins College, Roanoke, VA, 1968. Judge, National Book Award in history, 1979. *Military service:* U.S. Army, artillery, 1940-44; became captain. U.S. Marine Corps, 1944-45.

MEMBER: American Academy of Arts and Letters, Society of American Historians, Fellowship of Southern Writers.

AWARDS, HONORS: Guggenheim fellowships, 1955, 1956, and 1957; Ford Foundation grant, 1963; Fletcher Pratt Award, 1964, for *The Civil War: A Narrative*; named distinguished alumnus, University of North Carolina, 1974; Dos Passos Prize for Literature, 1988; Charles Frankel Award, 1992; St. Louis Literary Award, 1992; Nevins-Freeman Award, 1992; honorary D.Litt. degrees from University of the South, 1981, Southwestern University, 1982, University of South Carolina, 1991, University of North Carolina, 1992, Millsaps University, 1992, Notre Dame University, 1994, Loyola University, 1999, and College of William and Mary, 1999.

WRITINGS:

NOVELS

Tournament, Dial (New York, NY), 1949.
Follow Me Down (also see below), Dial (New York, NY), 1950.
Love in a Dry Season (also see below), Dial (New York, NY), 1951.
Shiloh, Dial (New York, NY), 1952.
Jordan County: A Landscape in Narrative (also see below), Dial (New York, NY), 1954.
Three Novels (contains *Follow Me Down, Love in a Dry Season,* and *Jordan County: A Landscape in Narrative*), Dial (New York, NY), 1964.
September September, Random House (New York, NY), 1979.
Child by Fever, Random House (New York, NY), 1995.
Ride Out, Modern Library (New York, NY), 1996.

OTHER

The Civil War: A Narrative, Random House (New York, NY), Volume 1: *Fort Sumter to Perryville,* 1958, Volume 2: *Fredericksburg to Meridian,* 1963, Volume 3: *Red River to Appomattox,* 1974, fortieth anniversary edition, Time-Life Books, 1998.
Jordan County: A Landscape in the Round (play), produced in Washington, DC, 1964.
A Novelist's View of History (nonfiction), 1981.
(Editor) *Chickamauga, and Other Civil War Stories* (short stories), Dell (New York, NY), 1993.

Stars in Their Courses: The Gettysburg Campaign (history), Random House (New York, NY), 1994.
The Beleaguered City: The Vicksburg Campaign, December 1862-July 1863 (originally published in Volume 2 of *The Civil War: A Narrative*), Modern Library (New York, NY), 1995.
The Correspondence of Shelby Foote and Walker Percy, edited by Jay Tolson, Center for Documentary Studies (New York, NY), 1997.
(Author of introduction) Anton Chekhov, *Early Short Stories, 1883-1888,* Modern Library (New York, NY), 1999.
(Author of introduction) Anton Chekhov, *Later Short Stories, 1888-1903,* Modern Library (New York, NY), 1999.
(Editor and author of introduction) Anton Chekhov, *Longer Stories from the Last Decade,* Modern Library (New York, NY), 1999.

ADAPTATIONS: Many of Foote's nonfiction writings, including *The Civil War: A Narrative, Stars in Their Courses,* and *The Beleaguered City,* have been adapted as audiobooks.

SIDELIGHTS: Although his novels have been favorably received, Shelby Foote is best known for his three-volume narrative history of the U.S. Civil War. Originally envisioned as a one-volume work, Foote's *The Civil War: A Narrative* grew into what critics have praised as a monumental project that took some twenty years to complete. In the *New York Times Book Review,* Nash K. Burger explained that after writing the Civil War novel *Shiloh,* "Mississippi-born Shelby Foote was asked by a New York publisher to write a short, one-volume history of that conflict. Foote agreed. It seemed a nice change of pace before his next novel. Now, twenty years later, the project is completed."

In Foote's work, the three volumes are divided up between the stages of the war, and appropriately titled *Fort Sumter to Perryville, Fredericksburg to Meridian,* and *Red River to Appomattox,* Noting the scope of Foote's almost three-thousand-word narrative, Burger praised *The Civil War* as "a remarkable achievement, prodigiously researched, vigorous, detailed, absorbing."

Other reviewers have voiced similar praise. In *Newsweek* Peter S. Prescott stated that "the result [of Foote's labor] is not only monumental in size, but a truly impressive achievement." Prescott added that "Foote the novelist cares less for generalizations about dialectics, men and motives than for creating 'the illusion that the observer is not so much reading a book as sharing an experience.'" According to M. E. Bradford in the *National Review,* in this endeavor Foote succeeds admirably. "There is, of course, a majesty inherent in the subject," noted Bradford of the U.S. Civil War, going on to note that "the credit for recovering such majesty to the attention of our skeptical and unheroic age will hereafter belong . . . to Mr. Foote."

Foote's account of the war is strictly a military one, detailing the battles, men, and leaders on both sides of the conflict. "The War itself . . . is indeed Foote's subject," Bradford remarked. "The *war,* the *fighting*—and not its economic, intellectual, or political causes." Lance Morrow echoed this summation in a *Time* review, noting that Foote's "attention is focused on the fighting itself—fortification, tactics, the strange chemistries of leadership, the workings in the generals' minds. Foote moves armies and great quantities of military information with a lively efficiency."

Critics have noted that although military histories concerning the U.S. Civil War abound, Foote's is among the most comprehensive, covering as it does the Union and Confederate Armies in both the eastern and western theaters of the war. Moreover, many reviewers have expressed admiration for the author's balanced and objective view of the still-somewhat divisive conflict. C. Vann Woodward commented in the *New York Review of Books* that "in spite of his Mississippi origins, Foote . . . attempts to keep an even hand in giving North and South their due measure of praise and blame." Burger agreed, adding that although Foote's chronicle begins and ends with reports on the activities of Confederate President Jefferson Davis, this introduction "is not indicative of any bias in favor of the South or its leader. . . . The complete work," Burger continued, "is a monumental, even-handed account of this country's tragic, fratricidal conflict."

In discussing Foote's concentration on the war itself and "therefore the persons who made, died in, or survived that conflict," Bradford asserted that it is not "an exaggeration to speak of the total effect produced by this emphasis as epic." Prescott concluded: "To read Foote's chronicle is an awesome and moving experience. History and literature are rarely so thoroughly combined as here; one finishes [the last] vol-

ume convinced that no one need undertake this particular enterprise again."

Foote became something of a national celebrity during the early 1990s for his on-camera commentary as part of documentary filmmaker Ken Burns's epic Public Television documentary *The Civil War,* which became something of a national event when it first aired in 1990. Sparked by his appearance on the cover of *Newsweek* magazine in the fall of that year, interest in Foote's work as an historian increased markedly, and his *The Civil War: A Narrative* received renewed interest among critics and general readers alike when it was made available as an audiobook. In addition to continuing to pen novels, in the mid-1990s Foote also collected short fiction of the Civil War period as *Chickamauga, and Other Civil War Stories,* and produced an in-depth history of one of the most dramatic battles of the war in *Stars in Their Courses: The Gettysburg Campaign.*

BIOGRAPHICAL AND CRITICAL SOURCES:

BOOKS

Carter, William C., editor, *Conversations with Shelby Foote,* University Press of Mississippi, 1995.
Phillips, Robert L., Jr., *Shelby Foote: Novelist and Historian,* University Press of Mississippi, 1992.
Tolson, Jay, *The Correspondence of Shelby Foote and Walker Percy,* Center for Documentary Studies, 1997.
White, Helen, and Redding S. Sugg, Jr., *Shelby Foote,* Twayne Publishers, 1982.

PERIODICALS

American Heritage, July-August, 1991.
Atlantic, May, 1952; December, 1963.
Book Week, December 15, 1963.
Chicago Sunday Tribune, November 16, 1958.
Christian Science Monitor, December 4, 1963.
Commonweal, January 9, 1959.
English Journal, September, 1992, Penny Turk, review of *Shiloh,* p. 98.
Library Journal, September 1, 1992, Michael Rogers, review of *Jordan County,* p. 220; March 1, 1995, Michael T. Fein, review of *Stars in Their Courses:*

The Gettysburg Campaign, p. 119; March 15, 1996, Barbara Mann, review of *The Beleaguered City: The Vicksburg Campaign,* p. 113.

Military Law Review, fall, 1994, pp. 275-279.

National Review, February 14, 1975.

Newsweek, December 2, 1974; January 30, 1978; October 8, 1990, Harry F. Waters, "Prime Time's New Star," p. 60.

New York Herald Tribune Book Review, July 16, 1950; October 21, 1951; April 6, 1952; May 2, 1954; November 23, 1958.

New York Review of Books, March 6, 1975.

New York Times, September 25, 1949; September 23, 1951; April 6, 1952; April 25, 1954; November 16, 1958; December 1, 1996.

New York Times Book Review, December 1, 1963; December 15, 1974; March 5, 1978.

Paris Review, summer, 1999, Donald Faulkner, interview with Foote, p. 48.

People, October 15, 1990, Michelle Greene, "The Civil War Finds a Homer in Writer Shelby Foote," p. 60.

San Francisco Chronicle, November 28, 1958.

Saturday Review, November 19, 1949; June 5, 1954; December 13, 1958.

Southern Literary Journal, fall, 2003, p. 21.

Time, July 3, 1950; January 27, 1975.*

*   *   *

FRIEL, Brian 1929-

PERSONAL: Born Bernard Patrick Friel, January 9, 1929, in Omagh, Tyrone, Northern Ireland; son of Patrick (a teacher) and Christina (MacLoone) Friel; married Anne Morrison, December 27, 1955; children: Paddy (daughter), Mary, Judy, Sally, David. *Education:* St. Columb's College, Derry, 1941-46; St. Patrick's College, Maynooth, 1946-49, B.A. 1949; St. Mary's Training College (now St. Joseph's College of Education), Belfast, graduate study, 1949-50. *Hobbies and other interests:* Reading, trout fishing, slow tennis.

ADDRESSES: Home—Drumaweir House, Greencastle, Donegal, Ireland. *Agent*—International Creative Management, 40 West 57th St., New York, NY 10019; Curtis Brown, 162-168 Regent St., London W1R 5TB, England.

CAREER: Playwright. Teacher at primary and post-primary schools in and around Derry, Northern Ireland, 1950-60; writer, 1960—. Tyrone Guthrie Theater, observer, 1963; cofounder of Field Day Theatre Company, 1980. Member of Irish Senate.

MEMBER: Irish Academy of Letters, Aosdana, National Association of Irish Artists, Irish Senate.

AWARDS, HONORS: Macauley fellowship from Irish Arts Council, 1963; Antoinette Perry ("Tony") Award nomination for best play, 1966, for *Philadelphia, Here I Come!,* and 1969, for *Lovers;* Christopher Ewart-Biggs Memorial Prize, British Theatre Association Award, and *Plays and Players* Award for best new play, all 1981, all for *Translations; Evening Standard* award for best play of the season, 1988, and New York Drama Critics Circle Award for best foreign play, 1989, both for *Aristocrats;* Olivier Award, 1991, for *Dancing at Lughnasa;* Writers' Guild of Great Britain Award, 1991; Tony Award for best play, 1992, for *Dancing at Lughnasa.* Litt.D., Rosary College (Chicago, IL), 1974, National University of Ireland, 1983, New University of Ulster, 1986, Queen's University, Belfast, 1992, Dominican College (Chicago, IL), Trinity College (Dublin), and Georgetown University.

WRITINGS:

PLAYS

The Francophile, produced in Belfast, 1960; produced as *The Doubtful Paradise,* Belfast, 1960.

The Enemy Within (three-act play; produced in Dublin, 1962), Proscenium Press, 1975.

The Blind Mice, produced in Dublin, 1963.

Philadelphia, Here I Come!, (produced in Dublin, 1964; produced on Broadway at Helen Hayes Theatre, 1966), Faber (London, England), 1965, Farrar, Straus (New York, NY), 1966.

The Loves of Cass McGuire (produced on Broadway at Helen Hayes Theatre, 1966), Farrar, Straus (New York, NY), 1967.

Lovers, (two one-act plays, *Winners* and *Losers;* produced in Dublin, 1967; produced on Broadway at Vivian Beaumont Theatre, 1968), Farrar, Straus (New York, NY), 1968.

Crystal and Fox (produced in Dublin, 1968; produced in Los Angeles at Mark Taper Forum, 1969; produced in New York, 1972), published with *The Mundy Scheme,* Farrar, Straus (New York, NY), 1970.

The Mundy Scheme (produced in Dublin, 1969; produced on Broadway at Royale Theatre, 1969), published with *Crystal and Fox,* Farrar, Straus (New York, NY), 1970.

The Gentle Island (two-act play; produced in Dublin, 1971), Davis-Poynter (London, England), 1973.

The Freedom of the City (two-act play; produced in Dublin, 1972; produced in Chicago at Goodman Theatre, 1974; produced on Broadway, 1974), S. French (New York, NY), 1974.

Volunteers (produced in Dublin, 1975), Faber (London, England), 1979.

Living Quarters (produced in Dublin, 1977), Faber (London, England), 1978.

The Faith Healer (produced in New York, 1979; produced at Royal Court Theatre, London, 1992), Faber (London, England), 1980.

Aristocrats (three-act play; produced in Dublin, 1979), Gallery Press (Oldcastle, County Meath, Ireland), 1980.

Translations (produced in Derry, 1980; produced at Manhattan Theatre Club, New York, 1981), Faber (London, England), 1981.

American Welcome (produced in New York, 1980), published in *The Best Short Plays 1981,* Chilton (Radnor, PA), 1981.

(Translator) *Anton Chekhov's "Three Sisters"* (produced in Derry, 1981), Gallery Press (Oldcastle, County Meath, Ireland), 1981.

The Communication Cord (produced in Derry, 1982; produced in Seattle, WA, 1984-1985), Faber (London, England), 1983.

Selected Plays of Brian Friel, Faber (London, England), 1984, Catholic University Press (Washington, DC), 1986.

(Adapter) *Fathers and Sons* (based on a novel by Ivan Turgenev), produced in London, 1987; produced in New Haven, CT, 1988.

Making History, produced in Derry, 1988; produced in London, 1988.

The London Vertigo: Based on a Play "The True Born Irishman; or, The Irish Fine Lady" by Charles Macklin, Gallery Press (Oldcastle, County Meath, Ireland), 1990.

Dancing at Lughnasa (produced in London, 1991), Faber (London, England), 1990, Dramatists Play Service (New York, NY), 1993.

A Month in the Country: After Turgenev, Gallery Press (Oldcastle, County Meath, Ireland), 1992, Dramatists Play Service (New York, NY), 1993.

Wonderful Tennessee, Gallery Press (Oldcastle, County Meath, Ireland), 1993.

Molly Sweeney, Gallery Press (Oldcastle, County Meath, Ireland), 1994, Penguin (New York, NY), 1995.

(Adapter) Anton Chekhov, *Uncle Vanya,* Gallery Press (Oldcastle, County Meath, Ireland), 1998.

Plays Two, Faber & Faber (New York, NY), 1999.

Give Me Your Answer, Do! (produced in London, 1997, produced in New York, 1999-2000), Plume (New York, NY), 2000.

Afterplay, produced in New York, NY, 2002.

The Yalta Game, (produced in Dublin, 2002), Gallery Press (Oldcastle, County Meath, Ireland), 2002.

RADIO PLAYS

A Sort of Freedom, produced by BBC Radio, 1958.

To This Hard House, produced by BBC Radio, 1958.

The Founder Members, 1964.

The Loves of Cass McGuire, 1966.

FICTION

A Saucer of Larks (stories), Doubleday (Garden City, NY), 1962.

The Gold in the Sea (stories), Doubleday (Garden City, NY), 1966.

Mr. Sing-Meines-Herzens-Freude, Verlag Agentur des Rauhen Hauses, 1966.

Selected Stories, Gallery Press (Oldcastle, County Meath, Ireland), 1979.

The Diviner: Brian Friel's Best Short Stories, Devin (Old Greenwich, CT), 1983.

(Editor) Charles McGlinchey, *The Last of the Name,* Blackstaff Press (Dover, NH), 1986.

Traduzioni e Altri Drammi, Bulzoni (Rome, Italy), 1996, Gallery Books, 1997.

Author of screen adaptation of his play *Philadelphia, Here I Come!,* c. 1970; also has written for British and Irish radio and television. Contributor of stories to periodicals, including *New Yorker.*

ADAPTATIONS: The Loves of Cass McGuire was produced on television in Dublin; *Dancing at Lughnasa* was adapted for film and released by Sony Pictures Classics, 1998.

SIDELIGHTS: One of Ireland's best-known playwrights, Brian Friel is noted for his deft use of language and his interest in Irish life and history. Cofounder of the Field Day Theatre Company in London's West End in 1980, Friel is considered a central figure in the resurgence of interest and appreciation for Irish-penned drama that took place in both England and the United States during the 1980s and 1990s. Among his best-known works for the stage are 1964's *Philadelphia, Here I Come!*, 1980's *Translations,* and *Dancing at Lughnasa,* first produced in 1990. The story of a hopeful but heretofore luckless Irishman who immigrates to the United States, *Philadelphia* was the first of many major stage successes for its author; it boasted a long run in New York City and was eventually adapted as a motion picture.

Taking place, as do most of Friel's works, in Ballybeg, a small, fictional town in County Donegal, Northern Ireland, *Philadelphia, Here I Come!* was the fourth play of Friel's to be produced; the first, a working-class drama called *A Doubtful Paradise,* was written in 1959, when its author was thirty. A graduate of St. Patrick's College who had abandoned early plans to join the priesthood, Friel had worked as a teacher in Londonderry while writing short stories and plays for both radio and the stage. In 1962 he left teaching to become a full-time writer after being encouraged by the reception of his short stories at the *New Yorker* magazine, wherein they were regularly published. In 1963, to increase his knowledge of the working theatre, Friel accepted an invitation from noted stage director Tyrone Guthrie to accompany him to the Minneapolis theater that bears his name. The experience as an observer of the great director paid off; Friel's next play, the humorous and sensitive *Philadelphia, Here I Come!* enjoyed a successful run in its author's native Northern Ireland, in London, and across the Atlantic in New York City.

In the play, twenty-seven-year-old Gar O'Donnell is preparing to board a plane for the United States, where he hopes to make a new life. Friel's portrayal of O'Donnell's duality—his public and private selves—through the use of two actors allows the playwright to expose, as Walter Kerr noted in a review of the play in the *New York Herald Tribune,* "the skipping, sassy, candid, tormenting back-talk all of us give ourselves when we know we are behaving like the chuckleheads we are, listening to the running argument we keep up with ourselves every furious, fumbled day of our lives."

Following his positive reception before international audiences, Friel increased his standing with such stage productions as *The Loves of Cass McGuire, The Freedom of the City,* and *Aristocrats,* first produced at Dublin's Abbey Theatre. The O'Donnells, an aristocratic Irish Catholic family in decline, serve as the focus of Friel's *Aristocrats,* which won the New York Drama Critics Circle award for best foreign play in 1989. In a multigenerational household in a rundown Georgian manse called Ballybeg Hall, the inner workings of the O'Donnell clan become exposed as friends, family, and outsiders gather to witness the wedding of the family's youngest daughter, Claire. Drawing numerous comparisons to the stage works of Anton Chekhov, *Aristocrats* earned overwhelming praise from critics, Edith Oliver calling it "an ironic, loving, imaginative, and all but faultless play" in her review of the Broadway production in the *New Yorker.* "One test of a good play is how much of a society it manages to put on stage," maintained *Guardian* critic Michael Billington, adding, "Friel gives us a comprehensive tour. . . . But [he] is less concerned with class-judgements than with the engrossing spectacle of decline; and, again, the Chekhovian parallel comes to mind in that the most dynamic characters are those with a hunger for life."

Friel's *Translations* was also widely welcomed, a "vibrant, deeply moving work of art in which everything seems to have come together for its author," according to *Chicago Tribune* critic Richard Christiansen. Set in 1833, as British authorities were in the process of mapping and renaming Ireland's old Gaelic towns, the play shows the beginning of the end of traditions and cultural identity and the roots of the modern divided Ireland. Sent to take part in the mapping of County Donegal, English Lieutenant Yolland falls in love with the countryside and with a young woman named Maire, who speaks only Gaelic, and their brief story plays out in tragic, inexorable parallel with that of Romeo and Juliet. Christiansen deemed the work "glorious," writing that in *Translations* Friel "found the theme, the period of history, the language and the passion to create a work that resonates with poetic metaphor, taking a specific incident and turning it into a profound and moving drama of universal meaning." *New York Post* critic Clive Barnes also had praise for *Translations* as a portrait of Ireland's loss of national identity, and commented that "This picture, this analysis of Ireland at a time conceivably of hope deferred if not lost, is full of that Hibernian gift of transforming a foreign reality into a native poetry."

Friel's *Dancing at Lughnasa* once again takes place in the town of Ballybeg, this time in the autumn of 1936, during the harvest festival honoring the ancient pagan god Lugh. It is a portrait of a woman-run household where itinerant father figures come and go, where Uncle Jack, recently dismissed from missionary service in Uganda after adopting the native religion, has come to live out his remaining years of ill-health, but where the five spinster Mundy sisters clearly hold sway. Narrated by Michael, the son of one of the sisters, the story revolves around the introduction of music to the house via a wireless radio. The wireless is broken—the music is sometimes present, sometimes not—but the intermittent intrusion of everything from Big Band sounds to torch songs to Irish folk tunes inspire the sisters to break away from the poverty of their lives and even contemplate attending the harvest dance. "It is hard to think of any play that has more explicitly honored women's work—manual, intellectual and spiritual—as the foundation upon which community survival is built," contended Margaret Spillane in the *Nation*. Drawing parallels between African and pre-Christian Celtic rituals as well as revisioning the role between the sexes, *Dancing at Lughnasa* also "seems to suggest the possibility of fusion rather than collision, of reconciliation rather than antagonism," commented S. F. Gallagher in a review in the *Irish Literary Supplement*.

While *Dancing at Lughnasa* became one of the most produced plays in the United States following its Broadway premiere, some critics were not so enthusiastic about *Wonderful Tennessee*. The play profiles a group of individuals awaiting a ferry to take them to an island off the Irish coast, a ferry that never arrives, and while *Lughnasa* is a play that reaffirms the joy existing in simple things, *Wonderful Tennessee* focuses on defeat. "Friel's play is about disappointment, nonfulfillment, both actual and symbolic," noted *Irish Literary Supplement* critic Robert Tracy. "None of his characters reach the island. Each is a study in failure." However, Tracy saw much of value in the play, notably the playwright's attempt to "move away from political drama, however implicit, and from his related—and Chekhovian—preoccupation with the use/misuse of language." *Wonderful Tennessee* "represents a new direction in Friel's work," maintained Tracy. "We can only wait, and cheer him on."

That new direction would be even more apparent in *Molly Sweeney*. A blind, forty-one-year-old woman from a small town, Friel's protagonist regains her sight at the hands of an alcoholic ophthalmologist experi-

menting with a new technique. Dispensing with modern stage techniques, the dialogue comes from three actors—Molly, her ophthalmologist, Paddy Rice, and husband, Frank—who share between them thirty-seven monologues from their seated position at center stage. In addition to outlining Molly and Frank's relationship up to the time of the surgery, these monologues also disclose the inner personality of each of the characters: creative, spiritual Molly; her unfocused but well-meaning, hyperactive husband; and Rice, whose belief extends only to the power of technology. Sightless from birth, Molly had achieved a great deal of success in her life. In fact, she had not sought out a cure for her blindness, but had meekly followed the wishes of Frank, who was in need of a new crusade to shield the growing knowledge that his life had produced little of actual achievement. The success of the operation comes as a surprise to all involved; the regaining of partial vision, even temporarily, now threatens to destroy Molly's heightened imaginative sense of both self and surroundings. The shock she experiences "raises fascinating intellectual and spiritual problems," explained John Lahr in the *New Yorker*. "In the material, sighted world, seeing is believing. But in the realm of faith, believing is *not* seeing; it is accepting the unknowable as fact."

"Stylistically, [Friel] moves away from naturalism, employing striking theatrical devices to shed a more intense light on his subject," commented Mel Gussow, characterizing Friel's body of work in the *New York Times Magazine*. "The plays take place at homecomings and leavings, reunions, and preludes to exile. Old worlds dissolve and traditional values are questioned. Language is of the utmost concern—not simply the lyrical language that elevates his plays, but in his commentary on communication. He illustrates the power of things spoken and unspoken, language as divider and bridge." June Schlueter expanded on this assessment in the *Dictionary of Literary Biography*, deeming the strengths of Friel's writing to be "sensitivity of characterization, authenticity of language, and an overall perceptivity." "These, coupled with his enduring commitment to dramatizing the Irish national character and dilemma," Schlueter concluded, "are responsible for Friel's deserved place among Ireland's most important contemporary playwrights."

Uncle Vanya is Friel's adaptation of another of Chekhov's plays. "Although fairly close to the Chekhov original, Friel's version is infused with a lyricism that turns the idle thoughts of Chekhov's idlers into artfully shaped soliloquies, which the actors then deliver with careful emphasis," wrote Charles Isherwood in *Variety*. Isherwood, writing in *Daily Variety,* also remarked that Friel's adaptation "is a bit too self-consciously eloquent, and a pointed tone of sarcasm is unnecessarily pervasive at times" throughout the play. In the story, Vanya and his niece, Sonya, suddenly find themselves facing the prospect of happiness after years of simple toil and existence. Vanya fancies the wife of Serebryakov, Yelena, and Sonya finds herself strongly attracted to Dr. Astrov. "Both affections are hopeless: Vanya's comically, Sonya's more tragically," Isherwood wrote.

Give Me Your Answer, Do! is "really about one's expectations of life, and life's inevitable disappointments—our present situations are merely substitutes for a set of other pains and disappointments we would have encountered on another road," wrote Jane Hogan in *Back Stage*. In the play, Tom and Daisy Connelly are a married couple with an autistic adult daughter. Tom writes well-respected but commercially unprofitable novels, and is courting a representative from the University of Texas, whom Tom thinks might be willing to pay handsomely for his archive. The representative visits, but the result is not what Tom expects. Ultimately, Hogan remarked, "The tiresome theme is of long-suffering women who have given up their careers and sublimated their wants for their men." Isherwood, again writing in *Variety,* observed, "The characters in *Give Me Your Answer, Do!* are drawn with depth and heart; their language, flecked with mordant wit, is robust yet natural. And the mood of nearly extinguished hope is carefully sustained. But in a play about a man struggling with writer's block, Friel himself seems merely to be marking time by falling back on familiar formulas."

In *Afterplay,* Friel combines characters from Chekhov plays, creating "a world where a character from one Chekhov play meets a character from another in 1920s Moscow—where Andrey, the brother from *Three Sisters,* meets Sonya from *Uncle Vanya,*" wrote Alastair Macaulay in the *Financial Times*. The characters interact, reminisce, and tell the stories of what happened to them after the end of their original plays. "Andrey pretends he is playing violin at the opera but in reality is busking for a living," wrote Bill Hagerty in the *Hollywood Reporter.* "Sonya obviously still pines for Astrov, which rules out any across-two-plays romance

that might have brought a flicker of happiness to this luckless pair." A reviewer in the London *Guardian* observed, "Far from depicting them as sad, middle-aged fantasists, Friel portrays Sonya and Andrey as people still sustained by unquenchable hope." The reviewer concluded, "The play gains from prior knowledge of Chekhov," but that within the relatively short seventy-minute running time, "it covers a huge emotional range and takes us close to the heart of Chekhov."

The Yalta Game is another Friel adaptation of Chekhov, this time of the short story "Lady with Lapdog." The Yalta game of the title "is invented by vacationers in the Crimea as a diversion from their ordinary lives," wrote William Pratt in *World Literature Today,* "a game played by imagining fantasy lives for others." The two characters of Friel's play, a middle-aged man (Gurov) and a young woman (Anna) with an imaginary dog, begin an affair at a small resort and continue it in the town where she lives with her husband. Though the affair fills their lives with excitement and a delight in the secretiveness of it, the play ends with them pledging continued loyalty but unsure how they'll be able to persist with their affair.

"Nowhere previously has Friel provided such a telling illustration of the idea that we live lives based on selected fictions," wrote Richard Pine in the *Irish University Review*. "In a sense, Gurov and Anna have no existence, since both deny the domestic contexts from which they have come to Yalta, and to which they return merely to endure long-distance-loving of a largely disembodied kind. The togetherness for which they yearn is, of course, impossible of realization," Pine commented. "This short, striking drama shows how much Friel the Irish playwright has in common with Chekhov the Russian playwright," Pratt concluded.

Friel has been notoriously shy of the spotlight that surrounds his success. "He has refused interviews many times and seldom poses for photographs, preferring anonymity to publicity," wrote William Pratt in *World Literature Today. Brian Friel in Conversation,* edited by Paul Delany, "removes some of the veil that has shrouded Friel up to now and presents him in his own words apart from his works," Pratt observed. Drawing on the infrequent published interviews and other documentary sources, Delany assembles a collection of works that portrays Friel as "a lively personality who enjoys frank discourse and witty remarks that could easily make him into a public figure if he chose that role," Pratt commented. Friel, however, reserves the spotlight for the actors in his plays, preferring to remain secluded with his wife, Anne, in his home in a village on the Donegal coast. "Overhearing his conversations, conveniently provided by this book, is a way of understanding better what he means," Pratt concluded.

BIOGRAPHICAL AND CRITICAL SOURCES:

BOOKS

Andrews, Elmer, *The Art of Brian Friel: Neither Reality nor Dreams,* St. Martin's Press (New York, NY), 1995.

Contemporary Dramatists, 6th edition, St. James Press (Detroit, MI), 1999.

Contemporary Literary Criticism,, Gale (Detroit, MI), Volume 5, 1976, Volume 42, 1987, Volume 59, 1990.

Dantanus, Ulf, *Brian Friel: The Growth of an Irish Dramatist,* Faber (London, England), 1987.

Delany, Paul, editor, *Brian Friel in Conversation,* University of Michigan Press (Ann Arbor, MI), 2000.

Dictionary of Literary Biography, Volume 13: *British Dramatists since World War II,* Gale (Detroit, MI), 1982.

Duncan, Dawn, John Countryman, and Susan C. Harris, editors, *Studies in the Plays of Brian Friel,* Nova University (Fort Lauderdale, FL), 1994.

Encyclopedia of World Biography, 2nd edition, Gale (Detroit, MI), 1998.

International Dictionary of Theatre, Volume 2: *Playwrights,* St. James Press (Detroit, MI), 1993.

Maxwell, D. E. S., *Brian Friel,* Bucknell University Press (Lewisburg, PA), 1973.

Modern British Literature, 2nd edition, St. James Press (Detroit, MI), 2000.

O'Brien, George, *Brian Friel,* Twayne (Boston, MA), 1990.

Peacock, Alan J., *The Achievement of Brian Friel,* Barnes & Noble Books (Lanham, MD), 1992.

Pine, Richard, *Brian Friel and Ireland's Drama,* Routledge (London, England), 1990.

Stade, George, and Sarah Hannah Goldstein, editors, *British Writers,* Supplement 5, Scribner (New York, NY), 1999.

PERIODICALS

America, September 24, 1966, pp. 359-360; January 29, 1994, p. 23.

Back Stage, July 16, 1999, Irene Backalenick, review of *The Freedom of the City,* p. 28; July 16, 1999, Irene Backalenick, review of *Uncle Vanya,* p. 30; July 30, 1999, review of *Aristocrats,* p. 31; October 15, 1999, Jane Hogan, review of *Give Me Your Answer, Do!,* p. 44; June 29, 2000, Madeleine Shaner, review of *A Month in the Country: After Turgenev,* p. 12; October 13, 2000, Martin F. Kohn, review of *Dancing at Lughnasa,* p. 29.

Chicago Tribune, September 24, 1982.

Commonweal, December 6, 1991, pp. 718-719.

Contemporary Review, April, 1995, p. 199.

Daily Telegraph (London, England), November 6, 2001, Dominic Cavendish, profile of Friel.

Daily Variety, January 20, 2003, Charles Isherwood, review of *Uncle Vanya,* pp. 6-7.

Economist, October 12, 2002, review of *Afterplay.*

English Review, April, 2002, Eileen Underhill, analysis of *Translations,* pp. 33-35.

Europe, July-August, 1999, p. 38.

Financial Times, March 15, 2002, Alastair Macaulay, review of *Afterplay,* p. 16.

Guardian (London, England), June 4, 1988; May 1, 1999, Fintan O'Toole, review of *The Faith Healer,* p. S4; November 29, 2001, review of *The Faith Healer,* p. 20; March 7, 2002, review of *Afterplay,* p. 23; September 18, 2002, review of *Uncle Vanya,* p. 16; September 20, 2002, review of *Afterplay,* p. 16.

Hollywood Reporter, October 1, 2002, Bill Hagerty, review of *Afterplay,* pp. 24-25.

Houston Chronicle, December 19, 2002, review of *Translations,* p. 7.

Irish Literary Supplement, fall, 1990, p. 12; spring 1994, pp. 17-18.

Irish University Review, spring-summer, 1999, Anthony Roche, "Friel and Synge: Towards a Theatrical Language," pp. 145-161; spring-summer, 2002, review of *The Yalta Game,* pp. 191-196.

Journal of Irish Literature, September, 1976, Robert B. Bennett, pp. 148-149.

Los Angeles Times, February 3, 1984; September 19, 1989.

Midwest Quarterly, spring, 2000, p. 264.

Modern Drama, fall, 1997, David Krause, review of *Dancing at Lughnasa,* pp. 359-373; winter, 1999, David Krause, "Friel's Ballybeggared Version of Chekhov," p. 634.

Nation, January 27, 1992, pp. 102, 104; March 4, 1996, pp. 33-35.

New Republic, January 27, 1992, p. 28.

New Statesman, May 22, 1981, Benedict Nightingale, review of *Translations,* pp. 23-24; September 10, 2001, Katherine Duncan-Jones, "Sisters Doing It for Themselves," review of *Three Sisters,* p. 42; December 17, 2001, Katherine Duncan-Jones, review of *The Faith Healer,* pp. 100-101; October 7, 2002, review of *Afterplay,* p. 45.

New Statesman & Society, January 14, 1994, p. 35.

Newsweek, November 4, 1991, Jack Kroll, review of *Dancing at Lughnasa,* p. 79.

New York, August 2, 1999, John Simon, "Bodies Politic," review of *The Freedom of the City,* pp. 57-58; August 9, 1999, John Simon, review of *Aristocrats,* pp. 52-53; October 18, 1999, John Simon, "Damaged Goods," review of *Give Me Your Answer, Do!* pp. 57-58.

New Yorker, May 8, 1989, Edith Oliver, review of *Aristocrats,* p. 104; November 4, 1991, pp. 95-97; July 19, 1993, p. 82; October 17, 1994, pp. 107-109; April 3, 1995, p. 98.

New York Herald Tribune, February 17, 1966.

New York Post, April 15, 1981; April 26, 1989.

New York Times, February 18, 1974, p. 32; April 7, 1979; December 11, 1979; April 15, 1981, pp. 264-265; February 24, 1983; November 12, 1983; April 26, 1989; April 30, 1989; June 9, 1999, James F. Clarity, review of *The Freedom of the City,* p. E2; July 4, 1999, Declan Kiberd, review of *The Freedom of the City* and *Dancing at Lughnasa,* p. AR1; July 9, 1999, Peter Marks, review of *Uncle Vanya,* p. E5; October 6, 1999, Ben Brantley, review of *Give Me Your Answer, Do!,* p. E1.

New York Times Book Review, October 17, 1999, Carol Peace Robins, review of *The Last of the Name,* p. 23.

New York Times Magazine, September 29, 1991, pp. 30, 55-61.

Saturday Review, March 5, 1996, Henry Hewes, review of *Philadelphia, Here I Come!,* p. 54.

Spectator, January 2, 1999, Patrick Carnegy, review of *A Month in the Country,* p. 1; September 21, 2002, Toby Young, review of *Uncle Vanya,* p. 56.

Sunday Telegraph (London, England), December 2, 2001, John Gross, review of *The Faith Healer.*

Sunday Times (London, England), March 28, 1999, profile of Brian Friel, p. 23; August 11, 2002, review of *Afterplay,* p. 12; September 15, 2002, profile of Brian Friel, p. 18; September 29, 2002, John Peter, review of *Afterplay,* p. 17.

Time, November 8, 1993, p. 91.

Times (London, England), May 9, 1983; July 11, 1987; June 4, 1988; December 7, 1988.

Times Educational Supplement, May 19, 2000, Aleks Sierz, review of *Translations,* p. FR127; July 13, 2001, Aleks Sierz, review of *Three Sisters,* p. 24.

Times Literary Supplement, April 19, 1963, p. 261; October 15, 1982; June 3, 1983; December 14, 2001, Robert Shore, review of *The Faith Healer,* p. 19; September 27, 2002, Katherine Duncan-Jones, review of *Uncle Vanya,* p. 19; October 4, 2002, Stephen Brown, review of *Afterplay,* p. 21.

Twentieth-Century Literature, fall, 2000, Karen M. Moloney, review of *Translations,* p. 285.

Vanity Fair, October, 1991, p. 128.

Variety, July 12, 1999, Charles Isherwood, review of *Uncle Vanya,* p. 46; July 19, 1999, Charles Isherwood, review of *The Freedom of the City,* p. 34; July 26, 1999, Charles Isherwood, review of *Aristocrats,* p. 42; October 11, 1999, Charles Isherwood, review of *Give Me Your Answer, Do!,* p. 162; August 27, 2001, Markland Taylor, review of *Philadelphia, Here I Come!,* p. 40; December 3, 2001, Matt Wolf, review of *The Faith Healer,* p. 38; September 30, 2002, Matt Wolf, review of *Uncle Vanya* and *Afterplay,* pp. 35-36.

Vogue, October, 1991, p. 174.

Wall Street Journal, October 6, 1999, Debra Jo Immergut, review of *Give Me Your Answer, Do!,* p. A20.

World Literature Today, summer, 1999, p. 445; autumn, 2000, William Pratt, review of *Brian Friel in Conversation,* p. 826; summer-autumn, 2002, William Pratt, review of *The Yalta Game,* p. 95.*

G

GLASS, Philip 1937-

PERSONAL: Born January 31, 1937, in Baltimore, MD; son of Benjamin C. (a record shop owner) and Ida (Gouline) Glass; married Jo Anne Akalaitis (a theater director; divorced); married Linda Burtyk, 1980 (divorced); married Candy Jernigan (an artist and set designer), 1991 (died, 1991); married Holly Critchlow; children: (first marriage) Juliet, Zachary; (fourth marriage) Cameron. *Education:* University of Chicago, A.B., 1956; Juilliard School of Music, M.S., 1964; studied composition with Nadia Boulanger in Paris, France, 1964-66; also studied with Indian performers Ravi Shankar and Alla Rakha.

ADDRESSES: Home—Cape Breton Island, Nova Scotia, Canada; and New York, NY. *Office*—Dunvagen Music Publishers, 632 Broadway, New York, NY 10012; fax: 212-473-2842. *E-mail*—info@dunvagen. com.

CAREER: Composer, musician, director, screenwriter, and performer. Composer-in-residence, Pittsburgh Public Schools, 1962-64; founder and electric organist, Philip Glass Ensemble, performing original music in concert tours throughout United States and Europe, 1968—; founder, Chatham Square Productions (record company), 1972; resident composer, Tyrone Guthrie Theatre, Minneapolis, MN, 1985-86. Also worked as a taxicab driver.

Film work: Music supervisor and transcriptionist, *Chappaqua,* Regional, 1967; music director, *Koyaanisqatsi,* New Yorker, 1982; dramaturgical consultant,

Philip Glass

Powaqqatsi, Cannon, 1988; director, *Anima Mundi* (documentary short film; also known as *The Soul of*

the World), 1991; creative musical supervisor and musical supervisor, *Closet Land,* Universal, 1991; song arranger, *Exposure,* 1991.

Film appearances: *Four American Composers,* Trans Atlantic Films, 1983; narrator, *A Composer's Notes: Philip Glass and the Making of an Opera (Akhnaten),* Michael Blackwell Productions, 1985; *Robert Wilson and the CIVIL warS* (documentary), Unisphere, 1987; music performer, *Christo in Paris* (documentary), 1990; as himself, *The Nova Convention Revisited* (also known as *The Nova Convention Revisited: William S. Burroughs and the Arts*), [video], 1998; keyboard artist, *The Truman Show,* Paramount, 1998.

Television appearances: "Einstein on the Beach: The Changing Image of Opera," *Great Performances,* Public Broadcasting Service (PBS), 1986; *Timeless Voices: The Gyuto Monks,* Discovery Channel, 1989; *Edgar Allan Poe: Terror of the Soul,* PBS, 1995; *Sessions at West 54th,* PBS, 1997; *Chuck Close: A Portrait in Progress,* PBS, 1998; interviewee, *Lou Reed: Rock and Roll Heart,* PBS, 1998.

Director of opera *1000 Airplanes on the Roof,* produced at Vienna International Airport, Vienna Austria, 1987. Appeared on stage in *Grace for Grace,* produced at Cathedral of St. John the Divine, New York, NY, 1991.

MEMBER: American Society of Composers, Authors, and Publishers; SACEM (France).

AWARDS, HONORS: Broadcast Music Industry Award, 1960; Lado Prize, 1961; Benjamin Award, 1961 and 1962; Young Composer's Award, Ford Foundation, 1964-66; Fulbright Composition grant, 1966-67; Foundation for Contemporary Performance Arts award, 1970-71; National Endowment for the Arts grant, 1974-75; Menil Foundation award, 1974; Obie Awards, special citations, 1975-76, for *Mabou Mines Performs Samuel Beckett,* and 1977-78, for *Einstein on the Beach;* Los Angeles Film Critics Association award, best music, 1983, for *Koyaanisqatsi;* named Musician of the Year, *Musical American,* 1985; Cannes International Film Festival award for best artistic contribution to a full-length film, 1985, for *Mishima;* Musician of the Year, *Musical America* magazine, 1985; named Lion of the Performing Arts, New York Public Library,

1987; Los Angeles Film Critics Association Award, Academy Award nomination, best original score, and Golden Globe nomination, 1997, all for *Kundun;* Golden Globe Award, best original score—motion picture, 1998, for *The Truman Show;* Academy Award nomination, best original score, 2002, for *The Hours.*

WRITINGS:

NONFICTION

Music by Philip Glass, Harper (New York, NY), 1987; new edition, with supplement published as *Opera on the Beach: On His New World of Music Theatre,* 1988.

COMPOSER OF MUSICAL STAGE PIECES

Music for Voices, produced at Mabou Mines Theatre, 1970.
Mabou Mines Performs Samuel Beckett, produced at Theatre for the New City, New York, NY, 1975.
Einstein on the Beach (opera), produced in Avignon, France, and throughout Europe, 1976; produced at Metropolitan Opera House, New York, NY, 1976; international tour, 1976; album, Nonesuch, 1993.
Dressed Like an Egg, produced at New York Shakespeare Festival, Public Theatre, New York, NY, 1977.
Dead End Kids, produced at New York Shakespeare Festival, Public Theatre, New York, NY, 1980.
Satyagraha (opera), produced in Rotterdam, The Netherlands, 1980; album, CBS Records, 1985; DVD, Image Entertainment, 2001.
The Panther, produced in 1980.
The Photographer: Far from the Truth (opera), produced in 1982; produced in New York, NY, 1983; album, CBS Records, 1983.
(With Robert Wilson and Maita di Discemi) *the CIVIL warS: a tree is best measured when it is down,* produced in 1982; adapted as a documentary, Unisphere, 1987; album, *the CIVIL warS: a tree is best measured when it is down: Act V, The Rome Section,* Nonesuch, 1999.
Samuel Beckett's Company, produced at New York Shakespeare Festival, Public Theatre, New York, NY, 1983.
Cold Harbor, produced at New York Shakespeare Festival, Public Theatre, New York, NY, 1983.

Glass Pieces (ballet from *Glassworks* and *Akhnaten*), produced by New York City Ballet, New York State Theatre, New York, NY, 1983.

(Composer of opening and closing music) *Suzanna Andler,* produced at South Street Theatre, New York, NY, 1984.

(Composer of incidental music) *Endgame,* produced by American Repertory Theatre, Cambridge, MA, 1984.

Akhnaten (opera), produced at Wurttemberg State Theatre, Wurttemberg, West Germany, 1984; album, CBS Records, 1987.

(With Robert Moran and Arthur Yorinks) *The Juniper Tree,* produced by American Repertory Theatre, Cambridge, MA, 1985.

"A Madrigal Opera," *An Evening of Micro-Operas,* produced at Mark Taper Forum, Los Angeles, CA, 1985.

(With Matthew Maguire and Molissa Fenley) *Descent into the Maelstrom* (theatre and dance piece; based on the Edgar Allan Poe story of the same name), Australian Dance Theatre, 1985; album, Orange Mountain Music, 2002.

The Making of the Representative for Planet 8 (three-act opera; based on the novel by Doris Lessing), produced in Amsterdam, The Netherlands, Houston, TX, Kiel, West Germany, and London, England, 1985-86.

One Thousand Airplanes on the Roof (opera; produced at Vienna International Airport, Vienna, Austria, 1987; produced at Beacon Theatre, New York, NY, 1988; album, Virgin, 1989), Gibbs-Smith (Salt Lake City, UT), 1989.

The Light, produced in Cleveland, OH, 1987.

The Fall of the House of Usher (two-act opera; based on the story by Edgar Allan Poe), produced by the Kentucky Opera and the American Repertory Theatre, Cambridge, MA, 1988.

Cymbeline, produced at New York Shakespeare Festival, Public/Newman Theatre, New York, NY, 1989.

Itaipu, produced in Atlanta, GA, 1989; album, *Itaipu/ The Canyon,* Sony, 1993.

Henry IV, Part I, produced at Public/Newman Theatre, New York, NY, 1991.

The Voyage (opera), produced at Metropolitan Opera House, 1992.

The Mysteries and What's So Funny?, produced at Joyce Theatre, New York, NY, 1992-93.

Orphee (opera), produced at the American Repertory Theatre, Cambridge, MA, 1992-93.

Woyzeck, produced at Public/Newman Theatre, New York, NY, 1992-93.

In the Summer House, produced at Vivian Beaumont Theatre, New York, NY, 1993.

Symphony No. 2, produced in New York, NY, 1994.

La Belle et la bete (opera), produced at the Next Wave Festival, Brooklyn Academy of Music, New York, NY, 1994; album, Nonesuch, 1995.

Prisoner of Love, New York Theatre Workshop, New York, NY, 1995.

Les Enfants terribles, produced in 1996.

Marriages between Zones Three, Four, and Five (opera; based on the work of Doris Lessing), produced in Heidelberg, Germany, 1997.

Monsters of Grace (opera), produced at Barbican Theatre, New York, NY, 1997.

White Raven, produced in Lisbon, Portugal, 1998; produced at Lincoln Centre, New York, NY, 2001.

In the Penal Colony, produced in 2000.

Galileo Galilei, produced at the Next Wave Festival, Brooklyn Academy of Music, 2002.

Music for the Elephant Man, produced in 2002.

The Sound of a Voice (based on two one-act plays by David Hwang), produced at American Repertory Theatre, Cambridge, MA, 2003.

OTHER MUSICAL PIECES AND SOUND RECORDINGS

Play, 1965.

String Quartet, 1966.

Brass Sextet, Mills Music, 1966.

In Again out Again (for two pianos), 1967.

One Plus One (for amplified tabletop), 1967.

Music in the Shape of a Square, 1967; album titled *Alter Ego—Music in the Shape of a Square,* Stradivarius, 2001.

Strung Out, 1967.

Arioso, String Orchestra, No. 2, Elkan-Vogel, 1967.

Red Horse Animation, 1968.

How Now, 1968.

Two Pages, 1968.

Gradus, 1969.

Music in Contrary Motion, 1969.

Music in Eight Parts, 1969.

Music in Fifths, 1969.

Music in Similar Motion, 1969.

Music with Changing Parts, 1970; album, Nonesuch, 1994.

Music in Twelve Parts, Dischi Ricordi, 1971-74, Nonesuch, 1996.

Another Look at Harmony, 1975.

The Lost Ones, 1975.

The Saint and the Football Player, 1975.

Knee Play No. 3, 1976.

Strung Out: For Amplified Violin, Dunvagen, 1976.

Modern Love Waltz, 1977.

North Star: Mark Di Suvero, Virgin, 1977, CBS Records, 1977.

Fourth Series Part I, 1978.

Music for a Performance/Reading by C. DeJong: Fourth Series, Part II, 1978.

Cascando, 1979.

Mercier and Camier, 1979.

Mad Rush: Fourth Series, Part III, 1979.

(With Lucinda Childs and Sol LeWitt) *Dance* (multimedia piece), 1979.

Dance No. 2, 1979.

Dance No. 4, 1979.

Dance Nos. 1 and 3, Tomato, 1980.

Vessels, 1981.

Facades, 1981.

Habeve Song, 1982.

Glassworks, CBS Records, 1982.

String Quartet No. 2: Company, 1983.

Floe, 1983.

The Olympian (for chorus and orchestra; used at the opening of the 1984 Olympics), Los Angeles, CA, 1984.

String Quartet No. 3: "Mishima," 1985; album, Chester, 1999.

Songs from Liquid Days, CBS Records, 1986.

Three Songs, 1986.

Kronos Quartet, Company, Nonesuch, 1986.

Concerto for Violin and Orchestra, 1987.

Dancepieces, CBS Records, 1987.

Dance Nos. 1-5, Sony, 1988.

The Canyon, 1988; album, *Itaipu/The Canyon,* Sony, 1993.

String Quartet No. 4: Boczak, 1989.

Solo Piano, CBS Records, 1989, Amsco, 1991.

Songs from the Trilogy, Sony, 1989.

Passages, Private Music, 1990.

Hydrogen Jukebox (based on the poetry of Allen Ginsberg), 1990; album, Nonesuch, 1993.

The Screens, Point Music, 1992.

Concerto for Three Ensembles, Dunvagen, 1992.

Low Symphony, Point Music, 1993.

Donald Joyce, Glass Organ Works, Catalyst, 1993.

Gidon Kremer, Violin Concerto, Deutsche Grammophon, 1993.

The Essential Philip Glass, Sony, 1993.

Echorus for Two Solo Violins & String Orchestra, 1994.

Two Pages/Contrary Motion/Music in Fifths/Music in Similar Motion, Nonesuch, 1994.

Jenipapo (also see below), 1995.

Melodies for Saxophone, 1995.

Symphony No. 3, 1995.

Kronos Quartet, String Quartets 2-5, Nonesuch, 1995.

T.E.C.C. Quartet, String Quartets 4-5, Beoton, 1996.

Heroes Symphony (based on the David Bowie album *Heroes*), 1996; album, Point Music, 1997.

Songs of Milarepa, 1997.

Days and Nights in Rocinha, 1997.

Glassmasters, Sony, 1997.

Gradus, 1998.

Symphony No. 2/Interlude from Orphee/Concerto for Saxophone Quartet and Orchestra, Nonesuch, 1998.

Arturo Stalteri, Circles, Materiali Sonori MASO, 1998.

Etudes for Piano, 1999; album titled *Etudes for Piano, Volume 1,* Orange Mountain Music, 2003.

String Quartet No. 5, Chester, 1999.

Jay Gottlieb, Piano Music, Pianovox, 1999.

Dance No. 2 for Organ, Chester Music, 1999.

Robert McDuffie, Violin Concerto, Telarc, 1999.

The Civil Wars, Rome Section, Nonesuch, 1999.

Aguas da Amazonia, Point Music, 1999.

Jeroen Van Veen, Minimal Piano Works, Piano Productions, 1999.

Concuto Fantasy for 2 Timpanists and Orchestra, 2000.

Symphony No. 5: Requiem, Bardo, Nirmanakaya, Nonesuch, 2000.

Adele Anthony, Violin Concerto/Prelude and Dance from Akhnaten/Company, Naxos, 2000.

Aleck Karis, Piano Music of Philip Glass, Roméo Records, 2000.

Symphony No. 3/Interludes from the Civil Wars/ Mechanical Ballet from the Voyage/The Light, Nonesuch, 2000.

Three Songs/Songs from Liquid Days/Vessels, Silva Classics, 2000.

Bruce Brubaker, Glass Cage, Arabesque Recordings, 2000.

Melodes for Saxophone, Chester, 2000.

Symphony No. 6 (Plutonian Ode), 2001.

Danussimo, 2001.

Voices for Organ, Didgeridoo, & Narrator, 2001.

Concerto for Cello and Orchestra, 2001.

Steffen Schleiermacher, Early Keyboard Music, MDG, 2001.

Music for Organ, Nimbus, 2001.

Philip on Film, Nonesuch, 2001.

Early Voice, Orange Mountain Music, 2002.

Concerto for Harpsichord and Chamber Orchestra, 2002.

Saxophone, Orange Mountain Music, 2002.

Tirol Concerto for Piano and Orchestra, Tyrol Tourist Board Special Edition, 2002.

Cello Octen Conjunto Ibérico, Glass Reflections, Ibérico Records, 2002.

Paul Barnes, Orphee Suite for Piano, Orange Mountain Music, 2003.

FILM SCORE COMPOSER, UNLESS OTHERWISE NOTED

Mark DiSuvero, Sculptor, Parrot Productions, 1977.

Koyaanisqatsi, MGM, 1982; album, Antilles, 1983, Nonesuch, 1998.

Breathless, Orion, 1983.

Four American Composers, Trans Atlantic Films, 1983.

Mishima: A Life in Four Chapters (also known as *Mishima*), Warner Bros., 1984; album, Nonesuch, 1985.

A Composer's Notes: Philip Glass and the Making of an Opera (Akhnaten), Michael Blackwell Productions, 1985.

Dead End Kids, Ikon, 1986.

Hamburger Hill, Artisan Entertainment, 1987.

Powaqqatsi, MGM, 1987; album, Nonesuch, 1988.

The Thin Blue Line (documentary), Anchor Bay, 1988; album, Nonesuch, 1989; *Music from the Thin Blue Line,* Orange Mountain Music, 2003.

(And song composer) *La Chiesa* (also known as *Cathedral of Demons, The Church, Demon Cathedral, Demons 3,* and *In the Land of the Demons*), Cecchi Gori, 1988.

Mindwalk, Paramount, 1990.

Anima Mundi (documentary short film; also known as *The Soul of the World*), Simitar, 1991; album, Nonesuch, 1993.

(Composer of songs) *Exposure,* 1991.

Merci, la vie, Orly Films/Cine Valse, 1991.

A Brief History of Time (documentary), Paramount, 1992.

Candyman, Columbia/TriStar, 1992; album titled *The Music of Candyman,* Orange Mountain Music, 2001.

Compassion in Exile: The Life of the 14th Dalai Lama (documentary), Wellspring, 1992.

Niki de Saint Phalle: Wer ist das Monster-du ode rich? (documentary; also known as *Figuren der Freude*), [Germany], 1994.

Jenipapo (also known as *The Inteview*), Boku Films/Ravina Films, 1994.

Candyman II: Farewell to the Flesh, MGM/UA, 1994.

The Secret Agent (also known as *Joseph Conrad's The Secret Agent*), Twentieth Century-Fox, 1996; album, Nonesuch, 1996.

Bent, Metro-Goldwyn-Mayer, 1996.

Kundun, Buena Vista, 1997; album, Nonesuch, 1997.

The Astronaut's Wife, New Line Cinema, 1998.

The Truman Show, Paramount, 1998; Milan Records, 1998.

Dracula, Universal, 1998; album, Nonesuch, 1999.

Si je t'aime. Prends garde a toi, Rezo Films, 1998.

The Source (documentary), Calliope Films, 1999.

The Eden Myth, Tuesday Night Movies, 1999.

The Hours, Paramount, 2002; album, Nonesuch, 2002.

(And screenwriter) *Naqoyqatsi* (documentary), Buena Vista, 2002; album, Sony, 2002.

The Fog of War, Columbia/TriStar, 2003; album, Orange Mountain Music, 2003.

Also composer of music for *Geometry of a Circle,* 1979, *Dialogue,* 1986, *Christo in Paris* (documentary), 1990, *Ballad of the Skeletons* (short film), 1996, *Absence Stronger Than Presence* (short documentary film), 1996, *Perfect Moment* (documentary), 1996, *The Man in the Bath,* 2001, *Diaspora,* 2001, *Notes,* 2001, *Passage,* 2001, and a new score for *Cenere,* Ambrosio Film.

MUSIC COMPOSED FOR TELEVISION

High Wire, Public Broadcasting Serve (PBS), 1986.

"Einstein on the Beach: The Changing Image of Opera," *Great Performances,* PBS, 1986.

"The Thin Blue Line," *American Playhouse,* PBS, 1988.

Timeless Voices: The Gyuto Monks, The Discovery Channel, 1989.

Peter Jennings Reporting: Guns, American Broadcasting Companies, Inc. (ABC), 1990.

"ConFusion in a Jar," *Nova,* PBS, 1990.

A Walk through Prospero's Library, 1991.

"The Cask of Amontillado," *Edgar Allan Poe: Terror of the Soul,* PBS, 1995.

Twyla Tharp: Oppositions, PBS, 1996.

Chuck Close: A Portrait in Progress, PBS, 1998.

Also composer of music for Alvin Ailey Dance Theatre, for choreographers Lar Lubovitch and Lucinda Childs, and for the Olympic Games, Los Angeles, CA, 1984, and Atlanta, GA, 1996.

SIDELIGHTS: Philip Glass is one of the most prolific and best-known avant-garde composers in the United States. His symphonies, operas, and film scores have made Glass known for his repetitive tonal techniques and his innovation within musical genres. With various libretticists, including Robert Wilson and David Henry Hwang, he has changed the face of opera with works such as *Einstein on the Beach, Satyagraha, Akhnaten,* and *The Voyage.* Glass's music has been an intricate part of acclaimed motion pictures, including *Koyaanisqatsi, Powaqqatsi, A Brief History of Time,* and *The Hours.* The composer has written about his works and his musical philosophy in *Music by Philip Glass.*

Glass, born in Baltimore, Maryland, has been surrounded by music his entire life. His parents owned a record store, from which he brought home records that did not sell—most of which were classical—and played them. Glass's interest in classical music predominated, but he exposed himself to many different types of music. He took flute lessons during his childhood, attended the famed Juilliard School of Music in New York City for his master's degree, and traveled to Paris in order to further his musical studies. While in Paris, Glass met renowned Indian sitar player Ravi Shankar who greatly influenced Glass's compositions. Glass continued to think about Eastern musical forms while traveling through Spain, North Africa, and Asia. He returned to New York and formed the Philip Glass Ensemble, which used wind instruments, keyboards, and other electronic devices to perform his compositions. Glass himself plays the electric organ with the group.

Though he has composed many pieces of music, *Einstein on the Beach* was Glass's first opera, created in collaboration with Robert Wilson. As the title implies, the work is meant to be a celebration of the life of famed atomic scientist Albert Einstein, but it is an extremely metaphorical celebration. There are images of trains, a scientist writing equations on a blackboard, a trial, and scenes of a white-haired man playing the violin, reportedly something Einstein enjoyed doing to relax. Of Glass's work as a composer on *Einstein on*

the Beach, Nation's Frank Rose remarked, "Unlike most Western composers, he uses rhythm as a base and adds harmony and melody later. His cyclically repeating rhythmic structures," the critic observed, "like Wilson's stage pictures, don't tell a story or lead anywhere in the customary sense, although they do have a powerful momentum." Rose concluded that "by purging their work of most of the conventional ingredients of music and drama, they create the possibility that something revelatory will happen, something transcendent and profound."

In *Satyagraha,* Glass examines the life of Hindu leader Mohandas Ghandi, focusing on his early experiences. The opera's words, sung in Sanskrit, are taken from the sacred Hindu text the *Bhagavad-Gita;* most audience members, therefore, must depend upon the visual tableaux presented for meaning. The scenes do, however, follow the subject of the opera more literally than do those of *Einstein on the Beach.*

Glass worked with Wilson on *the CIVIL warS: a tree is best measured when it is down. the CIVIL warS* is twelve hours long, and includes characters such as Mary Lincoln, the Earth Mother, Robert E. Lee, Hercules, and a Hopi named Snow Owl. Peter G. Davis of *New York,* who heard only the fifth act performed, reported that "one critic has already proclaimed the work [as a whole] a masterpiece, with the structural coherency of a Mozart string quartet and the tightly knit musical and verbal images of a Wagner opera." Davis, however, called *CIVIL warS* "a turkey, one that would not look especially appetizing even with fancy stage dressing."

Glass's *Akhnaten,* tells the story of the Egyptian pharaoh who temporarily converted his nation to monotheism. Glass also celebrates Akhnaten and his queen, the famed beauty Nefertiti, as the first romantic couple of history. Though much of the opera is sung in ancient languages, including Egyptian and Hebrew, a spoken commentary is provided in the language of the audience. The centerpiece of the opera, the text for which is Akhnaten's actual *Sun Hymn,* is always translated into the native language of the audience as well. In his *Music by Philip Glass,* the composer asserts that he chose Akhnaten as an admirable historical figure because the pharaoh "changed his (and our) world through the force of his ideas and not through the force of arms."

Though Paul John Frandsen, reviewing *Akhnaten* in *Musical Quarterly,* admitted that his training as an

Egyptologist prevented him from completely embracing the opera, he did praise "the 'sound' of the music," and "its repetitive nature." He also noted that these, along with "the fascination with ancient Egypt . . . do have their attractions." An *Opera News* critic, discussing an audio recording of *Akhnaten,* cited the "visionary power" of the *Akhnaten* as well as "the breadth and sweep of the enterprise." Years after it was first produced, *Akhnaten* still enraptures audiences. *American Record Guide*'s Peter Catalano wrote, "Choosing Akhnaten as a dramatic subject, adding the staged stylizations, exotic language, and powerful theatrical sensibility, Glass achieves a monumental artistic creation." John Rockwell wrote in the *New Republic,* "His music sets up a mood that hypnotically seduces one into contemplation."

In the early 1990s Glass was commissioned to write an opera in honor of the five hundredth anniversary of explorer Christopher Columbus's arrival in the New World. Though it did contain some content about Columbus, the resulting opera *The Voyage* (for which David Henry Hwang provided the libretto) was more concerned with the overall concept of exploration than with Columbus's specific achievement. Scenes of Viking explorers are included, as are scenes of future space travelers and alien contact. One of the characters in *The Voyage* is a wheelchair-bound scientist modeled on Stephen Hawking, whom Glass met while working on the score for the film version of Hawking's book, *A Brief History of Time.* Concerns about the ambiguity of modern attitudes toward Columbus—revisionist trends have painted him as everything from a heroic explorer to the man responsible for initiating centuries of exploitation of Native Americans—prompted Glass and Hwang to include what James R. Oestreich in the *New York Times Magazine* labeled a "poignant epilogue," in which "Columbus's failings are acknowledged, in line with the current widespread devaluation of his achievements, but ultimately resolved in contemplation of the final seductive journey of death." Michael Walsh, reviewing *The Voyage* in *Time,* was reserved in his praise of the work, but noted that the work "lowers, thunders and rages—it begins with the same six-note figure that opens Wagner's *Die Walküre*—vividly reflecting Hawking's visions of terror and wonder and Columbus's dark and stormy night of the soul." Walsh concluded, "If in the end the opera, like its hero, doesn't land where it was headed, sometimes it is indeed better to travel than to arrive."

Another opera Glass has helped to create is *The Making of the Representative for Planet 8,* which uses the avant-garde science-fiction novel of the same title by Doris Lessing as its libretto. William Albright, reviewing a performance in *Opera News,* praised its "hypnotic repetition of simple patterns, its harmonies and rhythms enriched by fragrant flowerings of melody." Glass also collaborated with Hwang and set designer Jerome Sirlin on *One Thousand Airplanes on the Roof,* the story of a man abducted by aliens after walking home a date. M., the protagonist, is the subject of scientific experiments by aliens during his captivity, and though the aliens do their best to make him forget his experience, he struggles to remember it and to inform the world of what has happened. Walsh, in another *Time* review, hailed the music for *One Thousand Airplanes on the Roof* as "one of [Glass's] most daring scores. From the arresting opening chords that symbolize the lurking spacemen . . . to the striking stretch of C-major that underpins poor M.'s longings for a girlfriend." Walsh noted that "this primal scream of angst surges and soars on an electric current of inspiration." Robert Baxter in *Opera News* judged Glass and his collaborators to have "merged sight, sound and word to create something unique and unforgettable."

In *The Sound of a Voice,* Glass joined with Hwang once again to bring two one-act operas to the stage, "The Sound of a Voice" and "Hotel of Dreams." The title piece is the story of an aging samurai who runs into a woman thought to be a witch. The second piece tells the story of a writer who develops a relationship with the madam of a brothel. Glass told Karen Campbell of *American Theatre* that *The Sound of a Voice* is "a kind of theatrical hybrid, straddling the line between what is traditionally considered opera and what is more commonly considered musical theatre." Richard Dyer of *Opera News* noted, "Glass writes traditionally and evocatively, with many bent notes and soulful sighings."

Glass's *Galileo Galilei,* which recounts the famous astronomer's life in reverse order, was met with mixed reviews upon its debut. However, *The White Raven,* which focuses on the explorations of Vasco da Gama, was better received. Writing in *New Criterion,* Patrick J. Smith commented, "Glass has, over the years, refined his music-making to a formula that communicates directly to the audience. . . . At times, he achieves a sort of austere beauty." A writer for the *Economist* noted, "The composer lulls listeners into thinking that little is changing, while subtly creating constant musical flux. . . . This confident subversion of what our ears expect is Mr. Glass's secret for remaining fresh."

Some of Glass's operas have used the minimalist tactic of showing the films of French director Jean Cocteau while singers perform a libretto consisting of the dialogue from these films. Glass has done both Cocteau's *Orphee* and his *La Belle et la bete* in this manner. *La Belle et la bete* is the classic tale of Beauty and the Beast. Glass received mixed response for his version of *La Belle et la bete;* though Davis, in another *New York* piece, conceded that "the idea" of Glass's treatment "is certainly original," he went on to note that "Glass has produced nothing but ninety minutes of prosy, mechanical patter that both destroys the movie's verbal poetry and undercuts its pictorial fantasy." However, in *Time,* Walsh observed that "everything comes together seamlessly," and declared that "the restless, relentless energy of the score—tempered, for the first time in Glass's career, by some fetching love music—pulls one into the film in a way that mere background music never could." A writer for the *Oxford Companion to Fairy Tales* wrote, "As an interpretation of the fairy-tale film, Glass's operatic score and media experiment stress the love story and the artist's inward journey towards creativity."

Glass's film scores have resulted in a more wide-scale recognition than his operas. In this genre, one of his most highly acclaimed efforts is his music for Godfrey Reggio's 1983 avant-garde documentary *Koyaanisqatsi.* Rising to cult status since its initial release, *Koyaanisqatsi* takes its title from a Hopi Native American word meaning "life out of balance." As Richard Corliss reported in *Time, Koyaanisqatsi* begins with a shot of a volcanic eruption and ends with the crash of a space vehicle to Earth. In between are many rapidly changing scenes depicting the effects of civilization upon mankind. According to Corliss, however, the "juxtaposition of nature (good) and civilization (bad) need not be taken too seriously." The critic went on to describe it as "ravishing." Tom O'Brien in *Commonweal* asserted that "few recent films have been more stirring." In 2003, Glass took the film and composition to Moscow, Russia. In an interview with a writer for *Europe Intelligence Wire,* Glass said *Koyaanisqatsi* "investigates the way the world is being transformed by the power of technology and it makes it a kind of critique in a way."

Glass also provided the score for Reggio's sequel to *Koyaanisqatsi, Powaqqatsi.* This film takes its title

from another Hopi word meaning "the sorcerer who steals from life." The format of *Powaqqatsi* is much like that of its predecessor, but this time Reggio focuses on the transformation of Third World cultures rather than that of the United States, as in *Koyaanisqatsi.* O'Brien described Glass's contribution to *Powaqqatsi,* writing, "Glass employs high soprano and tenor lines of a Peruvian children's choir; he blends his minimalist lyricism with indigenous instruments (especially some superb Andean flutes) and Amerindian, African, Asian, and Middle Eastern motifs." The reviewer explained, "Glass's major theme, superbly celebratory, is announced early, matching Reggio's shots of traditional ways of life, before a deluge of details documenting the squalor linked to progress." Randy Pitman, critiquing a video release of *Powaqqatsi* in *Library Journal,* called it "a feast for the eyes and ears" and went on to "highly" recommend it. The final installment in the "Qatsi" series is *Naqoyqatsi.* Jack Sullivan, in *American Record Guide,* commented on the soundtrack for the film, writing, "Glass's aesthetic works best with opera and film; by themselves, his pulsing, looping arpeggios can seem mechanical and monotonous especially when they run on for several movements, as they do here, but when yoked with images, they take on a mysterious life."

Glass provided the music for the documentary film *A Brief History of Time,* which featured the synthesized narration of Stephen Hawking, who wrote the book on which it is based and who has made great contributions to knowledge about the origins of the universe. Though the film version discusses Hawking's scientific contributions, it also tells viewers the story of his life, incorporating interviews with many of his family members and friends. According to Stanley Kauffmann, reviewing the motion picture in the *New Republic,* it "is more about the man than the work." Kauffmann reported that, unlike the high science to which he has devoted his life, "Hawking's personal story is within the grasp of all, and grasp is the right word: it grips." The critic also complimented Glass's work on the film in particular, judging that the score "has an apt spacy feeling." *A Brief History of Time* was directed by Earl Morris, with whom Glass also worked on the documentary about the death penalty appeals system, *The Thin Blue Line.*

In addition to documentaries, Glass's compositions provide the background to the other contemporary movies such as *Candyman, Candyman II: Farewell to* the *Flesh, Hamburger Hill,* about the Vietnam War, and *Kundun,* about the life of the Dalai Lama. His music for *The Truman Show* earned him a Golden Globe award, and his original score for the film *The Hours* was nominated for an Academy Award. Glass told David Mermelstein of *Daily Variety,* that the three subjects of *The Hours* "are so powerful that you might wonder what they have to do with each other." He explained, "It was my view that the music would provide coherence to something which otherwise might be moving out of the center. I wanted something that would bring you back to the center."

Glass told Harry Sumrall in *Smithsonian* that he has never held a "high art-low art set of standards." He explained, "I've spent my life in the avant-garde. But I think that every art from is honorable, and I never look down on anyone who enjoys what they're doing."

BIOGRAPHICAL AND CRITICAL SOURCES:

BOOKS

Baker's Dictionary of Musicians, centennial edition, Schirmer Books (New York, NY), 2001.

Baker's Dictionary of Opera, Schirmer Books (New York, NY), 2000.

Contemporary Composers, St. James Press (Chicago, IL), 1982.

Contemporary Musicians, Volume 1, Gale (Detroit, MI), 1989.

Contemporary Theatre, Film, and Television, Gale (Detroit, MI), Volume 6, 1989, Volume 26, 2000.

Dictionary of Twentieth-Century Culture, Volume 1: *American Culture after World War II,* Gale (Detroit, MI), 1994.

Encyclopedia of Contemporary American Culture, Routledge (New York, NY), 2001.

Glass, Philip, *Music by Philip Glass,* Harper (New York, NY), 1987.

International Directory of Opera, St. James Press (Detroit, MI), 1993.

Kostelanetz, Richard, editor, *Writings on Glass: Essays, Interviews, Criticism,* University of California Press (Berkeley, CA), 1997.

Maycock, Robert, *Glass: A Portrait,* Sanctuary (London, England), 2002.

Oxford Companion to Fairy Tales, Oxford University Press (New York, NY), 2000.

Penguin International Dictionary of Contemporary Biography, from 1900 to the Present, Penguin Reference, 2001.

Potter, Keith, *Four Musical Minimalists: La Monte Young, Terry Riley, Steve Reich, Philip Glass,* Cambridge University Press (New York, NY), 2000.

Richardson, John, *Refractions of Masculinity: Ambivalence and Androgyny in Philip Glass's Opera "Akhnaten" and Selected Recent Works,* University of Jyväskylä, 1995.

Richardson, John, *Singing Archaeology: Philip Glass's Akhnaten,* University Press of New England (Hanover, NH), 1999.

PERIODICALS

Advocate, December 9, 1997, pp. 77-78.

America, April 11, 1998, pp. 20-21.

American Record Guide, July-August, 1992, pp. 254-255; September-October, 1992, p. 108; January-February, 1993, pp. 35-36, 180; March-April, 1993, pp. 41-42; July-August, 1993, pp. 93-94; September-October, 1993, p. 54; March-April, 1994, pp. 100, 187; May-June, 1994, pp. 66-67; March-April, 1995, pp. 35-36; July-August, 1995, p. 114; November-December, 1995, pp. 122-123; September-October, 1996, pp. 124-125; March-April, 1997, pp. 139-140; July-August, 1997, p. 115; September-October, 1997, pp. 48-49; March-April, 1999, Rob Haskins, review of "Glass: *Circles, Koyaanisqatsi,*" p. 135; September, 1999, "Glass: *The Civil Wars, Act V,*" p. 155; January, 2000, Stephen D. Chakwin, Jr., "Glass: *Dracula,*" p. 98; January, 2000, Richard S. Ginell, "*Kronos Quartet,* Glass: *Dracula,*" p. 37; May, 2000, Peter Catalano, "Boston Lyric Opera: Glass *Akhnaten,*" p. 44; January, 2001, Charles McCardell, "Glass: *Dracula* Revisited," p. 52; September-October, 2002, John von Rhein, "*Galileo Galilei:* New Glass Opera Mostly Old Hat," p. 34; January-February, 2003, Rob Haskins, review of *Descent into the Maelstrom,* p. 133; March-April, 2003, Jack Sullivan, "Glass: *Naqoyqatsi,*" p. 106; March-April, 2003, Jack Sullivan, "Glass: *Itaipu* and *Salonen:* Jaderlund Songs," p. 106.

American Theatre, October, 2003, Karen Campbell, "In the Realm of the Voices: Composer Philip Glass Sets Two David Hwang Plays to Plangent Music," p. 103.

Americas, September-October, 1992, pp. 3-4.

Artforum International, summer, 1999, Susan Morgan, "Las Horas de Belen—A Book of Hours," p. 152.

Atlantic Monthly, July-August, 2001, David Schiff, "In Glass's House: More a Classicist Than an Avant-Gardist," p. 171.

Audio, May, 1988, pp. 97-98; May, 1997, p. 184.

Billboard, July 10, 1999, Bradley Bambarger, "Classical Keeping," p. 43; July 21, 2001, Steve Smith, "Philip on Film: Glass Continues to Score," p. 13; December 7, 2002, Steve Smith, "The Classical Score," p. 14.

Booklist, January 1, 1994, p. 838.

California, June, 1988, pp. 128-129.

Chicago, October, 1988, p. 24; June, 2001, Mary Abowd, "Breaking the Sound Barrier," p. 22.

Christian Science Monitor, October 22, 1999, "What Music They Make!," p. 15.

Commonweal, May 20, 1988, pp. 304-305.

Connoisseur, February, 1991, pp. 40-41; May, 1991, p. 17.

Consumers' Research Magazine, August, 1988, p. 43.

Daily Variety, December 9, 2002, Shalini Dore, "*The Hours* Hosts Glass," p. 33; January 6, 2003, David Mermelstein, "Philip Glass, *The Hours:* Bare Minimum for Maximum Effect," p. A10.

Dance Magazine, November, 1992, pp. 93-95; May, 1995, pp. 80-81.

Economist (U.K.), August 18, 2001, review of *White Raven,* p. 74.

Economist (U.S.), August 18, 2001, "Not All Ravens Are White," p. NA.

Entertainment Weekly, December 4, 1992, p. 66; October 11, 1996, p. 92; December 22, 1997, pp. 81-82; May 1, 1998, p. 66.

Europe Intelligence Wire, November 1, 2002, "Space Odyssey: Celebrated Chicago-based Writer Mary Zimmerman Has Teamed Up with Composer Philip Glass to Tell the Story of Galielo—Backwards," p. NA; November 4, 2002, "Opera: *Galileo Galilei*"; November 28, 2003, "Philip Glass Takes Move to Moscow."

Financial Times, July 16, 2001, Martin Bernheimer, "Through a Glass Darkly Opera New York," p. 14.

High Fidelity, July, 1988, pp. 61-62; January, 1989, p. 69.

Horizon, June, 1988, pp. 36-37.

Independent, May 22, 2001, Phil Johnson, "A Reputation for Repetition," p. S12.

Insight on the News, December 17, 2001, Ann Geracimos, "Cosmic Classic: A New Symphony by Philip Glass Celebrates the World's Major Religions," p. 33.

Library Journal, March 1, 1988, p. 68; September 15, 1990, p. 113; August, 1994, p. 152; May 1, 1997, p. 107.

Los Angeles Times, May 3, 2001, Josef Woodard, "Music Review: Polite Cross-Cultural Exchange in Glass' Pleasant *Screens,*" p. F54; July 16, 2001, Mark Swed, "Opera Review: New Worlds Ripe for Exploration; Lincoln Center Festival Gives U.S. Premieres of *White Raven* and *Luci Mie Traditrici,*" "Fresh Examples of the Genre," p. F2; October 25, 2001, Mark Swed, "Music Review: They Shoot, Glass Scores; Composer Deftly Melds Live Music with Short Works by Filmmakers," p. F55; June 25, 2002, Mark Swed, "Opera Review: Seeing the Big Spin; In His New Opera, *Galileo Galilei,* Philip Glass Unravels the Tale of the Great Astronomer in Backward Order," p. F1; October 18, 2002, Jon Burlingame, "Movie Review: Striking *Naqoyqatsi* Rounds out Trilogy," p. E19.

Maclean's, August 31, 1992, p. 42.

Magazine of Fantasy and Science Fiction, April, 2000, Barry N. Malzberg, review of *The Voyage,* p. 162.

Musical Quarterly, summer, 1993, pp. 241-267.

Music Week, November 10, 2001, review of *Philip on Film,* p. 10; July 27, 2002, Adam Woods, review of *Glass Reflections,* p. 28.

Nation, March 16, 1985, pp. 313-315; November 21, 1988, pp. 542-544.

National Review, January 26, 1998, pp. 52-53.

New Criterion, November, 2002, Patrick J. Smith, "Concert Notes," p. 58.

New Internationalist, January-February, 2002, Louise Gray, "Mantra Mix," p. 46.

New Republic, September 14, 1987, pp. 32-33; April 15, 1991, pp. 27-29; September 28, 1992, pp. 28, 30; April 10, 2000, John Rockwell, "Broken Glass: The Ups and Downs of Repetition," p. 29.

New Statesman & Society, September 6, 1991, p. 32; February 14, 1997, p. 40.

Newsweek, October 26, 1992, p. 62.

New York, June 4, 1984, p. 81; December 14, 1987, p. 78; May 16, 1988, pp. 110-111; July 31, 1989, p. 65; February 19, 1990, p. 72; May 27, 1991, p. 69; July 29, 1991, p. 59; September 14, 1992, pp. 76-77; October 26, 1992, pp. 91-92; June 7, 1993, p. 57; February 28, 1994, p. 117; November 28, 1994, pp. 86-87; January 2, 1995, p. 71; November 18, 1996, pp. 116-117; December 9, 1996, pp. 87-88; May 19, 1997, pp. 69-70; November

10, 1997, pp. 67-68; October 23, 2000, Peter G. Davis, review of *Symphony No. 5,* p. 98; June 18, 2001, Logan Hill, "His Glass Is Half Full," p. 64; July 30, 2001, Peter G. Davis, review of *White Raven,* p. 51; October 21, 2002, Peter G. Davis, "Bad Science," p. 54.

New Yorker, September 3, 1984, p. 81; September 5, 1988, pp. 76-78; March 11, 1991, pp. 76-77; October 26, 1992, pp. 125-129.

New York Times, March 14, 1998, p. B17; April 17, 1998, p. B30; January 10, 1999, K. Robert Schwarz, "Symphonic Film Score, Antisymphonic Symphony," p. AR33; October 28, 1999, Allan Kozinn, "Dracula Hears Philip Glass and Gets Thirsty," p. B5; December 25, 1999, "BAM Season Celebrates Philip Glass and Weill," p. C10; March 3, 2000, Anthony Tommasini, "Soaring in a Concert on Flight," p. B38; March 23, 2000, Allan Kozinn, "Philip Glass Explores Landscape on Film," p. B1; July 5, 2000, "Glass's Latest Symphony to Open New Wave Festival," p. B6; October 4, 2000, Allan Kozinn, "Glass Puts Everything into New Symphony," p. B1; November 23, 2000, Paul Griffths, "What the Timpanists Had to Say for Themselves," p. B3; June 10, 2001, Joanne Akalaitis, "Adapting the Horrors of Kafka Story to Suit Glass's Music," p. AR5; July 28, 2001, Allan Kozinn, "Scores by Philip Glass for Films from Five Countries," p. A15; December 16, 2001, Jon Pareles, review of *Philip on Film: Filmworks by Philip Glass,* p. AR35; October 3, 2002, Allan Kozinn, "A Heretical Astronomer Rethinking His Revolution," p. B1; October 18, 2002, Stephen Holden, "Technology's March, Surreal and Grim," p. B23; December 2, 2002, Allan Kozinn, "For Philip Glass, It's All about Endurance, Not Virtuosity," p. B5.

New York Times Magazine, October 11, 1992, pp. 22, 26, 28.

Opera, October, 2001, Martin Bernheimer, "Glass: *White Raven,*" p. 1250; December, 2001, Barry Emslie, "Glass: *Einstein on the Beach,*" p. 1460; January, 2002, Horst Koegler, "Glass: *The Fall of the House of Usher,*" p. 78; April, 2002, Christopher Norton-Welsh, review of *Satyagraha,* p. 429.

Opera News, January 16, 1988, p. 39; March 26, 1988, p. 38; June, 1988, pp. 8-11; December 24, 1988, pp. 36-37; March 4, 1989, p. 41; March 18, 1989, p. 35; April 1, 1989, p. 58; December 8, 1990, pp. 62-63; October, 1992, pp. 10-12, 38- 41; January 2, 1993, p. 37; May, 1993, pp. 50-51; November, 1993, p. 45; February 18, 1995, p. 4; March 30,

1996, pp. 8-9, 28-31; August, 1996, p. 46; May, 1999, "From around the World: New York City," p. 82; January, 2003, William R. Brawn, review of *Galileo Galilei,* p. 81; September, 2003, "From around the World: Cambridge, MA," p. 93.

Opera Quarterly, autumn, 2000, David McKee, review of *The Civil Wars: A Tree Best Measured When It Is Down,* p. 706.

People, September 7, 1992, p. 19.

Sarasota Herald Tribune, January 29, 1999, Richard Storm, "Glass *Monsters* Is Clear, but Simple," p. 25; December 24, 2000, "Glass Shines in No. 5," p. G3.

School Library Journal, October, 1987, p. 65.

Sensible Sound, February, 2000, Karl W. Nehring, review of *Robert McDuffie, Violin Concerto,* p. 49.

Smithsonian, November, 2003, Harry Sumrall, "Master Glass: From Opera Halls to Neighborhood Movie Theaters, Philip Glass Attracts an Enormous Audience—Many of Whom Never Listened to Classical Music," p. 100.

Spectator, November 9, 2002, Michael Tanner, "Time to Reflect," p. 92.

Stereo Review, March, 1988, p. 98; March, 1989, pp. 120-121; May, 1989, pp. 120-121; September, 1992, p. 93; December, 1993, p. 129; September, 1995, pp. 106-107; April, 1997, p. 96.

Stereo Review's Sound and Vision, October, 1999, "Dracula Revived," p. 146.

Texas Monthy, September, 1988, pp. 133-134.

Theatre Journal, October, 2001, Christine C. Mather, review of *In the Penal Colony,* p. 491.

Time, October 17, 1983, p. 90; August 1, 1988, p. 58; July 2, 1990, p. 54; October 26, 1992, p. 80; April 19, 1993, p. 66; December 19, 1994, p. 72; December 9, 1996, p. 85; December 22, 1997, pp. 81-82; October 23, 2000, Terry Teachout, review of *Symphony No. 5,* p. 90.

Variety, October 19, 1992, p. 166; June 14, 1993, p. 60; August 9, 1993, p. 34; December 15, 1997, pp. 57-58; March 1, 1999, David Rooney, review of *The Eden Myth,* p. 86; June 25, 2001, Robert Hofler, review of *In the Penal Colony,* p. 30; July 1, 2002, Chris Jones, review of *Galileo Galilei,* p. 36.

Wall Street Journal, May 12, 1998, p. A20; July 24, 2002, Joel Henning, "Opera: *Galileo Galilei* from Zimmerman and Glass," p. D13.

Whole Earth, summer, 1997, p. 73.

Worldsources Online, November 21, 2003, "Glass in the Window to Europe."

ONLINE

Glass Pages, http://www.glasspages.com/ (March 16, 2003), "Philip Glass on the Web."

Philip Glass Web site, http://www.philipglass.com/ (March 3, 2004), film works, discography, news, and biography.

Schirmer Web site, http://www.schirmer.com/ (April 9, 2001), "Philip Glass Biography."*

*   *   *

GORDIMER, Nadine 1923-

PERSONAL: Born November 20, 1923, in Springs, Transvaal, South Africa; daughter of Isidore (a jeweler) and Nan (Myers) Gordimer; married Gerald Gavronsky, March 6, 1949 (divorced, 1952); married Reinhold H. Cassirer (owner and director of art gallery), January 29, 1954; children: (first marriage) Oriane Taramasco; (second marriage) Hugo, one stepdaughter. *Education:* Attended private schools and the University of the Witwatersrand.

ADDRESSES: Agent—Russell and Volkening, Inc., 50 West 29th St., New York, NY 10001.

CAREER: Writer. Ford Foundation visiting professor, under auspices of Institute of Contemporary Arts, Washington, DC, 1961; lecturer, Hopwood Awards, University of Michigan, Ann Arbor, 1970; writer in residence, American Academy in Rome, 1984; has also lectured and taught writing at Harvard, Princeton, Northwestern, Columbia, and Tulane universities; has been goodwill ambassador of the United Nations Development Programme.

MEMBER: International PEN (vice president), Congress of South African Writers, Royal Society of Literature, American Academy of Arts and Sciences (honorary member), American Academy of Literature and Arts (honorary member).

AWARDS, HONORS: W. H. Smith and Son Commonwealth Literary Award, 1961, for short story collection *Friday's Footprint and Other Stories;* Thomas Pringle Award, English Academy of South Africa, 1969; James

Nadine Gordimer

Tait Black Memorial Prize, 1973, for *A Guest of Honour;* Booker Prize for Fiction, National Book League, 1974, for *The Conservationist;* Grand Aigle d'Or, 1975; CNA awards, 1974, 1979, 1981, and 1991; Neil Gunn fellowship, Scottish Arts Council, 1981; Commonwealth Award for Distinguished Service in Literature, 1981; Modern Language Association of America award, 1982; Nelly Sachs Prize, 1985; Premio Malaparte, 1986; Bennett Award, *Hudson Review,* 1986; Benson Medal, 1990; Commandeur de l'Ordre des Arts et des Lettres (France), 1991; Nobel Prize for literature, Nobel Foundation, 1991; rejected candidacy for Orange Award in 1998 because the award was restricted to women writers; Booker Prize long-list nomination for *The Pickup,* 2001; Commonwealth Writers Prize, Africa Region, best book category for *The Pickup.* Awarded honorary degrees from University of Leuven, 1980, Smith College, City College of the City University of New York, and Mount Holyoke College, all 1985, Harvard University, Columbia University, Yale University, and York University, England, 1987, New School for Social Research, 1988, University of the Witwatersrand, South Africa, University of Cape Town, South Africa, University of Cape Town, South Africa, Cambridge University, 1991, Oxford University, 1994, University of Durban-Westville, and Ben Gurion University, 1996.

WRITINGS:

NOVELS

The Lying Days, Simon & Schuster (New York, NY), 1953, published with new introduction by Paul Bailey, Virago (New York, NY), 1983.
A World of Strangers, Simon & Schuster (New York, NY), 1958.
Occasion for Loving, Viking (New York, NY), 1963, published with new introduction by Paul Bailey, Virago (New York, NY), 1983.
The Late Bourgeois World, Viking (New York, NY), 1966.
A Guest of Honour, Viking (New York, NY), 1970.
The Conservationist, J. Cape (London, England), 1974, Viking (New York, NY), 1975.
Burger's Daughter, Viking (New York, NY), 1979.
July's People, Viking (New York, NY), 1981.
A Sport of Nature (Book-of-the-Month Club dual selection), Knopf (New York, NY), 1987.
My Son's Story, Farrar, Straus & Giroux (New York, NY), 1990.
None to Accompany Me, Farrar, Straus & Giroux (New York, NY), 1994.
Harald, Claudia, and Their Son Duncan, Bloomsbury (New York, NY), 1996.
The House Gun, Farrar, Straus (New York, NY), 1998.
The Pickup, Bloomsbury (New York, NY), 2001.

SHORT STORIES

Face to Face (also see below), Silver Leaf Books (Johannesburg, South Africa), 1949.
The Soft Voice of the Serpent and Other Stories (contains many stories previously published in *Face to Face*), Simon & Schuster (New York, NY), 1952.
Six Feet of the Country (also see below), Simon & Schuster (New York, NY), 1956.
Friday's Footprint and Other Stories, Viking (New York, NY), 1960.
Not for Publication and Other Stories, Viking (New York, NY), 1965.
Livingstone's Companions, Viking (New York, NY), 1971.

Selected Stories (contains stories from previously published collections), Viking (New York, NY), 1975, also published as *No Place Like: Selected Stories,* Penguin (London, England), 1978.
Some Monday for Sure, Heinemann Educational (London, England), 1976.
A Soldier's Embrace, Viking (New York, NY), 1980.
Town and Country Lovers, Sylvester & Orphanos (Los Angeles, CA), 1980.
Six Feet of the Country (contains stories from previously published collections selected for television series of same title), Penguin (New York, NY), 1982.
Something Out There, Viking (New York, NY), 1984.
Reflections of South Africa: Short Stories, Systime, 1986.
Crimes of Conscience: Selected Short Stories, Heinemann, 1991.
Jump and Other Stories, Farrar, Straus (New York, NY), 1991.
Why Haven't You Written?: Selected Stories, 1950-1972, Viking (New York, NY), 1993.
Loot: And Other Stories, Farrar, Straus (New York, NY), 2003.

OTHER

(Compiler and editor, with Lionel Abrahams) *South African Writing Today,* Penguin (New York, NY), 1967.
African Literature: The Lectures Given on This Theme at the University of Cape Town's Public Summer School, February, 1972, Board of Extra Mural Studies, University of Cape Town (Cape Town, South Africa), 1972.
The Black Interpreters: Notes on African Writing, Spro-Cas/Ravan (Johannesburg, South Africa), 1973.
On the Mines, photographs by David Goldblatt, C. Struik (Cape Town, South Africa), 1973.
(Author of appreciation) *Kurt Jobst: Goldsmith and Silversmith; Art Metal Worker,* G. Bakker (Johannesburg, South Africa), 1979.
(With others) *What Happened to "Burger's Daughter"; or, How South African Censorship Works,* Taurus (Johannesburg, South Africa), 1980.
Lifetimes under Apartheid, photographs by David Goldblatt, Knopf (New York, NY), 1986.
The Essential Gesture: Writing, Politics and Places, edited and introduced by Stephen Clingman, Knopf (New York, NY), 1988.

(With Hugo Cassirer) *Berlin and Johannesburg: The Wall and The Colour Bar*, television documentary film.

Three in a Bed: Fiction, Morals, and Politics, Bennington College (Bennington, VT), 1991.

(With Ruth Weiss) *Zimbabwe and the New Elite,* Tauris (Johannesburg, South Africa), 1993.

Writing and Being: The Charles Eliot Norton Lectures, Harvard University Press (Cambridge, MA), 1995.

Living in Hope and History: Notes from Our Century, Farrar, Straus (New York, NY), 1999.

Also author of television plays and documentaries, including *A Terrible Chemistry,* 1981, *Choosing for Justice: Allan Boesak,* with Hugo Cassirer, 1985, *Country Lovers, A Chip of Glass Ruby, Praise,* and *Oral History,* all part of *The Gordimer Stories* series adapted from stories of the same title, 1985. Contributor to periodicals, including *Atlantic, Encounter, Granta, Harper's, Holiday, Kenyon Review, Mother Jones, New Yorker, Paris Review,* and *Playboy. New York Times,* syndicated columnist, January, 2003—. Gordimer's novels, short stories, and essays have been translated into twenty-five languages and are available in audio cassette form.

Indiana University, Lilly Library, houses a collection of Gordimer's papers.

ADAPTATIONS: Screenplays for four of the seven television dramas based on her own short stories, collectively titled *The Gordimer Stories,* 1981-82; *City Lovers,* based on Gordimer's short story of the same title, was filmed by TeleCulture Inc./TelePool in South Africa in 1982.

SIDELIGHTS: "Nadine Gordimer has become, in the whole solid body of her work, the literary voice and conscience of her society," declared Maxwell Geismar in the *Saturday Review.* In numerous novels, short stories, and essays, she has written of her South African homeland and its apartheid government—under which its blacks, coloreds, and whites suffered for nearly half a century. "This writer . . . has made palpable the pernicious, pervasive character of that country's race laws, which not only deny basic rights to most people but poison many relationships," maintained Miriam Berkley in *Publishers Weekly.* Others, like Judith Chettle of the *World and I,* were more critical, noting that Gordimer "has adroitly over the years

written books that drew world attention to the political situation in South Africa. Never jailed or exiled (though some books were briefly banned in the 1970s), Gordimer came to be regarded as the preeminent recorder of life under apartheid. Books like *Burger's Daughter* and *The Conservationist* gained her an international audience," but adding the caveat: "In these books, Gordimer astutely described the liberal politics of white and mostly English-speaking South Africa. She was much less incisive in dealing with those Afrikaners supporting the regime and was least successful in describing the blacks."

However, Gordimer's insight, integrity, and compassion inspire critical admiration among many. "She has mapped out the social, political and emotional geography of that troubled land with extraordinary passion and precision," commented Michiko Kakutani of the *New York Times,* observing in a later essay that "taken chronologically, her work not only reflects her own evolving political consciousness and maturation as an artist—an early lyricism has given way to an increased preoccupation with ideas and social issues—but it also charts changes in South Africa's social climate." One of only nine women so recognized, she was honored with the Nobel Prize in literature for her novels in 1991—a sign of the esteem in which the literary world holds her work.

When she began, Gordimer was only one of a number of novelists working in South Africa after World War II. "Some of the writers, like [Alan] Paton, turned to nonfiction or political work; even more, most notably [Peter] Abrahams and Dan Jacobson, expatriated," explained John Cooke in *The Novels of Nadine Gordimer: Private Lives/Public Landscapes.* "By the early sixties Gordimer was almost the only member of the postwar group to continue producing fiction from within the country. That she should be the survivor was not altogether surprising, for she was in essential ways more a product of South Africa than her contemporaries. She attended university at home, not in England as colonial writers so regularly have; she did not travel abroad until she was thirty."

"Gordimer seemed particularly unsuited to prosper as a writer in her arid land," Cooke continued, "because of the disjunction between her temperament and the situation she confronted. More than any of her contemporaries, Gordimer was initially drawn to private themes." Her novels and short stories are, at bottom, about complicated individuals caught in awkward or impossibly complex situations. "Her writing [is] so subtle that it forces readers to find their way back from her works into her mind," remarked Firdaus Kanga in the *Times Literary Supplement;* "her characters are powerful precisely because you cannot sum them up in a line or even a page."

Much of Gordimer's fiction focuses upon white middle-class characters. It frequently depicts what Geismar described as "a terrified white consciousness in the midst of a mysterious and ominous sea of black humanity." But the "enduring subject" of her writing has been "the consequences of apartheid on the daily lives of men and women, the distortions it produces in relationships among both blacks and whites," noted Kakutani. Her first novel, *The Lying Days,* is drawn from her personal experience and tells about a young woman who comes into contact with the effects of apartheid when she has an affair with a social worker. *A World of Strangers* is about the efforts of a British writer to bring together his white intellectual friends and his black African intellectual friends. In *Burger's Daughter,* considered by some to be her best novel, Gordimer examines white ambivalence about apartheid in the person of Rosa, who can no longer sustain the antiapartheid cause of her imprisoned Afrikaner father after his death. This work, like several others before it, was banned in South Africa, but the ban was quickly removed due to the critical attention the novel had attracted in the West. The story of the banning and unbanning of *Burger's Daughter* is related in *What Happened to "Burger's Daughter"; or, How South African Censorship Works,* published in 1980.

Both *The Lying Days* and *A World of Strangers* end with a note of hope for a better future for South Africans. Gordimer's later novels, however, take a more pessimistic tone. *A Guest of Honour,* which won the James Tait Black Memorial Prize in 1973, tells of the return of Colonel James Bray to his African homeland. Bray had been exiled by the previous government for his espousal of black revolutionary ideology. Upon his return, however, Bray discovers that the new revolutionary government is just as corrupt and self-interested as the previous government was. When he speaks out publicly against the new government, it targets him for assassination. *The Conservationist,* awarded the Booker Prize (England's highest literary honor) the following year, tells about the uneasy relationship between a white landowner

and black squatters who have settled on his estate, bringing up the question of "whose land is it anyway?" "Beginning with *A Guest of Honour,*" Cooke concluded, "Gordimer's novels are informed by a tension between . . . two impulses: she at once observes her world from without and envisions it from within. Through this double process, the fruit of her long apprenticeship, Gordimer creates masterful forms and shapes despite the 'low cultural rainfall' of her world."

These forms and shapes also appear in Gordimer's short fiction. *Jump and Other Stories*—published shortly before the author received the Nobel Prize—contains stories that approach her favorite themes in a variety of ways. She tells about a white man out for a jog, who is caught up in a black gang-killing and is saved by a black woman who shelters him. "A single truth is witnessed," wrote John Edgar Wideman in the *New York Times Book Review,* "a truth somehow missing in most fiction by white Americans that purports to examine our national life. No matter how removed one feels oneself from the fray, race and race relations lie at the heart of the intimate, perplexing questions we need to ask of ourselves: Where have I been? Where am I going? Who am I?" "Ms. Gordimer can be a merciless judge and jury," Wideman concluded. "Her portraits obtain a Vermeer-like precision, accurate and remorseless, with no room for hope, for self-delusion, no room even for the small vanities of ego and self-regard that allow us to proceed sometimes as if at least our intentions are honorable."

The Swedish Academy had considered Gordimer as a Nobel Prize nominee for years before she finally received the award in 1991. Several commentators, while congratulating her on her accomplishment, noted that the struggle against apartheid remained unfinished. "On the day of the announcement that Nadine Gordimer would receive the 1991 Nobel Prize for literature, a tribute to the complex and intimate stories she has written about racism's toll on people's lives in her native South Africa," wrote Esther B. Fein in the *New York Times,* "Nelson Mandela still did not have the right to vote." Mandela had been released from his political prison, but the basic tenets of apartheid prevented him from exercising the rights of citizenship. When South African president F. W. De Klerk announced that the policy of separation would end, reviewers wondered where the Nobel laureate would turn her attention. "With apartheid finally ended," Diana Jean Schemo declared in the *New York Times,* "the novelist waxes exultant over a sense of renewal in her homeland; the urgency is gone, but the turn of mind remains."

"For the whole of her literary career, Gordimer has grappled with the intricacies and distortions of life under a certain political system, a specific regime of oppression," noted Diane Simon in the *Nation.* With the ending of apartheid and the enfranchisement of South African blacks, critics scanned Gordimer's fiction for evidence of how this supremely political writer's focus would change. Her novel, *None to Accompany Me,* looks at the fortunes of two families— one black, one white—as they move into the new, postapartheid, era. "The repressions, the curle laws and persecutions, the campaigns of resistance, the exiles, the detentions, the bannings and brutalities—all these horrors of the past are finished," observed Sonya Rudikoff in the book *African Writers,* continuing: "What remains is the damage done to society and to personal relations." "*None to Accompany Me* is a sustaining achievement, proving Gordimer once again a lucid witness to her country's transformation and a formidable interpreter of the inner self," Anne Whitehouse commented in *Tribune Books.* While some viewed this work as a step away from the public themes of her earlier novels and short stories, Simon observed that all of Gordimer's main characters are actively involved in the political life of the new South Africa.

By contrast, Gordimer's second postapartheid novel, *The House Gun,* while it also explores the relationships between blacks and whites in the newly transformed South Africa, is arguably more concerned with the politicization of her characters' personal lives. The Lindegards are an affluent white couple who learn that their only son, Duncan, has committed a murder using a gun intended to protect the house from thieves. They hire a black lawyer to represent him, and begin the painful process of emerging out of the sheltered lives they have created. Through these events, Gordimer explores the question, "Does a violent society provoke violence in nonviolent individuals?" "The story deftly brings home a tricky truth," remarked Walter Kirn in *Time:* "Peace can be as perilous as war, and even more confusing to negotiate," especially when it is a peace that follows bitter internal strife. The novel's other underlying question, which asks if the level of violence in South Africa is higher than in Europe because of its large black population or because of the way blacks

have long been treated by racist whites, is the "question that haunts Gordimer's novel," according to Jack Miles in the *New York Times Book Review.* Miles described *House Gun* as an "elegantly conceived, flawlessly executed novel." While Michiko Kakutani in the *New York Times* dubbed the novel "little more than a courtroom thriller, dressed up with some clumsy allusions to apartheid's legacy of violence and the uses and misuses of freedom," *Library Journal* reviewer Edward B. St. John contended that *House Gun* is "much more ambitious" than the courtroom dramas of Scott Turow or John Grisham, adding that "Gordimer's trademark prose style . . . seems especially well suited to capturing the moral ambiguities of South African life." "Gordimer's great fiction has always personalized the political," observed Hazel Rochman in *Booklist,* but in this novel, the author "moves in the opposite direction, taking the personal intimacy of family, friend, and lover into the glare of the public sphere."

Gordimer's turn of mind reaches out in two directions: politically, she follows the fortunes of other first-class "third-world" writers such as Egyptian Naguib Mahfouz, Nigerian Chinua Achebe, and Israeli Amos Oz. "Her attention is turned on writers whose work seems most engaged in the questions that have absorbed her for much of her life," Schemo wrote, "how justice, wealth, power and freedom are parceled out in a society, and the repercussions for its people." In the essays collected in *Living in Hope and History: Notes from Our Century,* the author addresses politics and morals, writers and culture, and first of all, life as a white liberal in South Africa. Here especially, Gordimer "speaks with the authority of the insider," according to Hazel Rochman in *Booklist,* "bearing witness to what it has been like, as a white citizen and writer, to live in Johannesburg" during the years of apartheid and through the upheavals that accompanied the transition to a postapartheid regime. Critics noted that Gordimer herself has frequently called her fiction more truthful than her nonfiction, and agreed that, as a reviewer for *Publishers Weekly* claimed, the pieces found in *Living in Hope and History* "shouldn't be expected to attain the nuance and depth of Gordimer's best fiction, but some of them are devastating."

Another novel, *The Pickup,* and a volume of short stories, *Loot: and Other Stories,* followed, pursuing further the complexity of individual struggles with racial and cultural differences in racist societies. A

Booklist reviewer called *The Pickup* "a compelling, unsentimental exploration of the paradox of privilege." Robert Ross in the *World and I* praised the novel, which, he noted, was published on the eve of the fall of the Twin Towers in New York: "underneath what might appear a less gloomy treatment of human experience, there lies a muted but strong concern with the dispossessed: those trapped in economic strife, the victims of racism, those affected by official corruption, and those on the move, facing the obstacles of immigration." The setting is that a young, disaffected woman from a wealthy white family meets an illegal Arab immigrant when her car breaks down. She becomes enthralled with the (to her) simplicity and connectedness of the home he is trying to escape, while he longs for the (to him) glittering cosmopolitan ease of the surroundings she is running from. Their love affair could be seen as a lighter side of Gordimer—a cross-cultural romance or a South African *Romeo and Juliet,* as several critics have observed—or, as Ross suggested, as an exploration of the contradictions that appear when one who has too much material ease and too little meaning in her life intertwines with another yearning towards the life she abhors. Gordon Houser, in the *Christian Century,* pointed out that in this novel Gordimer again shows that she is looking further into the world for her themes following the end of apartheid. He wrote, Gordimer "moves outward to the complexities of the global community, where people seek refuge from poverty and hopelessness by going to more prosperous countries. She juxtaposes Abdul's desperate desire to escape economic chaos with Julie's desire for stability and a loving family." An *Entertainment Weekly* reviewer commented, "Gordimer, deploying the finest kind of irony and attuned to the tiniest gestures, spins an eloquent tale about the ways in which romance ratifies self-image."

Loot, includes both "fragments of crystallized insight" and three longer pieces, one almost a novella, according to Chettle. Gordimer, remarked *Spectator*'s Sebastian Smee, "still displays a natural short-story writer's feeling for the intimate moments and quiet epiphanies that can alter people's lives." He also, however, found her writing style to be "lazily allusive and unkempt" and reading the stories "a pleasureless slog" because of her convoluted prose, but he recommended parts of "Karma," "Mission Statement," and "Generation Gap," a tale about the break-up of a marriage from the point of view of the grown-up children. Carmen Callil in the *New Statesman,* however, argued that "you have to sit up straight to read her, open your mind, extend your understanding, watch every word. It's worth it." She continued, "In 'Mission Statement', a middle-aged Englishwoman, Roberta Blayne, who works for an international aid agency of the Clare Short kind, falls into an affair with the deputy director of land affairs, Gladwell Shadrack Chabruma, in some unnamed African state, the sort of country that has old hospitals 'still known by the name of a deceased English Queen.' Gordimer can capture bodies, black and white, in a word, and sexual attraction in a sentence, as when Roberta sees her lover's torso and its 'gleaming beauty, sweat-painted, of perfectly formed muscle, the double path below pectorals, left and right, of smooth ribbing beneath lithe skin. Black. Simply Black.' The ironic ending of their love affair is perfectly conceived." Callil noted: "In Gordimer's Africa, too much has happened for easy endings. Her Europeans, her whites, are as soulless as their predecessors. What followed apartheid, after all, was AIDS: today's relics of 'imperial compassion' tend what they have produced—the AIDS children, the 'rags of flesh and bone,' 'the new-born-to-die'." "The Gordimer of these stories inhabits a stern world."

Chettle was one critic who saw Gordimer struggling to find a new voice since the fall of apartheid. She stated: "While Gordimer's [work] will continue to be read as distilled portraits of a particular society that behaved in a particular way at a particular time, her characters have often been more articulate vehicles for ideas than vivid creations who strut their stuff off the pages and into our hearts." This presents, in Chettle's view, a problem: "Gordimer . . . has valiantly, if with mixed success, been trying to make the necessary adjustments. Her latest book, *Loot,* a collection of ten short stories, exemplifies these adjustments as it describes moments of transition when lives are changed by insight or action. The stories typically reflect both Gordimer's weaknesses and strengths. She has a reporter's eye for the defining detail, but the characters themselves are often disembodied shades, held hostage to the workings out of the authorial intellect rather than following the wayward devices of their own hearts." She especially found the long story, "Karma" a "long mediation (more an intellectual than spiritual examination)." However, Chettle engagingly described stories whose characters "all share moments of abrupt change, signaled often by the acquisition of what is suddenly, or long, desired." Callil, though, found "Karma" to be "as good as anything she has written. Complex and inventive, it depicts worlds within worlds, yet each life recounted is vividly rooted in family and neighbourhood. The history and stories of her country and ours weave in and out of each episode as a wandering soul is born, again and again, sometimes female, sometimes male (it is always better to be male), reaching eventually a view that seems to be Gordimer's own. For our misdeeds, in whatever human form we take, 'we are condemned to live forever.' And so the villainy continues."

Gordimer herself once told interviewer Beth Austin in the *Chicago Tribune:* "I began to write, I think, out of the real source of all art, and that is out of a sense of wonderment about life, and a sense of trying to make sense out of the mystery of life. That hasn't changed in all the years that I've been writing. That is the starting point of everything that I write."

BIOGRAPHICAL AND CRITICAL SOURCES:

BOOKS

Bardolph, Jacqueline, editor, *Telling Stories: Postcolonial Short Fiction in English,* Rodopi (Amsterdam, Netherlands), 2001.

Bazin, Nancy Topping, and Marilyn Dallman Seymour, editors, *Conversations with Nadine Gordimer,* University Press of Mississippi (Jackson, MS), 1990.

Brodsky, Joseph, *New Censors: Nadine Gordimer and Others on Publishing Now,* Cassell Academic, 1996.

Brownley, Martine Watson, *Deferrals of Domain: Contemporary Women Novelists and the State,* St. Martin's Press (New York, NY), 2000.

Chapman, Michael, editor, *The Drum Decade: Stories from the 1950s,* University of Natal Press (Pietermaritzburg, South Africa), 1989.

Clingman, Stephen, *The Novels of Nadine Gordimer: History from the Inside,* University of Massachusetts Press (Amherst, MA), 1992.

Cooke, John, *The Novels of Nadine Gordimer: Private Lives/Public Landscapes,* Louisiana State University (Baton Rouge, LA), 1985.

Cox, C. Brian, editor, *African Writers,* Scribner (New York, NY), 1997, pp. 277-290.

Driver, Dorothy, Ann Dry, Craig MacKenzie, and John Read, *Nadine Gordimer: A Bibliography of Primary and Secondary Sources, 1937-1992,* Hans Zell, 1994.

Dubbeld, Catherine Elizabeth, *Reflecting Apartheid: South African Short Stories in English with Socio-Political Themes, 1960-1987: A Select and Annotated Bibliography,* South African Institute of International Affairs, 1990.

Ettin, Andrew Vogel, *Betrayals of the Body Politic: The Literary Commitments of Nadine Gordimer,* University Press of Virginia (Charlottesville, VA), 1993.

Foster, John Burt, Jr., and Wayne Jeffrey Froman, editors, *Thresholds of Western Culture: Identity, Postcoloniality, Transnationalism.* Continuum (New York, NY), 2002.

Hardwick, Elizabeth, *Sight Readings,* 1998.

Head, Dominic, *Nadine Gordimer,* Cambridge University Press (New York, NY), 1995.

Kamm, Antony, *Biographical Companion to Literature in English,* Scarecrow (Lanham, MD), 1997, pp. 215-216.

King, Bruce, editor, *The Later Fiction of Nadine Gordimer,* St. Martin's Press (New York, NY), 1993.

Lentricchia, Frank, and Andrew DuBois, editors, *Close Reading: The Reader,* Duke University Press (Durham, NC), 2003.

Mwaria, Cheryl B., Silvia Federici, and Joseph McLaren, editors, *African Visions: Literary Images, Political Change, and Social Struggle in Contemporary Africa.* Praeger (Westport, CT), 2000.

Nell, Racilia Jilian, *Nadine Gordimer: Novelist and Short Story Writer: A Bibliography of Her Works and Selected Criticism,* University of the Witwatersrand, 1964.

Newman, Judie, *Nadine Gordimer,* Routledge (New York, NY), 1990.

Newman, Judie, editor, *Nadine Gordimer's "Burger's Daughter": A Casebook,* Oxford University Press (New York, NY), 2003.

Nyman, Jopi, and John A. Stotesbury, editors, *Postcolonialism and Cultural Resistance,* Faculty of Humanities, University of Joensuu (Joensuu, Finland), 1999.

Smith, Rowland, editor, *Critical Essays on Nadine Gordimer,* G. K. Hall (Boston, MA), 1990.

Wagner, Kathrin, *Rereading Nadine Gordimer,* Indiana University Press (Bloomington, IN), 1994.

Yelin, Louise, *From the Margins of Empire: Christina Stead, Doris Lessing, Nadine Gordimer,* Cornell University Press (Ithaca, NY), 1998.

Yousaf, Nahem, editor, *Apartheid Narratives,* Rodopi (Amsterdam, Netherlands), 2001.

PERIODICALS

Africa News Service, July 19, 2001, p. 1008200u3067.

Alternation: Journal of the Centre for the Study of Southern African Literature and Languages, 2000, p. 29.

America, October 31, 1981, p. 264; December 15, 1984, p. 410; November 18, 1989, p. 361; June 6, 1992, p. 518; December 12, 1998, p. 15.

Anglophonia: French Journal of English Studies, 2000, p. 179.

Atlanta Journal-Constitution, November 28, 1999, p. K8; October 7, 2001, p. F5.

Atlantic Monthly, January, 1960; October, 1994, p. 131; February, 1998.

Atlas, January, 1980, p. 30.

AUMLA: Journal of the Australasian Universities Language and Literature Association, November, 2001, p. 135.

Austin American-Statesman, January 25, 1998, p. D6.

B. A. S.: British and American Studies/Revista de Studii Britanice si Americane, 1999, p. 73; 2001, p. 71.

Booklist, October 1, 1958; January 10, 1960; August, 1992, p. 2022; June 1, 1994, p. 1862; September 15, 1995, p. 129; October 15, 1997, p. 362; August, 1999, p. 2025; September 1, 1999, p. 57; July 2001, p. 1949; January 1, 2002, p. 761; January 1, 2003, p. 807.

Boston Herald, May 18, 2003, p. 040.

Bulletin of Bibliography, Volume 36, 1979; Volume 42, number 1, 1985.

Business Week, September 8, 1980, p. 17.

Canadian Forum, February, 1984, p. 17; April, 1989, p. 27.

Cardozo Studies in Law and Literature, fall, 2001, p. 299.

Chicago Sunday Tribune, September 21, 1958.

Chicago Tribune, May 18, 1980; December 7, 1986; November 12, 1987; October 4, 1991.

Chicago Tribune Book World, September 9, 1979; June 7, 1981; July 29, 1984; December 11, 1988, pp. 8-9; September 25, 1994, section 14, pp. 1, 9.

Christian Century, May 26, 1982, p. 642; Nov 21, 2001, p. 33.

Christian Science Monitor, January 10, 1963; November 4, 1971; May 19, 1975; September 10, 1979.

CLA Journal, December 2001, p. 187.

Commentary, February, 1992, p. 51.

Commonweal, October 23, 1953; July 9, 1965; November 4, 1966; December 5, 1980, p. 702; November 30, 1984, pp. 662, 667-668; March 10, 1989, p. 150.

Contemporary Literature, spring, 2000, p. 554.

Cosmopolitan, August, 1981, p. 24.

Courier-Mail (Brisbane, Australia), March 18, 2000, p. W09; December 29, 2001, p. M05.

Critical Survey, 1999, p. 64.

Critique: Studies in Contemporary Fiction, winter, 1998, p. 115; winter, 1999, p. 161.

Current Writing: Text and Reception in Southern Africa, April, 2001, p. 49.

Daily Telegraph (London, England), September 15, 2001; May 31, 2003, p. 02; June 7, 2003, p. 09.

Daily Telegraph (Surry Hills, Australia), March 28, 1998, p. 110.

Denver Post, May 25, 2003, p. EE-02.

Detroit News, September 2, 1979; June 7, 1981; May 31, 1989.

Economist (U.K.), September 15, 2001, p. 94.

Editor and Publisher, December 9, 2002, p. 25.

Encounter, August, 1971; February, 1975.

English in Africa, May, 2002, pp. 27, 55.

English Journal, March, 1990, p. 70.

Entertainment Weekly, January 24, 1992, p. 52; November 4, 1994, p. 69; October 5, 2001, p. 128.

Estudios de Asia y Africa, September-December, 2000, p. 475.

Evening Standard (London, England), September 10, 2001, p. 50.

Explicator, summer, 1998, p. 213.

Extrapolation, spring, 1992, pp. 73-87.

Financial Times, March 14, 1998, p. 5.

Glamour, November, 1990, p. 174.

Globe and Mail (Toronto, Ontario, Canada), July 28, 1984; June 6, 1987; January 5, 1991; October 5, 1991.

Guardian (London, England), October 27, 2001, p. 6; October 12, 2003, p. 30; January 25, 2003, p. 7; February 28, 2003, p. 23; April 19, 2003, p. 7; May 22, 2003, p. 8; July 5, 2003, p. 27.

Harper's, February, 1963; April, 1976; November, 1990, p. 27.

Houston Chronicle, February 15, 1998, p. 26.

Hudson Review, spring, 1980.

Independent (London, England), November 17, 1999, p. 5.

Independent on Sunday (London, England), February 1, 1998, p. 31; February 21, 1999, p. 13; September 9, 2001, p. 15; June 8, 2003, p. 16.

Insight on the News, January 9, 1995, p. 27.

Interview, December, 1988, p. 140.

Irish Times (Dublin, Ireland), November 2, 2002, p. 62; June 14, 2003, p. 60.

Journal of Southern African Studies, 1999, p. 633.

Journal of Modern Literature, winter, 2001-2002, p. 50.

Kenyon Review, summer-fall, 1998, p. 94.

Library Journal, September 1, 1958; September 1, 1980, p. 1751; March 15, 1981, p. 680; December, 1985, p. 99; March 1, 1987, p. 70; April 15, 1987, p. 98; January, 1988, p. 41; July, 1988, p. 70; October 15, 1988, p. 91; May 15, 1990, p. 120; November 1, 1990, p. 124; August, 1991, p. 149; March 1, 1993, p. 122; April 1, 1993, p. 148; August, 1994, p. 1989; February 1, 1995, p. 114; September 1, 1995, p. 176; November 1, 1997, p. 115; August 2001, p. 161; March 1, 2003, p. 121.

London Magazine, April-May, 1975.

Los Angeles Times, July 31, 1984; December 7, 1986; May 4, 2003, p. R-12.

Los Angeles Times Book Review, August 10, 1980; April 19, 1987; April 3, 1988; April 2, 1989; October 28, 1990.

Maclean's, August 3, 1981, p. 43; November 2, 1981, p. 21; August 13, 1984, p. 52; June 1, 1987, p. 50; November 14, 1994, p. 104.

Modern Fiction Studies, summer, 1987; spring, 2000, p. 139.

Mother Jones, June, 1984, p. 56; December, 1988, p. 50.

Ms., July, 1975; June, 1981, pp. 41, 90; July, 1984, p. 33; September, 1987, p. 28.

Nation, June 18, 1971; August 18, 1976; January 3, 1981, p. 22; June 6, 1981, p. 226; June 25, 1983, p. 809; May 2, 1987, p. 578; May 30, 1987, p. 731, December 26, 1988, p. 726; December 17, 1990, p. 777; October 16, 1995, p. 431; March 2, 1998, p. 25; December 13, 1999, p. 36.

National Review, December 25, 1981, p. 1561.

New Leader, June 29, 1981, p. 17; June 25, 1984, p. 18; April 20, 1087, p. 18.

New Orleans, December, 1984, p. 87; November, 1985, p. 31.

New Republic, May 18, 1987, p. 33; November 28, 1988, p. 28; October 24, 1994, p. 34.

New Statesman, May 16, 1980, p. 751; September 11, 1981, p. 18; March 23, 1984, p. 27; April 10, 1987, p. 27; December 4, 1987, p. 30; September 10, 2001, p. 55; June 23, 2003, p. 50.

New Statesman and Nation, August 18, 1956.

New Statesman and Society, September 23, 1988, p. 35; December 15, 1989, p. 39; September 21, 1990, p. 40; September 16, 1994, p. 38.

Newsweek, May 10, 1965; July 4, 1966; March 10, 1975; April 19, 1976; September 22, 1980; June 22, 1981, p. 78; July 9, 1984, p. 71; August 4, 1986, p. 29; May 4, 1987, p. 78; October 1, 1990, p. 40; October 14, 1991, p. 40.

New York, August 25, 1980, p. 54; June 22, 1981, p. 64; February 3, 1986, p. 40; October 22, 1990, p. 119.

New Yorker, June 7, 1952; November 21, 1953; November 29, 1958; May 12, 1975; June 22, 1981, p. 114; June 29, 1987, p. 87.

New York Herald Tribune Book Review, May 25, 1952; October 4, 1953; October 21, 1956; September 21, 1958; January 10, 1960; April 7, 1963.

New York Review of Books, June 26, 1975; July 15, 1976; October 23, 1980, p. 46; August 13, 1981, p. 14; July 16, 1987, p. 8; March 30, 1989, p. 12; November 21, 1991, p. 27; December 5, 1991, p. 16; December 1, 1994, p. 12.

New York Times, June 15, 1952; October 4, 1953; October 7, 1956; September 21, 1958; May 23, 1965; October 30, 1970; September 19, 1979; August 20, 1980; November 8, 1990, p. 8; May 27, 1981; December 28, 1981; July 9, 1984; January 14, 1986; April 22, 1987; December 28, 1987; October 5, 1990; January 1, 1991; October 4, 1991, pp. A1, C28; October 10, 1991, p. C25; December 8, 1991, p. 22; September 16, 1994, p. C31; November 28, 1994, pp. C11, C15; January 16, 1998, pp. B43, E49; November 14, 1999, p. WK1; October 9, 2001, p. E7; May 10, 2002, p. A4; May 4, 2003, p. 8; May 8, 2003, p. A11.

New York Times Book Review, January 10, 1960; September 11, 1966; October 31, 1971; April 13, 1975; April 18, 1976; August 19, 1979; August 24, 1980, pp. 7, 31; December 7, 1980, p. 51; June 7, 1981, pp. 26, 226; February 7, 1982, p. 38; August 8, 1982, p. 23; December 5, 1982, p. 75; June 24, 1984, p. 40; July 29, 1984, p. 7; August 16, 1984, p. 3; February 16, 1986, p. 29; August 31, 1986, p. 20; May 3, 1987, pp. 1, 22; July 19, 1987, p. 1; November 27, 1988, p. 8; October 21, 1990, pp. 1, 21; December 2, 1990, p. 81; June 2, 1991, p. 21; September 29, 1991, p. 7; September 25, 1994, p. 7; December 24, 1995, p. 11; October 6, 1996, p. 102; January 16, 1998; February 1, 1998, p. 10; December 16, 2001, p. 10; December 23, 2001, p. 14; January 6, 2002, p. 18; January 13, 2002, p. 22; June 2, 2002, p. 23; October 20, 2002, p. 28; May 4, 2003, p. 8.

Observer (London, England), November 21, 1999, p. 13.

Paris Review, summer, 1983.

People, March 26, 1984, p. 104; August 20, 1984, p. 15; January 5, 1987, p. 18; May 4, 1987, p. 22; October 18, 1991, p. 14; October 21, 1991, p. 52; January 19, 1998, p. 37.

Plain Dealer (Cleveland, OH), September 30, 2001, p. J9.

Playboy, January, 1992, p. 32.

Progressive, January, 1982, p. 53; January, 1992, p. 30.

Publishers Weekly, June 27, 1980, p. 79; April 20, 1984, p. 82; May 23, 1986, p. 99; March 6, 1987; April 10, 1987, p. 80; November 6, 1987, p. 40; September 30, 1988, p. 54; August 17, 1990, p. 53; August 30, 1991, p. 69; October 18, 1991, p. 14; July 11, 1994, p. 61; August 14, 1995, p. 63; November 11, 1996, p. 66; October 20, 1997, p. 52; March 16, 1998, p. 21; August 16, 1999, p. 66; July 16, 2001, p. 155.

Record (Bergen County, NJ), December 19, 1997, p. 013.

Research in African Literatures, spring, 2000, p. 95.

Roanoke Times, March 10, 2002, p. 6.

Rocky Mountain News (Denver, CO), December 27, 1998, p. 1E.

St Louis Post-Dispatch, March 29, 1998, p. E5.

St. Petersburg Times, December 30, 2001, p. 4D.

San Francisco Chronicle, May 26, 1952; November 9, 1953; January 24, 1960; January 11, 1998, p. 3; December 12, 1999, p. 5.

Saturday Review, May 24, 1952; October 3, 1953; September 13, 1958; January 16, 1960; May 8, 1965; August 20, 1966; December 4, 1971; March 8, 1975; September 29, 1979; May, 1981, p. 67.

School Library Journal, May, 2000, p. 194.

Scotland on Sunday (Edinburgh, Scotland), June 1, 2003, p. 4.

Scotsman (Edinburgh, Scotland), September 15, 2001, p. 11; June 14, 2003, p. 8.

Seattle Post-Intelligencer, January 27, 1998, p. D2; August 22, 1998, p. D2.

Seattle Times, February 1, 1998, p. M2; July 24, 1998, p. E1; September 9, 2001, p. J12; April 13, 2003, p. L8.

Sewanee Review, spring, 1977.

Spectator, February 12, 1960; June 7, 2003, p. 45.

Star-Ledger (Newark, NJ), February 22, 1998, p. 006; January 9, 2000, p. 004; October 14, 2001, p. 004; April 6, 2003, p. 004.

Sunday Telegraph (London, England), Sept 16, 2001; June 1, 2003.

Sunday Times (London, England), September 23, 2001, p. 42; June 15, 2003, p. 44.

Tikkun, January-February, 1990, p. 67; May-June, 1995, pp. 76, 79.

Time, October 15, 1956; September 22, 1958; January 11, 1960; November 16, 1970; July 7, 1975; August 11, 1980, p. 70; June 8, 1981, p. 79; July 23,

1984, p. 95; April 6, 1987, p. 76; October 29, 1990, p. CT12; October 14, 1991, p. 91; January 19, 1998, p. 66.

Times (London, England), December 16, 1982; March 22, 1984; April 2, 1987; September 6, 1990; October 14, 2000, p. 18; September 5, 2001, p. 15; September 22, 2001, p. 20.

Times Literary Supplement, October 30, 1953; July 13, 1956; June 27, 1958; February 12, 1960; March 1, 1963; July 22, 1965; July 7, 1966; May 14, 1971; May 26, 1972; January 9, 1976; July 9, 1976; April 25, 1980; September 4, 1981; March 30, 1984; April 17, 1987; September 23-29, 1988; October 4, 1990; October 11, 1991, p. 14; April 1, 1994, pp. 10-11.

Tribune Books (Chicago, IL), April 26, 1987; December 11, 1988, pp. 8-9; October 14, 1990; September 25, 1994, pp. 1, 9.

U.S. News and World Report, January 27, 1986, p. 65; May 25, 1987, p. 74.

Village Voice, September 17, 1980.

Voice Literary Supplement, September, 1984.

Wall Street Journal, January 20, 1998, p. A16.

Washington Post, December 4, 1979; January 30, 1998, p. D03; February 8, 1998, p. X15; August 5, 2001, p. T08; September 30, 2001, p. T09.

Washington Post Book World, November 28, 1971; April 6, 1975; August 26, 1979; September 7, 1980; May 31, 1981; July 15, 1984; May 3, 1987; November 20, 1988; October 2, 1994.

Washington Times, February 1, 1998, p. 6; May 4, 2003, p. D06.

Weekend Australian (Sydney, Australia), March 28, 1998, p. R29; March 11, 2000, p. R13; November 24, 2001, p. B06.

Wilson Library Journal, February, 1994, p. 94.

World and I, November, 1998, p. 277; March, 2002, p. 245; July, 2003, p. 219.

World Literature Today, autumn, 1984; spring, 1992, pp. 390-391.

World Press Review, October, 1987, p. 61.

World Watch, July-August, 2002, p. 17.

Yale Review, winter, 1982, p. 254; winter, 1988, p. 243.

ONLINE

Atlantic Online, http://www.theatlantic.com/ (February 9, 2000), interview with Gordimer.

BBC Audio Interviews, http://www.bbc.co.uk/bbcfour/ (October 18, 1998).

Gifts of Speech, http://gos.sbc.edu/ (December 7, 1991), Nobel lecture.

University Scholars Programme, National University of Singapore, http://www.scholars.nus.edu.sg/post/sa/ (March 10, 2004), Gordimer page.

South African Review of Books, http://www.uni-ulm.de/ (November-December 1993), "Nadine Gordimer at 70."

United Nations Development Programme—South Africa, http://www.undp.org.za/ (March 10, 2004), biography of Gordimer.*

* * *

GOYTISOLO, Juan 1931-

PERSONAL: Born January 5, 1931, in Barcelona, Spain; immigrated to France, 1957. *Education:* Attended University of Barcelona and University of Madrid, 1948-52.

ADDRESSES: Home—Marrakesh, Morocco. *Agent*—c/o Author Mail, Serpent's Tail, 4 Blackstock Mews, London N4 2BT, England.

CAREER: Writer. Worked as reporter in Cuba, 1965; associated with Gallimard Publishing Co., Paris, France. Visiting professor at universities in the United States.

AWARDS, HONORS: Numerous awards for *Juegos de manos;* Premio Europalia, 1985.

WRITINGS:

NOVELS

Juegos de manos, Destino (Barcelona, Spain), 1954, 4th edition, 1969, translation by John Rust published as *The Young Assassins,* Knopf (New York, NY), 1959.

Duelo en el paraíso, Planeta (Barcelona, Spain), 1955, reprinted, Destino (Barcelona, Spain), 1981, translation by Christine Brooke-Rose published as *Children of Chaos,* MacGibbon & Kee (London, England), 1958.

El Circo (first novel in "Mañana efímero" trilogy; title means "The Circus"), Destino (Barcelona, Spain), 1957, reissued, 1982.

Fiestas (second novel in "Mañana efímero" trilogy), Emece, 1958, Destino (Barcelona, Spain), 1981, translation by Herbert Weinstock published as *Fiestas,* Knopf (New York, NY), 1960.

La Resaca (third novel in "Mañana efímero" trilogy; title means "The Undertow"), Club del Libro Español (Paris, France), 1958, J. Mortiz (Mexico City, Mexico), 1977.

La Isla, Seix Barral (Barcelona, Spain), 1961, reprinted, 1982, translation by Jose Yglesias published as *Island of Women,* Knopf (New York, NY), 1962, published as *Sands of Torremolinos,* J. Cape (London, England), 1962.

Señas de identidad (first novel in "Alvaro Mendiola" trilogy), J. Mortiz (Mexico City, Mexico), 1966, translation by Gregory Rabassa published as *Marks of Identity,* Grove (New York, NY), 1969, reprinted, Serpent's Tail (New York, NY), 2003.

Reivindicación del conde don Julián (second novel in "Alvaro Mendiola" trilogy), J. Mortiz (Mexico City, Mexico), 1970, Catedra (Madrid, Spain), 1985, translation by Helen R. Lane published as *Count Julian,* Viking (New York, NY), 1974.

Juan sin tierra (third novel in "Alvaro Mendiola" trilogy), Seix Barral (Barcelona, Spain), 1975, translation by Helen R. Lane published as *Juan the Landless,* Viking (New York, NY), 1977.

Makbara, Seix Barral (Barcelona, Spain), 1980, translation by Helen R. Lane, Seaver Books (New York, NY), 1981.

Paisajes despues de la batalla, Montesinos (Barcelona, Spain), 1982, translation by Helen R. Lane published as *Landscapes after the Battle,* Seaver Books (New York, NY), 1987.

Las Virtudes del pájaro solitario, Seix Barral (Barcelona, Spain), 1988, translation published as *The Virtues of the Solitary Bird,* 1993.

La Cuarentena, Mondadori (Madrid, Spain), 1991, translation by Peter Bush published as *Quarantine,* Dalkey Archive Press (Normal, IL), 1994.

Cuaderno de Sarajevo, Aguilar (Madrid, Spain), 1993, translation by Helen R. Lane published as *State of Siege,* City Light Books (San Francisco, CA), 2002.

La Saga de los Marx, Aguilar (Madrid, Spain), 1993, translation published as *The Marx Family Saga,* City Lights Books (San Francisco, CA), 1999.

Argelia en el vendaval, Aguilar (Madrid, Spain), 1994.

El Sitio de los sitios, Alfaguara (Madrid, Spain), 1995.

El Universo imaginario, Espasa Calpe (Barcelona, Spain), 1997.

Cogitus interruptus, Seix Barral (Barcelona, Spain), 1999.

Carajicomedia: De Fray Bugeo Montesino y otros pajaros devario plumaje y pluma, Seix Barral (Barcelona, Spain), 2000, translation published as *A Cock-eyed Comedy,* Serpent's Tail (New York, NY), 2002.

SHORT STORIES

Para vivir aquí (title means "To Live Here"), Sur (Buenos Aires, Argentina), 1960, reprinted, Bruguera (Barcelona, Spain), 1983.

Fin de fiesta: Tentativas de interpretacion de una historia amorosa, Seix Barral (Barcelona, Spain), 1962, translation by Jose Yglesias published as *The Party's Over: Four Attempts to Define a Love Story,* Weidenfeld & Nicolson (London, England), 1966, Grove (New York, NY), 1967.

Aproximaciones a Gaudí en Capadocia, Mondadori (Madrid, Spain), 1990.

Las Semanas del jardí; un círculo de lectores, Alfaguara (Madrid, Spain), 1997, translation by Peter Bush published as *The Garden of Secrets: As Written Down,* Serpent's Tail (New York, NY), 2002.

Estambul otomano, Planeta (Barcelona, Spain), 1989, translation published as *Marrakesh Tales,* Serpent's Tail (New York, NY), 2000.

TRAVEL NARRATIVES

Campos de Nijar, Seix Barral (Barcelona, Spain), 1960, Grant & Cutler (London, England), 1984, translation by Luigi Luccarelli published as *The Countryside of Nijar* in *The Countryside of Nijar* [and] *La Chanca,* Alembic Press (Plainfield, IN), 1987.

La Chanca, Librería Española, 1962, Seix Barral (Barcelona, Spain), 1983, translation by Luigi Luccarelli published as *The Countryside of Nijar* [and] *La Chanca,* Alembic Press (Plainfield, IN), 1987.

Pueblo en marcha: Instantaneas de un viaje a Cuba (title means "People on the March: Snapshots of a Trip to Cuba"), Librería Española (Paris, France), 1963.

Cronicas sarracinas (title means "Saracen Chronicles"), Iberica (Barcelona, Spain), 1982.

OTHER

Problemas de la novela (literary criticism; title means "Problems of the Novel"), Seix Barral (Barcelona, Spain), 1959.

Las Mismas palabras, Seix Barral (Barcelona, Spain), 1963.

Plume d'hier: Espagne d'aujourd'hui, compiled by Mariano José de Larra, Editeurs Français Reunis, 1965.

El Furgon de cola (critical essays; title means "The Caboose"), Ruedo Iberico, 1967, reprinted, Seix Barral (Barcelona, Spain), 1982.

España y los españoles, Editorial Lumen (Barcelona, Spain), 1969.

(Author of prologue) Jose Maria Blanco White, *Obra inglesa,* Formentor, 1972.

Obras completas (title means "Complete Works"), Aguilar (Madrid, Spain), 1977.

Libertad, libertad, libertad (essays and speeches), Anagrama (Barcelona, Spain), 1978.

(Author of introduction) Mohamed Chukri, *El Pan desnudo* (title means "For Bread Alone"), translation from the Arabic by Abdellah Djibilou, Montesinos (Barcelona, Spain), 1982.

Coto vedado (autobiography; also see below), Seix Barral (Barcelona, Spain), 1985, translation by Peter Bush published as *Forbidden Territory: The Memoirs of Juan Goytisolo,* North Point Press (San Francisco, CA), 1989.

(Author of commentary) Omar Khayyam, *Estances,* translated into Catalan by Ramon Vives Pastor, del Mall (Barcelona, Spain), 1985.

Contracorrientes, Montesinos (Barcelona, Spain), 1985.

En los reinos de taifa (autobiography; title means "Realms of Strife: The Memoirs of Juan Goytisolo, 1956-1982"; also see below), Seix Barral (Barcelona, Spain), 1986.

Space in Motion (essays), translation by Helen R. Lane, Lumen Books (New York, NY), 1987.

De la ceca a la meca, Alfaguara (Madrid, Spain), 1997.

Cartas de Americo Castro a Juan Goytisolo, 1968-1972: El Epistolario, Pre-Textos (Valencia, Spain), 1997.

(With Sami Naïr) *El Paeje del vida: Integración o rechazo de la emigración en España,* Aguilar (Madrid, Spain), 2000.

Paisajes de guerra con Chechnia al fondo (articles; formerly published in *El País*), Aguilar (Madrid,

Spain), 1996, translation published as *Landscapes of War,* City Lights Books (San Francisco, CA), 2001.

Pájaro que ensucia su propio nido, Galaxia Tugenberg (Barcelona, Spain), 2001.

Telón de boca, Aleph (Barcelona, Spain), 2003.

España y sus ejidos, Hijos de Mule-Rubio (Madrid, Spain), 2003.

Forbidden Territory and Realms of Strife: The Memoirs of Juan Goytisolo (translations of *Coto vedado* and *En los reinos de taifa*), edited by Peter Bush, Verso (New York, NY), 2003.

Also author of *Disidencias* (essays), 1977. Work represented in collections and anthologies, including *Juan Goytisolo,* Ministerio de Cultura, Direccion General de Promocion del Libro y la Cinematografia, 1982. Contributor to periodicals, including *Ínsula* and *El País.*

SIDELIGHTS: "Juan Goytisolo is the best living Spanish novelist," wrote John Butt in the *Times Literary Supplement.* The author, as Butt observed, became renowned as a "pitiless satirist" of Spanish society during the dictatorship of Generalissimo Francisco Franco, who imposed his version of conservative religious values on the country from the late 1930s until his death in 1975. Goytisolo, whose youth coincided with the rise of Franco, had a variety of compelling reasons to feel alienated from his own country. He was a small child when his mother was killed in a bombing raid, a casualty of the civil war Franco instigated to seize power from a democratically elected government. The author then grew up as a bisexual in a country dominated, in Butt's words, by "frantic machismo." Eventually, said Goytisolo in his memoir *Coto vedado* (*Forbidden Territory*), he became "that strange species of writer claimed by none and alien and hostile to groups and categories."

In the late 1950s, when his writing career began to flourish, Goytisolo left Spain for Paris and remained in self-imposed exile until after Franco died. The literary world was greatly impressed when Goytisolo's first novel, *Juegos de manos* (*The Young Assassins*), was published in 1954. Goytisolo was identified as a member of the Spanish "restless generation" but his first novel seemed as much akin to Fedor Dostoevski as it did to America's Jack Kerouac. The plot is similar to Dostoevski's *The Possessed:* a group of students

plot the murder of a politician but end up murdering the fellow student chosen to kill the politician. Some reviewers saw the theme as the self-destructiveness and hedonism of the smug and self-righteous.

Duelo en el paraíso (*Children of Chaos*) is seen as a violent extension of *The Young Assassins.* Like Anthony Burgess's *A Clockwork Orange* and William Golding's *Lord of the Flies, Children of Chaos* focuses on the terror wrought by adolescents. The children have taken over a small town after the end of the Spanish Civil War causes a breakdown of order.

Fiestas begins a trilogy referred to as "Ephemeral Morrow" (after a famous poem by Antonio Machado). Considered the best volume of the trilogy, this novel follows four characters as they try to escape life in Spain by chasing their dreams. Each character meets with disappointment in the novel's end. *El Circo,* the second book in the "Ephemeral Morrow" trilogy, was deemed by critics as too blatantly ironic to succeed as a follow-up to *Fiestas.* It is the story of a painter who manages a fraud before being punished for a murder he didn't commit. The third book, *La Resaca,* was also a disappointment, the novel's style considered too realistic to function as a fitting conclusion to the trilogy.

After writing two politically oriented travelogues, *Campos de Nijar* (*The Countryside of Nijar*) and *La Chanca,* Goytisolo returned to fiction and the overt realism he had begun in *La Resaca.* Unfortunately, critics have implied that both *La Isla* (*Island of Women*) and *Fin de fiesta* (*The Party's Over*) suffer because they ultimately resembled their subject matter, a small world of intellectuals who operate in a vacuum.

Goytisolo abandoned his realist style after *The Party's Over. Señas de identidad* (*Marks of Identity*), about an exile who returns to his native Barcelona after the Spanish Civil War, is the first in a trilogy that includes *Reivindicación del conde don Julián* (*Count Julian*) and *Juan sin tierra* (*Juan the Landless*). *Count Julian* has been widely considered as Goyitsolo's masterpiece to date. In it, the novelist uses techniques borrowed from James Joyce, Celine, Jean Genet, filmmaker Luis Bunuel, and painter Pablo Picasso. *Count Julian* is named for the legendary Spanish nobleman who betrayed his country to Arab invaders in the Middle Ages. In the shocking fantasies of the novel's narrator, a modern Spaniard living as an outcast in Africa, Julian returns to punish Spain for its cruelty and hypocrisy. Over the course of the narration, the Spanish language itself gradually transforms into Arabic. Writing in the *New York Times Book Review,* Carlos Fuentes called *Count Julian* "an adventure of language, a critical battle against the language appropriated by power in Spain. It is also a search for a new/old language that would offer an alternative for the future." Reviews of *Juan the Landless* were generally less favorable than those of either *Marks of Identity* or *Count Julian,* an *Atlantic* critic suggesting that the uninformed reader begin elsewhere with Goytisolo.

Even after the oppressive Franco regime was dismantled in the late 1970s, Goytisolo continued to write novels that expressed deep alienation by displaying an unconventional, disorienting view of human society. *Makbara,* for example, is named for the cemeteries of North Africa where lovers meet for late-night trysts. "What a poignant central image it is," wrote Paul West in the *Washington Post Book World,* "not only as an emblem of life in death . . . but also as a vantage point from which to review the human antic in general, which includes all those who go about their daily chores with their minds below their belts." The characters Goytisolo "feels at home with," West declared, "are the drop-outs and the ne'er do wells, the outcasts and the misfits." In *Paisajes despues de la batalla* (*Landscapes after the Battle*), the author moves his vision of alienation to Paris, where he had long remained in exile. This short novel, made up of seventy-eight nonsequential chapters, displays the chaotic mix of people—from French nationalists to Arab immigrants—who uneasily coexist in the city. "The Paris metro map which the protagonist contemplates . . . for all its innumerable permutations of routes," explained Abigail Lee in the *Times Literary Supplement,* "provides an apt image for the text itself." *Landscapes after the Battle* "looked like another repudiation, this time of Paris," Butt wrote, adding: "One wondered what Goytisolo would destroy next."

Accordingly, Butt was surprised to find that the author's memoir of his youth, published in 1985, had a markedly warmer tone than the novels that had preceded it. "Far from being a new repudiation," the critic observed, *Forbidden Territory* "is really an essay in acceptance and understanding. . . . Gone, almost, are the tortuous language, the lurid fantasies, the dreams of violation and abuse. Instead, we are given a mov-

ing, confessional account of a difficult childhood and adolescence." Goytisolo's recollections, the reviewer concluded, constitute "a moving and sympathetic story of how one courageous victim of the Franco regime fought his way out of a cultural and intellectual wasteland, educated himself, and went on to inflict a brilliant revenge on the social system which so isolated and insulted him."

In *Las Virtudes del pájaro solitario* (*The Virtues of the Solitary Bird*), Goytisolo explores the Christian, Jewish, and Moorish heritage of Spain and the hybrid mysticism that emerged from the intermingling of the three religions, particularly as expressed in the writings of Saint John of the Cross and Arabian poet Ibn al Farid. Goytisolo juxtaposes the persecution of Saint John with a contemporary narrator who entertains imaginary conversations with the sixteenth-century saint while living in exile and suffering from AIDS. Mirroring the author's own political oppression and departure from Franco's Spain, the book "is also the story of the independent thinker throughout history, flushed out by those fearful of 'contaminating ideas,'" observed a *Publishers Weekly* reviewer. Jack Byrne noted in the *Review of Contemporary Fiction* that Goytisolo's version of the martyred saint's verse "modernize[s], while not sanitizing, the horror of heresy—theological, political, social, moral—wherever and whenever it appears." Amanda Hopkinson wrote in the *Times Literary Supplement* that "Goytisolo expects to be read as a parable of our time, with all its complexities and obscurities. This is not prose, at least as conventionally punctuated, it is poetry full of rhapsodic psalms and oriental mysticism."

Goyitsolo's *Quarantine,* another complex, experimental novel, follows the spiritual wandering of a recently deceased female writer whose soul, according to Islamic tradition, must embark on a forty-day journey to eternal rest. Through an unnamed narrator, Goytisolo likens this spiritual quarantine to the creative writing process, whereby an author remains in isolation for a time to summon memory and the imagination. In effect, the fictional author's meditations on death and writing become the story itself as he imagines his own death, encounters the soul of his dead friend among angels and a Sufi mystic, and considers parallels to Dante's *Divine Comedy.* Jack Shreve noted in a *Library Journal* review that Goytisolo "multiplies levels of interpretation in order to 'destabilize' the reader." Goytisolo also interjects a strong antiwar theme through surreal news reports that describe the carnage of the Persian Gulf War.

In his novel *La Saga de los Marx* (*The Marx Family Saga*), Goytisolo tackles the political theme of the fall of communism in Europe and the West's reaction it. The wry, satirical, and funny story focuses on Albanian refugees in an Italian resort who are searching for a paradise called "Dallas" and who are confronted by locals outraged at their presence. The family is, in essence, a reincarnation of Karl Marx and his family, all living in a type of historical limbo, watching the televised crumbling of the system the father of communism created. Sophia A. McClennen, writing in the *Review of Contemporary Fiction,* said the novel "provides a brutally vivid characterization of the intricacies of social commitment in a world which consumes more television than literature." *New Statesman* contributor Abigail Lee Six commented, "*The Marx Family Saga,* like most of Goytisolo's recent fiction, is very funny as it makes serious literary and sociopolitical points."

Goytisolo's *The Garden of Secrets* tells the story of the young poet Eusebio, who is confined by his family in a psychiatric center and diagnosed as schizophrenic. Eusebio ultimately escapes and flees Franco's Spain. A reading group later tries to arrange the various facts of the poet's case, each telling their own respective versions of the story. Writing in the *Review of Contemporary Fiction,* Thomas Hove noted that Eusebio resembles Goytisolo in many biographical aspects and went on to note that "his story develops the author's frequent Joycean theme of exile as both liberation and alienation." Writing in *Library Journal,* Jack Shreve called *The Garden of Secrets* an "intriguing collective portrait by one of Spain's foremost writers."

Goytisolo tackles the Roman Catholic Church and its secret society Opus Dei in his satirical novel *Carajicomedia: De Fray Bugeo Montesino y otros pajaros de vario plumaje y pluma* (*Cock-eyed Comedy*). The novel includes a wide cast of historical characters, including Roland Barthes, Jean Genet, and a character who keeps popping up throughout the centuries under different guises to expose the hypocrisy of the Spanish priesthood. Writing in *Library Journal,* Nelly S. Gonzalez noted that in Goyitsolo's "parody of our times, humor and cynicism are omnipresent but unexaggerated, and nobody escapes Goytisolo's mordant wit."

The siege of Sarajevo is the setting for Goytisolo's *Cuaderno de Sarajevo* (*State of Siege*), which centers on the mystery surrounding the disappearance of a Spanish visitor's corpse. The missing visitor has left behind various writings signed "J. G." The novel is made up of these and other texts, including stories and poems, police reports, and testimonies by people who saw or knew the vanished man. Writing in *Booklist,* Frank Sennett noted that the novel has "all the earmarks of magic realism" and concluded that the story is "effective in underscoring the tragic absurdity of sieges whose victims can only guess at the rationale of their persecutors." *Review of Contemporary Fiction* contributor Megan A. McDowell noted that in *State of Siege* "Goytisolo exposes the most basic quality of consciousness that both feeds on and creates literature, the part that spawns violence and madness, humor and language."

In 2003, the author's two memoirs were published together in English translation as *Forbidden Territory and Realms of Strife: The Memoirs of Juan Goytisolo.* Describing the work as "literary history up close," a *Publishers Weekly* contributor noted that "style is king here, and it is wonderful, infiltrating Goytisolo's chronological narrative like one of his characters." Nedra Crowe Evers, writing in *Library Journal,* commented that the memoir's lack of an index is the book's only drawback and added, "The writing is powerful but never crude; many passages are, quite simply, beautiful."

BIOGRAPHICAL AND CRITICAL SOURCES:

BOOKS

Amell, Samuel, editor, *Literature, the Arts, and Democracy: Spain in the Eighties,* Fairleigh Dickinson University Press (Madison, NJ), 1990.
Contemporary Literary Criticism, Gale (Detroit, MI), Volume 5, 1976, Volume 10, 1979, Volume 23, 1983.
Epps, Bradley S., *Significant Violence: Oppression and Resistance in the Later Narrative of Juan Goytisolo,* Clarendon (New York, NY), 1996.
Gazarian Gautier, Marie-Lise, *Interviews with Spanish Writers,* Dalkey Archive Press (Normal, IL), 1991.
Goytisolo, Juan, *Forbidden Territory,* translation by Peter Bush, North Point Press (San Francisco, CA), 1989.

Pope, Randolph D., *Understanding Juan Goytisolo,* University of South Carolina Press (Columbia, SC), 1995.

Schwartz, Kessel, *Juan Goytisolo,* Twayne (New York, NY), 1970.

Schwartz, Ronald, *Spain's New Wave Novelists, 1950-1974: Studies in Spanish Realism,* Scarecrow Press (Lanham, MD), 1976.

PERIODICALS

Atlantic, August, 1977.
Best Sellers, June 15, 1974.
Booklist, October 1, 2002, Frank Sennett, review of *State of Siege,* p. 301.
Journal of Spanish Studies, winter, 1979, pp. 353-364.
Kirkus Reviews, March 1, 1994, p. 234.
Lettres Peninsulares, fall-winter, 1990, pp. 259-278.
Library Journal, October 1, 1990, p. 89; March 1, 1994, p. 117; December, 2000, Jack Shreve, review of *The Garden of Secrets,* p. 187; August, 2001, Nelly S. Gonzalez, review of *Cock-eyed Comedy,* p. S34; July, 2003, Nedra Crowe Evers, review of *Forbidden Territory and Realms of Strife: The Memoirs of Juan Goytisolo,* p. 80.
Los Angeles Times Book Review, January 22, 1989.
Nation, March 1, 1975.
New Republic, January 31, 1967.
New Statesman, July 19, 1991, p. 38; December 17, 1993, p. 46; August 9, 1996, Abigail Lee Six, review of *The Marx Family Saga,* p. 47.
New York Times Book Review, January 22, 1967; May 5, 1974; September 18, 1977; June 14, 1987; July 3, 1988; February 12, 1989.
Publishers Weekly, November 30, 1992, p. 48; March 7, 1994, p. 55; May 19, 2003, review of *Forbidden Territory and Realms of Strife,* p. 64.
Review of Contemporary Fiction, fall, 1993, p. 213; fall, 1999, Sophia A. McClennen, review of *The Marx Family Saga,* p. 176; January 8, 2001, Maya Jaggi, "Juan Goytisolo" (interview with author), p. 42; fall, 2001, Thomas Hove, "Landscapes of War: From Sarajevo to Chechnya," p. 197; spring, 2003, Megan A. McDowell, review of *State of Siege,* p. 148.
Saturday Review, February 14, 1959; June 11, 1960; June 28, 1969.
Texas Quarterly, spring, 1975.
Times Literary Supplement, May 31, 1985; September 9, 1988; May 19, 1989; November 17, 1989; July 12, 1991, p. 18.

Washington Post Book World, January 17, 1982; June 14, 1987.
World Press Review, April, 1994. p. 51.

ONLINE

Juan Goyitsolo Web site, http://www.cnice.mecd.es/tematicas/juangoyitsolo (April 15, 2004).*

*   *   *

GREEN, Sheila Ellen 1934-
(Sheila Greenwald)

PERSONAL: Born May 26, 1934, in New York, NY; daughter of Julius (a manufacturer) and Florence (Friedman) Greenwald; married George Green (a surgeon), February 18, 1960; children: Samuel, Benjamin. *Education:* Sarah Lawrence College, B.A., 1956. *Politics:* Democrat. *Religion:* Jewish.

ADDRESSES: Home—175 Riverside Dr., New York, NY 10024. *Agent*—Harriet Wasserman Literary Agency, 137 East 36th St., New York, NY 10016.

CAREER: Writer and illustrator.

MEMBER: PEN, Authors League.

AWARDS, HONORS: Notable Children's Book citations, American Library Association, 1981, for *Give Us a Great Big Smile, Rosy Cole;* Junior Library Guild Selection, 1983, for *Will the Real Gertrude Hollings Please Stand Up?,* 1989, for *Rosy's Romance,* 1990, for *Mariah Delany's Author-of-the-Month Club,* 1997, for *Rosy Cole: She Grows and Graduates,* and 2003, for *Rosy Cole's Worst Ever, Best Yet Tour of New York City;* Parents' Choice selection, 1985, for *Rosy Cole's Great American Guilt Club.*

WRITINGS:

SELF-ILLUSTRATED FICTION; UNDER NAME SHEILA GREENWALD

A Metropolitan Love Story, Doubleday (New York, NY), 1962.
Willie Bryant and the Flying Otis, Grosset (New York, NY), 1971.

Sheila Ellen Green

The Hot Day, Bobbs-Merrill (Indianapolis, IN), 1972.

Miss Amanda Snap, Bobbs-Merrill (Indianapolis, IN), 1972.

Mat Pit and the Tunnel Tenants, Lippincott (Philadelphia, PA), 1972.

The Secret Museum, Lippincott (Philadelphia, PA), 1974.

The Secret in Miranda's Closet, Houghton Mifflin (Boston, MA), 1977.

The Mariah Delany Lending Library Disaster, Houghton Mifflin (Boston, MA), 1977.

The Atrocious Two, Houghton Mifflin (Boston, MA), 1978.

All the Way to Wits' End, Little, Brown (Boston, MA), 1979.

It All Began with Jane Eyre; or, the Secret Life of Franny Dillman, Little, Brown (Boston, MA), 1980.

Give Us a Great Big Smile, Rosy Cole, Little, Brown (Boston, MA), 1981.

Blissful Joy and the SATs: A Multiple-Choice Romance, Little, Brown (Boston, MA), 1982.

Will the Real Gertrude Hollings Please Stand Up?, Little, Brown (Boston, MA), 1983.

Valentine Rosy, Little, Brown (Boston, MA), 1984.

Rosy Cole's Great American Guilt Club, Little, Brown (Boston, MA), 1985.

Alvin Webster's Sure Fire Plan for Success and How It Failed, Little, Brown (Boston, MA), 1987.

Write On, Rosy!: A Young Author in Crisis, Little, Brown (Boston, MA), 1988.

Rosy's Romance, Little, Brown (Boston, MA), 1989.

Mariah Delany's Author-of-the-Month Club, Little, Brown (Boston, MA), 1990.

Here's Hermione: A Rosy Cole Production, Little, Brown (Boston, MA), 1991.

Rosy Cole Discovers America!, Little, Brown (Boston, MA), 1992.

My Fabulous New Life, Browndeer Press (San Diego, CA), 1993.

Rosy Cole: She Walks in Beauty, Little, Brown (Boston, MA), 1994.

Rosy Cole: She Grows and Graduates, Orchard Books (New York, NY), 1997.

Stucksville, Dorling Kindersley (New York, NY), 2000.

Rosy Cole's Worst Ever, Best Yet Tour of New York City, Melanie Kroupa Books/Farrar, Straus & Giroux (New York, NY), 2003.

ILLUSTRATOR; UNDER NAME SHEILA GREENWALD

Marie L. Allen, *Pocketful of Poems,* Harper (New York, NY), 1957.

Carol Ryrie Brink, *The Pink Motel,* Macmillan (New York, NY), 1959.

Florence Laughlin, *The Little Leftover Witch,* Macmillan (New York, NY), 1960.

Jean Lee Latham, *The Man Who Never Snoozed,* Macmillan (New York, NY), 1961.

Miriam Dreifus, *Brave Betsy,* Putnam (New York, NY), 1961.

Grace V. Curl, *Come A-Witching,* Bobbs-Merrill (Indianapolis, IN), 1964.

Laura H. Fisher, *Amy and the Sorrel Summer,* Holt (New York, NY), 1964.

Barbara Rinkoff, *The Remarkable Ramsey,* Morrow (New York, NY), 1965.

Hila Colman, *The Boy Who Couldn't Make Up His Mind,* Macmillan (New York, NY), 1965.

Anne Mallet, *Who'll Mind Henry?,* Doubleday (New York, NY), 1965.

1977, review of *The Secret in Miranda's Closet,* p. 15; February, 1978, review of *The Mariah Delany Lending Library Disaster,* p. 93; September, 1978, review of *The Atrocious Two,* p. 9; December, 1979, review of *All the Way to Wits' End,* p. 70; September, 1980, p. 10; July, 1981, p. 193; April, 1982, review of *Blissful Joy and the SATs: A Multiple-Choice Romance,* p. 148; December, 1983, review of *Will the Real Gertrude Hollings Please Stand Up?,* pp. 67-68; January, 1985, review of *Valentine Rosy,* pp. 84-85; January, 1986, review of *Rosy Cole's Great American Guilt Club,* p. 86; January, 1988, Betsy Hearne, review of *Alvin Webster's Surefire Plan for Success,* p. 90; January, 1989, Roger Sutton, review of *Write On, Rosy!,* p. 121; July, 1989, Roger Sutton, review of *Rosy's Romance,* p. 276; September, 1991, Deborah Stevenson, review of *Here's Hermione: A Rosy Cole Production,* p. 11; January, 1993, Deborah Stevenson, review of *Rosy Cole Discovers America!,* p. 146; January, 1995, Deborah Stevenson, review of *Rosy Cole: She Walks in Beauty,* p. 165; November, 1997, Deborah Stevenson, review of *Rosy Cole: She Grows and Graduates,* p. 86; January, 2001, Fern Kory, review of *Stucksville,* p. 182.

Christian Science Monitor, November 8, 1972, Dorothy H. Kelso, review of *Mat Pit and the Tunnel Tenants,* p. B4; May 1, 1974, David Willis, review of *The Secret Museum,* p. F3; October 15, 1980, Elizabeth Muthur, review of *It All Began with Jane Eyre,* pp. B1, B6-B7; November 1, 1985, Lyn Littlefield Hoopes, review of *Rosy Cole's Great American Guilt Club,* p. B7.

Five Owls, November, 1990, review of *Mariah Delany's Author-of-the-Month Club,* p. 37; May, 1993, Mary Lou Burket, review of *Rosy Cole's Great American Guilt Club,* p. 106; November, 1993, Susan Patron, review of *My Fabulous New Life,* pp. 38-39.

Horn Book, February, 1978, review of *The Mariah Delany Lending Library Disaster,* p. 45; February, 1980, Ann A. Flowers, review of *All the Way to Wits' End,* p. 55; August, 1980, review of *It All Began with Jane Eyre,* p. 407; August, 1981, review of *Give Us a Great Big Smile, Rosy Cole,* pp. 421-422; August, 1982, review of *Blissful Joy and the SATs,* p. 412; August, 1983, review of *Will the Real Gertrude Hollings Please Stand Up?,* p. 443; January, 1985, review of *Valentine Rosy,* p. 50; January, 1986, review of *Rosy Cole's Great American Guilt Club,* p. 58; March, 1988, review

of *Alvin Webster's Surefire Plan for Success,* p. 201; March, 1989, review of *Write On, Rosy!,* p. 233; September, 1989, review of *Rosy's Romance,* p. 647; July, 1990, Pat Scales, review of *Mariah Delany's Author-of-the-Month Club,* p. 77; November, 1991, review of *Here's Hermione,* p. 735; July-August, 2003, Roger Sutton, review of *Rosy Cole's Worst Ever, Best Yet Tour of New York City,* pp. 457.

Journal of Reading, December, 1982, M. Jean Greenlaw, review of *Blissful Joy and the SATs,* pp. 274-277.

Kirkus Reviews, April 1, 1971, review of *Willie Bryant and the Flying Otis,* p. 365; March 15, 1972, review of *The Hot Day,* p. 320; August 1, 1972, review of *Miss Amanda Snap,* p. 856; September 15, 1972, review of *Mat Pit and the Tunnel Tenants,* p. 1098; March 1, 1977, review of *The Secret in Miranda's Closet,* p. 223; March 15, 1978, review of *The Atrocious Two,* p. 305; December 15, 1979, review of *All the Way to Wits' End,* p. 1430; June 1, 1980, review of *It All Began with Jane Eyre,* p. 717; July 1, 1981, review of *Give Us a Great Big Smile, Rosy Cole,* p. 800; November 15, 1987, review of *Alvin Webster's Surefire Plan for Success,* p. 1627; December 15, 1988, review of *Write On, Rosy!,* p. 1811; August 1, 1991, review of *Here's Hermione,* p. 1010; November 15, 1993, review of *My Fabulous New Life,* p. 1461; December 15, 1994, review of *Rosy Cole: She Walks in Beauty,* p. 1569; October 15, 1997, review of *Rosy Cole: She Grows and Graduates,* p. 1581; October 15, 2000, review of *Stucksville,* p. 1485; July 1, 2003, review of *Rosy Cole's Worst Ever, Best Yet Tour of New York City,* p. 910.

Language Arts, November, 1977, Ruth M. Stein, review of *The Secret in Miranda's Closet,* p. 947; January, 1979, Ruth M. Stein, review of *The Atrocious Two,* p. 51; December, 1993, review of *Rosy Cole Discovers America!,* p. 681.

Library Journal, June 15, 1971, Cary M. Ormond, review of *Willie Bryant and the Flying Otis,* p. 2130; June 15, 1972, Susanne Gilles, review of *The Hot Day,* p. 2230; November 15, 1972, review of *Miss Amanda Snap,* p. 3796.

Publishers Weekly, August 7, 1972, review of *Miss Amanda Snap,* p. 50; December 4, 1972, review of *Mat Pit and the Tunnel Tenants,* p. 62; March 25, 1974, p. 56; March 19, 1982, review of *Blissful Joy and the SATs* p. 71; July 19, 1991, review of *Here's Hermione,* p. 56; August 23, 1993, review of *My Fabulous New Life,* p. 72; October 16, 2000, review of *Stucksville,* p. 76.

Saturday Review, August 19, 1972, Karla Kuskin, review of *The Hot Day,* p. 61.

School Librarian, August, 1989, Gillian Gross, review of *Will the Real Gertrude Hollings Stand Up?,* p. 104; May, 1990, Derek Lomas, review of *The Mariah Delany Lending Library Disaster,* p. 64.

School Library Journal, May, 1974, Jean C. Halloway, review of *The Secret Museum* p. 55; May, 1977, Carolyn Johnson, review of *The Secret in Miranda's Closet,* p. 61; November, 1977, Christine McDonnell, review of *The Mariah Delany Lending Library Disaster,* p. 56; December, 1979, Liza Bliss, review of *All the Way to Wits' End,* pp. 85-86; March, 1981, p. 108; September, 1981, Marilyn Kaye, review of *Give Us a Big Smile, Rosy Cole,* p. 125; August, 1983, p. 65; December, 1984, Phyllis Graves, review of *Valentine Rosy,* p. 80; January, 1986, Ruth Semrau, review of *Rosy Cole's Great American Guilt Club,* p. 67; January, 1988, Susan L. Rogers, review of *Alvin Webster's Surefire Plan for Success,* pp. 74-75; January, 1989, David Gale, review of *Write On, Rosy!,* p. 77; August, 1989, Sylvia S. Marantz, review of *Rosy's Romance,* pp. 139-140; November, 1991, Jana R. Fine, review of *Here's Hermione,* p. 96; December, 1991, Joy Fleishhacker, review of *Mariah Delany's Author-of-the-Month Club,* p. 114; January, 1993, Cheryl Cufari, review of *Rosy Cole Discovers America!,* p. 98; October, 1993, Connie Tyrrell Burns, review of *My Fabulous New Life,* p. 124; January, 1995, Maggie McEwen, review of *Rosy Cole: She Walks in Beauty,* p. 106, 108; November, 1997, Anne Knickerbocker, review of *Rosy Cole: She Grows and Graduates,* p. 82; October, 2000, Ashley Larsen, review of *Stucksville,* p. 125; November, 2003, JoAnn Jonas, review of *Rosy Cole's Worst Ever, Best Yet Tour of New York City,* p. 95.

Voice of Youth Advocates, January, 1982, Susan B. Madden, review of *Blissful Joy and the SATs,* p. 33; October, 1983, Micki S. Nevett, review of *Will the Real Gertrude Hollings Please Stand Up?,* p. 202; June, 1994, Susan Dunn, review of *My Fabulous New Life,* p. 82.

ONLINE

Sheila Greenwald Home Page, http://www.sheila greenwald.com (January 12, 2004).

GREENE, Graham (Henry) 1904-1991

PERSONAL: Born October 2, 1904, in Berkhamsted, Hertfordshire, England; died of a blood disease, April 3, 1991, in Vevey, Switzerland; son of Charles Henry (a headmaster); married Vivien Dayrell Browning, 1927; children: one son, one daughter. *Education:* Balliol College, Oxford, B.A., 1925. *Religion:* Roman Catholic.

CAREER: Writer. *Times,* London, England, subeditor, 1926-30; film critic for *Night and Day,* c.1930s; *Spectator,* London, film critic, 1935-39, literary editor, 1940-41; with Foreign Office in Africa, 1941-44; Eyre & Spottiswoode Ltd. (publishers), London, director, 1944-48; Indo-China correspondent for *New Republic,* 1954; Bodley Head (publishers), London, director, 1958-68. Member of Panamanian delegation to Washington for signing of Canal Treaty, 1977.

AWARDS, HONORS: Hawthornden Prize, 1940, for *The Power and the Glory;* James Tait Black Memorial Prize, 1949, for *The Heart of the Matter;* Catholic Literary Award, 1952, for *The End of the Affair;* Boys' Clubs of America Junior Book Award, 1955, for *The Little Horse Bus;* Antoinette Perry ("Tony") Award nomination for best play, 1957, for *The Potting Shed;* Pietzak Award (Poland), 1960; D.Litt., Cambridge University, 1962; Balliol College, Oxford, honorary fellow, 1963; Companion of Honour, 1966; D.Litt., University of Edinburgh, 1967; Shakespeare Prize, 1968; named chevalier, Legion d'Honneur (France), 1969; John Dos Passos Prize, 1980; medal of City of Madrid, 1980; Jerusalem Prize, 1981; Grand Cross of the Order of Vasco Nunez de Balboa (Panama), 1983; named commander, Order of Arts and Letters (France), 1984; named to British Order of Merit, 1986; named to Order of Ruben Dario (Nicaragua), 1987; Royal Society of Literature Prize; honorary doctorate, Moscow State University, 1988.

WRITINGS:

FICTION, EXCEPT AS NOTED

Babbling April (poems), Basil Blackwell (London, England), 1925.
The Man Within, Doubleday (New York, NY), 1929.

The Name of Action, Heinemann (London, England), 1930, Doubleday (New York, NY), 1931.

Rumour at Nightfall, Heinemann (London, England), 1931, Doubleday (New York, NY), 1932.

Orient Express, Doubleday (New York, NY), 1932, published as *Stamboul Train,* Heinemann (London, England), 1932.

It's a Battlefield, Doubleday (New York, NY), 1934, with new introduction by author, Heinemann (London, England), 1970.

The Basement Room, and Other Stories, Cresset (London, England), 1935, title story revised as "The Fallen Idol" and published with *The Third Man* (also see below), Heinemann (London, England), 1950.

England Made Me, Doubleday (New York, NY), 1935, published as *The Shipwrecked,* Viking (New York, NY), 1953, reprinted under original title, with new introduction by author, Heinemann (London, England), 1970.

The Bear Fell Free, Grayson & Grayson (London, England), 1935.

Journey without Maps (travelogue; also see below), Doubleday (New York, NY), 1936, 2nd edition, Viking (New York, NY), 1961, reprinted, 1992.

This Gun for Hire (also see below), Doubleday (New York, NY), 1936, published as *A Gun for Sale,* Heinemann (London, England), 1936.

Brighton Rock, Viking (New York, NY), 1938, with new introduction by author, Heinemann (London, England), 1970, reprinted, 1981.

The Confidential Agent (also see below), Viking (New York, NY), 1939, with new introduction by author, Heinemann (London, England), 1971.

Another Mexico, Viking (New York, NY), 1939, reprinted, 1982, published as *The Lawless Roads* (also see below), Longmans, Green (London, England), 1939.

The Labyrinthine Ways, Viking (New York, NY), 1940, published as *The Power and the Glory,* Heinemann (London, England), 1940, Viking, 1946, with new introduction by author, Heinemann, 1971, reprinted, Penguin (New York, NY), 2003.

British Dramatists (nonfiction), Collins (London, England), 1942, reprinted, Folcroft (Folcroft, PA), 1979.

The Ministry of Fear (also see below), Viking (New York, NY), 1943.

Nineteen Stories, Heinemann (London, England), 1947, Viking (New York, NY), 1949, revised and expanded edition published as *Twenty-one Stories,* Heinemann, 1955, Viking (New York, NY), 1962.

The Heart of the Matter, Viking (New York, NY), 1948, with new introduction by author, Heinemann (London, England), 1971, reprinted, Penguin (New York, NY), 1999.

The Third Man (also see below), Viking (New York, NY), 1950, reprinted, 1983.

The Lost Childhood, and Other Essays, Eyre & Spottiswoode (London, England), 1951, Viking (New York, NY), 1952.

The End of the Affair, Viking (New York, NY), 1951, reprinted, Penguin (New York, NY), 1991.

The Quiet American, Heinemann (London, England), 1955, Viking (New York, NY), 1982, reprinted, Penguin (New York, NY), 2002.

Loser Takes All, Heinemann (London, England), 1955, Viking (New York, NY), 1957.

Our Man in Havana (also see below), Viking (New York, NY), 1958, with new introduction by author, Heinemann (London, England), 1970.

A Burnt-out Case, Viking (New York, NY), 1961.

In Search of a Character: Two African Journals, Bodley Head (London, England), 1961, Viking (New York, NY), 1962.

Introductions to Three Novels, Norstedt (Stockholm, Sweden), 1962.

The Destructors, and Other Stories, Eihosha (Tokyo, Japan), 1962.

A Sense of Reality, Viking (New York, NY), 1963.

The Comedians, Viking (New York, NY), 1966.

(With Dorothy Craigie) *Victorian Detective Fiction: A Catalogue of the Collection,* Bodley Head (London, England), 1966.

May We Borrow Your Husband?, and Other Comedies of the Sexual Life, Viking (New York, NY), 1967.

Collected Essays, Viking (New York, NY), 1969.

Travels with My Aunt, Viking (New York, NY), 1969.

(Author of introduction) Al Burt and Bernard Diederich, *Papa Doc,* McGraw-Hill (New York, NY), 1969.

A Sort of Life (autobiography), Simon & Schuster (New York, NY), 1971.

Graham Greene on Film: Collected Film Criticism, 1935-1940, Simon & Schuster (New York, NY), 1972, published as *The Pleasure Dome,* Secker & Warburg (London, England), 1972.

The Portable Graham Greene (includes *The Heart of the Matter,* with a new chapter; *The Third Man;* and sections from eight other novels, six short stories, nine critical essays, and ten public statements), Viking (New York, NY), 1972, updated and revised, Penguin (New York, NY), 1994.

The Honorary Consul, Simon & Schuster (New York, NY), 1973, reprinted, 2000.

Collected Stories, Viking (New York, NY), 1973.

Lord Rochester's Monkey, Being the Life of John Wilmot, Second Earl of Rochester, Viking (New York, NY), 1974.

The Human Factor, Simon & Schuster (New York, NY), 1978, reprinted, Knopf (New York, NY), 1992.

Dr. Fischer of Geneva; or, The Bomb Party, Simon & Schuster (New York, NY), 1980.

Ways of Escape, Simon & Schuster (New York, NY), 1981.

Monsignor Quixote, Simon & Schuster (New York, NY), 1982.

J'accuse: The Dark Side of Nice, Bodley Head (London, England), 1982.

Getting to Know the General: The Story of an Involvement, Simon & Schuster (New York, NY), 1984.

The Tenth Man, Bodley Head (London, England), 1985.

(Author of preface) *Night and Day* (journalism), edited by Christopher Hawtree, Chatto & Windus (London, England), 1985.

Collected Short Stories, Penguin (London, England), 1988.

The Captain and the Enemy, Viking (New York, NY), 1988.

Yours, etc.: Letters to the Press, 1945-1989, edited by Christopher Hawtree, Reinhardt (New York, NY), 1989.

Reflections (essays), Viking (New York, NY), 1990.

The Graham Greene Film Reader: Reviews, Essays, Interviews, and Film Stories, Applause Theatre Book Publishers (New York, NY), 1994.

A World of My Own: A Dream Diary, Reinhardt (New York, NY), 1994.

The Last Word and Other Stories, Penguin (New York, NY), 1999.

PLAYS

(With Terrence Rattigan) *Brighton Rock* (screenplay), 1947.

The Fallen Idol (screenplay; based on Greene's short story "The Basement Room"), 1949.

(With Carol Reed) *The Third Man: A Film* (screenplay; based on Greene's novel; produced, 1950), Simon & Schuster (New York, NY), 1968.

The Living Room (two-act; produced in London, England, 1953), Heinemann (London, England), 1953, Viking (New York, NY), 1957.

The Potting Shed (three-act; produced in New York, NY, 1957; produced in London, England, 1958), Viking (New York, NY), 1957.

The Complaisant Lover (produced in London, England, 1959), Heinemann (London, England), 1959, Viking (New York, NY), 1961.

Our Man in Havana (screenplay; based on Greene's novel), 1960.

Three Plays, Mercury Books, 1961.

Carving a Statue (two-act; produced in London, England, 1964; produced in New York, NY, 1968), Bodley Head (London, England), 1964.

The Comedians (screenplay; based on Greene's novel), 1967

The Return of A. J. Raffles (three-act comedy; based on characters from E. W. Hornung's *Amateur Cracksman;* produced in London, England, 1975), Simon & Schuster (New York, NY), 1976.

Yes and No [and] *For Whom the Bell Chimes* (comedies; produced in Leicester, England, 1980), Bodley Head (London, England), 1983.

Collected Plays, Vintage (London, England), 2002.

OMNIBUS VOLUMES

Three: This Gun for Hire; The Confidential Agent; The Ministry of Fear, Viking (New York, NY), 1952.

The Travel Books: Journey without Maps [and] *The Lawless Roads,* Heinemann (London, England), 1963.

Triple Pursuit: A Graham Greene Omnibus (includes *This Gun for Hire, The Third Man,* and *Our Man in Havana*), Viking (New York, NY), 1971.

Works also published in additional collections.

JUVENILE

This Little Fire Engine, Parrish (London, England), 1950, published as *The Little Red Fire Engine,* Lothrop, Lee & Shepard (New York, NY), 1952.

The Little Horse Bus, Parrish (London, England), 1952, Lothrop, Lee & Shepard (New York, NY), 1954.

GREENE

The Little Steamroller, Lothrop, Lee & Shepard (New York, NY), 1955.

The Little Train, Parrish (London, England), 1957, Lothrop, Lee & Shepard (New York, NY), 1958.

The End of the Party, Creative Education (Mankato, MN), 1993.

EDITOR

The Old School (essays), J. Cape (London, England), 1934.

H. H. Munro, *The Best of Saki,* 2nd edition, Lane (London, England), 1952.

(With brother, Hugh Greene) *The Spy's Bedside Book,* British Book Service (London, England), 1957.

(And author of introduction) Marjorie Bowen, *The Viper of Milan,* Bodley Head (London, England), 1960.

The Bodley Head Ford Madox Ford, 2 volumes, Bodley Head (London, England), 1962.

(And author of epilogue) *An Impossible Woman: The Memories of Dottoressa, Moor of Capri,* Viking (New York, NY), 1976.

(With Hugh Greene) *Victorian Villainies,* Viking (New York, NY), 1984.

Contributor to books, including *Twenty-four Short Stories,* Cresset (London, England), 1939; *Alfred Hitchcock's Fireside Book of Suspense,* Simon & Schuster, 1947; and *Why Do I Write?,* Percival Marshall, 1948. Contributor to *Esquire, Commonweal, Spectator, Playboy, Saturday Evening Post, New Statesman, Atlantic, London Mercury, New Republic, America, Life,* and other publications.

ADAPTATIONS: Screenplays based on Greene's books and stories include *Orient Express,* 1934; *This Gun for Hire,* 1942; *The Ministry of Fear,* 1944; *The Confidential Agent,* 1945; *The Smugglers,* 1948; *The Heart of the Matter,* 1954; *The End of the Affair,* 1955, 2000; *Loser Takes All,* 1957; *The Quiet American,* 1958, 2002; *Across the Bridge,* 1958; *Our Man in Havana,* 1959; *The Power and the Glory,* 1962; *The Living Room,* 1969; *The Shipwrecked,* 1970; *May We Borrow Your Husband?,* 1970; *The End of the Affair,* 1971, 2000; *Travels with My Aunt,* 1973; *England Made Me,* 1973; *A Burned-out Case,* 1973; *The Human Factor,* screenplay by Tom Stoppard, directed by Otto Preminger, 1980; *Beyond the Limit,* 1983; and *Strike It Rich* (based on the novella *Loser Takes All*), 1990. Several of Greene's novels have been adapted as audiobooks.

SIDELIGHTS: Graham Greene is among the most widely read of all major English novelists of the twentieth century. Yet Greene's popular success—which David Lodge in the book *Graham Greene* held partly responsible for a "certain academic hostility" toward the British author—came neither quickly nor easily. Of Greene's initial five novels, the first two were never published, and two others, *The Name of Action* and *Rumour at Nightfall,* sold very poorly. In his first autobiographical volume, *A Sort of Life,* Greene lamented that, in his earliest novels, he did not know "how to convey physical excitement": the ability to write a "simple scene of action . . . was quite beyond my power to render exciting." Even as late as 1944, Greene confessed in his introduction to *The Tenth Man,* he had "no confidence" in sustaining his literary career.

Greene's string of literary failures drove him to write *Stamboul Train,* a thriller he hoped would appeal to film producers. The novel, filmed two years later as *Orient Express,* is recognized by critics as Greene's coming-of-age work. Writing in a taut, realistic manner, Greene sets *Stamboul Train* in contemporary Europe; gathers a train load of plausibly motivated characters; and sends them on their journey. Retaining such stock melodramatic devices as cloak-and-dagger intrigue, flight and pursuit, hair-breadth escapes, and a breakneck narrative pace, Greene shifts the focus away from the conventional hero—the hunter—and onto the villain and/or ostensible villain. What emerges is less a formula than a set of literary hardware that Greene would use throughout the rest of his career, not just to produce further entertainments, but to help give outward excitement to his more morally centered, more philosophical novels.

Stamboul Train is the first of several thrillers Greene referred to as "entertainments"—so named to distinguish them from more serious novels. In his next two such entertainments, *A Gun for Sale*—originally published in the United States as *This Gun for Hire*—and *The Confidential Agent,* Greene incorporates elements of detective and spy fiction, respectively. He also injects significant doses of melodrama, detection, and espionage into his more serious novels *Brighton Rock, The Power and the Glory*—published in the United States as *The Labyrinthine Ways*—*The Heart of the Matter, The End of the Affair, The Quiet American, A Burnt-out Case, The Comedians, The Honorary Consul,* and *The Human Factor.* Indeed, so greatly did Greene's entertainments influence his other novels that, after 1958, he dropped the entertainments label.

Intrigue and contemporary politics are key elements of Greene's entertainments, and in at least two of his thrillers Greene eulogizes the tranquility of European life prior to World War I. "It was all so peaceful," Dr. Hasselbacher muses about Germany in *Our Man in Havana,* "in those days. . . . Until the war came." And Arthur Rowe, dreaming in *The Ministry of Fear,* notes that his mother, who "had died before the first great war, . . . could [not] have imagined" the blitz on London of the second. He tells his mother that the sweet Georgian twilight—"Tea on the lawn, evensong, croquet, the old ladies calling, the gentle unmalicious gossip, the gardener trundling the wheelbarrow full of leaves and grass"—"isn't real life any more." Rowe continues: "I'm hiding underground, and up above the Germans are methodically smashing London to bits all round me. . . . It sounds like a thriller, doesn't it, but the thrillers are like life . . . spies, and murders, and violence . . . that's real life."

Suffering, seediness, and sin are also recurring motifs that typify Greene's work. When, in one of the very early novels Greene later disowned, a character moans, "I suffer, therefore I am," he defines both the plight and the habit of mind of many protagonists who would follow him. In *A Burnt-out Case* Dr. Colin sees suffering as a humanizing force: "Sometimes I think that the search for suffering and the remembrance of suffering are the only means we have to put ourselves in touch with the whole human condition." Colin also adds what none of Greene's other characters would dispute: "suffering is not so hard to find."

Greene's characters inhabit a world in which lasting love, according to the narrator of the story "May We Borrow Your Husband?," means the acceptance of "every disappointment, every failure, every betrayal." By Greene's twenty-second novel, *Doctor Fischer of Geneva; or, The Bomb Party,* suffering has become a sufficient cause for having a soul. When the narrator of *Doctor Fischer of Geneva* tells his wife, "If souls exist you certainly have one," and she asks "Why?," he replies, "You've suffered." This statement may well sound masochistic—"Pain is part of joy," the whiskey priest asserts in *The Power and the Glory,* "pain is a part of pleasure"; but as Greene wrote in the essay "Hans Andersen," it is really the "Catholic ideal of the acceptance of pain for a spiritual benefit." This ideal is behind the saintly Sarah's striking statement in *The End of the Affair:* "How good You [God] are. You might have killed us with happiness, but You let us be with You in pain."

According to Kenneth Allott and Miriam Farris Allott in their book *The Art of Graham Greene,* "Seediness . . . seems to Greene the most honest representation of the nature of things." One recurring character embodying this trait in Greene's fiction, for example, appears as early as the opening chapters of *The Man Within.* From the "shambling," bored priest in that novel who sniffles his way through the burial service for Elizabeth's guardian; to the wheezing old priest smelling of eucalyptus at the end of *Brighton Rock;* to the whiskey priest in *The Power and the Glory;* to the broken-down Father Callifer in *The Potting Shed* with his "stubbly worn face," "bloodshot eyes," and "dirty wisp of a Roman collar," Greene anoints a small cathedral of seedy priests. In his critical study *Graham Greene,* Francis Wyndham summarized an objection whose validity each reader must judge for himself: "Some find [Greene's] continual emphasis on squalor and seediness . . . overdone."

Also typical of Greene's characters is their predilection for sin. Greene "seems to have been born with a belief in Original Sin," John Atkins suggested in his *Graham Greene,* and certainly the author's characters have been tainted by it. Raven in *A Gun for Sale* is but one of many Greene protagonists who "had been marked from birth." Another is the whiskey priest's illegitimate daughter in *The Power and the Glory:* "The world was in her heart already, like the small spot of decay in the fruit." Likewise, D. the "confidential agent": "Give me time," he thinks, "and I shall infect anything." Atkins "can almost hear [Greene's] teeth gnashing at those who omitted to sleep with someone else's wife or husband . . . it is difficult to read Greene's fiction without sensing a contempt for sinlessness." Atkins concluded: Greene's "concern with sin has become so intense he finds a life without sin to be devoid of meaning." But George Orwell's witty complaint about Greene in *The Collected Essays, Journalism, and Letters of George Orwell* is the best known. Labeling his subject the leader of the "cult of the sanctified sinner," Orwell declares that Greene shows a Catholic's "snobbishness" about sin: "There is something *distingue* in being damned; Hell is a sort of high-class nightclub, entry to which is reserved for Catholics only."

Although Greene's conversion to Catholicism has generated an intense critical debate, only five or six of his more than twenty novels actually focus on the faith: *Brighton Rock, The Power and the Glory, The Heart of the Matter*—the so-called "Catholic trilogy"—*The End of the Affair, Monsignor Quixote,* and, perhaps, *A Burnt-out Case.* In exploring Catholicism in his fiction, Greene eschewed propaganda. He noted in *Ways of Escape,* his second volume of autobiography, that he was "not a Catholic writer but a writer who happens to be a Catholic." That is, Catholicism does not provide a dogma he wishes to promulgate in his novels but instead supplies a framework within which he can measure the human situation. "I'm not a religious man," Greene once told *Catholic World* interviewer Gene D. Phillips, "though it interests me. Religion is important, as atomic science is."

Despite the attention paid his Catholicism, Greene explained to Phillips that religion occupied only "one period" of his writing career: "My period of Catholic novels was preceded and followed by political novels." Greene's first successful novels were written in the 1930s. In *Ways of Escape* Greene defines the mid-1930s as "clouded by the Depression in England . . . and by the rise of Hitler. It was impossible in those days not to be committed, and it is hard to recall details of one's private life as the enormous battlefield was prepared around us." Greene's earlier political novels are set in Europe, usually in England, but more recent political novels move from one Third-World trouble spot to another even as they explore the author's characteristic themes: commitment, betrayal, corruption, sin, suffering, and the nature of human sexuality, often against a backdrop of Catholicism.

In both religion and politics Greene opposed the dogmatic and the doctrinaire, sided against those who sacrifice the corrupt but living human spirit for a grand but bloodless thesis. For example, in *Monsignor Quixote,* however much the good-natured priest and the equally good-natured communist politician quibble, both reject the intellectual rigidities of those whose commitment to their respective causes is ideologically absolute. Politics and religion, then, are closely related. *Monsignor Quixote* is at once political and religious in nature; and, while nobody denies that *The Power and the Glory* is one of Greene's Catholic works, it can also be studied as a political novel.

Not only a novelist, Greene wrote in more than a dozen other genres, including novellas, short stories, plays, radio plays, screenplays, essays, memoirs, biographies, autobiographies, travel books, poetry, and children's literature. Although Greene made his mark primarily in the novel form, his stories, plays, and nonfiction prose have all attracted critical consideration.

About the short-story genre, Greene wrote in *Ways of Escape:* "I remain in this field a novelist who happens to have written short stories." Unfailingly modest in appraising his own literary efforts, Greene said in an introductory note to his *Nineteen Stories,* "I am only too conscious of the defects of these stories. . . . The short story is an exacting form which I have not properly practised." He dismissed his stories as "merely . . . the by-products of a novelist's career." However true this evaluation might be for *Nineteen Stories,* and however correct Lodge might be in calling the short story a "form in which [Greene] has never excelled," some of Greene's stories do merit reading. Even John Atkins, who in *Graham Greene* concurred with Lodge that the "short story is not one of Greene's successful forms," conceded that the four newer works in the expanded collection *Twenty-one Stories* "show an improvement" over those in the earlier volume. And in *Ways of Escape* Greene registered contentment with "The Destructors," "A Chance for Mr. Lever," "Under the Garden," and "Cheap in August": "I have never written anything better than" these works, he declared.

Less distinguished than his fiction, Greene's dramas provided him with, if nothing else, diversion. He recorded—indeed, almost bragged about—his lifelong attempt to escape depression and boredom, starting with Russian roulette as a teenager and culminating in a career as a restless, wandering novelist who, when his mainstay got boring, tried to escape by shifting genres. Writing plays, he declared in *Ways of Escape,* "offered me novelty, an escape from the everyday": "I needed a rest from novels."

As with Greene's short fiction, critics have not been overly enthusiastic about the novelist's plays, although *The Complaisant Lover* attracted some applause. Philip Stratford, in his book *Faith and Fiction,* called it an "outstanding and original achievement," while to Atkins it ranks as "vital as many of the Restoration comedies." Of Greene's plays overall, Smith pointed to a "curious lack . . . of memorable characters," a quality not shared with Greene's novels. On the whole most critics agreed with Lodge's assessment that "it does not seem likely that Greene will add a significant chapter to the history of British drama." Despite this dismissal, Greene's plays—which include *The Living Room, The Potting Shed,* and *Carving a Statue*—remained in print decades after their first mid-twentieth-century productions.

Greene's nonfiction prose, though not widely analyzed, has been more appreciated. Metaphorical and speculative, his travel books are distinctly literary, and record spiritual no less than physical journeys. Greene's first travel book, *Journey without Maps,* is representative of his work in the genre. Believing Africa to be "not a particular place, but a shape, . . . that of the human heart," Greene imagined his actual trip as, simultaneously, a descent, with Sigmund Freud as guide, into the collective soul of humanity in a quest of "those ancestral threads which still exist in our unconscious minds." Greene finds in Africa "associations with a personal and racial childhood"; and when in the end he returns to civilization, the conclusion he draws about his experience affirms the "lost childhood" theme about which he so frequently wrote: "This journey, if it had done nothing else, had reinforced a sense of disappointment with what man had made out of the primitive, what he had made out of childhood."

The essay collection *Reflections,* which brings together various nonfiction pieces such as film reviews, travel essays, and examinations of communism, Catholicism, and major literary figures, as well as *A World of My Own: A Dream Diary,* which presents dreams Greene recorded throughout his life, provide readers with greater insight into the novelist. Malcolm Bradbury, writing in the *New York Times Book Review,* concluded of the latter volume: "It's not surprising that the strange tales told here—and they do emerge as tales, not as random notes on disconnected, chaotic events—are as powerful as his fiction, and interweave with it. Greene's *World of My Own*—a carefully organized and edited selection from his dream diaries, which he made and introduced himself, just before his death—is equally the world of his novels, his distinctive, adventurous life as an author, his enigmatic character as a man."

Not surprisingly, commentators frequently turn to Greene's nonfiction pieces to aid their understanding of his fiction. "Fresh and stimulating," as Wyndham noted, the author's essays throw "much light on [Greene's] own work as a novelist." But the essays are worth reading in their own right. Atkins contended that "when Greene's criticism is gathered together we

realize how very good it is," that Greene "has unerring good judgment in all literary matters. He can always be relied upon to see through falsity and to detect the ring of truth in others." Atkins went so far as to maintain that Greene's "criticism is much more free of fault than his fiction."

From 1935 to 1940 Greene wrote film reviews for the *Spectator* and in 1937 performed the same service for *Night and Day.* These reviews have been collected in *The Graham Greene Film Reader,* which also includes reviews of film books, interviews, lectures, letters, scripts he wrote for short documentaries, film stories, and film treatments. "What provides pleasure in these musings on the movies," noted Pat Dowell in the *Washington Post Book World,* "is the glittering nuggets of a prose stylist who writes of the young Bette Davis's 'corrupt and phosphorescent prettiness' or pens a hilariously exasperated description of the unintentionally magnificent surrealism of *The Garden of Allah.*" Writing in the *New Republic* Stanley Kauffmann commented, "Overall, this assemblage of Greene's criticism is a boon."

In addition, more than twenty of his own novels and stories have been filmed, some with his own screenplays. Furthermore, Greene wrote original screenplays, including the 1949 classic *The Third Man.* It is, then, understandable that to the *Paris Review* interviewers he called himself a "film man."

Greene's cinematic prose method is evident in his first successful novel, *Stamboul Train.* Creating this work admittedly with one eye on the film camera, Greene intersperses passages of extended narrative with brief cuts from one character or group of characters to another. This device both sustains the novel's full-throttle pace by generating a sense of motion—appropriate to a story whose center is a speeding express train—and, with great economy, evokes the stew of humanity thrown together at a railway station or on a train. The union of film and fiction is even pondered in *Stamboul Train* by the character Q. C. Savory, who seems to describe Greene's own ambition to incorporate aspects of film into his fiction: "One thing the films had taught the eye, Savory thought, the beauty of the landscape in motion, how a church tower moved behind and above the trees, how it dipped and soared with the uneven human stride, the loveliness of a chimney rising towards a cloud and sinking behind the further cowls. That sense of movement must be conveyed in prose."

Although acclaimed for his work in various genres, it is as a novelist that Greene remains most respected. Indeed, some critics have cited him as the leading English novelist of his generation; in Lodge's view, among the British novelists who were Greene's contemporaries, "it is difficult to find his equal." Smith's evaluation—that Greene navigated "one of the more remarkable careers in twentieth-century fiction"—may seem by some to be understated when considered alongside the judgment of a *Times Literary Supplement* reviewer that Greene follows in the tradition of writers like Henry James, Joseph Conrad, and Ford Madox Ford. But it was, perhaps, Wyndham who came closest to explaining Greene's sustained popularity when he stated, simply, "Everything [Greene wrote] is readable."

BIOGRAPHICAL AND CRITICAL SOURCES:

BOOKS

Allain, Marie-Françoise, *The Other Man: Conversations with Graham Greene*, Bodley Head (London, England), 1983.

Allen, Walter, *The Modern Novel*, Dutton (New York, NY), 1965.

Allott, Kenneth, and Miriam Farris Allott, *The Art of Graham Greene*, Hamish Hamilton (London, England), 1951, Russell & Russell, 1965.

Atkins, John, *Graham Greene*, Roy, 1958.

Bestsellers 89, Issue 4, Gale (Detroit, MI), 1989.

Boardman, Gwenn R., *Graham Greene: The Aesthetics of Exploration*, University of Florida Press, 1971.

Cassis, A. F., *Graham Greene: An Annotated Bibliography of Criticism*, Scarecrow (Metuchen, NJ), 1981.

Contemporary Literary Criticism, Gale (Detroit, MI), Volume 1, 1973, Volume 3, 1975, Volume 6, 1976, Volume 9, 1978, Volume 14, 1980, Volume 18, 1981, Volume 27, 1984, Volume 37, 1986, Volume 70, 1992, Volume 72, 1992.

DeVitis, L. A., *Graham Greene*, Twayne (New York, NY), 1964.

Dictionary of Literary Biography, Gale (Detroit, MI), Volume 13: *British Dramatists since World War II*, 1982, Volume 15: *British Novelists, 1930-1959*, 1983, Volume 77: *British Mystery Writers, 1920-1939*, 1989.

Dictionary of Literary Biography Yearbook: 1985, Gale (Detroit, MI), 1986.

Duraan, Leopoldo, *Graham Greene: An Intimate Portrait by His Closest Friend and Confidant*, Harper (San Francisco, CA), 1994.

Duraan, Leopoldo, *Graham Greene: Friend and Brother*, HarperCollins (London, England), 1994.

Evans, R. O., editor, *Graham Greene: Some Critical Considerations*, University of Kentucky Press (Lexington, KY), 1963.

Falk, Quentin, *Travels in Greeneland: The Cinema of Graham Greene*, Quartet (London, England), 1984.

Gordon, Hayim, *Fighting Evil: Unsung Heroes in the Novels of Graham Greene*, Greenwood Press (New York, NY), 1997.

Greene, Graham, *A Sort of Life*, Simon & Schuster (New York, NY), 1971.

Greene, Graham, *Our Man in Havana*, Viking (New York, NY), 1958, with new introduction by author, Heinemann (London, England), 1970.

Greene, Graham, *The Graham Greene Film Reader: Reviews, Essays, Interviews and Film Stories*, Applause Theatre Book Publishers (New York, NY), 1994.

Greene, Graham, with A. F. Cassis, *Graham Greene: Man of Paradox*, Loyola University Press (Chicago, IL), 1994.

Hill, William Thomas, *The Search for Dwelling and Its Relationship to Journeying and Wandering in the Novels of Graham Greene*, International Scholars Publication, 1998.

Hoskins, Robert, *Graham Greene: An Approach to the Novels*, Garland (New York, NY), 1998.

Hynes, Samuel, editor, *Graham Greene: A Collection of Critical Essays*, Prentice-Hall (New York, NY), 1973.

Kermode, Frank, *Puzzles and Epiphanies*, Chilmark (New York, NY), 1962.

Kunkel, Francis L., *The Labyrinthine Ways of Graham Greene*, Sheed (London, England), 1959.

Living Writers, Sylvan Press, 1947.

Lodge, David, *Graham Greene*, Columbia University Press (New York, NY), 1966.

Malamet, Elliott, *The World Remade: Graham Greene and the Art of Detection*, P. Lang (New York, NY), 1998.

Mauriac, François, *Great Men*, Rockliff, 1952.

Mesnet, Maire-Beatrice, *Graham Greene and the Heart of the Matter*, Cresset (London, England), 1954.

Miller, Robert H., *Graham Greene: A Descriptive Catalog,* University of Kentucky Press (Lexington, KY), 1979.

Mueller, Walter R., *The Prophetic Voice in Modern Fiction,* Association Press, 1959.

Newby, P. H., *The Novel: 1945-1950,* Longmans, Green (London, England), 1951.

O'Faolain, Dean, *The Vanishing Hero,* Atlantic Monthly Press (Boston, MA), 1956.

Pendleton, Robert, *Graham Greene's Conradian Masterplot: The Arabesques of Influence,* St. Martin's Press (New York, NY), 1996.

Prescott, Orville, *In My Opinion,* Bobbs-Merrill (Chicago, IL), 1952.

Reed, Henry, *The Novel since 1939,* Longmans, Green (London, England), 1947.

Rostenne, Paul, *Graham Greene: Temoin des temps tragiques,* Juilliard, 1949.

Shelden, Michael, *Graham Greene: The Enemy Within,* Random House (New York, NY), 1994.

Sherry, Norman, *The Life of Graham Greene,* Viking (New York, NY), Volume 1: *1904-1939,* 1989, Volume 2: *1939-1955,* 1995.

Stratford, Philip, *Faith and Fiction,* University of Notre Dame Press, 1964.

Vann, Jerry Donn, *Graham Greene: A Checklist of Criticism,* University of Kentucky Press (Lexington, KY), 1970.

Watts, Cedric Thomas, *A Preface to Greene,* Longman (London, England), 1997.

West, W. J., *The Quest for Graham Greene,* St. Martin's Press (New York, NY), 1998.

Wobbe, R. A., *Graham Greene: A Bibliography and Guide to Research,* Garland (New York, NY), 1979.

Wyndham, Francis, *Graham Greene,* Longmans, Green (London, England), 1955.

Zabel, Morton Dauwen, *Craft and Character in Modern Fiction,* Viking (New York, NY), 1957.

PERIODICALS

America, January 25, 1941.

Atlantic, July-August, 2002, Peter Godman, "Graham Greene's Vatican Dossier," p. 84.

Booklist, April 15, 1999, Mary McCay, review of *The Third Man,* p. 1542.

British Heritage, February-March, 2002, Barbara Roisman-Cooper, "Graham Greene: The Man behind the Mask," p. 48.

Catholic World, December, 1954, pp. 172-175; August, 1969, pp. 218-221.

College English, October, 1950, pp. 1-9.

Explicator, spring, 2003, David Robertson, "Greene's 'Jubilee,'" p. 168.

First Things, November, 1999, Robert Royal, "The (Mis)Guided Dreams of Graham Greene," p. 16.

Globe and Mail (Toronto, Ontario, Canada), September 29, 1984.

Kliatt, July, 2002, Janet Julian, review of *The Comedians,* p. 49.

Library Journal, February 1, 1999, p. 138; July, 2001, p. 149; January, 2002, Nancy Pearl, review of *The End of the Affair,* p. 188.

Life, February 4, 1966.

London Magazine, June-July, 1977, pp. 35-45.

Los Angeles Times, September 25, 1980; January 2, 1981; March 20, 1985.

Los Angeles Times Book Review, October 23, 1988; October 23, 1994.

Modern Fiction Studies, autumn, 1957, pp. 249-288.

New Republic, December 5, 1994, p. 30.

New Statesman, November 27, 2000, John Gray, "A Touch of Evil," p. 51; December 3, 2001, Maureen Freely, "On Graham Greene's *The Quiet American,*" p. 55.

New Yorker, April 11, 1994, p. 46.

New York Review of Books, March 3, 1966; June 8, 1995; June 22, 1995; February 13, 2003, Pico Iyer, review of *The Quiet American,* p. 19.

New York Times, February 27, 1978; May 19, 1980; January 18, 1981; September 24, 1982; October 25, 1984; March 4, 1985; June 6, 1985; October 17, 1988; January 17, 1995.

New York Times Book Review, January 23, 1966; January 8, 1995.

Playboy, November, 1994, p. 32.

Renascence, winter, 1999, p. 133; fall, 2002 (special Greene issue).

Smithsonian, June, 2002, Bob Cullen, "Heart of the Matter: Graham Greene's Letters to His Paramour, Catherine Walston, Trace the Hazy Line between Life and Fiction," p. 112.

Southwest Review, summer, 1956, pp. 239-250.

Time, September 20, 1982.

Times (London), September 6, 1984; September 7, 1984; March 14, 1985; February 5, 1990.

Times Literary Supplement, January 27, 1966; March 28, 1980; March 15, 1985.

Washington Post, April 3, 1980; September 20, 1988.

Washington Post Book World, May 18, 1980; October 16, 1988; March 12, 1995.

World Press Review, December, 1981, pp. 31-32; April, 1983, p. 62.

OBITUARIES:

PERIODICALS

Detroit Free Press, April 4, 1991.
Guardian (London, England), April4, 1991.
New York Times, April 4, 1991.
Time, April 15, 1991.*

*   *   *

GREENWALD, Sheila
    See GREEN, Sheila Ellen

*   *   *

GREGORIAN, Vartan 1934-
    (V. Herian)

Vartan Gregorian

PERSONAL: Born April 8, 1934, in Tabriz, Iran; immigrated to the United States, 1956; son of Samuel B. (a government employee) and Shushanik G. (Mirzaian) Gregorian; married Clare Russell, March 25, 1960; children: Vahe, Raffi, Dareh (sons). *Education:* Collège Armenien, Beirut, Lebanon, diploma (Armenian studies), 1955; Stanford University, B.A., 1958 (with honors), Ph.D., 1964. *Hobbies and other interests:* Movies, concerts, chess, Armenian music, travel, walking, reading.

ADDRESSES: Office—Office of the President, Carnegie Corporation of New York, 437 Madison Ave., Floor 27, New York, NY 10022-7001.

CAREER: Worked as a reporter in Beirut, Lebanon, c. 1956; Stanford University, Stanford, CA, assistant foreign student adviser, 1959-60; University of California—Berkeley, instructor in Armenian history and culture, 1960; San Francisco State College (now University), San Francisco, CA, instructor, 1962-64, assistant professor, 1964-66, associate professor of history, 1966-68; University of California—Los Angeles, visiting associate professor of history, 1968; University of Texas—Austin, associate professor, 1968-70, professor of history, 1970-72; University of Pennsylvania, Philadelphia, professor of history and Tarzian Professor of

Armenian and Caucasian History, 1972-80, faculty assistant to president and provost, 1973-74, dean of Faculty of Arts and Sciences, 1974-78, provost, 1978-80; New York Public Library, New York, NY, president, 1981-89; New School for Social Research (now New School University), New York, NY, professor, 1984-89; New York University, New York, NY, professor of history and Near Eastern studies, 1984-89; Brown University, Providence, RI, president and professor of history, 1989-97; Carnegie Corp., New York, NY, president, 1997—. Chair of board of visitors, Graduate School and University Center, City University of New York, 1984-90; member of board of trustees, Museum of Modern Art, 1994. Member of board of directors, International League of Human Rights, 1984-97, Institute for Advanced Study, 1987, J. Paul Getty Trust, 1988, Institute for International Education, 1989-95, Aaron Diamond Foundation, 1990-97, Brookings Institutions, 1994-97, Aga Khan University, 1995, Human Rights Watch, 1996, McGraw-Hill Companies, Cell Therapeutics, Inc.; member, Bill and Melinda Gates Foundation; advisor, Annenberg Foundation.

MEMBER: International Federation of Library Associations (cochair of program committee, 1985), Academy of Arts and Sciences (fellow), American

Philosophical Society, American Antiquarian Society, American Historical Association (program chair, 1972), Association for the Advancement of Slavic Studies (program chair of Western Slavic Conference, 1967), Mid-East Studies Association, Council for Foreign Relations, Grolier Club, Round Table, Century Association, Phi Beta Kappa.

AWARDS, HONORS: Social Science Research Council fellowship, 1960; Ford Foundation foreign area fellowship, 1960-62; American Council of Learned Societies-Social Science Research Council fellowship, 1965-66, 1971-72; American Philosophical Society grants, 1965, 1966; E. H. Harbison Distinguished Teaching Award, Danforth Foundation, 1968; John Simon Guggenheim fellowship, 1971-72; Cactus Teaching award, 1971; American Council of Education fellowship, 1972-73; Golden Medal of Honor, City and Province of Vienna, Austria, 1976; Silver Cultural Medal, Italian Ministry of Foreign Affairs, 1977; award of distinction, Phi Lambda Theta and Phi Delta Kappa, 1980; First Distinguished Humanist award, Pennsylvania Humanities Council, 1983; National Fellowship award, Fellowship Commission (Philadelphia, PA), 1984; Gold Medal, National Institute for Social Sciences, 1985; decorated Officier de l'Ordre des Arts et des Lettres (France), 1995, and Grand Oficial Ordem Infante D. Henrique (Portugal), 1995; Distinguished Service to the Arts award, Third St. Music School Settlement, 1997; Distinguished Service to Public Education award, New York Academy of Public Education, 1998; Friends of the Arts award, Town Hall, 1998; National Humanities Medal, United States government, 1998. Honorary degrees from Boston University, 1983, Brown University, 1984, Jewish Theological Seminary, 1984, State University of New York, 1985, Johns Hopkins University, 1987, New York University, 1987, University of Pennsylvania, 1988, Dartmouth College, 1989, Rutgers University, 1989, City University of New York, 1990, Tufts University, 1994, University of Aberdeen, University of Illinois, and the Juilliard School. Also recipient of honors from Urban League, League of Women Voters, Players Club, PEN-American Center, Literacy Volunteers of New York, American Institute of Architects, and Charles A. Dana Foundation; has received additional honors from the city and state of New York, the states of Massachusetts, Texas, Pennsylvania, and Rhode Island, and the cities of Fresno, CA; Austin, TX; Providence, RI; and San Francisco, CA.

WRITINGS:

(Editor) Simon Vratzian, *Hin Tghter Nor Patmutian Hamar* (title means "Old Papers for the New History"), [Beirut, Lebanon], 1962.
(Editor) Simon Vratzian, *Kianki Oughinerov* (memoirs), Volume 5, [Beirut, Lebanon], 1966.
The Emergence of Modern Afghanistan: Politics of Reform and Modernization, 1880-1946, Stanford University Press (Stanford, CA), 1969.
Carved in Sand: A Report on the Collapse of the Rhode Island Share and Deposit Indemnity Corporation, State of Rhode Island (Providence, RI), 1991.
New York Public Library Desk Reference, Hungry Minds, 1993.
(Editor) *Censorship: Five Hundred Years of Conflict,* Oxford University Press (New York, NY), 1997.
The Road to Home: My Life and Times (memoir), Simon & Schuster (New York, NY), 2003.
Higher Education in an Age of Specialized Knowledge (sound recording), 2003.
Islam: A Mosaic, Not a Monolith, Brookings Institution Press (Washington, DC), 2003.

Contributor, sometimes under pseudonym V. Herian, to encyclopedias and to journals in United States, Iran, and Lebanon.

SIDELIGHTS: Born the son of Armenian parents in a city in northern Iran, Vartan Gregorian has turned his love of books and education into a distinguished career that has included positions as a history professor, president of Brown University and the New York Public Library, and president of the prestigious Carnegie Corporation of New York, whose goal is to award grants to worthy educational and cultural causes. Those familiar with Gregorian, who speaks Persian, English, Armenian, Turkish, Arabic, and French, know him as an erudite man whose love of learning has never stopped, and he has made it his mission in life to spread his values in education to his adopted country, America. Not only has he done this in the classroom as a teacher of history and world cultures, but Gregorian has astounded many observers with his abilities in fundraising. As president of the New York Public Library during the 1980s, he was able to increase the library's budget by nearly twofold while restoring the system's main library at a cost of $42 million. As president of Brown University, he raised $537 million.

In 1997 Gregorian became president of Carnegie Corporation, switching his role from fundraiser to fund-granter. The transition turned out to be a surprising one for him. As he told Bruce Cole in an interview for *Humanities,* "People think that giving away money is an easy job. Actually, it's harder than raising money, as you well know, because you have so many excellent projects that compete for funding. The issue is, I tell our staff: Are we going to be an incubator or an oxygen tank? Foundations have to be in the idea business, not the need business. Everyone has needs. And finally, we have to prepare the next generation of leaders, scholars, and thinkers."

Throughout Gregorian's career, his concern for the state of education in the United States has remained a common theme. He has become increasingly worried about America's deemphasizing studies in the humanities, which has been replaced by the desire to learn marketable skills, and he is concerned by the failure of high schools to prepare students for college so that they often spend the first two years at universities trying to catch up to where they should be. As he told Cole: "I'm worried about what's happening. Consciously or unconsciously, there has emerged a perception in the United States that somehow liberal arts should be for elite institutions and that your community colleges and your big state universities and others should concentrate on careers rather than on learning, per se. The higher the tuition goes up, the more parents tend to say, 'What's the earning power of a degree going to be?' That worries me. Our democracy may have an aristocracy of talent, as Jefferson said—which is fine—but we don't want everyone else to be left out. Something like that seems to be happening, though."

Gregorian added, "Similarly, for science to become an elective rather than central would also be a great loss. As a person who cheated himself by not taking science courses, I'm very conscious of how the sciences are sometimes relegated to the periphery of the liberal arts. Furthermore, we're doing something wrong when we say, it doesn't matter how much knowledge there is, you're going to be educated in four years by hook or crook, by condensation or summary. Now, more than ever, the university has to teach you how to learn to learn, and to teach you not only what you know, but also what you don't know. As a matter of fact, at one time I thought of giving a diploma that said, 'Con-

gratulations for knowing this much, and now we instruct you to learn for the rest of your life,' just to make the point that we are sending the graduate into the world with a map, with a compass, with a Geiger counter, with a hunting license, to go and learn."

In 2003 Gregorian published his memoirs, *The Road to Home: My Life and Times.* Here, he takes the time to acknowledge all the family members, friends, and others who helped him get where he is today, while relating his "rags-to-riches" story, as one *Publishers Weekly,* reviewer called it. The critic, while feeling that the later parts of the book, in which Gregorian describes his achievement, are somewhat overly detailed and dry, appreciated the parts in which Gregorian's love of literature "opens a doorway to history and to Persian and Armenian literature." The reviewer also enjoyed the author's "sense of wonder" as he relates stories of his early days in the United States. Peter Gay, in *New York Times Book Review,* praised the memoir as a "full account of a worthwhile life that has rewarded thousands of students and more thousands of readers. If the word had not been so badly debased in our time, I would call [Gregorian] a civilian hero."

Among Gregorian's other writings are books on Middle Eastern affairs, including *The Emergence of Modern Afghanistan: Politics of Reform and Modernization, 1880-1946* and *Islam: A Mosaic, Not a Monolith,* which attempt to explain Arabic culture to western audiences.

BIOGRAPHICAL AND CRITICAL SOURCES:

PERIODICALS

American Libraries, August, 2003, Cathleen Bourdon, "Up Close and Personal," p. 96.
Chronicle of Higher Education, March 29, 1989, Lawrence Biemiller, "The Unruly Schedule and Unpredictable Syntax of Vartan Gregorian," p. A3.
New York, January 16, 1984, Jennifer Allen, "The Library's Social Lion: On the Go with Gregorian," p. 34.
New Yorker, November, 1986, Art Plotnick, "Library Vartanization; or, the New Supra-Chiefs: If You've Got a Vartan Gregorian, It Works; Otherwise . . . ," p. 736.
New York Times Book Review, September 21, 2003, Peter Gay, "The Lion King," p. 14.

New York Times Magazine, December 14, 1997, Claudia Dreifus, "It Is Better to Give Than to Receive," p. 52.

Publishers Weekly, May 5, 2003, review of *The Road to Home: My Life and Times,* p. 214.

Rolling Stone, March 21, 1991, Norman Atkins, "The Making of the President," p. 63.

ONLINE

Humanities, http://www.neh.fed.us/news/humanities/ (September-October, 2003), Bruce Cole, "A Conversation with Vartan Gregorian."

H-J

HARUF, Kent 1943-

PERSONAL: Surname rhymes with "sheriff"; born February 24, 1943, in Pueblo, CO; son of Louis A. (a Methodist preacher) and Eleanor V. (a teacher and homemaker; maiden name, Shaver) Haruf; married Virginia K. Koon (divorced); married Cathy Dempsey; children: Sorel, Whitney, Chaney (daughters). *Education:* Nebraska Wesleyan University, B.A., 1965; University of Iowa, M.F.A., 1973.

ADDRESSES: Home—P. O. Box 1580, Salida, CO 81201. *Agent*—Peter Matson, Sterling Lord Literistic, 65 Bleecker St., New York, NY 10012.

CAREER: Worked odd jobs, including farm laborer, construction worker, rural paper route carrier, hospital orderly, railroad worker, librarian, and orphanage house parent; served in the Peace Corps in Turkey, 1965-67; taught high school English in Wisconsin and Colorado, 1976-86; Nebraska Wesleyan University, Lincoln, assistant professor, 1986-91; Southern Illinois University, Carbondale, associate professor, 1991-2000.

AWARDS, HONORS: PEN/Hemingway Foundation Special Citation, 1985; American Library Notable Books Award, 1985; Whiting Writer's Award, Mrs. Giles Whiting Foundation, 1986, for *The Tie That Binds;* Maria Thomas Award, 1991; National Book Award finalist in fiction, 1999, Mt. Plains Booksellers Award, 2000, *Salon.com* Award, 2000, Alex Award, 2000, *New Yorker* Fiction Award finalist, 2000, *Los Angeles Times* Fiction Award finalist, 2000, *Book Sense* Award finalist, 2000, 10th Colorado Evil Companions

Kent Haruf

Literary Award, 2002, and OneBook-AZ 2003 award, nominated for the Dublin IMPAC 2001 Literary Award, all for *Plainsong.*

WRITINGS:

NOVELS

The Tie That Binds, Holt (New York, NY), 1984.

215

Where You Once Belonged, Summit Books (New York, NY), 1991.

Plainsong, Knopf (New York, NY), 1999.

Eventide, Knopf (New York, NY), 2004.

Also contributor of short stories to periodicals, including *Puerto del Sol, Grand Street, Prairie Schooner,* and *Gettysburg Review.* Stories have appeared in *Best American Short Stories,* Houghton Mifflin (Boston, MA), 1987; and *Where Past Meets Present,* University of Colorado Press (Boulder, CO), 1994.

ADAPTATIONS: Haruf's short story "Private Debts/ Public Holdings" was adapted into a short film by Nancy Cooperstein for Chanticleer Films, 1987. CBS has acquired an option for TV rights to *Plainsong* and *The Tie That Binds. Plainsong* has been adapted for audio.

SIDELIGHTS: The son of a Methodist minister, Kent Haruf was born and raised in the flatlands of northeastern Colorado, an environment that provides the background for his fiction. Haruf's career path to his longtime ambition of writing was a slow and convoluted one, involving attendance at several universities, a stint in the Peace Corps in Turkey (where he penned his first short stories), and numerous odd jobs, including being a janitor while he waited for the Iowa Writers Workshop to "take pity on him," as he told *Denver Post* interviewer Nancy Lofholm. After graduating from the prestigious University of Iowa Writers Workshop at the age of thirty, Haruf again worked construction and shelved library books in Colorado, then taught high-school English while he slowly developed his writing. He did not make his first appearance in print, a short story in a literary magazine, until eleven years later at the age of forty-one. That same year, 1984, his first novel was published. Speaking with John Blades of *Publishers Weekly,* Haruf described Holt, the fictional town that provides the setting for his novels, as his own "little postage stamp of native soil." Holt is a small Colorado farming community, close to the Kansas and Nebraska borders and more akin to the rural environments of those states than it is to cosmopolitan Denver to the west. Blades noted: "Along with its surrounding farms and homesteads, Holt has proved as fertile—and will perhaps be as inexhaustible—for Haruf's fiction as the apocryphal Yoknapatawpha County was for Faulkner's."

Haruf's first novel, *The Tie That Binds,* chronicles the long, hard life of Edith Goodnough, born near the turn of the twentieth century. Edith's story is told by Sand-

ers Roscoe, the son of the man Edith loved but refused to marry, giving up her chance at happiness to care for a tyrannical crippled father. *The Tie That Binds* garnered Haruf several honors, including the 1986 Whiting Writer's Award. The novel was praised by critics as well; Ruth Doan MacDougall in the *Christian Science Monitor* observed that Haruf's "characters live, and the voice of his narrator reverberates after the last page: humorous, ironic, loving." Chris Wall in the *Los Angeles Times Book Review* hailed *The Tie That Binds* as "an impressive, expertly crafted work of sensitivity and detail, absent the hokum that usually accompanies sad tales of simple women and their domineering fathers." Haruf also won accolades from Perry Glasser in the *New York Times Book Review.* The critic declared that the author's "work is rooted in a sense of place; his eye and ear are faithful to his subject." The novel brought him "a $25,000 Whiting Award, a PEN/ Hemingway citation, and a job teaching freshman composition at Nebraska Wesleyan," according to Blades.

Haruf followed *The Tie That Binds* with his 1991 work, *Where You Once Belonged.* This book centers on Jack Burdette, a villainous former high school football hero who manages to ruin many lives in his home town of Holt, Colorado. Narrating Jack's story is a man with a stake in the events, newspaper editor Pat Arbuckle. Richard Eder in the *Los Angeles Times Book Review* offered a laudatory assessment of *Where You Once Belonged,* calling it "taut and deadly," and applauding the "disciplined economy" of "Haruf's writing." The critic concluded that the author's second novel is a "stirring and remarkable book." A *Publishers Weekly* reviewer called the book a "deeply affecting novel," and noted that "not a word is wasted in [Haruf's] brooding drama." A commentator for *Kirkus Reviews* observed that Haruf "does a beautiful job of capturing small-town life."

Haruf wrote his first two novels by conventional means. With his third he tried a radically different approach. Removing his glasses and placing a stocking cap (not wool) over his eyes, he typed his first draft blind on an old manual typewriter. Haruf's aim, as related by Blades, was "to achieve freshness and spontaneity without being distracted by the sight of words on the page." Haruf also told the *Boston Herald*'s Rosemary Herbert, "Unlike the computer, which needs another command to make the work go on paper, the typewriter is more simple, direct. Something about the sound of the keys hitting makes an obvious connection between what you think and the results you get." The result was *Plainsong,* a novel subsequently lauded by critics even more highly than Haruf's earlier books. Even before its publication, *Plainsong* began drawing special attention. According to Daisy Maryles of *Publishers Weekly,* "Knopf's enthusiasm for [the novel] began last spring with the manuscript being passed around in-house; for a while, it was the most photocopied manuscript on Knopf's fall list." On the basis of editorial response to the book, a larger first printing was planned, along with increased publicity that included a twelve-city tour for Haruf.

In the epigraph to *Plainsong,* Haruf states that the title of the book refers to the "simple and unadorned" vocal melodies, sometimes sung by alternating voices, that have been used in Christian churches for centuries. The novel tells the story of six major characters and several subsidiary ones, and like a plainsong, the action is related from alternating perspectives of different characters in different chapters. Once again the setting is Holt, Colorado, and its environs. The plot begins with three separate tales that ultimately intertwine. A pregnant teenager, Victoria Roubideaux, is kicked out of her home by her mother; a local high school history teacher, Tom Guthrie, is abandoned by his wife and left to raise his two young sons alone; and two elderly bachelor brothers, Harold and Raymond McPherson, have consigned themselves to an isolated existence on their cattle ranch miles from town. "Although the intersection of these three sets of lonely lives might normally have all the melodramatic makings of a provincial soap opera," noted Michiko Kakutani in the *New York Times,* "Mr. Haruf orchestrates their convergence with such authority and grace that their stories materialize before the reader's eyes without a shred of contrivance."

Writing in a lean prose style that several reviewers compared to that of Hemingway, Haruf portrays the lives of his characters from the fall of one year through the spring of the next, often using images from the natural world and the changing seasons to complement the changes they experience. "A fugue upon weather and light plays throughout the novel," observed Verlyn Klinkenborg in a glowing review of the novel for the *New York Times Book Review,* while Donna Seaman of *Booklist* commented: "Haruf's narrative voice is spare and procedural, and his salt-of-the-earth characters are

reticent almost to the point of mannerism until it becomes clear that their terseness is the result of profound shyness and an immensity of feeling. Haruf's unforgettable tale is both emotionally complex and elemental, following, as it so gracefully does, the cycle of life, death, and rebirth." London *Observer* critic, Selina Mills remarked, "Many American writers such as Cormac McCarthy have handled the subject of Midwest prairie towns and uncommunicative inhabitants before. Fiction, too, has often relied on musical form for narrative structure. Haruf, however, offers a fresh approach by creating layers, which intensify and deepen as the novel progresses, alternating between each character's life at every chapter. Like the 'unadorned melody' in the book's epigraph, the prose is simple and understated." Christian Stayner for the *Christian Science Monitor* described the characters as "richly-written." Although less overcome with the power of *Plainsong* than most reviewers, Robin Nesbitt of *Library Journal* nevertheless found it to be both "lyrical and well crafted" and a "tight narrative about how families can be made between folks who are not necessarily blood relatives [that] makes for enjoyable reading."

Knopf's confidence in *Plainsong* was justified when the novel became a National Book Award finalist and appeared on the *Publishers Weekly* best-seller lists, prompting further paperback reprints of Haruf's earlier novels. Discussing with Blades his "sudden" success at the age of fifty-six, Haruf noted: "This country's crazy in terms of fame and what people think it means. They expect a writer to be something between a Hollywood starlet and the village idiot. . . . Fame is very seductive and can be very dangerous if you're trying to get your work done." Lofholm quoted him on his success: "Haruf said writing has gotten more difficult: 'Your standards change. You want to do something better than you've done before.' He knows he's succeeded when a *New York Times* review calls *Plainsong* 'a novel foursquare, so delicate and lovely, that it has the power to exalt the reader.' But Haruf said he really knows he's made it when an eastern plains dairy farmer stabs his finger onto the cover of *A Tie That Binds* and says 'now that is exactly right'."

BIOGRAPHICAL AND CRITICAL SOURCES:

BOOKS

Contemporary Literary Criticism, Volume 34, Gale (Detroit, MI), 1985.

PERIODICALS

Arizona Republic (Phoenix, AZ), April 2, 2003, p. E1.

Atlanta Journal-Constitution, March 30, 2000, p. D2.

Austin American-Statesman, October 10, 1999, p. K6.

Booklist, August, 1999, Donna Seaman, review of *Plainsong,* p. 1986; January 1, 2000, p. 819; April 1, 2000, p. 1449.

Boston Herald, December 15, 2000, p. 051, interview.

Christian Science Monitor, December 7, 1984, p. B12; October 21, 1999, p. 13.

Denver Post, October 17, 2001, p. F-01.

Entertainment Weekly, November 5, 1999, Megan Harlan, "The Week," p. 76.

ISLE: Interdisciplinary Studies in Literature and Environment, winter, 2003, p. 185.

Kirkus Reviews, November 15, 1989, pp. 1618-1619.

Library Journal, October 1, 1984, review of *The Tie That Binds,* p. 1861; January, 1990, Joseph Levandoski, review of *Where You Once Belonged,* p. 148; September 1, 1999, Robin Nesbitt, review of *Plainsong,* p. 232; July 2000, p. 162.

Los Angeles Times Book Review, January 27, 1985, p. 4; February 11, 1990, pp. 3, 7.

Milwaukee Journal Sentinel, November 15, 1999, p. 1E.

News & Record (Piedmont Triad, NC), November 14, 1999, p. H5.

Newsweek, October 4, 1999, Jeff Giles, "The Heart of the Country," p. 67.

New York Review of Books, October 21, 1999, Joyce Carol Oates, "Wearing out the West," p. 30.

New York Times, October 8, 1999, pp. B45, E47; December 1, 1999, pp. B4, E1.

New York Times Book Review, January 6, 1985, Perry Glasser, review of *The Tie That Binds,* p. 16; October 3, 1999, p. 7.

Observer (London, England), May 14, 2000, p. 12.

Publishers Weekly, August 24, 1984, review of *The Tie That Binds,* p. 74; December 1, 1989, Sybil Steinberg, review of *Where You Once Belonged,* p. 47; August 2, 1999, review of *Plainsong,* p. 70; October 25, 1999, Daisy Maryles, "This Novel Just Sings," p. 19; November 1, 1999, review of *Plainsong,* pp. 46, 59, John Blades, "Kent Haruf: Home on the Plains," p. 59; February 7, 2000, p. 22; September 4, 2000, p. 24.

Rocky Mountain News (Denver, CO), February 27, 2000, p. 2E.

School Library Journal, June, 2000, p. 173.

Seattle Post-Intelligencer, November 8, 1999, p. E2.

Star-Ledger (Newark, NJ), December 12, 1999, p. 004.

Time, October 25, 1999, Elizabeth Gleick, review of *Plainsong,* p. 130.

Times (London, England), April 22, 2000, p. 22; April 28, 2001, p. 16.

Wall Street Journal, October 8, 1999, p. W10; October 11, 1999, p. B1.

ONLINE

January Magazine.com, http://www.januarymagazine. com/ (November 1999), review of *Plainsong.*

PageOneLit.com, http://www.pageonelit.com/ (March 9, 2004), interview with Haruf.

PeaceCorpsWriters.com, http://www.peacecorps writers.org/ (March 4, 2004), interview with Haruf,

Random House Web site, http://www.randomhouse. com/ (March 9, 2004), interview with Haruf.*

*   *   *

H. D.
  See DOOLITTLE, Hilda

*   *   *

HELFORTH, John
  See DOOLITTLE, Hilda

*   *   *

HERIAN, V.
  See GREGORIAN, Vartan

*   *   *

JANES, J(oseph) Robert 1935-

PERSONAL: Born May 23, 1935, in Toronto, Ontario, Canada; son of Henry F. (in public relations) and Phyllis (an artist; maiden name, Hipwell) Janes; married Gracia Joyce Lind (a social and environmental activist and project coordinator), May 16, 1958; children: Anne Janes Stewart, Peter, Catherine Janes Damianoff, John.

J. Robert Janes

Education: University of Toronto, B.A.Sc., 1958, M.Sc., 1967; further graduate studies at McMaster University, Queen's University, and Brock University.

ADDRESSES: Home and office—P.O. Box 1590, 261 King St., Niagara-on-the-Lake, Ontario L0S 1J0, Canada. *E-mail*—jrjanes@sympatico.ca.

CAREER: Mobil Oil of Canada, petroleum engineer in Alberta and Saskatchewan, 1958-59; Ontario Research Foundation, Toronto, Ontario, Canada, research engineer in minerals beneficiation, 1959-64; high school geology, geography, and mathematics teacher in Toronto, 1964-66; Ontario Research Foundation, field researcher in geology, 1966; Brock University, St. Catharines, Ontario, Canada, lecturer in geology, 1966-67, 1968-70; Ontario Science Centre, Toronto, earth scientist, 1967-68; full-time writer, 1970—. Consulting field geologist; lacrosse coach.

MEMBER: International Crime Writers, Crime Writers of Canada, Crime Writers of America, Crime Writers Association (U.K.), Historical Novel Society (U.K.).

AWARDS, HONORS: Grants from J. P. Bickell Foundation, Canada Council, and Ontario Arts Council; thesis award from Canadian Institute of Mining and Metallurgy, 1958; Hammett Prize nominee, North American Branch of the International Association of Crime Writers, 2003, for *Flykiller.*

WRITINGS:

FICTION; FOR YOUNG ADULTS

The Odd-Lot Boys and the Tree-Fort War, illustrated by Alfie Muhammad, Scholastic (Richmond Hill, Ontario, Canada), 1976.
Theft of Gold, Scholastic (Richmond Hill, Ontario, Canada), 1980.
Danger on the River, Clarke, Irwin (Toronto, Ontario, Canada), 1982.
Spies for Dinner, Collins (Toronto, Ontario, Canada), 1984.
Murder in the Market, Collins (Toronto, Ontario, Canada), 1985.

NONFICTION; FOR YOUNG PEOPLE

Rocks, Minerals, and Fossils, Holt, Rinehart & Winston Canada (Toronto, Ontario, Canada) 1973.
Earth Science, Holt, Rinehart & Winston Canada (Toronto, Ontario, Canada), 1974.
Geology and the New Global Tectonics, Macmillan (Toronto, Ontario, Canada), 1976.
(With Denis Cooke, Charles Hopkins, and John D. Hoyes) *Searching for Structure,* two volumes, Holt, Rinehart & Winston Canada (Toronto, Ontario, Canada), 1977.
The Great Canadian Outback, Douglas & McIntyre (Vancouver, British Columbia, Canada), 1978.
(With J. D. Mollard) *Airphoto Interpretation and the Canadian Landscape,* Energy, Mines, and Resources Canada (Ottawa, Ontario, Canada), 1984.

FICTION; FOR ADULTS

The Toy Shop, General Publishing (Don Mills, Ontario, Canada), 1981.
The Watcher, General Publishing (Don Mills, Ontario, Canada), 1982.

The Third Story, General Publishing (Don Mills, Ontario, Canada), 1983.

The Hiding Place, Paperjacks (Markham, Ontario, Canada), 1984.

The Alice Factor, Stoddart (Toronto, Ontario, Canada), 1991.

Mayhem, Constable (London, England), 1992, published as *Mirage,* D. I. Fine (New York, NY), 1992, published as *Mayhem,* Soho Press (New York, NY), 1999.

Carousel, Constable (London, England), 1992, D. I. Fine (New York, NY), 1993.

Kaleidoscope, Constable (London, England), 1993, Soho Press (New York, NY), 2001.

Salamander, Constable (London, England), 1994, Soho Press (New York, NY), 1998.

Mannequin, Constable (London, England), 1994, Soho Press (New York, NY), 1998.

Dollmaker, Constable (London, England), 1995, Soho Press (New York, NY), 2002.

Stonekiller, Constable (London, England), 1995, Soho Press (New York, NY), 1997.

Sandman, Constable (London, England), 1996, Soho Press (New York, NY), 1997.

Gypsy, Constable (London, England), 1997.

Madrigal, Victor Gollancz (London, England), 1999.

Beekeeper, Orion Books (London, England), 2001.

Flykiller, Orion Books (London, England), 2002.

OTHER

Geology (television script), first broadcast by Metro Educational Television Authority, 1966.

Author of fifteen resource kits comprising teaching guides and slide sets for Holt, Rinehart & Winston Canada (Toronto, Ontario, Canada), 1972. Contributor of articles and stories to Canadian magazines and newspapers, including *Canadian, Canadian Children's Annual, Globe and Mail,* and *Winnipeg Free Press.*

Theft of Gold has been translated into Norwegian. Other works have been translated into German, Japanese, and Turkish.

SIDELIGHTS: J. Robert Janes is best known as a writer of mystery novels for young people and adults, but he started his writing career with science textbooks and teaching materials. His original profession was

that of geologist and mining engineer, and he still thinks of himself as a field geologist. "Occasionally I'm asked why I gave up well-paying jobs for the constant stress of never knowing if and when I'd be paid and if it would be enough to meet the bills," he once told *CA.* "There isn't any answer except that I've always wanted to write stories."

Janes added, "I was the middle son of three boys and no doubt that helped because, being lonely and left to myself a lot, I used and developed my imagination. Mother was a very fine artist, very creative, a superb cook, and the epitome of what the Great Depression and small-town Ontario could teach a person. That, too, helped so much, for she made me see things as an artist would. . . . I think story all the time and want only to work in that medium. In a sense, then, one crosses a threshold and wishes only to be totally involved in the work. It feeds itself and expands until the time is filled and there is no longer time enough for all one wants to do."

Janes's first published work of fiction was *The Odd-Lot Boys and the Tree-Fort War,* a story about five boys who foil a real estate developer's plans for the vacant lot where they have erected their tree fort. His other works for young adults include *Danger on the River, Spies for Dinner,* and *Murder in the Market.* These stories are set in the southern part of Canada's Ontario province, including the city of Toronto and the Niagara Peninsula. Reviewers have praised these novels for their fast-paced mystery plots and realistic quintet of recurring characters. James Gellert, writing in *Canadian Children's Literature,* observed that the novels deal with loyalty and friendship as well as "more topical issues, including the threat to the environment of toxic waste in *Danger on the River,* and space-age industrial espionage in *Spies for Dinner.*" In *Murder in the Market,* the mystery plot brings the teenage protagonists into contact with occultists, jewel thieves, and a variety of other dangerous types. In this novel, Janes "succeeds in offering his audience an evocative atmosphere, highly spiced action, and a relatively accurate depiction of teenage life," Gellert commented.

Since the early 1980s, Janes has focused almost exclusively on writing novels for adults, especially his series of detective-mystery, psychological thrillers that are set in German-occupied France during World War II. Janes's interest in writing about Europe during World

War II grew out of his boyhood friendship with a Belgian youth whose family had fled to Canada. "I'm fascinated by the tapestry of the Occupation," he told *Maclean's* magazine. "How when you pull one thread everything starts to unravel." His series began with *Mirage* (also published as *Mayhem*) and includes *Kaleidoscope, Mannequin, Stonekiller, Beekeeper,* and numerous other titles. The novels feature a pair of detectives as protagonists: Jean-Louis St-Cyr, a Frenchman, and Hermann Kohler, a German who is skeptical of his government's policies. "They are thrown together in the battle against common crime when officially sanctioned crime was rampant," Janes once told *CA.* "They get on because they have to and become friends in spite of it all. The novels are great fun with a fantastic background, and truly wonderful characters, because that's what it's all about. They have lots of suspense and pace. They're thrillers, really."

These novels "have few rivals" when it comes to quality, remarked Reamy Jansen in the *Bloomsbury Review.* The two detectives are "sympathetic" characters, the critic wrote, with a strong and believable friendship that "acts as a counterweight to the sadistic and greedy alliances that set the crimes in motion." The stories, Jansen added, have moral complexity and a well-drawn historical background, and "the dimension of Janes's knowledge throughout the series is impressive." At the same time, Janes has an ambivalent attitude toward research, having once told *CA* that "too much factual stuff tends to form an obstacle to the flow of the story." Some reviewers have commented that Janes's stories have no problem with flow; indeed, Jansen observed, "The charged and desperate situations of Janes's novels are aptly joined by a careening narrative frenzy." Meanwhile, critics have praised his attention to detail as well. In a review of *Salamander* for Toronto's *Globe and Mail,* Margaret Cannon explained that Janes's period details "never intrude on the story. They just build and enhance it." *Booklist* contributor David Pitt observed that *Kaleidoscope* leaves readers "feeling as though we've traveled back in time."

Janes is a busy and disciplined writer, generally working eight hours a day, six days a week. "Generally I work all the time—that is to say, while I used to have hobbies and holidays, I have not had them in a very long time," he once told *CA.* "Virtually everything I do is connected with my writing, the project I'm on, the one I'm about to begin, and those I want to do but can never seem to get the time for. I'm not complaining. This is simply the way it is. For others it will be vastly different." He writes rough drafts in longhand, then types them at the end of his workday, and once a book is finished, he goes through the whole manuscript and makes corrections before sending it on to his publisher. His dedication to writing is such that he is "cursed," he once told *CA,* "by always having to think about the book I'm writing, or the one I will do next, or the one after that. If anyone tells you that this is fun—forget it! It is lovely sometimes to be able to write every day. There are the highs and lows as in any other job. But it is absolute hell most times."

BIOGRAPHICAL AND CRITICAL SOURCES:

PERIODICALS

Bloomsbury Review, January-February, 1999, Reamy Jansen, "Nom de Dieu!—Verdammt!," p. 8.

Booklist, October 1, 2001, David Pitt, review of *Kaleidoscope,* p. 301.

Canadian Children's Literature, Volume 48, 1987, James Gellert, "How I Spent My Summer Mystery," pp. 93-95.

Chicago Tribune, February 23, 2003.

Globe and Mail (Toronto, Ontario, Canada), May 21, 1994, Margaret Cannon, review of *Salamander,* p. C17.

Maclean's, September 2, 2002, Brian Bethune, "Prophets without Honour," p. 48.

New York Times, December 9, 2001.

Wall Street Journal, December 6, 2001.

K

KOCH, Kenneth 1925-2002

PERSONAL: Surname is pronounced "coke"; born February 27, 1925, in Cincinnati, OH; died of leukemia, July 6, 2002, in New York, NY; son of Stuart J. and Lillian Amy (Loth) Koch; married Mary Janice Elwood, June 12, 1954 (died, 1981); married Karen Culler, December 29, 1994; children: Katherine. *Education:* Harvard University, A.B., 1948; Columbia University, M.A., 1953, Ph.D., 1959.

CAREER: Rutgers University, Newark, NJ, lecturer, 1953-58; Brooklyn College (now of the City University of New York), Brooklyn, NY, lecturer, 1957-59; Columbia University, New York, NY, assistant professor, 1959-66, associate professor, 1966-71, professor of English and comparative literature, beginning 1971. Director of Poetry Workshop at New School for Social Research (now New School University), 1958-66. Exhibitions of Koch's collaborative work were held at the Ipswich Museum, England, 1993, at the Tibor de Nagy Gallery, New York, NY, 1994, and at Guild Hall, East Hampton, NY, 2000. *Military service:* U.S. Army, 1943-46.

MEMBER: American Academy of Arts and Letters.

AWARDS, HONORS: Fulbright fellow, 1950-51, 1978, and 1982; Guggenheim fellow, 1960-61; grant from National Endowment for the Arts, 1966; Ingram Merrill Foundation fellow, 1969; Harbison Award, 1970, for teaching; Frank O'Hara Prize, 1973, for *Poetry;* Christopher Book Award and Ohioana Book Award, both 1974, both for *Rose, Where Did You Get That Red?;* National Institute of Arts and Letters award, 1976; Award of Merit for Poetry, American Academy and Institute of Arts and Letters, 1986; National Book Critics Circle nomination, 1988, for *One Thousand Avant-garde Plays;* Bollingen Prize, Yale University, 1995; Rebekah Johnson Bobbitt National Prize for Poetry, Library of Congress, 1996, for *One Train: Poems;* named chevalier, Ordre des Arts et des Lettres (France), 1999; National Book Award finalist, 2000, for *New Address;* Levinson Prize, *Poetry,* 2000.

WRITINGS:

POETRY

Poems, Tibor de Nagy Gallery (New York, NY), 1953.
Ko; or, A Season on Earth (also see below), Grove (New York, NY), 1959.
Permanently, Tiber Press, 1960.
Thank You and Other Poems, Grove (New York, NY), 1962.
Poems from 1952 and 1953 (limited edition), Black Sparrow Press (Santa Barbara, CA), 1968.
The Pleasures of Peace and Other Poems, Grove (New York, NY), 1969.
When the Sun Tries to Go On, Black Sparrow Press (Santa Barbara, CA), 1969.
Sleeping with Women (limited edition), Black Sparrow Press (Santa Barbara, CA), 1969.
The Art of Love, Random House (New York, NY), 1975.
The Duplications (also see below), Random House (New York, NY), 1977.

The Burning Mystery of Anna in 1951, Random House (New York, NY), 1979.

Days and Nights, Random House (New York, NY), 1982.

Selected Poems, 1950-1982, Random House (New York, NY), 1985.

On the Edge, Viking (New York, NY), 1986.

Seasons on Earth (includes *Ko; or, A Season on Earth* and *The Duplications*), Penguin (New York, NY), 1987.

Selected Poems, Carcanet (Manchester, England), 1991.

One Train: Poems, Knopf (New York, NY).

On the Great Atlantic Rainway: Selected Poems, 1950-1988, Knopf (New York, NY), 1994.

Straits: Poems, Knopf (New York, NY), 1998.

New Addresses: Poems, Knopf (New York, NY), 2000.

Sun Out: Selected Poems, 1952-1954, Knopf (New York, NY), 2002.

A Possible World, Knopf (New York, NY), 2002.

FICTION

(With Alex Katz) *Interlocking Lives,* Kulchur Foundation (New York, NY), 1970.

The Red Robins (also see below), Random House (New York, NY), 1975.

Hotel Lambosa and Other Stories, Coffee House Press (Minneapolis, MN), 1993.

NONFICTION

Wishes, Lies, and Dreams: Teaching Children to Write Poetry, Chelsea House (New York, NY), 1970.

Rose, Where Did You Get That Red?: Teaching Great Poetry to Children, Random House (New York, NY), 1973.

I Never Told Anybody: Teaching Poetry Writing in a Nursing Home, Random House (New York, NY), 1977, revised edition, Teachers and Writers Collaborative (New York, NY), 1997.

(With Kate Farrell) *Sleeping on the Wing: An Anthology of Modern Poetry, with Essays on Reading and Writing,* Random House (New York, NY), 1981.

(With Kate Farrell) *Talking to the Sun: An Illustrated Anthology of Poems for Young People,* Metropolitan Museum of Art/Holt (New York, NY), 1985.

The Art of Poetry (literary criticism), University of Michigan Press (Ann Arbor, MI), 1996.

Making Your Own Days: The Pleasures of Reading and Writing Poetry, Scribner (New York, NY), 1998.

PLAYS

Little Red Riding Hood, produced in New York, NY, 1953.

Bertha (also see below), produced in New York, NY, 1959; produced as an opera, music by Ned Rorem, 1971.

Pericles (also see below), produced off-Broadway, 1960.

The Election (also see below), produced in New York, NY, 1960.

George Washington Crossing the Delaware (also see below), produced off-Broadway, 1962.

The Construction of Boston (also see below), produced off-Broadway, 1962; produced in Boston as an opera, music by Scott Wheeler, 1990-91.

Guinevere; or, The Death of the Kangaroo (also see below), produced in New York, NY, 1964.

The Tinguely Machine Mystery; or, The Love Suicides at Kaluka (also see below), produced in New York, NY, 1965.

The Moon Balloon (also see below), produced in New York's Central Park, 1969.

The Artist (opera; based on poem of the same title), music by Paul Reif), produced in New York, NY, 1972.

A Little Light, produced in Amagansett, NY, 1972.

The Gold Standard (also see below), produced in New York, NY, 1975.

Rooster Redivivus, produced in Garnerville, NY, 1975.

The Red Robins (based on novel of the same title; produced in New York, NY, 1978), Theatre Arts, 1979.

The New Diana, produced in New York, NY, 1984.

A Change of Hearts (opera; also see below), produced in New York, NY, 1985.

Popeye among the Polar Bears, produced in New York, NY, 1986.

(With composer Marcello Panni) *The Banquet,* produced in Bremen, Germany, 1998.

OMNIBUS VOLUMES; PLAYS

Bertha and Other Plays (also see below; includes *Bertha, Pericles, George Washington Crossing the Delaware, The Construction of Boston, The Return* of Yellowmay, The Revolt of the Giant Animals, The Building of Florence, Angelica, The Merry Stones, The Academic Murders, Easter, The Lost Feed, Mexico, Coil Supreme, The Gold Standard, and *Guinevere; or, The Death of the Kangaroo*), Grove (New York, NY), 1966.

A Change of Hearts: Plays, Films, and Other Dramatic Works, 1951-1971 (also see below; contains *Bertha and Other Plays, A Change of Hearts, The Tinguely Machine Mystery; or, The Love Suicides at Kaluka, The Moon Balloon, E. Kology, Without Kinship, Youth, The Enchantment,* and the film scripts *Because, The Color Game, Mountains and Electricity, Sheep Harbor, Oval Gold, Moby Dick, L'École normale, The Cemetery, The Scotty Dog,* and *The Apple*), Random House (New York, NY), 1973.

One Thousand Avant-garde Plays (produced in New York, NY, 1987), Knopf (New York, NY), 1988.

The Gold Standard: A Book of Plays, Knopf (New York, NY), 1996.

OTHER

(Editor, with others, and author of introduction) Joseph Ceravolo, *The Green Lake Is Awake: Selected Poems,* Coffee House Press (Minneapolis, MN), 1994.

Contributor to *Penguin Modern Poets 24,* Penguin, 1974; contributor of fiction, poetry, and plays to magazines, including *Art and Literature, Locus Solus, Poetry, Raritan, Grand Street,* and *New York Review of Books.* Member of editorial board of *Locus Solus,* 1960-62.

Koch's works have been translated into French and Italian.

ADAPTATIONS: The Art of Love was adapted for the stage by Mike Nussbaum and produced in Chicago, IL, 1976.

SIDELIGHTS: Prize-winning author Kenneth Koch published numerous collections of poetry, avant-garde plays, and short fiction while also serving as one of the nation's best-known creative writing teachers during a career that spanned over five decades. Associated with the New York School of poetry for most of

his career, Koch used surrealism, satire, irony, and an element of surprise in many of his poems. However, "his satires are more than mere jokes," explained Roberta Berke in her book *Bounds out of Bounds: A Compass for Recent American and British Poetry:* "They have a serious purpose of literary and social criticism." Koch explored an assortment of emotions in his poetry, but in an era seemingly dedicated to deep seriousness he refused to relinquish lightness or a sense of humor. According to Phoebe Pettingell in the *New Leader,* Koch's works "convey his perennial freshness in at least two senses of that word: novelty and cheekiness. He has a subtle grasp of the nuances of language as well as a gift for hilarious parody, and behind his casual, friendly manner there is formidable technique and learning."

During his career, Koch was called "the funniest serious poet we have," by David Lehman in *Newsweek.* Although Peter Stitt maintained in the *Georgia Review* that the author's "greatest commitment as a poet is to not making very much sense, to not taking things very seriously," other critics contend that Koch's poetry has an underlying seriousness and have praised his imagination and originality. Koch's "playfulness, in tone and technique, has often caused him to be underrated," stated *Salmagundi* contributor Paul Zweig. "But it is just his great capacity for humor, based on so much more than mere irony, that makes him important. He has reclaimed the humorous for serious writers of poetry and for that we are in his debt." David Lehman, in his book *The Last Avant-Garde,* commented that Koch "had the misfortune to be a protean comic genius at the moment when the lyric poem [was] the be-all and end-all of verse and [was] mistakenly held to be incompatible with the spirit of comedy."

Koch himself once addressed the idea of comic poetry in an interview with Jordan Davis, published in Koch's *The Art of Poetry.* "Some readers think of a poem as a sort of ceremony—a funeral, a wedding—where anything comic is out of order. They expect certain feelings to be touched on in certain conventional ways. Dissociation, even obscurity, may be tolerated, but only as long as the tone remains solemn or sad enough." Koch continued, "There may be a perfectly serious poem, a good poem . . . and some other person writes a parody of it and one line of the parody may have more truth than the whole original poem, or at least be freer to reach the intoxicating heights that sometimes seem where truth is from."

Koch is credited as being one of the founders of the New York School of poetry, which came into existence in the 1950s. At the time, the poets who were working within the "school"—including John Ashbery, Frank O'Hara, and Koch, among others—hardly considered themselves trend-setters. The name "New York School" was coined for them by Donald Allen for an anthology he was editing in the late 1950s, and it suggested a spirit of novelty and experimentation that well suited its young practitioners. "The so-called New York School assembled its own outsider identity from some of the same sources as the Beats: an urban male savvy, sometimes inflected with Jewish and gay sensibilities, and an openness to avant-garde work in other media," explained Christopher Benfey in the *New Republic.* According to Benfey, Koch was "a conspicuous member of the New York School, often chronicling its exploits and mourning its losses." *Dictionary of Literary Biography* contributor Michael Adams observed that Koch "characterized the New York School style as 'antitraditional, opposed to certain heavy uses of irony and symbolism.'" Adams also quoted Koch as saying, "I think we may have been more conscious than many poets of the surface of the poem, and what was going on while we were writing and how we were using words."

Like other poets of the New York School, Koch used stream-of-consciousness in his writing and stressed the importance of the present moment and the ordinary. Pettingell, concluded that pop references and personal asides notwithstanding, Koch's work continues to stand the test of time quite well. "Today, Robert Lowell and Allen Ginsberg are looking pretty hoary to the students of Generation X, and Eliot seems as remote as the late Victorian authors," the critic maintained. "The joke is that those bards of the passing scene, Ashbery and Koch, continue to flourish. Indeed, today they appear to exemplify the tenets of postmodernism."

Koch's first book of poetry, titled simply *Poems,* first sparked the critical debate over the seriousness of his work. Finding the book "tasteless, futile, noisy and *dull,*" Harry Roskolenko further contended in *Poetry* that "Koch writes lazy verse and is precious and puerile." This negative review prompted a rebuttal from writer Frank O'Hara, who asserted in *Poetry* that Koch "has the other poetic gift: vivacity and go, originality of perception and intoxication with life. Most important of all, he is not *dull.*" *Washington Post Book World* contributor Michael Lally agreed, claiming that

"Koch's work is always entertaining and usually enlightening." The poems in Koch's debut work cover a diversity of subjects; F. W. Dupee claimed in the *New York Review of Books* that "Koch is fond of making poetry out of poetry-resistant stuff. Locks, lipsticks, business letterheads, walnuts, lunch and fudge attract him; so do examples of inept slang, silly sentiment, brutal behavior and stereotyped exotica and erotica." Employing the bizarre humor of surrealism and the techniques of abstract expressionism, Koch crafted poems that emphasize form and sound. The words Koch selects to present his subjects surge together "like an express train of exuberant sounds," observed *Poetry* contributor David Lehman, adding that "the poet takes a great deal of delight in the sounds of words and his consciousness of them; he splashes them like paint on a page with enthusiastic puns, internal rhymes, titles of books, names of friends . . . and seems surprised as we are at the often witty outcome."

Koch seemed to thrive on the intensity in writing a new poem, and many of his verses deal with the poetic imagination and the act of creation. *Poetry* contributor Paul Carroll explained: "Koch celebrates that splendid faculty with which men make poetry. His poems embody the poetic imagination as it rejoices in the ebullience of its health and freedom, its fecundity, its capacity for endless invention, its dear, outlandish ability to transform everyday, pragmatic reality into an Oz or a tea-party at the March Hare's house, its potency in, possibly, achieving a bit of immortality as a result of having brought forth some children of the soul." In the title poem in *The Pleasures of Peace and Other Poems,* Koch presents this theme of the creative mind at work through Giorgio Finogle and another poet. Both poets are writing a poem about the pleasures of peace, and thus find themselves competing against one another. This is but one example of the author's "celebration of the excitement of the imagination as it begins to create," according to Carroll.

In *The Art of Love,* Koch's "voice is unperturbed, offering serene and careless advice on the arts of love and poetry for those who have ears and can hear," explained Paul Wilner in the *Village Voice.* Writing in *Poetry,* J. D. McClatchy referred to the book as an "erotic romp," and Wilner further described it as "updating Ovid by reinventing the alphabet of emotion." Zweig added that Koch's "humor has an edge of satire; his ebullient absurdity slides into an original form of social and cultural criticism, as in 'The Artist' and

'Fresh Air,' both enormously funny epics about the impossibility of art." In the poem "The Art of Love," Koch parodies several advice-giving documents and tries to "enable both poet and reader to distance feelings, ideas, experiences, so as to perceive them strangely, freshly, as if they were rare or even alien curiosities, *objets d'art,* perhaps, in some great Bloomingdale's of the imagination," asserted Sandra M. Gilbert in *Poetry.* The drawback to this form of presentation is that detachment can filter in. *Shenandoah* contributor Conrad Hilberry observed, for instance, that Koch's verse, "like pop art, present great simplicity but maintain so much ironic distance that they make the ordinary reader uneasy." However, Aram Saroyan maintained in the *New York Times Book Review* that the poems in *The Art of Love* embody "the ability to move the reader, plain but beautiful language that should appeal to a wide audience, a general graciousness of spirit that has long been an unremarked-on hallmark of Koch's writing, and last but not least, outright wisdom."

"Every book of poems by . . . Koch seems to be a new beginning, a starting over, a trying-out of new voices, styles and idioms," observed John Boening in his *World Literature Today* review of *Days and Nights.* This collection contains a wide variety of poems, in which, explained Mark Hillringhouse in the *American Book Review,* "Koch has paid more attention to physical detail and places his emotions directly and concretely into the poem." The poems encompass such subjects as love, aging, loneliness, the past, and the future. One of the pieces, "To Janice," is "moving, intimate, smiling, tender, touching and inventive," according to Boening, who added that it alone "is worth the price of the book." And the title poem, "Days and Nights," is phrased in such a way so as to evoke "a whole spectrum of emotions; from lost time to old friends, to travels and defeats to fears of writing itself," asserted Hillringhouse. "Koch sets out to explore a new landscape that is honest to the act of writing and to the process of the imagination."

On the Edge consists of two lengthy poems, "Impressions of Africa" and "On the Edge," the second being "more ambitious, ranging widely over the facts and fiction of . . . Koch's life," in the words of *New York Times Book Review* correspondent John Ash. The poem moves back and forth between past and present, according to Denis Donoghue in *Commonweal,* with "memories and currencies of sentiment jostling one

another within the strong propriety of the cadence." *Washington Post Book World* contributor Peter Davison viewed the allusions the poem relies on as "calculated to exclude outsiders, to make the non-belonger feel stupid, to make the reader ransack for a footnote." Ash, however, viewed the book as taking "great risks," and claimed that "we cannot do better" than appraise the work according to Koch's "own demanding criteria, set out in his *Art of Poetry.* Does it astonish? Is it sufficiently modern? Is it written in his own voice? Is it devoid of 'literary, "kiss-me-I'm-poetical" junk'? Is it 'serious without being solemn, fresh without being cold'? The answer, in all cases, must be affirmative."

The poem "Seasons on Earth" and two of Koch's previously published comic epics, "Ko; or, A Season on Earth" and "The Duplications," comprise *Seasons on Earth.* The book provides readers with "a poetic memoir that glances back at the time during which he wrote the earlier poems, a genre at which Koch's discursive talents have proved particularly masterful," explained Gary Lenhart in the *American Book Review.* Lenhart added that the title poem continues the mastery of the narrative, "but new urgencies threaten to move the poet away from the strict adherence to form characteristic of the earlier poems." Adams described *Ko; or A Season on Earth* as "a comic epic modeled partially after Byron's *Don Juan* and Ariosto's *Orlando Furioso*" that "details the misadventures of a group of outlandish characters who flit about from continent to continent, reality to unreality." Among other things, the poem relates the story of Ko, a Japanese college student who comes to the United States to play baseball. Lenhart says that the poem "is bursting with the exuberance of a sensuous young poet impatient with the literary world."

In the *Washington Post Book World,* Terence Winch regarded "The Duplications" as "something of a nonsense epic whose seriousness lies more in the demonstration of Koch's impressive technical skill than in the narrative itself." There are many "duplications" in the poem, maintained Winch, but the most important ones are the rhymes. And although the poem is a narrative, Winch also suggested that the way in which Koch's mind works and the language he uses deserve more attention than the actual story. His "work is important for its singularity as for its exuberant invention, inspired fluency, and histrionic imagination," concluded Lenhart.

Koch's mature works increasingly demonstrated the poet's willingness to experiment in a variety of forms.

In 1994 he released two poetry collections, following his 1993 volume of short-short stories. All three books earned significant critical response, with the poetry collections cited as factors in awarding Koch the Bollingen Prize. In a review of Koch's work in Chicago's *Tribune Books,* Paul Hoover hailed the poet as "an extravagant improviser, natural formalist and borscht-belt comedian. His poems have daring, ease and sprezzatura; they are formally accomplished without pomposity." Hoover cited the collection *On the Great Atlantic Rainway* for displaying Koch as "a poet of intimacy and size, lyricism and intelligence. Because his work is lighthearted, it has been accused of triviality. Yet in poems like his hilarious polemic, 'Fresh Air,' Koch shows the fiercely moral nature of the true satirist."

In *Straights* Koch contributes not only poems but prose and even a fugue; still, the poems on themes of aging, seasonal change and "the loss of the sacred in everyday life" most accurately characterize the volume. *Straits* was viewed as a somewhat mixed bag, according to *Poetry* reviewer Ben Howard, although Koch's most successful entries feature a "sophisticated wit and stylistic panache," both of which "illuminate their subjects." Noting an autobiographical bent in the collection, a *Publishers Weekly* contributor remarked upon perceiving "glimpses of the man behind the curtain" in the collection.

Koch reaches even deeper into his own life for the stuff of *New Addresses* and *A Possible World.* Autobiographical in focus, the two collections would prove to be Koch's last gift to readers; he was by now engaged in the battle against leukemia that would ultimately end his life in July of 2002. A *Publishers Weekly* reviewer, praising *New Addresses* as the poet's finest work to date, discussed with Koch its autobiographical elements. "One poem led to another," Koch explained. Examining his life as it revealed itself in the poems of *New Addresses,* the poet also came to terms with a pivotal moment in his life: his military service during World War II. "I'd never really been able to write [about the war] because it's like being psychotic to be in a war. You're walking around with a gun . . . and they shoot you!" However, from a distanced perspective, the mature poet found that treating the war as a character, like any other person, "enabled me to get some of the feelings back, like the crazy idea that I couldn't be killed because I had to write." Containing "Bel Canto," "Variations on Home and Abroad," and "A Memoir," as well as a number of short verses expressing the author's love of travel, *A Possible World* "displays Koch's verve and light touch," according to a *Publishers Weekly* contributor, although the overall mood of the collection "is unmistakably colored by requiem."

Koch also wrote many short plays that critics have praised for equal measures of parody, satire, and irony. As Koch once commented in his interview with Davis, "I like plays that are astounding in some way—that make convincing what is unusual and even, seemingly, impossible." Denis Donoghue suggested in a *New York Review of Books* essay that in *Bertha and Other Plays,* "Koch implies in his smiling way that nothing is too silly to be said or sung, provided we know exactly how silly it is." In the *New York Review of Books,* Stephen Spender described the plays in *A Change of Hearts: Plays, Films, and Other Dramatic Works, 1951-1971* as being "written in a variety of styles, parodying other styles." Koch is extremely inventive, concluded Spender, "and has the funniness which comes out of exuberant vitality."

Koch's *One Thousand Avant-garde Plays* described as "a pure act of poetic invention" by David Lehman in the *Washington Post Book World.* The cast of characters in these plays includes Lord Byron, Bozo, Olive Oyl, a Chinese cook, Little Red Riding Hood, Watteau, and hippopotami. "These brief plays are not fragments but full-blown dramas distilled to the action at the heart of each," asserted Lehman, concluding that "one can only applaud [Koch's] insistence on making plays that are at once intelligent and entertaining."

In an online interview with John Tranter for *Jacket,* Koch once praised "the genius in contemporary theatre. Most of the genius . . . seems to be in the directors. I'm not sure I can tell genius in an actor; there seems to be some there too. But the texts of contemporary plays I've seen have not seemed to me to be of the same quality—most of them—as that of the work of the best directors."

Aside from writing poetry, Koch also devoted his time to teaching poetry to children and to the elderly. In 1968 he began his experiment with children at P.S. 61, a New York City elementary school. His *Wishes, Lies, and Dreams: Teaching Children to Write Poetry* describes how writing became exciting for these students and includes some of the student poetry that resulted from Koch's instruction. *Saturday Review* contributor Herbert Kohl considered the work "perhaps the best book I have read portraying the joy and excitement young people experience when writing in a happy place where people care about their work."

Although the students in Koch's class wrote some exceptional poetry, Koch didn't stop there. As John Gardner explained in the *New York Times Book Review,* "The children themselves felt a need for something more. Koch's response was to shift the experiment to 'teaching great poetry to children,' thus broadening the tradition available to them." The record of this experiment and its tremendous results is *Rose, Where Did You Get That Red?: Teaching Great Poetry to Children.* Koch also worked with the residents of Manhattan's American Nursing Home, and *I Never Told Anybody: Teaching Poetry Writing in a Nursing Home* was the result. As well as collecting his students' poems, the book presents what a *Time* reviewer described as a "highly readable account of how he coaxed his students along." At first unresponsive, the elderly and infirm students learned "to summon and repeat words joyfully, to exaggerate enthusiastically, to celebrate contrasts, to become immersed in nature, to imagine all sorts of places, to put themselves into many different kinds of shoes," wrote Robert Coles in the *New York Times Book Review.*

"I seem to go on being influenced, and encouraged, by what I read," Koch once noted of his work as a poet. For his part, Koch also served as an influence to the writers who have followed in his wake. "Koch's poetry remains an underrated treasure, arousing discipleship and high ardor wherever the spirit of the New York school is strong and ignored wherever not," Lehman noted in his book. Bernard F. Dick in *World Literature Today* observed that the author's body of work depicts "a poet's progress, beginning with self-conscious experimentation in the usual way of finding a voice and ending with a voice as distinctive and resonant as the ones that echo through the poetry." Dick added that Koch's poems "attest to a creative power and its gradual refinement, as life and art, the playful and the profound."

BIOGRAPHICAL AND CRITICAL SOURCES:

BOOKS

Berke, Roberta, *Bounds out of Bounds: A Compass for Recent American and British Poetry,* Oxford University Press (Oxford, England), 1981.

Cohen, Sarah Blacher, editor, *Comic Relief: Humor in Contemporary American Literature,* University of Illinois Press (Champaign, IL), 1978.

Contemporary Dramatists, 6th edition, St. James Press (Detroit, MI), 1999.

Contemporary Literary Criticism, Gale (Detroit, MI), Volume 5, 1976, Volume 8, 1978, Volume 44, 1987.

Contemporary Poets, 7th edition, St. James Press (Detroit, MI), 2001.

Dictionary of Literary Biography, Volume 5: *American Poets since World War II,* Gale (Detroit, MI), 1980.

Diggory, Terence, and Stephen Paul Miller, *The Scene of My Selves: New Work on New York School Poets,* National Poetry Foundation, 2001.

Dupee, F. W., *"The King of Cats" and Other Remarks on Writers and Writing,* Farrar, Straus (New York, NY), 1965.

Howard, Richard, *Alone with America: Essays on the Art of Poetry in the United States,* Atheneum (New York, NY), 1969.

John Ashbery and Kenneth Koch: A Conversation, Interview Press, 1965.

Koch, Kenneth, *The Art of Love,* Random House (New York, NY), 1975.

Koch, Kenneth, *New Addresses: Poems,* Knopf (New York, NY), 2000.

Lehman, David, *The Last Avant-Garde,* Doubleday (New York, NY), 1998.

PERIODICALS

American Book Review, May, 1984, Mark Hillringhouse, review of *Days and Nights;* November-December, 1986; May, 1989, Gary Lenhart, review of *Seasons on Earth;* February, 1994, pp. 12, 19.

American Poetry Review, November-December, 1995, review of *On the Great Atlantic Rainway: Selected Poems, 1950-1988* and *One Train.*

Booklist, May 15, 1993, p. 1674; October 1, 2002, Donna Seaman, "A Poet's Fond Farewell," p. 296.

Commonweal, November 29, 1985, Dennis Donoghue, review of *On the Edge.*

Comparative Literature Studies, June, 1980.

Georgia Review, fall, 1985.

New Leader, January 30, 1995, pp. 14-15.

New Republic, August 2, 1969; March 13, 1995, Christopher Benfey, pp. 39-42.

Newsweek, September 16, 1985.

New York Review of Books, May, 1963, F. W. Dupee, review of *Poems;* October 20, 1966, Denis Donoghue, review of *Bertha and Other Plays;* September 20, 1973, Stephen Spender, review of *A Change of Hearts;* August 14, 1980; April 8, 1993, p. 36; January 16, 2003, Charles Simic, review of *Sun Out: Selected Poems, 1952-1954,* p. 13.

New York Times, November 21, 1970; April 10, 1977; January 19, 1978; January 12, 1979; February 7, 1995.

New York Times Book Review, February 11, 1968; December 23, 1973, John Gardner, review of *Rose, Where Did You Get That Red?: Teaching Great Poetry to Children;* September 28, 1975, Aram Saroyan, review of *The Art of Love;* April 10, 1977, Robert Coles, review of *I Never Told Anybody: Teaching Poetry Writing in a Nursing Home;* April 20, 1986, John Ash, review of *On the Edge;* June 4, 2000, Ken Tucker, "You Talking to Me?."

Poetry, March, 1955, Harry Roskolenko, review of *Poems;* June, 1955, Frank O'Hara, review of *Poems;* September, 1969; November, 1971; August, 1976, J. D. McClatchy, review of *The Art of Love;* August, 1978; April, 2000, Ben Howard, review of *Straits,* p. 32.

Publishers Weekly, April 5, 1993, p. 71; May 30, 1994, p. 45; April 27, 1998, review of *Straits,* p. 17; March 27, 2000, review of *New Addresses,* p. 71; September 23, 2002, review of *A Possible World* and *Sun Out,* p. 68.

Review of Contemporary Fiction, fall, 1993, pp. 221-222.

Sagetrieb, spring, 1993, p. 131.

Salmagundi, spring-summer, 1973.

Saturday Review, March 20, 1971, Herbert Kohl, review of *Wishes, Lies, and Dreams.*

Shenandoah, spring, 1978, Conrad Hilberry, review of *The Art of Love.*

Studies in Short Fiction, winter, 1995, pp. 102-105.

Time, April 4, 1977, review of *I Never Told Anybody.*

Times Literary Supplement, February 20, 1987.

Tribune Books (Chicago, IL), July 9, 1995, p. 6.

Village Voice, May 18, 1972; December 20, 1973; November 24, 1975, Paul Wilner, review of *The Art of Love.*

Washington Post Book World, August 3, 1975; April 17, 1977; January 12, 1986; April 13, 1986; August 28, 1988, Terence Winch, review of *Seasons on Earth;* January 1, 1995, David Lehman, review of *One Thousand Avant-garde Plays,* p. 8.

World Literature Today, winter, 1984, John Boening, review of *Days and Nights;* winter, 1994, Bernard F. Dick, review of *Hotel Lambosa and Other Stories,* p. 142; autumn, 1995, pp. 800-801.

Yale Review, July, 1985.

ONLINE

Jacket Online, http://www.jacket.zip.com/ (March 17, 1989), John Tranter, "Very Rapid Acceleration: An Interview with Kenneth Koch."

OBITUARIES:

PERIODICALS

Los Angeles Times, July 9, 2002, p. B10.

New York Times, July 8, 2002, p. A16.

Times (London, England), July 29, 2002.

ONLINE

International Herald Tribune Online, http://www.iht.com/ (July 9, 2002).*

*   *   *

KOCH, Stephen 1941-

PERSONAL: Surname is pronounced "coke"; born May 8, 1941, in St. Paul, MN; son of Robert Fulton (a lawyer) and Edith (Bayard) Koch. *Education:* Attended University of Minnesota, 1959-60; City College of the City University of New York, A.B., 1962; Columbia University, M.A., 1965. *Religion:* Episcopalian. *Hobbies and other interests:* Films and filmmaking.

ADDRESSES: Home—432 Lafayette St., New York, NY 10003. *Agent*—Maxine Groffsky, 2 Fifth Ave., New York, NY 10011.

CAREER: Writer. Columbia University, New York, NY, instructor in fiction writing, 1977-98.

MEMBER: Phi Beta Kappa.

Stephen Koch

WRITINGS:

Night Watch (novel), Harper, 1969.

Stargazer: Andy Warhol's World and His Films, Praeger, 1972.

The Bachelor's Bride (novel), M. Boyars (New York, NY), 1986.

(Author of essays, with Thomas Sokolowski) *Peter Hujar,* Grey Art Gallery and Study Center, New York University (New York, NY), 1990.

Double Lives: Spies and Writers in the Secret Soviet War of Ideas against the West, Free Press (New York, NY), 1994, published as *Double Lives: Stalin, Willi Munzenberg and the Seduction of the Intellectuals,* Welcome Rain (New York, NY), 2001.

The Modern Library Writer's Workshop: A Guide to the Craft of Fiction, Modern Library (New York, NY), 2003.

Author and host of "Eye-to-Eye," a television series for the Public Broadcasting System. Contributor of articles and reviews to literary journals.

SIDELIGHTS: Stephen Koch, who taught creative writing at New York City's Columbia University, has

written in several genres. He is the author of novels as well as nonfiction works, the latter of which include a biography of pop-culture artist Andy Warhol, a book about spies and intellectuals during the cold war, and a guide to writing that focuses on teaching the basics in a workshop format.

One of Koch's earliest books, *Stargazer: Andy Warhol's World and His Films,* is a biography of artist Andy Warhol and a critique of his films. The book is a small classic study of how Warhol created his own public image couched in a strange and impassive persona. Koch had been interested in Warhol's film work for several years and wrote a 1971 article about the film *Chelsea Girls* for *Artforum International.* The article became a central chapter in *Stargazer.* In a September, 2001, article in *Artforum International,* contributor Eric C. Banks noted that Koch's article firmly placed Warhol's work in context. Banks noted, "The filmmaker is seen to lay claim to the strong current of modernism in the avant-garde cinema of the period, a claim that entails both continuity with and development of the work of exemplary predecessors and a squaring with the aesthetic issues of the day. That Koch did so with style was no mean feat."

Koch is also the author of two widely translated novels, 1969's *Nightwatch* and 1986's *The Bachelor's Bride.* The latter novel takes place in New York's Greenwich Village and SoHo in the late 1960s. The story revolves around a talented painter, Mel Dworkin, whose work explodes onto the New York art scene but who has dubious moral values and manipulates people. As told through the eyes of the character Jason Phillips, an art historian and critic, the book provides an inside look at a time when Pop and New Wave art and design in New York had reached its pinnacle in terms of popularity and cultural influence.

Koch later turned his attention to the Russian Revolution and the ensuing ideological battle between the United States and the Soviet Union, which to led the cold war of the 1950s and beyond. In *Double Lives: Spies and Writers in the Secret Soviet War of Ideas against the West,* later published as *Double Lives: Stalin, Willi Munzenberg and the Seduction of the Intellectuals,* Koch talks about "soft" Soviet penetration into the West by manipulating key government, public, and private figures and institutions. He outlines how longtime German Communist Willi Munzenberg helped to orchestrate an army of agents to bolster the

Communist cause by "persuasion." In a review on the American Enterprise Institute Web site, Mark Falcoff wrote, "In Koch's telling, Munzenberg's particular genius was to recognize how ostensibly nonpolitical attitudes and impulses among Western intellectuals, clergy, artists, and also society leaders, businessmen, and politicians could be put to use for covert Soviet purposes."

After teaching writing for twenty-one years at Columbia University and serving for a time as the writing department chairman, Koch left Columbia and subsequently published a guide about the writing craft. In *The Modern Library Writer's Workshop: A Guide to the Craft of Fiction,* Koch takes his years of teaching experience and the wisdom of other great writers concerning their craft and produces a book for both beginners and professionals who want to get back to the basics. In an article for the *Writer,* Chuck Leddy called the book "accessible, concise and highly informative." Leddy quoted Koch as saying the book is "an effort to assemble and integrate what I believe amounts to something like a consensus among writers about the basics of their craft." In the guide, Koch covers everything from making the time to write to grappling with the concepts and complexities of plot, character, and structure and conflict. Herbert E. Shapiro, writing in *Library Journal,* noted, "This very readable book will appeal not only to serious fiction writers but also to all students of literature."

BIOGRAPHICAL AND CRITICAL SOURCES:

BOOKS

Koch, Stephen, *The Modern Library Writer's Workshop: A Guide to the Craft of Fiction,* Modern Library (New York, NY), 2003.

PERIODICALS

Artforum International, September, 2001, Eric C. Banks, "September 1971," p. 52.
Booklist, April 15, 2003, Kristine Huntley, review of *The Modern Library Writer's Workshop,* p. 1422.
Library Journal, February 15, 2003, Herbert E. Shapiro, review of *The Modern Library Writer's Workshop,* p. 145.
Writer, October, 2003, Chuck Leddy, review of *The Modern Library Writer's Workshop,* p. 44.

ONLINE

American Enterprise Institute, http://www.aei.org/ (January 1, 1994), Mark Falcoff, review of *Double Lives: Spies and Writers in the Secret Soviet War of Ideas against the West.*
Freedom Daily, http://www.fff.org/freedom/0794e.asp/ (July, 1994), Richard M. Ebeling, review of *Double Lives.**

*   *   *

KRAKAUER, Jon 1954-

PERSONAL: Born 1954, in Brookline, MA; son of Lewis Krakauer (a physician) and an art teacher; married Linda Moore, 1980. *Education:* Hampshire College, MA, early 1980s. *Hobbies and other interests:* Mountain climbing.

ADDRESSES: Agent—Doubleday, 1745 Broadway, New York, NY 10019. *E-mail*—ddaypub@random house.com.

CAREER: Journalist. Contributing editor to *Outside* magazine. Worked previously as a carpenter and commercial fisherman.

AWARDS, HONORS: National Magazine Award nominee for an article that formed the basis of *Into the Wild;* American Library Association Best Books for Young Adults citation, 1998, for *Into Thin Air.*

WRITINGS:

Eiger Dreams: Ventures among Men and Mountains (essay collection), Lyons & Burford (New York, NY), 1990.
(Photographer) David Roberts, *Iceland: Land of the Sagas* (travelogue), Abrams (New York, NY), 1990.
Into the Wild (nonfiction), Villard (New York, NY), 1996.
Into Thin Air: A Personal Account of the Mount Everest Disaster, Villard (New York, NY), 1998.
(Editor) Roland Huntford, *The Last Place on Earth: Scott and Amundsen's Race to the South Pole,* revised edition, Random House (New York, NY), 1999.

Jon Krakauer

(Editor) Gaston Rebuffat, *Starlight and Storm: The Conquest for the Great North Faces of the Alps,* Random House (New York, NY), 1999.

(Editor) Francis Parkman, *La Salle and the Discovery of the Great West,* Random House (New York, NY), 1999.

(With David F. Breashears) *High Exposure: An Enduring Passion for Everest and Unforgiving Places,* Simon & Schuster (New York, NY), 2000.

(Editor) Tim Severin, *The Brendan Voyage, Volume 1,* Random House (New York, NY), 2000.

(Editor) Chauncey Loomis, *Weird and Tragic Shores, Volume 1,* Random House (New York, NY), 2000.

(Editor) Robert Dunn, *The Shameless Diary of an Explorer,* Random House (New York, NY), 2001.

Under the Banner of Heaven: A Story of Violent Faith, Doubleday (New York, NY), 2003.

Contributor to several books, including foreword to *The Mountain of My Fear,* by David Roberts, Mountaineers Books, 1991; foreword to *Escape Routes: Further Adventure Writings of David Roberts,* by David Roberts, Mountaineers Books, 1997; introduction to *Touching My Father's Soul: A Sherpa's Journey to the Top of Everest,* by Jamling Tenzing Norgay with

Broughton Coburn, Harper San Francisco, 2001; and preface to *In the Land of White Death: An Epic Story of Survival in the Siberian Arctic,* by Valerian Albanov, introduction by David Roberts, expanded edition, Random House, 2001. Contributor to periodicals, including *Smithsonian, Outside,* and *Playboy.*

ADAPTATIONS: Into Thin Air was adapted for television by TriStar Television and broadcast on ABC-TV, 1997. It was also adapted into an audiocassette read by Krakauer by BAD, 1997.

SIDELIGHTS: Jon Krakauer is a journalist whose highly praised writings on mountain climbing and other sports combine the knowledge of the insider with the writer's sense of dramatic and well-timed storytelling. Born in Brookline, Massachusetts, in 1954, Krakauer was two years old when his family moved to the more rugged locale of Corvallis, Oregon; he began mountain climbing at the young age of eight. Krakauer's father, who led the hike up Oregon's ten-thousand-foot South Sister Mountain, was an acquaintance of climber Willi Unsoeld, who had been a member of the first American expedition to Mount Everest in 1963. As a boy, Krakauer idolized Unsoeld and fellow climber Tom Hornbein, and he dreamed of being like them and ascending to the summit of Everest some day.

Krakauer eventually attended Hampshire College in Massachusetts during the early 1970s. While at school, he met climbing writer David Roberts, who regaled him with stories of the excellent climbing in Alaska. In a *People* interview with William Plummer, Krakauer said, "I became a climbing bum. I worked as a carpenter in Boulder, Colorado, five months of the year, climbed the rest." In 1974, Krakauer climbed the Alaskan Arrigetch Peaks in the Brooks Range, ascending three peaks that had previously been unexplored. As a result, the American Alpine Club asked Krakauer to write about the climbs for its journal; this was the first article Krakauer wrote. Three years later, he published an article on climbing the Devil's Thumb in the British magazine *Mountain.* This article paid well enough for Krakauer to decide to become a freelance writer, and in 1983 he quit doing carpentry work and became a full-time writer.

"I have never received any formal training as a writer," Krakauer commented in *Outside Online.* "Whenever I read something that moves me, I re-read it many times to try and figure out how its author has worked his or her magic. . . . Like any craft, the longer and harder you work at your writing, the more likely you are to get better at it." Krakauer drew on his own experience to write his articles, using his carpentry experience to write about architecture for *Architectural Digest* and his experience as a commercial fisherman to write on commercial fishery for *Smithsonian.* He sent out about ten query letters a week, asking various editors if they were interested in his articles, and getting enough positive responses back to make a living. "I wanted to pay the bills, so I worked really hard," he wrote in an online *Bold Type* interview.

In the late 1970s, Krakauer met Linda Moore, a student at the University of Colorado at Denver, and married her in 1980. Moore, who was also a climber, thought Krakauer would stop climbing because of the risks involved. Although he promised her he would quit, he was unable to tear himself away from the mountains, and as he said in an *Outside Online* interview, "I came within a millimeter of wrecking our marriage. So, then we went through a bunch of years when climbing was a big issue. Now it is less of an issue. It is how I make my living, to no small degree. . . . It's a huge part of who I am, and I wouldn't be a writer if it wasn't for climbing, and Linda understands that and she accepts it."

As his writing career progressed, Krakauer found that he wrote best when he focused on outdoor subjects. His first book, *Eiger Dreams,* was a collection of magazine articles, which originally appeared in *Outside* and *Smithsonian.* Krakauer wrote about his own experiences climbing Mount McKinley, the North Face of the Eiger in Switzerland, and many other mountains, and tried to answer the question of why anyone would risk death by climbing these peaks. In the *New York Times Book Review,* Tim Cahill wrote, "The reader who knows little about climbing will learn much from *Eiger Dreams,* but Mr. Krakauer has taken the literature of mountains onto a higher ledge. His snow-capped peaks set against limitless blue skies present problems that inspire irrefutable human experiences: fear and triumph, damnation and salvation. There is beauty in his mountains beyond that expressed in conventional sermons. His reverence is earned, and it's entirely genuine."

In 1992, editors at *Outside* asked Krakauer to write about the life and death of Christopher McCandless, a twenty-four-year-old honors graduate who, prompted

by the writings of Leo Tolstoy, decided to give away all his possessions and go to the wilderness to experience transcendence. McCandless renamed himself Alex Supertramp and wandered through the American West, eventually reaching Alaska. Near Alaska's Denali National Park, he hiked into the bush, planning to live off the land. He carried with him only a .22 shotgun, a bag of rice, and some books. Four months later, his body was found: he had starved to death. Near the body was a desperate note in which he begged to be saved.

Krakauer used McCandless's journals and postcards, as well as interviews with those who knew him, to reconstruct the last two years of McCandless's life and write an article about it. However, McCandless's story fascinated Krakauer, and he expanded the article into a book, *Into the Wild.* In his introduction to the book, Krakauer wrote, "I was haunted by the particulars of the boy's starvation and by vague, unsettling parallels between events in his life and those in my own." Like McCandless, Krakauer had hitchhiked to Alaska in his early twenties. There, he set off into the wilderness to climb the Devil's Thumb, a forbidding peak, ignoring the pleas of family and friends that it was a foolhardy, dangerous undertaking. "The fact that I survived my Alaskan adventure and McCandless did not survive his was largely a matter of chance; had I died on the Stikine Icecap in 1977, people would have been quick to say of me, as they now say of him, that I had a death wish. . . . I was stirred by the mystery of death; I couldn't resist stealing up to the edge of doom and peering over the brink. The view into that swirling black vortex terrified me, but I caught sight of something elemental in that shadowy glimpse, some forbidden, fascinating riddle."

Although McCandless's death was commonly greeted with derision or apathy by Alaskans, who pointed to the arrogance inherent in his ill-equipped and untutored attempt to live off the land, Krakauer presented a sympathetic portrait of the young man and his yearnings. He wrote in the introduction to the book that in trying to understand McCandless, "I inevitably came to reflect on other, larger subjects as well: the grip wilderness has on the American imagination, the allure high-risk activities hold for young men of a certain mind, the complicated, highly charged bond that exists between fathers and sons." In the *New York Times Book Review,* Thomas McNamee wrote that as Krakauer "picks through the adventures and sorrows of Christopher McCandless's brief life, the story becomes painfully moving. Mr. Krakauer's elegantly constructed narrative takes us from the ghoulish moment of the hunters' discovery [of McCandless's body] back through McCandless's childhood, the gregarious effusions and icy withdrawals that characterized his coming of age, and, in meticulous detail, the two years of restless roaming that led him to Alaska. The more we learn about him, the more mysterious McCandless becomes, and the more intriguing."

Krakauer's next book, *Into Thin Air,* was also the result of a request by *Outside.* Asked to write about the increasing commercialization of Mount Everest climbing expeditions, Krakauer joined a climbing team led by Rob Hall, who had previously ascended the peak seven times. In the article that preceded the book, "Into Thin Air," Krakauer wrote that although he had previously abandoned his childhood dream of climbing the mountain, "When the call came to join Hall's expedition, I said yes without even hesitating to catch my breath. Boyhood dreams die hard, I discovered, and good sense be damned."

In *Outside* online Krakauer noted that at base camp, situated at an altitude of 17,600 feet, he saw that "there's a lot of inexperienced people here—and many people would say I'm one of them—and that's sort of scary. There's a lot of people here who shouldn't be here. And maybe I shouldn't be here. . . . People who wouldn't have the time and the experience—but they have the money—can do this."

He added that when he finally reached the summit of Everest, "straddling the top of the world, one foot in Tibet and the other in Nepal, I cleared the ice from my oxygen mask, hunched a shoulder against the wind, and stared absently at the vast sweep of earth below. I understood on some dim, detached level that it was a spectacular sight. I'd been fantasizing about this moment, and the release of emotion that would accompany it, for many months. But now that I was finally here, standing on the summit of Mount Everest, I just couldn't summon the energy to care." He also noted, "Reaching the top of Everest is supposed to trigger a surge of intense elation: against long odds, after all, I had just attained a goal I'd coveted since childhood. But the summit was really only the halfway point. Any impulse I might have felt toward self-congratulation was immediately extinguished by apprehension about the long, dangerous descent that lay ahead."

As Krakauer began the long, arduous descent down the mountain, a winter storm struck, stranding several climbers behind him. Krakauer managed to reach the safety of his camp in the darkness of the storm and the coming night, and he thought the other climbers would be close behind him. He was unaware that one of his teammates was already dead and that twenty-eight climbers were still on the mountain, struggling for their lives. It was a struggle that eight climbers, including Hall, lost. Krakauer, haunted by guilt because he was unable to do anything to save any of those who died, wrote about the trek for *Outside,* but as in *Into the Wild,* he wanted to explore the events more deeply than a relatively short magazine piece would allow. He expanded the article into the best-selling book *Into Thin Air: A Personal Account of the Mount Everest Disaster.* In the book, he wrote, "Days later . . . people would ask why, if the weather had begun to deteriorate, had climbers on the upper mountain not heeded the signs? Why did veteran Himalayan guides keep moving upward, leading a gaggle of amateurs . . . into an apparent death trap? Nobody can speak for the leaders of the two guided groups involved, for both men are now dead. But I can attest that nothing I saw early on the afternoon of May 10 suggested that a murderous storm was about to bear down on us."

The book was roundly criticized by friends and families of the climbers who died, as well as by other climbers who survived; they accused Krakauer of profiting off others' tragedy and of being too judgmental of the actions of the survivors. However, in *Outside,* Krakauer defended himself, commenting, "In writing the book I tried very hard to recount the events truthfully, in an even-handed, sympathetic manner that did not sensationalize the tragedy or cause undue pain to friends and families of the victims." In a discussion with *Outside* writer Mark Bryant, Krakauer said, "Plenty of people have said to me, 'Who are you to assess someone else's role or lack of experience or skill?' But I'm a working journalist, and I was there, and I was there to do a job—to tell what happened as best I could. I certainly feel that some people are hurt by my assessments, but somebody needed to step up and tell what went on up there."

Critics, on the other hand, praised the book, and readers kept it on the best-seller list for months. In *Forbes,* James M. Clash wrote, "Every once in a while a work of nonfiction comes along that's as good as anything a novelist could make up. Krakauer's new book . . . fits the bill." In the *New York Times Book Review,* Alastair Scott wrote that Krakauer "has produced a narrative that is both meticulously researched and deftly constructed. Unlike the expedition, his story rushes irresistibly forward." *Sports Illustrated* writer Ron Fimrite commented, "In this movingly written book, Krakauer describes an experience of such bone-chilling horror as to persuade even the most fanatical alpinists to seek sanctuary at sea level. Not that they're likely to do so."

In order to write the book, Krakauer filled up nine notebooks with detailed notes and observations. He told a *Boldtype* interviewer, "I sort of take notes the way photographers take photos. You just sort of scattershot everything, because you never know what's going to prove invaluable when you get back down. . . . The only time I didn't take notes was on summit day. I tried at 27,600 feet . . . but they're basically illegible, and they make no sense because my brain wasn't working [as a result of the low oxygen level at that altitude]." He also said that while writing the book, "I wanted more than anything else to show the complexities and ambiguities of this tragedy. . . . I wanted to tell the story in its full complexity."

In 2003, Krakauer departed from his series of books about the outdoors and people's passion for nature to discuss another kind of passion: religious fanaticism. *Under the Banner of Heaven: A Story of Violent Faith* examines the lives of polygamy-practicing Mormons who live in remote areas of the American West. According to Matthew Flamm in *Entertainment Weekly,* Krakauer said he wanted to understand "the terrible things people do . . . in the name of God."

Krakauer told Bryant, "I guess I don't try to justify climbing, or defend it, because I can't. There's no way to defend it, even to yourself, once you've been involved in something like this disaster. And yet I've continued to climb. I don't know what that says about me or the sport other than the potential power it has. What makes climbing great for me, strangely enough, is this life and death aspect. It sounds trite to say, I know, but climbing isn't just another game. It isn't just another sport. It's life itself."

BIOGRAPHICAL AND CRITICAL SOURCES:

PERIODICALS

Booklist, April 1, 1997, review of *Into Thin Air: A Personal Account of the Mount Everest Disaster,* p. 1276; March 15, 1998, review of *Into Thin Air,* p. 1211; April 1, 1998, review of *Into Thin Air,* p. 1311.

Choice, October, 1997, review of *Into Thin Air,* p. 334.

Christian Century, February 18, 1998, Jon Magnuson, review of *Into Thin Air,* p. 170.

Commonweal, December 4, 1998, review of *Into Thin Air,* p. 24.

Economist, September 6, 1997, review of *Into Thin Air,* pp. 17-18.

Entertainment Weekly, April 25, 1997, David Hochman, "Cliff Notes," pp. 40-43; May 2, 1997, review of *Into Thin Air,* p. 50; December 26, 1997, review of *Into Thin Air,* p. 150; April 17, 1998, review of *Into Thin Air,* p. 67; November 12, 1999, review of *Into Thin Air,* p. 73; February 21, 2003, Matthew Flamm, review of *Under the Banner of Heaven: A Story of Violent Faith,* p. 153.

Far Eastern Economic Review, August 7, 1997, review of *Into Thin Air,* p. 56.

Forbes, May 19, 1997, James M. Clash, review of *Into Thin Air,* p. 291.

Journal of the American Medical Association, April 14, 1999, Rollin James Hawley and Frederick L. Glauser, review of *Into Thin Air,* p. 1341.

Kirkus Reviews, February 1, 1990, p. 159; March 1, 1997, review of *Into Thin Air,* p. 357.

Kliatt, September, 1997, review of *Into Thin Air,* p. 29; September, 1997, review of *Into the Wild,* p. 3; May, 1998, review of *Into Thin Air,* p. 28; September, 1998, review of *Into Thin Air,* p. 4; March, 1999, p. 63.

Library Journal, November 15, 1995, p. 96; April 1, 1997, review of *Into Thin Air,* p. 117; September 15, 1997, p. 120.

London Review of Books, January 1, 1998, review of *Into Thin Air,* p. 31.

Los Angeles Times Book Review, September 3, 1995, p. 9.

Maclean's, June 23, 1997, review of *Into Thin Air,* p. 60.

New Statesman, August 22, 1997, Peter Gillman, review of *Into Thin Air,* p. 44.

Newsweek, April 21, 1997, review of *Into Thin Air,* p. 76.

New Yorker, May 12, 1997, review of *Into Thin Air,* p. 101.

New York Review of Books, August 14, 1997, review of *Into the Wild,* p. 59.

New York Times, January 4, 1996, p. C17; May 6, 1997.

New York Times Book Review, June 10, 1990, Tim Cahill, "Travel," p. 48; March 3, 1996, Jon Krakauer, "Adventures of Alexander Supertramp," p. 29; March 2, 1997, review of *Into Thin Air,* p. 28; May 18, 1997, Alastair Scott, review of *Into Thin Air,* p. G11; June 1, 1997, review of *Into Thin Air,* p. 39; July 13, 1997, review of *Eiger Dreams: Ventures among Men and Mountains,* p. 28; December 7, 1997, review of *Into Thin Air,* p. 12; April 12, 1998, review of *Into Thin Air,* p. 24; May 31, 1998, review of *Into Thin Air,* p. 50.

Observer (London, England), March 8, 1998, review of *Into the Wild,* p. 15.

Outside, January, 1993, Jon Krakauer, "Death of an Innocent"; February, 1996; September, 1996, Jon Krakauer, "Into Thin Air"; May 20, 1997, Mark Bryant, "Everest a Year Later: False Summit."

People, February 12, 1996, p. 35; June 2, 1997, William Plummer, review of *Into Thin Air,* pp. 53-57.

Publishers Weekly, February 20, 1990, p. 73; October 19, 1990, p. 44; November 6, 1995, p. 76; March 17, 1997, review of *Into Thin Air,* p. 63; May 5, 1997, p. 20; July 14, 1997, p. 18; September 22, 1997, p. 28.

Quill & Quire, March, 1999, review of *Into Thin Air,* p. 52.

San Francisco Review, January, 1997, review of *Into Thin Air,* p. 48.

School Library Journal, August, 1990, p. 178; November, 1997, review of *Into Thin Air,* p. 150; December, 1997, review of *Into Thin Air,* p. 29.

Sports Illustrated, May 12, 1997, Ron Fimrite, review of *Into Thin Air,* p. 18.

Time, April 21, 1997, John Skow, review of *Into Thin Air,* p. 123; December 29, 1997, review of *Into Thin Air,* p. 155.

Times Literary Supplement, December 26, 1997, review of *Into Thin Air,* p. 6.

Tribune Books (Chicago, IL), March 23, 1997, review of *Into Thin Air,* p. 6.

Voice of Youth Advocates, April, 1998, review of *Into Thin Air,* p. 37.

Wall Street Journal, May 29, 1997, review of *Into Thin Air,* p. A16.

Washington Post Book World, February 23, 1997, review of *Into Thin Air,* p. 12.

Whole Earth Review, winter, 2001, review of *Into Thin Air,* p. 69.

ONLINE

Bold Type Web site, http://www.randomhouse.com/ boldtype/ (May 28, 2003), interview with Krakauer.

BookPage.com, http://www.bookpage.com/ (November 10, 2003), Alden Mudge, review of *Into Thin Air.*

International Network on Personal Healing, http:// www.meaning.ca/bookstore/ (April, 1998), Jamie Leggatt, review of *Into Thin Air.*

Outside Online, http://www.outside.com/ (April 15, 1996), Jon Krakauer, "Into Thin Air."*

L

LAWRENCE, D(avid) H(erbert Richards) 1885-1930

(Jessie Chambers, Lawrence H. Davison)

PERSONAL: Born September 11, 1885, in Eastwood, Nottinghamshire, England; died of tuberculosis, March 2, 1930, in Vence, France; son of John Arthur (a coal miner) and Lydia (a schoolteacher; maiden name, Beardsall) Lawrence; married Frieda von Richthofen Weekley, July 13, 1914. *Education:* Nottingham University College, teacher training certificate, 1908. *Hobbies and other interests:* Oil painting.

CAREER: Writer. Worked as a manufacturer's clerk, 1899; pupil-teacher, 1902-06, first at Eastwood British School, then at Ilkeston, Derbyshire; Davidson Road School, Croydon, England, junior assistant master, 1908-11.

AWARDS, HONORS: James Tait Black Memorial Prize, Edinburgh University, 1921, for *The Lost Girl.*

WRITINGS:

NOVELS

The White Peacock, Duffield, 1911, revised edition edited by Andrew Robertson, introduction by Melvyn Bragg, Viking (New York, NY), 1984, reprinted, 1995.

The Trespasser, M. Kennerley (New York, NY), 1912, revised edition edited by Elizabeth Mansfield, Viking (New York, NY), 1983, revised with Elizabeth Mansfield, Penguin (New York, NY), 1994.

Sons and Lovers, M. Kennerley (New York, NY), 1913, reprinted, Dover (Mineola, NY), 2002, edited with an introduction and notes by Keith Sagar, Penguin, 1981, with notes by Helen and Carl Baron, Penguin (New York, NY), 1994, with notes by David Trotter, Oxford University Press (New York, NY), 1995, published as *Sons and Lovers: A Facsimile of the Manuscript,* edited with an introduction by Mark Schorer, University of California Press (Berkeley, CA), 1977, expanded edition edited by Helen and Carl Baron, Cambridge University Press (New York, NY), 1992, with an introduction by Geoff Dyer, Modern Library (New York, NY), 1999.

The Rainbow, Methuen (London, England), 1915, expurgated edition, B. W. Huebsch (New York, NY), 1916, reprinted edition edited with an introduction and notes by John Worthen, Penguin, 1981, reprinted, with Mark Kinkead-Weekes, Penguin (New York, NY), 1995.

Women in Love, privately printed (New York, NY), 1920, M. Secker (London, England), 1921, T. Seltzer (New York, NY), 1922, with foreword by Lawrence, introduction by Richard Aldington, Penguin, 1983, expanded edition edited by David R. Farmer, Lindeth Vasey, and John Worthen, Cambridge University Press (New York, NY), 1987, reprinted, Modern Library (New York, NY), 2002.

The Lost Girl, M. Secker (London, England), 1920, T. Seltzer (New York, NY), 1921, edited by John Worthen, Viking (New York, NY), 1982, with an introduction by Jeffrey Meyers, Bantam Books (New York, NY), 1996, with an introduction by Lee Diegel, Modern Library (New York, NY), 2003.

Aaron's Rod, T. Seltzer (New York, NY), 1922, new edition, Viking (New York, NY), 1972.

The Captain's Doll: Three Novelettes (contains *The Captain's Doll, The Fox* [also see below], and *The Ladybird*), T. Seltzer (New York, NY), 1923, published as *The Ladybird. The Fox. The Captain's Doll,* M. Secker (London, England), 1923, reprinted, Penguin, 1994.

Kangaroo, T. Seltzer (New York, NY), 1923, new edition, introduction by Richard Aldington, Viking (New York, NY), 1974, edited by Bruce Steele and with a new introduction, Penguin (New York, NY), 1997.

(With M. L. Skinner) *The Boy in the Bush,* T. Seltzer (New York, NY), 1924, facsimile reprint, Southern Illinois University Press (Carbondale, IL), 1971, edited and with introduction and notes by Paul Eggert, Penguin (New York, NY), 1996.

St. Mawr, Knopf (New York, NY), 1925, expanded edition published as *St. Mawr, together with The Princess* (also see below), M. Secker (London, England), 1925.

The Plumed Serpent (Quetzalcoatl), Knopf (New York, NY), 1926, with an introduction by William York Tindall, 1951.

Sun, expurgated edition, E. Archer, 1926, unexpurgated edition, Black Sun Press (Paris, France), 1928.

Lady Chatterley's Lover, privately printed, G. Orioli (Florence, Italy), 1928, W. Faro, 1930, expurgated edition, Knopf (New York, NY), 1932, unexpurgated edition, Heinemann (London, England), 1956, with an introduction by Mark Schorer, Grove (New York, NY), 1959, published as *The Complete and Unexpurgated Edition of Lady Chatterley's Lover* (includes decision by Federal Judge Frederick van Pelt Bryan) Pyramid Books (New York, NY), 1959, published with Lawrence's preface, "A Propos of Lady Chatterley's Lover" (also see below), Heinemann (London, England), 1982, reprint of third manuscript version, preface by Archibald MacLeish, introduction by Schorer, Modern Library (New York, NY), 1983, published as *Lady Chatterley's Lover; A Propos of Lady Chatterley's Lover,* Penguin (New York, NY), 1994, with an introduction by Kathryn Harrison, Modern Library (New York, NY), 2001, with an introduction by Geoff Dyer, New American Library (New York, NY), 2003.

The Escaped Cock, Black Sun Press (Paris, France), 1929, published as *The Man Who Died,* Knopf (New York, NY), 1931, reprinted, Ecco Press, 1994, expanded edition published in two volumes, Black Sparrow Press, 1973.

The Virgin and the Gypsy, Knopf (New York, NY), 1930, reprinted, Random House (New York, NY), 1984.

The First Lady Chatterley, Dial Press (New York, NY), 1944, published as *The First Lady Chatterley: The First Version of Lady Chatterley's Lover,* foreword by Frieda Lawrence, Heinemann (London, England), 1972.

The Fox, Sphere (London, England), 1971.

John Thomas and Lady Jane, Viking (New York, NY), 1972, published as *John Thomas and Lady Jane: The Second Version of Lady Chatterley's Lover,* Heinemann (London, England), 1972).

Mr. Noon (unfinished; portions previously published in *A Modern Lover* [also see below]), edited by Lindeth Vasey, Cambridge University Press (New York, NY), 1984.

Quetzalcoatl: The Early Version of "The Plumed Serpent," Black Swan, 1995, edited with an introduction by Louis L. Martz, New Directions (New York, NY), 1998.

SHORT FICTION

The Prussian Officer and Other Stories, Duckworth (London, England), 1914, B. W. Huebsch (New York, NY), 1916, edited by John Worthen, introduction by Melvyn Bragg, Viking (New York, NY), 1984, reprinted, Oxford University Press (New York, NY), 1995.

England, My England and Other Stories, T. Seltzer (New York, NY), 1922, reprinted, Books for Libraries Press, 1972.

Glad Ghosts (also see below), E. Benn (London, England), 1926

The Woman Who Rode Away and Other Stories (includes "Sun," "The Woman Who Rode Away," and "The Man Who Loved Islands"), Knopf (New York, NY), 1928, revised, Berkley Publishing (New York, NY), 1995.

Rawdon's Roof (also see below), Elkin Mathews & Marrot, 1928.

Love among the Haystacks, and Other Pieces, reminiscence by David Garnett, Nonesuch Press (London, England), 1930, Viking (New York, NY), 1933, edited by John Worthen and with an introduction by Keith Cushman, Penguin (New York, NY), 1996.

The Lovely Lady (includes "The Rocking-Horse Winner"), M. Secker (London, England), 1932, Viking (New York, NY), 1933, reprinted, Books for Libraries Press, 1972.

A Modern Lover, Viking (New York, NY), 1934, reprinted in *A Modern Lover and Other Short Stories,* Oxford University Press (New York, NY), 1995.

A Prelude (first published under pseudonym Jessie Chambers in the *Nottingham Guardian*), Merle Press, 1949.

Complete Short Stories, three volumes, Heinemann (London, England), 1955, published as *The Collected Short Stories of D. H. Lawrence,* 1974, Viking (New York, NY), 1961.

The Horse Dealer's Daughter, School of Art Press (Oxford, England), 1963.

The Rocking-Horse Winner, edited by Dominick P. Consolo, C. E. Merrill, 1969.

The Princess and Other Stories, Penguin (London, England), 1971.

The Mortal Coil and Other Stories, edited by Keith Sagar, Penguin (London, England), 1971.

You Touched Me, illustrated by Sandra Higashi, Creative Education, Inc., 1982.

Four Short Novels, Franklin Library (Franklin Center, PA), 1984.

Erotic Works, edited by Claire Booss and Christopher Busa, Gramercy Books (New York, NY), 2003.

Selected Stories, edited and with an introduction by James Wood, Modern Library (New York, NY), 1999.

POETRY

Love Poems and Others, Duckworth (London, England), 1913, M. Kennerley (New York, NY), 1915.

Amores, B. W. Huebsch (New York, NY), 1916.

Look! We Have Come Through!, Chatto & Windus (London, England), 1917, B. W. Huebsch, 1918, published as *Look! We Have Come Through! A Cycle of Love Poems,* introduction by Frieda Lawrence, illustrated by M. Adam, Ark Press (Dulverton, England), 1958, with woodcuts by Felix Hoffman, Humanities Research Center, University of Texas (Austin, TX), 1971.

New Poems, M. Secker (London, England), 1918, B. W. Huebsch, 1920, reprint of Secker edition, Haskell House, 1974.

Bay, Beaumont, 1919.

Tortoises, T. Seltzer (New York, NY), 1921, published as *Tortoises: Six Poems,* introduction by Jefferson Hunter, illustrated with wood engravings by Alan James Robinson, Cheloniidae Press (Williamsburg, MA), 1983.

Birds, Beasts, and Flowers, T. Seltzer (New York, NY), 1923, reprinted, Haskell House, 1974.

The Collected Poems of D. H. Lawrence, Volume I: *Rhyming Poems,* Volume II: *Unrhyming Poems,* M. Secker (London, England), 1928, published in one volume, 1932.

Pansies, Knopf (New York, NY), 1929, expanded edition privately printed, 1929.

Nettles, Faber (London, England), 1930.

Last Poems, edited by Richard Aldington and Giuseppe Orioli, G. Orioli (Florence Italy), 1932, Viking, (New York, NY) 1933, reprinted, Scholarly Press, 1971.

The Ship of Death and Other Poems, M. Secker (London, England), 1933.

Fire and Other Poems, foreword by Robinson Jeffers, note by Frieda Lawrence, Grabhorn Press, 1940.

The Complete Poems of D. H. Lawrence, collected and edited with an introduction and notes by Vivian de Sola Pinto and Warren Roberts, Heinemann (London, England), 1964, Viking (New York, NY), 1971.

D. H. Lawrence: Poems Selected for Young People, Viking (New York, NY), 1967.

The Body of God, Ark Press (Dulverton, England), 1970.

D. H. Lawrence: Selected Poetry and Non-Fictional Prose, Routledge (New York, NY), 1990.

No One Else Is Lawrence!: A Dozen of D. H. Lawrence's Best Poems, Harbour Publishing (Madeira Park, British Columbia, Canada), 1998.

Snake and Other Poems, Dover Publications (Mineola, NY), 1999.

PLAYS

The Widowing of Mrs. Holroyd: A Drama in Three Acts (produced in London, England, 1926; also see below), M. Kennerley (New York, NY), 1914, edited and with an introduction by Simon Trussler, Oxford University Press (New York, NY), 2001, with foreword by John Worthen, Pine Street Books (Philadelphia, PA), 2002.

Touch and Go: A Play in Three Acts (first produced in Oxford, England, 1979), T. Seltzer (New York, NY), 1920.

David (first produced in London, England, 1927), Knopf (New York, NY), 1926, reprinted, Haskell House, 1974.

A Collier's Friday Night (first produced in London, England, 1973), privately printed, 1940, Norwood Editions (Norwood, PA), 1976.

Complete Plays, Heinemann (London, England), 1965, Viking (New York, NY), 1966.

The Daughter-in-Law, first produced in London, England, at Royal Court Theatre, 1967.

The Fight for Barbara, first produced in London, England, 1967.

Plays (contains *The Widowing of Mrs. Holroyd, David, The Married Man, The Daughter-in-Law, The Fight for Barbara, Touch and Go, The Merry-Go-Round, A Collier's Friday Night, Altitude,* and *Noah's Flood*), introduction by Malcolm Elwin, Heron Books, 1969.

Plays, edited by Hans-Wilhelm Schwarze and John Worthen, Cambridge University Press (New York, NY), 1999.

TRAVEL SKETCHES

Twilight in Italy, B. W. Huebsch (New York, NY), 1916, published as *Twilight in Italy and Other Essays,* Cambridge University Press (New York, NY), 1995.

Sea and Sardinia, T. Seltzer (New York, NY), 1921, new edition, introduction by Richard Aldington, Viking (New York, NY), 1963.

Mornings in Mexico, Knopf (New York, NY), 1927, new edition, introduction by Ross Parmenter, G. M. Smith (Salt Lake City, UT), 1982.

Etruscan Places, Viking (New York, NY), 1932, reprinted, 1963.

D. H. Lawrence and New Mexico, G. M. Smith (Salt Lake City, UT), 1982.

Sketches of Etruscan Places and Other Italian Essays, Cambridge University Press (New York, NY), 1992.

D. H. Lawrence and Italy, with an introduction by Anthony Burgess, Penguin (New York, NY), 1997.

D. H. Lawrence in Italy and England, edited by George Donaldson and Mara Kalnins, St. Martin's Press (New York, NY), 1998.

NONFICTION

(Under pseudonym Lawrence H. Davison) *Movements in European History,* Oxford University Press (Oxford, England), 1921, published under name D. H. Lawrence, 1925, reprinted, 1971.

Psychoanalysis and the Unconscious (also see below), T. Seltzer (New York, NY), 1921.

Fantasia of the Unconscious (also see below), T. Seltzer (New York, NY), 1922.

Studies in Classic American Literature (essays), T. Seltzer (New York, NY), 1923, new edition, Penguin, 1977.

Reflections on the Death of a Porcupine and Other Essays, Centaur Press (Philadelphia, PA), 1925, Indiana University Press, 1963.

Pornography and Obscenity, Faber (London, England), 1929, Knopf (New York, NY), 1930, published as *Pornography and Obscenity: An Essay,* Alicat Book Shop, 1948.

Assorted Articles, Knopf (New York, NY), 1930, reprinted, Books for Libraries Press, 1968.

Apocalypse (also see below), G. Orioli (Florence, Italy), 1931, with an introduction by Richard Aldington, Viking (New York, NY), 1932, reprinted, 1966.

We Need One Another (two essays; originally published in *Scribner's*), illustrations by John P. Heins, Equinox, (London, England) 1933, reprinted, Haskell House, 1974.

Phoenix: The Posthumous Papers of D. H. Lawrence, edited with an introduction by Edward D. McDonald, Viking (New York, NY), 1936, reprinted, 1972.

Sex, Literature, and Censorship: Essays, edited by Harry T. Moore, Twayne (New York, NY), 1953.

Selected Literary Criticism, Heinemann (London, England), 1955.

The Symbolic Meaning: The Uncollected Versions of Studies in Classic American Literature, edited by Armin Arnold, preface by Harry T. Moore, Centaur Press (Philadelphia, PA), 1962.

Phoenix II: Uncollected, Unpublished, and Other Prose Works, edited with an introduction and notes by Warren Roberts and Harry T. Moore, Viking (New York, NY), 1968.

D. H. Lawrence on Education, Penguin Education (Harmondsworth, England), 1973.

Lawrence on Hardy and Painting: Study of Thomas Hardy [and] *Introduction to These Paintings* (essays; originally published in *Phoenix,* 1936), Heinemann Educational (London, England), 1973.

Study of Thomas Hardy and Other Essays, Cambridge University Press (New York, NY), 1985.

Selected Works, Gramercy (New York, NY), 1994.

Apocalypse and the Writings on Revelation, edited by Mara Kalnins, Penguin (New York, NY), 1996.

Selected Critical Writings, edited with an introduction and notes by Michael Herbert, Oxford University Press (New York, NY), 1998.

Psychanalysis and the Unconscious; and, Fantasia of the Unconscious, Cambridge University Press (New York, NY), 2003.

Late Essays and Articles, edited by James T. Boulton, Cambridge University Press (New York, NY), 2004.

Introductions and Reviews, edited by N. H. Reeve and John Worthen, Cambridge University Press (New York, NY), 2004.

LETTERS

The Letters of D. H. Lawrence, edited with an introduction by Aldous Huxley, Viking (New York, NY), 1932.

D. H. Lawrence: Reminiscences and Correspondence, edited by Earl Brewster and Achsah Brewster, M. Secker (London, England), 1934.

D. H. Lawrence's Letter to "The Laughing Horse," privately printed, 1936.

Letters to Bertrand Russell, edited by Harry T. Moore, Gotham Book Mart (New York, NY), 1948.

Selected Letters, introduction by Aldous Huxley, Penguin (London, England), 1950, reprinted, 1996.

Eight Letters to Rachel Annand Taylor, foreword by Majl Ewing, Castle Press, 1956.

Collected Letters, edited with an introduction by Harry T. Moore, two volumes, Viking (New York, NY), 1962.

Lawrence in Love: Letters to Louie Burrows, edited with an introduction and notes by James T. Boulton, University of Nottingham (Nottingham, England), 1968.

The Quest for Rananim: D. H. Lawrence's Letters to S. S. Koteliansky, 1914 to 1930, edited with an introduction by George J. Zytaruk, McGill-Queen's University Press (Montreal, Quebec, Canada), 1970.

Letters from D. H. Lawrence to Martin Secker, 1911-1930, privately printed (London, England), 1970.

The Centaur Letters, introduction by Edward D. Mc-Donald, Humanities Research Center, University of Texas (Austin, TX), 1970.

Consciousness, privately printed by the Press of the Pegacycle Lady, 1974.

Letters to Thomas and Adele Seltzer, edited by Gerald M. Lacy, Black Sparrow Press, 1976.

The Letters of D. H. Lawrence, Cambridge University Press (New York, NY), Volume I: *September, 1901-May, 1913,* edited by James T. Boulton, 1979, Volume II: *June, 1913-October, 1916,* edited by George J. Zytaruk and Boulton, 1982, Volume III: *October, 1916-June, 1921,* edited by Boulton and Andrew Robertson, 1984, Volume IV: *1921-1924,* edited by Boulton, Elizabeth Mansfield, and Warren Roberts, 1987, Volume V: *1924-1927,* edited by Boulton and Lindeth Vasey, 1989, Volume VI: *March, 1927-November, 1928,* edited by James and Margaret Boulton, 1991, Volume VII: *November, 1928-February, 1930,* edited by J. Boulton and Keith Sager, 1994.

The Letters of D. H. Lawrence and Amy Lowell, 1914-1925, edited by E. Claire Healey and Keith Cushman, Black Sparrow Press, 1985.

The Selected Letters of D. H. Lawrence, edited by James T. Boulton, Cambridge University Press (New York, NY), 1996.

OTHER

(Translator) A. F. Grazzini, *The Story of Doctor Manente,* G. Orioli (Florence, Italy), 1919.

(Translator) Giovanni Verga, *Mastro-Don Gesualdo,* T. Seltzer (New York, NY), 1923.

(Author of introduction) Maurice Magnus, *Memoirs of the Foreign Legion,* M. Secker (London, England), 1924.

(Author of foreword) *A Bibliography of the Writings of D. H. Lawrence,* Norwood Editions (Norwood, PA), 1925.

(Translator) Giovanni Verga, *Little Novels of Sicily,* T. Seltzer (New York, NY), 1925, reprinted, Steerforth Italia (South Royalton, VT), 2000.

Reflections on the Death of a Porcupine and Other Essays, Centaur Press (Philadelphia, PA), 1925.

(Translator) Giovanni Verga, *Cavalleria Rusticana,* J. Cape (London, England), 1928.

My Skirmish with Jolly Roger, Random House (New York, NY), 1929, revised edition published as *A Propos of Lady Chatterley's Lover, Being an Essay Extended from "My Skirmish with Jolly Roger,"* Mandrake Press, 1930, reprinted, Haskell House, 1973, published as *A Propos of Lady Chatterley's Lover,* M. Secker (London, England), 1931.

The Paintings of D. H. Lawrence, introduction by Lawrence, privately printed for subscribers only, Mandrake Press, 1929.

D. H. Lawrence's Unpublished Foreword to "Women in Love," 1919, preface by Nathan van Patten, Gelber, Lilienthal, 1936.

The Portable D. H. Lawrence, Viking Press (New York, NY), 1947.

Life, Ark Press (Surrey, England), 1954.

The Later D. H. Lawrence: The Best Novels, Stories, Essays, 1925-1930, University of Nottingham (Nottingham, England), 1968.

Lawrence on Hardy and Painting: Study of Thomas Hardy, Knopf (New York, NY), 1973.

Ten Paintings, Carcanet (Manchester, England), 1982.

The Sayings of D. H. Lawrence, Duckworth (London, England), 1995.

Work represented in anthologies and collections. Contributor of works in a variety of genres to periodicals, including the *Adelphi, Dial, English Review, Equinox,* and *Vanity Fair.*

ADAPTATIONS: A number of Lawrence's works have been adapted for film, including the novels *Sons and Lovers, Women in Love, Kangaroo,* and *Lady Chatterley's Lover,* and the short novel *The Fox.* Works adapted for other media include *The Fox,* which was adapted as a play, and *Lady Chatterley's Lover,* which was released as a sound recording.

SIDELIGHTS: During most of his career as a writer, D. H. Lawrence sparked controversy, and debate continues to characterize discussion of his life and work. Personally, his elopement with Frieda von Richthofen Weekley, the wife of another man, branded him an interloper. His peripatetic existence, marked by frequent changes of residence, country, and continent, earned Lawrence a reputation as a bohemian. Moreover, his personality, capable alternately of charm and malice, provoked extreme reactions from others. Professionally, his work defied not only the conventional artistic norms of his day but also its political, social, and moral values. In his foreword to *D. H. Lawrence and Human Existence* by Father William Tiverton, T. S. Eliot criticized Lawrence for "express[ing] his insights in the form least likely to make them acceptable to most of his contemporaries."

In particular, the sexual explicitness of many of Lawrence's books and paintings inflamed contemporary public opinion and resulted in several notorious court cases on charges of obscenity and pornography. As late as 1985 Lydia Blanchard, in *D. H. Lawrence's "Lady": A New Look at "Lady Chatterley's Lover,"* defended Lawrence against such accusations by as-

sociating him with "the battle against prudery and censorship, with the fight both to destroy the sexual restrictions of the Victorian age and to affirm the phallic reality of the body." Shortly after Lawrence's death, a London *Times* writer regretted that Lawrence "confused decency with hypocrisy, and honesty with the free and public use of vulgar words." However, in the *Nation and Athenaeum,* E. M. Forster lauded him as "the greatest imaginative genius of our generation."

The scope of Lawrence's "imaginative genius" was large. Best known as a novelist and short-story writer, he was also a notable poet and essayist. In *D. H. Lawrence: Novelist,* F. R. Leavis called him "an incomparable literary critic." According to Jeffrey Meyers in *D. H. Lawrence and the Experience of Italy,* his letters are "the greatest in English since [John] Keats and [Lord] Byron"; and his travel books "shift[ed] the center of interest from the external world to the self." In addition, Lawrence completed seven plays, of which two—*The Widowing of Mrs. Holroyd* and *David*—were staged during his lifetime. He also painted, especially during the last few years of his life, finding in that practice, as he noted in an essay collected in *Assorted Articles,* "a form of delight that words can never give."

Leavis described the strength of Lawrence's prose as "an infallible centrality of judgment" stemming from "an unfailingly sure sense of the difference between that which makes for life and that which makes against it, of the difference between health and that which tends away from health." Along the same lines, Richard Ellmann wrote in an essay for *The Achievement of D. H. Lawrence,* that "Lawrence wrote his poetry, and much of his prose, as a healer." Ironically, he spent most of his life in poor health, fighting tuberculosis of the lungs, which at last proved fatal.

Frail from birth, David Herbert Richards Lawrence was the fourth of five children born to Arthur John Lawrence, a coal miner, and Lydia Beardsall Lawrence, a former schoolteacher whom Lawrence described as "superior" in an autobiographical sketch from *Assorted Articles.* Lawrence grew up where he was born, in Eastwood, a Nottinghamshire mining village in the Midlands of England. Late in life he confessed, in an autobiographical fragment published in *Phoenix:* "Nothing depresses me more than to come home to the place where I was born, and where I lived my first twenty years." Physical want and constant bickering between his parents plagued his childhood. In "Discord in Childhood," a lyric poem about those early years, Lawrence described his parents' respective voices as "a slender lash / Whistling she-delirious rage, and the dreadful sound / Of a male thong booming and bruising."

In *The Priest of Love,* biographer Harry T. Moore noted: "Even more than in the case of other intensely autobiographical authors, [Lawrence's] life helps to illuminate his writings." Lawrence's most widely read novel, *Sons and Lovers,* is an autobiographical account of his youth, "a purgation become the successful work of art," claimed Seymour Betsky in *The Achievement of D. H. Lawrence.* In a letter dated November 14, 1912, Lawrence referred to the "battle . . . between the mother and the girl, with the son as object," which rages at the center of the novel. It represents Lawrence's divided feelings for his own mother and for Jessie Chambers, the "Miriam" of the novel and many of the early poems, whom Lawrence met when he was sixteen. Like Paul Morel in the novel, the adolescent Lawrence "knitted together with his mother in perfect intimacy." Consequently, when he came into contact with women, theorized Chambers in *D. H. Lawrence: A Personal Record,* there was "a split." In a November 14, 1912, letter Lawrence described the novel, and by implication the personal story it tells, as "a great tragedy."

Not only *Sons and Lovers* but also many of his other novels and tales have some connection with Eastwood and its adjacent countryside and with the people he knew there. Lawrence's first novel, *The White Peacock,* "idealized" his family, friends, and their immediate surroundings according to Emile Delavenay in his biography *D. H. Lawrence: The Man and His Work.* Lawrence's acknowledged masterpieces, *The Rainbow* and *Women in Love,* drew upon life in Eastwood and on Lawrence's own experience and that of friends and acquaintances, who frequently served as the originals on which he modeled his characters. Even his last major novel, *Lady Chatterley's Lover,* returned to the Midlands, one of Lawrence's enduring symbols, for its setting. "There the natural beauty . . . comes up against industrial ugliness," wrote Moore in *The Priest of Love.* This ironic juxtaposition became one of the most prevalent themes in Lawrence's work.

Soon after he broke into the literary world, Lawrence met Edward Garnett, a reader for a publishing firm. With Garnett's encouragement, Lawrence had exten-

sively revised his first novel, *The Trespasser,* before its publication. Garnett's sensitive criticism also helped Lawrence to complete *Sons and Lovers* and to put together his first book of verse, *Love Poems and Others.* As a tribute to Garnett, whom the young writer regarded as both father and brother, Lawrence dedicated *Sons and Lovers* to him. Interestingly, Lawrence was at first angry and bitter at the significant editing Garnett did to his original manuscript for the book. Feeling that the book's length and its frank sexual language would make it unpublishable, Garnett altered numerous passages and cut the length of the manuscript by more than 2,000 lines. Despite his original feelings, Lawrence eventually expressed gratitude and praise for Garnett's editing of the manuscript. The original, unedited version was not published until 1992, when Cambridge University Press produced a new, copyrighted version of the full manuscript.

Productive as they were artistically, these years were filled with personal crises. As Lawrence wrote in the foreword to *Collected Poems,* first came the "long illness and then the death of my mother; and in the sick year after, . . . I almost dissolved away myself, and was very ill." Because of his near-fatal illness, Lawrence gave up his teaching position and decided to live entirely on the earnings from his writing. He also terminated his relationships with several women, all of whom appear in his early fiction and poetry: Jessie Chambers, Helen Corke, and Louie Burrows—the "Beloved" of the poems and Lawrence's fiancée for almost two years. Then in April, 1912, on the eve of his departure for the continent, Lawrence met Frieda Weekley, the German-born, aristocratic wife of a professor at the University of Nottingham. In a letter to her written soon after their meeting, Lawrence called her "the most wonderful woman in all England." Scarcely one month later, Frieda eloped with Lawrence to Germany, leaving her husband and three small children behind. Thus began the unconventional, wandering life of the next twenty years that took the Lawrences—they married two years later, following Frieda's divorce—first to Italy, back to England during World War I, then to Sicily, Ceylon, Australia, the United States, Mexico, and finally once more to the Mediterranean.

Lawrence completed the final version of *Sons and Lovers* in Italy, where he and Frieda lived from 1912 to 1914. Although Lawrence later denied any intentional use of Freudian theories in writing the novel, early readers were quick to identify Freudian elements in the book. Alfred Booth Kuttner used Freudian theory to discuss the novel in an article for *Psychoanalytic Review,* the first important psychoanalytic study of Lawrence's work. Going one step further, John Middleton Murry, Lawrence's best friend during the war years, justified his theory, through references to *Sons and Lovers,* that Lawrence himself suffered from the Oedipus complex. In *Son of Woman,* his biography of Lawrence, Murry said of protagonist Paul Morel and by implication of Lawrence: "All unconsciously his mother had roused in him the stirrings of sexual desire. . . . He felt for his mother what he should have felt for the girl of his choice." However, Dorothy Van Ghent rejected the dominant Freudian interpretation of the novel, proposing in *D. H. Lawrence: A Collection of Critical Essays* that its central conflict originates in the clash between "the creative life force witnessed in the independent objectivity of things" and the "human attempt to distort and corrupt that selfhood." In Van Ghent's view, the novel alerts readers to "'the drift toward death' which Lawrence thought of as the disease syndrome of his time and of Europe."

Critical reactions to *Sons and Lovers* ranged from high praise to condemnation. Typical of the diverse reviews, a *Manchester Guardian* contributor judged the book "an achievement of the first quality," while in the *Nation* a critic warned of "boredom" and found the plot "commonplace and decadent." In contrast, *Love Poems and Others,* published the same year, won uniformly high praise. Ezra Pound asserted in *Poetry* that "there is no English poet under forty who can get within shot of him. . . . He has brought contemporary verse up to the level of contemporary prose."

Much that Lawrence wrote in Italy was about England, but he variously recorded his impressions of Italy in sketches later published as *Twilight in Italy, Sea and Sardinia,* and *Etruscan Places,* as well as in fiction—most extensively in *The Lost Girl* and *Aaron's Rod,* poetry, essays, and numerous letters. Referring to Italy, Meyers noted that "the sympathetic people, the traditional life, and especially the pagan, primitive element revitalized Lawrence and inspired his astonishing creative achievement. . . . Lawrence's discovery of Italy was also a discovery of himself."

Out of this period came *The Prussian Officer and Other Stories,* Lawrence's first collection of tales.

Delavenay stressed that these works placed Lawrence "in the front rank of contemporary English short story writers." R. E. Pritchard commented in *D. H. Lawrence: Body of Darkness* that "in their revised form, [these stories] mark the beginning of the 'true,' unmuffled Lawrence." Looking forward to his later writing, they transcend "conventional understanding of morality, personality, and even life . . . in search of the dark reality buried in the body, where consciousness, individuality, and sexuality are absorbed in the nonhuman source of life." In *D. H. Lawrence at Work: The Emergence of "The Prussian Officer" Stories,* Keith Cushman stressed the importance of this volume to understanding Lawrence's artistic development. As Janice Hubbard Harris wrote in *The Short Fiction of D. H. Lawrence,* "The individual tales, from 1907 to 1928, constitute a steady program of imaginative acts, each story having the potential to inspire Lawrence toward new projects or warn him of likely dead ends."

Also at this time, Lawrence began "The Sisters"—also called "The Wedding Ring" in manuscript—which after many drafts became *The Rainbow* and *Women in Love.* In *D. H. Lawrence: Novelist,* Leavis claimed that these two novels prove Lawrence to be "the greatest kind of artist" and represent "a supreme creative achievement." Because of these works, the critic identified Lawrence as "one of the major novelists of the English tradition." Leavis aggressively championed Lawrence as a novelist in *Scrutiny* in the early 1950s; until that time, as Hoffman and Moore pointed out, Lawrence's "new, bold, experimental, and anti-traditional writing made it difficult for critics to place him."

In an attempt to explain his unconventional novelistic style to a skeptical Garnett, Lawrence cautioned in a letter of June 5, 1914, "You mustn't look in my novel for the old stable ego of the character. There is another ego, according to whose action the individual is unrecognizable. . . . Don't look for the development of the novel to follow the lines of certain characters: the characters fall into the form of some other rhythmic form." In *The Achievement of D. H. Lawrence,* Mark Schorer defined this "other rhythmic form" as a series of "separate episodes, and these only sporadically developed as 'scenes.' Yet these are meant to form a pattern of psychic relationships, a pattern of psychic movement with a large *general* rhythm, but without the objective or rationalized frame of the old novel." Like many other readers of the time, Garnett preferred the more conventional *Sons and Lovers* to Lawrence's later novels.

Shortly after the publication of *The Rainbow,* Scotland Yard seized over a thousand copies of the book from the publisher and printer. The book was an "orgy of sexiness," according to a 1915 reviewer in *Sphere.* As stated in his introduction to Lawrence's *Apocalypse,* Richard Aldington believed that the underlying motives for the suppression of the book were "that [Lawrence] denounced War. And [Frieda was] German." Whatever the reason, "after the suppression of *The Rainbow* in 1915, Lawrence acquired a bad newspaper reputation as a writer of supposedly salacious books," commented Hoffman and Moore in *The Achievement of D. H. Lawrence.* Consequently, although Lawrence completed *Women in Love* by 1916, publishing it proved impossible for four more years.

Lawrence published little during the years he spent in England between 1914 and 1918. His increasingly poor health was exacerbated by the English climate and the psychological pressure caused by the suspicions with which others regarded Frieda's German nationality and the couple's outspoken opposition to World War I. The military authorities threatened the ailing Lawrence with conscription, calling him periodically for medical examinations. Moreover, Lawrence found himself "very badly off" financially, as he confessed often in letters during these years. His writing brought him little income. Only books of verse, most of which he had written much earlier, appeared during this time: *Amores*; *Look! We Have Come Through!*; *New Poems*; and *Bay.*

Socially, Lawrence and Frieda formed many close if volatile friendships during the war years. John Middleton Murry and Murry's wife, Katherine Mansfield, who shared with them what Lawrence referred to in a letter of March 8, 1916, as a "Blutbruderschaft" (blood-brother relationship), even joined the Lawrences at their cottage in Cornwall until, as Delavenay reported, the Murrys "were embarrassed by the violence of [Lawrence's] quarrels with Frieda." Lawrence also socialized with a number of aristocrats interested in him because of his writing, among them Lady Cynthia Asquith and Lady Ottoline Morrell, both of whom appear as characters in Lawrence's fiction. Through Lady Ottoline, Lawrence made the acquaintance of the circle later known as the Bloomsbury group; he became intimate for a short time with Bertrand Russell before

philosophical differences divided them, and also met American poet Amy Lowell, who made Lawrence a present of his first typewriter.

With the help of Lady Cynthia, the daughter-in-law of England's prime minister, Lawrence hoped to immigrate to the United States, where he planned to found a colony of like-minded individuals to be called "Rananim." Lawrence wrote on January 18, 1915, "I want to gather together about twenty souls and sail away from this world of war and squalor and found a little colony where there shall be no money but a sort of communism as far as the necessaries of life go, and some real decency." To prepare for emigration, Lawrence began reading American authors and writing critical essays on them. These were published in 1923 as *Studies in Classic American Literature,* described by Gamini Salgado in *A Preface to Lawrence* as "a milestone in the serious study of early American writers such as [Herman] Melville, [Nathaniel] Hawthorne, [James Fenimore] Cooper and [Edgar Allan] Poe." Lawrence also began articulating in prose some of the psychological and philosophical insights, implicit in his novels and poetry, on which his new community would be based.

In a letter to Russell dated December 8, 1915, Lawrence put forth his idea that there is a seat of consciousness in man other than the brain and the nervous system: "There is a blood-consciousness, which exists in us independently of the ordinary mental consciousness." For Lawrence, the tragedy of modern life was that "the mental and nerve consciousness exerts a tyranny over the blood-consciousness, and that will has gone over completely to the mental consciousness and is engaged in the destruction of blood-being or blood-consciousness." In this letter, as in the novels and poems he wrote at the time, Lawrence stressed the importance of the male-female "sexual connection" in rousing the blood-consciousness of the individual. "Blood knowledge comes either through the mother or through the sex," he declared. Lawrence formulated these ideas systematically in *Psychoanalysis and the Unconscious* and *Fantasia of the Unconscious,* along with his theories about male-female relationships and the nature of women.

When he was writing *The Rainbow* and *Women in Love,* Lawrence declared in a letter of April 17, 1913: "I can only write what I feel pretty strongly about: and that, at present, is the relation between men and women. After all, it is *the* problem of today, the establishment of a new relation, or the readjustment of the old one, between men and women." In *Psychoanalysis* Lawrence emphasized the importance of integrity to the individual, the couple, and society: "A soul cannot come into its own through that love alone which is unison. If it stress the one mode, the sympathetic mode, beyond a certain point, it breaks its own integrity, and corruption sets in in the living organism. On both planes of love, upper and lower, the two modes must act complementary to one another, the sympathetic and the separatist. It is the absolute failure to see this that has torn the modern world into two halves, the one half warring for the voluntary, objective, separatist control, the other for the pure sympathetic. The individual psyche divided against itself divides the world against itself and an unthinkable progress of calamity ensues unless there be a reconciliation." Lawrence further cautioned in *Fantasia* that "sex as an end in itself is a disaster: a vice. But the ideal purpose which has no roots in the deep sea of passionate sex is a greater disaster still. And now we have only these two things: sex as a fatal goal, which is the essential theme of modern tragedy: or ideal purpose as a deadly parasite." The only solution, according to Lawrence, is "to keep the sexes pure. And by pure we don't mean an ideal sterile innocence and similarity between boy and girl. We mean pure maleness in a man, pure femaleness in a woman. . . . Women and men are dynamically different in everything."

Such statements, together with Lawrence's presentation of women and of sexuality in his fiction, have provoked conflicting points of view on his basic attitudes to women. Indeed, wrote Hilary Simpson in *D. H. Lawrence and Feminism*, "attacks on Lawrence's misogyny and praise for his sensitive portrayals of femininity have coexisted since the inception of the critical debate." Anaïs Nin thought that Lawrence had a "complete realization of the feelings of women. In fact, very often he wrote *as a woman* would write." In Nin's opinion, expressed in *D. H. Lawrence: An Unprofessional Study*, it was "the first time that a man has so wholly and completely expressed woman accurately." However, in *Son of Woman*, Murry expressed another view of Lawrence's aim in both art and life: "to annihilate the female insatiably demanding physical satisfaction from the man who cannot give it her—the female who has thus annihilated him." Kate Millet less personally attacked Lawrence in *Sexual Politics* as "a counterrevolutionary sexual politician." Even though Lawrence often chose a fe-

male as the main protagonist in his fiction, such as Ursula in *The Rainbow* or Kate in *The Plumed Serpent*, Faith Pullin complained in *Lawrence and Women* that "Lawrence is an extremely egotistical writer. In his portraits of women, he is usually defining some aspect of himself, rather than attempting the creation of the other sex. Many critics have argued that Lawrence was the androgynous artist and therefore attuned to the inner experience of both sexes. . . . [But his] main object was always to examine the male psyche and to use his women characters to that end." Implicitly disagreeing in the same book, Smith saw such female identification as going back deep into Lawrence's childhood and suggested that "his physical weakness as a child caused him to be cast in a feminine role, by himself perhaps as much as by others." Simpson, who noted the "extent to which Lawrence used women as actual or potential collaborators, and women's writing as source material," cited as examples, among others, his borrowing of Helen Corke's diaries to write *The Trespasser* and his collaboration with the Australian writer Mollie Skinner on *The Boy in the Bush* (1924). In a further essay from *Lawrence and Women*, Moore theorized that "Lawrence regarded love—and women—in a way that can only be called religious." Moore added that the woman who knew Lawrence best, Frieda Lawrence, commented, "In his heart of hearts, I think he always dreaded women, felt that they were in the end more powerful than men."

The related idea of male friendship preoccupied Lawrence as well: "Friendship should be a rare, choice, immortal thing, sacred and inviolable as marriage. Marriage and deathless friendship, both should be inviolable and sacred: two great creative passions, separate, apart, but complementary: the one pivotal, the other adventurous: the one, marriage, the centre of human life; and the other, the leap ahead." So Lawrence proposed in an essay of the period, "Education of the People," published only after his death in *Phoenix.* He explored the passion of male friendship most fully in *Women in Love,* in the relationship of Rupert Birkin and Gerald Crich. In *Son of Woman,* Murry equated Lawrence with his character Birkin, labeling both "phallic failures." As Moore reported in *The Priest of Love,* although Murry later denied that "what is generally understood by the word homosexuality" applied to Lawrence, the suspicions he aroused have persisted. In his biography of Lawrence, Moore dismissed, as Frieda had, what he termed "the common charge of homosexuality" against him and suggested instead that he manifested a "compensatory urge, an identification of a frail body with a strong, through a vicarious athleticism."

These concerns shaped the themes, symbols, and relationships depicted in Lawrence's mature fiction and poetry. Schorer pointed out that the struggle of mental versus blood consciousness manifests itself in Lawrence's mature fiction. In *Women in Love,* for example, it appears as a battle between "Will" and "Being" and between an impulse for death on the one hand and life on the other. "Will"—which may be either sensual or spiritual, a death impulse in either case—said Schorer, "fights 'Being,' that integration of total self which is life. Will is the integration of the drive of the ego toward power, toward domination; it has its inverse in the desire to be overpowered, to be dominated, to yield everything to dissolution. Will is mechanical, and its symbol is therefore the machine; its historical and social embodiment is an industrial society that lives by war. Being is the integration of life forces in total and complete self-responsibility. Its historical embodiment lives in the future."

"In comparison with what came before and after, the works of the period between the war and Lawrence's arrival in America are clearly of a lower order," contended Keith Sagar in *The Art of D. H. Lawrence.* "It is widely accepted that the full-length novels of the period—*The Lost Girl, Aaron's Rod,* and *Kangaroo*—are inferior to *The Rainbow* and *Women in Love.*" Ironically, as Moore pointed out in *The Priest of Love, The Lost Girl,* brought Lawrence "the only official recognition he ever received during his lifetime: the James Tait Black Prize of Edinburgh University."

Aaron's Rod, Kangaroo, and *The Plumed Serpent,* most of which Lawrence wrote in a month while living in Mexico, comprise the "leadership" novels, or "novels of power," as Meyers called them. In them, Lawrence, soured by his experience of war, expressed "scorn for the degenerate mob, hatred of socialism and revolution, belief in discipline, respect for authority, and admiration for a strong and physically attractive leader." Such attitudes led Bertrand Russell and scholars like William York Tindall to regard Lawrence as sympathetic to fascism. Yet, as Meyers pointed out, Lawrence soon revised his desire for a "natural aristocracy" in which "he who is most alive, intrinsically, is King." Lawrence admitted, "I've hated democracy since the war. But now see I'm wrong calling for an aristocracy. What we want is a flow of life from one

to another." Meyers refuted the claim that Lawrence shared any sympathy with the Adolf Hitlers and Benito Mussolinis of the world: "The ideas that grew out of the war were certainly antidemocratic, for Lawrence was an elitist who despised the ignorant masses. But they were not Fascist: that totalitarian, nationalistic and racist movement, founded in Milan in 1919, did not yet exist when Lawrence first formulated his ideas." Moreover, as Meyers argued, Lawrence renounced his belief in leadership and authority and radically changed his political ideas in the last five years of his life.

Early in his career, in a letter dated February 9, 1914, Lawrence regretted that "in England, people have got the loathsome superior knack of refusing to consider me a poet at all. 'Your prose is so good,' say the kind fools, 'that we are obliged to forgive you your poetry.' How I hate them." "The claim that Lawrence is a poet of real stature is still contentious," Sagar declared in *The Art of D. H. Lawrence.* In *The Double Agent: Essays in Craft and Elucidation,* R. P. Blackmur saw in Lawrence's verse "the ruin of great intentions"; he found it flawed by the "fallacy of the faith in expressive form." Vivian de Sola Pinto admitted in his introduction to Lawrence's *Complete Poems* that "like [William] Wordsworth, [Lawrence] wrote a good deal of bad poetry." Nevertheless, he saw even Lawrence's "bad poems" as important because "they are the experiments of a major poet groping his way towards the discovery of a new kind of poetic art." Salgado commented in *A Preface to Lawrence:* "The fact that Lawrence is without question a great poetic novelist has had the unfortunate effect that his poetry has been either neglected, patronized, or dismissed. With the exception of anthology pieces such as 'Snake' and 'Piano' very few of Lawrence's poems are anything like as well known as they deserve to be."

Lawrence himself, recognizing that his poetry defied the formal conventions of his day, frequently invited his readers to regard it differently from other poetry. In the published preface to *Collected Poems,* he warned that the poems "hang together in a life," thus encouraging the reader to regard them as autobiography. As Aldington said in his introduction to *Last Poems and More Pansies,* "With Lawrence the book is not conceived as something made, something apart from the author, but as a prolongation of his own life." Lawrence defended his experiments in verse with a poetic theory that distinguished "poetry of the present" from "poetry of the beginning and poetry of the end." The latter sort of verse manifests "exquisite finality" and "perfection," as he explained in "Poetry of the Present," his introduction to *New Poems*. Like the poetry of Walt Whitman, he maintained, his own poetry is of the first, or "present," type: it is "never finished. There is no rhythm which returns upon itself, no serpent of eternity with its tail in its own mouth. There is no static perfection." Lawrence wanted to "get rid of stereotyped movements and the old hackneyed associations of sound or sense." He desired to "break the stiff neck of habit" in his verse. As a result, concluded Graham Hough in *The Dark Sun: A Study of D. H. Lawrence*, Lawrence's poems "are so independent of literary tradition that the ordinary categories will hardly serve us." At its best, Hough affirmed, "no one sensitive to the rhythms of English speech can fail to observe the lovely fluidity of movement" of Lawrence's verse.

At Kiowa Ranch, near Taos, New Mexico, a gift to Frieda from Lawrence's flamboyant patroness Mabel Dodge Luhan, Lawrence completed works that reflected his setting: the novelette *St. Mawr* and various short stories, among them "The Princess" and "The Woman Who Rode Away." Harris said of the short fiction of this period, that Lawrence's "accomplishments include . . . carving out a new kind of story in the visionary tales by blending realism and exemplum; and pointing the way out of realism toward fabulation."

Like most of Lawrence's work at the time, *St. Mawr* and the full-length novel *The Plumed Serpent* were poorly received by readers in England; the American public and press were more receptive. In reference to the latter book, Sagar wrote in *The Art of D. H. Lawrence* that *The Plumed Serpent* "has been mauled by the critics from Frieda, who called it 'desiccated swelled head,' onwards. . . . The wholesale condemnation it has received is indicative, it seems to me, of far deeper failings in the critics than in the book; a failure in imaginative range and flexibility; a failure to meet the basic critical challenge, the challenge to enter wholly, if only temporarily, into the fictional world." Leavis admitted in *D. H. Lawrence: Novelist* that he found the book hard to finish, and Eliseo Vivas condemned it in *D. H. Lawrence: The Failure and Triumph of Art* as propaganda instead of the prophecy Lawrence intended. As reported by Moore in *The Priest of Love*, Mexican philosopher Jose Vasconcelos praised the novel as "one of the best books of fantasy ever written about Mexico."

Lawrence spent most of his last five years in Italy, near Florence, and in southern France, where he died. His steadily deteriorating health altered his habits little: he traveled frequently, changed residences many times, and wrote as prolifically as ever. He also translated several works from Italian into English. During this time he composed some of his most famous short stories, among them "The Rocking Horse Winner," "Sun," and "The Man Who Loved Islands." Venting his spleen against the censors and critics of his work, he delighted in writing the satiric poems collected in *Pansies* and *Nettles*. In addition, he extensively revised the early poetry for inclusion in *Collected Poems*, arranging it to tell the story of his creative urge, which he personified as his "demon." Several important manuscripts survived him, in particular, those published as *Last Poems, Etruscan Places*, and the religious treatise *Apocalypse* (1932). For the most part, however, Lawrence limited himself to shorter forms, often dashing off reviews of books and articles on diverse topics for the income they brought him. He also took up painting again, which he found less taxing than writing. Nevertheless, he found the time and energy to compose two longer fictional works, *Lady Chatterley's Lover* and *The Escaped Cock*.

Indeed, Lawrence not only wrote three versions of *Lady Chatterley's Lover*, he also arranged for the private printing and distribution of the unexpurgated edition. Unlike most of Lawrence's books, it sold briskly and made money for him. Yet, as Squires and Jackson pointed out, "unable to obtain a copyright, Lawrence watched, helpless at first, as pirated editions appeared—and profits disappeared. Not until May 1929 did he combat the pirates with his inexpensive Paris edition of the novel."

Even more than *The Rainbow, Lady Chatterley's Lover* has been the subject of intense controversy. Until 1959 and 1960 respectively the unexpurgated edition of the novel could not be legally published and distributed in the United States and England. Critical debate has been intense since it first appeared. In *D. H. Lawrence: Novelist*, Leavis classed it among Lawrence's "lesser novels" because of its "offenses against taste." According to Squires and Jackson: "Its literary reputation is not yet secure; the scent of pornography clings. Too, a novelist's early work often seems more accessible to readers than does the late work, which is typically darker, more complex, more deeply shaded with ideology."

Recalling his earlier statements on blood-knowledge, Lawrence explained the ideas that shaped the novel in "A Propos of 'Lady Chatterley's Lover'": "In fact, thought and action, word and deed are two separate lives which we lead. We need, very sincerely, to keep a connection . . . and this is the real point of the book. I want men and women to be able to think sex, fully, completely, honestly and cleanly. . . . Life is only bearable when the mind and body are in harmony, and there is a natural balance between them, and each has a natural respect for the other." Lawrence maintained here, as he had earlier, that dependence on mental knowledge to the exclusion of blood-knowledge leads to most of the "tragedies" of the modern world, chiefly a "mechanization" of life. Far from being obscene, *Lady Chatterley's Lover* celebrates the creative power of togetherness, "which is religious and poetic," he asserted.

In *The World of the Major Novels,* Scott Sanders agreed with Lawrence's assessment: "In tracing the sources of human violence to the desire for mastery and the illusion of separateness, Lawrence was echoing a view common to many of the world's religions." Put briefly, Sanders wrote, what the characters of the novel and all modern people confront is "the choice between the way of power and the way of love. . . . What we are shown in the history of Lady Chatterley's loving is the education of one woman's consciousness. . . . In proportion as we are drawn into her loving and altered by it, we are forced to realize along with her that there is no ultimate basis for distinctions between classes, between races, between nations, or between humankind and the rest of nature."

In his introduction to *Selected Letters of D. H. Lawrence,* Aldous Huxley quoted part of a letter written by Lawrence on February 24, 1913, at the start of his writing career: "I often feel one ought to be able to pray before one works—and then leave it to the Lord. Isn't it hard work to come to real grips with one's imagination—throw everything overboard. I always feel as though I stood naked for the fire of Almighty God to go through me—and it's rather an awful feeling. One has to be so terribly religious to be an artist." Huxley, who knew Lawrence well in the last years of his life, commented, "Conversely, he might have added, one has to be terribly an artist, terribly conscious of 'inspiration' and the compelling force of genius, to be religious as Lawrence was religious."

Religious themes, symbols, and allusions occur throughout Lawrence's work, but especially at the end.

Impounded during the London exhibition in 1928 for indecency and immorality, Lawrence's paintings often evidence, in fact, religious themes; he regarded these works as sacred, as his frequent references to them in letters make plain. *The Escaped Cock,* a story of resurrection, and *Apocalypse,* which Lawrence worked on during the last months of his life, treat religious topics explicitly. The story of the risen Christ who in his wanderings meets and mates with the goddess Isis exemplifies many of the ideas set forth in *Apocalypse.* In his introduction to that book, Aldington admitted that "from the point of view of scholars Lawrence's book may be quite worthless as an interpretation of the Book of Revelation." He found it interesting "not as the revelation of John of Patmos, but as the revelation of Lawrence." In *Apocalypse* as in *The Escaped Cock,* Lawrence condemned all religion at the time of Christ as having turned from "the old worship and study of vitality, potency, power, to the study of death and death-rewards, death-penalties, and morals. All religion, instead of being a religion of *life,* here and now, became a religion of postponed destiny, death, and reward *afterwards,* 'if you are good.'" In his last works, including his poems and paintings and many of his shorter pieces, the underlying message matches that of *Apocalypse:* "What we want is to destroy our false, inorganic connections, especially those related to money, and reestablish the living organic connection, with the cosmos, the sun and earth, with mankind and nation and family." The Etruscan people, revealed to Lawrence through their art and architecture, summed up his conception of life, according to Aldington in the introduction to *Apocalypse:* "Nations of men and women living an intense, physical life without too much intellect and hatred. And in Etruria at any rate the women enjoyed great liberty and consideration, while the idea of sex and sexual desire as shameful things had never been thought of."

Because of his rapidly deteriorating physical condition, Lawrence reluctantly agreed to hospital care one month before he died; he entered a sanatorium near Vence, in southern France. In *The Priest of Love* Moore revealed that Lawrence's doctor, commenting on his famous patient's refusal to rest, even when hospitalized, said that "those very qualities which gave Lawrence such keen perception and such passionate feeling made it quite impossible for him to submit for any length of time to a restricted sanatorium existence." "I'm better in a house," Lawrence wrote in a letter dated February 21, 1930. The day before he died, he dragged himself from the nursing home to a rented villa and died there during the evening of March 2, 1930. Although Lawrence was buried in Vence, five years later Frieda arranged for the cremation of his remains, which she then transported to Kiowa Ranch. They are interred in the small chapel Frieda built to hold them and that she decorated with Lawrence's personal symbol: the rising phoenix.

Since his death, several of Lawrence's rough drafts and early versions of later published works have been found and published. One example is *Mr. Noon,* which combines fictional elements with travel writing in an autobiographical story about an English man's illicit affair with a married German woman and their travels through Italy. Not discovered until 1972, the story was finally published in 1984. *Quetzalcoatl,* meanwhile, represents an early version of Lawrence's 1926 novel *The Plumed Serpent.* Critics noted that the early version is significantly different than the highly mythical and theoretical finished story.

More important than these rough manuscripts is the voluminous correspondence Lawrence produced during his brief life. Totaling more than 5,500 letters, the collection was published in seven volumes by Cambridge University Press. The letters reveal the author's keen interest in his business affairs; his tender relations with his two sisters; his wanderings of America and Europe during the 1920s; and the enormous battle he waged against tuberculosis during the final years of his life, as he gradually realized that he would not live very long. Indeed, during these final years, Lawrence's letters represent a significant portion of his literary output, leading some critics to define the collected letters as one of his major works. *Modern Language Review* contributor Philip Hobsbaum, for instance, noted that the letters mark Lawrence as, next to Lord Byron, "the best correspondent in the language." Similarly, *Times Literary Supplement* reviewer Valentine Cunningham commented, "This collection, surely, ranks among the very best gatherings of modern literary letters." Lawrence biographer John Worthen, writing in the *Spectator,* concluded that the seven volumes of letters "stand clear now as perhaps Lawrence's single greatest achievement as a writer."

BIOGRAPHICAL AND CRITICAL SOURCES:

BOOKS

Aldington, Richard, *Portrait of a Genius, But . . . ,* Heinemann (London, England), 1950.

Balbert, Peter, *D. H. Lawrence and the Phallic Imagination,* St. Martin's Press (New York, NY), 1989.

Beal, Anthony, *D. H. Lawrence,* Oliver & Boyd (London, England), 1961.

Becket, Fiona, *D. H. Lawrence: The Thinker As Poet,* St. Martin's Press (New York, NY), 1997.

Blackmur, R. P., *The Double Agent: Essays in Craft and Elucidation,* Arrow Editions, 1935.

Brett, Dorothy, *Lawrence and Brett: A Friendship,* Lippincott (Philadelphia, PA), 1933.

Brewster, Earl, and Achsah Brewster, *D. H. Lawrence: Reminiscences and Correspondence,* M. Secker (London, England), 1934.

Britton, Derek, *Lady Chatterley: The Making of the Novel,* Unwin Hyman (London, England), 1988.

Bynner, Witter, *Journey with Genius: Recollections and Reflections concerning the D. H. Lawrences,* J. Day, 1951.

Carswell, Catherine, *The Savage Pilgrimage,* Chatto & Windus (London, England), 1932.

Cavitch, David, *D. H. Lawrence and the New World,* Oxford University Press (Oxford, England), 1969.

Chambers, Jessie (under pseudonym E. T.) *D. H. Lawrence: A Personal Record,* J. Cape (London, England), 1935.

Clarke, Colin, *River of Dissolution: D. H. Lawrence and English Romanticism,* Routledge & Kegan Paul (London, England), 1969.

Clark, L. D., *Dark Night of the Body,* University of Texas Press (Austin, TX), 1964.

Clark, L. D., *The Minoan Distance: The Symbolism of Travel in D. H. Lawrence,* University of Arizona Press (Tucson, AZ), 1980.

Corke, Helen, *Lawrence and Apocalypse,* Heinemann (London, England), 1933.

Corke, Helen, *D. H. Lawrence's Princess: A Memory of Jessie Chambers,* Merle Press, 1951.

Corke, Helen, *D. H. Lawrence: The Croydon Years,* University of Texas Press (Austin, TX), 1965.

Cowan, James C., editor, *D. H. Lawrence: An Annotated Bibliography of Writings about Him,* 1982.

Cushman, Keith, *D. H. Lawrence at Work: The Emergence of "The Prussian Officer" Stories,* University Press of Virginia, 1978.

Cushman, Keith, and Jackson, Dennis, editors, *D. H. Lawrence's Literary Inheritors,* St. Martin's Press (New York, NY), 1991.

Daleski, H. M., *The Forked Flame: A Study of D. H. Lawrence,* Faber (London, England), 1965.

Delany, Paul, *D. H. Lawrence's Nightmare: The Writer and His Circle during the Years of the Great War,* Basic Books (New York, NY), 1978.

Delavenay, Emile, *D. H. Lawrence: The Man and His Work; The Formative Years, 1885-1919,* Heinemann (London, England), 1972.

Dictionary of Literary Biography, Gale (Detroit, MI), Volume 10: *Modern British Dramatists, 1900-1945,* two volumes, 1982, Volume 19: *British Poets, 1880-1914,* 1983, Volume 36: *British Novelists, 1890-1929: Modernists,* 1985, Volume 162: *British Short-Fiction Writers, 1915-1945,* 1996.

Draper, R. P., editor, *D. H. Lawrence: The Critical Heritage,* Routledge & Kegan Paul (London, England), 1970.

Driskill, Richard T., *Madonnas and Christs, Maidens and Knights: Sexual Confusion in the Bildungsromans of D. H. Lawrence and André Gide,* P. Lang (New York, NY), 1997.

Dyer, Geoff, *Out of Sheer Rage: Wrestling with D. H. Lawrence,* North Point Press, 1998.

Eggert, Paul, and John Worthen, *Lawrence and Comedy,* Cambridge University Press (New York, NY), 1996.

Ellis, David, *D. H. Lawrence, Dying Game, 1922-1930,* Cambridge University Press (New York, NY), 1997.

Engelhardt, Dorthe G. A., *L. N. Tolstoy and D. H. Lawrence: Cross-Currents and Influence,* P. Lang (New York, NY), 1996.

Farr, Judith, editor, *Twentieth-Century Interpretations of "Sons and Lovers": A Collection of Critical Essays,* Prentice-Hall (New York, NY), 1970.

Feinstein, Elaine, *Lawrence and the Women: The Intimate Life of D. H. Lawrence,* HarperCollins (New York, NY), 1993.

Ford, George H., *Double Measure: A Study of the Novels and Stories of D. H. Lawrence,* Holt (New York, NY), 1965.

Franks, Jill, *Revisionist Resurrection Mythologies: A Study of D. H. Lawrence's Italian Works,* P. Lang (New York, NY), 1994.

Freeman, Mary, *D. H. Lawrence: A Basic Study of His Ideas,* University of Florida Press, 1955.

Gilbert, Sandra M., *Acts of Attention: The Poems of D. H. Lawrence,* Cornell University Press (Cornell, NY), 1972.

Goodheart, Eugene, *The Utopian Vision of D. H. Lawrence,* University of Chicago Press (Chicago, IL), 1983.

Gordon, David J., *D. H. Lawrence As a Literary Critic,* Yale University Press (New Haven, CT), 1966.

Green, Martin, *The von Richthofen Sisters: The Triumphant and the Tragic Modes of Love: Else and Frieda von Richthofen, Otto Gross, Mar Weber,* and D. H. Lawrence, in the Years 1870-1970, Basic Books (New York, NY), 1974.

Gregory, Horace, *Pilgrim of the Apocalypse,* Viking (New York, NY), 1933.

Hagen, Patricia L., *Metaphor's Way of Knowing: The Poetry of D. H. Lawrence and the Church of Mechanism,* P. Lang (New York, NY), 1995.

Hamalian, Leo, *D. H. Lawrence and Nine Women Writers,* Associated University Presses, 1996.

Harris, Janice Hubbard, *The Short Fiction of D. H. Lawrence,* Rutgers University Press, 1984.

Hochman, Baruch, *Another Ego: The Changing View of the Self and Society in the Work of D. H. Lawrence,* University of South Carolina Press, 1970.

Hoffman, Frederick J., and Harry T. Moore, editors, *The Achievement of D. H. Lawrence,* University of Oklahoma Press (Norman, OK), 1953.

Holbrook, David, *Where D. H . Lawrence Was Wrong about Woman,* Bucknell University Press, 1992.

Hough, Graham, *The Dark Sun: A Study of D. H. Lawrence,* Duckworth (London, England), 1956.

Howe, Marguerite Beede, *The Art of the Self in D. H. Lawrence,* Ohio University Press, 1977.

Joost, Nicholas and Alvin Sullivan, *D. H. Lawrence and the Dial,* Southern Illinois University Press (Carbondale, IL), 1970.

Kalnins, Mara, editor, *D. H. Lawrence: Centenary Essays,* Bristol Classical Press, 1986.

Kearney, Martin F., *The Major Short Stories of D. H. Lawrence: A Handbook,* Garland (New York, NY), 1998.

Kermode, Frank, *D. H. Lawrence,* Viking (New York, NY), 1973.

Kinkead-Weekes, Mark, *D. H. Lawrence: Triumph to Exile,* Cambridge University Press (New York, NY), 1996.

Kinkead-Weekes, Mark, editor, *Twentieth-Century Interpretations of "The Rainbow": A Collection of Critical Essays,* Prentice-Hall (New York, NY), 1971.

LaChapelle, Dolores, *D. H. Lawrence: Future Primitive,* University of North Texas Press, 1996.

Lawrence, Ada, and G. Stuart Gelder, *Young Lorenzo: The Early Life of D. H. Lawrence,* G. Orioli (Florence, Italy), 1932.

Lawrence, D. H., *Last Poems and More Pansies,* introduction by Richard Aldington, G. Orioli (Florence, Italy), 1932.

Lawrence, D. H., *Selected Letters,* introduction by Aldous Huxley, Penguin (Harmondworth, England), 1950, reprinted, 1996.

Lawrence, D. H., *Complete Poems,* introduction by Vivian de Sola Pinto, Heinemann (London, England), 1967.

Lawrence, Frieda, *Not I, but the Wind,* Rydal Press, 1934.

Leavis, F. R., *D. H. Lawrence: Novelist,* Chatto & Windus (London, England), 1955.

Leavis, F. R., *Thought, Words, and Creativity: Art and Thought in Lawrence,* Chatto & Windus (London, England), 1976.

Lewiecki-Wilson, Cynthia, *Writing against the Family: Gender in Lawrence and Joyce,* Southern Illinois University Press (Carbondale, IL), 1994.

Luhan, Mabel Dodge, *Lorenzo in Taos,* Knopf (New York, NY), 1932.

Mandell, Gail Porter, *The Phoenix Paradox: A Study of Renewal through Change in the "Collected Poems" and "Last Poems" of D. H. Lawrence,* Southern Illinois University Press (Carbondale, IL), 1984.

Marshall, Tom, *The Psychic Mariner: A Reading of the Poems of D. H. Lawrence,* Viking (New York, NY), 1970.

McDonald, Edward D., *A Bibliography of the Writings of D. H. Lawrence,* Centaur, 1925.

Meyers, Jeffrey, *D. H. Lawrence: A Biography,* Knopf (New York, NY), 1990.

Meyers, Jeffrey, *D. H. Lawrence and the Experience of Italy,* University of Pennsylvania Press, 1982.

Meyers, Jeffrey, editor, *D. H. Lawrence and Tradition,* Athlone (London, England), 1985.

Meyers, Jeffrey, editor, *The Legacy of D. H. Lawrence,* Macmillan (New York, NY), 1987.

Miko, Stephen J., editor, *Twentieth-Century Interpretations of "Women in Love": A Collection of Critical Essays,* Prentice-Hall (New York, NY), 1969.

Miko, Stephen J., *Toward "Women in Love": The Emergence of a Laurentian Aesthetic,* Yale University Press (New Haven, CT), 1971.

Miller, Henry, *The World of Lawrence: A Passionate Appreciation,* John Calder, 1996.

Millet, Kate, *Sexual Politics,* Abacus, 1972.

Montgomery, Robert E., *The Visionary D. H. Lawrence: Beyond Philosophy and Art,* Cambridge University Press (New York, NY), 1994.

Moore, Harry T., editor, *A D. H. Lawrence Miscellany,* Southern Illinois University Press (Carbondale, IL), 1959.

Moore, Harry T., *The Intelligent Heart,* Farrar, Straus (New York, NY), 1954.

Moore, Harry T., *The Life and Works of D. H. Lawrence,* Twayne (New York, NY), 1951.

Moore, Harry T., *Poste Restant: A Lawrence Travel Calendar,* University of California Press (Berkeley, CA), 1956.

Moore, Harry T., *The Priest of Love: A Life of D. H. Lawrence,* Farrar, Straus (New York, NY), 1974.

Murfin, Ross C., *The Poetry of D. H. Lawrence: Texts and Contexts,* University of Nebraska Press, 1983.

Murry, John Middleton, *Son of Woman: The Story of D. H. Lawrence,* J. Cape (London, England), 1931.

Murry, John Middleton, *Reminiscences of D. H. Lawrence,* J. Cape (London, England), 1933.

Nehls, Edward, *D. H. Lawrence: A Composite Biography,* University of Wisconsin Press (Madison, WI), Volume I, 1957, Volume II, 1958, Volume III, 1959.

Nin, Anaïs, *D. H. Lawrence: An Unprofessional Study,* Edward W. Titus, 1932.

Niven, Alastair, *D. H. Lawrence: The Novels,* Cambridge University Press (Cambridge, England), 1978.

Oates, Joyce Carol, *The Hostile Sun: The Poetry of D. H. Lawrence,* Black Sparrow Press, 1973.

Panichas, George, *Adventure in Consciousness: The Meaning of D. H. Lawrence's Religious Quest,* Mouton (Hague, Netherlands), 1964.

Partlow, Robert B., Jr., and Harry T. Moore, editors, *D. H. Lawrence: The Man Who Lived,* Southern Illinois University Press (Carbondale, IL), 1980.

Pinion, Frank, *A D. H. Lawrence Companion,* Macmillan (London, England), 1978.

Pinto, Vivian de Sola, *D. H. Lawrence: Prophet of the Midlands,* University of Nottingham (Nottingham, England), 1951.

Polhemus, Robert M., *Erotic Faith: Being in Love from Jane Austen to D. H. Lawrence,* University of Chicago Press (Chicago, IL), 1990, pp. 279-306.

Poplawski, Paul, *Language, Art and Reality in D. H. Lawrence's "St. Mawr": A Stylistic Study,* Edwin Mellen Press (Lewiston, NY), 1996.

Poplawski, Paul and John Worthen, *D. H. Lawrence: A Reference Companion,* Greenwood Press (New York, NY), 1996.

Powell, Lawrence Clark, *The Manuscripts of D. H. Lawrence,* Los Angeles Public Library (Los Angeles, CA), 1937.

Preston, Peter, *A D. H. Lawrence Chronology,* St. Martin's Press (New York, NY), 1994.

Pritchard, R. E., *D. H. Lawrence: Body of Darkness,* Hutchinson University Library (London, England), 1971.

Rice, Thomas Jackson, *D. H. Lawrence: A Guide to Research*, Garland Publishing (New York, NY), 1983.

Roberts, Warren, *A Bibliography of D. H. Lawrence*, Hart-Davis, 1963, revised edition, 1982.

Rolph, C. H., editor, *The Trial of Lady Chatterley*, Penguin (London, England), 1961.

Ross, Charles, *The Composition of "The Rainbow" and "Women in Love,"* University Press of Virginia, 1979.

Ross, Charles, and Dennis Jackson, *Editing D. H. Lawrence: New Versions of a Modern Author*, University of Michigan Press (Ann Arbor, MI), 1995.

Rylance, Rick, editor, *Sons and Lovers*, St. Martin's Press, 1996.

Sagar, Keith, *The Art of D. H. Lawrence*, Cambridge University Press (Cambridge, England), 1966.

Sagar, Keith, *D. H. Lawrence: A Calendar of His Works*, Manchester University Press (Manchester, England), 1979.

Sagar, Keith, *The Life of D. H. Lawrence*, Methuen (London, England), 1980.

Sagar, Keith, editor, *A D. H. Lawrence Handbook*, Barnes & Noble, 1982.

Salgado, Gamini, *D. H. Lawrence: "Sons and Lovers,"* Edward Arnold, 1966.

Salgado, Gamini, *A Preface to Lawrence*, Longman (London, England), 1982.

Salgado, Gamini, and G. K. Das, editors, *The Spirit of D. H. Lawrence: Centenary Studies*, Macmillan (London, England), 1988.

Sanders, Scott, *The World of the Major Novels*, Viking (New York, NY), 1973.

Scherr, Berry J., *D. H. Lawrence's Response to Plato: A Bloomian Interpretation*, P. Lang (New York, NY), 1995.

Short Story Criticism, Volume 4, Gale (Detroit, MI), 1990.

Simpson, Hilary, editor., *D. H. Lawrence and Feminism*, Northern Illinois University Press, 1982.

Smith, Anne, editor, *Lawrence and Women*, Vision, 1978.

Spender, Stephen, editor, *D. H. Lawrence: Novelist, Poet, Prophet*, Weidenfeld & Nicolson (London, England), 1973.

Spilka, Mark, *The Love Ethic of D. H. Lawrence*, Indiana University Press, 1955.

Spilka, Mark, editor, *D. H. Lawrence: A Collection of Critical Essays*, Prentice-Hall (New York, NY), 1963.

Squires, Michael, *The Creation of "Lady Chatterley's Lover,"* Johns Hopkins University Press (Baltimore, MD), 1983.

Squires, Michael, and Dennis Jackson, editors, *D. H. Lawrence's "Lady": A New Look at "Lady Chatterley's Lover,"* University of Georgia Press, 1985.

Srivastava, U. N., *Symbolism in the Novels of D. H. Lawrence*, [Delhi, India], 1994.

Sword, Helen, *Engendering Inspiration: Visionary Strategies in Rilke, Lawrence, and H. D.*, University of Michigan Press (Ann Arbor, MI), 1995.

Tedlock, E. W., Jr., *The Frieda Lawrence Collection of D. H. Lawrence Manuscripts*, University of New Mexico Press, 1948.

Tedlock, E. W., Jr., *Frieda Lawrence: The Memoirs and Correspondence*, Heinemann (London, England), 1961.

Tedlock, E. W., Jr., *D. H. Lawrence, Artist and Rebel: A Study of Lawrence's Fiction*, University of New Mexico Press, 1963.

Tedlock, E. W., Jr., *D. H. Lawrence and "Sons and Lovers": Sources and Criticism*, New York University Press (New York, NY), 1965.

Tindall, William York, *D. H. Lawrence and Susan His Cow*, Columbia University Press (New York, NY), 1939.

Tiverton, Father William (pseudonym of Martin Jarrett-Kerr), *D. H. Lawrence and Human Existence*, foreword by T. S. Eliot, Rockliff, 1951.

Twentieth-Century Literary Criticism, Gale (Detroit, MI), Volume 2, 1979, Volume 9, 1983, Volume 16, 1985, Volume 33, 1989, Volume 48, 1993.

Vivas, Eliseo, *D. H. Lawrence: The Failure and the Triumph of Art*, Northwestern University Press, 1960.

Widmer, Kingsley, *The Art of Perversity: D. H. Lawrence's Shorter Fiction*, University of Washington Press, 1962.

Widmer, Kingsley, *Desire and Negation: Dialectical Legacy of D. H. Lawrence*, Southern Illinois University Press (Carbondale, IL), 1991.

Worthen, John, *D. H. Lawrence and the Idea of the Novel*, Rowman & Littlefield (New York, NY), 1979.

Worthen, John, *D. H. Lawrence: The Early Years, 1885-1912*, Cambridge University Press (New York, NY), 1991.

PERIODICALS

Academy, March 18, 1911.
Antioch Review, winter, 1990, p. 114.
Athenaeum, June 1, 1912.

Atlantic, October, 1992.

Cambridge Quarterly, June, 2001, p. 133.

College Literature, fall, 2003, Eric P. Levy, "Ontological Incoherence in *Women in Love,*" p. 156.

Critical Survey, September, 2002, p. 14.

D. H. Lawrence Review.

English Literature in Translation, January, 1991, p. 119; March, 1992, p. 332; January, 1994, p. 114; February, 1994, p. 215.

Essays in Criticism, October, 1971, pp. 347-364.

Explicator, spring, 2002, Hal Blythe, "Lawrence's *The Odor of Chrysanthemums,*" p. 154; fall, 2002, p. 41.

Journal of Modern Literature, summer, 2000, Christopher Pollnitz, "D. H. Lawrence's Last Poems," p. 503; fall, 2001, Erwin R. Steinberg, "D. H. Lawrence: Mythographer," p. 91; summer, 2002, Brad Buchanan, "Oedipus in Dystopia: Freud and Lawrence in Aldous Huxley's *Brave New World,*" p. 75.

London Review of Books, December 5, 1991, p. 14; September 10, 1992, p. 12.

Los Angeles Times Book Review, March 15, 1987, p. 10; December 27, 1987, p. 2.

Manchester Guardian, July 2, 1913.

Midwest Quarterly, winter, 2002, Jae-Kyung Koh, "D. H. Lawrence's World Vision of Cultural Regeneration in *Lady Chatterley's Lover,*" p. 86.

Modern Language Review, July, 1991, p. 685; April, 1993, p. 435.

Mosaic, winter, 1988, pp. 1-11.

Nation, July 12, 1913, April 26, 1947.

Nation and Athenaeum, March 29, 1930.

New England Review, spring, 2003, p. 18.

New Statesman & Society, September 4, 1992, p. 40.

New York Review of Books, April 21, 1994, p. 29; December 5, 2002, Doris Lessing, review of *The Fox,* p. 18.

New York Times, November 29, 1992.

Observer, June 21, 1987, p. 24; August 30, 1992, p. 50.

Poetry, July, 1913.

Psychoanalytic Review, July, 1916.

Quill & Quire, August, 1987, p. 35.

Renaissance and Modern Studies, Volume 1, 1957.

Review of English Studies, November, 1993, p. 612; February, 2000, John Lyon, review of *Women in Love,* p. 160; February, 2002, Howard J. Booth, "D. H. Lawrence and Male Homosexual Desire," p. 86; May, 2002, p. 285; August, 2002, p. 461.

Sewanee Review, summer, 2001, Mark Kinkead-Weekes, "D. H. Lawrence: 'A Passionately Religious Man,'" p. 379.

Southern Humanities Review, spring, 1985, pp. 117-131.

Spectator, July 3, 1993, p. 27.

Sphere, October, 1915.

Studies in the Novel, spring, 1990, pp. 67-81; summer, 2000, Alan W. Friedman, "D. H. Lawrence: Pleasure and Death," p. 207; fall, 2002, p. 282.

Times (London, England), March 4, 1930.

Times Literary Supplement, May 29, 1987; October 16, 1987, p. 1142; November 17, 1989, p. 1260; September 13, 1991, p. 12; September 11, 1992, p. 20; July 23, 1993, p. 4; August 11, 1995, p. 23.*

*   *   *

LESSAC, Frané 1954-

PERSONAL: Given name is pronounced "Fra-*nay*"; born June 18, 1954, in Jersey City, NJ; daughter of Arthur J. (a comedian) and Estelle (a travel agency owner; maiden name, Siegel) Lessac; married Mark Greenwood (a musician), April 19, 1986; children: Luke, Cody. *Education:* Attended New School for Social Research (now New School University), 1973, University of Southern California, 1974, and University of California—Los Angeles, 1975-76.

ADDRESSES: Home—Western Australia. *Office*—c/o Artbeat Publishers, P.O. Box 1110, Fremantle, West Australia 6160, Australia. *Agent*—Marcia Wernick, Sheldon Fogelman Agency, 10 East 40th St., Ste. 3800, New York, NY 10016.

CAREER: Filmmaker, artist, and illustrator, 1983—. *Exhibitions:* Fowler Mills Gallery, Los Angeles, CA, 1980, 1982; Courtyard Gallery, Montserrat, 1981; Exhibition de Intercaribe de Peniture, Guadeloupe, 1981; Gallerie Antoinette, Paris, France, 1981; Centre des Arts et de la Culture, Guadeloupe, 1982; Bankside Gallery, London, England, 1983, 1984; Libertys Gallery, London, 1983; Sugar Mill, Montserrat, 1984, 1986; Barbican Center, London, 1984; Brixton Art Gallery, London, 1984; Chelsea Manor Street Gallery, London, 1984; Rona Gallery, London, 1984; Craft and Folk Art Museum, Los Angeles, 1985; Metropolitan Museum of Art, New York, NY, 1985; Riverside Studios, London, 1985; Commonwealth Institute, London, 1986; Yellow Poui Art Gallery, Grenada, 1987; Vanessa Devereux Gallery, London, 1987; Harmony Hall,

Frané Lessac

Antigua, 1989, 1991, 1993, 1995, 1996, 1998, 2003; Broughton House Gallery, Cambridge, England, 1990; Centrespace Gallery, London, 1991; Society of Illustrators, New York, NY, 1991, 1992, 1994, 1995; Perth Galleries, Perth, Australia, Australian Naive Gallery, Sydney, Australia, Every Picture Tells A Story, Los Angeles, and Santa Monica Heritage Museum, Los Angeles, all 1992; Barry Stern Gallery, Sydney, 1994; Children's Literature Centre, Fremantle, 1995, 2002; Kimberly Kreations, Broome, Australia, 1995; A-Shed Gallery, Fremantle, Australia, 1996; Perth Mint, Perth, 1999; Catanach's Gallery, Broome, Moore's Building, Fremantle, and Fremantle Arts Centre, Fremantle, all 2000; CBC National Conference, Perth, Australia, 2002; Australian National Maritime Museum, Sydney, 2003. Work is also included in many private collections worldwide.

MEMBER: Society of Children's Book Writers and Illustrators (assistant regional advisor, West Australia).

AWARDS, HONORS: Children's Book of the Year, Island of St. Martin's, 1984, and Books for Children selection, Library of Congress, 1985, both for *The*

Little Island; Notable Trade Book in Social Studies, National Council for the Social Studies/Children's Book Council (NCSS/CBC), 1989, and Book Show Award, American Institute of Graphic Arts, 1990, both for *Caribbean Canvas;* Editor's Choice citation, American Library Association, Parents' Choice Gold Award, and Notable Trade Book in Social Studies, NCSS/CBC, 1989, all for *The Chalk Doll* by Charlotte Pomerantz; Reading Magic Award, *Parenting Magazine,* and Notable Trade Book in Social Studies, NCSS/CBC, 1990, both for *The Bird Who Was an Elephant* by Alpeh Kamal; 100 Best Books selection, New York Public Library, Children's Books of the Year citation, Bank Street College, and Notable Trade Book in Social Studies, NCSS/CBC, 1993, all for *Caribbean Carnival: Songs of the West Indies* by Irving Burgle; Notable Trade Book in Social Studies, NCSS/CBC, 1994, for *Caribbean Alphabet;* Notable Children's Book citation, Language Arts/National Council of Teachers, and Américas Children's and Young Adult Literature commendation, both 1994, both for *Not a Copper Penny in Me House: Poems from the Caribbean* by Monica Gunning; Children's Book of Distinction finalist, "Emphasis on Reading List" citation, state of Alabama, and Notable Trade Book in Social Studies, NCSS/CBC, Notable Books for Children, American Library Association, and Notable Book for a Global Society Award, all 1996, all for *The Distant Talking Drum: Poems from Nigeria* by Isaac Olaleye; Book of the Year, Bank Street College, 1996, and Notable Trade Book in Social Studies, NCSS/CBC, 1997, both for *O Christmas Tree* by Vashanti Rahaman; Sydney Taylor Award for Younger Readers, for *Queen Esther Saves Her People* by Rita Golden Gelman; Top Ten Science Books citation, *Booklist,* and Notable Trade Book in Social Studies, NCSS/CBC, both 2000, both for *On the Same Day in March: A Tour of the World's Weather* by Marilyn Singer; West Australia Premier's Book Award, 2002, for *The Legend of Moondyne Joe* by Mark Greenwood.

WRITINGS:

My Little Island, Lippincott (Philadelphia, PA), 1984, published as *The Little Island,* Macmillan Caribbean (London, England), 1984.

The Dragon of Redonda, Macmillan Caribbean (London, England), 1986.

Caribbean Canvas, Macmillan Caribbean (London, England), 1987, Lippincott (Philadelphia, PA), 1989.

(With husband, Mark Greenwood) *Caribbean Alphabet* Macmillan Caribbean (London, England), 1989, Tambourine Books (New York, NY), 1994.

(Compiler and illustrator) *Camp Granada: Sing-Along Camp Songs,* Holt (New York, NY), 2003.

ILLUSTRATOR

Charlotte Pomerantz, *The Chalk Doll,* Lippincott (Philadelphia, PA), 1989.

Aleph Kamal, *The Bird Who Was an Elephant,* Cambridge University Press (Cambridge, England), 1989, Lippincott (Philadelphia, PA), 1990.

Barbara Ker Wilson, *The Turtle and the Island: A Folktale from Papua New Guinea,* Lippincott (Philadelphia, PA), 1990.

Marilyn Singer, *Nine o'Clock Lullaby,* HarperCollins (New York, NY), 1991.

Irving Burgle, compiler, *Caribbean Carnival: Songs of the West Indies,* Tambourine Books (New York, NY), 1992.

Monica Gunning, *Not a Copper Penny in Me House: Poems from the Caribbean,* Wordsong (Honesdale, PA), 1993.

Eric Maddern, *The Fire Children: A West African Creation Tale,* Dial (New York, NY), 1993.

Jan Wahl, *Little Gray One,* Tambourine Books (New York, NY), 1993.

Patricia Zelver, *The Wonderful Towers of Watts,* Tambourine Books (New York, NY), 1994.

Mark Greenwood, *Outback Adventure,* Plantagenet Press (Fremantle, West Australia), 1994.

Lee Bennett Hopkins, *Good Rhymes, Good Times: Original Poems,* HarperCollins (New York, NY), 1995.

Isaac Olaleye, *The Distant Talking Drum: Poems from Nigeria,* Wordsong (Honesdale, PA), 1995.

Mark Greenwood, *Our Big Island,* Plantagenet Press (Fremantle, West Australia), 1995.

Vashanti Rahaman, *O Christmas Tree,* Boyds Mills Press (Honesdale, PA), 1996.

Rita Golden Gelman, *Queen Esther Saves Her People,* Scholastic (New York, NY), 1998.

Marilyn Singer, *On the Same Day in March: A Tour of the World's Weather,* HarperCollins (New York, NY), 2000.

Mark Greenwood, *The Legend of Moondyne Joe,* Cygnet Books (Crawley, WA), 2002.

Mark Greenwood, *The Magic Boomerang,* Artbeat Publishers (Fremantle, West Australia), 2002.

Laura Krauss Melmed, *Capital! Washington D.C. from A to Z,* HarperCollins (New York, NY), 2003.

Barbara Ker Wilson, *Maui and the Big Fish,* Frances Lincoln (London, England), 2003.

WORK IN PROGRESS: Island Counting 1 2 3, for Candlewick Press (Cambridge, MA), publication expected in 2005; *Monday on the Mississippi,* by Marilyn Singer, for Holt (New York, NY), publication expected in 2005; *New York, New York! The Big Apple from A to Z,* by Laura Melmed, for HarperCollins (New York, NY), publication expected in 2005; *Look at the Clouds,* by Anne Rockwell, for HarperCollins (New York, NY).

SIDELIGHTS: A children's book author, illustrator, and internationally respected artist, Frané Lessac has lived around the world with her family, and her environment is often reflected in her works. Born in the United States, the author/illustrator has also called home the island of Montserrat and the continent of Australia. In her book *Caribbean Alphabet,* written with her husband, Mark Greenwood, Lessac relies on her gouache paintings and naïve style to illustrate sights, sounds, and activities from the Caribbean. Each letter represents some aspect of Caribbean culture and island life, from familiar activities such as fishing and kite flying to less well-known pursuits such as limbo dancing. Unfamiliar terms such as agouti, Junkanoo, and dasheen are explained in a pictorial glossary. "Each picture has its own little narrative on this celebratory island tour—fun, fluid, and imaginative," remarked a *Publishers Weekly* reviewer. Lessac's color selections and style allow all the colors of the island to "glow from the inside," wrote Mary Harris Veeder in *Tribune Books.*

Lessac also compiled and illustrated *Camp Granada: Sing-Along Camp Songs.* The book gathers the lyrics to more than thirty well-known songs sung over the years in summer camps and get-togethers. Well-known songs such as "If You're Happy," "Hello Muddah, Hello Faddah (Camp Granada)," and "Kum Ba Yah" are included, as well as lesser-known tunes such as "Found a Peanut" and "Ship Titanic." The book even includes the lyrics to "Taps," the melancholy tune played as days in camp draw to a close. Marge Loch-Wouters, writing in *School Library Journal,* remarked on Lessac's "folksy, lush gouaches," while a *Publishers Weekly* reviewer commented that Lessac's pictures "add to the homey humor." Todd Morning, in a

Booklist review, noted that the book "offer[s] an amusing glimpse of the community and landscape that make up camp life."

Lessac is also very active as an illustrator for other authors' books and stories. *Nine o'Clock Lullaby,* written by Marilyn Singer, answers a curious children's question. While they are getting ready to go to bed in Brooklyn, New York, what are kids in other parts of the world doing? The book's vignettes show children dancing in Puerto Rico, drawing water at dawn in India, getting a snack in the early hours in London, and more. The book serves as a "primer on time and the time zones, as an introduction to foreign cultures, and as a rhythmic, pleasing lullaby," commented a *Publishers Weekly* reviewer.

Eric Maddern's *The Fire Children: A West African Creation Tale* is a retelling of how spirit people Kwaku Ananse (a male) and Aso Yaa (a female) end up on earth and create the people of the world. One day, when sky god Nyame is looking down at the earth through a trapdoor in the moon, Kwaku Ananse and Aso Yaa, who live inside him, crawl out his mouth to have a look, too. But Nyame sneezes and propels the two spirit people to the surface of the earth. After a while, Aso Yaa becomes lonely and convinces Kwaku Ananse to help her make clay figures like themselves. When Nyame visits, which he does often, Kwaku Ananse and Aso Yaa take the clay figures out of the fire and hide them, fearing that Nyame will disapprove or be angry. The frequent firing and hiding result in many different figures with many different shades of color—the longer they stayed in the fire, the darker they became. The two spirit people breathed life into their clay creations, and the newly created humans wandered over the earth, established their cities and towns, and started their own families. This accounts for the varying skin tones among the people of earth—and no matter their color, Kwaku Ananse and Aso Yaa cherished each of their fire children equally. A *Publishers Weekly* critic remarked that the book is "elegantly told" and "gorgeously illustrated." *School Library Journal* reviewer Lyn Miller-Lachmann stated that "Lessac's gouache illustrations, which combine West African designs with her own characteristic style, work well with the text." Ellen Fader, writing in *Horn Book,* commented that Lessac's "ocher, brown, and blue-toned gouache paintings in a naïve style enhance and expand upon the story's folkloric quality."

The story of Simon Rodia, an artist and sculptor, is told in *The Wonderful Towers of Watts,* by Patricia Zelver. Rodia, an Italian immigrant, lived in the impoverished Los Angeles neighborhood of Watts. Over the course of more than thirty-three years, Rodia collected pieces of cast-off material, broken tiles from the factory where he worked and things that other people had thrown away, then used those items to construct three multicolored towers. The intricate, colorful towers were Rodia's life's work, "bearing witness to one man's dream of beauty," observed a *Publishers Weekly* reviewer, and they still stand in Watts today. Lessac's illustrations contain "the gaudy beauty of his achievement," observed the *Publishers Weekly* reviewer, and Corrine Camarata, writing in *School Library Journal,* remarked that "Lessac's familiar gouache paintings fill the pages with soft, rich colors."

Isaac Olaleye's *The Distant Talking Drum: Poems from Nigeria* is a collection of fifteen verses about Nigeria, the African rain forest, and the surrounding areas in Africa. Set largely in a Nigerian farming village, the free-verse poems tell simple but evocative stories of daily village life, including the making of a spicy but delicious soup, the effects of a sudden rainstorm, farming activities, doing laundry by the stream, going to the marketplace, and more. Lessac's illustrations "provide a perfect complement to the appealing poetry," remarked Dot Minzer in *School Library Journal.* Sheilamae O'Hara, writing in *Booklist,* called Lessac's paintings "as colorful and exuberant as the poems they complement," while *Horn Book*'s Maeve Visser Knoth commented that Lessac's "many brilliant colors" and "flat, folk-art style" combine "to complete the picture of a vital, lively village."

Young Anslem longs for snow and a "real" Christmas tree in his West Indies village in Vashanti Rahaman's *O Christmas Tree.* When a boat carrying pine trees arrives in port, Anslem is excited to finally be able to have a real tree—but he is bitterly disappointed when he discovers that the trees have dried out in transit and all the needles have fallen off, leaving only the scraggly limbs and twigs underneath. But Anslem comes to realize that the true meaning of Christmas does not require a tree and that there are plenty of other festive items and activities on the island—including the popular Christmas flower poinsettias—to make any Christmas a real one. Lessac's "artwork bursts with splashes of red poinsettia and showcases breezy island backgrounds," remarked a *Publishers Weekly* reviewer. *School Library Journal* reviewer Jane Marino observed that the illustrations are "filled with the colors and culture of the islands," and *Booklist* reviewer Susan Dove Lempke stated that "Lessac's cheerful folk-art paintings are delicately detailed."

Queen Esther Saves Her People, penned by Rita Golden Gelman, examines the background of the Jewish holiday Purim. Gelman retells the biblical story of Esther, who was taken into the court of the Persian King Ahasuerus. When Esther finds out about the prime minister's plot to kill all the Jews in the land, she risks her own life to warn the king and save her people. The Purim holiday celebrates Esther's courage each spring. *Booklist* reviewer Ilene Cooper remarked on the intricate illustrations, such as the cover painting of Esther "holding a tiny, almost unnoticeable white bird in her hand." A *Publishers Weekly* reviewer commented that Lessac's illustrations "are steeped in details," such as realistic Persian clothing, luxurious courtyard scenes, and fruit trees, "that provide a distinct sense of time and place."

Similar in construction to *Nine o'Clock Lullaby,* Marilyn Singer's *On the Same Day in March: A Tour of the World's Weather* provides an examination of the weather occurring in different parts of the world on the same March day. The book covers seventeen locations, including New York City, Paris, the Nile Valley, Darjeeling, Northern Kenya, and more. From tornadoes in the Texas panhandle to bitter snowstorms in Antarctica, rains in Africa and sunshine in Barbados, children are introduced to concepts of meteorology and climatology, and shown how drastically different weather can happen at the same time around the world. Reviewer Jody McCoy, writing in *School Library Journal,* remarked on the book's "carefully crafted, childlike illustrations" and "succinct, engaging text," while Michael Cart, writing in *Booklist,* commented on how Lessac's paintings "colorfully show us the way the weather and the world look."

In *Capital! Washington D.C. from A to Z,* Lessac and author Laura Krauss Melmed offer readers a tour of the U.S. capital. Arranged alphabetically, the book includes text and illustrations on the Air and Space Museum, the National Zoo, the Smithsonian Institution, the Lincoln Memorial, the Capitol Building, the Kennedy Center, the Holocaust Museum, Gallaudet University, and other important places. Each illustration is accompanied by a short paragraph that provides additional description and elaboration on the subject pictured. A *Kirkus Reviews* critic noted that Lessac's

"cheery folk-arty illustrations present thumbnail details with as much energy as broad landscapes," further commenting that "the illustrations work well with the prose explications" of the sights and scenery of Washington. Kathleen Odean, writing in *Booklist,* remarked that "this attractive offering will find its main audience among parents and teachers introducing D.C. to children."

Lessac once told *CA:* "My aim is to produce multicultural, nonsexist books for children, to break down racial barriers, and educate at the same time. I also want children to be aware of our precious environment.

"When I was at school, the art teachers considered me unteachable. Because my lines were never straight and my paintings didn't have dimension, the art teachers told me that they were wrong. My school wasn't progressive enough to recognize my work as a legitimate art form. Sometimes I even climbed in through the classroom window after school to change my grade in the professors' book.

"At the age of eighteen, I headed for film school in California. My aim was to make films about 'primitive' tribes before they were swamped by Western culture. Initially, I borrowed camera equipment and, given film, took off on the long road in the American Southwest, documenting a rodeo team, a long-distance trucker, and even the birth of a baby.

"Then in 1978, I moved from California to the small Caribbean island of Montserrat, and, stunned by its visual beauty, I concentrated on painting the old style West Indian architecture and its peoples. The locals would say to me, 'You live in de cement house, no worry de hurricanes,' and my feelings were torn as the houses were torn down. I wish there was a house museum. The beautiful images of Montserrat were the inspiration for my book of paintings, *The Little Island.*

"Montserrat is also the home of the one of the world's finest recording studios, Air Studios, which attracts an extraordinary number of international musicians and producers. These people become patrons of my paintings, and my work is now in private collections worldwide.

"In 1987, I published *Caribbean Canvas,* a collection of works, painted on my . . . travels to Barbados, Grenada, Antigua, Palm Island, and St. Kitts. This is aimed at a more extensive audience and also includes poetry by Caribbean writers.

"*The Dragon of Redonda* is a fairy tale endorsed by the 'real' King of Redonda. *The Bird Who Was an Elephant* is my favorite book. How could a bird become an elephant? Children will understand this, of course. But grown-ups, who always need explanations, may need to know that in India it is believed that we have many lives and that when we die, we can become another human being—or an animal. So this is the story of the bird."

BIOGRAPHICAL AND CRITICAL SOURCES:

PERIODICALS

Belles Lettres, spring, 1995, Bettina Berch, review of *Caribbean Canvas,* p. 60.

Booklist, October 1, 1992, Julie Corsaro, review of *Caribbean Carnival: Songs of the West Indies,* p. 331; July, 1993, Janice Del Negro, review of *The Fire Children: A West African Creation Tale,* p. 1971; September 15, 1993, Julie Corsaro, review of *Little Gray One,* p. 162, and Quarash Ali, review of *Not a Copper Penny in Me House: Poems from the Caribbean,* pp. 153-154; May 1, 1994, Carolyn Phelan, review of *The Wonderful Towers of Watts,* p. 1605; June 1, 1994, Hazel Rochman, review of *Caribbean Alphabet,* p. 1827; January 1, 1995, Sheilamae O'Hara, review of *The Distant Talking Drum: Poems from Nigeria,* p. 824; July, 1995, Hazel Rochman, review of *Good Rhymes, Good Times: Original Poems,* p. 188; September 1, 1996, Susan Dove Lempke, review of *O Christmas Tree,* p. 137; March 1, 1998, Ilene Cooper, review of *Queen Esther Saves Her People,* p. 1138; February 15, 2000, Michael Cart, review of *On the Same Day in March: A Tour of the World's Weather,* p. 1116; February 1, 2003, Kathleen Odean, review of *Capital! Washington, D.C. from A to Z,* pp. 998-999; March 1, 2003, Todd Morning, review of *Camp Granada: Sing-Along Camp Songs,* p. 1195.

Entertainment Weekly, Leonard S. Marcus, review of *Not a Copper Penny in Me House,* p. 73.

Horn Book, September-October, 1993, Ellen Fader, review of *The Fire Children,* pp. 610-611; March-April, 1995, Maeve Visser Knoth, review of *The Distant Talking Drum,* p. 211.

Kirkus Reviews, November 15, 2002, review of *Capital! Washington, D.C. from A to Z,* p. 1698.

New York Times Book Review, January 12, 1986; June 18, 1989; June 5, 1994, review of *The Wonderful Towers of Watts,* p. 30; January, 2003, review of *Capital! Washington, D.C. from A to Z,* p. 16.

People, November 28, 1994, review of *The Wonderful Towers of Watts,* pp. 35-36.

Publishers Weekly, March 30, 1990, review of *The Bird Who Was an Elephant,* p. 62; March 1, 1991, review of *Nine o'Clock Lullaby,* pp. 72-73; October 5, 1992, review of *Caribbean Carnival,* p. 72; June 7, 1993, review of *The Fire Children,* p. 69; July 5, 1993, review of *Not a Copper Penny in Me House,* p. 73; August 9, 1993, review of *Little Gray One,* p. 476; May 9, 1994, review of *The Wonderful Towers of Watts,* p. 72, and review of *Caribbean Alphabet,* p. 72; December 19, 1994, review of *The Distant Talking Drum,* p. 54; July 3, 1995, review of *Good Rhymes, Good Times,* pp. 60-61; September 30, 1996, review of *O Christmas Tree,* p. 90; December 22, 1997, review of *Queen Esther Saves Her People,* p. 54; January 25, 1999, review of *Not a Copper Penny in Me House,* p. 98; January 24, 2000, review of *On the Same Day in March,* p. 311; June 16, 2003, review of *Camp Granada,* p. 73.

Reading Teacher, October, 1995, review of *Caribbean Canvas,* p. 156.

School Library Journal, August, 1990, Marilyn Iarusso, review of *The Bird Who Was an Elephant,* pp. 130-131; January, 1991, Patricia Dooley, review of *The Turtle and the Island: A Folktale from Papua New Guinea,* p. 87; July, 1991, Patricia Dooley, review of *Nine o'Clock Lullaby,* p. 64; November, 1992, Lyn Miller-Lachmann, review of *Caribbean Carnival,* pp. 83-84; August, 1993, Lyn Miller-Lachmann, review of *The Fire Children,* p. 160; December, 1993, Ellen D. Warwick, review of *Not a Copper Penny in Me House,* p. 105; March, 1994, Liza Bliss, review of *Little Gray One,* p. 210; July, 1994, Lyn Miller-Lachmann, review of *Caribbean Alphabet,* p. 96; September, 1994, Corinne Camarata, review of *The Wonderful Towers of Watts,* p. 212; February, 1995, Dot Minzer, review of *The Distant Talking Drum,* p. 92; August, 1995, Sally R. Dow, review of *Good Rhymes, Good Times,* p. 135; October, 1996, Jane Marino, review of *O Christmas Tree,* p. 39; April, 2000, Jody McCoy, review of *On the Same Day in March,* p. 126; June, 2003, Marge Loch-Wouters, review of *Camp Granada,* p. 130.

Skipping Stones, April-May, 1996, review of *The Distant Talking Drum,* p. 31.

Tribune Books (Chicago, IL), June 12, 1994, Mary Harris Veeder, review of *Caribbean Alphabet,* p. 9.

ONLINE

Artbeat Publishers: Home Page of Frané Lessac, http://www.artbeatpublishers.com/ (March 18, 2004).

*   *   *

LIVELY, Penelope (Margaret) 1933-

PERSONAL: Born March 17, 1933, in Cairo, Egypt; daughter of Roger Low (a bank manager) and Vera Greer; immigrated to England, 1945; married Jack Lively (a university teacher), June 27, 1957; children: Josephine, Adam. *Education:* St. Anne's College, Oxford, B.A. (with honors), 1956. *Hobbies and other interests:* Gardening, landscape history, talking, listening.

ADDRESSES: Agent—David Higham Associates, 5-8 Lower John St., Golden Square, London W1F 9HA, England.

CAREER: Writer.

MEMBER: Society of Authors, PEN, Royal Society of Literature (fellow).

AWARDS, HONORS: Children's Spring Book Festival Award, *Book World,* 1973, for *The Driftway;* Carnegie Medal, and Hans Christian Andersen Award list, both 1973, both for *The Ghost of Thomas Kempe;* Whitbread Award, 1976, for *A Stitch in Time;* Booker-McConnell Prize shortlist, 1977, for *The Road to Lichfield,* and 1984, for *According to Mark;* Southern Arts Literary Prize, 1978, for *Nothing Missing but the Samovar and Other Stories;* Arts Council of Great Britain National Book Award, 1979, for *Treasures of Time;* Whitbread Award shortlist and Booker-McConnell Prize, both 1987, both for *Moon Tiger;* honorary D.Litt., Tufts University, 1990, and Warwick University, 1998; honorary fellow, Swansea University, 2002; Order of the British Empire, 1989, for contributions to literature; Commander of the British Empire, 2002; *The Ghost of Thomas Kempe, The House in Norham Gardens, A Stitch in Time,* and *Fanny's Sister* were all *Horn Book* honor books; *The House in Norham Gardens* was an American Library Association Notable Book.

Penelope Lively

WRITINGS:

FOR CHILDREN

Astercote, illustrated by Antony Maitland, Heinemann (London, England), 1970, Dutton (New York, NY), 1971.

The Whispering Knights, illustrated by Gareth Floyd, Heinemann (London, England), 1971, Dutton (New York, NY), 1976.

The Wild Hunt of Hagworthy, illustrated by Juliet Mozley, Heinemann (London, England), 1971, illustrated by Robert Payne, Pan Books (New York, NY), 1975, published as *The Wild Hunt of the Ghost Hounds,* Dutton (New York, NY), 1972, illustrated by Jeremy Ford, Puffin Books (New York, NY), 1984.

The Driftway, Heinemann (London, England), 1972, Dutton (New York, NY), 1973.

The Ghost of Thomas Kempe, illustrated by Antony Maitland, Dutton (New York, NY), 1973.

The House in Norham Gardens, Dutton (New York, NY), 1974.

Boy without a Name, illustrated by Ann Dalton, Parnassus Press (Berkeley, CA), 1975.

Going Back, Dutton (New York, NY), 1975.

A Stitch in Time, Dutton (New York, NY), 1976.

The Stained Glass Window, illustrated by Michael Pollard, Abelard-Schumann (London, England), 1976.

Fanny's Sister, illustrated by John Lawrence, Heinemann (London, England), 1976, new edition, illustrated by Anita Lobel, Dutton (New York, NY), 1980.

The Presence of the Past: An Introduction to Landscape History, Collins (London, England), 1976.

The Voyage of QV66, illustrated by Harold Jones, Heinemann (London, England), 1978, Dutton (New York, NY), 1979.

Fanny and the Monsters, illustrated by John Lawrence, Heinemann (London, England), 1979, enlarged edition, 1983.

Fanny and the Battle of Potter's Piece, illustrated by John Lawrence, Heinemann (London, England), 1980.

The Revenge of Samuel Stokes, Dutton (New York, NY), 1981.

Fanny and the Monsters and Other Stories (contains *Fanny's Sister, Fanny and the Monsters,* and *Fanny and the Battle of Potter's Piece*), Puffin Books (New York, NY), 1982.

Uninvited Ghosts and Other Stories, illustrated by John Lawrence, Heinemann (London, England), 1984, Dutton (New York, NY), 1985.

Dragon Trouble, illustrated by Valerie Littlewood, Heinemann (London, England), 1984, Barron's (New York, NY), 1989.

A House Inside Out, illustrated by David Parkins, Deutsch (London, England), 1987, Dutton (New York, NY), 1988.

Debbie and the Little Devil, illustrated by Toni Goffe, Heinemann (London, England), 1987.

Judy and the Martian, Simon & Schuster (London, England), 1992.

The Cat, the Crow, and the Banyan Tree, illustrated by Terry Milne, Candlewick Press (Cambridge, MA), 1994.

Good Night, Sleep Tight, Candlewick Press (Cambridge, MA), 1995.

Two Bears and Joe, Viking (New York, NY), 1995.

One, Two, Three, Jump!, M. K. McElderry Books (New York, NY), 1998.

In Search of a Homeland: The Story of the Aeneid, illustrated by Ian Andrews, Delacorte Press (New York, NY), 2001.

Also author of *The Disastrous Dog.* Contributor to children's magazines, including *Horn Book* and *Junior Bookshelf.*

ADULT FICTION

The Road to Lichfield, Heinemann, (London, England), 1977, Penguin (New York, NY), 1983.

Nothing Missing but the Samovar and Other Stories, Heinemann (London, England), 1978.

Treasures of Time, Heinemann (London, England), 1979, Doubleday (Garden City, NY), 1980.

Judgement Day, Heinemann (London, England), 1980, Doubleday (New York, NY), 1981, reprinted, Grove Press (New York, NY), 2003.

Next to Nature, Art, Heinemann (London, England), 1982, Penguin (New York, NY), 1984.

Perfect Happiness, Heinemann (London, England), 1983, Dial Press (Garden City, NY), 1984.

Corruption and Other Stories, Heinemann (London, England), 1984.

According to Mark: A Novel, Beaufort Books (New York, NY), 1984.

Pack of Cards (short stories, including "Nothing Missing but the Samovar" and "Corruption"), Heinemann (London, England), 1986, Penguin (New York, NY), 1988.

Moon Tiger, Deutsch (London, England), 1987, Grove Weidenfeld (New York, NY), 1988.

Passing On, Deutsch (London, England), 1989, Grove Weidenfeld (New York, NY), 1990.

City of the Mind, HarperCollins (New York, NY), 1991.

Cleopatra's Sister, HarperCollins (New York, NY), 1993.

Heat Wave, HarperCollins (New York, NY), 1996.

The Five Thousand and One Nights, Fjord Press (Seattle, WA), 1997.

Beyond the Blue Mountains, Viking (New York, NY), 1997.

Spiderweb, HarperCollins (New York, NY), 1999.

The Photograph, Viking (London, England), 2001, Viking (New York, NY), 2003.

OTHER

Boy Dominic (television play; three episodes), Yorkshire TV, 1974.

Time out of Mind (television play for children), BBC-TV, 1976.

(Author of introduction) Ivy Compton-Burnett, *Father and His Fate,* Oxford University Press (New York, NY), 1984.

(Author of introduction) Ivy Compton-Burnett, *Manservant and Maidservant,* Oxford University Press (New York, NY), 1987.

(Author of introduction) Edith Wharton, *The Age of Innocence,* Virago (London, England), 1988.

(Author of introduction) Lewis Carroll, *Alice in Wonderland,* Everyman (London, England), 1993.

Oleander, Jacaranda: A Childhood Perceived (memoir), HarperCollins (New York, NY), 1994.

(Author of introduction) Willa Cather, *My Antonia,* Everyman (London, England), 1996.

(Author of introduction) *The Mythical Quest,* British Library (London, England), 1996.

A House Unlocked (memoir), Viking (New York, NY), 2001.

Also contributor to books, including *My England,* Heinemann (New York, NY), 1973. Contributor of short stories and articles to periodicals, including *Encounter, Vogue, Cosmopolitan, Good Housekeeping, Literary Review,* and *Quarto.* Reviewer for newspapers and author of television and radio scripts. Many of Lively's writings have been translated into other languages.

ADAPTATIONS: Several of Lively's books have been adapted as audiobooks, including *House Inside Out,* Chivers Press, 1988. *The Ghost of Thomas Kempe* was adapted for television by ABC-TV, 1979.

SIDELIGHTS: Penelope Lively, author of more than forty books for children and adults, has distinguished herself as a writer of both juvenile and adult books in a career spanning over thirty years. She has won such prestigious awards as the Booker-McConnell Prize and the Whitbread Award. *Publishers Weekly* contributor Amanda Smith considered Lively "one of England's finest writers," and added that her novels are "characterized by intelligence, precision and wit." Sheila A. Egoff, in her *Thursday's Child: Trends and Patterns in Contemporary Children's Literature,* wrote that Lively "has an uncannily accurate and honest recall of what it is like to be a child in a world made for adults." As to her adult fiction, a *Times Literary Supplement* reviewer commented that Lively conveys "a prose that is invariably as precise as it is unostentatious."

Lively began writing children's books while raising her two children, Josephine and Adam. Writing stories for children was a convenient way to express her interests. Lively's first published novel, *Astercote,* explored her fascination with deserted medieval villages. Although the book was criticized for its lack of living characters and convincing dialogue, reviewers also found it intriguing and exciting. Lively published two subsequent juvenile novels, *The Whispering Knights* and *The Driftway. The Driftway* follows Paul and his tag-along sister as he runs away from his stepmother and a charge of shoplifting. He comes across an old road which has been used for thousands of years by various travelers. These travelers have left messages from the past, which Paul is able to see and interpret with the help of a cartdriver named Bill. Margery Fisher, editor of *Growing Point,* explained that each "interlude reflects part of Paul's situation and brings him a step nearer to understanding himself and his family." The characters from the past make him aware that "there is more than one point of view to every story, and he takes the first steps away from the morbid self-absorption of childhood towards feeling sympathy for others," concluded a *Times Literary Supplement* reviewer. Some writers such as John Rowe Townsend felt that the point of the story is weakened because the book as a whole lacks a strong storyline—the reader never does find out what happens to Paul and his sister. However, *Junior Bookshelf* contributor Aneurin R. Williams expressed her belief that, overall, "Lively writes well, exceeding by far the style and effect of" her earlier work. *The Driftway* won the Children's Spring Book Festival Award in 1973.

Lively's best-received juvenile book, *The Ghost of Thomas Kempe,* offers a light approach to the coming-of-age theme. The author uses one of her favorite devices in this book: the ghost. The purpose of Thomas Kempe's character, explained Lively in *Junior Bookshelf,* is to explore "the memory of places and the memory of people, and the curious business that we are all of us not just what we are now but what we have been." Putting this another way, *Children's Literature in Education* contributor Judith Armstrong wrote that this book "is concerned with different aspects of the same person, the person [James] might have been, or might still become, had he not encountered the ghost of his potential self." The story involves a boy's visitation by the spirit of a sorcerer from Stuart England. At first, the ghost seems only mischievous, but slowly becomes more and more menacing. James learns through the ghost what wickedness is, and is only able to put Kempe to rest by learning to recognize and cope with the wickedness within himself. Many critics agreed that *The Ghost of*

Thomas Kempe is a well-written children's book. David Rees, author of *The Marble in the Water: Essays on Contemporary Writers of Fiction for Children and Young Adults,* felt that the book is of such high quality because for the first time "the author is completely sure of her own abilities, and the writing has a positiveness that derives from the author's pleasure in her awareness of these abilities."

Rees had even higher praise for *A Stitch in Time,* Lively's Whitbread Award winner. "*A Stitch in Time* is probably Penelope Lively's most important and memorable book," he declared. "Not only is its exploration of the significance of history and memory more profound than in any other of her novels, but the unfolding of the story is very fine." As *Times Literary Supplement* reviewer Ann Thwait noted, the story does not have a great deal of plot action, since most of this action occurs unobtrusively within the mind of Marie, the main character. Marie, who is spending her vacation with her parents in an old Victorian house in Lyme Regis, discovers a sampler made in 1865 by a girl named Harriet. The sampler provides a link to the past which Marie senses through such things as the squeaking of a swing and the barking of a dog, neither of which exist near the house at the present; they are only echoes of the past. The tension in the story lies in Marie's suspicion that something tragic has happened to Harriet, a belief supported by the lack of any pictures in the house of Harriet as an adult. Though the mystery is eventually solved, the real message of the book is summarized by the owner of the old house when he sagely remarks: "Things always could have been otherwise. The fact of the matter is that they are not." This declaration, explained Terry Jones, a contributor to *Children's Literature in Education,*"finally ends Maria's 'vague imaginings' and completes one part of her education. . . . She leaves the Regency house determined to acquire 'some new wisdom about the way things are.' She grows, and the reader grows with her."

"*The Voyage of QV66* is a radical departure from all of Lively's earlier books," contended Alan McLay in the *Dictionary of Literary Biography.* At some unspecified time in the future, a cataclysmic event has wiped out the earth's human population. Animals have taken the place of humans, taking on speech and other human skills. For this tale, Lively has brought together six animals, including Pal, the dog, and Stanley, the monkey, to take a voyage to London in the boat *QV66.* In

following the animals along their journey, the book "views human nature and civilization from a wry, ironic perspective," noted McLay. He continued, "Readers are invited to laugh at the ways in which the animals imitate human behavior but are also exposed to the caustic comments made about humans, especially their habits of eating animals and killing one another with sharp sticks." In the end, the six voyagers find that the world has not changed; animals have simply replaced humans in carrying out the same human follies. Even so, as McLay pointed out, "The little group of animals on the QV66 . . . represents the virtues of friendship, loyalty, and community and offers hope for the future."

Lively continued to write children's books throughout the 1980s, including such titles as *The Revenge of Samuel Stokes, Uninvited Guests and Other Stories,* and *A House Inside Out.* In 1993, she published another tale of animals who carry on like people. *The Cat, the Crow and the Banyan Tree* portrays two friends, the cat and the crow, who live beneath the banyan tree, where they spend their time telling stories to each other. Critics have described the tales told by cat and crow as whimsical, imaginative, delightful, but potentially confusing for children. A reviewer for *Publishers Weekly* observed that "Lively's narrative percolates with rhythm" and focuses interestingly on the process of storytelling itself.

Although she continued to write for children, in the late 1970s, after writing children's books for almost a decade, Lively decided it was time to change her primary focus. "I began to feel that I was in danger of writing the same children's books over and over again," she explained in *Publishers Weekly.* "More than that, I'd exhausted the ways in which I could explore my own preoccupations and interests within children's books." In writing for an older audience, the author has maintained her interest in the past and memory, but has followed a different approach. Her adult characters consider memory "in the context of a lifetime rather than in the context of history," explained Lively in *Horn Book.* These later works no longer deal with how the past can teach one to mature so much as how it can change one's perspective or philosophy of life.

Lively's first novel for adults, *The Road to Lichfield,* is a complex tale about what happens to a married history teacher named Anne Linton when her conceptions about her childhood family life are suddenly altered. While going through her dying father's papers, she discovers that he was involved in an affair similar to her own extramarital relationship. "As everything in her life swings and changes, her father dies, her love is choked off, and only the road [between her present life in Cuxing and her childhood memories of Lichfield] remains permanent," summarized Jane Langton in the *Dictionary of Literary Biography.* "There is nothing very original about the plot" of *The Road to Lichfield,* noted John Mellors in the *Listener,* but the "book is lifted out of the ordinary by the author's treatment of her two main themes: continuity and memory."

In Lively's Booker-McConnell Award-winning story *Moon Tiger,* the "true center is no less than history itself—the abiding backdrop across which mere human beings flutter," said Anne Tyler in the *New York Times Book Review.* It is "the transitoriness of all human happiness and indeed of all human life" which is the concern of a respected historian, Claudia Hampton, as she considers her life from the vantage point of her deathbed, explained Francis King in a *Spectator* article. In this book, a complex interweaving of flashbacks takes the reader on a voyage through the dying historian's life, including a sojourn in World War II Egypt, where Claudia finds brief happiness with a tank commander, who is later killed in action. "Her image for their love," wrote Richard Eder of the *Los Angeles Times Book Review,* "is the moon tiger—a spiral coil of punk that burns slowly through the night beside their bed to keep away mosquitoes and that leaves only ash in the morning."

Parallel to this image are the last lines of the book in which Claudia passes away: "The sun sinks and the glittering tree is extinguished. The room darkens again. . . . And within the room a change has taken place. It is empty. Void. It has the stillness of a place in which there are only inanimate objects; metal, wood, glass, plastic. No Life." The denouement marks the end of, in Eder's words, Claudia's "long postponed search for herself." For some critics, like Martha Duffy of *Time* magazine, the flashbacks involved in her search become "overdrawn" after a while. However, many reviewers concurred with *Times Literary Supplement* contributor J. K. L. Walker, who wrote: "Lively's ingenious, historically informed handling of [the story] is a considerable achievement and Claudia Hampton herself a formidably reflective and articulate protag-

onist." It is a tale told from the most widely encompassing perspective possible for a human being, a study of one character's entire lifetime memory and how she regards it. Writing in the *New York Times Book Review,* Jay Parini commented: "In that inventive re-creation of life in Egypt during World War II, an evocative mixture of memory and desire, Ms. Lively established herself as a novelist of the first rank." Although Lively bases most of *Moon Tiger* upon the memory of a single character, exploring this favorite subject in depth, the author admitted to herself in *Horn Book:* "I don't imagine that I am ever going to find the answer to the questions prompted by the workings of memory; all I can do is pose these questions in fictional form and see what happens."

Aisling Foster, in the *Times Literary Supplement,* viewed Lively's novel *Heat Wave* as "all about the power of love: protective maternal love, promiscuous sexual love, the nurturing love of Mother Nature and our love of animals and countryside which is both benign and exploitative." Set in the English countryside, the novel explores themes that have interested Lively in past works: history in the context of the present, and myth versus reality. The main protagonist is Pauline, a fifty-five-year-old freelance copy-editor who worries that her daughter will repeat her own mistakes. "Most importantly," commented a reviewer in *Publishers Weekly,* Lively "creates a convincing picture of obsessive sexual love tainted by jealousy and misery, and of the kind of maternal love that carries its own implacable mandates." While all this transpires, England is in the grip of some uncharacteristic weather. "The tension mounts as temperatures rise," observed Donna Seaman in *Booklist,* "but Lively keeps cool as she leads us to a surprise denouement—her impeccable prose delectably restrained, her humor neat and vicious, and her articulation of emotional states keen and vivifying." "The novel makes clear," in the estimation of *People*'s Joanne Kaufman, "that Lively knows well the topography of the human heart."

In *A House Unlocked* Lively explores her memories of her ancestral home Golsoncott in Somerset, England, which was originally bought by her grandparents in 1923. In 1995 the family had to sell the house after Lively's aunt died, and as Lively told Robert McCrum in the *Observer,* "My children and I were all heartbroken." They spent a great deal of time reminiscing about the house, until Lively realized "that I had this memory house and would never lose it." However, the book considers the loss of the house, and is an elegy to the era that the house embodied, as well as to the people who lived in it. A *Publishers Weekly* reviewer wrote that the book "unlocks more than the house and its century."

In the *Dictionary of Literary Biography,* Ruth P. Feingold remarked, "Over the course of her career Penelope Lively has produced an astonishing quantity of well-crafted, sometimes brilliant work. . . . The structural complexity of her texts is matched by their intellectual and moral rigor: seldom possessed of neat resolutions, her adult novels in particular tend to illustrate her view that 'I have never come to terms with life, and I wouldn't wish anyone else to do so; if fiction is to help at all in the process of living, it is by illuminating its conflicts and ambiguities.'"

BIOGRAPHICAL AND CRITICAL SOURCES:

BOOKS

Children's Literature Review, Volume 7, Gale (Detroit, MI), 1984.

Contemporary Literary Criticism, Gale (Detroit, MI), Volume 32, 1985, Volume 50, 1989.

Dictionary of Literary Biography, Gale (Detroit, MI), Volume 14: *British Novelists since 1960,* 1983, Volume 161: *British Children's Writers since 1960,* 1996, Volume 207: *British Novelists since 1960, Third Series,* 1999.

Egoff, Sheila A., *Thursday's Child: Trends and Patterns in Contemporary Children's Literature,* American Library Association (Chicago, IL), 1981.

Ellis, Alec, and Marcus Crouch, editors, *Chosen for Children: An Account of the Books Which Have Been Awarded the Library Association Carnegie Medal, 1936-1975,* 3rd edition, American Library Association (Chicago, IL), 1977.

Moran, Mary Hurley, *Penelope Lively,* Twayne (New York, NY), 1993.

Rees, David, *The Marble in the Water: Essays on Contemporary Writers of Fiction for Children and Young Adults,* Horn Book (Boston, MA), 1980, pp. 185-198.

St. James Guide to Children's Writers, 5th edition, St. James Press (Detroit, MI), 1999.

Townsend, John Rowe, *A Sounding of Storytellers: New and Revised Essays on Contemporary Writers for Children,* Lippincott (New York, NY), 1979.

PERIODICALS

Belles Lettres, spring, 1992, pp. 26-29.

Booklist, March 15, 1994, p. 1322; June 1, 1995, p. 1787; August, 1996, p. 1854; February 15, 1998, p. 1027; October 15, 2000, Karen Harris, review of *Spiderweb,* p. 471; March 1, 2002, Donna Seaman, review of *A House Unlocked,* p. 1084.

Book Report, March, 2002, review of *In Search of a Homeland,* p. 69.

Books for Keeps, November, 2001, review of *In Search of a Homeland,* p. 27; January, 2002, review of *The Driftway,* p. 22.

Bulletin of the Center for Children's Books, June, 1999, review of *One, Two, Three, Jump,* p. 358.

Chicago Tribune Book World, August 9, 1981; May 15, 1988.

Children's Bookwatch, January, 2002, review of *In Search of a Homeland,* p. 1.

Children's Literature, number 18, 1990, pp. 53-67.

Children's Literature in Education, summer, 1978, pp. 59-66; autumn, 1981.

Children's Literature Quarterly, winter, 1984-85, pp. 157-64; fall, 1985, pp. 114-16.

Encounter, May, 1981.

Globe and Mail (Toronto, Ontario, Canada), November 14, 1987; October 6, 2001, review of *A House Unlocked,* p. D23.

Growing Point, July, 1972; July, 1973.

Horn Book, June, 1973; August, 1973; February, 1978; April, 1978; March, 1999, p. 164; fall, 1999, review of *One, Two, Three, Jump,* p. 237.

International Fiction Review, January, 2001, Nora Foster Stovel, review of *Spiderweb,* p. 115.

Journal of the Short Story in English, autumn, 1989, pp. 103-111.

Junior Bookshelf, September, 1972; June, 1974.

Kirkus Reviews, February 1, 1999, review of *Spiderweb,* p. 170; February 1, 2002, review of *A House Unlocked,* p. 161.

Library Journal, November 1, 1997, p. 130; October 1, 1999, Richard Oloizia, review of *Spiderweb,* p. 160; April 1, 2002, Ravi Shenoy, review of *A House Unlocked,* p. 129; April 1, 2003, review of *The Photograph,* p. 498.

Listener, August 4, 1977.

Los Angeles Times Book Review, April 17, 1988; April 25, 1999, review of *Spiderweb,* p. 23.

New Statesman, May 8, 1987, p. 23; October 2, 1987, p. 31; April 23, 1993, p. 33; June 3, 1994, p. 44; January 20, 2003, Amanda Craig, review of *The Photograph,* p. 51.

New Statesman and Society, April 12, 1991, p. 35.

New Welsh Review, spring, 1990, pp. 36-38.

New Yorker, November 18, 1991, p. 134; June 14, 1993, p. 99.

New York Times Book Review, April 17, 1988, p. 9; May 21, 1989, p. 13; February 11, 1990, p. 12; February 17, 1991, p. 7; September 1, 1991, p. 6; April 25, 1993, p. 7; June 12, 1994, p. 32; March 19, 1995, p. 19; June 11, 1995, p. 43; March 3, 1996, p. 25; April 11, 1999, review of *The Road to Lichfield* and *Pack of Cards and Other Stories,* p. 40.

Observer, April 25, 1993; November 14, 1999, review of *Spiderweb,* p. 15; August 26, 2001, review of *A House Unlocked,* p. 16.

People, July 25, 1994, p. 26; January 13, 1997, p. 28.

Publishers Weekly, November 13, 1987; February 12, 1988, p. 71; March 25, 1988, pp. 47-48; February 3, 1989, p. 97; May 21, 1989; December 1, 1989, p. 48; November 23, 1990, p. 56; February 11, 1990; June 21, 1991, p. 53; February 8, 1993, p. 76; March 7, 1994, p. 61; March 14, 1994, p. 73; April 10, 1995, p. 61; July 1, 1996, p. 41; May 26, 1997, p. 68; February 1, 1999, review of *Spiderweb,* p. 72; March 15, 1999, review of *One, Two, Three, Jump,* p. 56; March 4, 2002, review of *A House Unlocked,* p. 67.

School Library Journal, February, 1988, p. 73; May, 1994, p. 99; June, 1995, p. 91; February 1, 1999, review of *Spiderweb,* p. 72; March 15, 1999, review of *One, Two, Three, Jump,* p. 56; July, 1999, review of *One, Two, Three, Jump,* p. 76.

Spectator, November 22, 1980; May 23, 1987; September 1, 2001, review of *A House Unlocked,* p. 35.

Time, May 2, 1988, p. 86.

Times (London, England), October 30, 1987.

Times Educational Supplement, September 10, 1999, review of *The House in Northam Gardens,* p. 31.

Times Literary Supplement, July 14, 1972; April 6, 1973; July 16, 1976; November 21, 1980; May 23, 1986; October 17, 1986; May 15, 1987; April 7, 1989; April 23, 1993; May 24, 1996, p. 27; November 9, 2001, review of *A House Unlocked,* p. 25.

Wall Street Journal, April 2, 1999, review of *Spiderweb,* p. W7.

Washington Post Book World, August 2, 1981; September 13, 1988.

Woman's Journal, December, 1999, review of *Spiderweb,* p. 18.

ONLINE

Observer, http://www.observer.co.uk/ (August 26, 2001), Robert McCrum, interview with Lively.

Penelope Lively Web site, http://www.penelopelively.net/ (May 28, 2003).

*   *   *

LOWRY, Lois (Hammersburg) 1937-

PERSONAL: Born March 20, 1937, in Honolulu, HI; daughter of Robert E. (a dentist) and Katharine (Landis) Hammersberg; married Donald Grey Lowry (an attorney), June 11, 1956 (divorced, 1977); married; second husband's name Martin; children: Alix, Grey (deceased), Kristin, Benjamin. *Education:* Attended Brown University, 1954-56; University of Southern Maine, B.A., 1972; graduate study. *Religion:* Episcopalian.

ADDRESSES: Home—205 Brattle St., Cambridge, MA 02138. *Agent*—Wendy Schmalz, Harold Ober Associates, 425 Madison Ave., New York, NY 10017.

CAREER: Freelance writer, children's author, and photographer, 1972—.

MEMBER: Society of Children's Book Writers and Illustrators, PEN American Center, Authors Guild, Authors League of America, MacDowell Colony (fellow).

AWARDS, HONORS: Children's Literature Award, International Reading Association (IRA), Notable Book Citation, American Library Association (ALA), state children's choice awards, Massachusetts and California, 1978, for *A Summer to Die;* Children's Book of the Year citation, Child Study Association of America, and ALA Notable Book citation, all 1979, all for *Anastasia Krupnik;* ALA Notable Book citation, 1980, and International Board on Books for Young People Honor List citation, 1982, both for *Autumn Street;* ALA Notable Book Citation, 1981, and American Book Award nomination (juvenile paperback category), 1983, for *Anastasia Again!;* ALA Notable Book Citation, 1983, for *The One-Hundredth Thing about Caroline;* Children's Book of the Year Citation, Child Study As-

Lois Lowry

sociation of America, 1986, for *Us and Uncle Fraud;* state children's choice award, New Jersey, 1986, for *Anastasia, Ask Your Analyst; Boston Globe-Horn Book* Award, Golden Kite Award, Society of Children's Book Writers and Illustrators, and Child Study Award, Children's Book Committee of Bank Street College, all 1987, all for *Rabble Starkey;* Christopher Award, 1988; Newbery Medal, ALA, National Jewish Book Award, and Sidney Taylor Award, National Jewish Libraries, all 1990, all for *Number the Stars;* Newbery Medal, 1994, for *The Giver;* Children's Choice citation, IRA/Children's Book Council, 1997, for *See You Around, Sam!*

WRITINGS:

JUVENILE NOVELS

A Summer to Die, illustrated by Jenni Oliver, Houghton Mifflin (Boston, MA), 1977.

Find a Stranger, Say Goodbye, Houghton Mifflin (Boston, MA), 1978.

Anastasia Krupnik, Houghton Mifflin (Boston, MA), 1979.

Autumn Street, Houghton Mifflin (Boston, MA), 1979.

Anastasia Again!, illustrated by Diane deGroat, Houghton Mifflin (Boston, MA), 1981.

Anastasia at Your Service, illustrated by Diane deGroat, Houghton Mifflin (Boston, MA), 1982.

Taking Care of Terrific, Houghton Mifflin (Boston, MA), 1983.

Anastasia, Ask Your Analyst, Houghton Mifflin (Boston, MA), 1984.

Us and Uncle Fraud, Houghton Mifflin (Boston, MA), 1984.

The One Hundredth Thing about Caroline, Houghton Mifflin (Boston, MA), 1985.

Anastasia on Her Own, Houghton Mifflin (Boston, MA), 1985.

Switcharound, Houghton Mifflin (Boston, MA), 1985.

Anastasia Has the Answers, Houghton Mifflin (Boston, MA), 1986.

Rabble Starkey, Houghton Mifflin (Boston, MA), 1987.

Anastasia's Chosen Career, Houghton Mifflin (Boston, MA), 1987.

All about Sam, illustrated by Diane deGroat, Houghton Mifflin (Boston, MA), 1988.

Number the Stars, Houghton Mifflin (Boston, MA), 1989.

Your Move, J. P.!, Houghton Mifflin (Boston, MA), 1990.

Anastasia at This Address, Houghton Mifflin (Boston, MA), 1991.

Attaboy, Sam!, illustrated by Diane deGroat, Houghton Mifflin (Boston, MA), 1992.

The Giver, Houghton Mifflin (Boston, MA), 1993.

Anastasia, Absolutely, Houghton Mifflin (Boston, MA), 1995.

See You Around, Sam!, Houghton Mifflin (Boston, MA), 1996.

Stay!: Keeper's Story, illustrated by True Kelley, Houghton Mifflin (Boston, MA), 1997.

Looking Back: A Book of Memories, Houghton Mifflin (Boston, MA), 1998.

Zooman Sam, Houghton Mifflin (Boston, MA), 1999.

Gathering Blue, Houghton Mifflin (Boston, MA), 2000.

Gooney Bird Green, illustrated by Middy Thomas, Houghton Mifflin (Boston, MA), 2002.

The Silent Boy, Houghton Mifflin (Boston, MA), 2003.

OTHER

Black American Literature (textbook), J. Weston Walsh (Portland, ME), 1973.

Literature of the American Revolution (textbook), J. Weston Walsh (Portland, ME), 1974.

(Photographer) Frederick H. Lewis, *Here in Kennebunkport,* Durrell (Kennebunkport, ME), 1978.

(And photographer) *Looking Back: A Photographic Memoir* (autobiography), Houghton Mifflin (Boston, MA), 1998.

Also author of introduction to *Dear Author: Students Write about the Books That Changed Their Lives,* Conari Press, 1995. Contributor of stories, articles, and photographs to periodicals, including *Redbook, Yankee,* and *Down East.*

ADAPTATIONS: Find a Stranger, Say Goodbye was made into the *Afterschool Special* "I Don't Know Who I Am," ABC-TV, 1980; *Taking Care of Terrific* was televised on *Wonderworks,* 1988; *Anastasia at Your Service* was recorded on audiocassette, Learning Library, 1984; *Anastasia Krupnik* was made into a filmstrip, Cheshire, 1987.

SIDELIGHTS: Lois Lowry is an award-winning author of young adult novels. Born in 1937 in Honolulu, Hawaii, Lowry's original birth name was Cena, after her Norwegian grandmother, but the elder Cena strongly objected to having her granddaughter bear that name— Lowry's name was quickly changed, and at eleven months of age, she was baptized Lois Ann. At the time of her birth, Lowry's father, a military dentist and career army officer, was stationed at Schofield Barracks near Pearl Harbor. The family separated with the onset of World War II; her father continued his duty in the military, and Lowry spent the duration of the war with her mother's family in the Amish Country of Pennsylvania. "I remember all these relatively normal Christmases with trees, presents, turkeys, and carols, except that they had this enormous hole in them because there was never any father figure," Lowry said in *Authors and Artists for Young Adults.* This deep sense of loss is "probably why I've written a terrific father figure into all of my books—sort of a fantasy of mine while growing up." Her grandmother wasn't especially fond of children, but her grandfather adored her, and Lowry escaped the absolute trauma of war under the shelter of his affection. Much later, Lowry's wartime experience inspired her fourth novel, *Autumn Street.* As an author, Lowry has often translated her life into fiction for the purpose of helping others who may have suffered under similar circumstances. She once commented that she gauges her success as a writer by her ability to "help adolescents answer their own questions about life, identity and human relationships."

Lowry's books have dealt with topics ranging from the death of a sibling and the Nazi occupation of Denmark, to the humorous antics of the rebellious Anastasia Krupnik, to futuristic dystopian societies. In her first novel, *A Summer to Die,* Lowry portrays an adolescent's struggle with her older sister's illness and eventual death. When the Chalmers family moves to the country for the summer, thirteen-year-old Meg and fifteen-year-old Molly are forced to share a room. Already jealous of her older sister, Meg becomes increasingly argumentative and resentful when her sister's recurring nosebleeds become the focus of her parents' attention. As her sister's condition deteriorates, Meg realizes that Molly is slowly dying of leukemia. For friendship, she turns to old Will Banks, a neighbor who encourages her interest in photography, and Ben and Maria, a hippie couple who invite Meg to take pictures at the birth of their child.

A Summer to Die was well received by critics. The "story captures the mysteries of living and dying without manipulating the reader's emotions, providing understanding and a comforting sense of completion," observed Linda R. Silver in *School Library Journal.* Tragically, Lowry's sympathy for Meg and Molly was drawn from life. Her older sister, Helen, died of cancer when Lowry was twenty-five. "Very little of [*A Summer to Die*] was factual," she once commented, "except the emotions." The author added, "When my mother read the book she recognized the characters as my sister and me. She knew that the circumstances in the book were very different, but the characters had great veracity for her."

Following her successful debut as a novelist, Lowry continued to explore challenging adolescent topics. She documented an adopted child's search for her biological mother in *Find a Stranger, Say Goodbye.* Although neither Lowry nor any of her children are adopted, she felt that the subject was important enough to be dealt with at length. She explained, "Maybe it's because of having watched my own kids go through the torture of becoming adults . . . that I think those kinds of issues are important and it's important to deal with them in a sensitive and compassionate way."

Memories of her childhood as well as her experiences as a parent have led Lowry to her most popular character: Anastasia Krupnik, the spunky, rebellious, and irreverent adolescent who stars in a series of books that began in 1979. "Until I was about twelve I thought my parents were terrific, wise, wonderful, beautiful, loving, and well-dressed," the author confessed. "By age twelve and a half they turned into stupid, boring people with whom I did not want to be seen in public. . . . That happens to all kids, and to the kids in my books as well." In the first book of the series, *Anastasia Krupnik,* the ten-year-old heroine faces numerous comic crises, including a crush on a boy who is continually dribbling an imaginary basketball, and the coming arrival of a baby sibling. With the passing of each crisis Anastasia gains new insight into herself; by the book's close she is prepared to move on to a new level of maturity. "Anastasia's feelings and discoveries should be familiar to anyone who has ever been ten," noted Brad Owens in the *Christian Science Monitor,* "and author Lois Lowry has a sensitive way of taking problems seriously without ever being shallow or leaning too far over into despair."

The broad audience appeal of the first "Anastasia" book prompted Lowry to write another novel featuring her diminutive heroine. "I have the feeling she's going to go on forever—or until I get sick of her, which hasn't happened yet. I'm still very fond of her and her whole family," Lowry remarked. Subsequent titles include *Anastasia Again!* and *Anastasia at Your Service,* in which a twelve-year-old Anastasia finds a summer job serving as maid to a rich, elderly woman, who turns out to be a classmate's grandmother. Anastasia must deal with the embarrassment of working for the family of a well-to-do peer. "Despite differences the girls become friends; and with the help of Anastasia's precocious brother Sam, they generate a plot that is rich, inviting, and very funny," noted Barbara Elleman in a *Booklist* review. The popular Anastasia went on to appear in numerous additional titles, including *Anastasia, Ask Your Analyst; Anastasia on Her Own; Anastasia Has the Answers;* and *Anastasia's Chosen Career.*

In 1990 Lowry received the Newbery Medal for her distinguished contribution to children's literature with *Number the Stars.* Based on a factual account, the story is set against the backdrop of Nazi-occupied Denmark. Ten-year-old Annemarie Johansen and her family are drawn into the resistance movement, shuttling Jews from Denmark into neutral Sweden. (During the Second World War this type of heroism ensured the survival of nearly all of Denmark's Jews.) Newbery

Committee Chair Caroline Ward was quoted by *School Library Journal:* "Lowry creates suspense and tension without wavering from the viewpoint of Annemarie, a child who shows the true meaning of courage." The book "avoids explicit description of the horrors of war, yet manages to convey without oversimplification the sorrow felt by so many people who were forced to flee their homeland," wrote a *Children's Literature Review* critic.

Lowry received the prestigious Newbery Medal a second time for her 1993 novel *The Giver.* In this radical departure from her previous works, Lowry creates a futuristic utopian world where every aspect of life—birth, death, families, career choices, emotions, even the weather—is strictly controlled in order to create a safe and comfortable community with no fear or violence. Jonas is twelve years old and is looking forward to an important rite of passage: the ceremony in which he, along with all children his age, will be assigned a life's vocation. Jonas is bewildered when he is skipped during the ceremony, but it is because he has been selected for a unique position. Jonas will become the new Receiver, the prestigious and powerful person who holds all the memories of the community. In his lessons with the old Receiver, whom Jonas calls the Giver, Jonas begins learning about the things—memories, emotions, and knowledge—that the community has given up in favor of peacefulness. At first, these memories are pleasant: images of snow, colors, feelings of love. But then Jonas encounters the darker aspects of human experience—war, death, and pain—and discovers that community members who are "Released" are actually being euthanized. This discovery leads Jonas to escape from the community with his young foster brother Gabriel. In an interestingly ambiguous ending, readers can decide for themselves whether the boys have safely reached "Elsewhere," been intercepted by their community's security forces, or died from hunger and exposure.

Gathering Blue, which a *Publishers Weekly* reviewer hailed as a "dark, prophetic tale with a strong medieval flavor," is a sequel, or companion piece, to *The Giver.* Rather than depicting a technologically advanced society, however, Lowry here describes a technologically primitive world in which, as she states in her author's note, "disorder, savagery, and self-interest" rule. As in *The Giver,* a child is chosen to play a special role in this society. Kira was born with a twisted leg—a condition that would normally have resulted in her being put to death as a baby. But she was somehow allowed to live. Kira sews beautifully, and is chosen to be The Threader, whose duty it is to create the robe of The Singer, a garment that depicts the history of the world and is used in the annual ritual of the Gathering. In this role, however, Kira begins to learn the dark secrets beneath her society's rules and must make a life-altering choice. Many reviewers praised the novel for its sensitive handling of serious themes. Kay Bowes in *Book Report* considered it "thought-provoking" and "challenging," while a *Horn Book* writer observed that it "shares the thematic concerns of *The Giver* . . . [but] adds a layer of questions about the importance of art in creating and, more ominously, controlling community." Ellen Fader, in *School Library Journal*, concluded that "Lowry has once again created a fully-realized world. . . . Readers won't forget these memorable characters or their struggles in an inhospitable world."

Lowry revisited the world of Anastasia and her family with *Zooman Sam*. Anastasia's little brother, Sam (also the hero of *Attaboy, Sam!* and *See You Around, Sam!*), is on the cusp of learning to read. Acquiring the skill will allow him to be someone special, he believes: specifically, the Chief of Wonderfulness. To help him along, his mother makes Sam a special "Zooman Sam" jumpsuit for him to dress up in during Future Job Day at his nursery school—there wasn't enough room on the garment to fit the word "zookeeper." With dreams of being a zookeeper, a special type of job indeed in a room full of kids dreaming of more mundane occupations, Sam finds out that his teacher will let him stand at the head of the circle and tell about a different zoo animal each day for six weeks. With his budding reading skills, Sam is delighted to take on the task and enjoys the attention that comes with it. "Lowry gets everything about Sam just right," wrote Stephanie Zvirin in *Booklist*. Roger Sutton, writing in *Horn Book*, observed that the author "spins interesting variations on her theme," and wraps the book up with "a swell (and well-prepared) surprise."

The title character in *Gooney Bird Greene* is the newest arrival to the second grade and the most eccentric person the other students have ever seen. Leaning toward flamboyant dress (a pair of cowboy boots and pajamas one day, a polka-dot shirt and tutu the next), Gooney Bird is also a master storyteller in a small package. She delights in relating tales of herself and her "absolutely true" adventures of how she flew in

from China on a flying carpet, how she got her "diamond earrings" (actually gumball machine trinkets) from a noble prince, and how she got her oddball name. Encouraged by her teacher, Gooney Bird spins out her tales, prompting the other students to create and tell their own stories. In the process, the entire class—and the book's reader—learns important lessons in storytelling and constructing a compelling and believable narrative. GraceAnne A. DeCandido, writing in *Booklist*, called *Gooney Bird Greene* a "laugh-out-loud chapter book," concluding that the character's first appearance is "quite a debut." The book's message and the "cleverly titled stories could spark children's interest in writing their own stories," wrote Janet B. Bair in *School Library Journal*. Critic Peter D. Sieruta, writing in *Horn Book* observed that Gooney Bird is "not always convincing as a character, but she's a fine storyteller, and her message to her classmates—that they, too, have stories to share—is a good one."

In *Silent Boy* Lowry returns again to a more solemn setting with the story of Katy Thatcher, her physician father, and their life in a small-town New England setting during the early part of the twentieth century. Peggy Stoltz, a local girl who helps on the Thatcher farm, is Katy's best friend. Peggy has a brother, Jacob, and a sister, Nell, who works on the farm next to the Thatcher farm. Jacob is considered an "imbecile," or "touched in the head," a gentle thirteen-year-old who never speaks but has a profound ability to handle and communicate with animals. Katy knits together a tenuous companionship with Jacob and begins to sense the wonder in his affinity with animals. Katy has trouble dealing with the realities of country life, with her pending tenth birthday, and with the arrival of a new baby in her family. Nell also expects a baby after a relationship with her employers' son. When Jacob disappears with Nell's unwanted and unnamed infant—and the baby turns up dead—Katy cannot believe the sensitive and gentle boy could commit an act of murder, even one that, in his mind, may have been completely acceptable or even desirable. Jacob is incarcerated in an asylum for the rest of his life, and Katy grows up to become a doctor like her father, reminiscing about Jacob and the tragedy of his life. "Lowry's graceful, lively prose is dense with historical details," remarked Gillian Engberg in *Booklist*. Ellen Fader, writing in *School Library Journal*, noted that "Lowry excels in developing strong and unique characters and in showing Katy's life in a small town that changes around her as the first telephones and automobiles arrive."

Lowry's story "balances humor and generosity with the obstacles and injustice of Katy's world," a *Publishers Weekly* reviewer observed, though "Jacob's story ends in a tragedy deftly foreshadowed," remarked a *Kirkus Reviews* critic.

Although Lowry's books have explored a variety of settings and characters, she finds one unifying theme among them. "All of them deal, essentially, with the same general theme: the importance of human connections," she wrote on the *Lois Lowry* home page. Lowry is a grandmother, and has experienced the joys of life as well as its deep tragedies, such as when her fighter-pilot son, Grey, was killed in a plane crash. Lowry recounts her lifetime of remembrances in *Looking Back: A Book of Memories*. More like a visit from a favorite friend than an autobiography, *Looking Back* is "much more intimate and personal than many traditional memoirs," wrote Barbara Scotto in *School Library Journal*. A *Publishers Weekly* reviewer observed that "a compelling and inspirational portrait of the author emerges from these vivid snapshots of life's joyful, sad, and surprising moments."

BIOGRAPHICAL AND CRITICAL SOURCES:

BOOKS

American Women Writers, 2nd edition, St. James Press (Detroit, MI), 2000.
Authors and Artists for Young Adults, Volume 32, Gale, Detroit, MI), 2000.
Beacham's Guide to Literature for Young Adults, Beacham Publishing (Osprey, FL), 1990, Volume 4, 1990, Volume 6, 1994.
Chaston, Joel D., *Lois Lowry,* Twayne (New York, NY), 1997.
Children's Literature Review, Gale (Detroit, MI), Volume 6, 1984, Volume 46, 1997, Volume 72, pp. 192-206.
Dictionary of Literary Biography, Volume 52: *American Writers for Children since 1960: Fiction,* Gale (Detroit, MI), 1987, pp. 249-261.
Green, Carol Hurd, and Mary Grimley Mason, editors, *American Women Writers,* Volume 5: *Supplement,* Continuum Publishing (New York, NY), 1994.
Lowry, Lois, *Looking Back: A Book of Memories,* Houghton Mifflin (Boston, MA), 1998.
St. James Guide to Young Adult Writers, 2nd edition, St. James Press (Detroit, MI), 1999.
Silvey, Anita, editor, *Children's Books and Their Creators,* Houghton Mifflin (Boston, MA), 1995.
Something about the Author Autobiography Series, Volume 3, Gale (Detroit, MI), 1986, pp. 131-146.

PERIODICALS

Book, May-June, 2003, review of *Gooney Bird Greene,* p. 31.
Booklist, October 15, 1979, Barbara Elleman, review of *Anastasia Krupnik,* p. 354; April 15, 1980, p. 1206; September 1, 1982, Barbara Elleman, review of *Anastasia at Your Service,* p. 46; September 1, 1987, pp. 66-67; March 1, 1989, p. 1194; March 1, 1990, Ilene Cooper, review of *Your Move, J. P.!,* p. 1345; April 1, 1991, Stephanie Zvirin, review of *Anastasia at This Address,* p. 1564; April 15, 1993, p. 1506; November 1, 1997, Ellen Mandel, review of *Stay!: Keeper's Story,* p. 472; November 1, 1998, Carolyn Phelan, review of *Looking Back,* p. 490; July, 1, 1999, Stephanie Zvirin, review of *Zooman Sam,* p. 1947; September 15, 1999, review of *Looking Back,* p. 254; June 1, 2000, Ilene Cooper, review of *Gathering Blue,* p. 1896; August 2001, Elaine Hanson, review of *Gathering Blue* (audio version), p. 2142; September 1, 2002, GraceAnne A. DeCandido, review of *Gooney Bird Greene,* p. 125; April 15, 2003, Gillian Engberg, review of *The Silent Boy,* p. 1462.
Book Report, May, 1999, review of *Looking Back,* p. 73; January 2001, Kay Bowes, review of *Gathering Blue,* p. 58.
Books for Keeps, January, 2002, review of *Gathering Blue,* p. 26.
Bulletin of the Center for Children's Books, January, 1980, Zena Sutherland, review of *Anastasia Krupnik,* p. 99; November, 1980, pp. 57-58; January, 1982, p. 90; May, 1984, Zena Sutherland, review of *Anastasia, Ask Your Analyst,* p. 169; December, 1984, p. 71; May, 1985, p. 70; October, 1988, pp. 46-47; March, 1990, Ruth Ann Smith, review of *Your Move, J. P.!,* p. 169; April, 1993, p. 257; September, 1995, Deborah Stevenson, review of *Anastasia, Absolutely,* pp. 20-21; November, 1996, p. 105; January, 1998, Janice Del Negro, review of *Stay!,* p. 165; January, 1999, Janice Del Negro, review of *Looking Back,* p. 174; September, 1999, review of *Zooman Sam,* p. 21.
Catholic Library World, September, 1999, review of *See You Around, Sam,* p. 33.

Children's Bookwatch, March, 1999, review of *Looking Back,* p. 6; December, 1999, review of *Zooman Sam,* p. 4; March, 2001, review of *Looking Back,* p. 8.

Christian Science Monitor, January 14, 1980, Brad Owens, review of *Anastasia Krupnik,* p. B6; March 1, 1985, Lyn Littlfield Hoopes, review of *Us and Uncle Fraud,* p. 65; May 1, 1987, Betsy Hearne, "Families Shaped by Love, Not Convention," pp. B3-B4.

Five Owls, April, 1989, pp. 59-60; September-October, 1993, Gary D. Schmidt, review of *The Giver,* pp. 14-15; March, 2001, review of *Gathering Blue,* p. 92.

Horn Book, August, 1977, Mary M. Burns, review of *A Summer to Die,* p. 451; June, 1978, p. 258; December, 1979, Ann A. Flowers, review of *Anastasia Krupnik,* p. 663; October, 1981, Mary M. Burns, review of *Anastasia Again!,* pp. 535-536; December, 1982, p. 650; June, 1983, p. 304; December, 1983, p. 711; June, 1984, pp. 330-331; September-October, 1985, Ann A. Flowers, review of *Anastasia on Her Own,* pp. 556-557; May-June, 1986, Mary M. Burns, review of *Anastasia Has the Answers,* pp. 327-328; July-August, 1987, Ann A. Flowers, review of *Rabble Starkey,* pp. 463-465; January, 1988, pp. 29-31; May-June, 1989, Mary M. Burns, review of *Number the Stars,* p. 371; March-April, 1990, Ethel R. Twitchell, review of *Your Move, J. P.!,* pp. 201-202; July-August, 1990, pp. 412-421; July-August, 1990, Shirley Haley-James, "Lois Lowry," profile of Lois Lowry; November-December, 1993, Patty Campbell, "The Sand in the Oyster," pp. 717-721; July-August, 1994, Lois Lowry, "Newbery Medal Acceptance," pp. 414-422, Walter Lorraine, "Lois Lowry," pp. 423-426; September-October, 1996, Roger Sutton, review of *See You Around, Sam!,* p. 597; January-February, 1998, Roger Sutton, review of *Stay!,* pp. 76-77; January, 1999, Peter D. Sieruta, review of *Looking Back,* p. 87; September, 1999, Roger Sutton, review of *Zooman Sam,* p. 613; September, 2000, Roger Sutton, review of *Gathering Blue,* p. 573; September-October, 2002, Peter D. Sieruta, review of *Gooney Bird Greene,* pp. 575-577.

Instructor, May, 1999, review of *The Giver,* p. 16; May, 1999, review of *See You Around, Sam,* p. 16; May, 2001, review of *The Giver,* p. 37.

Journal of Youth Services in Libraries, fall, 1996, pp. 39-40, 49.

Junior Bookshelf, August, 1979, Mary Hobbs, review of *A Summer to Die,* pp. 224-225; August, 1980, p. 194.

Kirkus Reviews, April 1, 1986, review of *Anastasia Has the Answers,* pp. 546-547; March 1, 1987, review of *Rabble Starkey,* p. 374; March 15, 1991, review of *Anastasia at This Address,* p. 396; March 1, 1992, p. 326; March 1, 1993, review of *The Giver,* p. 301; October 15, 1997, review of *Stay!,* p. 1584; July 15, 1999, review of *Zooman Sam,* p. 1135; March 15, 2003, review of *The Silent Boy,* p. 472.

New York Times Book Review, February 28, 1982, p. 31; April 11, 1982, p. 27; August 5, 1984, p. 14; September 14, 1986, p. 37; May 21, 1989, Edith Milton, "Escape from Copenhagen," p. 32; October 31, 1993, Karen Ray, review of *The Giver,* p. 26; January 14, 1996, Michael Cart, review of *Anastasia, Absolutely,* p. 23; October 15, 1998, review of *Looking Back,* p. 1534; February 14, 1999, review of *Looking Back,* p. 27; November 19, 2003, Elizabeth Spires, review of *Gathering Blue,* p. 57.

Observer (London, England), October 21, 2001, review of *Gathering Blue,* p. 16.

Publishers Weekly, February 21, 1986, interview with Lowry, pp. 152-153; March 13, 1987, p. 86; November 8, 1985, review of *Switcharound,* p. 60; July 28, 1997, review of *Stay!,* p. 75; August 24, 1998, review of *Looking Back,* p. 58; April 5, 1999, review of *Stay!,* p. 243; September 13, 1999, review of *Zooman Sam,* p. 85; July 31, 2000, review of *Gathering Blue,* p. 96; March 24, 2003, review of *The Silent Boy,* p. 76; March 24, 2003, Ingrid Roper, "Picturing the Turn of the 20th Century," interview with Lowry, p. 77.

Reading Teacher, March, 2001, review of *Gathering Blue,* p. 638.

School Librarian, February, 1995, pp. 31-32.

School Library Journal, May, 1977, Linda R. Silver, review of *A Summer to Die,* pp. 62-63; May, 1978, p. 77; April, 1980, Marilyn Singer, review of *Autumn Street,* pp. 125-126; March, 1981, p. 109; October, 1981, Marilyn Kaye, review of *Anastasia Again!,* p. 144; October, 1983, Kathleen Brachmann, review of *The One Hundredth Thing about Caroline,* p. 160; May, 1984, p. 82; November, 1984, p. 133; August, 1985, p. 68; February, 1986, Maria B. Salvadore, review of *Switcharound,* p. 87; May, 1986, p. 94; September, 1987, Dudley B. Carlson, review of *Anastasia's Chosen Career,* p. 180; August, 1988, Trev Jones, review of *All about Sam,* p. 96; March, 1989, Louise L. Sherman, review of *Number the Stars,* p. 177; January, 1990, p. 9; May, 1992, Marcia Hupp, review of

Attaboy, Sam!, p. 114; October, 1996, Starr La-Tronica, review of *See You Around, Sam!,* p. 102; October, 1997, Eva Mitnick, review of *Stay!,*, p. 134; September, 1998, Barbara Scotto, review of *Looking Back,* p. 221; September, 1999, review of *Zooman Sam,* p. 193; August 2000, Ellen Fader, review of *Gathering Blue,* p. 186; May, 2001, review of *Gathering Blue* (audio version), p. 75; November, 2002, Janet B. Bair, review of *Gooney Bird Greene,* pp. 129-130; April, 2003, Ellen Fader, review of *The Silent Boy,* pp. 164-165.

Signal, May, 1980, pp. 119-122.

Voice of Youth Advocates, August, 1985, p. 186; April, 1988, p. 26; August, 1993, p. 167; December, 1995, p. 304; April, 1999, review of *Looking Back,* p. 76; August, 1999, review of *Looking Back,* p. 164; April, 2001, review of *Gathering Blue,* p. 12.

Washington Post Book World, May 9, 1993, p. 15.

ONLINE

Books 'n' Bytes, http://www.booksnbytes.com/ (May 28, 2003), Harried Klausner, review of *Gathering Blue.*

Houghton Mifflin Web site, http://www.houghtonmifflin books.com/ (May 28, 2003).

Lois Lowry Web site, http://www.loislowry.com (May 28, 2003).

Rambles Web site, http://www.rambles.net/ (May 28, 2003), Donna Scanlon, review of *Gathering Blue.**

*   *   *

LUDLUM, Robert 1927-2001
(Jonathan Ryder, Michael Shepherd)

PERSONAL: Born May 25, 1927, in New York, NY; died of a heart attack, March 12, 2001, in Naples, FL; son of George Hartford (a businessman) and Margaret (Wadsworth) Ludlum; married Mary Ryducha (an actress), March 31, 1951 (died, 1996); married second wife, Karen, 1997; children (first marriage): Michael, Jonathan, Glynis. *Education:* Wesleyan University, B.A., 1951. *Politics:* Independent.

CAREER: Writer, 1971-2001. Actor on Broadway and on television, 1952-60; North Jersey Playhouse, Fort Lee, NJ, producer, 1957-60; producer in New York, NY, 1960-69; Playhouse-on-the-Mall, Paramus, NJ, producer, 1960-70. *Military service:* U.S. Marine Corps, 1944-46.

MEMBER: Authors Guild, Authors League of America, American Federation of Television and Radio Artists, Screen Actors Guild.

AWARDS, HONORS: New England Professor of Drama Award, 1951; awards and grants from American National Theatre and Academy, 1959, and from Actors' Equity Association and William C. Whitney Foundation, 1960; Scroll of Achievement, American National Theatre and Academy, 1960.

WRITINGS:

The Scarlatti Inheritance, World Publishing (New York, NY), 1971, reprinted, Armchair Detective Library (New York, NY), 1990.

The Osterman Weekend, World Publishing (New York, NY), 1972, reprinted, Armchair Detective Library (New York, NY), 1991.

The Matlock Paper, Dial (New York, NY), 1973.

(Under pseudonym Jonathan Ryder) *Trevayne,* Delacorte (New York, NY), 1973.

(Under pseudonym Jonathan Ryder) *The Cry of the Halidon,* Delacorte (New York, NY), 1974.

The Rhinemann Exchange, Dial (New York, NY), 1974.

(Under pseudonym Michael Shepherd) *The Road to Gandolfo,* Dial (New York, NY), 1975, reprinted under name Robert Ludlum, Bantam (New York, NY), 1982.

The Gemini Contenders, Dial (New York, NY), 1976.

The Chancellor Manuscript, Dial (New York, NY), 1977.

The Holcroft Covenant, Richard Marek, 1978.

The Matarese Circle, Richard Marek, 1979.

The Bourne Identity, Richard Marek, 1980.

The Parsifal Mosaic, Random House (New York, NY), 1982.

The Aquitaine Progression, Random House (New York, NY), 1984.

The Bourne Supremacy, Random House (New York, NY), 1986.

The Icarus Agenda, Random House (New York, NY), 1988.

The Bourne Ultimatum, Random House (New York, NY), 1990.

The Road to Omaha, Random House (New York, NY), 1992.

The Scorpio Illusion, Bantam (New York, NY), 1993.

Three Complete Novels: The Ludlum Triad, Wings Books, 1994.

The Apocalypse Watch, Bantam (New York, NY), 1995.

The Matarese Countdown, Bantam (New York, NY), 1997.

(With Gayle Lynds) *Robert Ludlum's The Hades Factor* (first novel in "Covert-One" series), St. Martin's Press (New York, NY), 2000.

The Prometheus Deception, St. Martin's Press (New York, NY), 2000.

(With Philip Shelby) *Robert Ludlum's The Cassandra Compact* (second novel in "Covert-One" series), St. Martin's Press (New York, NY), 2001.

The Sigma Protocol, St. Martin's Press (New York, NY), 2001.

The Janson Directive, St. Martin's Press (New York, NY), 2002.

(With Gayle Lynds) *Robert Ludlum's The Paris Option* (third novel in "Covert-One" series), St. Martin's Press (New York, NY), 2002.

The Tristan Betrayal, St. Martin's Press (New York, NY), 2003.

(With Gayle Lynds) *Robert Ludlum's The Altman Code* (fourth novel in the "Covert-One" series), St. Martin's Press (New York, NY), 2003.

ADAPTATIONS: The Rhinemann Exchange was adapted as a television miniseries by NBC, 1977; *The Osterman Weekend* was filmed by EMI, 1980; *The Holcroft Covenant,* directed by John Frankenheimer and starring Michael Caine, was filmed in 1985; *The Bourne Supremacy,* read by Michael Prichard, was released on cassette tape by Books on Tape, 1986; an abridged version of *The Bourne Identity,* read by Darren McGavin, was released on cassette tape by Bantam, 1987, and a television film of this title, written by Carol Sobieski, directed by Roger Young, and starring Richard Chamberlain, was broadcast in 1988; *The Icarus Agenda,* read by Michael Prichard, was released on cassette by Books on Tape, 1988; *The Bourne Ultimatum,* read by Michael Prichard, was released on cassette by Books on Tape, 1990; *The Road to Omaha,* read by Joseph Campanella, was released by Random House, 1992; *The Scarlatti Inheritance* was filmed by Universal Pictures; a feature film of *The Bourne Iden-*

tity, with a screenplay by Tony Gilroy and William Blake Herron, directed by Doug Liman, and starring Matt Damon, was released by Universal Pictures in 2002; *The Bourne Supremacy,* with screenplay by Gilroy and Brian Helgeland, directed by Paul Greengrass, and starring Damon, was released by Universal in 2004. Eric Van Lustbader has authored another book featuring the Bourne character, *The Bourne Legacy,* published by St. Martin's Press in 2004.

SIDELIGHTS: Suspense novelist Robert Ludlum "has his share of unkind critics who complain of implausible plots, leaden prose, and, as a caustic reviewer once sneered, an absence of 'redeeming literary values to balance the vulgar sensationalism,'" Susan Baxter and Mark Nichols noted in *Maclean's.* "But harsh critical words have not prevented Robert Ludlum . . . from becoming one of the most widely read and wealthiest authors in the world." In fact, with sales of his books averaging 5.5 million copies each, Ludlum was "one of the most popular . . . authors [writing] in the English language," Baxter and Nichols concluded.

Authorship came as a second career for Ludlum. Having grown up in a well-to-do family in the suburbs of New York City, he left home as a teenager to pursue an acting career, then served in the Marines during World War II before going to college to study fine arts. He worked as an actor doing theater, television films, and commercial voice-overs and found success as a producer before writing his first published novel at age forty-two—he had written one novel while in his teens, but the manuscript disappeared one night when he was carousing in San Francisco. "Ludlum's acting career accustomed him to rude reviews, and he often said that his theatrical training helped him to create the complicated plots which marked his writing," observed an obituary writer in the *Times* of London. His most notable theatrical production, Bill Manhoff's *The Owl and the Pussycat,* featured then-unknown actor Alan Alda, who later gained fame for his role in the television series *M*A*S*H.* The play was performed at Playhouse-on-the-Mall in Paramus, New Jersey, the country's first theater in a shopping center, which Ludlum opened in 1960. After serving as producer at the Playhouse for ten years, Ludlum found himself bored and frustrated with the pressures of theater work. Finally, he gave in to his wife's admonition to try his hand at writing.

The Scarlatti Inheritance, Ludlum's first novel, was written around an old story idea and outline, drafted years earlier and finally fleshed out when he left the theater. Based on Ludlum's curiosity at the wealth of one group of Germans during that country's economic collapse and skyrocketing inflation following World War I, *The Scarlatti Inheritance* follows several financiers, including some Americans, who fund Hitler's Third Reich. The book set the pattern for Ludlum's career: the story of espionage and corruption became a best-seller. Criticism of *The Scarlatti Inheritance* also foreshadowed that of future works. In the *Dictionary of Literary Biography Yearbook: 1982,* Patricia L. Skarda described the novel as having a "somewhat erratic pace and occasionally melodramatic characterizations" but being nonetheless "a thrilling, compelling tale"—pronouncements typical of each of Ludlum's novels.

In his next work, *The Osterman Weekend,* a television reporter is convinced by the CIA that his friends are involved in a conspiracy to control the world economy and agrees to gather evidence against them, but finds himself in over his head when his wife and children are threatened. Though several reviewers considered the book's ending disappointing, William B. Hill, writing in *Best Sellers,* noted, "If the ending is a bit weak, it is chiefly because it lets the rider down off a very high horse." Skarda pointed out that the story "exposes the inadequacies of American intelligence operations and our deepest fears that our friends cannot be trusted." Government agents again use a civilian as an investigator in a situation beyond his expertise in *The Matlock Paper.* Professor Matlock is pushed "into an untenable and dangerous situation" while snooping around campus for information on a group of crime bosses, Kelly J. Fitzpatrick related in *Best Sellers.* "The climax is effective," Fitzpatrick wrote, "and leaves the reader wondering, 'Can it be so?'" Newgate Callendar remarked in the *New York Times Book Review,* "The basic situation is unreal—indeed, it's unbelievable—but a good writer can make the reader suspend his disbelief, and Ludlum is a good writer."

Trevayne and *The Cry of the Halidon,* both written under the pseudonym Jonathan Ryder, feature protagonists who discover they were hired not for their skills, but in hopes that they would be unable to uncover the truth about their employers. Andrew Trevayne, appointed to investigate spending by the U.S. Defense Department, uncovers a company so powerful that even the president of the United States is controlled by it. "There is no doubt that big business exerts an

inordinate amount of pressure," Callendar observed in a *New York Times Book Review.* "But how much pressure? Who is really running the country?" Reviewing *The Cry of the Halidon,* in which a young geologist is sent to Jamaica to conduct an industrial survey and winds up in the crossfire of British Intelligence, the corporation that hired him, and various underground factions, Callendar called Ludlum's writing style "rather crude and obvious," and commented that Ludlum "is not very good at suggesting real characters, and his hero is a cutout composite of a number of sources." A reviewer for *Publishers Weekly* found that, early on in *The Cry of the Halidon,* "cleverness ceases to look like a virtue and becomes an irritant. If the writing were as rich or subtle as the plot is involved the reader might more happily stay the course . . . , but the writing is in fact rather bare."

Ludlum's final pseudonymous offering—this time writing as Michael Shepherd—was *The Road to Gandolfo,* "a strange, lurching amalgam of thriller and fantasy," in the opinion of *Library Journal* contributor Henri C. Veit. Involving the pope, the Mafia, and the U.S. Army, the book is intended to be funny, but falls short, Veit continued. A *Publishers Weekly* reviewer similarly noted that the book "comes crammed with zaniness and playful characters, but, unhappily, neither asset produces comedy or the black humor indictment of the military mind the author intended."

The Rhinemann Exchange contains "one extremely ingenious plot gimmick," according to the *New York Times Book Review*'s Callendar, in which the United States and Germany arrange a trade—industrial diamonds for Germany, a weapons guidance system for the United States. Despite the author's "commonplace and vulgar style apparently much relished by his vast audience," Veit predicted in a *Library Journal* piece that the book would be a success. In a critique of the audio version of *The Rhinemann Exchange,* a *Publishers Weekly* contributor believed Ludlum fans "will find exactly what they're looking for—in a format already quite familiar." A secret with devastating consequences, described by Irma Pascal Heldman in the *New York Times Book Review* as "absolutely within the realms of authenticity and fascinating to contemplate," is the key to *The Gemini Contenders.* Twin brothers, compelled by their father's deathbed wish to find a hidden vault containing a volatile document, unleash the secret on the world. Despite criticizing the plot, characters, and period detail of *The Gemini Con-*

tenders, reviewer T. J. Binyon commented in the *Times Literary Supplement* that Ludlum "has the ability to tell a story in such a way as to keep even the fastidious reader unwillingly absorbed."

In *The Chancellor Manuscript,* Ludlum returned to remaking history as he had in *The Scarlatti Inheritance.* FBI director J. Edgar Hoover's death is found to be an assassination, not the result of natural causes as was previously believed. The murder was carried out to prevent Hoover from releasing his secret files, which, *Christian Science Monitor*'s Barbara Phillips noted, "contain enough damaging information to ruin the lives of every man, woman and child in the nation." A group of prominent citizens joins forces to retrieve the files but find half have already been stolen. An unsuspecting decoy is deployed, as in many other Ludlum stories, to lead the group to the thieves. The message of *The Chancellor Manuscript* is familiar to Ludlum fans, as the book "seems to justify our worst nightmares of what really goes on in the so-called Intelligence Community in Washington," Richard Freedman remarked in the *New York Times Book Review.*

The Bourne Identity, which introduces a trilogy of books, follows Jason Bourne, a spy who awakens in a doctor's office with amnesia; the story is played out as a remarkable number of killers and organizations attempt to finish Bourne off before he realizes his true identity. "Some of Mr. Ludlum's previous novels were so convoluted they should have been packaged with bags of bread crumbs to help readers keep track of the plot lines," Peter Andrews mused in the *New York Times Book Review.* "But *The Bourne Identity* is a Ludlum story at its most severely plotted, and for me its most effective." The second volume, *The Bourne Supremacy,* forces Bourne to face his past when his wife is kidnapped. The final story in the "Bourne" trilogy, *The Bourne Ultimatum,* finds Bourne drawn into one last battle with his arch-enemy, the Jackal. The *Los Angeles Times Book Review*'s Don G. Campbell praised the third "Bourne" book as an example of "how it *should* be done," concluding that "in the pulsetingling style that began so many years ago with *The Scarlatti Inheritance,* we are caught up irretrievably." After Ludlum's death, Eric Van Lustbader added to the Bourne series with *The Bourne Legacy,* published by St. Martin's Press in 2004.

A woman comes back from the dead and a spy in the White House threatens humanity's continued existence in *The Parsifal Mosaic.* "Certainly, millions of entranced readers tap their feet in time to his fiction, and I'm positive this new adventure will send his legions of fans dancing out into the streets," Evan Hunter remarked in the *New York Times Book Review.* "Me? I must be tone-deaf." A world takeover is again imminent in *The Aquitaine Progression,* this time at the hands of five military figures. "Ludlum's hero, Joel Converse, learns of a plot by generals in the United States, Germany, France, Israel and South Africa to spawn violent demonstrations. Once the violence bursts out of hand, the generals plan to step in and take over," Charles P. Wallace wrote in the *Los Angeles Times Book Review. The Icarus Agenda* features a similar plot. This time, five wealthy, powerful figures arrange the election of the next United States president. "There is a sufficient amount of energy and suspense present in *The Icarus Agenda* to remind the reader why Mr. Ludlum's novels are best sellers," Julie Johnson commented in the *New York Times Book Review.* "Ludlum is light-years beyond his literary competition in piling plot twist upon plot twist," Peter L. Robertson observed in Chicago's *Tribune Books,* "until the mesmerized reader is held captive, willing to accept any wayward, if occasionally implausible, plotting device."

In *The Road to Omaha,* Ludlum departs from the seriousness of his espionage thrillers with a follow-up to *The Road to Gandolfo* that continues that novel's farcical tone. The Hawk and Sam, Ludlum's heroes in *Gandolfo,* return to fight the government for a plot of land legally belonging to an Indian tribe. In a review of the audio version of *The Road to Omaha,* a *Publishers Weekly* reviewer noted, "Hardcore Ludlum fans may be taken aback at first, but they stand to be won over in the listening."

The Scorpio Illusion returned to more familiar Ludlum territory: terrorism, international intrigue, mayhem, and death. In this novel, Amaya Bajaratt, a beautiful Basque terrorist, ignites a plot to assassinate the leaders of Israel, England, France, and the United States. Supported in her plot by a secret society of assassins known as the Scorpios, Bajaratt ventures to the United States to carry out the prize murder—the assassination of the U.S. president. The killer runs into resistance in the form of Tye Hawthorne, a former Naval intelligence officer, who is the only person capable of stopping the scheme. *The Apocalypse Watch,* Ludlum's next novel, covers similar serious territory, as a well-funded group of neo-Nazis attempts to create a Fourth Reich and achieve world domination. This intricately plotted novel features Harry Latham, who infiltrates the evil group only to be implanted with a memory chip of false information about prominent supporters of the group. When Harry is killed by the neo-Nazis, his brother, Drew, must pick up the fight against the group. Aided by the beautiful and mysterious Karin de Vries, Drew dodges assassination attempts and thwarts the neo-Nazis' ploy for world-domination.

The key elements of Ludlum's books—corruption in high places, elaborate secret plans, and unsuspecting civilians drawn into the fray—are what kept Ludlum fans waiting for his next offering. His writing, characterized by the liberal use of exclamation points, italics, sentence fragments, and rhetorical questions, was called crude by some critics, but others acknowledged that the style is popular with millions of readers and has proven difficult to duplicate, leaving Ludlum with little copycat competition. Still, reviewers often pointed to Ludlum's use of mixed metaphors and illogical statements as serious flaws in his books. Horror novelist Stephen King, in a somewhat tongue-in-cheek review of *The Parsifal Mosaic* for the *Washington Post Book World,* highlighted some of Ludlum's "strange, wonderful, and almost Zen-like" thoughts: "'We've got . . . a confluence of beneficial prerogatives.' 'What I know is still very operative.' 'I'll get you your cover. But not two men. I think a couple would be better.'"

Robert Ludlum's The Hades Factor, written with Gayle Lynds, is the first novel in Ludlum's "Covert-One" series. Lt. Col. Jonathan Smith, a doctor and former espionage operative, is involved in biomedical research concerning deadly viruses. He is warned by an old friend—now an FBI agent—that his life is in danger. Within short order, his fiancé, also a virus researcher, is dead and Smith is forced underground after sidestepping several plots to kill him. The "doomsday" virus, unleashed by a shadowy enemy, kills three people in diverse locations within the United States, and Smith amasses his own secret force of experts in computer hacking and covert operations to stop those who are behind the virus and want to kill him. "The book reads fast," wrote Randy Michael Signor in *Book,* with "characters [who] are in service to plot, and plot [that] is in service to sales." Ronnie H. Terpening liked the book more, writing in *Library Journal* that *The Hades Factor* is "a top-notch international thriller" with "dev-

astating double-crosses, gutwrenching twists, fast-paced action, [and] pressure that ratchets up to an explosive conclusion."

In *The Prometheus Deception,* evil forces once again attempt to take over the world. Stopping them is Nick Bryson, a retired spy who is shocked to discover that the top-secret agency he worked for—the Directorate—for twenty years was a front for the Russians. The CIA turns to him for help in dismantling the organization, which is planning terrorist attacks on the West in the form of anthrax outbreaks, train derailments, and airplane explosions. Bryson comes to suspect that the attacks are not the work of the Directorate, but rather another shadowy intelligence agency, the Prometheans. As Bryson narrowly escapes many hair-raising situations, he comes to doubt everything the CIA has told him as well. A reviewer for *Publishers Weekly* wrote that Bryson "is a dynamo and lots of fun to watch in action," but thought Ludlum's concern that "technology will soon allow for surveillance on a scale that grossly infringes on personal privacy" gets drowned out by the nonstop action of the plot. David Pitt of *Booklist* commented that *The Prometheus Deception* "should keep even the most experienced readers guessing." But some reviewers found the book more substantial than that. Michael Lollar of the Memphis *Commercial Appeal* took the book's focus on privacy invasion rather seriously. "Ludlum creates a scenario in which seemingly benign mergers and acquisitions mean that a single corporation can delve into every aspect of a person's life," Lollar wrote. "Life insurance, health insurance, medical records, credit records and banking records all are merely subsidiary operations easily retrieved at corporate headquarters." Lollar concluded that by the end of the novel, readers "will be left with the chilling feeling that just because you're paranoid doesn't mean they aren't out to get you."

In *Robert Ludlum's The Cassandra Compact,* the second "Covert-One" novel, this time written with Philip Shelby, Lt. Col. Jonathan Smith returns, hot on the heels of a plot to steal the deadly smallpox virus from a decrepit Russian laboratory. In true Ludlum fashion, the conspiracy proves to be worldwide, and Smith chases the virus from Venice back across the Atlantic Ocean, and finally meets up with it in Nevada, after the space shuttle lands with several dead astronauts aboard—all victims of smallpox. A reviewer for *Publishers Weekly* noted that the plot is not as complex as some of Ludlum's previous novels, but "the cinematic chase through changing landscapes and mounting body count gives the book its rapid pace, while insider politics, tradecraft and technical wizardry lend an extra kick."

The "Covert-One" series has continued after Ludlum's death, with Lynds fleshing out his outlines in *Robert Ludlum's The Paris Option* and *Robert Ludlum's The Altman Code. The Paris Option* finds Smith on the trail of a missing French scientist and trying to avert nuclear war. A *Kirkus Reviews* contributor termed it "tops in the series," with Lynds's "cloth-of-velvet moods" balancing Ludlum's "multidimensional paranoid sensibility." *The Altman Code* deals with biological trade involving Iraq and China. Despite some unfortunate dialogue, this novel "provides plenty of action and intrigue," a *Publishers Weekly* reviewer remarked. When Ludlum died, he left behind outlines for many more novels, which his publisher said will be finished by others and released under Ludlum's name; these include five to ten "Covert-One" books and a few stand-alone titles. He also left one near-complete manuscript, *The Sigma Protocol,* which was given a few final touches and published in 2001. In this book Anna Navarro is a government agent assigned to a top-level case concerning a plot to murder the conspirators of a long-ago plan to steal a large amount of gold. Ben Hartman is an unsuspecting businessman who uncovers the truth about his billionaire parents and the death of his twin brother in a plane crash that Ben survived. It is the kind of book "in which the hero is just about to get an explanation for what's happening when the person he's talking to is silenced by an assassin's bullet," commented Chris Barsanti in *Book.* David Pitt of *Booklist* found *The Sigma Protocol* to contain "refreshing" differences from some of Ludlum's work, although it is nevertheless full of the author's characteristic action and plot twists. Pitt complimented Ludlum for "developing a smoother style" in his later books, with "characters that felt real and dialogue that didn't sound so obviously contrived."

At the time of his death, Ludlum was "probably the world's most read writer," according to an obituary in the *Economist,* with conservative estimates of 200 million copies of his books in print. He published over twenty novels in thirty years, writing at a pace of 2,000 words a day. "His apocalyptic messages were a part of the thriller tradition that dates back at least to

Sherlock Holmes," the *Economist* writer continued. Journalist Bob Woodward, writing in the *Washington Post Book World,* summarized the media's view of Ludlum in a review of *The Icarus Agenda:* "Ludlum justifiably has a loyal following. Reviews of most of his previous books are critical but conclude, grudgingly, that he had another inevitable best-seller." In a review of *The Bourne Identity* for the *Washington Post Book World,* Richard Harwood wrote, "Whether reviewers are universally savage or effusive seems irrelevant: the book is bound to be a best-seller. *The Bourne Identity . . .* is already on both the national and *Washington Post* best-seller lists and the damned thing won't officially be published [for three more days]. So much for the power of the press." Despite reviewers' advice, readers voiced their approval of Ludlum in sales figures. As Baxter and Nichols noted in *Maclean's,* "For all his imperfections, Ludlum manages—by pumping suspense into every twist and turn in his tangled plots and by demanding sympathy for well-meaning protagonists afflicted by outrageous adversity—to keep millions of readers frantically turning his pages."

BIOGRAPHICAL AND CRITICAL SOURCES:

BOOKS

Bestsellers 89, Issue 1, Gale (Detroit, MI), 1989.
Bestsellers 90, Issue 3, Gale (Detroit, MI), 1990.
Contemporary Literary Criticism, Gale (Detroit, MI), Volume 22, 1982, Volume 43, 1988.
Dictionary of Literary Biography Yearbook: 1982, Gale (Detroit, MI), 1983.
Greenberg, Martin H., editor, *The Robert Ludlum Companion,* Bantam (New York, NY), 1993.

PERIODICALS

Best Sellers, April 15, 1973, p. 41; April, 1972, p. 5.
Book, September, 2000, Randy Michael Signor, a review of *Robert Ludlum's The Hades Factor,* p. 75; November-December 2001, Chris Barsanti, a review of *The Sigma Protocol,* p. 69.
Booklist, April 15, 1995, Mary Frances Wilkens, a review of *The Apocalypse Watch,* p. 1452; August 2000, David Pitt, a review of *The Prometheus Deception,* p. 2074; September 15, 2001, David Pitt, a review of *The Sigma Protocol,* p. 164.

Christian Science Monitor, March 31, 1977, p. 31.

Commercial Appeal (Memphis, TN), October 29, 2000, Michael Lollar, "Big Brother Scenario Relevant in Light of Technology Today," p. H1.

Kirkus Reviews, August 15, 2001, Donald Newlove, "Bob the Ghost," p. 1141; May 15, 2002, review of *Robert Ludlum's The Paris Option.*

Knight-Ridder/Tribune Service, February 22, 1995, Fred Tasker, "Robert Ludlum, Bestselling 'Storyteller,' Unfazed by Critics or Fame."

Library Journal, October 1, 1974, p. 2504; April 1, 1975, pp. 694-695; September 1, 2000, Ronnie H. Terpening, a review of *The Prometheus Deception,* p. 250; October 15, 2001, Ronnie H. Terpening, a review of *The Sigma Protocol,* p. 108.

Los Angeles Times Book Review, March 11, 1984, p. 3; March 23, 1986, p. 3; March 18, 1990, p. 8.

Maclean's, April 9, 1984, pp. 50-52.

New Republic, November 25, 1981, p. 38; September 20, 1982, p. 43.

New York, May 9, 1988, pp. 74-75.

New Yorker, June 20, 1988, pp. 90-92; October 2, 2000, James Surowiecki, "The Financial Page: Lessons from Ludlum," p. 62.

New York Review of Books, May 8, 1986, pp. 12-13.

New York Times, March 13, 1978, p. C19.

New York Times Book Review, January 28, 1973, p. 20; May 6, 1973, p. 41; August 4, 1974, p. 26; October 27, 1974, p. 56; March 28, 1976, p. 18; March 27, 1977, p. 8; April 8, 1979, p. 14; March 30, 1980, p. 7; March 21, 1982, p. 11; April 22, 1984, p. 14; March 9, 1986, p. 12; March 27, 1988, p. 16; June 20, 1993, p. 16.

Publishers Weekly, April 8, 1974, p. 76; February 10, 1975, p. 52; March 1, 1991, pp. 49-50; March 2, 1992; April 19, 1993, p. 48; April 17, 1995, review of *The Apocalypse Watch,* p. 37; May 29, 1995, p. 37; April 24, 2000, review of *Robert Ludlum's The Hades Factor,* p. 58; August 28, 2000, a review of *The Prometheus Deception,* p. 50; April 2, 2001, review of *Robert Ludlum's The Cassandra Compact,* p. 38; May 5, 2003, review of *Robert Ludlum's The Altman Code,* p. 198.

Times Literary Supplement, October 1, 1976, p. 1260.

Tribune Books (Chicago), February 28, 1988, p. 7.

Washington Post Book World, March 23, 1980, p. 3; March 7, 1982, p. 1; February 21, 1988, p. 1.

ONLINE

Ludlum Books Web site, http://www.ludlumbooks.com/ (April 28, 2004).

OBITUARIES:

PERIODICALS

Economist, March 31, 2001, p. 1.

Guardian (London, England), March 14, 2001, John Williams, p. 22.

Independent (London, England), March 14, 2001, p. S6.

New York Times, March 13, 2001, p. A22; March 14, 2001, Douglas Martin, "Robert Ludlum, Bestselling Suspense Novelist, Dies at 73," p. A23.

Times (London, England), March 14, 2001, p. 25.*

M

MACHOTKA, Pavel 1936-

PERSONAL: Born August 21, 1936, in Prague, Czechoslovakia (now Czech Republic); son of Otakar (a professor) and Jarmila (a social worker; maiden name, Mohr) Machotka; married Hannelore Gothe, April 6, 1963 (divorced, December, 1980); married Nina Hansen, September 10, 1989; children: (first marriage) Danielle, Julia. *Ethnicity:* "White." *Education:* University of Chicago, A.B., 1956; Harvard University, M.A., 1958, Ph.D., 1962. *Politics:* Democrat.

ADDRESSES: Home—Loc. Bacciana, 06014 Montone (PG), Italy. *Office*—Department of Psychology, Social Sciences II, University of California—Santa Cruz, Santa Cruz, CA 95064. *E-mail*—pavel@machotka. com.

CAREER: Harvard University, Cambridge, MA, instructor in social relations, 1962-65; University of Colorado, Medical Center, Denver, assistant professor, then associate professor of clinical psychology, 1965-70; University of California—Santa Cruz, associate professor, then professor of psychology, beginning 1970, provost of College V, 1976-79, chair of Academic Senate, 1992-94. Also exhibits works as a professional painter. Precinct worker for local Democratic party, 1968.

MEMBER: International Informatization Academy (Moscow; academician, 1996—), American Psychological Association (fellow; member of Division on Psychology and the Arts; president, 1978-79), American Psychological Society (fellow), Société Paul Cézanne, Czechoslovak Society of Arts and Sciences (vice president, 1992-93).

Pavel Machotka

AWARDS, HONORS: Woodrow Wilson fellow, 1956; Fulbright fellow, 1958-60; named honorary professor, Perm State Institute of Arts and Culture, Perm, Russia, 1997; honorary D.H.C., Charles University, 1998.

WRITINGS:

(With D. G. Langsley, D. M. Kaplan, and others) *The Treatment of Families in Crisis,* Grune (New York, NY), 1968.

(With J. P. Spiegel) *Messages of the Body,* Grune (New York, NY), 1968, revised and condensed edition published as *The Articulate Body,* Irvington (New York, NY), 1982.

The Nude: Perception and Personality, Free Press (New York, NY), 1974.

Cézanne: Landscape into Art, Yale University Press (New Haven, CT), 1996.

(Editor, with L. Dorfman, L. Martindale, and others) *Emotion, Creativity, and Art,* Perm State Institute of Art and Culture (Perm, Russia), 1997.

Style and Psyche: The Art of Lundy Siegriest and Terry St. John, Hampton Press (Cresskill, NJ), 1999.

Pavel Machotka: Light, Form, and Sensuality, Galleria LaLoggia (Sansepolcro, Italy), 2002.

Painting and Our Inner World: The Psychology of Image Making, Kluwer Academic Publishers (New York, NY), 2003.

Contributor to periodicals, including *Empirical Studies of the Arts, Journal of Personality and Social Psychology, Leonardo, Journal of Experimental Psychology, American Journal of Psychiatry,* and the Czech journal *Aesthetica.*

WORK IN PROGRESS: Cézanne: The Painter's Art.

SIDELIGHTS: Pavel Machotka once told *CA:* "I write when I have something to say: to report on some psychological research I have done, or to report discoveries made about a painter such as Cézanne. Articles are for a professional audience and written in the style of each field; books, on the other hand, which I prefer to write, are in my own voice and directed at the informed reader, and have as their purpose to reveal as much about myself as about my subjects, but that is inadvertent and only the effect of my having found a voice in which to write.

"In my psychological writings I have been influenced especially by Freud, particularly the case histories in which he reveals a novelist's sensitivity to his characters. My aim is ultimately to understand 'people' as against 'subjects,' and his respect for the individual's complex nature is a model worth following. In my writings on Cézanne, there have been three influences: John Rewald by his hardheaded and scrupulous respect for facts, and Roger Fry and Lawrence Gowing by their painterly sensitivity and linguistic elegance.

"I am quite fluent when writing about psychology; perhaps it is because I have done it so much. More difficult—slower, more subject to revision and elaboration—has been writing about Cézanne. His art is too important to give anything less than one's best, and one's best includes perception, sensitivity, respect for facts, and above all precise yet evocative language.

"The roots of writing are not always accessible, and some may go back quite far, but I do recall early in my life wanting to make some major contribution to the psychology of aesthetics and to understanding Cézanne. I think *The Nude: Perception and Personality* and *Cézanne: Landscape into Art,* respectively, come closest to realizing that. Other major writings have been responses to discoveries—usually unplanned."

More recently Machotka added: "Two books on creativity came from my contact with painters and research into the dynamics of image-making in ordinary people: *Style and Psyche: The Art of Lundy Siegriest and Terry St. John* and *Painting and Our Inner World: The Psychology of Image Making.* Another unplanned book was an art book about my paintings, with a large number of reproductions and a critical essay by an Italian critic. That one responded to a one-man show I had in Sansepolcro, Italy. Now, I am following up my earlier work on Cézanne with a full-scale critical study of his work."

*   *   *

MARCH, Carl
    See FLEISCHMAN, (Albert) Sid(ney)

*   *   *

MARKLE, Sandra L(ee) 1946-

PERSONAL: Born November 10, 1946, in Fostoria, OH; daughter of Robert (a general foreman) and Dorothy (a secretary; maiden name, Sauler) Haldeman; married William Markle (a programmer/analyst), August 10, 1968; children: Scott, Holly. *Education:* Bowling Green State University, B.S. (magna cum laude), 1968; graduate study at Ohio University, 1970-71, and University of North Carolina, 1973-74.

Sandra L. Markle

ADDRESSES: *Home*—Atlanta, GA. *Office*—Compu-Quest Inc., 366 South Main St., Bartlett, IL 60103-4423. *Agent*—Carolyn Krupp, IMG-Bach, 22 East 71st St., New York, NY 10021. *E-mail*—markle@compuquill.com.

CAREER: Nonfiction author and curriculum designer. Teacher at elementary schools in Woodville, OH, 1968-69, Athens, OH, 1969-71, and Asheville, NC, 1971-79; Chapel Hill Middle School, Douglasville, GA, science teacher, 1979-80. CompuQuest, Inc., Bartlett, IL, founder, 1997, and director of the Kit & Kaboodle Curriculum Pilot, 1997-99; freelance writer, 1980—. Developer of online learning programs, including *On-line Expedition: Antarctica* and *On-line Expedition: New Zealand.* Presenter at teacher workshops and science assembly programs; science consultant for publishers and educational television. Presenter and scriptwriter for television series, including *Science Shop,* WLOS-TV, 1978, and *Ms. Whiz,* WANX-TV, 1979-80; planner of television specials.

MEMBER: Authors Guild, National Association of Science Writers.

AWARDS, HONORS: Outstanding Book selection, National Science Teachers Association, for *Exploring Winter;* Pick of the List selection, American Booksellers Association, 1991, for *Outside and inside You,* 1995, for *Outside and inside Snakes,* and 1997, for *Outside and inside Bats;* Best Books selection, National Council of Teachers of English, and Children's Book of the Year selection, Children's Book Committee at Bank Street College of Education, both 1993, for *Outside and inside Trees;* Young Adults Choice Book, International Reading Association, 1994, and Society of School Librarians International Honor Book, 1998, both for *The Fledglings;* Outstanding Science Trade Books for Children, National Science Teachers Association/Children's Book Council, 1995, for *Outside and inside Spiders, Outside and inside Birds,* and *Science to the Rescue,* 1999, for *Outside and inside Kangaroos,* and 2003, for *Growing Up Wild: Penguins;* Notable Books selection, American Library Association, 1995, for *Outside and inside Birds;* selected participant, Authors and Artist Program in Antarctica, National Science Foundation, 1996, and 1998-99; Best of Children's Nonfiction, Georgia Author of the Year Awards, 1997, for *Discovering Graph Secrets,* 1998, for *Outside and inside Bats,* 1999, for *Outside and inside Alligators,* and 2000, for *Outside and inside Kangaroos;* Women of the Year selection, Women in Technology International, 1999; Parents' Choice recommended book, 2000, for *Down, down, down in the Ocean;* Children's Book of the Year selection, Children's Book Committee at Bank Street College of Education, 2002, for *Growing Up Wild: Wolves.*

WRITINGS:

NONFICTION

Kids' Computer Capers: Investigations for Beginners, illustrated by Stella Ormai, Lothrop (New York, NY), 1983.

The Programmer's Guide to the Galaxy, illustrated by Stella Ormai, Lothrop (New York, NY), 1984.

(And illustrator; with husband, William Markle) *In Search of Graphics: Adventures in Computer Art,* Lothrop (New York, NY), 1984.

(And illustrator) *Digging Deeper: Investigations into Rocks, Shocks, Quakes, and Other Earthy Matters,* Lothrop (New York, NY), 1987.

(And illustrator) *Science Mini-Mysteries,* Atheneum (New York, NY), 1988.

(And illustrator) *Power Up: Experiments, Puzzles, and Games Exploring Electricity,* Atheneum (New York, NY), 1989.

The Young Scientists' Guide to Successful Science Projects, Lothrop (New York, NY), 1990.

Earth Alive!, Lothrop (New York, NY), 1991.

(And illustrator) *The Kids' Earth Handbook,* Atheneum (New York, NY), 1991.

Discovering Science Secrets, Scholastic/Lucky (New York, NY), 1992.

Discovering More Science Secrets, Scholastic/Lucky (New York, NY), 1992.

Science in a Bag, Scholastic/Lucky (New York, NY), 1993.

(And illustrator) *Math Mini-Mysteries,* Atheneum (New York, NY), 1993.

A Rainy Day, illustrated by Cathy Johnson, Orchard Books (New York, NY), 1993.

Science: Just Add Salt, Scholastic (New York, NY), 1994.

Science to the Rescue, Atheneum (New York, NY), 1994.

Science in a Bottle, illustrated by June Otani, Scholastic/Lucky (New York, NY), 1995.

Measuring Up: Experiments, Puzzles, and Games Exploring Measurement, Atheneum (New York, NY), 1995.

What Happens Next?, Longstreet Press (Atlanta, GA), 1995.

What Happens Next?: Two, Longstreet Press (Atlanta, GA), 1996.

Creepy, Crawly Baby Bugs, Walker (New York, NY), 1996.

Creepy, Spooky Science, illustrated by Cecile Schoberle, Hyperion (New York, NY), 1996.

Icky Squishy Science, Hyperion (New York, NY), 1996.

Science Surprises, Scholastic/Lucky (New York, NY), 1996.

Still More What Happens Next?, Longstreet Press (Atlanta, GA), 1996.

A Hole in the Sky: Investigating the Ozone Problem, Sierra Club, 1997.

Discovering Graph Secrets: Experiments, Puzzles, and Games Exploring Graphs, Atheneum (New York, NY), 1997.

Super Science Secrets: Exploring Nature through Games, Puzzles, and Activities, Longstreet (Atlanta, GA), 1997.

Gone Forever!: An Alphabet of Extinct Animals, illustrated by Felipe Dávalos, Simon & Schuster (New York, NY), 1998.

Windy Weather Science, Scholastic/Lucky (New York, NY), 1998.

Weird, Wacky Science, Hyperion (New York, NY), 1998.

Super Cool Science: South Pole Stations Past, Present, Future, Walker (New York, NY), 1998.

Down, down, down in the Ocean, illustrated by Bob Marstall, Walker (New York, NY), 1999.

After the Spill: The Exxon Valdez Disaster, Then and Now, Walker (New York, NY), 1999.

Super Science Magic, illustrated by Jamie Smith, Scholastic (New York, NY), 2001.

Really Wild Animals: Sea Babies, Scholastic (New York, NY), 2002.

Can You Believe?: Insects, illustrated by Jo-Ellen C. Bosson, Scholastic (New York, NY), 2002.

Can You Believe?: Hurricanes, illustrated by Jo-Ellen C. Bosson, Scholastic (New York, NY), 2002.

Can You Believe?: Volcanoes, illustrated by Jo-Ellen C. Bosson, Scholastic (New York, NY), 2002.

Amazing Human Body, illustrated by Jo-Ellen C. Bosson, Scholastic (New York, NY), 2002.

Amazing Earth: Earthquakes, illustrated by Jo-Ellen C. Bosson, Scholastic (New York, NY), 2002.

Predators, illustrated by Jo-Ellen C. Bosson, Scholastic (New York, NY), 2003.

Grow a Giant Beanstalk, and Fifteen More Amazing Plant Projects, illustrated by Eric Brace, Scholastic (New York, NY), 2003.

Build a Room Alarm, and Sixteen More Electrifying Projects, illustrated by Eric Brace, Scholastic (New York, NY), 2003.

Build a Rocket Boat, and Eighteen More Wild Wind Projects, illustrated by Eric Brace, Scholastic (New York, NY), 2003.

Make Fake Blood, and Fifteen More Spooky Special Effects, illustrated by Eric Brace, Scholastic (New York, NY), 2003.

Spiders: Biggest! Littlest!, photographs by Simon Polard, Boyds Mills Press (Honesdale, PA), 2004.

Snakes: Biggest! Littlest!, photographs by Simon Polard, Boyds Mills Press (Honesdale, PA), 2004.

Rescues, Lerner (Minneapolis, MN), 2005.

Chocolate: A Sweet History, illustrated by Charise Mericle Harper, Grosset & Dunlap (New York, NY), 2005.

"SEASON OF SCIENCE" SERIES; SELF-ILLUSTRATED

Exploring Winter, Atheneum (New York, NY), 1984.

Exploring Summer, Atheneum (New York, NY), 1987.

Exploring Spring, Atheneum (New York, NY), 1990.

Exploring Autumn, Atheneum (New York, NY), 1991.

"OUTSIDE AND INSIDE" SERIES

Outside and inside You, Simon & Schuster (New York, NY), 1991.

Outside and inside Trees, Simon & Schuster (New York, NY), 1993.

Outside and inside Spiders, Simon & Schuster (New York, NY), 1994.

Outside and inside Birds, Simon & Schuster (New York, NY), 1994.

Outside and inside Snakes, Simon & Schuster (New York, NY), 1995.

Outside and inside Sharks, Atheneum (New York, NY), 1996.

Outside and inside Bats, Atheneum (New York, NY), 1997.

Outside and inside Alligators, Atheneum (New York, NY), 1998.

Outside and inside Kangaroos, Atheneum (New York, NY), 1999.

Outside and inside Dinosaurs, Atheneum (New York, NY), 2000.

Outside and inside Rats and Mice, Atheneum (New York, NY), 2001.

Outside and inside Big Cats, Atheneum (New York, NY), 2002.

Outside and inside Giant Squids, Atheneum (New York, NY), 2003.

Outside and inside Killer Bees, Walker (New York, NY), 2004.

"PIONEERING" SERIES

Pioneering Space, Atheneum (New York, NY), 1992.

Pioneering Ocean Depths, Atheneum (New York, NY), 1995.

Pioneering Frozen Worlds: Polar Region Exploration, Atheneum (New York, NY), 1996.

"GROWING UP WILD" SERIES

Growing Up Wild: Bears, Atheneum (New York, NY), 2000.

Growing Up Wild: Wolves, Atheneum (New York, NY), 2001.

Growing Up Wild: Penguins, Atheneum (New York, NY), 2002.

"ANIMAL PREDATORS" SERIES

Polar Bears, Carolrhoda Books (Minneapolis, MN), 2004.

Owls, Carolrhoda Books (Minneapolis, MN), 2004.

Lions, Carolrhoda Books (Minneapolis, MN), 2004.

Killer Whales, Carolrhoda Books (Minneapolis, MN), 2004.

Great White Sharks, Carolrhoda Books (Minneapolis, MN), 2004.

Crocodiles, Carolrhoda Books (Minneapolis, MN), 2004.

Wolves, Carolrhoda Books (Minneapolis, MN), 2004.

OTHER

Primary Science Sampler, Learning Works, 1980.

Science Sampler, Learning Works, 1980.

Computer Tutor: An Introduction to Computers, illustrated by Bev Armstrong, Learning Works, 1981.

Computer Tutor Junior, illustrated by Bev Armstrong, Learning Works, 1982.

Weather/Electricity/Environmental Investigations, Learning Works, 1982.

The Fledglings (young adult novel), Bantam (New York, NY), 1992.

A Mother's Journey, Charlesbridge (Watertown, MA), 2004.

Author of books for instructors, including *Instructor's Big Book of Health and Safety,* 1985; *Hands-on Science,* 1988; and *Creative Science Classrooms,* 1991. Also author of "Natural Wonder Notebook," a monthly column in *Instructor,* and "The Learning Center," a monthly column in *Teaching and Computers.* Creator, "Kit and Kaboodle" elementary science curriculum. Contributing editor, *Teaching and Computers,* 1983—. Contributor to magazines, including *Cricket, Highlights for Children, Jack and Jill, Ranger Rick, 3-2-1 Contact, Woman's Day, Macintosh Buyer's Guide, PC World, Early Childhood Teacher, Classworks, Big, Parenting, Family Fun, Instructor, National Geographic for Kids, Time for Kids,* and *Learning.*

WORK IN PROGRESS: More science books for children.

SIDELIGHTS: Sandra L. Markle, who once worked as a science teacher, now devotes much of her time to creating science books for children. With books on animals, science experiments, computers, exploration, geology, and other specific topics to her credit, she has also become a sought-after science education consultant. "Few writers have quite the handle Markle does on how kids think about science," wrote a *Kirkus Reviews* critic in a review of *Icky Squishy Science.*

Critics have identified more than one reason for Markle's success as a science writer for children. First, Markle carefully pairs science with fiction. *The Programmer's Guide to the Galaxy,* which frames instruction about computer BASIC programming within an adventure story, was lauded by R. Scott Grabinger in *Voice of Youth Advocates* as "fun," "instructional," and an "excellent book for beginning and intermediate BASIC programmers." Second, Markle writes about science in a lucid, straightforward manner. Reviewing *Digging Deeper: Investigations into Rocks, Shocks, Quakes, and Other Earthy Matters,* which educates children about geography while showing them how to construct volcanoes and conduct other projects, Beth Ames Herbert commented in *Booklist:* "Markle's light-handed touch makes even technical jargon unintimidating." *A Rainy Day* explains such question-prompting things as how a cloud forms and why umbrellas are shaped the way they are. Janice Del Negro remarked in *Booklist* that *A Rainy Day* uses "a picture book format with strong visual narrative." Finally, in books like *Icky Squishy Science* and *Creepy, Spooky Science,* Markle encourages children to learn about science as they do something they love: get their hands dirty.

Markle's love of science is infectious, a fact that also makes her books so effective. She once told *CA,* "I can't believe the opportunities writing provides me! . . . I was able to travel to the South Pole—something I'd always dreamed of doing—and was transported by helicopter to spend a few hours as the only human in the midst of a penguin rookery. I've also spent a few days behind the scenes with the Ringling Brothers Barnum & Bailey Circus, been up in the Good Year Blimp, and lots more. Each new project brings new adventures. I always think of myself as the eyes and ears and fingers of all the young readers that will eventually be sharing my experiences through my books and magazine articles."

Many of Markle's books are published in series or thematically related groups. The "Outside and inside" books provide children with a scientific understanding of some of their favorite plants and creatures. *Outside and inside Sharks,* for example, explains how a shark's body works to make it a good hunter. *Outside and inside Snakes,* which, according to Karey Wehner in *School Library Journal,* is a "remarkably perceptive introduction to the ever-fascinating slitherer," discusses the anatomy, bodily functions, habits, and life cycle of the snake. "Succinctly written," Wehner explained in *School Library Journal, Outside and inside Spiders* "offers more detail on body functions than is currently available in other books." *Booklist* critic Chris Sherman described *Outside and inside Birds* as an "introduction to avian anatomy" that "will fascinate browsers," while a *Kirkus Reviews* critic asserted that young readers will "be captivated by her clear and detailed discussion" of everything rodent in *Inside and outside Rats and Mice.* Citing *Outside and inside Kangaroos* for particular praise, an *Appraisal* contributor noted that this book, like others in the series, "is full of intriguing science details and questions which encourage the reader to predict the reasons for adaptations and habits."

One of the "Outside and inside" books takes a look at a familiar creature: the healthy human child. *Outside and inside You* includes questions, suggestions, answers, and comparisons illustrated with close-up photos, X-rays, and computer-generated images that provide young readers with the opportunity to understand their bodies, right down to the skin, muscles, bones, and major organs. Stephanie Zvirin of *Booklist* described Markle's text as "accessible," commenting that the author's "clear explanations are rooted in children's everyday experience." The "Outside and inside" books, with color photos, also include glossaries, indexes, and pronunciation guides.

Another group of books by Markle that focuses on animals is the "Growing Up Wild" series, which started with 2000's *Growing Up Wild: Bears.* In this series designed for readers in grades two to four, full-color photographs accompany a clearly written text that describes the life of several species. In *Growing Up Wild: Bears,* readers meet a day-old black bear cub, two young polar bears, and young grizzlies fishing for salmon. The volume on wolves describes the challenges a young wolf must overcome to reach its first birthday and also explains life in a wolf pack, where play and sleep are balanced with hunting and learning to identify predators. Markle presents *Growing Up Wild: Wolves* through the eyes the young animals, "an appealing angle that makes use of the experiences of young readers," according to a *Horn Book* contributor. Praising the same volume in *Kirkus Reviews,* a critic noted that Markle's selection of facts is "perfectly designed to interest young readers," going on to remark that the author adds "intimate details" aimed to "astonish and intrigue" young imaginations.

In *Growing Up Wild: Penguins,* as in *Growing Up Wild: Wolves,* the author does not hide the fact that life in the wild is harsh and survival is not guaranteed, a fact that *Horn Book* contributor Danielle J. Ford claimed made the books noteworthy. Ford found "an element of tension" runs through *Growing Up Wild: Penguins* due to the fact that the Adelie penguin chicks are constantly hunted by shore birds. *Booklist* contributor Kay Weisman commended Markle for her "clearly written, succinct text" and her "especially detailed picture of the [penguin's] infancy period."

Markle's "Pioneering" books allow children to witness the scientific exploration of faraway worlds and encourage them to use their own scientific skills. In *Pioneering Frozen Worlds: Polar Region Exploration,* Markle follows scientists working in the North and South Poles and explains how they live and work. She describes the experiments the scientists are conducting and includes notes and suggestions for minor experiments that can help children better understand the rugged climate. *Pioneering Space* tells about space travel, space equipment, and future space colonization. It provides instructions for two experiments (one on rocket power and another on hydroponics systems). "This timely, attractively illustrated treatment of space exploration will excite young readers," Margaret M. Hagel commented in *School Library Journal.*

The "Season of Science" series, which Markle illustrated herself with line drawings, explains seasonal changes as well as traditional seasonal activities. The books provide a variety of lessons, science experiments, crafts, and games for children. A number of historical facts, mythical stories, riddles, and jokes are also included. *Exploring Spring,* for example, shows readers how to identify flowers and teaches them about egg development. Gayle Berge explained in *School Library Journal* that *Exploring Summer* could "provide an entire summer of . . . growing in scientific knowledge." "The number of winter tidbits assembled here is amazing," *School Library Journal* contributor Jeffrey A. French wrote in a review of *Exploring*

Winter. These seasonal books are designed to make learning fun, and Markle's style reflects this. As Hazel Rochman pointed out in a review of *Exploring Autumn* for *Booklist,* "Markle isn't afraid to be lyrical . . . or silly."

In 1989, an oil tanker named the *Exxon Valdez* crashed near Prince William Sound, Alaska, spilling thousands of gallons of oil into the water and creating an ecological disaster for the region's wildlife. In *After the Spill: The Exxon Valdez Disaster, Then and Now,* Markle returns readers to the scene of the accident ten years later and studies the aftereffects. Dividing the book into sections with titles such as "What Happened to the Animals?" and "Did the Oil Spill Affect People Too?," she explains how local birds, fish, and otters fared, and also explains the economic impact to the area and lists new regulations that have been implemented to prevent such a catastrophe from occurring again. An *Appraisal* reviewer commended the "wealth of practical experience" Markle brings to her task and praised the author for being able "to anticipate the questions and interests of her readers." Citing its "child-friendly format, and attractive photos," *School Library Journal* reviewer Dawn Amsberry commended the "clear, journalistic style" of *After the Spill,* while Deborah Stevenson maintained in the *Bulletin of the Center for Children's Books* that the photo-filled volume will give readers an enhanced "understanding of the different kinds of impact such an event can have."

Although most of Markle's books are nonfiction, she is also the author of an award-winning novel, *The Fledglings.* In this story, Kate's mother is killed by a drunk driver, leaving the fourteen-year-old protagonist an orphan. She is faced with the prospect of living with the family of her disagreeable uncle and aunt when she learns that her paternal grandfather is still alive. Although this grandfather has refused to care for her, Kate runs away to Cherokee, North Carolina, to find him. At first, her grandfather does not welcome her. Gradually, however, Kate earns his trust and comes to learn about her Cherokee heritage and life in the forest. In addition, Kate helps fight illegal poaching and cares for a fledgling eagle, prompting a *Publishers Weekly* reviewer to praise her "pluck and resourcefulness in daunting surroundings," finding Markle's story "fun to read."

Markle has not kept her talents reserved for the realm of text. She worked on television programs for many years and has since moved into cyberspace through an online science curriculum she has developed. "I've been communicating via the Internet and my special project called Online Expeditions," she once told *CA*. "The Internet is perfect for me because now I'm able to share what's happening in real time—including digitized pictures—even from places as remote as an icebreaker in the middle of the Ross Sea off the coast of Antarctica."

BIOGRAPHICAL AND CRITICAL SOURCES:

BOOKS

Markle, Sandra L., *After the Spill: The Exxon Valdez Disaster, Then and Now,* Walker (New York, NY), 1999.

PERIODICALS

American Scientist, November-December, 1997, Cynthia Harris, review of *Icky, Squishy Science,* p. 557.

Appraisal, spring-summer-fall, 2000, review of *After the Spill: The Exxon Valdez Disaster, Then and Now,* pp. 68-69, and *Outside and inside Kangaroos,* pp. 69-70.

Booklist, December 15, 1987, Beth Ames Herbert, review of *Digging Deeper: Investigations into Rocks, Shocks, Quakes, and Other Earthy Matters,* pp. 710-711; July, 1990, p. 2091; March 15, 1991, Stephanie Zvirin, review of *Outside and inside You,* p. 1494; November 1, 1991, Hazel Rochman, review of *Exploring Autumn,* p. 514; January 1, 1992, p. 827; March 1, 1993, Janice Del Negro, review of *A Rainy Day,* p. 1233; November 1, 1994, Chris Sherman, review of *Outside and inside Birds,* p. 504; May 1, 1996, p. 1501; October 1, 1997, Sally Estes, review of *Outside and inside Bats,* p. 320; March 15, 1998, Carolyn Phelan, review of *Super Cool Science: South Pole Stations Past, Present, Future,* p. 1238; June 1, 1998, Kathleen Squires, review of *Gone Forever!: An Alphabet of Extinct Animals,* p. 1722; December 1, 1998, Helen Rosenberg, review of *Outside and inside Alligators,* p. 681; August, 1999, Carolyn Phelan, review of *After the Spill,* p. 2054; January 1, 2000, Shelle Rosenfeld, review of *Outside and inside Kangaroos,* p. 914; May 15, 2000, Ellen Mandel, review of *Growing Up Wild: Bears,* p. 1746; December 1, 2000, Carolyn Phelan, review of *Out-*

side and inside Dinosaurs, p. 702; April 1, 2001, Carolyn Phelan, review of *Growing Up Wild: Wolves,* p. 1462; September 15, 2001, Shelle Townsend-Hudson, review of *Outside and inside Rats and Mice,* p. 220; December 15, 2001, Kay Weisman, review of *Growing Up Wild: Penguins,* p. 728; September 15, 2003, Terry Glover, review of *Outside and inside Giant Squids,* p. 233; October 1, 2003, Lauren Peterson, review of *Outside and inside Big Cats,* p. 314.

Bulletin of the Center for Children's Books, September, 1992, pp. 18-19; February, 1996, p. 196; April, 1998, Deborah Stevenson, review of *Super Cool Science,* p. 288; July, 1999, Deborah Stevenson, review of *After the Spill,* pp. 395-396.

Horn Book, March-April, 1991, pp. 216-217; January-February, 1998, Elizabeth S. Watson, review of *Outside and inside Bats,* p. 93; November, 1999, Marilyn Bousquin, review of *Outside and inside Kangaroos,* p. 759; September, 2000, review of *Outside and inside Dinosaurs,* p. 597; March, 2001, review of *Growing Up Wild: Wolves,* p. 231; September, 2001, review of *Outside and inside Rats and Mice,* p. 612; May-June, 2002, Danielle J. Ford, review of *Growing Up Wild: Penguins,* p. 347; July-August, 2003, Danielle J. Ford, review of *Outside and inside Big Cats,* p. 482.

Kirkus Reviews, April 1, 1987, p. 555; July 1, 1989, p. 994; August 15, 1992, p. 1064; March 15, 1994, review of *Outside and inside Spiders,* p. 399; January 15, 1996, p. 136; April 18, 1996, review of *Icky Squishy Science,* p. 230; January, 1998, review of *Gone Forever!,* p. 115; February 15, 2001, review of *Growing Up Wild: Wolves,* p. 262; August 1, 2001, review of *Outside and inside Rats and Mice,* p. 1128; November 15, 2001, review of *Growing Up Wild: Penguins,* p. 1613; June 1, 2003, review of *Outside and inside Big Cats,* p. 807.

Publishers Weekly, June 8, 1992, review of *The Fledglings,* p. 64; March 8, 1993, p. 77.

Reading Teacher, May, 2002, review of *Outside and inside Dinosaurs,* p. 782.

School Library Journal, November, 1984, Jeffrey A. French, review of *Exploring Winter,* p. 126; April, 1987, Gayle Berge, review of *Exploring Summer,* p. 100; January, 1988, p. 82; October, 1988, p. 157; February, 1993, Margaret M. Hagel, review of *Pioneering Space,* p. 101; June, 1994, Karey Wehner, review of *Outside and inside Spiders,* p. 141; June, 1995, Karey Wehner, review of *Outside and inside Snakes,* p. 122; March, 1996, Melissa Hudak, review of *Outside and inside Sharks,*

p. 212; May, 1996, p. 124; October, 1996, p. 136; April, 1997, Karey Wehner, review of *Creepy, Crawly Baby Bugs*, p. 128; July, 1997, Kathryn Kosiorek, review of *Science Surprises*, p. 85; September, 1997, Cynthia M. Sturgis, review of *Super Science Secrets: Exploring Nature through Games, Puzzles, and Activities*, p. 206; November, 1997, Margaret Bush, review of *Outside and inside Bats*, pp. 130, 132; March, 1998, Jody McCoy, review of *Discovering Graph Secrets: Experiments, Puzzles, and Games Exploring Graphs*, p. 236; April, 1998, John Peters, review of *Super Cool Science*, p. 120; May, 1998, Marilyn Payne Phillips, review of *Gone Forever!*, p. 134; November, 1998, Anne Chapman Callaghan, review of *Outside and inside Alligators*, pp. 107-108; September, 1999, Dawn Amsberry, review of *After the Spill*, p. 238; November, 1999, Patricia Manning, review of *Down, down, down in the Ocean*, p. 146; December, 1999, Sally Bates Goodroe, review of *Outside and inside Kangaroos*, pp. 154-155; May, 2000, Randi Hacker, review of *Growing Up Wild: Bears*, p. 163; November, 2000, Patricia Manning, review of *Outside and inside Dinosaurs*, p. 173; September, 2001, Susan Scheps, review of *Growing Up Wild: Wolves*, p. 218; November, 2001, Cynthia M. Sturgis, review of *Outside and inside Rats and Mice*, p. 147; March, 2002, Margaret Bush, review of *Growing Up Wild: Penguins*, p. 218; August, 2003, Patricia Manning, review of *Outside and inside Big Cats*, p. 182; December, 2003, Doris Losey, review of *Outside and inside Giant Squids*, p. 172.

Voice of Youth Advocates, April, 1985, R. Scott Grabinger, review of *The Programmer's Guide to the Galaxy*, p. 66; December, 1993, p. 324.*

*   *   *

MATHE, Albert
See CAMUS, Albert

*   *   *

McCLURE, Michael (Thomas) 1932-

PERSONAL: Born October 20, 1932, in Marysville, KS; son of Thomas and Marian (Dixie Johnston) McClure; married Joanna Kinnison, 1954 (divorced); married Amy Evans (a sculptor); children: Katherine Jane.

Michael McClure

Ethnicity: "Scotch Irish." *Education:* Attended University of Wichita, 1951-53, and University of Arizona, 1953-54; San Francisco State College, B.A., 1955. *Hobbies and other interests:* "The biological sciences."

ADDRESSES: Home—3200 Burnell Dr., Oakland, CA 94602. *Agent*—Denise Enck, Empty Mirror Books Agency, P.O. Box 972, Mukilteo, WA 98275-0972.

CAREER: California College of Arts and Crafts, Oakland, assistant professor, 1962-77, associate professor, beginning 1977, became professor of humanities. *Ark II/Moby I*, editor, 1957; *Journal for the Protection of All Beings*, coeditor, 1961; State University of New York at Buffalo, lecturer, 1979; Pierson College, Yale University, associate fellow, 1982. Member of board of directors, Drylands Institute, Tucson, AZ.

MEMBER: Sons of Anacreon.

AWARDS, HONORS: National Endowment for the Arts grants, 1967 and 1974; Guggenheim fellowship, 1973; Alfred Jarry Award, Magic Theatre, 1973; Rockefeller fellow for the theatre, 1975; Obie Award for best play, *Village Voice*, 1979, for *Josephine, the Mouse Singer;* California Arts Council Berkeley Stage Company award, 1980; Pushcart Prize for Poetry, 1991; Award for Lifetime Achievement in Poetry, National Poetry Association, 1993; Pen West Josephine Miles Award, 1994 for *Simple Eyes;* Bay Area Book Reviewers Award for Poetry, for *Touching the Edge: Dharma Devotions from the Hummingbird Sangha.*

WRITINGS:

POETRY

Passage, Jonathan Williams (Big Sur, CA), 1956.

Peyote Poem, Semina, 1958.

For Artaud, Totem Press (New York, NY), 1959.

Hymns to St. Geryon, and Other Poems, Auerhahn Press (San Francisco, CA), 1959.

Dark Brown, Auerhahn Press (San Francisco, CA), 1961.

The New Book/A Book of Torture, Grove (New York City),York, NY), 1961.

Ghost Tantras, privately printed, 1964, Four Seasons Foundation (San Francisco, CA), 1969.

Two for Bruce Conner, Oyez (Kensington, CA), 1964.

Love Lion, Lioness (poem poster), Oyez (San Francisco, CA), 1964.

Double Murder! Vahrooooooohr!, Semina, 1964.

Poisoned Wheat, Oyez (San Francisco, CA), 1965.

Mandalas, Dave Haselwood (San Francisco, CA), 1965.

Unto Caesar, Dave Haselwood (San Francisco, CA), 1965.

Dream Table, Dave Haselwood (San Francisco, CA), 1965.

(With Bruce Conner) *(The Mandala Book),* Dave Haselwood (San Francisco, CA), 1966.

Hail Thee Who Play: A Poem, Black Sparrow Press (Santa Barbara, CA), 1968, revised edition, Sand Dollar Press (Berkeley, CA), 1974.

Muscled Apple Swift, Love Press, 1968.

Love Lion Book, Four Seasons Foundation (San Francisco, CA), 1968.

The Sermons of Jean Harlow and the Curses of Billy the Kid, Four Seasons Foundation (San Francisco, CA), 1969.

Plane Pomes, Phoenix Book Shop (New York, NY), 1969.

Oh Christ God Love Cry of Love Stifled Furred Wall Smoking Burning, Auerhahn Press (San Francisco, CA), c. 1969.

Hymns to St. Geryon [and] *Dark Brown,* Cape Goliard Press (London, England), 1969, 3rd edition, Grey Fox Press (San Francisco, CA), 1982.

The Surge: A Poem, Frontier Press (Columbus, OH), 1969.

Lion Fight, Pierrepont Press (New York, NY), 1969.

Star, Grove (New York, NY), 1970.

99 Theses, Tansy Press (Lawrence, KS), 1972.

The Book of Joanna, Sand Dollar Press, 1973.

Transfiguration, Pomegranate Press (Cambridge, MA), 1973.

Rare Angel (writ with raven's blood), Black Sparrow Press (Los Angeles, CA), 1974.

September Blackberries, New Directions (New York, NY), 1974.

Solstice Blossoms, Arif Press (Berkeley, CA), 1974.

Fleas (189-195), Aloe Editions, 1974.

A Fist-Full (1956-1957), Black Sparrow Press (Los Angeles, CA), 1974.

On Organism, Institute of Further Studies (Buffalo, NY), 1974.

Flea 100, Frank Hallman, 1975.

Jaguar Skies, New Directions (New York, NY), 1975.

Man of Moderation: Two Poems, Frank Hallman, 1975.

Antechamber, Poythress Press, 1977, revised edition published as *Antechamber and Other Poems,* New Directions (New York, NY), 1978.

Fragments of Perseus, New Directions (New York, NY), 1983.

Fleas (180-186), Les Ferriss, 1985.

Selected Poems, New Directions (New York, NY), 1986.

Rebel Lions, New Directions (New York, NY), 1991.

Simple Eyes and Other Poems, New Directions (New York, NY), 1994.

Three Poems, introduction by Robert Hunter, Penguin Poets (New York, NY), 1995.

(Contributor) Jay DeFoe, *Selected Works, 1952-1989,* The Gallery, 1996.

Huge Dreams: San Francisco and Beat Poems, Penguin (New York, NY), 1999.

Rain Mirror, New Directions (New York, NY), 1999.

Plum Stones: Cartoons of No Heaven, O Books (Oakland, CA), 2002.

Also author of *Thirteen Mad Sonnets,* (Milan, Italy), 1965. McClure's poems have also been recorded on *Ghost Tantras* (audiocassette), S Press (Germany),

1982, and *Love Lion* (compact disc and audiocassette), Shanachie Records, 1993, and appear on *Howls, Raps and Roars: Recordings from the San Francisco Poetry Renaissance* (compact disc and audiocassette), Fantasy Records, 1993.

McClure's poetry has been translated into German, French, and Yugoslavian.

PLAYS

!The Feast!, produced in San Francisco, CA, 1960.

Pillow, produced in New York City, 1961.

The Blossom; or, Billy the Kid (produced in New York City, 1964), Great Lakes (Brighton, MI), 1967.

The Beard (produced in San Francisco, 1965), privately printed, 1965, revised edition, Grove (New York, NY), 1967.

The Shell (produced in San Francisco, 1975), Cape Goliard Press (London, England), 1968.

The Cherub (produced in Berkeley, CA, 1969), Black Sparrow Press (Los Angeles, CA), 1970.

The Charbroiled Chinchilla: The Pansy, The Meatball, Spider Rabbit, produced in Berkeley, 1969.

The Brutal Brontosaurus: Spider Rabbit, The Meatball, The Shell, Apple Glove, The Authentic Radio Life of Bruce Conner and Snoutburbler, produced in Berkeley, 1970.

Gargoyle Cartoons (contains *The Shell, The Pansy, The Meatball, The Bow, Spider Rabbit, Apple Glove, The Sail, The Dear, The Authentic Radio Life of Bruce Conner and Snoutburbler, The Feather,* and *The Cherub;* produced in Philadelphia, PA, 1970), Delacorte (New York, NY), 1971.

The Growl, produced in Berkeley, 1971.

Polymorphous Pirates: The Pussy, The Button, The Feather, produced in San Francisco, 1972.

The Mammals (contains *The Blossom, The Feast,* and *Pillow*), Cranium Press, 1972.

McClure on Toast, produced in Los Angeles, 1973.

The Pussy, The Button, and Chekhov's Grandmother; or, The Sugar Wolves, produced in New York, 1973.

The Grabbing of the Fairy (produced in Los Angeles, 1973), Truck Press, 1978.

Music Piece, produced in San Francisco, 1974.

Gorf; or, Gorf and the Blind Dyke (produced in San Francisco, 1974), New Directions (New York, NY), 1976.

One Acts by Michael McClure, produced in New York, 1974.

The Derby, produced in Los Angeles, 1974, new version produced in New York, 1981.

General Gorgeous, produced in San Francisco, 1975.

Sunny-Sideup: The Pink Helmet and The Masked Choir, produced in Los Angeles, 1976.

Range War, produced in Tucson, AZ, 1976.

Two for the Tricentennial: The Pink Helmet and The Grabbing of the Fairy, produced in San Francisco, 1976.

Goethe: Ein Fragment, produced in San Francisco, 1978.

Minnie Mouse and the Tap-Dancing Buddha, produced in San Francisco, 1978.

Josephine, the Mouse Singer (adaptation of a story by Franz Kafka; produced in New York at the W.P.A. Theatre, 1978), New Directions (New York, NY), 1980.

The Red Snake, produced in San Francisco, 1979.

The Mirror, produced in Los Angeles, 1979.

Coyote in Chains, produced in San Francisco, 1980.

The Beard and VKMTS, Grove (New York, NY), 1985, produced by Living Theater (New York, NY), 1999.

Also author of television documentary *The Maze,* 1967, and of radio play, *Music Peace,* 1974.

OTHER

Meat Science Essays, City Lights (San Francisco, CA), 1963, revised edition, 1966.

(With Frank Reynolds) *Freewheelin' Frank, Secretary of the Angels,* Grove (New York, NY), 1967.

Little Odes, Poems, and a Play, "The Raptors," Black Sparrow Press (Los Angeles, CA), 1969.

The Mad Cub (novel), Bantam (New York, NY), 1970.

The Adept (novel), Delacorte (New York, NY), 1971.

Scratching the Beat Surface (essays), North Point Press (Berkeley, CA), 1982, published as *Scratching the Beat Surface: Essays on New Vision from Blake to Kerouac,* with photographs by Larry Keenan, Penguin (New York, NY), 1994.

Isamu Noguchi at Gemini, 1982-1983 (art monograph), Gemini Press (Greensboro, NC), 1983.

Specks, Talon Books (Vancouver, BC, Canada), 1985.

(With Francesco Clemente) *Testa Coda* (art criticism), Rizzoli Books (New York, NY), 1991.

(With Bruce Conner) *Adventures of a Novel,* Limestone (Kingston, Ontario, Canada), 1991.

Lighting the Corners on Nature, Art, and the Visionary: Essays and Interviews, College of Arts and Sciences, University of New Mexico (Albuquerque, NM), 1993.

Rain Mirror, New Directions (Albuquerque, NM), 1993.

Touching the Edge: Dharma Devotions from the Hummingbird Sangha, Shambhala (Boston, MA), 1999.

Camping Wyoming, WigRaf, 1999.

Contributor to *"Forest Beatnike" and "Urban Thoreaus,"* P. Lang, 2000 and to anthologies, including *The Beat Scene,* Corinth, 1960; *The Poetics of the New American Poetry,* Grove (New York, NY), 1964; *The San Francisco Poets,* Ballantine (New York, NY), 1971; and *The Portable Beat Reader,* Viking (New York, NY), 1992. Contributor to magazines, including *Beatitude, Big Table, Black Mountain Review, Chicago Review, City Lights Journal, Conjunctions, Grand Street, Imago, Jabberwocky, Kulchur, Life, Nation, Poetry, Rolling Stone, Semina Two, Vanity Fair, Yugen,* and *Zyzzyva.*

ADAPTATIONS: Poems from *September Blackberries* were adapted for video by McClure and his former wife, Joanna, KQED-TV, 1973; *The Blossom* was filmed by George Herms; *Love Lion* was adapted as a video performance of poetry with piano by McClure and keyboardist Ray Manzarek, Mystic Fire Video/Island Visual Arts, 1991.

WORK IN PROGRESS: The Red Snake (play); *Dear Being* (poetry); *I Like Your Eyes Liberty,* music and poetry CD, with composer Terry Riley.

SIDELIGHTS: Poet Michael McClure, drawing inspiration from both biology and mysticism, sees writing as a process whereby the body and mind can be united; the term he coined for this union is "spiritmeat"; as a writer for *Jack* noted, "If [Jack] Kerouac was the Beat Generation's first priest, then McClure was the Beat 'spiritmeat.' Generation's first biologist." A reviewer for the *Times Literary Supplement* called McClure's work "one of the more remarkable achievements in recent American literature, a record of a man's attempt to find the terms he needs for a vital balance, for some kind of homeostasis of body and psyche." "It is this fusion of mind and body as a single principle that is

the particular stamp of the man," wrote David Kherdian in *Six Poets of the San Francisco Renaissance: Portraits and Checklists,* "and it is this concept that has determined the flow of his work, which is of constant change, growth, and expansion."

McClure was born in Marysville, Kansas, but grew up in Seattle, Washington. He first began writing in the 1950s, moved to San Francisco in 1954, and came to public attention as one of San Francisco's Beat poets. Influenced not only by such literary figures as Theodore Roethke and Charles Olson, but by the prevailing ideas in biology and other natural sciences, McClure's poetry is meant to be an expression of the whole individual. "For McClure," Kherdian wrote, "there can be no distinction between the man and the writer, one being condemned to serve the other nor can there be a differentiation between the mind and the body, for if the mind is in error it will be reflected by a gesture of the body." McClure explained that "a poem is as much of me as an arm. Measure, line, etc. is interior and takes an outward shape, is not predestined or logical but immediate."

In *Meat Science Essays,* McClure develops some of his ideas about poetry and biology. He speaks of the need for humankind to be aware of its animal nature. This awareness results in the "intellect as we know it [subsiding] and mammalian intelligence acknowledgment of the senses as organs of knowing [returning]," wrote Michael Lynch in *Parnassus.* Writing in the *Dictionary of Literary Biography,* William R. King pointed out that McClure sees the Beat movement as an "intense awakening of a 'bio-alchemical' consciousness" and calls for human beings "to achieve the clearest perceptions and to attune themselves to the inner voice or genetic being (the voice of the universe, which speaks from many centers) in order to transform society and restore the planet." From this biological awareness, then, an essentially mystical revelation emerges. "To McClure," King wrote, "the universe all that can be sensed or intuited is in a sense the messiah, leading us to witness its miraculous unfolding."

McClure's writing seeks to be an expression of the enlightened state of consciousness he hypothesizes. His work is, above all, a personal expression rather than a form of communication with an audience. Speaking in *Scratching the Beat Surface* of how he came to this approach, McClure stated that "communication was not as important to me as expression. To speak and move was the most important thing." Mc-Clure carries this idea to the physical structure of his poetry. His poems are centered on the page and move across and down in a flowing motion meant to approximate the actual speaking voice. Influenced by poet Charles Olson and his theory of projective verse and by the painter Jackson Pollock, who created action painting, McClure sees a poem as "a calligram of the moment of creation or experience, an artifact entirely representing the perceptions it contains in a highly compressed image," King explained. As McClure told Jhan Hochman and Todd Grimson of the *Portland Review,* "What we write, or what we paint, or what we sing or do, must actually, literally, be an extension of ourselves, or it is meaningless."

McClure's poetic language combining biblical phrasing, scientific terms, mantras, and meaningless yet powerful sounds gives his poetry a freewheeling energy that has been praised by many critics. Francis Crick, writing in *Margins,* observed, "What appeals to me most about [McClure's] poems is the fury and imagery of them. I love the vividness of his reactions and the very personal turns and swirls of the lines." Similarly, Robert Peters commented in *Margins* that "McClure's writing is like action painting: spontaneous. The reader is to re-experience the excitement McClure felt writing the poems. The energy . . . is as important as any direct poetic statement the reader might receive, of a traditional sort. . . . McClure's beast (mammal) language is LOVE: we are to form these strange sounds with abandon and pleasure, with love-explosives, love-verbal-fun-ejaculations." At its best, Geoffrey Thurley wrote in Lee Bartlett's book *The Beats: Essays in Criticism,* McClure's poetry "achieves a poise and a sinewy delicacy rarely to be found in recent American writing."

McClure's plays also display an intense energy. In the tradition of such avant-garde playwrights as Antonin Artaud, McClure's work combines wildly divergent elements into dreamlike sequences. Featuring the characters Billy the Kid and Jean Harlow, who meet in the hereafter, *The Beard* explores American sexual attitudes as embodied in two cultural representatives of sex and violence. As Richard Gilman wrote in his *Common and Uncommon Masks: Writings on Theatre, 1961-1970,* "The whole point of the couple's being dead and legendary is that they may now serve as exemplary figures of the American confusion between orders of being, of our perpetual conversion of sexual-

ity into one kind of art, the popular mythology of archetypal surrogates, the blonde bombshell, the steely outlaw and the consequent depletion of the sexual by being turned into emblem and shady metaphor." *The Beard* brought McClure notoriety from its first productions in San Francisco and Berkeley, California, in 1965. In 1968, because of the simulated sex act at the play's end, the members of the cast were arrested and carted off to jail at each performance on fourteen consecutive nights. (The play was later judged not obscene when finally brought to trial.) A production in Los Angeles was also met with police resistance, but the New York performance of *The Beard* won Obie awards for its director and lead actress.

Critical reaction to *The Beard* was generally favorable, with the play's "offensive" material deemed integral to its message. The language, the *Newsweek* reviewer admitted, is "without question the 'filthiest' ever heard on a commercial stage in the English-speaking nations." According to the reviewer, "McClure raises profanity to a comic passion. He has written a brilliant little monster of a play." *Nation* reviewer Harold Clurman, while judging *The Beard* "inconsequential as art," nevertheless found the play "a mockery of sex, a 'milestone' on the road to nonentity. We need not despise it. It shows us that our myths . . . are in the process of dissolution."

McClure won the coveted Obie Award for *Josephine, the Mouse Singer,* a play produced in New York in 1980. Unusual in that all the characters are mice, the play concerns the singer Josephine, who defends the freedom of the artist in modern society. It is in "the tradition of the fable, with all the grace and poise of [seventeenth-century French poet Jean de] la Fontaine along with his social astuteness," wrote Peter Clothier in the *Los Angeles Times Book Review.*

Speaking of McClure's work as a playwright, Mel Gussow of the *New York Times* called him "something of a comic-book fantasist, projecting larger-than-life images on an imaginary silver screen." But Arthur Sainer acclaimed him as "one of the best playwriting minds now working in America" and found *The Beard* to be "a small masterpiece." Speaking to *Portland Review*'s Hochman and Grimson, McClure defined the relationship between his poetry and plays this way: "They're quite different and they're complementary. And they certainly come from different aspects of my character; poetry being subjective, [it has to] do with perception, and theatre being a social probing more like doing sculptures with bodies to create hallucinations on stage, to see the effect of the reflection of my hallucinations on the universe and on other people. I *think* with my poetry, and I *experience* with my poetry, and I'm really *probing* with my theatre."

In the author's note to *Rebel Lions,* a poetry collection published in 1991, McClure commented frankly on his own career and on how he creates his poems. He called poetry "a muscular principle" and noted that he had centered his recent poems in order to give them a "body language on the page." Of his use of lines written in capital letters, he noted: "The poem on the page troubled me because it seemed like such a thing of beauty, I wanted to remind the reader that it was, in fact, an object, and a seductive object because it was so close to being alive. By putting lines of capital letters in the text of the poem there was a disruption of the allure of the poem and a reminder that it was a made thing."

In the same note, McClure discussed his collaboration with keyboardist Ray Manzarek of the rock group The Doors, who played piano while McClure read his poems. McClure noted that some of his more recent works "High Heels," "Foreman and Ali," and "Czechoslovakia" were written with "this artistic symbiosis in mind." Performing his poetry has long been a hallmark of McClure's art. In the *Dictionary of Literary Biography,* King noted that "at each stage of his progress, [McClure] has assumed the mantle of bard and stepped forward as a poet-singer, giving testimony and witness to the times. He has read to college students and Zen monks, at rock concerts, at the Library of Congress, and to lions." An interesting bit of trivia about McClure's career is the fact that he wrote the lyrics to the song "Lord, Won't You Buy Me a Mercedes-Benz," which was made popular by singer Janis Joplin.

In 1998, McClure was in a nearly fatal airplane crash; the event precipitated a depressed period in his life. He wrote about that time in *Rain Mirror.* According to John Sakowitz in *Metro Active,* the book "tells about this dark night of the soul, and later, of his recovery from depression." *Plum Stones: Cartoon of No Heaven,* like McClure's *Touching the Edge,* incorporates Buddhist thinking. Of *Plum Stones,* Jack Foley wrote in *Also Preview,* "The Buddhist stance and the wonderful specificity which is always an aspect of McClure's writing give the book a texture which is fresh and

new." The book contains deliberate repetition, as lines from earlier poems become the seeds of later ones; according to Foley, this technique successfully conveys the idea that "any single direction [is] essentially illusory."

Whether his poems are spontaneous or carefully reworked, McClure points out that he uses repetition to give his work energy. It is this energy and heightened awareness in *Rebel Lions* that many critics comment upon. Anne Waldman observed in a dust-jacket blurb for the book, "There is in [McClure's] poetry what Marianne Moore demands, and what many others misunderstand, the raw and the genuine willingness of unwearied senses to be what they perceive." Norman Mailer commented upon the singularity of McClure's work in his blurb, observing, "McClure is one of the few poets in America who has always been his own voice, and that voice is like no other." On his Web site, McClure noted, "When I speak of things or events I have usually experienced them. It is good fortune to have friends who have shown me eagles and serpentine cliffs and trees flowering with morning glories." And in *Contemporary Poets,* he commented, "Poetry is a muscular principle, an athletic song or whisper of fleshly thought. We can be as serious as blue black gloom or bright as a buttercup in the dawn. The spirit of poetry is hope we send out from the expanding helix of our lives. With poetry we can meet an old perception on a mountaintop or in a subway or view a new perception loping in the distance like a wolf or glimmering like an opal in the twilight."

McClure told *CA:* "I am a projective poet and my physical breath and my bodily energy are integral to the creation of poetry. I was walking one day in a forest near Gloucester with Charles Olson, the inventor of projective verse. Charles sat down on a stump under a tree and mimed writing a projective poem in the air, flourishing a broken branch in his hand as if it were a pen. I believe that language is most important as a means of the restructuring of thought and also for thinking itself. At the deepest level communication is not the most important aspect of language. Stephane Mallarme stated, 'Poetry is the language of a state of crisis.' That's right.

"One reason we love poetry is because we discover the inspirations of other poets, their illuminations light us up and prove that we can recognize our own inspirations, and not bluntly and quietly allow them to pass. Biology and the biological aspects of nature fascinate me for similar reasons. Certainly life is a state of crisis.

"As artists we are hungry to use the instruments of our art to enrich, and to make our self-experience more myriad-minded. With the invention of Projective Verse there came a means of vividly experiencing the field our energies and senses. I believe this is the way D. H. Lawrence rejoiced in his poetry. It is something like what I find in Percy B. Shelley and in William Blake and the visionary Japanese master Dogen and in Meister Eckhart. It is what I hear in the piano music of Thelonius Monk—and Monk does it with great elegance. This is the way that I experience Jackson Pollock's paintings."

BIOGRAPHICAL AND CRITICAL SOURCES:

BOOKS

A Bibliography of the Auerhahn Press and Its Successor, Dave Haselwood Books, Poltroon Press (Berkeley, CA), 1976.

Allen, Donald M., editor, *The New American Poetry, 1945-1960,* Grove (New York, NY), 1960.

Bartlett, Lee, editor, *The Beats: Essays in Criticism,* McFarland (Jefferson, NC), 1981.

Bartlett, Lee, *The Sun Is but a Morning Star,* University of New Mexico Press (Albuquerque, NM), 1989.

Bertholf, Robert J., and Ian W. Reid, editors, *Robert Duncan: Scales of the Marvelous,* New Directions (New York, NY,) 1979.

Clements, Marshall, *A Catalog of Works by Michael McClure, 1957-1965,* Phoenix Bookshop (New York, NY), 1965.

Contemporary Dramatists, 6th edition, St. James Press (Detroit, MI), 1999.

Contemporary Literary Criticism, Gale (Detroit, MI), Volume 6, 1976, Volume 10, 1979.

Contemporary Poets, 7th edition, St. James Press (Detroit, MI), 2001.

Cook, Bruce, *The Beat Generation,* Scribner (New York, NY), 1971.

Davidson, Michael, *The San Francisco Renaissance,* Cambridge University Press (New York, NY), 1989.

Dictionary of Literary Biography, Volume 16: *The Beats: Literary Bohemians in Postwar America,* Gale (Detroit, MI), 1983.

Ferlinghetti, Lawrence, and Nancy Peters, *Literary San Francisco: A Pictorial History from Its Beginnings to the Present Day,* City Lights/Harper (New York, NY), 1980.

Gilman, Richard, *Common and Uncommon Masks: Writings on Theatre, 1961-1970,* Random House (New York, NY), 1971.

Kahn, Douglas, *Noise, Water, Meat: A History of Sound in the Arts,* MIT Press (Cambridge, MA), 1999.

Kherdian, David, *Six Poets of the San Francisco Renaissance: Portraits and Checklists,* Giligia Press (Aurora, OR), 1967.

Leary, Paris, and Robert Kelly, editors, *A Controversy of Poets,* Anchor Books (New York, NY), 1965.

Lipton, Lawrence, *The Erotic Revolution,* Sherbourne Press (Los Angeles, CA), 1965.

McClure, Michael, *Lighting the Corners on Nature, Art, and the Visionary: Essays and Interviews,* College of Arts and Sciences, University of New Mexico (Albuquerque, NM), 1993.

Meltzer, David, *The San Francisco Poets,* Ballantine (New York, NY), 1971.

Morgan, Bill, *The Beat Generation in San Francisco: A Literary Tour,* City Lights Books (San Francisco, CA), 2003.

Phillips, Rod, *"Forest Beatniks" and "Urban Thoreaus": Gary Snyder, Jack Kerouac, Lew Welch, and Michael McClure,* P. Lang (New York, NY), 2000.

Philips, Rod, *Michael McClure,* Boise State University (Boise, ID), 2003.

Smith, Richard Cándida, *Utopia and Dissent: Art, Poetry, and Politics in California,* University of California Press, (Berkeley, CA), 1995.

Stephenson, Gregory, *The Daybreak Boys,* Southern Illinois University Press (Carbondale, IL), 1990.

PERIODICALS

Berkeley Gazette, July 8, 1982.

Big Table, spring, 1960.

Bloomsbury Review, November, 1999, review of *Rain Mirror,* p. 24.

Booklist, May 1, 1978; March 15, 1999, Donna Seaman, review of *Touching the Edge,* p. 1278.

Books, September, 1967; October, 1967.

Book World, August 15, 1971.

Christian Century, January 17, 1968.

Credences, number 1, 1980.

Kerouac Connection, spring, 1994, Mitchell Smith, interview with McClure, pp. 31-38.

Kirkus Reviews, September 15, 1999, review of *Rain Mirror,* p. 1445.

Los Angeles Free Press, February 2, 1982.

Los Angeles Times, November 16, 1993, p. F8.

Margins, March, 1975, "Michael McClure Symposium."

Nation, November 13, 1967, p. 508; July 20, 1970.

Newsweek, November 6, 1971.

New York Times, October 3, 1981.

New York Times Book Review, June 20, 1971; October 31, 1999, review of *Rain Mirror,* p. 25.

Parnassus, spring-summer, 1976.

Poetry Information, spring, 1975.

Portland Review, Volume 28, number 1, 1982.

Publishers Weekly, April 25, 1994, p. 65; July 31, 1995, p. 75; March 29, 1999, review of *Touching the Edge* and *Huge Dreams,* p. 100; April 12, 1999, review of *Touching the Edge,* p. 71.

Rain Taxi, fall 1999, Wayne Atherton, review of *Touching the Edge.*

Review of Contemporary Fiction, fall, 1990, S. E. Gontarski, interview with McClure, pp. 116-123.

San Francisco Review of Books, December, 1977.

San Francisco Theatre, summer, 1977.

Show, May, 1970.

Sulfur, spring, 1996, p. 163.

Times Literary Supplement, March 25, 1965, "This Is Geryon."

Village Voice, October 5, 1967; November 2, 1967; November 16, 1967; January 22, 1970; January 3, 1974.

Yugen, number 7, 1961.

ONLINE

AlsoPreview.com, http://www.alsopreview.com/ (May 29, 2003), Jack Foley, interview with McClure.

Empty Mirror Books, http://www.emptymirrorbooks.com/ (July 15, 2003).

Jack Magazine, http://www.jackmagazine.com/ (May 29, 2003).

Metro Active, http://www.metroactive.com/papers/ (December 19, 2000), John Sakowitz, profile of McClure.

Michael McClure Home Page, http://www.thing.net/~grist/l&d/mcclure/mcclure.htm (August 13, 2004).

McClure-Manzarek.com, http://www.mcclure-manzarek.com/ (May 29, 2003).

OTHER

Third Mind (video documentary), 1997.

*   *   *

McCULLOCH, John Tyler
See BURROUGHS, Edgar Rice

*   *   *

McDONALD, Megan 1959-

PERSONAL: Born February 28, 1959, in Pittsburgh, PA; daughter of John (an ironworker) and Mary Louise (a social worker; maiden name, Ritzel) McDonald; married Richard Haynes. *Education:* Oberlin College, B.A., 1981; University of Pittsburgh, M.L.S., 1986.

ADDRESSES: Home—Sebastopol, CA. *Agent*—c/o Author Mail, Candlewick Press, 2067 Massachusetts Ave., Cambridge, MA 02140.

CAREER: Children's book author and librarian. Carnegie Library, Pittsburgh, PA, children's librarian, 1986-90; Minneapolis Public Library, Minneapolis, MN, children's librarian, 1990-91; Adams Memorial Library, Latrobe, PA, children's librarian, 1991-94; storyteller and freelance writer.

MEMBER: American Library Association, Society of Children's Book Writers and Illustrators.

AWARDS, HONORS: Children's Choice Book, International Reading Association/Children's Book Council (CBC), 1991, and *Reading Rainbow* book selection, Public Broadcasting System, both for *Is This a House for Hermit Crab?;* Notable Children's Trade Book in the Field of Social Studies, National Council for the Social Studies/CBC, 1992, for *The Potato Man;* Judy

Megan McDonald

Blume Contemporary Fiction Award, Society of Children's Book Writers and Illustrators, 1993, for *The Bridge to Nowhere;* Carolyn W. Field Award, 1993, for *The Great Pumpkin Switch;* Garden State Children's Book Award for Younger Fiction, 2003, for *Judy Moody;* other honors include Keystone State Award, American Booksellers Association Pick-of-the-Lists selection, and *School Library Journal* Best Books of the Year citation.

WRITINGS:

FOR CHILDREN

Is This a House for Hermit Crab?, illustrated by S. D. Schindler, Orchard (New York, NY), 1990.

The Potato Man, illustrated by Ted Lewin, Orchard (New York, NY), 1991.

Whoo-oo Is It?, illustrated by S. D. Schindler, Orchard (New York, NY), 1992.

The Great Pumpkin Switch, illustrated by Ted Lewin, Orchard (New York, NY), 1992.

Insects Are My Life, illustrated by Paul Brett Johnson, Orchard (New York, NY), 1995.

My House Has Stars, illustrated by Peter Catalanotto, Orchard (New York, NY), 1996.

Tundra Mouse: A Storyknife Book, illustrated by S. D. Schindler, Orchard (New York, NY), 1997.

The Bone Keeper, illustrated by G. Brian Karas, DK Ink (New York, NY), 1999.

The Night Iguana Left Home, illustrated by Ponder Goembel, DK Ink (New York, NY), 1999.

Bedbugs, illustrated by Paul Brett Johnson, Orchard (New York, NY), 1999.

Lucky Star, illustrated by Andrea Wallace, Golden Books (New York, NY), 2000.

Reptiles Are My Life, illustrated by Paul Brett Johnson, Orchard (New York, NY), 2001.

Ant and Honey Bee, illustrated by Tom Payne, Candlewick Press (Cambridge, MA), 2001.

Shining Star, illustrated by Andrea Wallace, Random House (New York, NY), 2003.

Penguin and Little Blue, illustrated by Katherine Tillotson, Atheneum (New York, NY), 2003.

Baya, Baya, Lulla-By-A, illustrated by Vera Rosenberry, Atheneum (New York, NY), 2003.

Beetle McGrady Eats Bugs!, illustrated by Jane Manning, Greenwillow (New York, NY), 2004.

FOR CHILDREN; "BEEZY" SERIES

Beezy, illustrated by Nancy Poydar, Orchard (New York, NY), 1997.

Beezy at Bat, illustrated by Nancy Poydar, Orchard (New York, NY), 1998.

Beezy Magic, illustrated by Nancy Poydar (New York, NY), Orchard, 1998.

Beezy and Funnybone, illustrated by Nancy Poydar, Orchard (New York, NY), 2000.

FOR CHILDREN; "JUDY MOODY" SERIES

Judy Moody, illustrated by Peter H. Reynolds, Candlewick Press (Cambridge, MA), 1999.

Judy Moody Gets Famous!, illustrated by Peter H. Reynolds, Candlewick Press (Cambridge, MA), 2002.

Judy Moody Saves the World!, illustrated by Peter H. Reynolds, Candlewick Press (Cambridge, MA), 2002.

Judy Moody Predicts the Future, illustrated by Peter H. Reynolds, Candlewick Press (Cambridge, MA), 2003.

Judy Moody, M.D., illustrated by Peter H. Reynolds, Candlewick Press (Cambridge, MA), 2004.

FOR YOUNG ADULTS

The Bridge to Nowhere (novel), Orchard (New York, NY), 1993.

Shadow in the Glasshouse, Pleasant Company (Middleton, WI), 2000.

The Sisters Club, American Girl (Middleton, WI), 2003.

All the Stars in the Sky: The Santa Fe Trail Diary of Florrie Mack Ryder, Scholastic (New York, NY), 2003.

ADAPTATIONS: In 2003, Candlewick Press published a *Judy Moody Mood Journal,* a blank book illustrated by Peter H. Reynolds, that was inspired by McDonald's "Judy Moody" series.

WORK IN PROGRESS: Stink: The Adventures of Incredible Shrinking Boy, illustrated by Peter H. Reynolds, for Candlewick Press (Cambridge, MA), publication expected in 2005; *When the Library Lights Go Out,* illustrated by Katherine Tillotson, for Atheneum (New York, NY), publication expected in 2005.

SIDELIGHTS: Megan McDonald brings her diverse experiences as a park ranger, bookseller, museum guide, librarian, and especially storyteller to her many picture books, beginning readers, and novels for children. In books like *Whoo-oo Is It?* and *Insects Are My Life,* as well as in young-adult novels and her popular "Beezy" and "Judy Moody" series of beginning readers, McDonald combines an extensive knowledge of nature with a love of storytelling. "Connecting children with books has always been the centerpiece of my life's work," McDonald once told *CA.* In an effort to combat the statistics that show more and more children reading at lower-than-desired levels, the former librarian views the books she writes as another step in the fight against illiteracy.

Among McDonald's most popular books are those she has written for her "Beezy" and "Judy Moody" chapter-book series designed for readers-in-training. The "Beezy" books feature a young girl and the stray dog she adopts and names Funnybone. Beezy grows up in Florida, and her life incorporates that region's characteristics—like hurricanes—but also the universal day-to-day experiences of childhood, in short vignettes designed for easy reading. In *Beezy,* the girl joins friends in a neighborhood baseball game, spends time with her grandmother, and begins her friendship with Funnybone, while in *Beezy and Funnybone,* new friends and new adventures—like jumping out of a hot-air balloon—enter the mix. *School Library Journal* reviewer Maura Bresnahan praised "the warm and friendly tone" of *Beezy and Funnybone* and considered it a good choice for readers who want "to practice their new skills."

In the "Judy Moody" series, McDonald introduces a spunky, somewhat chameleon-like heroine. Third-grader Judy Moody approaches what life hands her with some trepidation but also with resilience and creativity, whether its vying for membership in the exclusive Toad Pee club or attempting to create the winning entry in her school's adhesive bandage contest. In *Judy Moody,* readers follow the series star on her first day back at school, which begins badly when there is no suitable T-shirt to wear, then begins to perk up due to the resourcefulness of McDonald's "entertainingly mercurial" protagonist, according to a *Publishers Weekly* contributor. The book's large, easy-to-read type was a hit with reviewers, among them *Booklist*'s Shelle Rosenfeld, who noted that McDonald's ability to tell her story from Judy's third-grade perspective enhances the "simple, expressive prose" and offers a healthy dose of "child-appealing humor." Also praising *Judy Moody Saves the World!,* Rosenfeld applauded that installment's "characteristically snappy, humorous prose" and "expressive, witty" line drawings by illustrator Peter H. Reynolds. Other volumes in the series include *Judy Moody Gets Famous!, Judy Moody Predicts the Future,* and *Judy Moody, M.D.*

Illustrated by S. D. Schindler, McDonald's first picture book, *Is This a House for Hermit Crab?,* has its roots in a puppet show the author hosted at Latrobe, Pennsylvania's Adams Memorial Library, where she then worked. "Its alliterative sounds, its rhythm and repetition worked so well with young children that I decided to write it as a picture book, in hopes that the story would find a wider audience," McDonald once explained to *CA.* In the story, a crab searches a rocky shoreline for a new home, finding the perfect abode in time to avoid becoming an afternoon snack for a crab-eating prickle-pine fish. Praising both its rhythmic text and its pastel illustrations, *Five Owls* contributor Margaret Mary Kimmel lauded McDonald's debut work as "a beautiful book to look at again and again, to repeat over and over." "Best of all," Carolyn Phelan pointed out in *Booklist,* "the writer knows when to ask questions to involve the children and when to stop."

After the success of *Is This a House for Hermit Crab?,* McDonald decided to collaborate with illustrator Schindler on a second nonfiction picture book, titled *Whoo-oo Is It?* This story revolves around a mother barn owl's attempt to sit on her eggs in peace, while all of nature seems to be intent on making noise. One particular sound—a strange noise that gradually gets louder—persists and is discovered to be the first young owlet pecking its way out of its shell. While the source of the noise, which begins at nightfall, is at first a mystery to listeners, "the final tender family scene will relieve any lingering concerns," according to *Horn Book* reviewer Elizabeth S. Watson. Praising the book, *Five Owls* critic Anne Lundin called *Whoo-oo Is It?* "a spirited book to read aloud, in a kind of celebration of life."

McDonald's *The Potato Man* and its sequel, *The Great Pumpkin Switch,* are based on stories her father told about what it was like growing up in Pittsburgh before the Great Depression of the 1930s. The gruff, old Potato Man, with his one good eye, rode through the streets on a wagon, "calling out a strange cry that sounded like 'Abba-no-potata-man', " McDonald once recalled. "When the children heard the cry, they became frightened and ran away. Because the story has its roots in the oral tradition of my own family, I tried to capture the feel, the setting, the language as I imagined it when the story was told to me as a young girl." In the book, a young boy—McDonald's father—tries to play tricks on Mr. Angelo, the Potato Man, but gets caught each time. When his hijinks cause him to be assigned extra chores at home, the boy decides to make his peace with the old peddler. Praising the story for its evocation of the past, *Horn Book* critic Mary M. Burns noted that the book's "text . . . sets forth conflict and solution without moralizing." In *The Great Pumpkin Switch,* the same mischievous boy and friend Otto smash his sister's prize pumpkin, by accident of course. Mr. Angelo comes to their rescue, replacing the smashed pumpkin with another just as good, in a story that *School Library Journal* contributor Susan Scheps maintained "will not seem the least old-fashioned to today's readers." The watercolor illustrations Ted Lewin contributes add greatly to the immediacy of *The Great Pumpkin Switch.* Describing the author's "warm, beautifully cadenced storytelling," a

Kirkus Reviews critic also commented favorably on the book's "engaging period details."

In the intriguingly titled *Insects Are My Life,* first-grader Amanda Frankenstein has a passion for bugs, much to the dismay of her friends and family. Not content merely to catch and collect dead bugs like most insect aficionados, Amanda thinks of her home as a bug sanctuary and invites her flying and crawling friends *inside* the house rather than shooing them out. She remains terribly misunderstood until the arrival of Maggie, the new girl in school, who happens to feel equally as passionate about reptiles. "McDonald's single-minded, sometimes naughty heroine evokes chuckles with her feisty independence," according to Margaret A. Bush in a review for *Horn Book,* while in *School Library Journal,* Virginia Opocensky dubbed "refreshing" McDonald's creation of "nonsqueamish female characters . . . willing to take on all adversaries in defense of their causes."

McDonald takes up Maggie's plight in a companion volume, *Reptiles Are My Life,* as the young reptile lover finds a kindred spirit in Emily, leaving bug-loving Amanda feeling left out. Finally, the three girls find a new camaraderie when Amanda saves the "Snake Sisters" from being called to the office for sticking out their tongues, in a book a *Kirkus Reviews* critic noted for its "sprightly writing" and focus on girls with unusual interests. *Childhood Education* contributor Jill Quisenberry praised McDonald's humorous text as "full of great insect and reptile references," while *School Library Journal* contributor Linda M. Kenton remarked that *Reptiles Are My Life* "accurately portrays the roller-coaster ride that some friendships take."

Other picture books by McDonald include *The Bone Keeper, The Night Iguana Left Home,* and *Penguin and Little Blue,* the last published in 2003. In *The Bone Keeper,* an ancient creature of the desert wanders in search of sun-baked bones, then returns to its cave to fashion these bones into a living creature. Told in verse, McDonald's "lyrical" and "evocative" tale was praised as "an original creation story of power and force" by *Bulletin of the Center for Children's Books* contributor Janice M. Del Negro, while in *School Library Journal,* Rosalyn Pierini dubbed *The Bone Keeper* "an eerie tale with mythical qualities."

McDonald serves up much more traditional picture-book fare in *The Night Iguana Left Home.* Readers commiserate with poor Alison Frogley of upstate New

York, who suddenly finds herself without her best friend, her pet iguana. "Iguanna," as the languid, sun-seeking reptile styles herself, has high-tailed it to Key West, Florida, but when the money runs out, the clever reptile finds a way to mail herself back north in a quirky picture book that *New York Times Book Review* contributor Jane O'Reilly dubbed "marvelously written . . . and gloriously illustrated" by Ponder Goembel. A *Horn Book* contributor praised the story's "slyly humorous balance of fantasy and realism" and styled *The Night Iguana Left Home* a tale that "will stir the imaginations of armchair travelers," while Gay Lynn van Vleck assured *School Library Journal* readers that McDonald's "inventive tale will guarantee grins."

Animals on the move are also the subject of *Penguin and Little Blue,* which finds two water park performers taking their show on the road and trying to make their hotel room in Kansas a little more Antarctic-like. Praising McDonald's pun-filled text, a *Publishers Weekly* reviewer cited *Penguin and Little Blue* as a story that "touts the importance of home and friends," while a *Kirkus Reviews* critic was caught up enough in the spirit of the story to claim that "young readers will flap their flippers at this tongue-in-cheek jaunt."

In addition to picture books and beginning readers, McDonald has penned several novels for older readers. *The Bridge to Nowhere,* a semi-autobiographical novel for young adults, introduces seventh-grader Hallie O'Shea, who is frustrated over her now-out-of-work father's inability to cope with the loss of his job. Depressed and withdrawn from the rest of the family, Mr. O'Shea spends his time in the basement, building metal sculptures, or driving off to his former job site, a still-unfinished bridge over the Allegheny river that he calls the "bridge to nowhere." Hallie's mother, meanwhile, becomes absorbed with worry about her husband, and older sister Shelley escapes to college, leaving the young teen to fend for herself. Things improve after Hallie meets Crane Henderson, a ninth grader for whom she soon develops a crush, but when her father attempts to commit suicide by driving off the unfinished bridge, the young couple's relationship is tested. Praising the book as a fine first effort for former picture-book writer McDonald, a *Kirkus Reviews* critic called *The Bridge to Nowhere* "unusually well crafted: accessible, lyrical, with wonderful natural dialogue" between parent and teen. Deborah Abbott pointed out in *Booklist* that the novel provides "realis-

tic characters, an attention-holding plot . . . and an upbeat ending."

Other novels by McDonald include *Shadows in the Glasshouse,* which follows the story of twelve-year-old Merry after she is forced to sail from London to the newly colonized Jamestown settlement to work for a glassblower. Taking place in 1621, the novel weaves together drama, mystery, and interesting information about life during that period of American history. Also in the genre of historical fiction is McDonald's 2003 novel *All the Stars in the Sky: The Santa Fe Trail Diary of Florie Mack Ryder.* Based on an actual diary of the mid-1800s, the book presents a fictionalized account of what life was like for a young teen who travels with her family from Independence, Missouri, to points southwest. Praising the book as a "solid entry" in Scholastic's "Dear America" series of fictional journals, a *Kirkus Reviews* contributor praised the story's young narrator as "a heroine readers will enjoy joining on her travels."

"Story can come from memory or experience," McDonald once explained to *CA.* "It seems to come from everywhere, and out of nowhere. In everything there is story—a leaf falling, the smell of cinnamon, a dog that looks both ways before crossing the street. The idea, the seed of a story, is implicit—but requires paying attention, watching, seeing, listening, smelling, eavesdropping. . . . To be a writer for children, I continue to believe in the transformative power of story that connects children with books."

BIOGRAPHICAL AND CRITICAL SOURCES:

BOOKS

Continuum Encyclopedia of Children's Literature, Continuum (New York, NY), 2001.
McDonald, Megan, *The Bridge to Nowhere,* Orchard (New York, NY), 1993.

PERIODICALS

Booklist, March 1, 1990, Carolyn Phelan, review of *Is This a House for Hermit Crab?,* p. 1347; April 1, 1993, Deborah Abbott, review of *The Bridge to Nowhere,* pp. 1424-1425; March 1, 1995, p. 1249;

April 15, 1999, Susan Dove Lempke, review of *The Bone Keeper,* p. 1531; November 1, 1999, John Peters, review of *The Night Iguana Left Home,* p. 540; July, 2000, Carolyn Phelan, review of *Beezy and Funnybone,* p. 2045, and Shelle Rosenfeld, review of *Judy Moody,* p. 2028; September 1, 2002, Shelle Rosenfeld, review of *Judy Moody Saves the World!,* p. 125; July, 2003, Gillian Engberg, review of *Shining Star,* p. 1899; August, 2003, Hazel Rochman, review of *Baya, Baya, Lulla-By-A,* p. 1990; September 15, 2003, Kay Weisman, review of *Judy Moody Predicts the Future,* p. 240; November 1, 2003, Lauren Peterson, review of *Penguin and Little Blue,* p. 502; December 1, 2003, Ellen Mandel, review of *The Sisters Club,* p. 677.

Bulletin of the Center for Children's Books, April, 1995, Deborah Stevenson, review of *Insects Are My Life,* p. 280; March, 1999, Janice M. Del Negro, review of *The Bone Keeper,* pp. 245-246.

Childhood Education, mid-summer, 2002, Jill Quisenberry, review of *Reptiles Are My Life,* p. 307.

Five Owls, July-August, 1990, Margaret Mary Kimmel, review of *Is This a House for a Hermit Crab?,* p. 105; May-June, 1992, Anne Lundin, review of *Whoo-oo Is It?,* p. 58.

Horn Book, March-April, 1990, p. 222; May, 1991, Mary M. Burns, review of *The Potato Man,* p. 318; May-June, 1992, Elizabeth S. Watson, review of *Whoo-oo Is It?,* p. 332; March-April, 1995, Margaret A. Bush, review of *Insects Are My Life,* p. 185; September, 1999, review of *The Night Iguana Left Home,* p. 596; September, 2001, review of *Judy Moody Gets Famous!,* p. 589.

Kirkus Reviews, January, 1992, p. 117; July 1, 1992, review of *The Great Pumpkin Switch,* p. 851; March 15, 1993, review of *The Bridge to Nowhere,* p. 374; July 15, 1999, review of *Bedbugs,* p. 1141; July 1, 2001, review of *Reptiles Are My Life,* p. 943; July 1, 2002, review of *Judy Moody Saves the World!,* p. 958; June 15, 2003, review of *Baya, Baya, Lulla-By-A,* p. 861; August 15, 2003, reviews of *The Sisters Club* and *All the Stars in the Sky: The Santa Fe Trail Diary of Florrie Mack Ryder,* p. 1076; September 1, 2003, review of *Penguin and Little Blue,* p. 1128.

New York Times Book Review, February 13, 2000, Jane O'Reilly, review of *The Night Iguana Left Home,* p. 27.

Publishers Weekly, December 14, 1990, p. 66; February 17, 1992, p. 62; September 29, 1997, p. 89; October 6, 1997, review of *Tundra Mouse,* p. 55;

February 1, 1999, review of *The Bone Keeper,* p. 84; October 4, 1999, review of *The Night Iguana Left Home,* p. 74; April 17, 2000, review of *Judy Moody,* p. 81; July 30, 2001, review of *Judy Moody Gets Famous!,* p. 85; June 30, 2003, review of *Baya, Baya, Lulla-By-A,* p. 77; August 25, 2003, reviews of *Penguin and Little Blue,* p. 63, and *The Sisters Club,* p. 65.

School Librarian, summer, 2002, Andrea Rayner, review of *Judy Moody,* p. 89.

School Library Journal, August, 1992, Susan Scheps, review of *The Great Pumpkin Switch,* pp. 143-144; March, 1995, Virginia Opocensky, review of *Insects Are My Life,* pp. 183-184; October, 1996, Sally R. Dow, review of *My House Has Stars,* pp. 102-103; November, 1997, p. 92; May, 1999, Rosalyn Pierini, review of *The Bone Keeper,* p. 93; September, 1999, Heide Piehler, review of *Bedbugs,* p. 194, Gay Lynn van Vleck, review of *The Night Iguana Left Home,* p. 195; July, 2000, Janie Schomberg, review of *Judy Moody,* p. 83; September, 2000, Maura Bresnahan, review of *Beezy and Funnybone,* p. 204; February, 2001, Kristen Oravec, review of *Shadows in the Glasshouse,* p. 118; August, 2001, Linda M. Kenton, review of *Reptiles Are My Life,* p. 156; October, 2001, Sharon R. Pearce, review of *Judy Moody Gets Famous!,* p. 124; March, 2002, Maura Bresnahan, review of *Lucky Star,* p. 194; November, 2003, Alison Grant, review of *Judy Moody Predicts the Future,* p. 106, Catherine Threadgill, review of *Penguin and Little Blue,* p. 107, Lee Bock, review of *All the Stars in the Sky,* p. 142, and Laurie von Mehren, review of *The Sisters Club,* p. 142.

ONLINE

Megan McDonald Home Page, http://www.megan mcdonald.net (January 19, 2004).*

*   *   *

McMILLAN, Terry (L.) 1951-

PERSONAL: Born October 18, 1951, in Port Huron, MI; daughter of Edward McMillan and Madeline Washington Tillman; married Jonathan Plummer, September, 1998; children (by Leonard Welch): Solomon Welch. *Education:* University of California, Berkeley, B.S., 1979; Columbia University, M.F.A., 1979.

ADDRESSES: Agent—c/o Author Mail, Viking Penguin, 375 Hudson St., New York, NY 10014.

CAREER: Writer. University of Wyoming, Laramie, instructor, 1987-90; University of Arizona, Tucson, professor, 1990-92.

MEMBER: PEN, Author's League.

AWARDS, HONORS: American Book Award, Before Columbus Foundation, 1987, for *Mama;* National Endowment for the Arts fellowship, 1988.

WRITINGS:

Mama, Houghton Mifflin (Boston, MA), 1987.

Disappearing Acts, Viking (New York, NY), 1989.

(Editor) *Breaking Ice: An Anthology of Contemporary African-American Fiction,* Viking (New York, NY), 1990.

(Author of introduction) Spike Lee, with Ralph Wiley, *By Any Means Necessary: The Trials and Tribulations of the Making of Malcolm X . . . including the Screenplay,* Hyperion (New York, NY), 1992.

Waiting to Exhale, Viking (New York, NY), 1992.

How Stella Got Her Groove Back, Viking (New York, NY), 1996.

A Day Late and a Dollar Short, Viking (New York, NY), 2001.

The Interruption of Everything, Viking (New York, NY), 2004.

Contributor to *Five for Five: The Films of Spike Lee,* Stewart, Tabori, 1991. Contributor of short stories to periodicals.

ADAPTATIONS: Waiting to Exhale was adapted for audio cassette, narrated by Terry McMillan, and as a motion picture starring Whitney Houston and Angela Bassett, Twentieth Century-Fox, 1996; *How Stella Got Her Groove Back* was adapted as a film starring Bassett, Whoopi Goldberg, Taye Diggs, and Regina King, Twentieth Century-Fox, 1998; *Disappearing Acts* was adapted for a film by Home Box Office, 2001; *A Day Late and a Dollar Short* was adapted for audio cassette, Penguin Audiobooks, 2001.

SIDELIGHTS: Terry McMillan's character-driven novels, most of them best-sellers, have drawn an audience of all ages, races, and genders. McMillan has a talent for confronting universal themes such as romantic commitment, family obligations, and relationships between parents and children, in ways that resonate in her readers' lives. To quote Anne Bowling in *Writer's Yearbook,* "The women McMillan crafts draw readers by the millions. These characters seem familiar enough to walk through your apartment door, drop a Coach bag on the coffee table and flop down on the couch for a chat." *Booklist* correspondent Vanessa Bush commended McMillan for her "distinctive style of unveiling the trials and mishaps of modern-day life for black folks." Loosely based on her own life experiences, such novels as *Waiting to Exhale* and *How Stella Got Her Groove Back* explore the many lifestyle issues facing educated, dynamic upper-class women as they seek happiness and self-definition through their work and their relationships.

For her portrayal of feisty, tough, black heroines, McMillan has been compared to acclaimed black women writers Alice Walker, Gloria Naylor, and Zora Neale Hurston. McMillan acknowledges the compliment, but asserted in the introduction to the 1990 short-story anthology *Breaking Ice,* which she edited, that her generation of black writers is "a new breed, free to write as we please . . . because of the way life has changed."

"McMillan has the power to be an important contemporary novelist," stated Valerie Sayers in the *New York Times Book Review* in 1989. By that time, McMillan had already garnered attention and critical praise for her first novel, *Mama,* which was published in 1987. Over the next five years predictions about the writer's future began to come true. In 1992 McMillan saw the publication of *Waiting to Exhale,* her third novel. Her publisher sent her on a twenty-city, six-week tour, and McMillan appeared on several popular television programs. As healthy sales of her novels, as well as the purchase of their film rights showed, the author's honest, unaffected writing style clearly struck a chord with the U.S. book-buying public.

McMillan grew up in Port Huron, Michigan, and discovered the pleasure of reading as a teenager while shelving books in a local library. As a student at a community college in Los Angeles, McMillan immersed herself in most of the classics of African-

American literature, and at age twenty-five she published her first short story. Eleven years after that, her first novel, *Mama,* was released by Houghton Mifflin.

McMillan was determined not to let her debut novel go unnoticed. Typically, first novels receive little publicity other than the press releases and galleys sent out by the publisher. When McMillan's publisher told her that they could not do more for her, she decided to promote the book on her own. She wrote over 3,000 letters to chain bookstores, independent booksellers, universities, and colleges. By the end of the summer of 1987 she had received several requests to do readings. McMillan then scheduled her own book publicity tour and let her publicist know where she was going.

Mama had started out as a short story. "I really love the short story as a form," explained McMillan in an interview with *Writer's Digest.* "Mama" was just one of several short stories McMillan had tried unsuccessfully to get into print. Then the Harlem Writer's Guild accepted her into their group and advised her that "Mama" really should be a novel and not a short story. After four weeks at the MacDowell artists colony and two weeks at Yaddo, McMillan had expanded her short story into a book of more than 400 pages. When her agent suggested certain revisions, McMillan questioned whether the woman truly understood what the book was about.

Frustrated by this and by other events taking place in her personal life, McMillan took things into her own hands and sent a collection of short stories to Houghton Mifflin, hoping to at least get some free editorial advice. McMillan was surprised when the publisher contacted her, not about the short stories, but about the novel she had mentioned briefly in her cover letter to them. She sent them pages from *Mama* and approximately four days later got word from the publisher that they loved it.

Mama tells the story of the struggle Mildred Peacock has in raising her five children after she throws her drunkard husband out of the house. The novel begins: "Mildred hid the ax beneath the mattress of the cot in the dining room." With those words, McMillan's novel becomes "a runaway narrative pulling a crowded cast of funny, earthy characters," stated Sayers in the *New York Times Book Review.* Because of McMillan's pro-

motional efforts, the novel received numerous reviews—the overwhelming majority of which were positive. Six weeks after *Mama* was published, it went into its third printing. Michael Awkward, reviewing the novel in *Callaloo,* deemed it a "moving, often hilarious and insightful exploration of a slice of black urban life that is rarely seen in contemporary black women's fiction."

Disappearing Acts, McMillan's second novel, tells the story of star-crossed lovers by alternating the narrative between the main characters. Zora Banks and Franklin Swift fall in love "at first sight" when they meet at Zora's new apartment, where Franklin works as part of the renovating crew. Zora is an educated black woman working as a junior high school music teacher; Franklin is a high-school dropout working in construction. In spite of the differences in their backgrounds, the two become involved, move in together, and try to overcome the fear they both feel because of past failures in love.

Writing in the *Washington Post Book World,* David Nicholson pointed out that although this difference in backgrounds is an old literary device, it is one that is particularly relevant to black Americans: "Professional black women complain of an ever-shrinking pool of eligible men, citing statistics that show the number of black men in prison is increasing, while the number of black men in college is decreasing. Articles on alternatives for women, from celibacy to 'man-sharing' to relationships with blue-collar workers like Franklin have long been a staple of black general interest and women's magazines." McMillan expressed her own thoughts on this issue in an article in *Essence.* "Maybe it's just me, but I'm finding it harder and harder to meet men. . . . I grew up and became what my mama prayed out loud I'd become: educated, strong, smart, independent and reliable. . . . Now it seems as if carving a place for myself in the world is backfiring. Never in a million years would I have dreamed that I'd be thirty-eight years old and still single."

Reviewers have commended McMillan for her ability to give such a true voice to the character of Franklin in *Disappearing Acts.* A reviewer for the *Washington Post Book World* called the novel "one of the few . . . to contain rounded, sympathetic portraits of black men and to depict relationships between black men and black women as something more than the relationship between victimizer and victim, oppressor and oppressed." In the *New York Times Book Review* another reviewer stated: "The miracle is that Ms. McMillan takes the reader so deep into this man's head—and makes what goes on there so complicated—that [the] story becomes not only comprehensible but affecting." Not only did McMillan's second novel win critical acclaim, it also was optioned for a film by Home Box Office. Although it also sparked a defamation suit brought by McMillan's former lover, who claimed that McMillan used him as the model for the novel's main male character, the New York State Supreme Court ultimately ruled in McMillan's favor.

Waiting to Exhale tells the stories of four professional black women who have everything except the love of a good man. The overall theme of the book is men's fear of commitment; a sub-theme is the fear of growing old alone. The novel hit a nerve with its readers, both male and female, as many readers seemed to identify with McMillan's characters. According to a *Los Angeles Times* writer, one black male reader proclaimed: "I think I speak for a lot of brothers. I know I'm all over the book. . . . All I can say is, I'm willing to learn. Being defensive is not the answer." That was precisely the response McMillan was hoping to get.

One issue that emerges from reviews of McMillan's books is her use of profanity, and *Waiting to Exhale* sparked the same criticism. One critic referred to the novel's protagonists as male-bashing stand-up comedians who use foul language. For McMillan, reproducing the profane language people actually use is her way of staying close to reality. As she told a *Publishers Weekly* interviewer: "That's the way we talk. And I want to know why I've never read a review where they complain about the language that male writers use!"

"Fans of McMillan's previous novels . . . will recognize McMillan's authentic, unpretentious voice in every page of *How Stella Got Her Groove Back,*" noted Liesl Schillinger in the *Washington Post Book World*. The story of a forty-something businesswoman whose life has been spent raising her son and working her way to success, *How Stella Got Her Groove Back* finds the resourceful, spunky protagonist off to Jamaica to shake up more than just a boring existence. Stella is determined to fill that empty place in her life where a permanent love interest should be, and a twenty-year-old Jamaican named Winston more than fits the bill.

She brings Winston back to the United States with her and, almost unbelievably, he is accepted by her eleven-year-old son as well as by her sisters, and life continues happily ever after. Although noting that McMillan's novel "is not deeper or more searching than the average sitcom, no more dramatically powerful than a backyard barbecue," Richard Bernstein cited *How Stella Got Her Groove Back* as "an irreverent, mischievous, diverting novel that at times will make you laugh out loud," in his *New York Times* review. Maxine Chernoff dubbed the novel "not quite serious enough for summer reading" in her review in Chicago's *Tribune Books*. Schillinger praised McMillan for realizing that "women are ready to read about themselves not only as schemers or sufferers, but as the adventurous heroes of their own lives."

A Day Late and a Dollar Short, published in 2001, had its genesis in the early 1990s, but McMillan was sidetracked by the deaths of her mother and her best friend, then by her marriage to Jonathan Plummer. The novel employs six first-person voices to explore the dynamics of one family as the beloved matriarch lies dying in the hospital. "All six voices—male and female, young and old—are fresh and vital, propelling conflict and exposing the strengths and foibles of the good but imperfect people," declared Jewell Parker Rhodes in the *Washington Post Book World*. Rhodes further characterized the novel as a "glorious" work that, "like the best fiction, helped illuminate corners of my own heart. Like a call-and-response chant, [McMillan's] strong characterization and plotting dared me not to laugh, cry and shout upon recognizing this glittering, complicated portrayal of African-American family life."

McMillan does not shy away from portraying the most devastating aspects of modern life in *A Day Late and a Dollar Short*. She tackles infidelity, drug and alcohol abuse, sexual abuse, and sibling rivalry, while allowing her characters to defend—and condemn—themselves through their own commentary. "The story was important to me," the author told a *Publishers Weekly* interviewer. "My hope for my readers is that broken relationships among family members might be looked at again." A *Publishers Weekly* contributor called *A Day Late and a Dollar Short* "a moving and true depiction of an American family, driven apart and bound together by the real stuff of life." In a review for *Book,* Andrea King Collier lauded the work, noting that, "In the hands of McMillan, the master of edgy, ensemble storytelling," the novel "has drama and snap."

With her string of best-sellers, McMillan has proven to be a "crossover" artist who, while writing exclusively about black characters, transcends the bounds of ethnic issues. McMillan's voice belongs to what has been described as "the New Black Aesthetic": one that does not deal with everything from the perspective of race. For example, her novel *The Interruption of Everything* tells the story of Marilyn Grimes, a consummate wife and mother of three grown children who is married to an average Joe. This scenario could aptly describe many women of any race, creed, or nationality. Although her life appears to be a good one, Marilyn has postponed many of her own dreams so long that she can no longer quite remember what they are. Feeling closed in by irrelevant demands, Marilyn sets out to reinvent her life.

As McMillan explained to *Writers Yearbook:* "Everything I write is about empowerment, regardless of what kind it is. It's always about a woman standing up for herself and her rights and her beliefs, and not worrying about what other people think. But one of the things I think fiction should not do is be didactic. I'm not here to preach, I'm not trying to be Gloria Steinem in disguise. I would prefer that you be affected, that by reading something you get a sense of empowerment, and hopefully if it's subtle enough you won't even know it happened."

Commenting on her motivation for writing, McMillan explained to a *Writer* contributor that she has a good reason to keep working. "I write because the world is an imperfect place, and we behave in an imperfect manner. I want to understand why it's so hard to be good, honest, loving, caring, thoughtful and generous. Writing is about the only way (besides praying) that allows me to be compassionate toward folks who, in real life, I'm probably not that sympathetic toward. I want to understand myself and others better, so what better way than to pretend to be them."

BIOGRAPHICAL AND CRITICAL SOURCES:

BOOKS

Authors and Artists for Young Adults, Volume 21, Gale (Detroit, MI), 1998.
Contemporary Black Biography, Volume 17, Gale (Detroit, MI), 1998.

Contemporary Literary Criticism, Gale (Detroit, MI), Volume 50, 1988, Volume 61, 1991.
Patrick, Diane, *Terry McMillan: The Unauthorized Biography,* St. Martin's Press (New York, NY), 1999.

PERIODICALS

Black Issues Book Review, January, 2001, Gwendolyn E. Osborne, review of *A Day Late and a Dollar Short,* p. 15.
Book, January, 2001, Andrea King Collier, review of *A Day Late and a Dollar Short,* p. 71.
Booklist, November 15, 2000, Vanessa Bush, review of *A Day Late and a Dollar Short,* p. 588.
Callaloo, summer, 1988.
Christian Science Monitor, January 11, 2001, "Waiting to Exhale in the Thin Atmosphere of Troubled Siblings," p. 18.
Cosmopolitan, August, 1989.
Detroit News, September 7, 1992.
Emerge, September, 1992; June, 1996.
English Journal, April, 1996, p. 86.
Esquire, July, 1988.
Essence, February, 1990; October, 1992; May, 1995, p. 52; June, 1996, pp. 50, 54.
Library Journal, January 1, 2001, Emily Jones, review of *A Day Late and a Dollar Short,* p. 155.
Los Angeles Times, February 23, 1987; October 29, 1990; June 19, 1992.
Mademoiselle, July, 1996, p. 77.
Newsweek, January 8, 1996, p. 68; April 29, 1996, pp. 76, 79.
New Yorker, April 29, 1996, p. 102.
New York Review of Books, November 4, 1993, p. 33.
New York Times, May 15, 1996, p. B5, C17.
New York Times Book Review, February 22, 1987; August 6, 1989; May 31, 1992; June 2, 1996, p. 21; February 4, 2001, Ruth Coughlin, review of *A Day Late and a Dollar Short,* p. 21.
New York Times Magazine, August 9, 1992.
People, July 20, 1992.
Publishers Weekly, May 11, 1992; July 13, 1992; September 21, 1992; May 6, 1996, p. 30; December 11, 2000, Diane Patrick, "Terry McMillan Is Back," p. 42; December 11, 2000, review of *A Day Late and a Dollar Short,* p. 65.
Time, January 8, 1996, p. 72; May 6, 1996, p. 77.
Tribune Books (Chicago, IL), September 23, 1990; May 31, 1992; May 5, 1996, p. 6.

Village Voice, March 24, 1987.

Wall Street Journal, April 11, 1991.

Washington Post, November 17, 1990; January 25, 2001, Linton Weeks, "Terry McMillan, Encompassing the Family Circle," p. C1.

Washington Post Book World, August 27, 1989; September 16, 1990; May 24, 1992; May 5, 1996, p. 1; February 11, 2001, Jewell Parker Rhodes, "The Price Club," p. 5.

Writer, August, 2001, interview with McMillan, p. 66.

Writer's Digest, October, 1987.

ONLINE

Voices from the Gaps, http://voices.cla.umn.edu/ (April 21, 2004), "Terry McMillan."

Writer's Yearbook, http://www.writersdigest.com/ (March 6, 2001), Anne Bowling, "Terry McMillan: 'Everything I Write Is about Empowerment.'"*

*   *   *

MERTON, Thomas (James) 1915-1968

PERSONAL: Born January 31, 1915, in Prades, Pyrennes-Orientales, France; brought to the United States, 1916; naturalized U.S. citizen, 1951; fatally electrocuted, December 10, 1968, in Bangkok, Thailand; son of Owen Heathcote (an artist) and Ruth (an artist; maiden name, Jenkins) Merton. *Education:* Attended Clare College, Cambridge, 1933-34; Columbia University, B.A., 1938, M.A., 1939.

CAREER: Instructor in English, Columbia University Extension Division, New York, NY, 1938-39, and St. Bonaventure University, Allegheny, NY, 1939-41; Abbey of Our Lady of Gethsemane, near Bardstown, KY, Roman Catholic monk of Cistercians of the Strict Observance (Trappists), 1941-68, ordained Roman Catholic priest as Father M. Louis, 1949, master of scholastics, 1951-55, monastic forester, beginning 1951, novice master, 1955-65, lived as a hermit on grounds of monastery, 1965-68. Artist; drawings exhibited in Louisville, KY; St. Louis, MO; New Orleans, LA; Milwaukee, WI; and Santa Barbara, CA, 1964-65.

MEMBER: Fellowship of Reconciliation.

AWARDS, HONORS: Mariana Griswold Van Rensselaer Award, 1939; citation from Catholic Press Association of the United States, 1948, for *Figures for an Apocalypse;* Catholic Literary Award, Gallery of Living Catholic Authors, 1949, for *The Seven Storey Mountain;* Catholic Writers Guild Golden Book Award for best spiritual book by an American writer, 1951, for *The Ascent to the Truth;* Columbia University Medal for Excellence, 1961; LL.D., University of Kentucky, 1963; Pax Medal, 1963; Religious Book Award, Catholic Press Association, 1973, for *The Asian Journal of Thomas Merton.*

WRITINGS:

POETRY

Thirty Poems (also see below), New Directions (New York, NY), 1944.

A Man in the Divided Sea (includes poems from *Thirty Poems*), New Directions (New York, NY), 1946.

Figures for an Apocalypse (also contains an essay), New Directions (New York, NY), 1948.

The Tears of Blind Lions, New Directions (New York, NY), 1949.

Selected Poems of Thomas Merton, Hollis Carter (London, England), 1950.

The Strange Islands: Poems (also see below), New Directions (New York, NY), 1957.

Selected Poems of Thomas Merton, New Directions (New York, NY), 1959, revised edition, 1967.

The Solitary Life, limited edition, Anvil Press (Lexington, KY), 1960.

Emblems of a Season of Fury (also contains prose and translations), New Directions (New York, NY), 1963.

Cables to the Ace; or, Familiar Liturgies of Misunderstanding, New Directions (New York, NY), 1968.

Landscape, Prophet, and Wild-Dog, [Syracuse, NY], 1968.

The Geography of Lograire, New Directions (New York, NY), 1969.

Early Poems: 1940-42, Anvil Press (Lexington, KY), 1972.

He Is Risen: Selections from Thomas Merton, Argus Communications (Niles, IL), 1975.

The Collected Poems of Thomas Merton, New Directions (New York, NY), 1977.

ESSAYS

What Is Contemplation? (also see below), Saint Mary's College, Notre Dame (Holy Cross, IN), 1948, revised edition, Templegate (Springfield, IL), 1981, expanded version published as *The Inner Experience: Notes on Contemplation,* edited and with an introduction by William H. Shannon, HarperSanFrancisco (San Francisco, CA), 2003.

Seeds of Contemplation, New Directions (New York, NY), 1949, revised and expanded edition published as *New Seeds of Contemplation,* New Directions (New York, NY), 1962, reprinted, Shambala (Boston, MA), 2003.

The Ascent to the Truth, Harcourt (San Diego, CA), 1951.

Bread in the Wilderness, New Directions (New York, NY), 1953.

No Man Is an Island, Harcourt (San Diego, CA), 1955.

The Living Bread, Farrar, Straus (New York, NY), 1956.

Praying the Psalms, Liturgical Press (Collegeville, MN), 1956, published as *The Psalms Are Our Prayer,* Burns & Oates (London, England), 1957, published as *Thomas Merton on the Psalms,* Sheldon Press (London, England), 1970.

The Silent Life, Farrar, Straus (New York, NY), 1957.

Thoughts in Solitude, Farrar, Straus (New York, NY), 1958.

The Christmas Sermons of Bl. Guerric of Igny (essay), Abbey of Our Lady of Gethsemane (Bardstown, KY), 1959.

Spiritual Direction and Meditation (also see below), Liturgical Press (Collegeville, MN), 1960.

Disputed Questions (also see below), Farrar, Straus (New York, NY), 1960.

The Behavior of Titans, New Directions (New York, NY), 1961.

The New Man, Farrar, Straus (New York, NY), 1962.

Life and Holiness, Herder & Herder (New York, NY), 1963.

Seeds of Destruction (also includes several letters), Farrar, Straus (New York, NY), 1964, abridged edition published as *Redeeming the Time,* Burns & Oates (London, England), 1966.

Seasons of Celebration, Farrar, Straus (New York, NY), 1965, published as *Meditations on Liturgy,* Mowbrays (London, England), 1976.

Mystics and Zen Masters (includes "The Ox Mountain Parable of Meng Tzu"; also see below), Farrar, Straus (New York, NY), 1967.

Zen and the Birds of Appetite, New Directions (New York, NY), 1968.

Faith and Violence: Christian Teaching and Christian Practice, University of Notre Dame Press (Notre Dame, IN), 1968.

The Climate of Monastic Prayer, Cistercian Publications (Kalamazoo, MI), 1969, published as *Contemplative Prayer,* Herder & Herder (New York, NY), 1969.

True Solitude: Selections from the Writings of Thomas Merton, Hallmark Editions (Kansas City, MO), 1969.

Three Essays, Unicorn Press (Greensboro, NC), 1969.

Opening the Bible, Liturgical Press (Collegeville, MN), 1970, revised edition, Liturgical Press (Collegeville, MN), 1983.

Contemplation in a World of Action, Doubleday (Garden City, NY), 1971, revised edition, University of Notre Dame Press (Notre Dame, IN), 1998.

The Zen Revival, Buddhist Society (London, England), 1971.

Thomas Merton on Peace, McCall (New York, NY), 1971, revised edition published as *The Nonviolent Alternative,* edited and with an introduction by Gordon C. Zahn, Farrar, Straus (New York, NY), 1980.

Spiritual Direction and Meditation; and, What Is Contemplation?, A. Clarke (Westhampstead, England), 1975.

Thomas Merton on Zen, Sheldon Press (London, England), 1976.

The Power and Meaning of Love (includes six essays originally published in *Disputed Questions*), Sheldon Press (London, England), 1976.

Ishi Means Man: Essays on Native Americans, foreword by Dorothy Day, Unicorn Press (Greensboro, NC), 1976.

The Monastic Journey, edited by Patrick Hart, Sheed, Andrews & McMeel (Mission, KS), 1977.

Love and Living, edited by Naomi Burton Stone and Patrick Hart, Farrar, Straus (New York, NY), 1979.

Thomas Merton on St. Bernard, Cistercian Publications (Kalamazoo, MI), 1980.

The Literary Essays of Thomas Merton, edited by Patrick Hart, New Directions (New York, NY), 1981.

Passion for Peace: The Social Essays, edited by William Henry Shannon, Crossroad Publishing (New York, NY), 1995.

(With Eberhard Arnold) *Why We Live in Community,* Plough (New York, NY), 1995.

The Springs of Contemplation: A Retreat at the Abbey Gethsemane, Ave Maria (Notre Dame, IN), 1997.

Mornings with Thomas Merton: Readings and Reflections, selected by John C. Blattner, Charis Books (Ann Arbor, MI), 1998.

Essential Writings, edited by Christine Bochen, Orbis Books (Maryknoll, NY), 2000.

Peace in the Post-Christian Era, edited by Patricia A. Burton, Orbis Books (Maryknoll, NJ), 2004.

AUTOBIOGRAPHIES

The Seven Storey Mountain, Harcourt (San Diego, CA), 1948, abridged edition published as *Elected Silence: The Autobiography of Thomas Merton,* with an introduction by Evelyn Waugh, Hollis Carter (London, England), 1949, fiftieth anniversary edition, HarperSanFrancisco (San Francisco, CA), 1999.

The Sign of Jonas (journal), Harcourt (San Diego, CA), 1953.

The Secular Journal of Thomas Merton, Farrar, Straus (New York, NY), 1959.

Conjectures of a Guilty Bystander (journal), Doubleday (Garden City, NY), 1966, 2nd edition, Sheldon Press (London, England), 1977.

The Asian Journal of Thomas Merton, edited by Naomi Burton Stone, Patrick Hart, and James Laughlin, New Directions (New York, NY), 1973.

Woods, Shore, Desert: A Notebook, May, 1968, with photographs by Merton, Museum of New Mexico Press (Santa Fe, NM), 1982.

A Vow of Conversation: Journals, 1964-65, edited by Naomi Burton Stone, Farrar, Straus (New York, NY), 1988.

Journals of Thomas Merton, Volume 1: *Run to the Mountain,* Volume 2: *Entering the Silence,* Volume 3: *A Search for Solitude,* Volume 4: *Turning toward the World: The Pivotal Years,* Volume 5: *Dancing in the Water of Life: Seeking Peace in the Hermitage,* Volume 6: *Learning to Love: Exploring Solitude and Freedom,* edited by Christine Bochen, Volume 7: *The Other Side of the Mountain: The End of the Journey, 1967-1968,* HarperSanFrancisco (San Francisco, CA), 1995-1998.

BIOGRAPHIES

Exile Ends in Glory: The Life of a Trappistine, Mother M. Berchmans, O.C.S.O., Bruce (Milwaukee, WI), 1948.

What Are These Wounds?: The Life of a Cistercian Mystic, Saint Lutgarde of Aywieres, Clonmore Reynolds (Dublin, Ireland), 1949, Bruce (Milwaukee, WI), 1950.

The Last of the Fathers: Saint Bernard of Clairvaux and the Encyclical Letter "Doctor Mellifluus," Harcourt (San Diego, CA), 1954.

LETTERS

Six Letters: Boris Pasternak, Thomas Merton, edited by Naomi Burton Stone, King Library Press, University of Kentucky (Lexington, KY), 1973.

(With Robert Lax) *A Catch of Anti-Letters,* Sheed, Andrews & McMeel (Mission, KS), 1978.

Letters from Tom: A Selection of Letters from Father Thomas Merton, Monk of Gethsemane, to W. H. Ferry, 1961-1968, edited by W. H. Ferry, Fort Hill Press (Scarsdale, NY), 1983.

The Hidden Ground of Love: The Letters of Thomas Merton on Religious Experience and Social Concerns, selected and edited by William Henry Shannon, Farrar, Straus (New York, NY), 1985.

The Road to Joy: The Letters of Thomas Merton to New and Old Friends, edited by Robert E. Daggy, Farrar, Straus (New York, NY), 1989.

The School of Charity: The Letters of Thomas Merton on Religious Renewal and Spiritual Direction, edited by Patrick Hart, Farrar, Straus (New York, NY), 1990.

The Courage for Truth: The Letters of Thomas Merton to Writers, edited by Christine M. Bochen, Farrar, Straus (New York, NY), 1993.

Witness to Freedom: The Letters of Thomas Merton in Times of Crisis, edited by William Henry Shannon, Farrar, Straus (New York, NY), 1994.

At Home in the World: The Letters of Thomas Merton and Rosemary Radford Ruether, edited by Mary Tardiff, Orbis Books (Maryknoll, NY), 1995.

Striving towards Being: The Letters of Thomas Merton and Czeslaw Milosz, edited by Robert Faggen, (New York, NY), 1997.

Thomas Merton and James Laughlin: Selected Letters, W. W. Norton (New York, NY), 1997.

When Prophecy Still Had a Voice: The Letters of Thomas Merton and Robert Lax, University Press of Kentucky (Lexington, KY), 2001.

Survival or Prophecy?: Letters of Thomas Merton and Jean Leclercq, Farrar, Straus (New York, NY), 2002.

LYRICS

Four Freedom Songs, G.I.A. Publications (Chicago, IL), 1968.

The Niles-Merton Songs: Opus 171 and 172, music by John Jacob Miles, Mark Foster Music (Champaign, IL), 1981.

For My Brother, Reported Missing in Action, 1943, music by Frank Ferko, E. C. Schirmer (Boston, MA), 2000.

EDITOR

What Ought I Do?: Sayings of the Desert Fathers, Stamperia del Santuccio (Lexington, KY), 1959, revised and expanded edition published as *The Wisdom of the Desert Fathers of the Fourth Century,* New Directions (New York, NY), 1961.

The Ox Mountain Parable of Meng Tzu, Stamperia del Santuccio (Lexington, KY), 1960.

(And contributor and author of introduction) *Breakthrough to Peace: Twelve Views on the Threat of Thermonuclear Extermination,* New Directions (New York, NY), 1962.

(And author of introduction) Mohandas Gandhi, *Gandhi on Non-Violence: Selected Texts from Gandhi's "Non-Violence in Peace and War,"* New Directions (New York, NY), 1965.

(And author of introductory essays) *The Way of Chuang Tzu,* New Directions (New York, NY), 1965, reprinted, Shambhala (Boston, MA), 2004.

(And author of introduction and commentary) Albert Camus, *The Plague,* Seabury (New York, NY), 1968.

TRANSLATOR

(From the French) Jean-Baptiste Chautard, *The Soul of the Apostolate,* Abbey of Our Lady of Gethsemane (Trappist, KY), 1946, new edition with introduction by Thomas Merton, Image Books (New York, NY), 1961.

(From the French) Saint John Eudes, *The Life and the Kingdom of Jesus in Christian Souls for the Use by Clergy or Laity,* P. J. Kennedy Sons (New York, NY), 1946.

(And author of commentary) *The Spirit of Simplicity Characteristic of the Cistercian Order: An Official Report, Demanded and Approved by the General Chapter together with Texts from St. Bernard Clairvaux on Interior Simplicity,* Abbey of Our Lady of Gethsemane (Trappist, KY), 1948.

(And author of preface) Cassiodorus, *A Prayer from the Treatise "De anima,"* Stanbrook Abbey Press (Worcester, England), 1956.

(And author of explanatory essay) Clement of Alexandria, *Selections from the Protreptikos,* New Directions (New York, NY), 1963.

(From the Latin; and author of introduction) Guigo I, *The Solitary Life: A Letter from Guigo,* Stanbrook Abbey Press (Worcester, England), 1963, published as *On the Solitary Life,* Banyan Press (Pawlet, VT), 1977.

(From the Spanish; with others) Nicanor Parra, *Poems and Antipoems,* edited by Miller Williams, New Directions (New York, NY), 1967.

Pablo Antonio Cuadra, *El Jaguar y la luna/The Jaguar and the Moon* (bilingual edition), Unicorn Press (Greensboro, NC), 1974.

OTHER

(Illustrator) *Cistercian Contemplatives: Monks of the Strict Observance at Our Lady of Gethsemane, Kentucky, Our Lady of the Holy Ghost, Georgia, Our Lady of the Holy Trinity, Utah—A Guide to the Trappist Life,* Abbey of Our Lady of Gethsemane (Trappist, KY), 1948.

Gethsemane Magnificat: Centenary of Gethsemane Abbey, Abbey of Our Lady of Gethsemane (Trappist, KY), 1949.

The Waters of Siloe (history), Harcourt (San Diego, CA), 1949, reprinted, 1979, revised edition published as *The Waters of Silence,* Hollis & Carter (London, England), 1950, deluxe limited edition, Theodore Brun Limited (London, England), 1950.

Silence in Heaven: A Book of the Monastic Life, Studio Publications/Crowell (New York, NY), 1956.

The Tower of Babel (play), [Hamburg], 1957, New Directions (New York, NY), 1958.

Monastic Peace, Abbey of Our Lady of Gethsemane (Trappist, KY), 1958.

Hagia Sophia (prose poems), Stamperia del Santuccio (Lexington, KY), 1962.

A Thomas Merton Reader, edited by Thomas P. McDonnell, Harcourt (San Diego, CA), 1962, revised and enlarged edition, Image Books (New York, NY), 1974.

Original Child Bomb: Points for Meditation to Be Scratched on the Walls of a Cave (prose poem), New Directions (New York, NY), 1962.

Come to the Mountain: New Ways and Living Traditions in the Monastic Life, Saint Benedict's Cistercian Monastery (Snowmass, CO), 1964.

The Poorer Means: A Meditation on Ways to Unity, Abbey of Our Lady of Gethsemane (Trappist, KY), 1965.

Gethsemane: A Life of Praise, Abbey of Our Lady of Gethsemane (Trappist, KY), 1966.

(Author of introductory essay) George A. Panichas, editor, *Mansions of the Spirit: Essays in Religion and Literature,* Hawthorn (New York, NY), 1967.

Christ in the Desert, Monastery of Christ in the Desert (Abiquiu, NM), 1968.

My Argument with the Gestapo: A Macaronic Journal, Doubleday (Garden City, NY), 1969.

A Hidden Wholeness: The Visual World of Thomas Merton, edited by John Howard Griffin, Houghton Mifflin (Boston, MA), 1970.

Cistercian Life, Cistercian Book Service (Spenser, MA), 1974.

(Author of introduction) John Wu, *The Golden Age of Zen,* 1975.

(Author of introduction) *Counsels of Light and Love,* Paulist Press (New York, NY), 1977.

Geography of Holiness: The Photography of Thomas Merton, edited by Deba Prasad Patnaik, Pilgrim Press (New York, NY), 1980.

Introductions East and West: The Foreign Prefaces of Thomas Merton, edited by Robert E. Daggy, Unicorn Press (Greensboro, NC), 1981, revised edition published as *Honorable Reader: Reflections on My Work,* Crossroad Publishing (New York, NY), 1989.

Blaze of Recognition: Through the Year with Thomas Merton: Daily Meditations, selected and edited by McDonnell, with illustrations by Thomas Merton, Doubleday (Garden City, NY), 1983, published as *Through the Year with Thomas Merton: Daily Meditations from His Writings,* Image Books (New York, NY), 1985.

Monks Pond: Thomas Merton's Little Magazine (collected issues), edited by Robert E. Daggy, University Press of Kentucky (Lexington, KY), 1989.

Thomas Merton: Preview of the Asian Journey, edited by Walter H. Capps, Crossroad Publishing (New York, NY), 1989.

Thomas Merton in Alaska: Prelude to the Asian Journal: The Alaskan Conferences, Journals, and Letters, New Directions (New York, NY), 1989.

Thomas Merton's Rewritings: The Five Versions of "Seeds/New Seeds of Contemplation" As a Key to the Development of His Thought, edited by Donald Grayson, Edwin Mellen Press (Lewiston, NY), 1989.

The Springs of Contemplation: A Retreat at the Abbey of Gethsemane, edited by Jane Marie Richardson, Farrar, Straus (New York, NY), 1992.

Thomas Merton, Spiritual Master: The Essential Writings, edited by Lawrence S. Cunningham, Paulist Press (New York, NY), 1992.

Ways of the Christian Mystics, Shambhala (Boston, MA), 1994.

Run to the Mountain: The Story of a Vocation, edited by Patrick Hart, HarperSanFrancisco (San Francisco, CA), 1995.

Thoughts on the East, New Directions (New York, NY), 1995.

Dialogues with Silence: Prayers and Drawings, edited by Jonathan Montaldo, HarperSanFrancisco (San Francisco, CA), 2001.

Seeds, edited with an introduction by Robert Inchausti, Shambhala (Boston, MA), 2002.

When the Trees Say Nothing: Writings on Nature, edited by Kathleen Deignan, illustrated by John Giuliani, Sorin Books (Notre Dame, IN), 2003.

Seeking Paradise: The Spirit of the Shakers, edited and with an introduction by Paul M. Pearson, Orbis Books (Maryknoll, NJ), 2003.

(Author of introduction) Alfred Delp, S.J., *Prison Writings,* Orbis Books (Maryknoll, NY), 2004.

Also author of numerous shorter works and pamphlets, including *A Balanced Life of Prayer,* 1951, *Basic Principles of Monastic Spirituality,* 1957, *Prometheus: A Meditation,* 1958, *Nativity Kerygma,* 1958, *Monastic Vocation and the Background of Modern Secular Thought,* 1964, and *Notes on the Future of Monasticism,* 1968. Contributor to books, including *New Anthology of Modern Poetry,* edited by Selden Rodman, revised edition, Modern Library (New York, NY), 1946; *The Happy Crusaders,* compiled by James E. Tobin, McMullen (New York, NY), 1952; and *J. F. Powers,* compiled by Fallon Evans, Herder & Herder (New York, NY), 1968. Contributor of book reviews, articles, and poetry to *New York Herald Tribune, New York Times Book Review, Commonweal, Catholic World,* and *Catholic Worker.* Editor, *Monks Pond* (quarterly), 1968. The largest collection of Merton's manuscripts is held at the Thomas Merton Studies Center, Bellarmine College, Louisville, KY.

ADAPTATIONS: The Tower of Babel, condensed and adapted by Richard J. Walsh, was televised by National Broadcasting Corporation (NBC-TV), 1957.

SIDELIGHTS: A monk who lived in isolation for several years, and one of the most well-known Catholic writers of the twentieth century, Thomas Merton was a prolific poet, religious writer, and essayist whose diversity of work has rendered a precise definition of his life and an estimation of the significance of his career difficult. Merton was a Trappist, a member of a Roman Catholic brotherhood known for its austere lifestyle and vow of silence in which all conversation is forbidden. Merton's accomplishments as an author are even more remarkable considering that when he entered the Trappist monastery in Kentucky in 1941, monks were allowed to write only two half-page letters four times a year and nothing more. In *The Seven Mountains of Thomas Merton,* biographer Michael Mott called Merton a "poet, writer, activist, contemplative, . . . reformer of monastic life, artist, [and] bridge between Western and Eastern religious thought." Indeed, Merton is credited with introducing the mysticism of Eastern spirituality to Western Christians.

The Seven Storey Mountain, an autobiography Merton published in 1948 when he was only thirty-three years old, is probably the book for which he is best remembered. It was an instant success, and even before its publication caused considerable excitement for its publisher. Looking for recommendations to print on the book's jacket, Robert Giroux, Merton's editor, sent galley proofs to Evelyn Waugh, Graham Greene, and Clare Boothe Luce for their opinions. According to Mott, Waugh responded that *The Seven Storey Mountain* "may well prove to be of permanent interest in the history of religious experience." Greene wrote that the autobiography has "a pattern and meaning valid for all of us." And Clare Boothe Luce declared, "It is to a book like this that men will turn a hundred years from now to find out what went on in the heart of men in this cruel century." These enthusiastic replies led publisher Harcourt, Brace to increase the first printing order from five thousand to twenty thousand copies and to order a second printing before publication.

Reviewers' praise of *The Seven Storey Mountain* confirmed Harcourt's suspicions that the book would be well received and talked about. In *Catholic World,* F. X. Connolly noted that Merton's autobiography "is bracing in its realism, sincere, direct and challenging. . . . *The Seven Storey Mountain* is a prolonged prayer as well as a great book." Commenting in the *New York Herald Tribune Weekly Book Review,* George Shuster wrote: "The fervor of [Merton's]

progress to the monastery of Gethsemane is deeply moving. It is a difficult matter to write about, but I think there will be many who, however alien the experience may remain to them personally, will put the narrative down with wonder and respect." George Miles observed in a *Commonweal* review that "the book is written simply; the sensory images of boyhood are wonderful, and the incisive quality of his criticism, that tartness of his humor have not been sentimentalized by Merton's entry into a monastery. . . . *The Seven Storey Mountain* is a book that deeply impresses the mind and the heart for days. It fills one with love and hope."

Reviewers and readers were moved by the intriguing story of Merton's undisciplined youth, conversion to Catholicism, and subsequent entry into the Trappist monastery. "With publication of his autobiography," noted Kenneth L. Woodward in *Newsweek,* "Merton became a cult figure among pious Catholics." According to Edward Rice in his biography *The Man in the Sycamore Tree: The Good Times and Hard Life of Thomas Merton: An Entertainment,* the book "was forceful enough to cause a quiet revolution among American Catholics, and then among people of many beliefs throughout the world." A *Time* writer reported that "under its spell disillusioned veterans, students, even teenagers flocked to monasteries across the country either to stay or visit as retreatants." As Richard Kostelanetz observed in the *New York Times Book Review,* Merton's "example made credible an extreme religious option that would strike many as unthinkable."

Rice theorized that the success of *The Seven Storey Mountain* was not only due to interest in Merton's story but also to the way events in his life reflected the feelings of a society recovering from the shock of world war. Explained Rice: What sets *The Seven Storey Mountain* apart from other books like it was "its great evocation of a young man in an age when the soul of mankind had been laid open as never before during world depression and unrest and the rise of both Communism and Fascism. . . . It became a symbol and a guide to the plight of the contemporary world, touching Catholics and non-Catholics alike in their deep, alienated unconsciousness."

The popularity of Merton's book resulted in profits, and the money Merton earned was used at the Abbey of Gethsemane for much-needed improvements and expansion. As Rice noted, however, it also "catapulted Merton into the eyes of the world," making a celebrity of a man who wanted to live in solitude. Without the publication of this autobiography, Mott wrote, it is possible "that Thomas Merton might have achieved . . . obscurity and oblivion." But that was not to be; for the rest of his life Merton was to deal with the consequences of having written such a popular book.

In the *Dictionary of Literary Biography,* Victor A. Kramer commented on the contradictory aspects of Merton's life and work, observing that "Merton's dual career as a cloistered monk and prolific writer, a career of silence yet one which allowed him to speak to thousands of readers world wide, was a paradox." The significance of this contrasting need in Merton for both silence and fellowship with the people outside the monastery walls "was a source of anxiety to Merton himself," explained Ross Labrie in the *Dictionary of Literary Biography Yearbook: 1981.* But according to Labrie, "It is one of the strongest centers of excitement in approaching his work as well as being one of the clearest ways to see his role in twentieth-century letters." James Thomas Baker agreed that the dichotomy of monk/writer in Merton's personality is an essential ingredient in his writing. As Baker stated in his *Thomas Merton: Social Critic,* "There was . . . an oriental paradox about his life and thought, the paradox of a monk speaking to the world, which gave it the quality that was uniquely Merton, and any other career would have robbed his work of that quality."

Due to the abundant autobiographical material Merton produced—at his death, he left 800,000 words of unpublished writings, mainly journals and letters, as well as hundreds of taped talks—a great deal is known about how he dealt with the anxiety produced by his paradoxical desire to be both a contemplative and a social activist. Mott's research revealed that by 1940 Merton was actually keeping two sets of journals, private journals handwritten in bound notebooks and the edited, typewritten journals he showed to others. In the late 1990s many of these journals were edited, resulting in the seven-volume *Journals of Thomas Merton.* Volume six, *Learning to Love: Exploring Solitude and Freedom* caused a small stir when journal entries revealed what Merton labeled an "affair" with a young nurse in 1966. The woman, identified only as "M," was the object of Merton's deep passion: "I have never seen so much simple, spontaneous, total love,"

he wrote, although stopping short of describing their relationship in sexual terms. As the book's editor, Christine Bochen, suggested in a *Knight-Ridder/Tribune News Service* article, "This journal needs to read as a chapter in Merton's story, but not a dominant one."

Merton's love of writing started early in his life, as Israel Shenker noted in the *New York Times.* "He wrote his first book at the age of ten," wrote Shenker, "and followed it with ten more unpublished novels." (One of these early novels was published posthumously as *My Argument with the Gestapo: A Macaronic Journal.*) By 1939, while teaching university extension classes at night, Merton's writing occupied most of his days. That same year, according to Mott, Merton also "wrote the first poem that would continue to mean something to him." Although Merton had already written quite a few poems, he explained in *The Seven Storey Mountain,* "I had never been able to write verse before I became a Catholic [in 1938]. I had tried, but I had never really succeeded, and it was impossible to keep alive enough ambition to go on trying."

Merton became well known as a poet during his first years in the monastery. His first book of poetry, 1944's *Thirty Poems,* includes poems composed before and after entering the abbey. According to Baker, Merton believed "the poetry which he wrote at that time was the best of his career." The book received favorable reviews, Robert Lowell writing in *Commonweal* that Merton is "easily the most promising of our American Catholic poets."

Merton's next book of poetry included all the selections from his first book plus fifty-six more written during the same period. This book, *A Man in the Divided Sea,* was equally praised by critics. Calling it "brilliant" and "provocative," *Poetry* critic John Nerber commented, "It is, without doubt, one of the important books of the year." In the *New Yorker* Louise Bogan wrote that although Merton "has not yet developed a real synthesis between his poetic gifts and his religious ones . . . the possibility of his becoming a religious poet of stature is evident."

Despite the stature of his religious writings and essays, the literary value of Merton's poetry has always been questioned. Writing in *Commonweal,* William Henry Shannon argued that Merton's poetry, consisting of "over a thousand pages," contained "a fair amount of . . . mediocre or just plain bad" writing, "but one will also find fine poetry there." Addressing the religious content of Merton's work, Therese Lent-foehr, writing in her *Words and Silence: On the Poetry of Thomas Merton,* explained that "only about a third of the poems might be viewed as having specific religious themes." Many of the other poems were accessible to a larger audience because Merton enjoyed writing about children, the natural world, and the larger world outside the monastery. In the 1960s he also wrote poems about social issues of the day.

After his poetry writing in the 1940s, Merton ceased writing poems in such quantities again until the 1960s. With his appointment in 1951 as master of scholastics, many of his works—such as *The Living Bread, No Man Is an Island,* and *The Silent Life*—expanded on ideas expressed in the monastery classes he conducted for the young monks studying for the priesthood.

Several critics, including Kramer and Baker, noted a change in Merton's writing sometime between the end of the 1950s and the early 1960s. Whereas Merton previously appeared to advocate isolation from society as the answer to the question of how a Christian should respond to the unspirituality of the world, his writing began to suggest the need to deal with social injustice through social activism. Baker explained, "By the mid-1960s [Merton's] attitude toward the world had changed so dramatically that Merton-watchers were speaking of the 'early Merton' and the 'later Merton' to distinguish between his two careers, the one as a silent mystic who celebrated the virtues of monastic life in glowing prose and poetry, the other as a social commentator."

Kramer cited three books in particular that demonstrate "the significant changes in awareness" in Merton's writing. The first of these books, 1949's *Seeds of Contemplation,* is entirely spiritual in focus. *New Seeds of Contemplation,* published in 1961 as a revised version of the same book, reflects what Kramer called Merton's "greater concern for the problems of living in the world." The third book, 1964's *Seeds of Destruction,* is a collection of essays on world problems, including racism. According to Kramer, the changing themes illustrated in these three books reflect Merton's movement from solitary monk in a monastery cell to social activist. While unable to join the sit-ins and protest marches of the 1960s, Merton was able to express his support for such activities with his writing.

Mott explained the change in Merton's style by noting that at the end of the 1950s, "after sixteen years of isolation from social issues, Merton was beginning to feel cut off from what he needed to know." Since radios, televisions, and newspapers were forbidden in the monastery, only chance readings of magazines and books brought to the abbey by Merton's friends enabled him to keep up with world events. Belatedly, he learned about the suffering caused by the U.S. atomic bomb attacks on Japan and the horrors of Nazi concentration camps. He learned of social injustice in Latin America by reading Latin-American poets, including Nicaraguan Ernesto Cardenal, who spent some time at the Abbey of Gethsemane himself in the late 1950s. As Mott explained, Merton "was unsure of himself, certain only that the time had come to move from the role of bystander . . . to that of declared witness." The works *Original Child Bomb: Points for Meditation to Be Scratched on the Walls of a Cave* and "Chants to be Used in Processions around a Site with Furnaces" are products of his awakening social conscience.

Merton's increasing concern with racial injustice, the immorality of war—particularly of the Vietnam conflict—and the plight of the world's poor caused increasing conflict with the monastic censors at Gethsemane. When originally confronted with the manuscript version of *The Seven Storey Mountain,* for instance, the censors rejected it because of the numerous references to sex and drinking it contained. Although the debate over *The Seven Storey Mountain* was eventually resolved, monastic censors once again grew concerned about Merton's writings on war and peace. Frustrated, Merton circulated some of his work in mimeographed form that came to be known as the "Cold War Letters." In 1962, Merton was forbidden by his superiors to write about war, but was allowed to write about peace.

Despite censorship and isolation, Merton became, according to Kenneth L. Woodward in *Newsweek,* "a prophet to the peace movement [and] a conscience to the counterculture." At the height of the Vietnam War, he welcomed a Vietnamese Buddhist monk to speak at the abbey, met with peace activist Joan Baez, corresponded with Catholic priest Daniel Berrigan, and planned a retreat for Dr. Martin Luther King, Jr., that was halted by King's assassination. Controversial comedian Lenny Bruce often closed his nightclub act by reading from an essay Merton wrote about German

Nazi leader Adolf Eichmann in which Merton questions the sanity of the world.

Much of Merton's increased public profile was observed after he began living as a hermit in a cabin located in the woods on the monastery grounds. Just as his desire to be removed from the world became greatest, so did his need to speak out on social problems. In his writings, he attempted to explain this paradox as much to himself as to others.

In *Best Sellers,* Sister Joseph Marie Anderson wrote that in Merton's *Contemplation in a World of Action,* the monk stresses "that the contemplative is not exempt from the problem of the world nor is the monastic life an escape from reality." In a review of Merton's *The Climate of Monastic Prayer,* a *Times Literary Supplement* critic noted, "Merton came to see that the monk is not exempt from the agonies of the world outside his walls: he is involved at another level." The reviewer offered this quote from Merton's book: "The monk searches not only his own heart: he plunges deep into the heart of that world of which he remains a part although he seems to have 'left' it. In reality the monk abandons the world only in order to listen more intently to the deepest and most neglected voices that proceed from the inner depth." According to Lawrence S. Cunningham, writing in *Commonweal,* Merton saw the contemplative as someone who "should be able to communicate . . . from the deep center or *ground* which is God."

Along with social activism, Merton became increasingly interested in the study of other religions, particularly Zen Buddhism. His books *Mystics and Zen Masters* and *Zen and the Birds of Appetite* reflect his love for Eastern thought. In the *New York Times Book Review,* Nancy Wilson Ross wrote, "In *Mystics and Zen Masters* [the author] has made a vital, sensitive and timely contribution to the growing worldwide effort . . . to shed new light on mankind's common spiritual heritage." She added: "Merton's reasons for writing this [book] . . . might be summed up in a single quotation: 'If the West continues to underestimate and to neglect the spiritual heritage of the East, it may well hasten the tragedy that threatens man and his civilization.'" In the *New York Times Book Review,* Edward Rice explained further that "Merton's first notion was to pluck whatever 'Christian' gems he could out of the East that might fit into the Catholic theological structure. Later he abandoned this attempt and accepted Buddhism, Hinduism and Islam on their own equally valid terms . . . without compromising his own Christianity."

Merton died in 1968, while attending an ecumenical conference in Bangkok, Thailand, his first extended journey outside the monastery walls since his entry in 1941. Ironically, his death came twenty-seven years to the day from when he first became a member of the Gethsemane community, and was the result of an electrical shock from a faulty fan.

Merton's writings on peace, war, social injustice, and Eastern thought created controversy both inside and outside the abbey. As J. M. Cameron remarked in the *New York Review of Books,* "Merton will be remembered for two things: his place . . . in the thinking about the morality of war. . . ; and his partially successful attempt to bring out, through study and personal encounter, what is common to Asian and West monasticism and . . . contemplative life." Rice agreed with this observation, noting in *The Man in the Sycamore Tree,* "It [was] the later writings on war and peace, nonviolence, race, . . . and above all on Buddhism, that show Merton at his best and most creative."

A man of great personal charisma, Merton symbolized, for many Catholics, the search for meaning in life in the aftermath of a cataclysmic war, the shock waves of which had shattered many cultural and social traditions and uprooted long-held values. Decades after his death, his works and life found additional relevance among a new generation of Catholics and non-Catholics, and his writings on war and peace from the 1960s were echoed in the U.S. Catholic bishops' statement on nuclear war published in the 1980s. The trajectory of his life, reveals, Monica Furlong maintained in her *Merton: A Biography,* "much about the twentieth century and, in particular, the role of religion in it."

Merton "has been prolific even in death," according to *U.S. Catholic* reporter Jim Forest, citing the many publications containing his essays, prayers, letters, and articles that continue to be published more than three decades after his tragic death. The fiftieth-anniversary edition of *The Seven Storey Mountain* was published in 1999. Other works released posthumously include *Dialogues with Silence: Prayers and Drawings,* which *Library Journal*'s Graham Christian applauded as casting "new and thought-provoking light on his finely written prayers," and *The Inner Experience: Notes on Contemplation,* a revision of Merton's 1948 book *What Is Contemplation?* In *Library Journal* Stephen Joseph praised *The Inner Experience* as an argument to make "contemplation . . . central to all aspects of life rather than just one more compartment." While noting the "rough" quality of the book due to its being still unfinished at Merton's death, a *Publishers Weekly* reviewer nonetheless cited *The Inner Experience* for providing "vivid examples of Merton's ability to make monastic disciplines intelligible and plausible even to secular readers."

Merton as *Something of a Rebel* is implied in the title of a biography of the spiritualist by William Shannon. Shannon's subject "was a unique monk," he stated. "One would have to go all the way back to the [twelfth] century—to St. Bernard—to find a monk whose writings were as influential as Merton's have been." But Merton "belonged to his own age," Shannon wrote. "He wrote in his own time in history, yet so much of what he wrote seemed to reach beyond the culture of his own time. He was supracultural, yet not ahistorical. By that I mean he was alive to the historical circumstances in which he lived, yet not so hemmed in by cultural restraints that he could not break through them."

The Thomas Merton Studies Center at Bellarmine College in Louisville, Kentucky, contains over 10,000 items related to Merton and some 3,000 of his manuscripts. The Merton Legacy Trust, devoted to gathering all future Merton scholarship, is also located at Bellarmine. The International Thomas Merton Society was founded in 1987 and reports a membership of over fifteen thousand.

BIOGRAPHICAL AND CRITICAL SOURCES:

BOOKS

Baker, James Thomas, *Thomas Merton, social critic; a study,* University Press of Kentucky (Lexington, KY), 1971.

Cunningham, Lawrence, *Thomas Merton and the Monastic Vision,* Eerdmans (Grand Rapids, MI), 1999.

Dictionary of Literary Biography, Gale (Detroit, MI), Volume 48, 1986, *Yearbook: 1981,* 1982.

Encyclopedia of World Biography, 2nd edition, Gale (Detroit, MI), 1998.

Forest, Jim, *Living with Wisdom: A Life of Thomas Merton,* Orbis Books (Maryknoll, NY), 1991.

Furlong, Monica, *Merton : a biography,* Liguori Publications (Liguori, MO), 1995.

Grayston, Donald, *Thomas Merton: The Development of a Spiritual Theologian,* E. Mellen (New York, NY), 1985.

Higgins, Michael W., *Heretic Blood: The Spiritual Geography of Thomas Merton,* Stoddart (New York, NY), 1998.

Inchausti, Robert, *Thomas Merton's American Prophecy,* State University of New York Press (Albany, NY), 1998.

The Intimate Merton: His Life from His Journals, edited by Patrick Hart and Jonathan Montaldo, HarperSanFrancisco (San Francisco, CA), 1999.

Kountz, Peter, *Thomas Merton As Writer and Monk: A Cultural Study, 1915-1951,* Carlson (Brooklyn, NY), 1991.

Lentfoehr, Therese, *Words and silence : on the poetry of Thomas Merton,* New Directions Pub. Corp. (New York, NY), 1979.

McInerny, Dennis Q., *Thomas Merton: The Man and His Works,* Cistercian Publications (Kalamazoo, MI), 1974.

Modern American Literature, 5th edition, St. James Press (Detroit, MI), 1999.

Mott, Michael, *The seven mountains of Thomas Merton,* Harcourt Brace (San Diego, CA), 1993.

Nouwen, Henri J. M., *Thomas Merton, Contemplative Critic,* Triumph (New York, NY), 1991.

Pennington, M. Basil, *Thomas Merton, Brother Monk: The Quest for True Freedom,* Continuum (New York, NY), 1997.

Religious Leaders of America, 2nd edition, Gale (Detroit, MI), 1999.

Rice, Edward, *The Man in the Sycamore Tree: The Good Times and Hard Life of Thomas Merton: An Entertainment,* Doubleday (Garden City, NY), 1970.

Shannon, William Henry, *"Something of a Rebel": Thomas Merton, His Life and Works: An Introduction,* St. Anthony Messenger Press (Cincinnati, OH), 1997.

Woodcock, George, *Thomas Merton, Monk and Poet: A Critical Study,* Douglas & McIntyre (Vancouver, British Columbia, Canada), 1978.

PERIODICALS

AB Bookman's Weekly, November 16, 1992, pp. 1832-1846.

America, October 25, 1969; November 24, 1984; October 22, 1988, pp. 277, 280, 288, 290; November 12, 1988, p. 387; October 21, 1989, p. 267; November 18, 1989, p. 358; February 3, 1990, p. 76; October 6, 1990, p. 218; October 27, 1990, p. 309; January 1, 1994, p. 6; February 11, 1995, p. 26; November 4, 1995, p. 33; April 13, 1996, p. 28; February 1, 1997, Robert Coles, "Secular Days, Sacred Moments," p. 6; February 15, 1997, Emilie Griffin, "Turning toward Lent: The Journals of Thomas Merton," p. 30; November 22, 1997, William Shannon, "Thomas Merton: To Russia with Love," p. 16; William Short, review of *Turning toward the World: The Pivotal Years,* p. 26; December 6, 1997, James Eudes Bamberger, review of *Thomas Merton and James Laughlin: Selected Letters,* p. 24; February, 21, 1998, Emilie Griffin, review of *"Something of a Rebel": Thomas Merton, His Life and Works: An Introduction,* p. 22; May 23, 1998, review of *Dancing in the Water of Life: Seeking Peace in the Hermitage,* p. 31; October 3, 1998, review of *The Other Side of the Mountain: The End of the Journey, 1967-1968,* p. 28; July 4, 1998, Anna Brown, review of *Learning to Love: Exploring Solitude and Freedom,* p. 22; March 4, 2000, Richard Hauser, "Father Louis up Close," p. 23.

American Book Review, March, 1990, p. 16.

Atlantic, May, 1949.

Best Sellers, November 15, 1970; April 15, 1971; August 15, 1973.

Bloomsbury Review, July, 1989, p. 23.

Book, December, 1998, review of *The Seven Storey Mountain,* p. 72.

Booklist, May 1, 1985, p. 1220; March 15, 1989, p. 1222; May 1, 1995, p. 1533; February 1, 1997, review of *Striving towards Being: The Letters of Thomas Merton and Czeslaw Milosz,* p. 909; July, 1997, Steve Schroeder, review of *Dancing in the Water of Life,* p. 1778; July, 1998, Steve Schroeder, review of *The Other Side of the Mountain,* p. 1835.

Books and Culture, November, 2000, Timothy Jones, "The Uncensored Merton," p. 25; January, 2001, Mark Galli, "The Romance of the Cloister," p. 34.

Boston Globe, August 22, 1993, p. B14; December 7, 1993, p. 19.

Boston Review, February, 1985.

Catholic Historical Review, January 1997, review of *At Home in the World: The Letters of Thomas Merton and Rosemary Radford Ruether,* p. 171.

Catholic World, October, 1948; November, 1948; October, 1949; December, 1949, pp. 198-203; June,

1950; November, 1951; March, 1953; June, 1955; February, 1957; July, 1958; November, 1960; August, 1961; April, 1962; May-June, 1990, pp. 126, 133; May, 1994, p. 148.

Chicago Tribune, January 27, 1985; May 22, 1992, p. C9.

Choice, December, 1997, review of *Thomas Merton and James Laughlin,* p. 638; September, 2001, W. C. Buchanan, review of *When Prophecy Still Had a Voice: The Letters of Thomas Merton and Robert Lax,* p. 136.

Christian Century, March 9, 1988, p. 242; March 22, 1995, p. 330; May 22, 1996, p. 570; July 30, 1997, Donald Grayson, review of *Turning toward the World,* p. 702; November 21, 2001, review of *Dialogues with Silence: Prayers and Drawings,* p. 47.

Christianity and Literature, summer, 2003, p. 557.

Church History, March, 1999, review of *The Other Side of the Mountain,* p. 230; June, 2001.

Columbia Literary Columns, November, 1989, pp. 18-30.

Commentary, April, 1965, pp. 90, 92-94.

Commonweal, June 22, 1945, pp. 240-242; December 27, 1946; August 13, 1948; April 15, 1949; October 14, 1949; October 26, 1951; February 27, 1953; May 13, 1955, pp. 155-159; July 6, 1956; June 9, 1961; March 16, 1962; April 19, 1963; March 12, 1965; January 10, 1969; October 17, 1969; February 27, 1970; January 22, 1971; October 12, 1973; February 3, 1978; November 18, 1983, pp. 634-637; October 19, 1984; February 28, 1986, p. 118; December 2, 1988, pp. 649-652; April 19, 1991, p. 270; February 25, 1994, pp. 26-28; September 9, 1994, p. 18; September 12, 1997, review of *Journals of Thomas Merton* and *Striving towards Being,* p. 36; March 12, 1999, review of *The Seven Storey Mountain,* p. 28.

Contemporary Literature, winter, 1973.

Critic, April, 1963; February, 1966; January, 1970; May, 1971; February 15, 1981.

Cross Currents, spring, 1999, George Kilcourse, Jr., "Thomas Merton's Contemplative Struggle: Bridging the Abyss to Freedom," p. 87; winter, 1999, Shaul Magid, "Monastic Liberation As Counter-Cultural Critique in the Life and Thought of Thomas Merton," p. 445.

Detroit Free Press, February 11, 1969.

First Things, February, 1997, Robert Royal, "The Several-Storied Thomas Merton," p. 34.

Hudson Review, spring, 1970, pp. 187-188; summer, 1978.

Journal of Pastoral Counseling, 2000, Marc Ricciardi, "As a Seed in the Cosmos," p. 155.

Journal of Religion, July, 1998, Robert Webster, "Thomas Merton and the Textuality of the Self," p. 387; January, 2000, Lawrence Cunningham, review of *The Other Side of the Mountain,* p. 141.

Kentucky Review, summer, 1987, pp. 1-145.

Kirkus Reviews, April 15, 1997, review of *Dancing in the Water of Life,* p. 619; May 15, 1998, review of *The Other Side of the Mountain,* p. 718.

Knight-Ridder/Tribune News Service, October 15, 1997, Art Jester, "Journal Relates 'Affair' of Famous Trappist Monk and Author Thomas Merton," p. 1015; December, 9, 1998, Art Jester, "Thirty Years after His Death, Noted Monk Thomas Merton Is Remembered," p. K4163.

Library Journal, June 1, 1997, Mark Woodhouse, review of *Dancing in the Water of Life,* p. 104; July, 1997, Mark Woodhouse, review of *Thomas Merton and James Laughlin,* p. 88; September 1, 1998, review of *The Seven Storey Mountain,* p. 224; October 15, 1999, Augustine Curley, review of *The Intimate Merton,* p. 76; January 1, 2001, Carolyn Craft, review of *When Prophecy Still Had a Voice,* p. 114; October 1, 2001, Graham Christian, review of *Dialogues with Silence,* p. 108; July, 2003, Stephen Joseph, review of *The Inner Experience: Notes on Contemplation and Prayer,* p. 87.

Los Angeles Times Book Review, December 14, 1980; December 30, 1984; October 13, 1985.

Motive, October, 1967.

Nation, November 6, 1948.

National Catholic Reporter, January 29, 1988, p. 7; July 14, 1989, p. 2; September 22, 1989, p. 17; April 12, 1991, p. 24; December 10, 1993, pp. 22-23; March 8, 1996, p. 14; May 9, 1997, William Graham, review of *The Springs of Contemplation: A Retreat at the Abbey of Gethsemane,* p. 14.

National Review, May 31, 1985, p. 42; December 5, 1994, p. 80; October 10, 2003, Peter Feuerherd, review of *The Inner Experience,* p. 4.

Negro Digest, December, 1967.

New Leader, March 24, 1997, Phoebe Pettingell, review of *Striving towards Being,* p. 13.

New Republic, October 4, 1948; September 12, 1949.

Newsweek, December 10, 1984.

New Yorker, October 5, 1946; October 9, 1948; October 8, 1949.

New York Herald Tribune Weekly Book Review, October 24, 1948.

New York Review of Books, February 11, 1965; April 10, 1969; September 27, 1979.

New York Times, March 18, 1945; October 3, 1948; March 20, 1949; September 18, 1949; March 26, 1950; September 23, 1951; February 8, 1953; March 27, 1955; March 11, 1956; July 10, 1969; December 10, 1984; December 20, 1984.

New York Times Book Review, October 3, 1948, pp. 4, 33; February 8, 1953, pp. 1, 30; February 14, 1965; April 17, 1966; July 2, 1967; March 30, 1969; March 15, 1970; March 14, 1971; July 8, 1973; February 5, 1978, p. 20; May 23, 1982, p. 15; December 23, 1984; September 17, 1989, p. 25; February 12, 1995, p. 22.

Our Sunday Visitor, January 25, 1987.

Parabola, February, 1991, p. 124.

Philosophy East and West, January, 1998, Frank Hoffman, review of *The Golden Age of Zen,* p. 165.

Poetry, February, 1945; December, 1946; October, 1948; July, 1950.

Publishers Weekly, December 7, 1984; April 14, 1997, review of *Dancing in the Water of Life,* p. 69; November 24, 1997, review of *Learning to Love,* p. 68; May 11, 1998, review of *The Other Side of the Mountain,* p. 65; September 28, 1998, review of *The Seven Storey Mountain,* p. 94; November 30, 1998, review of *Thoughts in Solitude,* p. 66; January 25, 1999, review of *Contemplation in a World of Action,* p. 89; October 1, 2001, review of *Dialogues with Silence,* p. 57; May 26, 2003, review of *The Inner Experience,* p. 65.

Renascence, winter, 1974; spring, 1978.

Saturday Review of Literature, October 9, 1948; April 16, 1949; September 17, 1949; February 11, 1950.

Sewanee Review, summer, 1969; winter, 1973; autumn, 1973.

Sojourners, January-February, 2002, review of *Dialogues with Silence,* p. 51.

Theology Today, April, 1999, Gary Commins, "Thomas Merton's Three Epiphanies," p. 59.

Thought, September, 1974.

Time, January 24, 1968; December 31, 1984.

Times Literary Supplement, December 23, 1949; May 22, 1959; February 12, 1970; May 5, 1972; August 14 1998, review of *Learning to Love* and *Dancing in the Water of Life,* p. 31.

U.S. Catholic, January, 1993, p. 20; December, 1993, p. 20; June, 1994, p. 33; April, 2000, Jim Forest, "Within Merton Within," p. 22.

Utne Reader, July-August, 2001, Craig Cox, "Passion Play," p. 98.

Virginia Quarterly Review, summer, 1968.

Wall Street Journal, June 4, 1985, p. 30.

Washington Post, September 4, 1969.

Washington Post Book World, December 16, 1984; June 30, 1985; March 30, 1997, review of *Striving towards Being,* p. 13; April 27, 1997, review of *Striving towards Being,* p. 13; December, 7, 1997, review of *The Seven Storey Mountain,* p. 8; December 27, 1998, Paul Hendrickson, "One of Us," p. F1.

Wilson Quarterly, summer, 1998, review of *Striving towards Being,* p. 107.

World Literature Today, spring, 1989, p. 311; summer, 1990, p. 469; autumn, 1997, Jerzy Maciuszko, review of *Striving towards Being,* p. 883.

ONLINE

American Catholic Online, http://americancatholic.org/ (September, 1997), William Shannon, "Thomas Merton: Something of a Rebel."

Thomas Merton Center Web site, http://www.merton. org/ (April 25, 2004).

Thomas Merton Page, http://edge.net/˜dphillip/Merton. html (February 25, 2002).

OBITUARIES:

PERIODICALS

Antiquarian Bookman, December 23-30, 1968.
Books Abroad, spring, 1969.
Detroit Free Press, December 11, 1968.
Newsweek, December 23, 1968.
New York Times, December 11, 1968.
Publishers Weekly, December 30, 1968.
Time, December 20, 1968.
Times (London), December 12, 1968.
Washington Post, December 12, 1968.*

*   *   *

MITTON, Tony 1951-

PERSONAL: Full name, Anthony Robert Mitton; born January 10, 1951, in Tripoli, Libya; son of Stanley (a social worker and former soldier) and Vera Eileen (Locke) Mitton; married Elizabeth Anne McKellar (a lecturer), January 19, 1991; children: Doris, Guthrie. *Education:* Cambridge University, B.A. (with honors),

Tony Mitton

1973. *Politics:* "Usually vote Labour." *Religion:* "Zen Buddhist influence." *Hobbies and other interests:* Poetry, story, song, folk culture, walking, baking, cookery, art, music.

ADDRESSES: Home—41 Sturton St., Cambridge CB1 2QG, England. *Agent*—Caroline Walsh, David Higham Associates, 5-8 Lower John St., Golden Sq., London W1R 4HA, England. *E-mail*—tonymitton@btinternet. com.

CAREER: Primary schoolteacher in Cambs Lea, England, 1975-85; special needs teacher, beginning 1986; currently freelance writer and poet.

MEMBER: Society of Authors.

AWARDS, HONORS: Nottinghamshire Children's Book Award, 1997, for *Royal Raps;* Silver Medal, Smarties Prize, age 6-8 category, 2000, and Best Toy Award, both for *The Red and White Spotted Handkerchief;* Experian Big Three Book Award, for *Robin Hood Raps.*

WRITINGS:

FOR CHILDREN

Nobody Laughed, Collins Educational (London, England), 1994.

(Reteller) *Three Tales from Scotland,* illustrated by Joe Rice, Collins Educational (London, England), 1995.

Mr. Marvel and the Cake, illustrated by Mandy Doyle, Heinemann Educational (Oxford, England), 1996.

Mr. Marvel and the Car, illustrated by Mandy Doyle, Heinemann Educational (Oxford, England), 1996.

Mr. Marvel and the Lemonade, illustrated by Mandy Doyle, Heinemann Educational (Oxford, England), 1996.

Mr. Marvel and the Washing, illustrated by Mandy Doyle, Heinemann Educational (Oxford, England), 1996.

Big Bad Raps, illustrated by Martin Chatterton, Orchard Books (London, England), 1996.

(Reteller) *The Three Billy Goats,* illustrated by Jenny Williams, Heinemann Educational (Oxford, England), 1996.

Playtime with Rosie Rabbit, illustrated by Patrick Yee, Simon & Schuster (New York, NY), 1996.

Bedtime for Rosie Rabbit, illustrated by Patrick Yee, Simon & Schuster (New York, NY), 1996.

Royal Raps, illustrated by Martin Chatterton, Orchard (London, England), 1996.

Dazzling Diggers (also see below), illustrated by Ant Parker, Kingfisher (New York, NY), 1997.

Rosie Rabbit's Birthday Party, illustrated by Patrick Yee, Simon & Schuster (New York, NY), 1997.

Rosie Rabbit Goes to Preschool, illustrated by Patrick Yee, Simon & Schuster (New York, NY), 1997.

Roaring Rockets (also see below), illustrated by Ant Parker, Kingfisher (New York, NY), 1997.

Monster Raps, illustrated by Martin Chatterton, Orchard (London, England), 1998.

Fangtastic Raps, illustrated by Martin Chatterton, Orchard (London, England), 1998.

Where's My Egg? A Flip-the-Flap Book, illustrated by Jane Chapman, Walker (New York, NY), 1998, 2nd edition, Candlewick Press (Cambridge, MA), 1999.

Spooky Hoo Hah!, illustrated by Oliver Postgate, Walker (New York, NY), 1998.

Flashing Fire Engines (also see below), illustrated by Ant Parker, Kingfisher (New York, NY), 1998.

The Magic Pot, illustrated by Mandy Doyle, Oxford University Press (New York, NY), 1998.

Plum (poetry), illustrated by Peter Bailey, Scholastic (New York, NY), 1998.

A Door to Secrets: Riddles in Rhyme, illustrated by David Parkins, Cambridge University Press (Cambridge, England), 1998.

The Seal Hunter, illustrated by Nick Malland, Hippo (London, England), 1998.

Terrific Trains (also see below), illustrated by Ant Parker, Kingfisher (New York, NY), 1998.

There's No Such Thing! A Flip-Flap Book, illustrated by Daniel Postgate, Candlewick Press (Cambridge, MA), 1999.

The Red and White Spotted Hankerchief, 2000.

Amazing Airplanes, illustrated by Ant Parker, Kingfisher (New York, NY), 2002.

Busy Boats, illustrated by Ant Parker, Kingfisher (New York, NY), 2002.

Down by the Cool of the Pool, illustrated by Guy Parker-Rees, Orchard Books (New York, NY), 2002.

Dinosaurumpus!, illustrated by Guy Parker-Rees, Orchard Books (New York, NY), 2003.

Amazing Machines (contains *Dazzling Diggers, Roaring Rockets, Flashing Fire Engines,* and *Terrific Trains*), illustrated by Ant Parker, Kingfisher (New York, NY), 2003.

Goodnight Me, Goodnight You, illustrated by Mandy Sutcliffe, Little, Brown (New York, NY), 2003.

Plum, illustrated by Mary GrandPré, Arthur A. Levine Books (New York, NY), 2003.

Riddledy Piggledy, illustrated by Paddy Mounter, David Fickling Books (New York, NY), 2004.

Spooky Hour (published in England as *Spookyrumpus*), illustrated by Guy Parker-Rees, Orchard Books (New York, NY), 2004.

The Tale of Tales, illustrated by Peter Bailey, David Fickling Books (New York, NY), 2004.

WORK IN PROGRESS: Various poetry, verse, and picture book projects; educational texts.

SIDELIGHTS: Tony Mitton once commented: "I was born in 1951 in North Africa, the son of a soldier. Until I was nine we lived mostly in Africa, Germany, and Hong Kong, so I didn't really get to know Britain until I was nearly ten. Most of my life I have worked as a primary school teacher. But for the last twelve years, I have only taught for half of the time. At first, I was busy being a parent for the other half of the time, when my children were very young. But now that they are a bit older and go to school, I spend at least two days a week working at my writing. I write poems and stories for school reading books and also for books you buy in the bookshops. I especially like writing in verse, using rhythm and rhyme. I also very much enjoy planning picture books and writing the words for them. But I need other people to do the pictures. I would like to learn to be an illustrator too, but I like working on the words so much that I don't think I'd make the time to practice. I think as time passes I may start to write more and teach less, if my writing keeps on doing well. But I like going in to school and I think I keep in touch with what a lot of children like by working with them. So for now it seems a good idea to keep on doing both jobs part-time.

"I live in a small house in the middle of Cambridge with my wife and two children, who are nine and thirteen as I write [this]. We also have a sweet cat called Tiggy. I like the town and many of the people, for it's the only place I've ever stayed for a long time. But my wife and I often wish we'd settled somewhere where there are better places for walking, like cliffs and hills with good views of the landscape.

"I honestly think that what I most like doing is writing poems, and working with words in verse. I love fiddling about until I've got it just right (though sometimes I can't). I've always loved reading poems and stories, though these days I find it harder to get proper time for reading, as I'm often busy writing. It's especially hard to find time to read longer books, like novels, so I have to choose carefully to find books that are really worth the time I give to them. I have a great interest in folk and fairy tales and legends, and when I was younger (in my teens) I used to spend a lot of time learning and singing folk and blues songs which I accompanied on the guitar. I think I learned a lot about verse and poetry from doing this, even though writing songs is not quite the same as writing poems.

"I'm not often stuck for ideas with my writing. More often I'm waiting to get the time to get on with something I want to write. Sometimes I get up very early in the morning and do one or two hours' writing while most other people are asleep. That's a very good time for me, as my mind's very fresh and clear and no one comes to interrupt. Sometimes, if I have a very good or strong idea, say for a poem, I get a bit frightened to

start on it, in case it doesn't turn out well. What I do then is just start writing things down and keep going at it, even if it doesn't go well to start with. That usually works.

"What else do I like doing? Cooking, baking cakes, social meals, and family life. As a family, we talk a great deal about all sorts of things. I love reading to my children and talking to my wife, who knows a lot about books, art, history, and lots more. If I had time to spare I'd like to be in a folk band and play traditional British and Irish folk music.

"When I was about nine, and rather miserable and lonely in a strict little boarding school, I stumbled on a novel during the enforced half-hour of reading after lunch. It was called *Prester John* and was by John Buchan. This is the first novel that I can remember reading for pleasure. It really gripped me. I remember the bereavement of finishing it and being unable to find anything that matched it for me then in power and style. I recently had a similar experience (thirty-seven years later) when I read the first two parts of Philip Pullman's 'His Dark Materials' trilogy (*Northern Lights* and *The Subtle Knife*). I'm now waiting for part three to come out, but I don't think Philip Pullman has finished writing it yet.

"My reading of poetry was galvanized by my brother putting a typed copy of a poem by W. B. Yeats up on our bedroom cupboard door. I must have been about thirteen at the time, and he would have been fifteen. The poem was, I believe, the much celebrated 'Lake Isle of Inisfree.' I liked it so much that I got hold of a copy of the Macmillan *Collected Poems of W. B. Yeats.* For a long time my favorite poem was 'The Song of Wandering Aengus.' I still love Yeats's lyric writing, and writing this paragraph has prompted me to get my copy down and dip into it again after a long gap."

Recently Mitton added: "Since writing the above piece about myself, I have become a full-time writer, and my children are both teenagers. The latest big excitement for me is starting to be published more prominently in the United States as a children's poet and picture book writer."

BIOGRAPHICAL AND CRITICAL SOURCES:

PERIODICALS

Booklist, January 1, 2003, Gillian Engberg, review of *Dinosaurumpus!,* p. 908; May 15, 2003, Grace-

Anne A. DeCandido, review of *Plum,* p. 1659; October 15, 2003, Jennifer Mattson, review of *Goodnight Me, Goodnight You,* p. 420.

Instructor, October, 2002, Liza Charlesworth, "Imagination Stretching," p. 37.

Junior Bookshelf, October, 1994, p. 166.

Kirkus Reviews, May 1, 2002, review of *Down by the Cool of the Pool,* p. 662; March 1, 2003, review of *Dinosaurumpus!,* p. 393; February 1, 2004, review of *The Tale of Tales,* p. 136.

Publishers Weekly, April 15, 2002, review of *Down by the Cool of the Pool,* p. 62; September 16, 2002, review of *Amazing Airplanes,* p. 71; January 6, 2003, review of *Dinosaurumpus!,* p. 57; February 17, 2003, review of *Plum,* p. 75; July 14, 2003, review of *Amazing Machines,* p. 78.

School Library Journal, May, 1997, pp. 108-109; July, 2002, Elaine Lesh Morgan, review of *Down by the Cool of the Pool,* p. 96; March, 2003, Dona Ratterree, review of *Dinosaurumpus!,* p. 200; May, 2003, Grace Oliff, review of *Plum,* p. 140; February, 2004, review of *Goodnight Me, Goodnight You,* p. 118.

N

NERUDA, Pablo 1904-1973

PERSONAL: Born Ricardo Eliezer Neftali Reyes y Basoalto, July 12, 1904, in Parral, Chile; name legally changed, 1946; died of heart failure during surgery, September 23, 1973, in Santiago, Chile; son of Jose del Carmen Reyes Morales (a railroad worker) and Rosa de Basoalto (a schoolteacher); married Maruca Hagenaar Vogelzang, 1930 (marriage ended); married Matilde Urrutia, 1951; children (first marriage): Malva Marina. *Education:* Attended Instituto Pedagogico (Santiago, Chile), c. early 1920s, and University of Chile, 1926. *Politics:* Communist. *Hobbies and other interests:* Sailing.

CAREER: Writer. Chilean consul to Rangoon, Burma, 1927, Colombo, Ceylon, 1929, and Batavia, Java, 1930, consul to Buenos Aires, Siam, Cambodia, Anam, and Madrid, early 1930s, and Mexico, 1941-44; elected to Chilean senate as Communist, 1945; self-exiled in Mexico, 1948-53; nominated for president on Chilean Communist Party ticket, 1970; Chilean ambassador to France, 1971-72. Founder and editor (with Manuel Altolaguirre) of *El Caballo verde para la poesía* (poetry periodical), 1935-36, and *Aurora de Chile,* 1938. Member of World Peace Council, 1950-73.

MEMBER: Union de Escritores Chilenos (president, 1959-73), Modern Language Association of America (honorary fellow), International PEN.

AWARDS, HONORS: Third prize, Juegos Florales competition, 1919, for "Communion ideal"; first prize for poetry, Instituto Pedagogico Students' Federation spring festival, 1921, for *La Canción de la fiesta;* honorary doctorate, University of Michoacan (Mexico), 1941; Premio Municipal de Literatura (Chile), 1944; Premio Nacional de Literatura (Chile), 1945; International Peace Prize, 1950; Lenin and Stalin Peace Prize, 1953; Litt.D., Oxford University, 1965; awarded Czechoslovakia's highest decoration, 1966; Nobel Prize in literature, 1971.

WRITINGS:

La Canción de la fiesta (poetry), Federacion de Estudiantes de Chile (Santiago, Chile), 1921.

Crepusculario (poetry), Nascimento (Santiago, Chile), 1923, 4th edition, Losada (Buenos Aires, Argentina), 1971.

Veinte poemas de amor y una canción desesperada, Nascimento (Santiago, Chile), 1924, definitive edition, 1932, 16th edition, Losada (Buenos Aires, Aregentina), 1972, translation by W. S. Merwin published as *Twenty Love Poems and a Song of Despair,* J. Cape (London, England), 1969, reprinted, Penguin (New York, NY), 2004.

El Habitante y su esperanza (prose; also see below), Nascimento (Santiago, Chile), 1925, 2nd edition, Ercilla (Santiago, Chile), 1939.

(With Tomas Lago) *Anillos* (prose poems; also see below), Nascimento (Santiago, Chile), 1926.

Tentativa del hombre infinito (poem; also see below), Nascimento (Santiago, Chile), 1926, new edition, Orbe (Santiago, Chile), 1964.

Prosas de Pablo Neruda (prose), Nascimento (Santiago, Chile), 1926.

El Hondero entusiasta, 1923-1924 (poetry; also see below), Ercilla (Santiago, Chile), 1933, 3rd edition, 1938.

Residencia en la tierra (poetry and prose), Arbol (Madrid, Spain), Volume I (1925-31), 1933, Volume II (1931-35), 1935, published in one volume, Losada (Buenos Aires, Argentina), 1944, 3rd edition, 1969, portions translated by Angel Flores as *Selected Poems,* privately printed, 1944, Volumes I and II translated by Flores as *Residence on Earth and Other Poems,* New Directions (New York, NY), 1946, revised edition, translated by Donald D. Walsh, 2004.

Poesías de Yillamediana presentadas por Pablo Neruda, Cruz y Raya (Madrid, Spain), 1935.

Homenaje a Pablo Neruda de los poetas españoles: Tres cantos materiales (poetry), Plutarco (Madrid, Spain), 1935, translation by Angel Flores published as *Tres cantos materiales: Three Material Songs,* East River Editions (New York, NY), 1948.

Sonetos de la muerte de Quevedo, presentados por Pablo Neruda, Cruz y Raya (Madrid, Spain), 1935.

España en el corazon: Himno a las glorias del pueblo en la guerra (poetry; first printed by Spanish Republican soldiers on the battlefront; also see below), Ercilla (Santiago, Chile), 1937, 2nd edition, 1938, translation by Richard Schaaf published as *Spain in the Heart: Hymn to the Glories of the People at War,* Azul Editions (Paris, France), 1993.

Las Furias y las penas (poetry), Nascimento (Santiago, Chile), 1939.

(With Emilio Oribe and Juan Marinello) *Neruda entre nosotros* (prose), A.I.A.P.E. (Montevideo, Uruguay), 1939.

Homenaje a García Lorca (prose), A.I.A.P.E. (Montevideo, Uruguay), 1939.

Chile os acoge (prose), [Paris, France], 1939.

Un Canto para Bolivar (poetry), Universidad Nacional Autonoma de México (Mexico City, Mexico), 1941.

(Contributor of poetry) *Presencia de García Lorca,* Darro (Mexico), 1943.

Nuevo canto de amor a Stalingrado (poem), Comité de ayuda a Rusia en guerra (Mexico), 1943.

Canto général de Chile (poem), privately printed, 1943, portions published as *El Mal y el malo,* P. Alcantara y V. Amaya (Peterborough, NH), 1974.

Cantos de Pablo Neruda (poetry), Hora del Hombre (Lima, Peru), 1943.

Cantico, La Gran Colombia (Bogota, Colombia), 1943.

Pablo Neruda: Sus mejores versos, La Grand Colombia (Bogota, Colombia), 1943.

Saludo al norte y Stalingrado, privately printed, 1945.

Carta a México, Fondo de Cultura Popular (Mexico City, Mexico), 1947.

Tercera residencia, 1935-1945 (poetry; includes *España en el corazon*), Losada (Buenos Aires, Argentina), 1947, 5th edition, 1971.

Viajes al corazon de Quevedo y por las costas del mundo (prose), Sociedad de Escritores de Chile (Santiago, Chile), 1947.

28 de Enero, Partido Comunista de Chile (Chile), 1947.

Los Heroes de carcon encarnan los ideales de democracia e independencia nacional, El Tranviario (Santiago, Chile), 1947.

La Verdad sobre las ruputuras (prose), Principios (Santiago, Chile), 1947.

La Crisis democratica de Chile, Hora del Hombre (Lima, Peru), 1947, translation published as *The Democratic Crisis of Chile,* Committee for Friendship in the Americas (New York, NY), 1948.

Dura elegia, Cruz del Sur (Santiago, Chile), 1948.

Himno y regreso, Cruz del Sur (Santiago, Chile), 1948.

Que despierte el leñador! (poetry), Coleccion Yagruma (Havanna, Cuba), 1948, translation published as *Peace for Twilights to Come!,* Jayant Bhatt for People's Publishing House (Bombay, India), 1950.

Alturas de Macchu-Picchu (poetry), Libreria Neira (Santiago, Chile), 1948, definitive edition, Nascimento (Santiago, Chile), 1954, translation by Nathaniel Tarn published as *The Heights of Macchu Picchu,* J. Cape (London, England), 1966, Farrar, Straus (New York, NY), 1967.

Coral de año nuevo para mi patria en tinieblas, privately printed, 1948.

Pablo Neruda acusa, Pueblos Unidos (Montevideo, Uruguay), 1948.

Y ha llegado el monento en que debemos elegir, privately printed, 1949.

Gonzalez Videla, el laval de America Latina: Breve biografia de un traidor, Fondo de Cultura Popular (Buenos Aires, Argentina), 1949.

Dulce patria, Pacifico (Santiago, Chile), 1949.

Neruda en Guatemala (prose), Saker-Ti (Guatemala), 1950.

Patria prisionera, Hora del Hombre (Lima, Peru), 1951.

A la memoria de Ricardo Fonseca, Amistad (Santiago, Chile), 1951.

Cuando de Chile, Austral (Santiago, Chile), 1952.

Poemas, Fundamentos (Buenos Aires, Argentina), 1952.

Los Versos del capitán: Poemas de amor (anonymously published until 3rd edition, 1963), privately printed (Naples, Italy), 1952, 7th edition, Losada (Buenos Aires, Argentina), 1972, translation by Donald D. Walsh published as *The Captain's Verses,* New Directions (New York, NY), 1972, reprinted, 2004.

Todo el amor (poetry), Nascimento (Santiago, Chile), 1953.

En su muerte, Partido Comunista Argentino (Buenos Aires, Argentina), 1953.

Poesía politica: Discursos politicos, two volumes, Austral (Santiago, Chile), 1953.

Las Uvas y el viento (poetry), Nascimento (Santiago, Chile), 1954.

Odas elementales (first volume of "Elementary Odes"; also see below), Losada (Buenos Aires, Argentina), 1954, 3rd edition, 1970.

Discurso inauguracion fundación Pablo Neruda, Universidad de Chile (Santiago, Chile), 1954.

Alli murio la muerte, Centro de Amigos de Polonia (Santiago, Chile), 1954.

Regreso la sirena (poetry), Centro de Amigos de Polonia, 1954.

Viaies (prose), Nascimento (Santiago, Chile), 1955.

Nuevas odas elementales (second volume of "Elementary Odes"; also see below), Losada (Buenos Aires, Argentina), 1956, 3rd edition, 1971.

Oda a la tipografía (poetry), Nascimento (Santiago, Chile), 1956.

Dos odas elementales, Losada (Buenos Aires, Argentina), 1957.

Estravagario (poetry), Losada (Buenos Aires, Argentina), 1958, 3rd edition, 1971, translation by Alastair Reid published as *Extravagaria,* J. Cape (London, England), 1972, Farrar, Straus (New York, NY), 1974.

Tercer libro de las odas (third volume of "Elementary Odes"), Losada (Buenos Aires, Argentina), 1959.

Algunas odas (poetry), Edicion del 55 (Santiago, Chile), 1959.

Cien sonetos de amor (poetry), Losada (Buenos Aires, Argentina), 1959, 6th edition, 1971, translation by Stephen J. Tapscott published as *One Hundred Love Sonnets,* University of Texas Press (Austin, TX), 1986.

Odas: Al libro, a las Americas, a la luz (poetry), Homenaje de la Asociacion de Escritores Venezolanos (Caracas, Venezuela), 1959.

Todo lleva tu nombre (poetry), Ministerio de Educacion (Caracas, Venezuela), 1959.

Navegaciones y regresos (poetry), Losada (Buenos Aires, Argentina), 1959.

(With Federico García Lorca) *Discurso al Alimon sobre Ruben Dario,* Semana Dariana (Nicaragua), 1959.

(With Pablo Picasso) *Toros: 15 lavis inedits,* Au Vent d'Arles (Paris, France), 1960.

Canción de gesta (poetry), Imprenta Nacional de Cuba (Havana, Cuba), 1960, 3rd edition, Siglo (Montevideo, Uruguay), 1968.

Oceana (poem), La Tertulia (Havana, Cuba), 1960, 2nd edition, 1962.

Los Primeros versos de amor (poetry), Austral (Santiago, Chile), 1961.

Las Piedras de Chile (poetry), Losada (Buenos Aires, Argentina), 1961, translation by Dennis Maloney published as *The Stones of Chile,* White Pine (Buffalo, NY), 1987.

Primer dia de la Sebastiana, privately printed, 1961.

Cantos ceremoniales (poetry), Losada (Buenos Aires, Argentina), 1961, 2nd edition 1972, published as *Ceremonial Songs,* Latin American Literary Review (Pittsburgh, PA), 1996.

Plenos poderes (poetry), Losada (Buenos Aires, Argentina), 1962, 2nd edition, 1971, translation by Alastair Reid published as *Fully Empowered: Plenos poderes,* Farrar, Straus (New York, NY), 1975, reprinted, New Directions (New York, NY), 1995.

(With Mario Toral) *Poema con grabado* (poetry), Isla Negra (Santiago, Chile), 1962.

La Insepulta de Paita (poetry), Losada (Buenos Aires, Argentina), 1962.

Con los catolicos hacía la paz, [Santiago, Chile], 1962, published as *Cuba: Los Obispos,* Paz y Soberania (Lima, Peru), 1962.

(With Nicanor Parra) *Discursos* (prose), Nascimento (Santiago, Chile), 1962.

Mensaje de paz y unidad, Internacionalismo proletario, [and] *El poeta de la revolucion* (addresses), Esclarecimiento (Lima, Peru), 1963.

(With Gustavo Hernan and Guillermo Atias) *Presencia de Ramon Lopez Yelarde en Chile,* Universitaria (Santiago, Chile), 1963.

Memorial de Isla Negra (poetry), Volume 1: *Donde nace la lluvia,* Volume 2: *La Luna en el laberinto,* Volume 3: *El Fuego cruél,* Volume 4: *El Cazador de raices,* Volume 5: *Sonata critica,* Losada (Buenos Aires, Argentina), 1964, translation by Alastair Reid published as *Isla Negra: A Notebook,* bilingual edition, Farrar, Straus (New York, NY), 1980.

Arte de párjaros, Sociedad de Amigos del Arte Contemporaneo (Santiago, Chile), 1966, translation by Jack Schmitt published as *The Art of Birds,* University of Texas Press (Austin, TX), 1985.

Una Casa en la arena (poetry and prose), Lumen (Barcelona, Spain), 1966, 2nd edition, 1969.

La Barcarola (poem), Losada (Buenos Aires, Argentina), 1967.

Fulgor y muerte de Joaquin Murieta: Bandido chileno injusticiado en California el 23 de julio de 1853 (play), Zig-Zag (Santiago, Chile), 1967, translation by Ben Belitt published as *Splendor and Death of Joaquin Murieta,* Farrar, Straus (New York, NY), 1972.

(With Miguel Angel Asturias) *Comiendo en Hungria* (poetry and prose), Lumen (Barcelona, Spain), 1968.

Las Manos del dia (poetry), Losada (Buenos Aires, Argentina), 1968, 2nd edition, 1970.

Aún: Poema, Nascimento (Santiago, Chile), 1969.

Fin de mundo (poem), Losada (Buenos Aires, Argentina), 1969.

La Copa de sangre (poetry and prose), privately printed, 1969.

La Espada encendida, Losada (Buenos Aires, Argentina), 1970, 2nd edition, 1972.

Las Piedras del cielo, Losada (Buenos Aires, Argentina), 1970, translation by James Nolan published as *Stones of the Sky,* Copper Canyon Press (Port Townsend, WA), 1987.

Discurso pronunciado con occasion de la entrega del premio Nobel de literatura, 1971, Centre de recherches hispaniques (Paris, France), 1972, translation published as *Toward the Splendid City: Nobel Lecture,* Farrar, Straus (New York, NY), 1974.

Cantos de amor y de combate (poetry), Austral (Santiago, Chile), 1971.

Geografia infructuosa (poetry), Losada (Buenos Aires, Argentina), 1972.

Cuatros poemas escritos en Francia, Nascimento (Santiago, Chile), 1972.

Libro de las odas, Losada (Buenos Aires, Argentina), 1972.

El Mar y las campanas: Poemas, Losada (Buenos Aires, Argentina), 1973, translation by William O'Daly published as *The Sea and the Bells,* Copper Canyon Press (Port Townsend, WA), 1988.

La Rosa separada (poetry), Losada (Buenos Aires, Argentina), 1973, translation by William O'Daly as *A Separate Rose,* Copper Canyon Press (Port Townsend, WA), 1985.

El Corazon amarillo (poetry), Losada (Buenos Aires, Argentina), 1974, translation by William O'Daly published as *The Yellow Heart,* Copper Canyon Press (Port Townsend, WA), 1990.

Elegia (poetry), Losada (Buenos Aires, Argentina), 1974, published as *Elegia: Obra postuma,* Seix Barral (Barcelona, Spain), 1976.

Incitacion al Nixonicidio y alabanza de la revolucion chilena (poetry), Grijalbo (Barcelona, Spain), 1974, translation by Steve Kowit published as *Incitement to Nixonicide and Praise for the Chilean Revolution,* Quixote (Houston, TX), 1974, 2nd edition, 1980.

Defectos escogidos (poetry), Losada (Buenos Aires, Argentina), 1974.

Oda a la lagartija (poem), P. R. Martorell (Camp Rico de Canovanas, Puerto Rico), 1974.

Jardin de invierno, Losada (Buenos Aires, Argentina), 1974, published as *Jardin de invierno: Obras postuma,* Seix Barral (Barcelona, Spain), 1977, translation by William O'Daly published as *Winter Garden,* Copper Canyon Press (Port Townsend, WA), 1986.

Libro de las preguntas, Losada (Buenos Aires, Argentina), 1974, translation by William O'Daly published as *The Book of Questions,* Copper Canyon Press (Port Townsend, WA), 1991.

Cartas de amor de Pablo Neruda (correspondence), compiled by Sergio Lorrain, Rodas (Madrid, Spain), 1974.

Confieso que he vivido: Memorias, Seix Barral (Barcelona, Spain), 1974, translation by Hardie St. Martin published as *Memoirs,* Farrar, Straus (New York, NY), 1977.

OMNIBUS VOLUMES

Seleccion (poetry), compiled by Arturo Aldunate, Nascimento (Santiago, Chile), 1943.

Coleccion residencia en la tierra: Obra poética, ten volumes, Cruz del Sur (Santiago, Chile), 1947-1948.

Canto général (poetry), Comite Auspiciador (Mexico), 1950, 5th edition in two volumes, Losada (Buenos Aires, Argentina), 1971.

Poesías completas, Losada (Buenos Aires, Argentina), 1951.

Los Versos mas populares (poetry), Austral (Santiago, Chile), 1954.

Los Mejores versos de Pablo Neruda (poetry), [Buenos Aires], 1956.

Obras completas, Losada (Buenos Aires, Argentina), 1957, 3rd edition published in two volumes, 1968.

El Habitante y su esperanza, El hondero entusiasta, Tentativa del hombre infinito, [and] *Anillos,* Losada (Buenos Aires, Argentina), 1957, 4th edition, 1971.

Antología, Nascimento (Santiago, Chile), 1957, 4th enlarged edition, 1970.

The Selected Poems of Pablo Neruda, edited and translated by Ben Belitt, Grove (New York, NY), 1961.

Poesías, selected by Roberto Retamar, Casa de las Americas (Havana, Cuba), 1965.

Antología esencial, selected by Hernan Loyola, Losada (Buenos Aires, Argentina), 1971.

Poemas immortales, selected by Jaime Concha, Quimantu (Santiago, Chile), 1971.

Obras escogidas (poetry), selected by Francisco Coloane, A. Bello (Santiago, Chile), 1972.

Antología popular 1972, [Santiago, Chile], 1972.

Pablo Neruda (includes poems, Nobel prize acceptance speech, interview, and chronologies), Noroeste (Buenos Aires, Argentina), 1973.

Poesía, two volumes, Noguer (Barcelona, Spain), 1974.

Neruda's Garden: An Anthology of Odes, Latin American Literary Review (Pittsburgh, PA), 1995.

Full Woman, Fleshly Apple, Hot Moon: Selected Poems of Pablo Neruda, translated by Stephen Mitchell, Harper (New York, NY), 1997.

The Essential Neruda: Selected Poems, edited by Mark Eisner, translation by Forrest Gander, City Light Books (San Francisco, CA), 2004.

OTHER ENGLISH TRANSLATIONS

Let the Splitter Awake and Other Poems (selected from *Que despierte el leñador!,* and *Canto général;* also see below), translated by Waldeen, Masses & Mainstream (New York, NY), 1950, reprinted, International Publishing (New York, NY, 1989, portions published as *Let the Rail-Splitter Awake,* 1951.

Twenty Love Poems: A Disdaining Song, translated by W. S. Merwin, Grossman (New York, NY), 1961.

Elementary Odes, translated by Carlos Lozano, G. Massa (New York, NY), 1961.

Bestiary/Bestiario: A Poem, translated by Elsa Neuberger, Harcourt (New York, NY), 1965.

Nocturnal Collection: A Poem, translated by Angel Flores, [Madison, WI], 1966.

We Are Many (poem), translated by Alastair Reid, Cape Goliard Press, 1967, Grossman (New York, NY), 1968.

Twenty Poems (selected from *Residencia en la tierra, Canto général,* and *Odas elementales*), translated by James Wright and Robert Bly, Sixties Press (Madison, WI), 1967.

Ben Belitt, editor, *A New Decade: Poems, 1958-1967,* translated by Belitt and Alastair Reid, Grove (New York, NY), 1969.

Pablo Neruda: The Early Poems, translated by David Ossman and Carlos B. Hagen, New Rivers Press (New York, NY), 1969.

Nathaniel Tarn, editor, *Selected Poems,* translated by Anthony Kerrigan and others, J. Cape (London, England), 1970, Delacorte (New York, NY), 1972.

New Poems, 1968-1970, edited and translated by Ben Belitt, Grove (New York, NY), 1972.

Residence on Earth (includes *Residencia en la tierra,* Volumes I and II, and *Tercera residencia*), translated by Donald D. Walsh, New Directions (New York, NY), 1973.

Five Decades: A Selection (Poems 1925-1970), edited and translated by Ben Belitt, Grove (New York, NY), 1974.

Passions and Impressions, translated by Margaret Sayers Peden, Farrar, Straus (New York, NY), 1982.

Windows That Open Inward: Images of Chile, translated by Alastair Reid and others, White Pine (Buffalo, NY), 1984.

Still Another Day, translated by William O'Daly, Copper Canyon Press (Port Townsend, WA), 1984.

The House at Isla Negra, translated by Dennis Maloney and Clark Zlotchew, White Pine (Buffalo, NY), 1988.

Late and Posthumous Poems, 1968-1974, edited and translated by Ben Belitt, Grove (New York, NY), 1989.

Selected Odes of Pablo Neruda, translated by Margaret Sayers Peden, University of California Press (Berkeley, CA), 1990.

2000, translated by Schaaf, Azul Editions (Paris, France), 1993.

Seaquake-Maremoto, translated by Dennis Maloney and Maria Giacchetti, White Pine (Buffalo, NY), 1993.

Pablo Neruda: An Anthology of Odes, edited by Yvette E. Miller, translated by Maria Giacchetti, Latin American Literary Review Press (Pittsburgh, PA), 1994.

Ferris Cook, editor, *Odes to Common Things,* translated by Ken Krabbenhoft, Little, Brown (Boston, MA), 1994.

Ferris Cook, editor, *Odes to Opposites,* translated by Ken Krabbenhoft, Little, Brown (Boston, MA), 1995.

En el corazón de un poeta (selección), introduction and notes by Esteban Llorach Ramos, Gente Nueva (Havana, Cuba), 1999.

Prólogos, Sudamericana (Santiago, Chile), 2000.

Oda a las flores de Datitla, (reproductions of pages of leaves and wildflowers, pressed and arranged by Matilde Neruda with handwritten verses by author), Sintesys (Santiago, Chile), c. 2002.

The Poetry of Pablo Neruda, edited and with an introduction by Ilan Stavans, Farrar, Straus (New York, NY), 2003.

On the Blue Shore of Silence : Poems of the Sea/ A la orilla azul del silencio, translations by Alastair Reid, paintings by Mary Heebner, Rayo (New York, NY), 2004.

OTHER

(Translator into Spanish) William Blake, *Visiones de las hijas de Albion y el viajero mental,* Cruz y Raya (Madrid, Spain), 1935.

(Translator into Spanish) William Shakespeare, *Romeo y Julieta,* Losada (Buenos Aires, Argentina), 1964.

(Translator into Spanish) *Cuarenta y cuatro* (Rumanian poetry), Losada (Buenos Aires, Argentina), 1967.

Pablo Neruda and Nicanor Parra Face to Face (speeches), E. Mellen Press (Lewsiton, NY), 1997.

Neruda at Isla Negra (prose poems), translations by Dennis Maloney and Clark M. Zlotchew, photographs by Milton Rogovin, foreword by Marjorie Agosin, afterword by Ariel Dorfman, White Pines Press (Freedonia, NY), 1998.

Pablo Neruda en Breve (poems), prologue by Nelson Osorio T., Universidad de Santiago (Santiago, Chile), 2001.

Also author of *Cartas de amor,* edited by Sergio Larrain, 1974; *Cartas a Laura,* edited by Hugo Montes, 1978; *Para nacer he nacido,* 1980; (with Hector Eandi) *Correspondancia,* edited by Margarita Aguirre, 1980; and *Poemas,* Horizonte. Also editor and translator of *Paginas escogidas de Anatole France,* 1924. Work represented in anthologies, including *Anthology of Contemporary Latin American Poetry,* edited by Dudley Fitts, New Directions (New York, NY), 1942; and *Modern European Poetry,* edited by Willis Barnstone, Bantam (New York, NY), 1966. Contributor to books, including *Neruda and Vallejo: Selected Poems,* compiled by Robert Bly, translated by Bly and others, Beacon Press (Boston, MA), 1971; *For Neruda, for Chile: An International Anthology,* edited by Walter Lowenfels, Beacon Press, 1975; *Three Spanish American Poets: Pellicer, Neruda, Andrade,* edited by Lloyd

Mallan, translated by Mary Wicker, Gordon Press (New York, NY), 1977; and *Macchu Picchu,* photographs by Barry Brukoff, translated by Stephen Kessler, prologue by Isabel Allende, Little, Brown (Boston, MA), 2001. Contributor of poems and articles to periodicals, including *Selva austral, Poetry, Nation, Commonweal, Canadian Forum,* and *California Quarterly.*

ADAPTATIONS: Some of Neruda's work has been recorded, including "Pablo Neruda Reads His Poems in Spanish," Spoken Arts, 1972; Rafael de Penagos reading "Poesías escogidas," Discos Aguilar, 1972; and *Loretta Pauker Reads Extended Excerpts of "Let the Rail Splitter Awake" [and] "The Dead in the Square,"* Khalan Records, 1973. Christopher Logue's *The Man Who Told His Love,* Middle Scorpion Press, 1958, is based on Neruda's poetry; Neruda's *Residencia en la tierra* was to music by Rudolph Holzmann as *Tres madrigales para canto y piano,* Argentina de Musica, 1946.

SIDELIGHTS: "No writer of world renown is perhaps so little known to North Americans as Chilean poet Pablo Neruda," observed *New York Times Book Review* critic Selden Rodman. Numerous critics have praised Neruda as the greatest poet writing in the Spanish language during his lifetime, although many readers in the United States have found it difficult to disassociate Neruda's poetry from his fervent commitment to communism. An added difficulty lies in the fact that Neruda's poetry is very hard to translate; his works available in English represent only a small portion of his total output. Nonetheless, declared John Leonard in the *New York Times,* Neruda "was, I think, one of the great ones, a Whitman of the South."

Born Ricardo Eliezer Neftali Reyes y Basoalto, Neruda adopted the pseudonym under which he would become famous while still in his early teens. He grew up in Temuco in the backwoods of southern Chile. Neruda's literary development received assistance from unexpected sources. Among his teachers "was the poet Gabriela Mistral, who would be a Nobel laureate years before Neruda," reported Manuel Duran and Margery Safir in *Earth Tones: The Poetry of Pablo Neruda.* "It is almost inconceivable that two such gifted poets should find each other in such an unlikely spot. Mistral recognized the young Neftali's talent and encouraged it by giving the boy books and the support he lacked at home."

By the time he finished high school, Neruda had published in local papers and Santiago magazines, and had won several literary competitions. In 1921 he left southern Chile for Santiago to attend school, with the intention of becoming a French teacher but was an indifferent student. While in Santiago, Neruda completed one of his most critically acclaimed and original works, the cycle of love poems titled *Veinte poemas de amor y una canción desesperada*—published in English translation as *Twenty Love Poems and a Song of Despair.* This work quickly marked Neruda as an important Chilean poet.

Veinte poemas also brought the author notoriety due to its explicit celebration of sexuality, and, as Robert Clemens remarked in the *Saturday Review,* "established him at the outset as a frank, sensuous spokesman for love." While other Latin American poets of the time used sexually explicit imagery, Neruda was the first to win popular acceptance for his presentation. Mixing memories of his love affairs with memories of the wilderness of southern Chile, he creates a poetic sequence that not only describes a physical liaison, but also evokes the sense of displacement that Neruda felt in leaving the wilderness for the city. "Traditionally," stated Rene de Costa in *The Poetry of Pablo Neruda,* "love poetry has equated woman with nature. Neruda took this established mode of comparison and raised it to a cosmic level, making woman into a veritable force of the universe."

"In *Veinte poemas,*" reported David P. Gallagher in *Modern Latin American Literature,* "Neruda journeys across the sea symbolically in search of an ideal port. In 1927, he embarked on a real journey, when he sailed from Buenos Aires for Lisbon, ultimately bound for Rangoon where he had been appointed honorary Chilean consul." Duran and Safir explained that "Chile had a long tradition, like most Latin American countries, of sending her poets abroad as consuls or even, when they became famous, as ambassadors." The poet was not really qualified for such a post and was unprepared for the squalor, poverty, and loneliness to which the position would expose him. "Neruda travelled extensively in the Far East over the next few years," Gallagher continued, "and it was during this period that he wrote his first really splendid book of poems, *Residencia en la tierra,* a book ultimately published in two parts, in 1933 and 1935." Neruda added a third part, *Tercera residencia,* in 1947.

Residencia en la tierra, published in English as *Residence on Earth,* is widely celebrated as containing "some of Neruda's most extraordinary and powerful poetry," according to de Costa. Born of the poet's feelings of alienation, the work reflects a world which is largely chaotic and senseless, and which—in the first two volumes—offers no hope of understanding. De Costa quoted Spanish poet García Lorca as calling Neruda "a poet closer to death than to philosophy, closer to pain than to insight, closer to blood than to ink. A poet filled with mysterious voices that fortunately he himself does not know how to decipher." With its emphasis on despair and the lack of adequate answers to mankind's problems, *Residencia en la tierra* in some ways foreshadowed the post-World War II philosophy of existentialism. "Neruda himself came to regard it very harshly," wrote Michael Wood in the *New York Review of Books.* "It helped people to die rather than to live, he said, and if he had the proper authority to do so he would ban it, and make sure it was never reprinted."

Residencia en la tierra also marked Neruda's emergence as an important international poet. By the time the second volume of the collection was published in 1935 the poet was serving as consul in Spain, where "for the first time," reported Duran and Safir, "he tasted international recognition, at the heart of the Spanish language and tradition. At the same time . . . poets like Rafael Alberti and Miguel Hernandez, who had become closely involved in radical politics and the Communist movement, helped politicize Neruda." When the Spanish Civil War broke out in 1936, Neruda was among the first to espouse the Republican cause with the poem *España en el corazon*—a gesture that cost him his consular post. He later served in France and Mexico, where his politics caused less anxiety.

Communism rescued Neruda from the despair he expressed in the first parts of *Residencia en la tierra,* and led to a change in his approach to poetry. He came to believe "that the work of art and the statement of thought—when these are responsible human actions, rooted in human need—are inseparable from historical and political context," reported Salvatore Bizzarro in *Pablo Neruda: All Poets the Poet.* "He argued that there are books which are important at a certain moment in history, but once these books have resolved the problems they deal with they carry in them their own oblivion. Neruda felt that the belief that one could write solely for eternity was romantic posturing." This new attitude led the poet in new directions; for many years his work, both poetry and prose, advocated an active role in social change rather than simply describing his feelings, as his earlier oeuvre had done.

This significant shift in Neruda's poetry is recognizable in *Tercera residencia,* the third and final part of the "Residencia" series. Florence L. Yudin noted in *Hispania* that the poetry of this volume was overlooked when published and remains neglected due to its overt ideological content. "Viewed as a whole," Yudin wrote, "*Tercera residencia* illustrates a fluid coherence of innovation with retrospective, creativity with continuity, that would characterize Neruda's entire career." According to de Costa, as quoted by Yudin, "The new posture assumed is that of a radical nonconformist. *Terra residencia* must, therefore, be considered in this light, from the dual perspective of art and society, poetry and politics."

"Las Furias y las penas," the longest poem of *Tercera residencia,* embodies the influence of both the Spanish Civil War and the works of Spanish Baroque poet Francisco Gomez de Quevedo y Villegas on Neruda. The poem explores the psychic agony of lost love and its accompanying guilt and suffering, conjured in the imagery of savage eroticism, alienation, and loss of self-identity. Neruda's message, according to Yudin, is that "what makes up life's narrative ('cuento') are single, unconnected events, governed by chance, and meaningless ('suceden'). Man is out of control, like someone hallucinating one-night stands in sordid places." Yudin concluded that, "Despite its failed dialectic, 'Las Furias y las penas' sustains a haunting beauty in meaning and tone" and "bears the unmistakable signature of Neruda's originality and achievement."

While some critics have felt that Neruda's devotion to Communist dogma was at times extreme, others recognize the important impact his politics had on his poetry. Clayton Eshleman wrote in the introduction to Cesar Vallejo's *Poemas humanos/ Human Poems* that "Neruda found in the third book of *Residencia* the key to becoming *the* twentieth-century South American poet: the revolutionary stance which always changes with the tides of time." Gordon Brotherton, in *Latin American Poetry: Origins and Presence,* expanded on this idea by noting that "Neruda, so prolific, can be lax, a 'great bad poet' (to use the phrase Juan Ramon Jimenez used to revenge himself on Neruda). And his change of stance 'with the tides of time' may not always be perfectly effected. But . . . his dramatic and

rhetorical skills, better his ability to speak out of his circumstances, . . . was consummate. In his best poetry (of which there is much) he speaks on a scale and with an agility unrivaled in Latin America."

Neruda expanded on his political views in the poem *Canto géneral,* which, according to de Costa, is a "lengthy epic on man's struggle for justice in the New World." Although Neruda had begun the poem as early as 1935—when he had intended it to be limited in scope only to Chile—he completed some of the work while serving in the Chilean senate as a representative of the Communist Party. However, party leaders recognized that the poet needed time to work on his opus, and granted him a leave of absence in 1947. Later that year, however, Neruda returned to political activism, writing letters in support of striking workers and criticizing Chilean President Videla. Early in 1948 the Chilean Supreme Court issued an order for his arrest, and Neruda finished the *Canto géneral* while hiding from Videla's forces.

"*Canto géneral* is the flowering of Neruda's new political stance," Don Bogen asserted in the *Nation.* "For Neruda food and other pleasures are our birthright—not as gifts from the earth or heaven but as the products of human labor." According to Bogen, *Canto géneral* draws its "strength from a commitment to nameless workers—the men of the salt mines, the builders of Macchu Picchu—and the fundamental value of their labor. This is all very Old Left, of course." Commenting on *Canto géneral* in *Books Abroad,* Jaime Alazraki remarked, "Neruda is not merely chronicling historical events. The poet is always present throughout the book not only because he describes those events, interpreting them according to a definite outlook on history, but also because the epic of the continent intertwines with his own epic."

Although, as Bizzarro noted, "In [the *Canto géneral*], Neruda was to reflect some of the [Communist] party's basic ideological tenets," the work itself transcends propaganda. Looking back into American prehistory, the poet examined the land's rich natural heritage and described the long defeat of the native Americans by the Europeans. Instead of rehashing Marxist dogma, however, he concentrated on elements of people's lives common to all people at all times. Nancy Willard wrote in *Testimony of the Invisible Man,* "Neruda makes it clear that our most intense experience of impermanence is not death but our own isolation among the living. . . . If Neruda is intolerant of despair, it is because he wants nothing to sully man's residence on earth."

"In the *Canto,*" explained Duran and Safir, "Neruda reached his peak as a public poet. He produced an ideological work that largely transcended contemporary events and became an epic of an entire continent and its people." According to Alazraki, "By bringing together his own odyssey and the drama of the continent, Neruda has simultaneously given to *Canto général* the quality of a lyric and an epic poem. The lives of conquistadors, martyrs, heroes, and just plain people recover a refreshing actuality because they become part of the poet's fate, and conversely, the life of the poet gains new depth because in his search one recognizes the continent's struggles. *Canto général* is, thus, the song of a continent as much as it is Neruda's own song."

Neruda returned to Chile from exile in 1953, and, said Duran and Safir, spent the last twenty years of his life producing "some of the finest love poetry in *One Hundred Love Sonnets* and parts of *Extravagaria* and *La Barcarola;* he produced Nature poetry that continued the movement toward close examination, almost still shots of every aspect of the external world, in the odes of *Navegaciones y regresos,* in *The Stones of Chile,* in *The Art of Birds,* in *Una Casa en la arena* and in *Stones of the Sky.* He continued as well his role as public poet in *Canción de geste,* in parts of *Cantos ceremoniales,* in the mythical *La Espada encendida,* and the angry *Incitement to Nixonicide and Praise for the Chilean Revolution.*"

At this time, Neruda's work began to move away from the highly political stance it had taken during the 1930s. Instead of concentrating on politicizing the common folk, Neruda began to try to speak to them simply and clearly, on a level that each could understand. He wrote poems on subjects ranging from rain to feet. By examining common, ordinary, everyday things very closely, according to Duran and Safir, Neruda gives us "time to examine a particular plant, a stone, a flower, a bird, an aspect of modern life, at leisure. We look at the object, handle it, turn it around, all the sides are examined with love, care, attention. This is, in many ways, Neruda . . . at his best."

In 1971 Neruda reached the peak of his political career when the Chilean Communist party nominated him for president. He withdrew his nomination, however, when he reached an accord with Socialist nominee Salvador Allende. After Allende won the election he reactivated Neruda's diplomatic credentials, appointing the poet ambassador to France. It was while Neruda was serving in Paris that he was awarded the Nobel Prize for literature, in recognition of his oeuvre. Poor health soon forced the poet to resign his post, however, and he returned to Chile, where he died in 1973—only days after a right-wing military coup killed Allende and seized power. Many of his last poems, some published posthumously, indicate his awareness of his death's approach. As Fernando Alegría wrote in *Modern Poetry Studies,* "What I want to emphasize is something very simple: Neruda was, above all, a love poet and, more than anyone, an unwavering, powerful, joyous, conqueror of death."

Commenting on *Passions and Impressions,* a posthumous collection of Neruda's prose poems, political and literary essays, lectures, and newspaper articles, Mark Abley wrote in *Maclean's,* "No matter what occasion provoked these pieces, his rich, tireless voice echoes with inimitable force." As Neruda eschewed literary criticism, many critics found in him a lack of rationalism. According to Neruda, "It was through metaphor, not rational analysis and argument, that the mysteries of the world could be revealed," remarked Stephen Dobyns in the *Washington Post.* However, Dobyns noted that *Passions and Impressions* "shows Neruda both at his most metaphorical and his most rational. . . . What one comes to realize from these prose pieces is how conscious and astute were Neruda's esthetic choices. In retrospect at least his rejection of the path of the maestro, the critic, the rationalist was carefully calculated." In his speech upon receiving the Nobel Prize, Neruda noted that "there arises an insight which the poet must learn through other people. There is no insurmountable solitude. All paths lead to the same goal: to convey to others what we are."

In 2003, thirty years after Neruda's death, an anthology of 600 of Neruda's poems arranged chronologically was published as *The Poetry of Pablo Neruda.* The anthology draws from thirty-six different translators, and some of his major works are also presented in their original Spanish. Writing in the *New Leader,* Phoebe Pettingell pointed out that, although some works were left out because of the difficulty in presenting them properly in English, "an overwhelming body of Neruda's output is here . . . and the collection certainly presents a remarkable array of subjects and styles." Reflecting on the life and work of Neruda in the *New Yorker,* Mark Strand commented, "There is something about Neruda—about the way he glorifies experience, about the spontaneity and directness of his passion—that sets him apart from other poets. It is hard not to be swept away by the urgency of his language, and that's especially so when he seems swept away."

BIOGRAPHICAL AND CRITICAL SOURCES:

BOOKS

Benson, Rachel, translator, *Nine Latin American Poets,* Las Americas, 1968.

Bizzarro, Salvatore, *Pablo Neruda: All Poets the Poet,* Scarecrow Press (Metuchen, NJ), 1979.

Bloom, Harold, editor, *Pablo Neruda,* Chelsea House (New York, NY), 1989.

Brotherton, Gordon, *Latin American Poetry: Origins and Presence,* Cambridge University Press (Cambridge, NY), 1975.

Burnshaw, Stanley, editor, *The Poem Itself,* Holt (New York, NY), 1960.

Contemporary Literary Criticism, Gale (Detroit, MI), Volume 1, 1973, Volume 2, 1974, Volume 5, 1976, Volume 7, 1977, Volume 9, 1978, Volume 28, 1984.

de Costa, Rene, *The Poetry of Pablo Neruda,* Harvard University Press (Cambridge, MA), 1979.

Duran, Manuel, and Margery Safir, *Earth Tones: The Poetry of Pablo Neruda,* Indiana University Press (Bloomington, IN), 1981.

Gallagher, David P., *Modern Latin American Literature,* Oxford University Press (Oxford, England), 1973.

García Lorca, Federico, *Obras completas,* Aguilar, 1964.

Neruda, Pablo, *Confieso que he vivado: Memorias,* Seix Barral (Barcelona, Spain), 1974, translation by Hardie St. Martin published as *Memoirs,* Farrar, Straus (New York, NY), 1977.

Neruda, Pablo, *Poemas humanos/ Human Poems,* translated by Clayton Eschelman, Grove (New York, NY), 1969.

Reiss, Frank, *The Word and the Stone: Language and Imagery in Neruda's "Canto général,"* Oxford University Press (Oxford, England), 1972.

Santi, Enrico-Mario, *Pablo Neruda: The Poetics of Prophecy,* Cornell University Press (Ithaca, NY), 1982.

Willard, Nancy, *Testimony of the Invisible Man: William Carlos Williams, Francis Ponge, Rainer Maria Rilke, Pablo Neruda,* University of Missouri Press (Columbia, MO), 1970.

PERIODICALS

Americas, March-April, 1991; September-October, 1991; September-October, 1992; July-August, 1995, p. 60.

Booklist, July, 2003, review of *The Poetry of Pablo Neruda,* p. 1858.

Books, June, 1966.

Books Abroad, winter, 1972, p. 49.

Book Week, May 28, 1967.

Encounter, September, 1965.

English Journal, September, 1987.

Evergreen Review, December, 1966.

Forum for Modern Language Studies, January, 1988.

Hispania, March, 1985, p. 55.

International Wildlife, May-June, 1987.

Library Journal, June 1, 2003, Jack Shreve, review of *The Poetry of Pablo Neruda,* p. 126.

Maclean's, February 7, 1983, p. 50.

Modern Poetry Studies, spring, 1974.

Nation, July 1, 1966; January 27, 1992, p. 95.

New Leader, July 3, 1967; July-August, 2003, Phoebe Pettingell, review of *The Poetry of Pablo Neruda,* p. 29.

New Statesman, June 4, 1965.

New Yorker, September 8, 2003, Mark Strand, "The Ecstasist," p. 091.

New York Review of Books, October 3, 1974; March 21, 1996, p. 16.

New York Times, June 18, 1966; August 1, 1966; March 4, 1977.

New York Times Book Review, July 10, 1966; May 21, 1967.

Poetry, June, 1947; February, 1963; October, 1967; June, 1968.

Publishers Weekly, October 23, 1995, p. 65.

Ramparts, September, 1974.

Saturday Review, July 9, 1966; November 13, 1971.

Washington Post, February 27, 1983, p. 4.

ONLINE

Nobel e-Museum, http://www.nobel.se/ (April 12, 2004), Pablo Neruda, "Towards the Splendid City" (Nobel Lecture, December 13, 1971).*

NORMAN, Marsha 1947-

PERSONAL: Born September 21, 1947, in Louisville, KY; daughter of Billie Lee (an insurance salesperson and realtor) and Bertha Mae (Conley) Williams; married Michael Norman (an English teacher; divorced, 1974); married Dann C. Byck, Jr. (a theatrical producer), November, 1978 (divorced); married Timothy Dykman; children: (third marriage) Angus, Katherine. *Education:* Agnes Scott College, B.A., 1969; University of Louisville, M.A.T., 1971.

ADDRESSES: Office—c/o The Tantleff Office, 375 Greenwich St., Suite 700, New York, NY 10013-2338.

CAREER: Playwright and producer. Teacher, Kentucky Department of Health, 1969-70, Jefferson County Public Schools, 1970-72, and Kentucky Arts Commission, 1972-76; book reviewer and editor for the *Louisville Times,* Louisville, KY, 1974-79; worked with disturbed children at Kentucky Central State Hospital; director at Actors Theatre of Louisville, 1980-81.

MEMBER: International PEN, Dramatists Guild, Writers Guild.

AWARDS, HONORS: American Theater Critics Association named *Getting Out* the best play produced in regional theatre during 1977-78; National Endowment for the Arts grant, 1978-79, for Actors Theatre of Louisville; John Gassner New Playwrights Medallion, Outer Critics Circle, and George Oppenheimer-*Newsday* Award, both 1979, both for *Getting Out;* Rockefeller playwright-in-residence grant, 1979-80, at the Mark Taper Forum; Susan Smith Blackburn Prize, Antoinette Perry (Tony) Award nomination for best play, Pulitzer Prize for drama, Columbia University Graduate School of Journalism, and Elizabeth Hull-Kate Warriner Award, Dramatists Guild, all 1983, all for *'Night, Mother;* Literary Lion Award, New York Public Library, 1986; Antoinette Perry (Tony) Award for best book of a musical, Antoinette Perry (Tony) Award nomination for best original score, 1991, and Drama Desk Award for best book of a musical, all 1991, all for *The Secret Garden;* also received grant from American Academy and Institute for Arts and Letters.

WRITINGS:

PLAYS

Getting Out, (two-act; first produced at Actors Theatre of Louisville, Louisville, KY, 1977; produced Off-

Marsha Norman

Broadway at Phoenix Theatre, 1978), Avon (New York, NY), 1977.

Third and Oak (contains the one-act plays *The Laundromat* and *The Pool Hall;* produced at Actors Theatre of Louisville, 1978), Dramatists Play Service (New York, NY), 1978, reissued in separate volumes as *Third and Oak: The Laundromat,* 1980, and *Third and Oak: The Pool Hall,* 1985.

It's the Willingness (teleplay), broadcast by Public Broadcasting Service (PBS), 1978.

Circus Valentine (two-act), produced at Actors Theatre of Louisville, 1979.

The Holdup (two-act; produced at Actors Theatre of Louisville, 1980), Dramatists Play Service (New York, NY), 1987.

In Trouble at Fifteen (teleplay), broadcast on NBC television program *Skag,* Lorimar Productions, 1980.

'Night, Mother (also see below; produced at American Repertory Theatre, Cambridge, MA; produced at Golden Theatre, New York, NY, 1983), Hill & Wang (New York, NY), 1982.

Traveler in the Dark (produced at the Mark Taper Forum, 1984), Dramatists Play Service (New York, NY), 1988.

The Laundromat (teleplay), produced for HBO, 1985.

Sarah and Abraham, produced at Actors Theater of Louisville, 1987.

Four Plays by Marsha Norman (collection), Theatre Communications (New York, NY), 1988.

(Author of book and lyrics) *The Secret Garden* (children's musical; produced by Virginia Stage Company, Norfolk, 1989), Warner Brothers (Secaucus, NJ), 1991.

Third and Oak: The Pool Hall (teleplay), produced on *American Playwrights Theatre: The One Acts,* Arts and Entertainment, 1989.

Face of a Stranger (teleplay; also known as *My Shadow*), CBS, 1991.

D. Boone (also see below), produced at Actors Theatre of Louisville, 1992, later retitled *Loving Daniel Boone.*

(Author of book and lyrics) *The Red Shoes,* produced at the Gershwin Theater, New York, NY, 1993.

Lunch with Lynn, produced at the Ensemble Studio Theatre, New York, NY, 1994.

Trudy Blue (produced at the Actors Theatre of Louisville, March, 1995; produced at MCC Theater, New York, NY, December 2, 1999), published in *Humana Festival '95: The Complete Plays,* Smith & Kraus (Newbury, VT), 1995.

Collected Plays (includes "Loving Daniel Boone," "Sarah and Abraham," "Getting Out," "Third and Oak," "Travelers in the Dark," "Circus Valentine," and "The Hold Up"), Smith & Kraus (Lyme, NH), 1997.

140, produced as part of *Love's Fire,* Guthrie Theater Lab, Minneapolis, MN, January 1, 1998; produced in London at the Barbican Center, 1998; produced at Joseph Papp Public Theater, June 19, 1998.

RCA, produced as part of *Fit to Print,* Bay Street Theater, Sag Harbor, NY, August, 1999.

Sisters, produced at the Broadway Playhouse, Sacramento, CA, November 7, 1999.

Take Flight (musical), staged reading at Eugene O'Neill Theater Center, Waterford, CT, August, 2001.

Last Dance, produced in New York, NY at Manhattan Theater Club, June 3, 2003.

SCREENPLAYS

'Night, Mother, Universal, 1986.

A Cooler Climate (adaptation of the novel by Zena Collier), produced for the Showtime network, 1999.

The Audrey Hepburn Story, ABC-TV, 2000.

Custody of the Heart (adaptation of the book by Barbara Delinsky), Lifetime, 2000.

Also author of unproduced screenplays *The Children with Emerald Eyes,* for Columbia, *The Bridge,* for Joseph E. Levine, *Thy Neighbor's Wife,* for United Artists, and *Medicine Woman.*

OTHER

The Jumbo Jelly Bean Journal, Courier-Journal/ Louisville Times (Louisville, KY), 1975.

The Fortune Teller (novel), Random House (New York, NY), 1987.

Also author of the musical *Shakers.* Work represented in anthologies, including *The Best Plays of 1978-1979: The Burns Mantle Yearbook of the Theatre,* edited by Otis L. Guernsey, Jr., Dodd (New York, NY), 1980; and *Selected from Contemporary American Plays: An Anthology,* New Readers Press, 1990. Contributor to educational journals and newspapers.

ADAPTATIONS: Getting Out was adapted as a television movie in 1994, starring Rebecca De Mornay.

SIDELIGHTS: Marsha Norman has established herself as a writer with a powerful message about ordinary people confronting extraordinary circumstances. She came to prominence with her debut drama, *Getting Out,* which was a huge success in 1979. In 1983 she won the Pulitzer Prize for her play *'Night, Mother.* Norman has continued to expand her horizons, writing screenplays and fiction in addition to her stage plays. In *Trudy Blue,* she explored the writer's psyche in a very personal way, for the main character is a writer who, like Norman, was misdiagnosed with a terminal illness. The play's protagonist, like Norman, finds that the experience gives her insight into what is really important to her.

Norman took the theater world by storm with *Getting Out.* A drama about a woman released from prison after an eight-year sentence and a lifetime of trouble, the play concentrates on the psychological changes of the character as she is transformed from a hate-filled child named Arlie into the rehabilitated woman,

Arlene. To contrast the two sides of her protagonist's personality, Norman used two actresses on the stage simultaneously. Critics hailed the innovative drama for its powerful dialogue and emotional honesty. In *Newsweek,* Jack Kroll praised *Getting Out* as a "superb first play . . . we see one of those before and after diptychs living right before our eyes, but this one blazes in the uncompromising light of truth." John Simon of *New York* declared: "No gesture is arbitrary, no syllable rings false. The language is the play's greatest asset: coarse-grained, unvarnished, often hateful, sometimes fumbling for tenderness, funny yet beyond laughter (except the hysterical kind), heartbreaking yet a stranger to tears. And always frighteningly true." In writing the play, Norman drew upon experiences she'd had while teaching disturbed children at a state hospital.

Norman's next two plays, *Third and Oak* and *Circus Valentine,* were written while she was playwright-in-residence at the Actors Theater in Louisville, Kentucky. *Third and Oak* consists of two one-act plays, "The Laundromat" and "The Pool Hall." The former features two women in a laundromat and the latter, two men in a pool hall, both pairs brought together out of loneliness. "Neither has the power of *Getting Out,*" observed Mary Ellen Miller in the *Dictionary of Literary Biography Yearbook,* "but both show Norman's ability to dramatize the ordinary in extraordinary fashion." *Circus Valentine,* a romanticized account of a traveling circus on the small-town circuit, was not well received by critics. Norman spoke with Allan Wallack of *Newsday* about its negative critical reception: "It was devastating. It took me about two years to recover from it and regain my confidence. . . . But the most wonderful result of failure was that ultimately I felt strengthened by it—that they [the critics] hated the play and I survived. That they had said everything awful that could be said. And I *still* wanted to write."

Norman's perseverance paid off in the form of a Pulitzer Prize in 1983 for her fifth play, *'Night, Mother.* A two-character drama, the play premiered at Harvard's American Repertory Theater starring Anne Pitoniak and Kathy Bates as Thelma and Jessie, a mother and daughter who spend a harrowing evening together in what turns out to be the last night of Jessie's life. "*'Night, Mother* reflects what I believe about the theater: Plays should deal with moments of crises," Norman commented in the *New York Times.* The crisis in *'Night, Mother* stems from Jessie's calm but deter-

mined announcement to her mother at the beginning of the play: "I'm going to kill myself." Her reasons are myriad: she's an overweight, plain woman who is afraid of going outside. She spends most of her time indoors caring for her self-indulgent, inept mother, gossiping about the neighbors, and eating junk food. Her husband has deserted her because she wouldn't quit smoking and her son is a petty thief. She was recently fired from her job in a hospital gift shop. In short, she neither enjoys nor controls her life and wants to end it. "I'm just not having a very good time, Mama," Jessie explains to Thelma. The rest of the play, Norman stated in the *New York Times,* "is the fight of their lives. We all know people who killed themselves. These suicides leave us hurt and wanting desperately to talk about it and understand." Norman has declined to elaborate on the incident in her own life that inspired the play, but she told Mel Gussow of the *New York Times Magazine,* "The play should not be seen as something from my life but as something from our lives. The best plays, the ones that last, are communal dreams."

Although Jessie spends the bulk of the play justifying her reasons for wanting to end her life, most critics contend that the drama is much more than simply a suicide story. "The play is about suicide only on its surface," observed Holly Hill of the *Times.* "Its subjects are perhaps the most difficult of all relationships—parent and child—and the definition of self." Miller sees the individual's right to choose as the drama's central concern. "It was not Norman's intention to judge the act of suicide in philosophical, religious, or social terms," Miller asserted. Instead, she wrote, the play is "about choice, about Jessie's decision to 'get off the bus,' because it is going nowhere she wants to be." Simon described the play's subjects as "suicide, love, and the meaning of life—as huge as they come; but they are treated with the specificity of threading a needle or choosing the right breakfast for your needs." Different interpretations of the play are to be expected, Simon added. "Believers and atheists, Freudians and anti-Freudians, rationalists and idealists, Marxists and capitalists, parents and children—everyone will have his or her interpretation of *'Night, Mother,*" he wrote. "Miss Norman may not provide any answers, but anyone who can serve up questions so brilliantly—in language that is only slightly, but finally appositely and awesomely, heightened—has more than earned that right," Simon concluded.

When she learned that *'Night, Mother* had won the prestigious Pulitzer Prize, Norman was vacationing by herself in a secluded cabin four hours north of San Francisco. Later, she told Gussow of the *New York Times:* "The Pulitzer seems like these redwood trees I've been sitting in all week. Enormous but very still at the center. I am thrilled." She continued: "I feel like someone just came into my room in my mind where I work and embroidered a big 'P' on the back of my typing chair. It may not change my life, but it will feel good to know it's back there."

In 1985, Norman wrote another play about ordinary people in a crisis situation entitled *Traveler in the Dark.* The cast of four consists of Sam, a famous surgeon; his wife, Glory; his son, Stephen; and his father Everett, a preacher. The focus of the play is Sam's attempt to deal with the death of a childhood friend on whom he unsuccessfully operated. During the course of the play, Sam's despair at death comes in conflict with his father's faith and his son's questioning. "Sam tries to put his rationality against the face of death," explained Norman in the *Los Angeles Times.* "There's this section of the play when young Stephen asks his dad, 'Is there a center of everything?' Sam replies, 'There was one, the Big Bang theory, but it blew up.' Stephen says, 'Everett says God lit the fire. Did he? Is there a God?' Sam answers, 'I think there is something out there. I want there to be a God, but I don't want it to be me.' That's the play: the incredible longing for God, while saying 'I don't want it to be me,'" Norman summarized.

Critics gave the *Traveler in the Dark* a lukewarm reception, praising it for its thoughtfulness and seriousness but questioning its lack of direction and pat ending. The play "makes large, dark gestures, but its tone is oddly cozy," wrote Dan Sullivan in the *Los Angeles Times.* "It is getting at something that isn't platitudinous, but platitudes are all that seem to come out." Richard Christiansen of the *Chicago Tribune* pointed out that the play shared some of *'Night, Mother*'s faults: "a hortatory argumentation, a schematic working out of a carefully set up problem and an ending that's too neatly wrapped up. But it's also a play that sincerely tries to grapple with the basic issues of human life and death, and it does so with stretches of powerful and moving dialogue." In the *Chicago Tribune,* Norman blamed the play's negative reviews on poor production and a shaky opening night that was "little better than a staged reading." Critics, she added, "didn't think I should write a play about a man."

In order to "escape the brutality of the theater," Norman told Hilary DeVries of the *Chicago Tribune,* she decided to try her hand at writing a novel. *The Fortune Teller* centers around Fay Morgan, a clairvoyant who is helping police solve a mystery involving twenty-seven kidnapped children. As she attempts to use her psychic powers to locate the missing youngsters, she becomes increasingly worried about her own nineteen-year-old daughter, whom she has envisioned running away with a rich but shallow boyfriend and leading a life of misery. While Fay tries to save her daughter from an unhappy future, she only succeeds in driving her further away. Despite her special gifts, Fay encounters the same obstacles as any mother who tries to spare her daughter the pain of making her own mistakes.

In the *New York Times Book Review,* Amy Hempel observed: "The mystic overlay is effective, and the feminist concerns that become key to the story are worth talking about. But the characters are rendered as just that—characters. Their ways and exchanges are so familiar that *The Fortune Teller* ends up being a quick read that does not linger or make us think." Comparing the novel unfavorably to *'Night, Mother,* Michiko Kakutani of the *New York Times* wrote: "Clearly the exchanges between the two women provide some of the best, most fully realized scenes in the novel, but while they occasionally promise to open into the sort of painful, revelatory talks that lent *'Night, Mother* its power, Ms. Norman never lets them develop fully." The novel, Kakutani concluded, feels "contrived and heavy-handed." In the *Detroit News,* Liza Schwarzbaum also drew a comparison between *The Fortune Teller* and Norman's Pulitzer Prize-winning drama, and found that the author traded "dramatic tension for fullness, a roundness like a wheel of fortune. . . . There is a roundness to this plot, a symmetry to the actions and relationships that is itself a kind of fortune telling."

Speaking of *The Fortune Teller* in the *New York Times Book Review,* Norman, too, compared writing to fortune-telling: "You look into someone's life, read where they have been and predict what will happen to them. What Fay does for her clients . . . I've done for characters my whole writing life." The novel, she continued, originated as a play, but eventually Norman realized there were too many characters to fit onstage and she "wanted to be able to include things like fire engines and sex, things you can't do onstage."

During her hiatus from the theater, Norman found herself, like many other established playwrights, being courted by Hollywood studios. "There are lots of opportunities there now for playwrights, and people are usually willing to trust our judgment," she remarked to Michael Bloom of the *New York Times*. Writing for a medium other than the theater provides an opportunity to reach the people she writes about, who Norman contends cannot always afford to go to the theater. "If I want to speak to them, I have to write in a different form," she told Bloom. One such opportunity Norman took advantage of was the chance to adapt her Pulitzer Prize-winning drama into a screenplay. The resulting movie garnered mixed reviews. "The structure of *'Night, Mother* is essentially a conceit built for the theater—two people talking in a room—and its power depends on the theater experience, the fact that you're watching flesh and blood and spittle and sweat ten rows away," observed Paul Attanasio in the *Washington Post*. "Adapting it would have required the kind of imagination that, apparently, was sorely missing." Jay Scott of the *Globe and Mail* also found the play's believability diminished in the film version, which he found "packed with tiny esthetic intermissions that weaken Norman's premise irreparably. . . . the illusion of real time and space that gave the play the power to persuade its audience that these were real people is disrupted." Janet Maslin of the *New York Times* found that despite a camera that is "constantly, annoyingly, in motion," the movie's momentum is maintained by the "urgency of Miss Norman's writing" and the persuasive performances of actresses Anne Bancroft and Sissy Spacek.

In 1988, three years after her last playwriting effort, Norman decided to return to the theater with an experimental workshop piece entitled *Sarah and Abraham*. "That's been my pattern—to get mad at the theater and go away for a while," she told DeVries. "I seem to write better from the outside," she added. As a workshop production, *Sarah and Abraham* was unreviewable and thus allowed Norman to try her hand at something "quite risky and bold" without fear of critical repercussions, she explained to DeVries. What was evident during the play's run, observed DeVries, was "the return of one of the country's most articulate and intelligent theatrical voices." *Sarah and Abraham,* she continued, "marks a new chapter in [Norman's] career."

The setting of the play is a regional theater, where actors are improvising and performing the biblical story of Sarah and Abraham. Using a play-within-a-play structure, Norman wove together the lives of the actors and the characters they play, with the theater owner representing God. The tone is more comic than that which had marked Norman's work previously, as she explores life in the theater, the plight of men overshadowed by successful women, and the right of women to make choices about childbearing and careers. The work sparked debate about whether it was a feminist or antifeminist statement, but its author preferred to let audiences draw their own conclusions about the meaning of what they saw.

According to Pamela Monaco, a contributor to the *Dictionary of Literary Biography, Sarah and Abraham* marked a "shift in Norman's writing toward plays with a greater mythic quality or fairy-tale aspect," which coincided with her "shift toward musical theater." This interest in musical theater was not new; her first attempt at writing for the stage was a children's musical about Thomas Edison. Her interest in writing more musical theater was in part a practical consideration, however. The author once declared that serious theater was dead in America. Monaco explained: "Unlike English theater, American society will not support plays that are not immensely popular and profitable, so in order for playwrights to make a living in America today, they must abandon serious theater. Although one can name several successful American playwrights who write straight plays, Norman contends she cannot make a living from that type of writing today, and she blames theater critics for some of this problem. A popular musical, on the other hand, will generate income for years."

Accordingly, she began work on a musical version of the classic children's novel by Frances Hodgson Burnett, *The Secret Garden*. Her adaptation was extremely successful, enjoying an almost two-year run at the St. James Theater in New York and winning Norman a Tony Award. The story concerns Mary Lennox, an English child who is orphaned while her parents are in India. Sent to Yorkshire to live with her uncle, the spoiled, unpleasant girl goes through a transformation mirroring that of a neglected garden she discovers. "In a classic story of death and rebirth, Mary restores the garden and in the process restores the family to health," related Monaco. A great popular success, the play was revived at many other locations across the United States after it closed in New York.

D. Boone, later retitled *Loving Daniel Boone,* was commissioned as part of the celebration of the state of

Kentucky's bicentennial. The plot concerns Flo, a cleaning woman in a historical museum. With few prospects for a modern lover, she travels through time to meet and assist Daniel Boone and his fellow frontiersmen after he is captured by Indians. She is accompanied by the museum's curator, Mr. Wilson; Hilly, Flo's assistant; and Rick, a married man who is nonetheless trying to woo Flo. The journey through time provides them all with a test of character. According to Monaco, at the time she wrote *Boone,* Norman "was no longer interested in domestic drama and wished to break away from the traditionally structured play. The few reviews called it a pleasant entertainment but questioned whether Norman's manipulation of history helped or hurt the creative process."

Norman tried an adaptation of another classic in 1998. *The Red Shoes* is her musical version of the 1948 movie about a ballerina caught between her love of dance and her love for a composer. In an attempt to give the story a more feminist slant, the dancer's suicide was changed to an accident. The show was not a success, closing after only three days and losing several million dollars.

Following this professional disaster, Norman became gravely ill and was diagnosed with lung cancer. The diagnosis turned out to be wrong, but before this was discovered, Norman experienced some profound insights about her life. As she told April Gornik in *Bomb Magazine,* "I was struck by this understanding that there really were only two things I wanted to know the outcome of: what my son, Angus, would look like as a man . . . and what would happen to the Madeline project, which was a movie script I was working on at the time and from which I was subsequently fired. So this leaves me with one decent curiosity about the future. I thought, There's something wrong here, regardless of how sick I turn out to be. I am not attached enough to my life, I am not living in a way I have respect for." This led her to write *Trudy Blue,* in which her lead character, a writer, goes through a similar experience. The character, Ginger, replays the past and fantasizes about past and future. When she learns she is not really going to die, she finds her life has changed anyway as a result of the realizations she has gone through, particularly those regarding her marriage and other relationships. According to Charles Isherwood in *Variety, Trudy Blue* is "an alternately playful and somber trip through the mind of an ailing writer" in this "whimsical comedy-drama." Isherwood

found that despite the original premise, the play does not catch "dramatic fire" until its "final minutes." Simi Horwitz, writing in *Back Stage,* pointed out that *Trudy Blue* is "both an extension of and departure from her previous works. . . . Mother-daughter relationships are a common concern for her, although in this instance, the story is told from Mom's side. Addressing the double self is a repeated theme. So is the conflict over remaining free and connected." And Patrick Butters, writing in the *Washington Times,* found that *Trudy Blue* "bores into one's soul with an intensity and humor that grab hold of the viewer."

Norman's stature in contemporary American theater puts her at "the crest of a wave of adventurous young women playwrights," declared Gussow. Throughout the highs and lows of her critical reception, the universality of Norman's themes continues to draw audiences from all over the world to her plays. *'Night, Mother* has been produced in thirty-two foreign countries, including Italy, Scandinavia and New Guinea. In each country, the characters of Jessie and Mama were altered only slightly to suit the archetypes of the particular culture. The feelings stirred by the play, however, remained the same no matter which language the characters were speaking. Norman explained the play's applicability around the world to Aljean Harmentz in the *New York Times:* "We all lose our children. You can live for a lifetime and not know what their life is to them. You think for a lifetime they belong to you, but they are only on loan."

The role of the playwright is one that Norman takes very seriously. "I almost see us as this battalion, marching, valiant, soldiers on the front lines, and we must not step on the mines," she told Gussow. "We are trying as best we can to clear the path, to tell you what's out there." As a woman, Norman is pleased with the emergence of women as major playwrights, a movement she helped launch. "Now we can write plays and not have people put them in a little box labeled 'women's theater,'" she continued. "It's a time of great exploration of secret worlds, of worlds that have been kept very quiet."

BIOGRAPHICAL AND CRITICAL SOURCES:

BOOKS

Brown, Linder Ginter, *Marsha Norman: A Casebook,* Garland (New York, NY), 1996.

Dictionary of Literary Biography, Gale (Detroit, MI), *Yearbook: 1984,* 1985, Volume 266: *Twentieth-Century American Dramatists, Fourth Series,* 2002.

Norman, Marsha, *'Night, Mother,* Hill & Wang (New York, NY), 1982.

PERIODICALS

American Theater, January, 2002, p. 60.

Back Stage, November 26, 1999, Simi Horwitz, review of *Trudy Blue,* p. 17; December 10, 1999, Victor Gluck, review of *Trudy Blue,* p. 48.

Booklist, June 1, 1998, Jack Helbig, review of *Love's Fire,* p. 1706; September 15, 1998, Jack Helbig, review of *Collected Plays,* p. 188.

Chicago Tribune, July 1, 1988; May 17, 1989; June 4, 1989.

Christian Science Monitor, May 3, 1991, John Beaufort, review of *The Secret Garden,* p. 14.

Commonweal, October 12, 1979; February 23, 1990, p. 117.

Detroit News, May 17, 1987.

Globe and Mail (Toronto, Ontario, Canada), September 20, 1986.

Library Journal, September 15, 1998, Howard E. Miller, review of *Collected Plays,* p. 80.

Los Angeles Times, January 17, 1985; January 25, 1985.

New Republic, July 7, 1979.

Newsday, May 8, 1983.

Newsweek, May 28, 1979; May 6, 1991, p. 69; December 27, 1993, p. 50.

New York, November 13, 1978; May 28, 1979; January 3, 1994, p. 64; July 20, 1998, John Simon, review of *Love's Fire,* p. 76; August 23, 1999, John Leonard, review of *A Cooler Climate,* p. 58.

New Yorker, May 13, 1991, pp. 84-85.

New York Times, May 17, 1979; May 27, 1979; June 8, 1979; September 15 1979; February 18, 1983; April 19, 1983; August 10, 1986; September 12, 1986; May 13, 1987; October 29, 1988; April 21, 1991, Alessandra Stanley, "Marsha Norman Finds Her Lost Key to Broadway," p. H5; April 26, 1991, Frank Rich, review of *The Secret Garden,* p. B1; May 31, 1998, Andrea Stevens, review of *Love's Fire,* p. AR4; June 23, 1998, Ben Brantley, review of *Love's Fire,* p. B1; July 5, 1998, Vincent Canby, review of *Love's Fire,* p. AR16; December 3, 1999, Anita Gates, "Thinking to Live, and Living to Think," p. B3; March 27, 2000, Anita Gates, review of *The Audrey Hepburn Story,* p. B8; June 4, 2003, Ben Brantley, review of *Last Dance,* p. E1.

New York Times Book Review, May 24, 1987, p. 10.

New York Times Magazine, May 1, 1983.

Post-Standard (Syracuse, NY), November 26, 2002, review of *Getting Out,* p. E4.

Saturday Review, September-October, 1983.

Star-Ledger (Newark, NJ), December 4, 1999, Michael Sommers, review of *Trudy Blue,* p. 44.

Times (London, England), May 5, 1983.

U.S. News and World Report, June 8, 1987, p. 78.

Variety, April 25, 1994, p. 26, February 19, 1992, p. 78; December 6, 1999, Charles Isherwood, review of *Trudy Blue,* p. 94.

Vogue, May 1987, p. 199.

Wall Street Journal, May 3, 1991, Edwin Wilson, review of *The Secret Garden,* p. A11; July 1, 1998, Donald Lyons, review of *Love's Fire,* p. A16.

Washington Post, April 30, 1983; October 13, 1986.

Washington Times, January 13, 2001, Patrick Butters, review of *Trudy Blue,* p. 2.

ONLINE

Bomb Magazine, http://www.bombsite.com/ (January 25, 2004), April Gornik, interview with Marsha Norman.*

O

O'NEILL, Eugene (Gladstone) 1888-1953

PERSONAL: Born October 16, 1888, in New York, NY; died of pneumonia, November 27, 1953, in Boston, MA; son of James (an actor) and Mary Ellen (Quinlan) O'Neill; married Kathleen Jenkins, October 2, 1909 (divorced, 1912); married Agnes Boulton (a writer), April 12, 1918 (divorced, 1929); married Carlotta Monterey (an actress), July 22, 1929; children: (first marriage) Eugene Gladstone, Jr.; (second marriage) Shane Rudraighe, Oona. *Education:* Attended Princeton University, 1906-07, and Harvard University, 1914-15. *Hobbies and other interests:* Swimming, fishing, boating.

CAREER: Playwright. New York-Chicago Supply Co. (mail order firm), New York, NY, secretary, 1907-08; prospector in Honduras, 1909-10; worked in father's theater company as assistant stage manager, 1910, and actor, 1912; sailor, and manual laborer in Buenos Aires, Argentina, 1910-11; *New London Telegraph,* New London, CT, reporter, 1912. Co-manager of Provincetown Players, beginning in 1923.

MEMBER: Authors League of America, American Academy of Arts and Letters, American Philosophical Society, National Institute of Arts and Letters, Dramatists Guild, Irish Academy of Letters.

AWARDS, HONORS: Pulitzer Prize, 1920, for *Beyond the Horizon,* 1922, for *Anna Christie,* 1928, for *Strange Interlude,* and 1957, for *Long Day's Journey into Night;* Gold Medal from National Institute of Arts and Letters, 1923; Litt.D. from Yale University, 1923; No-

bel Prize in literature, 1936; New York Drama Critics Circle Award, and Antoinette Perry Award for Best Play, both 1957, both for *Long Day's Journey into Night,* 1957; Antoinette Perry Award nomination for Best Play, 1959, for *A Touch of the Poet.*

WRITINGS:

PLAYS

Thirst and Other One-Act Plays (contains *Fog* [first produced in New York, NY, at Playwrights' Theatre, January 5, 1917], *Recklessness, Thirst* [first produced in Provincetown, MA, at Wharf Theatre, August, 1916], *Warnings,* and *The Web*), Gorham Press (Boston, MA), 1914.

Bound East for Cardiff (one-act; first produced in Provincetown, MA, then in New York, NY, at Playwrights' Theatre, 1916), published in *The Provincetown Plays, First Series,* F. Shay (New York, NY), 1916, revised version published in *The Moon of the Caribbees and Six Other Plays of the Sea,* 1919.

Before Breakfast (one-act; first produced in New York, NY, 1916), published in *The Provincetown Plays, Third Series,* F. Shay (New York, NY), 1916; published in *The Complete Works of Eugene O'Neill* (also see below), 1924.

The Sniper (one-act; first produced in New York, NY, 1917), published in *Lost Plays of Eugene O'Neill,* 1950.

In the Zone (one-act; first produced in New York, NY, 1917), published in *The Moon of the Caribbees and Six Other Plays of the Sea* (also see below), 1919.

The Long Voyage Home (one-act; first produced in New York, NY, 1917), published in *Smart Set*, October, 1917; published in *The Moon of the Caribbees and Six Other Plays of the Sea*, 1919; published in *The Long Voyage Home and Other Plays*, Dover (New York, NY), 1995.

Ile (one-act; first produced in New York, NY, 1917), published in *Smart Set*, May, 1918; published in *The Moon of the Caribbees and Six Other Plays of the Sea*, 1919.

The Rope (one-act; first produced in New York, NY, 1918), published in *The Moon of the Caribbees and Six Other Plays of the Sea*, 1919.

The Moon of the Caribbees (one-act; first produced in New York, NY, 1918), published in *Smart Set*, August, 1918; published in *The Moon of the Caribbees and Six Other Plays of the Sea*, 1919.

Gold (four-act; preliminary version of Act Four first produced as *Where the Cross Is Made* in New York, 1918; complete work first produced in New York, NY, 1921), Boni & Liveright (New York, NY), 1921, extensively revised version published in *The Complete Works of Eugene O'Neill*, 1924.

The Dreamy Kid (one-act; first produced in New York, NY, 1919), published in *Theatre Arts*, January, 1920; published in *Contemporary One-Act Plays of 1921 (American)*, Stewart Kidd (Cincinnati, OH), 1922; published in *The Complete Works of Eugene O'Neill*, 1924.

The Moon of the Caribbees and Six Other Plays of the Sea (contains *Bound East for Cardiff*, *Ile*, *In the Zone*, *The Long Voyage Home*, *The Rope*, and *Where the Cross Is Made*), Boni & Liveright (New York, NY), 1919.

Beyond the Horizon (three-act; first produced on Broadway, 1920), Boni & Liveright (New York, NY), 1920, reprinted, Dover (New York, NY), 1996.

Anna Christie (four-act; preliminary version produced as *Chris* in Atlantic City, NJ, 1920, and published as *Chris Christophersen*, Random House (New York, NY), 1982; final version first produced in New York, NY, 1921), published in *The Hairy Ape, Anna Christie, and The First Man*, 1922; published as *Anna Christie*, Dover (Mineola, NY), 1998.

Exorcism (one-act; later destroyed by the author), first produced in New York, NY, 1920.

The Emperor Jones (eight scenes; first produced in New York, 1920), published in *Theatre Arts*, January, 1921, revised version published in *The Emperor Jones, Diff'rent, and The Straw*, published as *The Emperor Jones*, Dover (Mineola, NY), 1997.

Diff'rent (two-act; first produced in New York, 1920), published in *The Emperor Jones, Diff'rent, and The Straw*, 1921.

The Straw (three-act; first produced in New London, CT, then New York, NY, 1921), published in *The Emperor Jones, Diff'rent, and The Straw*, 1921.

The Emperor Jones, Diff'rent, and The Straw, Boni & Liveright (New York, NY), 1921.

The First Man (four-act; first produced in New York, NY, 1922), published in *The Hairy Ape, Anna Christie, and The First Man*, 1922.

The Hairy Ape (eight scenes; first produced in New York, NY, 1922), published in *The Hairy Ape, Anna Christie, and The First Man*, 1922.

The Hairy Ape, Anna Christie, and The First Man, Boni & Liveright (New York, NY), 1922.

Welded (three-act; first produced in Baltimore, MD, 1924, then New York, NY at Thirty-ninth Street Theatre, 1924), published in *All God's Chillun Got Wings and Welded*, 1924, extensively revised version published in *The Complete Works of Eugene O'Neill*, 1924.

The Ancient Mariner (adapted from "Rime of the Ancient Mariner" by Samuel Taylor Coleridge; first produced in New York, 1924), published in *The Unknown O'Neill*, 1988.

All God's Chillun Got Wings (two-act; first produced in New York, NY, 1924), first published in *American Mercury*, February, 1924; published in *All God's Chillun Got Wings and Welded*, 1924.

All God's Chillun Got Wings and Welded, Boni & Liveright (New York, NY), 1924.

Desire under the Elms (three-act; first produced in New York, NY, 1924), published in *The Complete Works of Eugene O'Neill*,, revised version published separately, Boni & Liveright (New York, NY), 1925.

(And selector) *The Complete Works of Eugene O'Neill* (contains revised versions of later plays), Boni & Liveright (New York, NY), 1924.

The Fountain (eleven scenes; first produced in New York, NY, 1925), published in *The Great God Brown, The Fountain, The Moon of the Caribbees, and Other Plays*, Boni & Liveright (New York, NY), 1926.

The Great God Brown (four-act; first produced in New York, NY, 1926), published in *The Great God Brown, The Moon of the Caribbees, and Other Plays*, Boni & Liveright (New York, NY), 1926.

Marco Millions (three-act; preliminary two-part, eight-act version published as *Marco's Millions* in *The Unknown O'Neill*, 1988 [also see below]; final version first produced on Broadway, 1928), Boni & Liveright (New York, NY), 1927.

Lazarus Laughed (four-act; preliminary version of Act I published in *The American Caravan: A Yearbook of American Literature,* Macaulay (New York, NY), 1927; final version first produced in Pasadena, 1928), Boni & Liveright (New York, NY), 1927.

Strange Interlude (nine-act; first produced on Broadway, 1928), Boni & Liveright (New York, NY), 1928.

Dynamo (three-act; preliminary version first produced on Broadway, 1929), final version, extensively revised, Boni & Liveright (New York, NY), 1929.

Mourning Becomes Electra (trilogy; contains *Homecoming, The Hunted,* and *The Haunted*; first produced on Broadway, October 26, 1931), Liveright (New York, NY), 1931.

Ah, Wilderness! (four-act; three-act stage version first produced in Pittsburgh, PA, then on Broadway, 1933), Random House (New York, NY), 1933.

Days without End (four-act; first produced in Boston, MA, 1933; produced in New York, NY, 1934), Random House (New York, NY), 1934.

The Iceman Cometh (four-act; first produced on Broadway, October 9, 1946), Random House (New York, NY), 1946, reprinted, Vintage (New York, NY), 1999.

A Moon for the Misbegotten (four-act; first produced in Columbus, OH, then in New York, NY, 1957), Random House (New York, NY), 1952, reprinted, Vintage (New York, NY), 2000.

Lost Plays of Eugene O'Neill contains one-acts *Abortion, The Movie Man, The Sniper,* and *A Wife for a Life* and three-act *Servitude*), introduction by Lawrence Gellert, New Fathoms Press (New York, NY), 1950.

Long Day's Journey into Night (four-act; first produced in Stockholm, Sweden, February 10, 1956; produced on Broadway, November 7, 1956), Yale University Press (New Haven, CT), 1956.

A Touch of the Poet (four-act; first produced in Stockholm, Sweden, 1957; produced on Broadway, 1958), Yale University Press (New Haven, CT), 1957.

Hughie (one-act; first produced in Stockholm, Sweden, 1958; produced on Broadway, 1964), Yale University Press (New Haven, CT), 1959.

More Stately Mansions (unfinished; edited versions first produced in Stockholm, Sweden, 1962; produced in Los Angeles, CA, 1967), Yale University Press (New Haven, CT), 1964, complete transcript published as *More Stately Mansions: The Unexpurgated Edition,* Oxford University Press (New York, NY), 1988.

The Calms of Capricorn (unfinished), transcription by Donald Gallup, Yale University Library (New Haven, CT), 1981, edited with additions by Gallup, Ticknor & Fields (New Haven, CT), 1982.

Eugene O'Neill: The Unfinished Plays contains *The Visit of Malatesta, The Last Conquest,* and *Blind Alley Guy*), edited and annotated by Virginia Floyd, Ungar (New York, NY), 1988.

The Unknown O'Neill (includes *The Personal Equation, Marco's Millions* [eight-act version], and *The Ancient Mariner,* with prose and poetry), edited by Travis Bogard, Yale University Press (New Haven, CT), 1988.

Eugene O'Neill: Complete Plays (includes *Bread and Butter, Now I Ask You,* and *Shell Shock*), Library of America (New York, NY), 1988.

Ten "Lost" Plays (includes *A Wife for a Life, Thirst, The Web, Warnings, Fog, Recklessness, Abortion, The Movie Man, Servitude,* and *The Sniper*), Dover (New York, NY), 1995.

Three Plays (includes *Desire under the Elms, Strange Interlude,* and *Mourning Becomes Electra*), Vintage (New York, NY), 1995.

Early Plays (includes *The Moon of the Caribbees, Bound East for Cardiff, The Long Voyage Home, In the Zone, Ile, Where the Cross Is Made, The Rope, Beyond the Horizon, The Straw, The Emperor Jones, Anna Christie,* and *The Hairy Ape*), edited and with an introduction by Jeffrey H. Richards, Penguin (New York, NY), 2001.

OTHER

(Author of introduction) Benjamin DeCasseres, *Anathema!,* Gotham (New York, NY), 1928.

(With Ralph Sanborn and Barrett H. Clark) *A Bibliography of the Works of Eugene O'Neill, together with the Collected Poems of Eugene O'Neill,* Random House (New York, NY), 1931.

Inscriptions: Eugene O'Neill to Carlotta Monterey O'Neill, privately printed, 1960.

Poems, 1912-1944, edited by Donald Gallup, Yale University Library (New Haven, CT), 1979, revised, Ticknor & Fields (New Haven, CT), 1980.

Work Diary, 1924-1943, edited by Donald Gallup, Yale University Library (New Haven, CT), 1981.

Eugene O'Neill at Work: Newly Released Ideas for Plays (notebooks), edited and annotated by Virginia Floyd, Ungar (New York, NY), 1981.

"The Theatre We Worked For": The Letters of Eugene O'Neill to Kenneth Macgowan, edited by Jackson R. Bryer, Yale University Press (New Haven, CT), 1982.

"Love, Admiration, and Respect": The O'Neill-Commins Correspondence, edited by Dorothy Commins, Duke University Press (Durham, NC), 1986.

"As Ever, Gene": The Letters of Eugene O'Neill to George Jean Nathan, Farleigh Dickinson University Press (Rutherford, NJ), 1987.

Selected Letters of Eugene O'Neill, edited by Travis Bogard and Jackson R. Bryer, Yale University Press (New Haven, CT), 1988.

The Last Will and Testament of an Extremely Distinguished Dog, illustrated by Adrienne Yorinks, Holt (New York, NY), 1999.

(With Agnes Boulton) *A Wind Is Rising: The Correspondence of Agnes Boulton and Eugene O'Neill,* edited by William Davies King, Associated University Presses (Cranberry, NJ), 2000.

Contributor to periodicals, including *Seven Arts* and *New York Times.* Associate editor and contributor to *American Spectator,* beginning 1932.

ADAPTATIONS: Anna Christie was adapted for film in 1923, and, starring Greta Garbo, 1930; *Strange Interlude* was adapted for film, starring Clark Gable, Metro-Goldwyn-Mayer (MGM), 1932; *The Emperor Jones* was adapted for film, starring Paul Robeson, United Artists, 1933; *Ah, Wilderness!* was adapted for film, starring Lionel Barrymore, MGM, 1935, and, as *Summer Holiday,* starring Mickey Rooney, MGM, 1948; *Bound East for Cardiff, The Moon of the Caribbees, In the Zone,* and *The Long Voyage Home* were adapted for film as *The Long Voyage Home,* directed by John Ford and starring John Wayne, United Artists, 1940; *The Hairy Ape* was adapted for film, starring William Bendix and Susan Hayward, 1944; *Mourning Becomes Electra* was adapted for film, starring Raymond Massey, Rosalind Russell, and Michael Redgrave, RKO, 1947; *Desire under the Elms* was adapted for film, starring Sophia Loren, Tony Perkins, and Burl Ives, Paramount, 1958; *Long Day's Journey into Night* was adapted for film, directed by Sidney Lumet and starring Ralph Richardson, Jason Robards, Katharine Hepburn, and Dean Stockwell, Embassy, 1962; *The Iceman Cometh* was adapted for film, directed by John Frankenheimer and starring Lee Marvin and Fredric March, 1973. *Before Breakfast* was adapted, with August Strindberg's *The Stronger,* for the stage by Stephen Kennedy Murphy as *The Mourning Show,* 2001. Several of O'Neill's plays have been adapted as audio books.

SIDELIGHTS: Eugene O'Neill wrote more than fifty plays, won the Nobel Prize and several Pulitzer prizes, and earned a place as the first American dramatist of lasting, international stature. His work culminated with *The Iceman Cometh* and *Long Day's Journey into Night,* two of the most powerful portraits of despair ever created for the stage. Despite such accomplishments O'Neill's reputation has always been mixed. The playwright, wrote Mary McCarthy in the *Partisan Review,* has not "the slightest ear for the word, the sentence, the speech." "[He] is no thinker," wrote director Eric Bentley in the *Kenyon Review.* "Look at the fruits of his thinking; his comparatively thoughtless plays are better." However, as biographer Frederic Carpenter observed in *Eugene O'Neill,* the playwright's primary goal was not to be an intellectual playwright but an emotional one. "Our emotions are a better guide than our thoughts," Carpenter quoted O'Neill as saying. "They are the deep undercurrent whereas our thoughts are often only the . . . surface reactions." Rarely successful as a poet or philosopher, O'Neill still excelled at conveying the anguish of being alive. O'Neill, wrote a *Time* reviewer, could "seize a blase Broadway crowd and wring it dry, half from fatigue, half from an emotional buffeting that no other American playwright ever inflicted on an audience. [He] could do what only a major artist can do: make his public share in the life of his private demons."

Until his mid-twenties O'Neill wrote little, but he encountered a great deal of pain that informed his later work. His torments began with his family, displayed as the Tyrone clan in *Long Day's Journey into Night.* So painful and personal was this work that O'Neill would not allow it to be made public until after he was dead—preferably, not for decades after. O'Neill's father, James, rose from poverty to become one of nineteenth-century America's most popular actors. Obsessed with financial security, he toured the country for years performing *The Count of Monte Cristo,* a crowd-pleasing melodrama of betrayal, suffering, revenge, and triumph. Critics bemoaned the waste of his artistic talent, and, too late, he came to agree. As a young man James wed Mary Ellen Quinlan, known as Mary Tyrone in *Long Day's Journey into Night* and as Ella during her lifetime. Born to wealth and educated in Catholic convent schools, Ella was ill prepared to marry an itinerant actor and became terribly isolated. While recovering from Eugene's birth, she became addicted to morphine. O'Neill's older brother, Jamie, was pampered as a child and became utterly irresponsible, fixated on his mother, and was unable to accept any other women but prostitutes. With his father's influence he gained minor acting roles, but heavy drinking often ruined his performances. Surrounded by such disappointment, O'Neill acquired what might be termed a "tragic sense of life": that people are doomed to suffer intensely, mocked by dreams they cannot attain. "None of us can help the things life has done to us," noted Tyrone. "They're done before you realize it, and . . . they make you do other things until at last everything comes between you and what you'd like to be, and you've lost your true self forever."

The young O'Neill shared his parents' transient way of life as he shuttled between hotels attended boarding schools. He noticed Ella's distractedness and feared she was going insane, but he did not learn of her addiction until he was fourteen years old. That year when the family gathered at their only real "home," a summer house in New London, Connecticut, Ella ran out of morphine and tried to drown herself. O'Neill promptly renounced his Catholic faith, since his mother's devotions had failed her. From then on, observers suggest, he considered himself an emotional outcast, seeking replacements for the mother and the God who had disappointed him. In *Long Day's Journey into Night* O'Neill appears as "Edmund," actually the name of his brother who died in infancy. "It was a great mistake my being born a man, I would have been much more successful as a sea gull or a fish," Edmund says. "As it is, I will always be a stranger who never feels at home, . . . who must always be a little in love with death." O'Neill began to flout his parents' proprieties, as Jamie taught him about drinking, prostitutes, and iconoclastic writers. He soon discovered Friedrich Nietzsche, the German philosopher who said Christianity was in decline and offered a new faith based on confidence in one's inner resources. O'Neill also valued the pessimism of Sweden's August Strindberg, whose plays mix love and hate as couples are joined in sexual desire and then battle each other for domination. For O'Neill, these plays were essentially his own family history.

After flunking out of Princeton University, O'Neill eloped with Kathleen Jenkins, one of the few "respectable" young women he knew. Overwhelmed by marriage, he refused to live with his wife and their infant son, Eugene Jr. O'Neill's father found him work in an office, in the theater, and in a Central American gold-mining expedition, but O'Neill proved unenthusiastic until his father agreed to pay his passage on a tramp freighter. Enlisted to help the sailors, O'Neill found he enjoyed the work and the companionship; moreover, observers suggest, the sea became like a new god to him, its vastness offering the promise that he could transcend his own existence. Ashore O'Neill continued to disintegrate. He identified morbidly with poor and rootless men, and after living in poverty in Buenos Aires he shipped back to New York City and moved into a wretched boardinghouse and barroom. To receive a divorce under New York law, he arranged with his wife that he should be caught by her attorney with a prostitute. He then attempted suicide, surviving to find that he had tuberculosis.

Sent to a sanitarium to recover from his illness, O'Neill reassessed his life and decided to become a playwright. In 1914 he published his first one-act plays—once again using money from his father. O'Neill's apprentice works are generally mediocre and melodramatic, but as Travis Bogard observed in *Contour in Time,* they display basic themes that would dominate his later writings. Characters are manipulated by forces beyond their control; families are racked by conflict; those who betray their true nature are destroyed. Of particular note is *Bound East for Cardiff,* a play whose plausibility, focus, philosophical undercurrents, and careful use of emotion give it genuine power. The play unfolds aboard the S.S. *Glencairn,* where sailors watch over a dying shipmate. As the men converse they realize how the sea has bound them together and influenced their lives. The play succeeds despite its minimal plot, underscoring that O'Neill could build effective works entirely around the psychological interactions of his characters. The philosophical issues arise naturally from the setting. *Bound East for Cardiff* is not only the first proof of O'Neill's skill as a dramatist: it is also one of the first successes in realistic American drama.

O'Neill's ambitions soon outstripped his talent. He developed an experimenter's fascination with theatrical techniques and a wide-ranging imagination that often seemed unable to develop an idea slowly, plausibly, and completely. Ignoring his natural flair for heartfelt emotion, O'Neill tried a new series of plays that would be more "impersonal," as Baker wished. The results, according to Bogard, are abhorrently shallow and mechanical: the worst is probably *Now I Ask You,* a drawing-room comedy that mocks the author's interest in Nietzsche. O'Neill's talent revived when he returned to the bars of New York, where he now often drank with the young intellectuals of Greenwich Village. His friends included Terry Carlin, an old anarchist whose search for personal freedom had ended in quiet resignation. In the summer of 1916 the two men visited Provincetown, Massachusetts, where Carlin introduced O'Neill to the Provincetown Players, a group of theater enthusiasts who hoped to create an audience for innovative American drama. They were anxious for producible scripts, and soon their summer theater—a shack on a Provincetown wharf—premiered *Bound East for Cardiff.* O'Neill had found his first appreciative audience, and when the Players returned to Greenwich Village for the winter they awaited more of his work.

Seemingly driven by his own pain, he continued to fill his plays with unhappy marriages, madness, and death; but, surprisingly, his most effective early works are "Dionysian" evocations of the mysterious power of the sea and of human dreams. Three such plays—*In the Zone, The Long Voyage Home,* and *The Moon of the Caribbees*—once more involve sailors of the *Glencairn.* In *Caribbees,* the author's longtime favorite, the ship anchors off a Caribbean port while music wafts from shore. The sailors smuggle women and liquor aboard and engage in an orgy of mindless pleasure and brawling. The only unhappy man is pining for a lost girlfriend and refuses to participate. Like most of O'Neill's early works, the *Glencairn* plays are simple one-acts, ideally suited to a small company like the Provincetown Players.

His success brought larger ambitions, and in 1918 O'Neill completed *Beyond the Horizon,* a full-length tragedy in which two brothers destroy themselves by ignoring their dreams. Robert Mayo, a young poet with wanderlust, decides to marry and tend the family farm; as a result his brother Andrew, who hoped to be a farmer, must work at sea. In the end, Andrew is embittered and Robert welcomes his own untimely death, hoping to find poetry and transcendence beyond the grave. O'Neill waited two years to open the work on Broadway, achieving national fame and his first Pulitzer when it appeared in 1920. James O'Neill saw the work shortly before he died, and his approval helped to reconcile father and son.

O'Neill's lyrical realism peaked with *Anna Christie,* a 1921 romance that is considered one of his most popular plays and O'Neill's second Pulitzer Prize winner in 1922. The title character, who falls into a life of prostitution on land, is redeemed by becoming a sailor's wife. Her fate confounds her immigrant father, a sailor who sent her inland to protect her from "dat old davil sea." O'Neill was disturbed to see his play become a happy-ever-after story, which he did not intend. Thereafter O'Neill ceased to celebrate the dreamers of everyday life. Instead, observed Bogard, he embraced the new American doctrine of "Art Theatre," which questioned not only the light entertainment of James O'Neill's day but also a half-century of realism as perfected by dramatists in Europe. Seeking truths that lay beneath everyday reality, Art Theatre encouraged playwrights to compose philosophical works and to explore unusual techniques of presenting plays.

Two of O'Neill's early Art Theatre plays were highly successful—a mixed blessing, Bogard noted, that encouraged his later excess. *The Emperor Jones* is a nightmarish monologue loosely inspired by the author's experience in the Central American jungle. Brutus Jones, a strong-willed black American laborer, takes control of a Caribbean island by exploiting the inhabitants' fear of magic and spirits. When his subjects revolt, he escapes to the jungle, but he is overcome with terror and has a series of hallucinations—culminating in the appearance of a crocodile god—that make him easy prey for the rebels. The play was a huge success for the Provincetown troupe and offered the first major dramatic role for black actors on the white-dominated stage. In a similar vein, *The Hairy Ape* shows the emotional collapse of a workingman who is fiercely proud of his ability to shovel coal for a steamship's engines. Derided by a prim woman passenger, he rages at society for making him feel freakish. He tries to express his despair to both rich churchgoers and poor revolutionaries, then becomes wholly irrational and is crushed to death when he seeks the friendship of a gorilla at the zoo. Both plays convey emotional chaos through an atmosphere of unreality—the churchgoers, for instance, behave like automatons—but both are also based on real people whom O'Neill met during his wayfaring days. Even when O'Neill made broad statements about the human condition, he needed a realistic context to be most effective.

Soon O'Neill's experiments were defeated by the scope of his own ambition: like Nietzsche, he wanted to resolve the world's religious unrest by finding a new faith. In a series of grandiose, almost unproducible works—including *Welded, The Fountain, The Great God Brown, Lazarus Laughed, Dynamo,* and *Days without End*—O'Neill portrayed various spiritual quests. In *Dynamo,* the alienated son of a minister embraces the false god of modern science, symbolized by an electrical power plant; in *Lazarus Laughed,* the biblical Lazarus arises from the dead to proclaim his freedom from the fear of mortality. Inspired by Art Theatre, O'Neill slighted realistic characterization in favor of his ideas. For dramatic power he used theatrical devices: a power-plant set for *Dynamo,* a booming laugh and crowds of followers for Lazarus, and an elevated poetic diction that he was ill-equipped to sustain. Repeatedly the plays failed even when the ideas were interesting. In *Welded,* for instance, playwright Michael Cape enacts the dilemma of O'Neill's second marriage—Cape wants a total spiritual union with his wife, while she fears for her individuality. "*Welded* is a finely conceived but over-intellectualized study, not a well-rounded three-dimensional drama about human beings," said biographer Barrett Clark in *Eugene O'Neill: The Man and His Plays.* "It is the skeleton of a possibly fine play."

Eventually O'Neill saw that Art Theatre had not served him well. "No more sets or theatrical devices as anything but unimportant background," he told Kenneth Macgowan, as recorded in *"The Theatre We Worked For": The Letters of Eugene O'Neill to Kenneth Macgowan.* "Hereafter I will write plays primarily as literature to be read—and the more simply they read, the better they will act."

O'Neill's most successful work had continued to come from his forays into realism. *Strange Interlude,* like *The Emperor Jones* and *The Hairy Ape,* combines artistic experiment with social reality. The play's dialogue is punctuated with "interludisms"—asides during which the characters describe their thoughts. This technique, O'Neill realized, was ideal for portraying the self-conscious intellectuals he had known in Greenwich Village. The play centers on Nina Leeds, modeled on the free-loving Louise Bryant. Nina searches narcissistically for the perfect man, and since he does not exist, she surrounds herself with men—a rich husband, an ambitious lover, a fatherly confidant, a son—each of whom gives her partial fulfillment. Eventually most of her men forsake her, and she realizes that life consists of quiet disappointment. As Carpenter ob-

served, O'Neill's artistic vision had grown more pessimistic since the days of *Anna Christie,* and he now wrote of dreams gone wrong. *Strange Interlude* is an astonishing nine acts long, designed to rival the intricacy of a novel. When the play debuted on Broadway—complete with a dinner break—it was a massive success, partly because of the sheer novelty of its psychological revelations. The play also won O'Neill yet another Pulitzer Prize, in 1928.

"Interludisms," O'Neill decided, were not a likely basis for more plays; historical drama, by contrast, became a lasting source of inspiration. As Bogard suggested, a period setting gave some much-needed structure to O'Neill's imaginings. *Desire under the Elms* reveals the passions beneath the calm surface of a nineteenth-century New England farm family. "God's hard, not easy!" cries old patriarch Ephraim Cabot, toughened by years of labor. Meanwhile his passionate new wife has an affair with her adult stepson; in the shocking finale, she kills the illicit offspring of the affair, then goes hand-in-hand with her lover to prison. *Desire under the Elms* was decried on moral grounds, but scandal only increased its popularity. Joseph Wood Krutch praised the play without trying to discover a redeeming social message. "The meaning and unity of [O'Neill's] work," he wrote in the *Nation,* "lies not in any controlling intellectual idea and certainly not in a 'message,' but merely in the fact that each play is an experience of extraordinary intensity."

In his next historical drama, *Mourning Becomes Electra,* O'Neill consciously seeks the intensity of ancient Greek tragedy. He adapts the "Oresteia" trilogy of Aeschylus—a tale of passion, murder, and divine retribution which suggested to O'Neill the family's buried relationships. For O'Neill, the psychology of family life, not the ancient gods, determines each character's fate. When General Ezra Mannon returns to his New England home after the U.S. Civil War, he is killed by his adulterous wife, Christine. Their daughter, Lavinia—"Electra" in the old Greek version—thirsts for revenge and, with reluctant help from her brother, Orin, she drives Christine to suicide. Brother and sister then make a futile effort to find peace in the dream-world of the South Seas. Soon they return to New England, where Orin kills himself and Lavinia confronts the ugly Mannon heritage by shutting herself inside the family homestead. When *Mourning Becomes Electra* debuted on Broadway in 1931, noted Carpenter, it garnered better reviews than any previous

O'Neill work; nevertheless, the play closed fairly quickly and was seldom revived. "The very logical perfection of its artistic design," Carpenter explained, "may constitute its greatest fault": the characters are so relentlessly grim that they may lose the sympathy of the audience.

By the early 1930s O'Neill had written many plays about troubled families and spiritual quests. Biographers generally agree that his inspiration was autobiographical: he wished to deal with his "private demons" by using his life experience to make broad statements about human nature. If O'Neill wrote too coldly in such plays as *Welded* and *Mourning Becomes Electra,* in other works he was probably too close to his subject. In 1920 he released *Exorcism,* a thinly veiled account of his suicide attempt, then withdrew the play and destroyed the scripts. He followed with *All God's Chillun Got Wings,* a symbolic account of his parents' marriage that shows a black man—"Jim"—and a white woman—"Ella"—who struggle to love each other despite their differences. Unfortunately O'Neill could not dramatize the pain of the relationship without resorting to melodrama and reduced both characters to unconvincing madness. Finally, from 1932 to 1943, he wrote several openly autobiographical plays that are considered his finest work. As director Robert Brustein observed in *The Theatre of Revolt,* the author "had to write badly in order to write well."

Success gave O'Neill the leisure to write as he wished. *Strange Interlude* made him wealthy. One morning in 1932, as he was mired in writing the philosophical drama *Days without End,* he awoke with the idea for a nostalgic comedy loosely based on his youth in New London. Within a month he completed *Ah, Wilderness!* The main character is Richard Miller, a good-natured seventeen-year-old who prompts a minor scandal by quoting "decadent" poetry to his girlfriend. Chastised by adults, he rebels by visiting a bar and a prostitute with a heart of gold. When he comes home drunk, his alcoholic Uncle Sid gently sees him to bed. Here images of O'Neill's tormented early years are transformed into figures of benevolence. Richard's father, for instance, is not based on the unhappy James O'Neill but on Fred Latimer, a hearty New London newspaper editor who shepherded the young O'Neill through a brief stint as a reporter. "It is as if," Carpenter observed, "the man who wrote the play were also watching over his characters to see that they did not follow his own dangerous path." *Ah, Wilderness!,*

wrote Brustein, "prefigures [O'Neill's] transformation into an objective dramatic artist": only a mature writer, in full control of his material, could turn painful memories into a comedy with a life of its own.

Though O'Neill lived for twenty years after *Ah, Wilderness!* debuted in 1933, it was the last successful premiere he would see. Both his pessimism and his philosophizing were unsuited to the America of the Great Depression and World War II, when audiences craved dramas of social activism or positive statements about the national character. After *Days without End* failed in 1934 he withdrew from the theater, more concerned with writing plays than seeing them produced. When he received the Nobel Prize in 1936, some found him unworthy, including *Saturday Review* critic Bernard De Voto. "What does he tell us, what does he show us, that we did not know before?" De Voto wrote. "Nowhere do we encounter the finality or the reconciliation of great art, nowhere is any fragment of human life remade for us in understanding."

O'Neill's first post-Nobel effort was the "Cycle," a projected cycle of eleven historical dramas called "A Tale of Possessors Self-Dispossessed." The saga would span American history, showing the gradual corruption of the country's idealism by greed. By 1939, after years of preparation, O'Neill was close to completing only one play, *A Touch of the Poet.* Frustrated and bored, he largely abandoned the "Cycle" in favor of his autobiographical dramas, beginning with *The Iceman Cometh.*

Set in a dingy New York barroom, *The Iceman Cometh* centers on a group of steady drinkers like those O'Neill knew in his youth. Barman Harry Hope is based on a Villager who spent much of his life secluded in lodgings upstairs from his saloon. The patrons include Larry Slade, whose eloquent pessimism recalls that of failed anarchist Terry Carlin. Each of the regulars comforts himself with a hopeless "pipe dream": a politician awaits his public, a black man awaits interracial brotherhood, and so on. Into their world comes traveling salesman Theodore Hickman ("Hickey"), a besotted old friend who has suddenly become bright-eyed and energetic. With a salesman's skill and a preacher's zeal, Hickey convinces his friends to abandon their delusions in the name of truth. Having thus made them miserable, he proves himself to be the most deluded of all. In one of the most famous monologues in American drama, Hickey explains that he has shed his own delusion—guilt—by killing his wife, whose patient suffering made him feel guilty. He is immediately arrested, after which the patrons resume their drinking and dreaming, having decided that Hickey is insane. "All the old truisms of morality and philosophy seem suddenly to crumble," as Carpenter observed: if even the bringer of "truth" is a madman, what is left to believe in? "To hell with the truth!" says Larry Slade. "The lie of a pipe dream is what gives life to the whole misbegotten mad lot of us, drunk or sober."

The Iceman Cometh has attracted more interest among literary critics than any other of O'Neill's works. Completed in 1940, it anticipates by a decade the flowering of existentialism, a philosophy holding that humanity must create its own sense of purpose in a godless and chaotic universe. By abjuring philosophy in favor of his own concrete experience, O'Neill had at last created an intellectual masterpiece. The seeming nihilism of *The Iceman Cometh,* Bogard speculated, may have inspired O'Neill to write *Hughie,* a more hopeful one-act on a similar theme. In the lobby of a cheap New York hotel, Erie Smith tells the new night clerk about his predecessor—Hughie—who enjoyed Erie's posturing tales about the world of high-stakes gambling. The clerk tries to ignore Erie but finally relents. A sympathetic ear on a lonely night, O'Neill seems to suggest, is the only hope one person can offer another.

Next O'Neill turned to *Long Day's Journey into Night,* the play he may have spent his life preparing to write. Abandoning his old experiments, O'Neill here observes the classic unities of time, place, and action, evoking years of misery in the events of a single day. The play is set in 1912 in his family's New London, Connecticut, summer house. As day begins the Tyrones try to be kind to each other, but ugly memories repeatedly emerge and inspire intensifying rounds of soul-searching, recrimination, and apology. The audience can hope that young Edmund may escape the family's despair, but the others are clearly trapped: James Tyrone, Sr. by fear of poverty and regret for his wasted talent; Jamie by decadence and self-hatred; Mary by morphine and memories of her innocent girlhood. Finally that night the men watch helplessly as Mary appears in a drug-induced stupor, dragging her old wedding gown and recalling her lost youth. The Tyrones "become larger than their own small lives," wrote John Chapman in the *New York Daily News.* "They become humanity, looking for something but not

knowing exactly what it is looking for." He declared: "This is O'Neill's most beautiful play. . . . And it is one of the great dramas of any time."

In contrast with Edmund's youthfulness, Jamie is the jaded villain of *Long Day's Journey into Night.* "Kid. . . . Be on your guard," Jamie says, confessing that he introduced Edmund to alcohol and prostitutes out of a resentful urge to destroy him. Perhaps wishing to show more compassion for Jamie, who drank himself to death when their mother died, O'Neill wrote an epilogue to the play titled *A Moon for the Misbegotten.* This play is set in 1923, as an exhausted, middle-aged Jamie meets a hulking Irish-American farm girl named Josie Hogan. To compensate for her ugliness Josie claims vast sexual experience, but as an old fraud Jamie understands her lies at once. The two spend a chaste night discussing their sorrows and regrets. After Jamie leaves, Josie pronounces a sad blessing: "May you have your wish and die in your sleep soon, Jim, darling. May you rest forever in forgiveness and peace." Though criticized for an excess of sentiment, *A Moon for the Misbegotten* moved even Mary McCarthy, who wrote in the *New York Times Book Review* that "this play exacts homage for its mythic powers, for the element of transcendence jutting up in it like a great wooden Trojan horse."

As O'Neill composed *A Moon for the Misbegotten* he struggled against an increasing tremor in his hands. By the time he completed the play in 1943, his hands were virtually useless, and he refused to dictate any new work to others. Having come to terms with his family, he wrote no more. His last years were as painful as anything he had known in his youth or created for the stage. Writing, biographers speculate, had been a crucial emotional outlet for him, and once deprived of it he lost the will to live. He disowned two children: Oona had married Charlie Chaplin, an actor as old as her father, and Shane had become an aimless heroin addict. Meanwhile Eugene, Jr. was unable to fulfill his early intellectual promise and committed suicide. Ill health compelled the O'Neills to sell their isolated California home in 1944; thereafter, to stay close to hospitals, they often lived in the sort of urban apartments O'Neill had hated ever since his father's days as a traveling actor.

While living in New York City in the mid-1940s O'Neill helped with rehearsals for *The Iceman Cometh* and *A Moon for the Misbegotten,* but both plays, in keeping with his fears, met with indifference from the general public. When *A Moon for the Misbegotten* failed during out-of-town tryouts he withdrew all his new work from further consideration, publishing the play only because he needed money. O'Neill and his third wife, Carlotta, moved briefly to a home on the Massachusetts shore and eventually to a Boston apartment where he stayed in seclusion. When he died in 1953, he seemed a figure from the distant theatrical past.

In the years since his death O'Neill's reputation quickly revived, virtually giving him a new career, as John Gassner observed in *O'Neill: A Collection of Critical Essays*. In 1956 director Jose Quintero, actor Jason Robards, and other newcomers staged an acclaimed Off-Broadway revival of *The Iceman Cometh*, and to an audience familiar with existentialism the play seemed contemporary and important. The American premiere of *Long Day's Journey into Night* premiered the same year, earning O'Neill his fourth Pulitzer in 1957 and confirming his status as America's greatest playwright. In his last plays, admirers declared, O'Neill transcended his stylistic weakness through the strength of his battered humanism. "He had the writer's one indispensable gift," wrote Joseph Wood Krutch in the *New York Times Book Review*. "He 'communicated'—the situation, the characters, and above all the depth of his concern with them." Krutch concluded: "An O'Neill who wrote better would have been a better O'Neill. But he will last longer and mean more than many who can, in the ordinary sense, write rings around him."

O'Neill's plays continue to be performed around the world. In 2003, on the fiftieth anniversary of the playwright's death, *A Long Day's Journey into Night* was revived on Broadway. As a critic writing for *United Press International* noted, "The journey of a splendid cast into the playwright's black night of oblivion is one that theater-goers will never forget, and this soul-searching revival of the most memorable of all of O'Neill's more than fifty plays is not to be missed." In reviewing O'Neill's life and work in the *Southern Review*, Romulus Linney pointed out how wrong contemporary literary critics were when they consigned O'Neill and his plays to the dustbin of literary history. Linney especially praised *A Long Day's Journey into Night* and noted, "Someone will no doubt know better, but I can't think of any other writer who labored in fields so traditional and then crowned his life's work with a masterpiece so utterly radical."

BIOGRAPHICAL AND CRITICAL SOURCES:

BOOKS

Alexander, Doris, *The Tempering of Eugene O'Neill*, Harcourt (New York, NY), 1962.

Atkinson, Jennifer McCabe, *Eugene O'Neill: A Descriptive Bibliography*, University of Pittsburgh Press (Pittsburgh, PA), 1974.

Authors in the News, Volume 1, Gale (Detroit, MI), 1976.

Berlin, Normand, *Eugene O'Neill*, Grove Press (New York, NY), 1982.

Berlin, Normand, *O'Neill's Shakespeare*, University of Michigan Press (Ann Arbor, MI), 1993.

Bloom, Harold, editor, *Eugene O'Neill: Modern Critical Views*, Chelsea House (New York, NY), 1987.

Bogard, Travis, *Contour in Time: The Plays of Eugene O'Neill*, revised edition, Oxford University Press (New York, NY), 1987.

Bowen, Crosswell, *The Curse of the Misbegotten: A Tale of the House of O'Neill*, McGraw Hill (New York, NY), 1959.

Brustein, Robert, *The Theatre of Revolt: An Approach to the Modern Drama*, Little, Brown (Boston, MA), 1964.

Cargill, Oscar, N. B. Fagin, and W. J. Fisher, editors, *O'Neill and His Plays: Four Decades of Criticism*, New York University Press (New York, NY), 1961.

Carpenter, Frederic I., *Eugene O'Neill*, revised edition, Twayne (New York, NY), 1979.

Clark, Barrett H., *Eugene O'Neill: The Man and His Plays*, Dover (New York, NY), 1947.

Concise Dictionary of American Literary Biography: The Age of Maturity, 1929-1941, Gale (Detroit, MI), 1989.

Dictionary of Literary Biography, Volume 7: *Twentieth-Century American Dramatists*, Gale (Detroit, MI), 1981.

Dubost, Thierry, *Struggle, Defeat, or Rebirth: Eugene O'Neill's Vision of Humanity*, McFarland (Jefferson, NC), 1996.

Egan, Leona Rust, *Provincetown As a Stage: Provincetown, the Provincetown Players, and the Discovery of Eugene O'Neill*, Parnassus Imprints, 1994.

Eisen, Kurt, *The Inner Strength of Opposites: O'Neill's Novelistic Drama and the Melodramatic Imagination*, University of Georgia Press, 1994.

Engel, Edwin A., *The Haunted Heroes of Eugene O'Neill*, Harvard University Press (Cambridge, MA), 1953.

Falk, Doris V., *Eugene O'Neill and the Tragic Tension: An Interpretive Study of the Plays,* Rutgers University Press (Rutgers, NJ), 1958.

Fleche, Anne, *Mimetic Disillusion: Eugene O'Neill, Tennessee Williams, and U.S. Dramatic Realism,* University of Alabama Press (Tuscaloosa, AL), 1997.

Floyd, Virginia, *The Plays of Eugene O'Neill: A New Assessment,* Ungar (New York, NY), 1984.

Frenz, Horst, *Eugene O'Neill,* Ungar (New York, NY), 1971.

Gallup, Donald Clifford, *Eugene O'Neill and His Eleven-Play Cycle: "A Tale of Possessors Self-Dispossessed,"* Yale University Press (New Haven, CT), 1998.

Gassner, John, editor, *O'Neill: A Collection of Critical Essays,* Prentice Hall (Englewood, NJ), 1964.

Gelb, Arthur, and Barbara Gelb, *O'Neill,* Harper (New York, NY), 1962.

Griffin, Ernest G., *Eugene O'Neill: A Collection of Criticism,* McGraw-Hill (New York, NY), 1976.

Manheim, Michael, *The Cambridge Companion to Eugene O'Neill,* Cambridge University Press (New York, NY), 1998.

Miller, Jordan Y., editor, *Playwright's Progress: O'Neill and the Critics,* Scott Foresman (Chicago, IL), 1965.

Miller, Jordan Y., *Eugene O'Neill and the American Critic: A Summary and Bibliographical Checklist,* Archon Books (Hamden, CT), 1973.

O'Neill, Eugene, *The Complete Works of Eugene O'Neill,* Boni & Liveright (New York, NY), 1924.

O'Neill, Eugene, *The Iceman Cometh,* Random House (New York, NY), 1946.

O'Neill, Eugene, *A Moon for the Misbegotten,* Random House (New York, NY), 1952.

O'Neill, Eugene, *Long Day's Journey into Night,* Yale University Press (New Haven, CT), 1956.

Pfister, Joel, *Staging Depth: Eugene O'Neill and the Politics of Psychological Discourse,* University of North Carolina Press (Chapel Hill, NC), 1995.

Raleigh, John Henry, *The Plays of Eugene O'Neill,* Southern Illinois University Press (Carbondale, IL), 1965.

Raleigh, John Henry, editor, *The Iceman Cometh: A Collection of Critical Essays,* Prentice Hall (Englewood Cliffs, NJ), 1968.

Reaver, J. Russell, editor, *An O'Neill Concordance,* Gale (Detroit, MI), 1969.

Sheaffer, Louis, *O'Neill: Son and Playwright,* Little, Brown (Boston, MA), 1968.

Sheaffer, Louis, *O'Neill: Son and Artist,* Little, Brown (Boston, MA), 1973.

Siebold, Thomas, *Readings on Eugene O'Neill,* Greenhaven Press (San Diego, CA), 1998.

Tiusanen, Timo, *O'Neill's Scenic Images,* Princeton University Press (Princeton, NJ), 1968.

Tornqvist, Egil, *A Drama of Souls: Studies in O'Neill's Supernaturalistic Technique,* Yale University Press (New Haven, CT), 1969.

Twentieth-Century Literary Criticism, Gale (Detroit, MI), Volume 1, 1978, Volume 6, 1982, Volume 27, 1988, Volume 49, 1994.

World Literature Criticism, Gale (Detroit, MI), 1992.

PERIODICALS

Commentary, June, 1993, p. 58.
Kenyon Review, July, 1952.
Nation, November 26, 1924, Joseph Wood Krutch, review of *A Moon for the Misbegotten.*
New York, September 5, 1994, p. 52.
New York Daily News, November 8, 1956, John Chapman, review of *Long Day's Journey into Night.*
New York Times Book Review, August 31, 1952; September 22, 1957, Mary McCarthy, review of *Long Day's Journey into Night;* July 6, 2003, Margo Jefferson, "Alone with O'Neill," p. 27.
Partisan Review, November, 1946.
Saturday Review, November 21, 1936.
Southern Review, autumn, 2002, Romulus Linney, "O'Neill," p. 842.
Time, November 15, 1968.
United Press International, May 20, 2003, "*Long Day's Journey* Revived on Broadway," p. 1008140w8579.
Wall Street Journal, May 22, 1996, p. A18.

OBITUARIES:

PERIODICALS

Newsweek, December 7, 1953.
New York Times, November 28, 1953.
Time, December 7, 1953.*

* * *

ORGEL, Doris 1929-
(Doris Adelberg; Suzanne Altman, a joint pseudonym)

PERSONAL: Surname is pronounced "Or-*gel*"; born February 15, 1929, in Vienna, Austria; immigrated to

Doris Orgel

the United States, 1940; daughter of Ernest (a textile company manager) and Erna (Ehrmann) Adelberg; married Shelley Orgel (a psychiatrist and psychoanalyst), June 25, 1949; children: Paul, Laura, Jeremy. *Education:* Attended Radcliffe College, 1946-48; Barnard College, B.A. (cum laude), 1950. *Politics:* Independent. *Religion:* Jewish. *Hobbies and other interests:* Spending time with her children and grandchildren; reading, especially about ancient Greek culture and mythology; bird watching; traveling; swimming; music.

ADDRESSES: Agent—c/o Writers House, 21 West 26th St., New York, NY 10010.

CAREER: Employed in magazine and book publishing, prior to 1955; writer and translator of children's books, 1955—; Bank Street College of Education, New York, NY, Writer's Lab conductor, 1985-94; Bank Street Publications and Media Group, New York, NY, senior staff writer and editor, 1991-94.

MEMBER: Authors Guild, Authors League of America, PEN, Society of Children's Book Writers and Illustrators.

AWARDS, HONORS: Lewis Carroll Shelf Award, 1960, for translation of *Dwarf Long-Nose; Book World* Children's Spring Book Festival first prize in picture book division, 1972, for *Little John;* Notable Book citation, American Library Association, for *A Certain Magic;* Golden Kite Honor Book Award, Society of Children's Book Writers and Illustrators, 1978, Sydney Taylor Book Award, Association of Jewish Libraries, 1979, and Honor Book, Phoenix Award, 1998, all for *The Devil in Vienna.*

WRITINGS:

FOR CHILDREN

Sarah's Room, illustrated by Maurice Sendak, Harper (New York, NY), 1963.

(Under name Doris Adelberg) *Grandma's Holidays* (poetry), illustrated by Paul Kennedy, Dial (New York, NY), 1963.

(Under name Doris Adelberg) *Lizzie's Twins* (poetry), illustrated by N. M. Bodecker, Dial (New York, NY), 1964.

The Good-Byes of Magnus Marmalade (poetry), illustrated by Erik Blegvad, Putnam (New York, NY), 1966.

Cindy's Snowdrops, illustrated by Ati Forberg, Knopf (New York, NY), 1966.

Cindy's Sad and Happy Tree, illustrated by Ati Forberg, Knopf (New York, NY), 1967.

In a Forgotten Place, illustrated by James McMullan, Knopf (New York, NY), 1967.

On the Sand Dune, illustrated by Leonard Weisgard, Harper (New York, NY), 1968.

Whose Turtle?, illustrated by Martha Alexander, World Publishing (New York, NY), 1968.

Phoebe and the Prince, illustrated by Erik Blegvad, Putnam (New York, NY), 1969.

Merry, Rose, and Christmas-Tree June, illustrated by Edward Gorey, Knopf (New York, NY), 1969.

Next Door to Xanadu, illustrated by Dale Payson, Harper (New York, NY), 1969, published as *Next-Door Neighbors,* Harper (New York, NY), 1979.

The Uproar, illustrated by Anita Lobel, McGraw-Hill (New York, NY), 1970.

The Mulberry Music, illustrated by Dale Payson, Harper (New York, NY), 1971.

Bartholomew, We Love You!, illustrated by Pat Grant Porter, Knopf (New York, NY), 1973, published as *Me, Emily, and the Cat,* Scholastic (New York, NY).

A Certain Magic, Dial (New York, NY), 1975.

Merry Merry Fibruary (poetry), illustrated by Arnold Lobel, Parents' Magazine Press (New York, NY), 1977.

The Devil in Vienna, Dial (New York, NY), 1978.

Risking Love, Dial (New York, NY), 1985.

My War with Mrs. Galloway, illustrated by Carol Newsom, Viking (New York, NY), 1985.

Whiskers, Once and Always, illustrated by Carol Newsom, Viking (New York, NY), 1986.

Midnight Soup and a Witch's Hat, illustrated by Carol Newsom, Viking (New York, NY), 1987.

Crack in the Heart, Fawcett (New York, NY), 1989.

Starring Becky Suslow, illustrated by Carol Newsom, Viking (New York, NY), 1989.

Nobodies and Somebodies, Viking (New York, NY), 1991.

The Mouse Who Wanted to Marry, illustrated by Holly Hannon, Bantam (New York, NY), 1993.

Button Soup, illustrated by Pau Estrada, Bantam (New York, NY), 1994.

(With Ellen Schecter) *The Flower of Sheba,* illustrated by Laura Kelly, Bantam (New York, NY), 1994.

The Spaghetti Party, illustrated by Julie Durrell, Bantam (New York, NY), 1995.

Two Crows Counting (a counting book), illustrated by Judith Moffatt, Bantam (New York, NY), 1995.

The Princess and the God, Orchard (New York, NY), 1996.

Don't Call Me Slob-O, Hyperion (New York, NY), 1996.

Friends to the Rescue, Hyperion (New York, NY), 1996.

We Goddesses: Athena, Aphrodite, Hera, DK Publishing (New York, NY), 1999.

My Mother's Daughter: Four Greek Goddesses Speak, illustrated by Peter Malone, Roaring Brook Press (Brookfield, CT), 2003.

STORIES AND FAIRY TALES; RETELLER

Clemens Brentano, *Schoolmaster Whackwell's Wonderful Sons: A Fairy Tale,* illustrated by Maurice Sendak, Random House (New York, NY), 1962.

Wilhelm Hauff, *The Heart of Stone: A Fairy Tale,* illustrated by David Levine, Macmillan (New York, NY), 1964.

Richard Wagner, *The Story of Lohengrin, the Knight of the Swan,* illustrated by Herbert Danska, Putnam (New York, NY), 1966.

Wilhelm Hauff, *A Monkey's Uncle,* illustrated by Mitchell Miller, Farrar, Straus & Giroux (New York, NY), 1969.

E. T. A. Hoffman, *The Child from Far Away,* illustrated by Michael Eagle, Addison-Wesley (Boston, MA), 1971.

Rudolf E. Raspe, *Baron Munchausen: Fifteen Truly Tall Tales,* illustrated by Willi Baum, Addison-Wesley (Boston, MA), 1971.

Theodor Storm, *Little John,* illustrated by Anita Lobel, Farrar, Straus & Giroux (New York, NY), 1972.

Jacob and Wilhelm Grimm, *Godfather Cat and Mousie,* illustrated by Ann Schweninger, Macmillan (New York, NY), 1986.

Next Time I Will: An Old English Tale, illustrated by Betsy Day, Bantam (New York, NY), 1993.

Ariadne, Awake!, illustrated by Barry Moser, Viking (New York, NY), 1994.

(With Emily Coplon and Ellen Schecter) *She'll Be Coming round the Mountain,* illustrated by Rowan Barnes-Murphy, Bantam (New York, NY), 1994.

(With Ellen Schecter, under joint pseudonym Suzanne Altman) *Worst Days Diary,* Bantam (New York, NY), 1995.

The Lion and the Mouse and Other Aesop Fables, Dorling Kindersley (New York, NY), 2000.

The Bremen Town Musicians and Other Animal Tales from Grimm, illustrated by Bert Kitchen, Roaring Brook Press (Brookfield, CT), in press.

Also reteller of Clemens Brentano's *The Tale of Gockel, Hinkel, and Gackeliah,* illustrated by Maurice Sendak, 1961.

TRANSLATOR

Wilhelm Hauff, *Dwarf Long-Nose,* illustrated by Maurice Sendak, Random House (New York, NY), 1960.

Walter Grieder, *The Enchanted Drum,* illustrated by Walter Grieder, Parents' Magazine Press (New York, NY), 1969.

Mira Lobe, *The Grandma in the Apple Tree,* illustrated by Judith Gwyn Brown, McGraw-Hill (New York, NY), 1970.

Elke Heidenreich, *Nero Corleone: A Cat's Story,* Viking (New York, NY), 1997.

Antije Damm, *Ask Me,* Roaring Brook Press (Brookfield, CT), 2003.

David Chotjewitz, *Daniel Half-Human and the Good Nazi,* Atheneum (New York, NY), 2004.

Contributor of reviews to *New York Times* and *Five Owls,* and of translations to *Cricket.* Several of her books have been published in various countries abroad.

ADAPTATIONS: The Disney film *A Friendship in Vienna* is based on *The Devil in Vienna.*

SIDELIGHTS: "As the field of children's books becomes increasingly mass-market-driven, gimmicky, and reductive," noted children's author Doris Orgel in the *St. James Guide to Young Adult Writers,* "I feel grateful that it remains possible to write out of inwardness and singularity, and still hope to stir responses in individual children." Orgel's inward and singular work has delighted children since her translation of Wilhelm Hauff's *Dwarf Long-Nose* was published with illustrations by Maurice Sendak in 1960. Along with her translated books, Orgel has retold stories, like E. T. A. Hoffman's *The Child from Far Away* and Aesop's fables, and written fanciful original stories for young children, some in verse (like *Sarah's Room, Grandma's Holidays,* and *Lizzie's Twins*), some in prose (like *Merry, Rose, and Christmas-Tree June*). Orgel has also penned perceptive books for older children and young adults, notably her *The Devil in Vienna,* a thought-provoking novel based on her childhood during Hitler's annexation of Austria, and numerous other novels in which contemporary urban youths face problems involving busy parents, divorce, the death of pets, and first sexual relationships. And for young readers with a passion for Greek mythology, Orgel's fresh approach brings ancient heroines and goddesses alive in such books as *Ariadne, Awake!, The Princess and the God* (a version of the Cupid and Psyche myth told in Psyche's voice), *We Goddesses: Athena, Aphrodite, Hera* (in which the goddesses tell their stories), and *My Mother's Daughter: Four Greek Goddesses Speak* (featuring the tales of Leto, Artemis, Demeter, and Persephone).

Born Doris Adelberg, the author spent the first part of her life in Vienna, where her father worked as the manager of a textile company. Her mother did not work, but, as Orgel noted in her *Something about the Author Autobiography Series* (*SAAS*) essay, "her active social life kept her almost as busy as a job would have done." The author told *CA,* that she "remembers wishing her mother had more time for her, making the times they spent together all the more precious." Other early memories of the author include, "finding a lost, scruffy kitten and being allowed to keep it; feeding lettuce leaves to Ira, my box turtle; playing exciting games with my older sister, Lotte; and always hungering for stories—I could never get enough."

Tired of pestering grown-ups to read to her, she taught herself to read when she was five, and from then on read avidly. Among her favorite books were Astrid Lindgren's *Pippi Longstocking,* Selma Lagerlof's *The Adventures of Nils,* and Hugh Lofting's "Dr. Doolittle" books. "My all-time favorite—I read it at least thirty times—was Rudyard Kipling's *The Jungle Book* (Volume I, not II)," she recalled in *SAAS.* She also started writing her own stories at quite a young age. Into a book of blank pages her mother gave her, Orgel wrote a "rambling episodic novel about dolls who came alive and had adventures (a subject I revisited in *Sarah's Room, Merry, Rose, and Christmas-Tree June,* and in *A Certain Magic*)," she said in *SAAS.*

In 1938, Hitler and his army entered Vienna. Orgel told *SAAS* readers how disastrously this event affected Jews in Austria. "Soon after the Nazis took over, notices 'Forbidden to Jews' appeared on benches, drinking fountains, and the entrances to parks and other public places. . . . The grocer on our corner no longer sold food to us or other Jews when there were 'Aryan' (non-Jewish) customers in the store. . . . Jewish men, my grandfather among them, were taken from their homes before daybreak, told to bring their toothbrushes, and forced to scrub anti-Nazi slogans off walls and sidewalks while Jew-hating onlookers jeered."

Her father lost his job. Her best friend, Lieselotte, was no longer allowed to play with her. She and her Jewish classmates were thrown out of their school. As the persecution worsened, many Jewish parents sent their children abroad to what they thought were safe havens. But Orgel's parents resolved to keep their family together, come what may. In the summer of 1938, thanks to a ruse, great courage, and good luck, they managed to gain entrance to what was Yugoslavia. "The older I grow," she remarked in *SAAS,* "the more acutely I am aware of the enormous risk this entailed. I now acknowledge what as an adolescent and young adult I went to great lengths to keep secret from myself: That we got out by a hair's breadth. That we easily might *not* have."

They stayed in Yugoslavia until the following spring. Orgel attended school in Zagreb, a bewildering experience because everybody spoke Croatian, "of which I couldn't understand a word," she told *CA*. In April, 1939, they traveled by train and boat to England. For a while, they lived in London, then in the country. "I loved it there," the author said. "I knew enough English to do well at school, make friends, and thrill to a whole new world of reading: Charles Kingsley's *Water Babies,* George Macdonald's *The Princess and the Goblin,* Lewis Carroll's *Alice in Wonderland,* Anna Sewell's *Black Beauty,* and Shakespeare's *Julius Caesar* and *A Midsummer Night's Dream.*"

In December, the family's quota numbers, which allowed them to enter America, came up. Meanwhile, World War II had begun. To avoid being torpedoed by German submarines, the British ship the family sailed on took a zigzag course, making the voyage extra long—twelve days. The author recounted to *CA* that she was seasick the entire time. They arrived in New York City in January, 1940, almost penniless and faced a difficult time. Her father searched for a job in vain, and her mother, who had once studied Greek, Latin, and law, supported the family, working as a cleaning woman. They lived on the fifth-floor in an apartment with cockroaches and bedbugs. To make matters worse, Orgel was assigned to the ninth grade when she should have been in the fifth. The other students laughed at her clothes and accent, and she could not keep up in math class.

In the fall, the family moved to St. Louis, Missouri, where they had relatives "who helped us get on our feet," the author recalled to *CA*. "But living in Missouri was a culture shock. Segregation was still in force. There were separate schools for whites and 'negroes' (as African Americans were called)." As Orgel wrote in *SAAS,* "It reminded us of Nazism." The family moved back to New York in 1941. Orgel was placed in the eighth grade, where she belonged. A teacher, Mrs. Elmendorf, praised her writing and encouraged her to keep on.

After high school, she entered Radcliffe College in Cambridge, Massachusetts. Along with the required courses, she took as many courses in German literature

as she could. "In hindsight, I believe I did this in order to win back the language of my childhood, which I'd started to forget," she commented.

In her freshman year at Radcliffe, the author met Shelley Orgel, then at Harvard. They fell in love. At the start of her junior year, she transferred to Barnard College in New York, where Shelley Orgel was at the New York University School of Medicine. The couple married, and Doris Adelberg became Doris Orgel.

After graduating from Barnard, she worked at jobs in book and magazine publishing until the first of her three children was born. From then on, she continued to work at home as a translator, reviewer, and writer. Orgel confided to *CA* that she has never regretted her decision to leave the world of jobs and stay home. "An unforeseen dividend came of my decision: I'd always known I'd be a writer but was vague about just what I'd write. And now I knew for certain: children's books!"

Reading aloud to her children, Orgel re-experienced her childhood delight in stories. That led to her first translation, *Dwarf Long-Nose* by Wilhelm Hauff, which her mother had read to her. *Dwarf Long-Nose* won the Lewis Carroll Shelf Award for excellence. Inventive retellings of other favorite stories from her childhood soon followed, among them Clemens Brentano's *The Tale of Gockel, Hinkel, and Gackeliah.* And before long, she was writing stories of her own. Some of these, *In a Forgotten Place* for instance, use fantasy elements to offset the realistic events. Others embroider on what she had dreamed up as a child. And many were inspired by her young children—*their* wishes, fears, and dreams.

Cindy's Sad and Happy Tree and *Cindy's Snowdrops* are among Orgel's earliest books. In *Cindy's Sad and Happy Tree,* an elm tree in Cindy's yard has died, and Cindy weeps. When her parents suggest that they plant another tree in its place, Cindy insists on a tree that looks as though it were sad. At the same time, the tree must comfort her. Cindy selects a weeping cherry tree and calls it a "weeping cheery tree." Barbara Gibson noted in *Library Journal* that Orgel portrays "a child's identification with nature" in a sensitive manner. In *Cindy's Snowdrops,* Cindy visits a nursery and buys seven snowdrop bulbs to plant. The blossoms appear on Cindy's birthday in March. *Horn Book* reviewer Mary Silva Cosgrave thought that readers would "share Cindy's pride and joy."

In *Merry, Rose, and Christmas-Tree June,* illustrated by Edward Gorey, Jane goes to visit her great aunt and misses her beloved dolls Merry and Rose. Given the chance to select any doll at a doll shop, Jane chooses an old doll that was first put up for sale several Christmases ago. The shop owner tells Jane that the newer dolls can do mechanical things, such as walk a few steps or cry a few tears. Even so, Jane chooses the old doll who cannot do any mechanical things but can dance and sing and eat and play and do everything Jane wants her to—via pretend, as all well-loved dolls can do. According to a reviewer in the *Bulletin of the Center for Children's Books,* Orgel "strikes a blow for imaginative play."

Gradually, Orgel's fiction began to portray characters with realistic problems in realistic settings. Many of these books for older readers draw on her own experiences. One of the main events in *Bartholomew, We Love You!,* in which a young girl trades her kitten for a box of chocolates shaped like spools of thread and other sewing items, comes from Orgel's childhood. A *Publishers Weekly* reviewer called this book a "gently understated and appealing story with convincing characterizations."

Another book based on Orgel's experiences recalls her life in Nazi Austria. Inge, the narrator and protagonist of *The Devil in Vienna,* is a combination of Orgel and her older sister. The book is written in the form of entries in a young girl's diary. Inge begins her story in 1938 when Hitler and his troops arrived in Austria and the Jews there faced degradation and persecution. Inge has one non-Jewish person she can count on— Lieselotte, her best friend. Although Lieselotte's father is a Nazi, she remains loyal to Inge. The girls maintain their friendship after their parents forbid them to meet, after Inge is sent to a school for Jews, and even after Lieselotte moves to Germany. When Inge's family confronts overwhelming bureaucratic obstacles to leaving the country, it is Lieselotte's uncle, a Catholic priest, who plays a crucial part in helping them escape.

Throughout the book, in what Virginia Haviland described in *Horn Book* as a "naturally exuberant, girlish style," Inge tells of joyous moments as well as the anxiety and losses. According to Zena Sutherland in the *Bulletin of the Center for Children's Books, The Devil in Vienna* is one of the better stories in "depicting the erosion, the tension, and the fear" of Jewish families in German-occupied lands. Matilda Kornfeld

observed in *School Library Journal* that the inclusion of reactions of all kinds of people like teachers and schoolmates to the situations in *The Devil in Vienna* "makes the evil of the period comprehensible on a preadolescent level."

Orgel offered a different perspective on this same historical milieu with *A Certain Magic,* in which a contemporary girl, discovering a diary her aunt Trudl kept in the 1930s, learns how hard things were for Trudl when she was young and of the way she fought to overcome her outsider status. On a trip to England with her parents, eleven-year-old Jenny decides to visits the places where her aunt stayed as a refugee before immigrating to the United States. Matilda Kornfeld, writing in *School Library Journal,* praised the pace of the book and the "individual and believable" characters, but thought that "most interesting are the themes of guilt and evil that motivate the story in terms that children can well understand." Similarly, for Mary M. Burns in *Horn Book,* the novel was a "suspenseful, contemporary story which explores in childlike terms the unity of past and present as well as the notion of evil."

Whether they are based on her childhood or not, Orgel's novels for children and young adults are convincingly written from the perspectives of her protagonists. In *Next Door to Xanadu,* Patricia, also known as "Fatsy Patsy," learns—with a little help from her parents—to deal with the loss of best friend Dorothy when that girl moves away. A critic for *Kirkus Reviews* felt that girls would "like [the book] enormously and there's every reason they should." A reviewer for *Horn Book* thought that Patricia relates her story "with spontaneity and conviction," while Sutherland, writing in the *Saturday Review,* found the same book "a completely natural, smoothly written story of two very real girls."

Orgel's four-book series about Becky Suslow, the daughter of a divorced and busy physician-mother, presents a convincing portrait of a young city girl with contemporary problems. Orgel introduces seven-year-old Becky in *My War with Mrs. Galloway.* Becky dislikes Mrs. Galloway, her family's new sitter and housekeeper, from the start. Mrs. Galloway is strict, takes precious time away from Becky's mother, and does not seem to respect Becky's beloved, pregnant cat, Whiskers. Becky finds ways to show her discontent— she draws an unkind picture of the woman and uses vanishing cream to try to make her disappear. She remains hostile to Mrs. Galloway until the woman helps Whiskers with the birth of her kittens and accepts one of the three for herself. In Becky, Charlotte W. Draper wrote in *Horn Book,* "Orgel has created another unmistakably contemporary child." Sutherland, writing in the *Bulletin of the Center for Children's Books,* noted that the "light humor and controlled writing make pleasant reading."

In *Whiskers, Once and Always,* Becky's cat Whiskers dies after a bad fall. Consumed with grief and anger, Becky blames her mother's boyfriend, a veterinarian who could not save the cat. Becky gets into trouble at school and even shuns her mother. To make things worse, after a friend tells Becky that at least her mother did not die, Becky keeps visualizing her mother dead. Becky's problems begin to subside only after the school principal helps her deal with her feelings, and she stops worrying about her mother. According to *Horn Book* reviewer Karen Jameyson, Orgel's "handling of the subject . . . is quite perceptive"; a *Publishers Weekly* critic commented that "[Becky's] complex feelings are sensitively portrayed." Similarly, a contributor for *Kirkus Reviews* called the novel a "brief story . . . packed with feelings and thoughts familiar to children who have experienced the death of a cherished pet." And Ginny McKee recognized in a *School Library Journal* review of *Whiskers, Once and Always,* "Orgel is a skillful writer."

Midnight Soup and a Witch's Hat presents Becky's relationship with her father. When Becky, who is almost nine years old, arrives to visit him in Oregon, she is surprised to find that Hope, the six-year-old daughter of her father's girlfriend, is also visiting. From Becky's perspective, Hope steals time away from her father. The "plot's resolution . . . should leave readers satisfied and hopeful," remarked Katharine Bruner in *School Library Journal.* A *Publishers Weekly* critic felt that the book's strength was "a gently probing style and Becky's spirited methods for working out things herself." "Orgel has a light touch and smooth narrative flow in her writing," noted Sutherland in the *Bulletin of the Center for Children's Books.* A critic for *Kirkus Reviews* also commended this continuation of the series, noting that the author "presents realistic, contemporary concerns and experiences with understanding, humor, and affection."

According to a critic in *Kirkus Reviews,* readers who enjoyed Orgel's previous books about Becky "will be delighted with this sequel," *Starring Becky Suslow.* The book begins as Becky and her best friends, Kyra and Melanie, enter fourth grade, and Rainbow Rothstein, who has acted in commercials, joins their class. After Rainbow's mother, a talent scout, invites Becky to audition for a television commercial, Becky's relationship with Kyra and Melanie begins to sour. Although Becky's first audition is a success, it takes the realization that the crayons she is endorsing are of poor quality and her failure at the callback to restore peace among the four girls. As Carrol McCarthy noted in *School Library Journal,* Orgel develops each character "as an individual, with a unique personality, problems, and expectations."

Risking Love, for high school readers, features Dinah Moskowitz in her first year of college at Barnard. When Dinah meets Gray, a senior biology major, she begins her first sexual relationship and later announces her plan to abandon college for a year and follow Gray to a job in the Everglades. At her father's suggestion, Dinah begins to see a psychotherapist, Dr. Schneck, and realizes that her parents' divorce taught her a haunting lesson: love may not be forever. Critical opinion of *Risking Love* varied. As *School Library Journal* contributor Rita S. Padden pointed out, the therapy sessions "comprise the major portion of the story," and even though the presentation of psychotherapy is accurately portrayed, she felt that readers will become impatient with some of the "pretentious and verbose conversations." Nancy C. Hammond, however, concluded in *Horn Book* that "the girl comes alive through her psychological vulnerability." A critic in *Publishers Weekly* described *Risking Love* as a "very good and potentially enlightening story."

In addition to writing original stories and novels, Orgel continues to retell traditional and ancient tales. Instead of just revisiting the usual versions of these stories, Orgel makes neglected characters come to life with their own personalities, desires, and concerns. In *Ariadne, Awake!,* for example, Orgel takes a character heretofore marginal to the tale of Theseus and the Minotaur and transforms her into the heroine of her own story. In a prologue, Orgel tells how Ariadne's father, King Minos, offended Poseidon, and how Poseidon caused his wife to fall in love with a bull. After giving birth to a half-human, half-bull offspring, the Minotaur, Ariadne's mother dies. The Minotaur survives to demand an annual meal of young Athenian men. In the body of the book, Ariadne narrates her story, beginning with her attempt and failure to be-friend her half-brother the Minotaur as a child. She then reveals how, at fifteen, she falls in love with one of the young men to be sacrificed, Theseus, and helps him escape from the Minotaur's labyrinth. Theseus kills the Minotaur and abandons Ariadne on the island of Naxos. There she goes through a time of mourning her lost love and ultimately wins a new love—the great god Dionysus whom she marries. In *Horn Book,* Mary M. Burns wrote that the story's "style is contemporary in feeling, reinforcing the concept that ancient tales have universal applications." Likewise, Patricia Dooley, writing in *School Library Journal,* thought that "the emotional heroine, and the romantic and sexual themes, may make this myth material more than palatable to middle-school readers." Other reviewers also praised the accessibility of Orgel's retelling. A critic for *Kirkus Reviews* called the book a "dramatic introduction to a fascinating myth," and *Booklist*'s Hazel Rochman concluded, "Orgel shows that the young woman's perilous journey is also a personal one of leaving home and transforming herself."

Orgel tackles another Greek myth in *The Princess and the God,* a retelling of the story of Cupid and Psyche—from Psyche's point of view. In the myth, the beautiful Venus sends her son, Cupid, to punish Psyche, a young princess of such renowned physical beauty that she is said to rival even Venus. Cupid, of course, falls in love with the young beauty; far from punishing her, he takes her for his wife with one stipulation: she must promise not to look at him when he comes to visit her at night. Unable to resist, however, Psyche gazes on her lover, and is thereby sentenced to terrible drudgery by the groom's mother, Venus. A contributor for *Kirkus Reviews* thought this novel was "one of Orgel's most lyrical, compelling works, . . . an epic love story at its center and adventure running through it like a stream." Hazel Rochman, writing in *Booklist,* elaborated on the theme of the tale: "Orgel makes it clear that this is a story about growing up and leaving home. Above all, it's about the transforming power of love." For Cheri Estes, writing in *School Library Journal,* "Psyche's quest is grippingly related." And reviewing the novella in the *New York Times Book Review,* David Sacks felt that Orgel "describes with dignity Psyche's experience of marriage," and went on to comment that the book "succeeds because it interprets Psyche's heart."

Orgel continues to breathe new life into Greek myth with *We Goddesses* and the 2003 *My Mother's Daugh-*

ter. Described as a "feminist perspective on the Greek myths" by Elaine Williams in the *Times Literary Supplement, We Goddesses* presents first person narratives from three different goddesses, Hera, wife of Zeus, Athena, goddess of wisdom, and Aphrodite, goddess of love. This "original approach to Greek mythology," as a contributor for *Publishers Weekly* called the book, has the goddesses in question presenting personal stories that bring their meanings in Greek culture to life for modern readers. Orgel also includes a pronunciation guide as well as an ongoing explanation of historical events and Greek locations, such as Mount Olympus. *Booklist*'s Carolyn Phelan felt that "this handsomely designed book" with "Orgel's rousing interpretations" would appeal to young "mythology fans."

Orgel employs the same first-person narrative in *My Mother's Daughter,* this time relating stories of two mother-daughter teams, the Titaness Leto and her daughter, Artemis, goddess of wild creatures and hunting, and the grain goddess Demeter and her daughter Persephone, who was carried off by Hades to be the queen of the underworld. For a critic writing in *Kirkus Reviews,* the result was "Xena: Warrior Princess, crossed with soap opera." The same reviewer, while noting that Orgel was attempting to "revitalize the appeal of these goddesses," thought that the result of her efforts "falls a bit flat." Similarly, Angela J. Reynolds, writing in *School Library Journal,* found that the "storytelling is stilted," but also commented that Orgel's "characters do come to life."

Speaking on the Children's Book Council Web site, Orgel explained the sources of her inspiration: "The ancient Greeks believed the Muse, a goddess of the arts, inspired (literally, breathed) words, whole songs into a poet's ear. For us now, inspiration comes from many sources. Encouragement can bring it on. Or someone we admire, an agent or an editor, suggests a topic, the topic catches on fire. . . . And for a blessed interval, before I face up to the problems and sheer hard work ahead, I bask in feeling certain that I'm in to something I was born to write."

BIOGRAPHICAL AND CRITICAL SOURCES:

BOOKS

Children's Literature Review, Volume 48, Gale (Detroit, MI), 1997.

St. James Guide to Young Adult Writers, 2nd edition, St. James Press (Detroit, MI), 1999.

Something about the Author Autobiography Series, Volume 19, Gale (Detroit, MI), 1995, pp. 193-209.

PERIODICALS

Booklist, October 15, 1977, Barbara Elleman, review of *Merry Merry Fibruary,* pp. 379-380; October 1, 1984, Stephanie Zvirin, review of *Risking Love,* p. 212; March 15, 1986, Irene Cooper, review of *Godfather Cat and Mousie,* p. 1086; December 1, 1986, Barbara Elleman, review of *Whiskers, Once and Always,* p. 581; November 15, 1987, Phillis Wilson, review of *Midnight Soup and a Witch's Hat,* p. 572; December 15, 1989, Denise Wilms, review of *Starring Becky Suslow,* pp. 843-844; January 15, 1990, Hazel Rochman, review of *Crack in the Heart,* p. 991; July, 1991, Leone McDermott, review of *Nobodies and Somebodies,* pp. 2045-2046; December 1, 1993, Hazel Rochman, review of *Next Time I Will,* p. 702; February 1, 1994, Carolyn Phelan, review of *The Flower of Sheba,* p. 1012; May 1, 1994, Hazel Rochman, review of *Ariadne, Awake!,* p. 1599; October 1, 1995, April Judge, review of *Two Crows Counting,* p. 329; January 1, 1995, Hazel Rochman, review of *The Spaghetti Party,* p. 828; February 1, 1996, Hazel Rochman, review of *The Princess and the God,* p. 926; January 1, 1997, Shelley Townsend-Hudson, review of *Don't Call Me Slob-O,* p. 860; September 15, 1997, John Peters, review of *A Cat's Story,* p. 235; October 15, 1999, Carolyn Phelan, review of *We Goddesses: Athena, Aphrodite, Hera,* p. 429; October 1, 2000, GraceAnne A. DeCandido, review of *The Lion and the Mouse,* p. 343; April 1, 2003, GraceAnne A. DeCandido, review of *Ask Me,* p. 1400.

Bulletin of the Center for Children's Books, December, 1969, review of *Merry, Rose, and Christmas-Tree June,* pp. 62-63; January, 1970, review of *Phoebe and the Prince,* p. 86; November, 1970, pp. 46-47; December, 1970, review of *The Uproar,* p. 64; January, 1972, review of *The Mulberry Music,* pp. 77-78; July-August, 1973, review of *Bartholomew, We Love You!,* p. 174; December, 1978, Zena Sutherland, review of *The Devil in Vienna,* p. 70; February, 1985, review of *Risking Love,* p. 114; April, 1985, Zena Sutherland, review of *My War with Mrs. Galloway,* pp. 153-154; October, 1986, Betsy Hearne, review of *Whiskers, Once and Always,*

p. 34; July-August, 1987, Zena Sutherland, review of *Midnight Soup and a Witch's Hat,* p. 216; July, 1991, Roger Sutton, review of *Nobodies and Somebodies,* p. 270; June, 1994, p. 330.

Horn Book, February, 1967, Mary Silva Cosgrave, review of *Cindy's Snowdrops,* p. 62; February, 1970, review of *Next Door to Xanadu,* pp. 42-43; April, 1972, Virginia Haviland, review of *The Mulberry Music,* p. 147; August, 1976, Mary M. Burns, review of *A Certain Magic,* p. 400; February, 1978, review of *Merry Merry Fibruary,* p. 62; February, 1979, Virginia Haviland, review of *The Devil in Vienna,* p. 70; March-April, 1985, Nancy C. Hammond, review of *Risking Love,* p. 187; May-June, 1985, Charlotte W. Draper, review of *My War with Mrs. Galloway,* pp. 312-313; January-February, 1987, Karen Jameyson, review of *Whiskers, Once and Always,* pp. 56-57; July, 1989, Carolyn K. Jenks, review of *Starring Becky Suslow,* p. 75; November-December, 1991, review of *Nobodies and Somebodies,* pp. 737-738; September-October, 1994, Mary M. Burns, review of *Ariadne, Awake!,* pp. 589-590; March, 2001, review of *The Lion and the Mouse,* p. 220.

Journal of Reading, October, 1979, M. Jean Greenlaw, review of *The Devil in Vienna,* p. 88; April, 1986, Jan Lieberman and Alice Stern, review of *Risking Love,* p. 689.

Kirkus Reviews, August 15, 1969, review of *Phoebe and the Prince,* p. 852; December 1, 1969, review of *Merry, Rose, and Christmas-Tree June,* and *Next Door to Xanadu,* pp. 1258-1259; July 1, 1970, review of *The Uproar,* p. 678; September 15, 1986, review of *Whiskers, Once and Always,* p. 1451; August 15, 1987, review of *Midnight Soup and a Witch's Hat,* p. 1243; October 15, 1989, review of *Starring Becky Suslow,* pp. 1533-1534; February 1, 1994, review of *The Flower of Sheba,* p. 148; April 15, 1994, review of *Ariadne, Awake!,* pp. 561-562; January 15, 1996, review of *The Princess and the God,* p. 140; April 1, 2003, review of *My Mother's Daughter: Four Greek Goddesses Speak,* p. 538.

Language Arts, January, 1986, Janet Hickman, review of *My War with Mrs. Galloway,* pp. 89-90; December, 1986, Janet Hickman, review of *Godfather Cat and Mousie,* p. 826.

Library Journal, June 15, 1967, p. 2454; January 15, 1968, Barbara Gibson, review of *Cindy's Sad and Happy Tree,* p. 284; October 15, 1968, p. 3958; October 15, 1969, review of *Merry, Rose, and Christmas-Tree June,* pp. 3848-3851; December,

15, 1969, Eleanor Glaser, review of *Phoebe and the Prince,* p. 4597; September 15, 1970, Sada Fretz, review of *The Uproar,* p. 3041; November 15, 1971, Rose S. Bender, review of *The Mulberry Music,* pp. 3903-3904; May 15, 1973, Linda Johnson, review of *Bartholomew, We Love You!,* p. 1683.

New Statesman, June 2, 1972, John Fuller, review of *Sarah's Room,* p. 762.

New York Times Book Review, May 20, 1973, review of *Bartholomew, We Love You!,* p. 10; December 17, 1978; p. 26; October 14, 1984, Marilyn Kaye, review of *Risking Love,* p. 16; August 4, 1985, review of *My War with Mrs. Galloway,* p. 21; June 16, 1996, David Sacks, review of *The Princess and the God,* p. 33.

Publishers Weekly, September 1, 1969, review of *Merry, Rose, and Christmas-Tree June,* p. 52; March 5, 1973, review of *Bartholomew, We Love You!,* p. 83; August 28, 1978, review of *The Devil in Vienna,* p. 394; January 4, 1985, review of *Risking Love,* p. 69; May 30, 1986, review of *Godfather Cat and Mousie,* p. 65; November 28, 1986, review of *Whiskers, Once and Always,* pp. 75-76; November 13, 1987, review of *Midnight Soup and a Witch's Hat,* p. 71; November 24, 1989, review of *Crack in the Heart,* p. 73; June 7, 1991, review of *Nobodies and Somebodies,* p. 66; October 18, 1991, review of *Sarah's Room,* p. 65; November 15, 1991, review of *Starring Becky Suslow,* p. 74; April 22, 1996, review of *The Princess and the God,* pp. 72-73; November 29, 1999, review of *We Goddesses,* p. 72; August 14, 2000, review of *The Lion and the Mouse,* p. 354.

Reading Teacher, March, 1995, review of *Ariadne, Awake!,* p. 513.

Saturday Review, September 13, 1969, Zena Sutherland, review of *Phoebe and the Prince,* pp. 36-37; May 9, 1970, Zena Sutherland, review of *Next Door to Xanadu,* p. 45.

School Library Journal, May, 1976, Matilda Kornfeld, review of *A Certain Magic,* pp. 62-63; February, 1978, Annabelle R. Bernard, review of *Merry Merry Fibruary,* p. 50; November, 1978, Matilda

Kornfeld, review of *The Devil in Vienna,* p. 66; December, 1984, Rita S. Padden, review of *Risking Love,* p. 93; September, 1985, Louise L. Sherman, review of *My War with Mrs. Galloway,* p. 138; May, 1986, Liza Bliss, review of *Godfather Cat and Mousie,* p. 83; December, 1986, Ginny McKee, review of *Whiskers, Once and Always,* p. 107; October, 1987, Katharine Bruner, review of *Midnight Soup and a Witch's Hat,* p. 128; December, 1989, Carrol McCarthy, review of *Starring Becky Suslow,* p. 102; August, 1993, Gale W. Sherman, review of *Next Time I Will,* p. 160; June, 1994, Patricia Dooley, review of *Ariadne, Awake!,* p. 152; February, 1995, Sharon McElmeel, review of *Button Soup,* pp. 78-79; February, 1996, Marilyn Taniguchi, review of *Two Crows Counting,* p. 88; April, 1996, Cheri Estes, review of *The Princess and the God,* p. 157; July, 1996, Blair Christolon, review of *Friends to the Rescue,* pp. 85-86; March, 1997, Cheryl Cufari, review of *Don't Call Me Slob-O,* p. 162; October, 2000, Ginny Gustin, review of *The Lion and the Mouse,* p. 151; March, 2003, Liza Graybill, review of *Ask Me,* p. 191; May, 2003, Angela J. Reynolds, review of *My Mother's Daughter,* p. 158.

Spectator, April 22, 1972, Ruth Marris, review of *Sarah's Room,* p. 624.

Teacher Librarian, June, 2000, Jessica Higgs, review of *We Goddesses,* p. 55.

Times Educational Supplement, November 10, 2000, Elaine Williams, review of *We Goddesses,* p. 23.

Times Literary Supplement, April 28, 1972, review of *Sarah's Room,* p. 483.

Voice of Youth Advocates, April, 1990, Rosemary Moran, review of *Crack in the Heart,* p. 32.

Washington Post Book World, December 21, 1969, Polly Goodwin, review of *Merry, Rose, and Christmas-Tree June,* p. 8.

ONLINE

Children's Book Council Web site, http://www.cbc books.org/ (January 14, 2004).

P

PARRY, Graham 1940-

PERSONAL: Born January 5, 1940, in Sutton, Cold-field, England; son of Herbert and Ida (Jones) Parry; married Barbara Henry, November 4, 1967. *Ethnicity:* "White." *Education:* Pembroke College, Cambridge, B.A. 1961, M.A., 1965; Columbia University, Ph.D., 1965.

ADDRESSES: Home—28 Micklefield Lane, Rawdon, Leeds, England. *Office*—Department of English and Literature, University of York, Heslington, York YO1 5DD, England; fax: 01904-433372. *E-mail*—gp8@ york.ac.uk.

CAREER: Columbia University, New York, NY, pre-ceptor, 1962-65; University of British Columbia, Van-couver, British Columbia, Canada, assistant professor, 1965-67; University of Leeds, Leeds, England, lecturer in English, 1967-76; University of York, Heslington, York, England, lecturer in English, beginning 1977, became Professor of Renaissance Literature. University of Toulouse, visiting professor,1972-73; City College of the City University of New York, visiting professor, 1975-76; Doshisha University, visiting professor, 1981-82, 1997-98; University of British Columbia, visiting professor, 1993-94.

MEMBER: Society of Antiquaries (fellow), York Bibliographical Society (chair, 1988—).

WRITINGS:

Lady Mary Wroth's Urania, Leeds Philosophical and Literary Society (Leeds, England), 1975.

Graham Parry

The Pre-Raphaelite Image: Style and Subject, 1848-1856, University of Leeds Press (Leeds, England), 1978.

Hollar's England: A Mid-Seventeenth Century View, Michael Russell (Salisbury, England), 1980.

"The Golden Age Restor'd": The Culture of the Stuart Court, 1603-1642, Manchester University Press (Manchester, England), 1981.

358

Seventeenth-Century Poetry: The Social Context, Hutchinson (Dover, NH), 1985.

The Seventeenth Century: The Intellectual and Cultural Context of English Literature, 1603-1700, Longman (London, England), 1989.

The Trophies of Time: English Antiquarians of the Seventeenth Century, Oxford University Press (Oxford, England), 1995.

The Life and Letters of John Talman, Walpole Society (London, England), 1997.

(Editor, with Joad Raymond) *Milton and the Terms of Liberty,* Boydell & Brewer (Woodbridge, England), 2002.

Contributor to periodicals, including *British Journal of Aesthetics, Notes and Queries,* and *Cambridge Quarterly.*

WORK IN PROGRESS: A book about the Arts of the Church in the time of William Laud.

SIDELIGHTS: Trained as a literary scholar, Graham Parry is considered an expert on the cultural history of the seventeenth century; his emphasis is on the first half of the century and, in particular, on that region of Jacobean culture where its arts met its politics through royal and aristocratic patronage. While Parry's *The Pre-Raphaelite Image: Style and Subject, 1848-1856* examines the nineteenth-century British Pre-Raphaelite movement in painting and poetry, it is his subsequent volume, *Hollar's England: A Mid-Seventeenth Century View,* in which the author demonstrates his area of expertise. *Hollar's England* focuses on the life and work of Bohemian-born etcher Vaclav Hollar (1607-1677), who settled in England during much of his career and painted well-known pictures of London before the great fire.

With his next book, *"The Golden Age Restor'd": The Culture of the Stuart Court, 1603-1642,* Parry takes on a more central subject: the cultural life of the court of James I. He deals with the masques, or stylized stage entertainments, that were produced by Ben Jonson and Inigo Jones, investigating their contents and their backgrounds to show how the development of the court's taste paralleled its belief in the divine right of kings, while making comparisons between Britain and imperial Rome. (The title of Parry's book was also the title of one of Jonson's masques, hence the archaic apostrophe.) Parry devotes one of his "most illuminat-

ing chapters," in the view of *Times Literary Supplement* reviewer Blair Worden, to the Earl of Arundel, a noted art collector. Worden, who called Parry "a courteous and exceptionally helpful guide" through this subject matter, described the book as "a distinguished and eloquent survey" of a corner of the seventeenth century: "Parry crosses disciplinary frontiers with unconventional enthusiasm, and controls a wide range of material with notable lucidity and economy. His book has long been needed."

The Shakespearean scholar A. L. Rowse, who reviewed *"The Golden Age Restor'd"* for the *Spectator,* remarked that it is "good on the literary side, informative with regard to the arts, less good on the historical and social background to it all." Rowse pointed out the relative absence of material on the music of the court of James I, a court which was notable for its contributions to that art. He did, however, note that Parry is "illuminating on the literature of the masques." Kevin Sharpe in the *New York Review of Books* felt that Parry's treatment oversimplifies the life and politics of the court, underestimates the degree of dissent allowable in such environments, and sympathizes too little with the king; however, he appreciated *"The Golden Age Restor'd"* as "a broad landscape: the details are hazy, but the picture is clear enough to encourage exploration."

Parry subsequently published *Seventeenth-Century Poetry: The Social Context.* The target audience for the volume is university students who need background for their readings of literature. As Julia Briggs pointed out in the *Times Literary Supplement,* Parry confines his subject to the first half of the seventeenth century and specifically to nine poets: Jonson, early Milton, and seven metaphysical poets. Briggs judged that the narrowing of range helps make *Seventeenth-Century Poetry* a "successful" work. The social context of the poetry is "sketche[d] in capably when appropriate," she stated, and the author makes "subtle recommendations" on the literature, such as a positive recommendation for metaphysical poet Richard Crashaw. "Parry's account is consistently temperate, lucid, and thoughtful," Briggs commented.

Parry then published *The Trophies of Time: English Antiquarians of the Seventeenth Century.* This volume follows a theme also visible in *"The Golden Age Restor'd"*: Parry's perception of art collecting and antiquarianism as a key to the culture of a historical period.

Parry told *CA:* "*The Life and Letters of John Talman* is about an early eighteenth-century antiquary and collector of prints and drawings. He lived in Rome for twenty years and was a focal point for travelers and collectors who were interested in the Italian art market.

"Interconnections between the arts have always been at the center of my interests, and this curiosity drives my current research, which is concerned with the architectural styles appropriate to the Church of England in the seventeenth century, and the return of the arts—painting, stained glass, sacred music, devotional poetry—to the service of the church after ninety years of austerity and iconophobia."

BIOGRAPHICAL AND CRITICAL SOURCES:

PERIODICALS

New York Review of Books, December 2, 1982, Kevin Sharpe, review of *"The Golden Age Restor'd":* *The Culture of the Stuart Court, 1603-1642,* pp. 43-45.

Spectator, December 19, 1981, A. L. Rowse, review of *"The Golden Age Restor'd,"* pp. 28-29.

Times Educational Supplement, June 13, 1986, p. 28; September 26, 1986, p. 29.

Times Literary Supplement, February 5, 1982, Blair Worden, review of *"The Golden Age Restor'd,"* p. 123; December 13, 1985, Julia Briggs, review of *Seventeenth-Century Poetry: The Social Context,* p. 1436.

*   *   *

PATRICK, John 1905-1995

PERSONAL: Birth name, John Patrick Goggan; name legally changed; born May 17, 1905, in Louisville, KY; died of an apparent suicide, November 7, 1995, in Delray Beach, FL; son of John Francis and Myrtle (Osborn) Goggan. *Education:* Attended Holy Cross College, St. Edward's College, St. Mary's Seminary, Harvard University, and Columbia University.

CAREER: Playwright and author of screenplays. National Broadcasting Corp. (NBC-Radio), San Francisco, CA, scriptwriter, 1933-36; freelance writer in

John Patrick

Hollywood, CA, 1936-38. Also appeared in several movies, including (as bartender) *Spoilers of the Forest,* 1957; (as Sgt. Malin) *Revolution,* 1985; (as seaman) *Buster,* 1988; and (as poker instructor) *Honeymoon in Vegas,* 1992. *Military service:* American Field Service, 1942-44; served as ambulance driver; became captain; served with Montgomery's Eight Army in Egypt and with the British Ninth Army in Syria.

MEMBER: Dramatists Guild.

AWARDS, HONORS: New York Drama Critics Circle Award for best American play of the year, Pulitzer Prize in drama, Antoinette Perry (Tony) Award, League of New York Theatres and Producers, Aegis Club Award, and Donaldson Award, *Billboard Magazine,* all 1954, all for *The Teahouse of the August Moon;* Screenwriters Guild Award and Foreign Correspondents Award, both 1957, both for *Les Girls;* D.F.A. from Baldwin-Wallace College, 1972; honored with Patrick Film Festival, in Virgin Islands, 1979.

WRITINGS:

PLAYS

Hell Freezes Over, first produced in New York, NY, at the Ritz Theatre, December 28, 1935.

The Willow and I (three-act; first produced in New York, NY, at the Windsor Theatre, December 10, 1942), Dramatists Play Service (New York, NY), 1943.

The Hasty Heart: A Play in Three Acts (first produced Off-Broadway at Hudson Theatre, January 3, 1945), Random House (New York, NY), 1945; published as *The Hasty Heart: Comedy-Drama in Three Acts,* Dramatists Play Service (New York, NY), 1945.

The Story of Mary Surratt: A Play in Three Acts (first produced on Broadway at Henry Miller's Theatre, February 8, 1947), Dramatists Play Service (New York, NY), 1947.

The Curious Savage (three-act; first produced on Broadway at Martin Beck Theatre, October 24, 1950), Dramatists Play Service (New York, NY), 1951.

Lo and Behold!: A New Comedy in Three Acts (first produced on Broadway at Booth Theatre, December 12, 1951), Samuel French (New York, NY), 1952.

The Teahouse of the August Moon: A Play (adapted from the novel by Verne J. Sneider; first produced on Broadway at Martin Beck Theatre, October 15, 1953), Putnam (New York, NY), 1952, Dramatists Play Service (New York, NY), 1957.

Good as Gold (three-act; adapted from the novel by Alfred Toombs), first produced on Broadway at the Belasco Theatre, March 7, 1957.

(With James Norman) *Juniper and the Pagans,* first produced in Boston, MA, at the Colonial Theater, December 10, 1959.

Everybody Loves Opal: A "Prank" in Three Acts (first produced on Broadway at Longacre Theatre, October 11, 1961), Dramatists Play Service (New York, NY), 1962.

Everybody's Girl: A Comedy in Three Acts (first produced in Miami, FL, 1967; produced in Albuquerque, NM, at the Albuquerque Little Theatre, September, 1968), Dramatists Play Service (New York, NY), 1968.

Scandal Point: A Play in Three Acts (first produced in Albuquerque, NM, at the Albuquerque Little Theatre, September, 1967; produced in Paramus, NJ, at the Paramus Playhouse, May 12, 1970), Dramatists Play Service (New York, NY), 1969.

Love Is a Time of Day (first produced on Broadway at Music Box, December 22, 1969), Dramatists Play Service (New York, NY), 1970.

Lovely Ladies, Kind Gentlemen (adapted from his play *The Teahouse of the August Moon;* music and lyrics by Stan Freeman and Franklin Underwood; first produced on Broadway at Majestic Theatre, December 28, 1970), Samuel French (New York, NY), 1971.

A Barrel Full of Pennies (two-act; first produced in Paramus, NJ, at the Playhouse on the Mall, May 12, 1970), Dramatists Play Service (New York, NY), 1971.

Opal Is a Diamond (first produced in Flat Rock, NC, at Flat Rock Playhouse, the State Theatre of North Carolina, July 27, 1972), Dramatists Play Service (New York, NY), 1972.

Roman Conquest: A Play in Three Acts (first produced in Berea, Ohio, at Baldwin-Wallace Summer Theatre [formerly Berea Summer Theatre], July 25, 1973), Samuel French (New York, NY), 1972.

Macbeth Did It (three-act; first produced in Flat Rock, NC, at Flat Rock Playhouse, the State Theatre of North Carolina, July, 1972), Dramatists Play Service (New York, NY), 1972.

The Savage Dilemma (first produced in Long Beach, CA, at Long Beach Community Theatre, May 19, 1972), Dramatists Play Service (New York, NY), 1972.

The Dancing Mice: A Drama in Three Acts (first produced in Berea, OH, at Baldwin-Wallace Summer Theatre, June, 1972), Dramatists Play Service (New York, NY), 1972.

Anybody Out There?, Dramatists Play Service (New York, NY), 1972.

Love Nest for Three, Samuel French (New York, NY), 1973.

Sex on the Sixth Floor: Three One-Act Plays (includes *Tenacity, Ambiguity,* and *Frustration;* first produced in 1974), Samuel French (New York, NY), 1973.

Opal's Baby: A New Sequel in Two Acts (first produced in Flat Rock, NC, at Flat Rock Playhouse, the State Theatre of North Carolina, June 26, 1973), Dramatists Play Service (New York, NY), 1974.

The Enigma (first produced in Berea, OH, at Baldwin-Wallace Summer Theatre, June 12, 1972), Dramatists Play Service (New York, NY), 1974.

A Bad Year for Tomatoes (first produced in North Royalton, OH, at the John Patrick Dinner Theatre at the You Are Cabaret Dinner Theatre, 1974), Dramatists Play Service (New York, NY), 1975.

Opal's Husband (first produced in Flat Rock, NC, at the Flat Rock Playhouse, the State Theatre of North Carolina, 1975), Dramatists Play Service (New York, NY), 1975.

It's Been Wonderful (first produced in Albuquerque, NM, at the Albuquerque Little Theatre, September, 1966), Dramatists Play Service (New York, NY), 1976, 1998.

Divorce, Anyone? (first produced in North Royalston, OH, at the John Patrick Dinner Theatre at the You Are Cabaret Dinner Theatre, 1975), Dramatists Play Service (New York, NY), 1976.

Suicide, Anyone? (first produced in St. Thomas, Virgin Islands, at the Fortuna Theatre Club, 1976), Dramatists Play Service (New York, NY), 1976.

Noah's Animals: A Musical Allegory (first produced in Berea, OH, at the Baldwin-Wallace Summer Theatre, 1975), Dramatists Play Service (New York, NY), 1976.

That's Not My Mother: Three One Act Plays (includes *Seniority, Redemption,* and *Optimism;* first produced in Saint Thomas, Virgin Islands, 1979), Samuel French (New York, NY), 1980.

People!: Three One Act Plays (includes *Boredom, Christmas Spirit,* and *Aptitude;* first produced in North Royalston, OH, at the John Patrick Dinner Theatre at the You Are Cabaret Dinner Theatre, October, 1976), Samuel French (New York, NY), 1980.

The Girls of the Garden Club: A Comedy in Three Acts (first produced in Berea, Ohio, at the Baldwin-Wallace Summer Theatre, July, 1979), Dramatists Play Service (New York, NY), 1980.

That's Not My Father!: Three One Act Plays (includes *Raconteur, Fettucine,* and *Masquerade;* first produced in Saint Thomas, Virgin Islands, at the Fortune Theatre Club, 1979), Samuel French (New York, NY), 1980.

Opal's Million Dollar Duck (first produced in St. Thomas, Virgin Islands, at the School of Performing Arts, September, 1979), Dramatists Play Service (New York, NY), 1980.

The Magenta Moth, Dramatists Play Service (New York, NY), 1983.

It's a Dog's Life (three one-act plays; includes *The Gift, Co-Incidence,* and *The Divorce;* first produced in New York, NY, 1980), Samuel French (New York, NY), 1984.

Danny and the Deep Blue Sea, first produced in Louisville, KY, 1984.

The Reluctant Rogue, or, Mother's Day, Dramatists Play Service (New York, NY), 1984.

Cheating Cheaters: A Comedy, Dramatist Play Service (New York, NY), 1985.

The Gay Deceiver: A Play in Three Acts, Dramatists Play Service (New York, NY), 1988.

The Doctor Will See You Now: Four One-Act Plays, Dramatists Play Service (New York, NY), 1991.

Dirty Ditties, Penguin (New York, NY), 1996, recorded by Dove Audio (Los Angeles, CA), 1996.

Also author of other plays, including *The Chiropodist, Compulsion, Confession, Empathy, Four Dogs and a Bone, The Gynecologist, Habit, Integrity, Loyalty, The Physician,* and *The Psychiatrist.*

SCREENPLAYS; ALL BY TWENTIETH CENTURY-FOX, UNLESS OTHERWISE INDICATED

(With Lou Breslow and David Silverstein) *15 Maiden Lane,* 1936.

(With Lou Breslow) *36 Hours to Kill,* 1936.

(With others) *Charlie Chan at the Racetrack,* 1936.

(With Katherine Kavanaugh and Edward T. Lowe) *Educating Father,* 1936.

(With Lou Breslow and Edward Eliscu) *High Tension,* 1936.

(With Lou Breslow) *The Holy Terror,* 1937.

(With Lou Breslow, Helen Logan, and Robert Ellis) *Big Town Girl,* 1937.

(With Lou Breslow) *Dangerously Yours,* 1937.

(With Lou Breslow) *Look Out, Mr. Moto,* 1937.

(With Robert Ellis and Helen Logan) *Born Reckless,* 1937.

(with Lou Breslow and Ben Markson) *Sing and Be Happy,* 1937.

(With Lou Breslow, Robin Harris, and Alfred Golden), *One Mile from Heaven* (adapted from the short story by Judge Ben Lindsey, "Little Colored White Cloud"), 1937.

(With Lou Breslow) *Midnight Taxi* (adapted from the short story by Borden Chase), 1937.

(With Lou Breslow) *Time Out for Romance,* 1937.

(With Lou Breslow) *International Settlement,* 1938.

(With Lou Breslow) *Mr. Moto Takes a Chance,* 1938.

(With Lou Breslow and Maurine Watkins) *Up the River,* 1938.

(With Lou Breslow) *Five of a Kind,* 1938.

(With Lou Breslow and Norman Houston) *Battle of Broadway,* 1938.

Enchantment (adapted from the novel *A Fugue in Time* by Rumer Godden), RKO, 1948.

The President's Lady (adapted from the novel by Irving Stone), 1953.

Three Coins in the Fountain (adapted from the novel by John Secondari), 1954.

Love Is a Many Splendored Thing (adapted from the novel by Han Suyin), 1955.

High Society (adapted from the play *The Philadelphia Story* by Philip Barry), Metro-Goldwyn-Mayer (MGM), 1956.

The Teahouse of the August Moon (adapted from the novel by Verne J. Sneider and the play by Patrick), MGM, 1956.

(With Tom Hubbard) *Daniel Boone, Trail Blazer,* Republic, 1957.

Les Girls (adapted from the novel by Vera Caspary), MGM, 1957.

(With Arthur Sheekman) *Some Came Running* (adapted from the novel by James Jones), MGM, 1958.

The World of Suzie Wong (adapted from the play by Paul Osborne based on the novel by Richard Mason), Paramount, 1960.

Parrish (adapted from the novel by Mildred Savage), Warner Bros., 1961.

Gigot (adapted from the story by Jackie Gleason), Seven Arts (Fox), 1962.

(With Marguerite Roberts) *The Main Attraction,* Seven Arts (MGM), 1963.

(With James Kennaway) *The Shoes of the Fisherman* (adapted from the novel by Morris L. West), MGM, 1968.

Also author (with Arthur Dales) of the teleplay *The Small Miracle* (adapted from the children's story by Paul Gallico) for "Hallmark Hall of Fame," NBC-TV, 1973. Author of more than eleven hundred radio plays for the series *Cecil and Sally* (produced 1929-1933). Scriptwriter for Helen Hayes's programs.

OTHER

Sense and Nonsense (poems), Samuel French (London, England), 1989.

Contributor to *The Best Short Stories, 1915-1917,* compiled by Edward J. O'Brien. Also created the covers for the *Growling Light* by Martha Conley, St. Martin's Press, 1993; and *Inches* by William Marshall, Warner/Mysterious Press, 1994. John Patrick's manuscript collection is held at Boston University.

SIDELIGHTS: John Patrick's career as a playwright took off slowly, but gained momentum as he continued to write. *Hell Freezes Over,* Patrick's first effort as a playwright, highlights an airship crash in Antarctica. The author's first play showed his inexperience at playwriting, for it was quickly a box-office disappointment. His second play, *The Willow and I,* takes place in 1900. Two sisters, opposite in appear-

ance and temperament, fall in love with the same man. When he chooses the kinder, gentler sister for marriage, the other sister intends to shoot herself and take her own life. The placid sister discovers her and tries to wrestle the gun away, but is scared when the gun fires in the tousle. She runs away and lives as a recluse for forty years, her mind locked on the horrible events that occurred on the day she was supposed to be married. In the *Dictionary of Literary Biography,* John Marion wrote, "The strange, haunting story is unique among Patrick's plays, and reveals depth not usually found in his work. Certainly it reflects his mastery of mood and atmosphere and prevents challenging roles." Despite some favorable critical opinion, *The Willow and I,* like *Hell Freezes Over,* never became popular, and so Patrick would wait for his success.

After a stint with the American Field Service following World War II, Patrick wrote *The Hasty Heart,* a play based in part on his experiences during World War II. He composed the play on a return voyage from North Africa to Virginia, writing on any scrap of paper he could obtain. He then entrusted a pilot friend with the disjointed manuscript, sneaking it off the ship to avoid military censorship of his work. *The Hasty Heart*'s protagonist is Lachlen McLachlen, a terminally ill Scottish sergeant who has been sent to a British military hospital to convalesce. While at the hospital, Lachlen is wary of the other patients, but slowly warms to their attempts at friendship. When he discovers, however, that the patients know he will soon die, Lachlen interprets their friendship as pity and feels humiliated. When Lachlen divulges his sentiments to them, the patients become angry, and Lachlen learns to trust and value companionship. *The Hasty Heart* was Patrick's first successful play, faring well both at the box office and in popular critical opinion. Christian M. Moe wrote in the *Cyclopedia of World Authors* that the play demonstrates "Patrick's premise that human interdependency is crucially important."

The comedic *The Curious Savage,* Patrick's next play, involves the elderly Mrs. Ethel P. Savage, whose stepchildren have committed her to a mental asylum to give them access to her wealth. At the play's end, Ethel, with the help of her fellow patients, enacts revenge on the greedy children. Though the play experienced only a short run on Broadway, it earned Patrick international renown, as well as a loyal community theater following.

By far the most popular of Patrick's works is *The Teahouse of the August Moon,* an adaptation of the novel by Verne J. Sneider. *The Teahouse* takes place on the small island Okinawa, which was occupied by American soldiers after World War II. Based on historical events, but with a fictionalized plot, the play satirizes the American military as soldiers bumble about in an effort to democratize the Asian natives. Captain Fishby is a young soldier who has been assigned to this particular mission, called "Plan B." Fishby begins to teach the Okinawan people the concepts of democracy, encouraging them to make choices for themselves, as Americans do. He has an interpreter, Sakini, to help him communicate with the island natives. The military's initial plan is to build a schoolhouse for the people of Okinawa, but as the villagers learn more about democracy, they decide that they don't want a schoolhouse, but a teahouse instead. After a vote, the teahouse prevails, and Captain Fishby relents, using the military-issued schoolhouse supplies to build a teahouse. The establishment centers on the beautiful Lotus Blossom, a geisha whom Fishby first mistakes for a prostitute. When the cultural misconception is corrected, and Fishby no longer disdains her, Lotus Blossom teaches him about the native culture. As the teahouse is built, Fishby becomes culturally assimilated, until he finds himself wearing sandals, eating local foods, participating in tea ceremonies, and walking around in his bathrobe, his crude version of the kimono.

Upon his arrival on the island, Fishby had also been instructed to help the villagers establish a local enterprise in which to sell their local goods. After they fail at marketing crafts, Fishby is introduced to an old sweet-potato brandy recipe. He decides that this is their ticket to enterprise and creates a distillery, which profits very well. Fishby seems to have fulfilled the requirements of "Plan B" until his superior officer, Colonel Purdy, arrives at the teahouse unexpectedly and sees Fishby in his bathrobe. Fishby is reprimanded and Purdy orders that the teahouse and distillery be destroyed. The villagers only pretend to destroy the structures, which ultimately profits Purdy when the village is named one of the most successful American democratization efforts of the military.

The international popularity of *The Teahouse* was largely due to the comic nature of the play, and foreigners' delight upon seeing Americans make fun of their own culture. Its other cultural implications, however, have become dated since the play was written, and many critics question the appropriateness of

producing it in more recent years. "Although extremely popular in the 1950s, this play became outdated by the 1970s when increased awareness of racial issues led the audience to recognize the stereotypes of Asian people in the play," wrote one *Drama for Students* contributor. Another *Drama for Students* contributor, David Kelly, wrote, "It is almost impossible for modern readers to view *Teahouse of the August Moon* without being uncomfortably aware that it promotes attitudes toward race, gender, and chemical abuse that we find inappropriate today." The play won many awards for Patrick in 1956, including a Pulitzer Prize in Drama and a Tony award.

In 1961, Patrick introduced audiences to Opal, a character who would appear several times in his plays, in *Everybody Loves Opal*. Opal Kronkie is a middle-aged woman who lives by herself in an aging mansion near a dump. Opal goes to the dump to collect little bits of junk that amuse her. When three criminals on the run come to her door in search of a place to hide, Opal opens her home to them, setting herself up for a string of comic attempts to take the woman's life and collect her insurance money. The criminals, Gloria, Bradford, and Soloman, try to make the ceiling fall on her head, but Opal happens to be in the basement. Then they try to set her house on fire, but Opal's policeman friend shows up to chat. After several other attempts, the trio gives up, unaware that Opal had plenty of money stashed all over the house, which she would have given to them had they only asked. Opal returns in *Opal Is a Diamond*, first produced in 1972, when Opal takes on a shady politician in his run for mayor. Opal has many supporters, and she manages to win over enough of the voting population to make her campaign a threat. Opal again becomes an unknowing victim, and laughs are plentiful as Opal inadvertently survives a dangerous situation once again.

In *Opal's Baby*, Opal is searching for treasures in the dump when she meets a man who is looking for a tire. The man, Norman, assumes that Opal is wealthy and claims to be a long-lost relative. He encourages his daughter-in-law, Verna, to shove a pillow under her shirt and pretend she is pregnant. The delighted Opal decides to leave all of her money to the new baby, leaving Norman and Verna with a complicated scheme to pull off. In 1975, Opal gets married in *Opal's Husband*, but she does not marry for love. Opal answers a personal ad in search of a husband for her friend Rosie, but when the man turns out to be a ninety-five-year-old nursing home escapee, Rosie is displeased. The man's daughter tries to send him back, where she wants him to live his final days quietly until death allows her to collect his inheritance, so Opal saves the man by marrying him. In *Opal's Million Dollar Duck*, the fifth and final Opal play, two actresses visit Opal's junk shop. When they see a painting depicting a dead mallard and an apple, the actresses, Desmond and Queenie, recall that a valuable painting recently went missing from a local art museum, and a sizeable award is offered for its return. Thinking that Opal's painting is the missing masterpiece, they try to persuade Opal to sell it to them, but Opal intends to give Rosie the painting for her birthday. When Rosie rejects the painting because it reminds her of her dead pet duck, Opal gives the painting to the actresses, who ecstatically run away before Opal can change her mind. They do not know, however, that the painting has already been returned to the museum, and that Opal's copy is worthless. Patrick offered many comic delights with Opal and other characters, having found his niche in playwriting—to enchant audiences into laughter.

Patrick was also a highly successful screenwriter and, later in life, a poet. Although he lived for many years in the Virgin Islands, he died in 1995 in Florida, apparently a suicide. His final poem, "A Suicide Note," was found with his body: "I won't dispute my right to die; I'll only give the reasons why; You reach a certain point in time When life has lost reason and rhyme."

BIOGRAPHICAL AND CRITICAL SOURCES:

BOOKS

Banham, Martin, editor, *The Cambridge Guide to World Theatre,* Cambridge University Press (Cambridge, England), 1988.

Benet, William Rose, *The Reader's Encyclopedia,* 2nd edition, Thomas Y. Crowell (New York, NY), 1965.

Berney, K.A., editor, *Contemporary American Dramatists,* St. James Press (London, England), 1994.

Berney, K.A., editor, *Contemporary Dramatists,* 5th edition, St. James Press (London, England), 1993.

Bradbury, Malcolm, and others, editors, *The Penguin Companion to World Literature. American Literature,* McGraw-Hill (New York, NY), 1971.

Burke, W. J. and Will D. Howe, *American Authors and Books,* 1640 to the present day, 3rd revised edition, revised by Irving Weiss and Anne Weiss, Crown Publishers (New York, NY), 1972.

Dictionary of Literary Biography, Volume 7: *Twentieth-Century American Dramatists,* Gale (Detroit, MI), 1981.

Drama for Students, Volume 13, Gale (Detroit, MI), 2001.

Haliwell, Leslie, *Halliwell's Filmgoer's Companion,* 9th edition, Scribner (New York, NY), 1988.

Hart, James D., *The Oxford Companion to American Literature,* 6th edition, Oxford Univesity Press (New York, NY), 1995.

Herzbeg, Max J., *The Reader's Encyclopedia of American Literature,* Thomas Y. Crowell (New York, NY), 1962.

Katz, Ephraim, *The Film Encyclopedia,* Thomas Y. Crowell (New York, NY), 1979.

Lane, Hana Umlauf, editor, *The World Almanac Book of Who,* World Almanac Publishers (New York, NY), 1980.

Legends in Their Own Time, Prentice Hall General Reference (New York, NY), 1994.

Magill, Frank N., *Critical Survey of Drama,* revised edition, seven volumes, Salem Press (Pasadena, CA), 1994.

Magill, Frank N., editor, *Cyclopedia of World Authors,* revised 3rd edition, five volumes, Salem Press (Pasadena, CA), 1997.

The New York Times Biographical Service, Volume 26, numbers 1-12, UMI (Ann Arbor, MI), 1995.

Perkins, George, and others, editors, *Benet's Reader's Encyclopedia of American Literature,* 1st edition, HarperCollins (New York, NY), 1991.

Room, Adrian, *Dictionary of Pseudonyms,* 3rd edition, McFarland (Jefferson, NC), 1998.

Stephens, Michael L., *Gangster Films,* McFarland (Jefferson, NC), 1996.

ONLINE

Guide to World Drama Web site, http://www.4-wall.com/ (January 29, 2004), "John Patrick."

Homeville: Bibliographic Resources Web site, http://users.ev1.net/~homeville/ (January 29, 2004), "Index of Short Stories from Edward J. O'Brien's *The Best Short Stories, 1915-1917.*"

Locus Magazine Web site, http://www.locusmag.com/ (January 29, 2004), "Locus Index to Science Fiction: Cover Artists."

Microsoft Network Entertainment Web site, http://entertainment.msn.com/ (January 29, 2004), "Celebrity Information: John Patrick."

Movies.com, http://movies.go.com/ (March 3, 2004), "John Patrick."

Play Database, http://www.playdatabase.com/ (March 3, 2004), summaries of John Patrick's plays.

OBITUARIES:

PERIODICALS

Chicago Tribune, November 10, 1995, section 3, p. 10.
Los Angeles Times, November 11, 1995, p. A34.
New York Times, November 9, 1995, p. B17.
Washington Post, November 10, 1995, p. D7.*

*   *   *

PUZO, Mario 1920-1999

PERSONAL: Born October 15, 1920, in New York, NY; died of heart failure, July 2, 1999, in Bay Shore, NY; son of Antonio (a railroad trackman) and Maria (Le Conti) Puzo; married Erika Lina Broske (deceased), 1946; children: Anthony, Joey, Dorothy, Virginia, Eugene. *Education:* Attended New School for Social Research (now New School University) and Columbia University. *Hobbies and other interests:* Gambling, tennis, Italian cuisine, dieting.

CAREER: Novelist. Variously employed as messenger with New York Central Railroad, New York, NY, public relations administrator with U.S. Air Force in Europe, administrative assistant with U.S. Civil Service, New York, NY, and editor-writer with Magazine Management. *Military service:* U.S. Army Air Forces during World War II; served in Germany; attained rank of corporal.

AWARDS, HONORS: Academy Award for best screenplay adapted from another medium, American Academy of Motion Picture Arts and Sciences, and Screen Award, Writers Guild of America, West, both 1972, both for *The Godfather,* and 1974, for *The Godfather: Part II;* Golden Globe Award for best screenplay, Hollywood Foreign Press Association, 1973, for *The Godfather,* and 1990, for *The Godfather: Part III.*

WRITINGS:

The Dark Arena, Random House (New York, NY), 1955, revised edition, Bantam (New York, NY), 1985.

The Fortunate Pilgrim, Atheneum (New York, NY), 1964, reprinted, Random House (New York, NY), 1997.

The Godfather (also see below), Putnam (New York, NY), 1969, new edition, with an introduction by Robert Thompson and by Peter Bart, New American Library (New York, NY), 2002.

Fools Die, Putnam (New York, NY), 1978.

The Sicilian, Linden Press/Simon & Schuster (New York, NY), 1984.

The Fourth K, Random House (New York, NY), 1991.

The Last Don, Random House (New York, NY), 1996.

Omerta, Random House (New York, NY), 2000.

The Family, completed by Carol Gino, Regan Books (New York, NY), 2001.

SCREENPLAYS

(With Francis Ford Coppola) *The Godfather* (based on Puzo's novel), Paramount, 1972.

(With Francis Ford Coppola) *The Godfather: Part II,* Paramount, 1974.

(With George Fox) *Earthquake,* Universal, 1974.

(With David Newman, Leslie Newman, and Robert Benton) *Superman* (based on the comic strip created by Jerry Siegel and Joel Shuster), Warner Bros., 1978.

(With David Newman and Leslie Newman) *Superman II,* Warner Bros., 1981.

(With Francis Ford Coppola) *The Godfather: Part III,* Paramount, 1990.

(With John Briley and Cary Bates) *Christopher Columbus: The Discovery,* Warner Bros., 1992.

OTHER

The Runaway Summer of Davie Shaw (juvenile), illustrated by Stewart Sherwood, Platt & Munk (New York, NY), 1966.

"The Godfather" Papers and Other Confessions, Putnam (New York, NY), 1972.

Inside Las Vegas (nonfiction), photographs by Michael Abramson, Susan Fowler-Gallagher, and John Launois, Grosset & Dunlap (New York, NY), 1977.

Contributor to books, including *The Immigrant Experience: The Anguish of Becoming an American,* edited by Thomas C. Wheeler, Dial (New York, NY), 1971;

contributor of articles, reviews, and stories to *American Vanguard, New York, Redbook, Holiday, New York Times Magazine,* and other publications.

Manuscript collection is held at Boston University, Boston, MA.

The Godfather has been translated into Russian.

ADAPTATIONS: A Time to Die, based on a story by Puzo, was adapted for film by John Goff, Matt Cimbert, and William Russel, Almi, 1983; *The Cotton Club,* based on a story by Puzo, Coppola, and William Kennedy, was adapted for film by Kennedy and directed by Coppola, Orion Pictures, 1984; *The Fortunate Pilgrim* was adapted for television as *Mario Puzo's The Fortunate Pilgrim,* NBC, 1988; *The Sicilian* was adapted for film by Steve Shagan and directed by Michael Cimino, Twentieth Century-Fox, 1989; *The Last Don* was adapted for television, CBS, 1997. Film rights to *The Family* were optioned, 2003.

SIDELIGHTS: Though some critics have dismissed his best-sellers for pandering too much to commercial tastes, Italian-American novelist and screenwriter Mario Puzo forever changed the way the world thought of the Mafia. His "Godfather" books and the films on which they were based have become undisputed classics of twentieth-century popular literature, garnering both popular and critical acclaim and setting a new standard for the fictional treatment of organized crime. As *Time* writer Karl Taro Greenfeld put it, Puzo's work "virtually created the Mafia as literary and cinematic subject."

Despite his eventual celebrity, Puzo's success was a long time coming. The son of immigrants who moved to the Hell's Kitchen area of New York City from their native Italy, Puzo had dreamed of being a writer since high school but had struggled for years to achieve a footing in the publishing world. After serving in the U.S. Army in World War II, he worked as a freelance writer while attending City College of New York on the G.I. Bill. During this period, he completed his first novel, *Dark Arena,* which was published in 1955. A second novel, *The Fortunate Pilgrim,* was published nine years later. Though these books received positive reviews, they were not commercial successes; Puzo earned a mere $6,500 from their com-

bined sales. Struggling to support his wife and five children, Puzo slipped into debt; fortunately, as he told a writer for *Time,* an incident in 1955 convinced him to change his priorities. "It was Christmas Eve and I had a severe gall-bladder attack." Puzo explained. "I had to take a cab to the Veterans Administration Hospital on 23rd Street, got out and fell into the gutter. There I was, lying there thinking: here I am, a published writer, and I am dying like a dog. That's when I decided I would be rich and famous."

Ten years later, Puzo got his chance to act on his goal. "Late in 1965 a Putnam editor stopped in at Magazine Management's offices, overheard Puzo telling Mafia yarns and offered a $5,000 advance for a book about the Italian underworld," a writer for *Time* reported. The result was *The Godfather,* and "the rest," that writer noted, "is publishing history." In *"The Godfather" Papers and Other Confessions,* Puzo stated that *The Godfather* was written "to make money . . . I was forty-five years old and tired of being an artist." Nevertheless, as Robert Lasson of the *Washington Post Book World* contended, "Puzo sat down and produced . . . a novel which . . . had enormous force and kept you turning the pages." *The Godfather* became the best-selling novel of the 1970s, outselling that decade's other blockbusters—such heavyweights as *The Exorcist, Love Story,* and *Jaws*—by millions of copies. It remained on the *New York Times* best-seller list for sixty-seven weeks, and was also a best-seller in England, France, Germany.

The Godfather details the rise of Don Vito Corleone, the fall of his sons Sonny and Michael, the Mafia's peculiar behavior code and honor system, and the violent power struggle among rival "families." To some reviewers, Puzo's tale is a symbolic treatment of the corruption of the American dream. Although not all critics viewed the novel so seriously, most, like Polly Anderson in *Library Journal,* felt that "the book is well written, suspenseful and explodes in a series of dramatic climaxes." *Newsweek* reviewer Pete Axthelm called Puzo "an extremely talented storyteller" and stated that *The Godfather* "moves at breakneck speed without ever losing its balance." And a critic for the *Saturday Review* contended that "Puzo has achieved the definitive novel about a sinister fraternity of crime."

Several reviewers have noted the realism and believability of the book's settings and characters. "He makes his frightening cast of characters seem human and possible," maintained a *Saturday Review* contributor, while in the same journal Vincent Teresa praised the author for portraying the Godfather as a fair and compassionate administrator of justice: "Puzo also showed the compassion of a don, the fair way Corleone ruled. That's the way most dons are. . . . If you go to a don. . . and you've got a legitimate beef . . . and it proves to be the truth, you'll get justice. That's what makes the dons so important in the mob. They rule fair and square."

Such remarks led some to speculate that Puzo's knowledge of the Mafia and its people was first-hand. The author, however, always denied any personal involvement with the Mob. In *"The Godfather" Papers and Other Confessions,* he explains that the book was based on research and anecdotes he heard from his mother and on the streets. Still, doubts persisted. Real-life underworld figures began approaching Puzo, convinced that he had some sort of link to organized crime. "After the book became famous, I was introduced to a few gentlemen related to the material," the author stated in *Time.* "They were flattering. They refused to believe that I had never had the confidence of a don."

While most critics praised *The Godfather* for its realism, some objected to the fact that Puzo presents his subjects sympathetically. These critics contended that because Puzo consistently justifies Don Vito's violent actions and solutions, certain readers would find the criminal leader and his family worthy of compassion and esteem. "The author has chosen to portray all Godfather's victims as vermin and his henchmen as fairly sympathetic," *Esquire*'s Barton Midwood asserted, "and in this way the book manages to glamorize both the murderer himself and the [imbalanced] economy in which he operates." In *Critical Inquiry,* John G. Cawelti voiced a similar complaint: "Throughout the story, the Corleone family is presented to us in a morally sympathetic light, as basically good and decent people who have had to turn to crime in order to survive and prosper in a corrupt and unjust society." Puzo was puzzled by readers' positive response to the Corleones, particularly Vito. As he put it in a *Publishers Weekly* interview with Thomas Weyr: "I was awfully surprised when people loved the Godfather so much. I thought I showed him as a murderer, a thief, a villain, a man who threw babies in the oven. . . . So I was astounded when I was attacked for glorifying the Mafia. It's a little tricky. I think it is a novelist's

job not to be a moralist but to make you care about the people in the book."

Though *The Godfather* was Puzo's commercial breakthrough, catapulting him to fame and fortune, the author did not consider the novel to be his best work. "'I wished like hell I'd written it better,'" *New York Times* obituarist Mel Gussow quoted Puzo as saying. "'I wrote below my gifts in that book.'" According to Gussow, Puzo felt his best book was his second novel, *The Fortunate Pilgrim,* the story of an Italian-American family in New York City that is based in Puzo's own background. Puzo claimed that he had intended to write about himself, but the character of Lucia Santa, based on his mother, became so strong that he made her the novel's focus.

After *The Godfather* and *"The Godfather" Papers and Other Confessions,* Puzo focused his attention on screenwriting, first as coauthor of *The Godfather* and *The Godfather: Part II,* then as coauthor of the films *Earthquake, Superman,* and *Superman II.* Special effects, rather than story or plot, highlight the last three films. Pauline Kael of the *New Yorker* commented: "You go to *Earthquake* to see [Los Angeles] get it, and it really does. . . . *Earthquake* is a marathon of destruction effects, with stock characters spinning through it." A *Time* movie reviewer found that *Superman,* for which Puzo wrote the first draft, is "two hours and fifteen minutes of pure fun, fancy and adventure."

Garnering far more serious attention were *The Godfather* movie and its sequels. The first film covers the period from the mid-1940s to the mid-1950s, when Michael takes command of the "family"; the second film charts the youth and early manhood of the original Godfather, Vito, and contrasts his coming-of-age with Michael's. Vincent Canby in the *New York Times* remarked that "the novel is a kind of first draft—an outline of characters and an inventory of happenings—that has only now been finished as a film." In a *New Yorker* review, Kael deemed *The Godfather* "the greatest gangster picture ever made," and praised the "metaphorical overtones that took it far beyond the gangster genre." Part II, according to Kael, is even more "daring" in that "it enlarges the scope and deepens the meaning of the first film." The critic maintained that "the second film shows the consequences of the actions of the first; it's all one movie, in two great big pieces, and it comes together in your head while you watch."

Although Puzo was given coauthor credit for both screenplays, Francis Ford Coppola's direction and interpretation are credited with imbuing the films with their "epic" quality. Coppola "turns *The Godfather: Part II* into a statement, both highly personal and with an epic resonance, on the corruption of the American dream and on the private cost of power," Paul D. Zimmerman wrote in *Newsweek*. Puzo would have been the first to agree. "'Coppola fought the battle for the integrity of the movies; if it weren't for him, they would have been '30s gangster pictures,'" the novelist once told Herbert Mitgang in a *New York Times Book Review* interview. "'*Godfather* is really his movie.'" Yet, Kael noted, "there was a Promethean spark" in Puzo's novel that afforded Coppola "an epic vision of the corruption of America." Kael added, "Much of the material about Don Vito's early life which appears in Part II was in the Mario Puzo book and was left out in the first movie, but the real fecundity of Puzo's mind shows in the way this new film can take his characters further along and can expand . . . the implications of the book."

In October of 1978 Puzo's long-awaited fourth novel, *Fools Die,* was published. The headlines and cover stories surrounding its publication began in June—four months before the first hardcover edition went on sale—when New American Library paid an unprecedented $2.2 million for the paperback rights, plus $350,000 for the reprint rights to *The Godfather.* In spite of the hoopla concerning this record-setting price, or perhaps because of it, critical reaction to *Fools Die* was mixed. "It seems a publishing event rather than a novel," Roger Sale opined in the *New York Review of Books.* In a *New Republic* review, Barbara Grizzuti Harrison offered a similar appraisal, claiming that "it is a publishing event (though hardly a literary one)." In the *Village Voice,* James Wolcott asked: "In all this commotion, a fundamental question has gone unasked. . . . Has anyone at Putnam actually *read* this book?"

The action of *Fools Die* moves from Las Vegas to New York to Hollywood, purporting to provide readers with "the inside skinny" on gambling, publishing, and movie-making, according to *Washington Post Book World* reviewer William McPherson. Harrison commented that "the events loosely strung together in this . . . book are meant to dramatize ambition, power, and corruption. I say *meant* to, because Puzo, through the offices of his narrator, John Merlyn, keeps remind-

ing the reader that these are his themes, as if we might otherwise forget." Geoffrey Wolff, in the *New Times,* expressed a corresponding complaint: "Because he won't trust a reader to remember the climaxes of a few pages earlier, he recapitulates the plot, as though *Fools Die* were a serial, or a television series." Wolff suggested that "perhaps Puzo doesn't trust a reader to remember what he has just written because he himself has such trouble remembering what he has just written." The critic went on to detail several contradictory descriptions given throughout the novel concerning characters' appearances, habits, and lifestyles.

Wolcott criticized the structure and syntax of *Fools Die* as well, noting, "The novel seems to have evolved from manuscript to book without anyone daring . . . to make sorely needed corrections." Wolff attacked the book's "slipshod craftsmanship," and *Newsweek*'s Peter S. Prescott bluntly stated, "Structurally, *Fools Die* is a mess."

Despite such less-than-favorable reviews, the novel was a popular success due to its entertainment value and Puzo's humor. "I had a fine time reading it," Prescott admitted of *Fools Die.* "Its many stories, developed at varying lengths, are slickly entertaining." A *Time* reviewer commented: "*Fools Die* contains the sort of mini-dramas and surprises that keep paperback readers flipping pages; a man wins a small fortune at baccarat and blows his brains out; a straightforward love affair turns baroque with kinky sex; an extremely cautious character makes a stupid and fatal error." Moreover, Prescott found, "Puzo here reveals an unsuspected talent for gross comedy. . . . In [the character] Osano, the most famous living American novelist, he has written an inspired caricature of our own dear Norman Mailer."

"'I wrote *Fools Die* for myself,'" Puzo once admitted to Mitgang. "'I wanted to say certain things about gambling, Las Vegas and the country.'" According to David Robinson of the *Times Literary Supplement,* the author was successful: "The first and best section of *Fools Die* is set in Las Vegas. Puzo's forte is the neodocumentary background; and . . . his portrayal of [that city] has the appearance of authenticity." The *Time* critic agreed: "Puzo's description of Las Vegas, its Strip, showgirls, characters, and the variety of ways one can lose money swiftly and painlessly, are carried off with brio. The green baize world of casino management has never seemed more professional, entertaining and lethal."

In 1984 Puzo, returned to the safer ground of Sicily, the Mafia, and the Corleone family with his novel *The Sicilian,* which Christopher Lehmann-Haupt in the *New York Times* claimed "might more aptly be designated *The Godfather, Part I I/II.*" Based on actual events in the 1950s, the novel tells the story of Salvatore Giuliano, a Robin Hood-style outlaw who, with the support of the church and the Mafia, terrorized the Sicilian aristocracy. *The Sicilian* begins as Michael Corleone is preparing to return to America after a two-year self-imposed exile in Sicily. Shortly before departure, Michael is ordered by his father to find Giuliano and bring him to America before the authorities catch up with him. It is during Michael's search that Giuliano's history is revealed, along with the history of the Mafia itself. "[*The Sicilian*] gives Mr. Puzo another chance to do what he seems to do best, which is to spin a yarn of treachery, violence, sex, sadism, revenge and bloody justice," wrote Lehmann-Haupt. "But it's also a little sad that [Puzo] has felt it necessary to return to his Italian gangsters. . . . Though *The Sicilian* is fun and compelling, it seems like an admission of defeat in a way."

Author Gay Talese was impressed by the detailed and accurate account of Giuliano's life and the events that made him into a hero. Writing in the *New York Times,* Talese deemed *The Sicilian* "a fine, fast-paced novel about Sicily in the mid-1940s that is historically useful and, given events there in the mid-1980s, hardly out of date." Lehmann-Haupt, too, praised Puzo's well-researched look at the birth and evolution of the Sicilian Mafia. However, he found the characters "a little undernourished" in comparison to the strong personalities that were immortalized in the Godfather movies. "Even the familiar characters seem pale compared with their movie counterparts," the critic judged.

In 1988, Puzo was once again approached by Coppola, who had developed an idea for continuing the "Godfather" saga, and less than a year later the screenplay for *The Godfather: Part III* was completed. Picking up twenty years after Part II leaves off, Part III shows Michael as the head of the tremendously rich and influential Corleone family. However, their influence extends in different directions now, for Michael has taken the family fortune out of gambling and is using it for more legitimate investments. In addition, he has donated hundreds of millions of dollars to the Catholic Church in an attempt to purchase his redemption. Michael, though, is losing control of the family: frail, stricken with diabetes, and reluctant to act against his enemies, he does not command the respect he once did. Eager to replace him as don is Vincent, the illegitimate son of Michael's dead brother, Sonny. Michael struggles to regain his hold on the Corleone family, simultaneously seeking to gain influence within the Vatican; all the while, rival families plot to destroy both him and his investments. The novel culminates with an international banking scandal and the assassination of Pope John Paul I.

When *The Godfather: Part III* was released on Christmas Day, 1990, sixteen years had passed since the last "Godfather" movie—enough time for critics and moviegoers to build almost insurmountable expectations for this newest installment. Michael Wilmington in the *Los Angeles Times* found Part III to be "not quite a fitting climax to a series that ranks among the American cinema's most remarkable sustained achievements." As Stuart Klawans observed in the *Nation: The Godfather: Part III* "turns out to be as good as a post-sequel can be. . . . [It] is less gripping than the first *Godfather* and less interesting as a narrative structure than the second." Yet these flaws become apparent only when Part III is compared to the previous "Godfather" films; when judged on its own, Klawans pointed out, "it gives and keeps giving and doesn't give out until you're sated with the hero's doom." Wilmington, too, ultimately described *The Godfather: Part III* as "one of the best American movies of the year—a work of high ensemble talent and intelligence, gorgeously mounted and crafted, artistically audacious in ways that most American movies don't even attempt."

Less than a month after the release of *The Godfather: Part III,* Puzo used the increased media attention to promote his political thriller *The Fourth K.* Set in the first decade of the twenty-first century, the novel details the events occurring during the presidency of Francis Xavier Kennedy, a distant cousin of John, Robert, and Edward and the fourth "K" of the novel's title. At the time of FXK's administration, terrorism is out of control: the pope is assassinated on Easter Sunday by a group of Middle Eastern radicals, and when the gunman is captured in New York, the terrorist leader—a man named Yabril—kidnaps and murders the president's daughter. Intended to demonstrate the ineffectiveness of the United States as a world power, these actions instead drive Kennedy to near-madness, prompting him to bomb the capital of Yabril's oil-rich native land. This evokes the wrath of the Socrates

Club, a California-based group of billionaire investors with significant oil interests. Meanwhile, a group of ultra-left-wing intellectuals detonate a small atomic bomb in Manhattan in an attempt to illustrate the danger of nuclear proliferation. R. Z. Sheppard noted in *Time,* "The aggressive ways in which FXK handles foreign and domestic threats to his presidency and his life allow Puzo to pull out all the stops." Ross Thomas, in the *Los Angeles Times,* proclaimed *The Fourth K* "a witty, sometimes wise, often mordant tale about the American politics of tomorrow. And if [Puzo's] intricately plotted tale offers more insight than hope, it is still fine entertainment, which is more than can be said of today's politics."

With *The Last Don,* written after recovering from quadruple-bypass heart surgery and a protracted convalescence, Puzo produced another crime-family novel, this time introducing a new family—the Clericuzio. E. Z. Sheppard praised the novel in *Time,* citing *The Last Don* as "headlong entertainment, bubbling over with corruption, betrayals, assassinations, Richter-scale romance and, of course, family values." Set in Long Island, Las Vegas, and Hollywood, the novel relates the aging Don Clericuzio's wish to convert the family's vast criminal empire into legitimate enterprises, including efforts to enter the Hollywood film industry. Puzo's satiric portrayal of Hollywood is especially acerbic—revealing, as several critics noted, the author's lingering resentment over earlier experiences with the studios.

Christopher Lehmann-Haupt, in the *New York Times,* pointed out several obvious similarities between *The Godfather* and *The Last Don:* "Like Michael Corleone in *The Godfather,* the protagonist of *The Last Don,* Cross De Lena, tries to escape the criminal workings of his family but ends being drawn into the vortex of its malignity. Like *The Godfather, The Last Don* is filled with bloody warfare and shockingly sadistic acts of vengeance." As Vincent Patrick wrote in the *New York Times Book Review,* "It is a measure of Mario Puzo's skill that after turning the last page of his rich and ebullient new novel, I was able to remember no fewer than thirty-five characters and recall clearly their backgrounds, motivations and roles in the convoluted plot and subplots." Patrick added that *The Last Don* is Puzo's "most entertaining read since *The Godfather.*"

Omerta, Puzo's final novel, can be seen as a "tying up of loose ends," according to *National Review* writer Victorino Matus. The critic noted that Puzo had told the Associated Press that the book would be "a life-ending book, for me and the Mafia. Then I'll be dead, the Mafia will be dead, and the public will be glad of it. They've had enough of both of us." Although the Mafia did not appropriately succumb, Puzo died shortly after completing the manuscript; *Omerta* was published posthumously in 2000, quickly making bestseller lists and attracting Hollywood attention. The title refers to the Sicilian code of honor that forbids revealing information about crimes that are considered private affairs; the novel, like much of Puzo's late work, shows how this code of honor is no longer respected, particularly among the new generation. The story focuses on the murder of an old don, Raymonde Aprile, whose three adult children have grown up unaware of their father's business. Before Aprile is able to realize his dream to legitimize his operations and retire, he is killed. As his nephew, Astorre, seeks revenge, the FBI is also on the case.

While Matus found much of *Omerta* disappointing in that he felt the novel lacks the epic sweep of *The Godfather,* as well as the earlier book's saturation with religious rites and symbols, he believed the book to be "far from a failure." Among its merits, he claimed, are its ability to show how the Mafia "is not all that different from other organizations" in its exploration of the generational decline facing the Mob at the end of the twentieth century. *New York Times Book Review* critic Michiko Kakutani also cited the theme of decline, but had little praise for the novel. Adopting a mock-Mobster voice in reviewing *Omerta,* Kakutani wrote: "Fact is, the more I think about it, the more this book gives me agita. God forbid that I should criticize the author of the great 'GF,' but I gotta be honest with you: the man has lost his touch."

Time contributor R. Z. Sheppard, however, was one of several critics who praised the novel for its exciting plot and page-turning pace, commenting that *Omerta* "has more tasty twists than a plate of fusilli." Reviewers for *Booklist, Library Journal,* and *Publishers Weekly* also expressed great enthusiasm for the book, while Richard Dyer in the *Boston Globe* opined that, though parts of the novel remain relatively undeveloped and dialogue and narrative voice are not wholly satisfactory, "*Omerta* touches on themes that are bigger than it is and that Puzo didn't have the time or the stamina to realize. But even when he falls back on formula, it's a satisfying formula. After all, he invented it."

Before his death, Puzo was working on yet another "mob" story, this one centered on the fifteenth-century Spanish Borgia family, which, according to a *Publishers Weekly* reviewer, the author considered to be the "original crime family." In his attempt to make a dynasty of his family, Cardinal Rodrigo Borgia manipulates the 1492 papal election to become the new Pope Alexander. He moves into the Vatican with mistress and children, makes his son a cardinal, and marries his unwilling children to offspring of influential families. David Nudo, writing for *Library Journal* called the Borgia family "part Clintons, part Kennedys, part Sopranos." He noted that the historical fiction, completed by Puzo's long-time companion, Carol Gino, after Puzo's death, reads more like a "soap opera than serious treatment of the troubled dynasty that influenced the Renaissance."

Despite the shortcomings critics have found in Puzo's later work, his contributions to American culture continue to be readily acknowledged. James B. Hall, in the *Dictionary of Literary Biography,* commented that Puzo, like the naturalistic writers of the early twentieth century, excelled at depicting street life and "the underbelly of social institutions." Hall cited Puzo's careful attention to narrative structures and his skill at exploring human nature as evidence of the writer's craft and understanding. Puzo's achievement, Hall concluded, mirrors that of many modern American writers who, despite early critical success, had to resort to commercial formulas to find a large audience. However indirect Puzo's route to literary fame, Hall concluded, the author's place as "an authentic American literary voice" is assured.

BIOGRAPHICAL AND CRITICAL SOURCES:

BOOKS

Contemporary Literary Criticism, Gale (Detroit, MI), Volume 1, 1973, Volume 2, 1974, Volume 6, 1976, Volume 36, 1986.

Green, Rose B., *The Italian-American Novel,* Fairleigh Dickinson University Press (Madison, NJ), 1974.

Kilber, James E., Jr., editor, *Dictionary of Literary Biography,* Volume 6: *American Novelists since World War II, Second Series,* Gale (Detroit, MI), 1980.

Madden, David, editor, *Rediscoveries,* Crown (New York, NY), 1972.

Puzo, Mario, *"The Godfather Papers" and Other Confessions,* Putnam (New York, NY), 1972.

Wheeler, Thomas C., editor, *The Immigrant Experience: The Anguish of Becoming an American,* Dial Press (New York, NY), 1971.

PERIODICALS

Booklist, April 1, 2000, Danise Hoover, review of *Omerta,* p. 1413.

Boston Globe, August 24, 2000, Richard Dyer, review of *Omerta,* p. D6.

Chicago Tribune, June 19, 1981.

Commonweal, May 6, 1955; June 4, 1965.

Critical Inquiry, March, 1975, John G. Cawelti, review of *The Godfather.*

Esquire, February, 1971, Barton Midwood, review of *The Godfather.*

Kirkus Reviews, May 15, 1996, p. 711.

Library Journal, April 1, 1969; May 1, 2000, David Nudo, review of *Omerta,* p. 154; September 2001, David Nudo, review of *The Family,* p. 235.

Life, July 10, 1970.

Los Angeles Times, February 14, 1987; October 23, 1987.

Los Angeles Times Book Review, January 13, 1991; July 21, 1996.

Maclean's, March 18, 1991.

McCall's, May, 1971.

Nation, June 16, 1969; January 7, 1991, Stuart Klawans, review of *The Godfather: Part III,* p. 22.

National Review, July 31, 2000, Victorino Matus, review of *Omerta.*

New Republic, November 18, 1978, Barbara Grizzuti Harrison, review of *Fools Die.*

Newsweek, March 10, 1969, Peter Axthelm, review of *The Godfather;* December 23, 1974, Paul D. Zimmerman, review of *The Godfather: Part II;* September 18, 1978, Peter S. Prescott, review of *Fools Die;* January 1, 1979.

New Times, October 2, 1978, Geoffrey Wolff, review of *Fools Die.*

New York, March 31, 1969; July 10, 2000, Daniel Mendelsohn, review of *Omerta,* p. 52.

New Yorker, December 12, 1974; December 23, 1974; February 11, 1991.

New York Herald Tribune Book Review, March 6, 1955.

New York Review of Books, July 20, 1972; October 26, 1978, Roger Sale, review of *Fools Die.*

New York Times, February 27, 1955; March 12, 1972; March 16, 1972; June 19, 1981; November 22, 1984, Christopher Lehmann-Haupt, review of *The Sicilian,* p. 21; June 5, 1986, "Puzo to Write *Godfather, Part III,*" p. 27; May 22, 1987; January 10, 1991, Christopher Lehmann-Haupt, review of *The Fourth K,* p. B2; July 25, 1996, Christopher Lehmann-Haupt, review of *The Last Don,* p. B2.

New York Times Book Review, January 31, 1965; February 18, 1979, Herbert Mitgang, interview with Puzo; January 13, 1991, John Kenneth Galbraith, review of *The Fourth K,* p. 7; July 28, 1996, Vincent Patrick, review of *The Last Don,* p. 9; June 27, 2000, Michiko Kakutani, review of *Omerta.*

New York Times Magazine, January 2, 2000, Jeffrey Goldberg, "Sammy the Bull Explains How the Mob Got Made," p. 14.

People, July 3, 1978.

Publishers Weekly, May 12, 1978; June 10, 1996, p. 83; July 5, 1999, p. 17; July 24, 2000, p. 19; September 4, 2000, p. 42; July 30, 2001, review of *The Family,* p. 55.

Saturday Review, February 26, 1955; January 23, 1965; March 15, 1969; January 20, 1973.

Time, March 13, 1971; December 16, 1974; August 28, 1978; November 27, 1978; January 14, 1991, R. Z. Sheppard, review of *The Fourth K,* p. 62; July 29, 1996, R. Z. Sheppard, review of *The Last Don,* p. 82; July 17, 2000, R. Z. Sheppard, review of *Omerta,* p. 75.

Times (London, England), May 3, 1985.

Times Literary Supplement, December 1, 1978, David Robinson, review of *Fools Die.*

Tribune Books (Chicago, IL), January 20, 1991.

TV Guide, August 28, 1999, p. 9.

Village Voice, September 4, 1978, James Wolcott, review of *Fools Die.*

Wall Street Journal, January 11, 1991. Todd Buchholz, review of *The Fourth K,* p. A8.

Washington Post, March 12, 1970; October 23, 1987; October 24, 1987.

Washington Post Book World, March 9, 1969; April 9, 1972; September 24, 1978, William McPherson, review of *Fools Die;* January 20, 1991.

World & I, March, 1991.

ONLINE

Official Mario Puzo Library, http://www.jgeoff.com/puzo/ (April 23, 2004).

Salon.com, http://www.salon.com/ (April 24, 2004).

OBITUARIES:

PERIODICALS

Entertainment Weekly, July 16, 1999, p. 46.

New York Times, July 3, 1999, p. A13.

People, July 19, 1999, p. 75.

Time, July 12, 1999, p. 21.*

R-S

RAWLS, (Woodrow) Wilson 1913-1984

PERSONAL: Born September 24, 1913, in Scraper, OK; died of cancer, December 16, 1984, in Marshfield, WI; son of Minzy O. and Winnie (Hatfield) Rawls; married Sophie Ann Styczinski (budget analyst for Atomic Energy Commission), August 23, 1958. *Education:* Attended schools in Oklahoma. *Religion:* Presbyterian.

CAREER: Became itinerant carpenter in teens and worked in Mexico, in South America, on the Alcan Highway in Alaska, on five of the major dam projects in the United States, in West Coast shipyards, for the Navy in Oregon, and for a lumber company in British Columbia. Writer, beginning 1959. Lecturer at numerous schools, colleges, and universities in many states. Speaker at educational conventions.

MEMBER: Authors Guild, Authors League of America, Idaho Parent-Teacher Association (honorary life member).

AWARDS, HONORS: Sequoyah Children's Book Award, Oklahoma Library Association, 1979, William Allen White Children's Book Award, Emporia State University, 1979, golden Archer Award, University of Wisconsin, Oshkosh, 1980, Maud Hart Lovelace Book Award, Friends of the Minnesota Valley Regional Library, 1980, and California Young Reader Medal Award, California Reading Association, California Library Association, California Media and Library Educators Association, and California Association of

Wilson Rawls

Teachers of English, Children's Book Award for the Older Child, North Dakota, all 1981, all for *Summer of the Monkeys;* Evansville Book Award—Division III, Evansville-Vanderburgh School Corporation, 1979, Michigan Young Readers Award—Division II, Michigan Council of Teachers of English, 1980, Children's Book Award for the Older Child, North Dakota, 1981,

Twelfth Annual Children's Book Award, Massachusetts, 1987, and Great Stone Face Award, New Hampshire, 1988, all for *Where the Red Fern Grows*.

WRITINGS:

Where the Red Fern Grows: The Story of Two Dogs and a Boy, Doubleday (Garden City, NY), 1961, published as *Where the Red Fern Grows: And Related Readings,* McDougal Littell (Boston, MA), 1996, published as *Where the Red Fern Grows: The Story of Two Dogs and a Boy: With Connections,* Holt, Rinehart, & Winston (Austin, TX), 2000.

Summer of the Monkeys, Doubleday (Garden City, NY), 1976.

Dreams Can Come True (sound recording), Reading Tree Productions (Springfield, MA), 1993.

The Wilson Rawls collection, which includes literary awards, taped interviews, manuscripts, and other materials, is maintained by the Archives and Collections Department of the Cherokee National Museum, Tahlequah, Oklahoma. *Summer of the Monkeys* has been published in French and German.

ADAPTATIONS: Where the Red Fern Grows was adapted for film by Doty-Dayton Productions, narrated by the author, 1974, and has been recorded on audiocassette by Recorded Books, 1994, and Listening Library, 1994. *Summer of the Monkeys* was adapted for film by Disney Educational Productions, 1999.

SIDELIGHTS: Wilson Rawls was so critical of his own writing that he destroyed his first five manuscripts, yet his novel *Where the Red Fern Grows* eventually became a classic of children's literature. He was born on the Cherokee Nation land in northeastern Oklahoma, where his mother, who was descended from the tribe, owned land on the Illinois River. Life on this farm with his many siblings formed the substance of his later fiction. As school was not available on a regular basis, the Rawls children were mostly educated by their mother. Rawls's interest in reading was sparked by his mother's reading Jack London's adventure story *Call of the Wild*. He later credited this book, which he read repeatedly, as the source of his inspiration to become a writer.

Coming of age during the Great Depression, Rawls left home at the age of sixteen and began drifting about the country looking for work. As he traveled he also wrote, storing his manuscripts in a trunk at the family's home in Albuquerque when he visited there. Eventually, he found work at the Atomic Energy Commission's site in the Arco desert in Idaho. There he met Sophie Styczinski, a budget analyst who became his wife. She was a college graduate, and Wilson felt somewhat embarrassed about his lack of formal learning. His embarrassment drove him to burn his unpublished works. Later, he told her what he had done, and of his continuing desire to be a writer. She not only encouraged him, but helped him to edit his work. A series of stories, "The Hounds of Youth," was published in the *Saturday Evening Post,* and in 1961, the work was adapted into book form as *Where the Red Fern Grows*.

Where the Red Fern Grows is largely autobiographical. The protagonist, Billy Colman, thinks back to his impoverished boyhood. Billy wished for some hounds, and worked persistently to save enough money to buy a pair of pups. He trains them to be prize-winning hunting dogs, and the three of them share numerous adventures. Both dogs lose their lives protecting their master from a mountain lion. The book was favorably reviewed, but sold few copies until several years after its publication. At that time, Rawls accepted an invitation to speak at a teachers' workshop. His remarks about his book impressed the teachers there that they read the novel, and urged their students to do so, too. *Where the Red Fern Grows* then enjoyed a huge groundswell in popularity. By 1974, it had even been adapted as a film.

Rawls's next book was more fanciful. *Summer of the Monkeys* is set in the early years of the twentieth century and tells the tale of a Oklahoma teenager, Jay Berry Lee, who stumbles upon a group of monkeys who have escaped from the circus. Lured by a reward, the teenager resolves to capture the monkeys, but this proves difficult to do. He finally captures the monkeys, but instead of buying himself a horse with the reward as he had planned, Lee gets far more satisfaction spending the money for an operation on his sister's leg.

Summer of the Monkeys was also well received, but it was as a speaker to teachers and students that Rawls was perhaps most influential. He eventually visited some two thousand schools in twenty-two states. He always brought his books along and emphasized that he had created the stories even without understanding proper grammar and spelling. "Children are always asking me what advice I can give them on trying to be a writer," Rawls once told *CA*, [and] "I always tell them to do a lot of reading, read and study creative writing, then start writing and keep writing. Someday they will make it if they don't give up."

BIOGRAPHICAL AND CRITICAL SOURCES:

PERIODICALS

Albuquerque Tribune (Albuquerque, NM), January 4, 1999, Jan Jonas, "Leaving His Mark," p. C1.

Best Sellers, June 1, 1961.

Booklist, February 15, 1992, review of *Summer of the Monkeys,* p. 1101; August, 1995, Nancy McCray, review of audio version of *Where the Red Fern Grows,* p. 1966; March 15, 1996, Barbara Baskin, review of audio version of *Where the Red Fern Grows,* p. 1306; April 15, 2000, Debra McLeod, review of movie version of *Summer of the Monkeys,* p. 1158.

Chicago Tribune, June 4, 1961.

Children's Literature in Education, June, 1995, review of *Where the Red Fern Grows,* pp. 135-150.

Deseret News, February 16, 1974.

Horn Book, January, 1996, Kristi Beavin, review of audio version of *Where the Red Fern Grows,* pp. 105-108.

Idaho Falls Post-Register, March 17, 1974.

Library Journal, February 1, 1961, pp. 612-613.

Milwaukee Journal, June 25, 1978.

Salt Lake Tribune, April 7, 1974.

School Library Journal, July, 1994, Penny Peck, review of *Dreams Can Come True,* p. 68; June, 1995, Linda W. Braun, review of *Where the Red Fern Grows,* p. 71; November, 1996, Linda W. Braun, review of *Where the Red Fern Grows,* p. 60.

Tulsa Daily World (Tulsa, OK), April 15, 1976.

Voice of Youth Advocates, October 1992, Jody McCoy, review of *Summer of the Monkeys,* p. 230.

Yakima Herald-Republic (Yakima, WA), March 24, 1974.

ONLINE

Idaho Falls Public Library, http://www.ifpl.org/rawls/ (February 13, 2004), Madelaine Love, "Dreams Can Come True" (biography of Wilson Rawls).

OBITUARIES:

PERIODICALS

Idaho Falls Post-Register, December 18, 1984.*

*   *   *

RYDER, Jonathan
See LUDLUM, Robert

*   *   *

SACHAR, Louis 1954-

PERSONAL: Surname is pronounced "*Sack*-er"; born March 20, 1954, in East Meadow, NY; son of Robert J. (a salesman) and Ruth (a real estate broker; maiden name, Raybin) Sachar; married Carla Askew, 1985; children: Sherre. *Education:* University of California, Berkeley, B.A., 1976; University of California, San Francisco, J.D., 1980. *Hobbies and other interests:* Softball, chess, rugby, watching the San Francisco Giants.

ADDRESSES: Home—Austin, TX. *Agent*—c/o Farrar Straus & Giroux, 19 Union Square W, New York, NY 10003-3304.

CAREER: Beldoch Industries (manufacturers of women's sweaters), Norwalk, CT, shipping manager, 1976-77; writer, 1977—; attorney, 1981-89.

MEMBER: Authors Guild, Authors League of America, Society of Children's Book Writers and Illustrators.

AWARDS, HONORS: Ethical Culture School Book Award, 1978, and Children's Choice, International Reading Association and Children's Book Council, 1979, both for *Sideways Stories from Wayside School;* Parents' Choice Award, Parents' Choice Foundation, 1987, Young Reader's Choice Award, Pacific Northwest Library Association, and Texas Bluebonnet Award, Texas Library Association, both 1990, and Charlie May Simon Book Award, Arkansas Elementary School Council, Georgia Children's Book Award, Uni-

Louis Sachar

versity of Georgia College of Education, Indian Paint-brush Book Award (Wyoming), Golden Sower Award, Iowa Children's Choice Award, Land of Enchantment Children's Book Award, New Mexico Library Association, Mark Twain Award, Missouri Association of School Librarians, Milner Award, Friends of the Atlanta-Fulton Public Library (Georgia), Nevada Young Reader's Award, and West Virginia Book Award, Wise Library, West Virginia University, all for *There's a Boy in the Girls' Bathroom;* Parents' Choice Award, 1989, Garden State Children's Book Award, New Jersey Library Association, 1992, and Arizona Young Reader's Chapter Book Award, 1993, all for *Wayside School Is Falling Down;* nominee, Golden Archer Award, 1996-97, Garden State Children's Book Award, 1998, Indiana Young Hoosier's Book Award, Massachusetts Children's Book Award, and Young Reader's Choice Award, all for *Wayside School Gets a Little Stranger;* National Book Award, 1998, Best Books list, *School Library Journal,* 1998, Fanfare list, *Horn Book,* Books in the Middle: Outstanding Titles of 1998, *Voice of Youth Advocates,* Blue Ribbons selection, *Bulletin of the Center for Children's Books,* and Newbery Medal, all 1999, Mark Twain Award, 2001, and Rebecca Caudill Young Readers' Book Award, 2002, all for *Holes.*

WRITINGS:

Sideways Stories from Wayside School, Follett (Chicago, IL), 1978, reprinted, Morrow Junior Books (New York, NY), 1998.

Johnny's in the Basement, Avon (New York, NY), 1981, reprinted, Morrow Junior Books (New York, NY), 1998.

Someday Angeline, Avon (New York, NY), 1983, reprinted, Morrow Junior Books (New York, NY), 1998.

There's a Boy in the Girls' Bathroom, Knopf (New York, NY), 1987.

Sixth Grade Secrets, Scholastic (New York, NY), 1987.

Wayside School Is Falling Down, Lothrop (New York, NY), 1989.

Sideways Arithmetic from Wayside School, Scholastic (New York, NY), 1989.

The Boy Who Lost His Face, Knopf (New York, NY), 1989.

Dogs Don't Tell Jokes, Knopf (New York, NY), 1991.

Monkey Soup, illustrated by Cat Bowman Smith, Knopf (New York, NY), 1992.

Wayside School Gets a Little Stranger, Morrow Junior Books (New York, NY), 1995.

Holes (adapted to a screenplay by Sachar and Brent Hanley, Disney, 2003), Farrar, Straus (New York, NY), 1998.

Stanley Yelnats' Survival Guide to Camp Green Lake, Dell Yearling (New York, NY), 2003.

"MARVIN REDPOST" SERIES

Marvin Redpost: Kidnapped at Birth?, illustrated by Neal Hughes, Random House (New York, NY), 1992.

Marvin Redpost: Why Pick on Me?, illustrated by Barbara Sullivan, Random House (New York, NY), 1993.

Marvin Redpost: Is He a Girl?, illustrated by Barbara Sullivan, Random House (New York, NY), 1993.

Marvin Redpost: Alone in His Teacher's House, illustrated by Barbara Sullivan, Random House (New York, NY), 1994.

Marvin Redpost: A Flying Birthday Cake?, illustrated by Amy Wummer, Random House (New York, NY), 1999.

Marvin Redpost: Class President, illustrated by Amy Wummer, Random House (New York, NY), 1999.

Marvin Redpost: A Magic Crystal?, illustrated by Amy Wummer, Random House (New York, NY), 2000.

Marvin Redpost: Super Fast, Out of Control!, illustrated by Amy Wummer, Random House (New York, NY), 2000.

ADAPTATIONS: Holes, Sideways Stories from Wayside School, and *Wayside School Gets a Little Stranger* are all available on audiocassette from Random House (New York, NY). *There's a Boy in the Girls' Bathroom* and *Wayside School Is Falling Down* are available on audiocassette from Listening Library. *There's a Boy in the Girls' Bathroom* has been adapted to a play and performed at the Old Courthouse Theatre in Charlotte, NC.

SIDELIGHTS: Though he graduated from law school, passed the bar exam, and practiced law part-time for a number of years, Louis Sachar is best known as the author of poignant, humorous stories for children and young adults. Sachar began his writing career with the zany *Sideways Stories from Wayside School.* The book is a collection of thirty stories, each one corresponding with a floor in the thirty-story Wayside School. The inspiration for *Sideways Stories from Wayside School* came from Sachar's experience as a teacher's aide while an undergraduate at University of California, Berkeley.

Sachar's popularity as an author of young adult and children's literature stems, in part, from his choice of characters. "The protagonists of his books are often outcasts who learn about themselves and gain social acceptance through their relationships with other children and adults," noted a *Children's Literature Review* contributor. In *Sideways Stories from Wayside School,* Sachar recounts the antics of teachers and students in a crazy, one-classroom-per-story school. The names of the students in the book are the actual names of children in the class where Sachar worked as a teacher's aide. Sachar even threw himself into the book, as the character of Louis, the yard teacher.

Wayside School Gets a Little Stranger, is another collection of wacky stories about what happens when Mrs. Jewls, the teacher on the thirtieth floor, goes on maternity leave. In her place are some of the most outrageous substitutes ever, including one whose third ear lets her read the children's thoughts. A *Publishers Weekly* reviewer predicted that readers will be "turn-

ing the pages eagerly, awaiting the next twist of plot or play on words. Sachar's supply of both seems inexhaustible." Reviewer John Sigwald of *School Library Journal* wrote that while the stories "lack a few strong characters to bind the slapstick and the absurd together," the book is "fun and full of the kind of 'grossness' that middle schoolers love." Sachar has authored other "Wayside" books, including *Wayside School Is Falling Down* and *Sideways Arithmetic from Wayside School.*

Sachar's novels *There's a Boy in the Girls' Bathroom, Someday Angeline,* and *Dogs Don't Tell Jokes* all feature protagonists who are outcasts, but who learn to accept themselves for who they are. In *Someday Angeline* an eight-year-old genius is out of place when she is bumped up to the sixth grade. *Dogs Don't Tell Jokes* is about Gary "Goon" Boone, a jokester who covers up how he really feels by telling jokes. Both characters overcome their awkwardness and become comfortable with who they are. A reviewer in *Publishers Weekly* remarked that *Dogs Don't Tell Jokes* has "strong, realistic characterization," and believed "Sachar's gracefully told story will please his longtime fans and gain him new followers as well."

Sachar achieved critical acclaim for *There's a Boy in the Girls' Bathroom,* in which fifth-grade class bully Bradley Chalkers is befriended by the new kid in class, Jeff Fishkin. Like the protagonists in other Sachar tales, Bradley is an outcast, disliked by his classmates. However, through his friendship with Jeff and the help of a school counselor, Bradley transforms himself into a more positive person, and even gets invited to a birthday party. The book won many awards, including the Parents' Choice Award.

A *Children's Literature Review* contributor considered *Holes* "the greatest critical success of Sachar's career." *Holes* tells the story of Stanley Yelnats, a boy who is sentenced to go to Camp Green Lake, a punishment camp for bad boys, after being falsely accused of stealing a star athlete's sneakers. The boys at the camp dig five-foot-by-five-foot holes in the dried up lake bed all day long, under the hot Texas sun. Stanley figures out that the Warden has her own motives for wanting the holes dug. As the book moves back and forth between past and present, a story about treasure, poisonous nail polish, yellow-spotted lizards, and a whole cast of crazy characters unfolds. A *Publishers Weekly* reviewer called *Holes* "a dazzling blend of social commentary, tall tale and magic realism." Roger Sutton remarked in *Horn Book,* "Sachar has shown himself a writer of humor and heart, with an instinctive aversion to the expected." Betsy Hearne, in *New York Times Book Review,* observed that Sachar "abandons conventional plot for a more innovative mix of realism and legend, with elements of mystery that keep the surrealistic events suspenseful."

In an interview with Joan Novelli of *Instructor,* Sachar said that he thinks so many kids relate to the character of Stanley in *Holes* because he isn't a hero. "He's a kind of pathetic kid who feels like he has no friends, feels like his life is cursed. And I think everyone can identify with that in one way or another," explained Sacher. In a *Writing!* interview, Sachar told Kate Davis, "You always have to imagine what your character would be feeling and thinking, to see yourself as the character. Then you try to come up with characteristics that are interesting to the reader." Anne Dingus, in *Texas Monthly,* commented on the "tightly woven plot" of *Holes* and said that "Sachar leaves not one thread untucked at novel's end." Sachar explained in *Writing!:* "Tying everything together neatly in the end wasn't hard, because I knew how everything was going to relate. The tricky part was getting all that stuff out in the story without the reader getting bored." Sachar cowrote the screenplay version of *Holes,* which was released by Disney in 2003.

Sachar has also achieved success with his "Marvin Redpost" series. The first book in the series, *Marvin Redpost: Kidnapped at Birth?* has nine-year-old Marvin questioning the origin of his birth. His red hair and blue eyes make him different from everyone else in his family, and Marvin becomes convinced that he is the long-lost son of the King of Shampoo. In *Marvin Redpost: Class President,* Marvin and his class receive a surprise visit from the President of the United States on the same day that everyone is wearing clothes with holes in them. Anne Knickerbocker commented in *School Library Journal:* "Through a perfect blend of humor and thoughtful prose, [Sachar] drives home the point of what good citizenship is without being didactic." In *Marvin Redpost: A Flying Birthday Cake,* the new kid in Marvin's class, Joe Normal, is actually an alien. A reviewer in *Horn Book Magazine* commended the story for its "smart, funny twist on the new-kid theme, reminding us that everyone feels alienated at one time or another."

Sachar's books blend social commentary with humor. His underdog characters often triumph in the end, and most of his works have a deeper meaning hiding beneath the surface of his witty writing. Though his works are mostly for children and young adults, critics believe that they are also amusing to adults. "I think what makes good children's books is putting the same care and effort into it as if I was writing for adults," Sachar explained in an interview with Elizabeth Farnsworth on *Newshour.* "I don't write anything, put anything, in my books that I'd be embarrassed to put in an adult book," he added. Sachar touched on the same subject in an interview with *Austin Chronicle* writer Barbara Strickland: "I just try to write books that are fun to read. That's my first goal with all my books, to make reading fun."

BIOGRAPHICAL AND CRITICAL SOURCES:

BOOKS

Authors and Artists for Young Adults, Volume 35, Gale (Detroit, MI), 2000.
St. James Guide to Children's Writers, 5th edition, St. James Press (Detroit, MI), 1999.
Writers for Young Adults, Supplement 1, Scribner (New York, NY), 2000.

PERIODICALS

Book, May, 1999, review of *Holes,* p. 89.
Booklist, September 1, 1983, Ilene Cooper, review of *Someday Angeline,* p. 91; November 1, 1987, Ilene Cooper, review of *Sixth Grade Secrets,* p. 484; May 1, 1989, Carolyn Phelan, review of *Wayside School Is Falling Down,* p. 1553; April, 1990, Carolyn Phelan, review of *Sideways Arithmetic at Wayside School,* p. 1645; July, 1991, Randy Meyers, review of *Dogs Don't Tell Jokes,* p. 2046; April 15, 1992, review of *Monkey Soup,* p. 1539; December 1, 1992, review of *Marvin Redpost: Kidnapped at Birth?,* p. 680; March 15, 1993, review of *There's a Boy in the Girls' Bathroom,* p. 1369; May 1, 1993, review of *Marvin Redpost: Why Pick on Me?,* p. 1592; September 1, 1993, review of *Wayside School Is Falling Down,* p. 73; November 15, 1993, review of *Marvin Redpost: Is He a Girl?,* p. 626; April 15, 1994, Mary Berman, audio book review of *Sideways Stories from Wayside School,* p. 1547; June 1, 1994, Hazel Rochman, review of *Marvin Redpost: Alone in His*

Teacher's House, p. 1822; March 1, 1995, p. 1273; April 1, 1997, review of *Sideways Arithmetic for Wayside School,* p. 1342; June 1, 1998, Bill Out, review of *Holes,* p. 1750; March 15, 1999, review of *Holes,* p. 1302, p. 1309, p. 1317; April 15, 1999, review of *Marvin Redpost: Class President,* p. 153; April 15, 2000, Jeanette Larson, review of *Wayside School Gets a Little Stranger,* p. 1561.

Book Report, November, 1991, review of *The Boy Who Lost His Face,* p. 65; May, 1999, Lee Gordon, review of *Holes,* p. 66.

Bulletin of the Center for Children's Books, April, 1987, Betsy Hearne, review of *There's a Boy in the Girls' Bathroom,* p. 155; October, 1987, p. 37; October, 1991, review of *Dogs Don't Tell Jokes,* p. 47; October 1992, review of *Marvin Redpost: Kidnapped at Birth?,* p. 52, February 1993, Deborah Stevenson, review of *Marvin Redpost: Why Pick on Me?,* p. 167; June, 1994, review of *Marvin Redpost: Alone in His Teacher's House,* p. 334; March, 1995, Deborah Stevenson, review of *Wayside School Gets a Little Stranger,* p. 248; September, 1998, review of *Holes,* p. 29; April, 1999, review of *Marvin Redpost: Class President,* p. 293.

Catholic Library World, September, 1999, review of *Holes,* p. 28.

Childhood Education, spring, 1992, review of *Dogs Don't Tell Jokes,* p. 176.

Children's Book Review Service, November, 1989, review of *The Boy Who Lost His Face,* p. 36; spring, 1992, review of *Monkey Soup,* p. 136; December, 1998, review of *Holes,* p. 47.

Christian Science Monitor, December 10, 1998, review of *Holes,* p. 17; March 22, 2001, review of *Holes,* p. 21; July 10, 2001, review of *Holes,* p. 20.

Cincinnati Post, July 19, 2000, "Book Draws Flak in Forest Hills," p. 14A.

Dallas Morning News, March 14, 1999, Pete Slover, "Writing for Young Folks Anything but Child's Play: Austin's Louis Sachar Takes His Craft Seriously," p. 47A.

Emergency Librarian, May-June, 1982, Joan McGrath, review of *Johnny's in the Basement,* p. 30.

Five Owls, fall, 2001, review of *Sideways Stories from Wayside School,* p. 8.

Guardian (London, England), Julia Eccleshare, review of *Holes,* p. 6.

Horn Book, September, 1998, Roger Sutton, review of *Holes,* p. 593-595; May, 1999, audio book review of *Holes,* p. 358; July, 1999, Louis Sachar, "Newbery Medal Acceptance," p. 410, Sherre Sachar

and Carla Sachar, "Louis Sachar," p. 418; January, 2000, review of *Marvin Redpost: A Flying Birthday Cake,* p. 83, and review of *Holes,* p. 43; November, 2000, Roger Sutton, review of *Marvin Redpost: Super Fast, Out of Control!,* p. 763.

Instructor, July, 1992, review of *Wayside School Is Falling Down,* p. 14; May, 1993, review of *Dogs Don't Tell Jokes,* p. 24; September, 1998, review of *Wayside School Is Falling Down,* p. 10; May, 1999, review of *Marvin Redpost: Alone in His Teacher's House,* p. 16, review of *Holes,* p. 16; January, 2001, Louis Sachar and Joan Novelli, "Settings Take You Places," p. 53.

Kirkus Reviews, February 1, 1987, review of *There's a Boy in the Girls' Bathroom,* p. 224; July 15, 1991, review of *Dogs Don't Tell Jokes,* p. 934; December 1, 1992, review of *Marvin Redpost: Why Pick on Me?,* p. 1508; April 15, 1995, review of *Wayside School Gets a Little Stranger,* p. 562; June 15, 1998, review of *Holes,* p. 900; March 15, 1999, review of *Marvin Redpost: Class President.*

Kliatt, July, 1999, audio book review of *Holes,* p. 50.

Learning, September, 1995, review of *Wayside School Gets a Little Stranger,* p. 81.

Library Talk, March, 1991, review of *Wayside School Is Falling Down,* p. 48; March, 1992, review of *Dogs Don't Tell Jokes,* p. 49; May, 1995, review of *Wayside School Gets a Little Stranger,* p. 41.

Los Angeles Times Book Review, August 8, 1999, review of *Sideways Stories from Wayside School,* p. 6.

Magpies, March, 2000, Helen Purdie, review of *Holes,* p. 8-9; March, 2002, review of *There's a Boy in the Girls' Bathroom,* p. 37.

New York Times Book Review, November 15, 1998, Betsy Hearne, review of *Holes,* p. 52; December 6, 1998, review of *Holes,* p. 93.

Parents, May, 1992, review of *Dogs Don't Tell Jokes,* p. 239; spring, 1993, review of *Sideways Stories from Wayside School,* p. 106.

Parents' Choice, September, 1995, review of *Wayside School Gets a Little Stranger,* p. 13.

Progressive, January, 2000, Anne-Marie Cusac, "Best Books of 1999," p. 35.

Publishers Weekly, August 12, 1983, reviews of *Johnny's in the Basement* and *Someday Angeline,* p. 67; August 28, 1987, review of *Sixth Grade Secrets,* p. 80; March 1, 1991, review of *The Boy Who Lost His Face,* p. 74; July 28, 1991, review of *Dogs Don't Tell Jokes,* p. 102; January 6, 1992, review of *Monkey Soup,* p. 64; July 20, 1992, review of *Marvin Redpost: Kidnapped at Birth?,*

p. 250-251; August 24, 1992, review of *Dogs Don't Tell Jokes,* p. 81; February 13, 1995, review of *Wayside School Gets a Little Stranger,* p. 78; January, 29, 1996, review of *Wayside School Gets a Little Stranger,* p. 101; July 27, 1998, review of *Holes,* p. 78; November 2, 1998, review of *Holes,* p. 51; July 12, 1999, audio book review of *Holes,* p. 29.

Reading Teacher, October, 1988, Sam Leaton Sebesta, review of *There's a Boy in the Girls' Bathroom,* p. 83; May, 1990, Lee Galda, review of *Wayside School Is Falling Down,* p. 671; October, 1992, review of *Dogs Don't Tell Jokes,* p. 139; October, 1993, review of *Monkey Soup,* p. 130; October, 1996, review of *Wayside School Gets a Little Stranger,* p. 138.

Riverbank Review, fall, 1998, p. 32.

School Librarian, spring, 2000, Dennis Hamley, review of *Holes,* p. 47; spring, 2002, review of *There's a Boy in the Girls' Bathroom,* p. 35.

School Library Journal, September, 1978, p. 147; December, 1981, Jack Forman, review of *Johnny's in the Basement,* p. 68; April, 1987, David Gale, review of *There's a Boy in the Girls' Bathroom,* p. 103; May, 1989, p. 111; October, 1989, p. 122; September, 1991, review of *Dogs Don't Tell Jokes,* p. 259; June, 1992, review of *Monkey Soup,* p. 102; March, 1993, Kenneth E. Kowen, review of *Marvin Redpost: Kidnapped at Birth?,* p. 186; January, 1994, review of *Sideways Stories from Wayside School,* p. 74; August, 1994, audio book review of *Wayside School Is Falling Down,* p. 68; April, 1995, John Sigwald, review of *Wayside School Gets a Little Stranger,* p. 136; September, 1998, Alison Follos, review of *Holes,* p. 210; December, 1998, review of *Holes,* p. 27; June, 1999, Anne Knickerbocker, review of *Marvin Redpost: Class President;* July, 1999, review of *Marvin Redpost: Class President,* p. 79; September, 1999, audio book review of *Holes,* p. 165.

Teacher Librarian, Susan Faust and Helen Wiley, "Bestseller K-12," p. 42.

Texas Monthly, September, 1999, Anne Dingus, review of *Holes,* p. 121.

Time, December 7, 1998, review of *Holes,* p. 220.

U.S. News & World Report, February 15, 1999, "Louis Sachar: Children's Book Author Wins 1999 Newbery Medal for *Holes,*" p. 12.

Voice of Youth Advocates, October, 1991, review of *The Boy Who Lost His Face,* p. 280; December, 1998, review of *Holes,* p. 360; February, 1999, review of *Holes,* p. 413.

Washington Post Book World, April 12, 1992, review of *Monkey Soup,* p. 6; May 7, 1995, Brigitte Weeks, review of *Wayside School Gets a Little Stranger,* p. 16.

Wilson Library Bulletin, June, 1993, review of *There's a Boy in the Girls' Bathroom,* p. 1993.

Writing!, September, 2002, "Louis Sachar's *Holes* Wins Readers' Choice Award for Teen Books," p. 3; November-December, 2002, Kate Davis, "'Paint a Picture for the Reader': A Conversation with Louis Sachar," p. 26.

ONLINE

About.com, http://childrensbooks.about.com/cs/ (November 14, 2003), Elizabeth Kennedy, "Louis Sachar, Author of *Holes* and Much More."

Austin Chronicle Online, http://www.austinchronicle.com/ (November 14, 2003), Barbara Strickland, "Louis Sachar: Top of His Class."

Carroll County Maryland Web site, http://www.carr.lib.md.us/authco/ (November 14, 2003), "Louis Sachar."

Children's Book Council Web site, http://www.cbcbooks.org/ (November 14, 2003), "Archives: Louis Sachar."

Public Broadcasting System Web site, http://www.pbs.org/ (November 14, 2003), Elizabeth Farnsworth, interview with Sachar.

Random House Web site, http://randomhouse.com/ (November 14, 2003), "Louis Sachar."

ReadIn.org, http://www.readin.org/ (November 14, 2003), "Louis Sachar."

Scholastic Web site, http://www.teacher.scholastic.com/ (November 13, 2003), "More Authors and Books, Louis Sachar, Biography and Interview Transcript."*

*   *   *

SAETONE
See CAMUS, Albert

*   *   *

SAID, Edward W. 1935-2003

PERSONAL: Surname is pronounced "sa-*eed*"; born November 1, 1935, in Jerusalem, Palestine; immigrated to United States, 1951; died of leukemia, September 25, 2003; son of Wadie A. (businessman) and

Hilda (Musa) Said; married second wife, Mariam Cortas, December 15, 1970; children: Wadie, Najla. *Education:* Princeton University, A.B., 1957; Harvard University, A.M., 1960, Ph.D., 1964. *Religion:* Anglican. *Hobbies and other interests:* Playing piano.

CAREER: Harvard University, Cambridge, MA, tutor in history and literature, 1961-63; Columbia University, New York, NY, instructor, 1963-65, assistant professor, 1965-68, associate professor of English, 1968-70, professor of English and comparative literature, 1970-77, Parr professor of English and comparative literature, 1977-89, Old Dominion Foundation professor of humanities, 1989-91, university professor, 1992-2002, chair of doctoral program in comparative literature. Center for Advanced Study, University of Illinois, Urbana, fellow, 1967-68; Harvard University, Cambridge, MA, visiting associate professor of comparative literature, summer, 1968, and visiting professor of comparative literature, winter, 1974; Center for Advanced Study in the Behavioral Sciences, Stanford University, Stanford, CA, fellow, 1975-76; Princeton University, Princeton, NJ, Christian Gauss lecturer in criticism, spring, 1977; Johns Hopkins University, Baltimore, MD, visiting professor of humanities, spring, 1979; University of Chicago, Chicago, IL, Carpenter professor, 1983; Yale University, New Haven, CT, visiting professor, fall, 1985; University of Toronto, Toronto, Canada, Northrop Frye visiting professor, fall, 1986. Member of Palestine National Council, 1977-91.

MEMBER: United Nations Organizations (consultant, 1982-83), American University of Beirut (international advisory board, 2001-02); American Academy of Arts and Sciences, American Philosophical Society (2000), Arab-American Anti-Discrimination Committee, Modern Language Association (president, 1999), Institute of Arab Studies (chairman of the board, 1980-83), American Comparative Literature Association, PEN (executive board member, 1988-98), Association of Arab-American University Graduates (vice president, 1971; member of board, 1972), New York Council on Foreign Relations, New York Institute for the Humanities, New York State Council for the Humanities (executive board), Century Association, Phi Beta Kappa

AWARDS, HONORS: Woodrow Wilson fellowship, Harvard University, 1958; Bowdoin Prize, Harvard University, 1963; Center for Advanced Study, University of Illinois, fellowship, 1967-68; Guggenheim fellowship, 1972-73; Lionel Trilling Awards, Columbia University, 1976 and 1994, for *Beginnings;* National Endowment for the Humanities senior fellowship, 1981; Rene Wellek Award in literary theory, American Comparative Literature Association, for *The World, the Text, and the Critic,* 1984; Janet Lee Stevens Award, University of Pennsylvania, 1987; Picasso Medal, 1994; Nonino Award, 1996; Sultan Owais Prize for Cultural Achievement, 1998; Spinoza Prize, 1999; Anisfeld-Wolf Book Award, 1999; Morton Dauwen Zabel Award, American Academy of Arts and Letters, 2000; National Book Critics Circle Award nomination, for *Orientalism; New Yorker* Award for nonfiction, 2000, for *Out of Place;* Lifetime Achievement Award, Lannan Foundation, 2001.

WRITINGS:

Joseph Conrad and the Fiction of Autobiography, Harvard University Press (Cambridge, MA), 1966.

Beginnings: Intention and Method, Basic Books (New York, NY), 1975.

Orientalism, Pantheon (New York, NY), 1978.

The Question of Palestine, Times Books (New York, NY), 1979, new edition, with new introduction and epilogue, Vintage (New York, NY), 1992.

(Editor) *Literature and Society,* Johns Hopkins University Press (Baltimore, MD), 1980.

Covering Islam: How the Media and the Experts Determine How We See the Rest of the World, Pantheon (New York, NY), 1981, revised edition, Vintage (New York, NY), 1997.

The World, the Text, and the Critic, Harvard University Press (Cambridge, MA), 1983.

(Author of foreword) Raymond Schwab, *Oriental Renaissance: Europe's Rediscovery of India and the East, 1680-1880,* Columbia University Press (New York, NY), 1984.

After the Last Sky: Palestinian Lives, photographs by Jean Mohr, Pantheon (New York, NY), 1986.

(Author of foreword) Johannes Fabian, *Language and Colonial Power: The Appropriation of Swahili in the Former Belgian Congo, 1880-1938,* University of California Press (Berkeley, CA), 1986.

(Editor and author of introduction) Rudyard Kipling, *Kim,* Penguin (New York, NY), 1987.

(Editor, with Christopher Hitchens) *Blaming the Victims: Spurious Scholarship and the Palestinian Question,* Verso, 1988.

(Author of foreword) Phyllis Bennis and Michel Moushabeck, editors, *Beyond the Storm: A Gulf Crisis Reader,* Olive Branch Press, 1991.

Musical Elaborations, Columbia University Press (New York, NY), 1991.

(Author of foreword) Richard Poirier, *The Performing Self: Compositions and Decompositions in the Languages of Contemporary Life,* Rutgers University Press (New Brunswick, NJ), 1992.

Culture and Imperialism, Knopf (New York, NY), 1993.

Representations of the Intellectual: The 1993 Reith Lectures, Pantheon Books (New York, NY), 1994.

The Pen and the Sword: Conversations with David Barsamian, Common Courage Press (Monroe, ME), 1994.

The Politics of Dispossession: The Struggle for Palestinian Self-Determination, 1969-1994, Pantheon Books (New York, NY), 1994.

Peace and Its Discontents: Essays on Palestine in the Middle East Peace Process, with a preface by Christopher Hitchens, Vintage (New York, NY), 1995.

(Author of preface) Hanna Mikhail, *Politics and Revelation: Mawardi and After,* Edinburgh University Press (Edinburgh, Scotland), 1995.

Out of Place: A Memoir, Knopf (New York, NY), 1999.

(With Sheena Wagstaff) *Mona Hatoum: The Entire World As a Foreign Land* (essays), Tate Gallery (London, England), 2000.

Edward Said Reader, edited by Moustafa Bayoumi and Andrew Rubin, Vintage (New York, NY), 2000.

End of the Peace Process: Oslo and After, Pantheon (New York, NY), 2000.

Reflections on Exile and Other Literary and Cultural Essays, Harvard University Press (Cambridge, MA), 2000.

Power, Politics, and Culture: Interviews with Edward W. Said, edited by Gauri Viswanathan, Pantheon (New York, NY), 2001.

(With Daniel Barenboim) *Parallels and Paradoxes: Explorations in Music and Society,* Pantheon (New York, NY), 2002.

Freud and the Non-European, introduction by Christopher Bollas, response by Jacqueline Rose, Verso (New York, NY), 2003.

(With David Barsamian) *Culture and Resistance: Conversations,* South End Press (Cambridge, MA), 2003.

From Oslo to Iraq and the Road Map, Pantheon (New York, NY), 2004.

Humanism and Democratic Criticism, Columbia University Press (New York, NY), 2004.

Also author or editor of pamphlets: coeditor with Fuad Suleiman of *The Arabs Today: Alternatives for Tomorrow,* Forum Associates, 1973; coauthor with Daniel Berrigan and Israel Shahak of *Arabs and Jews: Possibility of Concord,* Association of Arab-American University Graduates (AAUG), 1974; coauthor with Ibrahim Abu-Lughod of *Two Studies on the Palestinians Today and American Policy,* AAUG, 1976; author of *Reaction and Counter-Revolution in the Contemporary Arab World,* AAUG, 1978, and *The Palestine Question and the American Context,* Institute for Palestine Studies, 1979; author, with others, of *A Profile of the Palestinian People,* Palestine Human Rights Campaign, 1983. Music critic for *Nation.* Contributor to anthologies; contributor of articles and reviews to *Kenyon Review, Nation, New York Times, Grand Street, New Statesman, London Review of Books, Raritan, Le Monde Diplomatique,* and other periodicals; contributor to Arabic-language newspapers in the Middle East and England.

SIDELIGHTS: A professor of English and comparative literature at Columbia University and an influential and provocative cultural critic until his untimely death in 2003, Edward W. Said remains best known to the general public as an astute commentator on Middle Eastern affairs and as a vocal and respected proponent of Palestinian national rights. His editorials on the Middle East appeared in major newspapers worldwide throughout his career, and he frequently appeared on national television news programs and talk shows. Writing in *Time* magazine, Robert Hughes described Said as one of American academia's "few public intellectuals—men or women whose views carry weight with general readers off-campus." *Israel Studies* contributor Alon Confino called Said "one of the premier political intellectuals of his generation, whose professional work has been fundamental to unmasking narratives of power and authority." Noting that Said gained stature as "a critic of Western power and its influence upon international politics and culture," *Free Inquiry* writer Norm Allen explained in Said's obituary that his 1978 book *Orientalism* "led to his remarkable career" as an advocate not only of the Palestinian people, but also of people in "India, Africa, Australia, and the Caribbean."

A Palestinian-American born in Jerusalem, Said grew up primarily in Cairo, Egypt, where his father owned a prosperous stationery business. The Said family also owned property in Jerusalem and Lebanon, but after the Arab-Israeli war of 1947-48 they were permanently exiled from Palestine. Said became one of hundreds of thousands of Palestinians who were made refugees during that and subsequent wars between Israel and its Arab neighbors. Unlike those of most refugees, however, Said's family was well to do, and he was educated at an exclusive private school in Cairo before completing his formal education in the United States.

A member of the Palestine National Council (P.N.C.), the Palestinians' parliament in exile, from 1977 to 1991, Said met many times with Palestine Liberation Organization (P.L.O.) chairman Yasir Arafat, and drafted the English version of the Palestinian declaration of statehood issued by the P.N.C. in 1988. While adamant in ascribing the persistence of the Palestinian-Israeli dispute to Israel's refusal to recognize Palestinian national rights, Said was widely regarded as a moderate; he was, Eqbal Ahmad reported in the *Nation*, "the first Palestinian writer to argue for the necessity of a full-scale political encounter between the Jews and the Palestinians 'whose past and future tie them inexorably together.'"

Said's unwavering advocacy of Palestinian rights did not prevented Said from criticizing Palestinian policies and leadership, however, and he was critical of the deals struck between the Palestinian authority and the Israeli government allowing for limited Palestinian autonomy in the Gaza Strip and portions of the West Bank in the early 1990s. He contended that the agreements gave the Palestinians too little authority over their own affairs while leaving Israel at liberty to pursue annexation of the bulk of the West Bank. In the *Nation* he lambasted the Palestinian authority leadership, and particularly Arafat, for following "undemocratic methods" in concluding agreements with Israel behind the backs of Palestinian representatives who were involved, with his blessing, in ongoing negotiations with Israeli authorities. The traditional Palestinian authority leadership, Said argued, not only displayed "incompetence and corruption," but failed "to mobilize the vast potential of its own people," and hence should "step aside." Said was also highly critical of the oppressiveness of other Middle Eastern regimes. While he denounced the United States' role in the 1991 Gulf War against Iraq, he was equally

outspoken in condemning the Iraqi regime of Saddam Hussein, whom he described in a *New Statesman* interview as "an appalling and dreadful despot."

While Said's writings cover a variety of topics, all evince a concern with the relationships between language and power. Several of Said's books and many of his shorter writings deal directly with the Palestinian issue. In *The Question of Palestine,* first published in 1979, he traces the history of the Palestinians and the Israeli-Palestinian conflict and argues that supporters of Israeli policies have distorted the record to make Palestinian efforts to obtain statehood appear irrational, evil, and unjustifiable. While Walter Laqueur, in the *New Republic,* dismissed the book as "another routine attack on Zionism and its dire consequences," in the *New York Times* Christopher Lehmann-Haupt suggested that *The Question of Palestine* "is as good a place as any for a Westerner to begin an attempt to understand" the Palestinian viewpoint. Said's 1988 anthology, *Blaming the Victims,* coedited with journalist Christopher Hitchens, presents a collection of studies exposing and analyzing cases of media misrepresentation of the Palestinian case. *After the Last Sky: Palestinian Lives,* published in 1986, combines a meditative essay by Said with photographs of Palestinians taken by Swiss photographer Jean Mohr. In a review in the *Nation,* Lesley Hazleton described *After the Last Sky* as "an extended voyage through the mind of exile" and "a beautifully written exploration of Palestinian identity and alienation."

Perhaps Said's most influential work, *Orientalism* examines European and U.S. representations of the peoples and societies of the Middle East. The author argues that traditional Western scholarship on the region, as well as popular and literary depictions of the Middle East, has created a stereotype of its cultures as irrational, unchanging, violent, and morally degenerate. Once rooted in Western perception, this stereotype has colored subsequent representations of the area, influencing the work of journalists, imaginative writers, and even scholars. Moreover, Said asserts, negative stereotypes of the "Orient" and its peoples have long been exploited to justify Western economic and political domination of the Middle East, and they continue to inform both popular attitudes and public policy toward the region.

Some Orientalist scholars were at first highly critical of Said's thesis. Bernard Lewis, in the *New York Review of Books,* charged him with lodging "reckless accusations" and making "arbitrary" and "capricious" use of information, while Albert Hourani, in a generally favorable review in the same publication, suggested that Said goes too far in generalizing about Orientalist scholars. However, John Leonard, writing in the *New York Times,* termed Said's argument "not merely persuasive, but conclusive." In an essay for the *Dictionary of Literary Biography,* John Kucich indicated that while *Orientalism* was "vigorously and sometimes abusively attacked by Islamic and Arabist specialists," it was also "welcomed by many specialists in related fields . . . as well as by those more generally interested in theories of representation, in the new historicism, or in imperialism itself." *Orientalism* quickly became a standard text in courses on postmodern literary theory and cultural studies, Scott Sherman describing the work in *Publishers Weekly* as "among the most influential works of critical theory in the postwar period."

Culture and Imperialism expands on the themes of *Orientalism,* "to describe," as Said states in the book, "a more general pattern of relationships between the modern metropolitan West and its overseas territories." In this study, published in 1993, Said explores the relationship between imperialism, as a defining feature of nineteenth- and twentieth-century Western culture, and Western art, particularly the novel. He also discusses the "culture of resistance," rejecting "nativism" or separatist nationalism in favor of "a more integrative view of human community and human liberation." Though characterizing the book as "dense, allusive . . . occasionally brilliant, often vexing and consistently provocative," Michiko Kakutani complained in the *New York Times* of its "hectoring tone" and worried that its author may be "trying to shoehorn examples into a rigid theoretical structure." Conversely, Robert Hughes, writing in *Time,* called *Culture and Imperialism* "the product of a culturally hypersaturated mind, moving between art and politics, showing how they do or might intermesh—but never with the coarse ideological reductiveness of argument so common in America nowadays." Michael Gorra in the *New York Times Book Review* praised Said's analysis of the complex interrelationships between imperialism and resistance. *Culture and Imperialism,* Gorra concluded, provides an "urgently needed synthesis of the work in a field that, more than any other critic, Edward W. Said has himself defined."

Notwithstanding his considerable output of book-length studies, Said's journalism and essays were per-

haps his most influential writings, and the most noted have been published in collections. *The World, the Text, and the Critic,* according to Kucich, attempts "to synthesize the two seemingly disparate bodies of [Said's] writing—that on literature and that on the Middle East." At the center of this synthesis lies Said's concept of "antithetical knowledge": the ability of a reader to counteract the constraints of orthodox thinking through a critical awareness of his or her own methods, interests, and cultural assumptions. Irwin Ehrenpreis, in the *New York Review of Books,* accused Said of inaccuracy and over-generalization in developing his arguments. In contrast, *Voice Literary Supplement* contributor Walter Kendrick found the essays partially successful, noting that "the diagnosis they offer" regarding the state of literary criticism in the late twentieth century "is accurate."

Both *The End of the Peace Process: Oslo and After* and *Reflections on Exile and Other Literary and Cultural Essays* assemble Said's writings on politics and literature. In a *New York Times Book Review* piece on *The End of the Peace Process,* Ethan Bronner called Said "one of the world's most eloquent advocates of the Palestinian cause," adding: "Few are as consistently devastating or as learned as Said in their condemnations." A *Publishers Weekly* correspondent summarized the book as "a potent analysis—one that refuses to follow a party line—of the complexities and stark realities of Middle Eastern politics." In his review, Bronner concluded of Said: "His voice, as heard in these essays, is deep, rich and courageous in what is often a scripted and dishonest international dispute." A *Kirkus Reviews* critic, reviewing *Reflections on Exile,* characterized Said as "one of the boldest and most articulate cultural theorists" of the late twentieth century, adding that the collection is "a fascinating exploration of post-colonialism as seen through the eyes of its progenitor."

Power, Politics, and Culture: Interviews with Edward W. Said collects interviews and panel discussions from the years 1976-2000. The book covers a wide range of topics, including the Palestinian-Israeli conflict and the peace process, the Gulf War, Middle East politics, literary criticism, cultural theory, opera, and travel drawn from a variety of publications, both in the United States and abroad. The book's editor, according to *Library Journal* reviewer Nader Entessar, "has captured Said's lifelong commitment to scholarship and political activism." A *Publishers Weekly* contributor noted, "These interviews trace [Said's] thoughtful perspectives and his unflinching candor about Middle Eastern politics." According to this reviewer, readers "interested in an overview of Said's ideas and oeuvre should start with this book." Entessar concluded of *Power, Politics, and Culture* that as an introduction to the writer's work, it "demonstrates the depth and breadth of Said's scholarship."

In the early 1990s Said was diagnosed with a virulent form of leukemia and began chemotherapy and other treatments in a battle that he would ultimately lose. This confrontation with his imminent mortality inspired him to write *Out of Place: A Memoir.* Even before the book's release, Said was attacked by critics, including *Commentary* essayist Justus Reid Weiner, who without having read the book accused Said of falsifying his background in order to make his sufferings as an expatriate more dramatic. In fact, when *Out of Place* was released, it revealed not only a truthful account of Said's peripatetic childhood, but also offered a candid account of his feelings of alienation, based not on physical suffering but on intellectual confusion about his place in the world. Confino wrote in *Israel Studies*: "A constant property links young Edward with the adult Said: the notion of out of placeness, of exile, as changeless, permanent features of his personality that existed before he could have known what the future had in store for him. Said thus becomes the intellectual par excellence, whose exile is not simply metaphoric, but both an objective reality (exiled from Palestine) and a subjective feeling (permanently out of place)."

Nation correspondent Ammiel Alcalay wrote of *Out of Place:* "Much as Zola galvanized public opinion in the Dreyfus affair, Said has lifted the Palestinian cause out of the apologetic and beleaguered discourse in which it had been embedded, to lend it universal dimensions. With the publication of *Out of Place,* these intellectual journeys and endeavors can finally be considered against the backdrop of other physical movements and psychological trials, as Said reaches back to recall a life lived before coming to such public, political consciousness." In the *New York Times Book Review,* Ian Buruma observed that "Said's efforts on behalf of Palestinians are admirable. But the hero emerging from his memoir is not the Palestinian activist so much as the alienated intellectual. . . . One finishes his book with the strong impression that Said presses the suffering of the Palestinian people into the service of his own credentials as an intellectual hero." Conversely, Confino concluded: "As a Palestinian, Said has written a testimony more eloquent than all his political writing; the personal is often more powerful than the purely political. . . . By attempting harder than most intellectuals to reflect on the very process of reflection, Said's memoir has movingly illuminated the composite and ambiguous condition of the modern intellectual who attempts to represent and explain the self while maintaining a vocation for the art of representing and explaining the society."

BIOGRAPHICAL AND CRITICAL SOURCES:

BOOKS

Contemporary Issues Criticism, Volume 2, Gale (Detroit, MI), 1984.

Dictionary of Literary Biography, Volume 67: *Modern American Critics since 1955,* Gale (Detroit, MI), 1988.

Parry, Benita, *Cultural Readings of Imperialism: Edward Said and the Gravity of History,* edited with Keith Ansell-Pearson and Judith Squires, St. Martin's Press (New York, NY), 1997.

Singh, Amritjit, and Bruce G. Johnson, editors, *Interviews with Edward W. Said,* University Press of Mississippi (Jackson, MS), 2004.

Sprinker, Michael, editor, *Edward Said: A Critical Reader,* Blackwell, 1993.

Xu, Ben, *Situational Tensions of Critic-Intellectuals: Thinking through Literary Politics with Edward W. Said and Frank Lentricchia,* P. Lang (New York, NY), 1992.

PERIODICALS

Antioch Review, spring, 2000, Grace A. Epstein, review of *Out of Place: A Memoir,* p. 244.

Atlantic, September, 2003, Christopher Hitchens, "Where the Twain Should Have Met," p. 153.

Booklist, July, 2001, Mary Carroll, review of *Power, Politics, and Culture: Interviews with Edward W. Said,* p. 1975; February 1, 2001, Mary Carroll, review of *Reflections on Exile and Other Literary and Cultural Essays,* p. 1035.

Canadian Journal of Law and Society, spring, 2002, Mikhael Elbaz, review of *Reflections on Exile and Other Literary and Cultural Essays,* pp. 190-191.

Christian Century, July 19, 2000, Marc H. Ellis, review of *End of the Peace Process: Oslo and After,* p. 762; November 15, 2003, James M. Wall: "Patriot Act: Two Giants for Justice Leave behind a Legacy of Activism and Patriotism," p. 45.

Commentary, August, 1989, Edward Alexander, "Professor of Terror," p. 49; September, 1999, Justus Reid Weiner, "'My Beautiful Old House' and Other Fabrications by Edward Said," p. 23; April, 2004, p. 21.

Grand Street, spring, 2002, "Daniel Barenboim and Edward W. Said: A Dialogue," pp. 46-59.

Hudson Review, winter, 2002, Bruce Bawer, "Edward W. Said, Intellectual," p. 620.

Israel Studies, fall, 2000, Alon Confino, "Remembering Talbiyah: On Edward Said's *Out of Place,*" p. 182.

Journal of Palestine Studies, spring, 2000, Ahdaf Soueif, review of *Out of Place,* p. 90; winter, 2002, Amr G. E. Sabet, "Focus on Edward Said," p. 86.

Kirkus Reviews, December 1, 2000, review of *Reflections on Exile and Other Literary and Cultural Essays,* p. 1667.

Library Journal, July, 2001, review of *Power, Politics, and Culture,* p. 111.

Middle East, February, 2002, Fred Rhodes, review of *Reflections on Exile and Other Literary and Cultural Essays,* p. 41.

Modern Language Quarterly, March, 2003, p. 97.

Nation, March 24, 1979, p. 309; March 22, 1980, Eqbal Ahmad, review of *The Question of Palestine,* p. 341; January 10, 1987, Lesley Hazelton, review of *After the Last Sky: Palestinian Lives,* p. 21; March 22, 1993, John Leonard, review of *Culture and Imperialism,* p. 383; September 20, 1993, pp. 269-270; February 14, 1994, pp. 190-193; September 8-15, 1997; September 20, 1999, Christopher Hitchens, "The Commentary School of Falsification," p. 9; December 20, 1999, Ammiel Alcalay, "Stop-Time in the Levant," p. 23.

National Review, April 26, 1993; August 9, 1999, David Pryce-Jones, "Corruption of the Best," p. 45.

New Criterion, January, 1999, Keith Windschuttle, "Edward Said's *Orientalism* Revisited," p. 30.

New Republic, November 29, 1975, p. 31; November 27, 1976, p. 29; December 15, 1979, p. 34; November 7, 1994, Michael Walzer, review of *Representations of the Intellectual: The 1993 Reith Lectures,* p. 38.

New Statesman, January 15, 1988, David Gilmour, review of *Blaming the Victims: Spurious Scholarship and the Palestinian Question,* p. 36.

New Statesman and Society, February 12, 1993, Paul Gilroy, review of *Culture and Imperialism,* pp. 46-47; March 3, 1994.

New York, January 23, 1989, p. 41; September 27, 1999, Emily Eakin, "Look Homeward, Edward," p. 48.

New York Review of Books, March 8, 1979, p. 27; June 12, 1980, Terrence Smith, review of *The Question of Palestine,* p. 42; May 27, 1982, Clifford Geertz, review of *Covering Islam: How the Media and the Experts Determine How We See the Rest of the World,,* p. 25; June 24, 1982, Anthony Lewis, "The Question of Orientalism," p. 49; January 19, 1984, Irvin Enrenpreis, review of *The World, the Text, and the Critic,* p. 37.

New York Times, December 1, 1978, p. C25; January 4, 1980, Christopher Lehmann-Haupt, review of *The Question of Palestine,* p. C20; March 9, 1993, Michiko Kakutani, review of *Culture and Imperialism,* p. C18.

New York Times Book Review, February 18, 1979, p. 3; January 20, 1980, Nicholas Bethell, review of *The Question of Palestine,* p. 7; July 26, 1981, Anthony Howard, review of *Covering Islam,* p. 7; February 27, 1983, John Bayley, review of *The World, the Text, and the Critic,* p. 11; November 9, 1986, Richard Ben Cramer, review of *After the Last Sky,* p. 27; February 28, 1993, Michael Gorra review of *Culture and Imperialism,* p. 11; June 26, 1994, David K. Shipler, review of *The Politics of Dispossession: The Struggle for Palestinian Self-Determination, 1969-1994,* p. 9; October 3, 1999, Ian Buruma, "Misplaced Person," p. 10; April 16, 2000, Ethan Bronner, "Voice in the Wilderness," p. 16; February 18, 2001, Martha C. Nussbaum, "The End of Orthodoxy: For Edward Said, Exile Means a Critical Distance from all Cultural Identities," p. 28.

Progressive, January, 2001, David Barsamian, review of *End of the Peace Process,* p. 35.

Sociological Analysis, winter, 1981, p. 382.

Publishers Weekly, September 6, 1999, Scott Sherman, "Edward Said: A Contested History," p. 74; March 27, 2000, review of *The End of the Peace Process,* p. 64; July 16, 2001, review of *Power, Politics, and Culture,* p. 176; August 26, 2002, review of *Parallels and Paradoxes: Explorations in Music and Society,* p. 52.

Spectator, March 16, 2002, Jonathan Sumption, review of *Reflections on Exile and Other Literary and Cultural Essays,* p. 46.

Tikkun, March-April, 1999, Mark LeVine, "An Interview with Edward Said," p. 11.

Time, June 21, 1993, Robert Hughes, "Envoy to Two Cultures," pp. 60-61.

Times Literary Supplement, June 12, 1987, p. 629; March 11, 1988, p. 267; November 29, 1991, p. 8.

Voice Literary Supplement, March, 1983, p. 17.

Washington Post, March 7, 1993, p. 1; October 26, 1999, John Lancaster, "Origin of an Outspoken Palestinian: Edward Said's Memoir Reveals the Personal Life behind the Political," p. C1.

Washington Post Book World, December 31, 1978, p. G7; September 18, 1988, p. 9.

World Literature Today, winter, 2000, Issa J. Boullata, review of *Out of Place,* p. 252.

ONLINE

Columbian University Web site, http://www.columbia.edu/ (April 24, 1998), Suzanne Trimel, "Edward Said."

Progressive Online, http://www.progressive.org/ (November, 2001), David Barsamian, "Edward Said Interview."

OBITUARIES:

PERIODICALS

College Literature, winter, 2004, p. 201.

Contemporary Review, November, 2003, p. 271.

Economist (U.S.), October 4, 2003, p. 84.

Free Inquiry, December, 2003, p. 23.

Nation, October 20, 2003, p. 4.

Newsweek, October 6, 2003, p. 8.

Research in African Literatures, spring, 2004, p. 6.

Spectator, October 22, 2003, p. 65.*

*   *   *

SETH, Vikram 1952-

PERSONAL: Surname is pronounced "sate"; born June 20, 1952, in Calcutta, India; son of Premnath (a consultant) and Leila (a judge) Seth. *Education:* Corpus Christi College, Oxford, B.A. (with honors), 1975, M.A., 1978; Stanford University, M.A., 1977; Nanjing University, China, graduate diploma, 1982.

Vikram Seth

ADDRESSES: Home—8 Rajaji Marg, New Delhi, India 110 011. *Office*—c/o Irene Skolnick Agency, 22 West 23rd St., 5th Floor, New York, NY 10010-5211; c/o Giles Gordon, Curtis Brown, 37 Queensferry St., Edinburgh EH2 4QS.

CAREER: Poet, novelist, and travel writer. Stanford University Press, Stanford, CA, senior editor, 1985-86.

AWARDS, HONORS: Thomas Cook Travel Book Award, 1983, for *From Heaven Lake: Travels through Sinkiang and Tibet;* Commonwealth Poetry Prize, Asian Region, 1985, for *The Humble Administrator's Garden;* Ingram Merrill fellowship, 1985-86; Quality Paperback Book Club New Voice Award and Commonwealth Poetry Prize, both 1986, for *The Golden Gate: A Novel in Verse;* Guggenheim fellowship, 1986-87; W. H. Smith Award, 1994, for *A Suitable Boy: A Novel;* Commonwealth Writer's Prize, 1994.

WRITINGS:

Mappings (poems), Writers Workshop (Calcutta, India), 1980.

From Heaven Lake: Travels through Sinkiang and Ti-bet, illustrated with own photographs, Chatto & Windus (London, England), 1983, Vintage (New York, NY), 1987.

The Humble Administrator's Garden (poems), Carcanet (Manchester, England), 1985.

The Golden Gate: A Novel in Verse, Random House (New York, NY), 1986.

All You Who Sleep Tonight: Poems, Knopf (New York, NY), 1990.

Beastly Tales from Here and There, illustrated by Ravi Shankar, Viking (New Delhi), 1992, HarperCollins (New York, NY), 1994.

(Translator) *Three Chinese Poets: Translations of Poems by Wang Wei, Li Bai, and Du Fu,* HarperPerennial (New York, NY), 1992.

A Suitable Boy: A Novel, HarperCollins (New York, NY), 1993.

The Poems, 1981-1994, Penguin (New York, NY), 1995.

Arion and the Dolphin, illustrated by Jane Ray, Dutton (New York, NY), 1995.

An Equal Music, Broadway Books (New York, NY), 1999.

SIDELIGHTS: Vikram Seth will "no doubt . . . be proclaimed the reinventor of narrative verse in America," predicted X. J. Kennedy in a review of *The Golden Gate: A Novel in Verse* for the *Los Angeles Times Book Review.* "I don't know when a versifier has proved better versed in verse-form than Seth," continued the reviewer, declaring that such mastery of poetry "probably hasn't been heard in English since Alexander Pope." Seth's studies in economics and literature, in addition to travel and residency in eastern Asia and west-coast America, have given him ample and uncommon background for his writings, and he has acquired a reputation as a skillful poet who exhibits unique cultural understanding in all of his works.

From Heaven Lake: Travels through Sinkiang and Ti-bet is Seth's account of his 1981 hitchhiking adventure from Nanjing University in eastern China through Tibet and Nepal to his home in Delhi, India. Seth tells of his episodes of loneliness, illness, and danger as well as the pleasures he took from visiting various civilizations, encountering interesting people along the way. Intermittently, he reflects—with both lament and satire—on the Chinese Cultural Revolution, the annihilation of Tibetan temples, and the treatment of foreigners by the Chinese. Mirsky noted that with his ability to read and speak Chinese, his attention to detail, and his acceptance of cultural differences, Seth is "a wonderful companion," able to manage better than the average tourist. "Very few foreigners have spent the night in Chinese truck parks and country inns," the reviewer added. "Few have had even a meal with a Chinese family. . . . Seth has, and he notices everything and tells us about it."

Seth conveys more of his cultural diversity through the medium of poetry in *The Humble Administrator's Garden.* Like his previous book, the collection of poems contains material gleaned from Seth's visits to both Eastern and Western countries. "Given the exotic nature of his background," noted Tom D'Evelyn in the *Christian Science Monitor,* the poet could have gone "toward the specialized feeling and idea, toward myth and cultural arcana, toward anthropology." Instead Seth goes in the other direction, continued the reviewer, choosing "to represent in his poems feeling of the widest applicability." Divided into three sections—on China, India, and California (with occasional references to England)—the book was hailed by Raymond Tong in *British Book News* as an "impressive" collection in which "a high level is generally maintained throughout."

As with *From Heaven Lake,* critics liked *The Humble Administrator's Garden* for the unassuming tone Seth presents in the work. Dick Davis in the *Listener,* for example, found the collection to be "modest, ordered, well-mannered and well-planned, with a trace of deprecatory self-pity." In his review in the *Times Literary Supplement,* Claude Rawson praised Seth's "fastidious probing language," noting that the work includes "small masterpieces of delicate verbal and emotional discipline, observant of pathos, of ironies of behaviour, of the unexpected small exuberances of life." Extolling Seth's talent as a disciplined poet, the critic observed that "Seth focuses on the mundane with unusual clarity," and he added that Seth "is one of the few young poets who has taken the trouble to learn, really learn, the disciplines of meter."

Seth's widest acclaim as a technically solid poet came with *The Golden Gate,* his 1986 verse novel, which many critics hailed as a tour de force. Containing nearly six hundred sonnets of iambic tetrameter, Seth's long narrative poem is set in present-day San Francisco and concerns the lives of young, urban professionals, or "yuppies." The story introduces John Brown, a twenty-six-year-old computer expert working for a defense contractor, who suddenly comes to the realization that his life is meaningless. He has lunch with his old girlfriend, Janet Hayakawa—a sculptor and a drummer in a punk-rock band called Liquid Sheep— after which Janet, unbeknownst to John, submits an advertisement on John's behalf to a lonely hearts column. The action is a catalyst for the presentation of *The Golden Gate*'s other characters: Liz Dorati, an attractive lawyer; Phil Weiss, a divorced single parent, philosopher, and peace demonstrator; and Ed, an advertising executive. In addition to incorporating timely concerns within the novel—such as a long scene at an antinuclear demonstration and a dialogue between two homosexual men on sex and celibacy—Seth places his characters in typically modern situations, such as singles bars and wine-making parties. Seth "knows these people inside out," noted Kennedy, and he consequently "conducts us on a psychological safari through five interesting souls."

Deemed "one of the curiosities of the season" by John Gross in the *New York Times, The Golden Gate* struck many critics as unusual in its portrayal of modern yuppies conveyed through narrative verse, a form that is a "throwback to our literary past," Raymond Mungo pointed out in the *New York Times Book Review.* Seth once told *CA* interviewer Jean W. Ross that he patterned the style of *The Golden Gate* after Russian poet Aleksandr Pushkin's *Eugene Onegin,* a work exhibiting intricately rhymed and metered sonnets. Expecting little, Seth found in reading *Eugene Onegin* that "I was reading it as I would read a novel. That was something that intrigued me, because the idea of a novel in verse had at first struck me as some curious hybrid, something that would not work. Here was something that *did* work, and that not only worked, but moved me and amused me and made me want to write something in a similar form set in my time and in a place that I knew." According to Alan Hollinghurst in the *Times Literary Supplement,* the Pushkin stanza is "a form whose inner counterpoint gives it both gravity and levity." Moreover, the reviewer judged the unconventionality of Seth's novel entirely appropriate, declaring, "It is hard to imagine a better vehicle for social verse narrative which aims to be both reflective and lightly comic."

It took Seth years to complete and publish his next novel, *A Suitable Boy,* described by Michele Field of *Publishers Weekly* as "the longest single-volume work

of English fiction since Samuel Richardson's *Clarissa* was published in 1747." At a dense 1,349 pages and weighing four pounds, *A Suitable Boy* is Seth's "magnum opus," according to Robert Worth of *Commonweal.* Seth completed several other works while *A Suitable Boy* was in progress: the poetry collections *Beastly Tales from Here and There* and *All You Who Sleep Tonight,* and the translation of a collection of Chinese poetry titled *Three Chinese Poets: Translations of Poems by Wang Wei, Li Bai, and Du Fu.*

A Suitable Boy is the story of the arranged marriage of Lata Mehra, an upper-class Indian woman rebelling against the traditional customs imposed upon her by her mother and Indian society at large. The widow Mehra, Lata's mother, is determined to find her daughter a husband of appropriate caste, color, religion, and financial stability—a "suitable boy." However, after attending her older sister's wedding at the beginning of the novel, Lata becomes skeptical of marriage and of the Indian traditions inherent in arranged matrimony. The plot centers on four families—the Mehras, Kapoors, Chatterjis, and Khans—yet Seth reaches beyond the limits of their experiences: "He chose to tell the whole story, producing for all time the whole world of Lata Mehra, with all the intermingled levels of North Indian culture," Schuyler Ingle remarked in the *Los Angeles Times Book Review.* While the action in *A Suitable Boy* takes place in the fictional northern city of Brahmpur in the 1950s, not long after India's 1947 independence from England, Seth describes in great detail the political, religious, and cultural shifts gripping postcolonial India in a multitude of subplots.

Reviews of the content of *A Suitable Boy* were mixed. *New Republic* reviewer Richard Jenkyns acknowledged the tendency of long books to "be spoken of, whether for praise or blame, in superlatives," which may seem to leave only one conclusion: "Since *A Suitable Boy* is not obviously a bad book, it must be a marvel. What we do not expect, with something so massive, is to speak in neutral, colorless terms: pleasant, mostly unpretentious, some pale charm, some gentle humor, readable but a bit flat and dull. But such, I think, is the judgment that we should return on this book." *Vanity Fair*'s Christopher Hitchens noted, "Those who aren't so keen on Seth's blockbuster say that it's more like [English writer John] Galsworthy than [Russian epic novelist Leo] Tolstoy, a jolly giant of a saga with lots of characters and speaking parts but no darkness or depth and no real consciousness of evil and suffering." Robert Towers, writing in the *New York Times Book Review,* found that "in his drive toward inclusiveness" the author "has sacrificed intensity," and he concluded, "In the end, *A Suitable Boy* succeeds less as a novel than as a richly detailed documentary focused upon a crucial era in the history of an endlessly fascinating country." *London Review of Books* contributor John Lanchester found, however, that the author succeeds in his quest for "complete transparency: all his energies are concentrated on making the prose a vehicle for the characters and the action." He further added, "The prose is intended not to distract. The resulting structural clarity is remarkable—you never don't know what's happening, why, where, and to whom. . . . It's a considerable technical feat." In the *Los Angeles Times Book Review,* Ingle noted the many hours required to read a novel of such length but concluded that "*A Suitable Boy* is a book that pays readers back, and richly, for their nightly effort."

As critics debated the issue of the book's length, some found it a hindrance, and others deemed it appropriate, though unwieldy. According to Jill Rachlin of *People,* although the author intended *A Suitable Boy* to be the first novel of a set of five, his first draft was close to two thousand pages. "After cutting it by a third," Rachlin reported, "he tried to divide it into two or three separate books. 'It didn't break in any right point,' he says with a laugh,'so I was stuck with this monster.'" In a *Newsweek* review, Laura Shapiro remarked, "Surprisingly, it makes very easy reading. What you can't do is *hold* the damn thing." She further observed, "Very few novels demand extraordinary length, and this isn't one of them. But Seth's publishers aren't entirely crazy: there is something strangely appealing about *A Suitable Boy.*" Pico Iyer, writing for the *Times Literary Supplement,* observed, "Every single page of *A Suitable Boy* is pleasant and readable and true; but the parts are better crafted, and so more satisfying, than the whole. . . . It is not immediately evident that its some 1,400 pages make it four times better than it would have been at 350." Yet Ingle found the book's length logical: "In a land of 900 million people, Seth seems to be saying, no one person can possibly be singled out: Their connections must be taken into account as well."

Arion and the Dolphin, a 1995 children's book based on Seth's libretto for an opera, is a blend of prose and verse that retells an ancient Greek legend: the story of a young musician whose life is saved by a dolphin. Cruel fisher folk imprison Arion and put his dolphin friend on display; the dolphin soon dies. Though the book is meant for children, its message that humans can find love, liberation, and mercy in the natural world may be overpowered for them by the sadness of the dolphin's death. The opera on which the book is based, with music by Alec Roth, was first performed in 1994 in Plymouth, England. A flyer from the Singapore opera, where the work was performed in 1996, notes that the cast totaled two hundred people, the most ambitious production ever undertaken by the company.

Seth's novel, *An Equal Music,* is a love story between Michael and Julia who are both immersed, by vocation, in the world of Western classical music. It is the story of a resurrected love between the two protagonists who meet by chance years later. Critics had mixed reactions to the work. Writing for *Time,* Elizabeth Gleick opined, "*An Equal Music* is almost unbearably sudsy, a huge disappointment for the legions of *A Suitable Boy* fans waiting to see what magic Seth could possibly spin next." However, Donna Seaman of *Booklist* was much more enthusiastic, writing "Seth has moved from the symphonic scope of his bestselling *A Suitable Boy* to a love story set to chamber music. . . . Replete with feverish drama and elegant characters, staccato dialogue, and sweeping emotions, Seth's irresistible novel is destined to please diverse readers as it artfully bridges the divide between popular and literary fiction."

BIOGRAPHICAL AND CRITICAL SOURCES:

BOOKS

Agarwalla, Shyam S., *Vikram Seth's "A Suitable Boy": Search for an Indian Identity,* Prestige Books, 1995.
Contemporary Literary Criticism, Gale (Detroit, MI), Volume 43, 1987, Volume 90, 1996.
Dictionary of Literary Biography, Volume 120: *American Poets since World War II, Third Series,* Gale (Detroit, MI) 1992, pp. 281-285.
Kirpal, Viney, editor, *The New Indian Novel in English,* Allied Publishers (New Delhi, India), 1990, pp. 91-100.
Contemporary Novelists, St. James Press (Detroit, MI), 1996.

Parker, Peter, editor, *A Reader's Guide to Twentieth-Century Writers,* Oxford University Press (Oxford, England), 1996.

Riggs, Thomas, editor, *Contemporary Poets,* St. James Press (Detroit, MI), 1996.

Serafin, Steven R., editor, *Encyclopedia of American Literature,* Continuum Publishing (New York, NY), 1999.

Stringer, Jenny, editor, *The Oxford Companion to Twentieth-Century Literature in English,* Oxford University Press (Oxford, England), 1996.

PERIODICALS

ACLALS Bulletin, 1989, Makarand R. Paranjape, "*The Golden Gate* and the Quest for Self-Realization."

American Poetry Revue, November-December, 1986, Marjorie Perloff, "'Homeward Ho!' Silicon Valley Pushkin."

Arkansas Philological Association, fall, 1996, Jay Curlin, "'The World Goes On': Narrative Structure and the Sonnet in Vikram Seth's *The Golden Gate.*"

Booklist, March 15, 1999, Donna Seaman, review of *An Equal Music,* p. 1261.

Books, summer, 1999, review of *An Equal Music,* p. 20.

British Book News, November, 1983; September, 1985.

Chicago Tribune, April 20, 1986; February 3, 1988.

Christian Science Monitor, August 21, 1985; June 10, 1999, review of *An Equal Music,* p. 16.

Commonweal, May 21, 1993, Robert Worth, review of *A Suitable Boy,* pp. 25-26.

Economist, May 15, 1999, review of *An Equal Music,* p. 12.

Entertainment Weekly, June 4, 1999, review of *An Equal Music,* p. 79.

Five Owls, January, 1996, p. 52.

Globe and Mail, May 15, 1999, review of *An Equal Music,* p. D16.

Horn Book Guide, fall, 1995, p. 281.

Island, winter, 1995, J. H. Walker, "Trunks of the Banyan Tree: History, Politics and Fiction."

Kirkus Reviews, March 15, 1999, review of *An Equal Music,* p. 404.

Library Journal, April 15, 1999, Shirley N. Quan, review of *An Equal Music,* p. 146.

Listener, December 5, 1985.

Literary Criterion, 1986, Rowena Hill, "Vikram Seth's *The Golden Gate.*"

London Review of Books, April 22, 1993, p. 9; April 29, 1999, review of *An Equal Music,* p. 15.

Los Angeles Times Book Review, April 6, 1986; May 23, 1993, pp. 4, 11; May 30, 1999, review of *An Equal Music,* p. 10.

New Republic, April 21, 1986, John Hollander, review of *The Golden Gate,* p. 32; June 14, 1993, Richard Jenkyns, review of *A Suitable Boy,* pp. 41-44; July 12, 1999, Karl Miller, review of *An Equal Music,* p. 44.

New Statesman, October 7, 1983, Kathy O'Shaughnessy, review of *From Heaven Lake: Travels through Sinkiang and Tibet,* p. 25; May 3, 1999, Tom Holland, review of *An Equal Music,* p. 58.

Newsweek, April 14, 1986, David Lehman, review of *The Golden Gate,* p. 74; May 24, 1993, Laura Shapiro, review of *A Suitable Boy,* p. 62; May 3, 1999, review of *An Equal Music,* p. 72.

New Yorker, July 14, 1986, Whitney Balliett, review of *The Golden Gate,* p. 82; June 7, 1999, David Denby, review of *An Equal Music,* p. 91.

New York Review of Books, July 15, 1999, review of *An Equal Music,* p. 20.

New York Times, April 14, 1986, John Gross, review of *The Golden Gate,* p. 18.

New York Times Book Review, May 11, 1986, Raymond Mungo, review of *The Golden Gate,* p. 11; May 9, 1993, Robert Towers, review of *A Suitable Boy,* pp. 3, 16; June 13, 1999, review of *An Equal Music,* p. 34.

Observer (London, England), September 12, 1993, p. 54; March 28, 1999, review of *An Equal Music,* p. 11; December 30, 2001, audio book review of *Beastly Tales from Here and There,* p. 14; January 27, 2002, review of *The Golden Gate,* p. 18; March 31, 2002, audio book review of *A Suitable Boy,* p. 16.

People, June 30, 1986, Cutler Durkee, review of *The Golden Gate,* p. 82; May 24, 1993, Jill Rachlin, review of *A Suitable Boy,* pp. 29-30.

Publishers Weekly, May 10, 1993, Michele Field, review of *A Suitable Boy,* pp. 46-47; June 26, 1995, review of *Arion and the Dolphin,* p. 106; April 12, 1999, review of *An Equal Music,* p. 53.

Rosyjska Ruletka, 1995, Roumiana Deltcheva, review of *The Golden Gate.*

School Library Journal, July, 1995, Cheri Estes, review of *Arion and the Dolphin,* p. 74.

Spectator, February 11, 1984; April 10, 1999, review of *An Equal Music,* p. 30.

Time, May 31, 1999, Elizabeth Gleick, review of *An Equal Music,* p. 98.

Times Literary Supplement, February 7, 1986; July 4, 1986; September 21-27, 1990, p. 1007; March 19, 1993, p. 20.

Vanity Fair, June, 1993, Christopher Hitchens, review of *A Suitable Boy,* pp. 36-40.

Wall Street Journal, May 14, 1999, review of *An Equal Music,* p. W9.

Washington Post, May 17, 1986.

Washington Post Book World, March 23, 1986; July 22, 1990, p. 4; December 2, 1990, p. 9; May 9, 1999, review of *An Equal Music,* p. 15.

Whole Earth Review, winter, 2001, review of *A Suitable Boy,* p. 6.

World Literature Today, spring, 1993, John Oliver Perry, review of *Beastly Tales from Here and There,* pp. 447-448.

ONLINE

Atlantic Unbound, http://www.theatlantic.com/ (June 23, 1999), interview with Seth.

Connect Online, http://www.connectmagazine.com/ (November 20, 2003), overview of Seth.

Emory University Web site, http://www.emory.edu/ (June 19, 2002), "Vikram Seth."

Four Elephants Web site, http://www.fourelephants. com/ (May 1, 2000), Samantha Brown, review of *An Equal Music.*

Illinois Institute of Technology Web site, http://www. iit.edu/ (November 20, 2003).

January Magazine, http://www.januarymagazine.com/ (November 20, 2003), interview with Seth.

Random House Web site, http://www.randomhouse. com/ (May, 2003).

Salon.com, http://archive.salon.com/ (May 13, 1999), Akash Kapur, review of *An Equal Music.*

Seattle Arts and Lectures Web site, http://www.lectures. org/seth.html/ (November 19, 2003), "Vikram Seth."

University of California, Santa Cruz Web site, http:// www.ucsc.edu/ (October 8, 2001), John Newman, overview of Seth.*

*   *   *

SHAFER, Byron E. 1947-

PERSONAL: Born January 8, 1947, in Hanover, PA; married; children: one son. *Education:* Yale University, B.A. (magna cum laude), 1968; University of California—Berkeley, Ph.D., 1979.

ADDRESSES: Office—Department of Political Science, 110 North Hall, University of Wisconsin—Madison, Madison, WI 53706; fax: 608-265-2663. *E-mail*—bshafer@polisci.wisc.edu.

CAREER: Russell Sage Foundation, New York, NY, resident scholar, 1977-84; Florida State University, Tallahassee, associate professor of political science, 1984-85; Oxford University, Andrew W. Mellon Professor of American Government and professorial fellow of Nuffield College, both 1985-2000, acting warden of Nuffield College, 2000-01; University of Wisconsin—Madison, holder of Glenn B. and Cleone Orr Hawkins chair of political science, 2001—.

MEMBER: American Political Science Association, American Historical Association, American Sociological Association, Organization of American Historians, National Conference of University Professors, Political Studies Association of the United Kingdom, British Association for American Studies, Phi Beta Kappa, Pi Sigma Alpha.

AWARDS, HONORS: American Political Science Association, E. E. Schattschneider Prize, 1980, for doctoral dissertation, Jack L. Walker Award, 1997, for the article "Primary Rules, Political Power, and Social Change," and Franklin P. Burdette Prize, 1990; prize from American Association and World Association of Public Opinion Researchers, 1991, for the article "Life and Death As Public Policy: Capital Punishment and Abortion in American Public Opinion."

WRITINGS:

Quiet Revolution: The Struggle for the Democratic Party and the Shaping of Post-Reform Politics, Russell Sage Foundation (New York, NY), 1983.

The Changing Structure of American Politics, Oxford University Press (Oxford, England), 1986.

Bifurcated Politics: Evolution and Reform in the National Party Convention, Harvard University Press (Cambridge, MA), 1988.

(With William J. M. Claggett) *The Two Majorities: The Issue Context of Modern American Politics,* Johns Hopkins University Press (Baltimore, MD), 1995.

The Two Majorities and the Puzzle of Modern American Politics, University Press of Kansas (Lawrence, KS), 2003.

Contributor to books, including *The Republican Revolution on Capitol Hill,* edited by Dean McSweeney and John E. Owens, Macmillan (Basingstoke, England), 1998. Contributor to periodicals, including *Electoral Studies, Journal of Politics, International Political Science Review, Corruption and Reform, Public Interest,* and *Journal of Law and Politics.*

EDITOR

(With James I. Lengle) *Presidential Politics: Readings on Nominations and Elections,* St. Martin's Press (New York, NY), 1980, 2nd edition, 1983.

(And contributor) *Is America Different? A New Look at American Exceptionalism,* Oxford University Press (Oxford, England), 1991.

(And contributor) *The End of Realignment? Interpreting American Electoral Eras,* University of Wisconsin Press (Madison, WI), 1991.

(And contributor) *Postwar Politics in the G-7: Orders and Eras in Comparative Perspective,* University of Wisconsin Press (Madison, WI), 1996.

(And contributor) *Present Discontents: American Politics in the Very Late Twentieth Century,* Chatham House (Chatham, NJ), 1997.

(And contributor) *Partisan Approaches to Post-War American Politics,* Chatham House, 1998.

(With Anthony J. Badger; and contributor) *Contesting Democracy: Substance and Structure in American Political History, 1775-2000,* University Press of Kansas (Lawrence, KS), 2001.

(And author of introduction) *The State of American Politics,* Rowman & Littlefield (Lanham, MD), 2002.

Member of editorial board, *Journal of American Studies,* 1986—, and *Journal of Policy History,* 1994—.

WORK IN PROGRESS: The Transformation of Southern Politics: Structural Change and Partisan Shifts in the Postwar South, with Richard G. C. Johnston; *Public Wishes: Issue Evolution, Policy Preferences, and Voting Behavior in Postwar American Politics,* with William J. M. Claggett; *Mapping the Political Landscape: Policy Positions and Social Coalitions in Postwar American Politics,* with Richard H. Spady.

BIOGRAPHICAL AND CRITICAL SOURCES:

PERIODICALS

Choice, April, 2002, P. D. Travis, review of *Contesting Democracy: Substance and Structure in American Political History, 1775-2000,* p. 1481; Novem-ber, 2002, T. M. Jackson, review of *The State of American Politics,* p. 555; November, 2003, H. L. Reiter, review of *The Two Majorities and the Puzzle of Modern American Politics,* p. 623.

History: Review of New Books, winter, 2004, Richard Jensen, review of *The Two Majorities and the Puzzle of Modern American Politics,* p. 45.

Journal of American History, June, 2003, Mark Wahlgren Summers, review of *Contesting Democracy,* pp. 214-215.

Journal of Southern History, August, 2003, Robert Griffith, review of *Contesting Democracy,* p. 676.

Perspectives on Political Science, winter, 2003, James R. Hurtgen, review of *Contesting Democracy,* p. 43.

*   *   *

SHANGE, Ntozake 1948-

PERSONAL: Born Paulette Linda Williams October 18, 1948, in Trenton, NJ; name changed 1971; pronounced "En-to-zaki Shong-gay"; daughter of Paul T. (a surgeon) and Eloise (a psychiatric social worker and educator) Williams; married second husband, David Murray (a musician), July, 1977 (divorced); children: Savannah. *Education:* Barnard College, B.A. (with honors), 1970; University of Southern California, Los Angeles, M.A., 1973, and graduate study. *Hobbies and other interests:* Playing the violin.

ADDRESSES: Home—402 McCarty C, P.O. Box 115900, Gainesville, FL 32611. *Agent*—c/o Author Mail, St. Martin's Press, 175 Fifth Ave, New York, NY 10010-7703.

CAREER: Writer, performer, and teacher. Faculty member in women's studies, California State College, 1973-75, Sonoma Mills College, 1975, University of California Extension, 1972-75, City College of the City University of New York, New York, NY, 1975, Douglass College, New Brunswick, NJ, 1978; University of Houston, Houston, TX, associate professor of drama, 1983-2001; University of Florida, professor, African American Studies Program and the Center for Women's Studies and Gender Research, 2000—. Visiting professor at DePaul University, visiting artist at Brown University, artist in residence, New Jersey State Council on the Arts, and creative writing instructor,

Ntozake Shange

City College of New York. Lecturer at Douglass College, 1978, and at many other institutions, including Yale University, Howard University, Detroit Institute of Arts, and New York University.

Dancer with Third World Collective, Raymond Sawyer's Afro-American Dance Company, Sounds in Motion, West Coast Dance Works, and For Colored Girls Who Have Considered Suicide (Shange's own dance company); has appeared in Broadway and off-Broadway productions of her own plays, including *For Colored Girls Who Have Considered Suicide/ When the Rainbow Is Enuf* and *Where the Mississippi Meets the Amazon.* Director of productions, including *The Mighty Gents,* produced by the New York Shakespeare Festival's Mobile Theatre, 1979, *A Photograph: A Study in Cruelty,* produced in Houston's Equinox Theatre, 1979, and June Jordan's *Lovers-in-Motion,* Houston, 1979, *The Issue* and *The Spirit of Sojourner Truth,* 1979. Actress in plays, including *The Lady in Orange,* New York, 1976, *Where the Mississippi Meets the Amazon,* New York, 1977, and *Mouths,* New York, 1981. Has given many poetry readings.

MEMBER: Actors Equity, National Academy of Television Arts and Sciences, Dramatists Guild, PEN American Center, Academy of American Poets, Poets and Writers, Women's Institute for Freedom of the Press, New York Feminist Arts Guild, Writers Guild.

AWARDS, HONORS: NDEA fellow, 1973; Obie Award, Outer Critics Circle Award, Audience Development Committee (Audelco) Award, Mademoiselle Award, and Tony, Grammy, and Emmy award nominations, all 1977, all for *For Colored Girls Who Have Considered Suicide/When the Rainbow Is Enuf;* Frank Silvera Writers' Workshop Award, 1978; *Los Angeles Times* Book Prize for Poetry, 1981, for *Three Pieces;* Guggenheim fellowship, 1981; Medal of Excellence, Columbia University, 1981; Obie Award, 1981, for *Mother Courage and Her Children;* Nori Eboraci Award, Barnard College, 1988; Lila Wallace-Reader's Digest Fund annual writer's award, 1992; Paul Robeson Achievement Award, 1992; Arts and Cultural Achievement Award, National Coalition of 100 Black Women (Pennsylvania chapter), 1992; Taos World Poetry Heavyweight Champion, 1992, 1993, 1994; Living Legend Award, National Black Theatre Festival, 1993; Claim Your Life Award, WDAS-AM/FM, 1993; Monarch Merit Award, National Council for Culture and Art; Pushcart Prize.

WRITINGS:

NOVELS

Sassafrass, Shameless Hussy Press (San Lorenzo, CA), 1976, revised edition published as *Sassafrass, Cypress, and Indigo,* St. Martin's Press (New York, NY), 1982.
For Colored Girls Who Have Considered Suicide/ When the Rainbow Is Enuf, Shameless Hussy Press (San Lorenzo, CA), 1976.
Betsey Brown, St. Martin's Press (New York, NY), 1985.
Liliane: Resurrection of the Daughter, St. Martin's Press (New York, NY), 1994.
If I Can Cook You Know God Can, Beacon Press, 1998.

FOR CHILDREN

Whitewash, illustrated by Michael Sporn, Walker (New York, NY), 1997.
Float Like a Butterfly: Muhammad Ali, the Man Who Could Float Like a Butterfly and Sting Like a Bee, Jump at the Sun (New York, NY), 2002.

Ellington Was Not a Street, Simon & Schuster (New York, NY), 2003.

Daddy Says, Simon & Schuster (New York, NY), 2003.

PLAYS

For Colored Girls Who Have Considered Suicide/ When the Rainbow Is Enuf: A Choreopoem, (first produced in New York, NY, at Studio Rivbea, July 7, 1975; produced off-Broadway at Anspacher Public Theatre, 1976; produced on Broadway at Booth Theatre, September 15, 1976), Shameless Hussy Press (San Lorenzo, CA), 1975, revised edition, Macmillan (New York, NY), 1976.

A Photograph: A Study of Cruelty (poem-play; first produced off-Broadway at Public Theatre, December 21, 1977; revised and produced as *A Photograph: Lovers in Motion* in Houston, TX, at the Equinox Theatre, November, 1979), S. French (New York, NY), 1981.

(With Thulani Nkabinde and Jessica Hagedorn) *Where the Mississippi Meets the Amazon,* first produced in New York, NY, at Public Theatre Cabaret, December 18, 1977.

From Okra to Greens: A Different Kinda Love Story; A Play with Music and Dance (first produced in New York, NY, at Barnard College, November, 1978), S. French (New York, NY), 1985, revised edition published as *Mouths,* The Kitchen, (New York, NY), 1981.

Boogie Woogie Landscapes (in *Poetry at the Public* series; produced at Shakespeare Festival (New York, NY), 1978; revised as *Black and White Two-Dimensional Planes,* produced at Sounds in Motion Studio Works, New York, February, 1979; revised and produced on Broadway, at Symphony Space Theater, 1979; produced in Washington, DC, at John F. Kennedy Center for the Performing Arts, 1980), St. Martin's Press (New York, NY), 1978.

Spell No.7: A Geechee Quick Magic Trance Manual (produced on Broadway at Joseph Papp's New York Shakespeare Festival Public Theater, July 15, 1979), published as *Spell No.7: A Theatre Piece in Two Acts,* S. French (New York, NY), 1981.

(Adapter) Bertolt Brecht, *Mother Courage and Her Children,* first produced off-Broadway at the Public Theatre, April, 1980.

Three Pieces: Spell No.7; A Photograph: Lovers in Motion; Boogie Woogie Landscapes, St. Martin's Press (New York, NY), 1981.

It Has Not Always Been This Way: A Choreopoem, (revision of *From Okra to Greens: A Different Kinda Love Story*), in collaboration with the *Sounds in Motion Dance Company,* Symphony Space Theater, (New York, NY), 1981.

Triptych and Bocas: A Performance Piece, (revision of *From Okra to Greens: A Different Kinda Love Story*) Mark Taper Forum (Los Angeles, CA), 1982

Three for a Full Moon [and] *Bocas,* first produced in Los Angeles, CA, at the Mark Taper Forum Lab, Center Theatre, April 28, 1982.

(Adapter) Willy Russell, *Educating Rita* (play), first produced in Atlanta, GA, by Alliance Theatre Company, 1982.

Three Views of Mt. Fuji (play), first produced at the Lorraine Hansberry Theatre, June, 1987, produced in New York, NY, at the New Dramatists, October, 1987.

Betsey Brown: A Rhythm and Blues Musical, produced in Philadelphia, PA, at American Music Theater Festival, 1989.

The Love Space Demands: A Continuing Saga, produced in New Brunswick, NJ, at Crossroads Theater, March 1992; in Philadelphia, PA, at Painted Bride Art Center, 1993.

Whitewash (video screenplay), First Run Features, 1994.

Author of the operetta *Carrie,* produced in 1981. Has written for a television special starring Diana Ross, and appears in a documentary about her own work for WGBH-TV (Boston).

POETRY

Melissa and Smith, Bookslinger (St. Paul, MN), 1976.

Natural Disasters and other Festive Occasions (prose and poems), Heirs International (San Francisco, CA), 1977.

A Photograph: Lovers in Motion: A Drama, S. French (New York, NY), 1977.

Nappy Edges, St. Martin's Press (New York, NY), 1978.

Some Men (poems), 1981.

A Daughter's Geography, St. Martin's Press (New York, NY), 1983.

From Okra to Greens, Coffee House Press (Minneapolis, MN), 1984.

Ridin' the Moon in Texas: Word Paintings (responses to art in prose and poetry), St. Martin's Press (New York, NY), 1987.

The Love Space Demands: A Continuing Saga, St. Martin's Press (New York, NY), 1991.

Three Pieces, St. Martin's Press (New York, NY), 1992.

I Live in Music, edited by Linda Sunshine, illustrated by Romare Bearden, Stewart, Tabori & Chang (New York, NY), 1994.

PROSE AND ESSAYS

See No Evil: Prefaces, Essays and Accounts, 1976-1983, Momo's Press (San Francisco, CA), 1984.

(Author of foreword) Robert Mapplethorpe, *The Black Book,* St. Martin's Press (New York, NY), 1986.

Plays, One, Methuen (London, England), 1992.

(Author of preface) Francoise Kourilsky and Catherine Temerson, editors, *Plays by Women, Book Two: An International Anthology,* Ubu Repertory Theater Publications (New York, NY), 1994.

(Contributor) Jules Feiffer, *Selected from Contemporary American Plays: An Anthology,* Literacy Volunteers of New York City (New York, NY), 1990.

(Editor) *The Beacon Best of 1999: Creative Writing by Women and Men of All Colors,* Houghton Mifflin (New York, NY), 1999.

Contributor to anthologies, including *Love's Fire: Seven New Plays Inspired by Seven Shakespearean Sonnets,* introduction by Mark Lamos, Quill, (New York, NY), 1998; *"May Your Days Be Merry and Bright" and Other Christmas Stories by Women,* edited by Susan Koppelman, Wayne State University Press (Detroit, MI), 1988; *New Plays for the Black Theatre,* edited by Woodie King, Jr., Third World Press (Chicago, IL), 1989; *Breaking Ice: An Anthology of Contemporary African American Fiction,* edited by Terry McMillan, Penguin Books (New York, NY), 1990; *Yellow Silk: Erotic Arts and Letters,* edited by Lily Pond and Richard Russo, Harmony Books (New York, NY), 1990; *Daughters of Africa: An International Anthology,* edited by Margaret Bushby, Pantheon (New York, NY), 1992; *Erotique Noire—Black Erotica,* edited by Miriam DeCosta-Willis, Reginald Martin, and Roseann P. Bell, Anchor (New York, NY), 1992; *Resurgent: New Writing by Women,* edited by Lou Robinson and Camille Norton, University of Illinois Press (Champaign, IL), 1992; *Wild Women Don't Wear No*

Blues: Black Women Writers on Love, Men, and Sex, edited by Marita Golden, Doubleday (New York, NY), 1993; and *Moon Marked and Touched by Sun: Plays by African-American Women,* edited by Sydne Mahone, Theater Communications Group (New York, NY), 1994.

Contributor to periodicals, including *Black Scholar, Third World Women, Ms.,* and *Yardbird Reader.*

ADAPTATIONS: A musical-operetta version of Shange's novel *Betsey Brown* was produced by Joseph Papp's Public Theater in 1986.

SIDELIGHTS: Ntozake Shange—originally named Paulette Williams—was raised with the advantages of the black middle class. Yet the roles she chose for herself—including war correspondent and jazz musician—were dismissed as "no good for a woman," she told Stella Dong in a *Publishers Weekly* interview. Frustrated and hurt after separating from her first husband, Shange attempted suicide several times before focusing her rage against the limitations society imposes on black women. While earning a master's degree in American Studies from the University of Southern California, she reaffirmed her personal strength based on a self-determined identity and took her African name, which means "she who comes with her own things" and she "who walks like a lion." Since then she has sustained a triple career as an educator, a performer/director, and a writer whose works draw heavily on her experiences of being a black female in America. "I am a war correspondent after all," she told Dong, "because I'm involved in a war of cultural and esthetic aggression."

Shange became famous for her play *For Colored Girls Who Have Considered Suicide/When the Rainbow Is Enuf.* A unique blend of poetry, music, dance and drama called a "choreopoem," it "took the theatre world by storm" in 1975 noted Jacqueline Trescott in the *Washington Post,* as it "became an electrifying Broadway hit and provoked heated exchanges about the relationships between black men and women. . . . Its form—seven women on the stage dramatizing poetry—was a refreshing slap at the traditional, one-two-three-act structures." Mel Gussow of the *New York Times* stated that "Miss Shange was a pioneer in terms of her subject matter: the fury of black women at their double subjugation in white male America."

In *For Colored Girls,* poems dramatized by the women dancers recall encounters with their classmates, lovers, rapists, abortionists, and latent killers. The women survive the abuses and disappointments put upon them by the men in their lives and come to recognize in each other, dressed in the colors of Shange's personal rainbow, the promise of a better future. As one voice, at the end, they declare, "i found god in myself / and i loved her / . . . fiercely." To say this, remarked Carol P. Christ in *Diving Deep and Surfacing: Women Writers on Spiritual Quest,* is "to say . . . that it is all right to be a woman, that the Black woman does not have to imitate whiteness or depend on men for her power of being." "The poetry," said Marilyn Stasio in *Cue,* "touches some very tender nerve endings. Although roughly structured and stylistically unrefined, this fierce and passionate poetry has the power to move a body to tears, to rage, and to an ultimate rush of love."

While some reviewers are enthusiastic in their praise for the play, others are emphatically negative. "Some Black people, notably men, said that . . . Shange broke a taboo when her *For Colored Girls* . . . took the theatre world by storm," Connie Lauerman reported in the *Chicago Tribune.* "[Shange] was accused of racism, of 'lynching' the black male." But the playwright does not agree. She told Lauerman, "Half of what we discussed in *For Colored Girls* about the dissipation of the family, rape, wife-battering and all that sort of thing, the U.S. Census Bureau already had. . . . We could have gone to the Library of Congress and read the Census reports and the crime statistics every month and we would know that more black women are raped than anyone else. We would know at this point that they think forty-eight percent of our households are headed by single females. . . . My job as an artist is to say what I see."

"Shange's poems aren't war cries," Jack Kroll wrote in a *Newsweek* review of the Public Theatre production of *For Colored Girls.* "They're outcries filled with a controlled passion against the brutality that blasts the lives of 'colored girls'—a phrase that in her hands vibrates with social irony and poetic beauty. These poems are political in the deepest sense, but there's no dogma, no sentimentality, no grinding of false mythic axes." Critic Edith Oliver of the *New Yorker* remarked, "The evening grows in dramatic power, encompassing, it seems, every feeling and experience a woman has ever had; strong and funny, it is

entirely free of the rasping earnestness of most projects of this sort. The verses and monologues that constitute the program have been very well chosen—contrasting in mood yet always subtly building."

Reviews of Shange's next production, *A Photograph: A Study of Cruelty,* were less positive, although critics were generally impressed with the poetic quality of her writing. "Miss Shange is something besides a poet but she is not—at least not at this stage—a dramatist," Richard Eder explained in a *New York Times* review. He continued, "More than anything else, she is a troubadour. She declares her fertile vision of the love and pain between black women and black men in outbursts full of old malice and young cheerfulness. They are short outbursts, song-length; her characters are perceived in flashes, in illuminating vignettes."

Shange's next play, *Spell No.7: A Geechee Quick Magic Trance Manual,* more like *For Colored Girls* in structure, elicited a higher recommendation from Eder. Its nine characters in a New York bar discuss the racism black artists contend with in the entertainment world. At one point, the all-black cast appears in overalls and minstrel-show blackface to address the pressure placed on the black artist to fit a stereotype in order to succeed. "That's what happens to black people in the arts no matter how famous we become. . . . Black Theatre is not moving forward the way people like to think it is. We're not free of our paint yet," Shange told Claudia Tate in *Black Women Writers at Work.* "On another level, *Spell No.7* deals with the image of a black woman as a neutered workhorse, who is unwanted, unloved, and unattended by anyone," noted Elizabeth Brown in the *Dictionary of Literary Biography.*"The emphasis is still on the experiences of the black woman but it is broadened and deepened, and it ventures more boldly across the sexual divide," Eder wrote in the *New York Times.* Don Nelson, writing in the *New York Daily News,* deemed the show "black magic. . . . The word that best describes Shange's works, which are not plays in the traditional sense, is power."

Shange's poetry books, like her theater pieces, are distinctively original. *Washington Post Book World* critic Harriet Gilbert believed *Nappy Edges,* containing fifty poems, is too long. However, Gilbert praised the author, saying, "Nothing that Shange writes is ever entirely unreadable, springing, as it does, from such an intense honesty, from so fresh an awareness of the beauty of sound and of vision, from such mastery of words, from such compassion, humor and intelligence." Alice H. G. Phillips related in the *Times Literary Supplement,* "Comparing herself to a jazzman 'takin' a solo, she lets go with verbal runs and trills, mixes in syncopations, spins out evocative hanging phrases, variations on themes and refrains. Rarely does she come to a full stop, relying instead on line breaks, extra space breaking up a line, and/or oblique strokes. . . . She constantly tries to push things to their limit, and consequently risks seeming overenthusiastic, oversimplistic or merely undisciplined. . . . But at its best, her method can achieve both serious humour and deep seriousness."

In her poetry, Shange takes many liberties with the conventions of written English, using nonstandard spellings and punctuation. Some reviewers feel that these innovations present unnecessary obstacles to the interested readers of *Nappy Edges, A Daughter's Geography,* and *From Okra to Greens: Poems.* Explaining her "lower-case letters, slashes, and spelling" to Tate, Shange said that "poems where all the first letters are capitalized" bore her; "also, I like the idea that letters dance. . . . I need some visual stimulation, so that reading becomes not just a passive act and more than an intellectual activity, but demands rigorous participation." Her idiosyncratic punctuation assures her "that the reader is not in control of the process." She wants her words in print to engage the reader in a kind of struggle, and not be "whatever you can just ignore." The spellings, she said, "reflect language as I hear it. . . . The structure is connected to the music I hear beneath the words."

Shange takes liberties with the conventions of fiction writing with her first full-length novel, *Sassafrass, Cypress, and Indigo.* "The novel is unusual in its form—a tapestry of narrative, poetry, magic spells, recipes and letters. Lyrical yet real, it also celebrates female stuff—weaving, cooking, birthing babies," related Lauerman. Its title characters are sisters who find different ways to cope with their love relationships. Indigo, the youngest sister, retreats into her imagination, befriending her childhood dolls, seeing only the poetry and magic of the world. The music she plays on her violin becomes a rejuvenating source for her mother and sisters. "Probably there is a little bit of all three sisters in Shange," Lauerman suggested, "though she says that her novel is not autobiographical but historical, culled from the experiences of blacks and from the information of my feelings."

Critics agree that Shange's poetry is more masterfully wrought than her fiction, yet they find much in the novel to applaud. Wrote Doris Grumbach in the *Washington Post Book World,* "Shange is primarily a poet, with a blood-red sympathy for and love of her people, their folk as well as their sophisticated ways, their innocent, loving goodness as much as their lack of immunity to powerful evil. . . . But her voice in this novel is entirely her own, an original, spare and primary-colored sound that will remind readers of Jean Toomer's *Cane.*" In Grumbach's opinion, "Whatever Shange turns her hand to she does well, even to potions and recipes."

In *The Love Space Demands,* a choreopoem published in 1991, Shange returned to the blend of music, dance, poetry and drama that characterized *For Colored Girls Who Have Considered Suicide.* "I've gone back to being more like myself," Shange explained to *Voice Literary Supplement* interviewer Eileen Myles. "I'm working on my poetry with musicians and dancers like I originally started." Described by Myles as "a sexy, discomfiting, energizing, revealing, occasionally smug, fascinating kind of book," *The Love Space Demands* includes poems on celibacy and sexuality, on black women's sense of abandonment by black men, on a crack-addicted mother who sells her daughter's virginity for a hit and a pregnant woman who swallows cocaine, destroying her unborn child, to protect her man from arrest. The lead poem of the book, "irrepressibly bronze, beautiful and mine," was inspired by Robert Mapplethorpe's photographs of black and white gay men. The artist's task, Shange told Myles, is "to keep our sensibilities alive. . . . To keep people alive so they know they can feel what is happening as opposed to simply trying to fend it off." "I would rather you not think about how the poem's constructed but simply be in it with me," she added. "That's what it's for, not for the construction, even for the wit of it. It's for actual, visceral responses."

Shange's novel *Liliane: Resurrection of the Daughter* again finds the author exploring the issues of race and gender in contemporary America. The protagonist, Liliane Lincoln, undergoes psychoanalysis in an attempt to better understand the events of her life, particularly her mother's decision to abandon Liliane and her father for a white man when Liliane was a child. As Clarence Major noted in the *Washington Post Book World,* the story is presented "through twelve monologue-performance pieces narrated in turn by

[Liliane] and her friends and lovers." Shange "offers a daring portrait of a black woman artist re-creating herself out of social and psychological chaos," remarked Kelly Cherry in the *Los Angeles Times Book Review.* Cherry added, "Shange has written a novel that manages to be both risky and stylish." While some reviewers praised the author for her lush and unusual prose, others felt that Shange's stylistic density occasionally "up-ends the narrative," in the words of *New Statesman and Society* reviewer Andrea Stuart. Nevertheless, commented Valerie Sayers in the *New York Times Book Review,* the book "is a dense, ambitious, worthy song." And Major concluded, "A standing ovation for Ntozake Shange. This is her finest work of fiction so far."

"In the tradition of M. F. K. Fisher," according to the publisher, *If I Can Cook You Know God Can* is a "generous banquet" of essays steeped in "lyrical originality and musical patois." These conversational essays take the reader to the tables of African Americans, Nicaraguans, Londoners, Barbadoans, Brazilians, and Africans. A *Booklist* reviewer noted that the recipes are interwoven with a "fervent, richly impassioned chronicle of African-American experience" that examines political turmoil and relates "how connections are made beyond issues of class or skin color."

In addition to poetry, novels, essays, and screenplays, Shange has taken on the field of children's literature with the publication of four books for children: *Whitewash, Float Like a Butterfly, Ellington Was Not a Street,* and *Daddy Says.* Receiving lukewarm praise and mixed critical reviews, Shange's children's fiction was not as well received among critics as her poetry. In a review of *Daddy Says* for the *School Library Journal,* Carol Edwards concluded, "Despite strong characters and a lively setting, this novel is disjointed and unsatisfying, which is a shame since Shange is clearly capable of portraying rivalry and competitive spirit realistically." However, a *Publishers Weekly* reviewer described *Float Like a Butterfly* a biographical tribute to boxer Muhammad Ali, as work that "nicely characterizes this modern-day hero, with poster-like illustrations and punchy text."

Shange as an editor is fully in her purview, as demonstrated by the positive critiques that greeted the release of *The Beacon Best of 1999,* a collection of poems, short stories, and essays written by lesser-known men and women of color. Vanessa Bush in *Booklist* called

it "an eclectic group of works, reflecting on racial and sexual relations in the context of everyday life and self-discovery." A *Publishers Weekly* reviewer claimed, "Shange has been careful not to surrender to ideology or dogma in her selection of material for this expansive collection, which deserves pride of place on the crowded shelf of literary anthologies." Shange defines the work of writers she profiled in *Beacon's Best* as "artful glimpses of life at the end of the twentieth century," which perhaps also describes Shange's work at its most acclaimed and creative.

BIOGRAPHICAL AND CRITICAL SOURCES:

BOOKS

Adell, Sandra, editor, *Dictionary of Twentieth-Century Culture,* Volume 5: *African American Culture,* Gale (Detroit, MI), 1996.

Andrews, William L., Frances Smith Foster, and Trudier Harris, editors, *The Oxford Companion to African American Literature,* Oxford University Press (New York, NY), 1997.

Arata, Esther Spring, editor, *More Black American Playwrights,* Scarecrow Press (Metuchen, NJ), 1978.

Authors and Artists for Young Adults, Volume 9, Gale (Detroit, MI), 1992.

Berney, K. A., editor, *Contemporary Dramatists,* St. James Press (London, England), 1993.

Berney, K. A., editor, *Contemporary American Dramatists,* St. James Press (London, England), 1994.

Berney, K. A., editor, *Contemporary Women Dramatists,* 5th edition, St. James Press (London, England), 1994.

Betsko, Kathleen, and Rachel Koenig, editors, *Interviews with Contemporary Women Playwrights,* Beech Tree Books, 1987.

Black Literature Criticism, Gale (Detroit, MI), 1992.

Brater, Enoch, editor, *Feminine Focus: The New Women Playwrights,* Oxford University Press (New York, NY), 1989.

Chevalier, Tracy, editor, *Contemporary Poets,* 5th edition, St. James Press (Chicago, IL), 1991.

Christ, Carol P., *Diving Deep and Surfacing: Women Writers on Spiritual Quest,* Beacon Press (Boston, MA), 1980.

Christian, Barbara T., *Black Feminist Criticism: Perspectives on Black Women Writers,* Pergamon Press (New York, NY), 1985.

Contemporary Literary Criticism, Gale (Detroit), Volume 8, 1978, Volume 25, 1983, Volume 38, 1986, Volume 74, 1993.

Coven, Brenda, *American Women Dramatists of the Twentieth Century,* Scarecrow Press (Metuchen, NJ), 1982.

Davis, Thadious M., and Trudier Harris, editors, *Dictionary of Literary Biography,* Volume 38: *Afro-American Writers after 1955: Dramatists and Prose Writers,* Gale (Detroit, MI), 1985.

Drama Criticism, Volume 3, Gale (Detroit, MI), 1993.

Easthope, Antony, editor, *Contemporary Poetry Meets Modern Theory,* University of Toronto Press (Toronto, Canada), 1991.

Geis, Deborah R., "Distraught at Laughter: Monologue in Shange's Theatre Pieces," in *Feminine Focus: New Playwrights,* Oxford University Press (New York, NY), pp. 210-225.

Green, Carol Hurd, and Mary Grimley Mason, editors, *American Women Writers,* Volume 5: Supplement, Continuum Publishing (New York, NY), 1994.

Halloway, Karla F. C., *Moorings and Metaphors: Figures of Culture and Gender in Black Women's Literature,* Rutgers University Press (Brunswick, NJ), 1992.

Hart, Lynda, *Making a Spectacle: Feminist Essays on Contemporary Women's Theatre,* University of Michigan Press (Ann Arbor, MI), 1989 .

Hine, Darlene Clark, editor, *Black Women in America: An Historical Encyclopedia,* Carlson Publishing (Brooklyn, NY), 1993.

Kester-Shelton, Pamela, editor, *Feminist Writers,* St. James Press (Detroit, MI), 1996.

Kirkpatrick, D. L., editor, *Contemporary Dramatists,* 4th edition, St. James Press (Chicago, IL), 1988.

Lester, Neal A., *Ntozake Shange: A Critical Study of the Plays,* Garland (New York, NY), 1995.

Magill, Frank N., *Critical Survey of Drama,* revised edition, Salem Press (Pasadena, CA), 1994.

Magill, Frank N., *Great Women Writers,* Henry Holt (New York, NY), 1994.

Magill, Frank N., *Survey of American Literature,* Marshall Cavendish (North Bellmore, NY), 1992.

Martin, Tucker, editor, *Modern American Literature,* Volume 6, third supplement, Continuum Publishing (New York, NY), 1997.

Modern American Literature, 5th edition, St. James Press (Detroit, MI), 1997.

Modern Black Writers, 2nd edition, St. James Press (Detroit, MI), 2000.

Olaniyan, Tejumola, *Scars of Conquest/Masks of Resistance: The Invention of Cultural Identities in African-American, and Caribbean Drama,* Oxford University Press (New York, NY), 1995.

Page, James A., and Jae Min Roh, compilers, *Selected Black American, African, and Caribbean Authors,* 2nd edition, Libraries Unlimited (Littleton, CO), 1985.

Peck, David, editor, *Identities and Issues in Literature,* Salem Press (Pasadena, CA), 1997.

Pendergast, Tom and Sara Pendergast, editors, *St. James Guide to Young Adult Writers,* 2nd edition, St. James Press (Detroit, MI), 1999.

Reinelt, Janelle, and Joseph Roach, *Critical Theory and Performance,* University of Michigan Press (Ann Arbor, MI), 1992.

Riggs, Thomas, editor, *Contemporary Poets,* 6th edition, St. James Press (Detroit, MI), 1996

Riggs, Thomas, editor, *Reference Guide to American Literature,* 4th edition, St. James Press (Detroit, MI), 2000

Robinson Lillian S., compiler and editor, *Modern Women Writers,* Continuum Publishing (New York, NY), 1996.

Schlueter, June, editor, *Modern American Drama: The Female Canon,* Fairleigh Dickinson University Press, 1990.

The Schomburg Center Guide to Black Literature, Gale (Detroit, MI), 1996.

Serafin, Steven R., editor, *Encyclopedia of American Literature,* Continuum Publishing (New York), 1999.

Shelton, Pamela L., editor, *Contemporary Women Poets,* St. James Press (Detroit, MI), 1998.

Smith, Valerie, Lea Baechler, and Walton Litz, *African American Writers,* Scribner (New York, NY), 1991.

Spradling, Mary Mace, editor, *In Black and White,* Gale (Detroit, MI), 1980.

Squier, Susan Merrill, editor, *Women Writers and the City: Essays in Feminist Literary Criticism,* University of Tennessee Press (Knoxville, TN), 1984.

Stringer, Jenny, editor, *The Oxford Companion to Twentieth-Century Literature in English,* Oxford University Press (New York, NY), 1996.

Tate, Claudia, editor, *Black Women Writers at Work,* Continuum (New York, NY), 1983.

Vaught, Jacqueline Brogan and Cordelia Chavez Candelaria, editors, *Women Poets of the Americas: Toward a Pan-American Gathering,* University of Notre Dame Press (Notre Dame, IN), 1999.

PERIODICALS

African American Review, spring, 1992, Neal A. Lester, "Ntozake Shange," pp. 322-325; summer, 1992, and Neal A. Lester, "Shange's Men: *For Colored Girls* revisited, and Movement Beyond," pp. 319-328 .

American Black Review, September, 1983; March, 1986.

Black American Literature Forum, winter, 1979, Henry Blackwell, "An Interview with Ntozake Shange," pp. 134-138; summer, 1981, Sandra Hollin Flowers, "*Colored Girls*: Textbook for the Eighties," p. 51; summer, 1983, Sandra L. Richards, review of *Spell No. 7,* pp. 74-75; fall, 1990; winter, 1990, Neal A. Lester, "At the Heart of Shange's Feminism: An Interview," pp. 717-730.

Black Issues Book Review, November-December, 2002, Clarence V. Reynolds, review of "For Colored Girls Who Have Considered Fairy Tales," p. 42; March-April, 2003, review of *Daddy Says,* p. 66.

Black Scholar, March, 1979; October, 1979, Robert Staples, "The Myth of Black Macho: A Response to Angry Black Feminists," pp. 24-33; March, 1981; December, 1982; July, 1985; winter, 1996, p. 68; summer, 1996, p. 67.

Booklist, April 15, 1987; May 15, 1991; January 1, 1998; October 15, 1999, Vanessa Bush, review of *The Beacon Best of 1999,* p. 410; June 1, 2001, review of *Betsey Brown,* p. 1837; March 15, 2003, Hazel Rochman, review of *Daddy Says,* p. 1317.

Boston Review, November 14, 1994, Laurel Elkind, review of *Lilliane: Resurrection of the Daughter,* p. 38.

Chicago Tribune, October 21, 1982.

Chicago Tribune Book World, July 1, 1979; September 8, 1985.

Christian Science Monitor, September 9, 1976; October 8, 1982; May 2, 1986.

College Language Association Journal, June, 1996, Jane Splawn, "Rites of Passage in the Writing of Ntozake Shange: The Poetry, Drama, and Novels," p. 1989; June 1986, Jane Splawn, "New World Consciousness in the Poetry of Ntozake Shange and June Jordan: Two African-American Women's Response to Expansionism in the Third World."

Cue, June 26, 1976.

Detroit Free Press, October 30, 1978; October 30, 1979, Laura Berman, "The Last Angry Woman? Playwright-Poet Isn't Running from the Rage That Inspires Her," p. C1.

Early Childhood Education Journal, fall, 1999, review of *Whitewash,* p. 36.

Entertainment Weekly, March 10, 1995, p. 65.

Essence, November, 1976; May, 1985, Marcia Ann Gillespie, "Ntozake Shange Talks with Marcia Ann Gillespie," pp. 122-123; June, 1985; August, 1991.

Freedomways, 1976, Jean Carey Bond, review of *For Colored Girls Who Have Considered Suicide,* pp. 187-191.

Horizon, September, 1977.

Journal of American Culture, fall, 1987, Jean Strandness, review of *Sassafrass, Cypress, and Indigo,* p. 11.

Journal of Ethnic Studies, spring, 1978, Erskine Peters, "Some Tragic Propensities of Ourselves: The Occasion of Ntozake Shange's *For Colored Girls Who Have Considered Suicide/When the Rainbow Is Enuf,*" pp. 79-85.

Kirkus Reviews, September 1, 1999, review of *The Beacon Best of 1999,* p. 69; September 1, 2002, review of *Float Like a Butterfly: Muhammad Ali, the Man Who Could Float Like a Butterfly and Sting Like a Bee,* p. 1320; December 1, 2002, review of *Daddy Says,* p. 1773.

Kliatt Young Adult Paperback Book Guide, January, 1989.

Library Journal, May 1, 1987; October 15, 1999, review of *The Beacon Best of 1999,* p. 70.

Los Angeles Times, October 20, 1982; June 11, 1985; July 28, 1987.

Los Angeles Times Book Review, August 22, 1982; October 20, 1982; January 8, 1984; July 29, 1984; June 11, 1985; July 19, 1987; December 18, 1994, p. 12.

Massachussetts Review, autumn, 1981, Andrea Benton Rushing, "For Colored Girls, Suicide or Struggle," pp. 539-550; winter, 1987, Brenda Lyons, "Interview with Ntozake Shange," pp. 687-696.

MELUS, fall, 1994, Barbara Frey Waxman, "Dancing out of Form, Dancing into Self: Genre and Metaphor in Marshall, Shange, and Walker," pp. 91-107.

Modern Drama, March, 1995, Timothy Murray, "Screening the Camera's Eye: Black and White Confrontations of Technological Representations," pp. 110-124; 1986, P. Jane Splawn, "Change the Joke[r] and Slip the Yoke: Boal's *Joker* System in Ntozake Shange's *For Colored Girls* and *Spell No. 7,*" pp. 386-398.

Mother Jones, January-February, 1995, p. 69.

Ms., September, 1976; December, 1977, "Ntozake Shange Interviews Herself"; June, 1985; June, 1987.

Newsday, August 22, 1976.

New Statesman, October 4, 1985.

New Statesman and Society, May 19, 1995, p. 37.

Newsweek, June 14, 1976; July 30, 1979.

New York Daily News, July 16, 1979.

New Yorker, June 14, 1976; August 2, 1976; January 2, 1978.

New York Times, June 16, 1976; December 22, 1977; June 4, 1979; June 8, 1979; July 16, 1979; July 22, 1979; May 14, 1980; June 15, 1980, Frank Rich, "*Mother Courage* Transplanted," p. D5; January 1, 1995, Valerie Sayers, "A Life in Collage," p. 38; September 3, 1995, Andrea Stevens, "*For Colored Girls* May Be for the Ages," p. H5.

New York Times Book Review, June 25, 1979; July 16, 1979; October 21, 1979; September 12, 1982; May 12, 1985; April 6, 1986; January 1, 1995, p. 6; October 15, 1995, p. 36; February 25, 1996, p. 32.

New York Times Magazine, May 1, 1983.

Phylon, fall, 1987, Elizabeth Brown-Guillory, "Black Women Playwrights: Exorcising Myths," pp. 229-239.

Plays and Players, June, 1985, Carole Woddis, review of *Spell No. 7,* pp. 230-248.

Publishers Weekly, May 3, 1985; November 14, 1994, review of *I Live in Music,* p. 65; January 1, 1996, p. 69; September 20, 1999, review of *The Beacon Best of 1999,* p. 65; September 16, 2002, review of *Float Like a Butterfly,* p. 68.

Saturday Review, February 18, 1978; May-June, 1985.

School Library Journal, February, 2003, Carol A. Edwards, review of *Daddy Says,* p. 148.

Social Studies, January, 2001, review of *Whitewash,* p. 39.

Studies in American Drama, 1989, "The Poetry of a Moment: Politics and the Open Forum in the Drama of Ntozake Shange," pp. 91-101, Neal A. Lester, "An Interview with Ntozake Shange," pp. 42-66.

Time, June 14, 1976; July 19, 1976; November 1, 1976.

Times (London, England), April 21, 1983.

Times Literary Supplement, December 6, 1985; April 15-21, 1988.

Umoja, spring, 1980, Linda Lee Talbert, "Ntozake Shange: Scarlet Woman and Witch/Poet," pp. 5-10.

Variety, July 25, 1979.

Village Voice, August 16, 1976, Michelle Wallace, "For Colored Girls, the Rainbow Is Not Enough," pp. 108-109; July 23, 1979; June 18, 1985.

Voice Literary Supplement, August, 1991; September, 1991.

Washington Post, June 12, 1976; June 29, 1976; February 23, 1982; June 17, 1985.

Washington Post Book World, October 15, 1978; July 19, 1981; August 22, 1982; August 5, 1984; February 5, 1995, p. 4.

Wilson Library Bulletin, October, 1990.

Women's Review of Books, November, 1985, Evelyn C. White "Growing Up Black," p. 11.

World Literature Today, summer, 1995, Deirdre Neilen, review of *Liliane: Resurrection of the Daughter,* p. 584.

ONLINE

Academy of American Poets Web site, http://www.poets.org/poets/ (February 21, 2001), "Ntozake Shange."

African American Literature Book Club Web site, http://aalbc.com/ (November 18, 2003), "Ntozake Shange."

Mother Jones.com, http://www.motherjones.com/ (January-February, 1995), "Rebecca Carroll, Back at You: Interview with Ntozake Shange."

Open Book Systems Web site, http://archives.obsus.com/obs/ (November 18, 2003), "Ntozake Shange."

University of Florida Web site, http://web.wst.ufl.edu/ (November 18, 2003), "Ntozake Shange."

Women of Color, Women of Words Web site, http://www.scils.rutgers.edu/~cybers/shange2.html/ (November 18, 2003), "Ntozake Shange."*

*   *   *

SHEPHERD, Michael
See LUDLUM, Robert

*   *   *

SIDDONS, (Sybil) Anne Rivers 1936-

PERSONAL: Born January 9, 1936, in Atlanta, GA; daughter of Marvin (an attorney) and Katherine (a secretary; maiden name, Kitchens) Rivers; married Heyward L. Siddons (a business partner and creative director), 1966; children: (stepsons) Lee, Kemble, Rick, David. *Education:* Auburn University, B.A.A., 1958; attended Atlanta School of Art, c. 1958. *Hobbies and other interests:* Swimming, cooking, reading, cats.

ADDRESSES: Home—3767 Vermont Rd. NE, Atlanta, GA 30319; (summer) Osprey Cottage, Brooklin, ME

Anne Rivers Siddons

04616. *Agent*—Jennifer Rudolph Walsh, William Morris Agency, 1325 Avenue of the Americas, New York, NY 10019.

CAREER: Writer. Worked in advertising with Retail Credit Co., c. 1959, Citizens & Southern National Bank, 1961-63, Burke-Dowling Adams, 1967-69, and Burton Campbell Advertising, 1969-74. Senior editor, *Atlanta*, 1964-67. Full-time writer, 1974—. Member of governing board, Woodward Academy; member of publications board and arts and sciences honorary council, Auburn University, 1978-83.

MEMBER: Chevy Chase Club, Every Saturday Club, Ansley Golf Club, Tri-Delt sorority.

AWARDS, HONORS: Alumna achievement award in arts and humanities, Auburn University, 1985; Georgia Author of the Year, 1988; honorary doctorate in Humanities, Oglethorpe University, 1991.

WRITINGS:

NOVELS

Heartbreak Hotel, Simon & Schuster (New York, NY), 1976.

The House Next Door (horror), Simon & Schuster (New York, NY), 1978.
Fox's Earth, Simon & Schuster (New York, NY), 1981.
Homeplace, Harper (New York, NY), 1987.
Peachtree Road, Harper (New York, NY), 1988.
King's Oak, Harper (New York, NY), 1990.
Outer Banks, HarperCollins (New York, NY), 1991.
Colony, HarperCollins (New York, NY), 1992.
Hill Towns, HarperCollins (New York, NY), 1993.
Downtown, HarperCollins (New York, NY), 1994.
Fault Lines, HarperCollins (New York, NY), 1995.
Up Island, HarperCollins (New York, NY), 1997.
Low Country, HarperCollins (New York, NY), 1998.
Nora, Nora, HarperCollins (New York, NY), 2000.
Islands, Harper Collins (New York, NY), 2004.

NONFICTION

John Chancellor Makes Me Cry (essays), Doubleday (New York, NY), 1975, HarperCollins (New York, NY), 1992.
Go Straight on Peachtree (guide book), Dolphin Books (New York, NY), 1978.

Contributor to *Gentleman's Quarterly, Georgia, House Beautiful, Lear's, Reader's Digest, Redbook,* and *Southern Living.*

ADAPTATIONS: Heartbreak Hotel was adapted as the film *Heart of Dixie,* Orion Pictures, 1989.

SIDELIGHTS: Novelist Anne Rivers Siddons identifies herself as an author of the South—an author of Atlanta in particular. "Everything I know and do is of here, of the South," she said in an interview in *Southern Living.* Her novels are most often concerned with the lives of Southern women; more recent books have occasionally transplanted these characters to other locales. Wherever they find themselves, however, Siddons's women must explore more than their surroundings: they must come to terms with their own lives and gain strength in the process. A *Booklist* reviewer once noted, "Siddons has had a solid winning streak with her seductive portrayals of plucky southern gals holding their own in alien territory. . . . What's intriguing about Siddons is how much she transcends the usual parameters of fluff fiction, both in terms of literary finesse and penetrating intelligence."

Oddly enough, the famed fiction writer's first book, *John Chancellor Makes Me Cry,* is a collection of essays. The book chronicles one year of her life in Atlanta, humorously reflecting on the frustrations and joys of day-to-day living—serving jury duty, hosting parties, and taking care of a husband suffering with the flu. The author's style in *John Chancellor Makes Me Cry* has been favorably compared to that of Erma Bombeck, whose own review of the book praised Siddons: "She is unique. She's an original in her essays that combine humor, intimacy, and insight into a marriage." Bombeck found the most "poignant and very real" chapter to be the one describing "the month [Siddons's] husband lost his job, her Grandmother died, a Siamese cat they were keeping for a friend was hit by a car, their house was burgled and their Persian cat contracted a fifty-dollar-a-week disease."

Siddons soon found a home in fiction. *The House Next Door,* Siddons's tale of an affluent couple whose lives are changed by the mysterious evils occurring in a neighboring house, was praised by Stephen King. In *Stephen King's Danse Macabre,* King's critique on the horror genre, King devoted an entire chapter to an analysis of *The House Next Door,* comparing it to Shirley Jackson's *Haunting of Hill House.* Siddons, in an interview in *Publishers Weekly,* called the book "something of a lark. It's different from anything I've ever written, or probably ever will. But I like to read occult, supernatural stories. Some of the world's great writers have written them, and I guess I wanted to see what I could do with the genre." In the *St. James Guide to Horror, Ghost, and Gothic Writers,* Brian Stableford called the book "a far more adventurous and interesting work than the rash of schlocky haunted-house movies which came soon after."

More recent Siddons novels, such as *Homeplace* and *Peachtree Road,* won greater favor with critics and became best-sellers. Noted Bob Summers in *Publishers Weekly, Homeplace* "struck a national chord" with its account of an independent Southern-born woman returning home after more than twenty years. *Peachtree Road* is Siddons's "love letter to Atlanta," according to *Chicago Tribune* contributor Joyce Slater. "Siddons does an admirable job of tracing the city's rebirth after World War II without idealizing it." Slater concluded that *Peachtree Road* is Siddons's "most ambitious [book] to date."

Siddons's first novel set outside the South, *Colony,* is the saga of the family of a Carolinian woman who has been transplanted by marriage into the Brahmin milieu of a coastal Maine retreat. As a young bride, heroine Maude Gascoigne detests her new summer home and its people, but with the passing decades she grows to love it enough to fight hard to pass it on to her granddaughter. Joan Mooney, writing in the *New York Times Book Review,* called Maude "a match for anything that's thrown her way—and plenty is." Others have also praised Siddons's development of character in *Colony.* A reviewer for *Publishers Weekly* deemed the novel "a page-turner by virtue of realistic characters who engage the reader's affection and concern," though *Booklist* contributor Denise Blank observed that "although her verbal artistry cannot be denied, Siddons never quite captures the feel of a place or a person—one is left with the impression of a very pretty painting that looks much like other very pretty paintings."

In her next novel, *Hill Towns,* Siddons again sends a Southern woman into new territory, this time even farther afield. Cat Gaillard suffers from what *Chicago Tribune* reviewer Joyce R. Slater termed "reverse acrophobia." She is only comfortable at heights that allow her to see for miles around her. She is also agoraphobic and is finally lured from a hermetic existence in her Appalachian lookout by an invitation to a wedding in Italy. Rome, Venice, and Tuscany have the expected loosening effect on Cat, though she and her husband "will not be corrupted by decadent Europeans, but by their fellow countrymen altered by extended sojourns abroad," according to Elaine Kendall in the *Los Angeles Times.* Among these are a famous expatriate painter and his wife, who work their separate wiles on Cat and her husband, Joe. Yet Cat pulls back from the brink. In the words of Slater, "Italy and the charismatic painter, Sam Forrest, are nearly Cat's undoing. Nearly."

Many reviewers identify Siddons's greatest strength in *Hill Towns* as her characterization. Writing for the *Washington Post,* Natalie Danford claimed that the author's "portrayals of people . . . are often stunning." Slater too praised Siddons in this regard, writing that she "sensitively describes the confusion of a woman who opts to travel from an existence of academic, almost Elysian perfection to one of the steamiest, most chaotic cities in the world."

Downtown, Siddons's 1994 novel set in the mid-1960s, is admittedly autobiographical. The circumstances that surround its main character, Smoky O'Donnell, a twenty-six-year-old ingenue with the dream and drive to succeed as a writer for Atlanta's trendiest magazine, mirror those of Siddons's own past. As a writer for *Downtown* magazine, Smoky sees the ups and downs of life in Atlanta at a time when "promises . . . hung in the bronze air like fruit on the eve of ripeness." For Smoky some of these promises are kept, but others, such as the promise that brightens within her growing awareness of the civil rights movement, are shot down as the decade approaches its close.

Critical reaction to *Downtown* was mixed. A reviewer for *Publishers Weekly* wrote of being "disappointed in [Siddons's] uninspired and often pretentious story line," and Jean Hanff Korelitz complained in the *Washington Post Book World* that Smoky's "responses are so predictable and her path to adulthood so well-worn that we can't escape feeling that we have already read this novel, that only the names and locations have been changed." Both reviewers nevertheless responded favorably to Siddons's evocation of the ambience of Atlanta in the 1960s.

One recurring theme in Siddons's work is the family crisis that forces a "comfortable" woman to assess the silent damage done by untreated psychic wounds. In *Fault Lines,* for instance, Merritt Fowler is caught in a series of midlife crises: her husband is a possibly philandering workaholic, her sixteen-year-old anorexic daughter, Glynn, is caught up in teenage rebellion, and her mother-in-law is afflicted with Alzheimer's and needs constant care. When Glynn runs away to her Aunt Laura's home in Northern California, Merritt follows, determined to save her daughter and herself. When Merritt, Laura, and Glynn unite, they take a trip to the Santa Cruz mountains in an attempt to leave their troubles behind. The trip marks a shift in Merritt's life as she begins to evolve out of the dutiful wife mindset. The earth shifts as well, and as the three women seek safety, they learn valuable lessons about themselves and each other. One reviewer wrote in *Contemporary Southern Writers,* "In *Fault Lines,* Siddons avoids fluff fiction with her excellent landscapes and characters, who are believable and for whom we care." Siddons's thirteenth novel, *Low Country,* reveals how socialite Caroline Venable is forced to choose between her marriage and privileged lifestyle and her deep devotion to Peacock Island, a wild, offshore island on which her grandfather had lived. Carol's husband of twenty-five years, Clay, owns a land-developing business and wants to turn her family's

native tribal settlement land into a theme park. When she discovers his plan, she must fight him to protect the beloved wild ponies that grace her island. She also struggles with the accidental drowning of her daughter, five years prior, and the desire to drink away her problems. "Familiar ground for the prolific Siddons . . . though her latest saga of the South replaces gothic melodrama with well-honed emotion," observed a *Kirkus* correspondent in a review of *Low Country.* The reviewer described the book as "a delicate, compelling tale, full of real feeling and lush description."

In a 1994 interview for the *Atlanta Journal & Constitution,* Siddons hinted that she was finished writing about Atlanta, although she toyed with the possibility of setting a future book in the nearby affluent enclave of Cobb County. Since then she has shown little inclination to cut her ties to the South, and—with hardcover and paperback sales in the millions—she has reason to stay the course. Stableford commended the author for her ability "to flay the skin of illusion from the moral pretensions of the American south" in her best work. In *Southern Living* Siddons commented, "I have found I can move anywhere in my fiction. If I take it from the point of view of a Southerner traveling there, it's still an honest point of view."

True to her word, Siddons's millennium novel *Nora, Nora* is set instead in the small, 1960s, segregated town of Lytton, Georgia. The main character is a twelve-year-old girl named Peyton McKenzie. Peyton endures many internal struggles, the biggest of which is the guilt she feels for "killing her mother" when she first came into the world. Peyton is a member of the Losers Club, whose other two members are the town grave keeper and the black housekeeper's handicapped son. It is only in this environment, and with this definition of herself, that she feels comfortable. Then her twenty-nine-year-old distant cousin Nora Findlay comes to Lytton to teach, and sets in motion the upheaval of Peyton's—and Lytton's—world. Nora is much different than anyone Peyton has known in her limited experience. Nora smokes, drinks, and engages in several other behaviors considered improper for a woman of her time, including advocating for drastic changes in the small town. Her bold red hair, pink Thunderbird convertible, and radical, integrated classrooms draw negative attention from Lytton citizens, who impatiently wait for Nora to self-destruct so they may be rid of her. But to Peyton, Nora's presence is a valuable one, as Peyton needs a catalyst to set her in motion and on the way to adulthood. Nora unearths qualities Peyton never realized she possessed: beauty, writing talent, and the possibility of a happy life. Nora removes Peyton's guilt and begins to teach Peyton how to love, beginning with herself. Even Peyton's father, who has lived in a shell since his wife's death, starts to come around under Nora's bright, nurturing glow. But darkness must inevitably fall, and Peyton starts to feel that Nora is hiding something unpleasant. When Nora's shocking secret is finally revealed, Peyton learns her most valuable lesson of love.

"Siddons's prose is so graceful, and lovely, that after diving in, the reader is carried along effortlessly and with great pleasure," praised Carol J. Bissett in a review of *Nora, Nora* for *Library Journal.* Bissett also pointed out the book's similarities and reference to Harper Lee's *To Kill a Mockingbird* and called the book "a completely satisfying and nourishing read, containing both style and substance." Not all critics were satisfied with Siddons's thematic distance from her previous novels. "Though Siddons doesn't deliver any thematic surprises in the well-worn genre," commented a *Publishers Weekly* reviewer, "she does offer a neatly competent and engrossing story that captures the reader's sympathies despite its quality of déjà vu, as she conjures up the social and racial attitudes of a small Southern town in the 1960s." In *Booklist,* Vanessa Bush described *Nora, Nora* as "a solid novel about growing up, daring to love, and weathering life's disappointments."

Though many reviewers have compared Siddons's writing and subject matter to those of Margaret Mitchell, Siddons doesn't see her writings as romanticized, but rather realistic. "It's like an old marriage or a long marriage," she once said about her relationship with the South and its portrayal in her novels. "The commitment is absolute, but the romance has long since worn off. . . . I want to write about it as it really is."

BIOGRAPHICAL AND CRITICAL SOURCES:

BOOKS

Contemporary Popular Writers, St. James Press (Detroit, MI), 1997.
Contemporary Southern Writers, St. James Press (Detroit, MI), 1999.

King, Stephen, *Stephen King's Danse Macabre,* Everest House (New York City), 1981.
St. James Guide to Horror, Ghost, and Gothic Writers, St. James Press (Detroit, MI), 1998.

PERIODICALS

Atlanta Journal & Constitution, October 9, 1988; July 14, 1991, p. N8; June 26, 1992, p. P1; June 28, 1992, p. N9; June 5, 1994, p. M1, p. N10.
Booklist, May 1, 1987, p. 948; July, 1988, p. 1755; August, 1990, p. 2123; June 1, 1991, p. 1843; November 15, 1991, p. 638; April 15, 1992, Denise Blank, review of *Colony,* p. 1643; March 15, 1993, p. 1369; May 1, 1993, p. 1548; February 15, 1994, Nancy McCray, sound recording review of *Heartbreak Hotel,* p. 1100; May 15, 1994, Donna Seaman, review of *Downtown,* p. 1645; May 15, 1995, Nancy McCray, sound recording review of *John Chancellor Makes Me Cry,* p. 1664; September 1, 1995, Joanne Wilkinson, review of *Fault Lines,* p. 7; April 15, 1997, Mary Frances Wilkins, review of *Up Island,* p. 1365; June 1, 1998, Brad Hooper, review of *Low Country,* p. 1671; June 1, 2000, Vanessa Bush, review of *Nora, Nora,* p. 1799; March 1, 2001, audiobook review of *Nora, Nora,* p. 1296.
Bookwatch, October, 1991, p. 6; August, 1992, p. 6.
Chicago Tribune, June 14, 1987; November 11, 1988, Joyce Slater, review of *Peachtree Road;* July 25, 1993, p. 6.
Chicago Tribune Book World, June 28, 1981.
Christian Science Monitor, July 1, 1994, p. 10.
Entertainment Weekly, November 3, 1995, Rebecca Ascher-Walsh, review of *Fault Lines,* p. 61; June 6, 1997, Vanessa V. Friedman, review of *Up Island,* p. 63; August 11, 2000, "The Week," review of *Nora, Nora,* p. 76.
Kirkus Reviews, April 1, 1987, p. 510; August 1, 1988, p. 1093; August 1, 1990, p. 1038; June 1, 1991, p. 692; May 1, 1992, p. 564; April 15, 1993, p. 484; May 1, 1994, p. 587; June 1, 1998.
Kliatt, spring, 1985, p. 18; July, 1994, p. 89; January, 1995, p. 52; March, 1995, p. 53; September, 2001, audiobook review of *Nora, Nora,* p. 54.
Library Journal, June 15, 1975, p. 1211; April 1, 1987, p. 165; August, 1990, p. 145; October 1, 1991, p. 159; September 15, 1992, p. 108; August, 1993, p. 178; October 15, 1993, p. 110; June 15, 1994, p. 97; November 15, 1994, p. 106; October 1,

1998, Mark Pumphrey, sound recording review of *Low Country*, p. 150; July, 2000, Carol J. Bissett, review of *Nora, Nora*, p. 143; October 1, 2000, Lane Anderson, review of *The House Next Door*, p. 176; January 1, 2001, Adrienne Furness, audio-book review of *Nora, Nora*, p. 186.

Locus, January, 1990, p. 52.

Los Angeles Times, September 3, 1993, p. E6.

Los Angeles Times Book Review, September 18, 1988, p. 10; September 16, 1990, p. 8; August 4, 1991, p. 3; October 3, 1993, p. 8; July 10, 1994, p. 14.

New York Times, September 16, 1989.

New York Times Book Review, April 13, 1975, p. 18; September 12, 1976; October 23, 1977; December 10, 1978; August 30, 1987, Robin Bromley, review of *Homeplace*, p. 20; August 14, 1988, p. 26; January 1, 1989, p. 14; November 4, 1990, Gene Lyons, "She Didn't Hate Herself in the Morning," p. 33; August 2, 1992, p. 20; December 10, 1995, Sarah Ferguson, review of *Fault Lines*.

People, September 16, 1991, Cynthia Sanz, "Ring out the Belles," pp. 101-102; May 5, 1997, review of *Up Island*, p. 194; June 9, 1997, Kim Hubbard, review of *Up Island*, p. 33; July 31, 2000, "Pages," Erica Sanders, review of *Nora, Nora*, p. 41.

Publishers Weekly, May 1, 1987, p. 55; August 5, 1988, p. 72; November 18, 1988, Bob Summer, interview with Siddons, pp. 55-56; November 3, 1989, p. 88; February 2, 1990, sound recording review of *Peachtree Road*, p. 50; August 3, 1990, Sybil Steinberg, review of *King's Oak*, p. 62; May 31, 1991, review of *Outer Banks*, p. 61; March 30, 1992, pp. 21-26; May 18, 1992, p. 57; May 25, 1992, review of *Colony*, p. 57; May 24, 1993, review of *Hill Towns*, p. 67; May 23, 1994, review of *Downtown*, pp. 76-77; August 14, 1995, review of *Fault Lines*, p. 69; May 5, 1997, review of *Up Island*, p. 194; May 25, 1998, review of *Low Country* p. 63; June 12, 2000, review of *Nora, Nora*, p. 52; July 31, 2000, Daisy Maryles, "Women, Women, Women," p. 21.

Reader's Digest, January, 1987, pp. 53-55.

Southern Literary Journal, spring, 1985, Lamar York, "From Hebe to Hippolyta: Anne River Siddons's Novels," pp. 91-99.

Southern Living, October, 1987, p. 96; March, 1991, p. 118; December, 1991, p. 83; September, 1994, Dianne Young, "Words of Home," pp. 100-102.

Town & Country, March, 1993, p. 76.

Tribune Books (Chicago, IL), June 14, 1987, p. 7; November 25, 1990, p. 4; July 25, 1993, p. 6.

USA Today, July 17, 1991, p. D5; August 1, 1991, p. D1.

Washington Post, August 3, 1987; July 28, 1991, p. July 13, 1993, p. E2.

Washington Post Book World, July 28, 1991, p. 1; June 12, 1994, Jean Hanff Korelitz, review of *Downtown*, p. 8; June 17, 2001, review of *Colony*, p. 4.

Woman's Journal, February, 1995, p. 13.

ONLINE

AllReaders.com, http://www.allreaders.com/ (November 17, 2003), Jennifer Kirkman, reviews of *Up Island*, *King's Oak*, *Fox's Earth*, *Colony*, *Nora, Nora*, and *Outer Banks*.

Book Haven, http://thebookhaven.homestead.com/ (November 17, 2003), Amy Coffin, review of *Nora, Nora*.

BookPage.com, http://www.bookpage.com/ (November 17, 2003), Lynn Hamilton, review of *Nora, Nora*; Alice Cary, "Anne Rivers Siddons Preserves Natural Treasures in *Low Country*" (interview).

BookReporter.com, http://www.bookreporter.com/ (November 17, 2003), "Anne Rivers Siddons."

Harper Collins Web site, http://www.harpercollins.com/ (November 17, 2003).*

*   *   *

SMITH, Kevin 1970-

PERSONAL: Born August 2, 1970, in Red Bank, NJ; son of Donald (a retired postal employee) and Grace Smith; married Jennifer Schwalbach, 1999; children: Harley Quinn (daughter). *Education:* Attended New School for Social Research (now New School University), New York, and Vancouver Film School, British Columbia, Canada.

ADDRESSES: Office—View Askew Productions, 69 Broad St., Red Bank, NJ 07701; c/o Jay and Silent Bob's Secret Stash, 35 Broad St., Red Bank, NJ 07701.

CAREER: Director, screenwriter, producer, and actor. Worked at Quick Stop, Leonardo, NJ, c. early 1990s. Filmmaker, 1993—. Cofounded View Askew Produc-

Kevin Smith

tion Company, Red Bank, NJ, with Scott Mosier. Owner of Jay and Silent Bob's Secret Stash (comic-book store), Red Bank, NJ.

Producer of films *Drawing Flies,* View Askew/Good Load Productions, 1996; and *A Better Place,* View Askew/Synapse, 1997. Executive producer of *Vulgar,* View Askew/Lions Gate, 1998; *Big Helium Dog,* View Askew, 1999; and, *Clerks Uncensored* (animated series), American Broadcasting Company (ABC), 2000. Coexecutive producer of *Good Will Hunting,* Miramax, 1997. Also executive consultant for the film *Tail Lights Fade,* Vidmark/Trimark, 1999. Film appearances include (as himself) *Mae Day: The Crumbling of a Documentary;* (as Silent Bob) *Clerks, Mallrats, Chasing Amy, Dogma, Scream 3,* Dimension, 2000, and *Jay and Silent Bob Strike Back;* (as narrator) *Starwoids,* Ventura, 2001; (as Martan Ingram) *Vulgar;* and (as morgue attendant Jack Kirby) *Daredevil,* Twentieth Century-Fox, 2003. Television appearances include "Rio Ghosto," *Space Ghost Coast to Coast,* Cartoon Network, 1998; (as himself) *Independent's Day,* Arts

and Entertainment (A&E), 1998; (as the voice of Silent Bob) *Clerks Uncensored,* ABC, 2000. Also finances an entertainment gossip Web site called *Movie Poop Shoot,* edited by Chris Ryall, directed a music video for the group *Soul Asylum,* and appeared in *Jay and Silent Bob's Video Stash,* MTV.

AWARDS, HONORS: Young Cinema Award, Cannes Film Festival, Deauville Film Festival Audience Award, Sundance Film Festival Filmmakers Trophy, all 1994, all for *Clerks;* Independent Spirit Award, best screenplay, 1998, for *Chasing Amy.*

WRITINGS:

SCREENPLAYS

(And director and producer) *Mae Day: The Crumbling of a Documentary,* 1992.
(And director and producer) *Clerks* (also see below), View Askew/Miramax, 1994.
(And director and producer) *Mallrats,* View Askew/Universal, 1995.
(Uncredited writer) *Overnight Delivery,* Warner Bros., 1996.
(And director and producer) *Chasing Amy* (also see below), View Askew/Miramax, 1997.
(And director and producer) *Dogma* View Askew/Columbia TriStar, 1998, Grove Press (New York, NY), 1999.
(Uncredited writer) *Coyote Ugly,* Touchstone, 2000.
(And director) *Jay and Silent Bob Strike Back,* View Askew/Dimension, 2001.
(And director) *Jersey Girl,* View Askew/Miramax, 2004.

Also wrote unpublished screenplay, *Superman Lives.*

BOOKS

(With John Pierson) *Spike, Mike, Slackers and Dykes: A Guided Tour across a Decade of American Independent Cinema,* Hyperion (New York, NY), 1996.
Clerks; and Chasing Amy: Two Screenplays, Hyperion (New York, NY), 1997.
Daredevil (Issues 1-6), Marvel (New York, NY), 1998-99.

Jay and Silent Bob: Chasing Dogma, with an introduction by Alanis Morissette, Oni Press (Portland, OR), 1999.

Clerks: The Comic Books, illustrated by Duncan Fegredo, Oni Press (Portland, OR), 2000.

(Writer) *Green Arrow: Quiver,* DC Comics (New York, NY), 2002.

(Writer) *Green Arrow: Sounds of Violence,* DC Comics (New York, NY), 2003.

Also author of comic books *Bluntman and Chronic,* Oni Press.

WORK IN PROGRESS: Set to write and direct a movie based on the comic book and television series, *The Green Hornet.* Also working on *Fletch Won,* a movie based on the series of *Fletch* novels by Gregory McDonald, and a feature-length film based on the *Clerks* animated series.

SIDELIGHTS: During his short stint at the Vancouver Film School in British Columbia, Canada, Kevin Smith and his film school partner, Scott Mosier, began working on a documentary about a transsexual. When the subject of the film disappeared, the duo created *Mae Day: The Crumbling of a Documentary,* a discussion of why their film failed. In 1993, at the age of twenty-three, writer-director Smith returned to filmmaking and appeared on the movie scene when his low-budget, black-and-white film *Clerks* made a splash at the Sundance Film Festival. The film revolves around a day in the work lives of two young male store clerks in New Jersey. Dante works at a Quick Stop convenience store and Randal works at a nearby video rental store. Smith made the film in three weeks, at the Quick Stop where he had been employed since he was nineteen, and with a budget of about $27,000, which he scrounged together by maxing out credit cards and selling his prized comic-book collection. Filming took place between 10:30 p.m. and 6 a.m., during the Quick Stop's off hours. Since the early days of his filmmaking career, Smith has enjoyed considerable success and has formed a dedicated cult following.

Critics had much to say about *Clerks* upon its release. "Smith's chatty, affectionate salute to brainy guys in brainless jobs exhibits a deadpan mastery of verbal comedy timing any veteran director might envy," commented David Ansen in *Newsweek,* adding that Smith has "a fine ear for his characters' needling small talk,

lovers' snits, smutty harangues and whiny obsessions." "Their talk is pretty filthy, but that's verisimilitude for you," remarked *Entertainment Weekly* reviewer Glenn Kenny, "and Smith never tries to wrest laughs from vulgarity alone." "It was unpretentious and funny. . . . The humor in *Clerks* is kind of dopey, in an innocent, adolescent sort of way," commented Witold Rybczynski in *Saturday Night.* Writing in *Film Comment,* Donald Lyons judged that "the boredom of a dull job is brilliantly evoked—brilliantly, because the evocation is never itself boring but is mainly visible in the eccentric behaviors it births and witnesses." "*Clerks* is smart enough to be about not Kevin Smith, budding filmmaker, but Kevin Smith, dead-end clerk. It takes the actual rhythms of a long day's job seriously, while not taking its heroes or itself without irony," he continued. "The key to *Clerks'* charm is that Smith obviously doesn't feel obligated to speak for his generation," maintained Kenny. "He seems content merely to write about characters he knows well. His clerks aren't constantly arguing about music or spouting arcane '70s references—they talk about their lives." Lyons commented that while *Clerks* is "beautifully acted," "the look of its black-and-white plainness never rises above Snapple-and-Drake's-donuts junkiness. Smith should learn that film, even in B&W, can be visually nourishing." Yet he concluded, "The thing is a joy." Likewise, Kenny decided that while *Clerks* is "hardly a feast for the eyes . . . it's a feat nonetheless."

With *Mallrats* Smith moved from independent writer-director to studio writer-director. This time, instead of a New Jersey convenience store, the action takes place in a mediocre New Jersey shopping mall. There two young men, Brodie and T.S., hang out, chase girls, and make jokes in what appear to be random scenes. *Mallrats* did not come close to enjoying the success of *Clerks.* "Filmmaker Kevin Smith's most notable achievement is to have proved that pop-culture inside jokes are now enough of a shared language that they can appeal to a mass audience," noted Ken Tucker in *Entertainment Weekly.* Like *Clerks, Mallrats* has lots of dialog and little action. "Plot be darned; it's the texture, coarse but colorful, that counts—the pungent bustle of the action and Smith's wackily convoluted dialogue," enthused Richard Corliss of *Time.* "The humor is gross-out but inoffensive, since it's rooted in whimsy, not malice. Smith finesses the sophomore jinx with sophomoric high jinks." According to Tucker, "whenever you're not chuckling, *Mallrats* leaves you wondering at the emotional emptiness of suburban youth culture, as well as at the complexity of it."

Smith's *Chasing Amy* is a romantic comedy about a comic-book artist, played by Ben Affleck, who falls in love with a lesbian artist, played by Joey Lauren Adams. Rob Edelman summarized it in the *International Dictionary of Films and Filmmakers,* writing, "As their stories unfold, *Chasing Amy* becomes a knowing examination of what it means to fall in love, and the sexual and emotional baggage that men and women bring to relationships in our modern era." *Chasing Amy* garnered wildly differing reviews. Although John Simon in the *National Review* praised the work for "a certain brio and some funny lines," he felt that Smith should not have cast his then girlfriend in the lead. "Although Smith deserves some credit for ingenuity, he doesn't have the skill to maintain a pleasurable sense of anticipation for an entire movie," observed Terrence Rafferty in the *New Yorker.* "What's disappointing about *Chasing Amy* is that Smith abandons his good comic premise halfway through the picture." Rafferty added, "The movie spends its first hour or so flirting ostentatiously with political incorrectness, then abruptly reverses field and runs away from the more controversial implications of its sexual comedy." On the other hand, Ansen found much to like. Remarking that "Smith startles us with raw emotional honesty," Ansen added, "Ultimately this funny, surprisingly moving love story is a devastating critique of the hetero male ego. . . .Who would have expected that Smith could write a female part with such passion and insight? . . . But whether discussing comics, cunnilingus or their deepest feelings, all of Smith's vibrant characters seduce us with their blunt and heartfelt eloquence."

Following *Chasing Amy,* Smith wrote and directed *Dogma* which, according to a writer for *Authors and Artists for Young Adults,* is meant "to poke some fun at the trappings of the Catholic church." The story focuses on a pair of angels named Bartleby and Loki who are banished from Heaven. The two are hatching a scheme to get back in, but their plan would end the world in the process. Enter the thirteenth apostle (omitted from the Bible because he was black), a celestial muse (in the form of a stripper), and an abortion clinic worker and lapsed Catholic (who also happens to be a descendant of Jesus), as the ragtag team picked to stop the apocalyptic plan. Because of its controversial religion-focused plot, *Dogma* received mixed reviews from critics. Some lambasted Smith, calling him a heretic, but according to a writer for *Newsmakers 2000,* Smith maintained "that the film grew out of a crisis of faith but helped him get back in touch with it." A *U.S.* *Catholic* reviewer, however, remarked, "This film contains as much sex and violence as found in the whole Bible and as much vulgarity as Chaucer."

A common thread uniting Smith's first four movies is a set of drugged-out slackers, one of whom spends his time pontificating on sex and drugs, while the other remains virtually silent. These characters, Jay (played by Jason Mewes) and Silent Bob (played by Smith himself), snuck their way into each of Smith's earlier films. In *Chasing Amy,* the duo becomes the basis for the main character's comic-book series, *Bluntman and Chronic.* In the star-studded *Jay and Silent Bob Strike Back,* Smith has the duo working their way to Hollywood to stop the production of a film based on *Bluntman and Chronic,* for which the two buddies are receiving no credit and no money. Jay and Silent Bob get tangled in many hilarious episodes along the way, but eventually land their slice of the pie. Eric Monder noted in *Film Journal International,* "From the title sequence onward, *Jay and Silent Bob Strike Back* constitutes a big in-joke for Kevin Smith about all his preoccupations: *Star Wars,* sex, comic strips, sex, his own films, sex, pop culture and . . . did I mention sex?" Monder continued, "Smith's work is as uneven as ever, but unlike in the past, the director gleefully surrenders any pretense toward making a 'good' or 'serious' film, and the effect is somewhat liberating." *Jay and Silent Bob Strike Back* marks Smith's fifth film in the so-called "New Jersey Chronicles," which includes *Clerks, Mallrats, Chasing Amy,* and *Dogma.* According to Mike Flaherty in *Entertainment Weekly,* "Smith has pledged that *Jay and Silent Bob [Strike Back]* would be their swan song, which would be a shame. [Jason] Mewes' comic potential alone is cause to hope he won't bogart such a promising franchise."

Jersey Girl focuses on the father-daughter relationship between single-dad Ollie Trinke and precocious seven-year-old Gertie. Smith based the relationship on that which he shares with his own daughter. Kirk Honeycutt of the *Hollywood Reporter* called *Jersey Girl* "a sentimental love story about an emotionally devastated man who must find the right way to love his young daughter." A writer for *USA Today* noted, "*Jersey Girl* is the most grown-up film yet for Smith, whose first movie *Clerks* put him at the vanguard of the 1990s wave of young independent filmmakers. The new movie has plenty of Smith's trademark character banter, but on a mature level, without the gross-out schtick of his previous work."

In addition to his onscreen endeavors, Smith has written a book and several comic books. He coauthored the book *Spike, Mike, Slackers and Dykes: A Guided Tour across a Decade of American Independent Cinema* with John Pierson. He wrote a four-issue comic-book miniseries, which he collected in *Jay and Silent Bob: Chasing Dogma*. The book fills in the adventures of Jay and Silent Bob between the films *Chasing Amy* and *Dogma*. Tony Chester of the *Concatenation: Science, Fact, and Fiction* Web site wrote in his review of the book, "This is a little gem of a comic, despite the word-heavy prose that is forgivable in film . . . but, which is not ideally suited to comics." Chester acknowledged, however, that "it is certain to be received warmly by fans of Smith's films." Other comic-book writings include issues in the *Daredevil* series, *Clerks: The Comic Books, Green Arrow: Quiver,* and *Green Arrow: Sounds of Violence*. Of *Green Arrow: Quiver,* Steve Raiteri remarked in *Library Journal,* "Smith puts his extensive knowledge of DC history to good use in this tale of the return of Oliver Queen, the original Green Arrow." Raiteri continued, "Smith's scripting shows great understanding of the characters and is full of humorous moments. . . . There's enough background for new fans, but longtime DC fans will especially appreciate Smith's many references to earlier stories and series."

As if directing movies, acting in several films, and writing screenplays, comics, and books, isn't enough, Smith owns Jay and Silent Bob's Secret Stash, a comic-book store in his hometown of Red Bank, New Jersey, where he often works behind the counter. He also owns, with Mosier, View Askew Productions, which is responsible for the production of all of Smith's movies. According to a writer for *Newsmakers 2000,* Smith "dreamed of making his own film ever since he saw *Jaws* at age five." Now that he is a well-known and accomplished director fulfilling his childhood dreams, Smith takes both the positive and negative criticism he receives in stride. In an interview with Ansen in *Newsweek,* Smith said, "Because I've made movies that pushed the edge of the envelope in the past, I get penalized when I make one that doesn't. Some people are, like, 'Well, it's not your riskiest move.' What am I, a stuntman? I got in the movies to tell the stories that I wanted to tell."

BIOGRAPHICAL AND CRITICAL SOURCES:

BOOKS

Authors and Artists for Young Adults, Volume 37, Gale (Detroit, MI), 2000.

International Dictionary of Films and Filmmakers, Volume 2: *Directors,* 4th edition, St. James Press (Detroit, MI), 2000.

Muir, John Kenneth, *An Askew View: The Films of Kevin Smith,* Applause Theatre and Cinema Books (New York, NY), 2002.

Newsmakers 2000, Issue 4, Gale (Detroit, MI), 2000.

Pierson, John, and Kevin Smith, *Spike, Mike, Slackers and Dykes: A Guided Tour across a Decade of American Independent Cinema,* Hyperion (New York, NY), 1996.

PERIODICALS

American Spectator, April, 1997, p. 68.
Billboard, February 16, 2002, Wes Orshoski, "Jay and Bob DVD: Another Final Bow: Dimension Issuing Two-Disc Set of Smith's Purposely Paper-Thin Comedy," p. 58.
Cosmopolitan, November, 1994, p. 24.
Entertainment Weekly, November 18, 1994, p. 79; May 19, 1995, pp. 68-71; June 23, 1995, pp. 26-29; September 29, 1995, p. 72; November 3, 1995, pp. 44-46; April 4, 1997, p. 64; April 11, 1997, p. 25; March 16, 2001, review of *Green Arrow,* p. 62; August 24, 2001, Jeff Jensen, "Mr. Smith Goes to Hollywood: The Voice behind Silent Bob Weighs in on His Return to *Mallrats* Culture," p. 104; September 7, 2001, Owen Gleiberman, "Smooth Mewes: As Half of the Dopey Duo in *Jay and Silent Bob Strike Back,* Jason Mewes Plays a Rebel without a Pause," p. 134; February 15, 2002, Mike Flaherty, "Chronic Gains: Kevin Smith's Raunchy *Jay and Silent Bob Strike Back* Is a Stoned-Cold Blast," p. 49; May 3, 2002, Jeff Jensen, "Don't Go 'Changing,'" p. 18; May 10, 2002, Owen Gleiberman, "Taste Dud: The Most Offensive Thing about *Vulgar* Is its Incompetence," p. 53; March 5, 2004, "*The Green Hornet,*" p. 46.
Film Comment, May-June, 1994, pp. 9-10.
Film Journal International, September, 2001, Eric Monder, review of *Jay and Silent Bob Strike Back,* p. 53.
Hollywood Reporter, August 20, 2001, Kirk Honeycutt, review of *Jay and Silent Bob Strike Back,* p. 9.
Interview, April, 1997, pp. 42-44; September, 2001, Kenneth M. Chanko, review of *Jay and Silent Bob Strike Back,* p. 100.
Library Journal, December, 1995, p. 112; September 1, 2002, Steve Raiteri, review of *Green Arrow: Quiver,* p. 151.

Maclean's, August 27, 2001, Brian D. Johnson, review of *Jay and Silent Bob Strike Back,* p. 48.

National Review, May 19, 1997, pp. 56-57.

New Republic, May 5, 1997, p. 24.

Newsweek, October 21, 1994, p. 68; April 7, 1997, p. 73; August 27, 2001, Devin Gordon, "A Phatty Boom Batty Flick: With His New Movie, Director Kevin Smith Says Thanks to Family, Friends, and Yes, Those Nutty Fans on the Web," p. 55.

New York, October 24, 1994, p. 41.

New Yorker, April 7, 1997, p. 97.

New York Times Book Review, February 4, 1996, p. 8.

People Weekly, November 7, 1994, p. 20; December 12, 1994, p. 156; August 27, 2001, Jason Lynch, "Chatter," p. 130; September 3, 2001, Leah Rozen, review of *Jay and Silent Bob Strike Back,* p. 37.

PR Newswire, February 19, 2004, "Miramax Films to Release Kevin Smith's *Jersey Girl* in Theaters on March 26, 2004; Ben Affleck and Liv Tyler Starrer to Expand on April 2nd and April 9th."

Rolling Stone, November 3, 1994, p. 104; April 17, 1997, p. 86.

Saturday Night, September, 1996, p. 110.

Time, November 6, 1995, p. 77; April 7, 1997, p. 76.

U.S. Catholic, February, 2004, review of *Dogma,* p. 46.

Variety, January 31, 1994, p. 4; October 16, 1995, p. 94; February 3, 1997, p. 46; May 24, 1999, Todd McCarthy, review of *Dogma,* p. 73; August 20, 2001, Scott Foundas, review of *Jay and Silent Bob Strike Back,* p. 23; July 1, 2002, David Bloom, "Helmer Delivers Biz Poop on New Web Site," p. 6.

ONLINE

Concatenation: Science, Fact, and Fiction, http://www.concatenation.org/ (January 16, 2003), Tony Chester, review of *Jay and Silent Bob: Chasing Dogma.*

Dogma Movie Web site, http://www.dogma-movie.com/ (January 16, 2003).

Hollywood Reporter, http://www.hollywoodreporter.com/ (March 17, 2004), Kirk Honeycutt, review of *Jersey Girl.*

Movie Poop Shoot, http://www.moviepoopshoot.com/ (March 25, 2004).

MSN Entertainment Web site, http://entertainment.msn.com/ (March 24, 2004), "Celebs: Kevin Smith."

Newsweek Web site, http://www.newsweek.com/ (March 29, 2004), David Ansen, "Chasing Kevin," interview with Kevin Smith.

ReelViews: Movie Reviews and Criticism, http://movie-reviews.colossus.net/ (March 25, 2004), James Berardinelli, review of *Jersey Girl.*

USA Today Web site, http://www.usatoday.com/life/ (March 25, 2004), "Ben and Jen Are Back, but It's Affleck's Show with *Jersey Girl.*"

View Askew Web site, http://www.viewaskew.com/ (March 24, 2004), information on Kevin Smith movies.*

*   *   *

SPARK, Muriel (Sarah) 1918-
(Evelyn Cavallo, a pseudonym)

PERSONAL: Born February 1, 1918, in Edinburgh, Scotland; daughter of Bernard and Sarah Elizabeth Maud (Uezzell) Camberg; married Sydney O. Spark, 1937 (divorced); children: Robin (son). *Education:* Attended James Gillespie's High School for Girls, Edinburgh, 1923-35; Heriot Watt College, 1935-37. *Religion:* Roman Catholic. *Hobbies and other interests:* Reading, travel.

ADDRESSES: Home—Italy. *Agent*—c/o Georges Borchardt, Inc., 136 East 57th St., New York, NY 10022; c/o David Higham Associates Ltd., 5-8 Lower John Street, Golden Square, London W1F 9HA, England.

CAREER: Writer. Employed in the Political Intelligence Department of the British government's Foreign Office, 1944-45; editorial assistant, *Argentor* (jewelry trade art magazine), 1946-47; general secretary, Poetry Society, 1947-49; editor of *Poetry Review,* 1947-49; editorial assistant, *European Affairs,* 1949-50; founder, *Forum* (literary magazine); part-time editor, Peter Owen Ltd. (publishing company).

MEMBER: PEN (honorary member), American Academy and Institute of Arts and Letters (honorary member), Society of Authors, Authors Guild, Royal Society of Edinburgh (honorary fellow).

AWARDS, HONORS: Observer short story prize, 1951, for "The Seraph and the Zambesi"; Prix Italia, 1962, for radio play adaptation of *The Ballad of Peckham Rye;* Yorkshire Post Book of the Year award, 1965, and James Tait Black Memorial Prize, 1966, both for

Muriel Spark

The Mandelbaum Gate; Order of the British Empire, 1967; Scottish Book of the Year award, 1987, for *The Stories of Muriel Spark;* First Prize, F.N.A.C. La Meilleur Recueil des Nouvelles Etrangeres, 1987, for the Editions Fayard translation of *The Stories of Muriel Spark;* Officier de l'Ordre des Arts et des Lettres, France, 1988, Commandeur, 1996; Bram Stoker Award, 1988, for *Mary Shelley;* Ingersoll T. S. Eliot Award, 1992; Dame, Order of the British Empire, 1993; David Cohen British Literature Prize, 1997; PEN International Gold Pen Award, 1998; Campion Award, Catholic Book Club, 2001.Honorary degrees, University of Strathclyde, 1971, University of Edinburgh, 1989, University of Aberdeen, 1995, Watt University, 1995, University of St. Andrews, 1998, and Oxford University, 1999.

WRITINGS:

FICTION

The Comforters (also see below), Lippincott (Philadelphia, PA), 1957.

Robinson, Lippincott (Philadelphia, PA), 1958.

The Go-Away Bird and Other Stories (short stories), Macmillan (London, England), 1958, Lippincott (Philadelphia, PA), 1960.

Memento Mori (also see below), Lippincott (Philadelphia, PA), 1959.

The Ballad of Peckham Rye (also see below), Lippincott (Philadelphia, PA), 1960.

The Bachelors, Macmillan (London, England), 1960, Lippincott (Philadelphia, PA), 1961.

Voices at Play (short stories and radio plays), Macmillan (London, England), 1961, Lippincott (Philadelphia, PA), 1962.

The Prime of Miss Jean Brodie (also see below), Macmillan (London, England), 1961, Lippincott (Philadelphia, PA), 1962.

A Muriel Spark Trio (contains *The Comforters, Memento Mori,* and *The Ballad of Peckham Rye*), Lippincott (Philadelphia, PA), 1962.

The Girls of Slender Means (also see below), Knopf (New York, NY), 1963.

The Mandelbaum Gate, Knopf (New York, NY), 1965.

Collected Stories 1, Macmillan (London, England), 1967, Knopf (New York, NY), 1968.

The Public Image, Knopf (New York, NY), 1968.

The Very Fine Clock (juvenile), Knopf (New York, NY), 1968.

The Driver's Seat, Knopf (New York, NY), 1970.

Not to Disturb, Macmillan (London, England), 1971, Viking (New York, NY), 1972.

The Hothouse by the East River, Viking (New York, NY), 1973.

The Abbess of Crewe (also see below), Viking (New York, NY), 1973.

The Takeover, Viking (New York, NY), 1976.

Territorial Rights, Coward (New York, NY), 1979.

Loitering with Intent, Coward (New York, NY), 1981.

Bang-Bang You're Dead and Other Stories, Granada (New York, NY), 1982.

The Only Problem, Coward (New York, NY), 1984, Franklin Library (Franklin Center, PA), 1984.

The Stories of Muriel Spark, Dutton (New York, NY), 1985.

A Far Cry from Kensington, Houghton Mifflin (Boston, MA), 1988.

Symposium, Houghton Mifflin (Boston, MA), 1990.

The Novels of Muriel Spark (selections), Houghton Mifflin (Boston, MA), 1995.

Reality and Dreams, Constable (London, England), 1996.

Open to the Public: New and Collected Stories, New Directions (New York, NY), 1997.

Aiding and Abetting (novel), Viking (New York, NY), 2000.

A Hundred and Eleven Years without a Chauffeur (limited edition of 26 copies; story previously appeared in the *New Yorker*), Colophon Press (London, England), 2001.
The Complete Short Stories, Viking (New York, NY), 2001.
All the Stories of Muriel Spark, New Directions (New York, NY), 2001.
The Ghost Stories of Muriel Spark, New Directions (New York, NY), 2003.

Also author of *The Small Telephone* (juvenile), 1993.

POETRY

The Fanfarlo and Other Verse, Hand and Flower Press (Kent, England), 1952.
Collected Poems 1, Macmillan (London, England), 1967, Knopf (New York, NY), 1968,
Going Up to Sotheby's and Other Poems, Granada (New York, NY), 1982.

NONFICTION

*Child of Light: A Reassessment of Mary Wollstonecraft Shelley,*Tower Bridge Publications, 1951, revised edition published as *Mary Shelley,* Dutton (New York, NY), 1987.
Emily Bronte: Her Life and Work, P. Owen (London, England), 1953.
John Masefield, Nevill (London, England), 1953, revised edition, Hutchinson (London, England), 1992.
The Essence of the Brontes, P. Owen (London, England), 1993.

EDITOR

(And author of introduction) *A Selection of Poems by Emily Bronte,* Grey Walls Press (London, England), 1952.
The Letters of Mary Shelley, Wingate (London, England), 1953.
The Letters of the Brontes: A Selection, University of Oklahoma Press (Norman, OK), 1954, published as *The Bronte Letters,* Nevill (London, England), 1954.
(Coeditor) *Letters of John Henry Newman,* P. Owen (London, England), 1957.

OTHER

Doctors of Philosophy (play; produced in London, 1962), Macmillan (London, England), 1963, Knopf (New York, NY), 1966.
Curriculum Vitae: An Autobiography, Houghton Mifflin (Boston, MA), 1993.

Also author of radio plays *The Party through the Wall,* 1957, *The Interview,* 1958, *The Dry River Bed,* 1959, *The Ballad of Peckham Rye,* 1960, and *The Danger Zone,* 1961. Contributor of short stories and poems to the *New Yorker,* and of poems, articles, and reviews to magazines and newspapers. Some writings appear under the pseudonym Evelyn Cavallo.

ADAPTATIONS: Several of Muriel Spark's novels have been adapted for the stage, film, and television. A dramatization of *Memento Mori* was produced on stage in 1964 and a version was televised by British Broadcasting Corporation (BBC) in 1992. Jay Presson Allen's dramatization of *The Prime of Miss Jean Brodie,* published by Samuel French in 1969, was first produced in Torquay, England, at the Princess Theatre beginning April 5, 1966, then in Boston at the Colonial Theatre from December 26, 1967, to January 6, 1968, and finally on Broadway at the Helen Hayes Theatre beginning January 9, 1968. Allen also wrote the screenplay for the 1969 film version of the same novel, a Twentieth Century-Fox production starring Maggie Smith. John Wood's dramatization of *The Prime of Miss Jean Brodie* was produced in London at Wyndham's Theatre in 1967, and on Broadway in 1968; a six-part adaptation of the novel appeared on public television in England in 1978 and in the United States in 1979. *The Driver's Seat* was filmed in 1972, and in 1974 *The Girls of Slender Means* was adapted for BBC television. *The Abbess of Crewe* was filmed and released in 1976 under the title *Nasty Habits.*

WORK IN PROGRESS: Spark's twenty-second novel, *The Finishing School,* will be published in English by Viking-Penguin, in German by Diogenes Verlag, and in French by Gallimard.

SIDELIGHTS: In a career spanning more than half a century, Scottish writer Muriel Spark has enlightened and entertained with her poetry, critical works, biographies, and editorial contributions, but most of all with her score of novels. These include such popular works as *The Prime of Miss Jean Brodie, Memento Mori, The Girls of Slender Means, The Ballad of Peckham Rye, Territorial Rights, Loitering with Intent, The Abbess of Crewe, Symposium, Reality and Dreams,* and *Aiding and Abetting,* many of which have been adapted for radio, the stage, television, or film. Often described as one of the best, yet one of the least appreciated, of today's novelists, Spark confounds those readers and critics who have an affinity for labels and categories. In granting her the 2001 Campion Award, the Catholic Book Club—as quoted on the author's Web site—praised Spark's singular achievement: "Themes universal to the human condition—good and evil, honor and duplicity, self-aggrandizement and self-pity and courage amid poverty—are incarnate in her writing with a sometime eerily familiar face. For good or bad, hers are characters that endure in our memory."

Spark had already achieved some recognition as a critic and poet when she entered what was virtually her first attempt at fiction, the short story "The Seraph and the Zambesi," in a 1951 Christmas writing contest sponsored by the London *Observer.* The fanciful tale of a troublesome angel who bursts in on an acting troupe staging a holiday pageant on the banks of Africa's Zambesi River, "The Seraph and the Zambesi" won top honors in the competition and attracted a great deal of attention for its unconventional treatment of the Christmas theme. Several other stories set in Africa and England followed; soon Spark's successes in fiction began to overshadow those in criticism and poetry.

With financial and moral support from author Graham Greene, Spark struggled for nearly three years to sort out the aesthetic, psychological, and religious questions raised by her conversion to Catholicism and her attempt at writing longer fiction. Drawing on the tenets of her new faith, which she believes is especially "conducive to individuality, to finding one's own individual point of view," the young writer formulated her own theory of the novel. According to Frank Kermode in his book *Continuities,* this theory suggests that "a genuine relation exists between the forms of fiction and the forms of the world, between the novelist's creation and God's." In essence, Spark sees the novelist as very God-like—omniscient and omnipotent, able to manipulate plot, character, and dialogue at will. Viewed in this light, Kermode and others contended, Spark's first novel, *The Comforters,* is obviously "an

experiment designed to discover whether . . . the novelist, pushing people and things around and giving 'disjointed happenings a shape,' is in any way like Providence."

Because Spark's Catholicism figures so prominently in *The Comforters* and subsequent works, it is "much more than an item of biographical interest," in the opinion of Victor Kelleher, who commented in *Critical Review:* "Spark does not stop short at simply bringing the question of Catholicism into her work; she has chosen to place the traditionally Christian outlook at the very heart of everything she writes. . . . [Her tales proclaim] the most basic of Christian truths: that all man's blessings emanate from God; that, in the absence of God, man is nothing more than a savage." Catharine Hughes makes a similar assessment of Spark's religious sentiment in an article in the *Catholic World.* The critic observed: "[Spark satirizes] humanity's foibles and incongruities from a decidedly Catholic orientation. One is conscious that she is a writer working within the framework of some of Christianity's greatest truths; that her perspective, which takes full cognizance of eternal values, is never burdened by a painful attempt to inflict them upon others."

At first glance, however, Spark's novels do not seem to reflect her strong religious and moral preoccupations. In terms of setting, for example, the author usually chooses to locate her modern morality tales in upper-class urban areas of England or Italy. Her "fun-house plots, full of trapdoors, abrupt apparitions, and smartly clicking secret panels," as novelist John Updike described them in a *New Yorker* article, focus on the often bizarre behavior of people belonging to a small, select group: elderly men and women linked by long-standing personal relationships in *Memento Mori;* unmarried male and female residents of the same London district in *The Bachelors;* students and teachers at a Scottish girls' school in *The Prime of Miss Jean Brodie;* servants on a Swiss estate in *Not to Disturb;* guests at a pair of neighboring Venetian hotels in *Territorial Rights.* The "action" in these stories springs from the elaborate ties Spark concocts between the members of each group—ties of blood, marriage, friendship, and other kinds of relationships. Commenting in her study of the author titled *Muriel Spark,* critic Patricia Stubbs observed that the use of such a technique reflects Spark's fascination with "the way in which the individual varies in different settings, or different company." "By taking this restricted group of protagonists," explained Stubbs, "[Spark] is able to create multiple ironies, arising from their connecting and conflicting destinies: by her selection of such a restricted canvas, she can display the many facets of her creatures' personalities, and the different roles which they, or society, decree they should play."

In the tradition of the intellectual novelist, Spark avoids florid descriptions of the physical world, preferring instead to concentrate on dialogue, on "the play of ideas and experiences upon the mind, and the interplay of minds upon each other," according to Joseph Hynes in his *Critical Essays on Muriel Spark*. Her characterizations are quick, sharp, and concise, and she teams her technical virtuosity with an elegant, acerbic wit and condescending attitude that most readers find highly entertaining. As Melvin Maddocks declared in *Life*: "Reading a Muriel Spark novel remains one of the minor pleasures of life. Like a perfect hostess, she caters to our small needs. In the manner available to only the best British novelists, she ordains a civilized atmosphere—two parts what Evelyn Waugh called creamy English charm, one part acid wit. She peoples her scene discriminatingly, showing a taste for interesting but not overpowering guests. . . . As the evening moves along, she has the good sense to lower the drawing-room lights and introduce a pleasantly chilling bit of tension—even violence—just to save us all, bless her, from the overexquisite sensibilities of the lady novelist."

The 1990 best-seller *Symposium* demonstrates the qualities to which Maddocks refers. It centers on Margaret Demien, a character whose wealthy mother-in-law dies while Margaret is away at a dinner party. Appearing to all as virtuous at first, Margaret openly expresses a more sinister intent. She is also connected to other mysterious deaths, so that when the guests receive news of the older woman's death, Margaret is a suspect. Peter Parker commented in the *Listener*, "This is a marvelous premise for a novel, and, as one would expect, Spark makes the most of opportunities for dark comedy. Against Margaret's willful attempt to become an instrument of evil is set an example of casual wickedness that unwittingly leads to mortal sin and provides the novel with a terrific final chapter. The book's epigraphs, taken from *Symposia* of Lucian and Plato, supply hints both of the book's resolution and of Spark's fictional method." The epigraphs also provide clues about the five couples at the dinner party,

who in some ways represent the varieties of love Plato defined. "But the real philosophical dialogue in *Symposium* is not about love nor is it explicitly argued. Rather, it takes place almost between the lines and concerns the mysteries of evil and suffering, destiny and predestination, guilt and intention," Nina King related in a *Washington Post Book World* review. A *Publishers Weekly* reviewer also remarked, "Spark's exquisitely balanced tone proves that the richest comedy is that which explores the darkest themes."

Yet, as Barbara Grizzuti Harrison reminded readers in a *New York Times Book Review* article, Spark is at heart "a profoundly serious comic writer whose wit advances, never undermines or diminishes, her ideas." Spark once explained to *Contemporary Authors* that the intent behind her "mischief" is to make a lasting impression on her readers: "Satire is far more important, it has a more lasting effect, than a straight portrayal of what is wrong. I think that a lot of the world's problems should be ridiculed, but ridiculed properly rather than, well, wailed over. People go to the theater, for instance, to see a play about some outrage or other, and then they come away feeling that they've done something about it, which they haven't. But if these things are ridiculed, it sticks and the perpetrators stop doing it. . . . I do believe in satire as a very, very potent art form."

Despite all that has been written about her and her fiction, Spark remains an enigma to most critics. Described as an artist, a serious and accomplished writer, a moralist engaged with the human predicament, wildly entertaining, and a joy to read, Spark has nevertheless, in Stubbs's opinion, "succeeded triumphantly in evading classification." Updike, too, contends that Spark possesses a truly exceptional talent—a talent that without a doubt makes her an unclassifiable "original." In fact, he declared in the *New Yorker*, Spark "is one of the few writers of the language on either side of the Atlantic with enough resources, daring, and stamina to be altering, as well as feeding, the fiction machine."

Spark produced *Curriculum Vitae: An Autobiography* in 1993, at the age of seventy-five, partly to correct critical misunderstandings and inaccuracies about her life, and partly to put together the facts about her life and her fiction. "So many strange and erroneous accounts of parts of my life have been written since I became well known," *New Leader* contributor Hope

Hale Davis quoted the author as saying, "that I felt it time to put the record straight." *Curriculum Vitae* covers the first thirty-nine years of Spark's life, up to the publication of her debut novel, *The Comforters.* It tells of her childhood in Edinburgh, daughter of a Jewish father and a Protestant English mother (whose accent mortified her daughter on more than one occasion). Spark also tells of her years at Gillespie's, where she studied under Christina Kay, who later served as the model for the title character in *The Prime of Miss Jean Brodie.* Unlike the fictional Brodie, however, Spark declares, Kay would never have manipulated her charges in an attempt to seduce a fellow teacher. *Curriculum Vitae* also covers Spark's time spent caring for her bedridden English grandmother; her unhappy marriage to and seven years in southern Rhodesia with the mentally disturbed Sydney O. Spark, who fathered her son, Robin; her war years in the propaganda wing of the British government; and her emergence as a powerful writer of fiction. "In her own fashion, reticent when she chooses but always free of invention," stated Helen Bevington in the *New York Times Book Review,* "Muriel Spark succeeds in her mission: she puts the record straight. With nearly half her life yet to consider, she will, I hope, tell us the rest of it."

Spark returned to the novel form in 1997 with *Reality and Dreams,* and again in 2000 with *Aiding and Abetting.* The former title features aging Tom Richards, a movie director recovering from a fall from a crane. His life is further set into a whirl by the disappearance of his younger daughter, plain-looking Miranda; this misfortune brings him and his wandering wife, Claire, together with Cora, his daughter by an earlier marriage, to try and find the second daughter, whom none of them has ever really accepted. Miranda turns up on a beach where Tom has earlier fantasized about a young girl, the subject of his last movie. Meanwhile, England is in the midst of economic crisis and redundancy. "The novel's awash with love, lust, disillusion, and banality," according to Dierdre Neilen, writing in *World Literature Today.* Neilen further commented that Spark's "writing compels the story forward, and the reader laughingly follows." Similarly, Francine Prose, writing in *People,* found the novel "witty [and] surprising," and advised readers to take this opportunity to sample Spark's voice: "elegant, wise, sympathetic, satiric—at once darkly sinister and brightly chipper." Gerda Oldham, writing in the *Antioch Review,* also thought Spark's "wit and irony" were the ingredients that make "her protagonist and his

extended family tick." Lynda Obst, writing in the *Los Angeles Times Book Review,* described as "masterful" the plot twist in which Marigold lures her father and mother to look for her. And for Lucy Ferriss, writing in the *St. Louis Post-Dispatch,* "the more we chortle at the absurdity of Tom's dreams and the sordidness of his reality, the more we recognize our own absurdity and sordidness, our own reality and dreams."

Aiding and Abetting deals with the actual case of Lord Lucan, a British peer who, while apparently attempting to kill his estranged wife, managed to kill the family nanny instead. When he finally attacked his wife, he botched that job as well, and he went missing. The first murder warrant for a peer was issued, but Lucan has never been found. "The Lucan story seems ready-made for Spark's enchanter's powers," wrote Robert E. Hosmer, Jr. in the *Chicago Tribune.* Hosmer went on to note that Spark "presents an imaginative reconstruction of Lucan's life after that ghastly night," and that she tells a "terrifying human story that cuts across boundaries of gender, race and class to reveal unsettling truths about who we are and how we can behave."

Spark's novel posits two fictional Lucans who visit a psychotherapist in Paris, eventually forming a dangerous and threatening trio when secrets are revealed about all three. *Booklist*'s Brad Hooper thought that this twenty-first novel "shows no diminishment of [Spark's] still-abiding qualities." According to Hooper, Spark created an "intelligent but, above all, entertaining novel of deception." A contributor for *Publishers Weekly* also noted Spark's strengths as a writer: "terse, astringent and blessed with a wicked satiric wit." For this same reviewer, the reader becomes "immersed in a puzzling maze" with the three main characters. Thomas Mallon, writing in the *Atlantic Monthly,* similarly praised Spark's "brilliant, addled novels—deceptive, dark little comedies that eventually veer off into bizarre supernaturalness." Mallon found these powers still at work in *Aiding and Abetting:* "The typical Spark novel has always been stimulatingly off its rocker, and on the strength of *Aiding and Abetting,* there's yet no need to start persuading Dame Muriel into hers." *Newsweek*'s Jeff Giles had mixed praise for the novel, calling it a "sly, intriguing—if not entirely nourishing—book," while *Time*'s Paul Gray dubbed it an "engaging game of rat and louse [that] concludes with a bit of poetic justice that is ghastly and richly appropriate." Sandra Cookson, writing in *World Litera-*

ture Today, had unconditional praise for *Aiding and Abetting,* noting that in it "Spark's prose is more tart, quirky, and spare than ever, her irony more relentless than in earlier novels."

In 2001 a limited edition of twenty-six copies of *A Hundred and Eleven Years without a Chauffeur* was published by Colophon Press. Each copy is signed and inscribed with a passage and a letter of the alphabet by Spark. The story previously appeared in the *New Yorker.* Further collections by Spark have appeared in the new millennium. *The Complete Short Stories* collects forty-one tales, many of them ghost tales, arranged according to theme rather than chronology. For Gabrielle Annan, reviewing the collection in the *Spectator,* the "neatest, wittiest, shortest, cleverest" of the ghost tales is "The Pearly Shadow," about a hallucination that is passed along like a cold. Religious stories as well as crime stories, ones set in Africa, and ones featuring a plucky female protagonist also find a place in the collection, which, in fact, is a mirror of Spark's artistic proclivities over the full span of her writing life. Reviewing the same collection in the *New Statesman,* Rebecca Abrams concluded that the "trademark" of all Spark's fiction, both novels and short stories, "is its lightness, the way it seems almost to shrug its shoulders at the people and lives it so piercingly brings to life."

BIOGRAPHICAL AND CRITICAL SOURCES:

BOOKS

Contemporary Literary Criticism, Gale (Detroit, MI), Volume 2, 1974, Volume 3, 1975, Volume 5, 1976, Volume 8, 1978, Volume 13, 1980, Volume 18, 1981, Volume 40, 1987, Volume 94, 1997.

Dictionary of Literary Biography, Gale (Detroit, MI), Volume 15: *British Novelists, 1930-1959,* 1983, Volume 139: *British Short-Fiction Writers, 1945-1980,* 1994.

Edgecombe, Rodney Stenning, *Vocation and Identity in the Fiction of Muriel Spark,* University of Missouri Press (Columbia, MO), 1990.

Enright, D. J., *Man Is an Onion: Reviews and Essays,* Chatto & Windus (London, England), 1972.

Hynes, Joseph, editor, *Critical Essays on Muriel Spark,* G. K. Hall (New York, NY), 1992.

Kemp, Peter, *Muriel Spark,* Elek, 1974, Barnes & Noble (New York, NY), 1975.

Kermode, Frank, *Continuities,* Random House (New York, NY), 1968.

Malkoff, Karl, *Muriel Spark,* Columbia University Press (New York, NY), 1968.

Page, Norman, *Muriel Spark,* St. Martin's Press (New York, NY), 1990.

Pearlman, Mickey, *Re-inventing Reality: Patterns and Characteristics in the Novels of Muriel Spark,* P. Lang (New York, NY), 1996.

Randisi, Jennifer Lynn, *On Her Way Rejoicing: The Fiction of Muriel Spark,* Catholic University of America Press (Washington, DC), 1991.

Short Story Criticism, Volume 10, Gale (Detroit, MI), 1992.

Sproxton, Judy, *The Women of Muriel Spark,* St. Martin's Press (New York, NY), 1992.

Sproxton, Judy, *Muriel Spark,* St. Martin's Press (New York, NY), 1994.

Stubbs, Patricia, *Muriel Spark,* Longman (London, England), 1973.

Whittaker, Ruth, *The Faith and Fiction of Muriel Spark,* Macmillan (London, England), 1978.

PERIODICALS

Antioch Review, winter, 1998, Gerda Oldham, review of *Reality and Dreams,* p. 116; spring, 2002, Barbara Beckerman Davis, review of *Aiding and Abetting,* p. 340.

Atlantic Monthly, February, 2001, Thomas Mallon, review of *Aiding and Abetting,* pp. 124-125.

Booklist, October 1, 2000, Brad Hooper, review of *Aiding and Abetting,* p. 292.

Catholic World, August, 1961, Catharine Hughes.

Chicago Tribune, June 19, 1997, Cassandra West, review of *Reality and Dreams,* p. 3; March 4, 2001, Robert E. Hosmer, Jr., review of *Aiding and Abetting,* p. 6; March 14, 2002, Sandy Bauers, review of *Aiding and Abetting,* p. B8.

Critical Review, number 18, 1976, article by Victor Kelleher.

Entertainment Weekly, March 30, 2001, Rebecca Ascher-Walsh, review of *Aiding and Abetting,* p. 64.

Library Journal, October 15, 2000, Barbara Love, review of *Aiding and Abetting,* p. 105.

Life, October 11, 1968, article by Melvin Maddocks.

Listener, September 20, 1990, Peter Parker, review of *Symposium.*

Los Angeles Times Book Review, June 8, 1997, Lynda Obst, review of *Reality and Dreams,* p. 10:2.

New Leader, May 17, 1993, Hope Hale Davis, review of *Curriculum Vitae,* p. 29.

New Statesman, October 1, 2001, Lisa Allardice, review of *Aiding and Abetting,* p. 80; October 15, 2001, Rebecca Abrams, review of *The Complete Short Stories,* pp. 56-57.

Newsweek, February 26, 2001, Jeff Giles, review of *Aiding and Abetting,* p. 71.

New Yorker, June 8, 1981, John Updike, review of *Loitering with Intent,* p. 148.

New York Times Book Review, May 31, 1981, Barbara Grizzuti Harrison, review of *Loitering with Intent,* p. 11; May 16, 1993, Helen Bevington, review of *Curriculum Vitae: An Autobiography;* March 11, 2001, Richard Eder, review of *Aiding and Abetting,* pp. 14-15.

People, August 25, 1997, Francine Prose, review of *Reality and Dreams,* p. 41; March 5, 2001, Joanne Kaufman, review of *Aiding and Abetting,* p. 51.

Publishers Weekly, October 26, 1990, review of *Symposium;* November 20, 2000, review of *Aiding and Abetting,* p. 44.

St. Louis Post-Dispatch, July 6, 1997, Lucy Ferriss, review of *Reality and Dreams,* p. F5.

Spectator, October 20, 2001, Gabrielle Annan, review of *The Complete Short Stories,* p. 53.

Time, March 12, 2001, Paul Gray, review of *Aiding and Abetting,* p. 90.

Village Voice, March 20, 2001, Charles McNulty, review of *Aiding and Abetting,* p. 66.

Virginia Quarterly Review, autumn, 1997, review of *Reality and Dreams,* p. 130.

Washington Post Book World, November 25, 1990, Nina King, review of *Symposium.*

World Literature Today, spring, 1997, Deirdre Neilen, review of *Reality and Dreams,* p. 373; summer, 2001, Sandra Cookson, review of *Aiding and Abetting,* p. 150.

ONLINE

David Higham Associates, http://www.davidhigham. co.uk/ (November 14, 2003).

Official Muriel Spark Web site, http://murielspark.com/ (November 14, 2003).

Penguin UK Web site, http://www.penguin.co.uk/ (November 14, 2003), Toby Litt, "Interview with Muriel Spark."*

SWENSON, May 1919(?)-1989

PERSONAL: Born May 28, 1919 (some sources say 1913), in Logan, UT; died December 4, 1989, in Ocean View, DE, (some sources say Bethany Beach, DE, or Salisbury, MD); daughter of Dan Arthur (a teacher) and Anna M. (Helberg) Swenson. *Education:* Utah State University, B.A., 1939.

CAREER: Poet, 1949-89. Formerly worked as an editor for New Directions, New York, NY; writer in residence at Purdue University, West Lafayette, IN, 1966-67, University of North Carolina, 1968-69 and 1974, Lothbridge University, Alberta, Canada, 1970, and University of California, Riverside, 1976. Lectured and gave readings at more than fifty American universities and colleges, as well as at the New York YM-YWHA Poetry Center, and San Francisco Poetry Center. Conductor of workshops at University of Indiana Writers Conference and Bread Loaf Writers Conference, Vermont. Participant at the Yaddo and Mac-Dowell colonies for writers.

MEMBER: Academy of American Poets (Chancellor, 1980), American Academy and Institute of Arts and Letters.

AWARDS, HONORS: Poetry Introductions Prize, 1955; Robert Frost Poetry Fellowship for Bread Loaf Writers' Conference, 1957; Guggenheim fellowship, 1959; William Rose Benet Prize of the Poetry Society of America, 1959; Longview Foundation award, 1959; Amy Lowell Traveling Scholarship, 1960; National Institute of Arts and Letters award, 1960; Ford Foundation grant, 1964; Brandeis University Creative Arts Award, 1967; Rockefeller Writing fellowship, 1967; Distinguished Service Medal of Utah State University, 1967; Lucy Martin Donnelly Award of Bryn Mawr College, 1968; Shelley Poetry Award, 1968; International Poetry Forum translation medal, 1972; National Endowment for the Arts Grant, 1974; National Book Award nomination, 1978, for *New and Selected Things Taking Place;* Academy of American Poets fellowship, 1979; Bollingen Poetry Award, 1981; MacArthur Award, 1987; National Book Critics Circle award nomination (poetry), 1987, for *In Other Words.* Honorary degrees from Utah State University, 1987.

WRITINGS:

POETRY

Another Animal, Scribner (New York, NY), 1954.
A Cage of Spines, Rinehart (New York, NY), 1958.

May Swenson

To Mix with Time: New and Selected Poems, Scribner (New York, NY), 1963.

Poems to Solve (for young adults), Scribner (New York, NY), 1966.

Half Sun, Half Sleep; New poems (new poems and her translations of six Swedish poets), Scribner (New York, NY), 1967.

Iconographs; Poems (includes "Feel Me"), Scribner (New York, NY), 1970.

More Poems to Solve, Scribner (New York, NY), 1971.

(Translator, with Leif Sjoberg) *Windows and Stones, Selected Poems of Tomas Transtromer* (translated from the Swedish), University of Pittsburgh Press (Pittsburgh, PA), 1972.

New and Selected Things Taking Place (includes "Ending"), Little, Brown (Boston, MA), 1978.

In Other Words, Knopf (New York, NY), 1987.

The Love Poems of May Swenson, Houghton Mifflin (Boston, MA), 1991.

The Complete Poems to Solve (for young adults), illustrated by Christy Hale, Macmillan (New York, NY), 1993.

Nature: Poems Old and New, Houghton Mifflin (Boston, MA), 1994.

The Centaur, illustrated by Barry Moser, Macmillan (New York, NY), 1994.

Nature: Poems Old And New, Houghton Mifflin (Boston, MA), 1994.

May out West: Poems of May Swenson, Utah State University Press (Logan, UT), 1996.

Dear Elizabeth: Five Poems and Three Letters to Elizabeth Bishop, afterword by Kirstin Hotelling Zona, Utah State University Press (Logan, UT), 2000.

The Complete Love Poems of May Swenson, Houghton Mifflin (Boston, MA), 2003.

OTHER

The Floor (one-act play), first produced under the program title *Doubles and Opposites* in New York at American Place Theater, May 11, 1966, on a triple bill with "23 Pat O'Brien Movies," by Bruce Jay Friedman, and "Miss Pete," by Andrew Glaze.

The Guess and Spell Coloring Book (for children), drawings by Lise Gladstone, Scribner (New York, NY), 1976.

(Selector of poems, with R. R. Knudson) *American Sports Poems,* Orchard Books (New York, NY), 1988.

Made with Words, edited by Gardner McFall, University of Michigan Press (Ann Arbor, MI), 1997.

CONTRIBUTOR

A Treasury of Great Poems, edited by Louis Untermeyer, Simon & Schuster (New York, NY), 1955.

New Poets 2, Ballantine (New York, NY), 1957.

New Poets of England America, edited by Donald Hall, Robert Pack, and Louis Simpson, Meridian (New York, NY), 1957.

A Country in the Mind, edited by Ray B. West, Angel Island Publications (Sausalito, CA), 1962.

Twentieth-Century American Poetry, edited by Conrad Aiken, Modern Library (New York, NY), 1963.

100 American Poems of the Twentieth Century, Harcourt (Orlando, FL), 1963.

The Modern Poets, edited by John Malcolm Brinnin and Bill Read, McGraw-Hill (New York, NY), 1963.

The New Modern Poetry, edited by M. L. Rosenthal, Macmillan (New York, NY), 1967.

Works represented in other anthologies. Poems also included in translation in anthologies published in Italy and Germany. Contributor of poetry, stories, and criticism to *Poetry, Nation, Saturday Review, Atlantic, Harper's, New Yorker, Southern Review, Hudson Review,* and other periodicals.

Swenson also produced sound recordings, including *May Swenson Reading Her Poems in New York City, March 15, 1958; The Experience of Poetry in A Scientific Age, 1964; May Swenson Reading Her Poems with Comment in the Recording Laboratory, May 12, 1969;* and *Julia Randall and May Swenson Reading and Discussing Their Poems in the Coolidge Auditorium, February 16, 1970.*

Swenson's work is included in the sound recording *Today's Poets: Their Poems, Their Voices,* Volume 2, Scholastic Records, 1968, and recordings for the Library of Congress, Spoken Arts Records, Folkways Records, and others. Her poems have been set to music by Otto Leuning, Howard Swanson, Emerson Meyers, Joyce McKeel, Claudio Spies, Lester Trimble, and Warren Benson.

SIDELIGHTS: During her prolific career, May Swenson received numerous literary awards and nominations for her poetry. Often experimental in both form and appearance, her poems earned her widespread critical acclaim. As Priscilla Long commented in the *Women's Review of Books,* "Swenson was a visionary poet, a prodigious observer of the fragile and miraculous natural world."

Swenson's poetry has been praised for its imagery, which is alternately precise and beguiling, and for the quality of her personal and imaginative observations. Swenson's poetry "exhibits . . . her continuing alertness to the liveliness of nature. Correspondences among all life forms pour from her work, confirming that nothing is meaningless. The universe's basic beauty and balance is the stuff and soul of her poems," observed *Los Angeles Times* reviewer Eloise Klein Healy.

Richard Howard emphasized in a *Tri-Quarterly* review that Swenson's enterprise is "to get out of herself and into those larger, warmer energies of earth, and to do so by liturgical means." Howard wrote: "When May Swenson, speaking in her thaumaturgical fashion of poetry, says that 'attention to the silence in between is the amulet that makes it work,' we are reminded, while

on other occasions in her work we are reassured, that there is a kind of poetry, as there used to be a kind of love, which dares not speak its name." Thus Swenson's "orphic cadences," her "siren-songs, with their obsessive reliance on the devices of incantation," are the means by which she seeks to "discover runes, the conjurations by which she can not only apostrophize the hand, the cat and the cloud in their innominate otherness, but by which she can, in some essential and relieving way, become them, leave her own impinging selfhood in the paralyzed region where names are assigned, and assume instead the energies of natural process."

Book Week contributor Chad Walsh noted: "In most of Miss Swenson's poems the sheer thingness of things is joyfully celebrated." Walsh called her "the poet par excellence of sights and colors." Stephen Stepanchev, author of *American Poetry since 1945,* also thought that Swenson's "distinction is that she is able to make . . . her reader see clearly what he has merely looked at before." Stepanchev, however, is one of the few critics to find her poems less than completely effective. "Miss Swenson," he wrote, "works in a free verse that is supple but rather prosaic, despite her picturemaking efforts."

Howard, writing of Swenson's development as a poet, stated that "from the first . . . Swenson has practiced, in riddles, chants, hex-signs and a whole panoply of invented sortilege unwonted in Western poetry since the Witch of Endor brought up Samuel, the ways not only of summoning Being into her grasp, but of getting herself out of that grasp and into alien shapes, into those emblems of power most often identified with the sexual." Of the more recent poems, Howard wrote: "They are the witty, resigned poems of a woman . . . eager still to manipulate the phenomenal world by magic, but so possessed, now, of the means of her identity that the ritual, spellbinding, litaneutical elements of her art, have grown consistent with her temporal, conditioned, suffering experience and seem—to pay her the highest compliment she could care to receive—no more than natural."

Reviewing *Half Sun, Half Sleep; New Poems, New York Times Book Review* contributor Karl Shapiro wrote: "[Swenson's] concentration on the verbal equivalent of experience is so true, so often brilliant, that one watches her with hope and pleasure, praying for victory all the way." *Poetry* reviewer William

Stafford observed: "No one today is more deft and lucky in discovering a poem than May Swenson. Her work often appears to be proceeding calmly, just descriptive and accurate; but then suddenly it opens into something that looms beyond the material, something that impends and implies. . . . So graceful is the progression in her poems that they launch confidently into any form, carrying through it to easy, apt variations. Often her way is to define things, but the definitions have a stealthy trend; what she chooses and the way she progresses heap upon the reader a consistent, incremental effect." And Shapiro offered this analysis of Swenson's achievement in this book: "The whole volume is an album of experiments . . . that pay off. It is strange to see the once-radical *carmen figuratum,* the calligraphic poem, spatial forms, imagist and surreal forms—all the heritage of the early years of the century—being used with such ease and unselfconsciousness."

Swenson herself wrote that the experience of poetry is "based in a craving to get through the curtains of things as they *appear,* to things as they are, and then into the larger, wilder space of things as they *are becoming.* This ambition involves a paradox: an instinctive belief in the senses as exquisite tools for this investigation and, at the same time, a suspicion about their crudeness." Swenson also noted: "The poet, tracing the edge of a great shadow whose outline shifts and varies, proving there is an invisible moving source of light behind, hopes (naively, in view of his ephemerality) to reach and touch the foot of that solid whatever-it-is that casts the shadow. If sometimes it seems he does touch it, it is only to be faced with a more distant, even less accessible mystery. Because all is movement—all is breathing change."

Among the "strategies and devices, the shamanism and sorcery this poet deploys," as Howard admiringly described them, is Swenson's use of the riddle in *Poems to Solve.* The book may be enjoyed by both children and adults; the poems here are another serious attempt to accommodate "the mystery that only when a thing is apprehended as something else can it be known as itself." Swenson wrote of these poems: "It is essential, of course, with a device such as this to make not a riddle-pretending-to-be-a-poem but a poem that is also, and as if incidentally, a riddle—a solvable one. The aim is not to mystify or mislead but to clarify and make recognizable through the reader's own uncontaminated perceptions."

Nature: Poems Old and New, published four years after Swenson's death, emphasized Swenson's sympathy for and identification with the outdoors. "Swenson was an unrelentingly lyrical poet," wrote Priscilla Long in the *Women's Review of Books,* "a master of the poetic line in which similar sounds accumulate and resonate so that the poem exists, beyond its meanings, as a rattle or a music box, or, in moments of greatness, a symphony." Her collection *Nature* is "so inward, independent, and intense, so intimate and impersonal at once," wrote *Yale Review* critic Langdon Hammer, that "it has been difficult to place in the field of contemporary poetry." Several other critics, however, identified the work as an appreciation of Swenson's profound talent, collecting the best of her work between two covers. "The poetry thinks, feels, examines," observed a *Publishers Weekly* contributor; "it's patiently, meticulously sensuous, and adventurously varied in form, much as nature is." "These poems, harvested from her life's work and arranged in this delightful format," stated Rochelle Natt in the *American Book Review,* "promote a lasting vision of Swenson's valuable contribution to American poetry."

BIOGRAPHICAL AND CRITICAL SOURCES:

BOOKS

Brinnin, John Malcolm, and Bill Read, editors, *The Modern Poets,* McGraw-Hill (New York, NY), 1963.

Contemporary Literary Criticism, Gale (Detroit, MI), Volume 4, 1975, Volume 14, 1980, Volume 61, 1990.

Contemporary Poets, St. Martin's Press (New York, NY), 1980.

Deutsch, Babette, editor, *Poetry in Our Time,* 2nd edition, Doubleday (New York, NY), 1963.

Dictionary of Literary Biography, Volume 5: *American Poets since World War II,* Gale (Detroit, MI), 1980.

Encyclopedia of American Literature, Continuum (New York, NY), 1999.

Hoffman, Daniel, editor, *The Harvard Guide to American Writing,* Belknap Press (Cambridge, MA), 1977.

Nemerov, Howard, editor, *Poets on Poetry,* Basic Books (New York, NY), 1966.

Poems for Young Readers: Selections from Their Own Writing by Poets Attending the Houston Festival of Contemporary Poetry, National Council of Teachers of English, 1966.

Stepanchev, Stephen, *American Poetry since 1945,* Harper (New York, NY), 1965.

Untermeyer, Louis, editor, *A Treasury of Great Poems, English and American,* Simon & Schuster (New York, NY), 1955.

PERIODICALS

American Book Review, September, 1995, p. 14.

Atlantic, February, 1968.

Booklist, June 1, 1993.

Book Week, June 4, 1967, Volume 4, number 30.

Book World, May 22, 1988, Thomas M. Disch, review of *In Other Words,* pp. 1, 14.

Christian Science Monitor, February 12, 1979.

Library Journal, June 15, 1994, Judy Clarence, review of *Nature: Poems Old and New,* p. 72.

Los Angeles Times, March 22, 1979.

New Republic, March 7, 1988, Mary Jo Salter, review of *In Other Words,* p. 40.

New York Times, March 19, 1979; June 16, 1987.

New York Times Book Review, September 1, 1963; May 7, 1967; February 11, 1979; June 12, 1988; January 19, 1992.

Poetry, December, 1967; February, 1979; February, 1993; November, 2001, Christian Wiman, review of *Nature,* p. 97.

Prairie Schooner, spring, 1968.

Publishers Weekly, May 30, 1994, review of *Nature,* pp. 46-47.

Tri-Quarterly, fall, 1966.

Twentieth Century Literature, summer, 1998, Kirstin Hotelling Zona, "A 'Dangerous Game of Change': Images of Desire in the Love Poems of May Swenson," p. 219.

Wilson Quarterly, winter, 1997, review of *May Swenson: Selected and Introduced by Anthony Hecht,* p. 105.

Women's Review of Books, January, 1995, pp. 8-9.

Yale Review, January, 1995, pp. 121-41.

ONLINE

Academy of American Poets Web site, http://www.poets.org/ (June 3, 2003), author profile.

University of Michigan Press Web site, http://www.press.umich.edu/ (June 3, 2003), review of *Made with Words.*

Utah State University Press Web site, http://www.usu.edu/usupress/ (June 3, 2003), reviews of *Dear Elizabeth: Five Poems and Three Letters to Elizabeth Bishop* and *May out West: Poems of May Swenson.*

OBITUARIES:

PERIODICALS

Chicago Tribune, December 10, 1989.

Los Angeles Times, December 14, 1989.

New York Times, December 5, 1989.

Washington Post, December 8, 1989.*

T-W

TASHJIAN, Janet 1956-

PERSONAL: Born June 29, 1956, in Providence, RI; daughter of Russell (a sales engineer) and Mariette (a homemaker; maiden name, Lajoie) Souza; married Douglas Tashjian (a medical consultant), December, 1985; children: Jake. *Education:* University of Rhode Island, B.A., 1978; Emerson College, M.F.A., 1994. *Politics:* "Progressive." *Religion:* Buddhist. *Hobbies and other interests:* Cooking, writing, playing with her son, writing, hiking, writing.

ADDRESSES: Agent—Jennifer Flannery, 1140 Wickfield Ct., Naperville, IL 60653.

CAREER: Writer, 1993—. Worked as a sales representative, sales manager, and sales consultant, 1978-93.

AWARDS, HONORS: Honor Book award, Women's National Book Association, 1998, for *Tru Confessions;* selection for "Best Books for the Teen Age," New York Public Library, 1998, for *Tru Confessions,* 1999, for *Multiple Choice,* and 2001, for *The Gospel according to Larry;* citation among best children's books, Bank Street College of Education, 1998, for *Tru Confessions,* 1999, for *Marty Frye, Private Eye,* and 2001, for *The Gospel according to Larry;* Children's Choice selections, Children's Book Council and International Reading Association, both 1998, for *Marty Frye, Private Eye;* Best of the Best selection, Chicago Public Library, and Pennsylvania Young Reader's Choice Award, both 1999, for *Multiple Choice;* Academic Excellence Award in Journalism, University of Rhode Island; DuPrey Fiction Award, Emerson College.

Janet Tashjian

WRITINGS:

JUVENILE FICTION

Tru Confessions, Henry Holt (New York, NY), 1997.
Marty Frye, Private Eye, Henry Holt (New York, NY), 1998.

Multiple Choice, Henry Holt (New York, NY), 1999.
The Gospel according to Larry, Henry Holt (New York, NY), 2001.
Fault Line, Henry Holt (New York, NY), 2003.
Vote for Larry, Henry Holt (New York, NY), 2004.

Contributor of essays, short stories, and poetry to various literary journals.

ADAPTATIONS: Tru's Confessions was adapted as a television movie, featuring Clara Bryant and Shia LeBeouf, broadcast by the Disney Channel in 2002. It later won a California Governor's Media Award for its portrayal of a youth with special needs.

SIDELIGHTS: Janet Tashjian once commented: "I was a journalism major in college, but when I graduated, I took a detour into sales and marketing. After spending fifteen years selling copy machines and computers, managing sales forces, and running training classes, I decided life was too short to spend another minute doing anything but what I really wanted to do, which was write. So I quit my job, bought a dozen spiral-bound notebooks and a pack of pens, and started writing.

"Eventually, I took some writing workshops, then found my way to the Masters in Fine Arts Program at Emerson College. Jack Gantos—*Rotten Ralph, Joey Pigza Swallowed the Key*—taught children's literature and writing there. On the first day of class, he told us in explicit detail about the neighborhoods he grew up in, his friends, teachers, et cetera. He remembered everything. (Of course, I found out later, he'd been keeping a diary since second grade.) I couldn't remember *that* much about growing up, but making stuff up seemed like more fun anyway. That night, I drove home and came up with the idea that would become *Tru Confessions*—a novel that explored what it would have been like for me to grow up with a special needs sibling the way my husband did.

"I wrote the book as a series-type mystery with Trudy and Eddie solving a local crime. I finished one, then wrote another. I sent them around to publishers and agents with no luck. One night about ten o'clock, I was sitting up with my infant son when I just started playing around on the computer. Trudy started talking to me, but not the Trudy I had spent all that time writing about. A new voice emerged, and she said she most certainly did *not* want to solve mysteries; she wanted her own television show, thank you very much. I wrote the first chapter that night and finished the new version book a few months later. Soon afterward, I got an agent who sold *Tru Confessions* to Henry Holt."

Tashjian's persistent process of improvement resulted in the publication of her first novel, *Tru Confessions.* Like its author, the story's heroine, Trudy, attempts resolutely to realize her dreams. Readers are allowed to get to know Tru by leafing through a printout of her computer journal. Complete with humorous headings and computer-penned pictures, the diary reveals Tru's thoughts and feelings as she struggles to realize her aspirations: to create her own television show and to "cure" her developmentally delayed brother, Eddie. Tru's two dreams merge when she enters a local cable television contest and is inspired to produce a documentary about Eddie. Janice M. Del Negro noted in the *Bulletin of the Center for Children's Books* that Tru begins her pursuit with "intense adolescent desires and youthful determination to just not admit defeat," but grows to have a more realistic understanding of the permanence of Eddie's disability, while keeping her sense of optimism about the future. However, while Del Negro suggested that Tru's previously convincing twelve-year-old voice matures too quickly and "near the end . . . the author's voice disconcertingly takes over," Cathryn M. Mercier asserted in *Five Owls* that "Tru's voice [has] an immediacy and lack of self-censorship that texture the entire novel." Also admiring the character, *Voice of Youth Advocates* reviewer Katie O'Dell Madison noticed that "the use of imaginative fonts, layout, and empty space lends authenticity" to the preteen point of view. A *Publishers Weekly* critic remarked, "Middle graders will laugh their way through Tru's poignant and clever take on everyday life; even the most reluctant of readers may tell their friends about this one."

Tashjian wrote: "The easy-reader, *Marty Frye, Private Eye,* came about because my friend's son used to laugh and laugh when I made up rhymes for him. I've always loved mysteries, so I made Marty a poet detective.

"I write every day, some days more than others. I try to get in a few turbo days a week. Writing is only a part of the process, though. I spend a lot of time rewriting, trying to polish each chapter, each scene, each sentence. I have several things going on at the same time—the first draft of a novel, a book in the final stages of editing, the outline for a screenplay, plus lots of ideas just waiting for me to get to them. Even when I'm not working, there's always something going on in my head, itching to get down on paper.

"When students ask me for advice I always say the same thing: 'Spend your life doing something you love.' Then act like what you're doing is the most important, sacred thing in the world, because it is. Find a teacher, a mentor, a group of people who want to improve their skills, too. Then practice, practice, practice. Devote yourself to your craft, and you will be greatly rewarded. As the comedy writer Larry Gelbart said, 'The meaning of life is beyond me. The best I can do is deal with it one word at a time.' Amen."

Recently Tashjian added: "I got the inspiration for my novel *Fault Line* while reading Naomi Wolf's *Promiscuities,* in which she writes about being physically abused by her boyfriend while in high school. I was shocked; if a leading feminist—a strong young woman from an educated family—was being beaten by her boyfriend, what chances did the average girl have? The next day, Harvard released a study in the *Journal of the American Medical Association* stating that one of every five teenage girls is physically abused by her boyfriend. I knew then that this was something I wanted to write about.

"It didn't interest me to show such a relationship in black-and-white terms. In Wolf's book, she described her boyfriend as a nice guy most of the time. This is one of the reasons why it becomes so difficult for girls and women to leave. I also wanted to write a novel that showed how easily we blame the victim for her situation. It was important for me to show both parties dealing with the issue of abuse. As much as the perpetrator's behavior is horrendous, I wanted to try and understand him. I thought it was important to balance a serious subject with some levity, so I set the story in the world of standup comedy, providing me (and the characters) with some much-needed respite.

"I have also handed in a sequel to *The Gospel according to Larry* titled *Vote for Larry.* It was a blast to hang out with Larry again. He's one of my favorite people in the world."

BIOGRAPHICAL AND CRITICAL SOURCES:

PERIODICALS

Booklist, January 1 and 15, 1998, pp. 816-817; November 1, 2001, Ilene Cooper, review of *The Gospel according to Larry,* p. 471; September 1, 2003, Ilene Cooper, review of *Fault Line,* p. 115.

Bulletin of the Center for Children's Books, January, 1998, Janice M. Del Negro, review of *Tru Confessions,* p. 180.

Five Owls, January-February, 1998, Cathryn M. Mercier, review of *Tru Confessions.*

Horn Book, January-February, 2002, Jennifer M. Brabander, review of *The Gospel according to Larry,* p. 84; September-October, 2003, Jennifer M. Brabander, review of *Fault Line,* p. 620.

Journal of Adolescent and Adult Literacy, April, 2002, Vashti Kenway, review of *The Gospel according to Larry,* p. 662.

Kirkus Reviews, October 1, 1997, p. 1538; October 15, 2001, review of *The Gospel according to Larry,* p. 1494; August 15, 2003, review of *Fault Line,* p. 1080.

Kliatt, July, 2003, Paula Rohrlick, review of *The Gospel according to Larry,* p. 27; September, 2003, Paula Rohrlick, review of *Fault Line,* p. 13.

Publishers Weekly, October 20, 1997, review of *Tru Confessions,* p. 77; December 3, 2001, review of *The Gospel according to Larry,* p. 61; September 1, 2003, review of *Fault Line,* p. 90.

Reading Today, August, 2000, Lynne T. Burke, review of *Tru Confessions,* p. 32.

School Library Journal, December, 1997, pp. 131-132; October, 2001, Francisca Goldsmith, review of *The Gospel according to Larry,* p. 172; October, 2003, Susan Riley, review of *Fault Line,* p. 180.

Stone Soup, July, 2000, Lauren Porter, review of *Multiple Choice,* p. 10.

Voice of Youth Advocates, December, 1997, Katie O'Dell Madison, review of *Tru Confessions,* p. 322.

*   *   *

WAISER, Bill
See WAISER, William Andrew

WAISER, William Andrew 1953-
(Bill Waiser)

PERSONAL: Born June 6, 1953, in Toronto, Ontario, Canada; son of Thaddeus and Jean (Ritchie) Waiser; married Marley English, August 22, 1975; children: Jess, Mike, Kate. *Education:* Trent University, B.A. (with honors), 1975; University of Saskatchewan, M.A., 1976, Ph.D., 1983. *Hobbies and other interests:* Canoeing, running, gardening.

ADDRESSES: Home—6 Arnason Cres., Saskatoon, Saskatchewan S7H 4MB, Canada. *Office*—Department of History, University of Saskatchewan, Arts Building, 9 Campus Drive, Saskatoon, Saskatchewan S7N 5A5, Canada; fax: 306-955-6348. *E-mail*—waiser@duke.usask.ca.

CAREER: University of Saskatchewan, Saskatoon, Saskatchewan, Canada, term lecturer, 1980-83, assistant professor, 1984-87, associate professor, 1987-90, professor of history, 1990—, graduate director, 1987-90, department head, 1995-98. Parks Canada, Prairie and Northern Regional Office, Yukon historian, 1983-84.

MEMBER: Canadian Historical Association (member of council, 1996-99), National History Society (Canada; member of board of directors, 2001—).

AWARDS, HONORS: Queen's fellowship, Canada Council; finalist for Governor-General's Literary Award for nonfiction, 1997, for *Loyal till Death: Indians and the North-West Rebellion.*

WRITINGS:

The Field Naturalist: John Macoun, the Geological Survey and Natural Science, University of Toronto Press (Toronto, Ontario, Canada), 1989.

Saskatchewan's Playground: A History of Prince Albert National Park, Fifth House Publishers (Saskatoon, Saskatchewan, Canada), 1989.

(Under name Bill Waiser; editor, with Dave De Brou) *Documenting Canada: A History of Modern Canada in Documents,* Fifth House Publishers (Saskatoon, Saskatchewan, Canada), 1992.

William Andrew Waiser

The New Northwest: The Photographs of the Frank Crean Expeditions, 1908-1909, Fifth House Publishers (Saskatoon, Saskatchewan, Canada), 1993.

Park Prisoners: The Untold Story of Western Canada's National Parks, 1915-1946, Fifth House Publishers (Saskatoon, Saskatchewan, Canada), 1995.

(Under name Bill Waiser; with Blair Stonechild) *Loyal till Death: Indians and the North-West Rebellion,* Fifth House Publishers (Calgary, Alberta, Canada), 1997.

(Under name Bill Waiser; with Paul Dederick) *Looking Back: True Tales from Saskatchewan's Past,* Fifth House Publishers (Calgary, Alberta, Canada), 2003.

(Under name Bill Waiser) *All Hell Can't Stop Us: The On-to-Ottawa Trek and Regina Riot,* Fifth House Publishers (Calgary, Alberta, Canada), 2003.

Chair of advisory board, *Canadian Historical Review,* 2000-03.

WORK IN PROGRESS: A centennial history of the province of Saskatchewan, Canada, completion expected in 2005.

SIDELIGHTS: William Andrew Waiser is the author of several books which cover aspects of Canadian history. One of his earliest books, *Saskatchewan's Playground: A History of Prince Albert National Park,* provides a history of the development of a Canadian national park. Waiser covers many of the issues and opposing viewpoints that had to be dealt with as the park developed over the years, and his chapters are formed around each of these issues. For example, one chapter covers the politics of park development and relates how supporters made great progress towards their goals by lobbying certain influential people. The book also covers park topics such as wildlife management and differing expectations for public use of the park. During the summer months of the 1930s area residents had adopted the habit of setting up shack-tent communities, or large enclaves of tents with wood walls and roofs, in the park. After World War II the Park Service began to change their management philosophy and attempted to get rid of the tents, which were no longer considered attractive. As Waiser relates, the disagreement was not fully settled, although some acceptable compromises were worked out. C. J. Taylor of the *Canadian Historical Review* found some of the coverage of the topic biased toward a human standpoint as opposed to a plant or animal frame of reference; for example, development is portrayed as positive. Taylor, however, called the park biography "among the best."

Waiser continued to explore the history of Canadian land use in *The New Northwest: The Photographs of the Frank Crean Expeditions, 1908-1909.* Crean, called a "hard drinking Irishman" by Gord Struthers of *Canadian Geographic,* was hired by the Canadian government to explore the possibility of land settlement in western Canada. Shortly after 1900, homesteading opportunities were becoming increasingly rare for immigrants to the country and the government was interested in finding other alternatives. Rumors circulated about land between Hudson Bay and the Rockies that was supposedly fertile for farming. Crean led two expeditions to the area and came back with positive but erroneous reports of the area's potential for agriculture—many of his conclusions were based on second-hand information and inaccurate photographs. The government enthusiastically received Crean's conclusions since they were what the government had been hoping to hear. Later forestry and soil reports actually showed the area to be poor for agricultural settlement.

In his review for *Canadian Geographic,* Struthers noted that he was impressed by the inclusion in the book of ninety-three black-and-white photographs from Crean's expeditions. While Struthers admitted that Waiser had relied on dull governmental reports for most of his information because Crean's journals were lost, Struthers called the book a "fascinating sliver of Western Canadian History." A *Canadian Literature* reviewer commented that the photographs portray "images of hard travel, of people in transition" which mirror the hopeful expectations prior to World War I.

Waiser continued on the topic of Canadian parks in *Park Prisoners: The Untold Story of Western Canada's National Parks, 1915-1946.* The book offers a unique view into park development labor methods and the creation of park facilities that many of today's visitors take for granted. In 1911 the first commissioner of parks, James Harkin, decided to use cheap labor to carry out park projects such as road improvements or facility construction. Many of those who were chosen to take part in this labor were society's undesirables, including the homeless, those without jobs, pacifists, foreign workers, and those who were considered subversive. According to Waiser these workers were housed in facilities akin to concentration camps. Workers were paid twenty-five cents per day, got little to eat, lacked warm clothing, and sometimes had to tramp miles through deep snow to get to work. Waiser's account of this time is based on research and actual interviews with people who were part of the park work camps.

R. W. Winks of *Choice* noted that a comparison by Waiser between the Canadian use of park labor and what other countries did to develop parks would have been of interest. Sid Marty of *Canadian Geographic* felt that the book gives surprising insights into Canadian classism and racism and called *Park Prisoners* a "lively, thought-provoking, and well researched history."

BIOGRAPHICAL AND CRITICAL SOURCES:

PERIODICALS

Beaver: Exploring Canada's History, February-March, 1997, p. 41.
Canadian Book Review Annual, 1995, p. 286.
Canadian Geographic, May-June, 1994, Gord Struthers, review of *The New Northwest: The Photographs of the Frank Crean Expeditions, 1908-*

1909, p. 100; May-June, 1996, Sid Marty, review of *Park Prisoners: The Untold Story of Western Canada's National Parks, 1915-1946,* pp. 93-94.

Canadian Historical Review, June, 1992, C. J. Taylor, review of *Saskatchewan's Playground: A History of Prince Albert National Park,* pp. 263-265; March, 1997, pp. 130-132.

Canadian Literature, summer, 1995, review of *The New Northwest,* pp. 165-166.

Canadian Materials, May, 1994, p. 89.

Choice, September, 1996, R. W. Winks, review of *Park Prisoners,* p. 200.

*   *   *

WALKER, Alice (Malsenior) 1944-

PERSONAL: Born February 9, 1944, in Eatonton, GA; daughter of Willie Lee and Minnie Tallulah (Grant) Walker; married Melvyn Rosenman Leventhal (a civil rights lawyer), March 17, 1967 (divorced, 1976); children: Rebecca. *Education:* Attended Spelman College, 1961-63; Sarah Lawrence College, B.A., 1965.

ADDRESSES: Home—Berkeley, CA. *Agent*—c/o Author Mail, Random House, 201 East 50th St., New York, NY 10022.

Alice Walker

CAREER: Writer. Wild Trees Press, Navarro, CA, cofounder and publisher, 1984-88. Has been a voter registration worker in Georgia, a worker in Head Start program in Mississippi, and on staff of New York City welfare department. Writer in residence and teacher of black studies at Jackson State College, 1968-69, and Tougaloo College, 1970-71; lecturer in literature, Wellesley College and University of Massachusetts—Boston, both 1972-73; distinguished writer in Afro-American studies department, University of California, Berkeley, spring, 1982; Fannie Hurst Professor of Literature, Brandeis University, Waltham, MA, fall, 1982. Lecturer and reader of own poetry at universities and conferences. Member of board of trustees of Sarah Lawrence College. Consultant on black history to Friends of the Children of Mississippi, 1967. Coproducer of film documentary *Warrior Marks,* directed by Pratibha Parmar, with script and narration by Walker, 1993.

AWARDS, HONORS: Bread Loaf Writer's Conference scholar, 1966; first prize, *American Scholar* essay contest, 1967; Merrill writing fellowship, 1967; MacDow-ell Colony fellowship, 1967, 1977-78; National Endowment for the Arts grant, 1969, 1977; Radcliffe Institute fellowship, 1971-73; Ph.D., Russell Sage College, 1972; National Book Award nomination and Lillian Smith Award from the Southern Regional Council, both 1973, both for *Revolutionary Petunias and Other Poems;* Richard and Hinda Rosenthal Foundation Award, American Academy and Institute of Arts and Letters, 1974, for *In Love and Trouble: Stories of Black Women;* Guggenheim fellowship, 1977-78; National Book Critics Circle Award nomination, 1982, and Pulitzer Prize and American Book Award, both 1983, all for *The Color Purple;* Best Books for Young Adults citation, American Library Association, 1984, for *In Search of Our Mother's Gardens: Womanist Prose;* D.H.L., University of Massachusetts, 1983; O. Henry Award, 1986, for "Kindred Spirits"; Langston Hughes Award, New York City College, 1989; Nora Astorga Leadership Award, 1989; Fred Cody Award for lifetime achievement, Bay Area Book Reviewers Association, 1990; Freedom to Write Award, PEN West, 1990; California Governor's Arts Award, 1994; Literary Ambassador Award, University of Oklahoma Center for Poets and Writers, 1998.

WRITINGS:

POETRY

Once: Poems (also see below), Harcourt (San Diego, CA), 1968.

Five Poems, Broadside Press (Highland Park, MI), 1972.

Revolutionary Petunias and Other Poems (also see below), Harcourt (San Diego, CA), 1973.

Goodnight, Willie Lee, I'll See You in the Morning (also see below), Dial (New York, NY), 1979.

Horses Make a Landscape Look More Beautiful, Harcourt (San Diego, CA), 1984.

Alice Walker Boxed Set—Poetry: Good Night, Willie Lee, I'll See You in the Morning; Revolutionary Petunias and Other Poems; Once, Poems, Harcourt (San Diego, CA), 1985.

Her Blue Body Everything We Know: Earthling Poems, 1965-1990 Complete, Harcourt (San Diego, CA), 1991.

A Poem Traveled down My Arm: Poem and Drawings, Random House (New York, NY), 2002.

Absolute Trust in the Goodness of the Earth: New Poems, Random House (New York, NY), 2003.

FICTION; NOVELS, EXCEPT AS NOTED

The Third Life of Grange Copeland, Harcourt (San Diego, CA), 1970.

In Love and Trouble: Stories of Black Women, Harcourt (San Diego, CA), 1973.

Meridian, Harcourt (San Diego, CA), 1976.

You Can't Keep a Good Woman Down (short stories), Harcourt (San Diego, CA), 1981.

The Color Purple, Harcourt (San Diego, CA), 1982.

Alice Walker Boxed Set—Fiction: The Third Life of Grange Copeland, You Can't Keep a Good Woman Down, and In Love and Trouble, Harcourt (San Diego, CA), 1985.

The Temple of My Familiar, Harcourt (San Diego, CA), 1989.

Possessing the Secret of Joy, Harcourt (San Diego, CA), 1992.

Everyday Use, edited by Barbara Christian, Rutgers University Press (New Brunswick, NJ), 1994.

By the Light of My Father's Smile, Random House (New York, NY), 1998.

The Way Forward Is with a Broken Heart, Random House (New York, NY), 2000.

Now Is the Time to Open Your Heart: A Novel, Random House (New York, NY), 2004.

FOR CHILDREN

Langston Hughes: American Poet (biography), Crowell (New York, NY), 1973, revised edition, illustrated by Catherine Deeter, HarperCollins (New York, NY), 2002.

To Hell with Dying, illustrations by Catherine Deeter, Harcourt (San Diego, CA), 1988.

Finding the Green Stone, Harcourt (San Diego, CA), 1991.

NONFICTION

In Search of Our Mothers' Gardens: Womanist Prose, Harcourt (San Diego, CA), 1983.

Living by the Word: Selected Writings, 1973-1987, Harcourt (San Diego, CA), 1988.

(With Pratibha Parmar) *Warrior Marks: Female Genital Mutilation and the Sexual Blinding of Women,* Harcourt (San Diego, CA), 1993.

Alice Walker Banned, with introduction by Patricia Holt, Aunt Lute Books (San Francisco, CA), 1996.

Anything We Love Can Be Saved: A Writer's Activism, Random House (New York, NY), 1997.

(With Francesco Mastalia and Alfonse Pagano) *Dreads: Sacred Rites of the Natural Hair Revolution,* Artisan (New York, NY), 1999.

OTHER

(Editor) *I Love Myself when I'm Laughing . . . and Then Again when I Am Looking Mean and Impressive: A Zora Neale Hurston Reader,* introduction by Mary Helen Washington, Feminist Press (New York, NY), 1979.

The Same River Twice: Honoring the Difficult; A Meditation of Life, Spirit, Art, and the Making of the film "The Color Purple," Ten Years Later, Scribner (New York, NY), 1996.

Contributor to anthologies, including *Voices of the Revolution,* edited by Helen Haynes, E. & J. Kaplan (Philadelphia, PA), 1967; *The Best Short Stories by*

Negro Writers from 1899 to the Present: An Anthology, edited by Langston Hughes, Little, Brown (Boston, MA), 1967; *Afro-American Literature: An Introduction,* Harcourt (San Diego, CA), 1971; *Tales and Stories for Black Folks,* compiled by Toni Cade Bambara, Zenith Books (New York, NY), 1971; *Black Short Story Anthology,* compiled by Woodie King, New American Library (New York, NY), 1972; *The Poetry of Black America: An Anthology of the Twentieth Century,* compiled by Arnold Adoff, Harper (New York, NY), 1973; *A Rock against the Wind: Black Love Poems,* edited by Lindsay Patterson, Dodd (New York, NY), 1973; *We Be Word Sorcerers: Twenty-five Stories by Black Americans,* edited by Sonia Sanchez, Bantam (New York, NY), 1973; *Images of Women in Literature,* compiled by Mary Anne Ferguson, Houghton Mifflin (Boston, MA), 1973; *Best American Short Stories: 1973,* edited by Margaret Foley, Hart-Davis, 1973; *Best American Short Stories, 1974,* edited by M. Foley, Houghton Mifflin (Boston, MA), 1974; *Chants of Saints: A Gathering of Afro-American Literature, Art and Scholarship,* edited by Michael S. Harper and Robert B. Stepto, University of Illinois Press (Chicago, IL), 1980; *Midnight Birds: Stories of Contemporary Black Women Authors,* edited by Mary Helen Washington, Anchor Press (New York, NY), 1980; and *Double Stitch: Black Women Write about Mothers and Daughters,* edited by Maya Angelou, HarperCollins (New York, NY), 1993.

Contributor to numerous periodicals, including *Negro Digest, Denver Quarterly, Harper's, Black World, Essence, Canadian Dimension,* and the *New York Times.* Contributing editor, *Southern Voices, Freedomways,* and *Ms.*

ADAPTATIONS: The Color Purple was made into a feature film directed by Steven Spielberg, Warner Bros., 1985.

SIDELIGHTS: Alice Walker "is one of the country's best-selling writers of literary fiction," according to Renee Tawa in the *Los Angeles Times.* "More than ten million copies of her books are in print." Walker has become a focal spokesperson and symbol for black feminism and has earned critical and popular acclaim as a major American novelist and intellectual. Her literary reputation was secured with her Pulitzer Prize-winning third novel, *The Color Purple,* which was transformed into a popular film by Steven Spielberg.

Upon the release of the novel in 1982, critics sensed that Walker had created something special. "*The Color Purple* . . . could be the kind of popular and literary event that transforms an intense reputation into a national one," according to Gloria Steinem of *Ms.* Judging from the critical enthusiasm for *The Color Purple,* Steinem's words have proved prophetic. Walker "has succeeded," as Andrea Ford noted in the *Detroit Free Press,* "in creating a jewel of a novel." Peter S. Prescott presented a similar opinion in a *Newsweek* review. "I want to say," he commented, "that *The Color Purple* is an American novel of permanent importance, that rare sort of book which (in Norman Mailer's felicitous phrase) amounts to 'a diversion in the fields of dread.'"

Jeanne Fox-Alston and Mel Watkins both felt that the appeal of *The Color Purple* is that the novel, as a synthesis of characters and themes found in Walker's earlier works, brings together the best of the author's literary production in one volume. Fox-Alston, in Chicago's *Tribune Books,* remarked: "Celie, the main character in Walker's third . . . novel, *The Color Purple,* is an amalgam of all those women [characters in Walker's previous books]; she embodies both their desperation and, later, their faith." Watkins stated in the *New York Times Book Review:* "Her previous books . . . have elicited praise for Miss Walker as a lavishly gifted writer. *The Color Purple,* while easily satisfying that claim, brings into sharper focus many of the diverse themes that threaded their way through her past work."

Walker was born in Eatonton, Georgia, a southern town where most African Americans toiled at the difficult job of tenant farming. Her writing reflects these roots, where black vernacular was prominent and the stamp of slavery and oppression were still present. When she was eight, Walker was accidentally shot in the eye by a brother playing with his BB gun. Her parents, who were too poor to afford a car, could not take her to a doctor for several days. By that time, her wound was so bad that she had lost the use of her right eye. This handicap eventually aided her writer's voice, because she withdrew from others and became a meticulous observer of human relationships and interaction.

An excellent student, Walker was awarded a scholarship to Spelman College in 1961. The civil rights movement attracted her, and she became an activist. In 1963 she decided to continue her education at Sarah

Lawrence College in New York, where she began to work seriously on writing poems, publishing several in a college journal. After graduation, she moved to Mississippi to teach and continue her social activism, and she met and married Melvyn Leventhal, a Jewish civil rights lawyer. The two became the only legally married interracial couple living in Jackson, Mississippi. After their divorce in 1976, Walker's literary output increased.

Walker coined the term "Womanist" to describe her philosophical stance on the issue of gender. As a Womanist, which is different from a feminist, she sees herself as someone who appreciates women's culture, emotions, and character. Her work often reflects this stance, and, paradoxically, the universality of human experience. Walker's central characters are almost always black women; Walker, according to Steinem, "comes at universality through the path of an American black woman's experience. . . . She speaks the female experience more powerfully for being able to pursue it across boundaries of race and class." This universality is also noted by Fox-Alston, who remarked that Walker has a "reputation as a provocative writer who writes about blacks in particular, but all humanity in general."

However, many critics recognize a particularly black and female focus in Walker's writings. For example, in her review of The Color Purple, Ford suggested that the novel transcends "culture and gender" lines but also refers to Walker's "unabashedly feminist viewpoint" and the novel's "black . . . texture." Walker does not deny this dual bias; the task of revealing the condition of the black woman is particularly important to her. Thadious M. Davis, in his Dictionary of Literary Biography essay, commented: "Walker writes best of the social and personal drama in the lives of familiar people who struggle for survival of self in hostile environments. She has expressed a special concern with exploring the oppressions, the insanities, the loyalties and the triumph of black women."

Walker's earlier books—novels, volumes of short stories, and poems—have not received the same degree of attention, but neither have they been ignored. Gloria Steinem pointed out that Meridian, Walker's second novel, "is often cited as the best novel of the civil rights movement, and is taught as part of some American history as well as literature courses." In Everyday Use, Barbara Christian found the title story— first published in Walker's collection In Love and Trouble:

Stories of Black Women— to be "pivotal" to all of Walker's work in its evocation of black sisterhood and black women's heritage of quilting. William Peden, writing in The American Short Story: Continuity and Change, 1940-1975, called this same collection "a remarkable book." David Guy's commentary on The Color Purple in the Washington Post Book World included this evaluation: "Accepting themselves for what they are, the women [in the novel] are able to extricate themselves from oppression; they leave their men, find useful work to support themselves." Watkins further explained: "In The Color Purple the role of male domination in the frustration of black women's struggle for independence is clearly the focus."

Some reviewers criticize Walker's fiction for portraying an overly negative view of black men. Katha Pollitt, for example, in the New York Times Book Review, called the stories in You Can't Keep a Good Woman Down "too partisan." The critic added: "The black woman is always the most sympathetic character." Guy noted: "Some readers . . . will object to her overall perspective. Men in [The Color Purple] are generally pathetic, weak and stupid, when they are not heartlessly cruel, and the white race is universally bumbling and inept." Charles Larson, in his Detroit News review of The Color Purple, pointed out: "I wouldn't go as far as to say that all the male characters [in the novel] are villains, but the truth is fairly close to that." However, neither Guy nor Larson felt that this emphasis on women is a major fault in the novel. Guy, for example, while conceding that "white men . . . are invisible in Celie's world," observed: "This really is Celie's perspective, however—it is psychologically accurate to her—and Alice Walker might argue that it is only a neat inversion of the view that has prevailed in western culture for centuries." Larson also noted that by the end of the novel, "several of [Walker's] masculine characters have reformed."

This idea of reformation, this sense of hope even in despair, is at the core of Walker's vision. In spite of the brutal effects of sexism and racism suffered by the characters of her short stories and novels, critics note what Art Seidenbaum of the Los Angeles Times called Walker's sense of "affirmation . . . [that] overcomes her anger." This is particularly evident in The Color Purple, according to several reviewers. Ford, for example, asserted that the author's "polemics on . . . political and economic issues finally give way to what can only be described as a joyful celebration of human spirit—exulting, uplifting and eminently universal." Prescott discovered a similar progression in the novel. He wrote: "[Walker's] story begins at about the point that most Greek tragedies reserve for the climax, then . . . by immeasurable small steps . . . works its way toward acceptance, serenity and joy."

Davis referred to this idea as Walker's "vision of survival" and offered a summary of its significance in Walker's work. "At whatever cost, human beings have the capacity to live in spiritual health and beauty; they may be poor, black, and uneducated, but their inner selves can blossom." This vision, extended to all humanity, is evident in Walker's collection *Living by the Word: Selected Writings, 1973-1987.* Although "her original interests centered on black women, and especially on the ways they were abused or underrated," *New York Times Book Review* contributor Noel Perrin believed that "now those interests encompass all creation." Judith Paterson similarly observed in *Tribune Books* that in *Living by the Word,* "Walker casts her abiding obsession with the oneness of the universe in a question: Do creativity, love and spiritual wholeness still have a chance of winning the human heart amid political forces bent on destroying the universe with poisonous chemicals and nuclear weapons?" Walker explores this question through journal entries and essays that deal with Native Americans, racism in China, a lonely horse, smoking, and response to the criticism leveled against both the novel and the film version of *The Color Purple.* Many of these treatments are personal in approach, and Jill Nelson found many of them trivial. Writing in the *Washington Post Book World,* Nelson commented, "*Living by the Word* is fraught with . . . reaches for commonality, analogy and universality. Most of the time all Walker achieves is banality." But Derrick Bell differed, noting in his *Los Angeles Times Book Review* critique that Walker "uses carefully crafted images that provide a universality to unique events." The critic further asserted that *Living by the Word* "is not only vintage Alice Walker: passionate, political, personal, and poetic, it also provides a panoramic view of a fine human being saving her soul through good deeds and extraordinary writing."

Harsh criticisms of Walker's work crested with the 1989 publication of her fourth novel, *The Temple of My Familiar.* The novel, featuring several of the characters of *The Color Purple,* reflects concerns hinted at in that novel and confronted directly in *Living by the*

Word: racism, a reverence for nature, a search for spiritual truths, and the universality referred to by reviewers Nelson and Bell. But according to David Gates in his *Newsweek* review, the novel "is fatally ambitious. It encompasses 500,000 years, rewrites Genesis and the Beatitudes and weighs in with mini-lectures on everything from Elvis (for) to nuclear waste (against)." David Nicholson of the *Washington Post Book World* felt that *The Temple of My Familiar* "is not a novel so much as it is an ill-fitting collection of speeches . . . a manifesto for the Fascism of the New Age. . . . There are no characters, only types representative of the world Walker lives in or wishes could be." In a similar vein, *Time*'s Paul Grey noted that "Walker's relentless adherence to her own socio-political agenda makes for frequently striking propaganda," but not for good fiction. Though generally disliked even by sympathetic critics, the novel has its defenders. Novelist J. M. Coetzee, writing in the *New York Times Book Review,* implored the reader to look upon the novel as a "fable of recovered origins, as an exploration of the inner lives of contemporary black Americans as these are penetrated by fabulous stories," and Bernard W. Bell, writing in the *Chicago Tribune,* felt that the novel is a "colorful quilt of many patches," and that its "stylized lovers, remembrances of things past, bold flights of fantasy and vision of a brave new world of cultural diversity and cosmic harmony challenge the reader's willingness to suspend disbelief."

A *Publishers Weekly* reviewer of Walker's 1991 children's story *Finding the Green Stone* said that "the tone is ethereal and removed . . . while the writing style, especially the dialogue, is stiff and didactic." But for Walker's collected poems, *Her Blue Body Everything We Know: Earthling Poems, 1965-1990 Complete,* a *Publishers Weekly* reviewer had high praise, characterizing Walker as "composed, wry, unshaken by adversity," and suggesting that her "strong, beautiful voice" beckons us "to heal ourselves and the planet."

Critics gave high praise to Walker's controversial fifth novel, *Possessing the Secret of Joy,* about the practice of female genital mutilation in certain African, Asian, and Middle Eastern cultures. Writing in the *Los Angeles Times Book Review,* Tina McElroy Ansa said that taking on such a taboo subject shows Walker's depth and range. The critic also felt that her portrait of the suffering of Tashi—a character from *The Color Purple*—is "stunning." "The description of the excision itself and its after effect is graphic enough to make one gag," but is the work of a thoughtful, impassioned artist, rather than a sensationalist, noted Charles R. Larson in the *Washington Post Book World.* And Donna Haisty Winchell wrote in her *Dictionary of Literary Biography* essay that *Possessing the Secret of Joy* is "much more concise, more controlled, and more successful as art" than *The Temple of My Familiar* and demonstrates an effective blend of "art and activism."

Walker's concerns about the international issue of female genital mutilation prompted her to further explore the issue, both on film and in the book *Warrior Marks: Female Genital Mutilation and the Sexual Blinding of Women,* written with documentary film director Pratibha Parmar. According to a *Publishers Weekly* contributor, *Warrior Marks* is a "forceful account" of how the two filmed a documentary on the ritual circumcision of African women.

In 1996 Walker produced *The Same River Twice: Honoring the Difficult; A Meditation of Life, Spirit, Art, and the Making of the film "The Color Purple," Ten Years Later.* The book focuses mainly on Walker's feelings about, and struggles with, the filming of *The Color Purple.* While having the book transformed into a film by Steven Spielberg was a high point in her life, it was also riddled with difficulties. First, Spielberg rejected Walker's screenplay of the book and implemented one with which Walker was not happy. In addition, the film itself was met with controversy and attacks on Walker's ideas—some people thought she had attacked the character of black people in general and black men specifically. Also at the time, Walker's mother was critically ill, while Walker herself was suffering from a debilitating illness that turned out to be Lyme disease. Included in the book are fan letters, reviews, and Walker's original version of the script. Francine Prose in Chicago's *Tribune Books* found fault with the book, feeling that Walker's protests about how things did not go her way ring of artistic posturing: "Walker seems to have so lost touch with the lives and sensibilities of ordinary humans that she apparently cannot hear how her complaints . . . might sound to the less fortunate, who have been less generously favored by greatness."

In 1998 Walker's sixth novel, *By the Light of My Father's Smile,* was published, a book again focusing on female sexuality. The main characters are the Robinsons, a husband-and-wife team of anthropologists,

and the story is told in flashback. Unable to secure funding for research in Mexico in the 1950s, the husband poses as a minister to study the Mundo, a mixed black and Indian tribe. The couple brings along their young daughter to this new life in the Sierra Madre. Sexuality is at the heart of the story, though the father reacts violently upon discovering that his daughter has become involved with a Mundo boy. This reaction has repercussions throughout the novel. Again, Walker experiments with points of view, even recounting the action through the eyes of the recently deceased patriarch of the Robinson clan. According to Prose, reviewing the novel in the *New York Times Book Review,* this novel deals with the "damaging ways in which our puritanical culture suppresses women's sexuality." However, Prose felt that in focusing on polemics, Walker's book became "deeply mired in New Age hocus-pocus and goddess-religion baloney." Prose also complained of "passages of tortuously infelicitous prose." Similarly, Nedhera Landers, writing in the *Lambda Book Report,* was disappointed to find "almost every character to be a two-dimensional stereotype."

Regardless of such criticism, however, Walker's literary reputation is secure. She continues to write in a variety of genres, from fiction to nonfiction and poetry. In 1997's *Anything We Love Can Be Saved: A Writer's Activism,* she details her own political and social struggle, while in the critically acclaimed short-story collection *The Way Forward Is with a Broken Heart,* she employs fiction in a "quasi-autobiographical reflection" on her own past, including her marriage to a Jewish civil rights lawyer, the birth of her daughter, and the creative life she built after her divorce. For Jeff Guinn, writing for the *Knight Ridder/Tribune News Service,* the thirteen stories plus epilogue of this collection "beautifully leavened the universal regrets of middle age with dollops of uplifting philosophy." A contributor for *Publishers Weekly* described the collection as a reflection on the "nature of passion and friendship, pondering the emotional trajectories of lives and loves." This same reviewer found the collection, despite some "self indulgence," to be both "strong . . . [and] moving." Adele S. News-Horst, reviewing the book in *World Literature Today,* found that it is "peopled by characters who are refugees, refugees from the war over civil rights, from the 'criminal' Vietnam-American War, and from sexual oppression." News-Horst further commented that the "stories are neither forced nor unnatural, and there is a sense of truth in all of them." And Linda Barrett Osborne, writing in the *New York Times Book Review,* called *The Way Forward* a "touching and provocative collection."

The versatile Walker returned to poetry with her 2003 collection *Absolute Trust in the Goodness of the Earth,* her first verse collection in more than a decade. Walker had, she thought, given up writing, taking time off to study Tibetan Buddhism and explore the Amazon. Inspired by the terrorist attacks of September 11, 2001, however, she began writing poems. Though just a few poems in *Absolute Trust* deal with the attacks on New York and Washington, D.C., the tragedy let Walker know that she was not yet done with writing. Guinn described the verse in the new collection as "choppy, with sparse clumps of words presented in odd, brisk rhythms." Such devices resulted, Guinn thought, in occasional "sophisticated thought in simple, accessible form." Short lines in free verse are the skeletons of most of the poems in the collection, many of them dealing with "social and environmental justice, and America's blinding ethnocentrism," as Kelly Norman Ellis described them in *Black Issues Book Review.* Ellis further praised the poems in the collection as "psalms about the human capacity for great good and . . . for unimagined brutality." A contributor for *Publishers Weekly* also commended this work, concluding that "readers across the country who cherished Walker's earlier poems will find in this new work exactly what they've awaited."

BIOGRAPHICAL AND CRITICAL SOURCES:

BOOKS

Allan, Tuzyline Jita, *Womanist and Feminist Aesthetics: A Comparative Review,* Ohio University Press (Athens, OH), 1995.
Bestsellers '89, Issue 4, Gale (Detroit, MI), 1989.
Black Literature Criticism, Volume 1, Gale (Detroit, MI), 1992.
Christian, Barbara, editor, *Everyday Use,* Rutgers University Press (New Brunswick, NJ), 1994.
Contemporary Literary Criticism, Gale (Detroit, MI), Volume 5, 1976, Volume 6, 1976, Volume 9, 1978, Volume 19, 1981, Volume 27, 1984, Volume 46, 1988, Volume 58, 1990, Volume 103, 1998.
Contemporary Novelists, 7th edition, St. James Press (Detroit, MI), 2001.
Dictionary of Literary Biography, Gale (Detroit, MI), Volume 6: *American Novelists since World War II, Second Series,* 1980, Volume 33: *Afro-American Fiction Writers after 1955,* 1984, Volume 143: *American Novelists since World War II, Third Series,* 1994.

Evans, Mari, editor, *Black Women Writers, 1950-1980: A Critical Evaluation,* Anchor (New York, NY), 1984.
Johnson, Yvonne, *The Voices of African American Women: The Use of Narrative and Authorial Voice in the Works of Harriet Jacobs, Zora Neale Hurston, and Alice Walker,* P. Lang (New York, NY), 1995.
Kaplan, Carla, *The Erotics of Talk: Women's Writing and Feminist Paradigms,* Oxford University Press (New York, NY), 1996.
Kramer, Barbara, *Alice Walker: Author of "The Color Purple,"* Enslow (Berkeley Heights, NJ), 1995.
O'Brien, John, *Interviews with Black Writers,* Liveright (New York, NY), 1973.
Peden, William, *The American Short Story: Continuity and Change, 1940-1975,* 2nd revised and enlarged edition, Houghton Mifflin (Boston, MA), 1975.
Prenshaw, Peggy W., editor, *Women Writers of the Contemporary South,* University Press of Mississippi (Jackson, MS), 1984.
St. James Guide to Young Adult Writers, 2nd edition, St. James Press (Detroit, MI), 1999.
Short Story Criticism, Volume 5, Gale (Detroit, MI), 1990.
Walker, Alice, *The Same River Twice: Honoring the Difficult; A Meditation of Life, Spirit, Art, and the Making of the film "The Color Purple," Ten Years Later,* Scribner (New York, NY), 1996.

PERIODICALS

Black Issues Book Review, March-April, 2003, Kelly Norman Ellis, review of *Absolute Trust in the Goodness of the Earth: New Poems,* p. 38.
Chicago Tribune, April 23, 1989, Bernard W. Bell, review of *The Temple of My Familiar.*
Detroit Free Press, August 8, 1982, Andrea Ford, review of *The Color Purple*; July 10, 1988; January 4, 1989.
Detroit News, September 15, 1982, Charles Larson, review of *The Color Purple.*
Knight Ridder/Tribune News Service, February 7, 2001, Ira Hadnot, review of *My Way Forward Is with a Broken Heart,* p. K1172; February 13, 2002, Sue Corbett, review of *Langston Hughes: American Poet,* p. K4900; March 12, 2003, Jeff Guinn, review of *Absolute Trust in the Goodness of the Earth,* p. K2933.
Lambda Book Report, December, 1998, Nedhera Landers, review of *By the Light of My Father's Smile,* p. 30.

Language Arts, November, 2002, Junko Yokota and Mingshui Cai, review of *Langston Hughes,* p. 152.

Library Journal, December, 1998, Nann Blaine Hilyard, review of *By the Light of My Father's Smile,* p. 172.

Los Angeles Times, April 29, 1981, article by Art Seidenbaum; April 18, 2003, Renee Tawa, "Alice Walker Ceased Writing, Then Started Anew. Don't Ask, Just Appreciate Wisdom Gained," p. E30.

Los Angeles Times Book Review, May 29, 1988, Derrick Bell, review of *Living by the Word: Selected Writings, 1973-1987;* July 5, 1992, Tina McElroy Ansa, review of *Possessing the Secret of Joy,* p. 4.

Ms., June, 1982, Gloria Steinem, "Do You Know This Woman? She Knows You," p. 35.

Newsweek, June 21, 1982, Peter S. Prescott, review of *The Color Purple,* p. 676; April 24, 1989, David Gates, review of *The Temple of My Familiar,* p. 74.

New York Times Book Review, May 24, 1981, Katha Pollitt, review of *You Can't Keep a Good Woman Down,* p. 9; July 25, 1982, Mel Watkins, review of *The Color Purple,* p. 7; June 5, 1988, Noel Perrin, review of *Living by the Word,* p. 42; April 30, 1989, J. M. Coetzee, review of *The Temple of My Familiar,* p. 7; October 4, 1998, Francine Prose, review of *By the Light of My Father's Smile,* p. 18; December 10, 2000, Linda Barrett Osborne, review of *The Way Forward Is with a Broken Heart,* p. 32.

Publishers Weekly, March 1, 1991, review of *Her Blue Body Everything We Know: Earthling Poems, 1965-1990 Complete,* p. 64; October 25, 1991, review of *Finding the Green Stone,* p. 66; October 25, 1993, review of *Warrior Marks: Female Genital Mutilation and the Sexual Blinding of Women,* p. 49; October 5, 1998, review of *By the Light of My Father's Smile,* p. 44; September 11, 2000, review of *The Way Forward Is with a Broken Heart,* p. 71; November 19, 2001, review of *Langston Hughes,* pp. 67-68; January 20, 2003, review of *Absolute Trust in the Goodness of the Earth,* p. 77.

Time, May 1, 1989, Paul Grey, review of *The Temple of My Familiar,* p. 69.

Tribune Books (Chicago, IL), August 1, 1982, Jeanne Fox-Alston, review of *The Color Purple;* July 17, 1988, Judith Paterson, review of *Living by the Word;* January 21, 1996, Francine Prose, review of *The Same River Twice,* p. 5.

Washington Post Book World, July 25, 1982, David Guy, review of *The Color Purple;* May 29, 1988, Jill Nelson, review of *Living by the Word;* May 7, 1989, David Nicholson, review of *The Temple of My Familiar,* p. 3; July 5, 1992, Charles R. Larson, review of *Possessing the Secret of Joy,* p. 1.

World Literature Today, spring, 2001, Adele S. Newson-Horst, review of *The Way Forward Is with a Broken Heart,* pp. 335-336.*

*   *   *

WELLS, Rebecca

PERSONAL: Born in Rapides, LA; father a self-employed businessperson; married Tom Schworer (a photographer). *Education:* Louisiana State University, B.A.; attended Naropa Institute.

ADDRESSES: Agent—Jonathan Dolger Agency, 49 East 96th St., No. 9B, New York, NY 10128.

CAREER: Playwright, actress, and author.

MEMBER: Performing Artists for Nuclear Disarmament (Seattle, WA; chapter founder, 1982).

AWARDS, HONORS: Western States Book Award for fiction, 1992, for *Little Altars Everywhere;* Adult Trade ABBY Award, 1999, for *Divine Secrets of the Ya-Ya Sisterhood.*

WRITINGS:

PLAYS

Splittin' Hairs (one-woman show), first produced at Seattle Repertory Theater in Seattle, WA; later toured the United States, 1983-84.

Gloria Duplex, first produced at Empty Space Uncommon Theatre in Seattle, WA, 1986-87.

NOVELS

Little Altars Everywhere, Broken Moon Press (Seattle, WA), 1992.

Divine Secrets of the Ya-Ya Sisterhood, HarperCollins (New York, NY), 1996.

Rebecca Wells

ADAPTATIONS: *Divine Secrets of the Ya-Ya Sisterhood,* a film based on the book by the same name and the book *Little Altars Everywhere* and written and directed by Callie Khouri, was released by Warner Brothers, 2002.

SIDELIGHTS: Rebecca Wells is the author of the best-selling novels, *Little Altars Everywhere* and *Divine Secrets of the Ya-Ya Sisterhood,* both of which center on loyalty among women in the South. Born in the rural parish of Rapides, Louisiana, and raised on a plantation, Rebecca Wells worked briefly as a waitress at Yellowstone National Park, studied writing with the poet Allen Ginsberg, then began a career in off-Broadway theater in New York before writing her first book. *Little Altars Everywhere* is a 1992 novel set in a small Louisiana town in the early 1960s, and stars the Walkers, led by the flamboyant Vivi and her outdoorsy husband, Shep, and their children, Siddalee, Little Shep, Lulu, and Baylor. In the first part of the book, Siddalee narrates several chapters, telling engaging and interesting stories about her family, and later in the book, the other children have their say. Their stories hint at misconduct and drunkenness, abuse and

hidden terrors, and even thirty years after the events took place, the family is still scarred. M. J. McAteer, in the *Washington Post Book World,* described the book as "a funny, eloquent and sad novel—her first—that easily leaps regional bounds." Mary B. Stuart, a reviewer for the *Curled Up with a Good Book* Web site, described *Little Altars Everywhere* as "a poignant, humorous, sad, heart-warming, heart-breaking novel that may very well, over time, be deemed an American classic, and a wonderful achievement by Rebecca Wells."

Divine Secrets of the Ya-Ya Sisterhood, published in 1996, tells the story of four aging Southern belles from Louisiana who have been friends ever since 1932, when they disrupted a Shirley Temple look-alike contest. The women made their first appearance in *Little Altars Everywhere,* and Vivi, the mother of the children in that book, is one of them. Her daughter Siddalee asks her mother about her friendships with the other women. Vivi gives her an old scrapbook about her friends, the "Ya-Yas," and the stories that unfold from this gift illuminate their past and their present relationship. *Booklist* reviewer Donna Seaman declared the book "a wonderfully irreverent look at life in small-town Louisiana from the thirties on up to the present through the eyes of the Ya-Yas, a gang of merry, smart, brave, poignant, and unforgettable goddesses." A *Publishers Weekly* reviewer was distracted by the "superficial characterization and forced colloquialisms," but most other critics responded to Wells's characterization with enormous enthusiasm. According to Sarah Van Boven in *Newsweek,* women all over the country have formed over a dozen "Ya-Ya clubs" of their own. Van Boven quotes fans as saying: "It gives me comfort just to see it up there on the shelf," and "It's inspiring to see the Ya-Yas reveling in their nonfamilial bond."

When *Divine Secrets of the Ya-Ya Sisterhood* was first released, the publisher did not view it as a best-seller, but it became one through word of mouth. When women started coming to Wells's book signings with stacks of copies for their mothers, sisters, and friends, she herself was surprised. "I didn't write the book because I had a group of friends like the Ya-Yas," she told Van Boven. "I think I wrote it because I wanted one." Readers identify deeply with the close-knit friends and the complicated mother-daughter relationship. At a reading, a fan once asked Wells if she was Sidda and her mother was Vivi. Before Wells could answer, another fan said, "No, I'm Sidda and my mother is Vivi." "The biggest blessing of the book has been meeting so many women who are loyal to each other," Wells told a writer for *People*. When asked how she feels about her characters inspiring women to "smoke, drink and never think," Wells smiled and said, "Well, that's just one part of the book. I say, 'Go, girl.'" A film adaptation of the book was released in 2002.

BIOGRAPHICAL AND CRITICAL SOURCES:

PERIODICALS

Bloomsbury Review, July, 1992, p. 12.

Booklist, June 1, 1996, Donna Seaman, review of *Divine Secrets of the Ya-Ya Sisterhood,* p. 1674; June 1, 1999, Whitney Scott, audio book review of *Little Altars Everywhere,* p. 1853.

Books, summer, 1999, review of *Divine Secrets of the Ya-Ya Sisterhood,* p. 21; summer, 2001, review of *Little Altars Everywhere,* p. 21.

Book Week, September 6, 1992, p. 9.

Christian Century, July 3, 2002, John Petrakis, movie review of *Divine Secrets of the Ya-Ya Sisterhood,* p. 43.

Daily Variety, May 10, 2002, Todd McCarthy, movie review of *Divine Secrets of the Ya-Ya Sisterhood,* p. 2.

Kliatt Young Adult Paperback Book Guide, March, 1999, audio book review of *Little Altars Everywhere,* p. 57; November, 1999, audio book review of *Divine Secrets of the Ya-Ya Sisterhood,* p. 52.

Library Journal, November 1, 1999, Beth Farrell, audio book review of *Little Altars Everywhere,* p. 142; November 1, 2002, Beth Farrell, audio book review of *Divine Secrets of the Ya-Ya Sisterhood,* p. 143.

Newsweek, July 6, 1998, Sarah Van Boven, review of *Divine Secrets of the Ya-Ya Sisterhood,* p. 71.

Observer (London, England), June 6, 1999, review of *Divine Secrets of the Ya-Ya Sisterhood,* p. 13.

People Weekly, October 5, 1998, "Divine Write," p. 87.

Publishers Weekly, June 29, 1992, review of *Little Altars Everywhere,* p. 58; April 8, 1996, review of *Divine Secrets of the Ya-Ya Sisterhood,* p. 57; February 22, 1999, Daisy Maryles, "Ya-Ya begins Two, Too," p. 20.

Romance Reader, February 4, 1999, review of *Divine Secrets of the Ya-Ya Sisterhood.*

Small Press, fall, 1992, p. 61.

Southern Living, November, 1992, p. 94.

Tribune Books (Chicago, IL), August 3, 1997, p. 8.

Washington Post Book World, September 6, 1992, p. 9.

Western American Literature, November, 1992, p. 282.

Women's Journal, July, 2001, review of *Little Altars Everywhere,* p. 16.

ONLINE

ApolloGuide.com, http://www.apolloguide.com/ (October 28, 2003), movie review of *Divine Secrets of the Ya-Ya Sisterhood.*

BookPage.com, http://www.bookpage.com/ (October 28, 2003), interview with Wells.

Curled Up with a Good Book Web site, http://www.curledup.com/ (October 27, 2003), Mary B. Stuart, review of *Little Altars Everywhere;* Denise M. Clark, review of *Divine Secrets of the Ya-Ya Sisterhood.*

January Magazine, http://www.januarymagazine.com/ (October 27, 2003), Monica Stark, review of *Divine Secrets of the Ya-Ya Sisterhood.*

Rebecca Wells Web site, http://www.ya-ya.com/ (October 27, 2003).

SouthCoast Today Online, http://www.southcoasttoday.com/ (October 27, 2003), Shana McNally, "You'd Know If You're 'Ya-Ya.'"*